The Good Britain Guide 2003

Edited by Alisdair Aird

Deputy Editor: Fiona Stapley

Associate Editors: Karen Fick, Robert Unsworth

Research Officer: Elizabeth Adlington

Additional Research: Emily Bone

Walks Consultant: Tim Locke

EBURY PRESS
LONDON

Please send reports to:

The Good Britain Guide
FREEPOST TN1569
WADHURST
E Sussex
TN5 7BR

This edition published in 2002 by
Ebury Press
Random House, 20 Vauxhall Bridge Road
London SW1V 2SA

www.randomhouse.co.uk

3 5 7 9 10 8 6 4 2

ISBN 0 09 188626 0

Typeset from author's disks by Textype Typesetters, Cambridge
Printed and bound in Great Britain by Cox and Wyman, Reading, Berks

Contents

INTRODUCTION

Britain is packed with all sorts of interesting and highly enjoyable ways of spending holiday time, whether it's just a day out, a short break, or a longer holiday. This *Guide* includes literally thousands of places worth visiting and things to do and see, and the variety is increasing every year – we have added over a hundred to this new edition. We have also tracked down 900 really nice places to stay in, all well placed to make the most of the areas they are in (about three dozen of these are new to this edition).

One alarming fact is that this year – against a background of near-zero inflation – so many holiday places have steeply increased their prices. Of the 1,918 independently owned attractions which charge for admission and which are included in this *Guide*, 722 have put up their prices. The average increase among these price-raisers is a whopping 16%. More than half the 414 places in our survey that are owned by national organisations (National Trust, National Trust for Scotland, English Heritage, Historic Scotland, and Cadw for Wales) also raised their prices, usually by 10%. The worst price-hike villain is a body which certainly ought to know better – the cost of a tour of the Houses of Parliament has more than doubled this year, up from £3.50 to £7.50. These price increases are hardly the way to attract more visitors, at a time when the British holiday industry is seriously worried about its future.

Another factor which weakens Britain's holiday appeal is an odd lack of integration. There are some good schemes which link attractions, places to stay and public transport, but these are usually confined to a few towns. More typical is the way that neighbouring attractions rarely seem even to harmonise their opening days. For instance, in Wisbech there are four places you might want to visit, but the only day you can catch them all open is on Wednesday.

Opening times are even more irritating. A great many places stay closed in the morning, so a visitor can't fill a day by going to one in the morning, having lunch nearby, then going to another in the afternoon. This means having to choose between them – so one of the places loses out, if not both (when you decide that it's not worth making the journey just for one).

Far too many places also close for half a year or so – even some which have so many visitors when they are open that they restrict entrance numbers then. This removes key attractions from many areas which would otherwise be very appealing low-season destinations.

On the plus side is the amazing number of establishments that not only stay open for the whole year, but are also absolutely free. This edition of the *Guide* includes over 600 free places, and among these are some of Britain's biggest draws.

AWARD WINNERS

Bird Centre of the Year is Flamingo Park Wildlife Encounter at Seaview on the Isle of Wight: see and even feed all sorts of other birds as well as the flamingos.

Boat Trip of the Year is the day trip to the island of Lundy, off North Devon – a real experience.

Farm Park of the Year is the Cotswold Farm Park at Kineton in Gloucestershire, an excellent value working farm, fascinating for children.

Aquarium of the Year is the National Marine Aquarium in Plymouth, with its giant new walk-through water world.

Adventure of the Year is Hawkstone Park Follies in Shropshire, a romantic fantasy world that's great to explore on a fine day.

Garden of the Year is Groombridge Place Gardens in Kent, beautiful to see, and unusual in having so much to enchant children.

Zoo of the Year is Chester Zoo, a sure-fire success as a family day out.

Railway of the Year is Snowdon Mountain Railway in Llanberis, North Wales: an enthralling ride up the highest mountain in Wales.

Tour of the Year is the National Coal Mining Museum in Middlestown, Yorkshire – and this fascinating half-day glimpse of life as a miner above and far below ground is completely free.

Discovery Centre of the Year is Birmingham's Thinktank, intriguing and entertaining for children of all ages (and adults aren't left out).

Castle of the Year is Warwick Castle, a magnificent building that's great fun to visit.

Theme Park of the Year is Thorpe Park in Surrey, a superb family treat with spectacular new rides and lots for younger children too.

Specialist Museum of the Year is the National Space Centre in Leicester, a deep probe into space with everything from full-size rockets to designing your own alien.

Living Museum of the Year is the Historic Quay in Hartlepool, Northumbria, a vivid full-scale re-creation of an 18th-century port.

Historic House of the Year is Blenheim Palace in Oxfordshire, magnificently opulent, in miles of parkland, and very well organised for visitors.

Gallery of the Year is the National Gallery of Scotland in Edinburgh, a great collection appealingly displayed, and its handsome building being extended to open with a blockbuster Monet exhibition later in 2003.

National Museum of the Year is the Imperial War Museum in London, fascinating on many levels and for all ages – another top day out that's completely free.

Visitor City of the Year is friendly medieval York, with masses of interesting things to see.

Newcomer of the Year is The Deep in Hull, Yorkshire: since its opening this hi-tech new exploration of the sea has been astonishing hundreds of thousands of visitors, an amazing success.

Family Attraction of the Year is the Ironbridge Gorge Museum in Shropshire, a remarkable living re-creation of industrial life over 100 years ago.

While we are handing out plaudits, here are two more. This year, we have been particularly impressed by the friendliness and helpfulness of all the people we dealt with in Scotland. And a word of praise for the thousands of volunteers helping to staff so many of the country's attractions, from little local museums to great historic buildings.

USING THE GUIDE

THE COUNTIES

England has been split alphabetically into county chapters. Scotland and Wales have each been covered in single chapters, and London appears immediately before them at the end of England.

WHERE TO STAY

In each section, hotels, inns and other places to stay such as farmhouses are listed alphabetically by town or village.

The price we show is the total for two people sharing a double or twin-bedded room with its own bathroom, for one night in high season. It includes full English breakfast (unless only continental is available, in which case we say so), VAT and any automatic service charge that we know about. So the price is the total price for a room for two people. We say if dinner is included in this total price. It is commonly included in some of the more remote places, especially in Cumbria and Scotland, and may also be in some other places where the quality of the food is a main attraction; in these cases, the establishment concerned does not normally offer B&B on its own. In some of the places we list, some or occasionally even all the bedrooms share bathrooms; we say if this is the case.

An asterisk beside the price means that the establishment concerned assured us that that price would hold until the end of summer 2003. Many establishments were unable to give us this assurance; it would be prudent to allow for an increase of around 5% by then.

A few hotels will do a bargain break price at weekends even if you're staying for just one night. If so, that's the price we give, and we show this with a w beside the price. Many more hotels have very good value short break prices, especially out of season, if you stay a minimum of at least two nights; if you plan to stay in one area rather than tour around, it's well worth asking if there's a special price for short breaks when you book. Many more hotels than previously now offer short-notice bargains which don't appear on their tariffs if they are underbooked on a particular night, so as to fill their rooms even at a discount. So, especially if you are not booking in advance, ask what price they can quote you for that particular night.

If we know that the back rooms are the quietest or the front ones have the best views or the ones in the new extension are more spacious then we say so. If you want a room with a sea view or whatever, you should always ask specifically for this, and check whether it costs extra.

If the hotel closes for any day or part of the year, we say so. But there may be unscheduled closures, and some go out of business altogether. So don't head off into an area where there are no nearby alternatives without checking by telephone first. We always mention a restaurant if we know the inn or hotel has one. Note that we always commend food if we have information supporting a positive recommendation. So a bare mention that food is served shouldn't be taken to imply a recommendation of the food.

WHERE TO EAT

The price in ordinary type is for one person having a typical three-course restaurant meal with half a bottle of wine, including any automatic service charge. So double it to get a meal for two. The second price, in bold type after the | , is for a more informal single-dish meal, if that's available.

We list any scheduled closing dates. Many of the restaurants we list are very popular, and without a booking you may find there's no room for you.

If you want a good meal out in any area, look at the places to stay as well as the restaurants, especially in country areas. When we praise a hotel or inn for its food, that means it's well worth consideration as a place for a good meal out. In some parts of the country, it's in these hotel restaurants that you'll find the best food.

Our brief mentions of places to eat in the text of the **To see and do** sections are based on our own inspections or firm recommendations from readers.

CHILDREN AND DOGS

We asked all hotels, restaurants and other places to stay in and eat at which have full entries in the *Guide* whether they allow children. If the entry doesn't mention children, that means the establishment has told us that it welcomes them, with no restrictions. If there are restrictions (either an age limit, or segregated early evening meals for them), we spell these out. We have found that very occasionally establishments turn out in practice to be more restrictive about children than they claim. And of course managements change, and so do their policies. If you are travelling with children, to avoid misunderstandings it's always worth checking ahead. Please let us know if you find any difference from what we say. We have picked out a few places to stay that are really special for families. We've marked these in the text with ☺, our good for families symbol. This year we also asked all places to stay whether they allowed dogs; we say if they do.

LOCATIONS

Generally, we list places to see (and hotels and restaurants) under the name of the nearest village or town. We use **BOLD CAPITALS** to name the locality, and **bold type** like this to name the establishment. If the village is so small that you probably wouldn't find it on a road map, we've listed it under the name of the nearest sizeable village or town instead.

Places well known in their own right – famous castles, great houses, for example – are shown in **BOLD CAPITALS** instead of the locality name. The maps use the same locality name as the text.

We include places in their true geographical locations – so if a village is actually in Buckinghamshire that's where we list it, even if its postal address is in Oxfordshire.

EUROPEAN HERITAGE OPEN DAYS

On European Heritage Open Days, many notable buildings will be open to the public which are normally closed. English National Heritage Weekend will be on 13–14 Sept, when over 2,000 properties will be open. As we went to press individual details are undecided, but if 2002 was anything to go by they will range from intriguing follies through all sorts of official and office buildings to even the Chancellor of the Exchequer's office. For more information ring (020) 7930 0914 or look at their web site: www.civictrust.org.uk. The Welsh Civic Trust run open establishments through the three last weekends of September, ring (029) 20 484606 for details. The Scottish equivalent, Doors Open Days, takes in over 700 properties and will run most weekends in September; ring (0141) 221 1466. During London Open House Weekend, 20–21 September, there will be free admission to over 500 buildings; anything from City Hall to private residences. For more details write to London Open House, PO Box 25361, London, NW5 1GY, or call (0207) 267 2070.

PRICES AND OTHER FACTUAL DETAILS

Information about opening times and so forth is for 2003. In some cases establishments were uncertain about these when the *Guide* went to press during the late summer of 2002; if so, we say in the text. (And of course there's always the risk of changed plans and unexpected closures.) When we say 'cl Nov–Mar' we mean closed from the beginning of November to the end of March, inclusive; however, when we say 'cl Nov–Easter' we mean that the establishment reopens for Easter.

Where establishments were able to guarantee a price for 2003, we have marked this with an asterisk. In many cases establishments could not rule out an unscheduled price increase, and current experience suggests that about half these places – ie, no asterisk against the price – will put up their prices by 10–15% in around April 2003.

🎟 OUR DISCOUNT VOUCHER

In this edition over 700 places to visit have a 🎟 symbol immediately after their name. These have said they will honour our discount voucher until the end of 2003 (or of course the end of their season, if they close earlier). To get the discount, you must hand one of the vouchers in at the admissions kiosk; there are six vouchers on the tearout card in the centre of the book. Usually, the discount is that one child will be admitted free for two adults paying the full price. Please also note the general conditions on the voucher itself, and in some instances we have spelt out different conditions in the text for an establishment. Note that the offer is generally not available on bank holidays or special event days.

NATIONAL TRUST

NT after price details means that the property is owned by the National Trust, and that for members of the Trust admission is free. There is a similar arrangement for properties owned by the National Trust for Scotland (NTS); the two Trusts have a reciprocal arrangement, so that members of one may visit the properties of the other free. Membership is therefore well worth while if you are likely to visit more than a very few properties in the year – quite apart from its benefit to the Trusts' valuable work. NT membership is £32.50 a year (£60 family membership); details from National Trust, PO Box 39, Bromley, Kent BR1 3XL, (0208) 315 1111. NTS membership is £32 (£53 family); details from National Trust for Scotland, 28 Charlotte Sq, Edinburgh EH2 4ET, (0131) 243 9300.

FRIENDS OF HISTORIC HOUSES

The Friends of Historic Houses Association has NT-style membership offering free entry to around 280 historic houses and gardens in private ownership throughout Britain – we recommend a high proportion of these. Membership is £28 a year (£40 for joint membership), so you only have to go to four or five houses and you've got your money back. Details from Historic Houses Association, Heritage House, PO Box 21, Baldock, Herts SG7 5SH, (01462) 896688.

ENGLISH HERITAGE

A similar membership scheme gives free access to those EH properties (about half) which charge admission. It costs £31.50 (£58.50 family). Details from English Heritage Membership Dept, PO Box 570, Swindon, SN2 2UR, (0870) 3331182. Cadw (for Wales) (029) 2050 0200: £26, (family £47), details from Cadw, Crown Building, Cathays Park, Cardiff, CF10 3NQ, and Historic Scotland (0131) 668 8600: £30 (family £53), details from Historic Scotland, Longmore House, Salisbury Place, Edinburgh, EH9 1SH, have similar schemes.

OTHER MONEY SAVERS

In the relevant sections we mention any notable travel bargains and other sight-seeing bargains we know of. The All Britain Pass is very popular with backpackers from overseas, for coach runs linking all the main tourist cities around Britain – a £159 ticket gets you the whole circuit, and you can get on or off at any stage for as long as you like – there's no time limit, and the drivers are very flexible; (0207) 373 7737.

MAP REFERENCES

Most place names are given four-figure map references, looking like this: NT4892. The NT means it's in the square labelled NT on the map for that area. The first figure, 4, tells you to look along the grid at the top and bottom of the NT square for the figure 4. The third figure, 9, tells you to look down the grid at the side of the square to find the figure 9. Imaginary lines drawn down and across the square from these figures should intersect near the locality itself. The second and fourth figures, the 8 and the 2, are for more precise pinpointing, and are really for use with larger-scale maps such as road atlases or the Ordnance Survey 1:50,000 maps, which use exactly the same map reference system. On the relevant Ordnance Survey map, instead of finding the 4 marker on the top grid you'd find the 48 one; instead of the 9 on the side grid you'd look for the 92 marker. This makes it very easy to locate even the smallest village.

DISABLED ACCESS

We always ask establishments if they can deal well with disabled people. We mention disabled access if a cautious view of their answers suggests that this is reasonable, though to be on the safe side anyone with a serious mobility problem would be well advised to ask ahead (many establishments tell us that this helps them to make any special arrangements needed). There may well be at least some access even when we or the establishment concerned have not felt it safe to make a blanket recommendation – again, well worth checking ahead. There are of course many places where we can't easily make this sort of assessment – particularly the less formal attractions such as churches, bird reserves, waterside walks, viewpoints. In such cases (which should be obvious from the context) the absence of any statement about disabled access doesn't mean that a visit is out of the question, it simply means we have no information about that aspect. We're always grateful to hear of readers' own experiences. An important incidental point: many places told us that they would give free admission to a wheelchair user and companion.

CHANGES DURING THE YEAR – PLEASE TELL US

Changes are inevitable during the course of the year. Managements change, and so do their policies. We very much hope that you will find everything just as we say. But if you find anything different, please let us know, using the report card in the middle of the book, the forms at the end of the book, or just a letter. This *Guide* depends very heavily indeed on readers reporting back to it. In that sense it's very much a collaborative venture: and the more people that send us reports, the better the book will be. So please do help us by telling us about places you think should be added to the book, or removed from it, or even just confirming that places still deserve their entry. We try to answer all letters (though there may be a delay – and between the end of May and October we put all letters aside until after the end of the hectic editorial rush). People who help us do get a special offer discount price on the next edition. There's a note on the sort of information we need at the back of the book, with report forms; and a tear-out report card in the middle of the book. For letters posted in Britain you don't need a stamp: the address is The Good Britain Guide, FREEPOST TN1569, WADHURST, E Sussex TN5 7BR. Alternatively you can use our web site, www.goodguides.com (see below) to send us reports.

Our web site combines material from *The Good Britain Guide* and its sister publication *The Good Pub Guide*. It additionally includes a day-by-day list of thousands of events that will be taking place this year.

SYMBOLS

For simplicity's sake we use just five symbols in the text:

☺ Good places for families to stay   ≹ Surface rail – former British Rail
⊖ London Underground   £⃞ Our special offer discount (see
                                        details above and tear-out card)

* indicating that a price is for 2003

Additionally, the map uses these two symbols:

🛏 places to stay
✗ places to eat

BEDFORDSHIRE

Particularly good for wildlife – some outstanding days out

Two of the best animal attractions in the whole country are in Bedfordshire. From the exciting Safari Park to the more sophisticated treasures of the county's finest stately home, Woburn Abbey has lots to keep a family occupied and is Bedfordshire's Family Attraction of the Year. Whipsnade Wild Animal Park has around 2,500 animals in lovely surroundings, as well as a children's farm, big adventure playground, and indoor discovery centre. On a smaller scale, there are good family-friendly farms at Slip End, Billington and (new to the *Guide* this year) Thurleigh. Bedford Butterfly Park at Wilden has quite a bit to keep children entertained.

Picturesque Old Warden has enough for a nicely varied day out, with its collection of vintage aeroplanes, unusual Swiss Garden, and birds of prey centre. Luton has a variety of attractions at Stockwood Craft Museum and Gardens, and pretty Bromham Mill has some good special events during the school holidays.

The museum at Lower Stondon has one of the largest private collections of vehicles in the country, and you'll find trains from all over the world at Leighton Buzzard museum. The Cecil Higgins Art Gallery in Bedford houses its impressive collection in a beautifully furnished Victorian mansion. Bird-lovers (and strollers) will appreciate the Lodge at Sandy, and Harrold and Odell Country Park; gardeners especially will find Wrest Park interesting.

Although the county's scenery is generally not memorable, there are some charming villages to stroll through, and Dunstable Downs have decent walking and remarkable views. The relative flatness is a boon to cyclists; a tourist board leaflet details good circular cycle routes. You can get this from local Tourist Information Centres, which have an especially wide range of helpful information. Other good leaflets cover year-round weekend activities, and guided walks through some of the prettier villages and countryside.

Where to stay

FLITWICK TL0234 **Flitwick Manor** *Church Rd, Flitwick, Bedford, Bedfordshire MK45 1AE (01525) 712242* **£218**, plus special breaks; 17 thoughtfully decorated rms. 17th-c country house surrounded by interesting gardens, with log fire in entrance hall, comfortable lounge and library, and smart restaurant with fine French wines and imaginative food using home-grown and local produce; tennis, putting, croquet; children over 12 in evening restaurant; dogs welcome in bedrooms

LEIGHTON BUZZARD SP9224 **Swan** *High St, Leighton Buzzard, Bedfordshire LU7 7EA (01525) 372148* **£65**, plus wknd breaks; 34 rms. Handsome Georgian coaching inn with pleasant lounge, relaxed bars, and attractive conservatory restaurant with English cooking; limited disabled access

SANDY TL1651 **Highfield Farm** *Tempsford Rd, Sandy, Bedfordshire SG19 2AQ (01767) 682332* **£55**; 10 rms (2 in former stables). Neatly kept whitewashed house

Bedfordshire

NORTHANTS

CAMBRIDGESHIRE

Shelton

Keysoe

Sharnbrook
Felmersham   Thurleigh   Colmworth

Harrold   Harrold Odell Country Park
Carlton   Milton Ernest   Wilden

Stevington

Turvey   A428   Bromham

Stagsden   Bedford   A603   Sandy   Potton

Biddenham   Sutton

BUCKS   A422   Elstow   Northill

SP   A421   Ickwell Green   TL
Houghton Conquest   Old Warden   Broom
Ireland

M1   Ampthill Park   Maulden Wood
13   A507   Clophill   A507
Aspley Guise   Flitwick   Lower Stondon
Silsoe
Pulloxhill

Woburn   A4012   Sharpenhoe Clappers
12   Sundon Hills Country Park
Toddington   Chalgrave

Leighton Buzzard   A5   HERTFORDSHIRE
Eggington   M1   A6
Billington   Dunstable   Luton
11
Dunstable Downs
Slip End   10
Whipsnade

0 Miles   5
0 Kilometres   8

(no smoking) set well away from A1 and surrounded by attractive arable farmland
with plenty of room for children to run around; warmly friendly, helpful owner,
open fire in comfortable sitting room, and communal breakfasts in pleasant dining
room; disabled access; dogs welcome in bedrooms ☺

WOBURN SP9433 **Bell** *21 Bedford St, Woburn, Milton Keynes, Buckinghamshire
MK17 9QB (01525) 290280* **£70**w; 24 attractively decorated rms, some with
antiques. Lovely friendly old inn, carefully restored, with beamed evening
restaurant, long narrow bar/dining area, good changing food, and well kept ales;
also, residents' own lounge and bar.

Please let us know what you think of places in the *Guide*. Use the report forms
at the back of the book, write us a letter or log on to www.goodguides.com

To see and do

Bedfordshire Family Attraction of the Year

WOBURN SP9632 **Woburn Safari Park** (off A4012, not far from M1, junction 13) Attractively set in 300 acres of Woburn Abbey's grounds, this well run park has a lot more to offer than simply its famous drive-through safari. They recently opened the much-anticipated Sea Lion Cove, a nicely landscaped breeding ground for Californian sea lions, with regular shows and feeding displays; underwater windows and raised walkways ensure a good view the rest of the time. There are as many activities and animals as at any comparable zoo, including a splendid walk-through monkey enclosure, with four different species, and an aviary where birds swoop down and feed from your hand. Other shows are based around the elephants or penguin-feeding, and it's these out-of-the-car features that many visitors to the park enjoy best. That said, it's hard to beat the thrill of spotting a lion or a tiger through the window of the family car, and if you're lucky, driving round you may spy zebra, rhinos and various types of antelope not too far from the other side of your windscreen. Of course the animals don't appear on demand, so a second circuit may show up completely different residents. You can drive round as many times as you like, but pick your day carefully: bank holidays and summer weekends can produce slow-moving traffic jams, so even though they lay on extra activities then, you might prefer to visit another day. Don't bring your dog, they're not allowed in the park – and nor are convertibles or soft-roofed cars. After they've been cooped up in the car, the various play areas are great for children: there's an indoor one shaped like Noah's Ark, a soft play area for younger visitors, and an outdoor Treetop Trail rather like an assault course. The toboggan run is popular, while swan-shaped boats on the lake appeal to those with more sedate tastes. A train runs between various points of the park. Between Apr and Oct they have birds of prey displays at weekends and school hols. There's easily enough here to fill a whole day, with lots under cover – though you'll get more out of it in dry weather. Meals, snacks, shop, disabled access; cl wkdys Nov–Feb; (01525) 290407; £12.50 adults, £9 children 3–15; tickets are a pound extra between late July and early Sept. Family tickets for two adults and two children or one adult and three children offer £2 savings.

AMPTHILL PARK TL0239
Former Hunting Ground of Henry VIII, surprisingly heathy but landscaped by Capability Brown, with lovely trees and a water-lily lake.

BEDFORD TL0549
Despite its long history, this is a straightforwardly modern town, but there are decent riverside gardens and a few nice buildings. The Corn Exchange (St Paul's Sq) has a bronze bust of Glenn Miller, who made many of his morale-boosting broadcasts from here. Lincolns (Goldington Green) is an interesting old place for lunch.
Bedford Museum (Castle Cl) Traditional museum next to the Cecil Higgins; cl Mon (exc bank hols), and 25 Dec; (01234) 353323; £2.10.

Cecil Higgins Art Gallery & Museum (Castle Cl) Bedford's outstanding attraction, this rewarding place boasts the kind of paintings most other museums can only dream about, inc great works by Turner, Constable, Rembrandt, Matisse, Picasso, and Dali. The Victorian mansion's beautifully furnished rooms make it look as if the family that lived here have just popped out – it's clear that careful thought has gone into the displays, and nothing seems unnatural or out of place. An extension has collections of local lace, most notably by Thomas Lester, and european glass and ceramics; changing exhibitions. Snacks, shop, disabled access; cl Mon (exc pm bank hols), 25–26 Dec, 1 Jan, Good Fri; (01234)

211222; *£2.10, free on Fridays.

John Bunyan Museum (Bunyan Meeting Free Church, Mill St) In the grounds of the church where John Bunyan was minister; stained-glass windows show scenes from *The Pilgrim's Progress*, and the bronze entrance doors are impressive. Visitors can walk through a series of tableaux of his life, and they've some of his possessions – there's also a trail around Bunyan-related sites in the town. Snacks, shop, disabled access; cl Sun, Mon, Good Fri, and Nov–Feb; (01234) 213722; free.

BILLINGTON SP9422

Mead Open Farm (Stanbridge Rd) Children enjoy themselves at this well arranged place, with trailer rides, indoor and outdoor play areas (inc one for under-3s), and a variety of hands-on activities such as egg collecting and pony grooming; falconry displays twice a month exc Jan. Meals, snacks, shop, disabled access; cl Weds–Fri Nov–Feb, 24–27 and 31 Dec, 1 Jan; (01525) 852954; *£4.25.

BROMHAM TL0050

Bromham Mill 🏚 (Bridge End) Picturesque working 17th-c watermill on River Ouse, with Sun and bank hol milling demonstrations (weather permitting), and a gallery with local art and crafts. Lots of events throughout the year, esp in school hols – phone for more information. Snacks and picnic area, shop, disabled access to ground floor only but they plan improvements; open Sun and bank hols, plus pm Weds–Sat Nov–Feb, daily in school hols; (01234) 824330; £1.25 (£2.50 Sun and bank hols). The Swan is a pleasant family dining pub.

COLMWORTH (BUSHMEAD) TL1160

Bushmead Priory Ruins of 12th-c Augustinian priory, well preserved, with medieval wall paintings and timber-framed roof. Open a few wknds in summer, ring to check times and prices; (01234) 376614; EH; free.

DUNSTABLE TL0221

Priory Church of St Peter (Church St) This remarkable priory church incorporates part of a 12th-c abbey (where Henry VIII's first marriage was annulled). Shop, disabled access; cl bank hols; free. The Old Sugarloaf (High St) is useful for lunch.

DUNSTABLE DOWNS TL0019

Very popular with kite-fliers and gliders at wknds or in summer; there's a countryside centre (open Apr–Oct, plus wknds Nov–Mar), two car parks, and lots of space to run around. The downs give great views from a spectacular escarpment path, amid ancient grasslands. They can be linked to a circuit incorporating Whipsnade village and the nearby Tree Cathedral – the best walk in Beds. **Five Knolls** is an important Bronze Age burial mound, excavated by Agatha Christie's husband Sir Max Mallowan and Gerald Dunning. The Horse & Jockey (A5183) is a useful family food pub.

ELSTOW TL0447

The county's finest village, with a very attractive core of fine old timbered houses by the green. Bunyan was baptised in the handsome church, which has an unusual detached tower and a 'Pilgrim's Progress' window. The Three Tuns at Biddenham is the closest good place for lunch.

Moot Hall Outstanding brick-and-timber medieval market house with a collection of John Bunyan's works (he was born nearby), and a reconstruction of his writing room. Shop; cl am, Mon (exc bank hols), Fri and Sat, and Oct–Mar; £1.

FELMERSHAM SP9957

A lovely church by a medieval tithe barn and attractive old houses, some thatched, with the River Ouse below. Nearby Pavenham is also pretty, with a stroll down to the river. The Fordham Arms at Sharnbrook has enjoyable food, and a play area in its big garden.

HARROLD SP9556

Pretty riverside village with 13th-c church and pack-bridge, and an early circular 19th-c lock-up on the village green. The Magpie is useful for lunch, and in Odell the Bell is good.

Harrold Odell Country Park (Carlton Rd) One for the bird-watchers; with a lake and nature reserve, it's especially good for waterfowl, particularly in winter. Bedfordshire CC publish a circular route incorporating three waymarked walks up to 13 miles long. Snacks, disabled access; visitor centre and wildlife hide; (01234) 720016; free.

LEIGHTON BUZZARD SP9224

Leighton Buzzard Railway ⊞ (Pages Park Station, Billington Rd) Good collection of locomotives from around the world, with a fleet of steam trains to trundle you through gently varied countryside. The Stonehenge Works terminus has industrial heritage displays and crafts shop. Snacks, shop, disabled access; open Sun and bank hol wknds Mar–Sept, wknds in Dec, and other days in school hols; (01525) 373888 for timetable; £5 (discount voucher not valid over Christmas). The Globe in Linslade is a nicely set canalside food pub, with pleasant nearby walks.

LOWER STONDON TL1535

Stondon Museum ⊞ (Station Rd) One of the largest private collections of vehicles in Britain, with around 400 exhibits in five halls. As well as the usual cars (decent collection of Rolls-Royces and Bentleys), bikes and military vehicles, most days they do guided tours around a replica of Captain Cook's ship the *Endeavour* (12, 2 and 3.30pm). Snacks, shop, disabled access; cl Christmas wk; (01462) 850339; *£5.

LUTON TL0820

Stockwood Craft Museum & Gardens (Stockwood Country Park, Farley Hill) Ideal for a restrained and uncomplicated day out. Besides a museum and several lovely period garden settings (inc a 17th-c knot garden and a Victorian cottage garden), there's a refreshingly witty sculpture garden, and an adjacent children's play area. Also here, the **Mossman Collection** concentrates on the history of horse-drawn transport from Roman times onwards with more than 70 vehicles – the Royal Mail coach is particularly noteworthy. Snacks, shop, disabled access; cl Mon (exc bank hols), wkdys Nov–Mar, 25–26 Dec, 1 Jan; (01582) 738714; free.

MAULDEN WOOD TL0638 Ancient woodland with a picnic site, marked walks and muntjac deer. The Star & Garter over in Silsoe has enjoyable home cooking.

OLD WARDEN TL1343 An attractive village, built deliberately quaintly in the 19th c, and especially worth visiting for the Shuttleworth Collection (a triple ticket which includes the Swiss Garden and the English School of Falconry is available for £12.50 – see below; not on special event days). The village church has a number of European wood carvings, inc some from the private chapel of Henry VIII's wife Anne of Cleves. The Hare & Hounds has imaginative food, and a play area in its nice garden.

English School of Falconry (splendidly positioned in the grounds of Shuttleworth Mansion) This Birds of Prey Centre makes a pleasant family day out, especially when the weather is fine. Over 300 birds are kept in settings similar to their natural surroundings, inc the rare king vulture, crested seriema and brahminy kite. Staff are helpful, and there are daily talks and flying demonstrations (10.30, 12.30, 2.30, plus 4pm in summer) as well as the chance to hold a bird; lots of aviaries inc the walk-through barn where the owls are free to fly around you. Snacks and pleasant picnic areas by the lake, shop, disabled access; cl 25–26 Dec, 1 Jan; (01767) 627527; £6.

Shuttleworth Collection Nearly 40 working historic aeroplanes covering the early history of aviation, from 1909 Bleriot to 1942 Spitfire in purpose-built hangars on a classic grass aerodrome. Several exhibits are the only surviving examples of their type, and it's worth trying to go on one on the days when some of them are flown (usually the first Sun of the month and Sat evenings, May–Oct; best to phone). Meals, snacks, shop, disabled access; cl Christmas wk; (01767) 627288; £6.

Swiss Garden ⊞ (part of Old Warden Park) Early 19th-c romantic wilderness garden, a nice place for a wander, with pretty vistas and colourful trees and shrubs. Meals, snacks, shop, disabled access; open Sun and bank hols Jan, Feb and Oct, plus pm Mar–Sept; (01767) 627666; £3.

SANDY TL1847

The Lodge (RSPB Nature Reserve) ⊞ The elegant 19th-c Tudor-style house is the RSPB's HQ, and though it isn't open to the public, it's surrounded by formal gardens, a wildlife garden, and a nature reserve covering 106 acres of heath, lake and woodland, with plenty of birds, animals and numerous trails of varying lengths. Perfect for watching birds undisturbed, but even if bird-spotting's not your thing, this is a relaxing place to explore, especially charming in spring when the woods are carpeted with bluebells. Snacks, good shop, some disabled access (and they've now got disabled parking); cl 25–26 Dec; (01767) 680541; *£3 (free for RSPB members). In the town the Kings Arms is good for lunch.

SHARPENHOE CLAPPERS
TL0629
Steep-sided downland with chalkland flora and butterflies, crowned with a fine beechwood and Iron Age hill fort; the area is owned by the National Trust and is laced with paths.

SHELTON TL0368
Pretty little cottages, hall and rectory grouped around the quite delightful church, with 13th-c work inside and a 14th-c font on seven legs. The St John Arms at Melchbourne is useful for something to eat, with a nice cottagey garden.

SILSOE TL0935
Wrest Park House & Gardens (off A6) Inspired by French chateaux, the 19th-c house has a few ornately plastered rooms open to visitors, but the enormous formal gardens are the main attraction. They go on for over 90 acres and give a good example of the changes in gardening styles between 1700 and 1850. Perhaps best of all is the Great Garden, designed by the Duke of Kent between 1706 and 1740 and later modified by Capability Brown, with lovely views down the water to the baroque pavilion. Light refreshments, shop, disabled access to grounds only (can be tricky in the grassy gardens); open wknds and bank hols Apr–Oct; (01525) 860152; £3.80; EH. The Star & Garter by the church has a good range of home-made food.

SLIP END TL0818
Woodside Farm & Wildlife Park 🎫 Good value friendly farm (much of it under cover) where children can collect eggs from the hen house, and have fun seeing and touching some of

the 250 different breeds of animals and birds. Their monkey house has particularly friendly lemurs and marmosets – some have been hand-reared. There are good indoor and outdoor play areas, and they've recently added a crazy golf course. You can buy feed for the animals from their very well stocked farm shop; tractor and pony and trap rides, trampolines and bouncy castles usually available during school holidays. Meals, snacks, indoor and outdoor picnic areas, shops, good disabled access; open daily (from 8am in summer), cl 25 Dec, 1 Jan; (01582) 841044; £3.50.

SUNDON HILLS COUNTRY PARK TL0528
Sheep-cropped downland with good views and marked walks (some quite steep).

SUTTON TL2247
Notable for its steeply humpbacked packhorse bridge; ironically, cars have to use a more ancient crossing, the shallow ford beside it. A decent pub nearby is named after John o' Gaunt, the village's former owner.

THURLEIGH TL0658
Thurleigh Farm Centre Bustling farm centre with decent indoor and outdoor play areas (inc an assault course for older children), as well as farm animals, nature trail, pedal tractors and quad bikes; special events throughout the year. Meals, snacks, farm shop; cl Mon–Tues, 25 Dec–Easter; £2.95 adults, £4.50 children. In the village the Jackal has good food (inc garden barbecues on Sun in summer).

TODDINGTON TL0029
Toddington Manor 🎫 (Park Rd, Toddington) Readers warmly recommend this well set place for its rare breeds centre and gardens, with pleached lime walk, herbaceous borders, and herb and rose gardens. Lovely woodland walks, one of the biggest vintage tractor collections in the country, and wknd cricket matches in front of the house. Children are given treasure hunt sheets, and nets and buckets for pond-dipping. Snacks, plant centre, limited disabled access; phone for opening times; (01525) 872576; £3.50. The village green is attractive,

with unusual carvings on the church.

WHIPSNADE TL0018

Tree Cathedral Tucked just off
the village road is this most unusual
war memorial, trees planted in the
plan of a cathedral in the 1930s,
with plantings continuing even
nowadays.

Whipsnade Wild Animal Park
Altogether 2,500 animals roam the
beautiful downs-edge parkland, from
tigers, giraffes and rhinos, to monkeys,
wallabies, peafowl and Chinese water
deer. It's an enormous place, and an
open-topped tour bus can take you
between the various stopping points
(or you can take your car, £8.50),
though it's more fun on their narrow-
gauge railway, which chuffs past herds
of Asian animals; their 17-acre elephant
paddock is the biggest in Europe, and
has recently gained the elephants from
London Zoo. There's a hands-on
children's farm, a big adventure
playground, an indoor discovery centre
and several daily demonstrations.
Whipsnade has an excellent record in
conservation and breeding, and their
successes have led to several species
being saved from extinction. Meals,
snacks, disabled access; cl 25 Dec;
(01582) 872171; *£11.50 plus an extra
£2 for the main car park. Children are
very welcome at the Farmers Boy in
nearby Kensworth.

WILDEN TL0954

Bedford Butterfly Park 🖼 (off B660
just N of town) Well organised place
with quite an emphasis on children, inc
a very good adventure playground with
a separate play area for younger
children. The hothouse is full of exotic
plants and flowers, as well as colourful
butterflies and caterpillars, ponds with
koi carp and water-lilies, and a
cascading waterfall. Children like the
bugs room with tarantulas, scorpions
and other creepy-crawlies, and they've
a new British butterfly enclosure and a
butterfly garden. Hay meadow nature
trail (most colourful in July), children's
quiz sheets from the gift shop. Snacks,

disabled access; cl Nov–Feb 14; (01234)
772770; £4.

WOBURN SP9632

Woburn Abbey & Deer Park One of
England's grandest stately homes –
everything from the lovely English and
French 18th-c furniture to the splendid
range of silver seems to have the edge
over most assemblages elsewhere, and
the art collection, taking in sumptuous
paintings by Rembrandt, Van Dyck and
Gainsborough, is outstanding (where
else can you see 21 Canalettos in just
one room?). The 3,000 acres of
surrounding parkland were landscaped
by Humphrey Repton, and today are
home to several varieties of deer. Swans,
ducks and other waterfowl on the lake;
pottery and huge antiques centre. Meals,
snacks, shop, disabled access (stairs to
gold and silver vaults); open wknds
Jan–Mar and Oct, daily Apr–end Sept;
(01525) 290666; £8.00. Readers
recommend the attractive drive into the
park through Froxfield, which has
masses of rhododendrons in Jun.

Woburn Safari Park *See separate
family panel on p.3.*

Other attractive villages include
Aspley Guise SP9335, spacious
Biddenham TL0249 (nice 12th-c church),
Broom TL1743, Clophill TL0837,
Eggington SP9525, Northill TL1546,
Sharnbrook SP9959 (interesting
specialist shops), Pulloxhill TL0634,
Turvey SP9452 (the interesting church
has Saxon origins) and Woburn Sands
(good wooded walks nearby) SP9235; all
have pubs we can recommend for lunch.
Carlton SP9555 is also pleasant. Ickwell
Green TL1545 nr Northill is well worth a
look, too, with its colourful thatched
houses around a broad green; Stagsden
SP9849 is attractive, with a good few
thatched houses, and strolls in the woods
nearby. Stevington SP9853 has a
handsomely restored windmill, and a
holy well opposite the handsome church.
Other churches worth investigating
include Chalgrave TL0027 and Potton
TL2449 (it's the gravestones that are
worth the visit).

Where to eat

HOUGHTON CONQUEST TL0441 **Knife & Cleaver** *The Grove* (01234) 740387 Civilised 17th-c dining pub with welcoming comfortable bar, blazing winter fire, attentive friendly service, smartly stylish bar food (lovely fresh fish and shellfish), over two dozen good wines by the glass, well kept real ales, good choice of whiskies, no smoking conservatory restaurant, and neat garden; good bdrms; cl Sun pm, 27–30 Dec; disabled access. £21.95|**£5.95**

IRELAND TL1341 **Black Horse** (01462) 811398 Busy and attractive beamed pub in lovely setting, with a good choice of imaginative food in sizeable lounge or family dining area, helpful friendly staff, and lots of tables in lovely front garden with play area; cl Sun pm, 25 Dec, 1 Jan. £23|**£5.25**

KEYSOE TL0763 **Chequers** *Pertenhall Rd* (01234) 708678 Friendly and unpretentious village local with two comfortably modernised beamed bars, consistently good food, well kept beer, and terrace and garden with children's play equipment; cl Tues; disabled access. £19|**£6.50**

MILTON ERNEST TL0156 **Strawberry Tree** *3 Radwell Rd* (01234) 823633 18th-c thatched cottage with low beams and open fires, very good interesting lunchtime and evening food using the best ingredients from a sensibly short menu in the no smoking dining room; cl Sun, Mon, Tues, 2 wks winter, 2 wks summer; disabled access. £44

WOBURN SP9533 **Paris House** *Woburn Park* (01525) 290692 Lovely black and white timbered house in Woburn's deer park, with a neat garden for pre-meal drinks, and serving enjoyable modern French food with exotic touches, and a mainly French wine list; cl Sun pm, Mon, all Feb; disabled access. £60

Special thanks to Mrs Y Champion, Judith Feline, Jenny and Michael Back, B and K Hypher

BERKSHIRE

The home of the monarchy and the world of Lego draw most people to Windsor and its surroundings, but some unique family attractions elsewhere have great appeal – and the west of the county has possibilities for quiet breaks

There's lots to do in pretty Windsor. Home of the sovereign for 900 years, Windsor Castle is inevitably very popular, while Legoland continues to delight its floods of visitors, and this year takes the title of Berkshire Family Attraction of the Year. Windsor Great Park is good for a pleasant stroll, and peaceful Savill Garden and the Valley Gardens are also both worth a visit. Eton is very close by – the museum covering its famous public school is interesting.

Younger children will enjoy Bucklebury Farm Park, and attractive Beale Park at Lower Basildon has lots of exotic birds and animals (and an interesting Palladian mansion nearby), while bird-watchers should head for Thatcham Moor. In Hampstead Norreys, the reconstructed rainforest is handy for cold days, and in fine weather, Wellington Country Park at Riseley (and more peacefully Trilakes Country Park and Fishery at Sandhurst) is a pleasant place to spend an afternoon. Look Out discovery park in Bracknell manages a very successful blend of hands-on science with nature and outdoor adventure.

Besides the world-famous Ascot, there are also fine racecourses at Newbury and Windsor, and you can watch racehorses being trained in Lambourn. There's plenty of boating activity, and easy towpath sauntering between Marlow and Henley – the best stretch of the Thames. The river does get very busy during the holidays, but it's idyllic on a fine early summer or autumn afternoon. Away from the Thames, there are also boat trips in Hungerford, Newbury and Kintbury.

The west of the county has a good range of walking possibilities, from gentle strolls to long hikes – with some comfortable and attractive places to stay in, and lots of good food. Its rolling downland and civilised small villages linked by pleasant minor roads make for scenic drives – the Lambourn Valley and Lambourn Downs, the B4009 and B4494, and the back road from Pangbourne to Aldworth are among the best.

Where to stay

BRAY SU9179 **Monkey Island** *Old Mill Lane, Bray, Maidenhead, Berkshire SL6 2EE (01628) 623400* **£190***, plus wknd breaks; 26 comfortable rms. Set on an island in the River Thames and reached only by footbridge or boat, this peaceful 18th-c former fishing lodge, built by the 3rd Duke of Marlborough, is made up of two smart white buildings surrounded by beautifully kept gardens with peacocks, ducks and geese; some fine original features such as an original painted ceiling in the lounge showing monkeys in 18th-c sporting gear, helpful friendly staff, and enjoyable food in restaurant overlooking the water; disabled access

HAMSTEAD MARSHALL SU4165 **White Hart** *Hamstead Marshall, Newbury, Berkshire RG20 0HW (01488) 658201* **£80**; 6 comfortable beamed rms in converted barn. Civilised country inn in quiet village with a log fire open on both sides of the L-shaped bar, a partly no smoking restaurant, good Italian food (the daily specials are the thing to go for), decent Italian wines, friendly service, and very pleasant walled garden; cl 25–26 Dec, 1 Jan, 3 wks summer

HUNGERFORD SU3369 **Bear Hotel** *41 Charnham St, Hungerford, Berkshire RG17 0EL (01488) 682512* **£93**w, plus special breaks; 42 comfortable, attractive rms with antiques and beams in older ones. Civilised hotel with fresh flowers, open fires, a fantastic huge clock, plentiful bar food, well kept real ales, and a relaxing restaurant; disabled access

HUNGERFORD SU3268 **Marshgate Cottage** *Marsh Lane, Hungerford, Berkshire RG17 0QN (01488) 682307* **£55***; 10 individually decorated rms. Family-run little hotel backing on to Kennet & Avon Canal, with residents' lounge and bar, super breakfasts, a friendly atmosphere, and seats overlooking water and marsh, and in sheltered courtyard; plenty to see nearby; disabled access; dogs by arrangement

LAMBOURN SU2977 **Lodge Down** *Ermin St, Lambourn Woodlands, Hungerford, Berkshire RG17 7BJ (01672) 540304* **£50***; 3 rms. Country house in lovely grounds with views over the gallops of Lambourn Downs, open fire in spacious elegant sitting room, friendly owners, and good breakfasts around communal table; visits to stables on request

MAIDENHEAD SU8880 **Fredricks Hotel & Restaurant** *Shoppenhangers Rd, Maidenhead, Berkshire SL6 2PZ (01628) 581000* **£250***; 37 luxurious rms, many with garden views. Smart red-brick hotel next to the greens of Maidenhead Golf Club, with champagne on arrival in reception with its stylishly modern chandeliers and marble waterfall; plush cocktail bar, fine professional cooking in luxurious restaurant, and good formal service from long-standing staff; lush winter-garden conservatory, and terrace where you can take meals in warm weather; cl Christmas/New Year; disabled access

STOCKCROSS SU4468 **Vineyard** *Stockcross, Newbury, Berkshire RG20 8JU*

(01635) 528770 **£257**, plus special breaks; 31 lovely big rms with garden views, sculpture, and antiques. Old hunting lodge with lots of modern art out in the grounds and in the public rooms, opulent country house-style furnishings, plants, lovely flower arrangements, newspapers and books, excellent food in restaurant, an exceptional wine list, and kind staff; indoor swimming pool and gym; disabled access

STREATLEY SU5980 **Swan at Streatley** *High St, Streatley, Reading, Berkshire RG8 9HR (01491) 878800* **£129**w, plus special breaks; 46 attractive rms, many overlooking the water. Well run, friendly riverside hotel with comfortable, relaxed lounges, consistently good food in attractive newly refurbished restaurant, popular leisure club with indoor swimming pool, restored Magdalen College Barge, and flower-filled gardens; disabled access

WINDSOR SU9277 **Oakley Court** *Windsor Rd, Water Oakley, Windsor, Berkshire SL4 5UR (01753) 609988* **£165***w, plus special breaks; 118 spacious, individually furnished rms. Splendid Victorian country-house hotel in 35 acres of grounds by the Thames with 9-hole golf course, croquet lawn, tennis, fishing, boating, and health club; log fires in the elegant lounges, a panelled library, and particularly good food in smart restaurant; used in 200 films, notably the 'St Trinians' series and Hammer 'Dracula' films; disabled access

YATTENDON SU5574 **Royal Oak** *The Square, Yattendon, Newbury, Berkshire RG18 0UG (01635) 201325* **£130***, plus special breaks; 5 pretty rms. Elegant and comfortable old inn in peaceful village, with fresh flowers and log fires in prettily decorated panelled bar and lounge, a relaxed atmosphere, interesting modern food, real ales, a good wine list, and a charming walled garden

---

Please let us know what you think of places in the *Guide*. Use the report forms at the back of the book, write us a letter or log on to www.goodguides.com

To see and do

Berkshire Family Attraction of the Year

WINDSOR SU9374 **Legoland** (B3022, 2m SW of town centre; shuttlebus from the station at Windsor & Eton Riverside, which connects with London Waterloo) Ever-expanding and truly imaginative, this hugely enjoyable place is undoubtedly one of the most exciting days out in the entire country for children under 12. It isn't cheap, but considering how much there is to see and do it's really not bad value, and you'd be hard pushed to find many places in the UK with so much verve and flair. You can save quite a bit off the entrance price by visiting outside peak season (avoiding school holidays can save a family of four £12 off the gate price), and it's cheaper still if you book in advance by phone (see below), or online at www.lego.com. Sorting out tickets in advance has other benefits too: you can avoid the queues at the gate and march straight in, and perhaps even avoid being turned away altogether, as they sensibly stop admissions once they feel it's too busy. It also means you can plan what you want to see before you arrive – essential for getting the best out of the place. The park is divided into several differently themed areas, with recent additions including a safari ride and the Hall of Fame, which has fun re-creations of celebrities, including of course the well known family that live next door. Other highlights include the driving school at Lego Traffic, the Rat Trap – a first-class labyrinth of wooden walkways, climbing nests and slides – a dragon-themed roller-coaster, and an excellent steep water chute. Children over 9 can create robots in the more sophisticated Mindstorms Centre (entrance is by timed ticket, so try to sort your slot out as soon as you arrive). The colourful Duplo Gardens appeal to younger children, while My Town has some jolly fairground rides and a circus. There's a virtual reality racing game, but best of all is Miniland, where 32 million bricks charmingly re-create European capitals in miniature, with moving vehicles, people and animals, and wonderful attention to detail (right down to the 'Mind the Gap' on the London Underground). They've recently added a Lego version of the London Eye, and an interactive racing circuit modelled on the track at Le Mans. You'll need a full day to stand even a chance of seeing everything (it stays open later in the summer holidays, so though you'll pay more, you'll get a couple of extra hours in the park); a two-day ticket (around £9 extra) helps to avoid rushing. Meals, snacks, good shops (you can leave your purchases and have them ready for pick-up as you leave), good disabled access; open daily mid-Mar–early Nov, phone for exact dates; (08705) 040404; £18.95 off peak (£15.95 children 3–15), £22.95 peak (£19.95).

ARBORFIELD SU7566
Henry Street Garden Centre
Specialist rose and bedding plant grower, with a well stocked garden centre. From Jun to Sept you can wander through the fragrant rose fields. Meals, snacks, shop, disabled access; cl 25–26 Dec, and Easter; (0118) 976 1223; free. The George & Dragon over at Swallowfield is good for lunch.

ASCOT SU9268
Royal Ascot Probably the most famous racecourse in the world, though most visitors spend as much time watching the people as the horses. The four-day Royal Meeting in mid-Jun is still one of the highlights of the English season; to try for admission to the Royal Enclosure, British citizens should apply to The Royal Enclosure Office, Ascot Racecourse, Ascot, SL5 7JN, foreign citizens to their embassy. For the other stands contact the racecourse; tickets must be booked in advance and are available from 1 Jan. Plenty of other top-class races throughout the year, when ticket prices range from £6 to £49 depending on the enclosure (the Silver Ring is the cheapest). Meals, snacks, shop, disabled

access; (01344) 876876 for dates. The Thatched Tavern at Cheapside is the best nearby place for lunch.

BISHAM SU8484

Bisham church Well worth a look; sitting on a seat in the churchyard by the Thames on a fine evening is rather special. The Rising Sun in nearby Hurley has good food.

BOULTER'S LOCK SU9082

An excellent starting-point for leisurely strolls by the River Thames (head upstream).

BRACKNELL SU8666

Look Out 🖼 (3m from centre; Nine Mile Ride, off B3430) This busy centre should satisfy both lively minds and legs. It's the starting point for 2,600 acres of woodland, but the main feature is the under-cover hands-on science centre. Visitors can enjoy climbing through a giant mole hole, try the Puzzle Carousel, or have a go at launching a miniature hydrogen rocket or a hot-air balloon. Mainly conifer plantations, the forest is full of nature trails and wildlife; you can hire mountain bikes (school hols and wknds only (01344) 874611; *£9 for two hours), the many tracks, some based on Roman roads, allow long if not varied walks and rides (one leading to an Iron Age hill fort). There are good views from the 22-metre look-out tower. Meals, snacks, shop, disabled access; cl 25–26 Dec; (01344) 354400; £4.50 (half price after 4pm, but shuts at 5). For those with any energy left, across the road the Coral Reef swimming pool complex is great for younger members of the family; the Wild Water Rapids are the best bit (cl 2 wks before Christmas; (01344) 862525; £5.70).

BUCKLEBURY SU5570

Bucklebury Farm Park (on the edge of village, signed from Hermitage off A34) Attractively set in the Pang Valley, this notably friendly and traditional little farm park is a good bet for under-12s into animals. As well as all the animals you'd expect, they've a big herd of red deer; a tractor-drawn trailer ride (included in the price) takes you right up to them, and some are even tame enough to feed – the deer calves are born in Jun. There's plenty going on: children can handle rabbits and guinea pigs in the pets' corner, bottle feed lambs and calves in spring, and visit Father Christmas and his reindeers at Christmas, and their pick-your-own strawberries are popular. It's a nice spot for simply ambling round – they own five acres of woodland (awash with bluebells in spring), and there's a two-mile way-marked walk across an ancient common. A decent enclosed adventure playground has climbing frames and a castle, and there's a cable slide for slightly older children. Snacks, disabled access, open daily mid-Mar–mid-Sept and Autumn half-term, plus wknds mid-Sept–Christmas; (0118) 971 4002; £4.25 adults, £3 children over 3. The Rowbarge down at Woolhampton is a good waterside family dining place.

COOKHAM SU8985

The village, leading down to the Thames, is attractive, and has several decent pubs, of which the very smart if expensive Bel & the Dragon, and Uncle Tom's Cabin at Cookham Dean, are our current favourites. There are plenty of opportunities in this area for **walks** combining the Thames with its hinterland, including great views from the chalk escarpment of Winter Hill. Cock Marsh (NT), by the Thames, is a fine lowland marsh, with breeding wading birds and wetland flora. Paths in this area are very well kept, and it is hard to lose the way seriously, although woodland walking sometimes means you have to keep your eyes skinned for arrow markers painted on trees.

Stanley Spencer Gallery (King's Hall) Cookham really made its mark on Spencer and his art: it was his birthplace and he spent most of his working life here. This rewarding little gallery has a good range of his unique work, with highlights including 'The Last Supper' and the curious unfinished 'Christ Preaching at Cookham Regatta'. Shop, disabled access; cl wkdys (exc bank hols) Nov–Easter; (01628) 471885; £1.

EASTHAMPSTEAD SU8667

Easthampstead church The church here has fine Pre-Raphaelite stained glass by William Morris, Edward Burne-Jones and others.

ETON SU9677

So close to Windsor it's pretty much

part of it, this has a restrained and decorous High St with a mix of interesting old shops and houses. Its glory is **Eton College**, the famous public school, whose stately Tudor and later buildings in graceful precincts are marvellously calm during the school's holidays. The Chapel is an outstanding late Gothic building in the Perpendicular style, and a museum tells the story of the school from its foundation in 1440 up to the present, with fascinating videos on life for pupils here today (inc Prince Harry). Bizarre information is turned up by the various historical documents – in the 17th c, for example, smoking was compulsory for all scholars as a protection against bubonic plague. The Brewhouse Gallery has some good changing exhibitions, and next door there's a collection of Egyptian antiquities. Shop, some disabled access; cl am in term-time, and all Oct–Mar; (01753) 671177; from £3.50 (guided tours from £4.50). The college runs residential courses in summer on a wide range of topics. Gilbeys (High St) does good imaginative light meals.

FINCHAMPSTEAD RIDGES SU7863
A steepish chunk of heather and pinewood, not big but with a good natural character, good views and sheltered picnic spots; the fine avenue of wellingtonias just above it is well worth seeing too. The Queens Oak in the village has good value food. To the N, Simons Wood NT woodland, with a walk to Heath Pool and Devil's Highway Roman road, now a track.

HAMPSTEAD NORREYS SU5376
Living Rainforest (B4009 slightly out of village) Readers are most impressed with this unusual and quite fascinating tropical rainforest reconstructed under glass, with thousands of weird-looking plants currently in danger of extinction. They're spread over two different areas, Lowland Tropical and Amazonica, each with its own climate and atmosphere. Particularly strange are the giant 8-ft lily pads (best from Jun–Oct), which start life the size of a pea, and the orchid collection is exceptional. Quite a few of these plants can't be seen anywhere else in Europe. Also rare monkeys, various fish, tarantulas, a chameleon and even a dwarf crocodile. As it's so warm, this is particularly handy on a cold day. Snacks, good shop (with plants for sale), mostly disabled access (though hard work in gravel car park); cl 25–26 Dec; (01635) 202444; £4.75. The White Hart has good value food.

HUNGERFORD SU3368
Attractive small town with some interesting antiques shops, inc a large arcade on the High St (01488) 683701; some general, others specialising in items as diverse as fireplaces, kitchen furnishings and billiard tables. The Kennet & Avon Canal Trust run **canal trips** from the Wharf; phone (01488) 683389 for details. The John o' Gaunt (High St) has a good choice of food.

INKPEN BEACON SU3562
The high escarpment between here and Walbury Hill gives some dramatic ridgeway walking; best reached from the minor road S of Inkpen (where the Swan is handy for lunch, and has a good adjoining organic farm shop). The gibbet on top of the hill is a macabre relic from highwayman days.
Immediately S lie some lovely rolling downlands laced with gentle and mostly well marked tracks, field paths and woodland paths.

KINTBURY SU3866
Horse-drawn barge trips 🔲 1½-hr trips along the restored Kennet & Avon Canal. Snacks, shop, disabled access by arrangement; open Apr–Oct; phone (01635) 44154 for a timetable; £5. The waterside Dundas Arms has good food (not Sun).

LAMBOURN SU3278
Quiet streamside racehorse-training village below the downs. The parish **Church of St Michael and All Angels** is worth a look (originally Norman, with Perpendicular additions), and the Hare & Hounds (on the B4000 S), with strong racing connections, is good for lunch.
Lambourn Trainers Association (Windsor House) Guided tours around this racehorse training centre; you meet individual horses and see them put through their paces. Wear suitable shoes, and you must make an appointment. Shop, disabled access; open 10–12am, daily exc Sun and bank hols; (01488) 71347; *£5 plus VAT.

Seven Barrows Up on the downs off the Lambourn–Kingston Lisle rd (OS Sheet 174 SU329827) this Bronze Age cemetery has at least 32 barrows – a spectacle even for the uninitiated.

LOWER BASILDON SU6178

Basildon Park (off A329) Elegant Bath stone Palladian mansion, with delicate plasterwork on the ceilings and walls, unusual Octagon Room, and intriguing collection of rare sea shells in the Shell Room. Outside are old-fashioned roses, a pretty terrace, and pleasant grounds beyond. The classical frontage is particularly impressive. Summer teas, light lunches, shop, disabled access to garden and grounds only; open pm Weds–Sun and bank hols, Apr–Oct; (0118) 9843040; £4.40, £2 grounds only; NT.

Beale Park 🖾 (Church Farm) Good, informative and expanding wildlife gardens, with a range of birds and mammals – many rare. Nearly all their animals were born here in conditions as close as possible to the wild; they've recently built a huge new owlery. The surroundings are beautiful, and there's plenty going on – attractions include a narrow-gauge railway, a model boat collection, paddling pools (a new play area is planned for 2003), and there are now animal handling sessions. Meals, snacks, shop, disabled access; cl 23 Dec–Mar; (0118) 984 5172; *£4.80. In summer there are short river cruises, and you can get a boat to here from Caversham Bridge in Reading (two hrs each way, (0118) 948 1088, £6 return).

MAIDENHEAD SU9081

Boating on the Thames Though busy in summer, this is a lovely stretch of the river, flowing through lively towns and villages, past grand houses in imposing grounds. Some idyllic reaches by steep quiet woodland have islets where you can picnic. A particularly pretty trip is from Wargrave to Henley to Medmenham Abbey to Hambleden, Hurley and Marlow Reach. A good shorter stretch is Cliveden Reach (the two miles between Cookham and Boulter's Lock). As well as motor launches, you can hire very attractive (not to mention silent and quite environmentally friendly) electric launches, though for the purists – and the energetic – only a rowing boat will

do. Kris Cruisers in Datchet have 6- to 12-seater motor boats for hire ranging from £96 to £249 a day – they do good mid-week discounts; (01753) 543930.

NEWBURY SU4667

Busy shopping town with some nice old parts, and interesting older buildings among the high street shops (less traffic-plagued since the opening of the notorious bypass). **St Nicolas** is a fine early 16th-c Perpendicular church with a magnificent pulpit. West Mills is the best evocation of the town's 18th-c prosperity, and leads to the attractively rejuvenated canal. **Boat trips** run Easter–end Sept from the old wharf, beyond the market square on the other side of the High St; phone (01635) 44154. The town has an excellent **racecourse**, with mid-week and wknd races all year; (01635) 40015 for dates, prices £5–£22.

Donnington Castle (just N off B4494) is the tall ruined medieval gatehouse of a much larger fortress destroyed in the Civil War. The nicely set canalside Lock Stock & Barrel, with suntrap balcony, has decent food all day.

West Berkshire Museum (The Wharf) Handsome museum housed in a 17th-c Cloth Hall and an 18th-c granary, good on the Civil War battles fought here, and on the development of ballooning, also local archaeology and history. Shop, disabled access to ground floor only; cl Weds (exc school hols), Sun and bank hols; free.

PADWORTH SU6067

Kennet & Avon Canal Visitor Centre (Aldermaston Wharf) In a nice little house beside the canal, exhibitions on the history and usage of the waterway, and useful information on things to do along its various stretches (of which some would say the Berkshire bits are the prettiest). Good trails and walks. Snacks (in picnic garden), shop, limited disabled access; cl Nov–mid-Mar; (0118) 971 2868; free. Nearby quietly placed **Padworth church** feels very ancient and peaceful, and the Round Oak has decent food. *See also Hungerford, Kintbury and Newbury entries for boat trips.* And besides other places we mention, there's good access from Marsh Benham SU4267, Thatcham SU5167 and Woolhampton SU5767, all of which have decent pubs. The railway makes a useful method of return, after a walk along the canal from Hungerford to Kintbury, for example.

PANGBOURNE SU6376

Pangbourne Meadow Traditional meadow by the Thames, scythed after flowering and seeding to preserve its wide range of wild flowers. The attractive riverside Swan has food all day, and the village has some decent shops; it was the home of Kenneth Grahame, who perhaps found inspiration around here for *The Wind in the Willows*.

READING SU7173

Berkshire's county town, largely 19th-c red brick, and not really a tourist town, but with museums worth visiting. The abbey ruins in Forbury Gardens are worth a look if passing. In West St, Vicars & Sons, an old-fashioned game butcher's established in the 19th c, is an interesting shop with good food. For the extravagant, a **balloon trip** gives a very different view of Berkshire; lift off from town-centre parks (weather permitting) in summer, dawn and dusk; (0208) 840 0108 for details; *£145. The 3Bs Bar in the airily redeveloped Town Hall arts/culture centre (Blagrave St) has decent snacks all day, and Sweeney & Todd (Castle St) has excellent value home-made pies.

Museum of English Rural Life (University of Reading, Whiteknights Park; 2m SE on A327, so you don't have to go into the busy centre) You won't find a better exploration of life in the English countryside over the last couple of centuries than this, taking in farm tools, rural crafts, and domestic room settings. Shop, disabled access; cl 1–2pm, all day Sun and Mon, and 25 Dec–1 Jan; (0118) 931 8661; £1. A £5 million lottery grant has recently been awarded to the museum to help it move nearer the town centre; they plan the move during 2004.

Museum of Reading (Blagrave St) In a showy neo-Gothic building, with hands-on displays, and a unique Victorian copy of the Bayeux Tapestry, displays range from biscuit tins back to Roman pottery. Meals, snacks (not Sun), shop, disabled access; cl Mon exc bank hols (open till 7pm, Thurs); (0118) 939 9800; free.

REMENHAM SU7682

A good start for gentle strolls along the Thames towpath, showing to full effect the river's nostalgic qualities of boating and Edwardian England. There are spectacular period riverside mansions towards Maidenhead. This reach is the course of the Henley regatta; you can instead start a walk from Henley itself (coming back over the bridge).

RISELEY SU7164

Wellington Country Park 🅿 (off B3349 Reading–Basingstoke) Plenty for families in this big country park; the 350 acres of meadows, woodland and lakes include marked nature trails, a miniature railway, deer park, a collection of small domestic animals, sandpit and an adventure playground. You can fish and hire rowing and pedal boats on the lake; caravan and camping facilities. Snacks, shop; cl wkdys Nov–Feb; (0118) 932 6444; £4.50. The George & Dragon at Swallowfield does good lunches.

SANDHURST SU8262

Trilakes Country Park and Fishery (Yateley Rd) Not just for fishermen, these attractive lakes and surrounding park and woodland have lots of animals (including alpacas) and birds, some of which you can feed. Pony rides for children on summer Suns; model railway and remote control boats. Meals, snacks, shop, limited disabled access; cl wkdys Nov–Mar; (01252) 873191; £2.50, £7.50 fishing (licence required). The nearby Bird in Hand at Little Sandhurst is useful for lunch.

SONNING SU7575

A charming village, with a pleasant walk through the churchyard and past the lovely **church** to the River Thames, and to Sonning Lock. The attractive old Bull is open all day on wknds.

STREATLEY HILL SU5580

The NT car park below here gives access to NT downland for fine views over the Thames Valley. The long-distance downs-top Ridgeway Path, one of the oldest tracks in England, follows surfaced farm roads in places hereabouts, but takes in some quiet countryside. The nearby Bell at Aldworth is a delightful country pub.

THATCHAM MOOR SU5066

Nature Discovery Centre Surprisingly, the largest area of inland freshwater reed beds in England; lots of birds (some rare), moths, and marshland and aquatic plants. Car park S of A4. The **Nature Discovery Centre** explains more about the environment with some hands-on exhibits, and has a good programme of special events; also two large adventure playgrounds. Snacks, shop, disabled access (limited inside); cl Mon, am in term-time, 25–26 Dec and 6–21 Jan; (01635) 874381; free. The Sun in the Wood at Ashmore Green just N has good food.

THEALE SU6271

Englefield House (A340) This historic house is open only to groups of 20 or more by appointment, but the attractive surrounding woodland is open to individuals, with interesting trees, water and formal gardens, and deer park. Some disabled access; open Mon all year, plus Tues–Thurs Apr–Oct; (0118) 930 2221; £3. Both the Bull and the Old Boot over at Stanford Dingley are enjoyable for lunch.

TWYFORD SU7975

Valley Vineyard (Stanlake Park, B3018) English wines made by a pioneering blend of tradition and technology. Snacks, shop; cl Sun am, 25 Dec–2 Jan; (0118) 934 0176; free. The Duke of Wellington in the village serves a wide choice of food.

VIRGINIA WATER SU9768

Very beautiful, particularly in autumn; the Long Walk gives glorious perspectives of Windsor Castle. Best access via Valley Gardens or Savill Garden car parks.

WALTHAM ST LAWRENCE SU8377

Shottesbrooke church A magnificent 14th-c building, unusually set in a park just E of Waltham St Lawrence – itself an attractive quiet village with an ancient centre, and tasty food in the handsome old Bell.

WINDSOR SU9676

Well worth an expedition (though a tremendous magnet for visitors), the town is dominated by its famous castle, the largest inhabited one in the world. The little streets to the S have many pretty timber-framed or Georgian-fronted houses and shops. The High St, by contrast, is wide and busy. You can walk by the Thames (for example, from Home Park, beyond the station); or across to Eton. The good evening racecourse is best approached by boat – shuttle services run from Barry Avenue Promenade; (01753) 865234 for race dates. The Two Brewers in pretty Park St is a good food pub, and in the quieter nearby Thames-side village of Old Windsor the Union has good bar food.

Frogmore House (Home Park) This lesser known former Royal residence is definitely worth catching on one of its few open days – phone (020) 7321 2233; shop; £5.20, no under-8s. It was a favourite with Queen Victoria, who is buried in a mausoleum in the grounds (open annually on Weds nearest to 24 May), alongside her beloved Albert.

Guildhall (High St, opposite Tourist Information Centre) Over 300 years old, it was designed by Sir Thomas Fitz and, after his death, completed by Sir Christopher Wren. Notice how the central columns don't quite reach the ceiling (tradition has it that the councillors of the time insisted that columns were necessary for safety, so Wren added some – an inch short of the ceiling to prove his plans were correct). Open 10–2 Mon (or Tues after a bank hol); (01628) 796422; free.

Legoland See separate family panel on p.12.

Savill Garden 🏛 (Wick Lane, Englefield Green – where the Fox & Hounds, no children, is a good lunch break) On the eastern edge of Windsor Great Park, 35 peaceful acres taking in woodland, a formal rose garden, rock plants, herbaceous borders and so forth, and punctuated with a number of rare trees, shrubs and perennials; they've recently opened a new garden in honour of the Jubilee. Perhaps best in spring, when there's a dazzling range of colours, but quite stunning at any time of year. Meals, snacks, good shop, plant sales, disabled access; cl 25–26 Dec; (01753) 847518; £5.50 Apr–May, £4.50 Jun–Oct, £3.25 Nov–Mar.

Valley Gardens Lovely for a relaxing stroll, with over 200 acres of woodland – 50 of which are devoted to rhododendrons, making this the largest planting of the species in the world.

Also an outstanding collection of trees and shrubs, a heather garden, waterfowl lakes, and attractive landscaping. It's free for pedestrians (the mile-long walk from Savill Garden is pleasant), though cars can enter by a gate on Wick Rd, Englefield Green, for a fee of £3.50, £5 Apr–May – change needed for the automatic barrier.

Windsor Castle A mass of towers, ramparts and pinnacles, this awesome palace is the official residence of the monarch, though it's changed considerably since William the Conqueror built his original wooden fort here. Henry II constructed the first stone buildings, inc the familiar Round Tower, but for many the highlight is the magnificent **St George's Chapel**, a splendid example of Perpendicular architecture, with intricate carvings on the choir stalls, fine ironwork, an amazing fan-vaulted ceiling, and the arms and pennants of every knight entered into the Order of the Knights of the Garter. This is closed Sun and occasional other dates, often at short notice – best to check on the number below. The **State Apartments**, used for ceremonial and official occasions, are decorated with carvings by Grinling Gibbons and ceilings by Verrio, and full of superb paintings from the Royal collection (inc notable Rembrandts and Van Dycks), porcelain, armour, and exceptionally fine furniture. This part may be closed when the Queen is in residence. Although everything is well signed, readers recommend buying a guidebook, and if you visit in one of their quieter periods the helpful staff take time to point out details you might not notice. Entrance to **Queen Mary's Doll's House**, an exquisite creation by Edwin Lutyens, built for Queen Mary in the 1920s, with perfectly scaled furniture and decoration, is also included in the general admission price. The approach to the castle has recently been enhanced by the creation of a new

Royal garden to celebrate the Golden Jubilee. It's designed to complement the castle rather than be an attraction in its own right, and when there are enough people they take groups round – ask at reception when you arrive. Shop (a new farm shop too), disabled access (exc Doll's House); occasionally closed for official events, so best to phone (020) 7321 2233; £11.50. The guards generally change daily Mon–Sat (alternate days only in winter), at 11 o'clock – again, phone for exact dates.

Windsor Great Park Miles of well maintained and peaceful parkland, so sensitively landscaped that it takes the occasional surprising find (statues, even a totem pole) to remind you that it's not natural. It's the only real prospect in this eastern part of the county for walks that'll make you feel genuinely exercised.

WOKINGHAM SU7865

California Country Park (B3016 S of Wokingham, turning R at Wick Hill opposite B3430) These woods and open spaces are very useful for young children to let off steam in.

Holme Grange Craft Village (Heathlands Rd, just SE) Craft centre with paintings, sculpture, rugs, traditional sweets and even a circus shop; children like the pygmy goats and chipmunks, and there's an aviary. Snacks, shops, disabled access; cl 25 Dec–1 Jan; (0118) 977 6753; free. Heathlands Rd has a couple of farm shops and pick-your-own plots; the nearby Crooked Billet (Honey Hill) is a friendly place for lunch.

Other attractive villages, all with decent pubs and pleasant local walks, include Aldworth SU5579, Aston SU7884, Bagnor SU4569 (with a well regarded theatre in a lovely old watermill), Bray SU9079, Chaddleworth SU4177, Datchet SU9876, Holyport SU8977, Hurley SU8283, Wargrave SU7878, Winterbourne SU4572 and Yattendon SU5574.

Where to eat

BOXFORD SU4271 **Bell** *Lambourn Rd (01488) 608721* Civilised and neatly kept mock Tudor village inn with long snug bar, a nice mix of racing pictures, smaller old advertisements, and interesting bric-a-brac, a rather smart restaurant, thoughtful modern cooking, well kept real ales, and great wines; bdrms; cl 26 Dec. £27|£5

BRAY SU9079 **Fat Duck** *1 High St (01628) 580333* Really innovative food cooked with immense care and based on traditional French cooking (some perfectly cooked more straightforward dishes as well) in this black and white former pub; a relaxed if slightly sophisticated feel, knowledgeable helpful staff, and a well chosen wine list; cl Sun pm, Mon, 2 wks Christmas; disabled access. £70/3-course lunch £27.75

BRAY SU9079 **Fish** *Old Mill Lane (01628) 781111* Converted pub with two stylish but relaxed rooms and a no smoking conservatory, candles and fresh flowers, particularly good fish dishes, lovely puddings, real ales, and a good wine list; cl Sun pm, Mon, 25 Dec, 1 Jan. £30|**£9.95**

BRAY SU9079 **Waterside Inn** *Ferry Road (01628) 620691* (Ferry Rd) In a lovely setting by the Thames, this enormously – and justifiably – popular restaurant is a very special place, and for many, the perfect dining experience; impeccable, classic French cooking beautifully presented inc superb puddings, wonderful petits fours, cosseting and helpful service, and a fine French wine list; a lovely place to stay, too; cl Mon, Tues (but open Tues evening during Jun, July, Aug); children over 7; disabled access. |**£45.50**

CHEAPSIDE SU9469 **Thatched Tavern** *Cheapside Rd (01344) 20874* Smartly civilised dining pub (not actually thatched!) with low old beams, polished flagstones, and a big inglenook, prettily set tables in three attractive dining rooms, a large choice of good food inc local game and fresh fish, well kept real ales, and polite friendly service; partial disabled access. £31|**£6.95**

ETON SU9677 **Gilbey's Bar and Restaurant** *82 High St (01753) 854921* Bustling wine bar with an airy and relaxed bar overlooking the High St, a restaurant and conservatory with bookable tables and friendly helpful staff, an elegant private dining room, imaginative modern food, and a super wine list; cl one wk Christmas. £26/2-course set menu £10.95|**£7.25**

LAMBOURN SU3275 **Hare & Hounds** *Ermin St (01488) 71386* Stylish dining pub in the heart of horse country, with friendly new owners who have carefully refurbished throughout – attractive pine chairs and tables in the several rooms that lead off narrow bar, imaginative food, well kept real ales, and decent wines. £24|**£7.25**

MARSH BENHAM SU4267 **Red House** *(01635) 582017* Attractively set smart thatched dining pub with comfortable bar, no smoking dining room, and front orangery restaurant, good carefully cooked food, well kept ales, decent wine list, lots of malt whiskies, and quite a few brandies and ports; seats on terrace and long lawns that slope down to water meadows and River Kennet; cl Sun pm, Mon; children must be well behaved and over 6 in restaurant; disabled access. £30.20|**£6.75**

PEASEMORE SU4577 **Fox & Hounds** *(01635) 248252* Tucked-away downland pub with hunting prints and fox masks in the two bars, a log-effect gas fire open to both rooms, a relaxed atmosphere, enjoyable bar food, singer/guitarist Fri evenings, and seats outside with far-reaching views; cl Mon, cl Tues–Fri ams. £26|**£5.50**

REMENHAM SU7682 **Little Angel** *Remenham Lane (01491) 574165* Cosy little restaurant with good seafood, splendid range of wines by glass, friendly, helpful service and big conservatory; also bar food and well kept real ales in old low-beamed and panelled bar; floodlit terrace; cl winter Sun pm; children must be well behaved. £28|**£10**

SWALLOWFIELD SU7364 **George & Dragon** *Church Rd (0118) 988 4432* Attractive, cottagey dining pub, cosily old-fashioned, with a smart décor of stripped beams, rugs on flagstones, red walls, good solid wooden furnishings, and a big log fire; good seasonal food inc imaginative daily specials; a no smoking dining conservatory; well kept real ales, decent wines, and friendly prompt service. £29|**£8**

WEST ILSLEY SU4782 **Harrow** *(01635) 281260* Popular white-tiled village inn overlooking duck pond and green, with enjoyable home-made bar food, no smoking dining area, real ales, a relaxed atmosphere, and big garden; no food winter Sun/Mon pms; children over 10; disabled access. £27|**£9**

Special thanks to B and K Hypher

BUCKINGHAMSHIRE

Plenty of enjoyable family outings, some unusual museums, lovely
Chilterns scenery, and grand houses and gardens

There are some splendid stately homes in Buckinghamshire. Claydon House at Middle Claydon has a wonderfully lavish interior, and Waddesdon Manor and Ascott at Wing are both rich testaments to the Rothschild alliance of wealth with taste. In contrast, Chenies Manor House and Hughenden Manor (home of Benjamin Disraeli) will appeal to those with subtler tastes. Bletchley Park has good and untouristy displays on the role of its codebreakers in World War II, as well as toy and military vehicle collections. For gardens, Stowe and Cliveden (at Taplow) are the best places to head for West Wycombe Park is another grand strolling ground, and the Hellfire Caves here are also worth a visit.

Top of a nice range of family attractions comes the Chiltern Open-Air Museum at Chalfont St Giles (a relaxing and enjoyable outing for a summer afternoon), and younger children will really like the themed rides at Gulliver's Land in Milton Keynes. Odds Farm Park at Wooburn Common and the Bucks Goat Centre at Stoke Mandeville will appeal to animal-lovers, and fans of Roald Dahl will enjoy the hands-on themed displays at the Roald Dahl Gallery in Aylesbury.

With endless scenic walking possibilities, the Chiltern Hills give the south of the county a special charm: quiet valleys, lovely tucked-away villages with pretty brick-and-flint houses. This scenery is at its best in spring and autumn through to November, when the beechwoods are at their most beautiful. Some of the best stretches of the Thames are in this area – the finest reaches of all are best seen from a boat. Coombe Hill, the highest point, is an excellent spot for kite-flying.

Where to stay

AYLESBURY SP7812 **Hartwell House** *Oxford Rd, Aylesbury, Buckinghamshire HP17 8NL (01296) 747444* **£235**, plus special breaks; 46 rms, some huge and well equipped, others with four-posters and fine panelling, inc ten secluded suites in restored 18th-c stables with private garden and statues. Elegant Grade I listed building with Jacobean and Georgian façades, wonderful decorative plasterwork and panelling, fine paintings and antiques, a marvellous Gothic central staircase, splendid morning room, and library, exceptional service, pricey wines, and excellent food; 90 acres of parkland with ruined church, lake and statues, and spa with indoor swimming pool, saunas, gym and beauty rooms, and informal restaurant; croquet, fishing; children over 8; good disabled access; dogs in Hartwell Court

HAMBLEDEN SU7886 **Stag & Huntsman** *Hambleden, Henley-on-Thames, Oxfordshire RG9 6RP (01491) 571227* **£68**; 3 attractive rms. Peaceful brick-and-flint pub opposite church in very pretty village surrounded by Chilterns beechwoods; compact half-panelled lounge, large fireplace, attractively simple public bar and cosy snug, good food, well kept real ales, and spacious pretty garden (summer barbecues); cl 25 Dec, 1 Jan; no children

Buckinghamshire

KINGSEY SP7406 **Foxhill** *Risborough Road, Kingsey, Aylesbury, Buckinghamshire HP17 8LZ (01844) 291650 £52*; 3 beamed rms with showers. Neatly kept white house with heated swimming pool and Wendy house in mature and pretty back garden, a duck-filled pond in front, carefully furnished rooms, enjoyable breakfasts in breakfast/sitting room, and helpful owners; cl Dec–Feb; children over 5

MARLOW SU8586 **Compleat Angler** *Bisham Rd, Marlow, Buckinghamshire SL7 1RG (01628) 484444 £205w*, plus special breaks; 64 pretty, individually furnished rms overlooking garden or river. Famous Thames-side hotel with comfortable panelled lounge, balconied bar, spacious beamed restaurant, imaginative food, and prompt service; tennis, croquet, coarse fishing, and boating; disabled access

TAPLOW SU9185 **Cliveden** *Taplow, Maidenhead, Berkshire SL6 0JF (01628) 668561* **£250** (plus £7 each paid to National Trust), plus special breaks; 39 luxurious, individual rms with maid unpacking service and a butler's tray. Superb Grade I listed stately home with gracious, comfortable public rooms, fine paintings, tapestries and armour, and a surprisingly unstuffy atmosphere; lovely views over the magnificent NT Thames-side parkland and formal gardens (open to the public); imaginative food in the two no smoking restaurants with lighter meals in the conservatory, friendly breakfasts around a huge table, and impeccable staff; pavilion with swimming pool, gym, etc.; tennis, squash, croquet, riding, coarse fishing, a new golf course 5 minutes away reached by chauffeur-driven car, and boats for river trips; they are kind to children; good disabled access ☺

WINSLOW SP7627 **Bell** *Market Sq, Winslow, Buckinghamshire MK18 3AB (01296) 714091* **£64**; 43 rms. Elegant black and white timbered inn with beams and open fires, plush hotel bar, all-day coffee lounge, enjoyable bar food, good lunchtime and evening carvery in restaurant; disabled access; dogs welcome in bedrooms

WOOBURN COMMON SU9087 **Chequers** *Kiln Lane, Wooburn Green, High Wycombe, Buckinghamshire HP10 0JQ (01628) 529575* **£77.50**w, plus special breaks; 17 stripped pine rms in mock-Tudor wing. Popular inn with unchanging traditional atmosphere in cosy low-beamed bar, standing timbers and alcoves, log fires and comfortable sofas, well kept real ales, good daily-changing food in busy dining room, nice breakfasts, and spacious garden

To see and do

Buckinghamshire Family Attraction of the Year

CHALFONT ST GILES TQ0193 **Chiltern Open-Air Museum** (Newland Park, Gorelands Lane) This collection of re-assembled historic buildings makes a relaxed, quietly instructive family trip out, free from queues, crowds, and overflowing car parks. The 30 or so buildings dotted around have been painstakingly dismantled and rebuilt here piece by piece to avoid demolition. That may not sound too exciting for children, but in fact a lot of effort is put into bringing the buildings and their heritage to life; you might come across historic cooking on an open hearth, or be able to join in brick- or candle-making (ring in advance for what's on when). During school holidays they have a whole range of hands-on activities and demonstrations designed with children in mind. And at any time the 45 acres of woods and parkland are a delight to explore; they happily encourage children to run around, and there's a decent children's playground. You can pick up themed guidesheets to the sculpture trail environmental trail, and pretty woodland walk at the ticket office. The buildings themselves are fascinating: structures as diverse as an Iron Age house (its design based on excavations in the area), Victorian farmyard complete with animals, intriguing oddities like the 18th-c well head and Edwardian public convenience, and a 1940s prefab, with useful displays on their original use. You can explore the site in a couple of hours, but even when there's nothing special going on it's easy to spend a fair bit longer; the site is ideal for a picnic. One 19th-c barn is a centre of the Hawk and Owl Trust, and though they don't keep any captive birds, they run regular demonstrations and after-school clubs, when you may be lucky enough to see some of the wild birds of prey that live in the grounds. As you'll spend most of your time outdoors, the museum isn't really a place to come in wet weather. Dogs are welcome on a lead. Snacks, picnic area, mostly disabled access; open Apr–Oct (and usually for events around Christmas); (01494) 87117; £5.50 adults, £3 children 5–16. A family ticket for two adult and two children is £15.

AMERSHAM SU9597
The older part, especially the High St, retains a number of well preserved buildings from several periods inc the charming Tudor-fronted Kings Arms, and the Crown, fronted by a Georgian façade, but containing some 16th-c wall paintings and original beams inside; both have good value bar food.

AYLESBURY SP8113
Buckinghamshire County Museum and Roald Dahl Children's Gallery (St Mary's Sq, Church St) Roald Dahl lived in Buckinghamshire for most of his life, and as well as having local history displays, this museum celebrates the connection with a gallery of hands-on displays that use Dahl's novels and characters to teach children about insects, light and any number of other topics; visitors can crawl through the tunnel of Fantastic Mr Fox, discover Willy Wonka's inventions, and even go inside the Giant Peach to find out what things look like under the microscope. Also a good collection of regional art and a walled garden. Snacks, shop, good disabled access; cl Sun am and 25–26 Dec (Dahl gallery cl until 3pm wkdys in term-time); (01296) 331441; museum free, £3.50 Dahl Gallery. The Kings Head is an almost unique Tudor inn around a courtyard, with a small crafts shop in the corner.

BEACONSFIELD SU9391
Bekonscot Model Village (Warwick Rd) This miniature portrayal of rural Britain in the 1930s includes scaled-down churches, castles, zoo and even a racecourse, as well as a gauge-1 model railway; train ride and play area. Snacks, shop, disabled access; cl end Oct–mid-Feb; (01494) 672919; £4.50. The Crown up at Penn (good views, interesting church) is a good family pub.

BLETCHLEY SP8633
Bletchley Park (turn off B4034 at Eight Bells pub, then right into Wilton Ave) Victorian mansion featured in the Robert Harris novel *Enigma*, where 12,000 men and women worked cracking German codes during World War II. It now has a series of genuine and untouristy wartime exhibitions and displays. Some of the codebreaking bits are a little technical, but there's plenty

more to see, inc a toy collection, landscaped grounds, wartime fire engines and military vehicles. Meals, snacks, shop, disabled access; usually open wknds and bank hols (plus wkdys for the guided tour at 2pm) Feb–Nov; (01908) 640404; £6. The Crooked Billet (Westbrook End, Newton Longville) has good food and wines.

BOARSTALL SP6214
Boarstall Duck Decoy Displays and working demonstrations of one of only three remaining 17th-c working duck decoys. Also woodland walks and nature trail. Open wknds and bank hols plus 4–7pm Weds, Apr–Aug bank hol; (01844) 237488; £2.10; NT. Brill is the nearest useful place for lunch.

BRADENHAM SU8396
This pretty village is surrounded by ancient woodland, with pleasant strolling possibilities.

BRILL SP6514
The **windmill** (usually open pm summer Suns) is in a magnificent position right on the edge of the Chilterns, with distant views across Oxfordshire; there's been a mill on this site for over 700 years. In the distinctive and quietly attractive village the Pheasant (with a view of the windmill) is good for lunch. There's a decent walk up nearby Muswell Hill, or along the ridge and down to Boarstall.

BUCKINGHAM SP6933
Quite a lot of attractive early 18th-c brick buildings, and much of the nostalgic charm of a once important town that has been eclipsed by rivals (in this case Aylesbury and Milton Keynes). The White Hart (Market Sq) is handy for a snack or coffee.
Old Gaol Museum 🔲 (Market Hill) Housed in an extraordinary early Gothic Revival gaol, this small local history museum has a good audio-visual show in an intact original cell and other exhibits in a glazed exercise courtyard; the Tourist Information Centre is in here too. Shop, disabled access; cl Sun; (01280) 823020; £1.50.

BURNHAM BEECHES SU9485
A supreme example of a Chilterns beechwood, splendid in spring and autumn colours, and with perhaps a glimpse of deer; maps are posted throughout the forest, but it is quite

easy to lose one's bearings. The main starting-point is at East Burnham Common car park, opposite the W end of Beeches Rd at Farnham Common. There are several decent pubs dotted around the forest.

CHALFONT ST GILES SU9893
Chiltern Open-Air Museum See *separate family panel on p.22.*
Milton's Cottage (Deanway) The writer brought his family to this timber-framed 16th-c cottage to escape the Plague in 1665, and while here completed *Paradise Lost* and began *Paradise Regained*. Displays of first editions, other rare books and memorabilia, and a charming cottage garden full of plants and flowers mentioned by Milton in his poetry. Shop, disabled access to ground floor; cl 1–2pm, all day Mon (exc bank hols), and Nov–Feb; (01494) 872313; £2.50. The nearby White Hart (Three Households) has decent food.

CHENIES TQ0198
Chenies Manor House Rewarding 15th-c house with Tudor rooms, tapestries, priest's hole, and newly discovered 16th-c cellars; the gardens include a physic garden, herbs and mazes. Home-made teas, shop (good for dried flowers and herbs), disabled access to gardens only; open pms Weds, Thurs and bank hol Mons Apr–Oct; (01494) 762888; £5 house and garden, £3 garden only. The neighbouring **church** has the rich family monuments of the Bedfords (viewed through a glass panel), 15th-c brasses, and a Norman font. The Red Lion is good for lunch.

CHESS VALLEY TQ0298
Shared between Bucks and Herts, this is miniature and unspoilt, and handily reached from Chalfont & Latimer station on the Metropolitan Underground line; Chenies and Latimer in Bucks, and Sarratt just over the Herts border, are the villages to head for.

CHETWODE SP6430
Chetwode church A handsome church, notable for its fine Early English windows.

CHILTERNS SU7295
The well wooded Chiltern Hills offer plenty of easy-going walks, with a good scattering of rural pubs and pretty villages, though sometimes you have to choose your path carefully to avoid the numerous suburban developments. Even so, it's easy to escape into idyllic landscapes which some rate above all others for wknd walks. The escarpment where the hills drop sharply down to the plain gives some very distant views, for instance from above Bledlow. The signposted Ridgeway takes in the most dramatic features.

CHURCH WOOD SU9786
On the edge of the immaculate village of Hedgerley (where the friendly old White Horse has decent food), this is a nature reserve managed by the RSPB, with over 80 species of birds in 34 acres.

COOMBE HILL SU8506
The highest point in the Chilterns, with its Boer War Memorial (an excellent place for views – and for kite-flying). Wendover Woods with some well marked nature trails are adjacent. The town of Wendover (the Red Lion Hotel here is walker-friendly) gives nearby access, or you can follow paths from Ellesborough and sneak views of Chequers, the Prime Minister's country retreat (emphatically private); an alternative path in is from Dunsmore.

DORNEY SU9279
Dorney Court 🏠 Engaging partly 15th-c timber-framed manor house with pleasant gardens and some very fine furniture, as well as the Elizabethan Palmer Needlework tapestry. The same family have lived here for over 450 years. In the 16th c they grew the first pineapple raised in England, and still have pick-your-own fruit and vegetables every day in season (usually daily Jun–Sept – discounts on Mon, Tues or Weds). Also plant centre, with plants from Blooms of Bressingham, and teas. Snacks, shop (at plant centre), some disabled access (ground floor only); open pm bank hols and preceding Suns in May, and daily pm in Aug exc Sat; (01628) 604638; £5. The village itself, the most southerly in the county, is known for its honey – its name means 'island of bumble bees'. The Palmer Arms is handy for lunch.

FAWLEY SU7684
Fawley Court Not the typical English stately home it appears to be; though it

does boast some fine Wyatt interiors and an elaborate ceiling by Grinling Gibbons, it's owned by a Polish religious order, and has a surprising museum dedicated to their homeland, particularly strong on Polish military history. The grounds (landscaped by Capability Brown) run down to the river, and you can stay here, B&B or half and full board. Snacks, shop, limited disabled access; open pm Weds, Thurs and Sun May–Oct (not Whitsun week or Easter); (01491) 574917; £4. The Walnut Tree has enjoyable food.

FINGEST SU7791

Fingest church This brick-and-flint church is famous for its huge Norman tower with a twin saddleback roof. The Chequers opposite is nice for lunch, and, below the landmark windmill to the N, this is a particularly delectable valley – try the road round through Turville.

FORTY GREEN SU9291

Royal Standard of England The pub stands out as a quite remarkable old building, full of interesting furniture – crowded at wknds, it's well worth a quiet prowl during the week.

HADDENHAM SP7408

St Tiggywinkles Visitor Centre ▣ (Aston Rd) This expanding visitor centre at this wildlife hospital has a new hedgehog museum, and a video system lets you watch the animals being treated without disturbing them. The gardens have enclosures for the animals that they can't release back into the wild, inc hedgehogs, ducks, badgers and foxes. Snacks, shop, disabled access; cl 25–26 Dec, plus wknds Christmas–Easter; (01844) 292292; £3.80. The Green Dragon (Church End; no under-7s) is a pleasant dining pub.

HAMBLEDEN SU7886

Thames walk The footbridge over the weir below the charming Chilterns village of Hambleden is attractive, and is the best starting point on the Buckinghamshire bank for riverside walks. The Stag & Huntsman is a very pleasant food stop.

HANSLOPE SP8046

Hanslope church Attractive in its own right, but the most striking feature is its unusually tall spire. The White Hart over at Stoke Goldington is good

value for lunch, with a footpath network on its doorstep.

HIGH WYCOMBE SU8693

Wycombe Museum (Castle Hill House, Priory Avenue) 18th-c house telling the history of the town's furniture industry, in pretty landscaped gardens; local history displays with hands-on exhibits. Snacks, shop; disabled access to ground floor; cl Sun am and all day bank hols; (01494) 421895; free.

HODGEMOOR WOODS SU9693 (W of Chalfont St Giles) This ancient woodland has three colour-coded nature trails, giving enjoyable walks of varying lengths.

HUGHENDEN SU8695

Hughenden Manor The home of Benjamin Disraeli until his death in 1881, this imposing house still has many of the ex-Prime Minister's books and other possessions, as well as related memorabilia, portraits of friends, and formal gardens; he's buried in the grounds. Meals, snacks, shop, some disabled access; open pm Weds–Sun and bank hols Apr–Oct, wknds only in March; surrounding woodlands open all year; special events and performances throughout the summer (01494) 755565; £4.50, garden only £1.60, NT. The Red Lion at Great Kingshill does good fish lunches.

IVINGHOE SP9416

Attractive old village giving its name to the beacon hill high above. The Rose & Crown does fresh bar lunches. This enclave is a fragment of Buckinghamshire almost encircled by Hertfordshire.

Ford End Watermill (Station Rd) 18th c, the only remaining working watermill with original machinery in the county. An unusual feature is the sheep wash, a special pool into which sheep were dropped and cleaned to make shearing easier. Shop, limited disabled access; open pm Easter Mon, then first Sun and bank hols May–Sept, with milling (water level permitting) 3–5pm on bank hols and second Sun in May; (01582) 600391; £1.20.

Ivinghoe Beacon This is a protruding finger of the Chilterns, and the finish of the long-distance Ridgeway Path which begins in Wiltshire. The slopes, too steep for ploughing, comprise woodland, scrub and unspoilt downland, with an Iron Age earthwork on top. From the beacon itself you look down over eight counties; the best views are northwards.

JORDANS SU9791

Jordans Interesting as a quiet tree-filled village built mainly this century in honour of the first 17th-c Quaker meeting place here – a simple, evocative building. The nearby Mayflower Barn is built with timbers from the famous ship.

LACEY GREEN SP8100

Lacey Green Smockmill (off A4010) The oldest surviving smockmill in the country, and indeed the third-oldest windmill of any type, built around 1650. It's been well restored. Open pm Sun and bank hols May–Sept; (01844) 343560; *£1.00. The Pink & Lily does good food – and has kept its little tap room much as Rupert Brooke enjoyed it.

LITTLE MISSENDEN SU9298

Pretty village with charming old timbered and tiled houses; the **church** has wall paintings from the 12th c and some pre-Norman traces. You can get good sandwiches at the attractive old Crown.

LONG CRENDON SP6909

The cottages in the High St are very pretty, some little changed since the village was a rich wool centre in the 15th c. The Angel is a good restaurant, and the Churchill Arms has decent pub food.

Courthouse A particularly lovely timber-framed building, early 15th c; probably built as a wool store. Open wknds and pm Weds (upper floor only), 23 Mar–Sept; (01494) 528051; £1; NT. There are snacks in the nearby church house.

LOWER WINCHENDON SP7312

This secluded old place has carefully restored houses and a charming, simple church – the walk over the hill to Upper Winchendon gives interesting views. The Crown in Cuddington has good interesting food.

MARLOW SU8586

Thames boating Marlow Reach is lively and attractive, and a good centre for trips in either direction. Salters (01865) 243421 operate 40-min cruises Apr–Sept. Snacks, some disabled access (boats can take wheelchairs on deck but no facilities); £4.40. The Compleat Angler right on the river is a fine place for lunch; on a humbler plane the Two Brewers back over the bridge and the Hare & Hounds out towards Henley are good bets.

MARSWORTH SP9114

Canalside walk Marsworth gives good towpath access to an imposing **flight of locks**. The cheery Red Lion has good value food.

MIDDLE CLAYDON SP7125

Claydon House The wonderfully over-the-top rococo décor is the prime attraction of this mainly 18th-c house (featured in BBC's *Vanity Fair* – quite a surprise given the classical simplicity of the exterior). Highlights are the carvings by Luke Lightfoot and the fantastic walls, ceilings and overmantels, though there are also portraits by Lely and Van Dyck, and mementoes of Florence Nightingale, a frequent guest. The original owner's tastes were considerably richer than his pockets, and his ambitious plans for the house eventually bankrupted him, though his family still live here. Meals, snacks, secondhand bookshop, disabled access to ground floor; open pm Sat–Weds Apr–Oct; (01296) 730349; £4.40; NT. The Old Thatched Inn over at Adstock has enjoyable food.

MILTON KEYNES SP8742

Britain's largest New Town is perhaps also the most successful example of the idea, with roads well laid out to keep traffic moving easily and well away from pedestrians, and plenty of greenery. Locals are proud of the remarkable number of public sculptures dotted around, from the endearing Wounded Elephant, to the famous concrete cows in a field on the N side of the H3 road (Monks Way, or A422) near the A5 junction. There's a swish shopping centre at Midsummer Boulevard (named for its alignment with the summer solstice), and in Avebury Boulevard a huge leisure and 16-screen cinema complex contains Europe's largest real-snow ski slope; (01908) 230260. Tucked around the city are various villagey corners, and the Old Beams (Osier Lane, Shenley Lodge) and canalside Black Horse at Great Linford

are both pleasant retreats for lunch.
City Discovery Centre (Bradwell
Abbey) Tells you all you could need to
know about the New Town
development (lots of slides, maps and
old photographs), in a 16th-c
farmhouse in the 17-acre grounds of a
former abbey. Also 14th-c barn and
chapel, medieval fishponds, herb
gardens, and nature trail. Meals, snacks,
shop, disabled access; open Mon–Fri
and some Sun pms, but best to phone in
advance to avoid large school groups;
(01908) 227229; free.
Gulliver's Land (Newlands, M1
junction 14) Most under-12s will
happily spend a day at this friendly
family-run place. Like its sister parks at
Matlock Bath and Warrington, it's
loosely based on Jonathan Swift's tale of
the shipwrecked surgeon taken
prisoner by the pint-sized population of
Lilliput. Most of the 30 or so rides and
attractions are scaled-down versions of
what you'd expect, but there are some
unusual ones: you can travel on musical
instruments and flying boots, or on a
water ride that whisks you through
waterfalls and whirlpools; good play
area for the under-5s. Most rides are
under cover, and they have special
events. Restaurants, cafés, shops,
disabled access; open wknds Easter–Jun
and Sept–Oct and daily Jun–Aug; best
to ring outside peak summer times as
they may also be open other days;
(01908) 609001; £8.80 adults and
children, includes unlimited goes on
everything all day. Free for children
under 90cm (they may not be able to go
on some rides).
Milton Keynes Gallery (900
Midsummer Blvd, Margaret Powell Sq)
Contemporary art gallery with changing
exhibitions, in a sleek modern building.
Shop, disabled access; cl Mon and bank
hols, and when they change their
exhibitions; phone (01908) 676900 to
check; free.
Milton Keynes Museum (McConnell
Drive, H2 Millers Way) Includes
Victorian and Edwardian room settings,
a school-room, a steam tram, print
shop and a transport hall; they have a
Victorian Christmas week (usually end
of Nov). Snacks, shop, disabled access;
usually open pm Weds–Sun,

Easter–Oct and wknds Nov–Easter but
phone to check; (01908) 316222; £3.50.
Willen Lakeside Park (Brickhill St)
Two lakes – one with water sports,
hotel and restaurant, and the other for
bird-watching; also a Japanese peace
pagoda built by Buddhist monks, turf
maze, and nature trail.
OLNEY SP8951
Pleasant stone-built small town with a
nice riverside stroll to the Robin Hood
at Clifton Reynes, and a Thurs market.
The Bull is HQ for the town's famous
Shrove Tuesday pancake race, first run
in 1445; the Swan (no under-10s) is our
current tip for lunch here.
Cowper and Newton Museum
(Market Pl) Enthusiastically run, in the
former home of hymn-writer William
Cowper. Several of his personal
possessions, manuscripts and poems
are on display, along with some
belonging to his friend John Newton,
curate of Olney and composer of
'Amazing Grace'. There's a notable
textiles exhibition, a restored period
summerhouse in the little garden, and
local history displays. Shop, limited
disabled access to building; cl 1–2, all
day Sun (exc pms July–Aug) and Mon,
and 23 Dec–Feb; (01234) 711516; £3.
PITSTONE SP9415
As well as a decent little **agricultural
museum** (shop, disabled access; open
2nd Sun of month and bank hols
May–Sept; (01582) 605464; £3) and an
interesting old **church**, this small village
has the oldest **windmill** in the country,
built in 1627; open pm 2nd Sun of
month and bank hols Jun–Sept; £1; NT.
You can hire canal boats for a day from
the Wharf (over the B489; phone
(01296) 661920) and there are pleasant
canal walks from there to the Red Lion
or White Lion at Marsworth.
QUAINTON SP7419
Bucks Railway Centre 🚂 (Quainton
Rd Station) One of the largest
collections of engines and rolling stock
we know of, with examples from all
over the world attractively displayed in
a restored country station; also vintage
steam-train rides, workshops,
miniature railway, and small museum.
Regular half-day steam driving courses
(not cheap at £160, but people come
away converted for life). Snacks, picnic

area, shop, disabled access; cl Mon (exc bank hols) and Tues, all Nov–Mar; (01296) 655720; *£5 (*£6 bank hols). Discount voucher not valid for Thomas the Tank Engine Events. Waddesdon is the closest good place for lunch.

Quainton Hill This prominent viewpoint is one of the main features on the 30-mile North Bucks Way, a long-distance footpath from Chequers Knap above Great Kimble to Wolverton in Milton Keynes; the Way also runs past Waddesdon.

Quainton Tower Mill 🖾 Particularly tall 19th-c mill on the edge of the village green; you can watch the continuing restoration work. Shop; open Sun 10–12.30; (01296) 655348; £1.

SHABBINGTON WOOD SP6210 (nr Oakley) Designated a Site of Special Scientific Interest because of its rich butterfly habitats; a special butterfly trail helps you to spot some of the 40-odd species here. The thatched Clifden Arms over in the attractive village of Worminghall has decent food and pretty gardens.

STEWKLEY SP8525
The **church** in this unusually long village has good examples of late Norman work; the Carpenters Arms has good value food.

STOKE MANDEVILLE SP8309
Bucks Goat Centre (Layby Farm, just off A4010) Goats galore as well as a pig, poultry, pony, donkeys, pets and a reptile house; you can feed the animals (they sell bags of cut-up vegetables in the shop). Many animals are under cover, so good for a rainy day. Also farm shop (with cheese and fudge made from goat's milk), and various others inc a specialist Korean furniture shop. Meals, snacks, disabled access; open daily; (01296) 612983; *£3. The Swan & Brewer on the green at Great Kimble has good value food.

Oak Farm Rare Breeds Park (off A41, E edge of Aylesbury) There's more to see at this friendly little working farm than you might think; you can get close to some of the animals (they sell bags of food), and there are walks and nature trails, play and picnic areas, and duck ponds. Snacks, shop, mostly disabled access; open daily (weather permitting) Easter–Oct;

(01296) 415709; £3. The Bell at Bierton has reliable food, esp fish.

STOKE POGES SU9783
Stoke Poges church The graveyard inspired Thomas Gray's elegy (he's buried here); the church itself has 17th-c stained heraldic glass in the 16th-c chapel.

STOWE SP6737
Stowe Landscape Gardens 🖾 Stunning gardens stretching over 350 acres, first laid out between 1713 and 1725. Capability Brown was head gardener for ten years, and the monuments and temples that adorn the grounds are by the likes of James Gibb, Sir John Vanbrugh and William Kent. There's a continuing programme of restoration, and in recent years they've planted thousands of new trees and shrubs. Several suitably grand events throughout the year, but at any time this is a spectacular place to visit, the scale of its artistry quite staggering. Meals, snacks, shop, disabled access (inc electric-powered cars at no extra charge); open Weds–Sun Mar–Dec; (01280) 822850; £4.80; NT. The house itself (a public school since 1923) is open pm daily (exc some wknds) during the Easter and summer hols (phone to check extra opening times (01280) 818000). You may feel it's outclassed by its surroundings, though it is very elegant from the outside; £3. The Wheatsheaf at Maids Moreton does good lunches, and the Queens Head at Chackmore is even handier.

TAPLOW SU9185
Cliveden Nearly 400 acres of lovely formal gardens, woodland and parkland overlooking the Thames. The magnificent house used to belong to the Astors and is now a luxury hotel (and extremely enjoyable as such), although non-resident visitors can see some of the rooms with their family portraits and elegant furnishings and décor. Meals, snacks, shop, disabled access; gardens open daily mid-Mar to Dec, house open only Thurs and Sun Apr–Oct, 3–5.30pm; (01628) 605069; *£6, house *£1 extra; NT. The village too is attractive.

TERRICK SP8408
Chiltern Brewery Small traditional brewery with a little museum, and

guided tours at noon every Sat (phone to book (01296) 613647; £3.50). Shop, disabled access; cl Sun, 25–26 Dec and 1 Jan; free.

THORNBOROUGH BRIDGE
SP7433
(A421) A 4½-mile walk starting and ending here, and well described in a leaflet from Bucks County Council, takes in a mill, the site of a medieval village, and the Buckingham Arm Canal. Leaflets from information centres, or from the County Hall, phone (01280) 823020.

WADDESDON SP7316
Waddesdon Manor One of the spectacular mansions built for Baron Ferdinand de Rothschild at the end of the 19th c. Plenty of rooms to see, each as lavish as the last, and filled with a dazzling array of furnishings, porcelain, portraits, and other objects; there's an unrivalled display of Sèvres china. The fabled wine cellars have huge vintage bottles, and a collection of labels designed or painted by some of the century's greatest artists. Quite splendid late Victorian formal gardens surround the house, and they still use the rococo-style aviary. A very satisfying place to visit, but it does get busy; they operate a timed ticket system for the house (can be bought in advance, but £3 booking charge), and recommend you get there by 2.30pm. Good meals, snacks, shops, disabled access; house open Weds–Sun and bank hol Mon 2 Apr–2 Oct, grounds 5 Mar–21 Dec; *£11 house and grounds, *£4 grounds only; NT.

WEEDON SP8018
This is a lovely little village, well worth walking around for the variety of its 17th- and 18th-c houses. The White Swan in nearby Whitchurch has decent food.

WEST WYCOMBE SU8394
The whole village was bought by the NT in 1929 when it was threatened with road-widening. It's still beleaguered by traffic, and you risk getting run over as you step back to admire the architecture along the village street – all the sites we mention are just off street. The busy George & Dragon is popular for lunch. A visit to the caves and village here can be easily combined with a walk

into the beechwoods just N; the pretty village of Bradenham makes a good objective for longer circular walks.
Hell Fire Caves 🖼 Great fun, these spooky old caves were extended in the 1750s by Sir Francis Dashwood to provide work for the unemployed. Legend has it that the Hell Fire Club he founded met in the tunnels for their drinking, whoring and sorcery. Once through the atmospheric Gothic entrance, the tunnels extend for about a third of a mile underground, and are filled with colourful models and tableaux. Underground café, shop; cl wkdys Nov–Feb; (01494) 533739; £3.75.

St Lawrence church On the site of an Iron Age fort, adapted by Dashwood, and crowned with a golden ball so big (it can seat six people) that it too served as a meeting-place for the Hell Fire Club. The view from the top of the tower is impressive.

West Wycombe Park 300 acres of beautifully laid-out parkland surround this splendid 18th-c Palladian house, parts of which are currently being restored. The magnificent rooms have a good collection of tapestries, furniture and paintings, and the Italianate painted ceilings are particularly notable. Disabled access to ground floor only, Braille guide; house and grounds open pm Sun–Thurs Jun–Aug, grounds also open pm Sun–Thurs Apr–May; (01494) 513569; £5, grounds only £2.60; NT.

WHITELEAF CROSS SP8204
A large ancient hill cross dug out of the chalk on the Chilterns escarpment, above which is a neolithic barrow. The Red Lion below is useful for lunch.

WING SP8922
Ascott Another Rothschild mansion, its black and white timbers and jutting gables quite a contrast to the luxuriant opulence of nearby Waddesdon. Once again it's crammed full of treasures, but it feels more like a home and less like a museum; indeed it's still lived in. Ming and K'ang Hsi porcelain, paintings by Hogarth, Rubens and Gainsborough, Dutch art by Hobbema, Cuyp and others, and French and Chippendale furniture. The 260-acre grounds have extensive gardens with rare trees and shrubs, and some intriguing astrological

topiary. House and grounds open pm Tues–Sun Apr and 6 Aug–13 Sept, gardens also open pm Weds and last Sun of month May–July, plus pm Weds 18 and 25 Sept, phone to check; (01296) 688242; £5.60 (£4 garden only), NT. **All Saints church** has a fine monument to Sir Robert Dormer (died 1552), a 10th-c apse, crypt and nave, and 12th-c font. The Stag over in yet another Rothschild village (Mentmore) has good food.

WINSLOW SP7627
Keach's Meeting House Fine example of a 17th-c dissenters' chapel; you'll need to get the key from Wilkinson's the estate agent on Market Sq, or from Mrs Longton (01296) 715746. The Bell is useful for lunch.

WOOBURN COMMON SU9189
Odds Farm Park Everything at this well organised place has been carefully designed with children in mind. They can go right up to the cattle, pigs, sheep and poultry, and join in daily activities such as bottle-feeding the lambs, hand-milking the goats and cows, or collecting the chickens' eggs. Good outdoor and indoor play areas (one especially for under-5s), and most pens and enclosures have signs written in a way that children can understand; many of the displays are instructive as well as fun. In winter most bits are under cover, though there are some days when not every activity will take place; they have regular special events, and in summer there are usually tractor and trailer rides. Meals, snacks (and picnic area), shop, disabled access; cl 25–26 Dec; (01628) 520188; £4.25 adults. The Falcon (Old Moor Lane) has decent food and an attractive garden.

Other attractive villages all with decent pubs, include Beachampton SP7737 (stream along main street), Bishopstone SP8010 (pleasant country walks), Bledlow SP7702 (great views; Norman church with early wall-paintings), Calverton SP7939, Cuddington SP7311, Denham TQ0386, Dinton SP7611, Great Missenden SP8901, Hedgerley SU9686, Hyde Heath SU9399, Ibstone SU7593, Little Hampden SP8503, Little Horwood SP7930, Marlow SU8586, Northend SU7392, Penn SU9193, Preston Bissett SP6529, Ravenstone SP8450, Speen SU8399, Stoke Hammond SP8829, Turville SU7690 (perhaps the most lovely valley of all here) and Worminghall SP6308.

Where to eat

EASINGTON SP6810 **Mole & Chicken** *Easington* (01844) 208387 Bustling country dining pub with very attractively furnished beamed bar, winter log fires, candles on tables and a relaxed atmosphere, particularly good imaginative food served by neatly dressed young staff, and a fine range of drinks; bdrms. £28|£9
GREAT HAMPDEN SP8401 **Hampden Arms** (01494) 488255 Comfortable two-room country pub by cricket green with civilised atmosphere, interesting reasonably priced food, real ales, quietly obliging service, and a tree-sheltered garden; good for nearby walks; partial disabled access. £20|£5.95
GREAT KINGSHILL SU8798 **Red Lion** *Missenden Rd* (01494) 711262 Little brick-and-flint cottage with simple furnishings, very fresh fish from Billingsgate served by friendly Spanish landlord and his staff, and good house wines; cl Sun pm, Mon, Christmas–New Year; disabled access. £20|£8
HADDENHAM SP7408 **Green Dragon** *8 Churchway* (01844) 291403 Civilised dining pub with imaginative food in its two attractively decorated high-ceilinged rooms, a French brasserie-type atmosphere, well chosen wines, real ales, a winter log fire, and seats out on the big sheltered terrace; cl Sun pm; disabled access. £27|£7.50
LITTLE HAMPDEN SP8503 **Rising Sun** (01494) 488393 Secluded upmarket dining pub surrounded by fine walks, with interesting food, a short but decent wine list, real ales, and an attractive terrace; bdrms; cl Sun pm, Mon, Tues pm; disabled access. £26.50|£4.95
MENTMORE SP9019 **Stag** *The Green* (01296) 668423 Pretty village pub with small civilised lounge bar, fresh flowers and open fire, well kept real ales in simple

public bar, and friendly service; nicely presented enjoyable food; seats on pleasant flower-filled terrace and in neat sloping garden. £19|£6

MOULSOE SP9141 **Carrington Arms** *Cranfield Rd* (01908) 218050 Well refurbished old brick house with comfortable traditional furnishings, meat and fish displayed in refrigerated glass case with friendly staff who guide you through what is on offer (it is then sold by weight and cooked on a sophisticated indoor barbecue), separate bar menu as well, an oyster bar, well kept real ales, and a good range of wines inc champagne by the glass; bdrms. £20|£5.50

PRESTON BISSETT SP6529 **White Hart** *Pound Lane* (01280) 847969 Friendly 18th-c thatched and timbered house with three cosy little rooms, traditional atmosphere and furnishings, tasty often interesting bar food inc lunchtime snacks, real ales and a dozen malt whiskies, and chatty helpful staff; best to book evenings; cl Mon and Tues am; children over 12. £21|£8

SKIRMETT SU7790 **Frog** (01491) 638996 Brightly modernised country inn with the atmosphere of a smart rural local, a mix of comfortable furnishings and open fire in neat beamed bar area, good popular interesting food, efficient service, no smoking restaurant, real ales and a fair range of wines, and lovely garden; bdrms; cl Sun pm from Nov–Easter Sun; disabled access. £25.50/2-course lunch £13.95

WADDESDON SP7416 **Five Arrows** *High Street* (01296) 651727 Rather grand small hotel – part of the Rothschild estate – with an informally pubby bar made up of several open-plan rooms, a relaxed but civilised atmosphere, Rothschild family portraits and old estate-worker photographs on the walls, sturdy furnishings on parquet flooring, newspapers and magazines, delicious imaginative food, a no smoking country house-style restaurant, a formidable wine list, well kept real ales, efficient service, and sheltered back garden; good bdrms; cl 25 Dec pm, 26 Dec. £26|£7.50

WEST WYCOMBE SU8394 **George & Dragon** *High St* (01494) 464414 Striking partly Tudor inn with a cheerful bustling atmosphere in rambling main bar, big log fire, popular food inc very good home-made pies, and big peaceful garden; bdrms (not Christmas, New Year or Easter). £21|£7

WOBURN SANDS SP9235 **Spooners** *61 High St* (01908) 584385 Smart, pretty restaurant with good value, highly enjoyable French and English cooking, and a welcoming atmosphere; good value snacks downstairs; cl Sun, Mon, 1 wk Aug, 1 wk Christmas; disabled access. £30 dinner|£8.95

Special thanks to Jenny and Michael Back

CAMBRIDGESHIRE

A good mix of attractions for all ages and most tastes, plus the city of Cambridge – great for a short visit, with plenty of interest and free-of-charge world-class museums

This is a good county for pottering around picturesque villages and towns – some with fine churches; Barrington, Fulbourn, Ickleton and Hemingford Grey are among the best. The quiet city of Ely with its graceful cathedral and unusual stained-glass museum is well worth visiting too. The countryside, though, is a bit monotonous – especially the north's flat silt fens and vast level fields. But there are those who love the misty bleakness in autumn, and this area has a lot to offer bird-watchers (especially at Wicken Fen, parts of Grafham Water, and Ramsey Heights). As part of an ambitious multi-million pound scheme to attract rare birds and wildlife by re-creating wetlands last seen in Roman times, around 2,000 acres of farmland and quarry works near Needingworth are to be flooded over the next few years. To the west, the land is drier and more rolling, with stone-built villages more reminiscent of Leicestershire.

Cambridge, one of the most attractive university cities in the world, is an extremely rewarding place to visit, with a cluster of interesting museums to browse around, beautiful colleges, gardens and churches to explore (and concerts to listen to), and good pubs too. The best time to go is during the university terms; in summer (when it is host to foreign-language students) its popularity with coach tours means that particular parts can get very crowded. A short bus ride away from the city, the Imperial War Museum Duxford will enthral anyone interested in aviation, and there's quite a bit for children there too.

Shepreth Wildlife Park is the year's top family attraction for the county, while Hamerton Zoo Park (good value, and handy when it's wet) and friendly Linton Zoo are also good places to take children; there's enough for families at stately Wimpole Hall to fill most of the day. You can go on picturesque trips to or from Peterborough on the Nene Valley Railway. Other attractions include the well organised prehistoric site at Flag Fen, and there are fine houses at Elton and Lode; at Waterbeach, you'll find a medieval abbey and a farming museum.

Where to stay

BASSINGBOURN TL3145 **Finch Farmhouse** *28 Fen Road, Bassingbourn, Royston, Hertfordshire SG8 5PQ (01763) 242019* **£45**; 3 light, pretty rms with views of river. Originally an alehouse for Irish farm workers, this Victorian house has an open fire in the sitting room, delicious imaginative food in the boldly decorated dining room (lunches are available on request), and friendly owners; children over 5
CAMBRIDGE TL4459 **Arundel House** *Chesterton Rd, Cambridge CB4 3AN (01223) 367701* **£103.90**; 105 comfortable rms, some overlooking the river. Carefully preserved terrace of fine early Victorian houses overlooking the River

Cam and parkland; comfortable, attractive bar with two fires, elegant restaurant, large and airy plant-filled conservatory, good imaginative food, and seats in the pleasant garden

CAMBRIDGE TL4359 **Cambridge Lodge** *139 Huntingdon Rd, Cambridge CB3 0DQ (01223) 352833* **£80**; 15 rms, 12 with own bthrm. Mock-Tudor house on the outskirts, with open fire in relaxed and comfortable lounge, friendly service, and good freshly prepared food in the popular oak-beamed restaurant; cl 27–30 Dec

DUXFORD TL4845 **Duxford Lodge** *Ickleton Rd, Duxford, Cambridge CB2 4RU (01223) 836444* **£115***; 15 good-sized, warm rms, 2 with four-posters. Carefully run late Victorian hotel in an acre of neatly kept landscaped gardens, with a welcoming, relaxed atmosphere, individually chosen modern paintings and prints, a restful little lounge, decent wines, enjoyable modern cooking in the airy newly refurbished no smoking restaurant, and good breakfasts; cl 24 Dec–1 Jan; dogs welcome in bedrooms

ELY TL5480 **Lamb** *2 Lynn Rd, Ely, Cambridgeshire CB7 4EJ (01353) 663574* **£95***; 32 comfortable rms. Pleasant, neatly kept old coaching inn near the cathedral, with two smart bars, enjoyable food in an attractive restaurant, very friendly staff, and good car parking; dogs welcome in bedrooms

HUNTINGDON TL2471 **Old Bridge** *1 High St, Huntingdon, Cambridgeshire PE18 6TQ (01480) 452681* **£145***, plus wknd breaks; 24 excellent rms with CD stereos and power showers. Creeper-covered Georgian hotel with pretty lounge, log fire in panelled bar, imaginative British cooking and extensive wine list in the no smoking restaurant and less formal lunchtime room (nice murals), and quick courteous service; riverside gardens; partial disabled access; dogs welcome in bedrooms

NEEDINGWORTH TL3571 **Pike & Eel** *Overcote Lane, Needingworth, St Ives, Huntingdon, Cambridgeshire PE17 3TW (01480) 463336* **£70**, plus wknd breaks; 9 rms. 17th-c inn in very peaceful riverside spot with spacious lawns and grounds by marina, roomy plush bar, big open fire and easy chairs in smaller room, glass-walled restaurant, carvery, real ale, good breakfasts, and friendly staff; disabled access

SIX MILE BOTTOM TL5857 **Swynford Paddocks** *Six Mile Bottom, Newmarket, Cambridgeshire CB8 0UE (01638) 570234* **£110**; 15 individually furnished rms with good bthrms. Gabled country house in neat grounds overlooking stud paddocks; carefully furnished, newly refurbished rooms with fresh flowers and log fires, a new conservatory Garden Room, a relaxed atmosphere, good food, and friendly service; tennis, putting, and croquet; disabled access; dogs welcome in bedrooms

STILTON TL1689 **Bell** *7 High St, Stilton, Peterborough, Cambridgeshire PE7 3RA (01733) 241066* **£89.50***; 19 rms. Elegant, carefully restored coaching inn with attractive rambling bars, big log fire, generous helpings of good food using the famous cheese (which was first sold from here), and seats in the sheltered cobbled and flagstoned courtyard; cl 25 Dec

WANSFORD TL0799 **Haycock** *London Rd, Wansford, Peterborough, Cambridgeshire PE8 6JA (01780) 782223* **£110**, plus special breaks; 50 attractively decorated rms. Old-fashioned golden stone inn with relaxed, comfortable, carefully furnished lounges and pubby bar; pretty lunchtime café, smart restaurant with good food, excellent wines and efficient friendly service; garden with boules, fishing and cricket; disabled access. The little village it dominates is attractive, with a fine bridge over the Nene, and a good antiques shop; dogs welcome in bedrooms

---

Please let us know what you think of places in the *Guide*. Use the report forms at the back of the book, write us a letter or log on to www.goodguides.com

To see and do

Cambridgeshire Family Attraction of the Year

SHEPRETH TL3948 **Shepreth Wildlife Park** (off A10, next to Shepreth railway station) Attractively laid out around three lakes, this genuine little animal centre started out as a wildlife sanctuary, and rescued animals and birds are still a major part of the mix. It's developed a lot since those early days, but not so much that it's lost its charm or real commitment to the residents: it's just that these days you're as likely to find mountain lions and tigers as you are deer or squirrels. Recent arrivals include a couple of otters, happily settled in their purpose-built enclosure, while other animals include an unusual albino wallaby, wolves, and plenty of prairie dogs, who've long since learned how to swim across from their island home and now pop up just about everywhere. Particular favourites are the big cat house, the tropical house, and the fantastic collection of spiders, ants and all sorts of creepy-crawlies so entertainingly presented in Bug City; there are over 2,000 creatures in here alone, with everything from a hard-working colony of leaf-cutter ants to a huge madagascar spitting cockroach. This section — and its aquatic-themed neighbour Waterworld – have a small extra charge. Younger visitors can pet rabbits and feed horses and koi carp (they sell bags of feed), and there are several well organised play areas, including one specially for toddlers with a sandpit, and an adventure fort for older children. They may do pony rides, and in August have an annual fun day with extra events and activities. Like most wildlife centres, it's best on a dry day, though there's plenty under cover so don't rule it out if it's raining; there are several picnic areas, so a visit can easily stretch towards a half day. If you're driving, the brown tourist signs for the park use its old name, Willersmill Wildlife Park, and the entrance isn't that well signed so keep an eye out. No dogs (except guide dogs). Meals and snacks (there's a rather jolly elevated treetop café), shop, disabled access; cl 25 Dec; (01763) 262226; £4.95, children over 2 £3.75. Bug City and Underwater World are an extra £1.95 (£1.25 children).

BARNACK TF0704
Barnack has interesting dotted-about clusters of stone-built houses, a windmill, a part-Saxon church, and a fine pub (the Millstone).

BARRINGTON TL3949
Superb village green surrounded by pretty timbered houses, an interesting church and a pleasant food pub, the Royal Oak; the nearby village of Foxton is especially interesting if you know the book *The Common Stream* by Rowland Parker (an intricate account of the village through the ages).

BOURN TL3255
Wysing Arts (Fox Rd) Lively arts centre in 11 acres of farmland, with contemporary art exhibitions and a continuous programme of events and workshops (see website www.wysing.demon.co.uk). Snacks, disabled access; cl Sun; (01954) 718881;

free, charges for workshops. The Duke of Wellington is a decent food pub.

BURWELL TL5866
Burwell church This handsome and airy building has a fine oak roof. The village also has a restored windmill. Nearby Swaffham Prior is another attractive village, and the Red Lion there does decent fresh food

CAMBRIDGE TL4458
Quieter than Oxford (which the colleges here were founded to escape), the centre is dominated by ancient and graceful university buildings, and you get a real sense of centuries of study. It still has the character of a small, old-fashioned market town; Cambridge's hi-tech light industry is kept firmly on the outskirts. Between the colleges and university buildings are numerous less imposing but attractive old buildings, often grouped together quite

picturesquely. The architecture has a striking diversity (continuous development of the colleges means that most have much-loved or maligned modern blocks), though isn't always shown off at its best, thanks to layers of muck and grime that rather spoil some of the libraries and faculty buildings. Happily, one of the most delightful parts of town, **The Backs**, where the river snakes through the colleges, always looks charming, with its delightful lawns, trees, college gardens, punts gliding past the weeping willows and grazing cattle opposite King's. Don't try to drive around town; there isn't really any parking, and apart from the pedestrianised centre there's a frustrating tangle of congested one-way streets. Head for one of the big out-of-town car parks and use the excellent park and ride system. If you don't plan to take a car at all, it's worth noting that the railway station is far from central, although there is a frequent bus service into the historic centre. For a first-time visit, the Tour Bus (about an hour) is a good introduction. Walking tours set off from the Tourist Information Centre (Wheeler St) four times a day in summer (£7.25 inc entrance to King's Chapel, last tour £6.25 inc entrance to St John's – best to book in advance; (01223) 457574). Cyclists will enjoy the towpaths here; nettle-free, and safe if you have children with you. Quite a few shops are that bit different and worth popping in to. In term-time, there are countless events; any college notice-board will show what's on. West Road concert hall has outstanding acoustics, while a concert in one of the smaller college chapels can be a charmingly intimate experience.

Cambridge colleges The colleges look private, but you can usually wander into the courtyards (access limited at exam time, and expect to be charged by many during the summer). Be warned though, college porters will get extremely agitated if you even look at the grass let alone accidentally step on it. Several of the dining halls and chapels are worth seeking out. The largest, finest and richest college is Trinity, where the imposing Great Court is usually open to the public, and

the Wren Library (open wkdys 12–2pm) in Neville's Court is definitely worth a visit. King's is probably the best known, with its magnificent chapel, and is pleasant to walk through. Gonville & Caius (pronounced 'keys') is small and slightly snooty, but very pretty. Queen's has a half-timbered courtyard and an eye-catchingly gaudy painted hall, as well as the famous Mathematical Bridge. Peterhouse is the oldest, founded in 1284; the buildings carry their years very gracefully, although these days its deer park is devoid of deer. Opposite, Pembroke's chapel is one of Wren's first buildings. St John's has the very photographed Bridge of Sighs. Jesus, a bit off the main beat, is huge and grandly impressive, and Emmanuel has notable gardens. Clare and Trinity Hall are smaller yet charming colleges, next to each other by The Backs.

King's College Chapel 🖾 The annual Festival of Nine Lessons and Carols has made the interior and something of the atmosphere familiar to most visitors, but you're still not fully prepared for the grandeur and scale of the fan-vaulted ceiling, or the miraculously preserved 16th-c stained glass. The overall effect is marred slightly by the unique dark oak screen added by Henry VIII, but the chapel's other famous feature – Rubens's *Adoration of the Magi* – is quite breathtaking. In term-time try to attend choral evensong (5.30pm Mon–Sat, Sun 10.30am and 3.30pm). Shop, disabled access; cl most of Sun during term-time, Advent, Easter Sun and 24 Dec–3 Jan – phone to check other times; (01223) 331212; £3.50.

Cambridge churches Of the many churches here, it's worth noting **St Bene't's**, one of the city's oldest, the popular **Holy Sepulchre** or Round Church (which has brass-rubbing), and **Great St Mary's** with its fine roof and good city views from the tower.

Fitzwilliam Museum (Trumpington St) This is a wonderful place, a grand and impressive building, crammed with more dazzling treasures than you could hope to examine in one visit. Downstairs are Greek, Egyptian, and Roman antiquities, while upstairs you'll

find furniture, sculpture and paintings by Titian, Canaletto and French Impressionists. Until they finish redeveloping the courtyard in 2004, only the Founder's Building will be open, so displays are limited to the highlights of collections, and there won't be any temporary exhibitions; no disabled access till then either. Shop opposite museum; cl Mon (exc bank hols) and am Sun, plus 23 Dec–1 Jan, Good Fri; (01223) 332900; free.

Cambridge & County Folk Museum (2–3 Castle St) Useful exploration of local life in a handsome 16th-c former inn near the river – a touch-screen database includes contemporary residents' diaries and 'virtual' city tours. Shop, disabled access to ground floor; cl Sun plus Mon Oct–Mar, 23 Dec–2 Jan and Good Fri; (01223) 355159; *£2.50.

Other Cambridge museums Most of the town's other museums have a rather academic bent, but are no less rewarding for that: the **Sedgwick Museum** (Downing St) is the university geology museum, with an outstanding collection of fossils, and rocks from Darwin's journey in HMS *Beagle*. The curator once proved that iguanadons were put together differently from how scientists had previously thought: the bones of his museum's 6-metre (20-ft) specimen have not been rearranged for historical reasons although theoretically, he claims, it is currently in agony. Shop, limited disabled access; cl 1–2pm, Sat pm, all Sun, Christmas–New Year, Easter; free. Down the same street is the **Museum of Archaeology & Anthropology**, home to a 15-metre (50-ft) totem pole (open Tues–Fri, pm-Sat, cl Christmas, Easter; free) and a **Museum of Zoology**, where a 21-metre (70-ft) whale skeleton hangs above the entrance inside (cl wknds and 1–2pm; free). The **Museum of Classical Archaeology** on Sidgwick Ave has one of the few surviving collections of casts of Greek and Roman sculpture (cl wknds; free), while the various scientific instruments and apparatus at the **Whipple Museum of Science** (Free School Lane) quickly make you thankful we need no longer rely on sundials and abacuses (open wkdys pm though best to check outside term; (01223) 330906; free). The **Scott Polar Research Institute** (Lensfield Rd) houses fascinating exhibits from the fateful polar expedition inc diaries, letters and clothing, also Inuit carving. Shop, disabled access; open pm Mon–Fri (exc bank hols), but phone to check; (01223) 336540; free. The exhibition centre at the towering and austere **University Library** (West Rd) has occasional displays of rare and ancient manuscripts; cl Sat pm and all Sun; free.

University Botanic Garden (Cory Lodge, Bateman St) Opened in 1846, and now covering 40 acres, with some marvellous mature trees, a rock garden which has alpine plants from the mountains of every continent, scented garden, water and winter gardens, and many rare plants inc nine National Collections. Rarely crowded, and very pleasant to stroll through. Tearoom (wknds only in winter), summer shop, disabled access; cl 25 Dec–1 Jan, (01223) 336265; *£2.50.

Kettle's Yard (Castle St) Lively arts centre with temporary exhibitions in the gallery and permanent displays in the avant-garde yet surprisingly welcoming house (you may sit in any of the chairs – some of which are more than 300 years old), taking in 20th-c paintings and sculptures (interesting St Ives connections), lovely 18th-c furniture and oriental carpets, and collections of shells and stones. In order to preserve the exact lay-out from when the gallery's founder Jim Ede lived here, the fresh lemon in the downstairs sitting-room has to be changed every two days. Lots of activities and workshops, several designed especially for the blind or hard of hearing. Devotees say the sunlight on winter afternoons illuminates the exhibits to extraordinary effect. Shop, disabled access (limited in house); cl am, all Mon (exc bank hol Mon), and bank hols; (01233) 352124; free.

Punting The only way to travel, though if your skills in this department were picked up in Oxford you'll find they do things a little back to front here. You can punt right along The Backs, and

even down to Grantchester, a pleasant little village still much as described in Rupert Brooke's poem of the same name, with the civilised Orchard Tea Gardens (lovely in summer – and does other drinks too, inc champagne) and three pubs. Hire punts from Scudamores on Mill Lane (01223) 359750 or other stations along the water; prices are generally around £12 an hour per punt (£8 per person if you require a chauffeur). Bumps races (several rowing eights start off in a line and have to catch up with the one in front) take place on the river in Feb, Jun and July.

Towpath walks From Magdalene Bridge right in Cambridge itself there's a pleasant walk by the towpath out into the meadows – tranquil, with only punts as far as the lock. Beyond that, you could walk as far as Ely, with oarsmen setting an altogether more vigorous tone – though the Ancient Shepherds at Fen Ditton might be a gentler target. Another pleasant stroll out from Cambridge – in the opposite direction – is the walk along the Cam to Grantchester.

Shopping There are lots of **secondhand bookshops** worth a look. Heffers children's bookshop is particularly good, and the general bookshops are as fine as you'd expect in this university town. Every Sat there's a **craft fair** on All Saints Gardens (opposite St John's College), and **Cambridge Contemporary Art** (Trinity St) has changing exhibitions of british contemporary artwork.

Snacks in Cambridge Many attractive snack places include Indigo Coffee House (St Edward's Passage – off King's Parade), Roof Garden (top floor of Arts Theatre – side entrance in St Edward's Passage), the tiny Little Tea Room (All Saints Green), Rainbow Café is good for vegetarian food (King's Parade), Dojo's – popular Chinese restaurant (off Mill Lane) and Hobbs Pavilion does fantastic pancakes. Decent **riverside pubs** include the Anchor (Silver St Bridge), Boathouse (Chesterton Rd), Fort St George (Midsummer Common) and Granta (Newnham Terrace). The best pubs away from the river are the smoke-free

Cambridge Blue (Gwydir St) and atmospheric Eagle (Bene't St).

CASTOR TL1298
Pleasantly relaxed ancient village with a fine **church** and several handsome thatched stone-built houses. The Fratelli is an attractive italian restaurant.

COTON TL4059
Cambridge American Cemetery
A beautiful and haunting tribute to the American servicemen and women who lost their lives in World War II, this covers 30 acres, framed by woodland to the west and south. The Portland stone memorial chapel has some intriguing features inc a map of air assaults over the Atlantic and stained-glass windows depicting the seals of the States arranged from left to right in the order that they entered the Union. Disabled access; cl 25 Dec and 1 Jan; (01954) 210350; free.

CROYDON TL3149
Croydon church Quietly charming, a proper country church with a timeless feel. The Queen Adelaide is a roomy and popular dining pub.

DEVIL'S DITCH TL5765
This miles-long ancient embankment lets you fuel a walk with speculations on whether it was built to fight off the Romans, or some centuries later to protect the riches of East Anglia from Midlands warlords. It's not much of a topographical feature, and is crossed by one or two very busy roads. A good start or finish might be the Dykes End pub in Reach, at its N end, with a wide range of food.

DUXFORD TL4546
Imperial War Museum Duxford (just off M11, junction 10) Unmissable for anyone interested in aviation, this big former airfield is a good deal more rewarding for children than you might expect. It's also home to Europe's best collection of military and civil aircraft, nearly 200 in all, from flimsy-looking bi-planes through Gulf War jets to current state-of-the-art front-line fighters. Children can clamber into the cockpits of some of them, pick up helmets and gunpacks, and there's an adventure playground. They also have a huge collection of tanks and military vehicles, and a naval collection inc midget submarines and helicopters. There are

several exhibitions with new ones all the time; a display on the Falklands War has recently been added, and they've begun a four-year project to re-house their British aircraft. The American Air Museum, a collection of US combat aircraft, is now in a remarkable building by Norman Foster. The site covers about a mile (a bus can take you between the different bits), and the preserved hangars, control tower and operations rooms have something of the atmosphere they must have had when this was a working base. Each year they have several dramatic air shows (extra charge), and some planes still fly on other days. A free bus runs every hour from and to Cambridge Station; it takes about 20 minutes. Meals and snacks (and plenty of space for picnics), shop, good disabled access; cl 24–26 Dec; (01223) 835000; *£8, children free. The Green Man close by at Thriplow is an interesting place for lunch.

ELTON TL0892
Elton Hall ⊞ From the back a splendid 'gothick' fantasy, this is a fascinating lived-in house dating back to Tudor times, with lovely furnishings, porcelain and paintings, inc works by 15th-c Old Masters, Gainsborough and Constable. The library has a Prayer Book that belonged to Henry VIII (his writing is inside), and the gardens are especially pleasant in summer when the roses are in bloom. Shop, adjacent garden centre and tearoom, disabled access to garden only; open pm first bank hol in May and Aug bank hol, pm Weds in Jun, pm Weds–Thurs and Sun July–Aug (phone to check); (01832) 280468; £5, £3 garden. The Black Horse nearby has good interesting food, and the attractive stone-built village has a lovely Saxon church.

ELY TL5480
Busy little market town with good shops and some lovely old buildings; it well repays a leisurely stroll. A Passport to Ely ticket allows you to visit the cathedral, Oliver Cromwell's House, Ely Museum and the Stained Glass Museum for £9. The Prince Albert (Silver St, nr cathedral) has a nice garden, and the Lamb (Brook St) is useful for lunch, too.

Ely Cathedral One of England's most striking, its distinctive towers dominating the skyline for miles; especially good views coming in on the Soham rd. Complete by the late 12th c, it was restored in a surprisingly sympathetic manner mainly in the mid-19th c. The façade, covered in blind arcading, is fantastic, but most remarkable perhaps is the Octagonal Tower, over 400 tons suspended in space without any visible means of support; it looks especially impressive from inside. The Lady Chapel has the widest medieval vault in the country, and the walls are carved with hundreds of tiny statues which were all brutally beheaded in the Reformation – look out for the controversial new life-sized statue of the Virgin Mary (some say it looks like the TV presenter Charlie Dimmock in a wet T-shirt). The splendid Norman nave seems even longer than it really is because it's so narrow. Also not to be missed are a couple of elaborately sculpted medieval doors. It's worth trying to catch the evensong here, 5.30pm daily exc Weds (Sun at 3.45pm). Meals, snacks, shop, disabled access; (01353) 667735; £4.

Ely Museum (Old Gaol, Market St) Displays inc fossils, Roman remains, original gaol cells and brewing in Ely. Shop; disabled access; usually cl two wks over Christmas and New Year; (01353) 666655; £2.

Oliver Cromwell's House (St Mary's St) Next to the unexpectedly grand Church of St Mary, this fine old house was the home of Oliver Cromwell and his family from 1636 until shortly before he became Lord Protector. Period furnished rooms, useful videos (one on the draining of the Fens), and information centre in the downstairs front room. Shop; usually cl 25–26 Dec, 1 Jan, best to check; (01353) 662062; £3.50.

Stained Glass Museum Housed in the cathedral's south triforium, this preserves fine medieval and modern stained glass, much of it rescued from redundant buildings and churches. Good displays on how the windows are made, and a bonus is the unusual view over the cathedral. Meals, snacks, shop; cl Sun am, 25, 26 Dec and Good Fri;

(01353) 660347; *£3.50.

FENGATE TL2199
Flag Fen Bronze Age Excavation
📷 (Fengate, 2m E of Peterborough) Fascinating and well organised prehistoric site. Remains of a wooden platform which crossed a shallow lake have been unearthed; from it Bronze Age settlers appear to have thrown all sorts of deliberately broken bronze objects as part of a ritual – some of the best finds (inc England's oldest wheel) are in the very good adjacent museum, and they've recently opened a new environmentally friendly Heritage Centre. In summer you should be able to watch archaeologists painstakingly uncovering more secrets, while reconstructed Bronze and Iron Age roundhouses help put the discoveries in context; peaceful lakeside walk and primitive breeds of sheep and pigs. Snacks, new shop, mostly disabled access; cl 24 Dec–2 Jan; (01733) 313414; £4, EH.

FULBOURN TL5155
This is an attractive largely thatched village, with a windmill on the Cambridge rd, a good farm shop with pick-your-own fruit, and a pretty church; the picturesque Bakers Arms is a popular lunch spot. A path takes you eastwards to the wooded line of the Fleam Dyke, a miles-long Dark Ages defence earthwork.

GODMANCHESTER TL2668
Wood Green Animal Shelter
(Kings Bush Farm) This well maintained rescue centre has wildlife and unwanted pets, water garden, oriental cattery, picnic site and playground; events most wknds. Meals, snacks, shop, disabled access; cl 25–26 Dec (01480) 830014; free (donations welcome). In Godmanchester itself there are a few interesting buildings, the Exhibition has good food, and you can stroll along the river to the lock.

GOG MAGOG HILLS TL4953
Not exactly a towering range, these are worth a passing visit; among tall trees you can trace the main rampart and ditch of **Wandlebury Iron Age fort**, and there are good views of the city's distant towers and spires.

GRAFHAM WATER TL1667
A regular haunt for some readers, this

has fishing, sailing, cycle hire, and a nature reserve with bird-watching hides and trails (you'll see a lot more birds in winter – don't forget the binoculars); exhibition centre. There's an attractive waterside path along the northern shore, and can take wheelchairs the whole way round. Snacks; (01480) 812154; free, £2 car parking charge. The Lion over in Buckden, an appealing coaching inn, has enjoyable food.

HAMERTON TL1481

Hamerton Zoo Park A firm favourite with some readers, and good value too, this dedicated and expanding centre has a splendidly varied collection of rare and endangered species from all over the world. There are over a 100 different species in over 15 acres of pretty countryside, from playful marmosets, gibbons, wolves and boa constrictors (and you can now see their Bengal tigers – one of them is white) to smaller animals such as tortoises and porcupines; they also have plenty of birds, and you can feed and stroke some of the animals. Talks from the keepers during feeding times at wknds and school holidays. Nearly a mile of covered walkways mean you can get between most of the animal houses without getting wet. Tearoom (cl in winter), small shop, disabled access; cl 25 Dec; (01832) 293362; £5.50. Their website, www.hamertonzoopark.com, usually has money-saving offers.

HEMINGFORD GREY TL2970

Charming village with a peaceful view of the church over the willow-bordered river (the odd church tower is the result of its spire being lopped off by an 18th-c storm); one stone house among the thatched brick ones is Norman and said to be England's oldest. The Cock has good value food, and nearby Hemingford Abbots is also pretty.

HUNTINGDON TL2371

After considerable recent growth the old centre now feels a bit sidetracked, but has one or two fine buildings such as the George, a particularly handsome Georgian coaching inn. The Old Bridge is a good civilised place for lunch.

Cromwell Museum (Grammar School Walk) Two of Huntingdon's MPs can claim to have run the country

for a while, and this commemorates the first. The restored Norman building is where the future Lord Protector went to school (as did Pepys), and many of his possessions are on display. Shop; cl 1–2pm all year, Mon, bank hols (exc Good Fri), plus am in winter (exc Sat), phone to check; (01480) 375830; free.

Hinchingbrooke Country Park (off B1514 W) Good for a walk, a run-about or picnic; guided walks or events most wknds. Snacks (wknds and school hols), disabled access; (01480) 451568; free.

Hinchingbrooke House (B1514 W) Now a school, this is where some reckon Cromwell and Charles I met as children. Snacks, disabled access; usually open pm Sun May bank hol–Aug bank hol; (01480) 375678; *£3. The Exhibition in Godmanchester is the best nearby place for lunch.

ICKLETON TL4944

This attractive village has a fine church, with Roman columns as bases for its arches, and interestingly carved pews. The churchyard is lovely, and around the church and small green are several beautiful old houses – often a good deal older than their Georgian refacing suggests. The John Barleycorn in Duxford is a good food pub.

ISLEHAM TL6474

Isleham church Attractive from the outside, but its best feature is its wonderful roof.

LEVERINGTON TF4411

Leverington church The tower and its spire are noteworthy, as is the very unusual two-storey 14th-c porch. The Woodmans Cottage over at Gorefield has decent food.

LINTON TL5648

Chilford Hall Vineyard (towards Balsham) A friendly 18-acre winery with interesting old buildings and tours at 11.30am, 2.30pm and 4pm. Meals, snacks, shop, disabled access; cl 23 Dec–Feb; (01223) 895625; £4.50 (inc tastings).

Linton Zoological Gardens (B1052, just off A604) This friendly family-run zoo has a firm emphasis on conservation and breeding. Residents include giant tortoises, snow leopards, a couple of Grevy's zebras, tigers, marabou storks and lemurs, all housed in enclosures as close to their natural habitats as possible. Family quiz trails all year round, talks, play area for smaller children, bouncy castle (weather permitting), picnic areas around the prettily landscaped grounds (some under cover). Snacks, shop, disabled access; cl 25–26 Dec; (01223) 891308; *£6. The PearTree at Hildersham does decent lunches.

LITTLE GIDDING TL1281
Little Gidding church Archetypal small-village country church, well worth a look inside; if it's closed, ask at the farmhouse.

LODE TL5362
Anglesey Abbey, Gardens and Lode Hill 🅰 All that remains of the original priory is a medieval undercroft, but the handsome 17th-c house has an engaging collection of clocks and eclectic range of furniture and paintings; it's definitely worth pausing at Constable's view of the Thames and the landscapes by Claude. The bookshelves in the library are made from Rennie's Waterloo Bridge. The lovely gardens were laid out from 1926 by the first Lord Fairhaven; a restored **watermill** still produces flour. Varied events and activities, inc highly regarded open-air theatre and jazz. Meals, snacks, shop, some disabled access; house open pm Weds–Sun and bank hols Apr–Oct, daily Jul–Aug (when it's open till 8 on Thurs), grounds open daily. Meals, shop and plant centre; (01223) 811200; *£6.40, *£4 grounds only (discount voucher not available on bank hols or special events days); NT. The Quy Mill at Stow cum Quy does enjoyable lunches.

MARCH TL4195
Pleasant country town, market day Weds and Sat; a good base for exploring the Fens. **St Wendreda's church** with its wonderful angel roof was described by Betjeman as being 'worth cycling 40 miles in a headwind to see'. The Acre (Acre Rd) has good home cooking.

PETERBOROUGH TL1998
Has preserved much of its long history and fine old buildings, though it expanded hugely in the mid-1970s and is now a thriving industrial town (with a good pedestrianised shopping centre). Handily, a network of cycleways,

footpaths and bridleways link tourist attractions and nature reserves with residential areas. Charters (by Town Bridge) is an enjoyable floating pub/restaurant in a converted barge.
City Museum and Art Gallery (Priestgate) Among other interesting exhibits are some unusual models made from fishbones by Napoleonic prisoners of war. Shop, disabled access; cl Mon and am Sun, plus am in term-time; (01733) 343329; free, charge when special exhibits shown.
Ferry Meadows Country Park (off A605 W of Peterborough) Useful for children to let off steam; 500 acres with play areas, two big lakes with water sports, fishing and boat trips, nature reserve, pony rides, miniature railway, and two golf courses and pitch and putt nearby. Visitor centre; snacks, shop, disabled access; (01733) 234443; free, parking charge wknds and bank hols Apr–Oct, £2.50. The Cuckoo at Alwalton out this way is a reliable dining pub.
Longthorpe Tower (Thorpe Rd, W of centre) 13th/14th-c fortified house with rare wall paintings (open pm wknds and bank hols Apr–Oct; £1.70, best to phone; EH.
Peterborough Cathedral One of the most dramatic in the country, its extraordinary west front a medieval masterpiece, with a trio of huge arches. Despite the damage inflicted by Cromwell, the richly Romanesque interior has preserved its original fabric to a remarkable degree; especially worth a look are the elaborately vaulted retro-choir and the fine early 13th-c painted wooden nave ceiling; an exhibition in the north aisle tells more about its history. Till Easter 2003 there may be restricted access to some parts, while smoke damage from a fire in 2001 is made good. Meals, snacks, shop, some disabled access; cl 25–26 Dec and am Sun (except for services); (01733) 345064; donations.
Railworld 🅰 (Oundle Rd) Friendly railway and environment exhibition centre with museum; wknd and bank hol snacks, shop, disabled access; cl wknds Nov–Feb, and 25 Dec–1 Jan; (01733) 344240; £3.50.
St Margaret's church (Fletton) On

the southern edge of Peterborough, this has some exceptionally fine little Anglo-Saxon sculptures.

PRICKWILLOW TL5982

Drainage Engine Museum 🏛 The story of water, pumping and fen drainage in the area since the last Ice Age, especially interesting when the engines are running; phone for dates. Snacks, small shop, disabled access; open Fri–Tues May–Sept, wknds and bank hols March–Apr and Oct; (01353) 688360; £2 (£3 when engines running).

PURLS BRIDGE TL4787

Recommended for diehard bird-watchers; there's an RSPB reserve off the B1093 with several hides (one with disabled access) and big mugs of coffee.

RAMSEY TL2984

Abbey Gatehouse The ruins of an ornate Gothic gatehouse with buttresses and friezes, along with the 13th-c Lady Chapel (all that's left of the abbey itself). Cl Nov–Mar; free. Some of the stone from the abbey is thought to have made up the nearby local history **museum** (open pm Thurs and Sun, Apr–Sept, other times by appointment; (01487) 815715; *£2). The Cross Keys at Upwood (where there's a windmill) has good value food.

RAMSEY HEIGHTS TL2384

Wood Walton Fen (off B1040 W of Ramsey) Quiet and peaceful nature reserve, developed around the overgrown remains of old brick pits and kilns; nature trails lead through several meadows and along a dyke, and you may spy some of the many small woodland birds from a hide overlooking a marshy area, with boardwalks over ponds for a closer look; parking in meadow nearest the lane.

RIVER OUSE TL2772

The stretch between St Ives and Hemingford Grey is a popular wknd stamping-ground, with **Houghton Mill** as a charming set piece – a lovely building in a pretty setting.

SHELFORDS, THE TL4552

The interlinked villages of Great and Little Shelford will reward a slow stroll for those with an eye for architectural detail, and even a quick drive through will show up several delightful timbered houses. The convivial Navigator (Little

Shelford) has good authentic thai food.

SHEPRETH TL3847

Docwra's Manor Gardens Tranquil gardens, at their best Apr–Jun but always with a variety of unusual plants. The best bit is perhaps the lovely intimate walled garden. Disabled access (although gravel paths may be hard work); open Weds and Fri, plus pm first Sun of month Apr–Oct; (01763) 261557; *£3. The Plough does generous pub lunches.

Shepreth Wildlife Park *See separate family panel on p.34.*

SOHAM TL5872

As well as a rather grand **church**, this has two surviving mills.

ST IVES TL3171

Pleasant little town, with a graceful church, small local museum (usually cl lunchtime, plus winter Sun), and walks by the curving river. There's an unusual tiny chapel on the old bridge, rising straight out of the water; key from museum. In the town, the Royal Oak does generous food, and the riverside Pike & Eel out at Needingworth is attractively placed for lunch.

ST NEOTS TL1860

Pleasant town next to the River Ouse with a large market place and a pleasant landscaped park; the medieval church of St Mary's is worth a look, and the Chequers near it has good value food. An interesting little museum (New St), in a former police station and Magistrate's Court, has a rare example of a 1907 cell block; other displays include the story of St Neot, local crafts and trades, and changing exhibitions by local artists; shop, disabled access; open Tues–Sun mid-Apr–Feb (cl during Jan school hols), Weds–Sun Mar–mid-Apr, best to check; (01480) 388788; *£1.50.

THORNEY TF2804

Rises from the flatlands like an island – which it was, when this was all half-submerged marsh. Much older than most villages in the area, it has a Norman-modified Saxon church on its green, and some interesting yellow-brick workers' houses put up by the Duke of Bedford. The friendly **Heritage Museum** has good displays, and organises tours of the village and abbey. Shop, disabled access (but no facilities); open pm wknds Easter–end

Sept; (01733) 270780; museum free, tours £1.50. The Rose & Crown does freshly made food.

THORNHAUGH TF0700

Sacrewell Farm and Country Centre (off A47) Based around an old working watermill, with demonstrations and displays of rural crafts, tools and machinery and discovery centre, as well as gardens, children's maze and nature trails, lots of animals. Pleasantly simple and undeveloped, this is a friendly well organised place. Meals, snacks, shop, disabled access; cl Christmas wk; (01780) 782254; £3.50. Wansford is very handy for lunch.

TRUMPINGTON TL4454

Trumpington church Attractive in its own right, but perhaps most famous for having the second-oldest memorial brass in England.

WANSFORD TL0997

Nene Valley Railway 15-mile round trip on steam trains through quiet countryside to Peterborough. Also a fine collection of steam locomotives and rolling stock, and a small museum. The railway is a favourite with film-makers. Meals and snacks on steam days, shop, disabled access; phone for train times (01780) 784404; £2 site admission (refundable against train fare), £10 for the train. It's easy to extend this into an all-day trip by breaking your journey at one of the country parks alongside stations en route, or by taking a stroll around Peterborough. At the Wansford end (pretty village), the Haycock is particularly good for lunch.

WATERBEACH TL4868

Denny Abbey & Farmland Museum ♿ (off A10) 12th-c Benedictine abbey with some impressive Norman remains and a 14th-c nuns' refectory. The museum focuses on farming and the county's rural history, with reconstructions of a village shop, kitchen and dairy, and there's a 1940s cottage; various workshops and events. Snacks and picnic area, shop, disabled access (limited in the abbey and cottage), and they'll lend you a wheelchair; open pm Apr–Oct; (01223) 860489; £3.60; EH. The Travellers Rest at Chittering has decent food.

WELCHES DAM TL4786

Ouse Washes Reserve (via Manea, off B1093 SE of March) The best time to visit is in winter when this RSPB reserve floods, and you can watch some of the thousands of ducks and swans from hides (one is wheelchair accessible) along the banks of the River Ouse; picnic areas, and an information centre where you can hire binoculars (cl 25–26 Dec); donations.

WHITTLESFORD TL4748

Whittlesford church The interior is a rich testament to the former agricultural wealth of this area.

WICKEN TL5670

Wicken Fen (Lode Lane) After an absence of over 60 years, otters have been spotted again at this, the last of the undrained fens. Sheathed underground in plastic to prevent its drying out, it is an outstanding area for bird-watching (there are hides). The marshy and open fen landscape is one of the oldest nature reserves in the country, originally safeguarded in 1899 as an example of what the fens were like before they were turned over to intensive agriculture. Beautiful at all times of year, it's home to a remarkable range of plants, insects, birds and other wildlife; some good trails (one for wheelchairs), along with the last fenland windpump (moved here from elsewhere), and tiny fen cottage (open Sun and bank hols Apr–Oct and some Weds in Aug, phone to check). Reserve open every day, visitor centre with snacks, shop and disabled access cl Mon exc bank hols, 25 Dec; (01353) 720274; *£3.80, £1.50 cottage only; NT. The Maids Head prettily set by the village green duckpond has good food.

WILLINGHAM TL4070

Willingham church Lots to notice here: outside are the fine tower and spire, and inside it has many early wall paintings, and some fine early screens. The old Three Tuns has good value home cooking (not Mon).

WIMPOLE TL3350

Wimpole Hall and Home Farm (off A603) The varied attractions at this huge estate can easily fill most of a day. Children like the working stock farm best, its thatched and timbered buildings designed by Sir John Soane when it was at the forefront of agricultural innovation. A restored barn houses machinery and tools from those days, and there are plenty of farm animals (with younger ones to pet and feed) inc various rare breeds; separate play areas for older and younger children. The mainly 18th-c house is one of the most striking mansions in East Anglia. Behind its imposing and harmonious Georgian façade is a lovely trompe l'oeil chapel ceiling, and rooms by James Gibbs and Sir John Soane. Perfect for a relaxing stroll, the gardens are good for spring daffodils, and vegetables grow in the restored walled garden. Best of all perhaps are the 360 acres of parkland, home to the National Walnut Collection, and designed by several different notable landscapers inc Capability Brown and Repton; the remains of a medieval village are under the pasture. Good programme of concerts and events in the hall or grounds. Meals, snacks, shops, some disabled access (not to house). Hall open pm Tues–Thurs and wknds mid-Mar to early Nov, plus bank hol and Fri pm in Aug. Farm open same times plus mornings, wknds in winter, and Fri in July and Aug; (01223) 207257; £9.50 hall, farm and garden (£6.40 hall, £4.90 farm, £2.60 gardens); NT. The surrounding park is open all year, with walkers welcomed free of charge to the extensive paths and tracks through its farmland and woodland, past a folly and up to a surprisingly elevated ridge path. The handsome Hardwicke Arms has decent food.

WISBECH TF4609
The North Brink along the River Nene has handsome Georgian houses (among them the Red Lion has decent food, and serves beer from the nearby brewery – see below – in fine condition).

Elgoods Brewery Museum and Gardens (North Brink) Watch traditional brewing methods in practice at this handsome 200-year-old brewery on the banks of the River Nene. Behind, four acres of gardens include a hot-house, lake and lawns leading to a maze. Snacks, shop, disabled access to gardens only; usually open pm Weds–Fri, Sun and bank hols May–Sept, brewery tours 2pm; (01945) 583160;

£6 brewery hall, £2.50 gardens only.

Octavia Hill Birthplace Museum
Commemorating the life and work of lesser known Victorian housing reformer Octavia Hill, five rooms in this Georgian house document her influence in modern life (her vigorous public campaigns to save recreational open space led to the foundation of the National Trust). The highlight is probably the re-created slum dwelling of 1861, though there are also some interesting tales about Octavia's eccentric family (until she was 13 her father kept Jeremy Bentham's skeleton in the corner of one room). Open pm wknds, Weds and bank hol Mon end Mar–Oct or by appointment; (01945) 476358; £2.

Peckover House ⓔ (North Brink) Lovely early 18th-c house with rococo decoration, restored Victorian library, and a two-acre Victorian garden with a pond, herbaceous borders, rose gardens, summer houses and glasshouses – where orange trees are still fruiting after 300 years. Meals and snacks when house open, shop, disabled access in garden; house and garden open pm Weds, wknds and bank hol Mon (plus Thurs May–Aug), garden open pm Sat–Thurs Apr–end Oct; (01945) 583463; £4, £2.50 garden only; NT.

Wisbech & Fenland Museum
(Museum Sq) Honest and thorough local history museum, with several early manuscripts, an exhibition on Thomas Clarkson and the slave trade, and a display on former times in fenland. Shop, good disabled access; cl Sun, Mon; (01945) 583817; free.

WOODHURST TL3375
Raptor Foundation ⓔ Sanctuary and breeding centre for over 300 birds of prey inc owls, buzzards, hawks and falcons, with flying displays three times a day; take your camera. Meals, snacks, shop, disabled access; cl 25 Dec, 1 Jan; (01487) 741140; *£2.50.

Other attractive villages include Alconbury Weston TL1776, Brampton TL2170, Eltisley TL2659, John Clare's Helpston TF1205, Elton TL0893, Glatton TL1585, Leighton Bromswold TL1175, Gamlingay TL2452, Great Abington TL5348, Great Chishill

TL4239 (well restored windmill), Holywell TL3370, Meldreth TL3746, Rampton TL4268, Ufford TF0904

(lovely area at bluebell time), Whittlesey TL2797 and Woodditton TL6659.

Where to eat

BYTHORN TL0575 **White Hart** *(01832) 710226* Civilised dining pub with a friendly welcome, several linked smallish rooms, magazines and cookery books to read, open fire, imaginative food in Bennett's Bistro, real ales, and a sensible wine list; cl Sun pm, Mon, New Year. £22|£7

CAMBRIDGE TL4557 **Browns** *23 Trumpington Street (01223) 461655* Cheerful and informal sizeable restaurant with cushioned wicker chairs and sofas, well spaced tables, candles, ceiling fans, big potted plants, a good range of enjoyable food, efficient helpful service, and tables on small front roadside terrace; branches in Bath, Brighton, Edinburgh, London, and Oxford. £22 ☺

CAMBRIDGE TL4559 **Twenty Two** *22 Chesterton Rd (01223) 351880* Simple and pretty candlelit evening restaurant in Edwardian house with imaginative modern cooking from a set menu, a fine wine list, and friendly service; no smoking; cl Sun, Mon, 1 wk Christmas; children over 10. £29.75

ELY TL5380 **Old Fire Engine House** *25 St Marys St (01353) 662582* Former fire station next to the cathedral, with good hearty English cooking inc nice puddings, an interesting wine list, simple furnishings and a relaxed atmosphere; large walled garden, also an art gallery; cl Sun pm, bank hols, 25 Dec–6 Jan. £28|£7.50

FEN DRAYTON TL3368 **Three Tuns** *High St (01954) 230242* Pretty thatched inn with two inglenook fireplaces and heavy Tudor beams and timbers in its unpretentious and cosy bar; well kept real ales, generous helpings of good reasonably priced food, and a neat back garden with children's play equipment; children until 8pm; disabled access. £21.50|£5.95

FORDHAM TL6270 **White Pheasant** *Market St (01638) 720414* Well converted, fresh-feeling dining pub with simple decorations, flowers in bottles on tables, farmhouse chairs on bare boards, and a cheerful log fire; creative food, generously served on big white plates, super daily specials, good house wines and well kept real ales; cl 25 and 26 Dec. £30|£4.95

FOWLMERE TL4245 **Chequers** *High St (01763) 208369* Civilised old coaching inn with smartly dressed waiters, ambitious food in galleried restaurant, good puddings, and excellent wines; two comfortably furnished rooms with an open log fire, some interesting photographs of local World War I and II airfields, and a no smoking conservatory overlooking the neat garden; cl 25 Dec; children in family room; disabled access. £24.50|£5.80

HEYDON TL4243 **King William IV** *Chrishall Rd (01763) 838773* Bustling village pub with nooks and crannies in rambling rooms, neatly kept agricultural implements on standing props, wall timbers and dark oak beams, and a log fire; notably interesting vegetarian dishes (plus some meaty dishes, too), well kept real ales, and friendly efficient staff; disabled access. £24|£7.50

KEYSTON TL0475 **Pheasant** *Village Loop Rd (01832) 710241* Pretty thatched former smithy, full of character, with a nice civilised atmosphere, a relaxed bar with informal service, a slightly more formal no smoking room with linen napkins, delicious imaginative food, a particularly good wine list, and real ales; cl 25 Dec pm; partial disabled access. £32/2-course lunch £11.75

KIMBOLTON TL0967 **New Sun** *20 High Street (01480) 860052* Nice old pub with low-beamed front lounge, standing timbers and exposed brickwork, armchairs and sofa by fireplace, well kept real ales, and dining room and bright, busy conservatory; good food inc interesting daily specials, and seats in very pleasant garden. £21|£6.95

MADINGLEY TL3960 **Three Horseshoes** *High St (01954) 210221* Thatched dining pub, smart and well run, with a relaxed and civilised atmosphere, open fire in the charming bar, and an attractive conservatory; very good imaginative food, well kept real ales, a thoughtful, but fairly priced wine list (many by the glass inc champagne), and efficient attentive service; pretty summer garden; cl Sun pm. £32|£8.50

MELBOURN TL3844 **Pink Geranium** *25 Station Rd* (01763) 260215 Very pretty 15th-c thatched cottage, pink inside and out, with consistently good sophisticated cooking; a cosy and relaxed atmosphere, a carefully chosen wine list with helpful notes, cottagey garden, and chauffeur service; good value set lunches, and cookery courses, too; cl Mon, 25–26 Dec. £50 dinner, £25.50 lunch

MELBOURN TL3844 **Sheene Mill** *39 Station Rd* (01763) 261393 Lovely late 17th-c River Mel watermill owned by celebrity chef Steven Saunders, just 200 yards from its sister restaurant, the Pink Geranium; relaxed and informal bar and conservatory, airy restaurant decorated in yellow and terracotta, with pretty blue dining chairs around yellow-clothed tables, and lovely gardens with seats on the terrace; delicious modern cooking inc vegetarian and fish dishes, and light lunches or snacks; bdrms; cl Sun pm, 25 Dec, 1 Jan; partial disabled access. £52

SUTTON GAULT TL4279 **Anchor** *Bury Lane* (01353) 778537 Very friendly, popular dining pub with gas lamps and candles in four heavily beamed rooms (two are no smoking), log fires and stripped pine furniture; delicious imaginative modern cooking (good value two-course wkdy lunches), very good wine list (10 by the glass), well kept real ales, helpful service, and riverbank tables; bdrms; cl 26 Dec; disabled access. £30/2-course wkdy lunch £7.95

Special thanks to Jenny and Michael Back

We welcome reports from readers

This *Guide* depends on readers' reports. Do help us if you can – in return, we offer a discount on the next edition to people who've helped us with reports for it. Tell us what you think about places already in it, and anything extra you think we should say about them. And send us your ideas for inclusion in the next edition: places to visit, eat at or stay in, attractive drives or walks, maybe even unusual shops you know of. Use the card in the middle, the report forms at the end, or just write – no stamp needed: *The Good Britain Guide*, FREEPOST TN1569, Wadhurst, E Sussex TN5 7BR. Or log on to www.goodguides.com

CHESHIRE

A county of great charm; wonderfully varied countryside, pretty villages, and a real diversity of attractions – from the Romans to the Space Age

With beautifully restored and preserved medieval buildings and plenty of things to do, Chester is ideal for a short break at any time of year. This city also boasts the incredible Chester Zoo (the biggest zoo in the country, with something new every year).

Other highlights for families include Blue Planet aquarium in Ellesmere Port with its dramatic walk-through tunnel and friendly staff (there's plenty to occupy families at the nearby Boat Museum too). Other notably enjoyable places to spend a sunny day are Arley Hall & Gardens (children especially like the tractor ride to nearby Stockley Farm), and Tatton Park in Knutsford, with its lovely grounds and working historic farm; older children enjoy the science centre (and there's an arboretum) at Jodrell Bank.

Quarry Bank Mill & Styal Estate at Styal is our Cheshire Family Attraction for this year (it puts real pleasure into finding out about the Industrial Revolution), and other good heritage centres include the Salt Museum in Northwich, and the three silk museums in Macclesfield. Lots of interactive displays at Catalyst in Widnes turn even chemistry into an adventure, and the motor museum at Mouldsworth has a splendid collection of cars.

With more of an appeal for adults are the fine hall and gardens at Lyme Park near Disley, splendid-looking Little Moreton Hall near Congleton and the unusual Adlington Hall; Norton Priory in Runcorn and Capesthorne Hall are worth a visit too. There are fine paintings at Tabley House, and in the summer Gawsworth Hall has outdoor plays and concerts. In fine weather, the gardens at Neston, Cholmondeley and Kettleshulme are pleasant places to while away a peaceful afternoon, and we've added this year Rode Hall Gardens at Scholar Green.

Cheshire's countryside is peppered with charming thatched and timbered villages. It ranges from the picturesque castle-topped wooded hills of the west, through the lush parkland, leafy lanes and meres (shallow lakes) of the central plain, to the rugged eastern Peak District – small steep stone-walled pastures, shaggy sheep, deep twisty valleys, austere moorland. An intricate network of canals takes in some of the most interesting countryside, with well maintained towpaths; in Northwich, a unique legacy of the canal era, the Anderton Boat Lift, has now been fully restored.

Please let us know what you think of places in the *Guide*. Use the report forms at the back of the book, write us a letter or log on to www.goodguides.com

Where to stay

BEESTON SJ5559 **Wild Boar Hotel** *Whitchurch Rd, Beeston, Tarporley, Cheshire CW6 9NW (01829) 260309* **£105.75**, plus special breaks; 37 rms with appealing touches such as fresh fruit. Striking timbered 17th-c former hunting lodge, much extended over the years, with relaxed and comfortable bars and lounges, enjoyable bar meals and formal beamed restaurant, and good helpful service; disabled access; dogs in ground floor bedrooms only

BICKLEY MOSS SJ5450 **Cholmondeley Arms** *Cholmondeley, Malpas, Cheshire SY14 8HN (01829) 720300* **£60***, plus special breaks; 2 rms with bath, 4 with showers. Airy converted Victorian schoolhouse close to castle and gardens (famously, Cholmondeley is pronounced 'Chumley'), with lots of atmosphere, very friendly staff, interesting furnishings, open fire, excellent imaginative bar food, and very good choice of wines; disabled access; dogs welcome anywhere

BROXTON SJ4754 **Egerton Arms** *Whitchurch Rd, Broxton, Chester, Cheshire CH3 9JW (01829) 782241* **£51.45**; 7 attractive rms. Welcoming neatly kept family inn with handsome big dark-panelled bar, enjoyable reasonably priced food in dining room, well kept real ales, decent wines by the glass, consistently friendly service, and garden with children's play area and pleasant country views

CHESTER SJ4065 **Castle House** *23 Castle St, Chester CH1 2DS (01244) 350354* **£50***, plus special breaks; 5 comfortable rms, 3 with own bthrm. Small carefully preserved 16th-c guest house in the middle of the city, with helpful friendly owners, and fine breakfasts; dogs welcome in bedrooms

COTEBROOK SJ5765 **Alvanley Armscho** *Cotebrook, Tarporley, Cheshire CW6 9DS (01829) 760200* **£60**; 7 rms. Handsome 400-year-old sandstone inn with pleasant beamed rooms (three areas are no smoking), big open fire, a chintzy little hall, shire horse décor (pictures, photographs, horseshoes, horse brasses, harness and bridles), generous helpings of good food, and a garden with lake and trout; shire horse stud next door opening Easter 2002; dogs welcome in bedrooms

FULLERS MOOR SJ4854 **Frogg Manor** *Nantwich Rd, Broxton, Chester CH3 9JH (01829) 782629* **£107**, plus special breaks; 7 lavishly decorated rms with thoughtful extras. Enjoyably eccentric Georgian manor house full of ornamental frogs and antique furniture, open fires and ornate dried-flower arrangements, a restful upstairs sitting room, cosy little bar, a large collection of 30s/40s records, and good English cooking in elegant dining room which leads to conservatory overlooking the gardens; disabled access; dogs welcome in bedrooms

HIGHER BURWARDSLEY SJ5257 **Pheasant** *Higher Burwardsley, Burwardsley, Chester, Cheshire CH3 9PF (01829) 770434* **£80**, plus special breaks; 10 rms in comfortably converted sandstone-built barn. Pretty, recently refurbished, half-timbered 17th-c inn on top of Peckforton Hills with marvellous views, an attractive bar with a huge log fire in the see-through fireplace, no smoking conservatory, and good modern cooking; lots of walks nearby; disabled access

HIGHER WYCH SJ4943 **Mill House** *Higher Wych, Malpas, Cheshire SY14 7JR (01948) 780362* **£44**; 2 rms. Very welcoming and friendly B&B in former farmhouse on the Welsh/English border, with relaxed atmosphere and good breakfasts – evening meals by arrangement; self-catering cottage; cl Dec

HOOLE SJ4167 **Hoole Hall** *Warrington Rd, Hoole, Chester, Cheshire CH2 3PD (01244) 408800* **£133.75**, plus special breaks; 97 well equipped rms, some no smoking. Extended and attractively refurbished 18th-c hall with five acres of gardens, good food in two restaurants, and friendly service; good disabled access; dogs welcome in bedrooms

KNUTSFORD SJ7479 **Longview** *51–55 Manchester Rd, Knutsford, Cheshire WA16 0LX (01565) 632119* **£69.50**w; 26 rms. Friendly Victorian hotel with attractive period and reproduction furnishings, open fires in original fireplaces, pleasant cellar bar, ornate restaurant, and good well presented food; cl Christmas–mid-Jan; dogs welcome in bedrooms

MACCLESFIELD SJ9271 **Sutton Hall Hotel** *Bullocks Lane, Sutton, Macclesfield,*

Cheshire SK11 0HE (01260) 253211 **£90**; 9 marvellous rms. Welcoming and secluded historic baronial hall, full of character, with stylish rooms, high black beams, stone fireplaces, suits of armour and so forth, friendly service, and good food; can arrange clay shooting/golf/fishing; dogs welcome in bedrooms

MOBBERLEY SJ7779 **Laburnum Cottage** *Knutsford Rd, Mobberley, Knutsford, Cheshire WA16 7PU (01565) 872464* **£57**; 4 pretty rms. Neatly kept and friendly no smoking country guest house in an acre of landscaped garden; relaxed atmosphere in comfortable lounge with books, a sunny conservatory, and very good food; disabled access (with prior notice); dogs by arrangement

MOLLINGTON SJ3869 **Crabwall Manor** *Parkgate Rd, Mollington, Chester CH1 6NE (01244) 851666* **£170***, plus special breaks; 48 very comfortable individually decorated rms. Partly castellated, largely 17th-c hotel in landscaped grounds with restful, attractive rooms, open fires, very good modern British cooking in elegant restaurant, and friendly professional service; leisure club; disabled access

POTT SHRIGLEY SJ9478 **Shrigley Hall** *Shrigley Park, Pott Shrigley, Macclesfield, Cheshire SK10 5SB (01625) 575757* **£120**, plus special breaks; 150 smart well equipped rms, some with country views. In over 260 acres of parkland, this impressive country house has a splendid entrance hall with several elegant rooms leading off, enjoyable food in the orangery and restaurant, and good service from friendly staff; championship golf course, fishing, tennis, and leisure centre in former church building; plenty to do nearby; disabled access; dogs welcome in bedrooms

PRESTBURY SJ9077 **White House** *The Village, Prestbury, Macclesfield, Cheshire SK10 4HP (01625) 829376* **£119***, plus wknd breaks; 11 individual, stylish and well equipped rms with antiques, in separate manor just a short walk from the restaurant. Carefully restored Georgian house with an exceptionally friendly and pretty restaurant, imaginative modern British cooking, thoughtful wine list and a spacious bar; breakfast in small conservatory lounge or in room; cl 25 Dec; children over 10

ROWTON SJ4464 **Rowton Hall** *Whitchurch Rd, Rowton, Chester CH3 6AD (01244) 335262* **£113.50**, plus wknd breaks; 38 attractive rms. 18th-c country house in eight acres of award-winning gardens with tennis courts and croquet lawn; conservatory lounge, comfortable bar, log fires, a relaxed atmosphere, and smart oak-panelled restaurant; swimming pool, gym, sauna and solarium; disabled access

SANDBACH SJ7560 **Old Hall** *High St, Sandbach, Cheshire CW11 1AL (01270) 761221* **£70**, plus special breaks; 12 comfortable rms. Fine Jacobean timbered hotel with lots of original panelling and fireplaces, relaxing refurbished lounge, friendly welcome, and popular, newly refurbished restaurant; disabled access; dogs welcome

SANDIWAY SJ5968 **Nunsmere Hall** *Tarporley Rd, Oakmere, Northwich, Cheshire CW8 2ES (01606) 889100* **£220**w inc dinner; 36 individually decorated rms. Luxurious lakeside hotel on wooded peninsula with elegantly furnished lounge and library, oak-panelled cocktail bar, very good modern cooking, and a warm welcome from courteous staff; children over 12 in evening restaurant; disabled access

TARPORLEY SJ5562 **Swan** *50 High St, Tarporley, Cheshire CW6 0AG (01829) 733838* **£69**; 16 rms. Well managed Georgian inn with a good mix of individual tables and chairs in attractive bar, well kept real ales, decent wines, and quite a few malt whiskies, good food from extensive menu, nice breakfasts, and friendly staff; limited disabled access

TILSTON SJ4650 **Tilston Lodge** *Tilston, Malpas, Cheshire SY14 7DR (01829) 250223* **£70***; 3 thoughtfully equipped rms, 2 with four-posters. Warmly friendly and beautifully restored Victorian house in 16 acres of grounds that include award-winning gardens, ponds, and a collection of rare breed farm animals; comfortable and attractive public rooms with original features, open fire in dining room, and good breakfasts with home-made jams and marmalades

WESTON SJ7352 **White Lion** *31 Main Rd, Weston, Crewe, Cheshire CW2 5NA (01270) 500303* **£68**, plus wknd breaks; 16 comfortable rms. Pretty 17th-c timbered inn with low beams (several no smoking areas), a friendly relaxed atmosphere, well kept real ales, and popular food; own bowling green, and they have a licence for civil marriages; cl Christmas, New Year and bank hols

WETTENHALL SJ6261 **Boot & Slipper** *Wettenhall, Winsford, Cheshire CW7 4DN (01270) 528238* **£48**; 4 attractive rms with showers. Cosily refurbished 16th-c coaching inn on small country lane, with low beams and open fire in quiet bars, a relaxed friendly atmosphere, and good breakfasts; children over 11

WHEELOCK SJ7558 **Grove House** *Mill Lane, Wheelock, Sandbach, Cheshire CW11 4RD (01270) 762582* **£60**; 8 rms with showers. Family-run Georgian restaurant-with-rooms, with relaxed homely atmosphere, quietly furnished lounge and restaurant, personal friendly service, and very good modern cooking in popular restaurant; plenty to do nearby; cl 22 Dec–3 Jan; dogs welcome in bedrooms

WORLESTON SJ6555 **Rookery Hall** *Main Rd, Worleston, Nantwich, Cheshire CW5 6DQ (01270) 610016* **£95**, plus special breaks; 45 individually decorated rms. Fine early 19th-c hotel in 38 acres of lovely parkland, with elegant lounges, log fires, intimate panelled restaurant with enjoyable food, and friendly service; disabled access; dogs in bedrooms in Coach House

To see and do

Cheshire Family Attraction of the Year

STYAL SJ8383 **Quarry Bank Mill & Styal Estate** A real favourite with readers, this is one of the best and most extensive places in the country to get to grips with the Industrial Revolution, and as you can easily spend most of a day here, it's also good value for money. The 18th-c cotton mill that's the centrepiece is still operational, so there's always plenty going on, with lively displays and demonstrations of cotton production spread over five floors, bringing vividly to life the factory conditions for mill-workers and their bosses. The most dramatic sight is the 50-ton waterwheel, the most powerful in Europe; it still turns every afternoon, very much the best time to visit if you have only half a day free, as that's when the steam engines are working too. Children have plenty to stimulate their interest: the Power gallery has multimedia displays illustrating how water and later steam were used to power the mill, there's a good film and lots of interactive exhibits (one on the restoration of the 1840 beam engine in the original engine house), and they have a very full programme of activities such as rope-making and dip-dyeing, particularly in the summer holidays (most are included in the ticket price, though you will need to pay extra – and book in advance – for their occasional more elaborate events such as scarecrow-making). Our favourite part isn't in the Mill at all – it's the Apprentice House in the village outside, where enthusiastic guides in period dress explain the lifestyle and 12-hour working days faced by the young pauper children who worked here. By the start of the 19th c 90 children were living here – half the mill's workforce. Children love discovering how grim their lives could have been back then, and are positively encouraged to pump water from the well, test out the straw-filled beds, and stir the porridge in the kitchen. There are timed tickets in operation here, so it makes sense to come here at the start of a visit if you can (though note the opening times, below). The garden has some rare fruit and vegetables. The surrounding village is nice to stroll around, with its carefully preserved workers' cottages, chapels and shop, and there are good woodland and waterside walks in the park, with plenty of space for picnics by the river. Meals, snacks, shop, disabled access; mill cl Mon Oct–Mar, Apprentice House and garden usually cl Mon all year (exc in summer hols), and Tues–Fri mornings in term-time; (01625) 527468; an all-in ticket is £6.50 (£3.70 children), with a family ticket for £16.50; a mill-only ticket is £5 (£3.40 children), with the family ticket £14.50; free to National Trust members. Parking in the estate car park is £2.50, with £1.50 of that refundable against entry to the mill.

Cheshire

LANCASHIRE, MERSEYSIDE

Warrington

Widnes

Runcorn

Daresbury

Grappenhall

Lymm

Little Bollington

Rostherne

Ellesmere Port

THE WIRRAL

Parkgate

Neston

Mollington

Hoole

Chester

Christleton

Rowton

Eccleston

Frodsham

Delamere Forest

Mouldsworth

Great Budworth

Marbury Country Park

Arley

Tabley

Plumley

Lower Peover

Northwich

Sandiway

Whitegate

Little Budworth

Cotebrook

Tarporley

Eaton

Wettenhall

Sandbach

Wheelock

Haslington

Crewe

Weston

Nantwich

Bridgemere

Audlem Wharf

SHROPSHIRE

Aldford

Tattenhall

Beeston

Bunbury

Worleston

Whartons Lock

Higher Burwardsley

Broxton

Burwardsley

Peckforton Hills

Raw Head

Cholmondeley

Farndon

Stretton

Tilston

Fullers Moor

Bickley Moss

Malpas

Wrenbury

Marbury

Higher Wych

NORTH-EAST WALES

0 Miles 5

0 Kilometres 8

ADLINGTON SJ9080

Adlington Hall 🔁 Home of the Legh family since 1315, some of the rooms in this unusual black and white timbered house with Georgian additions show the hunting song written by family friend Handel on a visit here. The impressive Tudor great hall has an original hammerbeam roof, huge Elizabethan windows and a gilded Father Smith organ (the largest 17th-c organ in the country). There's a fine yew walk and lime avenue planted more than 300 years ago in the Capability

& MANCHESTER

8　　　　　9

0

Disley

M56 ⑦ Poynton

Styal Middlewood Way

Mobberley Kettleshulme

Adlington

Knutsford Prestbury Bollington

Kerridge Hill

Nether Alderley Pott Shrigley

Capesthorne **Macclesfield**

Jodrell Teggs Nose Country Park

Bank

Lower Withington Gawsworth A54

Swettenham

Macclesfield

Canal

Congleton Cloud

Astbury

Hassall Green

Scholar Green Mow Cop

⑯

Barthomley

STAFFORDSHIRE

Brown-style 18th-c gardens. Snacks, shop, limited disabled access; open pm Weds Jun–Aug; (01625) 820201; *£4.50. The Windmill over at Whiteley Green is a useful family pub with a big garden.

ARLEY SJ6780
Arley Hall & Gardens and Stockley Farm ⊞ The dramatic-looking house is Victorian Jacobean, but the same family have lived on the estate for over 500 years, so there are older furnishings and mementoes. Outside, the charming grounds include walled, scented, and herb gardens, shrub rose collection and a more informal woodland area; also an interesting private chapel. Meals, snacks, shop and nursery, disabled access; open Tues–Sun mid-Apr–Sept (hall open pm Tues and Sun); (01565) 777353; £4.50 grounds and gardens, hall £2.50 extra. From the car park, tractor and trailer rides take you to nearby **Stockley Farm**, a friendly working dairy farm that's ideal for children; £4.30; (01565) 777323.

ASTBURY SJ8461
This is a delightful village, and its church is well worth a look – graceful detached spire, spectacular roofing, rich carving. The Egerton Arms is a charming pub.

AUDLEM WHARF SJ6543
For walkers, a good access point for the **Shropshire Union Canal** which threads through this area, giving interesting stretches for strolls; just outside the village is an impressive flight of over a dozen locks.

BARTHOMLEY SJ7752
This charming village has lots of thatch, black and white timbering, quiet up-and-down lanes, a fine church, and a delightfully unspoilt pub, the White Lion.

BEESTON SJ5459
Beeston Castle Well worth the steep climb, this ruined 13th-c fortress gives wonderful views from its perch on a dramatic crag; Richard II is said to have left treasure buried here. Good exhibition covers site's 4,000-year history; special events in summer. Snacks, shop; cl 25 Dec and 1 Jan; (01829) 260464; £3, EH. The pub of the same name, handy for the canal, does good value generous food.

BOLLINGTON SJ9377
Bollington is well worth a stroll: handsome stone milltown buildings, unchanged 19th-c shops and houses, and overhead a great stone aqueduct

and its later rival the railway viaduct. The Church House is a useful pub, and on the E edge of town the Poachers (Ingersley Rd) or Redway (Kerridge) are good start points for the viewpoint Kerridge Hill (crowned by a curious folly known as White Nancy). You can also pick up the long-distance Gritstone Trail for walks among high stone-walled pastures.

BRIDGEMERE SJ7243
Bridgemere Garden World (A51) A garden-lover's paradise – 25 acres of gardens (inc the WI cottage garden), plants, glasshouses, and garden furniture, with more plants in more varieties than anywhere else in Britain (indoor and outdoor), and professional help on hand for any sort of query. There's an art and crafts shop and an aquatics area. Best to visit in the morning before the coach parties arrive. Good meals and snacks, excellent shop, disabled access; cl 25 and 26 Dec; (01270) 521100; free.

BUNBURY SJ5758
Bunbury has pretty cottages around its 14th-c church, a well restored 19th-c watermill, and an excellent dining pub, the Dysart Arms.

BURWARDSLEY SJ5257
Cheshire Candle Workshops Popular demonstrations of candle-making and other crafts, and a big craft shop. Meals, snacks, disabled access; cl 25 Dec and winter Mons; (01829) 770401; free. The Pheasant is good for lunch, with great views.

CAPESTHORNE SJ8473
Capesthorne Hall 18th-c family home of the Bromley-Davenports, who have lived on the site since Domesday; fine paintings include Lowry's unusual interpretation of the house's striking exterior, and there's a good collection of Roman and Greek busts and vases. Also lovely Georgian chapel and 60 acres of gardens and woodland. Snacks, disabled access; open pm Weds, Sun and bank hols Apr–Oct; (01625) 861221; *£6.50, *£4.00 garden and chapel only. The Blacksmiths Arms at Henbury (A537 towards Macclesfield) is a decent family dining pub, if you don't want the longer trip to the Dog over at Peover Heath.

CHESTER SJ4066

A great place for a visit, Chester was the site of an important fort in Roman times, and later plentiful river traffic kept it rich; nowadays, it's a cheerful bustling place with interesting shops, and lots of places to eat and drink. The old centre is ringed by a medieval **town wall** that's more complete than any other in Britain. You can walk the whole way round, enjoying marvellous views; there are usually summer exhibitions, and music festivals for you to visit along the way. Partly because of the limit set by the wall, the centre of town is easy to get around on foot, not too big, and with the main streets pretty much free of cars (there may be a few buses), although in summer the sheer number of tourists and shoppers can still make them appear congested. Guided walks leave the Chester visitor centre on Vicars Lane at 10.30am daily, and also 2.15pm May–Oct; £3.50. If you're driving in, you'll be shunted round to one of the big car parks, and you may have to queue a while to get a space, so it's best to use the park and ride on the major approach roads. Chester's racecourse, the Roodee, is the oldest in Britain; it still has fashionable races Mar–Sept, with lively family events in Aug (01244) 304600. The quaint Albion (Park St) and canalside Old Harkers Arms (Russell St) both have good food.

Chester Castle 🏰 Though now largely moated by car parks and occupied by civil servants, this has some impressive buildings, both medieval and grand-manner late 18th-c, although only a few rooms are open to the public. The **Military Museum** here is worth a visit; it covers the history of the Cheshire Regiment, with new interactive displays, re-creations and dioramas; (01244) 327617. Shop, disabled access; cl 22 Dec–2 Jan; *£2.

Chester Cathedral Not unlike an ordinary church at first glance, this is far more impressive inside, with some marvellous medieval carving in and above the choir stalls, and some fine vaulting. Many of the former abbey buildings survived the Reformation, so the precincts still include peaceful arcaded flagstoned cloisters, a medieval chapter house, and older Norman parts inc a refectory – brought back into use as an excellent café (which even has a resident pianist Tues, Fri lunchtimes). Handel first rehearsed *The Messiah* here in 1742, and they show a copy of his marked score. All the carved bosses have been gilded, and a model of the cathedral has a Braille text. Shop, disabled access; cl for Sun am services (up to 12.30pm); (01244) 324756; donation suggestion. There are quiet cobbled Georgian lanes around Abbey Sq, behind the cathedral a little way down Northgate.

Chester viewpoints The tree-shaded Groves look out to the medieval bridge over the River Dee – very photogenic and a pleasant place for a stroll or picnic. Several companies offer boat trips on the river from here; (01244 325394); from £4, Mar–Sept. The bridge at the N end of Northgate gives a close view of the so-called Bridge of Sighs over the canal far below.

Chester Zoo 🔄 (A41, 2m N) The biggest and undoubtedly one of the best zoos in Britain, constantly developing and improving. Its several thousand animals are housed in spacious near-natural enclosures (their jaguar enclosure is the best in Europe, and they've recently improved the rhino enclosure) spread over 80 acres of glorious gardens, with 11 miles of pathways. More than 200 of the species here are classed as rare or endangered, and they put a great deal of effort into breeding, so there's usually quite a range of baby animals. Highlights include the splendidly laid out Chimpanzee Island, the komodo dragons and amazon parrots in the Islands in Danger tropical habitat, and the remarkable free-flying bat cave. There's a full programme of feeding sessions throughout the day, and smaller children can pet the animals at the well organised farm. A waterbus can ferry you between the attractions (£1.50), and an overhead train zips around the grounds (£1.80 mid-July–Aug, £1.50 rest of year). Meals, snacks, shops, good disabled access, tactile maps and Braille guides; cl 25 Dec; (01244) 380280; *£11.

Dewa Roman Experience (Pierpoint Lane, off Bridge St) Re-creation of Chester's Roman heyday, with the sights, sounds and smells of streets, fortresses, and even bathhouses. It starts off as though you're on board a Roman galley, and at the end is an exhibition of Roman, Saxon and medieval relics found on the site. Shop, disabled access; cl 25–26 Dec; (01244) 343407; £3.95.

Grosvenor Museum (Grosvenor St) This interesting museum breathes life into all sorts of detail about Chester and its surroundings; an unexpected highlight is the gallery of huge Roman tombstones. A conservatory shop leads to a Georgian house with restored Georgian and Victorian rooms, an art gallery, and displays of locally made silver and furniture; interactive computers and good changing exhibitions. Good disabled access – touch-screen computers give wheelchair visitors a virtual view of the exhibits upstairs, and there are large print and Braille labels. Cl Sun am, Good Fri, 24–26 Dec and 1 Jan; (01244) 402008; free.

Roman Chester Recent research has led to speculation that Emperor Vespasian foresaw a key role for Chester at the heart of an enlarged province of Britannia. This would help to explain the city's grandiose walls, constructed with unusually large sandstone blocks in a manner designed to impress, with imposing ornamental gateways. Other remains include some broken Roman columns from the fortress baths in a neat and peaceful garden running outside the city walls by the Newgate. Nearby is the excavated part of a very large Roman amphitheatre – probably big enough to seat nearly 5,000 people. Other relics can pop up in unexpected places: Spud-U-Like (Bridge St) and Miss Selfridge (Northgate St) show off well preserved sections of hypocaust.

The Rows Giving Chester's heart a magnificently Tudor look, these are sets of timbered two-storey shops with open upper arcaded galleries, radiating from the central Cross. Parts are thought to be at least 700 years old. Besides being attractive to look at and charming to walk through, they form the heart of the city's shopping centre (and include a useful pub, the Boot, on

Eastgate Row N). Watergate is one of the finest stretches, with some of Chester's most glorious timber-framed buildings, though more fine buildings jetty out over the pavement in Lower Bridge St (for instance, the late 17th-c Falcon, once a house used by the Duke of Westminster's ancestors but now a well restored pub), and in St Werbergh St off Eastgate (built in the 1890s, despite their Elizabethan look).

CHOLMONDELEY SJ5351
Cholmondeley Castle Gardens Very pretty to stroll through, with acres of colourful ornamental gardens around elegant castle buildings (not open). Also fine woodland and lakeside walks, llamas and entertaining pygmy goats among the rare breeds, and an ancient private chapel. Snacks, shop and plant centre, limited disabled access; open Sun, Weds, Thurs and bank hols (exc Good Fri) Apr–Sept, but best to check; (01829) 720383; £3. The Cholmondeley Arms is excellent for lunch.

CHRISTLETON SJ4465
Though now almost part of Chester, this is still very much a distinct village, with a classic green, pond with a nesting swan, almshouses, and medieval packhorse bridges. The Ring o' Bells and Cheshire Cat both have decent food.

CLOUD SJ9063
There are good hilly walks here, and the craggy summit, with steep drops to the Cheshire Plain, gives grand views; the Coach & Horses at Timbersbrook is a useful nearby pub.

CONGLETON SJ8358
Little Moreton Hall (Scholar Green; A34 S) One of Britain's best-preserved half-timbered buildings, its splendid black and white exterior pretty much unchanged since it was built in 1580, and covered with such a profusion of lines the effect is almost dizzying. The inside, though largely unfurnished, has some interesting features too, especially the wainscoted Long Gallery, Great Hall and chapel. There's a re-creation of a typical 17th-c knot garden – and make sure you don't miss the built-in dog kennel. Regular open-air theatre and concerts. Meals, snacks, shop, disabled access to ground floor

only; open pm Weds–Sun and bank hols Apr–Oct, then wknds Nov–Dec, but phone to confirm; (01260) 272018; price is usually around £5; NT. The Brownlow Inn nearby is popular for lunch. **Heritage Narrow Boats** at Kent Green have electric narrow boats to hire by the day; cl Dec; (01782) 785700; £80 wkdys for up to 12 people (£95 wknds) – very satisfying, gliding along in silence.

CREWE SJ7055
A 19th-c railway town, smartened up a lot in the last decade or two, with bargains in the market, a pedestrianised centre, colourful Queens Park and useful foyer restaurant in the Victorian theatre.

Railway Age (Vernon Way) A museum with a wide range of locomotives from electric through to steam, along with models, miniature and standard-gauge railways and other displays. Shop (not always open), some disabled access; usually cl Nov to mid-Feb; (01270) 212130; £3.50 wkdys, £4.50 wknds (when there's more going on). The Crown (Earle St) is handy for something to eat, with a model shop nearby.

DARESBURY SJ5882
Daresbury church The 'Alice in Wonderland' stained-glass window commemorates Lewis Carroll, who was born here. There are attractive canalside strolls, and the Ring o' Bells is good for lunch.

DELAMERE FOREST SJ5571
Several square miles of mainly coniferous plantation, with some older oak and other woodland, inc plenty of open stretches and picnic places, and some small stretches of reedy water. A section of the 30-mile **Sandstone Trail** long-distance path takes in much of the best bits, with good access from several places inc Delamere and Hatchmere, and decent prettily placed pubs in both villages.

DISLEY SJ9682
Lyme Park ⊞ You might recognise this wonderful country estate, outside the pleasant hillside village of Disley, from the recent TV series *The Forsyte Saga*. The Hall at its centre is a magnificent blend of Elizabethan, Georgian and Regency architecture and

styles. Tours are unguided, so you can take your time looking at the intricate carvings, and lovely tapestries, paintings and furniture. There's a particularly grand staircase, and a fine collection of English clocks. Around the house are 17 acres of Victorian gardens with orangery, sunken dutch garden and wilderness garden, and a sprawling ancient park with a newly restored hunting tower, herds of red deer and nature trails inc one suitable for wheelchairs. Pleasant walk down to the canal. Meals, snacks, shop, disabled access (to part of the house only); house open pm Fri–Tues Apr–Oct, garden open Apr–Oct, plus wknds Nov; the park is open all year; (01663) 766492; £3.50 per car to go in the park, then £5.50 house and garden, £2.50 garden only; NT. The White Horse is a useful food stop (with OAP lunch days). The long-distance **Gritstone Trail** starts from the park and runs along the western flanks of the Peak District. It's well marked and offers a few days' walking of the highest quality.

EATON SJ5763
Eaton is a classic Cheshire village, with picture-postcard combinations of thatch, stone and timbering. The Red Lion (open all day) has good reasonably priced food.

ECCLESTON SJ4162
This romantically eclectic estate village was built for the Duke of Westminster, with a richly expansive sandstone church that's a culmination of Victorian ecclesiastical architecture.

ELLESMERE PORT SJ4174
Blue Planet 🔳 (off A5117 nr M53, junction 10) One of Britain's most stunning aquariums, and though it does get busy, it's all very efficiently organised. The most obviously dramatic feature is the 71-metre (233-ft) walk-through tunnel, surrounded by sharks, stingray, and three and a half million gallons of water; a moving walkway lets you trundle along gawping without having to look where you're going. Knowledgeable staff (many of them marine biologists) are on hand to answer questions, and they give talks throughout the day. They have good shows in the Aquatheatre, where you can watch divers feeding the creatures;

they use underwater microphones to chat with the audience while they do it. The main displays re-create water environments from around the world, and touchpools give children the chance to handle starfish and the like. As well as fish they have reptiles and insects, and their encounter sessions can introduce you to everything from toads and hissing cockroaches to toxic frogs; also several film and slide shows, and free face painting. Meals, snacks, shop, good disabled access; cl 25 Dec; (0870) 4448440; £7.25 adults; they do various family tickets. Nearby on this S edge of town is the huge factory outlet shopping village, **Cheshire Oaks**.
Boat Museum 🔳 (South Pier Rd) Nicely set in a historic dock complex, a huge floating collection of canal boats, as well as steam engines, a blacksmith's forge, workers' cottages, stables, big indoor exhibitions, and boat trips. Meals, snacks, shop, disabled access; cl Thurs and Fri Nov–Mar, 25–26 Dec and perhaps some other days over Christmas; (0151) 355 5017; *£5.50. Parts of the surrounding dock have been redeveloped with craft workshops and the like. The Woodlands (Chester Rd) is a useful pub/restaurant (with its own bowling green).

FARNDON SJ4154
Charming rustic two-mile riverside walk from car park by arched Dee bridge; the Nags Head is useful for lunch.

FRODSHAM SJ5075
Foxhill Arboretum (off B5393, S of Frodsham). Begun in 1962, this includes a mix of rare conifer and broadleaf trees, from dawn redwood and Spanish firs to native elms. Be careful though, some of the steeper paths can be very slippery; shop, (01928) 739189; £2. As we went to press, the arboretum was going through a change of management and future arrangements were uncertain, so phone to check. Netherton Hall (A56 Frodsham–Helsby) has good food all day.

GAWSWORTH SJ8969
Gawsworth Hall 🔳 Exceptionally pretty timbered manor house dating back to Norman times, the former home of Mary Fitton, possibly the Dark

Lady of Shakespeare's Sonnets; plenty of fine furniture, stained glass, pictures and sculptures. In summer the open-air theatre has a well chosen range of concerts and plays; good gardens and park too. Snacks, shop, disabled access to gardens; open pm Sun and bank hols 18 Apr–5 Oct (pm daily 9 Jun–Aug); (01260) 223456; £4.50. The village has fine houses in parkland, ponds, an interesting church, and an unusual unspoilt farm pub, while the Sutton Hall Hotel over at Sutton Lane Ends is quite handy for lunch.

GRAPPENHALL SJ6386
This attractive village is worth a visit for the grinning cat on its church tower, which inspired Lewis Carroll; the Parr Arms by the church has good home cooking, and there are peaceful canalside strolls here.

GREAT BUDWORTH SJ6677
In attractive rich countryside, this is a quaint purpose-built estate village; the church is imposing (as is the George & Dragon pub), and there are many pretty cottages.

HASLINGTON SJ7358
Lakemore Country Park (Lane End Farm) Readers enjoy this country park with rare breeds inc miniature donkeys and endangered birds of prey. Nature trails link five man-made lakes; pets' corner, outdoor and indoor playgrounds – extra charge for children's rides. Open Weds–Sun Apr–Oct and daily during school hols; (01270) 253556; £3.95. The friendly Fox nearby has decent food.

JODRELL BANK SJ7970
Jodrell Bank Centre & Arboretum (off A535, nr M6 junction 18) Plenty to do at this lively place which, unusually for a working research establishment, welcomes visitors. The centrepiece is still the huge radio telescope, the second largest in the world and as big as the dome of St Paul's, but they also have a fun science centre with eight galleries examining subjects as diverse as plants, prisms and planets with hands-on displays and exhibitions; regular shows in the Planetarium (over-5s only). The 2,500 varieties of tree and shrub in the 35-acre arboretum are quite a contrast to the indoor exhibits, and there's also an Environmental Discovery Centre

and nature trails. Busy programme of events and special activities. Meals and snacks (the café has fine views of the telescope), picnic area, shop, good disabled access (outside too); (01477) 571339; cl Mon Nov–mid-Mar, and 23–27 and 31 Dec, 1, 6–10 Jan; £5. The Olde Red Lion at Goostrey is quite handy for lunch.

KERRIDGE HILL SJ9477
Above Bollington, and with fine views, this is topped by the curious folly known as White Nancy. Good walks here, and to the E – where the quaint Highwayman pub (B5470 N of Rainow) also has good views, and is handy for the long-distance Gritstone Trail path.

KETTLESHULME SJ9879
Dunge Valley Gardens (off B5470) Colourful gardens in Peak District countryside, esp good for rhododendrons, acers, magnolias (May, Jun), roses and unusual perennials. Lunches, teas, plant sales, limited disabled access; cl Sept–Feb (exc plant sales by appointment) and Mon exc bank hols; (01663) 733787; *£3. The Crag at nearby Wildboarclough does decent food, and fits in well with a walk to the Three Shires Head and the summit of Shutlingsloe.

KNUTSFORD SJ7578
Despite obvious present-day prosperity and some rather heavy traffic, this has a pleasantly old-world feel, with lots of striking Georgian and other period buildings. It might seem strangely familiar to you if you've read Mrs Gaskell's *Cranford* – its alias.
Tatton Park On Knutsford's northern edge, a busy estate with a handsome neo-classical Georgian mansion at its centre. Magnificent collection of furnishings, porcelain and paintings (inc two Canalettos) in the opulent State rooms, and restored kitchens and servants' quarters; the Tudor Old Hall hints at the long history of the estate. The lovely grounds boast an Edwardian rose garden, Italian and Japanese gardens, orangery and fern house, leading to a big country park with mature trees, lakes, signposted walks and deer and waterfowl; you can fish or take a carriage ride. There's also a Home Farm that works as it did 60 years ago, with vintage machinery and

rare breeds of animals; children's playground. You could easily spend most of an undemanding day here (good family activities in summer school hols), or take a carload for a picnic in the park. Meals, snacks, shop, some disabled access; park and gardens open all year (exc winter Mons and 25 Dec), rest cl Mon (exc bank hols), all Oct–Mar (exc farm open pm wknds), Tudor Hall open pm wknds Apr–Sept, mansion open pm Tues–Sun Apr–Sept, and some wknds in Dec – best to check; (01625) 534400; entry to park £3.80 per car (free for cyclists and pedestrians), then £3 for the mansion or gardens, farm or Tudor Hall. A ticket allowing entry for any two attractions is £4.60; NT (though as the site is managed by the county council members still have to pay for all exc the mansion and garden).

LITTLE BOLLINGTON SJ7286
This peaceful hamlet gives strolls by the Bridgewater Canal and in Dunham Massey deer park; the Swan With Two Nicks is a very pleasant refreshment stop.

LITTLE BUDWORTH SJ5867
Cheshire Herbs Award-winning specialist herb nursery growing and selling over 400 different varieties from agrimony to yellow melilot. Shop, disabled access; cl 24 Dec–3 Jan; (01829) 760578; free. The Shrewsbury Arms has good value food.

Little Budworth Common This country park is a strong (and oddly refreshing) contrast to most of this area's richly manicured countryside: poor wild heath with young bogs and scrawny birch woods.

LOWER PEOVER SJ7474
Many people's favourite Cheshire village: cobbled lanes, glorious 14th-c black and white timbered church, quiet watermeadows and a fine pub, the Bells of Peover.

LOWER WITHINGTON SJ8169
Welltrough Dried Flowers (signed off A535) Helpful and friendly dried and silk flowers specialist based on a working arable farm. Snacks, shop, disabled access; cl 25–27 Dec, 1–3 Jan; (01477) 571616; free. The Black Swan is a pleasant country dining pub. Further along the A34 at Marton is a simple

14th-c shingle-roofed black and white timbered **church** in unpromising surroundings; readers recommend the adjacent **craft centre**, where a farm shop sells local ice-cream.

LYMM SJ6887
There are pretty cottages in The Dingle, and you can take **boat trips** on the Bridgewater Canal, for example from the new Admiral Benbow pub at Agden Wharf. The walk up to the lake at Lymm Dam is a pleasant stroll, and the Spread Eagle (Eagle Brow) has good value food.

MACCLESFIELD SJ9173
Away from the modern shopping streets are plenty of fine old buildings associated with the early industrial revolution and the silk industry; the weavers' cottages on Paradise St with their wide garret windows are of special note. You can buy a joint ticket to the two silk museums and Paradise Mill (£6 for three, £4 for two). Behind St Michael's church is a more ancient core with quaint little cobbled alleys, the famous 108 steps, and fine views across the town to the Pennines. The tea shop at Arighi Bianchi furniture shop (Silk Rd) is highly recommended. The Sutton Hall Hotel just S is best for lunch.

Hare Hill (off B5087 NW of Macclesfield) Acres of lovely parkland with walled garden, pergola, fine spring flowers, and rhododendrons and azaleas in May. Some disabled access; open Weds–Thurs, Sat–Sun and bank hols Apr–Oct plus daily during May; (01625) 584412; £2.50 (car park £1.50 but refundable when enter garden); NT. A footpath leads to Alderley Edge.

Paradise Mill (Park Lane) Enthusiastic guides, many of whom are former silk workers, take you around and demonstrate the silk production process on the mill's restored handlooms – room settings give a good idea of 1930s working conditions. Good disabled access; tours are 11.30, 12.30, 2.30 and 3.30; cl am Sun, 25–26 Dec and 1 Jan; (01625) 618228; £3. Nearby the new **Park Green Silk Museum** is housed in what used to be the art school, where silk designers were trained; displays on the properties of silk and design, and lots of historic machinery; cl am Sun; 25–26 Dec and 1

Jan; £3.

Silk Museum Heritage Centre
(Roe St) Formerly a Sunday school for children who worked in the silk mills, this heritage centre now houses a good silk museum with audio-visual displays, changing exhibitions and some fine examples of the end product; there's also a re-created schoolroom and a weaver's cottage. Snacks, shop, some disabled access (and audio guides); (01625) 613210, £2.90.

West Park Museum (Prestbury Rd) Small museum with a decent range of decorative arts (inc works by local bird artist Charles Tunnicliffe), and some interesting Egyptian antiquities. Adjacent West Park is pleasant and has one of the largest bowling greens in the country. Shop; cl am, all day Mon (exc bank hols), 25–26 Dec, 1 Jan; free.

MACCLESFIELD CANAL SJ8965
With good more or less level towpath walks, this tracks through fine high countryside from the Cheshire county boundary nr Disley to pass Bollington, Macclesfield and Congleton, with plenty of access points. One of the most interesting places is S of the A54 just W of its junction with the A523, where a staggering flight of 10 locks leads down to a sturdily elegant iron aqueduct.

MALPAS SJ4847
The most striking thing in this attractive place is the extraordinarily uplifting ceiling in its 14th-c hilltop **church**. There's also a fragmentary castle ruin nearby, as well as pretty cottages and almshouses, and some grander buildings.

MARBURY SJ5645
Some delightful landscapes open up in this village, with its attractive church, lake, wood and canal surroundings. The Swan is pleasant for lunch.

MARBURY COUNTRY PARK
SJ6576
With some quiet short walks, this gives on to the extensive **Budworth Mere**, with sailing, and herons, ducks, grebes and coots pottering around the rushes. The George & Dragon at Great Budworth is good for lunch.

MIDDLEWOOD WAY SJ9482
A sort of linear country park near Macclesfield, this runs along a former railway; attractively bordered with wild flowers and trees, with cycle tracks (bicycle hire at Lyme View Café (01625) 850985; £5 for 3 hours) and horse rides (around £10 an hour (01625) 872656); several decent pubs in Bollington, one at Whiteley Green. The pleasant stretches around the Poynton inclines are underrated, and the Boars Head here has good value food (all day wknds).

MOBBERLEY SJ7979
Hillside Bird Oasis (Damson Lane, Beech Hill) Excellent private collection of wildfowl with rare species such as white-headed stifftail and the Abyssinian black duck, as well as aviaries of softbills, flamingos and other exotic birds. Children should enjoy the penguin pool, and they have a pair of white wallabies. Under-cover picnic area, snacks, shop; open Apr–Oct exc Thurs plus Nov–Mar Sun and Weds; (01565) 873282; £4.50. The **church** has a magnificently carved Tudor rood screen. The Roebuck, Bulls Head and Church Inn, all welcoming children, are handy for lunch.

MOULDSWORTH SJ5070
Mouldsworth Motor Museum ⊞
(Smithy Lane) Splendid changing collection of cars, everything from vintage MGs to gleaming Ferraris. It's an especially friendly place, and you really don't have to be a car fiend to enjoy it – the 1930s art deco building and its grounds are very attractive in themselves, and there's plenty to amuse children, with quizzes, play areas and space to run around. There's also a collection of unusual teapots, many from the 1920s and 30s. Disabled access; open pm Sun Feb–end Nov, plus pm Weds July and Aug, best to check; (01928) 731781; £3. The Boot over at Boothsdale nr Willington is a good nearby dining pub (food all day wknds).

MOW COP SJ8557
Right on the Staffs border is a shaggy steep hill with a castellated folly on top, and a rock pinnacle left by former quarrying; views over Cheshire (the village just behind, which is in Staffs, is a reminder of the contrast with Cheshire's richness). Worth a look if passing.

NANTWICH SJ6552
A pedestrian-only centre protects the

splendid 14th-c **church**, with its exceptional carved choir-stalls; look out for the devil forcing open a nun's mouth, and the wife threatening her husband with a ladle. Much of the town, destroyed by a firestorm in 1583, was rebuilt then in intricate black and white timbering, and with countless window-boxes in flower in spring and summer is a fine sight esp around the centre. Quite a few decent antiques shops, and the picturesque Crown (High St) has good value lunchtime food. As most of south Cheshire's roads seem to intersect at the town, traffic can be a problem. Just N of town Reaseheath College (B5074) has a huge maize maze; open daily in school summer hols; (01270) 613215; £3.50; they also have lambing wknds in March.

Firs Pottery (Aston; A530 towards Whitchurch) Friendly place organising one-day pottery workshops (half-days for children). Booking essential; (01270) 780345; £28 for a day course, inc lunch, tea and coffee (£12 children, during school hols). A good shop sells all sorts of useful pots; disabled access to ground floor only. The nearby Bhurtpore has good food and an excellent range of real ales. Readers enjoy the vast array of different flavours of ice-cream available at **Snugbury's Ice-Cream Farm** (Hurleston, A51 N); cl 25–26 Dec and 1 Jan.

Hack Green Secret Nuclear Bunker 🖭 (off A530 S of Nantwich; Baddington) Built in the 1950s, this concrete labyrinth would have hidden civil servants and military commanders in the event of a nuclear war. An ordinary utility building on the surface, inside is crammed with gadgets and interactive displays conjuring up a picture of what life would be like during nuclear fall-out – you can even view the original TV broadcasts that would have been transmitted on all channels before a strike; children's trail. Meals, snacks, shop, disabled access; cl Dec; (01270) 629219; £5.30. The Aston at Bhurtpore is quite handy for lunch.

Stapeley Water Gardens (A51 about a mile SE) The world's largest and best-regarded water-garden centre, with display pools full of over 350 sorts of water-lily (at their best Jun–Sept), fountains and waterfalls, various gardens, and coldwater and tropical fish (as well as eels, piranhas and stingrays, they've now got black-tip reef sharks too). A huge heated glasshouse has palms and parrots, and in the animal room there are monkeys, creepy-crawlies, a crocodile and lots of different frogs. Plenty for fishermen, a pet centre, and frequent special events. Meals, snacks, shop, disabled access; cl 25 Dec and Easter Sun; (01270) 623868; gardens free; £3.85.

NESTON SJ3075

Ness Botanic Gardens Liverpool University's extensive collection of specimen trees and shrubs, herbaceous plants, renowned heather, rock, rose and water gardens; visitor centre, good children's adventure playground, and picnic area. Meals, snacks, shop and plant sales (not over Christmas), wheelchair route; cl 25 Dec; (0151) 353 0123; £4.70. The Boathouse and Red Lion in nearby Parkgate are good for a light lunch.

NETHER ALDERLEY SJ8476

Nether Alderley Mill Lovely 15th-c watermill with carefully preserved atmosphere, and restored working waterwheels. The Victorian machinery still grinds flour (water supplies permitting). Open pm Weds, Sun and bank hols Apr and Oct, Tues–Sun Jun–Sept; (01625) 584412; £2; NT. Nearby Alderley Edge SJ8677 (not to be confused with the straggling suburban settlement named after it) rises high out of the plain, with good walks through the woodland and fine views of the higher hills to the E.

NORTHWICH SJ6876

Anderton Boat Lift (just N of town) This is one of the great monuments of the canal era, a vast 1875 structure that was the only one of its kind ever built in Britain. Recently restored with grants of almost £7m from the Lottery and English Heritage, it once again lifts crafts more than 15 metres (50ft) between sections of the Trent and Mersey canal; boats enter a water-filled tank (or 'caisson') counterbalanced by another, and gravity does most of the work. There's a temporary visitor centre (the permanent one should be ready by Easter 2003), and you can go up the lift in a specially designed glass-topped boat. Meals, snacks, shop, disabled access; phone for information as they were unsure of opening times and prices as we went to press; (01606) 786777; free.

Salt Museum ⊞ (London Rd) Cheshire is the only British county to produce salt on a large scale, and much of it comes from this area. This interesting museum has the industry pretty well covered; microscopes let you see the intricacy of each crystal. Snacks, shop, limited disabled access; cl am wknds, all day Mon (exc bank hols and in Aug), 24–26 Dec; (01606) 41331; £2.25. You can follow the Salt Heritage Trail around some of the other buildings. From the Quay there are cruises down the river. The Smoker at Plumley (A556 E) is a reliable dining pub.

PARKGATE SJ2879
Once a more important port than Liverpool, this interesting village is the country's only inland seaside resort, the Dee estuary having retreated since its palmy days at the end of the 18th and early 19th c. There's an eerie charm in sitting in the Boathouse or Red Lion on the 'Promenade', looking out over the marshes to the distant waters and the Welsh hills on the far side. A similar sense of stranded time can be had at the Harp by the ruined marshside quay near Little Neston; you can walk between the two (and on to Ness Gardens at Ness) along the Dee estuary 'coastal' path.

PECKFORTON HILLS SJ5256
These are tracked by a particularly fine section of the 30-mile **Sandstone Trail**, with splendid views of real and real-looking romantic castles, and good pubs usefully placed at Bulkeley and Higher Burwardsley. The Trail offers very varied scenery, following the romantically wooded sandstone ridges, crags and outcrops stretching from Overton on the edge of Frodsham in the N (the church here is pretty, and the Ring o' Bells is a most attractive pub, with Mersey views) to the Shropshire border S of Malpas (the ancient Bell o' the Hill pub nr Tushingham down there is another good stop).

POYNTON SJ9183
Brookside Garden Centre
(Macclesfield Rd) A splendid miniature railway chuffs its way through an authentically detailed circuit in a pretty garden setting to a replica West Country station, packed with railway memorabilia; there's also a pottery. Parking is not always easy. Meals, snacks, shop, disabled access (not train); railway runs wknds all year (exc in Christmas hols) plus Weds Apr–Sept and daily mid-July–Aug, best to check; (01625) 872919; train £1, garden centre free. A mile away at Higher Poynton, Coppice Fruit Farm has **pick-your-own**, and the Boars Head does enjoyable food (all day wknds).

PRESTBURY SJ9077
Very prosperous-feeling now, with leafy surroundings, good shops, and for refreshment the smart Legh Arms and homelier Admiral Rodney. There are pleasant riverside walks to the S, along the Bollin.

RAW HEAD SJ5154
From the A534 nr Harthill a section of the 30-mile Sandstone Trail ascends Raw Head, the most spectacular natural feature of the central Cheshire ridge, with sandstone cliffs weathered into bizarre shapes, and a cave to explore. The Pheasant at Higher Burwardsley is a pleasant nearby haven.

ROSTHERNE SJ7483
As well as charming brick cottages along its quaint cobbled pavement, this picture-postcard village gives a lovely view over one of the county's broadest meres from the graveyard of its attractive timbered church.

RUNCORN SJ5481
Apart from Norton Priory, this New Town has some enjoyable surprises – such as the Sunday-afternoon **miniature train rides** in the Park on Stockham Lane (Halton), popular with children; Easter–Sept, 50p. There are views from the nearby ruins of **Halton Castle** up on its grassy hill.

Norton Priory Museum and Gardens ⊞ (Tudor Rd, Manor Park) Lovely 12th-c priory that developed into a now demolished Georgian country house, with exhibitions on medieval monastic life, and sculpture inc a twice-lifesize sandstone statue of St Christopher, said to be carved by a member of the priory 600 years ago.

There are beautiful woodland gardens and an enchanting 18th-c walled garden. Meals, snacks, shop, disabled access; cl am, 24–26 Dec, 1 Jan, walled garden cl am, and Nov–Mar; (01928) 569895; £3.95.

SANDIWAY SJ6070
Blakemere Craft Centre (Chester Rd) Top-notch craft centre based around restored Edwardian stable block, with interesting range of goods in the 30 shops, aquatic and falconry centre, garden centre and indoor play area. Wknd craft fairs, meals, snacks, disabled access; cl Mon (exc bank hols); (01606) 883261; free.

SCHOLAR GREEN SJ8157
Rode Hall Gardens In a Repton landscape, this fine house has been in the same family since it was first built in the early 18th c (though it's been extensively remodelled inside since then); the large gardens include a stylish rose garden, a working Victorian walled kitchen garden, and a grotto and ice-house. Snacks, poor disabled access (steps up to house, pebbled walkways in garden); house open pm Weds and bank hols, garden open pm Tues–Thurs plus bank hols) end Mar–Sept; (01270) 873237; £5 house and garden, £3.50 garden only.

STRETTON SJ4453
Stretton Watermill Working watermill in lovely countryside, which still produces corn, powered by two ancient wheels. Snacks, shop, some disabled access; cl am, all Mon and Oct–Mar (open wknds Apr and Sept); (01606) 41331; £1.90. The Cock o' Barton up on the A534 is quite useful for lunch (and a good base for walks – as is the Farndon Arms in the attractive Dee-side village of Farndon).

STYAL SJ8383
Quarry Bank Mill & Styal Estate
See separate family panel on p.51.
The Ship is pleasant for lunch.

SWETTENHAM SJ8067
One of Cheshire's tucked-away comfortable villages – rich paddocks with wrought-iron fences, daffodils in spring in a dell by an old mill, a good dining pub (the Swettenham Arms) behind the partly 13th-c church.

TABLEY SJ7177
Cuckoo Land 🏠 (Old School House, Nether Tabley) The friendly owners will take you on a guided tour of this huge collection of cuckoo clocks, all made in the Black Forest. They currently have over 550 rare and beautiful clocks, most of them working; five working historic fairground organs are among the other mechanisms on show, as well as a collection of vintage motorcyles. Phone for an appointment; shop, disabled access; (01565) 633039; £4.50.

Tabley House 🏠 (off A5033) The only Palladian house in the North-West, with a splendid collection of paintings. Sir John Fleming Leicester (whose family lived at Tabley for over 700 years) was the first great collector of British art, and though plans to turn his home into a National Gallery came to nothing, most of the works he assembled are still here, inc pictures by Turner, Reynolds, Henry Thompson and James Ward. Snacks, shop, very good disabled access (though they prefer notice); open Apr–Oct, pm Thurs–Sun and bank hols; (01565) 750151; £4. The Smoker at Plumley is good for lunch.

TARPORLEY SJ5562
Largely bypassed and quietly attractive, with very individual shops inc antiques shops, and a fine pub (the Rising Sun).

TATTENHALL SJ5059
Cheshire Farm Ice Cream 🏠 (Drumlan Hall Farm) Watch the cows being milked then sample over 30 flavours of the delicious end product. They've a new birds of prey rescue centre, a play barn, hedgehog care centre and rare breeds corner. Meals, snacks, shop, disabled access; usually cl two wks in Jan, but phone to check; (01829) 770995; free (when you buy one ice-cream you can get another free with our discount voucher). The Calveley Arms at nearby Handley has good imaginative food.

TEGGS NOSE COUNTRY PARK SJ9472
Cheshire's hilly eastern edge forms part of the Peak District, and offers some grand views westwards towards North Wales. This country park has a useful summer information centre, and good walks with far views, punctuated by relics of the former quarrying here. By

the turn off the A537, the Setter Dog is a good pub. From the park, a well marked track – actually part of the long-distance Gritstone Trail – heads off S into the **Macclesfield Forest**, with steep deep green pine plantations around neatly walled small reservoirs; on the far side of this the isolated Leathers Smithy E of Langley is a warmly welcoming moorside refuge with superb views, and the Stanley Arms tucked away at Bottom of the Oven is also good.

WARRINGTON SJ5990
Gulliver's World (Old Hall) Theme park very similar to its sister parks in Milton Keynes and Matlock Bath (see **Buckinghamshire and Derbyshire** chapters), with rides and entertainment aimed at the under-12s. Meals, snacks, shop, disabled access; open wknds Sept–Nov, daily Apr–Aug, phone to check; (01925) 444888; £7.50.
Warrington Museum and Gallery (Bold St) The geology and botany galleries contain hands-on displays and a 'breathing' model dinosaur. Other weird and wonderful exhibits include a model mermaid, a cannibal's flesh hook, an Egyptian mummy, a toy-packed nursery, and lots of beetles and other creepy-crawlies. Snacks, shop, disabled access; cl Sun and bank hols; (01925)442392; free. The Ferry at Fiddlers Ferry down by the Mersey off the A562 at Penketh is prettily placed for lunch.

WHARTONS LOCK SJ5360
With a handy family dining pub nearby, this is a good place for walks along the **Shropshire Union Canal**; this is a charming section, winding through the lifting bridge by it.

richly wooded farming country below Beeston Castle.

WHITEGATE SJ6168
An interesting village, with thatched houses around the village green, fragmentary remains of what was once the biggest Cistercian monastery in the whole of England opposite its church, and a lakeside walk along a nearby derelict railway. The Plough on Beauty Bank (towards Foxwist Green) is a pleasant old pub.

WIDNES SJ5183
Catalyst (Mersey Rd) This centre explores the chemical industry and how it affects our lives. Put like that it doesn't sound too gripping, but children who enjoy museums where you poke, press and push things will really get a lot out of it. It's all presented in a splendidly enjoyable way, with interactive games and displays such as Apples and Maggots, where you battle against maggots, gales and floods to grow a successful crop of apples, or the Game of Health, which involves travelling from the past to the present without falling victim to any deadly diseases. A glass lift whisks you up to a rooftop Observatory with splendid views. There's an adjacent waterside park, with wildlife and brightly coloured fishing boats. Meals, snacks, shop, disabled access; cl Mon exc bank and school hols, 24–26 Dec, 1 Jan; (0151) 420 1121; £4.65.

WRENBURY SJ5947
Canal walks The pretty **Llangollen Branch** is a relaxing canal for gentle waterside walks, with access at Wrenbury for example; the good Dusty Miller dining pub here has an interesting

Where to eat

ALDFORD SJ4158 **Grosvenor Arms** *Chester Rd (01244) 620228* Sizeable but friendly Victorian pub, attractively decorated, with big panelled library and several quieter rooms, airy conservatory, good interesting food from a daily-changing menu, well kept real ales, lots of New World wines (and malt whiskies), and large Sun-trap terrace by neat lawn; best to get there early; cl 25 Dec, pm 1 Jan; disabled access. £23.85|**£6.50**
BOLLINGTON SJ9377 **Mauro's** *88 Palmerston St (01625) 573898* Friendly Italian restaurant with lots of good pasta, excellent fresh fish and lovely puddings; cl Sun, Mon, 25–26 Dec; disabled access. £25|**£5.70**
BUNBURY SJ5758 **Dysart Arms** *Bowes Gate Rd (01829) 260183* By the village

church, this neat former farmhouse has a civilised, old-fashioned atmosphere, log fires, lots of antique furniture, cosy alcoves, a no smoking library area, well kept ales and house wines, interesting food, friendly service, and tables in lovely elevated big garden; cl 25 Dec; children over 10 in evenings; disabled access. £23|**£5.95**

CHESTER SJ4066 **Brasserie 10/16** *10–16 Brookdale Place* (01244) 322288 Good modern brasserie food in light and airy, simply decorated two-floored restaurant; interesting Mediterranean/British dishes, lovely puddings, good value wines, an open kitchen, and friendly helpful service; disabled access. £29.55|**£4**

CHESTER SJ4166 **Old Harkers Arms** *I Russell St* (01244) 344525 Attractive conversion of an early Victorian canal warehouse with lofty ceiling, tall windows and well spaced tables and chairs, lots to look at, a comfortably busy atmosphere, friendly efficient staff, a changing choice of nicely presented food inc interesting sandwiches, well kept real ales, and New World wines; no food Fri pm; children until 7.30pm; disabled access. £19.50|**£6.50**

COTEBROOK SJ5765 **Fox & Barrel** *Foxbank* (01829) 760529 Well run bar and restaurant with a lively friendly atmosphere, interestingly furnished snug areas, a very big log fire, extensive no smoking candlelit dining area, and huge helpings of tasty, interesting bar food; real ales, decent choice of wines, jazz Mon pm. £27|**£8.50**

DARESBURY SJ5782 **Ring o' Bells** (01925) 740256 Roomy pub with plenty of places to sit inc no smoking dining rooms and a down-to-earth part for walkers; reasonably priced and interesting daily specials, well kept real ales, 12 wines by the glass, a dozen malts, efficient, friendly service, and roaring fire; tables in long, partly terraced garden; this is an attractive village where Lewis Carroll's father was vicar; disabled access. £21|**£6.80**

HASSALL GREEN SJ7758 **Brindley's Lockside Restaurant** *Canal Centre* (01270) 762266 200-year-old house with tearoom offering breakfasts, snacks, lunches, cream teas, and evening restaurant – and you can sit on the lawn and watch the narrow-boats going through the locks; gift shop and towpath walks; bdrms; cl winter Sun pm. £21|**£4.95**

KNUTSFORD SJ7578 **Belle Epoque Brasserie** *60 King St* (01565) 633060 Popular restaurant-with-rooms decorated in art nouveau style with lavish drapes, marbled pillared alcoves, and smartly set tables, enthusiastic friendly staff and lovely modern cooking; cl Sun pm, Mon am; children over 12. £30|**£7.95**

PLUMLEY SJ7176 **Smoker** *Chester Rd* (01565) 722338 Popular thatched 16th-c pub with open fires and comfortable sofas in three well decorated connecting rooms, good swiftly served food, a wide choice of whiskies, well kept real ales, and friendly service; big garden; disabled access. £22|**£7.95**

Special thanks to Jenny and Michael Back, Leo and Barbara Lionet

CORNWALL

Ideal holiday country, from sandy family resorts through picturesque creeks, coves and quaint fishing villages to wild majestic cliffs and bleak moors; masses of family attractions, some spectacular gardens, a fine choice of places to stay in

Fantastic beaches and delightful seaside villages and towns are Cornwall's biggest attraction. With 500 miles of coastal walks here, many carefully preserved by the National Trust, it is easy to find breathtaking beauty throughout the county. The pretty south coast is very sheltered, with some fine places to stay. East of the Lizard point are plenty of interesting little coves, winding estuaries and creeks rich in bird life, and boat trips from almost every harbour.

For family beach holidays, the north coast is ideal, with an almost continuous line of resort developments, and lots of family attractions within easy travelling distance. The pretty harbour town of St Ives (which has two good art galleries), the quaint working fishing town of Padstow with its attractive slate houses, and Cornwall's biggest resort, bustling Newquay, are all superb for a lively holiday.

Heading a great range of family outings are Flambards theme park near Helston, Land's End (both of these easily fill a day), and – Cornwall's top family attraction this year – the new National Maritime Museum in Falmouth. Energetic children will get a kick out of the adventure play area at Dobwalls. Dairyland near Newquay (a firm family favourite) and Hayle's colourful Paradise Park (HQ of the World Parrot Trust) are entertaining, and there's an expanding animal centre at Trecangate. Newquay Zoo, the monkey sanctuary near Looe, the otter park at North Petherwin and the seal sanctuary at Gweek (the largest in Europe) all have plenty to interest wildlife-lovers.

Magnificent gardens are another great draw: because of its climate Cornwall can produce exotic plants unlike those elsewhere in England. Among many fine gardens are Lanhydrock (the house too is impressive), the Lost Gardens of Heligan in Mevagissey, and the two great gardens at Mawnan Smith; we've this year added Lamorran House Gardens in St Mawes. Cornwall is also home to the Eden Project, luring record numbers of visitors to this ambitious project – housed in the biggest greenhouse in the world. Cotehele near Calstock is Cornwall's most splendid house, and St Michael's Mount has a uniquely memorable setting. The Minack Open-Air Theatre at Porthcurno is an enchanting place to see a play.

There are some dramatic cliffy stretches of coast, interspersed with fine sandy beaches, especially on the Penwith peninsula (the part west of Marazion/St Ives), culminating in a spectacular range of cliffs from Treen to Land's End. Penwith, with its rugged windswept moorland, ruined tin mine buildings and overgrown stone walls, has lots of visible prehistoric remains – Bronze Age burial chambers and standing stones, Iron Age hill forts and village sites, and ancient stone crosses. Our pick of the best are Men an

Tol, Chun Castle, Chun Quoit and Lanyon Quoit (all near Morvah), Ballowal (see Pendeen entries), the Iron Age village sites of Chysauster and Carn Euny (the latter near Sancreed), Zennor Quoit, and the Merry Maidens (near Lamorna).

Another stretch of wild Cornwall is up towards Devon, north of commercialised Tintagel – with high cliffs, dramatic surfing beaches and plenty of wildlife. Port Isaac and Boscastle are the pick of this part's few settlements.

The inland parts of the county are largely treeless, with rolling pastures and moorland. Windswept Bodmin Moor is the county's most untouched inland area (Lakeside Adventure Park, Potters Museum of Curiosity, and Daphne du Maurier's Jamaica Inn give a lively contrast here). In the more exposed spots, the towering alloy propellers of the new wind farms are becoming a striking landscape feature.

In high summer, there's lots of traffic on the narrow roads (and some serious parking problems). Even then you can easily escape the hordes, and out of season, Cornwall comes into its own, with lots to do, a very relaxed pace and attractive prices. Late May and early June is an ideal time for a short break here, with relatively few other visitors. In spring (the best time for gardens) and early summer, the tall hedged banks which block the view from many byroads compensate by being virtual walls of wild flowers. September and October is seal pup time.

It is worth mentioning that not many of the roads actually follow the coast – great for walkers, but disappointing for drivers and cyclists. A Cornish Rail Rover ticket is good value for eight days (which don't have to be consecutive) of unlimited train journeys throughout the county for around £40.50 (less out of summer); you can also get a ticket for three days; phone (0845) 748 4950 for details. Much of Cornwall is covered by a surprisingly good bus network, and for a county-wide bus timetable and map, contact the Cornish Tourist Board, (01872) 322900.

The Isles of Scilly are ideal for a really quiet and relaxing holiday, with Penzance the quickest jumping-off point.

Where to stay

BODINNICK SX1352 **Old Ferry** *Bodinnick, Fowey, Cornwall PL23 1LX* (01726) 870237 **£65**; 12 comfortable and spacious rms, most with own bthrm and river views. 400-year-old inn in lovely situation overlooking Fowey estuary; back flagstoned bar partly cut into the rock, real ales, comfortable residents' lounge with French windows opening on to a terrace, and decent food in both bar and little evening restaurant; quiet out of season

BOTALLACK SW3632 **Botallack Manor** *Botallack, St Just-in-Penwith, Penzance, Cornwall TR19 7QG* (01736) 788525 **£50***; 3 rms. Blissfully quiet and friendly 17th-c local granite manor on working farm, with a medley of furnishings in reading room, good breakfasts with home-baked bread, and safe walled garden; no pets; marvellous cliff walks, ruined mines and small coves

BURYAS BRIDGE SW4427 **Rose Farm** *Chyenhal, Buryas Bridge, Penzance, Cornwall TR19 6AN* (01736) 731808 **£50***, plus winter breaks; 3 delightfully furnished rms. Relaxed, informal and friendly 200-year-old farmhouse tucked away

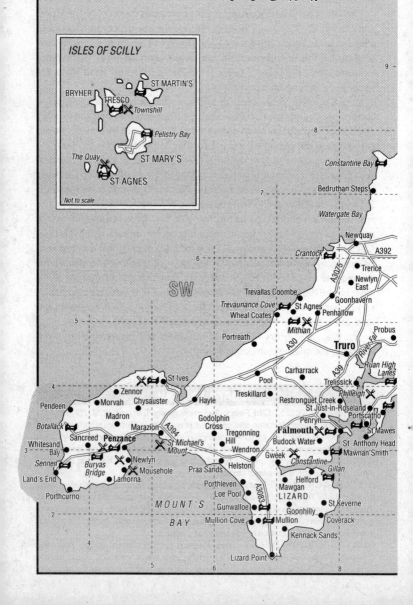

Cornwall

ATLANTIC

OCEAN

ISLES OF SCILLY

BRYHER
ST MARTIN'S
TRESCO
Townshill
Pelistry Bay
The Quay
ST MARY'S
ST AGNES

Not to scale

9

8

Constantine Bay

Bedruthan Steps

7

Watergate Bay

Newquay
A392
Crantock
SW
Trerice
Newlyn East
6
Trevallas Coombe
A3075
Trevaunance Cove
St Agnes
Goonhavern
Wheal Coates
Penhallow
5
Mithian
Probus
Portreath
A30
Truro
River Fal
Carharrack
Ruan High Lanes
St Ives
Pool
Trelissick
4
Zennor
Treskillard
A39
Philleigh
Morvah
Chysauster
Hayle
Restronguet Creek
Pendeen
Godolphin Cross
St Just-in-Roseland
Portscatho
Madron
Penryn
St Mawes
Botallack
Marazion
A394
Tregonning Hill
Falmouth
Whitesand Bay
Sancreed
Penzance
St Michael's Mount
Budock Water
St Anthony Head
Mawnan Smith
Sennen
Newlyn
Wendron
Gweek
Constantine
Gillan
Land's End
Buryas Bridge
Mousehole
Helston
Helford
Porthcurno
Lamorna
Praa Sands
Mawgan
LIZARD
3
Porthleven
Loe Pool
A3083
Goonhilly
St Keverne
Gunwalloe
MOUNT'S
Mullion Cove
Mullion
Coverack
2
BAY
Kennack Sands

Lizard Point

Morwenstow

Bude

DEVON

SS

Crackington Haven

Maxworthy

Boscastle

Tintagel

North Petherwin

Port Isaac

Delabole

Camelford

Altarnun

Launceston

Trelights

Polzeath

St Kew

Treburley

Rock

BODMIN MOOR

Padstow

Kit Hill

Little Petherick

Wadebridge

A390

Tredinnick

Callington

Calstock

Bodmin

St Neot

St Cleer

A38

Dobwalls

Liskeard

Pillaton

Lanhydrock

Braddock

Lanlivery

Restormel

A38

Roche Rock

Luxulyan

Trecangate

Duloe

St Germans

Saltash

Eden Project

Lanreath

A387

St Blazey

Golant

Langtelos Highway

St Martin

A374

Torpoint

St Austell

Polkerris

Bodinnick

Looe

Charlestown

Fowey

Lansallos

Polperro

Porthallow

Kingsand/Cawsand

Mevagissey

SX

Veryan

Caerhays

Portloe

Carne Beach

Dodman Point

Gerrans Bay

ENGLISH CHANNEL

0 Miles 10

0 Kilometres 16

down remote country lane, with excellent breakfasts around big table; can see lots of animals (working farm), and children love it; cl 24–25 Dec ☺

CARNE BEACH SX0655 **Nare Hotel** *Carne Beach, Veryan, Truro, Cornwall TR2 5PF (01872) 501279* **£252** inc afternoon tea, plus special breaks; 36 lovely rms to suit all tastes – some stylish ones overlook garden and out to sea. Attractively decorated and furnished hotel in magnificent clifftop position with secluded gardens, outdoor and indoor swimming pools, tennis, sailboarding, and fishing; antiques, fresh flowers and log fires in the airy, spacious day rooms, very good food in two restaurants (one is new this year, with a more relaxed atmosphere), wonderful breakfasts, and run by staff who really care; ideal for quiet family hols, with safe sandy beach below; disabled access; dogs welcome in bedrooms ☺

CONSTANTINE BAY SW8674 **Treglos Hotel** *Constantine Bay, Padstow, Cornwall PL28 8JH (01841) 520727* **£95**, plus special breaks; 42 light rms, some with balcony. Quiet and relaxed hotel close to good sandy beach, and in the same family for 30 years; comfortable traditional furnishings, log fires, good food, friendly helpful staff, sheltered garden plus playground and adventure equipment, indoor swimming pool, table tennis, table football, and pool table, and children's playroom with electronic games; lovely nearby walks; self-catering apartments; cl mid-Nov–mid-Mar; children over 7 in restaurant; disabled access; dogs welcome in bedrooms ☺

CRACKINGTON HAVEN SX1496 **Manor Farm** *Crackington Haven, Bude, Cornwall EX23 0JW (01840) 230304* **£60***; 4 pretty rms. Lovely Domesday-listed, no smoking manor surrounded by 25 acres of farmland and carefully landscaped gardens; antiques in four lounges, a log fire, a house-party atmosphere, big breakfasts, and a delicious 4-course dinner at 7pm; cl 25 Dec; no children

CRANTOCK SW7760 **Crantock Bay Hotel** *West Pentire, Crantock, Newquay, Cornwall TR8 5SE (01637) 830229* **£73***, plus special breaks; 33 comfortable rms, most with coastal views. In a lovely setting on the West Pentire headland, facing the Atlantic and a huge sheltered sandy beach, this relaxed and informal hotel has been run by the same friendly family for 50 years; four acres of grounds, an indoor swimming pool, toddlers' pool, sauna and exercise room, all weather tennis court, a putting course, and children's play area; two lounges, bar lounge and restaurant, enjoyable food using local produce, and nice afternoon teas; cl early Nov–end Jan; families most welcome; lots to do nearby; disabled access and facilities; dogs welcome away from public rooms ☺

FALMOUTH SW7932 **Penmere Manor** *Mongleath Rd, Falmouth, Cornwall TR11 4PN (01326) 211411* **£102**, plus special breaks; 37 spacious rms. Run by the same owners for 29 years, this quietly set Georgian manor has five acres of subtropical gardens and woodland, heated outdoor swimming pool, giant chess, croquet, and leisure centre with indoor swimming pool, gym, sauna, and woodland fitness trail; particularly helpful friendly staff, an evening pianist, and enjoyable food in restaurant and informal bar; cl 24–27 Dec; dogs welcome in bedrooms

FOWEY SX1251 **Fowey Hall** *Fowey, Cornwall PL23 1ET (01726) 833866* **£160**; 24 rms inc 11 suites and 4 pairs of interconnecting rms. Fine Gothic-style mansion in five acres of grounds overlooking the harbour and run along the same lines as their other hotels – Woolley Grange, Bradford-on-Avon, Moonfleet Manor at Fleet, and Old Bell, Malmesbury; marble fireplaces, baroque plasterwork, panelling, antiques, big potted plants, two enjoyable restaurants, marvellous facilities for children inc supervised nursery, and covered swimming pool, croquet, and badminton; dogs welcome away from eating areas ☺

FOWEY SX1251 **Marina Hotel** *17 Esplanade, Fowey, Cornwall PL23 1HY (01726) 833315* **£100**, plus special breaks; 13 rms, several with lovely views (some with balcony). Friendly Georgian hotel in fine position overlooking Fowey River and open sea (private access from secluded walled garden); comfortable lounge/reading room, cheerfully decorated bar, attractive dining room overlooking the water, good food (super fresh fish and shellfish), and helpful service; disabled access

GERRANS BAY SW8938 **Pendower Beach House** *Ruan High Lanes, Truro,*

Cornwall TR2 5LW (01872) 501241 **£164** inc dinner, plus special breaks; 14 rms. Family-run hotel dating back to 16th c in eight acres by lovely sandy beach, with superb sea and coastal views, and plenty of seats on sunny terrace; a relaxed, friendly atmosphere in attractive and comfortable rooms, good food in cosy restaurant (super fresh local fish and shellfish), and tennis court; cl Nov–Feb; disabled access; dogs welcome in bedrooms

GILLAN SW7825 **Tregildry** *Gillan, Manaccan, Helston, Cornwall TR12 6HG (01326) 231378* **£144*** inc dinner, plus special breaks; 10 attractive rms with fine views over Falmouth Bay. Elegantly furnished hotel in four acres of grounds with private access to the cove below; spacious comfortable lounges, fresh flowers, books and magazines, a restful atmosphere, very good food in attractive restaurant, enjoyable breakfasts, and kind, courteous service; cl Nov–Feb; children over 8; dogs welcome in bedrooms

GUNWALLOE SW6522 **Halzephron** *Gunwalloe, Helston, Cornwall TR12 7QB (01326) 240406* **£72**; 2 cosy rms. 500-year-old former smugglers' inn run by knowledgeable and friendly Cornish landlady, with imaginative food in bar areas and bistro-style restaurant, open fire, and fine views of Mounts Bay; lots of walks, nearby beaches, golf, and boating; cl 25 Dec; no children for accommodation (allowed in pub)

LISKEARD SX2460 **Well House** *St Keyne, Liskeard, Cornwall PL14 4RN (01579) 342001* **£110**, plus special breaks; 9 individually designed rms with fine views. Light and airy Victorian country house, recently redecorated, with warm, friendly owners, courteous staff, comfortable drawing room, cosy little bar, and particularly good food and fine wines in dining room overlooking terrace and lawns; three acres of gardens with hard tennis court, swimming pool and croquet lawn; children over 8 in evening restaurant; dogs welcome in bedrooms

LITTLE PETHERICK SW9172 **Old Mill Country House** *Little Petherick, Wadebridge, Cornwall PL27 7QT (01841) 540388* **£64***, plus special breaks; 4 rms. 16th-c corn mill in lovely riverside gardens with waterwheel and other original features, enjoyable breakfasts in beamed dining room, lounges, and attentive service; plenty of places nearby for evening meals; cl Nov–Mar; no children

LOOE SX2251 **Talland Bay Hotel** *Porthallow, Looe, Cornwall PL13 2JB (01503) 272667* **£110**, plus special breaks; 22 charming rms with sea or country views. Down a little lane between Looe and Polperro, this restful partly 16th-c country house has lovely subtropical gardens just above the sea; comfortable drawing room with log fire, smaller lounge with library, fresh flowers, courteous service, good food in pretty oak-panelled dining room, and pleasant afternoon teas; heated outdoor swimming pool, putting, croquet; cl Jan; children over 5 in evening restaurant (high tea for younger ones); dogs welcome in bedrooms

MAWNAN SMITH SW7828 **Meudon Hotel** *Mawnan Smith, Falmouth, Cornwall TR11 5HT (01326) 250541* **£200** inc dinner, plus special breaks; 29 well equipped comfortable rms in separate wing. Run by the same caring family for over 36 years, this is an old stone mansion with a newer wing, in beautiful subtropical gardens laid out 200 years ago by R W Fox; fine views from the dining room, comfortable lounge with log fire and fresh flowers, good English cooking, and old-fashioned standards of service; cl 3–31 Jan; disabled access; dogs welcome in bedrooms

MAXWORTHY SX2492 **Wheatley Farm** *Maxworthy, Launceston, Cornwall PL15 8LY (01566) 781232* **£48**, plus special breaks; 4 attractive rms with showers. In the same family for five generations, this working dairy farm has comfortable, pretty furnishings, log fires, good 4-course evening meals using local produce in spacious dining room, and hearty breakfasts; cl Nov–end Jan; self-catering cottages, safe children's play area, animals to visit, and pony rides

MITHIAN SW7450 **Rose-in-Vale Country House Hotel** *Mithian, St Agnes, Cornwall TR5 0QD (01872) 552202* **£99**, plus special breaks; 18 pretty rms inc 2 suites. Secluded and quietly set Georgian house in four acres of neatly kept gardens, with comfortable spacious day rooms, a friendly atmosphere, helpful, long-standing local staff, and good food in enlarged dining room; ducks on ponds, a trout steam, outdoor swimming pool, badminton, and croquet, plus a sauna and solarium; children over 7 in evening in public rooms and restaurant (high tea for smaller ones); cl Jan–Feb; disabled access; dogs welcome in bedrooms

MULLION SW6818 **Meaver Farm** *Meaver Rd, Mullion, Helston, Cornwall TR12 7DN (01326) 240128* **£50**, plus special breaks; 3 individual rms with super bthrms. 17th-c stone farmhouse (no longer a working farm), with good Aga-cooked breakfasts in beamed kitchen, log fire, plants and antiques in sitting room, and friendly helpful owners; dogs welcome

MULLION SW6718 **Polurrian Hotel** *Mullion, Helston, Cornwall TR12 7EN (01326) 240421* **£130** inc dinner, plus special breaks; 39 rms, some with memorable sea view. White clifftop hotel in lovely gardens with path down to sheltered private cove below, a restful atmosphere in the comfortable lounges and bright cocktail bar, fresh flowers, good food using fresh local ingredients (pianist and sea views in the dining room), enjoyable breakfasts, leisure club with heated swimming pool, and heated outdoor pool, badminton, tennis, mini-golf, squash and croquet; particularly good for families; disabled access; dogs welcome ☺

PADSTOW SW9175 **Treverbyn House** *Station Rd, Padstow, Cornwall PL28 8DA (01841) 532855* **£60**; 5 rms with lovely views over the Camel estuary. Carefully restored Edwardian house opposite the famous Seafood Restaurant, with friendly owners, open fires in comfortable public rooms, and good breakfasts; cl Christmas; disabled access

PENZANCE SW4730 **Abbey Hotel** *Abbey St, Penzance, Cornwall TR18 4AR (01736) 366906* **£105**, plus winter breaks; 7 charming rms. Stylish little 17th-c house close to harbour with marvellous views, a relaxed atmosphere in comfortable drawing room full of flowers, fine paintings and antiques, a good set menu in small restaurant, and pretty garden; cl 1 wk Christmas; children over 7 in dining room; dogs welcome in bedrooms

PENZANCE SW4730 **Georgian House Hotel** *20 Chapel Street, Penzance, Cornwall TR18 4AW (01736) 365664* **£46**; 11 comfortable rms, most with own bthrm. Warmly friendly little hotel, once the home of the Mayor of Penzance and close to the harbour and shopping centre, with helpful owner and staff, very good breakfasts in attractive dining room, reading lounge, and private parking; cl Christmas– mid-Jan; dogs welcome in bedrooms

PENZANCE SW4729 **Summer House** *Cornwall Terrace, Penzance, Cornwall TR18 4HL (01736) 363744* **£65**, plus special breaks; 5 charming rooms with fresh flowers and antiques. In a mews 50 metres from the sea, this Regency restaurant-with-rooms (flooded with light by a curving glass tower) has a relaxed, informal atmosphere, lots of cheerful yellows and blues, wooden floors, comfortable sofas and local paintings, and wonderful Mediterranean-style food (the owner/chef worked in some top London restaurants); pretty walled garden; cl Jan, part Feb; children over 13

PILLATON SX3663 **Weary Friar** *Pillaton, Saltash, Cornwall PL12 6QS (01579) 350238* **£50**, plus special breaks; 12 rms. Pretty 12th-c inn by church in pleasantly remote village; lots of character in its four knocked-together rooms (one no smoking), attractive furnishings, well kept real ales, and good food in both bar and restaurant; children over 10

PORT ISAAC SX0080 **Port Gaverne Hotel** *Port Gaverne, Port Isaac, Cornwall PL29 3SQ (01208) 880244* **£80**, plus special breaks; 15 comfortable rms. Lovely place to stay and an excellent base for area (dramatic coves, good clifftop walks, and lots of birds); big log fires in well kept bars, relaxed lounges, decent bar food, good restaurant food, and fine wines; also, restored 18th-c self-catering cottages; cl 5 Jan–12 Feb; children over 7 in restaurant; dogs anywhere except dining room

PORTLOE SW9339 **Pine Cottage** *Portloe, Truro, Cornwall TR2 5RB (01872) 501385* **£70**; 2 rms. Charming old house in pretty garden just a few hundred yards from the harbour of this unspoilt fishing village; open fire, books and honesty tray in cosy sitting room, particularly good food using fresh local produce and a thoughtful little wine list in light, spacious dining room, super breakfasts (they will make up picnics and packed lunches, too), and warmly friendly owner; cl Christmas; babies welcome, but children over 9; disabled access.

ROCK SW9375 **St Enodoc Hotel** *Rock, Wadebridge, Cornwall PL27 6LA (01208) 863394* **£165***, plus special breaks; 19 individually designed rms with lovely views. Quietly set hotel overlooking the Camel estuary and next to two 18-hole golf courses; stylish Mediterranean décor with plenty of paintings and fresh flowers, delicious modern cooking in bar and split-level restaurant, a relaxed informal atmosphere, a gym, sauna and billiards room, and heated swimming pool in big garden; good for families with playroom, table tennis, table football, TV and video, and quite a few other facilities; lovely nearby beaches and walks; cl Jan–mid-Feb ☺

RUAN HIGH LANES SW9039 **Crugsillick Manor** *Ruan High Lanes, Truro, Cornwall TR2 5LJ (01872) 501214* **£80**, plus special breaks; 3 rms. One of the loveliest houses in Cornwall, this Queen Anne manor is extended from a pre-Elizabethan farmhouse and surrounded by a big quiet garden with wooded valley views; log fire in drawing room with Napoleonic ceiling, candlelit dinners in 17th-c dining room using home-grown produce where possible, fine breakfasts, and charming owners; self-catering cottages in grounds – excellent disabled access, and children welcome (but must be over 12 in main house); house cl Christmas (self-catering open then); dogs anywhere in cottages, not in bdrms in house

SALTASH SX3957 **Erth Barton** *Elmgate, Saltash, Cornwall PL12 4QY (01752) 842127* **£70**; 3 rms. Lovely old manor house with its own chapel, peaceful rooms with lots of books, pictures and big fireplaces, good enjoyable food, bird-watching in the surrounding estuaries, and riding (you can bring your own horse); children over 12; dogs welcome anywhere

SENNEN SW3425 **Lands End Hotel** *Sennen, Penzance, Cornwall TR19 7AA (01736) 871844* **£130**, plus special breaks; 33 elegant airy rms, many with splendid sea views. Comfortable hotel right on the clifftop with fine sea views, good food in attractive conservatory-style restaurant, elegant seating areas, informal bar with lots of malt whiskies, and helpful staff; lots to do nearby; cl end Oct–1 Mar; dogs welcome in bedrooms

ST BLAZEY SX0655 **Nanscawen Manor House** *Prideaux Road, St. Blazey, Par, Cornwall PL24 2SR (01726) 814488* **£80***; 3 spacious, pretty rms overlooking the garden. Extended 16th-c house in five acres of lovely grounds and gardens with an outdoor swimming pool and whirlpool spa, and a sunny terrace; big sitting room with honesty bar, friendly helpful owners, enjoyable breakfasts in light conservatory (plenty of places nearby for evening meals), and a relaxed atmosphere; no smoking; the Eden Project is close by; children over 12

ST IVES SW5437 **Countryman** *Old Coach Rd, Trink, St Ives, Cornwall TR26 3JQ (01736) 797571* **£65***, plus special winter breaks; 6 rms. Small friendly no smoking hotel in two acres of gardens; comfortable lounge, bright flower-filled conservatory, and cosy restaurant; walks, golf and Tate Gallery nearby; children over 9

ST IVES SW5040 **Garrack** *Burthallan Lane, St Ives, Cornwall TR26 3AA (01736) 796199* **£131***, plus winter breaks; 20 rms, some in more modern wing. Friendly hotel in two acres of gardens with wonderful sea views, cosy lounges with antiques, books and open fires, a family room, good food inc fresh shellfish, helpful staff, and indoor leisure centre; disabled access; dogs welcome in bedrooms

ST MARTIN SX2755 **Bucklawren Farm** *St Martin, Looe, Cornwall PL13 1NZ (01503) 240738* **£50***, plus special breaks; 6 rms. Spacious farmhouse on 500-acre beef and arable working farm with coastal and sea views, croquet and putting in the big garden, large homely lounge, south-facing sun lounge, and enjoyable food in restaurant; cl Dec–end Feb; children over 5; disabled access

ST MAWES SW8433 **Rising Sun** *The Square, St Mawes, Truro, Cornwall TR2 5DJ (01326) 270233* **£64.50***; 8 rms. Small attractive hotel in popular picturesque waterside village, with harbour views, large comfortable lounge bar area, airy conservatory, charming terrace; dogs welcome in bedrooms

ST MAWES SW8432 **Tresanton** *Lower Castle Rd, St Mawes, Truro, Cornwall TR2*

5DR (01326) 270055 **£235**, plus special breaks; 26 rms all with individual furnishings and sea views. Hidden away behind a discreet entrance, with elegant terraces (heating for cool weather), little bottom bar, steps up to the main building and its stylish lounge with deeply comfortable sofas and armchairs, big bowls of flowers, log fire, daily papers and sophisticated but relaxed atmosphere; excellent food, a fine wine list, and friendly informal service; several boats for hire inc the beautiful 48-ft yacht *Pinuccia*

TREVAUNANCE COVE SW7251 **Driftwood Spars** *Trevaunance Cove, St Agnes, Cornwall TR5 0RT (01872) 552428* **£68**; 15 attractive, comfortable bdrms, some with sea view, 8 in separate building. Friendly family-owned hotel dating from the 17th c and just up the road from the beach and dramatic cove; woodburner in comfortable lounge, main bar with large open fire, upstairs gallery, beamed ceilings, helpful staff, and enjoyable food; live music wknds; cl 25 Dec; dogs welcome anywhere

To see and do

Cornwall Family Attraction of the Year

FALMOUTH SW8032 **National Maritime Museum Cornwall** 🆓 (Discovery Quay) The opening of this ambitious new centre was still eagerly awaited as we went to press, but we make no apology for enthusiastically recommending it before we've seen it: the inventive displays have been designed in a splendidly entertaining way, very much with children in mind, and it's likely to be a hugely rewarding half-day out for boat enthusiasts and landlubbers alike. In a spectacular new building dominating the waterfront, it sets out to explore all things relating to boats and the sea, and particularly the importance of the sea to Cornwall. The National Small Boat Collection is on permanent loan from the museum's better known branch in Greenwich, and every year around 40 different boats will be shown across the various galleries. In one, imaginatively put together minute-long audio-visual shows will tell the story behind individual boats, including ones used for leisure, racing and rescue; sometimes the whole gallery will for a short time be transformed into one scene – a regatta, say, or an estuary in deep fog. A definite highlight will be the tidal gallery, built below sea level with big glass windows to dramatically show the patterns of the tide; you should be able to get a good look at local sealife too – builders constructing this gallery were fascinated to watch a cormorant sweep down in front of them to catch a passing fish. Many of the exhibits will be hands-on: an interactive water science gallery is firmly aimed at children, while other interactives will explain aspects of navigation and meteorology. At the top of the building's lighthouse-like tower, telescopes and push-button exhibits will reveal more about the surrounding area. Older visitors with a serious interest in all things nautical won't be left out: some galleries are packed with resources and information that could keep enthusiasts fascinated for weeks. There will also be demonstrations of traditional ship-building techniques. When we last spoke to them an exact opening date still hadn't been announced, but they should be open by the time this book hits the shops – best to check on their website www.nmmc.co.uk for the latest information. Meals, snacks, shop, good disabled access; cl 25 Dec; *£5.90, *£3.90 children over 5.

Please let us know what you think of places in the *Guide*. Use the report forms at the back of the book, write us a letter or log on to www.goodguides.com

ALTARNUN SX2281

Altarnun church The church has an enchanting set of 16th-c carved bench ends, much humanity and humour. The unpretentious Rising Sun just N is good value. Nearby **Wesley's Cottage** just off A30 at Trewint, the world's smallest Methodist place of worship, has a room set out as it would have been in 1744.

BEDRUTHAN STEPS SW8469 (off B3276 Newquay–Padstow) The scenic highlight of this stretch of coast: gigantic rock pillars towering over a rocky beach; NT car park nearby.

BODMIN SX0766

Bodmin & Wenford Railway 🖼 (General Station, St Nicholas St) Restored steam locomotives take you back to the glory days of the Great Western Railway when hordes of holiday-makers travelled this route to the sun. As well as enjoying the view, you can stop off for pleasant woodland walks. Main line connection at Bodmin Parkway station. Snacks, shop, disabled access; cl Jan–late Mar, and Nov, with a limited service in Apr, May, Oct and Dec; (runs daily Jun–Sept) – best to phone for train times; (01208) 73666; from £5 (discount voucher not valid for special events).

Bodmin Gaol (Berrycoombe Rd) The former county prison, built in 1778, with spooky underground dungeons; the Crown Jewels were stored here in World War I. Meals and snacks (pub on site), shop; (01208) 76292; £3.90. There's a sacred well in the churchyard of St Petroc's church.

Pencarrow 🖼 (Washaway, 3m N of Bodmin off A389) Notable 18th-c house with fine paintings and furniture, rococo ceiling in the music room, and, perhaps the highlight, 50 acres of lovely formal and woodland gardens with over 700 different rhododendrons and an acclaimed conifer collection. Also marked trails, children's play area, peacocks, chickens and other birds, craft centre and ancient British encampment. Meals, snacks, shop, limited disabled access; house open Sun–Thurs Apr–Oct; gardens open daily; (01208) 841369; *£6, garden only *£3. On the way out, the Borough Arms is good value for lunch.

BODMIN MOOR SX1875

Cornwall's highest part, this granite upland is something like a miniature Dartmoor, though not as richly endowed for walking as its Devon counterpart. Although largely pathless and bleak, it does have its own character, with gnarled tors, wind-bent trees, prehistoric traces, granite walls and lonely lakes. Good views from the main A30 (generally better than the side roads). One of the most accessible bits is around Minions, on the south side of the moor. Amid disused quarries here, you can park near the Hurlers stone circles, and stroll an old quarry track to a striking weathered rock formation, the Cheesewring (resembling a great stack of cheeses); excellent views E to Dartmoor and N over the centre of Bodmin Moor. Just S of Minions at Darite, Trethevy Quoit is the area's best antiquity – a megalithic tomb complete with capstone. Also grand views from the summit of Rough Tor (pronounced Roe Tor), reached from a signed car park off the A39 nr Camelford, looking towards Brown Willy, the highest point in Cornwall. Riding is popular on the moor, and quite a few stables on or around it cater for all levels of riding ability.

Lakeside Adventure Park 🖼 (off A30 just S) Barn owls and red squirrels are among the animals being reintroduced at this family-oriented place; also rare breeds of birds, poultry, indoor and outdoor pets, adventure play areas, under-cover assault course, museum, and lakeside walks. Snacks, shop, some disabled access; cl end Sept–Apr; (01208) 821469; £4.95. About a mile away, Dozmary Pool is one of two Cornish lakes that claim to be where a legendary arm rose from the depths and reclaimed Excalibur (the other is Loe Pool near Porthleven), and it's an easy starting point for Bodmin Moor.

Potters Museum of Curiosity 🖼 In the little complex that's sprung up around Jamaica Inn, the pub immortalised by Daphne du Maurier, this is a bizarre Victorian collection of stuffed animals and other assorted oddities. Not content with displaying them in cases, Mr Potter constructed elaborate tableaux around the bodies brought to him by local farmers, with the animals positioned as if they were tiny humans. Guinea-pigs play cricket, rabbits sit in a classroom, and squirrels carouse in a pub in this weird little world – the Kittens' Wedding has to be seen to be believed. Meals, snacks, shop, limited disabled access; cl Jan; (01566) 86838; £2.50. The pub itself is still atmospheric despite the developments. The A30, incidentally, has better views of the moor than any of the byroads.

BOSCASTLE SX0991
Pretty harbour with 16th-c pier squeezed into a rocky creek, cottages converted from warehouses, gift shops, a witchcraft museum; the Napoleon (a stiff climb) is nice for lunch. The cliffs nearby afford some fascinating views. Not far from here at Trevalga, Tredole Farm will arrange coastal or country **horse and pony trekking** (inc a 3-hr ride to a pub); non-riders welcome; (01840) 250495; from £15. Nearby **St Juliot church** was restored by Thomas Hardy in his career as an architect; he described the area later in *A Pair of Blue Eyes*.

BRADDOCK SX1662
Braddock church Hardly striking as a building, but well worth visiting for its handsome wood carvings.

BUDE SS2106
A popular area for surfing, with great beaches beyond the dunes; Sandy Mouth slightly N has clean water for bathing. Otherwise it's an unremarkable resort, though the Bude and Stratton Museum (The Wharf) is a decent rainy-day retreat (shop, disabled access; open daily Easter–Sept; 50p) – placed by the lock at the seaward end of the Bude Canal (now navigable for only two miles to Helebridge). The Falcon Hotel does good value quick food. The carved bench ends up at Poughill church (pronounced poffle) are entertaining; the Preston Gate is a decent pub there.

BUDOCK WATER SW7730
Penjerrick Garden Peaceful 15-acre garden with some huge trees, created 200 years ago by the Fox family who were also responsible for Glendurgan at Mawnan Smith. The upper garden (good sea views from here) contains a notable collection of rhododendrons as well as camellias, azaleas, tree ferns and bamboos, while the wilder valley garden has ponds and tree ferns dating back almost to the original planting of the garden; open pm Weds, Fri and Sun Mar–Sept; (01872) 870105; £2.

CAERHAYS SW9741
Caerhays Castle Gardens 🏰
Revered by gardening cognoscenti, these magnificent spring gardens are beautifully set around the back of a striking castle, with lovely coastal views. Renowned especially for their rhododendrons, magnolias and camellias, they're easily combined with a visit to the better known Lost Gardens of Heligan. Tearoom, limited disabled access; garden open Mar–May, castle open pm Mon–Fri 17 Mar–9 May; (01872) 501310; £4.50. Depending on where you're coming from, the Crown over at St Ewe and the Kings Arms at Tregony up on the main road are handy for lunch.

CALLINGTON SX3769
Dupath Holy Well (off A388 S) In a 15th-c chapel, the best-preserved of Cornwall's many holy wells, its unappetising water said to cure whooping cough. The town is not in itself remarkable, but the Coachmakers Arms is a good lunch stop.

CALSTOCK SX4268
Cotehele (1m W by footpath, 6m by road) Tucked away in a network of twisting roads high above the Tamar, this rambling granite house has hardly changed since being built in the late 15th c; there's no electricity, so the dark rooms – with fine furniture, armour and tapestries – have an authentically medieval atmosphere. Outside are lovely terraced gardens, a medieval dovecote, restored watermill, and miles of peaceful woodland walks. Down at Cotehele Quay a National Maritime Museum outpost shows the quay's history, and the last of the Tamar ketch-rigged barges has been restored here; there's a little art gallery too. Meals, snacks (tearoom in pleasant riverside setting with good cream teas), shop, some disabled access; house cl Fri and Nov–Mar, mill as house (but cl am and open Fri July–Aug), garden open daily all year; (01579) 351346; £6.40,

£3.60 garden and mill only; NT. Pleasant walks along the Tamar from the village. The unusual Who'd Have Thought It at St Dominick is good for lunch.

CAMELFORD SX1083

Locals will tell you this is the site of Camelot, and send you a mile N to the otherwise unremarkable Slaughter Bridge, where Arthur supposedly fell at his last battle. The friendly Darlington does food at almost any time.

British Cycling Museum ⊞ (The Old Station – B3266 N) Comprehensive collection of more than 400 bicycles, tricycles and even a five-wheeled Hen and Chickens bike, ranging from an original 1819 hobby-horse through boneshakers and penny-farthings to the hi-tech bikes of today. The couple who run it met through cycling, and really know their stuff. Outside is a sculpture made up of old bicycles. Shop, disabled access; usually cl Fri and Sat, and 25 Dec; (01840) 212811; £2.75.

North Cornwall Museum and Gallery ⊞ (The Clease) Good exploration of regional life over the past century, with displays of cider-making and farming, and collections of pottery and even early vacuum cleaners. Shop; cl Sun and Oct–Mar; (01840) 212954; £1.50.

CARHARRACK SW7341

Carharrack Methodist church Has an exhibition on Cornish Methodism and John Wesley, who preached at the octagon chapel that used to stand here; disabled access; open by appointment; (01209) 820381; free. Wesley preached more regularly at nearby **Gwennap Pit**, a spectacular grass ampitheatre, which still has services (usually spring bank hol, 3pm Suns in July and Aug and perhaps other times), and a visitor centre. Shop, snacks, disabled access; centre usually only cl lunchtimes, Sat pm, and end Sept–Apr, though best to check; (01209) 821390. The peaceful grass amphitheatre itself is open all the time; free. The Fox & Hounds at Lanner is good for lunch.

CHARLESTOWN SX0351

A picturesque working china clay port, with sailing ships as well as modern cargo boats; it's much used as a film/TV setting. Two square-rigged sailing ships,

stars of many films inc *1492: Conquest of Paradise* may be in the harbour. The **Shipwreck & Heritage Centre** (Quay Rd) has an exhibition about the *Titanic* and is good for local history (cl Nov–Feb; (01726) 69897; £4.95). The waterside Harbour Inn (Pier House Hotel) is useful for lunch.

CHYSAUSTER SW4735

Chysauster Ancient Village (off B3311 N of Gulval, where the Coldstreamer is a well run dining pub) Highly evocative Iron Age site, perched on a windy hillside: remains of eight courtyard houses grouped beside what might be Britain's oldest village street give an idea of Celtic life almost 2,000 years ago. The site is also notable for its large untreated meadow, popular with wild birds, and, depending on the season, bright with bluebells, heather or unusual orchids. Snacks, shop; cl Nov–Mar; (07831) 757934; £1.80; EH.

COVERACK SW7818

An attractive coastal village, with a decent pub. A rewarding walk takes you down to Black Head and beyond, or to Lowland Point, for dramatic views of The Manacles – striking offshore rocks.

CRACKINGTON HAVEN SX1496

A really nice beach here, with plenty of rock pools; the 'Crackington formation' creates fissures and arches in the rocks that were treacherous to sailors. With a superbly sited family dining pub, the Coombe Barton, to set you up (or reward you afterwards), there's also a good walk to **High Cliff**, Cornwall's loftiest.

DELABOLE SX0884

Gaia Energy Centre ⊞ On the country's first wind farm, this hi-tech visitor centre is designed to promote green issues; you can get a close-up look at the 30-metre wind turbines, and see lots of examples of alternative energy ranging from waterwheels and wave power to futuristic hydrogen fuel cells; cl 24–25 and 31 Dec and 1 Jan. Meals, snacks and picnic area, shop, disabled access; (01840) 214101; £4.95.

DOBWALLS SX2165

Dobwalls Family Adventure Park (off A38) This place started life as a miniature railway, and the two miles of scaled-down American-style railroad are still very much the hub of activity;

ten different steam and diesel trains chuff up and down the track, and there's an accompanying video. Active visitors may prefer to head straight for their extensive adventure play area full of ropes, aerial walkways and so on; in a pleasant woodland setting, it's got sections for children at both ends of the age range. The skydome, a complex climbing frame of latticed ropework, is particularly unusual. Three costumed bears provide unsophisticated entertainment for younger visitors, and, for an extra £2.50, a children's driving school lets over-5s drive a tiny London bus and take a driving test. Next door an art gallery specialises in birds and animals. Meals, snacks, shop, some disabled access; open Easter–Oct, but may be cl occasional dates Sept–Oct, wknds only Nov–Easter; (01579) 320325; £6.95; a week-long ticket for two people (ie an adult and one child) is £13.50, three people £20, and four people £26. Under-2s are free. After 2.30pm on Fri and Sat, you can get tickets valid for just that afternoon for £3.50.

DODMAN POINT SX0039
Reached from Gorran Haven (where the Llawnroc Hotel does good value food inc local fish), or one of the closer car parks – for instance, at Hemmick Beach – this allows a round walk mainly along clifftops.

EDEN PROJECT SX0554
Eden Project This mammoth £86 million project is now fully opened, if not completely finished: several features will be better in the next few years when they will have had the chance to grow a bit more. Originally intended to be the world's largest greenhouse, it's like a space-age version of Kew Gardens, focusing on how plants from around the world affect us all. The 35-acre site is a conversion of an old china clay pit: you start in a visitor centre perched on the edge of the pit, from where you'll have your first view of the place's most dramatic features, the huge conservatories (called biomes) that look like domes made from a silvery bubblewrap. Constructed with massive hexagonal panels that slot together like a giant Meccano set, these are interesting to walk through,

particularly the bigger Humid Tropics Biome, which effortlessly fits in a re-created rainforest, lagoon and 25-metre waterfall, with all the plants you'd expect to find in that kind of environment (and perhaps some birds and insects too). The colourful Warm Temperate Biome features plants from the Mediterranean and California (which need to grow a bit), while gardens outside show what you'd find in a temperate climate like that of Britain, or the Himalayas. Displays explain how people live in various climates, and how plants are used for food, medicine, and to make everything from tyres to toothpaste. As well as display boards, points are also made more inventively with art, sculpture, or music; adventure trails have hands-on activities and workshops for children, but don't expect elaborate play areas or computer displays. It's a well organised place (though at peak times it does get extremely crowded), and the friendly staff are ready to explain things in an accessible and interesting way. Meals, snacks, good shops, good disabled access and facilities; cl 24–25 Dec; (01726) 811911; £9.80 adults (you can usually buy fast track tickets from St Austell Tourist Information Centre). The Kings Arms at Luxulyan is a handy retreat.

FALMOUTH SW8132
The county's biggest town has a huge natural harbour full of sailing boats of every description, big sea-going ships, little passenger ferries (to St Mawes and Truro – great fun) and boat trips (2-hr trip *£6.50; (01326) 374241) – or head for the Prince of Wales Pier; they've also got a summer road train that stops at all the town's main attractions (around £5 for an all-day ticket). It's also a busy but pleasant shopping centre, with some nice old-fashioned streets, ships' chandlers and a good bustling atmosphere, though surprisingly few sea views. Broad avenues of spiky-leaved dracaena trees away from the centre give it quite a foreign feel; they hope to have introduced a new park and ride and even a park and float by summer 2003. The Quayside and Chain Locker by the inner harbour do useful food, and the

Warehouse is an enjoyable waterside restaurant. The A39 here from Truro can be tiresomely slow.

National Maritime Museum Cornwall See separate family panel on p.74.

Pendennis Castle (1m SE of Falmouth) Superb views from this well preserved fort, one of Henry VIII's chain of coastal defences; displays of firearms and uniforms in the museum, a hands-on discovery centre and World War II guardroom with cells. Meals (Apr–Oct), snacks, shop, some disabled access; cl 24–26 Dec, 1 Jan; £4; EH.

FOWEY SX1251
(pronounced 'Foy') Steep, lively and bustling, in an exceptional riverside position, with pretty views from up the hill on either side, some interesting shops in its maze of quaint alleys and tiny lanes, and a choice of good value food pubs – King of Prussia, Ship and Galleon. The harbour has yachts to ocean-going ships, also car ferry to Bodinnick, and foot ferry to Polruan, the similarly steep little harbourside hamlet opposite – less interesting, but with lovely views of Fowey (both have decent pubs). **St Catherine's Castle** is a ruined stronghold built by Henry VIII, restored mid-19th c; free. The NT owns most of the coastline in these parts, so count on clean beaches; just around from the harbour, the secluded cove at Lantic Bay (reached by a steep coastal path) is particularly nice. A popular circular route takes walkers across on the Bodinnick car ferry, then takes the path through the steep creekside woods round to Polruan, and comes back on the other foot ferry.

GODOLPHIN CROSS SW6031
Godolphin House You can watch restoration in progress at this 15th-c house of the Earls of Godolphin, well known for its colonnaded front; the gardens date back to Tudor times, and there's a display of wagons in the old stables. Snacks, shop; open Tues, Thurs and Fri 21–27 Apr, Thurs–Fri and pm Sun May, Jun and Sept, plus Tues July–Aug; (01736) 762409; £3. There's free access to the estate, which is owned by the NT and has splendid views as well as over 400 archaeological features. The Queens Arms down at

Breage does decent food.

GOLANT SX1254
This waterside village has its attractions – particularly the **church**, unusual for its complete 15th-c fittings. The Fishermans Arms is a pleasant water's-edge pub.

GOONHAVERN SW7853
World in Miniature The world's landmarks at a fraction of the normal cost – and size; and some much larger dinosaurs. Beautiful gardens with thousands of plants, and children's fairground rides, and they've a new maze. Meals, snacks, shop, disabled access; cl Nov–Easter; (01872) 572828; £5.

GOONHILLY SW7221
Goonhilly Earth Station This eerily space-age international telecoms complex dominates the flat hinterland of the Lizard peninsula, a startling sight in the heart of Cornwall. You can operate one of their tracking dishes in the visitor centre, and there are guided tours of the site (which is a nature reserve), film show, and free internet surfing. A well presented, interesting and genuinely exciting place, though probably not ideal for younger children. Meals, snacks, shop, disabled access; usually cl Dec–Mar, plus Fri and Sat in Nov – best to check at beginning and end of season; (0800) 679593; £5. The B3293 past here and the byroad to Kuggar are unusual for Cornish roads, in giving some quite distant views.

GUNWALLOE SW6620
St Winwaloe This romantic little 15th-c church is set amongst the sand dunes in Church Cove; its detached bell tower (usually half-buried in blown sand) is actually built into the cliff. North of here, the beach at Halzephron has been the scene of many shipwrecks (the name means 'Hell's cliff' in Cornish); it's popular with treasure-hunters.

GWEEK SW7027
National Seal Sanctuary ▣
Britain's largest marine mammal rescue centre, this provides a home for dozens of injured or orphaned seals (all with their own names and character traits) that they hope to be able to release back into the wild. They've underwater observatories, a sea lion pool, and a pair

of otters too now; also woodland walks and a nature trail, play area, donkeys, ponies and goats, and an audio-visual display. Snacks and summer barbecues, shop, disabled access; cl 25 Dec; (01326) 221361; £7.50. The Gweek Inn is a handy nearby family pub, and the Trengilly Wartha at Nancenoy is excellent for lunch, with a nice walk down to Scotts Quay on the creek.

HAYLE SW5536
Paradise Park ⊞ The World Parrot Trust's HQ, with some of the beautiful and sometimes rare residents shown to spectacular effect in the huge Parrot Jungle, a splendid mix of waterfalls, swamps and streams. You can try feeding lorikeets in the Australian aviaries (nectar for sale in the shop), there's a new toucan aviary, and lots of other exotic birds and numerous animals inc miniature horses, pygmy goats and red pandas, some of which you can feed at the Fun Farm. Daily free-flying bird show (usually at 12.30), summer bird of prey displays (not Sat exc July– Aug), entertaining penguin and otter feeding shows, children's quiz trails, big play area, and a narrow-gauge railway gently rattling through the park. Adults may prefer the tropical plants in the Victorian walled garden (lovely clematis arches in May) or the pub that brews its own real ale. The park has initiated a scheme to reintroduce the rare chough to its native countryside, and you can also see red squirrels. Meals, snacks, shop (and plant sales), mostly disabled access; (01736) 751020; £6.99, return tickets usually available.

HELFORD SW7526
There's an undemanding coast path E to **Dennis Head** and beyond. This NE part of the Lizard is appreciably leafier, with some intricate coves.

HELSTON SW6527
Pleasantly quiet, hilly town that livens up for its famous annual Furry Dance in early May. Worth a visit if passing, the folk museum in the Old Market Place has a a new costume gallery; shop, disabled access; cl Sun and bank hols; £2. The simple Blue Anchor pub has a 15th-c working brewhouse which you can usually look around at lunchtime; the best food nearby is at the

Halzephron at Gunwalloe, off the A3083 S – a good road with views, and usually signs of action from the Culdrose helicopter base.
Flambards Village Theme Park (off A394, S edge of village) A clear cut above the average, this beautifully kept leisure park appeals to adults as much as children, and you could easily spend a day here. One of the best parts is the very good reconstructed Victorian village, which now has over 50 authentically furnished and stocked houses, shops and settings, complete with cobbled streets, carriages and other period pieces. Also a state-of-the-art time travel exhibition from the Big Bang to the present day, a life-size 'Britain in the Blitz' street, a collection of aircraft, adventure playground and play areas, beautiful gardens, displays on topics from wedding fashions to antique prams, and rides to suit all ages. Meals, snacks, shop, disabled access; cl Mon in May, Mon and Fri Apr, Sept and Oct, all Nov–Easter; (01326) 564093; £11.95.
Trevarno Estate & Gardens (off B3303 NW) There are some lovely walks around a tranquil lake with Victorian boathouse, through a yew tunnel, and in a wood full of bluebells in spring. Also here, the **National Museum of Gardening** has been moved to a bigger purpose-built building; tracing the development of gardening from the 18th c, the collection includes lots of antique gardening equipment and memorabilia. The attractive conservatory has a fountain, and serves good value snacks and cream teas; various workshops inc soapmaking. Meals, snacks, shop, some disabled access; (01326) 574274; *£4.75, £1.50 museum only.
KENNACK SANDS SW7316
(just E of Kuggar) One of the cleanest beaches in Britain, with beautifully clear water; it can get crowded.
KINGSAND/CAWSAND SX4350
Appealing seaside village with higgledy-piggledy charm, nr great cliff walks, notably S to Rame Head, which juts far out at the E end of Whitsand Bay; it is capped by a primitive hermitage chapel. Also easy access on foot to Mount Edgcumbe Country Park. The Halfway House in the village has good local fish.

Rame Head Jutting far out at the E end of Whitsand Bay, this is capped by a primitive **hermitage chapel** – a worthwhile walk from Kingsand.

KIT HILL SX3771
(off the A390 N of Callington) With a huge chimney stack and mine shafts, this gives breezy walks, and impressive views across to Dartmoor.

LAMORNA SW4424
The cove is pretty, with good walks along the coast path; there's a nice view of the Merry Maidens stone circle from the B3315 just W, a Bronze Age stone circle, reputedly 19 local girls turned to stone for dancing on Sunday. **Lamorna Pottery** also has a garden with acclaimed cream teas; meals, snacks, shop, disabled access; cl 25–26 Dec; (01736) 810330; free. The Lamorna Wink is pleasant for lunch, with interesting warship memorabilia.

LAND'S END SW3425
Land's End The most westerly point of England, with wild and blustery walks along dramatic clifftops, and on a clear day views out as far even as the Isles of Scilly. You'll be lucky if you're able to stand and contemplate it on your own, though – the 200-acre site has been extensively developed for families over the years, and it's become almost like a theme park, with 'multi-sensory experiences', farm animals, a sound and light show, amusement arcades, gift shops, craft centres, burger bars and plenty to amuse children. The exhibitions and hi-tech displays are a useful enough introduction to the folklore of the area, there's also a Wildlife Trust hut, and an RSPB observation hide has information on the coastline's wildlife. Meals, snacks, shopping arcade, good disabled access; cl 24–25 Dec; (01736) 871501; £10 for all attractions. However, there's no need to go in or buy a ticket if you just want the views, as a public right of way goes through here to Land's End itself. The same goes for the fine cliff walks in both directions – the one to Sennen is short and sweet (good family beach at Sennen Cove), but it's even better in the other direction: the eight-mile clifftop walk to Treen encompasses two natural arches (one in Nanjizal, the first bay after Land's End), stupendous views

and three wonderfully remote beaches (in Nanjizal, Porthgwarra and Porthcurno – this last has the best swimming opportunities).

LANHYDROCK SX0863
Lanhydrock House This splendid old house has a staggering 50 rooms to look at; the highlight is the Long Gallery, with its magnificently illustrated Old Testament scenes – it's one of the few original 16th-c parts left, as a disastrous fire in the 19th c resulted in major changes and refurbishments. Do leave time to explore the pretty formal gardens (glorious around May) and grounds with Victorian coach house stables; it's a lovely walk down to the river and back through the woods. Good meals and snacks, shop and plant sales, disabled access; house cl Mon (exc bank hols) and Nov–Mar; (01208) 73320; £7, £3.80 grounds only; NT. The Crown down at Lanlivery is most enjoyable for lunch, in a Jane Austen village setting.

LANREATH SX1856
Pretty village with some remarkable woodwork in its exceptional medieval **church**.
Folk Museum 🏛 Most fun for its summer demonstrations and workshops – corn dolly making (Mon), Cornish pasty crimping (Weds) and egg decorating (Fri); all activities 2–4pm. Snacks, shop, disabled access; cl Nov–Easter; (01503) 220321; £2.50.

LANSALLOS SX1751
Lansallos church The attraction here is inside the church – the ancient carved bench ends, each individual but all sharing a style.

LANTEGLOS HIGHWAY SX1453
Lanteglos Highway church A curiosity, Perpendicular but not – subsidence has left the arches at drunken angles.

LAUNCESTON SX3285
Once Cornwall's capital, this is the most attractive inland town in Cornwall, with winding old hillside streets and an untouristy feel; the White Hart does popular food.
Launceston Castle Set on a Norman motte, the ruined 12th- and 13th-c hilltop castle is substantial and commanding – it was captured four times during the Civil War. Snacks,

shop, limited disabled access; cl Nov–Mar exc Fri–Sun, 24–26 Dec and 1 Jan; (01566) 774911; £2; EH.

Launceston Steam Railway 19th-c locomotives running on a 2-ft gauge line along the trackbed of the old North Cornwall Railway, through 2½ miles of scenic valley – open carriages on sunny days; also transport museum. A network of footpaths leads off from Newmills Station. Snacks, bookshop, disabled access; open Easter, a week after Good Fri, Jun Sun–Weds, July–Sept daily (exc Sat), phone to check; (01566) 775665 for times; £5.50, 50p extra for dogs.

Lawrence House (Castle St) Georgian house with useful displays on the town's past; shop, disabled access to ground floor; cl wknds and Oct–Mar; (01566) 773277; free.

Trethorne Leisure Farm ⊞ (Kennards House, off A30 3m W of Launceston) 140-acre farm (with plenty under cover) good for children, who can milk a cow, play with the rabbits, take a pony ride or bottle-feed the lambs. Also roller-blading, ten-pin bowling, good 18-hole golf course and driving range, assault course and big indoor and outdoor play areas. Meals, snacks, shop, disabled access; cl Sun (exc golf) and 25–26 Dec; (01566) 86324; £4.95.

LIZARD SW7012

This peninsula S of Helston is famous as the most southerly part of mainland Britain, and though the inland parts can be rather flat and dull and not really worth extended walks, the coastline is more attractive. The National Trust have improved the area around Lizard Point, the southern tip, in recent years, and it's a good start for bracing cliff walks in either direction, with uplifting views. Readers very much enjoy exploring the Lizard's dramatic western and eastern edges. The W side has mighty cliffs, with roads down to beautiful Mullion Cove and Kynance Cove. The E side is more sheltered and lusher, with wooded creeks: ensconced in a cove here, Cadgwith is a picturesque steep village with photogenic fish stores, thatched cottages, and a good pub. A rewarding short stroll on the coast path leads S to

Chynhalls Point past the aptly named Devil's Frying Pan, where the waves foam into a spectacular collapsed cavern. Lizard village itself is pretty uninspiring (the Top House is a very civilised pub, and a shop has interesting local serpentine rock carvings), but is well placed for longer walks encompassing Church Cove to the E. It's also a lovely walk NW along the coast to Kynance Cove, a wonderful little tidal beach below the spectacular cliffs (or a shorter walk down from the Kynance Cove car park), with huge rocks, caves and sandy coves. On top and inland the Lizard is disappointing: a big flat peninsula, although the Goonhilly satellite station is a remarkable landmark.

Wireless Station (Bass Point – 10 mins walk from Housel Bay Hotel) The two wooden huts and aerial mast here are thought to be the oldest surviving purpose-built wireless station in the world; in 1901 it was from here that Marconi proved that radio waves could travel around the curvature of the earth when he received signals from the Isle of Wight. You can see a replica of the equipment he used, and find out how an amateur radio works; the friendly and knowledgeable volunteers will happily tell you more. Shop, open pm Weds Oct–May, plus pm Sun Jun, pm Sun and Tues–Fri July–Sept, though best to check; (01326) 290384; donations.

LOE POOL SW6424

Cornwall's largest lake, a haven for waterfowl, is blocked from the sea by a shingle bank called Loe Bar (only breeding place of the rare sandhill rust moth – and favourite place of worship of a German evangelical sect); a path leads round the lake and through the NT-owned Penrose estate. There's a coast walk from here to Gunwalloe fishing cove.

LOOE SX2553

Seaside resort packed with tourist shops, teashops and pubs, but with a nice easy-going atmosphere even in high season. The old fishing village with its picturesque harbour and narrow little back streets is now immersed in tourism, and is the main shark-fishing place (on 'shark-fishing' trips you watch others doing the catching). From the quay there are summer **boat trips**, the easiest out to nearby St George's Island. The Olde Salutation has plenty of atmosphere and good simple food; the Smugglers is a decent friendly restaurant, and the quayside Trawlers has very good unusual seafood.

Monkey Sanctuary (signed off B3253 at No Man's Land, just E of Looe) A fascinating place; established in 1964, its wooded grounds are home to a colony of Amazonian woolly monkeys. All were born here, and talks by staff give an intriguing insight into the dynamics and politics of the monkey community. Meals, snacks, shop, disabled access (though some bits are quite steep); cl Fri, Sat, and Oct–week before Easter; (01503) 262532; £4.

LUXULYAN SX0558
The village has an attractive church, and from the village you can walk along the valley to the S, and explore the area's industrial archaeology, most of it tucked away in the woods; 19th-c granite quarrying left a huge viaduct, inclines and water courses. The Kings Arms has decent food.

MADRON SW4431
Trengwainton Garden (B3312) The name in Cornish means 'Farm of the Spring', and it does always seem to be spring at this lovely place, the climate favouring plants not usually found outside in England. Magnolias, azaleas, rhododendrons, unusual southern hemisphere trees and shrubs inc a delightful tree-fern grotto, walled gardens, good views to Mounts Bay and the Lizard. Cream teas, shop, interesting plant sales, some disabled access; open Sun–Thurs (and Good Fri) Mar–Oct (01736) 362297; £3.90; NT. The King William IV has enjoyable food.

MARAZION SW5130
St Michael's Mount There's something particularly awe-inspiring about this medieval castle, rising majestically from the sea. On gloomy or stormy days the picturesque silhouette seems even more dramatic. The little island is reached by ferry (it doesn't go in bad weather), or at low tide on foot along a causeway; the walk up to the castle, still the home of the family which acquired it in 1660, is quite steep. Fine

Chippendale furniture, plaster reliefs, armour and paintings. Summer meals, snacks, shop; open (tide and weather permitting) wkdys and some wknds Apr–Oct, and Mon, Weds and Fri only Nov–Mar, phone to check; (01736) 710507; *£5; NT (members have to pay at wknds). The extensively redeveloped Godolphin Arms has popular food.

MAWGAN SW7223
Trelowarren This manor house is worth a look for its elaborate Strawberry Hill 'gothick chapel' (usually open pm Weds and bank hols Mar–Dec), and the surrounding estate (open all the time) has plenty going on in summer inc woodland walks, craft shops and pottery, campsite, Thurs evening entertainments, and good meals in the New Yard Restaurant; cl Jan–Feb (01326) 221224; £1.50 per car.

MAWNAN SMITH SW7728
This sheltered coastal village is pretty, and the Red Lion is good for lunch. From nearby Mawnan a fine if blowy stretch of the coast path takes you around Rosemullion Head and on N to Maenporth, where there's a sheltered sandy cove with decent modern pub/restaurant.

Glendurgan Garden Lovely sub-tropical garden in valley above Helford River, started by Alfred Fox in 1820; fine shrubs from all over the world, mature trees, walled garden and restored laurel maze. Shop, snacks; cl Sun, Mon (exc bank hols), Good Fri, and Nov to mid-Feb; (01326) 250906; £4; NT.

Trebah Garden 🖼 Next to Glendurgan, this is a gorgeous steeply wooded ravine garden much enjoyed by readers. It can feel as if you've strayed into a benign, exclusive jungle, with huge subtropical tree ferns and palms, giant gunnera, lots of blue and white hydrangeas, 100-year-old rhododendrons, and some fine rare trees. Several activities for children, and at the bottom end a private beach on the Helford River – good for a picnic or secluded swim. New restaurant with home-made snacks and meals, shop (plants for sale), disabled access (electric buggies are available); (01326) 250448; £5 (half price with a Truronian bus ticket).

MEVAGISSEY SX0144

This fishing village is great fun, and still packed with Cornish character, despite commercialisation and sizeable modern outskirts. At its most fetching around the knot of streets at the little working harbour (which has a parking charge of £1 in winter and £2 to £2.50 in the summer months), with hillside cottages looking over it. The Fountain (down an alley by the post office) has a good harbourside atmosphere, the local male voice choir enliven the Kings Arms (Fore St) on Mon, and the waterside Mr Bistro and Sharks Fin do mainly fresh fish.

Folk Museum Run by enthusiastic staff, this decent local museum in an 18th-c boat-builder's shed on East Quay has a comprehensive wartime exhibition; shop, disabled access to ground floor only; cl Nov–Easter; £1.

Lost Gardens of Heligan (off B2373, just NW) The televised restoration of these gardens, neglected and forgotten from 1914 to 1991, made them among Britain's best known. Some very fine mature trees, Victorian walled gardens, lots of rhododendrons, lakes, and impressive collection of tree ferns, bamboos and palms. It's a friendly place, and they're more than happy to talk about their work. Meals, snacks, shop/nursery, disabled access; cl 24–25 Dec; (01726) 845100; £6. The Crown at St Ewe is good for lunch.

World of Model Railways (Meadow St) Over 50 model trains trundling through a realistic little world that takes in Cornish china clay pits, ski resorts, fairgrounds, towns and country. Shop, disabled access; open daily Mar–Oct, Sun and school half-term Nov–Feb; (01726) 842457; £3.15.

MORVAH SW4035

Wonderfully rugged scenery both inland and along the coast here: the moors nearly reach the sea, and in a few miles walkers can take in the cliff path, the moors close to the ruin of Ding Dong Mine, the prehistoric stone hoop of Men an Tol, the inscribed stone of Men Scryfa, and the Iron Age hillfort of Chun Castle (Cornwall's best preserved hillfort, with many stones still in place), which looks down to the mushroom-shaped Bronze Age burial chamber of Chun Quoit. Lanyon Quoit, a very photogenic prehistoric burial chamber sometimes called the Giant's Table, reassembled after a storm toppled it in the early 19th c, is beside the road from Madron.

MORWENSTOW SS2015

The **church**, in an idyllic setting, has Norman arches and 16th-c bench ends, with shipwrecked sailors' headstones in the graveyard. A driftwood shack built for contemplation by a Victorian parson over the impressive cliffs is preserved by the NT. The Bush is an interesting very ancient pub, and the rectory tearoom is delightful.

MOUSEHOLE SW4626

Attractive working fishing village with steep little roads – too many summer visitors, but lovely out of season, with spectacular Christmas lights in the little harbour; the Old Coastguard has good interesting food and a lovely shoreside garden.

MULLION SW6719

This attractive village has a popular family pub (the Old Inn) and a possibly unique feature in its church – a dog flap. You can hire bicycles at Atlantic Forge; £5 half-day, £7 a day (and wetsuits too; £5); (01326) 240294 – open Easter–late Sept, phone to check at other times. This is a good way to explore the Lizard.

MULLION COVE SW6617

This dramatic fusion of rock, sand and sea is most rewardingly reached by a there-and-back walk along the cliff from Porth Mellin; for the energetic, the extension S to Kynance Cove is outstanding.

NEWLYN SW4629

Cornwall's busiest working fishing port – it's great fun watching the boats come in – and home to the last working **Salt Pilchard Works**, a tour of which passes a surprisingly entertaining hour or so; shop; cl wknds (exc by appointment) and Nov–Mar; (01736) 332112; £3.25. There's an unusual art deco swimming pool, and an excellent and occasionally rather avant-garde **Art Gallery** (New Rd) in a lovely coastal setting with fine views; changing exhibitions every five weeks (cl Sun, 25–26 Dec and 1 Jan; (01736) 363715; donations). At Christmas the fishermen decorate the harbour and its boats with spectacular lights. The Tolcarne, with a new sea wall terrace (and parking), is useful for lunch.

NEWLYN EAST SW8655

Lappa Valley Steam Railway and Leisure Park 15-inch gauge steam train trips through pretty countryside to an old lead mine. It's surrounded by parkland with lakes, woodland walk, a maze, and play areas; a section of the old branch line leads to a nine-hole golf course. Meals, snacks, shop, some disabled access; cl Nov–Easter, and some days in Oct – best to check train times; (01872) 510317; £6.50, covers fare and all attractions exc golf. The backstreet Pheasant has good home cooking.

NEWQUAY SW8261

England's surfing capital, this thorough-going seaside resort has a cheery young feel. It has excellent safe golden beaches below breezy cliffs; Crantock Beach is the best and least crowded, with great views from the Bowgie family pub up on West Pentire headland. Fistral Beach is reckoned by some to be the best surfing beach in Europe; a couple of surfing schools here can get beginners started. There's no shortage of souvenir shops, an alcohol-free zone declared on the streets, theme parks on the edge, and older houses around the harbour. The sea-view Fort Hotel (Fore St) has decent family food all day.

Blue Reef Aquarium 🅰 (Towan Promenade) This has more than 30 living displays inc a see-through tunnel which creates the illusion of walking along the sea bed, while bubble windows bring you face to face with fish, sea-horses and sharks; also Mediterranean underwater display and Caribbean tropical reef, regular talks and feeding displays. Meals, snacks, shop, some disabled access; cl 25 Dec; (01637) 872134; £4.95, £14.95 family ticket.

Dairyland 🅰 (A3508 4m SE) Much expanded since it first opened over 20 years ago, this bustling dairy farm is a huge favourite with families. Its showpiece remains the daily milking sessions, when cows step aboard a bizarre merry-go-round milking machine and are milked to the strains of

classical music. Also well labelled nature trails, farm park, rural bygones; there's even an opportunity to milk Clarabelle the cyber cow, and plenty of other activities for children. Meals, snacks, shop, disabled access; cl Nov–Mar; (01872) 510246; £5.50. The Plume of Feathers down at Mitchell is a good dining pub.

Holywell Bay Fun Park 🅰 (off A3075 SW) Active children should enjoy the go-karts, bumper boats, rides, indoor play area, golf; meals, snack, shop, disabled access; cl Nov–Easter; (01637) 830095; separate charges for various attractions (discount voucher gives 10 tokens free when you buy £20 worth of tokens). A short walk away, **Holywell Bay** is one of the area's more sheltered beaches, with a 70-year-old shipwreck, and a cave visible at low tide; the Smugglers Den at Cubert is a nice pub.

Newquay Zoo (Trenance Leisure Park, off A3075 Edgcumbe Ave) The emphasis is very much on conservation here, with many exotic animals in natural enclosures inc monkeys, penguins and lions, as well as gardens, and summer activities. Feeding displays are well timetabled so there's something to see throughout the day, and there's also a children's farm, play areas, and a maze. Meals, snacks, shop, disabled access; cl 25 Dec; (01637) 873342; £5.95. **Water World**, a lively fun pool, is just up the road; (01637) 853829.

Tunnels Through Time (St Michaels Rd) A 40-minute rainy day diversion, with re-created figures and scenes from history and myth inc King Arthur, smugglers and pirates, past punishments for drunken husbands and nagging wives, and some gory torture scenes. Snacks, shop; open Sun–Fri (plus Sat school and bank hols) Easter–autumn half-term; (01637) 873379. £3.80.

NORTH PETHERWIN SX2889

Tamar Otter Park Friendly place breeding otters, then releasing them back into the wild; it's fun to watch the attractive asian short-clawed otters playing. Three species of deer roam free, and there are waterfowl lakes, wallabies, and nature trails. The otters are fed at noon and 3pm. Snacks, shop, some disabled access; cl Nov–Mar; (01566) 785646; £5. The Countryman at Boyton is a handy lunch stop.

PADSTOW SW9175

Quaint streets, old buildings clustered around the working fishing harbour, and attractive slate houses. The quayside **Lobster Hatchery Visitor Centre** has viewing tanks and displays inc some interactive ones; shop, disabled access; cl Sun mid-Sept–Apr plus 24–26, 31 Dec and 1 Jan; £2.50; (01841) 533877. Rick Stein's restaurants draw the crowds (you'll need to book well in advance) and the Golden Lion and (wknds only, winter) London Inn are useful for lunch. The Camel estuary, popular for sailing, has gentle dreamy scenery with lots of little boats, while the Camel trail is good for walkers and cyclists. Plenty of lovely clean beaches near here (though no beaches in the town itself); Constantine Bay is the best, and well liked by surfers. The B3276 has the best roadside coastal views in this part of Cornwall. **Prideaux Place** Still a lived-in family home, this fine old house has changed little since it was built in the late 16th c. Highlights include the elegant ceilings, atmospheric library and the intricate biblical tableaux in the Great Chamber. Notable concerts and special events in the grounds. Cream teas, shop, disabled access to ground floor only; cl am, Fri and Sat, Oct–Easter, and 2 wks after Easter–late May, best to check; (01841) 532411; £6, gardens only £2. **Shipwreck, Rescue and Heritage Centre** (South Quay) A friendly museum not far from the town's little harbour, with relics and tales of the plentiful shipwrecks along this coast, and a decent collection of diving equipment with exhibits dating back to 1740; you can also clamber on board an old lifeboat, and have a go at remote-control boats (50p). Snacks, shop, disabled access; open Mar–Oct; (01726) 69897; £4.95.

PENDEEN SW3834

Geevor Tin Mine (Boscaswell) You get a good idea of what mining was really like at this nicely undeveloped tin mine (readers tell us the changing rooms are especially evocative), which was working until 1990; you can explore the mine's surface, a guided tour takes you underground, and there's a small museum. Meals, snacks, shop, limited disabled access; cl Sat Easter–end Oct (exc on Sat near bank hols), plus Sun Nov–Easter; (01736) 788662; £6. The Radjel has good value food.

Levant Mine (B3306, 1m W) The coast path goes right through this ghostly wasteland of abandoned buildings, mine shafts and rubble; in the midst of it all is the clifftop engine house, restored and powered by the oldest steam engine in Cornwall (built 1840), all explained by knowledgeable and enthusiastic staff – if someone is available they'll take you on a tour of the site. Shop, some disabled access; open Fri all year, Easter and May bank hol Mon, Weds, Thurs and Sun in Jun, daily exc Sat July–Sept, Tues in Oct, phone to check; steaming Mar–Sept only; (01736) 786156; £4; NT. The nearby Pendeen Watch lighthouse is worth a look, and not far down the coast (forking left to Carn Gloose off the Cape Cornwall road out of St Just) is Ballowal, an extraordinarily complex Bronze Age burial mound above the sea, with local tales of fairies and dancing lights.

PENHALLOW SW7650

Cornish Cyder Farm Traditional working cider farm producing scrumpy, country wines and jam, with seasonal demonstrations, and friendly horses, rabbits, goats, pigs and donkeys. Also cider museum with ancient presses, and hives of the bees needed for pollination; guided tour £5 (inc a tractor trailer ride). Meals, snacks, shop (with samples of everything they make), disabled access; cl 23 Dec–14 Jan, wknds mid-Jan to Mar; (01872) 573356; free. The Miners Arms at Mithian is handy for lunch.

PENRYN SW7834

Appealing waterside town, quite sizeable, with pretty Tudor, Jacobean and Georgian houses.

PENZANCE SW4730

The area's main shopping centre, a pleasantly relaxed town by the sea with a wealth of appealing 18th- and 19th-c terraces and squares, and two palm-shaded parks. The prettiest part is Chapel St, where there's an absorbing Maritime Museum (neck-craningly low ceilings in its shiplike interior), and the extravagantly designed early 19th-c Egyptian House deserves a passing look; the Turks Head is a good pub. Harris's restaurant in New St has good local fish. On the pier they've one of the few operational lido swimming pools left in the country; filled with seawater, it's only a little warmer than the sea (cl mid-Sept–May, and perhaps at other times for cleaning; £2). In summer you can take boat trips around the coastline, and there are ferry trips to the Isles of Scilly (phone (08457) 105555; from £35–£72 return), or you can take a helicopter flight across; best to book (01736) 362341; £108 return, £72 day return – ask about special offers. You can't get to the islands on Sun.

National Lighthouse Centre (Old Buoy Store, Wharf Rd) Easy to spot thanks to the big buoys outside, this has an excellent collection of lighthouse equipment, and a good audio-visual display on what it was like to live in one; a typical room is reconstructed, with original curved furniture. Many of the staff are ex-lighthouse personnel so a good source of information – and there is a lighthouse opposite. Shop, disabled access; cl Nov–Apr; (01736) 360077; £3.

Penlee House Gallery & Museum 🖼 (Morrab Rd) In pleasant Penlee Park, this Victorian house mainly shows paintings by the Newlyn School. Meals, snacks, shop, disabled access; cl Sun, 25–26 Dec, 1 Jan; £2 (free Sat).

POLKERRIS SX0952
Little seaside hamlet – scarcely more than the good waterside inn – with terrific view, almost even better in winter, across St Austell bay from well restored ancient quay.

POLPERRO SX2150
Almost unbelievably pretty, tiny streets around a very quaint sheltered fishing harbour, little cottages perched on rocks – once a busy smuggling place, now some enjoyable craft shops tucked away, one or two tourist attractions, oddities like the shell-encrusted Shell House, and unspoilt harbourside fishermen's locals (the Blue Peter and

Three Pilchards); the Crumplehorn Mill does decent food. The beaches around here are some of England's cleanest. It gets very busy in summer, with little electric buses (or horse and cart) shuttling in from the out-of-village car park. A sensible alternative to sweating out summer traffic jams in the village itself is to park instead in Talland Bay, for an easy one-mile walk along the coast to enter this harbour feeling you've earned it.

Land of Legend & Model Village (The Old Forge, Mill Hill) A useful enough distraction for children, with three model railways, and a scaled-down version of Polperro. Shop, some disabled access; cl Nov–Easter; (01503) 272378; £2.50.

POLZEATH SW9378
The village itself, facing the mouth of the Camel estuary, is unremarkably modern, but a lovely path N rounds the rocky headland at Rumps Point, all of which can be walked round in an hour or so. To the S the coastal path heads through the dunes beyond Brea Hill (worth diverting inland to St Enodoc church, burial place of John Betjeman) to Rock – with the option of walking along the beach at low tide. Useful seasonal foot passenger ferry from Rock to Padstow.

POOL SW6741
Cornish Engines (A3047) Developing site based around two big beam engines, originally used for pumping water from tin and copper mines; visitor centre with interactive and audio-visual displays. Shop, disabled access; open Sun–Fri Apr–Sept, phone for winter opening; (01209) 315027; £5; NT. The Cornish Choughs (at Treswithian, just off the far end of the Camborne bypass) has interesting food inc good fresh fish.

PORT ISAAC SX0080
Delightful steep fishing village, a favourite with many: tiny streets, and houses hanging high over the pretty harbour – the Golden Lion's terrace overlooks it. Park at the top and walk down (at low tide you can park on the beach). There are some particularly fine stretches of cliffs for walking around here, and just up the coast Port Gaverne is a beautiful NT cove.

PORTHALLOW SX2251

This is snugly set above a little fishing harbour with a beautifully set pub, the Five Pilchards. A friendly little **vineyard** here has self-guided tours, free samples of their wines and cider, and a particularly tasty birch country wine; open Mon–Sat (cl 1–2pm) Easter–Oct; (01326) 280050.

PORTHCURNO SW3822

Porthcurno's lovely silver sands – among Cornwall's best beaches – are the property of the National Trust, in common with so much of the coastline round here. If you walk their length, be careful not to get cut off by high tide. There's no problem if you stick to the coast path, which is exciting in either direction. A mile E it reaches Treryn Dinas, arguably the most stunning of Cornwall's headlands, capped by the precariously balanced Logan Rock. From here, the Logan Rock pub at Treen is a short lunchtime diversion across fields.

Minack Theatre & Visitor Centre There are few better backdrops for plays than the one at this famous little open-air theatre – dramatic cliffs and blue sea stretching into the distance make this a magical setting. Varied summer season, and an exhibition on the life of Rowena Cade, the remarkable woman who built the theatre, cut into these steep cliffs, with her own hands. Tickets go on sale in May, but aren't for particular seats – if you've booked you'll still need to get there early to bag the best. Evening shows are more atmospheric. Shows are cancelled only in extreme conditions, so take a waterproof. Snacks, shop, disabled access to café and exhibition; performances May–Sept, exhibition cl during matinées, and 25–26 Dec; (01736) 810181; shows *£7, exhibition *£2.50. **Museum of Submarine Telegraphy** Don't be put off by the name – this museum housed in the secret wartime communications centre in underground tunnels is a good deal more interesting than you'd think. Shop, disabled access, cl Sat Apr–Oct (exc July–Aug and before a bank hol), phone for winter opening times; (01736) 810966; £4.

PORTHLEVEN SW6225

Pretty working fishing village; the Ship, built into the cliffs, is a good pub, and the long stretch of rocky beach S is a good walk if the surf's not beating in too fiercely.

PORTLOE SW9339

Tiny unspoilt village wedged into a precipitous cove, with splendid cliff walks in rugged scenery, and stiffish climbs on to Nare Head; good teashop, and good value bar lunches in the Ship.

PORTREATH SW6545

A good base for long bracing clifftop walks, with enjoyable food at the Basset Arms; along this whole section of coast, between St Ives Bay and Trevose Head (nr Padstow), the coast path is rich in rugged views, and very rewarding to those with sturdy legs. Newly opened for walkers and riders, the 11-mile Coast-to-Coast Trail links Portreath to Devoran following two mineral tramways (once a vital communication and transport link between copper and tin mines in West Cornwall); ask for a leaflet at local tourist information centres.

Cornish Goldsmiths (Tolgus Mill) You can watch goldsmiths at work, and there are a few gold-related displays inc the chance to see what your weight in gold looks like; also James Bond car and a working pottery; children's activities in summer. Meals, snacks, large jewellery shop; cl 25 Dec, 1 Jan, Easter Sun; (01209) 218198; free. Tricky Dickies up on Tolgus Mount has good value food.

PORTSCATHO SW8735

Very sheltered fishing village with a picturesque little harbour, and some fine nearby beaches – excellent for families. Virtually the whole of Gerrans Bay around here is good easy walking, with some lovely clifftop stretches; there's a good sandy stretch at Pendower Beach.

PRAA SANDS SW5828

A popular summer family beach. Worth strolling along the coast SE for half a mile to Rinsey Head (car park): here by the coast path are two magnificently sited ruined tin and copper mine buildings, Wheal Prosper and Wheal Trewavas, both now maintained as landmarks by the NT.

PROBUS SW9247

Trewithen (off A390 between Probus and Grampound, where the Dolphin has good value food) Justly famous landscaped gardens, with many rare trees and shrubs. The early 18th-c house is a little unfairly overshadowed by what's outside, and is an interesting obviously lived-in family home. Snacks, rare plants for sale, disabled access; gardens open Mar–Sept (cl Sun exc Apr and May), house open only Mon and Tues pms Apr–July (plus Aug bank hol); (01726) 883647; gardens £4.25, house another £4.50, combined £6.50.

RESTORMEL SX1060

Restormel Castle Very well preserved Norman castle with notable round keep and fine views over Fowey Valley. Lots of flowers in spring. Snacks, shop; cl Nov–Mar; (01208) 872687; £1.90; EH. The Royal Oak in Lostwithiel (Cornwall's capital in the 13th c) is good for lunch.

RESTRONGUET CREEK SW8137

Though the waterside village is mainly of no great age, its pub the Pandora has a lovely location – you can park in Mylor Bridge for a leisurely two-mile waterside walk there and back (though parking can be difficult in summer), or drive all the way.

ROCHE ROCK SW9959

This small but picturesque crag is worth the short walk from the B3274, with a 14th-c ruined ivy-covered chapel built into it, and a ladder up (decent pub nearby, past the station).

SANCREED SW4129

Carn Euny Ancient Village Dating from the 1st c, substantial traces of a little village of stone courtyard houses, and a 'fogou' – a 20-metre underground passage leading to a circular chamber of unknown purpose (some very minor roads to get here); free access.

ST AGNES SW7150

A former mining town, now with a holiday role; some attractive steeply terraced cottages, fine cliff scenery nearby, and great views from the St Agnes Beacon hilltop, just W of town. The Railway Inn has some interesting collections, and there are good surfing beaches nearby at Trevaunance Cove and Chapel Porth (NT).

Presingoll Barns (Penwinnick Rd) Craft centre with demonstrations of glass painting, candle and fudge-making, good picnic areas. Meals, snacks, shop, limited disabled access; cl 25–26 Dec; (01872) 553007; free (a small charge for candle-dipping).

ST ANTHONY HEAD SW8431

On the E side of the Fal estuary, by the **Zone Point lighthouse**, this has superb views, and easy walks along low, level cliffs; parking at the head itself, or near Porth Farm on the way down.

ST AUSTELL SX0352

The centre of the china clay industry and a busy modern shopping town. Holy Trinity **church** has a fine tower and interesting font, and you can tour the **St Austell Brewery** on Trevarthian Rd (booking recommended – (01726) 66022; £4, inc beer samples, children over 8 only).

Pine Lodge Gardens (Holmbush) are well worth a visit: the 30 acres include an arboretum, fernery, herbaceous borders, Japanese garden, and several ponds and water features (the lake has black swans); tearoom, plant sales, disabled access; open 12 Apr–Oct; (01726) 73500; *£4.50. The area N is a strange bleak moonscape of whitish spoil heaps with metallic blue lakes dotted among them; the B3279 St Stephen–Nanpean gives some of the best views over this.

China Clay Museum 🖼 (B3274 N of St Austell – you don't have to go into the town) Interestingly restored 19th-c clayworks showing the 250-year history of china clay production. Working waterwheels and other equipment, steam locomotives, nature trails with a spectacular viewpoint over a huge clay pit, children's adventure trail and picnic areas. Snacks, shop; cl Nov–Mar, best to check; (01726) 850362; *£5 (a good value family ticket gets 2 adults and up to 4 children in for £13). The Bugle Inn (A391) does food all day.

ST CLEER SX2568

Trevethy Quoit This is a very photogenic megalithic tomb, its massive stones now left high and dry by a fall in the soil level over thousands of years. The Crows Nest down near Darite is handy for lunch.

ST GERMANS SX3657

St Germans church Wonderful Norman doorway and particularly fine east window; worth a look if you're passing this waterside village. There's a good view towards Port Eliot, a stately home designed by John Soane (not open).

ST IVES SW5039

A pretty place, despite the summer crowds, with its attractive working harbour and narrow streets and alleys (the cobbled Fore St is the prettiest). It has good wide beaches, and plenty of bird life along the Lelant Saltings (the Old Quay House there, sharing its car park with the RSPB reserve, has good value food). Besides the Blue Fish, the waterside Sloop (interesting pictures for sale) is reliable for lunch, and the Pedn Olva overlooking Porthminster beach has enjoyable modern food. The best beach for surfers is Porthmeor slightly N, while in the other direction the B3306 to Land's End has great coast and moorland views. Out of season, when the caravan and camp sites are empty, the magnificent sands around St Ives Bay are well worth walking, with good cliff walks to the west.

Barbara Hepworth Museum and Sculpture Garden 🖼 (Porthmeor Beach) This tranquil escape from the holiday hordes, devoted to the artist's work and life, has sculptures in the house, studio and subtropical garden, as well as photographs and letters. Shop; cl Mon Nov–Feb, and 24–26 Dec; (01736) 796226; *£3.75. Other works by Hepworth are dotted about the town.

Tate Gallery St Ives (Porthmeor Beach) St Ives's famous popularity with artists is best explored at this gallery, which can take a lot of the credit for the town's tourism boom. Works by the familiar St Ives School names are regularly joined by displays of 20th-c art with a Cornish connection. It's an impressive building, outside and in, fully exploiting its spectacular cliffside setting – views are best from the café. Meals, snacks, shop, disabled access; cl Mon Nov–Feb and in Oct for re-hanging; (01736) 796226; £4.10.

ST JUST-IN-ROSELAND SW8435

An unspoilt spot, with its church in an idyllic creekside setting; the steep graveyard, described by John Betjeman as 'perhaps the most beautiful churchyard on earth', is like a lost subtropical garden – well worth a visit on a quiet sunny day, or in spring with the baby rooks blethering and the smell of wild garlic. The churchyard paths are full of stones inscribed with words of wisdom, which almost steal the show.

ST KEVERNE SW7921

Set around a little square, this is a pleasant village, with a lovely little **working farm** just S at Tregellast Barton, undeveloped and tranquil, with pleasant walks through woods and meadows, afternoon milking (4.30), and a good farm shop with samples of their unusually flavoured ice-cream such as apricot or marzipan; (01326) 280479; free. The Three Tuns has good food, and there's a good walk to Lowland Point.

ST KEW SX0276

Delightful quiet leafy village with old-fashioned feel; the St Kew Inn is a nice place for a meal.

ST MAWES SW8433

Very pretty harbourside and estuary views, a long waterfront to stroll along, clean bathing waters, a foot-passenger ferry to Falmouth and other boat trips (full of yachtsmen and others in summer, lots of guesthouses). The 16th-c **castle** is remarkably well preserved and has a decent audio tour (Mon–Tues Nov–Mar; £2.90; EH). On the hillside, and with good views out to sea, **Lamorran House Gardens** is a four-acre Mediterranean garden with lots of different species inc a large collection of palms; open Weds, Fri and perhaps first Sat in month Apr–end Sept; (01326) 270800; £4. The Rising Sun has good value food. Readers recommend taking the ferry across to St Anthony-in-Roseland for some remote and unspoilt views and walks. The King Harry chain-drawn car ferry on the B3269 N of St Mawes is a favourite family crossing, and on the way the Roseland at Philleigh is a charming pub.

ST NEOT SX1867

The village **church** is well known for its early stained glass, and also has an unusual stone vault in the south porch. Nearby ancient remains include the five impressive **Brown Gelly Barrows** and some hut circles, halfway to Bolventor. The London Inn is a good lunch spot.

TINTAGEL SX0588

King Arthur's Great Halls 🖼 (Fore St) Far from being a light-hearted romp, Arthurian legends are treated very earnestly here, and there's no denying the impressive craftsmanship, esp in the 72 stained glass scenes. The best bit though is the tour's light show, which is narrated by Robert Powell and gives the outline of the legend. Decent shop, disabled access; cl 2nd Sat in Oct and 25 Dec, limited opening hours in winter; (01840) 770526; £3.

Old Post Office Full of character, one room in this small saggy slate-roofed 14th-c manor was used as a post office in the 19th c; shop; cl Nov–Mar; (01840) 770024; £2.30; NT.

Tintagel Castle Forgetting the myths and legends, these dramatic 12th- and 13th-c ruins have a spectacular setting and unrivalled views. A good start is from Rocky Valley, a craggy valley leading from the B3263 to the sea. Try to come out of season, when the crowds are fewer and the mist and crashing waves add a touch of mystery. There's quite a lot of climbing involved, and the often steep steps among the crags can be slippery in wet weather. As for King Arthur, latest theories suggest he was a Shropshire lad, but a small exhibition makes the most of the Cornish case, inc the recently found Arthnou stone, a 1,400-year-old inscribed slate naming the hero. Shop; cl 24–26 Dec and 1 Jan; (01840) 770328; £3; EH. In summer, a Land Rover can ferry you to the site from the village (a tourist trap since the 19th c) at regular intervals throughout the day. The Old Malthouse is a useful food stop, and the parish **church** is worth a look.

TORPOINT SX4156

Antony House (2m NW) A pleasant ferry ride from Devonport in Plymouth, this is the finest Classical house in Cornwall, little changed since the early 18th c, with interesting contents and paintings in its panelled rooms; also riverside grounds redesigned by Humphrey Repton, a dovecote, topiary and woodland and knot gardens. Tearoom, shop, some disabled access to ground floor only; open pm Tues–Thurs and bank hols Apr–Oct, plus Sun Jun–Aug; (01752) 812191;

*£4.60, grounds only £2.40, woodland garden £3.60 (woodland garden and grounds £3.90); NT. If instead you go by road (it's a long way round), the B3247 takes you past the Finnygook at Crafthole, a useful dining pub.

Mount Edgcumbe 🖼 (B3247 E of Kingsand) The family seat of the Edgcumbes, who left their old house at Cotehele and opted for a more fashionable pile here in the 18th c, only to see it destroyed in the last war by a stray bomb. Now faithfully rebuilt, with period furniture; the main attraction is the surrounding spread of lovely gardens and parkland, divided into English, French and Italian sections, with great views to Plymouth. Free eco-bus running when house and gardens open. Meals, snacks, shop, disabled access; house cl Mon (exc bank hols), Tues, and Oct–Mar (but park and gardens open then, free); (01752) 822236; £4.50. It's a short walk up from the Plymouth pedestrian ferry to Cremyll, where the charmingly furnished Edgcumbe Arms has decent food.

TRECANGATE SX1759

Porfell Animal Land 🖼 Delightfully unspoilt and friendly, this expanding centre has deer, wallabies, racoons, lemurs, meerkats and a capybara called Bart, as well as rabbits, guinea-pigs, goats, ducks and chickens in 15 acres of sloping fields and woodland. Readers very much enjoy the peaceful and remote feel. Snacks, shop, disabled access; cl wkdys 27 Dec–Good Fri; (01503) 220211; £4. The Ship over at Lerryn is fairly handy for lunch and often has good watercolours for sale; the stepping stones over the river there are a hit with children, and good circular walks are signposted from the car park.

TREDINNICK SW9270

Shires 🖼 Far more to this busy complex than just the magnificent horses: there's a children's farm, a haunted castle, an exhibition of rural antiquities, nature trails, watermill and working craftsmen, and very big indoor and outdoor adventure playgrounds inc animated animal shows. The horses are displayed in an indoor arena, and you can see them being groomed in their stables – along with Shetland ponies.

Lots for all ages, but ideal for children. Meals, snacks, shop, disabled access; cl Nov–Mar; (01841) 540276; £7.50. The Ring o' Bells at St Issey is handy for lunch.

TREGONNING HILL SW6029
Takes only a few minutes to climb but has an impressive view; here in 1746 William Cookworthy made the first discovery of china clay in England, and went on to make porcelain.

TRELIGHTS SW9879
Long Cross Victorian Gardens 🏛
Slightly inland at Trelights (but with good views down to the sea), the prettily restored gardens by the Long Cross Hotel, intricately hedged against the sea winds, have interesting granite and water features, a maze, and playground and pets' corner for children. Meals, snacks, plant sales (not Nov–Easter), disabled access; (01208) 880243; *£1.80 (donations only in winter).

TRELISSICK SW8339
Trelissick Garden 🏛 (B3289)
Woodland park with beautifully kept gardens of camellias, magnolias and hydrangeas, also subtropical garden and other unusual plants; good views of the King Harry Passage and over to Pendennis Castle. There's a pretty orchard, and good walks in the surrounding woodland. Meals, snacks, shop, disabled access; cl am Sun, and Nov–mid-Feb; (01872) 862090; £4.50; NT. The NT have four holiday cottages on the estate. The Punch Bowl & Ladle at Penelewey on the King Harry Ferry rd is popular for lunch.

TRERICE SW8458
Trerice House Pretty Elizabethan house with unusual Dutch-style gables, and elaborate plasterwork ceilings in the magnificent Hall and Great Chamber. Fine furnishings from the 17th and 18th c, notable paintings, early embroideries, Oriental and English porcelain, and in the grounds an unusual collection of lawnmowers; lovely colourful gardens with Cornish fruit trees. Snacks (in a barn with activities for toddlers), shop, very good disabled access; cl Sat and Tues (exc cl Sat only 15 Jul–11 Sept), and Nov–Mar; (01637) 875404; £4.50; NT. The Two Clomes at Quintrel Downs is quite handy for lunch.

TRESKILLARD SW6739
Shire Horse Farm & Carriage Museum 🏛 Refreshingly uncommercialised; most displays are indoors, and there are working blacksmith's and wheelwright's shops. Snacks, shop, disabled access; cl Sat and Nov–Good Friday; (01209) 713606; £4.50.

TREVALLAS COOMBE SW7351
Blue Hills Tin Streams 🏛 Tours of this family-run outfit include demonstrations of the tinner's ancient craft. Snacks (summer only), shop, disabled access; cl Sun (bookings only Nov–Mar), and 24 Dec–2 Jan; (01872) 553341; £4. The ancient Miners Arms at Mithian is good for lunch.

TRURO SW8244
A busy but civilised town with good shops. Lemon St is a particularly fine Georgian street, and Boscawen St is cobbled; bustling Lemon Quay has recently been developed into a pleasant piazza and shopping area; the adjacent covered farmers' market is open on Sats. The **cathedral** is one of the newer Anglican ones, designed in 1880 in Early English style and finished in 1910; the handsome twin spires of the west front pop up dramatically from behind shops and houses; meals, snacks, shop. The **Royal Cornwall Museum** (River St) tells tales of local characters such as Black John of Tetcott, an 18th-c dwarf whose party piece was apparently tying mice together by their tails, swallowing them whole, and then pulling them up again; also archaeology, natural history, Egyptian and textile galleries. Meals, snacks, shop, disabled access; cl Sun and bank hols; (01872) 272205; £4. Just outside the centre, **Bosvigo** (Bosvigo Lane) is a charming plantsman's garden, with most colour Jun–Sept; small nursery; open Thurs–Fri Mar–Sept; (01872) 275774; £3. The City (Pydar St) and Old Ale House (Quay St) are popular for lunch.

VERYAN SW9139
Lovely village famous for its five devil-proof thatched round houses; also a water garden sheltered by holm oaks. The New Inn has good value food.

WADEBRIDGE SW9673
The disused railway track between Wadebridge and Padstow is a level six

miles along the edge of the Camel estuary, with banks of wild flowers, birds, and lovely views between cuttings – you can walk or cycle (bike hire at either end (01208) 813050; £8 day – best to book in summer), or picnic on the small beaches at low tide. Those with less energy could park at Wadebridge, walk to Padstow, have lunch and get the bus back. You might then walk on through scenic countryside beyond Bodmin (worth stopping at Helland pottery, just by the path at Helland Bridge).

WENDRON SW6831
Poldark Mine & Heritage Centre
The underground post box in this 18th-c tin mine is the deepest in Britain. Varied enough to interest most members of the family, with plenty of children's amusements, an underground tour of the mine, a museum, a film on the history of Cornish mining, a working beam engine, and gardens. Meals, snacks, craft shops, limited disabled access; phone for winter opening hours, cl Jan–Feb; (01326) 573173; guided tour £5.75, entry free.

WHEAL COATES SW6949
One of the most photogenic **mine ruins** on the Cornish coast; for walkers, the diversion up St Agnes

Beacon is well worth it for the commanding views.

WHITESAND BAY SW3526
Long expanses of wonderfully clean sands below the cliffs here give good walks, stretching away N of Sennen Cove (very popular with surfers; the Old Success here has a great view).

ZENNOR SW4538
The church here is best seen in its granite landscape from the hills above. The Tinners Arms is useful for lunch, and the hostel in the adjacent former chapel doubles as a tearoom. Around here you can walk for miles without seeing another soul; a striking objective is Zennor Quoit, with its enormous leaning capstone, on the hillside to the SE. Gurnards' Head juts dramatically into the Atlantic, and the hotel near it on the B3306 is a good base for cliff walks (with unusual bar snacks).
Wayside Folk Museum Readers have had a lot of fun at this little local history museum, with its chatty descriptions and information scattered through the exhibits; children's quiz trails. Teas, shop (specialising in Cornish books and crafts); cl Nov–wk before Easter and Sat (exc summer school and bank hols); (01736) 796945; £2.50.

Where to eat

CONSTANTINE SW7328 **Trengilly Wartha** *(01326)* 340332 Well run tucked-away inn with a woodburner in the relaxed and civilised bar, a bright no smoking family conservatory, a thoughtful wine list with 20 by the glass (they also operate a retail business), very good imaginative food, a fine range of changing real ales, 40 malt whiskies, and a pretty, landscaped garden; nice bdrms; no food 25 or 31 Dec. £32|£7

DULOE SX2358 **Olde Plough House** *(01503)* 262050 Very neatly kept pub with lovely slate floor in both communicating bar rooms, three woodburners, a mix of pews and chairs, good interesting food inc fishy specials and steaks cooked on hot stones, real ales, sensibly priced wines, and attentive service; cl 25–26 Dec pms; disabled access. £21|£4.95

FALMOUTH SW8135 **HMS Ganges** *Mylor Yacht Harbour (01326) 374320* Not actually a ship though obviously named after one, this friendly little restaurant looks across the River Fal and specialises in fresh fish and seafood – they also serve breakfast for the many yachtsmen who sail in; good choice of wines from around the world at reasonable prices, and helpful service; cl Sun pm (open then in July/Aug), cl Jan and bank hols; disabled access. £29|£5.95

FOWEY SX1251 **Food for Thought** *4 Town Quay (01726) 832221* Carefully run quayside evening restaurant with generous helpings of attractively presented food inc fine fish and some simple as well as other elaborate dishes, and lovely puddings; cl Sun, cl Jan/Feb; children must be well behaved. £21.95

LANLIVERY SX0759 **Crown** *(01208)* 872707 Pretty 12th-c inn with friendly licensees, a rambling series of rooms with open fires and a chatty atmosphere, good food using home-grown and local produce, well kept real ales, and a nice garden; disabled access. £19.50|**£5.95**

MITHIAN SW7450 **Miners Arms** *(01872)* 552375 Secluded Tudor pub with lots of character, fine old furnishings and warm winter fires, popular food, a no smoking dining room, real ales, and friendly service. £23|**£6.95**

MOUSEHOLE SW4626 **Cornish Range** *6 Chapel St (01736) 731488* Very friendly and neatly kept restaurant with a relaxed atmosphere and carefully cooked food inc plenty of good local fish dishes and enjoyable puddings; smart new bdrms; cl winter Mon, Tues; partial disabled access. £29.50

MOUSEHOLE SW4726 **Old Coastguard** *The Parade (01736) 731222* Attached to a comfortable hotel, this notable seaside bar is bright and spacious with a relaxed, cheerful feel, modern furnishings on the wood-strip floor, good modern paintings, fresh flowers and potted plants, and lower dining area overlooking Mounts Bay; good enterprising, mainly modern food, well kept real ales, a decent choice of wines, and thoughtful choice of juices; seats on decking by attractive garden that leads to the sea. £22.50|**£8**

NEWLYN SW4628 **Smugglers** *12–14 Fore St (01736) 331501* In a fine setting on the edge of the fishing-boat harbour, this simply furnished little restaurant has candles on pine tables, a friendly atmosphere, and an interesting menu inc delicious fresh fish and super puddings; also does coffee and light lunches in high season; cl Mon–Weds in winter; partial disabled access. £25

PADSTOW SW9175 **Seafood Restaurant** *Riverside (01841) 532700* Airy quayside restaurant so famous for its wonderfully fresh seafood straight from the boats that you have to book far in advance; good puddings, nice cheeses, a long, interesting and fairly priced wine list, and friendly service; conservatory for aperitifs; smart, comfortable bdrms; cookery school courses; they also own Rick Stein's Café; cl 1 May, 22–26 Dec; children over 4. Lunch £36, dinner £60

PADSTOW SW9175 **St Petroc's** *4 New St (01841) 532700* Attractive little hotel (under the same ownership as the Seafood Restaurant) with a cheerfully and informally decorated dining room, good quickly served food from a short bistro-type menu (plenty of fish), a sensible wine list, and friendly atmosphere; bdrms; cl 1 May, 1 July, Christmas; children over 4. Lunch £24.75, dinner £60

PENZANCE SW4730 **Harris's** *46 New St (01736) 364408* Long-standing and boldly decorated cosy restaurant in a narrow cobbled street, with good enjoyable food using local produce (the freshest fish and shellfish), well liked puddings, and a decent wine list; cl Sun, Mon in winter (open Mon pm in summer), cl 3 wks in winter. £28|**£7.50**

PHILLEIGH SW8739 **Roseland** *(01872)* 580254 Friendly little 17th-c pub just up the hill from the King Harry ferry, with good popular home-made food, well kept real ales, several small interesting rooms, old photographs and a good winter fire; disabled access. £19|**£6**

POLPERRO SX2051 **Kitchen** *The Coombes (01503) 272780* Cottagey, informal no smoking evening restaurant with really enjoyable interesting food inc vegetarian and daily-changing fresh fish dishes (lovely fresh lobster and crab), and good value wines; cl Mon, Oct–Easter; children over 12. £25

POLPERRO SX2051 **Plantation Café** *The Coombes (01503) 272223* Popular beamed teashop with good, totally home-made food inc lovely soups and cream teas, a wide choice of interesting teas inc herbal and fruit, lunchtime sandwiches, and evening meals (in season); cl Sat (but open then in July/Aug), cl winter wkdys (but open Christmas period), Jan/Feb (but open Feb half-term); disabled access.

ST IVES SW5140 **Porthminster Beach Café** *(01736)* 795352 Bustling, popular café open all day for morning coffee with home-baked pastries, cream teas, light lunches and more substantial evening meals offering good Mediterranean-style cooking (nice daily specials) using local produce, and a wide choice of coffees and teas; kind to children; may cl Nov–Mar. £25

ST KEW SX0276 **St Kew Inn** *(01208) 841259* Handsome stone-built pub with welcoming new owners, nice old-fashioned furnishings in neatly kept bar, good popular food, and peaceful garden; lovely church next door. £21.25|**£6.25**

ST MICHAEL'S MOUNT SW5130 **Sail Loft** The Harbour *(01736) 710748* Converted boat house with enjoyable home-made cakes, Cornish cream teas, more substantial meals, and friendly service; no smoking; cl 31 Oct–mid-Mar; disabled access. £20|**£4.30**

TREBURLEY SX3477 **Springer Spaniel** *(01579) 370424* Main-road pub with good interesting food, friendly service, well kept real ales, good wines by the glass, relaxed and simply furnished bars and attractive no smoking restaurant. may cl 4 days over Christmas. £24|**£6.95**

Isles of Scilly

Charmingly unspoilt, the islands, about 28 miles W of Land's End, are a great place for utter relaxation. They have beautiful scenery, an almost subtropical climate, and a variety of shorelines giving excellent coastal walks. In a lazy day you can comfortably walk round the largest, St Mary's, which is just six square miles. Tresco and St Agnes are the other main populated ones, though that means small undeveloped communities rather than any towns or big settlements. There are over 200 islands and islets in all, some just strange-shaped rocks jutting out of the sea, their only visitors seals, dolphins and puffins.

You can get there from Penzance by ferry (around £37 day return) or more spectacularly by helicopter, a 20-minute ride with really beautiful views of the Cornish coast and of the islands (return fares start from about £80). The islands also have their own little airline Skybus which leaves from Land's End, Newquay, Exeter and even Bristol several times a day. The trip from Land's End is quickest and cheapest (from around £60 day return; no flights Sun); (0845) 710 5555 for details.

Where to stay

PELISTRY BAY SV9211 **Carnwethers Country House** *Carnwethers, Pelistry Bay, St Mary's, Isles of Scilly TR21 0NX (01720) 422415* **£120*** inc dinner – good value weekly terms, too; 9 rms. Well run no smoking country guesthouse nr very fine beach, with an acre of lovely gardens, heated swimming pool, and croquet, lounge with helpful books about the islands, well stocked bar, good freshly cooked set 4-course dinner using local produce served at 6.30pm, sound wine list, and games room with pool table and table tennis; sauna; lots of coastal walks; cl Oct–mid-Apr; children over 10; dogs welcome in bedrooms

ST AGNES SV8808 **Coastguards** *St Agnes, Isles of Scilly TR22 0PL (01720) 422373* **£69** inc dinner; 3 rms in separate cottages, with views of the sea. Peacefully set former coastguard cottages with open fire, interesting artefacts, and sea views in the sitting room, enjoyable homely dinners and breakfasts, friendly, helpful owners, and big garden; no smoking; cl Nov–Mar; children over 12; dogs welcome in bedrooms

ST MARTIN'S SV9116 **St Martin's on the Isle** *Lower Town, St Martin's, Isles of Scilly TR25 0QW (01720) 422092* **£170**, plus special breaks: 30 attractively decorated rms, most with fine sea views. Welcomed by the friendly manager as you step off the boat, you find this stone-built hotel set idyllically on a white sand beach, with stunning sunsets; comfortable, light and airy split-level bar-lounge with doors opening onto the terrace, lovely flower arrangements, genuinely friendly professional staff, sophisticated food in main restaurant (lighter lunches in the bar), and a fine wine list; they are particularly kind to children, with buckets and spades to borrow, videos, and high tea for under-12s (they must be over 12 in evening restaurant); fine walks (the island is car free), launch trips to other islands, and good bird-watching; small swimming pool; cl Nov–end Feb; disabled access; dogs welcome in bedrooms ☺

TRESCO SV8915 **Island Hotel** *Tresco, Isles of Scilly TR24 0PU (01720) 422883* **£128** inc dinner; 48 rms, many with balconies and terrace overlooking gardens or sea. Tiny private island, renowned for its wonderful subtropical Abbey Gardens and reached by helicopter or boat – hotel tractor-drawn bus (no cars allowed though bike hire available) takes you to spacious, very friendly modern hotel with colonial-style bar, fine food and wine, panoramic views, swimming pool, and private beach; cl Nov–Feb

To see and do

BRYHER SV8715
A tiny quiet place, even by Scilly standards. The South bay has lots of wild flowers, and Watch Hill has wonderful views. The Hell Bay Hotel is good value.

ST AGNES SV8708
The most south-westerly community in the British Isles, joined to a smaller island called Gugh by a sandbar, awash at high tide. The sheltered cove here is especially popular. The 17th-c lighthouse is the second oldest in Britain. The views from here out to the rocks and islets are very atmospheric, especially when you remember more ships have been wrecked here than anywhere comparable in the world.

ST MARTIN'S SV9315
A narrow rocky ridge with flowers stretching down to the main attraction – the extensive beaches, very popular for picnics. There's a diving school, and the St Martin's Hotel has lovely sunset views.

ST MARY'S SV9010
The hub of Scilly Isles life, though its centre, Hugh Town, is little more than a village by mainland standards. Most ferries and planes arrive here, and you can get **pleasure cruises** from the Quay out to the bird and seal colonies on the outer islets and islands; there are fishing trips from here too.

There's a **museum**, and 9-hole golf course with fine views. The Bishop & Wolf is a pleasant pub, and the Atlantic Hotel has a good pub part. Up in the N at Bant's Carn there's a burial chamber and ancient village. Back down S, walk out to Penninis Head for good views of the Wolf and Bishop's Rock lighthouses. Just along the coast is Star Castle Hotel.

TRESCO SV8915
The highlight here is the amazing **subtropical garden** around the grounds of the abbey, begun in 1834, which, despite storms, contains a magnificent collection of exotic plants, bananas even. Also in these grounds is **Valhalla**, a collection of carved figureheads from wrecked ships, many dating back to the 17th c. Helicopters from Penzance land just outside the garden gate, so it's possible (though not cheap) to come here just for a day. The southern parts of the island are mainly sandy, but in the north it's more wild and rugged, with the remains of the castles of both Charles I and Oliver Cromwell, and a cave known as the Piper's Hole. Cycling and walking are real pleasures – not least because there aren't any cars. The New Inn, embellished with a mystery cargo of pine planking which washed ashore a while back, has good food inc seafood.

Where to eat

ST AGNES SV8708 **Turks Head** *The Quay (01720) 422434* Idyllically placed pub (a pleasant place to stay) with outstanding views over sweeping bay, enjoyable food in simple pine-panelled bar inc legendary huge locally made pasties, afternoon teas, evening barbecues, real ales, and decent wines; you can walk down to the slipway and sit right on the shore – or enjoy the wonderful views from seats on the lawn; children must be well behaved; cl Nov–Mar. £20|£6.50

TRESCO SV8915 **New Inn** *Townshill (01720) 423006* Just up from the harbour, this popular inn has a chatty, cosy bar, a main room with comfortable old sofas, banquettes, planked partition seating, and farmhouse chairs and tables, a few standing timbers, boat pictures, a large model sailing boat, a collection of old telescopes, and plates on the delft shelf; an airy dining extension has plenty of seats and tables on the blue wooden floors, cheerful yellow walls, and doors to the terrace; enjoyable food (more elaborate at night) with daily specials and afternoon tea, well kept real ales, good wines, and proper coffee; bdrms. £24|£6.95

With special thanks to Dr Venetia Stent, Jenny and Brian Seller, Ian Downes, B and K Hypher, J Black, Prof R J Harrison

We welcome reports from readers

This *Guide* depends on readers' reports. Do help us if you can – in return, we offer a discount on the next edition to people who've helped us with reports for it. Tell us what you think about places already in it, and anything extra you think we should say about them. And send us your ideas for inclusion in the next edition: places to visit, eat at or stay in, attractive drives or walks, maybe even unusual shops you know of. Use the card in the middle, the report forms at the end, or just write – no stamp needed: *The Good Britain Guide*, FREEPOST TN1569, Wadhurst, E Sussex TN5 7BR. Or log on to www.goodguides.com

CUMBRIA

Some of Britain's finest scenery; outstanding access to open country – ideal for outdoor activities, with lots of interesting places to visit, and excellent places to stay

The most beautiful scenery is concentrated thickly around the central area, especially around the towns of Ambleside and Windermere. Both places are quite intensively developed for visitors and very busy in summer; Keswick too has lots going on for all ages. These parts really come into their own at quieter times of year. Cockermouth to the NW has plenty of attractions to fill a rainy day.

Each lake has its own character, and the landscape around them varies greatly too. Windermere, the longest and busiest, has always been a favourite; it's picturesquely dotted with villas built by Victorian magnates, and has masses of accommodation on its E side. Ullswater approaches the grandeur of Scottish lochs, and has some excellent (if not cheap) places to stay right by the lake shore. Buttermere and Crummock Water also have scenery on the grand scale. Derwent Water wavers charmingly between highland and lowland in flavour, and its islands and manageable proportions make it a favourite for idle boating and bankside strolls. Coniston Water, quite well wooded, also appeals to both boaters and walkers, with some fine views – in some ways it's a smaller and quieter version of Windermere. Wastwater, England's deepest lake, is austere, surrounded by towering screes. Bassenthwaite is altogether gentler, lowland in feel. Some much smaller lakes, notably Grasmere, Rydal Water and Elterwater, are idyllic.

The best coastal scenery is around Morecambe Bay. The W coast is untouristy, with miles of unfrequented beaches. If you like wandering we'd recommend the villages of Hawkshead, Troutbeck (the preserved 'statesman's' farm here is interesting), Cartmel, and Hutton-in-the-Forest.

There's also plenty in Cumbria for families who prefer more constructed entertainment. Favourite outings include the South Lakes Wild Animal Park at Dalton-in-Furness and, for tamer creatures, the Lakeland Sheep & Wool Centre in Cockermouth; the Lakeland Wildlife Oasis at Milnthorpe is an intriguing cross between a museum and a zoo, and there's a well thought-out aquarium at Newby Bridge.

Holker Hall & Gardens, the winner of our Family Attraction Award for Cumbria this year, tops a list of family-friendly great houses, while Muncaster Castle & Owl Centre (children like the maze and the birds best), Mirehouse near Bassenthwaite and Dalemain at Dacre are also good bets. Fine stately homes, with a special appeal for gardeners, include Sizergh Castle and Levens Hall. A lot of Cumbria's great houses have been in the same family for centuries, and this seems to add to their appeal.

Among a good range of museums and heritage centres, the Rheged centre at Penrith (Europe's largest grass-covered building) is especially worth a mention, and children like the interactives and reconstructions at Tullie House in Carlisle. You can learn how weather forecasts are put together at the heritage centre in Whitehaven, and a trip to Sellafield in Seascale is more interesting than you might think. Kendal continues a very good value ticket scheme for its three interesting museums. One of England's oldest and most enjoyable railways is in Ravenglass.

In summer the literary trail is heavily trodden. The main Wordsworth focus is on Grasmere, Rydal and Cockermouth, while admirers of Ruskin head for the museum at Coniston (his house Brantwood, across the water, has a more general appeal). If Beatrix Potter is more your style, you'll find her paintings in Ambleside and Hawkshead (young children enjoy the re-creations at the World of Beatrix Potter in Windermere).

The National Trust control over a quarter of the land in the Lake District National Park, and this dominant influence means that preservation of and access to the countryside is first-class (and it's an area where membership of the Trust really pays off in terms of free admission). You could stay here for weeks every year of your life and never walk the same path twice – so our walks suggestions are just initial pointers. Also, many of our places to stay (and there's an excellent choice – lots serve really good food too) have been chosen for the grand walks right from their doorsteps, and are strong on peace and quiet.

For a quiet break with plenty of walking, the Langdales, particularly Great Langdale, and Borrowdale are outstanding. The west is even quieter, separated from the central Lake District by high ridges with tortuous roads over the few passes. British rock-climbing was born over here, with England's highest mountain, Scafell Pike, surrounded by other awesome peaks – serious walking country.

Another area where, even in summer, you can count on peace and quiet is the part east of the M6 – one of England's least-known areas. Though overshadowed by the Lake District proper it has a lot of charm, as well as some excellent value places to stay in. Quiet river valleys shelter below more awesome open country and high moors, and there are some attractive and untouristy places to visit. Much of the high country is too bleak and boggy for most walkers, but moorland roads give drivers good views (eg A683 Kirkby Lonsdale–Kirkby Stephen, B6260 Tebay–Appleby, B6413 Lazonby–Brampton, A689 Brampton–Alston). The railway crossing the moors between Carlisle and Settle is perhaps the best way of all for seeing this unusual part of England.

Lakeland generally is at its best out of season. May (sheets of wild flowers on the hills) and June are ideal: more sun, no crowds. The views are often clearest (and the ground firm and dry for walkers) in October and November. In the summer holidays and at other peak times crowds make the best places less enjoyable. For all but the hardiest expert outdoorsmen, winter up here is too bleak for pleasure – unless you plan to stay indoors. Whenever you come bring something waterproof – the Lake District has more annual rainfall than any other part of the country.

Public transport in the Lakes is good and works well for round-trip long walks. Local information leaflets offer plenty of choice of well guided walks; information too from National Park visitor services (015394) 46601, and from the National Trust (015394) 35599. Many places offer horse riding, and bicycles can be hired by the day in the main towns (considering the scenic grandeur, you can cycle for a surprisingly long way, at least in the central area, without having to struggle up steep hills).

Where to stay

ALSTON NY7646 **Lovelady Shield Country House** *Nenthead Rd, Alston, Cumbria CA9 3LF (01434) 381203* **£180** inc dinner, plus special breaks; 12 rms, though they hope to add 2 more. In a lovely setting with River Nent running along bottom of garden (tennis and croquet), this handsome country house has a tranquil atmosphere, courteous staff, log fires in comfortable rooms (no smoking in sitting room or restaurant), and very good food inc fine breakfasts; children over 7 in evening restaurant; dogs welcome in bedrooms

AMBLESIDE NY3703 **Rothay Manor** *Rothay Bridge, Ambleside, Cumbria LA22 0EH (015394) 33605* **£130**, plus special breaks; 17 attractive rms (many overlooking garden) inc 3 suites. Family-run Regency country house in neatly kept mature grounds, with open fires and fresh flowers in quietly civilised and comfortable day rooms, very good English food in no smoking dining room, a thoughtful wine list, super big breakfasts, and helpful friendly service; free use of nearby leisure club, and walking, cycling and sailing close by; cl 3 Jan–7 Feb; good disabled access

AMBLESIDE NY3804 **Rowanfield Country House** *Kirkstone Rd, Ambleside, Cumbria LA22 9ET (015394) 33686* **£79***w, plus special breaks. 8 rms, 3 with own sitting area. Charming carefully restored Lakeland house looking across Lake Windermere to distant hills, with a woodburner in the comfortable and attractively furnished sitting room, super breakfasts (good nearby restaurants for evening meals), and friendly owners; cl Dec–mid-Feb, but open Christmas and New Year; children over 8

AMBLESIDE NY3703 **Wateredge Inn** *Borrans Rd, Ambleside, Cumbria LA22 0EP (015394) 32332* **£90**, plus special breaks; 21 good comfortable, recently refurbished rms. Beautifully placed, warmly welcoming inn with neat gardens running down to Lake Windermere (embarkation point for cruising the lake); light airy bar (with fine views) and lounge, good meals in no smoking beamed dining area (more lovely views and candlelit at night), and excellent service; may cl 2 wks Jan; disabled access; dogs welcome in bedrooms

APPLEBY NY6920 **Appleby Manor** *Roman Rd, Appleby, Cumbria CA16 6JB (01768) 351571* **£114***, plus special breaks; 30 well equipped rms in original house (the nicest), coach house annexe or modern wing. Very friendly family-run hotel with fine views over Appleby Castle and Eden Valley, log fires in two of the three comfortable lounges, relaxed bar with wide range of whiskies, excellent service, good interesting food in panelled restaurant, and leisure centre; enjoyed by families; cl 24–26 Dec; disabled access; dogs welcome in bedrooms ☺

BARBON SD6282 **Barbon Inn** *Barbon, Carnforth, Cumbria LA6 2LJ (015242) 76233* **£65**; 10 simple but comfortable rms, some with own bthrm. Small friendly village inn in quiet spot below fells, with relaxing bar, traditional lounge, good meals in candlelit dining room, and helpful service; dogs by prior arrangement

BASSENTHWAITE LAKE NY2032 **Armathwaite Hall Hotel** *Bassenthwaite Lake, Keswick, Cumbria CA12 4RE (017687) 76551* **£180***; 42 rms. Turreted 17th-c mansion in 400 acres of deerpark and woodland; handsome public rooms with lovely fireplaces, fine panelling, antiques, paintings and fresh flowers, good French and English cooking, a super wine list, and helpful staff; snooker room, croquet, pitch-and-putt, tennis court, indoor swimming pool, gym and beauty salon, fishing and riding, archery and clay pigeon shooting, and jogging and mountain-bike tracks; disabled access ☺

BASSENTHWAITE LAKE NY1930 **Pheasant** *Bassenthwaite Lake, Cockermouth, Cumbria CA13 9YE* (017687) 76234 **£130**, plus special breaks; 16 newly refurbished rms. Civilised hotel with delightfully old-fashioned pubby bar, restful lounges with open fire, antiques, fresh flowers and comfortable armchairs, and interesting gardens merging into surrounding fellside woodlands; cl 25 Dec; children over 8; disabled access; dogs in bar and in Garden Lodge bedrooms

BRAMPTON NY5760 **Farlam Hall** *Hallbankgate, Brampton, Cumbria CA8 2NG* (016977) 46234 **£250** inc dinner, plus special breaks; 12 comfortable rms. Charmingly Victorian (though parts are much older) and very civilised country house with log fires in spacious lounges, excellent attentive service, good 4-course dinner using fine china and silver, marvellous breakfasts, and peaceful spacious grounds with croquet lawn and small pretty lake; cl 25–30 Dec; children over 5; dogs welcome except in restaurant

BUTTERMERE NY1716 **Bridge** *Buttermere, Cockermouth, Cumbria CA13 9UZ* (017687) 70252 **£120** inc dinner, plus special breaks; 21 recently refurbished rms. Comfortable hotel surrounded by some of the best steep countryside in the county, with beamed bar, open fire and deep armchairs in sitting room, good food in bar and no smoking restaurant, real ales, decent malt whiskies, and a friendly atmosphere; self-catering also; children over 7 in dining room; dogs welcome in bedrooms

CARLISLE NY4055 **Number Thirty One, Howard Place** *31 Howard Pl, Carlisle, Cumbria CA1 1HR* (01228) 597080 **£90**; 3 well equipped individually decorated rms. Carefully restored no smoking Victorian townhouse with a relaxed informal atmosphere, open fire and plenty of books in the cosy lounge, delicious interesting food using the best local produce, breakfast with home-baked bread, home-made preserves and home-made Cumbrian sausages, and helpful courteous owners; cl 1 Nov–1 Mar; no children

CASTERTON SD6279 **Pheasant** *Casterton, Carnforth, Lancashire LA6 2RX* (015242) 71230 **£76**, plus special breaks; 10 comfortable rms, most with countryside views, and several newly refurbished. Small civilised inn with pleasant atmosphere, good food in no smoking panelled dining room, cheerful staff, and small but sound wine list; cl 25–26 Dec; disabled access; dogs welcome

CROOK SD4395 **Wild Boar** *Crook, Windermere, Cumbria LA23 3NF* (015394) 45225 **£115**; 36 rms. Comfortable well run extended hotel with period furnishings and log fires in its ancient core, attentive service, and good food in no smoking dining room; free access to nearby leisure club and discounts on watersports; children's club at sister hotel, The Lowwood; dogs welcome

CROSBY ON EDEN NY4459 **Crosby Lodge** *High Crosby, Crosby on Eden, Carlisle, Cumbria CA6 4QZ* (01228) 573618 **£120***, plus special breaks; 11 spacious rms (2 in stable conversion). Imposing and carefully converted country house in attractive mature grounds, with comfortable and appealing individual furnishings, enjoyable home-made food using local produce in no smoking restaurant, friendly long-established owners, and nice surrounding countryside; cl Christmas/New Year; limited disabled access; dogs by arrangement

DENT SD7686 **Sportsmans** *Cowgill, Dent, Sedbergh, Cumbria LA10 5RG* (01539) 625282 **£47**, plus winter breaks; 6 rms with shared bthrm. Unassuming comfortable pub notable for its wonderful position in Dentdale by the River Dee overlooking the Settle–Carlisle railway, and walks in all directions; open log fires, real ales, and good value home-made food; dogs welcome in bedrooms

DERWENT WATER NY2618 **Hilton Keswick Lodore** *Borrowdale, Keswick, Cumbria CA12 5UX* (017687) 77285 **£143***, plus special breaks; 71 well equipped rms. Long-standing but well updated big holiday hotel with lots of facilities in 40 acres of lakeside gardens and woodlands, comfortable day rooms, elegant restaurant, leisure club, tennis and squash, outdoor swimming pool, and games room; particularly well organised for families with NNEB nannies and so forth; self-catering house too; dogs welcome in bedrooms ☺

DOCKRAY NY3921 **Royal** *Dockray, Penrith, Cumbria CA11 0JY (017684) 82356*
£64, plus special breaks; 10 rms. Friendly family-run hotel with open fires in big
modernised open-plan bar, good value hearty meals, and well kept beers; in fine
spot between hills and lake with walks from the doorstep; children must be well
behaved; dogs welcome in bedrooms

ELTERWATER NY3204 **Britannia Inn** *Elterwater, Ambleside, Cumbria LA22 9HP*
(015394) 37210 **£80**, plus special breaks; 9 rms. Simple charmingly traditional pub
in fine surroundings opp village green, with a happy friendly atmosphere (it does get
very busy at peak times), hearty home cooking inc superb breakfast, comfortable no
smoking lounge and bustling bar, real ales, and Sun evening quiz; fine walks all
around; cl 25–26 Dec; dogs in bars and bdrms

FAR SAWREY SD3895 **Sawrey** *Far Sawrey, Ambleside, Cumbria LA22 0LQ*
(015394) 43425 **£63**, plus special breaks; 18 rms. Friendly hotel well placed at the
foot of Claife Heights, with simple pubby and smarter bars, friendly staff, good
straightforward food, and seats on pleasant lawn; cl Christmas; kind to children;
partial disabled access; dogs welcome in bedrooms

GARRIGILL NY7441 **Ivy House** *Garrigill, Alston, Cumbria CA9 3DU (01434)*
382501 **£44***, plus special breaks; 3 rms. 17th-c farmhouse in fine scenery on
Alston Moor, with a comfortable guest lounge, open fire and plenty of books, games
and newspapers, helpful welcoming owners, and good breakfasts plus packed
lunches and evening meals (which must be booked in advance); they also offer llama
treks with instructions on how to handle and befriend them (children must be over
12 for this); dogs welcome

GRASMERE NY3308 **Swan** *Keswick Rd, Grasmere, Ambleside, Cumbria LA22 9RF*
(015394) 35551 **£138**, plus special breaks; 38 rms, most with fine views. Smart and
friendly 17th-c hotel in beautiful fell-foot surroundings, with beams and inglenooks,
elegant no smoking dining room, enjoyable food, and attractive garden; lovely
walks; partial disabled access; dogs anywhere except restaurant

GRASMERE NY3307 **Wordsworth Hotel** *Grasmere, Ambleside, Cumbria LA22*
9SW (015394) 35592 **£140***, plus special breaks; 37 comfortable, pretty rms. Well
run hotel, right in village next to the churchyard where Wordsworth is buried;
stylish lounges and airy restaurant overlooking landscaped gardens, a relaxed
conservatory and popular pubby bar, friendly service, enjoyable food inc super
buffet lunch, mini-gym, and sauna; good disabled access

GRIZEDALE SD3394 **Grizedale Lodge** *Hawkshead Hill, Grizedale, Ambleside,*
Cumbria LA22 0QL (015394) 36532 **£75***, plus special breaks; 8 no smoking rms.
Friendly, comfortable B&B hotel in the middle of the magnificent Grizedale Forest
with lots of walks from the front door, lounge bar, and hearty breakfasts in
attractive breakfast room; children over 5; disabled access; dogs welcome in
bedrooms

HAWKSHEAD NY3501 **Drunken Duck** *Barngates, Hawkshead, Ambleside,*
Cumbria LA22 0NG (015394) 36347 **£110**, plus special breaks; 13 comfortable rms.
Attractive 17th-c Lakeland inn alone in 60 hillside acres, with several cosy mainly no
smoking beamed rooms, open fires, distant views of Lake Windermere, home-
brewed ales, over 50 malt whiskies, and good interesting lunchtime food (more
elaborate in the evening); fishing in private tarn; cl 25 Dec pm; limited disabled
access

HAWKSHEAD SD3498 **Highfield House** *Hawkshead Hill, Ambleside, Cumbria*
LA22 0PN (015394) 36344 **£100***, plus winter breaks; 11 pretty rms. Welcoming
Victorian country house in spacious woodland garden with fine views (good walks
from the door), open fire in comfortable lounge, cosy bar, and enjoyable food inc
packed lunches, children's high tea, and good breakfasts; cl Jan; dogs welcome in
bedrooms

IREBY NY2335 **Overwater Hall** *Ireby, Carlisle, Cumbria CA5 1HH (017687)*
76566 **£100**, plus special breaks; 12 recently refurbished rms. Relaxed and friendly
family-run hotel, partly castellated, in 18 acres of gardens and woodland, with log

fire in elegant comfortable drawing room, good imaginative food in cosy dining room, and lots of walks; cl 2 wks from 3 Jan; children over 5 in restaurant (high tea 5 pm); partial disabled access; dogs in bdrms and one lounge

KENDAL NY5401 **Low Jock Scar** *Selside, Kendal, Cumbria LA8 9LE (01539) 823259* **£60***; 5 rms, most with own bthrm. Relaxed and friendly little country guesthouse in six acres of garden and woodland, with residents' lounge, and good home cooking (picnic lunches on request); no smoking; cl Nov–mid-Mar; children over 12; dogs welcome in bedrooms

KESWICK NY2623 **Shu-le-Crow Cottage** *7 Penrith Rd, Keswick, Cumbria CA12 4HF (017687) 75253* **£50***; 3 attractive rms. Pink-washed no smoking 18th-c cottage with plenty of original features, cheerful owners who can advise on local walks, and super breakfasts (vegetarian options); plenty of places to eat nearby; cl Christmas

KESWICK NY2421 **Swinside Lodge** *Newlands, Keswick, Cumbria CA12 5UE (017687) 72948* **£100**, plus special breaks; 7 comfortable rms. Victorian hotel in own grounds surrounded by wonderful unspoilt scenery at the foot of Cat Bells, and a few minutes from shores of Derwent Water; hearty breakfasts and super home-made evening meals in candelit dining room, helpful friendly service, and two relaxing sitting rooms; children over 10

KIRKCAMBECK NY5269 **Cracrop Farm** *Kirkcambeck, Brampton, Cumbria CA8 2BW (016977) 48245* **£55**; 4 rms with showers, overlooking garden and open fields. Friendly Victorian farmhouse on 425 acres with very good marked farm trails (they are keen on conservation), comfortable homely rooms, good traditional breakfasts (other food arranged in advance) and games room and sauna; no smoking; children over 12

LANGDALE NY2806 **Old Dungeon Ghyll** *Great Langdale, Ambleside, Cumbria LA22 9JY (015394) 37272* **£78**, plus special breaks; 14 rms, some with shared bthrm. Friendly, simple and cosy walkers' and climbers' inn dramatically surrounded by fells, wonderful views and terrific walks; cosy residents' lounge and popular food – best to book for dinner if not a resident; cl Christmas; dogs welcome away from dining room

LINDALE SD4180 **Greenacres Country Guest House** *Lindale, Grange-over-Sands, Cumbria LA11 6LP (015395) 34578* **£52***, plus special breaks; 4 appealing rms. Charming 19th-c cottage with friendly atmosphere, pretty sitting room, conservatory, log fire, good home-made food and big breakfasts in cosy dining room, and packed lunch on request; kind to families and will set aside the whole house for family parties; cl Christmas and New Year ☺

LITTLE LANGDALE NY3103 **Three Shires** *Little Langdale, Ambleside, Cumbria LA22 9NZ (015394) 37215* **£70**, plus special breaks; 10 rms. Family-run stone-built country inn with beautiful views, comfortably refurbished residents' lounge, separate walkers' bar with real ales, decent food, and pretty gardens; cl mid-week during Dec/Jan

LORTON NY1522 **New House Farm** *Lorton, Cockermouth, Cumbria CA13 9UU (01900) 85404* **£88**, plus special breaks; 5 rms with wonderful hillside views. Friendly no smoking 17th-c house (not a working farm) in 15 acres, with beams and rafters, flagstones, open fires, and three residents' lounges, very good food inc game and fish caught by owner, home-made scones and preserves, a thoughtful wine list – and lots of walks; children over 6; dogs welcome in bedrooms

MUNGRISDALE NY3630 **Mill Hotel** *Mungrisdale, Penrith, Cumbria CA11 0XR (017687) 79659* **£85**; 9 rms, most with own bthrm. Very friendly small streamside hotel beautifully placed in lovely valley hamlet hidden away below Blencathra, with open fire in cosy and comfortable sitting room, good imaginative 5-course evening meals, and a small carefully chosen wine list; cl Nov–beginning Mar; they are kind to children; disabled access; dogs welcome in bedrooms

POOLEY BRIDGE NY4521 **Sharrow Bay** *Pooley Bridge, Penrith, Cumbria CA10 2LZ (017684) 86301* **£300** inc dinner, plus special breaks; 26 lovely rms with antiques, books, and games. Country-house hotel in quiet idyllic spot by Ullswater with lovely views of the lake and mountains, and showing the years of loving care the owners put into its distinctive style, furnishings and décor; unobtrusively attentive service and excellent English cooking in the two contrasting dining rooms; cl early Dec–beginning Mar; no children; disabled access

RYDAL WATER NY3406 **White Moss House** *White Moss, Ambleside, Cumbria LA22 9SE (015394) 35295* **£138** inc dinner, plus special breaks; 6 thoughtfully furnished and comfortable little rms in main house plus separate cottage let as one unit with 2 rms. Bought by Wordsworth for his son, this attractive stripped-stone country house – set in charming mature grounds overlooking the lake – is a marvellously relaxing place to stay, with owners who have been there for over 20 years, a comfortable lounge, excellent fixed-price 5-course meals in pretty no smoking dining room, a fine wine list, and exemplary service; free fishing and free use of local leisure club; cl Dec–Jan; no toddlers; dogs in cottage

SEATOLLER NY2413 **Seatoller House** *Borrowdale, Keswick, Cumbria CA12 5XN (017687) 77218* **£59**; 10 spotless, comfortable rms. Friendly house-party atmosphere in 17th-c house that has been a guesthouse for over 100 years, with self-service drinks and board games in comfortable lounges (no TV), and good no-choice fixed-time hearty dinner (not Tues) served at two big oak tables; packed lunches; two acres of grounds and many walks from doorstep (house is at the foot of Honister Pass); cl end Nov–Mar; dogs welcome

TALKIN NY5557 **Hullerbank** *Talkin, Brampton, Cumbria CA8 1LB (016977) 46668* **£48***; 3 rms. Comfortable and very friendly no smoking Georgian farmhouse in unspoilt countryside, with a relaxed atmosphere in homely lounge, enjoyable breakfasts, and packed lunch on request; cl Dec–Jan; children over 12

THIRLMERE NY3117 **Dale Head Hall** *Thirlmere, Keswick, Cumbria CA12 4TN (017687) 72478* **£85**, plus special breaks; 12 pretty rms, most with lake views, and 7 in new wing. Peaceful partly 16th-c country house in lovely lakeside grounds, with comfortable lounges, log fire, cheerful owners, and home-cooked food using produce grown in own walled garden; children over 10 for evening meals; cl Jan

TIRRIL NY5026 **Queens Head** *Tirril, Penrith, Cumbria CA10 2JF (01768) 863219* **£60***, plus special breaks; 7 lovely rms, most with own bthrm. Bustling very welcoming inn with flagstones and bare boards in the bar, spacious back restaurant (mostly no smoking), low beams, black panelling, inglenook fireplace and old-fashioned settles in older part, good interesting food inc snacks and OAP specials, and well kept real ales (inc their own brews); babies welcome but older children must be over 13; dogs welcome except in restaurant

WASDALE HEAD NY1607 **Wasdale Head Hotel** *Wasdale Head, Seascale, Cumbria CA20 1EX (019467) 26229* **£90**; 9 simple but warmly comfortable pine-clad rms, with 3 more luxurious ones in farmhouse annexe. Old flagstoned and gabled walkers' and climbers' inn in magnificent setting surrounded by steep fells, with civilised day rooms, popular home cooking, good wine list, huge breakfasts, and cheerfully busy public bar; steam room; self-catering cottages; partial disabled access

WATERMILLOCK NY4421 **Leeming House** *Watermillock, Ullswater, Penrith, Cumbria CA11 0JJ (017684) 86622* **£148**, plus special breaks; 40 cosseting rms, many with beautiful views. Well run extended hotel in 20 acres of quiet lakeside grounds, with log fires in comfortable lounges, cosy panelled bar, fine food in lovely no smoking dining room, and good courteous service; boating and fishing; high teas for young children; good provision for disabled; dogs welcome in bedrooms

WATERMILLOCK NY4321 **Old Church Hotel** *Watermillock, Penrith, Cumbria CA11 0JN (017684) 86204* **£165***, plus special breaks; 10 rms, some with lovely Ullswater view. Attractive 18th-c Lakeland house peacefully placed in waterside gardens, with log fires and individual furnishings in civilised day rooms, kind service, and excellent English dinners at 8pm in attractive dining room; no smoking; rowing/windsurfing boats; cl Dec–Feb

WATERMILLOCK NY4523 **Rampsbeck Country House** *Watermillock, Penrith, Cumbria CA11 0LP (017684) 86442* **£100**, plus special breaks; 20 attractive rms, some with balconies. 18th-c hotel in 18 acres by Lake Ullswater with extensive lake frontage; open fire in the cosy sitting room, French windows into the garden from the plush, comfortable lounge, friendly attentive staff, and carefully prepared food in the attractive dining room; croquet; lots to do nearby; cl Jan–mid-Feb; children over 8 in dining rm; dogs welcome in bedrooms

WINDERMERE SD4097 **Fir Trees** *Lake Rd, Windermere, Cumbria LA23 2EQ* *(015394) 42272* **£68***; 9 attractive spotless rms inc 2 family ones. Well run and comfortable no smoking Victorian house with an informal relaxed atmosphere, antiques, fine prints and fresh flowers, warmly helpful service (detailed suggestions of what to do), and good hearty breakfasts and vegetarian meals by prior arrangement; children over 5

WINDERMERE SD4295 **Gilpin Lodge** *Crook Rd, Windermere, Cumbria LA23 3NE (015394) 88818* **£110**, plus special breaks; 14 marvellous rms with lots of space, sitting areas, super bthrms, and fine views. Impeccably run country house hotel with lovely gardens and grounds that take in ponds, woodlands and moor; big peaceful sitting rooms with antiques, fresh flowers, magazines, and open fires (no formal bar or reception desk), delicious food in three charming restaurant rooms, exceptional breakfasts and afternoon teas, and genuinely friendly, professional but unpretentious staff; free use of nearby Parklands Country & Leisure Club; children over 7; partial disabled access

WINDERMERE NY3801 **Langdale Chase Hotel** *Windermere, Cumbria LA23 1LW (015394) 32201* **£150**; 27 rms, many with marvellous lake view. Welcoming family-run hotel in lovely position on the edge of Lake Windermere with water-skiing and bathing from the hotel jetty; tennis, croquet, putting and rowing, afternoon tea on the terraces, gracious oak-panelled rooms with antiques, paintings, fresh flowers, open fires, very good food (huge breakfasts, too), and friendly service; disabled access; dogs welcome

WITHERSLACK SD4384 **Old Vicarage** *Witherslack, Grange-over-Sands, Cumbria LA11 6RS (015395) 52381* **£75** inc dinner, plus special breaks; 14 individually decorated rms – some in the modern Orchard House are more spacious and have their own woodland terraces. Late Georgian vicarage in five acres of peaceful gardens and woodland, with two comfortable lounges, a log fire, good interesting food in cosy restaurant inc home-made bread, cakes and preserves, and hearty breakfasts; tennis and lots of surrounding walks; dogs welcome in bedrooms. Coffee shop, gift shop, disabled access; cl 25 Dec; (015395) 30153; £5.75. The nicely set Swan has decent food.

To see and do

Cumbria Family Attraction of the Year

CARK-IN-CARTMEL SD3577 **Holker Hall & Gardens** With its opulently built and furnished mansion, first-class gardens, and entertaining motor museum, this busy estate easily has enough to keep most families occupied for the bulk of the day. The house dates back to the early 16th c (and has been in the same family ever since), but the present building is mainly Victorian, constructed after a disastrous fire destroyed much of the original. Despite its beauty, it has an appealingly unstuffy feel, and remains very much a family home. But it still has some splendidly grand features: look out in particular for the stunning staircase, where each baluster has a unique design. Impressive as they are, the rooms are rather eclipsed by what's outside: the glorious 25-acre formal and woodland gardens are among the best in the county, with spectacular water features, a sunken garden, rhododendron and azalea arboretum, and rare plants and shrubs. A potting shed has an exhibition on garden history, and there's a very good nursery. The motor museum – not huge, but very appealingly presented – has a good collection of cars, bikes, tractors, and all sorts of related equipment and memorabilia, from enamel signs through models to petrol pumps. Perhaps most interesting is the display on Donald Campbell's world record-breaking attempts, with a full-size replica of the ill-fated Bluebird. Children enjoy the 125-acre deer park, and are given a Discovery Card when they arrive at the estate to help them explore; there's also an adventure playground for under-12s, and a picnic area. Dogs on a lead are welcome in the park. There's a good Garden Festival towards the end of May; opening times may vary slightly then. Meals, snacks, shop, disabled access; cl Sat, and Nov–Mar; (015395) 58328. An all-in ticket is £8.25 (£4.65 children over 6), or they do just about every other possible ticket combination: house and garden only is £6.50 (£3.95 children), motor museum and garden only £6.90 (£4.20), or a garden only ticket £3.95 (£2.25 children).

ABBEY TOWN NY1751 **Holme Cultram** (B5302 Wigtown–Silloth) Remains of formidably rich Cistercian abbey – extraordinarily grand for this quiet village. The New Inn at Blencogo has good food – must book, on (016973) 61091.

ALSTON NY7146 This interesting little well weathered Pennine market town is the highest of its kind in England, with a surprising number of pubs up and down its very steep cobbled main street (the Angel is best), and a couple of craft shops; readers recommend Stokoe House Ceramics (Market Pl) and Blueberries restaurant nearby. *Oliver Twist* was filmed here, and a leaflet from the gallery below marks the main sites. **Gossipgate Gallery** (The Butts) Local art and crafts, with changing exhibitions, a good big shop, and a garden with a tea

terrace, and cultivated flowers planted alongside their wild ancestors; disabled access (though no facilities); cl 1–2pm, Jan–mid-Feb, Mon (exc bank hols) and Tues, and other days in winter, best to phone at beginning and end of season; (01434) 381806; free. **Hartside Nursery** (A686 W of Alston) Beautifully placed alpine nursery with small streamside garden and rare plants for sale; it's quite a draw for birds and wildlife. Some disabled access with notice; cl am wknds and bank hols, Nov to mid-Mar (exc by appointment); (01434) 381372; free. **South Tynedale Railway** The chief attraction around here, giving leisurely rides through the beautiful scenery of the South Tyne valley, behind preserved steam and diesel locomotives from here and abroad. Teas, shop, disabled access by arrangement; open wknds and bank hols Easter–Oct, daily July–Aug (exc most Mons and Fridays in July), and some wknds in Dec – best to ring for timetable; (01434) 381696; fares from £4.

AMBLESIDE NY3704

A busy holiday-oriented shopping town inc excellent outdoor equipment shops strung along its central one-way system, with the quaintest information centre in the Lakes – the little NT shop in the tiny stone Bridge House over Stock Ghyll by the main car park. Above Stock, the old milling quarter, lying just uphill from here, has cottagey charm and is at the beginning of the road up to Kirkstone; ½m farther is the entrance to verdantly set Stock Ghyll Force waterfall. Waterhead is the northern ferry terminal on Lake Windermere, and close by are the scant remains of Galava Roman Fort (free access). Traditional glass blowing at Adrian Sankey, Rydal Rd; good demonstrations and shop; (015394) 33039. Hayes Garden World (Lake Rd) is a big garden centre in landscaped gardens; café, disabled access (only on ground floor).

Armitt Ambleside Museum Decent local history museum with the largest collection of Beatrix Potter's watercolours, plus works by local artists, photographers, several original manuscripts by local writers, and numerous archaeological remains. Shop, disabled access; cl 25–26 Dec; (015394) 31212; £2.50.

Brockhole (A591 S of Ambleside, or launch from town pier) National Park information centre in country house with well landscaped gardens and attractive lakeshore grounds; also audio-visual show, exhibitions, and adventure play area. Special talks and events all year. Meals, snacks, shop, disabled access; visitor centre cl Nov–Mar, gardens and grounds open all year; (015394) 46601; free, but charge for parking (£4 all day, £3 for half day).

Stagshaw Garden (Waterhead, just S) Hillside woodland garden with lovely lake views, mature camellias, rhododendrons, magnolias and heathers; best in spring. Open daily Apr–Jun then by appointment July–Oct; (015394) 35599; free; NT. Parking is very limited.

APPLEBY NY6820

An attractive riverside village; the main street, rising from the harmonious 12th-c church to the castle, is still a grand sight despite the cars, with a good few handsome buildings inc a lovely courtyard of almshouses. Pleasant strolls by the River Eden. The Royal Oak is enjoyable for lunch.

Appleby Castle Conservation Centre This interesting place has one of the best-preserved Norman keeps in the country (the rest of the buildings are later additions); terrific views from the ramparts. The Clifford family lived here for nearly 700 years, though they moved later to the grander house next door (as we went to press the Great Hall was closed for renovations, but they hope it will be open again by the middle of 2003). Attractive grounds with a big collection of birds, waterfowl and farm animals, in a lovely setting above the river, children's play area. Meals, snacks, shop, limited disabled access; usually open Easter–end Sept but best to check; (017683) 53823; £5.

ARNSIDE SD4578

A good start for the 20-min train trip along the N shore of Morecambe Bay to Ulverston: long viaducts, stupendous views. The Ship at nearby Sandside also has glorious views.

ARNSIDE KNOTT SD4577

Medium-sized wooded limestone hill, easily walked up from Arnside, with a highly rewarding view across Morecambe Bay to the southern Lakeland fells.

ASKHAM NY5123

Idyllically dozy limestone village with greens and broad verges; actually in the Lake District, but more reminiscent of the Yorkshire Dales. Pleasant pastoral walk skirting the spooky ruin of Lowther Castle and heading along the River Lowther to Whale, then on to Helton and back to Askham. The Queens Head is useful for lunch.

BARBON SD6282

An unpretentious village given appeal by its fine setting, just below the fells; the road from here to Dent via Gawthrop leads through lonely Barbondale, dominated by the Barbon Fell. The Barbon Inn is good.

Cumbria

BORDERS

DUMFRIES & GALLOWAY

Kirkcambeck

44 *Crosby on Eden*

Brampton

43 **Talkin Tarn**

Carlisle *Talkin*

NX *Dalston* *Wetheral*

Abbey Town *Armathwaite*

Staffield

Torpenhow *Caldbeck* *Little Salkeld*

Ireby *Langwathby*

Maryport *Hesket Newmarket* **41** **Penrith**

Bassenthwaite Lake *Binsey* **Skelton** **40**

Cockermouth *Bassenthwaite* *Mungrisdale* **Stainton**

Skiddaw *Brougham*

Workington **A66** *Applethwaite* **A66** *Tirril* *Yanwath*

Thornthwaite *Dacre* *Pooley Bridge*

Lorton **Keswick** *Watermillock*

Thornthwaite Forest *Dockray* *Askham* *Lowther*

Loweswater *Derwent Water* *Ullswater*

Crummock Water *Thirlmere* *High Street* *Bampton*

Whitehaven *Dalehead* *Borrowdale* *Helvellyn*

Ennerdale Water *Stonethwaite* *Hawes Water*

St Bees *Buttermere* *Honister Pass* *Seatoller* *Fairfield* *Shap*

Egremont *Seathwaite* *Grasmere*

Wasdale Head *Gt Langdale* *Rydal Water* *Rydal*

Beckermet *Elterwater* *Wansfell Pike*

Gosforth *Wast Water* *Little Langdale* **Ambleside**

Seascale *Wasdale* *Hardknott Pass* *Troutbeck*

Boot *Tarn Hows* **Windermere**

Ravenglass *Eskdale* *Coniston* *Hawkshead* *Latterbarrow* **Kendal**

Duddon Valley *Coniston Water* *Far Sawrey* *Crook*

Grizedale *Near Sawrey* *Crosthwaite*

Broughton Mills *Graythwaite* *Brigsteer*

Swinside *Gümmers How* *Sizergh*

Broughton-in-Furness *Lakeside* *Levens*

Finsthwaite *Cartmel Fell*

Newby Bridge *Witherslack* *Milnthorpe*

Millom *Lindale*

Haverigg Point *Ulverston* *Cartmel* *Grange-over-Sands* **Beetham**

Lindal-in-Furness **Cark-in-Cartmel** *Arnside*

Dalton-in-Furness **A590** *Bardsea* *Arnside Knott*

Flookburgh *Humphrey Head Point*

Barrow-in-Furness *Gleaston*

Walney Island **MORECAMBE BAY SANDS**

Piel Island **LANCS**

6   7   8   9

NORTHUMBERLAND

Hadrian's Wall

A69

A689

NY

Alston

A686

Melmerby

Garrigill

DURHAM

Maiden Way

Temple Sowerby

Dufton

High Cup Nick

A66

Appleby

Crosby Ravensworth

Brough

39

A685

38

Winton

Ravenstonedale

Mallerstang

Howgill Fells

A684

Sedbergh

Dent

Barbon

Casterton

Kirkby Lonsdale

NORTH YORKSHIRE

0 Miles   10

0 Kilometres   16

BARROW-IN-FURNESS SD1969

The town shows the effects of the virtual collapse of shipbuilding in this country, on which it depended. The **railway** from here to Whitehaven hugs the coast and has good views, missed by the road, though in the other direction the A5087 to Ulverston has fine views across Morecambe Bay. The cheerful Black Dog out past Dalton-in-Furness is a good stop.

Dock Museum (North Rd) Futuristic-looking museum exploring how Barrow developed from a tiny hamlet to the biggest iron and steel centre in the world, before becoming renowned for shipbuilding; displays range from simple fishing boats to model submarines and rare Vickers ship models; also interactive displays and an adventure playground. Snacks, shop, good disabled access; cl Mon (exc bank hols), plus Tues Nov–Mar and 25–26 Dec; (01229) 894444; free.

Furness Abbey (slightly NE, towards Dalton) Impressive warm sandstone Norman remains of the one-time second richest monastery in England, with lovely arched cloisters, peaceful lawns, and views of pretty valley. Small museum, shop, disabled access; cl Mon and Tues in Nov–Mar, 24–26 Dec, and 1 Jan; (01229) 823420; £2.80; EH.

Sandscale Haws (SD1875) These dunes are protected as a **nature reserve**.

BASSENTHWAITE NY2332

Attractive close-set little village – the 12th-c parish church is three miles S; the Sun is a decent pub. You can also hire rowing boats on Bassenthwaite Water.

Mirehouse (off A591 S) The family that still live in this modest 17th-c house once had excellent literary connections, so the fine rooms have mementoes of Wordsworth, Carlyle and Tennyson among others. They frequently have informal piano recitals (guests are welcome to sit by the fire and listen), and on Weds in Jun, July and Sept they usually have lace-making demonstrations. Interesting garden (bee/butterfly plants) with changing poetry exhibitions in the verandah, as well as peaceful lakeshore grounds, lakeside church, and woods with well thought-out adventure play areas. Lots to do, with a surprising number of activities for children, also a trail, secret drawers, and dolls to play with – they may even be allowed to sound the big dinner gong. Generous Cumbrian home cooking in ex-mill tearoom, disabled access; open Apr–Oct, house pm Sun and Weds, garden daily; (017687) 72287; £4, garden only £2.

BASSENTHWAITE LAKE NY2032

Trotters World of Animals (Coalbeck Farm, B5291, signed from A591 and A66 as Trotters and Friends) The range of animals at this 25-acre site really is wide, from rare breeds of pigs, cattle and goats, through birds of prey, lizards and snakes, to otters, llamas and gibbons. Throughout the day, at certain times, you might be able to bottle-feed a baby goat, cuddle the rabbits, or have a hawk fly down to your wrist, and helpful uniformed staff are on hand to answer questions. For an extra charge they usually have trailer rides or pony rides; there's an adventure playground, and plenty of space for a picnic. Quite a few things are under cover, and in winter they keep up a full range of indoor activities. Their birds of prey centre has the region's only breeding golden eagles and caracaras. Meals, snacks, shop, disabled access; cl wkdys Nov to mid-Feb, and 25 Dec, 1 Jan; (017687) 76239; *£4.75. The Pheasant just S is an attractive place to stop and have lunch.

BEETHAM SD4979

Heron Cornmill and Papermaking ⊞ Well organised working watermill dating from 1096, though the current building is 18th c; baking exhibition. Displays about the paper-making industry are in a converted barn next door. Shop; cl Mon (exc bank hols), and Oct–Easter; (015395) 65027; *£2. Beetham itself is attractive, with an interesting **church**, and the Wheatsheaf is good for lunch. A woodland walk leads to the Fairy Steps with rewarding views over the bay.

BINSEY NY2235

A pathless lump of a hill, but with splendid views of the Lakes and Solway Firth (and into Scotland) by virtue of its geographical isolation.

BOOT NY1801

The steam railway from Ravenglass ends here, at Dalegarth Station, and Dalegarth Falls here are lovely. The Burnmoor Inn, very well placed for walkers, has good value food; the Bower House further down Eskdale at Eskdale Green is also good.

Eskdale Watermill Guided tours of working 16th-c oatmeal mill, with a picnic area nr waterfalls. Snacks, shop; cl Mon and all Oct–Mar (exc wknds in Oct); (019467) 23335; £1.50.

BORROWDALE NY2517

Good views from the B5289 of what is many people's favourite Lakeland base for walks, with good paths along or just above the wooded River Derwent; impregnable-looking Castle Crag is a splendid mini-peak to head for, reached in about 30min from Grange (which has a useful teashop). Close to the road are the Bowder Stone (a huge boulder with a ladder up to the top), and the Lodore Falls (behind Lodore Hotel). For prized walks see Seathwaite entry, and Watendlath under Derwent Water. The Flock Inn tearoom at Yew Tree, Rosthwaite is excellent, with good generous home-made food, and the Langstrath at Stonethwaite (run by a direct descendant of huntsman John Peel) makes a beautifully placed base.

BRAMPTON NY5563

Lanercost Priory (brown signs from town) Impressive and extensive remains of Norman priory, built with stone recycled from Hadrian's Wall. Shop, some disabled access; cl Nov–Mar; £2.30; EH. The nave, picturesquely framed by an arch, was restored in the 18th c as a red sandstone church, and has stained glass by William Morris and Burne-Jones. The Abbey Bridge Inn by the priory has decent food.

BROUGH NY7914

Brough Castle Classic ruined Norman fortress, in a romantic setting on moors above the village, with great views; free. The Golden Fleece is useful for lunch.

BROUGHAM NY5329

Brougham Castle (off A6 S of Penrith) A sturdy Norman ruin on steep lawns above riverside sheep pastures; climb to the top of the keep for the best view. Traces of Roman remains too, with a small exhibition of tombstones. Snacks, shop, disabled access; cl Nov–Mar; £2.20 (01768) 862488; EH. The Gate Inn at Yanwath has good food.

Brougham Hall Craft Centre 🖼 15 different craft workshops inc metal workers, furniture restoration, smoked foods and home-made chocolates, in the attractive stone courtyard of a 15th-c Hall. Plenty to see around the house and grounds inc Cromwellian chapel and a collection of dolls and doll's houses. Meals, snacks, shop, disabled access; cl 25 Dec; (01768) 868184; £2.

BROUGHTON-IN-FURNESS SD2187
Small town with a villagey feel, and a handsome sloping square lined with Georgian houses. A handy base for exploring the Duddon and other quieter Lakeland valleys; for an exciting high-altitude drive, head NW over Corney Fell to Corney. The Manor Arms in Broughton does popular snacks.

BUTTERMERE NY1815
A splendid varied flat walk circles the lake, with glorious views, plenty of safe opportunities for children aged 6 or more to let off steam, and even a tunnel; weather has to be really savage to spoil it. Parking at Gatescarth. The Bridge Hotel in the village is good for lunch; in summer you can hire **rowing boats**; (017687) 70233; from £6.

Ceiling of the Lakes The green slatey fells N of Buttermere offer keen walkers superlative routes along high ridges: Whiteless Pike, Causey Pike, Crag Hill and Grasmoor are among the most exciting points.

Hay Stacks To the south of Buttermere and high above it, this is a challenging walk, but a rewarding one for the enjoyable views, continuing on to Fleetwith Pike.

Rannerdale Knotts Modest-sized hill reached via Low Bank from Buttermere village, a grand vantage point and a good alternative to the much loftier summits around it; splendid views of Crummock Water and the hills surrounding it.

CALDBECK NY3239
The grave of John Peel (of 'Do ye ken John Peel' fame) can be found in the churchyard here, and the Oddfellows Arms has good generous food. There's a pretty drive to attractive Mungrisdale; alternatively, a pleasant stroll to a peaceful spot with a waterfall called the Howk.

CARK-IN-CARTMEL SD3577
Holker Hall & Gardens See separate family panel on p.106. The nearby Engine has good home-made food.

CARLISLE NY3956
Cumbria's only city, not an obvious holiday destination, but plenty to interest the visitor, with several quietly attractive old buildings (and a very helpful visitor centre in one of them, the Old Town Hall). **St Cuthbert's church** is remarkable for its mobile pulpit. The Kings Head (Fisher St) does good value snacks, and there's good home cooking in the Black Lion out at Durdar, where the attractively placed racecourse has meetings every month exc July; telephone (01228) 522973 for dates.

Carlisle Castle This extensive medieval fortress, rather gaunt and forbidding, is surprisingly well kept considering its violent history. Interesting period furnished rooms, a portcullised gatehouse, lots of staircases and passages, and centuries of prisoners' carved graffiti in the dungeons; good views from the ramparts. Snacks, shop, limited disabled access; cl 24–26 Dec; (01228) 591922; £3.20; EH.

Carlisle Cathedral This unpretentious abbey church, founded in 1122 and severely damaged in the Civil War, has fine stained glass; try to go on a bright morning when the sunlight comes streaming colourfully through the east window. Also medieval carvings inc the Brougham Triptych, painted panels and stonework, and crypt treasury. Meals, snacks, good shop (some tasty local foods), disabled access (exc to restaurant); access may be restricted during services (01228) 535169; free but donations encouraged.

Guildhall Museum (Green Market) A handsomely restored medieval timbered hall; worth a look inside if passing – some displays inc interesting

Guild silver. Cl am, and Mon (exc bank hols) and all Nov–Easter; free.

Settle–Carlisle railway Running up Ribbledale and into the Cumbrian Pennines, stopping at Dent Station, Garsdale Head, Kirkby Stephen, Appleby, Langwathby and other Eden Valley villages, this is a memorable 70 miles of grand scenery, best from Appleby to Settle; (08457) 484950 for times and fares.

Solway Aviation Museum ⌨ (Aviation House, Carlisle Airport; A689 towards Brampton) Exhibits inc several aircraft, Whittle's prototype jet engines and various displays on local airports used as wartime air bases. Meals, snacks, shop, disabled access (not to aircraft); open Sun Apr–Oct, wknds Jun and Sept, Fri–Sun July–Aug, best to check; (01228) 573823; £3.

Tullie House (Castle St) Great fun: dramatic displays of Border history, using state-of-the-art techniques of sight, sound and smell. Children especially find lots to do, from exploring mine tunnels to trying out a Roman crossbow; the ground floor has a more conventional art gallery/museum. The Millennium Gallery contains archaeology and mineral displays, a local art exhibition, and two discovery walls (one you explore by opening doors, windows and letterboxes, and when you crouch close to the other one you can hear local stories). Meals, snacks, shop, good disabled access; cl am Sun in winter, 25–26 Dec, 1 Jan; (01228) 534781; £5.

CARTMEL SD3778
Picturesque little alleys lead off the delightfully harmonious central square – esp the one out through the former **Priory gatehouse**. The **Priory church**, which towers massively over the village, is an interesting mix of architectural grandeur from 12th to 16th c, inc fine carving. Lots of arts and crafts in the village, and Cartyhing and Penrith fudge. The picturesque Kings Arms does reasonably priced food, and the Mallard has very good cakes and coffee. The village can get particularly busy in summer.

CARTMEL FELL SD4189
In a wonderful tucked-away country location, **St Anthony's church** here has interesting early pews and a fine triple-decker pulpit. Arthur Ransome lived nearby when he wrote *Swallows and Amazons*. The Hare & Hounds at nearby Bowland Bridge has decent food, and the road here from Winster (where the Brown Horse is a popular dining pub) is very pretty.

CASTERTON SD6279
Brontë fans will want to see **Casterton School**; attractive Pre-Raphaelite stained glass and paintings in the **church** result from enthusiastic Brotherhood holidays here. The Pheasant is good.

COCKERMOUTH NY1130
Quietly attractive riverside town, just outside the Lake District proper, but a good base for the western fells, with a distinctive character of its own and a good wide range of places to visit. The comfortable Trout does good food.

Castlegate House (Castlegate) Friendly lived-in Georgian house opposite the castle, home to changing exhibitions of modern art, with Adam ceiling, warming winter fires, and sculpture in the walled garden. Sales of paintings, disabled access; cl Thurs, am Sun, and all Jan–Feb; (01900) 822149; free.

Jennings Brewery ⌨ Tours of traditional Castle Brewery, where the water for brewing is still drawn from the well that supplied the castle at the time of the Norman Conquest. Shop; tours 11am and 2pm Mar–Oct – booking advisable; cl Sun (exc July–Aug when they do extra tours); (01900) 821011; £4.50. No under-12s.

Lakeland Sheep & Wool Centre ⌨ (off A5086 slightly S) Along with an entertaining live show starring 19 different species of sheep (and sometimes a few geese), they also hold shearing demonstrations and sheepdog trials at this friendly place, and they've recently acquired Jersey cows; the adjacent exhibition is a worthwhile introduction to the area. Meals, snacks, shop, disabled access; centre cl 2 wks in Jan, shows usually Mar–Oct but best to phone first; (01900) 822673; show *£4, exhibition free.

Printing House (next to Wordsworth House) This working print museum has a good range of historic presses and equipment; you can try out various printing methods. Shop, disabled access; cl Sun, and Christmas–Easter; (01900) 824984; £2.75. The Norham opposite is a good teashop.

Toy & Model Museum 🖼 (Market Pl) Good expanding collection of mainly British toys from the 20th c; shop, limited disabled access to ground floor; cl Dec–Jan exc by appointment; (01900) 827606; £3.

Wordsworth House (Main St) The poet's happy childhood home, a restored 18th-c town house with fine furniture, pictures by friends and contemporaries, good original panelling, and walled garden above river. Worth a visit in its own right as well as for its Wordsworth associations, and interesting to see how different it is from the places he lived in later on. Meals, snacks, shop, some disabled access (not to house); cl wknds (exc Sats Jun–Aug or before bank hols), and Nov–Mar; (01900) 824805; £3.50; NT.

CONISTON SD2997
Unpretentious former mining village turned resort, at the foot of its mountain, the Old Man, and spreading towards Coniston Water. From Spoon Hall there's pony trekking on the fells above; cl Nov–Easter; (015394) 41391; from £12 an hour. The Sun is good for lunch.

Brantwood Ruskin's rambling Victorian house round on the E side of the lake, with lots of his furniture, books and paintings. It's appealingly unstuffy, but the real attraction is the surroundings and setting, especially the very extensive informal hillside woodland gardens (best in late May/Jun). Good hour's walk on nature trail, and breathtaking views of lake and fells. Meals, snacks, good shop, disabled access (grounds steep in places); cl Mon and Tues mid-Nov to mid-Mar and 25–26 Dec; (015394) 41396; £4.50, £2 gardens only.

Coniston Water An opulent Victorian **steam yacht** sails daily Easter–Oct, from Coniston Pier and Brantwood; (015394) 41288 for times – best to ring between 9 and 10.30am or you're likely to get the answerphone;

£4.80 for a 45-min trip. Or hire rowing or other boats from the boating centre run by the National Parks, 15 mins' walk from the village; usually cl Nov–Mar but worth ringing; (015394) 41366; rowing boats from £5 an hour (£1 each extra person), motorboats from £10.

Coniston Water walks There's a lovely path on the W side, S of Coniston; you can combine this walk with one on a higher-level route along the Walna Scar 'Road' (an ancient hard track closed to through traffic) beneath the **Old Man of Coniston**, the outstanding viewpoint of the vicinity. Climb the Old Man from Coniston, go up past the remains of copper mines, and return down the Walna Scar Road.

Ruskin Museum 🖼 Eclectic mix of displays inc some interactive ones in this very friendly museum, from local architecture, geology and lace-making to a video of Donald Campbell's water speed record attempts, Swallows and Amazons, and a virtual tour of local copper mines; also audio guides in several languages. Naturally, much is given over to the eponymous Victorian philosopher, inc a look at his watercolours, essays, and even his funeral pall. His elaborately biographical memorial is in the nearby churchyard. Shop, disabled access; cl Mon–Tues mid-Nov to mid-Mar, 24–26 Dec and 1 Jan; (015394) 41164; £3.50.

CRUMMOCK WATER NY1518
The scenery is less rewarding than around neighbouring Buttermere, but it's not to be sniffed at. A good start for a walk is the car park by **Lanthwaite Wood**, off the B5289 towards Loweswater at the N end; there's a pretty view from the hill above the wood. You can hire rowing boats on this lake (015394) 35599, and if you're keen to swim in one of the lakes this is probably the best.

DACRE NY4726
Dalemain Historic House & Gardens 🖼 A medieval, Tudor and Georgian house, so an appealing variety of periods and style. Some rooms are grand, others are charming, with splendid furnishings and paintings and some bits for children to enjoy too. Particularly interesting Chinese Room with hand-painted wallpaper. There are

deer in the carefully landscaped **park** with mountain views. Atmospheric restaurant in a medieval hall, shop, plant centre, limited disabled access; cl Fri and Sat, and mid-Oct to Sun before Easter; (017684) 86450; £5.50, £3.00 grounds; discount voucher not valid for special events. The village **church** has pre-Norman sculpture, and quaint medieval stone bears in the graveyard. The Horse & Farrier has good value food.

DALEHEAD NY2215

From Howtown there's a good walk up Martindale (where the **church** has attractive primitive stonework), then up over the fells to Bedafell Knott and down into Patterdale; hard work, but gorgeous views, also buzzards and ring ouzels.

DALTON-IN-FURNESS SD2273

The village has a rather austere square castle; the Black Dog (Broughton Rd) has good value hearty food (all day wknds).

South Lakes Wild Animal Park (Crossgates) Very much enjoyed by readers, this committed and expanding wildlife centre is well placed for fine views of the entire Furness peninsula. The highlight is still watching their Sumatran and Amur tigers clamber up a 6-metre (20-ft) vertical pole to hunt their meat (daily at 2.30). Also fun is the chance to hand-feed their big collection of kangaroos, the only place you can do this outside Australia. Gathered together according to the continents they hail from, residents include rhinos, giraffe and cheetahs, with lots of smaller creatures such as meerkats, pandas, coatis and porcupines; they've recently aquired spectacle bears. A four-acre section has wallabies and emus waiting to be fed (children especially like this bit), and their regular talks are interesting and informative; play area, and a miniature railway (Apr–Sept). Meals, snacks, shop, disabled access; cl 25 Dec; (01229) 466086; £7. Admission is reduced Nov–Feb.

DENT SD7087

Inside the modern outskirts is a delightful cobbled village, a rewarding end to an attractive drive – though now on the tourist trail, so busy in summer. During its heyday the town had a thriving knitting industry – Robert Southey even referred to the incessant knitters of Dent. The welcoming Sun brews its own beer, and the church is well worth a look; the views from the churchyard are spectacular. Dentdale has easy to middling walks, in the shadow of Whernside.

DERWENT WATER NY2523

With all its inlets and islets, a pleasant place for pottering about in boats. It has gorgeous lakeside scenery, romantic little islets, ancient woodland, a variety of mountain backdrops. You can hire rowing boats and launches in Keswick (017687) 72263. Regular launches run all year from Keswick to half a dozen points around the lake. Walks along the lake's W shore, best reached from car parks off the back road between Grange and Swinside, can be combined with the more demanding walk up Cat Bells for the superb views of the lake. It looks equally magnificent from the E side at Friar's Crag (by the lakeside, a level stroll out from Keswick), Castlehead Wood (just S of Keswick), and Walla Crag (a more adventurous climb from the NT car park at Great Wood, an area teeming with red squirrels).

Watendlath This lovely lost village is little more than a tarn, a farm and a very modest café. A narrow road climbs from the B5289 by Derwent Water, but the village makes a very rewarding destination for a walk over the hills – for instance from Rosthwaite, where the Scafell is a fine walkers' local.

DUDDON VALLEY SD2296

A favourite starting point for rather more demanding walks, either by the river or up into the heights, with the Newfield Inn at Seathwaite a good base (food all day). Outstanding scenic drives along the valley, and then along the Wrynose and Hard Knott passes.

DUFTON NY6926

High Pennines Over to the E of the Lakes, these have few walking routes and are extremely bleak: this is the reserve of the dedicated peat-bog enthusiast. An easy way to get an idea of the remoteness of these hills is to walk along paths encircling **Dufton Pike** from Dufton (the Stag has good food).

EGREMONT NY0110

Dominated by its very ruined Norman

castle; as so often, the gatehouse is the best preserved part. **Lowes Court Gallery** Georgian house with local arts and crafts for sale, disabled access; cl Sun, pm Weds and pm wkdys Jan–Feb; (01946) 820693; free.

Florence Mine Heritage Centre (A595 just SE of Egremont) Based around the last working iron ore mine in Europe. Tours of the pit (wknds and bank hols at noon – phone for wkdy times), and visitor centre with reconstructions of pit life at the start of the last century. Snacks, shop, disabled access to visitor centre; (01946) 820683; £6.50 pit tour, £2 visitor centre (£1 if you buy ticket to pit tour).

ELTERWATER NY3204
Idyllically placed village, with lake views. The Britannia is a favourite place for lunch. The B5343 past here gives awesome mountain views; you can keep on a poorer steeper road, passing pretty Blea Tarn, and coming back down through Little Langdale.

ENNERDALE WATER NY1016
One of the quietest lakes, with nearby slopes densely cloaked in conifer plantations, so it's not to everyone's taste. Gentle walks by the lake (no boating), with glimpses of high peaks above, and Ennerdale is virtually car-free. The Shepherds Arms at Ennerdale Bridge does enjoyable food, and has a frequently updated weather forecast blackboard. The road S from Ennerdale Bridge to Calder Bridge gives outstanding views of fells and coast.

ESKDALE NY1700
Excellent for walks, esp around Boot. Here, a prime objective is the **Stanley Ghyll Force** waterfall, approached by a series of bridges and visible from a dizzying view-platform high above. From Trough House Bridge car park nr the waterfall you can walk along one side of the river to Doctor Bridge, then return the other side, for an easy route – with delectable views throughout. Other walks take you up towards the open fells (the landlord of the Burnmoor Inn is helpful with route suggestions). You can use the Ravenglass & Eskdale railway as part of a round trip.

FAIRFIELD NY3511
Rewarding for determined fell-walkers, climbed by a horseshoe layout of ridges from Rydal.

FAR SAWREY SD3895
Between the ferry here and the Wray Castle estate to the N can be found the cream of Windermere's waterside strolls, along the lake's W shore. The estate is a large NT tract with public access. The forested slope rising from this shore has several well signposted routes, with Far Sawrey and Near Sawrey villages, and Latterbarrow, worthwhile objectives for circular walks. The Sawrey Hotel serves simple, generous lunchtime food.

FINTHSWAITE SD3788
Stott Park Bobbin Mill (just N) In coppiced woodland, this former water-and-steam mill made wooden cotton reels from 1835 right up to 1971; enthusiastic guides give excellent demonstrations of 19th-c industrial techniques. The mill is still powered by steam Tues–Thurs: the lathes look lethal. Snacks, shop, disabled access; cl Nov–Mar; (015395) 31087; £3.20; EH. The Swan at Newby Bridge is attractively set for lunch.

FLOOKBURGH SD3675
This peaceful village has excellent potted local shrimps. In Winder Lane **Lakeland Miniature Village** has over 100 buildings made from Coniston slate; disabled access; (015395) 58500; *£3. The Engine in nearby Cark has good home cooking.

GLEASTON SD2671
Gleaston Watermill Well restored working watermill in peaceful surroundings, with a pleasant streamside walk and apiary tours (am Sat); it's also the site of archaeological digs, and you can watch bees in their observation hive. Enjoyable meals and snacks, shop specialising in all things piggy, some disabled access; cl Mon (exc bank hols); (01229) 869244; £2.50. The ruins of a partly built medieval castle are nearby, and the General Burgoyne at Great Urswick is a cosy refreshment stop.

GOSFORTH NY0603
The churchyard has a 10th-c carved **cross**, one of Britain's finest; there are more ancient carved hogback tombstones in the church. The working **pottery** may let you try making a pot

(only in school hols); good shop. Open Fri–Sat May–Sept, phone in winter; (01946) 725296.

GRANGE-OVER-SANDS SD4077

This sedately old-fashioned resort, with several good cafés along the High St and a long promenade, is the start for summer guided walks over **Morecambe Bay Sands**, oddly other-worldly; glistening tidal flats, quick-stepping patrols of wading birds, distant hills, grisly tales of people and horses sucked under – a guide really is essential; phone Cedric Robinson (the official guide, appointed by the Queen), who's been doing it for almost 40 years, on (015395) 32165 for times. **Hampsfield Fell** From the town, a pleasant and not too steep walk up through the woods to the modest, flattish summit, giving terrific views over the Bay from its limestone pavements and summit 'hospice' inscribed with 19th-c words of wisdom.

GRASMERE NY3407

The pretty village swarms with visitors in summer, most of them here to see **Dove Cottage** – still much as Wordsworth had it in his most creative years (he completed *The Prelude* here), with sister Dorothy's journals and his extensive cottage garden. Informative guided tours cope well with the bustle, but in early morning (opens 9.30) out of season you may get some space to yourself. The place always was crowded; barely big enough for two, with the poets' children and friends it often had a dozen or more people living here. The adjoining **Wordsworth Museum**, included in the price, has changing exhibitions and possessions of the poet and his family and friends, as well as a reconstructed Lakeland kitchen and contemporary art gallery. Meals, snacks, shop, limited disabled access; cl mid-Jan to mid-Feb, 24–26 Dec; (015394) 35544; £5.50 museum and house, £2.75 museum only. Wordsworth is buried in the graveyard of the pebbledashed old church, which is better inside then outside. Sarah Nelson's gingerbread shop by the church is wonderfully old-fashioned. The Travellers Rest (A591) is our current pick for lunch. The lake itself, with Rydal Water and Elterwater, is the very heart of picturesque Lakeland. All three are famous for their lovely settings, and there are pleasant walks all around; you can even link all three together in a long afternoon's walk filled with glorious views. The walk up the good track to Easedale Tarn from Grasmere quickly gets you away from all the crowds, into a fine valley; the lake itself is romantically situated below rocks.

GRAYTHWAITE SD3791

Graythwaite Hall Gardens (2m N of Lakeside) Well kept late Victorian garden, strong on rhododendrons and late-spring shrubs. Open Apr–Jun; (015395) 31248; £2.

GREAT LANGDALE NY2806

Dominated by the awesome Langdale Pikes, this is the area's main centre for more serious fell-walking in grand scenery. One very popular shorter walk here is up the good track to Stickle Tarn, from the car park by the Stickle Barn (useful for refreshments), and Bow Fell and Crinkle Crags are two longer fell walks. Wainwrights, in the not specially graceful settlement of Chapel Stile off the B5343, another useful refreshment place, is particularly well liked by our readers as a base for walks along here.

GRIZEDALE SD3394

Grizedale Forest Park Visitor Centre Woodland trails from short strolls to half-day walks, punctuated by 90 or so forest-based sculptures. These trails are good when rain cuts off more open views; the sculptures are set in various spots throughout the forest (map from visitor centre). Lots of other activities too: exhibitions, gallery, good information centre, orienteering, bike hire (it's an ideal area for cycling), and adventure play area. In all, six or seven square miles of mixed woodland to get lost in. Meals, snacks, shop, some disabled access; cl a few wks over Christmas and beginning of Jan; (01229) 860373; parking from £2. The Eagles Head at Satterthwaite (some winter closures) is good value for lunch, and the back roads through this area are quiet and pleasant.

GUMMERS HOW SD3988

An easy 20-min climb from the road, for a fine lake view of Windermere.

HADRIAN'S WALL NY5664
Surviving traces of this far less known western section of the Roman wall can be reached on well signed paths from the lanes between the A69 and B6318 N of Brampton. For the Birdoswald Roman fort at Gilsland, see Northumbria chapter.

HARDKNOTT PASS NY2101
Hardknott Roman Fort Quite well preserved and interestingly restored, but most notable for its breathtakingly lonely position high in the mountains; magnificent views to sea and even the Isle of Man. The drive up here is not for the faint-hearted – it's very steep and twisting, through this pass and Wrynose Pass, but the scenery makes it worthwhile; the Woolpack Inn at Bleabeck just W is good value.

HAWKSHEAD SD3598
Don't miss this virtually unchanged Elizabethan Lakeland village, with sturdy outside walls, and sheltered flower-filled inner courtyards. Though very popular with summer visitors, even at its busiest it has a pleasantly foreign 'different' feel, and the fact that cars are kept out helps a lot. The church has some eye-catching early 18th-c murals. The best nearby pub for lunch is the Drunken Duck up at Barngates. Trout **fishing** and **boat hire** on nearby Esthwaite Water, the largest stocked lake in the region; (015394) 36541; day permit £18, plus boat hire £30.
Beatrix Potter Gallery (Main St) A generous annually changing selection of the original illustrations of *Benjamin Bunny* and other favourites, as well as rather different more acutely (almost acidly) observed drawings. A timed ticket system keeps it uncrowded – during holiday periods you may have to wait to get in. Shop; cl Thurs, Fri, and Nov–Mar; (015394) 36355; £3; NT.
Old Grammar School Museum Founded in 1585, this is now a museum worth poking your nose into, if only to see where Wordsworth carved his name on a desk (he attended 1779–1787). Shop, limited disabled access; cl 12.30pm–1.30pm, Sun am, and Nov–Mar; £2.

HELVELLYN NY3415
This famous Lakeland landmark is most easily (and crowdedly) tackled from Thirlmere, but much more exciting when reached from Glenridding and Striding Edge, where the path follows a narrow rocky edge (mild scrambling needed – best ascended rather than descended; return via Swirral Edge or one of the other paths) above a great post-glacial corrie; it's a day's hard walking, for perhaps the grandest and certainly the most popular of all Lakeland panoramas, with dramatic ridges leading off for miles.

HIGH CUP NICK NY7426
A great scoop in the ridge of the Pennines, this is one of the most dramatic features in the whole of the range, well worth the long but easily followed walk from the pretty village of Dufton, where the welcoming Stag has good value food.

HIGH STREET NY4515
One of Lakeland's great fell walks, this is a Roman ridge road, reached best from Hawes Water reservoir (the hotel here is a good stop).

HONISTER PASS NY2213
From the top of the pass, stout-hearted and well equipped walkers can tackle Brandreth, and perhaps head on via Windy Gap for the least taxing ascent of **Great Gable**. Even if you decide not to go the whole way, the views in clear weather are spectacular.

HOWGILL FELLS SD6897
Bold 2,000-footers, tough going even for hardened walkers; the easiest walks into them are up Winder from Sedbergh, and from the A683 N of Sedbergh to majestic **Cautley Spout** waterfall.

HUMPHREY HEAD POINT SD3874
This ½-mile-long headland protruding into the sea gives walkers stunning views of Morecambe Bay.

KENDAL SD5192
A real town as opposed to a tourist centre, busy, with hectic traffic, but lots of small closes leading off the main street, some of them attractively restored to give a feel of what the place was like in the 18th-c heyday of the wool-weaving industry. The mint cake that takes its name comes in a surprising number of varieties. If you visit Abbot Hall Art Gallery & Museum, Kendal Museum or Lakeland Life, entry to the other two is £1. **Brewery Arts**

Centre (Highgate) has good changing events and exhibitions, café, bar, and landscaped garden; (01539) 725133 for what's on. The child-friendly Olde Fleece (Highgate) does inexpensive food all day, and Alexanders (Castle Green Hotel, high over the town) is good. **Webbs Garden Centre** (Burneside Rd) is big, with lots of plants; decent café, disabled access.

Abbot Hall Art Gallery & Museum (Kirkland) Beautifully restored Georgian house with an art collection that reflects Kendal's importance in the 18th c as the centre of an artists' school, inc works by Ruskin, Turner, Constable, and esp George Romney; also changing exhibitions. Meals, snacks, shop, disabled access; cl Sun, and Christmas–mid-Feb; (01539) 722464; £3.50.

Kendal Castle Ruin on a small hill on E edge of town, reputedly the birthplace of Henry VIII's wife Katherine Parr. There's little more now than parts of the outer wall with some towers – but children enjoy it, and there are fine views. A humble building associated with it is the **Castle Dairy** (Wildman St), an unspoiled Tudor house with some period furniture, inc the oldest bed the V&A have ever recorded. It's a restaurant but they are happy to let people look around.

Kendal Museum (Station Rd) One of the oldest museums in the country, this traditional place takes a comprehensive look at local and natural history, geology and archaeology; one display is devoted to the work of Alfred Wainwright, the walkers' guru. Shop, disabled access to ground floor only; (01539) 721374; cl Sun and 25 Dec to mid-Feb; *£3.50.

Lakeland Life (behind Abbot Hall, Kirkland) Lovingly re-created period rooms, shops and workshops, and an almost palpable feel of the past. Subjects as diverse as shoemaking, Arthur Ransome, and the Arts and Crafts movement. Meals, snacks, shop, some disabled access; cl Sun, and end Dec to mid-Feb; (01539) 722464; £3.50.

Quaker Tapestry Exhibition 🖼 (Friends Meeting House, Stramongate) Bayeux-style tapestry history of the Quaker movement, also embroidery demonstrations. Meals, snacks, shop, disabled access; cl Sun (plus Sat Nov–Dec) and all Jan–Mar; (01539) 722975; £3.25.

KESWICK NY2623 The tourist centre of the northern Lakes, handy for Derwent Water, with lots of Victorian villas (many of them now guesthouses and small hotels) outside quite a traditional centre, with small cobbled closes running off the main streets. It's full of breeches, boots and backpacks in high season, with good outdoor equipment shops, and is a routine stop on coach tours. The Dog & Gun and interesting old George Hotel are very popular for lunch, with the Pheasant out towards Crosthwaite also good value (and giving a pleasant walk up to the ancient church of St Kentigern). The **Wild Strawberry** (Main St) is a useful café in a quaint building, and further out on this road Greta Hall, now part of a school, is where the poets Coleridge then Southey lived. **Lakeside Tea Gardens** (Lake Rd) have home-baking, lots for children, pleasant modern furniture and crockery inside and in garden with trees and chaffinches; cl wknds in Jan. George Fisher (Borrowdale Rd) is a good big outdoors shop. The Theatre by the Lake seats 400 people; cl some Suns; box office (017687) 74411. The back road around Swinside is pretty, and in clear weather is worth following up the gauntly formidable Keskadale Pass.

Cars of the Stars Motor Museum 🖼 (Standish St) Unusual collection of cars from film and TV dating back to Laurel & Hardy's Model T Ford, taking in Chitty Chitty Bang Bang, the Batmobile and cars used by James Bond, the Flintstones, Postman Pat and even Del Boy's van. Shop, disabled access; cl Jan, and wkdays in Dec; (017687) 73757; £3.50.

Castlerigg stone circle (just E) This neolithic monument is well preserved, and gives photogenic perspectives of the mountains (the best times for pictures are morning and evening); take a map to identify the peaks it aligns with. There's a brief explanation of the stones' history. NT.

Dodd Wood (off A591 N) Marked

walks through the woods, or on open hillside, with Bassenthwaite views.

Keswick Museum and Art Gallery ⌖ (Fitzpark, Station Rd) Thoroughly traditional; the Poets Corner stands out. Shop, disabled access; cl Nov–Mar; (017687) 73263; £1.

Pencil Museum (Southey Works) Alongside the Derwent pencil factory, this surprisingly interesting museum has some unexpected exhibits inc, at 7.91 metres (26ft), the world's longest pencil. Shop, disabled access; cl 25–26 Dec, and 1 Jan; (017687) 73626; £2.50.

Teapottery (Central Car Park Rd) You can watch craftsmen at work on these often fantastical teapots, and a short video explains the process. New café, shop, disabled access to ground floor only; cl 25–26 Dec, 1 Jan; (017687) 73983; free.

KIRKBY LONSDALE SD6178 Small and usually quiet town of considerable character, interesting old yards and ginnels and good country shops; it's more lively on Thurs country-market day. Behind the fine **church** of St Mary is a pretty stretch of the River Lune, good for walking or just lazing about – even swimming if it's hot. Along here 87 steps lead up to Ruskin's View, a beautiful panorama over the Lune Valley, appealing countryside little visited by tourists. The Snooty Fox has good food. The lovely Devil's Bridge over the River Lune just below the town dates from the 12th c.

LAKESIDE SD3787 **Lakeside & Haverthwaite Railway** A 3½-mile steam trip running up to Haverthwaite. There's a small collection of steam and diesel locomotives. Meals, snacks, shop, disabled access; cl Nov–Easter (exc Christmas special wknds in Dec); (015395) 31594 for times; £4.10 return. The White Hart at Bouth does good food (not Mon/Tues lunch).

LANGWATHBY NY5734 **Eden Ostrich World** ⌖ (Langwathby Hall Farm) There are quite a few animals to see at this friendly farm inc alpacas, wallabies, zebras, emus, rare breeds, and of course ostriches, and you can feed some of the animals; also a maze, riverside walks, and indoor and outdoor play areas. Meals, snacks, shop, disabled access; open daily Mar–Oct, phone in winter; (01768) 881771; *£4.50.

LATTERBARROW SD3699 A mere hillock in comparison to the great Lakeland fells, but elevated enough above a relatively low-lying area to give views over Windermere and Langdale.

LEVENS SD4985 **Levens Hall** (A6) Impressive Elizabethan mansion based around older core, with fine carved oak chimney-pieces, ceiling plasterwork, spanish leather panelling, period furnishings and interesting paintings. The magnificent **topiary gardens** in their original layout of 1692 are perhaps the highlight, the fantastic shapes really standing out against the ancient grey stone of the house. Traction **steam engine** (in steam bank hols and summer Suns), play area, grand beech trees, and deer park. Snacks, plant sales, shop, disabled access to grounds only; open Sun–Thurs (house cl am) Apr to mid-Oct but best to ring to check; (015395) 60321; £6.50, £5 for grounds only. The Hare & Hounds is handy for lunch.

LINDAL-IN-FURNESS SD2576 **Colony Country Store** View the candlemakers at work then browse among the vast array of candles in the shop; disabled access; cl 25–26 Dec and 1 Jan; (01229) 461102. Chandlers Café next door has good value home-made food.

LITTLE SALKELD NY5737 **Long Meg and Her Daughters** There's access off the lane N to this quaintly named **stone circle**. Also worth a visit if you're passing, the **Watermill** is a bustling bright pink 18th-c watermill which produces 11 sorts of organic flour; they usually do guided tours Mon, Tues and Thurs (11,12, 2.30 and 3.30), and they also hold bread-making and cookery courses. Organic café; cl wknds; (01768) 881523; free. The Highland Drove in Great Salkeld does good inventive food.

LOWTHER NY5323 **Lakeland Bird of Prey Centre** Hawks, eagles, owls, buzzards and falcons in the huge Victorian walled garden at Lowther Castle, with flying displays at 2 and 4pm. Teas, shop, disabled access; cl Nov–Feb; (01931) 712746; £5.

MAIDEN WAY NY6433

The back road from Langwathby on the A686 through Skirwith to Kirkland leads to this **Roman road**, amazingly still sound for walkers after all those centuries. It plunges northwards into the bleak high Pennines, giving a great feeling of solitude. There are other walks from the clusters of farms along the foot of the Pennines between here and Appleby.

MALLERSTANG NY7800

This area, which the B6259 S of Kirkby Stephen runs through, has a lot of charm as a place for a short break. Lady Anne's Way, a lonely walk, runs down the valley passing the romantic ruin of Pendragon castle, supposedly once the home of King Arthur's father.

MARYPORT NY0337

Senhouse Museum ⊞ (The Battery, Sea Brows) Impressive collection of Roman military altar stones and inscriptions, dug from the former fort next door from the 1570s onwards, making it one of the oldest collections of antiquities in the country; also other artefacts inc a Celtic serpent stone. Snacks, shop, disabled access; usually open Tues, Thurs–Sun and bank hols Apr–Jun, daily July–Oct, Fri–Sun Nov–Mar; (01900) 816168; £2.

MILLOM SD1779

Not much of a town, but there's an interesting **church**, and **ruined castle** around what's now a farm (A5093 N: ask at the house for permission to look round the ruins). The Duddon Pilot (Borwick Rails) has good value food. S of the town a broad lagoon built to protect former mineworks is now a bird reserve (also home to natterjack toads), the loneliness exaggerated out of season when the nearby unsmart but enjoyable little resort of Haverigg SD1678 (great beaches, good sailing and fishing) has closed down; the Harbour Inn has good cheap food, good walks in the wildflower dunes.

Haverigg Point This huge stretch of impressive **dunes** is a high point on this section of coast, but virtually the whole length from Ravenglass down to Hodbarrow Point is good for breezy seaside walks – lots of long beaches, deserted except in high season.

MILNTHORPE SD5078

Lakeland Wildlife Oasis ⊞ (Hale, A6 S) Millions of years of evolution flash before your eyes at this lively jungle house, a fascinating cross between zoo and museum. Interactive displays alongside the brightly coloured and unusual fish, birds, insects and animals, and woodland where children can crawl along tunnels overlooking the meerkat enclosure. Activities include fossil rubbing and an animal rubber-stamping trail. Meals, snacks, shop, disabled access; cl 25–26 Dec; (015395) 63027; £5.50. The B5282 to Arnside has quiet estuary and mountain views.

NEAR SAWREY SD3795

Hill Top Small-roomed typically Cumbrian 17th-c farmhouse, kept exactly as it was when owned by Beatrix Potter, who wrote many of her stories here; with the royalties from her books, she bought a lot of Lake District land and gave it to the NT. Shop, disabled access to ground floor by prior arrangement; cl Thurs and Fri, and all Nov–Mar (015394) 36269; £4.50, £7 combined ticket with Beatrix Potter Gallery; NT. The old-fashioned NT-owned Tower Bank Arms (with nicely furnished bedrooms) is pictured in *The Tale of Jemima Puddle-Duck*.

NEWBY BRIDGE SD3787

Aquarium of the Lakes By the steamer stop, this imaginatively laid out aquarium-style centre vividly demonstrates the story of a local river. You can walk in see-through tunnels along a re-created lake bed, with the area's animals (inc otters), insects, birds and plants all around, and there's a water lab with microscopes for close-up examinations of tadpoles, larvae and even plankton; audio-visual display and good views of the lake. Snacks, shop, disabled access; cl 25 Dec; (015395) 30153; £5.75. The nicely set Swan Hotel is a very comfortable refreshment stop (snacks all day).

PENRITH NY5130

The biggest town in Lakeland, which has been very much a northern country town rather than a tourist place; but it's likely to become less obviously the centre of a traditional farming community following the recent closure of its Sat livestock market (though for the time being the Tues farmers' market will continue). Genuinely traditional Lakeland shops sell real fudge and toffee, rich cakes (Greggs), local cheeses (Grahams), tasty Cumberland sausages (Cranstons), local antiquarian books, and cheap and sturdy country clothes. John Norris (Victoria Rd) is the outstanding fishing/outdoor-wear shop, with something for everyone at good prices. A **museum** on Middlegate is a useful introduction to the area, and the George does decent lunches.

Penrith Castle Built in the 14th c as a defence against Scottish raids, and the home of Richard III when he was Duke of Gloucester. The ruins are surrounded by a park; free.

Rheged Discovery Centre (Redhills, A66/A592 W) Named after the Celtic kingdom which once stretched from Strathclyde to Cheshire, this vast development, set right into a hillside, is Europe's largest grass-covered building. They show three films a day on a cinema screen the size of six double-decker buses, while a separate video display takes a look at contemporary life through the eyes of six local people. Also a permanent mountaineering exhibition, changing exhibitions of local art (some of it for sale), an in-house potter, workshops, indoor children`s play area, and specialist shops and restaurants promoting local produce. The huge glass atrium gives views across to the High Pennines. Meals, snacks, shop, disabled access; cl 25 Dec; (01768) 868000; cinema or exhibition £5.50, £9.45 for both. The Kings Arms at Stainton is handy for a good lunch.

St Wilfred's church (B6262 E of Eamont Bridge) A striking exception to the usual Lakeland rule of simplicity in churches, filled with magnificent furnishings inc continental treasures; candlelit. The nearby Gate Inn at Yanwath has good food.

Wetheriggs Pottery (Clifton Dykes, signed off A6 S) Interesting and very smart working pottery – one of the oldest in the country – with 19th-c steam engine and equipment; children can try their hands at the wheel, and

there's a play area and birds of prey. Meals, snacks, shop, disabled access; cl Tues, plus Weds Sept–Easter, 25–26 Dec, and 1 Jan; (01768) 892733; free (exc Aug, £2.50).

PIEL ISLAND SD2363
Small island shared by a basic inn and a grand 14th-c ruined fortress commanding Barrow Harbour and Morecambe Bay. It's reached by ferry (by arrangement only in winter) from Roa Island nr Barrow, subject to tides; (01229) 833609/870156.

RAVENGLASS SD0896
Pretty sailing harbour by the well sheltered Esk estuary; in summer a local fishing boat sells freshly caught fish on the shore. The Ratty Arms does interesting food. The so-called **Walls Castle** just outside the village is actually a Roman bath house; its walls stand taller than any other building of its age so far north.

Muncaster Castle & Owl Centre
🄲🄱 (A595, 1m E) The same family have lived in the elegant house since 1208, and will continue to do so as long as a magical glass drinking bowl remains intact. Extended over the centuries (esp the 19th) from its original tower, it still feels very lived-in, and the rich furnishings and décor include some fine Elizabethan furniture and embroidery. There's an entertaining audio tour, and young children will especially like the underground maze (you can advance only by answering questions about the environment). Muncaster is the HQ of the World Owl Trust, and they have over 180 birds from 50 different species; an interpretation centre has closed circuit TV of nesting owls. There are talks and flying displays at 2.30pm, and you can watch wild herons being fed (every afternoon Mar–Nov, weather permitting). The lovely 77-acre grounds are particularly rich in species rhododendrons and have unusual trees, nature trails, adventure play area and lots of rescued birds of prey. Various special events. Meals, snacks, shops, good plant centre, mostly disabled access; castle open daily (exc Sat) beginning Mar–Oct, garden and owl centre open all year; (01229) 717614; £7.50 for everything, £5.50 for the garden, owl centre and maze.

Ravenglass & Eskdale Railway 🎫
England's oldest narrow-gauge steam trains, lovingly preserved, with open carriages chugging up seven miles of unspoilt valley to Dalegarth; admirers say it's the most beautiful train journey in England. Cafés each end, and at Ravenglass a small museum and audio-visual display; free. Shop, disabled access (with notice); open daily end Mar–beginning Nov, trains many winter weekends, phone to check; (01229) 717171; £7.80 return. Enjoyable 3-hr summer walk back from Boot (walks booklets from stations).

RAVENSTONEDALE NY7203
The village is notable more for its pleasant riverside scenery than for its buildings – apart from the unspoilt **church** which escaped Victorian refitting; longitudinal pews, three-decker pulpit, steeply pitched gallery (steep stairs up), and fine E window memorial to Fothergill family (one was last female Protestant martyr to be burned at the stake). Choose a bright day for best light.

RYDAL NY3606
Rydal Mount 🎫 (A591)
Wordsworth's sister Dorothy described Rydal as a paradise when the family moved here from Grasmere in 1813; they stayed for the rest of their lives. The house itself is quite modest, with family portraits and period furniture, and it's what's outside that really stands out – the good-sized garden is still much as the poet laid it out, consciously picturesque, with original ideas that people are still rediscovering today. The setting is lovely, overlooking mountains and lakes; they often have readings of the poetry it inspired. Shop, limited disabled access; cl Tues Nov–Mar, 25 Dec, 8 Jan–1 Feb; (015394) 33002; *£4. Decent campsites nearby. The Glen Rothay Hotel does decent lunches, and Dora's Field beside it has lots of daffodils.

SEASCALE NY0204
Sellafield Visitor Centre (off A595)
Not everyone approves of the pro-nuclear PR, but children certainly enjoy the lively hands-on approach to the industry at this nuclear power visitor centre, now imaginatively redesigned by the Science Museum using the latest interactive technology. Meals, snacks, shop, disabled access; cl 25 Dec; (019467) 27027; free. Seascale itself has a pleasant beach, and a singularly scenic golf course, where every hole offers views of the sea or the mountains; the third tee ironically puts Sellafield into the same frame as a ring of prehistoric stones.

SEATHWAITE NY2109
Packhorse track Determined fell-walkers enjoy the unspoilt packhorse track from Seathwaite (just off the B5289 in Borrowdale) over **Styhead Pass** down into Wasdale. The summit of the pass is a start point for a fiercely dramatic route up Scafell Pike. More easily reached is the Taylorgill Force waterfall.

SEDBERGH SD6390
Hardy small town at the foot of the Howgill Fells, with a helpful Yorkshire Dales National Park Centre on Main St (wknds only Nov–Easter; (015396) 20125). The Dalesman is good for lunch.
Holme Farm 🎫 (Middleton, just SW of Sedbergh) 2pm tours of traditional hill farm, with plenty of young animals and nature trail. They do occasional evening tours with badger watch. Shop, disabled access; cl Oct–Feb exc by arrangement; (015396) 20654; *£2.50. You can camp here (£5).

SHAP NY5514
Shap Abbey (left towards Keld off A6 going N out of village) The best feature is the unspoilt and undeveloped riverside seclusion; the abbey itself is ruined, but you can trace the 13th-c layout in some detail. Nearby **Keld Chapel** is a lonely untouched shepherds' church in a riverside hamlet, and the gated Swindale road signed off the Bampton road nr Rosgill is pretty. The Greyhound has good unfussy food.

SIZERGH SD4888
Low Sizergh Barn Popular with readers for its fresh farm foods, and other local produce inc damson beer and Morecambe Bay shrimps. A nature trail around the organic-minded dairy farm highlights its conservation work. The tearoom, upstairs in a 17th-c barn well worth visiting anyway for its glorious array of local and organic

produce, country crafts and clothes, overlooks the milking parlour and makes a fine place for lunch. Meals, snacks, shop; cl 25–26 Dec and 1 Jan; (015395) 60426; free.

Sizergh Castle Lovely country house surrounded by two lakes, over the centuries harmoniously extended from its original sturdy 14th-c tower by the family who have lived here for generations. Fine Tudor and Elizabethan carving, panelling and furniture, Jacobite relics, and terraced gardens surrounding a grand flight of steps down to the water. Lots to interest a gardener, inc an enormous rock garden, Japanese maples, water garden, wild flowers, and daffodils in the apple orchard; the autumn colours are lovely. Snacks, shop, disabled access to garden and ground floor of house; open pm Sun–Thurs Apr–Oct; (015395) 60070; *£5, *£2.50 garden only; NT.

SKELTON NY4635

Hutton-in-the-Forest (B5305) Some say this formidable mansion was the castle of the Green Knight of Arthurian legend. Grandly extended in the 17th c from its 14th-c peel tower core, then castellated more recently, it has a magnificent panelled gallery. A terraced garden runs down to the lake; there's an 18th-c walled formal garden, and a more romantic Victorian garden with grand trees, dovecot and woodland nature walk. Tearoom, shop; garden open daily (exc Sat), house open pm Thurs, Fri and Sun 18 Apr–28 Sept, plus Easter wknd and all bank hols; (01768) 484449; £4.50, £2.50 garden only.

SKIDDAW NY2629

One of Cumbria's four 3,000-footer peaks, but more accessible than many lesser ones – quite an easy haul up from Applethwaite (just N of Keswick), for far-ranging views.

ST BEES NX9712

In the old centre of this coastal village (the starting point for the extremely popular 190-mile Coast to Coast Walk across three National Parks to Robin Hood's Bay in Yorkshire), St Bees Priory stands on a 7th-c Augustinian site; now just the church remains, rather done over in the 19th c but a magnificent Norman doorway survives. Close by, you can glimpse the 16th-c

part of St Bees School, quite Oxbridgey in character. The Queens does good generous home cooking.

Cliffs and birds The cliff path between Whitehaven and St Bees is the best part of the Cumbrian coast for walkers and bird-watchers (each town has a railway station). From the beach car park NW of St Bees an easy walk takes you up the nature-reserve sandstone headland, famous for its bird life, and with magnificent sea and hill views.

STAFFIELD NY5342

Nunnery Walks These private paths through old woodland take you through a lovely Eden Valley river gorge with waterfalls and quiet pools; teas. There are other good free walks in this delightfully wooded sheltered valley, for instance from Armathwaite and Wetheral. The Eden Valley has the handy reputation of staying dry when it's pouring over in Lakeland.

STAINTON NY4827

Alpaca Centre 🏫 The first centre for these fleecy Andean animals in Britain; you can view them in their paddocks, from the tearoom, or get up close on a field walk and hear them humming (£1). Snacks, shop, disabled access; cl 25–26 Dec, 1 Jan; (01768) 891440; free. The Kings Arms is good for lunch.

SWINSIDE SD1688

Swinside Stone Circle Not that much visited, but definitely one of the best prehistoric sites in Lakeland: it's a bit of a trek to reach and worth combining with the drive over spectacular Corney Fell, which gives views of the coast and the Duddon Valley. Take the side turn to Millom, leading to a lone house called Cragg Hall, from where it's a 15-min walk.

TALKIN TARN NY5457

Lovely lake with partly wooded shores, peaceful mountain views, plenty of space for strolling; nature trail, orienteering and rowing boats; disabled access, teas. The village is pretty; the Blacksmiths Arms does enjoyable meals.

TARN HOWS SD3299

So popular a beauty spot that it has its own one-way system to get to it; this is a gorgeously photogenic small lake, particularly beautiful on a still clear autumn day, or early in the morning before the crowds have arrived.

TEMPLE SOWERBY NY6128

Acorn Bank Garden (off B6412 N)
Richly planted terraced and walled
garden with 250 varieties of medicinal
and culinary herbs, clematis, unusual old
fruit trees, and herbaceous borders; the
steep wild garden drops down to the
stream. The wheel of the restored mill
down here turns at wknds when there
is a volunteer. This is a lovely spot at
daffodil time. Meals, snacks, shop,
disabled access; cl Tues, and Nov–Mar;
(017683) 61893; £2.50; NT. Under new
owners, the handsome Kings Arms
does enjoyable food. The B6412 to
Lazenby and then the back road
through the Eden Valley to
Armathwaite and on up to Wetheral
gives delicious quiet views.

THIRLMERE NY3213
At the geographical heart of the Lake
District, a lake enlarged into a
reservoir, but mostly naturalistic.
Looks its best from the unclassified
road around its W side; here short
stretches of lakeside path look across
to the massive slopes of Helvellyn. On
the main road the Kings Head is a useful
lunch spot.

THORNTHWAITE NY2225

Thornthwaite Galleries Fine art,
pottery and other crafts, as well as teas,
summer try-your-hand-at-it
demonstrations, and a play area. Snacks,
shop, disabled access (but no facilities);
usually cl Tues, Mon–Thurs in Nov, and
all Dec–Feb; (017687) 78248; free. The
Coledale Inn at Braithwaite is useful for
lunch.

THORNTHWAITE FOREST
NY2124
The first-ever Forestry Commission
plantation: walks through it, and up to
the fells above (with lake and mountain
views), are best started with a visit to
the Whinlatter Visitor Centre (B5292
above Braithwaite); this has good
explanatory forestry displays, and in
2002 attracted over 70,000 visitors
anxious to watch the progress on their
live web-cam of two osprey chicks (two
of only three to have hatched in England
for 150-years), shop, forest maps, teas.

TORPENHOW NY2039

Torpenhow church A formidable
Norman building, striking in itself but
worth looking at closely, for the even
older Roman masonry.

TROUTBECK NY4002

Townend The perfectly preserved
home of a comfortably off, very
traditional farming family who lived
here for 300 years till the 1940s, the
house showing little change over all that
time. Solid simple unshowy comfort,
and a sensible, down-to-earth and
entirely self-sufficient layout. This is one
of several such beautifully placed
'statesmen's' farms making up this
lovely village strung along the steep
valley below high fells. Braille guide; cl
am, all day Mon (exc bank hols) and Sat,
and Nov–Mar; (015394) 32628; £3; NT.

ULLSWATER NY4421
Here elegant Victorian steamers
converted to diesel run between
Pooley Bridge, Howtown and
Glenridding; disabled access, cl
Dec–Mar. Motor boats can be hired
from Ullswater Marina at
Watermillock, (017684) 86415, cl
Nov–Mar, and the sailing school at
Glenridding has a range of canoes and
sailing dinghies for hire – some
experience of sailing necessary to hire a
sailboat, though they do give
introductory lessons and courses –
(017684) 82541; cl winter. Mountain
bikes, rowing and other boats can be
hired from Tindals in Glenridding;
(017684) 82393; around £6 per hour,
motorboats around £15, mountain
bikes from £10 for a half day.

Aira Force Waterfall This is the
best-known walk on Ullswater's W side
– a pleasant if rather populated stroll of
a mile or so from the car park on the
A592 just NE of the A5091 junction,
through NT lakeshore woods to the
waterfalls themselves, and the gothick
folly of Lyulph's Tower, with
Wordsworth's daffodils a bonus in
spring; experts have recently expressed
concern that the original wild daffodils
(thought to have been introduced by
the Romans) are being contaminated by
more aggressive cultivars sold by
garden centres. Above here,
Gowbarrow Park has the best lake
views on this side. Aira Force is a 20-
metre (65-ft) waterfall, at its best after
rain or on a misty morning; tearoom
and shop, parking £2 for 4 hours. The

Royal Hotel at Dockray (open all day) is a pleasant handy refuge.

Ullswater walks The E shore is outstanding; there are many different views, with a rewarding combination of waterside stretches and higher ground giving more sweeping vistas. On the best and most popular stretch, Howtown–Patterdale–Glenridding, you will meet quite a few other people in summer (when it can be combined with the steamer for a round trip; best to take the steamer on the way out in case the service is cancelled). The Howtown Hotel is a useful stop, and Hallin Fell nearby gives an aerial view of the lake.

ULVERSTON SD2878

This town holds the bizarre double claim of being the birthplace of both pole-vaulting and the Quaker movement (no wonder it went on to produce Stan Laurel). Readers recommend Chandler's Country Café (London Rd); the Farmers Arms (Market Pl) has good food and seems very much the welcoming heart of the town.

Conishead Priory (Priory Rd) There's a unique Buddhist Temple in the grounds of this eye-catching early 19th-c Gothic mansion; guided tours of the mansion £2; phone for opening times; snacks, shop, disabled access; (01229) 584029.

Lakes Glass Centre ⌨ (Oubas Hill) Watch the craftsmen blowing, cutting and engraving. The factory shop is good value, with cheap seconds. Meals, snacks, shop, disabled access; cl 25–26 Dec and 1 Jan (no glassmaking on Sun); (01229) 584400; £2.

Laurel & Hardy Museum (Upper Brook St) In Stan Laurel's home town, with delightfully informally presented mementoes and all-day films. Shop, disabled access; cl Jan; (01229) 582292; *£2.50.

Swarthmoor Hall ⌨ Elizabethan manor known as the 'powerhouse of the early Quaker movement', after George Fox was sheltered here in 1652. The interior has been lovingly restored with 17th-c furnishings. Guided tours 2.30pm Thurs, Fri and Sun mid-Mar to mid-Oct; (01229) 583204; *£2.50.

WALNEY ISLAND SD1869

Over the bridge from Barrow, this has some long roads of low houses but is mostly a windswept sweep of duney grass, very offshore-feeling; nature reserves at both ends, with excellent bird-watching and interesting plants. The George has decent food.

WANSFELL PIKE NY3904

Gained by a path from Ambleside, this is toylike in size compared with the bigger fells, but the view is as good as from many more imposing peaks.

WASDALE NY1808

The start for many magnificent fell walks, inc the ascents of Great Gable and Scafell Pike; one less taxing walk is straight up the head of the valley to the summit of Black Sail Pass and back. Apart from around the interesting churchyard, it's not so good for gentle strolls, and parking at Wasdale Head can be a problem in summer or at holiday times. Besides the Wasdale Head Hotel, the Strands lower down is a useful stop for food.

WATERMILLOCK NY4422

The **church** is worth stopping at for its evocative photographs of all its 1930s parishioners. **Sailing dinghies** can be hired by competent sailors from Ullswater Marina here. The cheerful Brackenrigg overlooking the lake has imaginative food.

WHITEHAVEN NX9718

Planned as an 18th-c industrial town and major port, this interesting place is being restored after its economic decline. The harbour is attractive at high tide (a bit dirty at low tide). Michael Moon's **bookshop** (Lowther St) has a vast and rewarding second-hand stock, the best in the Lakes; cl Sun, bank hols, and Weds Jan–Easter. There are some other interesting shops in side streets, and Sal Madges (Duke St) has cheap food; if you plan to visit the Rum Story and the Beacon, it's worth getting a joint ticket (£7.50). Just S at Sandwith, the Lowther Arms, with good homely food and accommodation, is handy for the coast-to-coast walk.

Beacon ⌨ (West Strand) Whitehaven's history is well covered here, but what really makes this friendly museum worth a look is the Met Office Weather Gallery on the top floor, full of hi-tech monitoring and recording equipment, and excellent hands-on displays explaining how weather forecasts are put together. The building itself is striking, with good views from the top floor over the town and harbour and even across to Scotland. Snacks, shop, disabled access; cl Mon (exc bank hols and school hols), and 25 Dec; (01946) 592302; £4.25. There's also a gallery, with changing exhibitions on the ground floor; free. They do heritage walks from here Tues and Sat afternoons; phone to book (01946) 852939; £3. Ask at the friendly Tourist Information Centre about the Quest (you complete ten different trails and answer questions, and are then entered into a prize draw; £6.95).

Rum Story Covers the history of rum, with quite a few re-creations from a slave ship and rum store to a prohibition-era FBI office. Meals, snacks, shop, disabled access; cl 25 Dec and 1 Jan; (01946) 592933; £4.50.

WINDERMERE SD4096
An extensive largely Victorian development of guest houses and small hotels spreads up between the older village of Bowness and the hillside station. It has a touristy feel right through the year, especially around the main street down to the steamer piers. In Bowness itself there is an inner core of narrower much older streets and buildings – one of the most ancient is the quaint Hole in t' Wall pub. **Horse riding** can be arranged from Wynlass Beck Stables (bottom of Patterdale Rd) from £18 an hour; (015394) 43811. The Tourist Information Centre on Victoria St has a useful range of locally produced crafts if you haven't time to look properly, and the Birdcage (College Rd) is a good **antiques shop** – mostly small things, esp lamps.

Blackwell Arts and Crafts House (Storrs Park, Bowness) This is one of England's most important surviving houses from the turn of the 20th c. It was designed by M H Baillie Scott as a holiday home for Mancunian brewer and twice Lord Mayor Sir Edward Holt, and is a fine example of Arts and Crafts movement architecture. Inspired by Lakeland surroundings, it has lots of attractive detail inc carved panelling, stained glass and intricate wrought ironwork. Upstairs are changing art and craft exhibitions, and they're replanting the small terraces outside. In a beautiful setting, the views from here are quite breathtaking. Good tearoom, shop, mostly disabled access; cl Christmas to mid-Feb; (01539) 722464; £4.50.

Holehird Gardens (A592 Kirkstone Pass rd) Lakeland Horticultural Society's hillside garden – ten acres of well grown plants, with three National Collections inc one of hydrangeas, extensive rock gardens, herbaceous borders and alpine houses; lovely lakeland views. Open all year; (015394) 46008; donation recommended (they rely on this to maintain the gardens).

Lake Windermere This is England's largest lake – the most popular boating lake in Cumbria – and also the easiest place to hire rowing boats and other craft. Lots of launches, of all sorts of shapes and sizes, run cruises of varying lengths from Bowness Bay, Ambleside and (not Nov–Mar) Newby Bridge. The pick of the sightseeing boat trips is the 45-min tour on the silent steam launch *Osprey*, though it's available only to visitors to the Steamboat Centre (see separate entry). For a treat, readers recommend the Sail 'n' Dine cruises, phone to book (015242) 74255; £45 inc a five-course meal and drinks. The pier at the S end of the lake is the terminus for the Haverthwaite steam railway. Rowing boats can be hired from the Bowness Bay Boating Co; from £3 an hour. They also have motorboats, and a number of launches – at least one of which is equipped to take disabled people; (015394) 43360 to check. Lake Holidays Afloat do motorboats too; (015394) 43415; from £14 an hour. A pleasant place to hire rowing boats (not Nov–Easter) is **Fell Foot Park** nr Newby Bridge, an 18-acre park with plenty of room for lakeside picnics; café and shop (cl Nov–Mar), some disabled access; (015395) 31273; parking charges (from £2); rowing boats £5 per hour for two people; NT. They can provide details of boating and fishing on other NT waters. Maples (Marina Village, Bowness) do day, wknd or longer cruises and courses on large sailing yachts; from *£135 a day.

Windsurfing or waterskiing can be arranged at Low Wood Water Sports Centre, Windermere; (015394) 39441. The chain ferry linking the ferry road below Bowness with the Hawkshead road below Far Sawrey is a utilitarian way of taking to the water; but though it runs every 20 mins and saves miles of driving, queues mean that it saves time only out of season.

Orrest Head A short steep walk (half-hour each way) from opposite the station, this gives spectacular views over the lake and the Pennines, lovely at sunset.

Steamboat Centre 🖼 (Rayrigg Rd) Nearly three dozen gleamingly restored graceful antique steamboats and a collection of motorboats, inc the 1850 steam launch *Dolly*, the oldest mechanically powered boat in the world. Also Arthur Ransome and Beatrix Potter boats, and they hold quite a few events like vintage boat rallies and model boat regattas. Snacks, shop, disabled access; cl Nov–mid-Mar; (015394) 45565; £3.50. For an extra £5 and weather permitting, there are stately 50-minute tours of the lake on the silent steam launch *Swallow* or motor launch *Water Viper*.

World of Beatrix Potter 🖼 (Old Laundry, Crag Brow, Bowness) Much enjoyed by young children, delightfully detailed re-creations of characters and scenes from *Peter Rabbit* and other tales. Some bits have smells, so you can get more of the atmosphere of Mrs Tiggy-Winkle's laundry or nasty old Mr McGregor's potting shed. Meals and snacks (in the Tailor of Gloucester's tearoom), shop, disabled access; cl 25 Dec, and 6–26 Jan; £3.75.

WORKINGTON NY0028 Heavily industrial and not at all a tourist town, but reaches a moment of unexpected cobblestone prettiness in Portland Sq, plus a few other streets of colour-washed terraced cottages; the Alamin Indian restaurant (Jane St) is good. In Curwen Park (on the NE edge of town) you can still see the ruinous hulk of **Workington Hall**; mansion not open but the grounds are; free.

Helena Thompson Museum (Park End Rd) Some antique and Georgian costumes, as well as pottery, silver, furniture and local history, in period surroundings. Bookshop, disabled access to ground floor only; cl Sun; (01900) 326255; free.

Other attractive villages in fine scenery, all with good pubs, include Armathwaite NY5146, Bampton NY5118, Bardsea SD3074, Beckermet NY0207, Brigsteer SD4889, Broughton Mills SD2290, Crosby Ravensworth NY6215 (Maulds Meaburn is also pretty), Dalston NY3650, Garrigill NY7441, Hesket Newmarket NY3438, Langwathby NY5734, Stonethwaite NY2613 and Wetheral NY4654. The comfortable Kirkstile Inn at Loweswater NY1222 deserves a mention for its glorious setting.

Where to eat

AMBLESIDE NY3704 **Glass House** *Rydal Rd (015394) 32137* Restored 15th-c mill, next to the owner's glass studio, with working waterwheel, lots of space, a relaxed and friendly atmosphere, imaginative food plus simpler set lunches, and a carefully chosen and reasonably priced wine list; cl 3 wks Jan; children over 5 in evening. £25

AMBLESIDE NY3704 **Sheila's Cottage** *The Slack (015394) 33079* 250-year-old cottage and converted barn run by the same owners for over 30 years, with very good and enjoyable food served all day inc popular afternoon teas; cl Tues–Weds pms Nov–Easter, cl 12 days in Jan; children over 8 in evening. £23|£5

APPLETHWAITE NY2725 **Underscar Manor** *(01768) 775000* Italianate Victorian house in wonderful position with panoramic views, a comfortable sitting room, two pretty restaurants with ornate drapes and lovely fresh flowers, very good beautifully presented classical cooking, and a mainly French wine list; smart dress; no smoking; bdrms plus time ownership apts, and health spa; cl 3 days after New Year; children over 12. £35.50 lunch, £40.50 dinner

ARMATHWAITE NY5046 **Dukes Head** *(016974) 72226* In an attractive village, this is a comfortable and friendly inn with a civilised lounge bar, a warm coal fire, good home cooking, well kept real ales, and decent wines; bdrms; cl 25 Dec; disabled access. £26|£5.95

CARTMEL FELL SD4189 **Masons Arms** (015395) 68486 Old-fashioned building (under new ownership this year) in unrivalled setting with wonderful views, several real ales, and very popular food; self-catering accommodation; cl 25 Dec. £24|£6

CROSTHWAITE SD4692 **Punch Bowl** (015395) 68237 Prettily set Lakeland inn with an interesting series of nicely furnished rooms, and concentrating very much on excellent food; a good pubby atmosphere, well kept real ales, and friendly service; bdrms; cl Sun pm, Mon, last wk Nov, 1st wk Dec, 1 wk Jan. £27/£9.95 2 courses

DENT SD7087 **Stone Close** Main St (015396) 25231 Cottagey 17th-c teashop with pine furniture on the flagstones, cast-iron ranges, beams, and local crafts, home-made meals served from mid-morning until early evening inc delicious cakes and pastries, and a relaxed friendly atmosphere; bdrms, plus self-catering cottage next door; cl mid-Jan–early Feb. £15|£4.50

KESWICK NY2623 **George** 3 St John's St (017687) 72076 Fine old inn with attractive traditional black-panelled side room with interesting Wordsworth connection, and a good log fire; open-plan main bar with old-fashioned settles and modern banquettes under Elizabethan beams, and daily newspapers to read; enjoyable, often interesting bar food, well kept real ales, and a no smoking restaurant. £19|£6.25

KESWICK NY2623 **Maysons** 33 Lake Rd (017687) 74104 Busy restaurant with an interesting range of highly enjoyable food inc good vegetarian dishes, nice salads, and yummy cakes; cl evenings Nov–Easter; partial disabled access. £15|£4.50

KIRKBY LONSDALE SD6178 **Snooty Fox** 33 Main St (015242) 71308 Rambling inn with plenty of interest in the various relaxed pubby rooms, good interesting food, a no smoking dining annexe, well kept beers, and pretty garden; cl 25 Dec pm; children must be well behaved. £24|£7

MELMERBY NY6137 **Village Bakery** (01768) 881515 Converted stone barn selling wonderful organic bread and cakes for cream teas, super breakfasts (until 11am) and good home-made lunchtime restaurant food using produce grown organically behind the bakery; craft gallery upstairs; cl 25–26 Dec, 1 Jan; disabled access. £18.70|£4.95

SEATOLLER NY2413 **Yew Tree** (017687) 77634 Set at the foot of a lovely valley, this restaurant was originally two 17th-c miners' cottages, and has fine oak beams, a slate floor, an open range and brick bread oven, lots of interesting old photographs and memorabilia, a super atmosphere, and good interesting food using local produce; cl Mon, Jan; disabled access. £20|£5

STONETHWAITE NY2613 **Langstrath** (017687) 77239 Small civilised inn surrounded by beautiful steep fells; neat simple bar, log and coal fire in big stone fireplace, simple furnishings and local pictures, well kept real ales, enjoyable bar food, and separate back restaurant. £20|£7.95

TROUTBECK NY4103 **Queens Head** (015394) 32174 Popular gabled 17th-c coaching inn with several rambling bar rooms, some fine antique carving, a log fire and woodburner, efficient staff, particularly good first-class bar food, and well kept real ales; bdrms; cl 25 Dec; disabled access. £22|£5.95

ULVERSTON SD3177 **Bay Horse Hotel and Restaurant** Canal Foot (out Past Glaxo) (01229) 583972 Civilised and nicely placed inn overlooking Morecambe Bay, with attractively presented, interesting food, well kept real ales and good wine list; bdrms; children in bar lounge only; cl Mon am; children over 12; disabled access. £45|£10

WINDERMERE SD4198 **Oregano** 4 High St (015394) 44954 Intimate well liked little evening restaurant with good Mediterranean-influenced English cooking, candlelit tables on wooden floors, a relaxed bistro-type atmosphere, and helpful service; good value set menus; cl Sun; children over 12. £28

WINDERMERE SD4096 **Porthole** *3 Ash St, Bowness (015394)* 42793 Long-established bustling bistro with consistently good meals (mainly Italian), genuinely personal service, simple furnishings, and decent wine – a reliably enjoyable evening out; cl Sat am, Mon am, Tues, Christmas–mid-Feb; limited disabled access. £30
YANWATH NY5127 **Gate Inn** *(01768) 862386* Unpretentious village local with really good inventive food, well kept real ales, obliging service, log fire in simple chatty bar, and no smoking dining room. £20|£6.95

Special thanks to Roger and Jenny Huggins, Mrs Y Champion, Helen Wharton

---

We welcome reports from readers

This *Guide* depends on readers' reports. Do help us if you can – in return, we offer a discount on the next edition to people who've helped us with reports for it. Tell us what you think about places already in it, and anything extra you think we should say about them. And send us your ideas for inclusion in the next edition: places to visit, eat at or stay in, attractive drives or walks, maybe even unusual shops you know of. Use the card in the middle, the report forms at the end, or just write – no stamp needed: *The Good Britain Guide*, FREEPOST TN1569, Wadhurst, E Sussex TN5 7BR. Or log on to www.goodguides.com

DERBYSHIRE

Great days out and glorious landscapes – plenty to fill a holiday at any age; very good places to stay in

Derbyshire is laced with remarkable underground caverns. The Heights of Abraham in Matlock Bath is the best one for families (the mining museum here too is worth a visit), spectacular Poole's Cavern in Buxton is Britain's longest show cave, and for other impressive caverns and interesting mines Castleton is the best place to head for.

One of Britain's richest pre-industrial areas, Derbyshire has more than its fair share of magnificent stately homes. Topping a list of family-friendly houses is Chatsworth, a wonderful day out with plenty to keep younger members of the family occupied. Sudbury Hall has an excellent museum of childhood. Other rewarding houses include the well preserved medieval manor house at Haddon Hall, Hardwick Hall (especially if you like tapestry), and, in contrast, the fascinating Calke Abbey. Eyam Hall (the village too is interesting) and Catton Hall (new to the *Guide* this year) are still very much family homes. The 18th-c Palladian mansion at Kedleston is a fine example of Robert Adam's work, and the gardens at Renishaw Hall (home of the famous Sitwell siblings) are beautiful.

Derbyshire played an important role in the Industrial Revolution (the mills between Cromford and Derby have recently been granted World Heritage status), and if industrial heritage is something you're interested in, you'll find plenty to keep you occupied. The 18th-c cotton-milling village of Cromford is a good place to head for, as is the new Belper Valley Visitor Centre; children like the hands-on displays in Derby's Industrial Museum.

Our Derbyshire Family Attraction Award this year goes to the American Adventure Theme Park at Ilkeston (a full day out – with lots for younger children), and there's another theme park in Matlock Bath. Crich Tramway Village (more than just trams) is another pleasant family outing, and Ripley is worth a stop if you're after a relaxed afternoon.

The best of the scenery is in the central area, more or less S of the A625, known as the White Peak. This limestone country, picturesquely cut by the intricate channels of the dales, has an abundance of generally gentle walking – it's rewarding for drivers too. High, flat pastures have small fields of rich grassland enclosed by silvery stone walls, clusters of often very photogenic pale stone farm buildings, and small old-fashioned villages. In summer the loveliest dales do have almost a crocodile of walkers snaking along them, though even then you can find quiet areas. Further north, up in the High Peak, the scenery becomes bleaker and more forbidding – daunting for all but the most committed walker, though exhilarating for drivers – the A6024, A628 (rather slow), A57, A5002, A624 and A625 all have outstanding views.

Where to stay

ASHBOURNE SK1746 **Callow Hall** *Mappleton Rd, Ashbourne, Derbyshire DE6 2AA (01335) 300900* **£130**, plus special breaks; 16 lovely well furnished rms, excellent bthrms. Quietly smart and friendly Victorian mansion up a long drive through grounds with fine trees and surrounded by marvellous countryside; comfortable drawing room with open fire, fresh flowers and plants, and period furniture, very good traditional food using home-grown produce, excellent breakfasts, and kind hosts; good private fishing; cl Christmas; disabled access; dogs welcome in bedrooms

ASHFORD IN THE WATER SK1969 **Riverside Country House Hotel** *Fennel St, Ashford in the Water, Bakewell, Derbyshire DE4 1QF (01629) 814275* **£125***, plus special breaks; 15 individually decorated pretty rms. Creeper-covered Georgian house in delightful village with attractive riverside gardens, a relaxed house-party atmosphere, antiques and log fires in cosy sitting rooms, good modern English cooking, and good service; children over 12; disabled access

BAKEWELL SK2272 **Hassop Hall** *Hassop, Bakewell, Derbyshire DE45 1NS (01629) 640488* **£98.90**, plus winter breaks; 13 gracious rms. Mentioned in the Domesday Book, in lovely parkland surrounded by fine scenery, this handsome hotel has antiques and oil paintings, an elegant drawing room, oak-panelled bar, good food and friendly service; tennis; no accommodation 3 nights over Christmas; partial disabled access; dogs welcome in bedrooms

BASLOW SK2572 **Cavendish Hotel** *Baslow, Bakewell, Derbyshire DE45 1SP (01246) 582311* **£160.10**, plus winter wknd breaks; 24 spotless, comfortable and individually furnished rms (varying in size). Charming hotel with magnificent views over Chatsworth estate, most attractive well furnished day rooms (some furnishings come from Chatsworth), an eclectic collection of the owner's pictures, open fires and fresh flowers, fine food in two restaurants, very courteous staff

BASLOW SK2572 **Fischer's Baslow Hall** *Calver Rd, Baslow, Bakewell, Derbyshire DE45 1RR (01246) 583259* **£150**, plus special breaks; 11 comfortable, pretty rms. Handsome Edwardian manor house with individually chosen furnishings and pictures, open fires, fresh flowers and plants, beautifully presented fine food using the best ingredients (some home-grown and lots of game and fish) in airy, no smoking dining room, and courteous attentive service; cl 25–26 Dec; no children

BIGGIN-BY-HARTINGTON SK1559 **Biggin Hall** *Biggin-by-Hartington, Buxton, Derbyshire SK17 0DH (01298) 84451* **£70**, plus special breaks; 19 spacious rms with antiques, some in converted 18th-c stone building and in bothy. Cheerfully run 17th-c house in quiet grounds with a very relaxed atmosphere, two comfortable sitting rooms, log fires, freshly cooked straightforward food with an emphasis on free-range wholefoods served at 7pm in the attractive dining room, and packed lunches if wanted; children 12 and over; limited disabled access; dogs welcome in bedrooms

BIRCH VALE SK0287 **Waltzing Weasel** *New Mills Rd, Birch Vale, High Peak, Derbyshire SK22 1BT (01663) 743402* **£75**; 8 lovely rms. Attractive traditional inn with open fire, some handsome furnishings, daily papers and plants in quiet civilised bar, very good food using the best seasonal produce in charming back restaurant (fine views), excellent puddings and cheeses, obliging service; children over 7 in restaurant; disabled access; dogs welcome

CASTLETON SK1582 **Bargate Cottage** *Market Pl, Castleton, Hope Valley, Derbyshire S33 8WQ (01433) 620201* **£50**; 3 well equipped rms. Lovely, beautifully restored old cottage with beams, an inglenook fireplace, delicious breakfasts, super packed lunches, and pretty terraced garden; no smoking; cl 24–25 Dec; children over 12

DOVE DALE SK1550 **Peveril of the Peak** *Thorpe, Ashbourne, Derbyshire DE6 2AW (08704) 008109* **£89**, plus special breaks; 46 rms. Relaxing hotel in pretty village with comfortable sofas and log fire in lounge, modern bar and attractive restaurant overlooking the garden, and good English cooking; tennis; wonderful walking nearby; disabled access; dogs welcome in bedrooms

GLOSSOP SK0593 **Wind in the Willows** *Derbyshire Level, Sheffield Rd, Glossop, Derbyshire SK13 7PT* (01457) 868001 **£105**; 12 individual rms with thoughtful extras. In five acres on the edge of the Pennines, this early Victorian house has a restful atmosphere in its tranquil traditionally furnished sitting rooms, log fires and antiques, enjoyable set dinners (the restaurant is not open to the general public), particularly good breakfasts, and charming helpful service; adjoining golf course; children over 10

GRINDLEFORD SK2478 **Maynard Arms** *Main Rd, Nether Padley, Grindleford, Hope Valley, Derbyshire S32 2HE* (01433) 630321 **£79***, plus special breaks; 10 rms. Comfortable hotel with log fire and good Peak District views from the first-floor lounge, smart welcoming bar, good choice of food, popular evening restaurant, and particularly attentive service; good walks nearby; dogs welcome in bedrooms

HATHERSAGE SK2281 **George** *Main Rd, Hathersage, Hope Valley, Derbyshire S32 1BB* (01433) 650436 **£120**, plus special breaks; 19 pretty rms (the back ones are quietest). Substantial and comfortably modernised old inn with attractive airy lounge, beamed friendly bar, popular food, and a neat flagstoned back terrace by rose garden; good walks all around; dogs welcome in bedrooms

HOPE SK1783 **Underleigh House** *Edale Rd, Hope, Castleton, Derbyshire S33 6RF* (01433) 621372 **£69***, plus special breaks; 6 thoughtfully decorated rms. In unspoilt countryside, this spotlessly kept converted barn has fine views from the comfortable sitting room, hearty breakfasts with good home-made preserves enjoyed around communal table in flagstoned dining room, friendly cheerful owners, attractive gardens; terrific walks on the doorstep, packed lunches can be arranged; cl Christmas and New Year; children over 12; dogs by arrangement

KIRK IRETON SK2650 **Barley Mow** *Kirk Ireton, Ashbourne, Derbyshire DE6 3JP* (01335) 370306 **£45**; 5 rms. Tall, Jacobean, walkers' inn with lots of woodwork in series of interconnecting bar rooms, a solid fuel stove in beamed residents' sitting room, and well kept real ales; close to Carsington Reservoir; cl Christmas wk; dogs in one ground-loor rm

MATLOCK SK3059 **Riber Hall** *Matlock, Derbyshire DE4 5JU* (01629) 582795 **£136**, plus special breaks; 14 lovely beamed rms with antiques, chocolates, and baskets of fruit. Elizabethan manor house in pretty grounds surrounded by peaceful countryside, with antiques-filled heavily beamed rooms, fresh flowers, two elegant dining rooms with enjoyable food and fine wines, and tennis and clay pigeon shooting; children over 10; dogs welcome in bedrooms

MONSAL HEAD SK1871 **Monsal Head Hotel** *Monsal Head, Buxton, Derbyshire DE45 1NL* (01629) 640250 **£50**, plus special breaks; 7 very good rms, some with lovely views. Comfortable and enjoyable small hotel in marvellous setting high above the River Wye, with horsey theme in bar (converted from old stables), freshly prepared decent food using seasonal produce, and good service; cl 25 Dec; dogs welcome in bedrooms

ROWLAND SK2172 **Holly Cottage** *Rowland, Bakewell, Derbyshire DE45 1NR* (01629) 640624 **£48***, plus special breaks; 2 pretty rms, shared bthrm. 200-year-old no smoking cottage on a quiet lane, surrounded by peaceful rolling countryside; new stone fireplace and woodburning stove in newly refurbished lounge, woodburner in panelled hall, attractive dining room and homely relaxed atmosphere, excellent breakfasts with home-made rolls, bread and preserves; lovely gardens, and friendly black Labrador; lots of walks; cl Nov–Feb

ROWSLEY SK2565 **Peacock** *Rowsley, Matlock, Derbyshire DE4 2EB* (01629) 733518 **£125**, plus special breaks; 16 comfortable rms. 17th-c country-house hotel by River Derwent (private fishing in season), with well kept gardens, friendly staff, interesting old-fashioned inner bar, spacious lounge, and very popular restaurant; dogs welcome in bedrooms

SHIRLEY SK2241 **Shirley Hall Farm** *Shirley, Ashbourne, Derbyshire DE6 3AS* (01335) 360346 **£52**; 3 rms. Timbered and part-moated farmhouse on family-run dairy and arable farm, with homely sitting room, and good breakfasts with home-made bread, jam and marmalade, and local organic sausages; private coarse fishing and lots of walks; nearby pub for evening meals; self-catering cottages

SHOTTLE SK3050 **Dannah Farm** *Bowmans Lane, Shottle, Belper, Derbyshire DE56 2DR (01773) 550273* £79*, plus special breaks; 8 rms with old pine and antiques, and some with private sitting rooms, four-posters, and whirlpool baths. Carefully restored and newly refurbished, friendly Georgian farmhouse with two comfortable sitting rooms, popular imaginative cooking in attractive no smoking dining room, and super breakfasts; hens, a nanny goat, hairy kune-kune pigs and farm cats; cl 24–26 Dec; partial disabled access

To see and do

Derbyshire Family Attraction of the Year

ILKESTON SK4444 **American Adventure Theme Park** (off A6007, signed from M1 junction 26) Perhaps understandably a little overshadowed by better-known Alton Towers nearby, this is a good alternative for those who want the theme park experience but don't want to shell out quite so much time or money. It's a more manageable size, and easy to get round in a day without getting lost or exhausted. The rides and attractions are all as you'd expect (there aren't too many surprises), with a few good white-knuckle rides to keep thrill-seekers happy, and, perhaps more unusually, lots for younger children, or those with less daredevil tastes, from gentler roller-coasters and a scaled-down swinging boat (there's a bigger, scarier one too) to carousels, a helter-skelter, and a huge indoor play area. As usual, many rides have height restrictions, but, usefully, these are all listed on the park's website (www.americanadventure.co.uk), along with other helpful information and statistics such as the rides' speeds, so you can plan in advance which are the most suitable. Older children with braver tastes will want to head for the Missile, a stomach-churning roller-coaster that twists and turns at unfeasible angles, before going the whole route again backwards, Nightmare Niagra, a triple log flume with a 13-metre (42-ft) drop at 62mph, and perhaps even the Sky Coaster, at 61 metres (200 ft) the UK's biggest freefall ride. Everything supposedly has an American theme, which at times can be a little flimsy (the Buffalo Stampede for example isn't exactly packed with buffalo), but none the worse for it. Live shows include a Wild West saloon and Mexican fiesta, and there's a big lake with pedaloes and a steamboat. A train travels round the lake between the various areas. A few things, like the crazy golf, have an extra charge, and watch out, there are plenty of other places to spend money: in places there seem almost as many food outlets and shops as there are rides. You can book tickets online: the prices are the same, but it avoids queuing on the day. Meals, snacks, shops, good disabled access; open Apr–early Nov; 0845 3302929; £13.99 adults and children over 12, £10.99 children under 12 but more than 1 metre tall (smaller children are free, but can't go on as many rides). A family ticket for two adults and two children is £42.50. Entry is usually cheaper on weekdays outside school holidays.

Derbyshire

YORKSHIRE

Renishaw
A619 **30** A619
A616 Creswell Crags
Bolsover
A632
29 A617
Hardstoft
M1
Hardwick Hall
28

SK

NOTTINGHAMSHIRE

Ilkeston

Dale Abbey
Stanton by Dale
25
M1
Shardlow
A6

LEICESTERSHIRE

ASHBOURNE SK1846
Southern gateway to the Peak District,
though quite separate in character; a
good few interesting Georgian and
earlier buildings (inc almshouses and
the 16th-c old grammar school) nr the
market place and along Church St. This
street leads to the elegantly
proportioned church, which has a
famous white marble statue of a
sleeping child. The Gingerbread Shop
sells the town's long-standing speciality,
and Smiths Tavern is good for lunch.
The B5056 towards Bakewell and
B5053 to Wirksworth have
characteristic views. You can hire
bicycles by the half-day or day from
Ashbourne Cycle Hire, Mapleton Lane;
(01335) 343156; £8 for half a day.
Derwent Crystal Centre (Shaw
Croft) Quality glassworks and
engravers, with demonstrations
(9am–2.30pm Mon–Thurs) and factory
shop. Disabled access; cl Sun, 25–26
Dec, 1 Jan; (01335) 345219; free.
Tissington Trail This path for walkers
and cyclists follows a disused railway
track from Ashbourne up to Parsley
Hay on the A515, where it joins the
similar **High Peak Trail** from Buxton
to near Cromford; branching off at
Roystone Grange is an archaeological
trail. You can hire cycles in Ashbourne,
or from Parsley Hay Cycle Hire, Parsley
Hay; (01298) 84493; 3 hours £8. This
has a particularly interesting finale from
Middleton Top engine house (cycle hire
here, too) to High Peak Junction,
dipping down a great incline past old
engine houses to reach the Cromford
Canal.

ASHFORD IN THE WATER
SK1969
An attractive main street in a village of
three bridges, inc Sheepwash Bridge
with its attached sheep enclosure; good
food in the Bulls Head.
Magpie Mine (2m SW, nr Sheldon)
Surface remains of a mine last worked
in 1958 and stabilised in the 1970s give a
good idea of a 19th-c lead mine; free.

BAKEWELL SK2168
The only town inside the Peak National
Park, and away from the traffic, this is a
civilised place, especially around the
church. You can still get those famous
tarts here, though there has been some

dispute over the original recipe – two shops have claimed rights to the authentic Bakewell Pudding, and the case even went to court. The handsome Rutland Arms has enjoyable food in its bar and restaurant.

Old House Museum (Cunningham Pl) Folk collection in a 16th-c house, still with its original wattle-and-daub interior walls and open-timbered chamber. Limited disabled access; open pm daily Good Fri–Oct, plus am July–Aug; (01629) 813642; £3.

BELPER SK3448
Derwent Valley Visitor Centre
Though it looks quite simple from the outside, this early 19th-c cotton mill was the most technically advanced building of its time, and is now a World Heritage Site. An exhibition inside traces the evolution of the machines which developed the factory system with examples from hand spinning wheels and a spinning jenny right up to 20th-c machines of mass production. You can find out more about the Belper man who took Britain's industrial plans to America, and they've a fine collection of silk and cotton stockings. Shop, disabled access; cl Mon and Tues (plus Wed Easter–Oct), and all Dec–Jan; (01773) 880474; £2. The Holly Bush over in Makeney has just the right sort of atmosphere.

BIRCHOVER SK2362
Starting point for an extraordinary walk over **Stanton Moor**, where among quarry workings and prehistoric burial mounds are the Nine Ladies stone circle, a folly tower and a huge boulder known as the Cork Stone, equipped with metal steps for the courageous and adorned with at least four centuries' worth of graffiti (the earliest we found was 1613); there are good views into Darley Dale from the edge of the escarpment. Behind the Druid Inn in Birchover are **Rowtor Rocks**, a gritstone outcrop into which a contemplative parson cut steps, benches and a stone armchair.

BOLSOVER SK4770
Bolsover Castle The original ruined castle dates back to the 12th c, but was rebuilt in 1613 as a spectacular mock castle – about 200 years ahead of this fashion. Battlements and turrets

outside, and inside allegorical frescoes, fine panelling and ornate fireplaces; visitor centre and restored fountain garden. Snacks, shop, some disabled access; cl Tues and Weds Nov–Mar, 24–26 Dec and 1 Jan; (01246) 823349; £6.20, inc Walkman tour. Just on the other side of the M1 at Sutton Scarsdale (and in fact looking down on the motorway) are the evocative ruins of a once-grand 17th-c hall.

BRADBOURNE SK2152
Appealing Dales village, with an ancient Saxon cross outside its **Norman church**.

BUXTON SK0572
England's highest market town, it's much changed but still has some handsome buildings dating from its days as a flourishing spa, with Georgian terraces (the Crescent is a noble Georgian streetscape), and a restored Edwardian opera house. St Ann's Well is the only direct reminder of its water-based heyday (you can take the water for free here, and it's naturally warm) though there are plans to revive the spa (which is underneath the tourist information centre) and the Crescent over the next few years. Many of the grander buildings come back to life during the town's excellent July festival. The Columbine (Hall Bank) and the Old Hall Hotel's wine bar (The Square) are good for food. An enjoyable self-guided walk takes you around the town's attractions inc the Pavilion Gardens, currently being restored; available from the Tourist Information Centre (The Crescent); 50p.

Buxton Museum & Art Gallery (Terrace Rd) A useful introduction to the area; shop, disabled access; cl Mon (exc bank hols) and winter Sun, 25–26 Dec and 1 Jan; £1.

Grin Low Woods (just S) Well landscaped, with mature woodland and the Victorian folly of Solomon's Temple (good views from the top), though it's not always open.

Poole's Cavern (Buxton Country Park, Green Lane) The best show cave in the Peak District and thought to be the longest in Britain, a spectacular natural limestone cavern in 100 acres of woodland, with well lit stalactites and stalagmites, and exhibitions on caves, woodland and Romans. As in other caverns, wrap up well. Snacks, shop, some disabled access with notice; cl Nov–Feb; (01298) 26978; £5.10.

CALKE SK3622

Calke Abbey One of the most rewarding NT properties in Britain, an unusual baroque mansion still in pretty much the same state as when the last baronet died here in 1924. You might expect the splendidly decorated rooms with their fascinating displays (inc an extensive natural history collection), but it's quite a surprise to find the more dilapidated corridors and areas where family possessions were just bundled together in heaps. This gives you a better appreciation of how the abbey was a much-loved family home – and of how things forgotten in the attic can quickly become social history. Also extensive parkland and walled gardens. Meals, snacks, shop, disabled access to ground floor; cl am Thurs, Fri, and Nov–Mar; (01332) 863822; £5.60, garden only £2.80 – there's a £2.70 vehicle charge on entering the park, refundable on entry to the house (which has a timed ticket system on busy days); NT. The nearby Saracens Head (Heath End Lane) has great value snacks.

CARSINGTON WATER SK2552

Britain's newest reservoir, already toning into the landscape as if it's been a lake for ever, is developing into a great place for inexpensive family outings; good visitor centre with interactive displays and a good safe play area, easy waterside walks (even with pushchairs or wheelchairs), bird hides, fishing, cycling, watersports inc kayaks and canoes. Meals, snacks, shop, disabled access; cl 25 Dec; (01629) 540696; car park charge, £2 all day. The Red Lion at Hognaston has good food, and the Miners Arms in Carsington is another useful stop.

CASTLETON SK1482

Very much geared to visitors, and filled with walkers and cavers in summer; plenty of cafés, and shops selling expensive worked pieces of the Blue John fluorspar that's found only in the nearby mine workings. The village's attractive dark stone buildings (one of the most impressive now a youth hostel) are dominated by the ruins of **Peveril Castle**, built high above in the 11th c – magnificent views. Shop, snacks; cl Mon and Tues in Nov–Mar, 24–26 Dec and 1 Jan; (01433) 620613; £2.40; EH. There's decent food at the Castle Hotel, Rose Cottage and George, and in the pretty nearby village of Hope the Cheshire Cheese is good. The B6061 to Sparrowpit (where the Wanted Inn is good value) has fine views. The most varied **walks** in the High Peak are found around Castleton and Hope. The great walk here takes in Castleton, the Lose Hill/Mam Tor ridge, the caves, and Winnats Pass; Mam Tor is so shaly and prone to landslips that it's dubbed the Shivering Mountain – the abandoned section of the A625 is a testament to the victory of the mountain over man. Cave Dale is an optional side trip from the back of Castleton. Quarrying has had an unfortunate effect on the local landscape in the area, and limits walks further afield, though there are some pleasant walks to be had in the gentler high pastures of the limestone country to the south.

Blue John Cavern & Mine ♿ (Buxton Rd) Containing eight of the 14 known veins of Blue John, this has been the main source of the precious stone for nearly 300 years. It's an impressive example of a water-worn cave, over a third of a mile long, with chambers 45 metres (150 ft) high. Snacks, craft shop; cl 25–26 Dec, 1 Jan; (01433) 620638; £6.

Peak Cavern ♿ Right in the village, this is the biggest natural cavern in the country and really does seem huge – the entrance hall is so large it used to house an entire village; there are no significant stalactites or stalagmites. From there it's a half-mile walk along subterranean passageways to the Great Cave, 45 by 27 metres (150 ft wide, 90 ft long). By the time you reach the Devil's Staircase you'll be nearly 140 metres (450 ft) underground. Rope-making demonstrations; Snacks, shop; cl wkdys Nov–Mar; (01433) 620285; £5.25.

Speedwell Cavern ♿ (Winnats Pass – declassified continuation of A6187 W of Castleton) Very atmospheric former lead mine, with 105 steps down to a half-mile underground boat trip along floodlit passages, finishing in a cathedral of a cavern with an impressive 'bottomless pit'. Great fun; there may be a queue. Shop, snacks; (01433) 620512; cl 25 Dec; £5.75.

Treak Cliff Cavern ☒ (off declassified continuation of A6187 W) Informative tours of one of the first Blue John mines, worked since 1750, with rich veins of the mineral and quite staggering stalactites and stalagmites. Well placed lights create spooky shapes and atmospheric shadows. The entrance is narrow, and it's quite steep, but readers like this even more than many of the other caverns nearby, and they hold regular special events. Snacks, shop; cl 24–26 and 31 Dec, and 1 Jan; (01433) 620571; £5.50.

CHAPEL-EN-LE-FRITH SK0580

Chestnut Centre ☒ (A625) Warmly recommended conservation park, concerned especially with breeding otters and barn owls, but other animals and birds of prey too. Good observation platforms. Snacks, shop; cl wkdys Jan and Feb; (01298) 814099; *£5.50. The Cross Keys has good food (all day Sun).

CHATSWORTH SK2670

(off B6012) This wonderful estate on the banks of the River Derwent has almost as much appeal for children as it has for adults. The first-class adventure playground is perhaps the highlight for younger visitors, and a working farmyard has plenty of opportunities to get close to cows, sheep, pigs and horses. The house itself has been home to the Duke of Devonshire's family for nearly 450 years. Sumptuously furnished, the 26 rooms on display show off a superb collection of fine arts, with memorable paintings by Rembrandt and Van Dyck, and a set of nine Regency bedrooms is also usually open for a small extra charge. Private guided tours are available by prior arrangement (extra charge). The gardens cover 100 acres; brass bands play on summer Sunday afternoons. The surrounding park was landscaped by Capability Brown, and covers 1,000 acres; well marked walks and trails. Good meals and snacks, shop, garden centre, disabled access to garden only; open Apr–21 Dec; (01246) 582204; £8 house and garden, £4.50 garden only, and a further £3.60 for the farm and adventure playground. Entry to the park is free (open all year). Car parking is £1. Also in the grounds, at Stud Farm, 1½ miles towards Pilsley, is one of England's best farm shops (they also have a branch in Pimlico, London). Around Chatsworth, **Edensor** is a very attractive estate village, and walkers have free access to the park W of the River Derwent; there is a delightful riverside walk at Calton Lees car park, N to Chatsworth bridge and Edensor. The B6012 (busy in summer) has pleasant views, and the Devonshire Arms at Beeley has decent food all day.

CHESTERFIELD SK3871

Not a tourist town, but its mainly 14th-c **church** has a really striking leaning spire, and is a rich building inside; the town **museum** (Corporation St) has the full angle on it; cl Weds and Sun; free. The ancient Rutland (Stephenson Pl, by the church) has decent food. The Victorian market hall has flourishing indoor and outdoor markets Mon, Fri and Sat (flea market Thurs, street entertainment summer Sats). The Chesterfield Canal has recently undergone its first phase of renovation giving up to five miles of towpath walks (forming part of the Trans-Pennine Trail), with a good Visitor Centre at Tapton Lock (cl wknds 25 Dec–Easter). From here you can hire out boats and canoes, take boat trips (disabled access; open Easter–Christmas), and they provide leaflets on walks, events and wildlife around the canal. Nearby **Grassmoor Country Park** is a pleasant place to stroll; fishing lake. The Derby Tup (Sheffield Rd) is an enjoyable ale house with good value simple food.

CRESWELL CRAGS SK5374

Beside Crags Pond, these form the basis of a short but attractive there-and-back walk through woodland.

CRICH SK3455

Crich Tramway Village (Matlock Rd) When you enter this enthusiastically run place, you're given an old penny (or half-penny for children), which you use to pay for unlimited rides on the lovingly restored vintage trams that run up and down a one-mile period street and beyond, through lovely parts of the Derwent Valley (familiar to viewers of *Peak Practice*). A comprehensive exhibition has more trams, from all over the British Isles and further afield. There are plenty of play areas: a big one outside, with bridges, ropes and balancing poles, and a tram-themed one inside with a section for under-5s. Nice walks through the surrounding woodland, and regular special events – it's particularly good fun in the run-up to Christmas. They've a new workshop viewing gallery (where you can watch the trams being restored). New pub and restaurant, picnic areas, disabled access (one tram has been adapted for wheelchairs, and they have a guide book in Braille); cl wkdys in Mar and Tues–Fri Nov–22 Dec (exc 2nd wk in Dec), best to check; (0870) 7587267; £7. The Cliff Inn nearby has great views.

CROMFORD SK2956

A good example of an 18th-c cotton-milling village, little developed after its original building, and rewarding to stroll through. Carefully preserved North St (1777) is the first true industrial street in Derbyshire. The old-fashioned Boat Inn has good value basic food. The canal is a quiet and attractive early Industrial Revolution setting with a restored steam-powered pumping house and a fine aqueduct over the river. Good walks along the canal and the High Peak Trail (see Ashbourne). The A5012 to Grangemill gives evocative views.

Cromford Mill (Mill Lane) Richard Arkwright established the world's first successful water-powered cotton mill here in 1771; the true beginning of the factory age, it's now a World Heritage Site. Meals, snacks, shops, limited disabled access; cl 25 Dec; (01629) 823256; site free, tours £2.

High Peak Junction Workshops Oldest surviving railway workshops in the world. The visitor centre includes exhibitions, a film and now an audio tour; snacks, shop; cl wkdys Oct–Mar; (01629) 822831; 60p.

CURBAR SK2575

The eastern edges of the Peak District include the abrupt ramparts of Curbar Edge and Froggatt Edge, popular with rock-climbers and easily accessible from the road. The Bridge Inn down at Calver has good value plain food and a big Derwentside garden. In this same area, Birchen Edge and Wellington's Monument are obvious objectives for walkers from the Robin Hood, on the A619 E of Baslow.

DALE ABBEY SK4338

Abbey ruins, Hermits Cave and remarkable All Saints church, part of which was formerly the village inn; the village is attractive, and over in Ockbrook the 18th-c Royal Oak does cheap lunches.

DARLEY DALE SK2762

Carriage Museum (Red House Stables) Collection of vehicles and equipment, some of which you can ride in. Also carriage rides – booking essential. Teas, disabled access; cl 25 Dec; (01629) 733583; £2.75.

Peak Rail 🎫 Private railway; trains run between here and Matlock, then on to Rowsley, and the eventual aim is to run as far as Buxton. Wknd restaurant car, shop, limited disabled access; usually open wknds all year, but best to check; (01629) 580381; £6.

DERBY SK3536

A big busy city, but not too daunting for a visitor to explore, with a pedestrianised centre, and several things worth visiting. It's got far more open spaces than you'd expect including England's first public park (donated to the city by a local mill owner, it's currently undergoing a £5 million restoration).

Derby Cathedral The 16th-c tower is the second highest church tower in the country; the nave was built in the 18th c. Bess of Hardwick is buried in the vaults, and there's a delightful early Georgian screen. Shop, disabled access; suggested donation £2. Nearby **St Mary's Chapel** is one of only six surviving bridge chapels still in use. The quaint nearby Olde Dolphin (Queen St) has bargain food all day.

Derby Museum & Art Gallery (The Strand) Stands out for its collections of porcelain, and paintings by local Joseph Wright. Shop, disabled access; cl Sun am and over the Christmas hols; (01332) 716669; free.

Heritage Centre (St Peter's

churchyard) Once a Tudor grammar school, now the start for good ghost walks through the city's tunnels and other themed tours (also from Old Gaol, Friargate) 7pm; cl Dec 24–26; booking essential, (01332) 299321; from £13 inc meal. Centre cl Sun and most bank hols; free.

Industrial Museum (Full St) This restored early 18th-c silk mill has a range of displays on local industries, a major collection of Rolls-Royce aero engines, and a Power Gallery with lots of hands-on displays. Shop, disabled access; cl am Sun and bank hols, and over Christmas – phone to check; (01332) 255308; free. The nearby Old Silk Mill is an interesting pub, open all day.

Pickfords House Museum (Friargate) Gives a very good idea of 18th-c domestic life, with period furnished rooms and Georgian garden; also costume display and a collection of toy theatres. Shop, disabled access to ground floor only, and video with subtitles; cl am Sun and bank hols, and around a wk over Christmas and New Year; (01332) 255363; free.

Q Gallery (Queen St) City-centre gallery showing contemporary visual art, photography and new media; shop, disabled access; cl am, and Sun–Tues, around 2 wks over Christmas, and between exhibitions – best to phone; (01332) 295858; free.

Royal Crown Derby Visitor Centre (Osmaston Rd) Cheerfully informative tours four times a day of a bone-china factory, celebrating 250 years of porcelain production. A museum traces the industry's development from its origins. Meals, snacks, shop (lots of bargain seconds), disabled access (exc museum); open daily, no tours wknds, bank hols or factory shut-down weeks; (01332) 712800; £4.95 (£2.95 without tour) – no under-10s on tours.

DOVE DALE SK1452
Shared between Derbyshire and Staffordshire, with the River Dove as the boundary, this is the most popular of all the dales. Partly wooded, it has a beautifully varied mixture of water, trees and pastures, and is lined with crags and curiously shaped outcrops of rock. The main access point is at the S end (where the scenery is at its most spectacular). A less crowded approach is to start from the quiet village of Alstonefield and walk down to the hamlet of **Milldale** (handy refreshment places on the Staffordshire side of the river are the Watts Russell Arms at Hopedale and George at Alstonefield). Or head further upstream towards **Beresford Dale, Wolfscote Dale** and **Biggin Dale** (nr Hartington). Useful nearby refreshment places are the Coach & Horses at Fenny Bentley and (to be found on the Staffordshire side) the Izaak Walton Hotel nr Ilam (cosier inside than it looks from out). Also try the Okeover Arms at Mapleton (with a domed church and a nice riverside walk to Thorpe.)'

EDALE SK1285
Famous as the start of the 256-mile Pennine Way to the Scottish border, with a good information centre, and decent food in the Old Nags Head. It tends to be packed with expectant long-distance walkers on Sunday mornings. For a taste of the Dark Peak proper, this can be the start for half-day walks that quite quickly take you up through the stone-walled pastures of the valley on to the edge of the dark plateau above. The track signed as the alternative Pennine Way route up Jacob's Ladder is easier to find, and has more to see (inc some strange weathered rocks and an ancient cross), than the official Pennine Way plod across a huge blanket bog.

ELVASTON SK4032
Elvaston Castle Country Park (B5010) 200 acres of lovely 19th-c landscaped parkland, with formal and Old English gardens, wooded walks, and wildfowl on the ornamental lake. Meals, snacks, shop, disabled access; (01332) 571342; car park 70p wkdys, £1.30 wknds. Shardlow is convenient for lunch.

EYAM SK2276
Attractive secluded village with a dark past: in the Great Plague sick villagers confined themselves here for fear of infecting people outside – plaques record who died where, and stones on the village edge mark where money was disinfected. The Miners Arms is very

good for lunch. Just up the B6521 at Upper Padley, **Padley Chapel** is an interesting 15th-c revival, effectively restored in 1933.

Eyam Hall 🏠 Sturdy-looking 17th-c manor house, still very much a family home, with furniture, portraits and tapestries, fine Jacobean staircase and impressive flagstoned hall; there's a small craft centre in the stables. Meals, snacks, shop, some disabled access; house open Weds–Thurs, Sun and bank hol Mon Jun–Aug, craft centre open daily exc Mon, and over Christmas and New Year; (01433) 631976; £4.25 – timed ticket system.

GOYT VALLEY SK0177
The well wooded valley with its three miles of reservoirs is a man-made landscape, but nonetheless charming for walks or picnics; sterner rambles up to the viewpoint of Shining Tor (also reached via a bracing ridge walk from a car park to the N). Reached off the A54 W of Buxton (one-way system operates; no access from A5002).

HADDON HALL SK2366
One of the most perfectly preserved medieval manor houses in England, still with its 12th-c painted chapel, 14th-c kitchen, and banqueting hall with minstrels' gallery. Perhaps because they're furnished with the original furniture and tapestries, some rooms can seem rather bare; a bright spot is Rex Whistler's painting of the house in the silver-panelled long gallery. It's a particularly pretty location in summer when the long terraced rose gardens are in full bloom. Several films and TV adaptations have had scenes shot here in recent years. Meals, snacks, shop; cl Mon–Weds in Oct, and all Nov–Mar; (01629) 812855; £5.90. The Lathkil Hotel up in Over Haddon is good for lunch, and nearby roads have attractive views.

HARDSTOFT SK4264
Herb Garden 🏠 (B6039, not far from M1 junction 29) Big main garden with lots of herbs and Old English roses, smaller gardens specialising in rare medicinal herbs, pot-pourri or lavender. Snacks, shop; cl Mon–Tues (exc bank hols and Easter) and mid-Sept to mid-Mar; (01246) 854268; £1. The comfortable Shoulder of Mutton has decent food.

HARDWICK HALL SK4663
The marriages of the redoubtable Bess of Hardwick couldn't necessarily be described as happy but she certainly did very well out of them, the fourth leaving her enough money to build this triumphant Elizabethan prodigy house. The beautifully symmetrical towers are crowned with the monogram ES, and there's an amazing expanse of glass (her sight was dimming). Also fine tapestries and needlework, large park, and gardens laid out in walled courtyard. They're restoring the huge and ancient Gideon tapestries which run the length of the 50-metre (167-ft) Long Gallery, a silk canopy, and the garden walls; a gazebo houses an exhibition on garden history; guided walks to stone mason's yard (Weds and Thurs at 11.30, 1.30 and 3). Meals, snacks, shop, disabled access to ground floor only; open pm Apr–Oct, garden cl Tues, house cl Mon, Tues and Fri (exc bank hols), hall cl am; £2 vehicle charge to enter the grounds; £6.40 house and garden, £3.40 garden only; NT. Not far from this 'new' house is the shell of Hardwick Old Hall, Bess's birthplace; (01246) 850431; £3. A joint ticket is available for both houses (£8.50). Also on the estate is a restored watermill (adult £2.10, NT). The park is attractive for walks, and nearby Hardwick Inn, also NT-owned, is good for lunch.

HARTINGTON SK1260
This attractive village has a good cheese shop selling local stilton, and the Devonshire Arms is a popular stop. Excellent valley floor walks into Beresford Dale and then on through Wolfscote Dale to the N end of Dove Dale.

HATHERSAGE SK2281
Charlotte Brontë wrote *Jane Eyre* here, and Little John's supposed grave is in the churchyard. Though somewhat suburban in character, it's a good village for walkers and climbers, with fine routes along the River Derwent towards Grindleford, and E through the moors and woods of the Longshaw Estate (nr the Fox House Inn up on the Sheffield road) and up to the dramatic Iron Age hill fort of Carl Wark. The riverside Plough (A622) is good for lunch.

HAYFIELD SK0387

This moorland village and its attractive nearby smaller sister Little Hayfield have good walks around them, both up towards Kinder Scout and to the Lantern Pike viewpoint in the opposite direction. There's also a popular walk or cycle ride – the Sett Valley Trail – along a hillside former railway to New Mills, looking down on the mill buildings by the River Sett. A handy bike shop does hire in Hayfield (Station Rd), and there's an information centre for the Trail; (01663) 746222. The Pack Horse is a popular dining pub, open all day.

ILKESTON SK4444

American Adventure Theme Park *See separate family panel on p.133.*

Shipley Country Park Medieval estate developed and landscaped in the 18th c, with 600 acres of woodland, lakes and fields; it`s a pleasant place to wander, with railway lines transformed into leafy walkways. Snacks, shop, disabled access; visitor centre cl 25 Dec; (01773) 719961; free.

INGLEBY SK3427

River Trent Good views of the formidable river from the big riverside garden of the John Thompson pub, which brews its own beer.

KEDLESTON SK3140

Kedleston Hall This 18th-c Palladian mansion is thought by many to be the finest example of Robert Adam's work – it's certainly the least altered. Interesting objets d'art, original furnishings, good collection of paintings, and a museum of items collected by Lord Curzon when he was Viceroy of India. Adam designed a charming boathouse and bridge in the park outside, which also has extensive formal gardens with marvellous rhododendrons, and long woodland walks. Meals, snacks, shop, disabled access; open pm Sat–Weds Apr–Oct, grounds also open am, and wknds Nov–Dec; (01332) 842191; £5.10, £2.30 grounds only; NT. The Joiners Arms in Quarndon does good value weekday lunches.

LADYBOWER RESERVOIR SK1788

One of a chain of impressive reservoirs, scenic enough to merit driving along; also the lane up to the car park by the Derwent Reservoir gives plenty of easy waterside-forest **walking** on the relatively sheltered stone-walled slopes of the upper parts of Derwent Dale, with access to the higher moors for better views – for example, up on to Win Hill, or on a kind day on to the formidable Derwent Moors to the E. The Yorkshire Bridge Hotel (A6013 towards Bamford) is a good refuge.

LATHKILL DALE SK1865

Charming combination of woods, steep pastures and well weathered signs of old mines; its short tributary Bradford Dale is also very good for walks. The large attractive village of Youlgreave makes a useful focal point for walkers; its church has windows by William Morris and Burne-Jones, and the 17th-c George has good home cooking.

LEA SK3258

Lea Gardens Beautiful woodland gardens with rhododendrons inc rare species and cultivars, azaleas and rock plants. Home-baked snacks, shop and garden centre, limited disabled access; open 20 Mar–Jun, other times by appointment; (01629) 534380; £3. The Tavern at Tansley is a decent dining pub.

LONGSTONES, THE SK1871

Little Longstone and nearby Great Longstone (where the new people in the White Lion are doing imaginative food) are charming steep stone-built villages, and the back road from Baslow through here to Tideswell is a pretty drive.

MATLOCK BATH SK2958

Pleasantly busy place, with lots to do. A spectacular wooded cliff looks across the lower roadside town to pastures by the Derwent; up the side of the gorge, quiet lanes climb steeply past 18th- and 19th-c villas. The Temple Hotel (Temple Walk) has great views and decent food.

Gulliver's Kingdom (1m S, off A6) Family theme park with chair lift and hectic rides, cave tour, and cowboy and ghost towns; it's aimed at the under-12s, so don't expect white knuckles. Meals, snacks, shops, limited disabled access; open wknds and school hols Easter–Sept; (01629) 580540; £6.80.

Heights of Abraham 🖾 Derbyshire is full of stunning show caverns, but few are as good for families, and none can boast as thrilling an introduction as the one here: cable cars whisk you up from the Derwent Valley to a 60-acre hilltop country park, with dramatic views over the ancient limestone gorge (not to mention a railway and the busy A6). At the end of the 5-minute trip a multi-media show explains how the rock was formed 325 million years ago, then guides escort you into the two show caverns. Outside are nature trails, nicely laid out woodland walks, the Prospect Tower to climb, and a few play areas (inc a maze, and a new playground aimed at the under-5s); usually clown shows or similar entertainments in summer. Good restaurant and café, limited disabled access; open most wknds mid-Feb to Easter (best to check), then daily mid-Mar to Oct; (01629) 582365; £7.30.

Matlock Bath Aquarium & Hologram A useful family attraction if you're staying in the area; cl wkdys Nov–Easter (exc school hols); (01629) 583624; £1.80.

Peak District Mining Museum (Temple Rd) Lively exploration of mining, with a unique early 19th-c water-pressure pumping engine, and interactive display on the pitfalls of working in a mine. Also tours of the old Temple Mine workings (£5, £9 for tour of museum and mine), and the chance to pan for minerals – in the past they've even found a tiny amount of gold. Snacks, shop, disabled access; cl 25 Dec; (01629) 583834; without tour £2.50, joint ticket to museum and mine £4.

MELBOURNE SK3825
This pleasant small town has a good relaxed feel and villagey lanes; the White Swan and Railway Hotel are good for lunch. The **church** of St Michael and St Mary is impressive, more like a cathedral than an ordinary parish church.

Melbourne Hall Behind its 18th-c façade, this grandly extended house dates back in part to the 13th c, and has twice been the home of prime ministers; fine pictures and furnishings. Glorious formal gardens with fountains, pools, and famous yew tunnel; interesting craft centre (open all year). Meals, snacks, shop, limited disabled access; Hall open pm daily in Aug (exc first three Mons), plus gardens open Weds, Sat, Sun and bank hol Mon pms Apr–Sept; (01332) 862502; £3 (with gardens, £5).

MIDDLETON BY WIRKSWORTH SK2755
Middleton Top Engine House Home to a beam engine built in 1829 to haul waggons up a steep incline on the Cromford & High Peak Railway. Snacks, shop; engine house open first wknd of month and bank hol wknds; visitor centre cl wkdys Oct–Easter; (01629) 823204; £1.20. The Olde Gate over at Brassington is highly recommended for a pub lunch (not Mon). And see Tissington Trail entry, under Ashbourne.

National Stone Centre 🆓 (Porter Lane) Surprisingly enjoyable centre, featuring 330-million-year-old tropical lagoons and limestone fossil reefs, as well as an exhibition, guided fossil trails, and, for an extra charge, activities like gem-panning or fossil-rubbing. Snacks, shop, some disabled access; cl 25–26 Dec and 1 Jan; (01629) 824833; £1.80.

MILLERS DALE SK1573
The B6049 N off the A6 SE of Buxton gives access to Millers Dale, just past the little village of that name (the Anglers Rest is a decent pub with great gorge views); upstream of Monsal Dale, this is rather less visited but also a lovely spot for walks – as is its continuation Chee Dale.

MONSAL DALE SK1771
This winding valley is the outstanding place for walks in this central part of the White Peak area, its pastoral quality emphasised by the disused limestone cotton mills along the way. It's especially lovely in May and June with wild flowers enriching the pastures along the broader stretches. Don't expect to have it to yourself. There's good access from the A6 a couple of miles towards Buxton from Ashford in the Water; and from Monsal Head (friendly hotel), where a disused railway viaduct (part of the Monsal Trail) adds interest.

MONSAL TRAIL SK1172
This outshines the other former railway-track walks in the Peak District, though like them is in parts more

exposed to the winds than walks down in the dales. It runs from Wye Dale E of Buxton to Coombs Road viaduct S of Bakewell. W of Millers Dale Station, the trail leaves the old railway and takes a stepping-stone route along the river beneath the towering cliffs of Chee Tor before rejoining the railway track.

MONYASH SK1566

2m S of this quiet village (good value home cooking at the Bulls Head) is the mysterious **Arbor Low** – the finest prehistoric site in the Peak District – a henge monument with a circular bank enclosing a fallen stone circle and inner sanctum; access via adjacent farmyard (honesty box).

OLD BRAMPTON SK3371

The village itself is attractive, and has one special curiosity: count the minutes between one and two o'clock on its church clock.

OLD WHITTINGTON SK3874

Revolution House (High St) Innocuous-looking thatched cottage where three conspirators met to plan their powerful part in the Revolution of 1688. Good audio-visual display, and period furniture. Shop, disabled access to ground floor only; open Easter–Sept and last 2 wks in Dec (exc 25–26); (01246) 345727; free. Just behind, the Cock & Magpie is handy for lunch.

OSMASTON SK2043

This village of pretty thatched cottages has a pleasant path through a lakeside park; the Shoulder of Mutton has good value food.

RENISHAW SK4378

Renishaw Hall Gardens 🖻 Beautiful series of Italianate gardens around a grand house, home to the Sitwell family since the mid-17th c. Laid out at the turn of the 20th c by Sir George Sitwell, grandfather of the present owner, they include sculptured yew hedges, carp-filled ornamental water features, a Gothic temple and hidden gardens. Below the gardens a lakeside walk leads past caves and through woodland. In the stable block, the **Museum of Sitwell Memorabilia** gives an insight into the colourful lives of Edith, Osbert and Sacheverell, the siblings who were at the centre of artistic developments in the 1920s; also a costume gallery, performing arts gallery, and an

exhibition on the artist John Piper, whose 'sombre and fiery genius' Osbert found 'peculiarly suited' to the Renishaw landscape. Meals, snacks, shop, disabled access; open Fri–Mon Easter–end Sept; (01246) 432310; £5, gardens/galleries and museum only £3. The civilised Sitwell Arms has decent food.

RIPLEY SK3947

Denby Pottery Visitor Centre (B6179 S) Guided factory tours (10.30–3.15 – not lunchtimes) show the intricate skills of potters and craftsmen, and give you the chance to make a frog and paint a plate. Big factory shop, children's play area and little museum. Meals, snacks, shops and garden centre, disabled access; cl 25–26 Dec; (01773) 740799; guided tours from £3.25, otherwise free. The Moss Cottage (A610 Nottingham rd) has a good carvery.

Midland Railway Centre 🖻 (Butterley Station, B6179 just N) Regular steam-train passenger service through country park, and developing railway museum. Meals, snacks, shop, disabled access; best to ring for train timetable, (01773) 570140; £7.95 (£8.95 bank hols and special events). It's good for families – not only are there a few farm animals on the adjacent farm (you can visit here free without having to go on the railway), but two children are admitted free with every adult. The Excavator on the A610 out at Buckland Hollow is a good value family dining pub.

ROWSLEY SK2565

Caudwell's Mill & Craft Centre Working 19th-c flour mill, powered by water turbines, with crafts such as glass-blowing, ceramics and wood-turning. Meals, snacks, shop; cl wkdys in Jan and 24–26 Dec, mill cl 24 Dec–1 Jan; (01629) 733185; mill £3, craft centre free. Rowsley also has an interesting **stone circle** called the Nine Ladies. Nearby Stanton in Peak is a lovely steep stone village overlooking this rich green valley; the Flying Childers has good value snacks (not Mon).

Peak Village Developing designer shopping village in the heart of the Peak District; also craft and other shops. Meals, snacks, disabled access; (01629)

735326; free. Also here (and useful to reward children with after a tedious morning's shopping), the **Wind in the Willows** attraction is based on the classic adventures of Toad, Mole, Ratty and Badger. The characters are brought to life with films, interactive displays and re-creations – children can climb into Toad's caravan, wander through the Wild Wood and creep along the passage to Toad Hall; they can also learn about real voles, moles, badgers and toads. Shop, disabled access; cl 25 Dec and Jan 29–31; (01629) 733433; £3.75.

SHARDLOW SK4430
Shardlow – canal basin Attractive, with some handsome former wharf buildings – one now an antiques warehouse, another, the Malt Shovel, a good pub.

SNAKE PASS SK1092
(A57 Glossop–Hathersage) The car park at the top of the pass is near the centre of the biggest of the NT's moorland holdings here, giving free access to the miles of Hope Woodlands (there aren't actually many trees). The dark moors of the High Peak are one of England's great wildernesses. But they have few easy circular routes for walkers, are largely very bleak indeed, and often consist of private grouse moor with no right of public access yet.

SOUTH WINGFIELD SK3754
Wingfield Manor (B5035) Substantial ruin with virtually complete banqueting hall, tower and undercroft. The 16th-c Babington Plot is thought to have been hatched here, leading to the final downfall of Mary, Queen of Scots. Snacks, shop, some disabled access; phone for opening times and prices; (01773) 832060. New people at the nearby Old Yew Tree are doing good value food.

SUDBURY SK1532
Sudbury Hall Individual but attractive Stuart mansion with elaborate carving, frescoes, murals and plasterwork in splendidly elegant rooms. It's worth a visit just for the excellent **National Trust Museum of Childhood**, which has a chimney climb for sweep-sized children, and a fine collection of toys and dolls. You can play with some exhibits, and at wknds the schoolroom

is staffed by an Edwardian teacher. Snacks, shop, some disabled access (bear in mind, car park is 400 yds from Hall); museum open pm (grounds all day) Weds–Sun 19 Mar–2 Nov plus a few wknds in Dec, Hall open pm Weds–Sun 2 Apr–3 Nov; (01283) 585305; £6.30 for everything, £3.90 house and grounds or museum only; NT.

SWADLINCOTE SK2015
Catton Hall You'll enjoy the guided tour of this classic Georgian house, designed by James Gibbs, and still with much of its original furniture and paintings. Catton has been in the same family since 1405, and you may even be taken around by one of the owners; it's right by the River Trent, with a formal garden and parkland, and a little chapel. Tours 1.30 and 3pm Mon Apr–Oct; (01283) 716311; £4.

TIDESWELL SK1575
In good walking country, this large and attractive village is almost a small town; its spacious 14th-c church is known as the Cathedral of the Peak. The George is good value, and the B6049 across Millers Dale has nice views.

TISSINGTON SK1752
The Peak District's most beautiful village, its broad main street wonderfully harmonious, with wide grass verges, handsome stone houses inc a Jacobean hall (open Tues–Thurs pm late Jun to late Aug; (01335) 352200; £5, gardens only, £2) and interesting church. The grey stone gardener's cottage is familiar from many calendars; garden centre, decent homely café.

TORRS RIVERSIDE PARK SJ9984
This deep gorge below New Mills is a good place to potter among the ivy-covered remains of former mills and other industrial relics; the canal basin has been restored over at Buxworth – the Navigation here is an enjoyable pub. The **Goyt Way** is a track heading N towards and beyond Marple, partly following the Peak Forest Canal – a pretty walk.

WIRKSWORTH SK2854
Wirksworth Heritage Centre (Crown Yard, Market Pl) Attractive old silk and velvet mill, with displays on quarrying and local customs such as well-dressing and clypping the church,

and children's activities. Meals, snacks, shop; cl Sun am, Mon (exc bank hols), plus Tues in Nov and mid-Feb–Easter, and all Dec–mid-Feb, but phone to check; (01629) 825225; £2. The town boasts a lot of restored old buildings; the Blacks Head (Market Pl) is a useful local pub.

Other attractive villages include Brassington SK2354, Coton in the Elms SK2415, Duffield SK3443, Earl Sterndale SK0967, Elton SK2261, Flagg SK1368, Ford SK4080, Holymoorside SK3469, Idridgehay SK2849, Kirk Ireton SK2650, Little Hucklow SK1678, Litton SK1675, Lullington SK2513, Mapleton SK1648 (domed church, nice riverside walk to Thorpe), Milton SK3126, Parwich SK1854, Pilsley SK2471, Repton SK3026, Ridgeway SK3551, Smisby SK3419, Stanton by Dale SK4638 and Stanton in Peak SK2464.

Decent country pubs perfectly placed for walkers include the Peacock at Barlow SK3474, Robin Hood at Baslow SK2572 (handy for the ridge of Baslow Edge), Barley Mow at Bonsall SK2858 (by the Limestone Way, landlord organises walks), Bowling Green at Bradwell SK1781 in Smalldale, Barrel on the ridge at Bretton SK2077, Church at Chelmorton SK1170, Beehive at Combs SK0478 (lovely valley), Packhorse at Crowdecote SK1065, Gate just W of Cutthorpe SK3273, Bridge at Ford SK4080, Grouse nr Froggatt Edge SK2577, Queen Anne at Great Hucklow SK1878, Miners Arms at Milltown SK3561, Bulls Head in pretty Monyash SK1566, Grouse at Nether Padley SK2577, Fox in Brookbottom at New Mills SJ9886, New Napoleon by Ogston Reservoir SK3761, Little Mill nr Rowarth SK0189 (particularly for Lantern Pike), Moon at Stoney Middleton SK2375, Queens Arms at Taddington SK1472 and Bulls Head at Wardlow SK1874 (for well wooded Cressbrook Dale).

Where to eat

BAKEWELL SK2168 **Byways** *Water Lane (01629) 812807* Olde-worlde tearoom with several separate areas, roaring log fire, well presented good value food from snacks to meals, and warmly friendly staff. £9|£3

BAKEWELL SK2168 **Renaissance** *Bath St (01629) 812687* Overlooking a little walled garden where fresh herbs are grown, this beamed restaurant serves imaginative French dishes inc gourmet specials and a fresh fish of the day, and delicious puddings; friendly service; cl Sun pm, Mon, 25 Dec–mid-Jan, first 2 wks Aug. £29.65|£5.99

BIRCHOVER SK2362 **Druid** *(01629) 650302* Civilised and pleasantly remote creeper-covered dining pub with huge choice of very popular interesting food (best to book), well kept real ales, and friendly service; bustling little bar with big coal fire, no smoking Garden Room, and spacious and airy two-storey dining extension; children must leave by 8pm; may cl Mon. £24.70|£9

BUXTON SK0673 **Coffee Bean Café** *50 Spring Gardens (01298) 27345* Small bustling café, long and narrow, with old tea and coffee advertisements, 15 types of coffee, all-day breakfasts, savouries and light lunches, and delicious cakes; cl evenings; disabled access.|£4

BUXWORTH SK0282 **Navigation** *(01663) 732072* Very welcoming extended pub by restored canal basin, with low-ceilinged rooms, plenty to look at, good fires, well kept real ales, good value generous food, and cheerful staff; tables on sunken flagstone terrace; disabled access. £20|£4.95

EYAM SK2276 **Miners Arms** *Water Lane (01433) 630853* Carefully refurbished pub with a restful atmosphere in its three little plush beamed rooms, good interesting lunchtime food served by attentive staff, well kept ales, and decent nearby walks; bdrms; no food Sun pm; disabled access. £21|£6.95

HOGNASTON SK2350 **Red Lion** *Main St (01335) 370396* Carefully renovated open-plan oak-beamed dining pub with a friendly welcome and relaxed atmosphere, attractive mix of candlelit tables on ancient flagstones, three open fires, a collection of teddy bears, well presented imaginative food (book at wknds), well kept real ales, and attentive staff; attractive bdrms; cl Mon am; children over 9. £23|£4.95

HOPE SK1783 **Cheshire Cheese** *Edale Rd (01433) 620381* 16th-c village pub with three cosy beamed rooms, each with its own coal fire, well kept real ales, a decent choice of house wines, good food (esp evenings), obliging service, and two small no smoking dining rooms. £16.50|£4.95

IDRIDGEHAY SK2848 **Black Swan** *Wirksworth Road (01773) 550249* Open-plan dining pub with bright airy simple décor, a relaxed, unhurried atmosphere, cheerful paintings, no smoking lower garden room, and small bar area with daily papers and real ale; generous and enjoyable food and prompt, polite service. £20.25/2-course lunch £8.95

MELBOURNE SK3825 **Bay Tree** *4 Potter St (01332) 863358* Small family-run cottagey restaurant with beams and simple furnishings, carefully presented popular food (Sun lunch is booked up weeks ahead), and thoughtful relaxed service; cl Sun pm, Mon. £24.40|£7

MILLTOWN SK3661 **Miners Arms** *(01246) 590218* Impeccably kept and comfortable stone-built dining pub with L-shaped layout, a back bar, and no smoking dining room; particularly good home-made food, well priced, with especially good interesting vegetables (a choice of half a dozen), and three sorts of potato, well kept real ales, decent value wines, and friendly efficient service. £19.25|£7.10

OVER HADDON SK2066 **Lathkil** *(01629) 812501* Comfortable inn with stunning views and plenty of surrounding walks; open fires, beams, partly no smoking dining area which doubles as an evening restaurant, enjoyable food and well kept real ales, and helpful service; children lunchtime only; cl 25 Dec. £19|£6.15

RIDGEWAY SK4081 **Old Vicarage** *Ridgeway Moor (0114) 247 5814* Big Victorian house in lovely gardens with a marvellously relaxing welcoming atmosphere, cosy sitting room for pre-dinner drinks and beautifully presented, quite exceptional cooking using home-grown produce in candlelit dining room or light and airy less formal conservatory; cl Sat am, Sun pm, Mon (though they will open then for private parties of over 10 people); disabled access. £51/3-course Sun lunch £33.34

WOOLLEY MOOR SK3661 **White Horse** *Badger Lane (01246) 590319* Popular old pub run by very friendly people – and much liked by locals; very good food using best local produce, lots of daily specials, decent wines and beers, conservatory, lovely view from garden (pleasant Ashover Valley walks), good play area; disabled access. £21|£7.25

Special thanks to Mrs J Davison

DEVON

Devon has so much to see and do, and such a wonderful variety of scenery, that we have divided it into three areas. South Devon, with Dartmoor, has the widest appeal of all, with a mass of interesting places to visit, and glorious vistas of coast and moor. East Devon is classic family holiday country, with Exeter a charming small city for a short break. North Devon, with Exmoor, is rewarding but less touristy than the other areas. There are some outstanding places to stay, at all price levels, and the food in this area is particularly good.

Some of the best views here are from trains; besides vintage steam trains puffing through gorgeous river valleys, the standard railway Devon Rover is a good deal, with unlimited train journeys in the area at a reduced rate for either eight days out of fifteen or any three days out of seven; phone (08457) 484950.

Exeter & East Devon

Good for seaside holidays, with plenty to keep families busy, and the appealing small city of Exeter

The coast has four main beach resorts, each quite different from the others. Exmouth, which doubles as a working port, is the liveliest and biggest. Seaton, quieter, is a more typical family resort, with much less of a beach. Budleigh Salterton, the quietest, is rather retiring and genteel. Sidmouth has the broadest all-round appeal: it's slightly busier, with a good deal of character as well as plenty for families. The prettiest coastal village is Branscombe.

Inland, coastal downs give a gently varied landscape of charming wooded valleys with views and high pastures between, and several attractive villages. N of the A30/A35 is more self-contained farmland, mainly well hedged traditional stock and dairy farms.

Exeter is well worth a visit or short stay: served by fast trains and the M5, it can be reached quickly from far away, and has unexpected highlights such as the Bill Douglas film centre, and underground medieval passages. Good roads bring other parts of Devon within comfortable reach for a day out.

Many of the family attractions we mention have a nice mix of activities for children. Crealy Adventure Park (rides and play areas as well as animals), the World of Country Life in Exmouth (from steam engines to safari rides through llama paddocks), and Farway Countryside Park (a good combination of animals and play areas) all cater well for families with varied tastes. The Pecorama Pleasure Gardens at Beer are especially good if you like railways, and Escot Aquatic Gardens at Ottery St Mary are worth a visit if you're passing; garden lovers should also head for East Budleigh and Killerton.

EXETER SX9292 **Edwardian Hotel** *30–32 Heavitree Rd, Exeter, Devon EX1 2LQ* (01392) 276102 **£56**, plus special breaks; 12 individually furnished rms, 4 with four-posters. Popular guest house close to cathedral and city centre, with pretty lounge, enjoyable breakfasts in attractive dining rooms, and warmly friendly and knowledgeable resident owners; plenty of places nearby for evening meals; cl 25–26 Dec; dogs welcome in bedrooms

EXETER SX9292 **Hotel Barcelona** *Magdalen Street, Exeter, Devon EX2 4HY* (01392) 281000 **£106**; 46 beautifully furnished rms with CD-player and video, and lovely bthrms. Stylishly modern, converted Victorian eye hospital filled with bright posters and paintings, a bar with 1950s-style furniture and fashionable cocktails, a smart but informal no smoking restaurant overlooking the big walled garden, with a wood-burning grill and wood-burning pizza oven plus other good-value contemporary choices, a nightclub showing 1950s films noir, and very helpful staff; disabled access; dogs welcome in bedrooms

EXETER SX9192 **St Olaves Court** *Mary Arches St, Exeter, Devon EX4 3AZ* (01392) 217736 **£123**w, plus special breaks; 14 lovely rms. Handsome Georgian-style house just 400 yds from the cathedral in its own walled garden, with a warm welcome from helpful friendly staff, comfortable rooms, enjoyable evening meals in candlelit restaurant, and good breakfasts; dogs welcome away from restaurant

GITTISHAM SY1497 **Combe House** *Gittisham, Honiton, Devon EX14 0AD* (01404) 540400 **£138**; plus winter breaks; 15 individually decorated pretty rms with lovely views. Peaceful Elizabethan country hotel in gardens with 700-year-old cedar of Lebanon, and walks around the 3,000-acre estate; elegant day rooms with antiques, pictures and fresh flowers, a happy relaxed atmosphere, very good food using some home-grown produce, and fine wines (the cellar is popular for wine tastings); can use the house for special occasions and meetings; dogs welcome in bedrooms

MEMBURY ST2703 **Lea Hill** *Membury, Axminster, Devon EX13 7AQ* (01404) 881881 **£70**; 4 individually furnished rms. Thatched, no smoking 14th-c longhouse in 8 acres of secluded grounds inc their own par 3, 9-hole golf course, and lovely views; comfortable beamed rooms with inglenook fireplaces, a convivial bar, relaxed and friendly owners, and nice breakfasts, morning coffee, and afternoon tea; self-catering, too; no children; dogs welcome in bedrooms

SIDFORD SY1489 **Blue Ball** *Sidford, Sidmouth, Devon EX10 9QL* (01395) 514062 **£70**; 6 rms, most with own bthrm, and with nice touches like free papers, fruit and fresh flowers. Welcoming thatched 14th-c inn run by the same family since 1912, with lovely winter log fire in low partly panelled lounge bar, heavy beams, lots of bric-a-brac, no smoking snug, very friendly service, and decent food inc hearty breakfasts

STOCKLAND ST2404 **Kings Arms** *Stockland, Honiton, Devon EX14 9BS* (01404) 881361 **£50**; 3 rms. Cream-faced thatched pub with elegant rooms, open fires, first-class food in bar and evening restaurant food (esp fish), and interesting wine list; skittle alley, live music Sat, Sun pm; cl 25 Dec; dogs welcome

WHIMPLE SY0497 **Woodhayes Country House Hotel** *Whimple, Exeter, Devon EX5 2TD* (01404) 822237 **£90**; 8 lovely spacious rms. Big Georgian country house in neat grounds, with comfortable quietly decorated lounges, open fires, flagstoned bar and pretty dining room, fine food, afternoon teas, and excellent breakfasts; croquet; cl 2 wks over Christmas and New Year

---

Please let us know what you think of places in the *Guide*. Use the report forms at the back of the book, write us a letter or log on to www.goodguides.com

To see and do

BEER SY2289

Rather cottagey resort village, still with fishing boats pulled up on the shingle beach (summer boat hire, too; (01297) 21998), a stream channelled down the main street, and good local fish in the nice old Dolphin. The village was famous from Roman times for its cavernous whitestone quarries, which can be visited, and the B3174 inland

passes lots of Bronze Age burial mounds. Fascinating coast path W to Branscombe Mouth, through the tumbled chalky mass of Hooken Undercliff.

Pecorama Pleasure Gardens 🔳

Fun for railway lovers, with models and train collections in the exhibition, and outside a miniature steam and diesel passenger line with stunning views of

East Devon

Stockland
Chardstock
Tytherleigh
Membury
Dalwood

A303
A30
A358
A35

DORSET

SY

A3052

Seaton ● Axmouth
Beer ●
● Dowland Cliffs

0 Miles   5

0 Kilometres   8

a lovely seaside valley. Branscombe, lying just inland, is linked to the coast path by other paths, and has the good Masons Arms in the main part of the village, as well as the NT Old Bakery tearoom opp the unique NT thatched smithy.

BROADCLYST SX9897
Pretty thatch-and-cob village, with a marvellous old church, picturesque outside, interesting in; the Red Lion beside it is owned by the NT.

CLYST ST MARY SY0090
Crealy Adventure Park (Sidmouth Rd) There's plenty to amuse children of all ages at this bustling family complex. The Magical Kingdom, a delightfully constructed area aimed mostly at under-7s, has play areas and a soaring gondola swing, while among the attractions to occupy older children are bumper boats, go-karts and a farm where you can milk the cows, and meet baby animals. Many of the attractions are indoors, inc some of the animals, and a very good varied adventure playground, with plenty of slides and things to swing on. There's also a family roller-coaster, new carousel and play ship, toddlers' garden play area, multicolour meadow, splash zone, pony rides and lakeside walks (they've recently planted an arboretum), and they have a wide range of special events and activities (usually on summer Suns). Meals, snacks, shop, disabled access; (01395) 233200; cl Mon and Tues during term-time Nov–Feb, 24–26 Dec and 1 Jan; £7.75; several family tickets available. If you don't want to eat in the park, the Half Moon is good value.

CULLOMPTON ST0207
The church is notable for its remarkable painted screen; the busy little town is appealing, and the farmers' market (Station Rd, 2nd Sat each month) was the prototype for the hundreds which now exist. The Merry Harriers at Westcott (B3181 S) has enjoyable food.

CULMSTOCK ST1013
The village has a handsome **church**, enjoyable food in the ancient waterside Culm Valley pub, and a pleasant riverside walk to Uffculme.

DALWOOD SY2499
Burrow Farm Gardens ▣ (half a mile or so off A35; turn off at Taunton

the bay. Also crazy golf, aviary, wooden maze and assault course, a multi-themed garden, and live entertainment. Meals, snacks, shop, mostly disabled access; cl Sat pm, Sun (exc Jun–Aug), and outdoor features cl Oct–Easter (exc Oct half-term); (01297) 21542; £4.75.

BRANSCOMBE SY1988
The **church** has a magnificently carved oak gallery, and a Norman tower with distinctive stair-turret. The village is notably pretty – a series of largely unspoilt thatched hamlets strung along

Cross sign) Part of this 7-acre site has been created from an ancient Roman clay pit, and there are spacious lawns, borders and unusual shrubs and trees, as well as a woodland garden, pergola walk with old-fashioned roses, and super views; also a rill garden, and a wildlife lake. Cream teas, snacks, nursery, disabled access; cl Oct–Mar; (01404) 831285; £3.50. The pretty Tuckers Arms is good for lunch.

DOWLAND CLIFFS SY2889
The steeply tumbled brambly wooded wilderness of this undercliff 3m E of Axmouth has numerous small birds.

EAST BUDLEIGH SY0684
Attractive and quietly placed cob and thatch village; the pleasant **church** has fascinating Jacobean carved pew ends – some grotesque, some hilarious, some frankly rude. The Sir Walter Raleigh has decent food.

Bicton College The gardens here are of great if rather specialised appeal; long monkey-puzzle avenue through parkland, rich collection of magnolias, camellias and flowering cherries, national pittosporum and agapanthus collections, and 17-acre arboretum with woodland garden. Snacks, plant centre; cl wknds Nov–Mar, 25 Dec and Good Fri; (01395) 568353; £2.50.

Bicton Park 63 acres of lovely gardens, shrubs, lakes and woodland. A futuristic-looking glass Palm House turns out to be early 19th c, and has a fine collection of tropical trees and plants; also fuchsia, geranium and orchid houses, bird garden, pinetum, magnificent Italian gardens, miniature train rides and nature trails. They've recently added a miniature golf course and extended the children's play area, and in 2003, you'll also be able to see a new film on the gardens. Meals, snacks, shop and plant centre, disabled access; cl 25 Dec; (01395) 568465; £4.75.

EXETER SX9292
Though large parts of the centre were devastated by World War II bombing, some choice streets and buildings survive, with picturesque partly Tudor narrow lanes leading from the mainly pedestrianised High St into the serene tree-shaded cathedral close. In the centre, modern shops are integrated into the old layout very discreetly. With many smaller churches, decent book and other shops, pubs and so forth nearby, this is a very pleasant part for browsing around, and there's a pleasantly easy-going atmosphere. Particularly attractive streets include Southernhay at the end of the close, and Stepcote Hill, a picturesque detour from Fore St. The Quay, beyond the streams of fast traffic on the ring road (there are quiet underpasses), has become lively and entertaining, with handsomely restored buildings, resurgent cafés and pubs (the Prospect and Port Royal are worth knowing), and craft shops and the like; the Old Quay House has a visitor centre with audio-visual show; (01392) 265213. Civilised pubs and wine bars with decent food include the sumptuous Imperial (New North Rd), Ship (14th c, Martins Lane) and Well House (The Close – cathedral view and Roman well). There are **boat trips** down the ship canal to Turf Locks; or you can walk down, passing the Double Locks (a favourite pub) and ending at the Turf Hotel looking out over the estuary. A range of daily free guided tours leave the Royal Clarence Hotel (Cathedral Cl) throughout the day (phone (01392) 265203 for details, or pick up a programme from the Tourist Information Centre, Paris St); there are good cycle paths into the countryside. The quickest way into the city from either the M5 or the A38 is to keep on round to the westbound A30 and go into the city from the Alphington roundabout. As part of the jubilee celebrations, Exeter is now one of 29 cities with a Lord Mayor, and by the end of 2003 the new HQ for the Meteorological Office will have been built on the outskirts; there's a thriving university.

Bill Douglas Centre (Old Library, Exeter University, Prince of Wales Rd) Display of almost 1,000 cinema-related objects amassed by the late film-maker Bill Douglas; includes film-star dolls, 19th-c optical toys, and oriental shadow puppets. Disabled access; cl all wknds and bank hols, 1–2 Jan, and a week over Easter; (01392) 264321; free (guided tours £2).

Exeter Cathedral England's finest example of Decorated Gothic architecture, with its magnificent nave soaring to the vaulted roof, and intricately carved choir stalls; the 13th-c misericords are thought to be the oldest in the country. It also boasts the longest unbroken Gothic vaulting in Europe, superbly atmospheric. Lots of colourfully embroidered cushions, chronologically illustrating english and local history. The façade has three tiers of sculpted figures, inc the Apostles. Meals, snacks, shop, disabled access; guided tours 11am and 2.30 (plus 12.30 July–Aug) wkdys, 11 Sat, 4 Sun Apr–Oct, or by appointment; £3 suggested donation.

Guildhall (High St) This medieval municipal building with its ornately colonnaded Elizabethan façade is one of the oldest still in use; it has displays of civic regalia and so on. Disabled access to ground floor only; cl 1–2pm, Sat pm (and all day Sats in winter), all day Sun and bank hols, during civic functions and over Christmas; (01392) 265700; free.

Royal Albert Memorial Museum (Queen St) Wonderful Gothic exterior, notable displays inside of regional silver, African carvings, archaeology, paintings, natural history and ethnology: three galleries include touch-screen computer displays and intriguing exhibits such as materials collected during Captain Cook's voyages. Snacks, shop, disabled access; cl Sun and bank hols; (01392) 665858; free.

St Nicholas's Priory (Mint Lane) 11th-c Benedictine monastery with unusual Norman undercroft, Tudor room and 15th-c kitchen. Shop, disabled access to ground floor only; open 2–4.30pm Mon, Weds and Sat Easter–Oct, occasionally cl for private functions; (01392) 665858; free.

Underground Passages 🔢 (entrance via Boots Arcade in High St) An unusual medieval attraction is this atmospheric network, built in the 14th c to bring water into the city; there's an introductory exhibition and video, then a guided tour of the passages themselves, still much as they were centuries ago. The guides can be very entertaining, and clearly enjoy their work. Flat shoes are recommended. Shop; cl 1–2pm (exc school hols), Sun Jun–Sept, plus Mon

Oct–May; (01392) 665887; £3 (£3.75 in summer).

EXMOUTH SY0080
Good family seaside holiday town, worth a visit for its lively harbour and marina, its long sandy beach, and its stately church. Summer cruise trips go from the harbour up to Topsham, (01395) 222144 for details; there are sea fishing trips from the landing stage (they supply rod and bait); (01395) 275882. The Seafood Restaurant (Tower St) has nothing but the freshest fish and shellfish; the Grove (attractive seafront garden and play area) is good value too.

A la Ronde (A376 2m N) Extraordinary 16-sided house, built around 1795 and decorated in part with feathers, seashells, seaweed and sand. A charmingly whimsical place, the outside looking not entirely unlike a giant biscuit barrel. Meals, snacks, shop, disabled access to ground floor only; cl Fri, Sat, and all Nov–Mar; (01395) 265514; *£3.80; NT.

Great Exmouth Model Railway (Sea Front) Home to the world's biggest 00 gauge model railway, nearly 1½ miles of track indoors. It took 14 years to build and is constantly updated – they're currently building a zoo; some of the detail is amazing, right down to the birds in the trees. Shop, some disabled access; cl mid-Sept–Easter; (01395) 278383; £2.

High Land of Orcombe Reached by the shore road E out of Exmouth and protected against campsite encroachment by its National Trust ownership, this gives walkers a short stroll with sea views.

World of Country Life (Sandy Bay) 40 acres of enjoyable family-based activities, with friendly animals (you can feed some of them, and there are usually babies to see), adventure playground and under-cover play areas, safari rides through deer and llama paddocks, and there's an owl centre; also reconstructed Victorian street, classic motorcycle collection, steam engines, crazy golf and quad bikes. Meals, snacks, shop, disabled access; cl Nov–Easter; (01395) 274533; £6.

FARWAY SY1896
Farway Countryside Park 🔢 (off

A3052 W of Colyford) Prettily set over 100 acres, this bustling place is home to a real jumble of animals. Children can feed calves and lambs twice a day, and other baby animals to pet include rabbits, chicks and guinea-pigs. Elsewhere you'll find more unusual creatures like pot-bellied pigs, as well as indoor and outdoor play areas, pony rides and a 9-hole pitch and putt course. Meals, snacks, shop, disabled access; open daily Apr–Oct, plus wknds and school hols in winter (exc 24–26 Dec and 1 Jan); (01404) 871367; £4.25, extra charge for golf and rides.

HEMBURY HILL FORT ST1103
A walk up from the A373 NW of Honiton, for good views.

HONITON ST1600
Some handsome Georgian buildings along this country town's long High St, and some interesting shops. The Red Cow is good value for lunch. Fine views from the A375 S.

Allhallows Museum 🆑 (High St) This refurbished 13th-c building has displays of Honiton lace, and lace-making demonstrations Jun–Aug. Shop; cl pm Sat, all Sun, and Nov–Mon before Easter; (01404) 44966; £2 (£3 Aug–Sept).

KILLERTON SS9700
Killerton House Best of all in spring, 15 acres of beautiful hillside gardens, shrub borders and planted beds, with an impressive avenue of beech trees. The 18th-c house has an annually changing costume exhibition in period furnished rooms, but it's the gardens that really give the place its special appeal. Meals, snacks, shop and plant centre, good disabled access (with buggies round the grounds); house cl Tues (exc Aug), plus Mon in Oct and 3 Nov–12 Apr (garden open daily); (01392) 881345; £5.40, £3.90 garden only; NT. The Three Tuns in Silverton has well prepared food, esp vegetarian, and there's a rewarding antiques centre at nearby Hele (towards Bradninch).

OTTERTON SY0785
Otterton Mill Centre 🆑 Working watermill still grinding flour for the bread, cakes and pies sold on the premises. Also craft workshops, display of local lace, and interesting evening events. Enjoyable meals and snacks,

shop, garden centre, some disabled access; cl 3 days over Christmas; (01395) 568521; £2 (free entry to wheelchair users). The village is pretty.

OTTERY ST MARY SY1095
Restrained small town – or extended village – with some attractive old buildings around its interesting twin-towered church. The circular **tumbling weir** by an 18th-c mill signed off Mill St is unusual, and photogenic. The London Inn is useful, and the Otter Nurseries (Gosford Rd) have good plants.

Cadhay (just NW) Beautiful Tudor and Georgian manor house, with fine timbered 15th-c roof in its Great Hall, and unusual Court of Sovereigns – a pretty courtyard with statues of various monarchs. Disabled access to garden and downstairs; open pm Tues–Thurs July–Aug, plus Sun and Mon spring and Aug bank hol; (01404) 812432; *£4.50.

Escot Aquatic Centre & Gardens 🆑 (Parklands Farm, Escot; off A30) Tropical and coldwater fish from koi carp to piranhas, as well as rabbits and other pets, otters (fed at 11am and 3pm), Victorian walled rose garden, wild boar enclosures, walks, views and parkland. Also wetlands and waterfowl park, birds of prey, play area and pet centre with all you'll need for any kind of pet, as well as the animals themselves. Meals, snacks, shop, some disabled access; cl Nov–Easter; (01404) 822188; £3.95.

SEATON SY2589
Pleasantly restrained family resort, with quite a long beach, the amusements you'd expect, and an attractive setting, with cliffs on either side – see Dowlands Cliffs for the interesting landslips to the E. Open-top trams run up the Axe valley to Colyton, where the Kingfisher is a good pub; back in town, the Fishermans (Marine Crescent) has decent cheap food all day. On the other bank of the river, Axmouth has pretty cottages, a Norman church, and near it the Ship, a nice pub doubling as an owl rescue centre.

SIDBURY SY1391
A pretty village, with a charming **church**; the Hare & Hounds (3m N, A375/B3174) has enjoyable food all day.

SIDMOUTH SY1287

Attractive old streets, very 18th c, running back from the seafront, and grander Regency buildings facing the sea. It was a fashionable upper-class resort in the early 19th c, and many of the town's buildings show undoubted architectural verve – there's very little seaside tat. The pebbly beach has fishing boats pulled up on it, and the town is protected by warm red sandstone cliffs; it stretches back along the river valley, though away from the sea the buildings are less interesting. The partly 14th-c Old Ship is the best pub here, and Sue's Pantry (High St) has tasty cakes and pastries. The dedicated **Donkey Sanctuary** is a useful free attraction for families, with an incredible number of donkeys; (01395) 578222; meals, snacks, shop, disabled access. The **Heritage Centre** (in a fine Regency house on Church St, cl am Mon and Sun and all Nov–Easter; £1) organises summer walking tours round the town, Tues and Thurs at 10.15 am.

Cliff walks The long stretch of red sandstone cliff between Sidmouth and Branscombe can be reached from either place (or, steeply but very prettily, from Salcombe Regis).

SILVERTON SS9502
An attractive village, with a particularly handsome **church**. The friendly old Three Tuns is good for lunch.

TOPSHAM SX9688
Old-world seaside village, good for a quiet potter. Its buildings show its past importance as a port – as do its large number of good pubs and inns. The Passage House is currently the best for food, and readers like the fresh fish at the Galley restaurant.

Topsham Museum (the Strand) This friendly little museum is crammed full of local and maritime history, and, more unexpectedly, has some Vivian Leigh memorabilia, and an exhibition on Thomas Hardy's cousin; also model and full-sized boats, period room re-creations and touch-screen computers. Good tearoom (the riverside garden is a nice place to enjoy one of their popular cream teas), disabled access; open pm wknds, Mon and Weds Apr–Oct; (01392) 873244; free.

UFFCULME ST0612
A large pleasant village above the Culm

River, with a magnificent carved screen in the attractive **church**. The B3397 to Culmstock and then the turn to Hemyock is a pretty drive; beyond at Clayhidon the Merry Harriers has good food, by a footpath to the Blackdown Hills visitor centre; (01823) 680280.

Coldharbour Mill Working Museum ⌨ You can watch every stage in the production of wool at this well restored 18th-c mill building (it was operated as a woollen factory by the same family for almost 200 years and is now run by enthusiastic volunteers). The 80-metre (264-ft) New World Tapestry, the biggest stitched embroidery in the world, is also here – it took 25 years of stitching to complete. Meals, snacks, shop, limited disabled access; cl 24 Dec–Feb; (01884) 840960; £5.50.

WILLAND ST0309
Diggerland ⌨ (B3181 N of Cullompton) The third and most recent of these unusual adventure parks. Under close supervision, children from 5 upwards can operate and drive real excavation equipment inc JCB diggers, dumpers and a fork-lift truck. Rides or drives last around five minutes, and children complete various challenges such as fishing a duck from a pond or knocking down skittles. Also pedal-power diggers, computer games and a video, bouncy castle, and a play area for under-6s. Meals, snacks, shop, disabled access. Cl wkdys in school term-time (exc bank hol Mon) and 25 Dec; (08700) 344437; £2.50 entrance fee, from £1.50 per ride or drive.

WOODBURY SY0387
Lonely heathland, fine views (off B3180 E) Miles of heath with some pinewoods, a place to get away from people even in high summer (red flags warn if there's firing on one section which is a shooting range). From the highest points, nr the road, there are far views along the coast and to Dartmoor. The wooded **hill fort** right by the road is worth a look, and it's a bit eerie tracing the ramparts through the beech trees. The village of Woodbury itself is attractive, and by the church the White Hart has good value food.

Other attractive villages, all with decent pubs, include seaside Axmouth

SY2591, Broadhembury ST1004, Butterleigh SS9708, Chardstock ST3004, Lympstone SX9984, Otterton SY0684, Salcombe Regis SY1488, Tytherleigh ST3103 and Upottery ST2007.

Where to eat

BRANSCOMBE SY1988 **Masons Arms** *(01297) 680300* Popular, well run inn with no smoking bar, two-sided woodburner, stripped original pine woodwork, low beams in main bar with massive central hearth, no smoking restaurant, particularly enjoyable imaginative food, well kept real ales inc summer beer festival, 14 wines by the glass, and outside tables under little thatched roofs; good bdrms, some with four-posters; self-catering cottages; disabled access. £29.50|**£8.95**

BROADHEMBURY ST1004 **Drewe Arms** *(01404) 841267* Excellent fresh fish in charming 15th-c pub with carved beams and handsome stone-mullioned windows in the bar, several other interesting rooms, lovely puddings, fine wines, well kept beers, and charming garden in attractive village (church worth a visit, nearby craft centre); cl Sun pm, 31 Dec; disabled access. £32|**£8.50**

CLAYHIDON ST1716 **Merry Harriers** *(01823) 421470* Warmly welcoming and charmingly laid out dining pub with comfortably cushioned pews and farmhouse chairs in several small linked areas, plenty of horsey and hunting prints and local wildlife pictures, lit candles in bottles, and a couple of warm woodburning stoves; good restaurany food using local venison, lamb, and duck, organic chicken, fresh fish from Brixham, and local cheeses and cream, ten enjoyable wines by the glass, well kept real ales, two pub dogs, and picnic-sets on a small terrace, with more in a sizeable garden; good walking area. £22|**£6.50**

CLYST HYDON ST0300 **Five Bells** *(01884) 277288* Charming spotless thatched pub, with long bar divided by standing timbers, lots of plates on shelves, sparkling brass and copper, fresh flowers and candles in bottles, very good popular food, warmly friendly service, and lovely cottagey gardens; cl pms 25-26 Dec; children in bar only (not in pretty evening restaurant). £35|**£8.95**

DALWOOD ST2400 **Tuckers Arms** *(01404) 881342* Delightful thatched medieval longhouse with fine flagstoned bar, lots of beams, log fire in inglenook, woodburner, a good mix of dining chairs, window seats and wall settles, huge collection of miniature bottles, well prepared enterprising bar food and lots of colourful hanging baskets; bdrms; no children; disabled access. £25|**£7.25**

EXETER SX9292 **Brazz** *10–12 Palace Gate (01392) 252525* Stylish, buzzy brasserie with elegant modern décor (inc interesting two-tier fish tank), enjoyable contemporary all-day food plus imaginative extras and rich puddings, a good range of drinks, friendly service, and a decent wine list; they are kind to children; cl 25 Dec; disabled access. £25|**£6.95**

EXETER SX9390 **Double Locks** *Canal Banks (01392) 56947* Friendly and very relaxed lock-side country pub, popular with students, with good simple bar food (all day), summer barbecues, and up to ten real ales; disabled access. £18|**£5.45**

EXETER SX9292 **Michael Caines at Royal Clarence** *Cathedral Yard (01392) 310032* Opposite the cathedral, this smart, no smoking and colourful restaurant in a historic hotel has a friendly relaxed atmosphere, helpful service, enjoyable artistically presented food inc good puddings, and a thoughtful wine list; there's also a stylish, airy café-bar; disabled access. £26.75/2-course lunch £16.50

TOPSHAM SX9688 **Georgian Tea Room** *35 High St (01392) 873465* 18th-c house with pretty embroidered tablecloths and fresh flowers, and good food all day – breakfasts, morning coffee, snacks, lunchtime meals inc a popular roast on Tues, Thurs and Sun, cream teas with home-made cakes and cookies, and a wide range of teas and coffees with home-made lemonade; no smoking bdrms; cl Weds, Christmas wk; partial disabled access|**£5.20**

South Devon & Dartmoor

**Lovely coastline from desolate beaches to the bustle of the
Torbay riviera, Dartmoor, charming villages, plenty of
family attractions, and beautiful places to stay in**

Dartmoor is a splendid brooding wilderness, with complete walking
freedom in most parts (you're not confined to footpaths), and all sorts of
points of interest – especially its tors (weirdly shaped rock excrescences)
and visible prehistoric remains. The National Park Authority website is
useful (www.dartmoor-npa.gov.uk) for information about guided walks,
transport and so forth; or you can phone (01822) 890414. Around its
edges, and delightful to explore, are intimate and picturesque valleys and
villages. There's a similar intimate appeal in the small coves, stretches of
cliff, sheltered boating creeks and estuaries cut deeply into the hills of the
S and W coast. Here, relaxed and welcoming small towns such as
Dartmouth and Totnes have plenty to see and do. Some of England's best
and cleanest beaches such as Slapton Sands are to be found here. A walk
along Lydford Gorge takes in some dramatic scenery.

Torbay and its English Riviera offer a complete contrast: spacious
promenades, low cliffs, bright gardens and palm trees. From tours of
ancient caves (the ones in the evening are the most atmospheric) to a re-
created Victorian street, Torquay itself has much to offer families besides
its sandy beaches; watch out for the new Living Coasts attraction due to
open in the summer.

The National Marine Aquarium, our Devon Family Attraction this year,
tops a great list of things to do in Plymouth. The recently reopened
Plymouth Dome (the city's past presented in a way that children enjoy),
the new Mayflower Centre (a very up-to-date introduction to Plymouth)
and Crownhill Fort (lots to explore – especially good when the weather's
fine) are just some of the others.

Families are spoilt for choice elsewhere too. The rides and animals at
Blackawton's Woodland Leisure Park, and the industrial re-creations at
Morwellham Quay, easily fill a pleasurable day. Excellent wildlife
attractions include pretty Paignton Zoo, and the bustling animal centre at
Buckfastleigh; young children love the miniature horses at
Moretonhampstead. There's plenty of scope for combining several
activities, say, catching a steam train to the enjoyable Butterfly Park &
Dartmoor Otter Sanctuary at Buckfastleigh, or swapping steam trains for
river boats between Dartmouth and Totnes.

Buckland Abbey will be more family-friendly in 2003, with a new
interactive room for children. Other splendid houses are Saltram at
Plympton, and the fine modern impostor Drogo at Drewsteignton;
Compton at Marldon is picturesque, while Okehampton is the county's
largest medieval castle. Popular Buckfast Abbey has the added attraction
of a good shop. For many, the gardens in Salcombe and Kingswear are

South Devon & Dartmoor

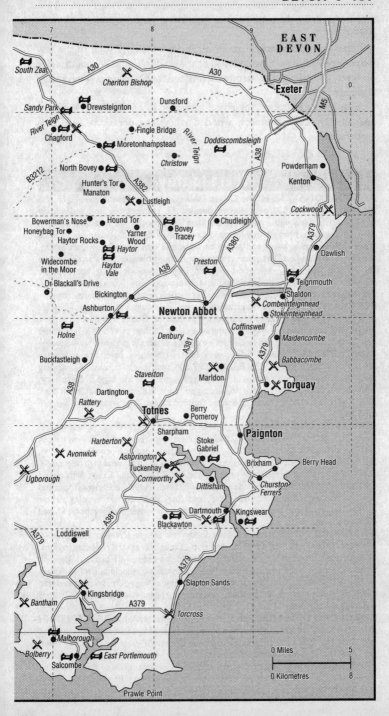

more of a draw than the houses; interesting gardens, too, at Newton Abbot.

Treats for adults include tours of Tuckers Maltings (one of the few working malthouses in the country) or the gin distillery in Plymouth; cider drinkers will prefer the farm at Dunsford, and there's a vineyard at Sharpham.

Away from Dartmoor, the inland landscape is made up largely of well hedged hilly pastures, steeply wooded valleys and occasional vivid red-earth fields.

Where to stay

ASHBURTON SX7270 **Holne Chase** *Ashburton, Newton Abbot, Devon TQ13 7NS* *(01364) 631471* **£150**, plus winter breaks; 17 comfortable and individually furnished rms, many with views over the Dart Valley, and some split-level suites in converted stables. Marvellously peaceful ex-hunting lodge of Buckfast Abbey in 70 acres with sweeping lawns and plenty of woodland walks, a mile of Dart fishing, shooting and riding on Dartmoor; cheerful welcoming owners, comfortable public rooms with log fires, very good modern English cooking using home-grown vegetables, and enjoyable breakfasts and afternoon teas (home-made breads, marmalades and so forth); children over 12 in evening restaurant; dogs welcome

BLACKAWTON SX8050 **Normandy Arms** *Blackawton, Totnes, Devon TQ9 7BN* *(01803) 712316* **£58***, plus special breaks; 4 pretty rms. Quaint friendly pub in quiet village, with cosy main bar, log fire, some interesting displays of World War II battle gear, generous food in bar and restaurant, real ales, and seats in garden; dogs welcome

BOVEY TRACEY SX8078 **Edgemoor Hotel** *Haytor Rd, Bovey Tracey, Newton Abbot, Devon TQ13 9LE (01626) 832466* **£99.50***, plus special breaks; 16 charming rms. Ivy-covered country house in neatly kept gardens on the edge of Dartmoor, with comfortable lounge and bar, log fires, good food in elegant restaurant; cl 1 wk after Christmas; children over 10; limited disabled access; dogs welcome away from food areas

BURGH ISLAND SX6443 **Burgh Island Hotel** *Burgh Island, Bigbury-on-Sea, Devon TQ7 4AU (01548) 810514* **£250** inc dinner; 19 suites all with sea views, most with balconies. Art Deco hotel (and 14th-c smugglers' pub) on private tidal island, reached by foot or hotel 4WD vehicles at low tide, by sea tractor at high tide; public rooms and suites all furnished in period style: 20s domed Palm Court with classic cocktail bar, glamorous 30s Ballroom, and sunny black and white Ganges Room and Terrace for enjoyable meals using the best local produce; Sat evening dinner dances; tennis court, snooker and table tennis, sea-water bathing pool; cl Jan; disabled access.

CHAGFORD SX7189 **Easton Court** *Sandy Park, Chagford, Newton Abbot, Devon TQ13 8JN (01647) 433469* **£140** inc dinner, plus special breaks; 8 redecorated rms. Creeper-clad, thatched and newly refurbished 15th-c house with beams, inglenook fireplace, granite walls, and big library (literary connections include Evelyn Waugh writing *Brideshead Revisited* here), cosy bar, charming sitting room, good breakfasts, delicious evening meals in candlelit restaurant; cl Jan; children over 12; dogs welcome in bedrooms

CHAGFORD SX7087 **Gidleigh Park** *Chagford, Newton Abbot, Devon TQ13 8HH (01647) 432367* **£410** inc dinner, plus winter breaks; 15 opulent and individual rms with fruit and flowers. Exceptional luxurious Dartmoor-edge mock Tudor hotel with deeply comfortable panelled drawing room, wonderful flowers, conservatory overlooking the fine grounds (40 acres, with walks straight up on to the moor), log fires, particularly fine cooking and a fine wine list, and caring staff; children over 7 in restaurant; dogs welcome in bedrooms

CHILLATON SX4381 **Tor Cottage** *Chillaton, Lifton, Devon PL16 0JE (01822) 860248* £130, plus special breaks; 4 carefully furnished rms, 1 in main house with own sitting rm, 3 garden rms with own log fire and private garden or terrace. Peaceful no smoking house in 18 acres of own valley with lots of wildlife, lovely gardens, enjoyable breakfasts in conservatory dining room or on terrace, a relaxed atmosphere, and outdoor heated swimming pool; restaurant booking service; no children; partial disabled access

DARTMOUTH SX8751 **Ford House** *44 Victoria Rd, Dartmouth, Devon TQ6 9DX (01803) 834047* £85, plus special breaks; 4 individually decorated rms. Nr the harbour, this Regency town house has a log fire in the comfortable drawing room, antiques, good interesting food using fresh local produce eaten around a big table, delicious breakfasts, helpful service, and sheltered garden; you can take over the whole house for a wknd party; cl Nov–Mar; dogs welcome

DARTMOUTH SX8850 **Gunfield Hotel** *Castle Road, Dartmouth, Devon TQ6 0JN (01803) 834571* £95; 10 rms with views of the river. In waterside gardens overlooking the estuary, this informal and friendly hotel has a convivial bar, cheerful staff, an attractive airy dining room serving enjoyable food, and an outside decked eating area overlooking the water; water taxi into Dartmouth, and their own motor-boats; dogs in bedrooms and on lead in bar

DARTMOUTH SX8751 **Royal Castle** *11 The Quay, Dartmouth, Devon TQ6 9PS (01803) 833033* £119.90, plus special breaks; 25 individually furnished rms. Well restored mainly Georgian hotel (part 16th c) overlooking the inner harbour – great views from most rooms; lively and interesting public bar with open fires and beams, quiet library/lounge with antiques, drawing room overlooking the quayside, winter spit-roasts in lounge bar, elegant upstairs seafood restaurant, decent bar food, and friendly staff; dogs welcome in bedrooms

DODDISCOMBSLEIGH SX8586 **Nobody Inn** *Doddiscombsleigh, Exeter, Devon EX6 7PS (01647) 252394* £70*; 7 rms, some in a Georgian manor house 150 yds down the road, and most with own bthrm. Friendly 16th-c pub with beams, heavy wooden furniture, and inglenook fireplace in the attractively furnished two-roomed lounge bar, an outstanding cellar running to 800 (fairly priced) wines and 250 malts, and popular food in bar and restaurant inc huge range of Devon cheeses; good views from garden, and the church is worth visiting for fine stained glass; cl 25–26 Dec; no children; dogs welcome

DREWSTEIGNTON SX7192 **Silkhouse** *Drewsteignton, Exeter, Devon EX6 6RF (01647) 231267* £60; 2 rms. Quietly set, rambling 16th-c longhouse named by the Huguenots who wove silk here; low beams, fine paintings, antiques and richly coloured fabrics and paintwork, a relaxed atmosphere, imaginative food in low-ceilinged dining room, and a really lovely garden with ponds and streams, lots of wildlife, and all-weather tennis court; horses welcome; no children; dogs welcome

EAST PORTLEMOUTH SX7537 **Gara Rock** *East Portlemouth, Salcombe, Devon TQ8 8PH (01548) 842342* £140 inc dinner; 17 rms, some can convert to family suites, and 20 self-catering apartments. Originally a coastguard station and look-out, with its own beach at the foot of the cliffs; marvellous for families with daily clubs and rooms for every age, baby-listening and sitting, acres of grassy garden with heated outdoor swimming pool and paddling pool, tennis, an adventure playground with wooden boat, various pets, lots of entertainments, children's menus, early suppers, and so forth; enjoyable food all day inc barbecues, helpful friendly staff, and an informal and relaxed atmosphere; lots to do nearby (though so much in the hotel, you might not leave the grounds); cl Dec–Jan; disabled access ☺

HAYTOR SX7777 **Bel Alp House** *Haytor, Newton Abbot, Devon TQ13 9XX (01364) 661217* £120*, plus special breaks; 8 spacious rms. Handsome Edwardian country house with elegant drawing room, comfortable sitting room, log fires and lots of fresh flowers and plants, friendly atmosphere, and fine careful cooking in pretty restaurant; wonderful views and peaceful garden; cl 21 Dec–12 Jan; disabled access; dogs welcome in bedrooms

HAYTOR VALE SX7777 **Rock** Haytor Vale, Newton Abbot, Devon TQ13 9XP (01364) 661305 **£85.50***, plus special breaks; 9 individual rms. Civilised old coaching inn on the edge of Dartmoor National Park, with good food (inc fresh fish), a nice mix of visitors and locals in the two rooms of the panelled bar, open fires, no smoking restaurant, courteous service, and big garden; walking, fishing, riding and golf nearby; cl 25 Dec; dogs welcome in bedrooms

HEXWORTHY SX6572 **Forest Inn** Hexworthy, Princetown, Yelverton, Devon PL20 6SD (01364) 631211 **£59**; 10 cosy, comfortable rms. Country inn in fine Dartmoor setting, popular with walkers and anglers; varied menu in both bar and restaurant, local ales, good choice of wines, and welcoming staff; cl Jan; dogs welcome

HOLNE SX7170 **Wellpritton Farm** Holne, Ashburton, Devon TQ13 7RX (01364) 631273 **£45***, plus special breaks; 5 pretty rms. Small, recently refurbished friendly Dartmoor farm set in 15 acres with horses, goats and chickens and lovely views from terrace and garden; comfortable sitting room, good, completely home-made evening meals using local produce, and enjoyable breakfasts; children under 5 by arrangement; dogs welcome in bedrooms

KINGSTON SX6347 **Dolphin** Kingston, Kingsbridge, Devon TQ7 4QE (01548) 810314 **£55***; 3 rms. Peaceful 16th-c inn with several knocked-through beamed rooms, a warmly welcoming atmosphere, a small no smoking area, very good home-made food, and real ales; swings for children in extensive gardens, and tracks down to the sea

KINGSWEAR SX8850 **Nonsuch House** Church Hill, Kingswear, Dartmouth, Devon TQ6 0BX (01803) 752829 **£90***; 3 big, comfortable rms overlooking the river to Dartmouth. Two Edwardian villas in a lovely hillside spot, with open fires and books in elegant sitting room, an airy conservatory overlooking the lovely, carefully tended garden (the owners are serious gardeners), enjoyable food using the freshest local produce, nice breakfasts, and warmly welcoming owners; no smoking; children over 10

LEWDOWN SX4586 **Lewtrenchard Manor** Lewdown, Okehampton, Devon EX20 4PN (01566) 783256 **£175**, plus special breaks; 9 well equipped rms with fresh flowers and period furniture. Lovely Elizabethan manor house in garden with fine dovecot and surrounded by peaceful estate with shooting, fishing and croquet; dark panelling, ornate ceilings, antiques, fresh flowers, and log fires, a friendly welcome, relaxed atmosphere, and candlelit restaurant with very good imaginative food; children over 8; partial disabled access; dogs welcome in bedrooms

LIFTON SX3885 **Arundell Arms** Fore St, Lifton, Devon PL16 0AA (01566) 784666 **£120**, plus special breaks; 28 well equipped rms, 5 in annexe over the road. Carefully renovated old coaching inn with 20 miles of its own waters – salmon and trout fishing and a long-established fly-fishing school; comfortable sitting room, log fires, super food in both bar and elegant restaurant, carefully chosen wines, and kind service from local staff; new eating area in attractive terraced garden; cl 4 days over Christmas; dogs allowed away from restaurant and river bank

MALBOROUGH SX7039 **Soar Mill Cove Hotel** Malborough, Salcombe, Devon TQ7 3DS (01548) 561566 **£218**, plus special breaks; 21 comfortable rms, some opening on to garden. Neatly kept single-storey building in idyllic spot by peaceful and very beautiful cove on NT coast (excellent walks), with lovely views, extensive private grounds, tennis/putting, and warm indoor pool; outstanding service, log fires, very good food (marvellous fish), and they are particularly kind to children of all ages: microwave, fridge, and so forth for little ones, own high tea or smaller helpings of most meals, fully equipped laundry, a play room, table tennis and snooker, swings, and donkey and pony; by Feb, a new restaurant, lounge and coffee shop will have opened; cl Jan; disabled access; dogs welcome in bedrooms ☺

MORETONHAMPSTEAD SX7386 **Great Sloncombe Farm** Moretonhampstead, Newton Abbot, Devon TQ13 8QF (01647) 440595 **£48***; 3 rms – the big double is the favourite. Lovely 13th-c farmhouse on a working dairy and stock farm, with friendly owners, carefully polished old-fashioned furniture in oak-beamed lounge, decent food, hearty breakfasts, log fires, a relaxed atmosphere, and good nearby walking and bird-watching; no smoking; children over 8; dogs welcome in bedrooms

NORTH BOVEY SX7483 **Gate House** *North Bovey, Newton Abbot, Devon TQ13 8RB* (01647) 440479 **£60***, plus special breaks; 3 charming rms. 15th-c thatched cottage in picturesque village, with huge granite fireplace in attractive beamed sitting room, breakfasts and candlelit evening meals in beamed dining room, tea with home-made cakes, friendly owners, and outdoor swimming pool in peaceful garden; plenty to do nearby; no children; dogs welcome in bedrooms

PRESTON SX8773 **Sampsons Farm** *Preston, Newton Abbot, Devon TQ12 3PP* (01626) 54913 **£65***, plus special breaks; 12 lovely, individual rms in farmhouse and converted barn and stable block. Thatched 14th-c longhouse with beams, panelling and big open fires in cosy sitting rooms, a very relaxed welcoming atmosphere, most enjoyable food in two popular dining rooms, good breakfasts, and lots of nearby walks; watercolour workshops; children over 3; good disabled access; self-catering too

SALCOMBE SX7338 **Tides Reach** *Cliff Rd, South Sands, Salcombe, Devon TQ8 8LJ* (01548) 843466 **£142**, plus special breaks; 35 rms, many with estuary views. Unusually individual resort hotel run by long-serving owners in pretty wooded cove by the sea, with airy luxury day rooms, big sea aquarium in cocktail bar, good restaurant food using fresh local produce, friendly efficient service, and squash, snooker, leisure complex, health area, and big heated pool; windsurfing, etc., beach over lane, and lots of coast walks; cl Dec–Jan; children over 8; dogs welcome in bedrooms

SANDY PARK SX7189 **Mill End** *Sandy Park, Chagford, Newton Abbot, Devon TQ13 8JN* (01647) 432282 **£120***, plus special breaks; 15 attractive rms with fine bthrms and views. Quietly set former flour mill with waterwheel in neatly kept grounds below Dartmoor with 600 yards of private salmon and trout fishing, access to miles of game fishing and still-water fishing on local lakes; comfortably refurbished lounges, carefully prepared interesting food, fine breakfasts, and cream teas on the lawn, and good service; cl Jan; partial disabled access; dogs welcome in bedrooms

SOUTH ZEAL SX6593 **Oxenham Arms** *South Zeal, Okehampton, Devon EX20 2JT* (01837) 840244 **£60**, plus special breaks; 8 rms. Grandly atmospheric old inn dating back to 12th c and first licensed in 1477 (a neolithic standing stone still forms part of the wall in the TV room); elegant beamed and panelled bar with chatty relaxed atmosphere and open fire, a wide choice of enjoyable food and wines, and charming ex-monastery small garden; dogs welcome away from dining room

STAVERTON SX7964 **Sea Trout** *Staverton, Totnes, Devon TQ9 6PA* (01803) 762274 **£74**; 10 cottagey rms. Comfortable pub in quiet hamlet nr River Dart with two relaxed beamed bars, log fires, popular food in bar and airy dining conservatory, and terraced garden with fountains and waterfalls; cl Christmas; disabled access; dogs welcome away from restaurant

STOKE GABRIEL SX8457 **Gabriel Court** *Stoke Gabriel, Totnes, Devon TQ9 6SF* (01803) 782206 **£84**, plus special breaks; 19 rms, some in former hay lofts. In a walled Elizabethan garden, this attractive family-run manor has quiet relaxing lounges (winter log fire), enjoyable traditional English food, and courteous helpful staff; outdoor heated swimming pool and croquet lawn; dogs welcome away from dining room

TEIGNMOUTH SX9372 **Thomas Luny House** *Teign St, Teignmouth, Devon TQ14 8EG* (01626) 772976 **£80***, plus special breaks; 4 pretty rms with flowers and books. Lovely little no smoking Georgian house nr fish quay; open fires in spacious, comfortable drawing room and elegant dining room, a relaxed friendly atmosphere, enjoyable food (plus free afternoon tea with home-made cake), and sunny walled garden; children over 12

TWO BRIDGES SX6274 **Prince Hall** *Two Bridges, Yelverton, Devon PL20 6SA* (01822) 890403 **£105**, plus special breaks; 8 attractive spacious rms. Surrounded by Dartmoor National Park, this tranquil, recently refurbished 18th-c country house is run by caring friendly owners and their helpful staff; lovely views from convivial bar, comfortable sitting room, and cosy dining room, open fires, very good evening meals, enjoyable breakfasts, and lots of fine walks; cl mid-Dec to mid-Feb; children over 10; dogs welcome

To see and do

Devon Family Attraction of the Year

PLYMOUTH SX4854 **National Marine Aquarium** (The Barbican) We've always liked this enthralling, world-class aquarium, which goes from strength to strength – this year they opened a huge new walk-through tank deeper than any in Europe. The size of a three-storey building, it's designed to show off the sort of creatures you'd find in the waters of the Mediterranean: countless fish swirl above your head, below your feet and on either side, and, of course, four brooding sharks are a more menacing and utterly compelling presence. Building the tank was quite a feat: behind all that glass are two and a half million litres of water, all of which had to be almost trickled into place to avoid cracking the glass. What used to be the shark tank now highlights life on a coral reef, but is still just as popular, thanks to its new resident, a loggerhead turtle called Snorkel. There's plenty more to see: thousands of splendidly coloured and curiously shaped individuals are shown in elaborate indoor reconstructions of their natural habitat, starting with a moorland stream and bog, and passing through an estuary before arriving at the sea shore. A real highlight is the largest collection of seahorse species in the world, and there are discovery pools for children to get a closer look at creatures like starfish. A changing programme of talks and demonstrations ranges from watching the sharks being fed (Mon, Weds and Fri as we went to press, though best to check the schedule in advance) to discovering why romantic seahorses not only mate for life but every morning perform a little dance for their partner. Quite a contrast to some of the older buildings nearby, the aquarium is ideal in any weather, and it's easy for two or three hours to fly by without your being aware of it. Meal and snacks (the café has nice views over Plymouth Sound), shop, disabled access; cl 25 Dec; (01752) 600301; *£8 adults, *£4.50 children 3–15. The family ticket – £22 for two adults and two children – offers better than usual savings (tickets allow same day re-entry). £10 joint ticket with the Mayflower Centre.

ASHBURTON SX7370
The most attractively individual of the ring of small towns around the edge of Dartmoor. The **River Dart Country Park** (Holne Park) is pleasant for walking or fishing, with adventure playgrounds for children. Snacks, shop; cl Oct–Mar; (01364) 652511; £5.75, dogs £1.50.
BANTHAM SANDS SX6643
A gentle walk from Bantham through dunes (good picnic spots) to the broad stretch of rivermouth sand facing Burgh Island. You can go on above the rocks S, for views of Bolt Tail and the coves between.
BERRY POMEROY SX8361
Berry Pomeroy Castle (off A385

just E of Totnes; keep on past village) Reputedly Devon's most haunted castle, hidden away on a crag over a quiet wooded valley. Appropriately spooky medieval gatehouse and walls around the ruins of an imposing and unexpected Tudor mansion, with an interesting 15th-c fresco inside; a new audio tour will tell you more about the castle and its inhabitants. The lawns in front are ideal for a picnic. Snacks; cl Nov–Easter; (01803) 866618; *£2.80; EH. The red sandstone 15th-c village **church** is worth a look on the way; odd monument in Seymour Chapel. The road through here from Ashburton via Littlehempston and on to Stoke Gabriel is a nice drive.

BICKINGTON SX7972

Gorse Blossom Railway Adventure Park Rides on 7½-inch gauge steam railway through acres of woodland; also nature trails and play areas. Meals, snacks, shop, some disabled access; as we went to press they were unsure of their opening times for 2003 so best to phone or check their website www.gorseblossom.com; (01626) 821361 to check times; £5.

BLACKAWTON SX8052

Woodland Leisure Park (off A3122) The emphasis is on fairly traditional good value family fun, and for children up to around 12 who like to charge around this is one of the best days out in Devon. The highlight for children at the upper end of the age range is the spiralling and plunging water-coaster Twister (there are several similar waterchutes nearby), and a very exciting toboggan run, the Tornado. Younger children are well looked after with a nicely put-together Wild West town aimed at the under-5s, and a little zoo with wallabies, llamas and foreign and exotic birds. Stacks of well thought out play areas range from a commando-style assault course to imaginative under-cover areas for toddlers. Five floors of indoor rides and activities include a ferris wheel, and the chance to drop well over 10 metres (40 ft) to experience weightlessness. Also a honey farm with millions of bees behind glass, a tractor yard, paddling pool, pedal karts; twice-daily falconry displays, and special events all year. Woodland walks, boating lake, and they have an adjacent caravan park. Meals, snacks, shop, disabled access; cl Nov to mid-Mar exc wknds and school hols; (01803) 712598; £6.70 adults and children (less in winter, when the water rides aren't open). The George and the Normandy Arms in the village are good pubs.

BOVEY TRACEY SX8178

An unassuming small Dartmoor-edge town; the Devon Guild of Craftsmen have a good varied **craft centre** at Riverside Mill (cl 24–26 Dec and 1 Jan; free). The **House of Marbles and Teign Valley Glass** (Pottery Rd) has demonstrations of glass-blowing at a factory specialising in marbles, with a fantastic array of these and some interesting marble runs in its museum inc, they claim, the largest marble run in the world. Meals, snacks, shop, disabled access; cl 25–26 Dec, 1 Jan and Easter Sun; no glass-blowing Sat end Sept–Easter, but best to check; (01626) 835358; free. The Cromwell Arms does generous food.

BRIXHAM SX9256

Busy fishing port, perhaps the prettiest of the Riviera resorts, with some attractive narrow streets on the hill above. Lots of activity (and summer seaside shops and cafés) in the harbour, inc a full-size reconstruction of Drake's *Golden Hind*, and summer boats around Tor Bay. The local history **museum** (Bolton Cross) has something of a maritime emphasis. Shop; usually cl Sun and Sat pm, all Nov–Easter (exc am Mon–Sat Feb–Mar); (01803) 856267; £1.50. The harbourside Blue Anchor has decent food inc local fish, and Shoalstone beach nr here has some of the cleanest bathing water in the UK.

Berry Head Tremendous coast, sea and shipping views from ex-quarry country park; squat lighthouse, formidable Napoleonic War battlements with cannon (and guardhouse café), nature trail takes in kittiwakes and guillemots on cliffs, uncommon plants.

Scabbacombe Head A blowy but rewarding day's walk from Brixham to Kingswear, 12 miles of stunning wild scenery (and some steep climbs), passing the oasis of Coleton Fishacre gardens.

BUCKFASTLEIGH SX7467

Buckfast Abbey Originally established in 1018, but after the Dissolution of the Monasteries left abandoned until 1882, when it was refounded by Benedictine monks. They then did most of the rebuilding work themselves, over a period of 32 years. It's now one of the most visited religious sites in Britain, with an interesting exhibition, and several services each day. Excellent shops sell not just their own famous tonic wine, but goods produced at other Benedictine monasteries around Europe, inc Bavarian beer, French cakes, and Irish linen; for many, this alone is worth a special journey. Good meals and snacks, disabled access; cl Good Fri and 24–26 Dec; (01364) 645500; free.

Butterfly Park & Dartmoor Otter Sanctuary 🖼 (Dart Bridge Rd) You can watch otters swimming and playing from an underwater viewing tunnel, or see them on land in the six big landscaped enclosures; summer feeding times (readers enjoy this part most) 11.30, 2 and 4.30pm. Also under-cover tropical garden with free-flying butterflies and moths. Meals, snacks, shop, disabled access; cl Nov–Feb; (01364) 642916; £4.95. Combined with a trip on the South Devon Railway (the trains stop here), this makes for a very pleasant day out. The nearby Dartbridge Inn is a popular family pub.

Pennywell 🖼 (Lower Dean, off A38 just S) Friendly and unfussy, with over 750 animals in 80 acres (and a new birds of prey centre), as well as lovely scenery, wildlife viewing hides, and barn owl demonstrations. Different events every half-hour so always something for children to get involved in, from milking and feeding to ferret racing and worm charming; also play areas, an assault course, go-kart ride, theatre, pony and donkey rides and an area where children can try out crafts like basket weaving. Meals, snacks, shop, disabled access; cl Nov–Feb half-term (phone for opening times over Christmas); (01364) 642023; £6.75.

South Devon Railway GWR steam train trips through lovely unspoilt scenery along the wooded River Dart (some of which is hard to see any other way). It stops just outside Totnes as well as at Staverton, and they do tickets combining it with a Dartmouth–Totnes river trip; also a small museum, play area and a chance to see the ongoing restoration of rolling stock. Shop, disabled access; trains normally run four times a day (more in the height of summer, less at other times); best to check dates; cl Nov–Mar (exc Santa trains at Christmas, booking essential); (01364) 642338 for timetable (or pick one up from local Tourist Information Centres); £6.80. The Dartbridge

opposite is a popular family dining pub.
BUCKLAND MONACHORUM
SX4866
Buckland Abbey 🖼 The home of Francis Drake until his death in 1596, and of his family until 1946. By spring 2003 they'll have modernised the three museum rooms: one room explores the abbey's history, another has objects associated with Drake (inc the famous drum said to sound whenever England is in danger), while a third has various interactive displays designed to catch children's interest. Also craft workshops, a brass rubbing centre, herb knot garden, thyme garden, an Elizabethan garden, good walks, and entertaining summer activities for children. Meals, snacks, shop, limited disabled access; cl Thurs, and Nov–Apr; (01822) 853607; *£5, *£2.70 grounds only; NT. The Drake Manor pub is a really nice village archetype.

Garden House Profusion of unusual plants beautifully laid out in a warm walled garden surrounding the picturesque ruin of a medieval vicarage; also a spring garden, quarry garden and wildflower meadow. Interesting plant sales, meals, teas, limited disabled access; cl mid-Nov–Feb; (01822) 854769; £4.

BURGH ISLAND SX6544
Connected at low tide by a causeway to Bigbury-on-Sea (undistinguished for much save its clean sandy beaches); spectacular cliffs on the seaward side, a true island and quite remote-seeming when the tide's in. At high tide an odd giant tractor-on-stilts wades back and forth with passengers. The Pilchard is a quaint seaview pub.

CHAGFORD SX7087
Appealing large village or small town right in the heart of Dartmoor, and an attractive jumping-off point for the moor; even the bank is thatched, and the two old-fashioned general stores are fun. The Ring o' Bells is good for lunch, the Bullers Arms is useful too, and for non meat-eaters, the small vegetarian Courtyard Café is recommended. If you eat at the luxury country-house hotel Gidleigh Park, you can stroll around their lovely grounds, with colourful woodland walks and water garden, and immaculate more

formal gardens.

CHUDLEIGH SX8678

Despite the 1807 fire which destroyed lots of the buildings, this is a pleasant old wool town with pretty cottages in narrow, winding lanes. In Fore St the Bishop Lacey and Old Coaching House both have decent food.

Rock Garden and Cave 🖼 Eight acres of wild gardens in an ancient quarry, populated by a good range of birds and wildlife. The cave has some interesting calcite formations, and they are still digging in search of legendary larger caverns. From the pretty neighbouring waterfall it's a short walk up Chudleigh Rock for dramatic vistas of the surrounding countryside and moors. Snacks, nursery, limited disabled access; cl a wk over Christmas and New Year; (01626) 852134; £2. You can arrange abseiling or caving on (01626) 852717.

Ugbrooke Park 🖼 (off A380 just SE) An interesting early example of the work of Robert Adam, in lovely Capability Brown parkland. Delightfully informal guided tours (2pm and 3.45pm). Teas, disabled access; open pm Sun, Tues, Weds, Thurs and bank hols mid-July to early Sept; (01626) 852179; £5.

DARTINGTON SX7862

Dartington Cider Press Centre (Shinners Bridge) Cluster of 16th- and 17th-c buildings with craft shops, farm foods, herbs and such, and restaurants, inc a good vegetarian one. The surroundings add a lot to the attraction, with nearby medieval great hall on photogenic lawned courtyard, sculpture gardens, street entertainers, and streamside nature trail. Disabled access; cl Suns Christmas–Easter, 25 Dec and 1 Jan; (01803) 864500; free. The Cott Inn is handy for lunch.

DARTMOOR SX5880

The National Park covers two very contrasting landscapes. One is the moor itself, one of England's most untouched and wild-seeming areas, a vast expanse rising to the highest points south of the Pennines. Then further E and S are the deep lush valleys of the Teign, Dart and other rivers, where stone-built houses crouch among sycamores and oaks. It's not an area

thick with indoor sights: the outdoors is the great attraction here (though unfortunately the massif is prone to sudden and prolonged bouts of mist and fog). The moor is punctuated with all sorts of interesting focal points and features (it's one of the most important areas for Bronze Age remains in Europe): strange wind-sculpted, eroded granite tors crowning many of the slopes; little streams threading over boulders; water-courses where leats (or miniature canals) curl carefully around the contours; abandoned and ruined tin-mine workings' wheel-houses; and shaggy ponies hoping for a hand-out (though it's an offence to feed livestock because it encourages them on to the roads). Good roads over the moor are the B3212 and B3357, and the back roads towards Ashburton off the B3344 just NW of Manaton. Villages within the national park (such as Chagford, North Bovey, Lustleigh and Widecombe) are well worth exploring: typically thatched white-plastered stone cottages clustered around an ancient stone church beside its church-house inn. The towns ringing the moor (and just outside the national park) have rather more facilities. A big chunk of NW Dartmoor is used by the Ministry of Defence for firing practice; during training the ranges are marked out by red flags and white posts by day and red lights at night; you can check times on (0800) 458 4868. Dartmoor is outstanding for walking, but mist can come down very suddenly, so on the open moor you must carry a compass, wear strong footwear, and carry spare clothing and food. A lot of the moor is a long way from the road, hence rather inaccessible. There are more paths for walkers than the right-of-way network suggests, but don't assume a right of way marked on the OS map will be visible on the ground (the black dashed lines on these maps are generally more reliable though not necessarily rights of way unless they are overprinted with a green line). Old mineral railways and cart tracks make for some good walkers' routes. There are plenty of things to head for, to give a moorland walk a sense of purpose – most obviously, one of the many tors of naked rock rising out of the moor (beware: the rounded rocks can be a good deal more slippery than they look). Villages and sights are described separately; the following is a list of scenic and archaeological highlights:

Bowerman's Nose SX7480 This quaint tor, looking snootily out over a patchwork of pastures, makes a pleasant objective for a Dartmoor walk.

Brentor church SX4780 (above back rd Lydford–Tavistock, just S of North Brent Tor) 12th-c St Michael de la Rupe is one of England's smallest churches, notable for its lonely hilltop position with remarkable coast and Dartmoor views.

Burrator Reservoir SX5568 This gives up to a five-mile walk in beautiful woodland and moorland surroundings. **Sheepstor church** nearby has interesting memorials to the Brookes family, former rajahs of Sarawak.

Clapper bridge SX6578 By the B3212 at Postbridge (enjoyable food from the East Dart Hotel) is a complete clapper bridge – an ancient stone packhorse bridge; there are other ruined examples nr Bellever (a mile S), and by the end of the B3357 at Dartmeet.

Devonport leat SX5975 This watercourse, still largely complete, was first engineered 200 years ago to give Devonport a water supply. A path largely along the gently graded channel takes in some remote scenery in southern Dartmoor, and makes getting lost quite difficult; it's easily reached off the B3212 NE of Yelverton.

Dr Blackall's Drive SX7073 This old carriage drive from Bel Tor Corner to near Poundsgate gives splendid views of the Dart Valley, and is among Dartmoor's finest paths for walkers.

Fingle Bridge SX7489 Beautifully sited bridge over the Teign, at the end of a minor road. From the pleasant Anglers Rest café/pub the lovely Fisherman's Path winds along a wooded stretch of the valley; you can return at high level on the Hunter's Path, passing near Castle Drogo, and gaining tremendous views.

Great Mis Tor SX5676 In the lonely terrain NW of Princetown (and Dartmoor Prison), this gives walkers panoramic views over much of the moor – it's within the Ministry of Defence range areas so look out for the red warning flags.

Haytor Rocks SX7577 This fortress-like collection of rocks makes a striking and popular objective for walks. Nearby abandoned granite quarries were served by an unusual 19th-c tramway with grooved-granite rails, linked with a canal to the coast – now an 18-mile walk down to Teignmouth called the **Templer Way.**

Hound Tor SX7478 Majestically monumental and a good destination for a walk, with an interesting excavated abandoned **medieval village** nearby.

Hunter's Tor SX7682 The ridge path to this landmark gives panoramic views of Lustleigh Cleave and the Bovey Valley.

Plym Valley SX5866 The upper valley of the Plym has numerous ancient sites, inc visible hut circles, stone rows and cairns.

Shovel Down SX6585 These open moorland expanses harbour some of Dartmoor's richest concentrations of **antiquities**. You'll need a map just to find the car park at Scorhill, SW of Gidleigh and W of Chagford; from there, a path brings you out on to the moor within sight of Scorhill stone circle. Close by are stone slab bridges over clear brooks; among the litter of rocks by one river is the Teign Tolmen, a natural boulder through which the water has gouged a perfectly circular hole. You can walk over to nearby Kes Tor, close to which is the Long Stone and a fine stone row of about 2500–1500BC.

Vixen Tor SX5474 Towering up from the bracken, this looks unclimbable, but is quite easily reached. This area of the **Walkham Valley** is relatively lush and green, and walkers can explore the old railway tracks which once served local quarries.

Yarner Wood SX7778 (nr Bovey Tracey) This National Nature Reserve has a good nature trail.

Yes Tor SX5890 On the NW of Dartmoor, this high landmark gives great views over Devon and Cornwall. This area of Okehampton Common is the highest terrain in southern England, though as in other Ministry of Defence areas, check for red flags.

DARTMOUTH SX8751

Charming waterside small town with many exceptional buildings, esp around the inner harbour. Though so popular, it's kept its own strong character, and stays very much alive through the winter. Cobbled Bayards Cove, with old fort and steep wooded hills behind, is particularly photogenic, as is pedestrianised Foss St. Markets Tues, Fri: Old Market is picturesque. The Royal Naval College is a striking building. Interesting shops, plenty of waterside seats, lots of action on the river. Parking in summer can be trying: best to use good park-and-ride on B3207 Halwell Rd. Enjoyable boat trips run from here to Totnes; (01803) 834488); £5.50 single, £7 return.

Dartmouth Castle (slightly SE of town, off B3205) Classic late 15th-c battlemented fortress, virtually intact, with cannon and later gun batteries (a video display shows it firing), and great views out into the Channel. Snacks, shop; cl winter lunchtimes, and all day Mon and Tues Nov–Mar, and 24–26 Dec and 1 Jan; (01803) 833588; £3.20; EH. In summer a little ferry leaves the South Embankment for here every 15 mins or so. Otherwise it's an enjoyable and fairly gentle 20-min walk from Dartmouth itself, though the immediate hinterland is unremarkable.

Dartmouth Museum 🖼 (Duke St) Well restored 17th-c timbered house, with mainly nautical displays; shop, some disabled access; cl Sun, 25–26 Dec, and 1 Jan; £1.50.

Newcomen Engine House (Royal Avenue Gdns) Huge steam-powered atmospheric beam-engine pump, thought to be the world's oldest, worked 1720–1913. Shop, disabled access; cl Sun Nov–Mar, 25–26 Dec and 1 Jan; (01803) 834224; free, donations welcome.

River trips to Totnes Pass some of Devon's prettiest scenery, much of which can't be seen on foot or by car (including where Agatha Christie lived); you can combine this with steam trains or a connecting bus back – which saves hearing the commentary a second time. You can also go on circular tours of the surrounding area, known as doing a

'Round Robin' (from £12) – an enjoyable way to spend an afternoon. Cl Jan–Feb; phone to check in winter (01803) 834488; £7 return to Totnes. Also quaint car and pedestrian ferries to Kingswear and the A379 (can be 2-hr car wait at peak summer times).

St Saviour's (Church Close) Lots of charming detail, well worth a look, inc altar, pulpit, painted rood screen, brasses on chancel floor, elaborate 14th-c hinges on S door.

DAWLISH SX9576

Old-fashioned small resort with modern developments and camps outside; red sandstone cliffs, waterside parks with black swans, small summer museum (open May–Sept; (01626) 888557; £2), prom, pier; the mainline railway cut through the cliffs right by the water is striking.

Dawlish Warren Sandy grassy spit (with golf course) largely blocking in Exe estuary, with glistening tidal flats full of wading birds, and dunes with some rare plants. In summer get well out to the point, to avoid the crowds and caravan parks; in winter it's splendidly wild and blowy there, with thousands of ducks, brent geese and waders (even avocets) congregating at high tide to wait till the mudflats show again. Shop, disabled access to visitor centre; visitor centre cl 1–2pm and wkdys Oct–Mar; free, guided nature walks £2; (01626) 863980 for times. The Boathouse is a good value family pub in a big seafront complex at the station end, near a large amusement arcade.

DREWSTEIGNTON SX7290

Castle Drogo Impressive granite castle, designed by Lutyens and built early last century as a bizarre and brilliantly inventive mixture of medieval style and 20th-c luxury, with cunningly disguised radiators and amazing details even in the kitchen and lavatory. Lovely grounds with yew hedges form an outer barbican. Good guided walks through the surrounding woodland, and super views – it's 275 metres (900 ft) up overlooking the gorge of the River Teign. Meals, snacks, shop; cl Nov–Mar, plus castle cl Fri (though garden, shop and tearoom still open); (01647) 433306; £5.70, garden and grounds only £2.90; NT. Down on the village square nr the church, the unspoilt Drewe Arms does good lunches. A well signposted minor road W takes you to **Spinster's Rock**, a well preserved neolithic burial chamber and the most easily accessible prehistoric feature in the area.

DUNSFORD SX8389

Brimblescombe Farm Cider (Farrants Farm, off B3212 W of Exeter) Cider is made here in the traditional way, which visitors often find fascinating. Parts of the farm pre-date Saxon times; shop; cl Nov–Easter; (01647) 252783; free (inc sample). In the village, the Royal Oak has generous home cooking.

ERMINGTON SX6353

Ermington church Notable for the crooked 14th-c stone spire above its tower – Victorian rebuilding kept the tilt. The Crooked Spire pub has enjoyable food, and the B3210 from Totnes is pretty.

KENTON SX9583

Kenton church A delightful church, its harmonious medieval sandstone masonry photographing well against blue sky; fine carving inside. In the pretty village the Dolphin does generous meals.

KINGSBRIDGE SX7344

Small town of character, with pretty cobbled lanes diving off steep Fore St, and arcaded shops; there are various markets (Tues–Thurs), and a farmers' market on the first Sat of the month. Interesting monuments in church, boats on tidal estuary (and ferry to Salcombe); the waterfront Crabshell is very popular for seafood. At the head of the nearby creek, pretty South Pool has a fairly interesting **church**, with a delightfully ghoulish story attached, and a good little pub, the Millbrook.

Cookworthy Museum of Rural Life (Fore St) Collection of rural artefacts from Victorian kitchen implements to 1930s farming equipment, housed in a 17th-c grammar school. Shop, some disabled access; cl Sun, and all Nov–Mar; (01548) 853235; £2.

KINGSTON SX6347

There are several walks from the village down to an unspoilt beach; the Dolphin has enjoyable food.

KINGSWEAR SX9051

Coleton Fishacre 🏠 (3m E, off Lower Ferry Rd at Tollhouse) D'Oyly Carte's romantic and lush subtropical garden, with 24 colourful acres dropping down to a pretty cove; formal terraces, walled garden with stream-fed ponds, unusual trees and shrubs and grassy woodland paths. Designed in the 1920s, the house reflects the Arts and Crafts tradition, but has a modern interior. Snacks, shop, limited disabled access to garden; open Weds–Sun and bank hols Apr–Oct; (01803) 752466; £3.80 (house £1.10 extra); NT. More ambitious marked paths beyond the gardens take you along the cliffs, showing how wild this part was before the garden was planted. The Paignton and Dartmouth Railway (described under Paignton) runs from here; the Ship has decent food.

LODDISWELL SX7248

If you cross the river by the lane towards Woodsleigh, there's a quiet walk upstream by riverside pastures and woods towards Topsham Bridge. The Loddiswell Inn has generous home cooking.

LUSTLEIGH SX7881

One of England's most attractive villages, with charming riverside walks in utterly unspoilt woodland around it, or up to Hunter's Tor on Dartmoor. Primrose Cottage has great cream teas, and the Cleave Inn is good.

LYDFORD SX5084

Lydford Gorge Spectacular gorge formed by the River Lyd cutting into the rock, causing boulders to scoop out potholes in the bed of the river. Walks along the ravine take you to dramatic sights such as the 27-metre (90-ft) White Lady Waterfall and the Devil's Cauldron whirlpool (summer crowds around this bit). Children like it but need to be watched carefully as paths can be narrow and slippery. There are also various family events organised throughout the year (phone for details). Meals, snacks (in ingeniously designed tearoom), shop, special path for the disabled; open Apr–Nov (and perhaps Fri–Sun in Dec); (01822) 820320; £3.80; NT. The forbidding ruined **castle** has a daunting 12th-c stone keep, its upper floor once used as a court, and the lower as a prison; free. The Dartmoor

Inn has excellent creative food.

MANATON SX7580

An attractive village, with the private riverside woodland around **Becky Falls Woodland Park** (B3344 to Bovey Tracey) useful enough for undemanding family walks if you don't plan to take advantage of the countryside proper (also rescued owls and birds of prey, animals for children to pet, and pony rides). Meals, snacks, shop, some disabled access; cl Nov–Feb; (01647) 221259; £5.20, £2 for pony rides. The prettily placed Kestor has decent food.

MARLDON SX8664

Compton Castle (1m N, off A3022; or off A381 at Ipplepen turnoff) Formidably fortified and rather picturesque 14th-, 15th- and 16th-c manor around courtyard with portcullised entrance, particularly interesting for its completeness. Shop, very limited disabled access; open Mon, Weds and Thurs Apr–Oct, cl 12.15–2pm; (01803) 875740; £2.90; NT. The Church House Inn is good for lunch.

MEAVY SX5367

This clear wooded river has some pleasant spots for strolling. Meavy itself (pronounced Mewy locally) is an attractive village with one of the oldest oak trees in Britain, and where the parish still owns the (good) pub, whose locals dance around the tree on New Year's Eve. Another useful pub for people walking in this valley is the Skylark at Clearbrook.

MODBURY SX6551

Attractive buildings esp in steep Church St, with photogenic church at top and pretty Exeter Inn at bottom. Brownston St is quite interesting too, with an ornate water conduit at the top.

MORETONHAMPSTEAD SX7184

Miniature Pony & Animal Farm (B3212 W) Very much geared towards younger children, with sociable miniature ponies and donkeys (go in spring and you'll probably see foals), pigs, rabbits, goats, and other small animals. Carefully supervised activities inc pony rides and animal feeding sessions, they've an adventure play area (and an indoor play area for toddlers), nature trail, trout lake, and picnic areas.

Meals, snacks, shop (with various arts and crafts), disabled access; (01647) 432400; cl Nov–Easter; *£6.

MORWELLHAM SX4470

Morwellham Quay Thriving and meticulously researched open-air museum in lovely countryside, with costumed guides convincingly re-creating the boom years when Morwellham was the greatest copper port in the Empire. You can watch the work of a cooper, assayer, coachmen and quay workers. Very popular in school hols – a visit can easily last all day. Meals, snacks, shop, disabled access limited (reduced admission price); cl Nov–Easter (exc maybe 2 wknds before Christmas for special events and 26 Dec–1 Jan – best to check); (01822) 832766; £8.90 (reduced price and operations in winter). The Ship (part of the centre) is good, with period waitresses and drinks.

NEWTON ABBOT SX8670

A working town rather than a holiday centre, but several interesting places here or nearby.

Bradley Manor (off A381 S) Peaceful 15th-c house nr stream through extensive wood-fringed grounds, quiet walks. Open pm Tues–Thurs Apr–Sept; (01626) 354513; £2.90; NT.

Orchid Paradise (Forches Cross, A382 N) Colourful place, with lots of rare and endangered species in elaborate indoor reconstructions of their natural habitats. Snacks, nursery and shop, some disabled access (but no facilities); cl winter bank hols; (01626) 352233; £2.

Plant World 🖼 (St Marychurch Rd; signed from Penn Inn roundabout) Unusual four-acre garden built and planted as a giant map of the world, with the countries containing their correct native plants, trees and flowers – many of them quite rare in this country, but flourishing in the mild Devon climate. Also plant centre (with seeds of some of the rarest plants), old-fashioned English garden and fine views from picnic area. Snacks; cl Oct–Mar; (01803) 872939; £2. The Linny in nearby Coffinswell is a charming old thatched pub.

Tuckers Maltings (Teign Rd) One of

the few remaining working malthouses in the country, and the only one open to the public – every year they produce enough malt for 20 million pints of beer. Tours show all aspects of malting (you can touch the grain and taste the malt); they also have their own brewery. There's a hands-on section for children. Snacks, shop with over 200 speciality bottled beers (open all year); open Mon–Sat (plus Sun July–Aug) Good Fri–Oct, last guided tour starts 3.30pm; (01626) 334734; £4.95 (inc sample of beer).

NEWTON FERRERS/NOSS MAYO SX5548
Picturesque twin villages on very sheltered rocky wooded creek of Yealm estuary; besides modern development, there are some charming whitewashed cottages – and lots of yachting in summer. The riverside Ship is a good place for a meal; beware of rising tides if you park on the slipway. There are attractive walks from here along the estuary, then beyond to Gara Point and exposed cliff; largely NT. This can be reached in sections via the Noss Mayo–Holbeton coastal ridge rd.

NORTH BOVEY SX7184
A delightful peaceful Dartmoor village, not usually invaded by tourists: oak-shaded green with mounting block, stone cross, pump, ancient cottages and attractive pub.

OKEHAMPTON SX5895
This bustling Dartmoor-edge working town has enterprising food in the Plymouth (West St), and a couple of things worth stopping for:
Museum of Dartmoor Life (West St) Well converted Victorian agricultural mill with interactive displays on local life, Tourist Information Centre and working craft studios next door. Tearoom, shop, some disabled access; cl Sun Easter–May, plus Sat Oct–Easter, 24 Dec–2 Jan but best to check; (01837) 52295; usually £2. The Plymouth nearby has enterprising food.
Okehampton Castle The tower on a steep grassy mound above the river is remarkable above all for the way it stays standing – a balancing act of ruined masonry zigzagging up into the sky. It's the biggest medieval castle in Devon, with sections dating from 11th–14th c;

good woodland walks. Snacks, shop; cl Nov–Mar; (01837) 52844; £2.50.

PAIGNTON SX8861
Largely a typical resort, with long promenade between good sandy beach and green; the little harbour is pretty, with working fishing boats as well as yachts. The original inland core has an attractive red sandstone church with some interesting buildings nearby, esp **Kirkham House**, a handsome sandstone Tudor merchant's house with lofty hall. The formal and subtropical lakeside gardens at **Oldway** are colourful; on summer wkdy mornings (not Sat) there are guided tours of some rooms in the Versailles-style colonnaded mansion at their centre; phone (01803) 557671; £1. Attractive Elberry Cove between Paignton and Brixham is altogether quieter. Decent places for lunch include the Embassy (Colin Rd), Inn on the Green (Esplanade Rd) and Ship (Manor Rd, not far from Preston beach).
Paignton & Dartmouth Steam Railway (Queens Park Station, Torbay Rd) One of the nicest such steam train trips we know of – GWR steam trains run from here right by the sea along the spectacular Tor Bay coast; the front Pullman coach is less crowded. You can combine this with a boat Dartmouth–Totnes, and bus Totnes–Paignton. Dining train available on some Suns, snacks, shop, disabled access; open Apr–Oct (daily Jun–Sept) and selected dates out of season (01803) 555872 for timetable; £6.60 return.
Paignton Zoo (St Michael's) Well run and shown, with over 1,300 animals and birds (many of them breeding) in 75 acres of beautifully planted surroundings; it's perhaps the country's most visually appealing zoo, and lays a decent emphasis on conservation. Also lakeside miniature railway, play area and splendid hands-on animal education centre for children. Lots of events and feeding displays throughout the day. Meals, snacks, shop, good disabled access; cl 25 Dec; (01803) 697500; £8.
Quaywest Waterpark (Goodrington Sands) Lively waterpark (the water is heated so worth considering even if the weather's not

that great) with a submarine themed play zone and a play pool for the under-5s as well as all the various slides (inc the highest and fastest flume in the country); go-kart rides too (£3) and regular Punch and Judy shows. Meals, snacks, shop; open daily in summer (exc in very bad weather); (01803) 555550; £7.95. Across the road at Ski West you can arrange jet ski rides, waterskiing, sailing and other watersports; (01803) 663243.

PLYMOUTH SX4753

Apart from the area around the Barbican most of the old parts of the city were destroyed in World War II; in parts it`s like lots of other busy modern towns. There are some interesting escapes from the bustle, and in places The Hoe has something of the feel of smaller seaside promenades, with great views out over the Sound; decent food from the Yard Arm (looking out in a suitably nautical style) and the Waterfront bar/restaurant. A statue of Drake is a reminder that he's supposed to have played his famous game of bowls here; there's still a bowling green close by. A tour bus can take you to the main attractions, though it's perhaps more fun on one of the **boat trips** run by Tamar Cruises from Mayflower Steps, off Madeira Rd, Barbican; (01752) 822105. There are also boats from here to the **Mountbatten Peninsula**, a former Ministry of Defence area now open to the public; you can walk along the breakwater, which goes right out into The Sound with views back towards the city. The ferries to Torpoint in Cornwall put Antony House and Mt Edgcumbe in very easy reach. The Notte Inn (Notte St) has enjoyable food.

Barbican Carefully restored since the war, a series of narrow twisty streets of old buildings W of working Sutton Harbour; photogenic – and evocative even in wet weather. New St is its oldest core. The Dolphin pub has original Beryl Cook paintings.

Barbican Glassworks The old fishmarket has been redeveloped as a visitor centre. You can watch glass-blowing demonstrations by Dartington Crystal, and there are exhibitions on the local area. Large shop, disabled access; cl

25 Dec, 1 Jan and Easter Sun; free.

Black Friars Distillery (60 Southside St) Photogenic home of Plymouth Dry Gin, now the only English gin still made in its original distillery, founded in 1793. The building itself dates back much further, and has had periods as a monastery and a prison; tours include demonstrations of production, a film of the city's history and, of course, a sample of the gin itself. Shop; open daily beginning Mar–24 Dec (though limited opening over Christmas and New Year so phone to check then), plus Sat Jan–Feb; (01752) 665292; *£2.75.

City Museum & Art Gallery (Drake Circus) Friendly museum with well shown collections of mostly West Country interest. Snacks, shop, good disabled access; cl Sun, Mon (exc bank hols) and 25–26 Dec; (01752) 304774; free.

Crownhill Fort (Crownhill Fort Rd, just N) The biggest and least altered of Plymouth's Victorian forts, though from the road it looks little more than a wooded hill. Used by the Army right up to 1986, it's been well restored by the Landmark Trust, with barrack rooms, underground tunnels, secret passageways, and lookout towers to explore; children can run around quite freely, and there's an adventure playground. You can stay here in a Victorian officer's flat (all year), and have the run of the place after dark. Snacks, shop, limited disabled access (lots of steep steps); cl Nov–Mar, but hours vary so phone to check; (01752) 793754; £4.75.

Elizabethan House (32 New St) Splendid timber-framed Tudor sea-captain's house with period furniture. Shop; cl Mons and Tues, and Oct–Easter; (01752) 304380; £1.10. There's an Elizabethan garden just down the road at number 39.

Mayflower Centre (Rope Walk, off Sutton Rd) Using display panels and touch screen computers, this new visitor centre charts the development of Sutton Harbour from a fishing port to a military base and trade centre. There's an interesting section on Drake's circumnavigation of the world and the Pilgrim Fathers, and they've models of the *Golden Hind* and

Mayflower. You begin at the top of the building, where a terrace has views over the city and harbour, and there's a short introductory film; various quizzes, and smell and touch tests (though lots of reading, so more suitable for older children). Shop, disabled access; cl 25 Dec; 01752 306330; £4, £10 joint ticket with the National Marine Aquarium. Ask about about their guided walks; £1.50.

Merchant's House (St Andrew St) Well restored 16th-c jettied house, telling the city's day-to-day history in displays themed on tinker, tailor, soldier, sailor; also early Victorian apothecary's shop and schoolroom. Shop; cl 1–2 pm, Sun, Mon (exc bank hols), and Oct–Easter; (01752) 304381; £1.10.

National Marine Aquarium *See separate family panel on p.164.*

Plymouth Dome (The Hoe) Reopened after extensive refurbishments, this state-of-the-art evocation of Plymouth's past and present is interesting and fun. Using feel-part-of-it technology, you can stroll along lively Elizabethan streets, dodge press gangs, meet Drake and the Pilgrim Fathers, and come bang up to date with satellite and radar monitoring of current harbour action and weather. Their new exhibition on the four Eddystone Rock lighthouses includes a virtual tour of Smeaton's Tower, and they've a new film about the Blitz. Snacks, shop, good disabled access; as we went to press they had not yet decided on their winter opening times so best to phone; (01752) 603300; £4.50, £6 with Smeaton's Tower.

Prysten House (Finewell St) The city's oldest house: austere late 15th-c granite building with galleried courtyard. Unpretentious but quite atmospheric restored rooms feature a model of 17th-c Plymouth, and several yards of an ambitious tapestry showing American colonisation. Cl wknds; (01752) 661414; £1.

Royal Citadel (The Hoe) Unrivalled views of the city and sea from the ramparts of this magnificent 17th-c battlemented fortress. The gateway is striking, and the barracked parade-ground is still in use. Disabled access

(though no facilities); admission by guided tour only at 2.30pm May–Sept (this may change – best to check); (01752) 266030; £3.

Smeaton's Tower (The Hoe) Colourfully striped 18th-c former Eddystone Rocks lighthouse, moved here 110 years ago and recently restored, with a good view from the top if you like steps. Phone for opening times (01752) 600608; £2, joint ticket with Dome available.

St Andrew's (St Andrew St) Bombed but lovingly restored, with stained glass by John Piper illustrating the city's history.

PLYMPTON SX5255

Saltram ⊞ (2m W, off A38/A379 at Marsh Mills roundabout) Magnificent mostly 18th-c mansion still with pretty much all the original contents, and notable for its unaltered Robert Adam rooms. George II furnishings, decoration and paintings (strong on Reynolds, who as a regular guest advised on which other pictures to buy), interesting period kitchen, stately garden with orangery, and parkland by wooded Plym estuary. Meals, snacks, shop, local art/crafts gallery, disabled access; house cl Fri and all Nov–Mar (gardens open all year, exc Fri), shop, gallery, and tearoom (wknds only) cl 21 Dec–Mar, best to check; (01752) 333500; £6.30, garden only £3.30; NT. The old town around St Maurice church is worth a look if you're here: attractive partly arcaded streets, very ruined motte and bailey castle, decent food at the George.

POWDERHAM SX9684

Powderham Castle ⊞ The ancestral home of the Earls of Devon, badly damaged in the Civil War but elaborately restored in the 18th and 19th c. The richly decorated state rooms were used in the film adaptation of *The Remains of the Day*. Spectacular rose garden, home to Timothy the 160-year-old tortoise, spring woodland garden, a secret garden designed for children with ducks, rabbits, guinea-pigs and chinchillas, and broad deer park with views over Exe estuary; there's also a miniature steam railway. Good guided tours, lots of special events, and a new country store. Meals, snacks, some disabled access; cl Sat, and Nov–Mar; (01626) 890243; £6.45. The ancient waterside Anchor at Cockwood has good seafood.

PRAWLE POINT SX7735

Impressive scenery: wind-blasted gorse, grass and thrift above low but fierce cliffs, lending itself to a round walk, with a useful network of green lanes leading inland to the village of East Prawle.

SALCOMBE SX7438

Steep narrow-streets fishing village, full of enjoyable holiday bustle in summer, with lots of souvenirs, bric-a-brac, boating shops, teashops and pubs overlooking sea, nearby beaches and coves. **Boat trips** and boat hire; (01548) 843818. The Fortescue and Victoria have decent food.

Bolt Head/Bolt Tail Six miles of one of the best coast-path sections, with remote exposed clifftops, glorious coves, far views, well preserved Iron Age earth ramparts on Bolt Tail; all NT. Best access is via Overbecks, Soar Mill Cove or Hope Cove.

Overbecks (South Sands; signed from Salcombe and Malborough) Named after the eccentric research chemist who lived here until 1937; among his possessions and inventions you can still see the Rejuvenator which he claimed 'practically renewed' his youth. For most the chief attraction is the luscious subtropical gardens, with terraced plantings among woodland, many rarities and plenty of palms and citrus fruits; outstanding late May–Jun for the magnolias, but worth a trip any time of year. Glorious views out to sea, also colourful statue garden, picnic belvedere and collections of dolls and lead soldiers. Snacks, shop; cl Sat (exc Aug), Fri in Oct, and all Nov–Mar (garden open all year); (01548) 842893; £4.40, £3.20 garden only; NT. Mill Bay nr here has one of the area's safest bathing beaches.

SHALDON SX9372

Interesting and colourful mix of seaside houses spanning 200 years of architectural fancy; some lovely corners esp down by water away from the centre, also much older cottages in Crown Sq. The Clifford Arms and London Inn have decent food. High grassy sandstone Ness overlooks the sea and Teignmouth, with a tunnel cut by the 19th-c landowner to a sheltered beach; the beautifully set Ness House up here is useful for food, too. There's a ferry from Teignmouth (exc 25 Dec, and times limited in winter), and the A379 to Maidencombe has sea views.

Wildlife Trust £ (Ness Drive) Specialist breeding centre for rare and endangered foreign birds, and small mammals inc monkeys. Shop; cl 25 Dec; (01626) 872234; £3.

SHARPHAM SX8158

Sharpham Vineyard £ Two self-guided trails (one alongside a river) take you through the vineyard at this attractive 500-acre estate that also includes a jersey dairy farm (not open to the public). Shop; cl Sun (exc Jun–Aug), and last wk in Dec–Feb; (01803) 732203; £2.50 (inc wine tasting).

SLAPTON SANDS SX8343

One of the finest beaches in the country, six miles of almost straight shingle N of the lighthouse at Start Point, backed by hills in the S and by road, shingle bank, lake (Slapton Ley nature reserve, marked nature trail) and marsh, then low cliffs, in the N. Good for out-of-season desolation, sheltered from W winds, with a storm-ruined village at Hallsands, and salvaged tank memorial to a US Normandy landings practice disaster at Torcross.

SOURTON SX5390

Highwayman An extraordinary pub, one bar recalling a galleon, the other a sort of fairy-tale fantasy, and the garden demonstrating yet more exuberant imagination – all meticulously done by the owners, not some brewery theme pub.

SOUTH WEST COAST PATH SX5446

The finest part of Devon's S coast for walkers is between Plymouth and Brixham – much of it quite unspoilt. In summer ferries cross the rivers (exc the River Erme S of Ermington, which you have to cross at low tide).

SPARKWELL SX5858

Dartmoor Wildlife Park & Westcountry Falconry Centre £ A variety of animals inc big cats (feeding time 3.30pm) in 30 acres of countryside. Also falconry centre with displays at 12pm and 4pm (Easter–Oct exc Fri, weather permitting), adventure playground and picnic area. Meals, snacks, shop, disabled access; (01752) 837209 (info line); £7.45. The Treby Arms has reliable modestly priced food.

STICKLEPATH SX6494

Finch Foundry No longer producing the sickles, shovels and tools for which it was known in the 19th c, but the waterwheels and machinery all still work, with regular demonstrations throughout the day. Snacks, shop; cl Tues, and Nov–end Mar; (01837) 840046; £3; NT. The very unpretentious thatched Devonshire Inn in the village is good value.

STOKE GABRIEL SX8457

Steep village above a sheltered side-pool of the Dart estuary, with 14th-c church (with ancient yew) and Church House (pleasant for lunch) perched prettily on a high cobbled terrace.

TEIGNMOUTH SX9473

A popular resort for family holidays, with good beaches, windsurfing and so on, some handsome 19th-c streets and active docks, and on French St a decent local history **museum** (cl Sun am, and Nov–Apr; (01626) 777041; £1). The riverside Ship (Queen St) has good food, all day in summer.

TORQUAY SX9163

The busiest of the area's resorts, good for evening strolling, with palm trees and rocks, promenades, colourful gardens, decorous guesthouses and huge hotels, broad Victorian streets and upmarket shops. The sheltered beaches around here are cleaner than many along this coast. Summer bustle centres around the attractive harbour, with lots of shops, boat trips, and an aquarium. In summer a **cliff railway** takes care of a dizzy swoop from Oddicombe Beach to the high wooded clifftop (01803) 328750. The quaint Hole in the Wall (Park Lane) and big smart London (Strand) do good value food. The waterfront between Princess Pier and Beacon Cove is currently undergoing a £21 million rejuvenation which should be completed by March 2004.

Bygones ⊞ (Fore St, St Marychurch) Enthusiastically reconstructed life-sized Victorian street, with well stocked period shops and rooms, model railway, and re-created World War I trench with sound effects and cooking smells. Open till 9pm (6pm Fri–Sun) July–Aug. Café, shop; cl 24–25 Dec; (01803) 326108; £4.50.

Cockington Winding lanes of olde-worlde thatched cottages and bric-a-brac/craft shops in sheltered village with millpond, etc., well preserved by Torbay Council; adjoining 500-acre park. The Drum pub (a useful stop) was designed to match by Lutyens in 1934. Terribly pretty, and very touristy in season, with open horse-drawn carriages.

Kents Cavern Showcaves (Ilsham Rd, Wellswood) The oldest directly dated archaeological site in Britain; continuing excavations often make scientists reconsider their theories about prehistoric life. Good guided tours really bring out the history of the caves, and colourful stalagmites and stalactites add to the eerie atmosphere. In summer they do spooky evening tours (booking essential). Very well presented, and definitely worth an hour or so if you're in the area. Special visits at Christmas. Summer meals, snacks, shop, disabled access (with prior notice); cl 25 Dec; (01803) 215136; £5.70, evening tours £6.30.

Living Coasts (Beacon Quay) This new aquatic visitor attraction sounds as though it will be well worth a visit when it opens in July. Despite having a serious message (how coastal habitats throughout the world are being threatened by man) it's going to be lively and interesting with plenty for children. Lots to see underwater and above-water as you make your way round the walkways (best of all some of the birds fly freely around you) inc penguins, puffins, seals or maybe sea otters, and even black rats (they'll be housed in a mock-up of a ship's hold). Phone Paignton Zoo for details; (01803) 697500.

Model Village ⊞ (Hampton Ave, Babbacombe) Hundreds of one-twelfth scale buildings in four acres of miniaturised landscape, beautifully done. Try coming at dusk between Easter and Oct, when the scenes are prettily floodlit. Meals, snacks, shop, good disabled access; cl 25 Dec; (01803) 315315; £5.80 – a little pricey, but it's probably the best of its type (you may also have to pay for parking). The beach here has safe bathing water, and the Cary Arms (Beach Rd) is good, with great views.

Torquay Museum (529 Babbacombe Rd) Includes galleries on the Devon farmhouse, plus finds from ancient local caves and local history. Shop; cl am Sun, and Christmas wk, phone for winter opening times; (01803) 293975; £3.

Torre Abbey (Kings Drive) As we went to press, plans for an extensive £7 million four-year restoration of the abbey and gardens hadn't yet been confirmed (they include a new entrance, better disabled access, and a new interactive family art gallery), so phone to check opening times. Some of the earlier parts of the abbey remain, inc the medieval barn, gatehouse, undercrofts and ruined Norman tower, but they've been eclipsed by the later house with its 18th- and 19th-c period rooms. The main feature is Devon's largest art gallery, and there's an Agatha Christie room full of possessions of the locally born author; also garden and palm house. Snacks, shop; probably open Easter–Jun; (01803) 293593; £3.

TOTNES SX8060

Busy in summer, but still keeping most of its charm then, particularly early in the morning. The picturesque Elizabethan area known as **The Narrows** is very atmospheric, esp along the High St down to the arch at the top of Fore St, with quaint pillared arcades (on Tues mornings May–Sept there's a little Elizabethan and craft market). There's a working harbour, and you can walk some way downstream on either side of the River Dart. Behind the church of St Mary's (which has a super rood screen), several rooms in the 11th-c **guildhall** may be open (wkdys mid-Oct–Easter); it was originally part of a Benedictine priory. Perhaps unexpectedly, Totnes has quite a New Age flavour; there's even a flotation tank to wash away city stresses. The Kingsbridge Inn (Leechwell St) has enjoyable food. The **South Devon Railway**, which stops here, is described under Buckfastleigh,

and the highly recommended river trips are described under Dartmouth.

Devonshire Collection of Costume (43 High St) Period costumes and accessories from the 18th c to the present, from ordinary work clothes to high fashion, with changing annual exhibitions. Shop; cl wknds, and Oct–May; £1.75.

Totnes Castle Part Norman, part 14th c, these classic circular remains were lucky enough to avoid any battles, so the keep is pretty much intact. There's a tree-shaded inner lawn, and lovely views of the town and down to the river. Snacks, shop; cl Nov–Mar; (01803) 864406; £1.80.

Totnes Museum (70 Fore St) Elizabethan merchant's house with galleried courtyard, herb garden, and display on the inventions of Totnes boy Charles Babbage, creator of one of the earliest computers. Shop; cl wknds, and Nov–Easter; (01803) 863821; £1.50.

TUCKENHAY SX8156

This gives a pretty one-mile stroll E along wooded Bow Creek, from the Maltsters Arms – good food here.

WEMBURY BAY SX5148

A walk here gives good views, starting from Wembury past the church at the start of NT clifftops; woods and pastures on opposite shore, Plymouth shipping in the distance.

WIDECOMBE IN THE MOOR SX7176

One of the most visited villages on Dartmoor, immortalised by the trip of Uncle Tom Cobbleigh and all to Widecombe Fair (the granite-carved village sign shows them all crowded on to their old grey mare); get here before lunchtime to avoid the coach parties. The **church**, known as the Cathedral of the Moors, has a distinctive disproportionately high tower. The adjoining 16th-c **church house**, now the church hall, is worth a look. Next door, the **Sexton's Cottage** is a NT and Dartmoor National Park information centre and gift shop; cl 24 Dec to mid-Feb. The Post Office Stores has good ice-cream and local honey. The well run reconstructed Olde Inne in the village is very popular with tourists, but for more of a Tom Cobbleigh flavour try the Rugglestone

Inn just S. The finest view over the village is from **Honeybag Tor**, to the north. The **Shilstone Rocks Riding Centre** organises horse-riding over Dartmoor, beginners welcome. Disabled access; (01364) 621281; from £17 an hour.

YEALMPTON SX5751
They open the stunning illuminated **Kitley caves** here only to small groups or individuals with a special interest in the subject; phone (01752) 880885 to book free guided tour. Above ground 50 acres of pretty woodland and riverside walks with many varieties of plants, shrubs and trees. The Volunteer does good food. Nearby is a good **farm shop**; (01752) 880925, and seasonal **pick-your-own** fruit and veg; (01752)

880688.

YELVERTON SX5167
Paperweight Centre (Buckland Terrace) Private collection of hundreds of glass paperweights, all sizes and designs, inc collectors' pieces. Extensive paperweight shop, disabled access; open wknds, daily Apr–Oct and 1–24 Dec though best to check; (01822) 854250; free. The Rock (A386) is a good family pub.

Other attractive villages, all with decent pubs, include Belstone SX6293, Christow SC8384, Churston Ferrers SX9056, Coffinswell SX8968, Denbury SX8168, waterside Dittisham SX8654, Holbeton SX6150, seaside Maidencombe SX9268, Malborough SX7039 and Stokeinteignhead SX9170.

Where to eat

ASHPRINGTON SX8157 **Durant Arms** *(01803) 732240* Friendly gable-ended dining pub opposite the church, with two attractive bar rooms, several open fires, good enjoyable bar food, well kept beers, and friendly service; cl pm 25 Dec; disabled access. £16|**£6.45**

AVONWICK SX7158 **Avon Inn** *(01364) 73475* Popular dining pub with comfortable fairly modern furnishings, a wide range of good Italian food inc lots of interesting pasta dishes, plenty of fish, and lovely puddings, good Italian wines, well kept real ales, and pleasant riverside garden; cl Sun, first wk Jan; children in restaurant only; disabled access. £23|**£6.50**

BABBACOMBE SX9265 **Tea Rose Tearooms** *49 Babbacombe Downs Rd (01803) 324477* Charming small tearoom with inside and outside tables in a garden opposite the sea, with waitresses in period dress, generous cream teas and snacks, and proper leaf tea; disabled access.|**£3.55**

BANTHAM SX6743 **Sloop** *(01548) 560489* Near a sandy beach (good for surfing), this 16th-c nautical village inn has good bar food inc lots of fish, hearty breakfasts, and decent beers and wines; comfortable bdrms, self-catering cottages; cl pms 25–26 Dec. £20|**£5**

BOLBERRY SX6939 **Port Light** *(01548) 561384* Popular even on dismal winter wkdys, this clifftop former RAF radar station (easy walk from Hope Cove) is warmly friendly, with good home-made food in attractive bar and restaurant, super sea views, woodburner, and good outdoor children's play area; bdrms; cl Mon am in early season, cl 1–10 Dec, and all Jan; disabled access. £20|**£6.50**

CHAGFORD SX6987 **22 Mill Street** *22 Mill Street (01647) 432244* Cheerfully decorated little restaurant with a relaxed, friendly atmosphere, plenty of loyal customers, highly enjoyable modern cooking, lovely puddings, and a carefully chosen wine list; cl Sun, am Mon and Tues, 2 wks Jan, 1 wk late May; children must be well behaved. £19.50 lunch, £27 dinner

CHERITON BISHOP SX7695 **Old Thatch** *(01647) 24204* Welcoming 16th-c inn with good bar food from big menu, interesting puddings, winter themed food evenings, beamed bar and big open stone fireplace, real ales from small independent breweries, and friendly service; bdrms; cl 25 Dec. £21|**£5.95**

COCKWOOD SX9780 **Anchor** *(01626) 890203* Friendly and very popular pub by the harbour with small low-ceilinged rambling rooms and lots of good fresh fish dishes – 30 ways of serving mussels, 12 of serving scallops, 10 of oysters, and so forth, no smoking restaurant, well kept real ales, 10 wines by the glass, and 50 malt whiskies; cl 25 Dec pm; disabled access. £25|**£5.95**

COMBEINTEIGNHEAD SX9271 **Coombe Cellars** (01626) 872423 Big bustling family pub with lots for children inc an indoor play area, their own menu, fun days with entertainment, outside play galleon and fenced-in playground; lovely estuary setting with tables on jetties and big terraces, a roomy and comfortable bar with plenty of nautical bric-a-brac, well kept ales, lots of wines by the glass, enjoyable food, and friendly efficient staff; disabled access. £21|**£7** ☺

CORNWORTHY SX8255 **Hunters Lodge** (01803) 732204 Welcoming and popular country local with a two-roomed low-ceilinged bar, cottagey restaurant with 17th-c fireplace, tasty lunchtime food and imaginative evening meals, well kept real ales, decent wines, and plenty of seats outside. £22|**£6**

DARTMOUTH SX8751 **Café Alf Resco** Lower Rd (01803) 835880 On three levels (the one on street level is partly open-air), this is a bustling, popular café with a friendly easy-going atmosphere, people dropping in all day to read the papers over a cappuccino, simple wooden furnishings, old newspapers decorating the ceiling, regular live jazz, a heated marquee with plenty of seats, and good hearty breakfasts (served all day), morning coffee and lunchtime snacks; bdrms; cl Mon, Tues, last 2 wks Feb; disabled access. £20|**£5**

DARTMOUTH SX8751 **Carved Angel** 2 South Embankment (01803) 832465 Black and white timbered restaurant, airy and attractive, overlooking the quay, with delicious meals using carefully chosen absolutely fresh produce – superb fish, impressive puddings and fine cheeses, wines in every price range, and a smart yet friendly atmosphere; no smoking; the cheerful (and much cheaper) **Carved Angel Café** at 7 Foss St, under the same owners, has very good simpler but imaginative food in the form of morning coffee, light lunches, afternoon tea, and wknd evening meals (they've just opened a new branch in Exeter, by the cathedral); main restaurant cl Sun pm, Mon am, 3 days Christmas; children welcome lunchtime (over 10 in evening); partial disabled access. £50

DARTMOUTH SX8751 **Cherub** 10 Higher St (01804) 832571 Dartmouth's oldest building (already 300 years old when Sir Francis Drake used it), this has a bustling bar, liked by locals, an upstairs dining room, decent food, and well kept ales; no children. £25|**£8**

GULWORTHY SX4473 **Horn of Plenty** (01822) 832528 On the edge of Dartmoor in quiet flower-filled gardens, this relaxed, refurbished Georgian no smoking restaurant-with-rooms has excellent carefully cooked food using top-quality local produce inc lovely puddings and cheeses (wonderful breakfasts, too), a good wine list, and vine-covered terrace for aperitifs; comfortable bdrms; cl Mon am, 24–26 Dec; children over 10 in evening restaurant; disabled access. £29.75 lunch, £45.75 dinner

HARBERTON SX7758 **Church House** (01803) 863707 Ancient village pub with magnificent medieval panelling, attractive old furnishings, generous helpings of interesting daily specials, well kept beers, and decent wines; bdrms; children in family room; pms 25, 26 Dec and 1 Jan. £23|**£7**

KINGSBRIDGE SX7443 **Crabshell** The Quay, Embankment Rd (01548) 852345 Famous old dining pub, very popular for its lovely waterside position and fresh local fish and shellfish – they also do picnics and take-aways; quick friendly staff, well kept real ales, decent wines, warm winter fire, and live music Thurs; cl 25 Dec pm; disabled access. £17.75|**£4.75**

LUSTLEIGH SX7881 **Primrose Cottage** (01647) 277365 Thatched 15th-c cottage by the old village church with seats in riverside garden, clotted cream teas, lovely home-made cakes and pastries, and tasty all-day light meals; cl Mon and Tues, cl Nov–Feb; disabled access|**£5.95**

LYDFORD SX5285 **Dartmoor Inn** (01822) 820221 The overall feel in the small bar here is of civilised but relaxed elegance: matt pastel paintwork in soft greens and blues, naïve farm and country pictures, little side lamps supplemented by candles in black wrought-iron holders, basketwork, dried flowers, fruits and gourds, and perhaps an elaborate bouquet of fresh flowers; limited choice of lunchtime bar snacks plus creatively cooked and beautifully presented restaur ry food using top-notch local produce; well kept real ales, an interesting and helpfully short wine list, and polite young staff; tables on terrace, with a track straight up on to the moors. £27|£7.50

MARLDON SX8663 **Church House** *(01803) 558279* Well run bustling pub with several different attractive bar areas and restaurant, candles on tables, bare boards, hops and dried flowers, imaginative daily-changing food, well kept real ales, ten wines by the glass, and seats outside; bdrms; children over 10 in evening. £26|£8

PLYMOUTH SX4754 **Chez Nous** *13 Frankfort Gate* (01752) 266793 Classic informal French evening bistro with long-serving owners, a red, white and blue colour scheme, careful cooking of fresh local produce, esp fresh fish and fine puddings, some distinguished wines, and friendly atmosphere; cl Sun, Mon, 3 wks Feb, 3 wks Sept; children over 12; partial disabled access. £50

RATTERY SX7461 **Church House** *(01364)* 642220 One of Britain's oldest pubs, with big open fires, friendly customers and staff, good bar food, decent wines and beers, fine malt whiskies, and nice dog and cats; peaceful setting; disabled access. £16.95|£5.50

TORCROSS SX8241 **Start Bay** *(01548) 580553* Notable and very popular fresh seafood generously served in busy thatched pub overlooking three-mile pebble beach; farm cider; family room; cl 25 Dec pm ; partial disabled access. £18|£5.95

TORQUAY SX9064 **Mulberry Room** *1 Scarborough Rd* (01803) 213639 Popular no smoking restaurant-with-rooms, with good innovative food using local produce, and very enjoyable home-made cakes and scones for afternoon tea; cookery demonstrations; bdrms; cl Mon, Tues (exc to residents), cl Weds–Thurs am; disabled access. £25|£4.50

TOTNES SX8060 **Greys Dining Room** *96 High St* (01803) 866369 No smoking Georgian house with pretty china on a handsome dresser and partly panelled walls, lots of teas plus herb and fruit ones, sandwiches, salads and omelettes as well as lots of cakes and set teas; cl Weds and Sun; no pushchairs and children must be well behaved; partial disabled access. £12|£6.50

TUCKENHAY SX8156 **Maltsters Arms** *(01803) 732350* Very well run creekside pub with enthusiastic friendly owners, particularly good interesting food – though they are keen to keep it as a pub where people also feel comfortable dropping in for a drink – well kept real ales, 12 wines by the glass, and relaxed, airy bars; seats by the water; super bdrms; open all day Sat and Sun and all day during summer hols; cl 25 Dec; disabled access. £23|£6

UGBOROUGH SX6755 **Anchor** *Letterburn St* (01752) 892283 Bustling, homely pub with log fire in the oak-beamed bar, comfortable partly no smoking restaurant, good food (you can eat from either the bar or restaurant menus and sit anywhere in the pub), courteous service, and well kept real ales; bdrms; disabled access. £23|£6.50

We welcome reports from readers

This *Guide* depends on readers' reports. Do help us if you can – in return, we offer a discount on the next edition to people who've helped us with reports for it. Tell us what you think about places already in it, and anything extra you think we should say about them. And send us your ideas for inclusion in the next edition: places to visit, eat at or stay in, attractive drives or walks, maybe even unusual shops you know of. Use the card in the middle, the report forms at the end, or just write – no stamp needed: *The Good Britain Guide*, FREEPOST TN1569, Wadhurst, E Sussex TN5 7BR. Or log on to www.goodguides.com

North Devon & Exmoor

**Outstanding coastal scenery, particularly below Exmoor;
easy to find peace and quiet even in summer**

Aside from the few resorts and the famously pretty Clovelly and Combe Martin, much of this area is still untouched by tourism, and long stretches of coastline remain almost empty all year round. Even Ilfracombe, the main resort, is not too touristy; pleasant and distinctive with plenty for families, it stays very much alive out of season. In contrast the lower-key beach resorts such as Woolacombe and Westward Ho! virtually shut down when the season's over, and then their marvellous beaches are perfect for lonely wanderings. Elsewhere there are fine bracing cliff walks, and there's a magnificent coastal path. Lundy Island is a windswept wilderness, and getting there adds to the fun.

For walkers (and drivers) Exmoor is full of interest, and quieter in summer than Dartmoor. Though part lies in Somerset, we've covered the whole of the moor area in this chapter (some places such as Dunster' within the boundary of the National Park but outside the moor itself, are described in the Somerset chapter). Some of the best parts of the Tarka Trail, a popular route for walkers and cyclists, are on and around the moor. Other inland areas are largely secluded farmland. The twisty wooded Taw Valley is pretty; the A377 gives drivers some good views here, though not quite so outstanding as the Exeter–Barnstaple rail journey, one of England's finest.

Despite its relatively undeveloped nature, there's no shortage of outings for families here. Young children appreciate the fairy-tale world at Watermouth Castle, and its sister park Once Upon A Time, at Woolacombe, even has its own driving school; Milky Way in Clovelly is very handy on a wet day. The sheep races and duck trials at the Big Sheep near Tiverton are great fun, and the combination of wildlife and dinosaurs at Combe Martin is a successful one. Exmoor Zoological Park (South Stowford) and Exmoor Falconry & Animal Farm (Allerford) will also please animal lovers.

At Torrington Heritage Centre the guides work hard to make children feel involved (good gardens nearby too), and at Bickleigh there's a mill and maze, as well as a castle. There's plenty to look at inside Arlington Court, and the gardens at the wonderfully ornate Knightshayes Court (Bolham) are glorious.

Where to stay

BRAUNTON SS4437 **Saunton Sands Hotel** *Saunton, Braunton, Devon EX33 1LQ (01271) 890212* **£156**; 75 light airy rms inc family rms, many with lovely sea views. Family-run hotel with stunning views over five miles of sandy beach and grounds with outdoor swimming pool (there's also an indoor swimming pool), and

North Devon & Exmoor

squash and tennis courts (Saunton Golf Club is on the doorstep); cocktail bar, comfortable terraced lounge, very good imaginative food and a thoughtful wine list in elegant dining room, and helpful polite staff; live music and entertainment; gym, sauna, and solarium; very good for families with full-time nursery, a full programme of entertainments, games room and junior putting green, and adventure area; partial disabled access ☺

BISHOP'S TAWTON SS5928 **Halmpstone Manor** *Bishops Tawton, Barnstaple, Devon EX32 0EA (01271) 830321* **£100**; 5 pretty rms. Quietly relaxing small country hotel with log fire in comfortable sitting room, enjoyable food in panelled dining room, good breakfasts, caring service, an attractive garden, and nice views; plenty to do nearby; cl Christmas, New Year, and Feb; dogs welcome

BUCKLAND BREWER SS4220 **Coach & Horses** *Buckland Brewer, Bideford, Devon EX39 5LU (01237) 451395* **£60**; 2 rms above bar (so could be noisy for children until 11.30pm). Welcoming well preserved 13th-c thatched village pub with cosy beamed bar, log fires in inglenook fireplaces, enjoyable food, dining room, and pleasant garden; partial disabled access; dogs in bar on lead

CADBURY SS9005 **Beers Farm** *Cadbury, Exeter, Devon EX5 5PY (01884) 855426* **£40**; 2 rms. Set in several acres with lovely views across to the Raddon Hills, this non-working farm is quiet and comfortable (and no smoking) with friendly, helpful owners and good breakfasts; packed lunches on request; garden plants for sale; lots to do nearby

CHITTLEHAMHOLT SS6520 **Highbullen** *Chittlehamholt, Umberleigh, Devon EX37 9HD (01769) 540561* **£150***, plus special breaks; 45 comfortable and elegant, often spacious rms in main building and various attractively converted outbuildings. Victorian 'gothick' mansion in huge wooded parkland and gardens with lots of wildlife, fishing (several beats), 9-hole golf course, indoor tennis court and swimming pool, table tennis, and squash court; consistently good food in intimate restaurant overlooking the valley, busy little bar, library, and relaxed informal service (no reception, you ring a bell and wait); children over 8

CLAWTON SX3499 **Court Barn Hotel** *Clawton, Holsworthy, Devon EX22 6PS (01409) 271219* **£66**, plus special breaks; 8 individually furnished rms. Charming, recently refurbished country house in five pretty acres with croquet, 9-hole putting green, small chip-and-putt course, and tennis and badminton courts; comfortable lounges, log fires, library/TV room, good service, imaginative food and award-winning wines (and teas), and a quiet relaxed atmosphere; they are kind to families; cl first 2 wks Jan; dogs welcome in bedrooms

HEDDON'S MOUTH SS6548 **Heddon's Gate Hotel** *Martinhoe, Parracombe, Barnstaple, Devon EX31 4PZ (01598) 763313* **£138.80** inc dinner, plus special breaks; 14 comfortable rms named for their original use and many with views. Victorian country house hotel in interesting large gardens on the edge of Exmoor, with marvellously relaxed and friendly atmosphere, comfortable sitting room with lovely views, good library/Victorian morning room, attractive dining room, very good home cooking inc 6-course dinners and proper afternoon tea, and friendly helpful service; cl Nov–Easter; children welcome if able to eat at 8pm (no special meals for them); disabled access in annexe cottage; dogs welcome away from dining room

LYNMOUTH SS7249 **Rising Sun** *Mars Hill, Lynmouth, Devon EX35 6EG (01598) 753223* **£99**, plus special breaks; 16 comfortable and cosy rms. Thatched 14th-c inn with lovely views over the little harbour and out to sea, oak-panelled dining room, beamed and panelled bar with uneven oak floors, good food and wines, charming terraced garden, and lots of nearby walks; children over 7; dogs welcome in bedrooms

LYNTON SS7249 **Highcliffe House** *Sinai Hill, Lynton, Devon EX35 6AR (01598) 752235* **£52***, plus special breaks; 6 well equipped attractive rms. Carefully decorated no smoking Victorian house with wonderful views over Lynton, the sea, and wooded countryside; two comfortable sitting rooms, good food in candlelit dining conservatory, and kind staff; cl mid-Dec–mid-Jan; no children

NORTHAM SS4528 **Yeoldon House** *Durrant Lane, Northam, Bideford, Devon EX39 2RL* (01237) 474400 **£90**, plus special breaks; 10 individually decorated rms. Quietly set hotel in two acres by the River Torridge, with a warmly friendly and relaxed atmosphere, a comfortable lounge, good food using local produce in the attractive dining room, and helpful service; lots to do nearby; cl Christmas; dogs welcome away from restaurant

OAKFORD SS9122 **Newhouse Farm** *Oakford, Tiverton, Devon EX16 9JE* (01398) 351347 **£50***, plus special breaks; 3 rms. 17th-c longhouse on edge of Exmoor, with a cottagey sitting room, beams, and country dining room serving home-made food inc good bread, pâtés and puddings, and using the best local ingredients; cl Christmas; no children

PORLOCK SS8846 **Oaks** *Doverhay, Porlock, Minehead, Somerset TA24 8ES* (01643) 862265 **£100***, plus special breaks; 9 airy and pretty rms. Particularly welcoming and spotless Edwardian country house looking down from Exmoor to Porlock Bay, with surrounding lawns and oak trees, a relaxed atmosphere and log fire in attractive lounge, and good unpretentious cooking in attractive no smoking restaurant; cl Nov–Mar; children over 8; dogs welcome in bedrooms

PORLOCK SS8846 **Seapoint** *Redway, Porlock, Minehead, Somerset TA24 8QE* (01643) 862289 **£52***, plus winter breaks; 3 rms. Surrounded by the Exmoor hills and with views of Porlock Bay, this no smoking Edwardian guesthouse has a comfortable sitting room with winter log fire, a friendly and relaxing atmosphere, enjoyable home-made food in candlelit dining room, and fine breakfasts; cl Dec–Jan; they are kind to children; dogs welcome away from dining area

SELWORTHY SS9346 **Hindon Farm** *Selworthy, Minehead, Somerset TA24 8SH* (01643) 705244 **£48***; 2 rms. Organic Exmoor farm of 500 acres with sheep, pigs, cattle, donkeys and ducks, lots of lovely surrounding walks inc award-winning conservation trail, riding (can bring your own horse), and mountain biking; games barn with table tennis and snooker, log fires, and fine breakfasts using their own eggs, bacon, honey, and bread; self-catering farmhouse wing plus cottage, and organic produce basket on arrival; organic farm shop also; children under 11 by arrangement in B&B; dogs welcome in bedrooms

SHEEPWASH SS4806 **Half Moon** *Sheepwash, Beaworthy, Devon EX21 5NE* (01409) 231376 **£80**, plus special breaks; 14 rms inc 5 newly refurbished ones in stables. Civilised heart-of-Devon hideaway in colourful village square with 10 miles of private salmon, sea trout and brown trout fishing on the Torridge, a neatly kept friendly bar, solid old furnishings and big log fire, good wines, lovely evening restaurant, lunchtime bar snacks; cl 20–27 Dec; limited disabled access; dogs welcome away from dining room

WEST BUCKLAND SS6630 **Huxtable Farm** *West Buckland, Barnstaple, Devon EX32 0SR* (01598) 760254 **£50***, plus special breaks; 6 rms. 16th-c farmhouse surrounded by carefully converted listed stone buildings, open fields, fine views, sheep, chickens, and pigs; candlelit dinner with wholesome home-made food using home-grown produce, home-made wine and bread, a relaxing sitting room, and beams, open fireplaces with bread ovens, and uneven floors; sauna, fitness room, tennis court, games room, and play area with swings, sandpit and Wendy house; good for families; cl Dec/Jan (but open New Year) ☺

WEST PORLOCK SS8746 **Bales Mead** *West Porlock, Somerset TA24 8NX* (01643) 862565 **£75***; 3 comfortable, recently refurbished rms with sherry, fresh flowers, and thoughtful little extras. This quiet and relaxing no smoking Edwardian house has lovely Exmoor views towards the sea, a particularly pretty garden, charmingly decorated sitting room with log fire and baby grand piano, super breakfasts (no evening meals), and friendly helpful owners; cl Christmas–New Year; no children

WOOLACOMBE SS4543 **Woolacombe Bay Hotel** *Woolacombe, Devon EX34 7BN* (01271) 870388 **£180**, plus special breaks; 64 rms. Carefully extended Victorian hotel in six acres by a splendid three-mile Blue Flag beach; quiet comfortable lounges, elegant high-ceilinged restaurant with chandeliers, bustling bistro for lighter lunches, two bars, and splendid facilities for children: indoor and outdoor pool (with flume), a children's club plus teenage activities, a crèche, discos and bands, board games and books, and billiard room, pool tables and table tennis; 9-hole approach golf, tennis, squash, and gym, sunbed, jacuzzi, and steam room; golf, riding and surfing nearby, and lovely unspoilt surrounding countryside; cl Jan–Feb ☺

To see and do

ALLERFORD SS9047
Pretty stone-built village with lovely packhorse bridge, and enthusiastic **West Somerset Museum of Rural Life** with occasional summer craft demonstrations; open wkds May–Oct and Suns during summer school hols; (01643) 862529; £1.50.
Exmoor Falconry & Animal Farm 🔊 Friendly place with animals to feed, twice-daily animal handling with snakes, lizards, rabbits, ferrets and parrots, and flying displays; special events all year such as hawk walks and clay-pigeon shooting. B&B in the 15th-c farmhouse, meals, snacks, shop, disabled access; cl Tues–Thurs Nov–Feb; (01643) 862816; £5.50.

APPLEDORE SS4630
A pretty centre of narrow cottagey streets off the quayside road which looks out over the Taw estuary, and ship- and boat-building in the yard just upstream. There's a pedestrian ferry over to Instow (depending on the tide) run by Tarka Cruises; (01237) 476191. Good value food and superb estuary views in the Royal George and the Beaver.
North Devon Maritime Museum (Odun House, Odun Rd) Good museum exploring a different topic in each room. Shop, disabled access to ground floor only; cl pm wkdys, am wknds, and Nov–Easter; (01237) 422064; £1.

ARLINGTON SS6140
Arlington Court (A39) From its Victorian heyday up to 1949 Rosalie Chichester filled this early 19th-c house with model ships, stuffed birds, holiday souvenirs – in fact anything she could get her hands on; her assemblages have been watered down since, but there's still quite a fascinating medley. The grounds have attractive landscaped gardens and a number of Shetland ponies and sheep, along with Victorian

garden and conservatory, woodland and lakeside nature trails, and an unusual collection of carriages and horse-drawn vehicles (rides available). There is also a batcave (you can watch rare lesser horseshoe bats on CCTV, and even zoom in on particular ones using a special joystick). Meals, snacks, shop, disabled access to ground floor only; cl Tues, and Nov–Mar; (01271) 850296; £5.60, garden only £3.50; NT. The Pyne Arms at East Down is nice for lunch.

BARNSTAPLE SS5533
The main regional shopping centre is pedestrianised, with a good deal of unforced charm in the older parts. Interesting buildings include an imposing 18th-c colonnaded arcade on the Great Quay, a lofty Victorian market hall (markets every day exc Sun), almshouses behind the church, more off the square by the long old stone bridge, and some interesting shops. It's still a working port, though in a very small way now. Panniers (Boutport St) has decent food all day. In summer you can hire bikes at the main railway station (01271) 324202; £9 a day; a good ride is the one along the disused rail track up to Torrington. The surviving mainline **Exeter–Barnstaple** line (known as the Tarka Line), mostly tracking along closer to the River Taw than the road does, is one of the finest of all train rides for scenery.
Art Hotel 🔊 (off B3230 towards Ilfracombe) There's an appealing blend of old and new at this friendly late Victorian hotel surrounded by woodland. Inside, the house is decorated with antiques and contemporary art, while new works are continually added to the evolving sculpture garden; they also run a programme of lectures, music recitals and poetry readings. Meals, snacks;

garden and gallery cl am Mon–Weds, and 15 Dec–15 Jan; (01271) 850262; *£3.50. The hotel has a tennis court and heated outdoor swimming pool; B&B £27.50 (wknd £32.50).

Barnstaple Heritage Centre ⊞ (Queen Anne's Walk) You pass through an ornate Georgian colonnade to reach this centre, which relates the 1,000-year history of the town with the help of computer and hands-on displays. Shop, disabled access; cl Sun, 25–26 Dec, 1 Jan; (01271) 373003; £2.50.

Disused railway paths Down at sea level sections of the former track from Barnstaple and Bideford can be walked or cycled (local bicycle hire (01271) 345182; £12 a day for an adult, £24 for 2 adults and 2 children). The best section is the one from Barnstaple through Instow and Bideford up to the Puffing Billy at the former Torrington Station. In autumn and winter particularly this gives close views of the wading birds massed on the tidal sands of the estuary, and year-round the section up to Torrington is very attractive. The longest cycle ride here is 28 miles without touching a road.

Marwood Hill Gardens (Marwood; off A361 towards Braunton) 18 well kept and colourful acres inc rare trees and shrubs, small lakes, extensive bog garden, clematis, camellias, alpines and eucalyptus, and national collections of astilbes (best in July) and tulbaghias. Snacks, plant centre, some disabled access; cl 25 Dec; (01271) 342528; £3. The Ring o' Bells at Prixford is very handy for lunch.

Museum of North Devon (The Square) Local history museum with interactives for children, and temporary exhibitions upstairs. Disabled access; cl Sun, Mon, a wk over Christmas and New Year, and bank hols; (01271) 346747; free.

BICKLEIGH SS9306

Bickleigh Castle Charming moated and fortified manor house, still very much a family home; the 11th-c chapel is said to be Devon's oldest complete building. Also medieval hall, armoury and guard room, Tudor bedroom, 17th-c farmhouse, and exhibitions on maritime history and the Civil War. All done with great enthusiasm, and with a fair bit to amuse children. A restaurant is open for evening meals (Thurs–Sat, booking essential), limited disabled access; open pm Weds and Sun Easter–Sept; (01884) 855363; *£4. The Fishermans Cot is a beautifully placed riverside dining pub.

Bickleigh Mill and Maize Maze ⊞ (Bickleigh Mill Farm) Bustling family-run place with a working waterwheel, resident potter, and an 11-acre maize labyrinth which can grow over head-height; you can also fish for trout (£10 inc rod hire and bait). Meals, snacks, shops, limited disabled access; open daily exc 25–26 Dec (maze late Jun–end Sept only); (01884) 855419; free (exc maze; £2).

BIDEFORD SS4526

Quiet hillside town now bypassed, with notable medieval bridge and some pleasant old streets, partly pedestrianised, behind the Quay. The day-trip boat for Lundy (a good long day) sails from here year round, though not every day, and only rarely in March; phone (01271) 863636 for times. One of the oldest streets is Bridgeland St, and up towards the top of Bridge St there are quite a few antiques or antiqueish shops. The Joiners Arms (Market Pl) has decent food, and the Vagabond Cavalier (Cooper St) does good value Italian meals.

Big Sheep ⊞ (A39, 2m W) Exuberant sheep centre, best known for its splendidly entertaining sheep steeplechasing (usually around 3.20pm), when sheep with knitted jockeys on their backs race 200 yards from their field towards the prize of extra food. Even better are the duck trials at midday, miniature sheepdog trials with the sheep replaced by ducks; there are more traditional sheepdog demonstrations too. Other events and displays take in everything from shearing and bottle-feeding to milking, with plenty of opportunities to get close to the animals (lambs are born throughout the year, so always some to cuddle). Decent adventure play area, lots under cover, and it's good value – tickets are valid for unlimited return visits for a week for £2. Home-made meals and snacks (good teas), shop, disabled access; usually open daily Easter–Dec, wknds Dec–Easter exc 3 wks over Christmas and New Year – but best to check; (01237) 472366; £5.95. The Thatched Inn family dining pub at Abbotsham is handy for lunch.

BOLHAM SS9615

Knightshayes Court Lovely woodland garden with acres of unusual even unique plants, esp lovely in spring but a glory at any time of year. Alpine and more formal gardens, ancient yew topiary, attractive walks, and good Exe Valley views; they hope by spring 2003 to have finished restoring the walled garden too. The spooky-looking house itself is extravagantly ornate Victorian gothick, with elaborate painted ceilings and décor and a restored minstrel's gallery. The original plans were even more over-the-top, but when the horrified owner saw them he sent the architect William Burges packing; though one room has recently been reconstructed as Burges intended it. Meals, snacks, shop and plant centre, disabled access; open 22 Mar–2 Nov (house cl Fri); (01884) 254665; £5.70, garden only £4.10; NT.

BRADWORTHY SS3213

A pleasant jumping-off point for walks, with some quiet local strolls on the common, or over by the Tamar Lake a couple of miles SW. The thatched Bradworthy Inn has good food.

Gnome Reserve ⊞ (West Putford, 2m E) One of the most delightfully silly places in the area, woodland and wildflower meadows populated by hand-painted and individually modelled pixies. They lend you gnome hats and fishing rods so that resident gnomes will think you're one of them. The setting is pretty (flowers and plants are labelled), and very small children love it. Shop, snacks, disabled facilities but limited access; cl Oct–20 Mar; (0870) 8459012; £2.45.

BRAUNTON BURROWS SS4532

This vast nature reserve expanse of great swelling dunes, grazed by little Soay sheep, is easily reached from the B3231 W of Braunton (red flags warn if there's shooting on the range in the southern part here). The Mariners Arms in South St in Braunton itself is a pleasantly untouristy pub, and the

Seafood Bistro (Caen St/Chalenors Rd) has friendly service and good fresh locally caught fish.

BROWNSHAMS, THE SS2825

These isolated farmhouses, now NT property, give walkers good quiet access to the woods, cliffs and clifftop farmland W of Clovelly.

BULL POINT SS4646

There's a lighthouse here, and dramatic cliff walks between here and Morte Point; Mortehoe makes a good start point, with an interesting church, and enjoyable food in the Chichester Arms.

CALVERLEIGH SS9214

An attractive village with a fine **church** and decent pub.

CHITTLEHAMPTON SS6127

Cobbaton Combat Collection ⊞ (off A377) Growing private collection of British and Canadian World War II vehicles, quite tightly packed under cover but looking ready for action; also mock-ups of wartime scenes, wartime memorabilia, and play area with Sherman tank. Summer snacks, shop, some disabled access; usually only cl wknds Nov–Easter but best to check in winter; (01769) 540740; £4.25. The Exeter Inn at Chittlehamholt has good food.

CHULMLEIGH SS6814

Lovely unspoilt village, and a good base for touring the coast and Taw Valley. The Globe has attractively priced home cooking.

CLOVELLY SS3124

One of Devon's most famous views, down the very steep old cobbled street, free from traffic and with flower-covered cottages either side, to the tiny harbour below. It's a delightful village, best appreciated out of season. At any time of year you'll have to park up at the top, outside the village, then pay £3.50 to pass through a turnstile, and walk down. The Red Lion is pleasantly placed down by the quay; if you can't face the climb back up, a Land Rover can drive you back from behind here (summer only, £1.60). Up towards the A39 is a big Iron Age hill fort, Clovelly Dykes, and along the coast the beachside hamlet of Bucks Mills is well worth a visit. The woods, cliffs and clifftops farmland W of Clovelly is attractive walking country. The moorland road down from Stibb Cross on the A388 via Woolfardisworthy is good, and the woodland Hobby Drive toll road is the area's best coast drive.

Clovelly Court These parkland gardens have tranquil sea views, and a fine walled garden and restored Victorian greenhouse. Meals, snacks, souvenir and book shop, disabled access. Cl 25 Dec; (01237) 431200; £3.50 (Land Rover ride to Court £1.60, return £2.50).

Milky Way ⌨ (Downland Farm) Plenty of action for families in this adventure park, and as it's one of the biggest covered attractions in the region it's handy for a rainy day. Games and rides are based on the theme of alien life – one of them, the fun Clone Zone ride, is interactive. Good big indoor and outdoor play areas (inc one for toddlers), an assault course and archery as well as mini golf, laser target shooting, birds of prey (twice-daily displays) and a little railway. There's also a new animal barn with lambs and kids for children to bottle feed, a chick hatchery, and you can watch ferret racing too; cl wkdys Nov–Apr (exc school hols), 25–26 Dec and 1 Jan; (01237) 431255; £6.50, may be reduced in winter when less is open.

COMBE MARTIN SS5846
A string of former smallholdings and cottages scattered down a lovely sheltered valley, with an odd pub, the Pack of Cards, built to celebrate a cards win – four floors, 13 doors, 52 windows. There's a little fishing harbour in the shingly cove between the cliffs, and the Fo'csle is useful for lunch.

Combe Martin Wildlife & Dinosaur Park ⌨ (A399) A good place for children, with plenty of animals and birds in over 30 acres of woodland, inc a pair of rare snow leopards, and meerkats in a huge desert enclosure. Also a dinosaur museum, and meticulously researched life-size dinosaurs, some of which move and roar – like the towering *Tyrannosaurus rex*. A themed train ride runs through the gardens, which have rare and tropical plants; there are wallabies to feed, daily falconry displays, and a recently added butterfly house. Meals,

snacks, shop; cl Nov–Easter; (01271) 882486; £10.

CROYDE SS4439
A magnet for surfers, this clean-sand village has a good family pub, the Thatched Barn. Baggy Point W of here has a path good enough for wheelchairs.

EGGESFORD SS6811
This quiet Taw Valley village has a 14th-c **church**, and a garden centre set in the walled garden of a ruined house; refreshments on a terrace with lovely views. A good base for inland walks (and a stop on the Barnstaple–Exeter rail line): in Flashdown Wood, up wooded Hayne Valley to Wembworthy, or through Heywood Wood, where the mound of the former castle gives good views (and there are picnic sets).

EXMOOR SS7739
(We include the Somerset part of the park here; Allerford and Lynton are listed separately, and Dunster is in the Somerset chapter.) Excellent walking, both inland and along the coast, and less busy than Dartmoor in summer. In some places it's been more tamed than Dartmoor – drained and resown with richer-growing grasses for better pasture. But it's still a wild place, with hawthorns and low oak trees bent and gnarled by the winds, and (unlike Dartmoor) wild deer. Where it drops away sharply to the sea, fast streams and rivers cut deeply into beautiful wooded valleys. Note that some of Exmoor's moorland paths have a disconcerting habit of fizzling out without warning. Exmoor is probably the part of Britain where hunting traditions are most deeply rooted. It's also rewarding territory for drivers, with plenty of good views; the B roads are generally less congested than others.

Dulverton SS9127 The main town for Exmoor is a civilised place, with a handsome old stone market house, and a fine bridge over the river which has cut this steeply wooded valley. The Lion Hotel is useful for lunch, and the area's main information centre is at the S end of Fore St; (01398) 323841.

Dunkery Hill SS8941 Exmoor's great ridge walk, with Dunkery Beacon as its high point surveying a huge chunk of

SW England and S Wales (as tramping boots have worn three feet off the top of the Beacon, walkers are asked to take a bag of stones and earth up to deposit there). It is easily walked from the nearby road; a handy place to leave the car is Webbers Post (which is also good for local pottering). It can also be incorporated into longer walks from Horner Woods or Luccombe.

Exford SS8538 Prettily set in a sheltered valley by a small streamside green; the church up the hill a bit is well worth a look. The Crown is good for lunch, and satisfying walking is to be had along the Exe to Winsford.

Heddon's Mouth Cleave SS6548 A secretive wooded combe running between rugged hills from the beautifully placed Hunters Inn to the sea – an easy walk which can be extended along the cliffs at two levels to Woody Bay to the E. W of Hunters Inn is the terraced walkway known as the Ladies Mile, along a charming valley nr Trentishoe.

Malmsmead Natural History Centre SS7947 Badgworthy Water is the focus of a walkers' path from Malmsmead which takes you into the very heart of Lorna Doone country – it gets wilder and more remote with every step southwards (the surrounding moors provide a handful of return routes). From the **Malmsmead Natural History Centre**, the Exmoor Natural History Society run leisurely two-hour strolls through the striking scenery every Weds mid-May–mid-Sept, plus Thurs in Aug, at 2pm; very enthusiastically done, and free (you can get a cup of tea afterwards for a small donation); Mr and Mrs Cornish have full details on (01984) 631859. The Exmoor Sandpiper at Countisbury up towards Lynton is a useful food stop.

Parracombe SS6644 A lovely little village worth visiting in its own right, but particularly interesting is **St Petroc's church**, one of the few churches to have an unspoilt medieval fabric completely untouched by Victorian restoration, all flagstones and Georgian box pews; this may be locked Nov–Easter, but key from custodian then. The interesting Fox & Goose has good food.

Porlock SS8846 Hilly village, with a lot of traffic, but some attractive cottages with distinctive lighthouse-like chimneys and thatched roofs.

Porlock Weir SS8647 This harbour tucked below wooded cliffs is much quieter than nearby Porlock, though it does get a lot of summer visitors; decent food at the thatched Ship. It has a pebbly beach and wooded cliffs to the W – you can walk this way to remote **Culbone church**, the smallest complete church in the country.

Selworthy SS9146 Gloriously unspoilt village, rated by some readers as the most attractive they've ever seen, with groups of white thatched cottages around a prettily planted hillside green looking out over Exmoor. The church is a gem, with a fine waggon-roof; Selworthy Beacon, some way above the village, is a four-way viewpoint nr a minor dead-end road that climbs steeply up from Minehead.

Tarka Trail This long-distance figure-of-eight signed path runs nearly 200 miles, linking Exmoor, Dartmoor and the N Devon coast, following the route of Henry Williamson's *Tarka the Otter* – and is most enjoyable with a copy of the book. One beautiful section is the route around **Pinkworthy Pond** and The Chains, reached from the car park a couple of miles along the B3358 E of Challacombe (where the Black Venus is good). It's even more popular with cyclists than walkers.

Tarr Steps SS8632 The River Barle's most famous feature, the finest of all the stone-and-slab clapper bridges for packhorses. The path along the river, which runs between Simonsbath and Dulverton, is uneven and surprisingly slow-going in places.

Watersmeet SS7448 Paths run eastward out of Lynton along the Lyn River to Watersmeet (1½m E), where the Hoaroak Water tumbles down to meet the East Lyn in a series of rocky cascades among steeply picturesque oak woods. There's a discreet NT refreshment pavilion here, cl Nov–Mar. Don't miss the wonderful return route on the Tarka Trail/Two Moors Way high above the valley to the S (some steep sections). Riverside paths head on further upstream, to the prettily set

Rockford Inn (a good base for walks – food finishes at 2). Just N of Watersmeet, the Foreland Cliffs are the highest in the country and have dramatic views.

Winsford SS9035 A quiet and attractive village below high hills, with the River Exe lacing through its countless bridges. The Royal Oak is good for lunch.

HARTLAND SS2424

Hartland Abbey ⬜ Fine old (and still lived in) house on the site of an Augustinian abbey, with elegant rooms (the drawing room is modelled on the House of Lords), paintings by Gainsborough and Joshua Reynolds among others, several interesting historic documents, exhibition of old photography, woodland walks and peacock-filled parkland. There's a restored Victorian fernery, an 18th-c walled garden, and a wild-flower walk leading to a peaceful cove. Cream teas, shop; house open pm Easter Sun and Mon, pms Weds, Thurs, Sun and bank hols (plus pm Tues July–Aug) Apr–6 Oct, garden open pm Sun–Fri Apr–6 Oct, best to check; (01237) 441264; £5, grounds only £3. The village has **craft shops** inc working pottery (01237) 441693, and Windsor chair maker (children's sizes too); (01237) 441590.

HARTLAND QUAY SS2324

Grand isolated spot at foot of toll road (no fee winter), on jagged coast which looks a dramatic cross between illustrations for geology textbooks and ones for a shipwreckers' manual. Down by the sea is a wonderfully maritime old inn (cl winter), and the **museum** covers four centuries of smuggling and shipwrecks – even big ships still go down here; cl Oct–Easter; (01273) 441218; £1. For walkers, the cliffs around here are much more dramatic than those at nearby Hartland Point (which also has a toll gate). Just S at Spekes Mill Mouth the sea-eroded valley leaves the river spewing down the cliff in a **seaside waterfall**.

Docton Mill ⬜ ((Milford)) Extensive and interesting sheltered streamside garden and new woodland plantation, largely naturalised, beside an ancient restored watermill. It's particularly attractive in spring. Snacks, (good cream teas), plant sales; cl Nov–Feb; (01237) 441369; £3.50 They have a couple of bedrooms you can stay in.

HATHERLEIGH SS5404

An attractive hillside village – even the church slopes – with a handsome inn (the George) and a good **pottery** (20 Market St).

ILFRACOMBE SS5147

Picturesque resort around busy harbour sheltered by high cliffs, with terraces of late Victorian boarding houses and small hotels looking out over it from their perches among the trees of the steep bay. There are period resort buildings and gardens, and even tunnels cut through the rock to a former Victorian bathing place. The 14th-c chapel above the harbour mouth has doubled as a lighthouse for over 450 years; the **lifeboat station** can be visited (donation requested). **Holy Trinity church** (Church St) is worth a look for its richly carved 15th-c waggon-roof, one of the most striking in the area. The ancient George & Dragon is a nice spot for lunch. In summer the paddle steamer *Waverley* or the traditional cruise ship *Balmoral* run cruises from the pier to Lundy, Minehead, and other places – even as far as Swansea. Bicclescombe Park (A361 just S) has a restored 18th-c **cornmill**; the Coach House nearby also has decent food. The best cliff walks are to the W of the town, towards Lee Bay.

Ilfracombe Museum ⬜ (Runnymede Gardens) Enthusiastic town museum, a bit like looking through someone's attic (cl pm, and wknds Nov–Mar; £1.50).

Old Corn Mill & Pottery (A399 just E) Well restored early 16th-c mill; pottery demonstrations, and the chance to throw your own pot. Cream teas, shop, disabled access to pottery and tearoom only; cl Nov–Mar; (01271) 863185; £2.50.

Old Railway This disused railway trail above Ilfracombe is popular with walkers and cyclists, with a tunnel, interesting plants, and attractive scenery inc the lakes of Slade Reservoirs. For a one-way walk it's best to do it in reverse, for better views – and it's downhill all the way; Red Bus 31 or 31A to Lee Bridge or Lee Cross (or to the Fortescue Hotel for a preliminary bracer); (0870) 608 2608 for bus information.

Watermouth Castle 🏰 This is a fine 19th-c structure overlooking the bay, transformed into a world of gnomes, goblins, trolls and fairy tales, with slides, carousels and a musical water show; also miniature golf, various rides and a maze. Very much for families, with young children the ones who'll enjoy it most. Snacks, picnic area, shop, disabled access; open Apr–Oct, but phone for times as they vary each week; (01271) 867474; £7.

INSTOW SS4728
At the mouth of the Torridge estuary, this has an expanse of tidal sands, with dozens of moored boats beached on them at low tide. The Boathouse has good food and views. Tapeley Park The very pretty Italianate garden with rococo features and walled kitchen garden is the main draw, though there's also a pets' corner, play area, and woodland walk. Lovely views down to the sea. Teas and snacks in period dairy, plant sales, some disabled access; cl Sat, and Nov to mid-Mar; (01271) 342558; £4, (house tours £2.50 – you need to give a week's notice).

KING'S NYMPTON SS6819
An attractive village with a fine **church** and decent pub.

LEE SS4846
This pretty village in a sheltered woody valley has an attractive ancient pub, the Grampus. There are good cliff walks between Lee Bay and Ilfracombe.

LUNDY DAY TRIPS SS1344
(boat from Bideford or, in summer, Ilfracombe) Well worth considering if you're in Devon for more than just a few days. The island's best known for the migrant birds that come here in spring and autumn, but the remoteness and loneliness are also a powerful draw – the permanent population is around a dozen. Lovely walks along its seven miles of formidably high cliffs, windswept rough pastures, small church, evocative castle ruins, two lighthouses (one the highest in Britain), wandering goats, small Soay sheep and ponies, and the chance of seeing seals (especially in autumn), the introduced small sika deer, and, in Apr and May, the

island's trademark puffins. Accommodation can be arranged through the Landmark Trust (01628) 825925. The Marisco Tavern is the place to eat. The return boat trip (1–2 hrs each way) is £25; (01271) 863636 for sailing times.

LYNTON SS7249
This beautifully placed hilltop village tucks into the wooded seaside gorge where the East and West Lyn tumble down to the sea. One way of getting down to its pretty harbourside extension, Lynmouth, is a 19th-c funicular cliff railway; £1.90 return. The most delightful walks in N Devon are around here. Lynton clearly shows its origins as a Victorian resort in one of the many areas then known as Little Switzerland, with hillside villas (now quiet boarding houses), photogenic corners and some older cottages. Craft shops and so forth; lots of trippers during the day in summer. The Olde Cottage Inne (B3234 – lovely walk up The Lynway from Sinai Hill) is useful for lunch, and the Rising Sun down by the harbour has a good restaurant. The Valley of Rocks is an easy (and enjoyable) walk from the village or you can get there by horse-drawn carriage; 50-minute round-trips leave from the cliff railway; £4 return; (01598) 753215; Watersmeet is also within reach.

Exmoor Boat Cruises Informative boat trips, with talks about sea birds and coastal geography, leave the harbour from 11am daily, but very much dependent on weather and tide, Apr–Oct; check when rough (01598) 753207; from £5 for a 40-min trip.

Glen Lyn Gorge Carefully restored after the tragic flood of 1952, with pretty walks and an exhibition on water power (the village uses hydro-electricity). Some disabled access. Exhibition cl Nov–Mar (reduced admission £2), gorge cl 3rd Weds in Jan, and in bad weather; (01598) 753207; £3. They have decent holiday flats and cottages in a peaceful setting.

Lyn & Exmoor Museum (Market St) In the old part of the upper village, this engagingly simple museum of local history is in an 18th-c cottage, with a scale model of the former Lynton–Barnstaple narrow-gauge railway (you can still walk much of its track bed). Shop; cl 12.30–2 pm, Sun am, Nov–Easter, and perhaps other times too, so best to check; (01598) 752225); free.

Valley of Rocks A great valley bowl with steep crags and pinnacles of rock dividing it from the sea (and a dreadful unscreened car park smack in the middle). It's reached by an easy coast path from Lynton, or by paths over Hollerday Hill (wooded, but opens out dramatically on top). The cliff-skipping goats here are ancient feral stock.

MOLLAND SS8028
An attractive village with classic box pews in its wonderfully untouched **church**, and good value food in the unspoilt London Inn beside it.

MUDDIFORD SS5535
Blakewell Trout Farm Good for experts and beginners, with a little pool where you're practically guaranteed a bite. Meals, snacks, shop, disabled access; cl 25 Dec; (01271) 344533; free. The Muddiford Inn is an inexpensive family pub.

NORTHAM BURROWS SS4430
Dunes, sand slacks and meres behind a pebble ridge, with the Atlantic rollers swinging in along the rock-strewn Saunton Sands beyond – deserted out of season and stimulating then for lonely walks; in summer a popular family beach.

ROADFORD LAKE SX4290
Trout fishing ▣ Serious trout fishing in this carefully landscaped reservoir; cl Oct–Mar; £13 day permit. Meals, snacks, shop, disabled access for fishing from bank; if you want a boat you will have to book 24hrs in advance; (01409) 211514.

SHEBBEAR SS4409
An interesting and attractive tucked-away village, with the odd Devil's Stone by the green (and a decent pub named after it), and a working wood-fired pottery; (01409) 281271.

SHEEPWASH SS4806
Quiet village with cob-and-thatch houses around the green; the Half Moon is useful for lunch. A mile N is Duckpool Cottage traditional wood-fired **pottery**.

SOUTH MOLTON SS7126
An attractive central square and imposing church – and its farming roots

show in the Thurs cattle market. The 18th-c Town Hall has a local history **museum** (cl Fri, Sun, and Dec–Feb, limited hours Sat, Weds; (01769) 572951; free), and monthly art-and-craft shows. The Corn Dolly (East St) is nicely decorated with its namesakes and is ideal for afternoon tea, while the Mill (cl Weds; off A361 at Bish Mill roundabout) is a pleasant family food pub.

Quince Honey Farm (North Rd) The biggest wild-bee farm in the world, with observation hives looking right into the centre of the colonies. Meals, snacks, shop (lots of honey and their own beeswax skin and hair care products); cl Nov–Easter (though shop stays open); (01769) 572401; £3.40.

SOUTH STOWFORD SS6540
Exmoor Zoological Park ▣ (off B3226 N of Bratton Fleming) Good-sized collection of rare and endangered creatures, many of which breed successfully throughout the year. Children can feed the smaller animals or play on the assault course, and there are good views from the well landscaped grounds; regular activities in summer inc bottle feeding, face painting and birds of prey displays. Snacks, shop, disabled access; cl 21–31 Dec; (01598) 763352; £5.25. The Old Station House at Blackmoor Gate is a pleasant dining pub.

TIVERTON SS9512
Formerly prosperous wool town, well worth wandering around; **St Peter's church** is magnificently decorated with rich carving, and other grand buildings include the Jacobean council offices. The four showrooms of the **Tiverton Craft Centre** showcase the work of over 170 local craftsmen (cl Sun). In summer there are 2½-hr **horse-drawn boat trips** along the attractively restored canal from the wharf; booking advisable, (01884) 253345; open Apr–Oct; £6.95. They also hire out rowing boats and motor-boats.

Tiverton Castle ▣ The handsome castle was built in 1106 as a Royal fortress dominating the River Exe, and still has its Norman tower and gatehouse, as well as one of the best assemblages of Civil War armour and arms; pretty gardens too. You can stay in apartments in the oldest parts of the building. Shop, disabled access to ground floor and garden; open pm Sun, Thurs and bank hol Mons Easter–Jun and Sept, pm Sun–Thurs July and Aug; (01884) 253200; £4.

Tiverton Museum of Mid-Devon Life 🆓 (Beck's Sq) A mid-19th-c school houses this large local history museum, with two waterwheels, an excellent railway gallery, a display on the work of the wheelwright, and a collection of farm waggons; shop, disabled access; cl Sat pm, Sun, and Christmas–3 Feb; (01884) 256295; £3.50.

TORRINGTON SS4919

Quiet dairy-farming town on a ridge above the River Torridge, with some attractive buildings inc 14th-c Taddiport Chapel (for a former leper colony), the imposing Palmer House, and a rather grand church built to replace the original blown up in the Civil War. There are good views from the neatly mown hill above the river, and other nearby strolls on the preserved commons surrounding the town. The Black Horse is useful for lunch.

Dartington Crystal 🆓 (Linden Cl) You can tour the factory (last tour 3.15pm); there's a useful visitor centre, and reputedly the biggest glass shop in the country. They get very busy on wet days in summer – best to phone and check tour availability. No tours wknds and bank hols, shop cl 25–26 Dec, Easter Sun; meals, snacks, disabled access (not to tour); (01805) 626242; £4.

Downes (A386 Torrington–Bideford, nr Monkleigh) Fine big woodland garden with interesting flowering trees and shrubs, lovely landscaped lawns, and great views. Wknd snacks, plant sales; open daily Easter–mid-Jun, then by appointment till Sept; (01805) 622244; £2.

RHS Garden Rosemoor 🆓 (off A3124 just S) A wonderful place, constantly being developed and updated by the Royal Horticultural Society; marvellous rare trees, shrubs, and other plants in charmingly landscaped sheltered woodland setting, rose, stream and bog gardens, foliage

and plantsman's garden, and trails for children. Meals, snacks, picnic area, shop, disabled access; cl 25 Dec; (01805) 624067; £5.

Torrington 1646 (South St car park) This lively heritage centre brings to life one of the lesser-known battles of the English Civil War, fought here in February 1646. Four or five actors, all in period clothes, and rarely stepping out of character, work hard to get children involved. The scene-setting first part is a fairly traditional exhibition of Civil War history, where you can try on a helmet or find out from touch-screens whether you'd have been a Cavalier or Roundhead. A video shows a large-scale reconstruction of the battle by the Sealed Knot. Small groups are ushered in and told to imagine they're back in the 17th c; the guide disappears and is replaced by a 17th-c local keen to usher you away from the battle to safety. He'll take you through various reconstructions and situations, until you get to the church. Outside, army stragglers will try to sell you their armour and weapons; they'll show you how to charge into battle, let you examine their swords, and may introduce you to period games. Finally you're shown around a reconstructed 17th-c garden. Teas, snacks, picnic area, shop, disabled access; cl Sun outside school hols, best to check winter opening times; (01805) 626146; £6, children £4.50.

UPTON PYNE SX9197

Appealingly unspoilt village, the basis of Barton in *Sense and Sensibility*.

WELCOMBE MOUTH SS2118

Rather a rough drive down, but an attractive spot, and the cliffs around have possibilities for wild coast walks.

WOOLACOMBE SS4843

The clean beach here is one of the best in Britain, and its Atlantic breakers now draw quite a few surfers. The Rock at Georgeham has good value food and a great conservatory for children, and the back rd to Mortehoe is scenic.

Once Upon a Time 🆓 (Old Station, B3343 inland) Run by the same people as Watermouth Castle in Ilfracombe, this is a super place for children up to about 11, with lots of rides and other activities; there's a driving school that

even offers tests. Snacks, shop, disabled access; open Apr–end Sept, but times and days vary so phone to check; (01271) 867474; £3, £5.50 children (discount voucher admits one adult free for one child ticket).
Other attractive villages with

decent pubs include Berrynarbor SS5646, Buckland Brewer SS4220, Iddesleigh SS5708, Knowstone SS8223, Thorverton SS9202 and Winkleigh SS6308.

Where to eat

BRAUNTON SS4836 **Squires Fish Restaurant** *Exeter Rd (01271) 815533* First-class fish and chip take-away and restaurant with really excellent fish, good wines, friendly service and attractive airy surroundings; cl Sun (but open school summer hols then), 25–26 Dec; disabled access. £9.70|**£3.70**

CHULMLEIGH SS6814 **Old Bakehouse** *South Molton St (01769) 580137/580074* Thatched 16th-c merchant's house with lots of beams, a flower-filled courtyard, and dining room serving morning coffee, light lunches and afternoon teas (plus breakfast and dinner for residents); bdrms. cl Mon, Christmas; children over 5; disabled access. £25|**£5.50**

COLEFORD SS7701 **New Inn** *(01363) 84242* Comfortable thatched 14th-c inn with good interesting food, an extensive wine list, well kept real ales, four nicely furnished areas, winter log fire, and attractive garden with seats on decking along the stream; bdrms; cl 25–26 Dec. £19.95|**£6.95**

DOLTON SS5712 **Union** *Fore St (01805) 804633* Relaxed and friendly old pub with good interesting genuinely home-made food using first-class produce, well kept real ales, and decent wines; comfortable little lounge, characterful lower bar with chatty drinking area and tables for eating, and charming owners; bdrms; cl Weds, 1st 2 wks Feb. £22|**£5**

PORLOCK SS8647 **Andrews on the Weir** *(01643) 863300* Victorian villa housing a restaurant-with-rooms overlooking the harbour; country house-style décor, imaginative modern British cooking using first-class local produce (the Exmoor hill lamb, fish freshly landed on the nearby quay, and west country cheeses, are excellent), lovely puddings, and a well chosen wine list; cl Sun pm, Mon, all Jan; children over 12. £43.50/2-course lunch £10.50

TIVERTON SS9512 **Four and Twenty Blackbirds** *43 Gold St (01884) 257055* Friendly teashop with beams, a mix of old tables and chairs, lots of interesting things to look at, and delicious food (all home-made); cl Sun.|**£3.75**

VIRGINSTOW SX3892 **Percy's Country Hotel and Restaurant** *(01409) 211236* Carefully renovated and interestingly designed restaurant-with-rooms in 16th-c longhouse set in 40 acres (which provide some of the organic produce used in the no smoking evening restaurant); good imaginative modern cooking (super bread and puddings) and a well chosen wine list; comfortable spacious bdrms; children over 12; disabled access. £37.50

WINKLEIGH SS6308 **Pophams** *Castle St (01837) 83767* Tiny bustling place for morning coffee and lunch – bring your own wine – with particularly good interesting food, and relaxed happy atmosphere; cl Sat–Weds, and Feb; no children. £30

WINSFORD SS9035 **Royal Oak** *(01643) 851455* Beautiful thatched inn in quiet spot with attractively furnished cosy bars, a smartly civilised atmosphere, enjoyable home-made bar and restaurant food, well kept real ales, and friendly staff; lots of surrounding walks; bdrms; disabled access. £27|**£8**

Special thanks to Dave Irving, Derek and Sylvia Stephenson, Karen Scott, Sharon Hicks

DORSET

Great for families, with attractions as varied as the coastline, from bustling Bournemouth to striking unspoilt fossil-strewn beaches; interesting towns, and some untouched countryside makes for rewarding walks

Ninety-five miles of coast between Orcombe Point in Devon and Old Harry Rocks in Dorset has recently been declared a World Heritage Site, because of its geological importance. This 'Jurassic Coast' is the first natural World Heritage Site in England, and gives Dorset some spectacular scenery. Striking coastal features include Lulworth Cove, the rugged Isle of Purbeck, Portland Bill, and the tremendous sweep of Chesil Beach and its great lagoon near East Fleet. A coastal path, often with magnificent views, runs the length of the county.

Interesting towns are another bonus. The classic seaside resort of Bournemouth has seven miles of good beaches, and a civilised and spacious spread of comfortable resort areas and leafy suburbs. Its close neighbours Poole (beautiful gardens and a fun water park) and Christchurch (interesting buildings and an appealingly eclectic museum) have much to offer in their own right. There's lots to keep families entertained in Weymouth, from staring at the fish in the excellent Sea Life Park to scrambling around Nothe Fort or getting some hands-on action at the good museums. Elegant Lyme Regis is smaller and more individual.

Dorchester has plenty to offer, from an eminent Dinosaur Museum, and the intriguing Tutankhamun Exhibition, to a cheery Teddy Bear Museum. There's plenty for Thomas Hardy fans here and elsewhere; his books (and films of them) are vividly conjured up by particular Dorset villages and tracts of countryside. Sherborne, Shaftesbury, Blandford Forum, and especially Wimborne Minster are smaller towns well worth visiting. Ask in the Tourist Information Centres about the Explorer ticket – a good buy here if you're going to be doing much travelling on buses.

Tremendous fun for younger children, the Alice in Wonderland Family Park in Hurn is our Dorset Family Attraction of the Year. Moors Valley Country Park on Ashley Heath is great for burning off energy, and, in contrast, Stapehill Abbey is just right for a relaxed afternoon. A satisfying range of animal attractions include Putlake Adventure Farm at Langton Matravers, Monkey World at Wool, the Dorset Heavy Horse Centre at Edmondsham, and well organised Farmer Palmers at Organford (fun for small children). Bird-lovers find the Swannery at Abbotsbury very rewarding (interesting sub-tropical gardens here too).

The lively Royal Signals Museum in Blandford Forum is worth a visit if military matters interest you, and the Tank Museum at Bovington Camp has quite a bit for families (Lawrence of Arabia's Clouds House is nearby). In Tolpuddle you can learn more about the eponymous martyrs, and there are superb paintings at impressive 17th-c Kingston Lacy house near Wimborne Minster. Nearby Knoll Gardens has lots of rare and exotic plants, while Chickerell, Beaminster and Minterne Magna Minterne Gardens are other good destinations for plant lovers. Forde Abbey at Thorncombe boasts a lovely house as well as beautiful gardens.

Inland, the countryside has a subtle understated appeal, with secluded valleys, narrow lanes threading through peaceful farmland and tucked-away villages (Milton Abbas best of all – a good day out). The central area's chalk uplands cut by intricate valleys give some splendid high viewpoints – not to mention the prehistoric giant cut into the hillside north of Cerne Abbas. In May the bluebell woods at Bere and Delcombe make lovely walks. The west's intimate farming country feels untouched by time, with ancient monuments such as the impressive earth ramparts of Eggardon Hill. The heathland W of Poole Harbour, partly planted with conifers, has a quite different character – largely flat tank training ground W of Weymouth, a more interesting roaming ground for nature-lovers towards Studland Bay with its fine beach. Off Poole, Brownsea Island is a good place to run around and explore, with lots of wildlife.

Where to stay

ABBOTSBURY SY5785 **Abbey House** *Church Street, Abbotsbury, Weymouth, Dorset DT3 4JJ (01305) 871330* **£70***; 5 pretty rms. Partly 15th-c house (said to have been the Abbey infirmary) with 17th and 18th-c additions, and set in gardens which slope down to the mill pond, behind which stands the impressive Abbey Tithe Barn, the largest in England; in the corner of the garden stands the only surviving Benedictine water mill in this country; comfortable, homely sitting room, reasonably priced and enticing lunches and teas in attractive country-style dining room, and friendly, efficient service

BOURNEMOUTH SZ1091 **Langtry Manor** *26 Derby Rd, Eastcliff, Bournemouth, Dorset BH1 3QB (01202) 553887* **£109.50**, plus special breaks; 27 pretty rms, some in the manor, some in the lodge. Built by Edward VII for Lillie Langtry, with lots of memorabilia, relaxed public rooms, helpful friendly staff, and good food inc Edwardian dinner every Sat evening; cl 1st 2 wks Jan; no children; disabled access; dogs welcome in bedrooms

BRIDPORT SY4691 **Britmead House** *West Bay Rd, Bridport, Dorset DT6 4EG (01308) 422941* **£64**, plus special breaks; 7 rms. Extended Victorian hotel with lots to do nearby, comfortable lounge overlooking garden, attractive dining room, good food, and kind helpful service; disabled access; dogs welcome in bedrooms

CHURCH KNOWLE SY9380 **Bradle Farmhouse** *Bradle, Wareham, Dorset BH20 5NU (01929) 480712* **£46**, plus special breaks; 3 spacious rms. Fine Victorian stone-built house on 550 acres of working farmland with long views, good breakfasts in homely dining room with its woodburner, and a relaxed friendly atmosphere; good nearby pub for meals; cl 25–26 Dec; children over 8

CORFE CASTLE SZ0080 **Knitson Old Farmhouse** *Knitson, Corfe Castle, Wareham, Dorset BH20 5JB (01929) 422836* **£40**; 3 no smoking rms, shared bthrm. Big ancient cottage on working farm with sheep and Jersey cows, large garden with hens and horses and children's play area; comfortable sitting room with flagstones and woodburner, and good evening food by arrangement using home-reared pork and lamb and free range eggs served in the spacious kitchen; they are kind to families

CORFE CASTLE SY9681 **Mortons House** *45 East Street, Corfe Castle, Wareham, Dorset BH20 5EE (01929) 480988* **£118**; 17 individual rms inc 2 suites.

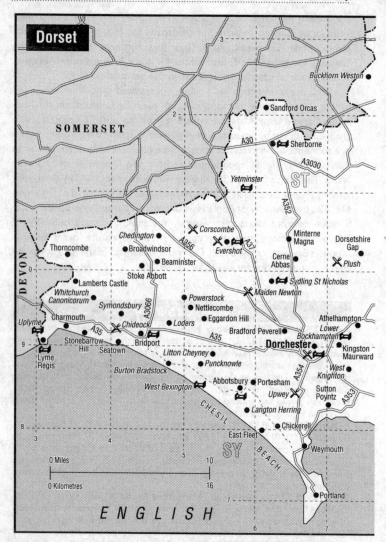

Dorset

SOMERSET

DEVON

Buckhorn Weston

Sandford Orcas

Sherborne

A30

A3030

Yetminster

ST

Corscombe

Chedington

Broadwindsor

Beaminster

A356

Evershot

A37

Minterne Magna

Dorsetshire Gap

Cerne Abbas

Plush

Thorncombe

Stoke Abbott

Sydling St Nicholas

Lamberts Castle

Whitchurch Canonicorum

Symondsbury

A3066

Powerstock

Nettlecombe

Maiden Newton

Charmouth

A35

Chideock

Loders

Eggardon Hill

Athelhampton

Uplyme

Stonebarrow Hill

Seatown

Bridport

A35

Bradford Peverell

Lower Bockhampton

Lyme Regis

Litton Cheyney

Puncknowle

Burton Bradstock

Dorchester

A354

Kingston Maurward

West Knighton

West Bexington

Abbotsbury

Portesham

Upwey

Sutton Poyntz

A353

CHESIL

Langton Herring

Chickerell

East Fleet

SY

Weymouth

BEACH

0 Miles   10

0 Kilometres   16

Portland

ENGLISH

Fine Elizabethan manor house in walled garden, with an oak-panelled drawing room, log fire, nice prints, and carved wooden friezes, the original stone fireplace in the entrance hall, very friendly, helpful staff and owners, delicious modern evening meals, and plenty to do nearby; no smoking; children over 5 in restaurant

DORCHESTER SY6990 **Casterbridge** *49 High East St, Dorchester, Dorset DT1 1HU (01305) 264043* **£75**, plus wknd breaks; 14 rms. Small Georgian hotel in town centre with modern annexe across little courtyard; elegant drawing room, cosy library, attractive dining room and conservatory, and good breakfasts; no evening meals (lots of nearby restaurants); best to book early as they are very popular; cl 25–26 Dec; disabled access

DORCHESTER SY6889 **Maiden Castle Farm** *Dorchester, Dorset DT2 9PR (01305) 262356* **£52***; 4 rms. Victorian farmhouse in 2 acres of gardens in the heart of Hardy country and set beneath the prehistoric earthworks from which the farm takes its name; views of the hill fort and countryside, and comfortable traditionally furnished sitting room which overlooks the garden; disabled access; dogs welcome in bedrooms

EAST KNIGHTON SY8185 **Countryman** *East Knighton, Dorchester, Dorset DT2 8LL (01305) 852666* **£70***; 6 rms. Attractively converted and much liked pair of old cottages with open fires and plenty of character in the main bar which opens into several smaller areas, no smoking family room, half a dozen real ales, imaginative, generously served food inc nice breakfasts and a hot carvery in large restaurant, and courteous staff; cl 25 Dec; dogs welcome

EVERSHOT ST5704 **Summer Lodge** *Evershot, Dorchester, Dorset DT2 0JR (01935) 83424* **£205**, plus special breaks; 18 big, individually decorated rms. Beautifully kept, peacefully set former dower house with lovely flowers in the comfortable and elegantly furnished day rooms, excellent food using the best local produce in most attractive restaurant overlooking pretty garden, delicious breakfasts and afternoon tea, and personal caring service; outdoor swimming pool, tennis and croquet; children over 7 in evening restaurant; partial disabled access; dogs welcome in bedrooms

GILLINGHAM ST7827 **Stock Hill Country House Hotel** *Wyke, Gillingham, Dorset SP8 5NR* (01747) 823626 **£240**inc dinner, plus special breaks; 8 lovely very comfortable rms. Marvellously relaxing carefully run Victorian manor house in 11 acres of wooded grounds, with antiques and paintings in opulent day rooms, particularly welcoming service, and excellent food in the no smoking restaurant using home-grown herbs and vegetables, local meat and fish; all-weather tennis court, croquet; children over 7

KINGSTON SY9579 **Kingston Country Courtyard** *West Street, Kingston, Corfe Castle, Wareham, Dorset BH20 5LH* (01929) 481066 **£52***; 10 rms in most attractive farm building conversions. A collection of stylish suites and apartments in beautifully decorated houses keeping much original character and charm, and with wonderful views over Corfe Castle, Arne Peninsula, and the Isle of Wight; enjoyable full English or continental breakfasts in Old Cart Shed dining room; self-catering too; lots to do nearby; cl Dec/Jan; good disabled access; dogs welcome in bedrooms

LOWER BOCKHAMPTON SY7290 **Yalbury Cottage** *Lower Bockhampton, Dorchester, Dorset DT2 8PZ* (01305) 262382 **£90**, plus special breaks; 8 rms overlooking garden or fields. Very attractive family-run 16th-c thatched house with a relaxed friendly atmosphere, and low beams and inglenook fireplaces in comfortable lounge and dining room; carefully cooked often imaginative food, good wines; cl Jan; dogs welcome in bedrooms

LYME REGIS SY3392 **Charnwood Guest House** *21 Woodmead Rd, Lyme Regis, Dorset DT7 3AD* (01297) 445281 **£50***, plus special breaks; 8 rms with showers. No smoking Edwardian house with covered verandah, recently modernised rooms, friendly owners who will help with walks and other local information, and decent breakfasts; children over 5

POOLE SZ0090 **Mansion House** *Thames St, Poole, Dorset BH15 1JN* (01202) 685666 **£120**, plus special breaks; 32 cosy rms with lots of little extras. Close to waterfront, this civilised old merchant's town house has a lovely sweeping staircase, antiques in the elegant residents' lounge, convivial cocktail bar, good food in the attractive restaurant, and courteous service

SHERBORNE ST6316 **Pheasants** *24 Greenhill, Sherborne, Dorset DT9 4EW* (01935) 815252 **£70**; 4 rms. Georgian town house with friendly staff, residents' lounge, and cottagey garden; no evening meals but plenty of places nearby; cl 2 wks Jan

STUDLAND SZ0383 **Knoll House** *Studland, Swanage, Dorset BH19 3AH* (01929) 450450 **£240**; inc lunch and dinner; 80 comfortable rms. Spacious, very well run hotel owned by the same family for over 40 years, in 100 acres with marvellous views of Studland Bay and direct access to the fine 3-mile beach; relaxed friendly atmosphere, particularly helpful staff, super food in dining room with windows overlooking the gardens, cocktail bar, TV lounge, and excellent facilities for families: attractive children's dining room (with proper food and baby food, microwave, own fridge, etc), well equipped play room, table tennis, pool and table football, heated outdoor pool, tennis courts, small private golf course, marvellous adventure playground, and nearby sea fishing, riding, walking, sailing and windsurfing; health spa; cl end Oct–Easter; children over 8 in evening dining room; disabled access; dogs welcome ☺

STURMINSTER NEWTON ST7711 **Plumber Manor** *Hazelbury Bryan Road, Plumber, Sturminster Newton, Dorset DT10 2AF* (01258) 472507 **£155**, plus special breaks; 16 very comfortable rms, some in nearby period buildings; many in the house itself overlook the peaceful, pretty garden and down the stream with herons and even maybe egrets. Handsome 17th-c, family-run house in quiet countryside, with warm fires, a convivial well stocked bar, attractive writing room/lounge, resident black Labradors, good interesting food inc tempting puddings in three dining rooms, nice breakfasts, a relaxed atmosphere, and exceptionally friendly helpful service; tennis; cl Feb; children welcome by prior arrangement; disabled access; dogs welcome in bedrooms

SYDLING ST NICHOLAS SY6399 **Lamperts Cottage** *Sydling St Nicholas, Dorchester, Dorset DT2 9NU (01300) 341659* **£44**; 3 little rms under the eaves, shared bthrms. Charming mainly no smoking 16th-c thatched cottage in unspoilt village, with friendly welcome from helpful owner, good breakfasts in beamed dining room with huge inglenook fireplace and bread oven, and pretty garden; children over 8; dogs welcome in bedrooms

UPLYME SY3194 **Amherst Lodge Farm** *Uplyme, Lyme Regis, Dorset DT7 3XH (01297) 442773* **£70**; 3 rms. Comfortable longhouse surrounded by 140 acres of gardens, woodlands, fields and seven lakes – rod room, trout fishing; relaxed friendly country-house atmosphere, oak-panelled lounge with fire, books and magazines, and enjoyable breakfasts; self-catering also; no children; cl Christmas

WAREHAM SY9287 **Priory Hotel** *Church Green, Wareham, Dorset BH20 4ND (01929) 551666* **£155**, plus special breaks; 18 very comfortable rms – the best being in the converted boathouse with its own landscaped gardens. Beautifully converted medieval buildings in four acres of carefully kept riverside gardens; two elegant lounges with antiques, delicious English cooking served in the converted Abbot's Cellar (exceptional English cheese board), and genuinely welcoming service; children over 8

WEST BEXINGTON SY5386 **Manor** *Beach Rd, West Bexington, Dorchester, Dorset DT2 9DF (01308) 897616* **£110**, plus special breaks; 13 cottagey rms. Handsome and civilised old stone hotel mentioned in Domesday Book in a pleasant setting not far from beach; relaxed informal atmosphere, comfortable lounge, popular pubby cellar bar, log fires, good bar food, excellent restaurant, and friendly service

WIMBORNE MINSTER SZ0199 **Beechleas** *17 Poole Rd, Wimborne, Dorset BH21 1QA (01202) 841684* **£79**, plus special breaks; 9 attractive, comfortable rms. Carefully restored Georgian house with open fires in cosy sitting room and charming dining room, airy conservatory overlooking walled garden, enjoyable Aga-cooked food using organic produce, nice breakfasts, and friendly helpful owners; lots to do and see nearby; cl 24 Dec–mid-Jan; disabled access; dogs welcome in bedrooms

YETMINSTER ST5910 **Manor Farmhouse** *High St, Yetminster, Sherborne, Dorset DT9 6LF (0800) 0566761 – free in UK* **£70**; 4 rms. Fine, carefully modernised, no smoking 17th-c building, with beams and oak panelling, inglenook fireplaces, helpful owners, and good fresh traditional cooking; no children; cl 26 Dec–6 Jan; disabled access

Dorset Family Attraction of the Year

HURN SZ1197 **Alice in Wonderland Family Park** (opposite Bournemouth Airport, signed from Christchurch junction on A338) A theme park based around the Lewis Carroll books could have been a recipe for disaster, but in fact this is an unexpectedly rewarding place for very young children (it won't really appeal to over-8s), put together with real thought and effort. It's grown quite a lot in the last few years, starting out as just the big, elaborate maze that still remains the centrepiece, with 5,200 bushes shaped into characters from the two Alice books. Around that have sprung up several gentle fairground rides such as spinning teacups, a caterpillar train, and flying elephants, along with junior go-karts, an astroslide and a bouncy castle. For many the highlight is the half-hour show that adapts the stories into something close to a pantomime; purists may bristle, but children love it. Performances are normally at 12 and 3 – usually indoors but out on the storytelling lawn when the weather's fine. The costumed performers wander around the grounds between shows. Other attractions include a number of farmyard animals and pets (including, of course, several white rabbits), croquet lawns, and indoor and outdoor play areas. In the summer holidays they usually have extra events and activities. Quite a few things are under cover, but it's best in dry weather. You certainly won't need a full day to do everything, but it's surprising how long some children can stretch it out. If you live close by, it's a good bet for birthday parties. Meals, snacks, picnic area, shop, some disabled access; open Easter–Oct (cl wkdys from mid-Sept, exc half-term); (01202) 483444; £5.85 adults and children. A family ticket (two adults, two children) is £22.

ABBOTSBURY SY5982
Delightful west country village of golden stone and thatch, beneath a breezy chalk escarpment (itself excellent walking country, with wide coastal views) and with several worthwhile places within easy walking distance – most famous are the unique ancient swannery and the gardens (see separate entries, joint ticket may be available). On prominent Chapel Hill, the green hillock grooved with the patterns of ancient field systems, stands 14th-c **St Catherine's Chapel** (usually open), with a bare earth floor; it belonged to the abbey, of which there are a few medieval fragments around the church. A huge medieval thatched **tithe barn** built for the abbey has children's play areas, some animals and a video on smugglers. Shop, disabled access; cl wkdys Nov–Feb (01305) 871817; £4.50. The Ilchester Arms is useful for lunch. From Abbotsbury you can stroll around Chapel Hill and on to the massive shingle bank of **Chesil Beach** (exhausting to walk any distance

along – see, too, East Fleet entry; swimming here is dangerous). Paths leading N from the village get lovely views from the chalk downs. The B3157 W also has fine views.
Abbotsbury Subtropical Gardens 20 acres of beautiful woodland with the very mild coastal climate letting rare and record-breaking plants and trees flourish. The central walled garden in spring is a mass of azaleas, camellias and rhododendrons. Also woodland trail, owls, and children's play area. Pleasant tearoom, shop and plant centre, some disabled access; cl Christmas–New Year; (01305) 871387; £5.50 summer.
Abbotsbury Swannery (Newbarn Rd) Another legacy of the former abbey, this is home to the only sizeable colony of swans in the world that can be seen during nesting time. The swan families quite happily come right up to visitors, and during the cygnet season (late May–Jun) you might see some of the hundreds of eggs hatching right next to you. All year there are mass feedings of the flock at noon and 4pm; they

sometimes choose a visitor to help, and it can be rather dramatic – certainly a far cry from the average trip to feed the swans. An ugly duckling trail keeps younger children amused, and there are interesting reed bed walks; also the country's oldest duck decoy, and an audio-visual show. No dogs. Restaurant (reached by a little bridge), shop, good disabled access; cl Nov to mid-Mar; (01305) 871858; £5.50. A joint ticket with the gardens is £9.

ARNE SY9788
Tucked away above the inlets of Poole Harbour, this backwater of a village has a good **toy museum**, Arne House; cl Oct–Easter, plus ams and all Mon and Sat Apr–Jun and Sept; (01929) 552018; £3. There's also a quiet beach and a nature trail.

ASHLEY HEATH SU1006
Moors Valley Country Park A great place for family adventures, with nearly 988 acres of forest. Plenty to do here when it's sunny, with river and lakeside walks, and nature trails inc a play one that children really enjoy, with various activities such as jumping across stepping stones and climbing into and sliding out of the snake pit or exploring the giant ant hill; there's an unusual treetop walkway. Also cycle hire, narrow-gauge steam railway, and 18-hole golf course. Meals, snacks, shop, disabled access; cl 25 Dec; (01425) 470721; £5 car parking charge (less after 4pm), 50p winter wkdys (£2.50 wknds then and also off-peak outside winter). The Old Barn Farm at Three Legged Cross is good value for family meals.

ATHELHAMPTON SY7794
Athelhampton House and Gardens (old A35) Readers love coming to this magnificent 15th-c house, built on the legendary site of King Athelstan's palace. The great hall has a fantastic roof, and throughout there are beautiful furnishings and contents, with some fine panelling. An added bonus are the acres of wonderful formal and landscaped gardens with rare plants, topiary and fountain pools. Meals, snacks, shop, disabled access; open daily (exc Sat) Mar–Oct; (01305) 848363; £6.25 house and gardens, £4.50 garden only (voucher admits two

adults for the price of one). The young Thomas Hardy helped design the church across the road. The Martyrs at Tolpuddle has decent home cooking.

BEAMINSTER SY5199
Mapperton Gardens (off B3163 E) Several delightful acres of terraced hillside gardens in grounds of a 17th-c manor house; specimen trees and shrubs, fountains, grottoes, fishponds, orangery, good walks and views. Occasional musical events in summer. Snacks, shop, some disabled access; cl am, and Nov–Feb; (01308) 862645; £3.50. In the town Pickwicks has good food.

BERE REGIS SY8494
Bere Regis church This boasts the finest timbered roof in Dorset, with extraordinary carved figures; 20p in a slot lights these up to remarkable effect. It also contains the Turberville tomb and window mentioned in *Tess of the D'Urbervilles*. The Drax Arms is good value for lunch.

BERE WOOD SY8794
At the W end of Bloxworth, this is a fine bluebell wood, at its best in May; the track can be followed right through to Bere Regis.

BLANDFORD FORUM ST8806
Georgian market town, rebuilt in 1731 after the older buildings were destroyed by fire – very interesting to walk round. The Crown Hotel (West St) does good value bar meals.
Cavalcade of Costume Museum (The Plocks) 250 years of fashion housed in Georgian Lime Tree House. Snacks, shop, disabled access to ground floor only; cl Tues, Weds, and mid-Dec to mid-Feb; (01258) 453006; £3.
Royal Signals Museum (Blandford Camp) A lively look at the history of army communications, with an exhibition on SAS codes and code-breaking, plus several interactive displays and fun trails for children. Snacks, shop, disabled access; cl wknds exc Mar–Oct, and 3 wks at Christmas – phone to check; (01258) 482248; £4.50.
BOURNEMOUTH SZ0890
A classic beach resort with neatly kept streamside gardens in the centre (various bands in summer), a pier (though they charge you 40p to stroll along it – the theatre at the end is

quaintly old-fashioned), long promenades below the low cliff, and miles of well organised sandy beach (no dogs in summer, when there are children's activities). The best beaches, with water safe for swimming and good wrist-band schemes to prevent children from getting lost, are from Durley Chine to Southbourne, and boat rides leave from next to the pier. All this, along with a mild climate, has made the town a favourite place to retire to, though it's also very popular with foreign language students and families; the town is currently working hard to attract younger visitors. Though it's a big, busy town surrounded by suburbs, with tall modern buildings and monumental traffic schemes, down by the sea all that seems far away, with features such as the IMAX cinema (Pier Approach), palm trees, Edwardian street furniture, and a camera obscura (Bournemouth Sq). Tethered balloon flights in Lower Gardens are a nice way to take it all in (£9.95, £7 before 10am; (01202) 314539); also here are miniature golf (queues in summer) and maybe Jumpzone (a clever modern take on trampolines, fascinating to watch; £5). The western residential suburbs of Westbourne and particularly Branksome Park are quiet, with pinetree valleys winding down to the sea; it's virtually impossible to tell here when Bournemouth becomes Poole. The West Beach Restaurant (Pier Approach) and Moon in the Square (Exeter Rd) are good value, and the Durley (Durley Chine) is a very well run beachside pub.

Hengistbury Head By far the best place close to Bournemouth for a stroll: not a long walk, but the feeling of space and views over Christchurch harbour and beyond are outstanding. It has traces of an Iron Age hill fort, and a good beach below.

Oceanarium (Pier Approach, West Beach) An impressive range of fish from all around the world, with an emphasis on the environment and conservation. Meals, snacks, shop, disabled access; cl 25 Dec; (01202) 311993; £5.85.

Russell-Cotes Art Gallery & Museum Victorian mansion with a good collection of 17th- to 20th-c paintings, ceramics and furnishings as well as exhibitions on Japanese art, and a story-telling gallery aimed at children. Café, shop, disabled access; cl Mon, 25 Dec, and Good Fri; (01202) 451800; free.

BOVINGTON CAMP SY8288
A military area, with army vehicles and the distant sound of firing practice much in evidence.

Tank Museum Enjoyed by a wider spectrum of readers than you might guess (and good on a wet day as it's all under cover), over 150 armoured fighting vehicles from 26 countries, some of which you can go inside, as well as a tank simulator, costumes, medals, weapons and videos, and a reconstructed World War I trench. Many of the tanks are put through their paces, complete with simulated gunfire (Tues and Thurs in summer hols); there are armoured vehicle rides on summer wkdys. There's an exhibition on Lawrence of Arabia, an assault course for children, and a new family activity trail. Meals, snacks and picnic areas, shop, disabled access; cl 16–26 Dec; (01929) 405096; £7.50.

Clouds Hill A mile or so up the road is this cottage where Lawrence of Arabia lived in relative obscurity as a private in the Tank Corps after his famous desert exploits. His sleeping bag, furniture and other memorabilia can be seen in the four ascetic little rooms on display (the re-created bathroom is covered in cork tiles, while the walls of a room upstairs are lined with aluminium foil). A new information centre and video will tell you more. Open Thurs–Sun pm and bank hols Apr–end Oct; (01929) 405616; £2.80; NT.

BRADFORD PEVERELL SY7191
New Barn Field Centre Authentic re-creation of Iron Age homestead, complete with animals and so on; also working potter, wildflower reserve and nature trails. Summer meals and snacks, shop, some disabled access; open Aug; (01305) 268865; £3.50.

BRIDPORT SY4692
Still the country's main rope producer, and its old harbour is now the busy fishing port of nearby West Bay, a restrained small resort (where the West Bay Hotel has good local

seafood). The Harbour Life Exhibition (Salt House) tells the story of the area with the aid of pictures, photographs and videos Shop, disabled access; cl Nov–Mar; (01308) 422807; £1.25).

Bridport Museum (South St) Usually has displays of rope and net making and loom weaving,and a new display on the Romans teaches you how to wear a toga. Free activity sheets for children; shop, disabled access to ground floor only; cl Sun, and Nov–Mar; (01308) 422116; £2.

BROADWINDSOR ST4302

Craft & Design Centre Good centre in former farm buildings; meals, snacks, shop, disabled access; cl 2–31 Jan; (01308) 868362; free. The White Lion has generous home cooking..

Pilsdon Pen Not a place for long walks, but ideal for those who want a rewarding view in a very short stroll – Dorset's highest point, capped by a hill fort, and looking over Lyme Bay and N towards the Mendips. It is reached within minutes from the layby on the B3164 2m SW. This rd to Birdsmoorgate and then the B3165 through Marshwood is an unspoilt scenic drive through a little-known valley

BULBARROW HILL ST7705

Memorable viewpoint on the narrow lanes just S of Woolland, esp on a summer evening with the sun going down over Somerset. Around here, a scenic drive runs from Piddletrenthide through Plush (the Brace of Pheasants is a very good lunchtime stop) and Mappowder to Hazelbury Bryan, then through Ansty and Melcombe Bingham, to turn right at Cheselbourne for Piddletrenthide again.

CERNE ABBAS ST6701

Famed above all for its prehistoric giant cut into the chalk above, giving no doubts as to his virility; best seen from the signed layby on the A352 N. The village itself is most attractive in its own right: a fine church, fragments of the old abbey, good pubs. There's a working **pottery** (cl Mons, phone Nov–Easter); (01300) 341865 on the way up to the giant; above it, the old Dorchester—Middlemarsh ridge road has some bracing views.

CHARMOUTH SY3693

The beach here is famous for fossil-hunting. A small museum exhibits locally found relics; open Easter–Sept, plus Oct half-term; (01297) 560772; free; good shop, hammers for hire. The George has good value food.

CHETTLE ST9513

Chettle House Fine baroque country house, with beautifully laid out gardens; various craft wknds and special events. Snacks, disabled access to garden only; open 1st Sun of month May–Oct, Easter Sun, and for special events, phone to check; (01258) 830209; £3. The Museum Hotel over in Farnham does good lunches.

CHICKERELL SY6580

Bennetts Water Gardens 🏫 (Putton Lane) Eight acres of landscaped lakes renowned for their summer water-lilies – over 150 varieties, plus a replica of Monet's famous bridge at Giverny; also a tropical house, and a museum covering the gardens and local history. Home-made teas, shop, disabled access; cl Mon, Sun in Sept (exc bank hols), and all Oct–Mar; (01305) 785150; *£4.95. The Red Barn on working Bagwell Farm (B3157 NW) does enjoyable lunches.

CHRISTCHURCH SZ1592

The E end of the Bournemouth complex, and the oldest part, with attractive Georgian brick buildings in its centre, a restored watermill, and a quay looking out over the yachting harbour, busy in summer. Beyond the harbour mouth, long beaches stretch off into Hampshire from the vast Mudeford car park; the Haven House family pub has an unrivalled spot by the sea here, there's an excellent fishmonger nearby, and the Ship in Distress is a good dining pub specialising in local seafood. Pleasant walking out of season. Stuarts Gardenland (A35 out of Christchurch) usually have a giant maize maze but as we went to press they were still seeking planning permission, so ask at the Tourist Information Centre; (01202) 471780.

Christchurch Castle & Norman House All that remains is a ruined keep, and the ruins of the Norman house probably used by the castle constable. It's quite well preserved, with one of the earliest chimneys in the country, and an ancient midden by a millstream; free; EH.

Christchurch Priory Magnificent medieval monastic church, at well over 90 metres (300 ft) the longest parish church in the country; very striking inside, with remarkable carving. The 'Miraculous Beam' apparently fitted in the roof only with divine assistance, so prompting the renaming of the borough to Christchurch (it used to be called Twynham). Shop, mostly disabled access; cl 25 Dec and Sun during services; (01202) 485804; donations. The church has a small museum open in the summer, and good views from the tower (£1, only when a member of staff is available) – though with 176 spiral steps you have to earn them.

Highcliffe Castle 🎟 Originally built in the 1830s using large quantities of medieval stonework from France. Externally fully restored, this fine example of Romantic Picturesque architecture could almost fool you into thinking it's still a stately home. Inside, any decorative features have been destroyed after two fires left it vulnerable to the weather, and it now houses a friendly exhibition centre with displays that change every three weeks. Snacks, shop, house cl end Dec–Mar; (01425) 278807; £1.50 (discount voucher admits one adult free for every adult paying full entry price).

Museum of Electricity (opposite Castle's Ironmongers, Bargates) In an Edwardian power station, this has a range of electrical exhibits from antique washing machines to power generators. A transport gallery houses vehicles as diverse as a 90-year-old Bournemouth tram, a 1970s electric car, and Sir Clive Sinclair's over-hopeful Sinclair C5; interactive displays, and demonstrations of early electrical experiments. Shop, some disabled access; cl am, wknds, and Oct–Easter (exc half-terms); (01202) 480467; *£2.30.

Red House Museum & Gardens 🎟 (Quay Rd) Georgian house with local history and archaeology, Victorian bygones, costumes, and a walled herb garden. Snacks, shop, disabled access to ground floor and herb garden only; cl Sun am, Mon (exc bank hols), Good Fri,

and 25 Dec–1 Jan; (01202) 482860; £1.50.

CORFE CASTLE SY9681 One of the most spectacular ruins in England, the spiky remains of the castle rise on a hill in a breach in the Purbeck ridge, above the village of the same name; superb views from its dramatic hilltop position. Until it was seized in the Civil War and blown up it was a veritable skyscraper; its demolition has left the masonry leaning at unlikely-looking angles, and there are remnants of portcullises and menacing murder holes. Much of the stone was re-used in buildings in the village. Meals, snacks, shop; cl 25–26 Dec; (01929) 481294; £4.40; NT. The Swanage Railway runs to here; a joint ticket is available (worth walking along the **Nine Barrow Down**, the Purbeck ridge from Swanage, for wonderful two-way views, then getting the train back); (01929) 425800. The bustling ancient Greyhound has popular food, all day in summer. Parking can be a problem here in summer; it's best to use the castle car park on the edge of the village. The road W through Church Knowle is pretty.

Corfe Castle Model Village In attractive gardens, with a faithful reconstruction of how the Norman castle looked before the Parliamentarians destroyed it in 1646. Cream teas, snacks, shop, disabled access (but no facilities); cl Nov–beginning Apr; (01929) 481234; £2.50.

CRANBORNE SU0513 A peaceful place, with the Fleur-de-Lys a good pub well known to Hardy and the subject of an entertaining poem by Rupert Brooke (framed inside).

Cranborne Manor Gardens Delightful 17th-c gardens originally laid out by Tradescant; Jacobean mount garden, herb garden, lovely river garden and avenues of beech and lime. Particularly attractive in spring. Snacks, shop and garden centre, disabled access (limited in gardens); gardens open Weds Mar–Sept, garden centre open daily all year; (01725) 517248; *£3.50. The B3078 has good country views, as does the minor rd crossing it to Three Legged Cross and the Gussages.

CRANBORNE CHASE ST9116

Shared between Dorset and Wiltshire, this offers good walking with some fine views, especially around Ashmore.

DELCOMBE WOOD ST7805
A lovely bluebell wood, sheets of colour in May; but the only public track just skirts the W edge of the wood.

DORCHESTER SY6990
Thriving though rather traffic-ridden county town (which features as Casterbridge in Hardy's novels), with busy shopping streets, Weds market, and several worthwhile antiques and print shops. Though most of the more attractive Georgian buildings are just out of the bustle, there are a few distinguished buildings on the main streets, inc the timbered building of **Judge Jeffreys' Lodgings** in High West St; he stayed here during his notorious Bloody Assizes (the Oak Room in Antelope Passage, with good teas and cakes, is the courtroom where the Monmouth rebels were tried). The trial of the Tolpuddle Martyrs also took place on High West St, in the **Old Crown Court**, preserved as a memorial; for an extra £1.50 you can look round some of the cells (open wkdy pms in summer). There are one or two traces of the Romans' occupation, inc the fragmentary remains of a town house behind the County Hall (which has a booklet on its history), and of an amphitheatre (Maumbury Rings), rather tucked away on Weymouth Ave. The Napper's Mite restaurant (South St), a former almshouse, is good value, and the Blue Raddle (Church St) is popular for pub lunches.

Dinosaur Museum (Icen Way) The best of Dorset's dinosaur-related exhibitions, a well displayed and entertaining collection very much designed with younger visitors in mind. There are full-size skeletons and reconstructions, lots of opportunities to handle bones, fossils and the like (not many exhibits have barriers), and fun activities such as Dinosaurs and You, where you put in your height and weight and the computer works out how you compare with a couple of dinosaurs. Look out for the intriguing Dinosaurid – a canadian expert's idea of what dinosaurs would have evolved

into if they hadn't become extinct. Shop, disabled access to ground floor only; cl 24–26 Dec; (01305) 269880; £4.75.

Dorset County Museum (High West St) Hardy's study from Max Gate has been reconstructed at this comprehensive museum (the largest Thomas Hardy collection in the world). The writer's gallery looks at the lives of Hardy and other Dorset novelists such as Sylvia Townsend Warner, with touch-screen computer displays. Also, dinosaur footprints and fossils in the geology gallery, and a new gallery devoted to the town. Shop, disabled access to ground floor only; cl Sun Nov–Apr, plus 25–26 Dec and Good Fri; (01305) 262735; £3.50. Along in High East St the Kings Arms Hotel is full of Hardy associations.

Dorset Teddy Bear Museum (Antelope House) Tucked away in an old coaching house behind a good teddy shop, a family of human-sized bears dwell in blissful oblivion to the outside world. You can snuggle up next to a dozing Grandpa on the chair, go upstairs to see Mother and her ever-increasing brood of baby bears, or head downstairs to the cellar, where the Dorset Teddy Bear Museum collection includes every kind of teddy imaginable; enthusiastically run, this is a must for all teddy lovers. Shop; cl 25–26 Dec; (01305) 263200; £2.95.

Hardy's Cottage (Higher Bockhampton, just off A35 3m E) All alone by a sandy track inside the edge of a forest, the thatched cottage where Thomas Hardy was born in 1840 hasn't changed much since. Shop, disabled access to ground floor only; cl Fri and Sat and all Nov–Mar; (01305) 262366; *£2.80; NT. The forest was heath in Hardy's day, but you can walk through the plantations SE of the cottage to find open heathland much as he knew it on Black Heath and Duddle Heath, parts of the 'untamed and untameable' Egdon Heath of his novels. From the Hardy's Cottage car park, it's a shortish walk to the cottage; a nature trail takes a slightly longer but prettier route via Thorncombe Wood. The 16th-c thatched Wise Man at West Stafford has good value food. See nearby

Stinsford and Max Gate for more Hardy associations.

Keep Military Museum (Bridport Rd) More interesting than most military museums, in handsome Victorian barracks gatehouse; splendid views from the battlements. Meals, snacks, shop, disabled access; cl Sun (exc July–Aug), plus two wks at Christmas; (01305) 264066; £3.

Maiden Castle (off A354 S; no access from bypass) Europe's most famous Iron Age fort, a series of massive grassy ramparts covering 47 acres, and once home to some 200 families; the Romans captured it after a particularly bloody battle. It's so vast that the tour of its grassy ramparts almost qualifies as a fully fledged walk; free.

Max Gate (Alington Ave, A351 1m E) Among the places associated with Thomas Hardy (who lived in Dorchester for most of his life), this is the house he designed and lived in from 1885 to his death in 1928, and where he wrote *Tess* and *Jude the Obscure*. You can see only the dining and drawing rooms (the study has been moved to the County Museum), but the gardens are fascinating, not least because they inspired so much of Hardy's poetry. Shop, disabled access; open pm Sun, Mon and Weds 2 Apr–29 Sept; (01305) 262538; £2.40; NT. The Trumpet Major food pub is very handy.

Stinsford (off A35 at E end of bypass) On the Thomas Hardy trail: he featured the village as Mellstock, and at the church his heart is buried beside the body of his first wife.

Tutankhamun Exhibition (High West St) Impressive exhibits re-creating the discovery of ancient treasures using a mix of sights, sounds and smells. Shop, disabled access; cl 24–26 Dec; (01305) 269571; £4.75.

DORSETSHIRE GAP ST7403
The downland W of Melcombe Bingham is attractive for walkers; the dry ground of the Gap comes as a pleasant surprise on those days when it seems as if all Dorset is turning to chalky mud. Despite the ultra-English charm of much of inland Dorset – chalk downs, sleepy thatched villages, clumps of beechwoods and fine views – the area is surprisingly little walked, so field

routes are often not obvious and careful map-reading is needed.

EAST FLEET SY6380
Interesting, particularly for the tiny ruined church which was wrecked by a legendary 1824 storm. Nearby Chesil Beach, its pebbles and boulders immaculately graded by millennia of storms, is emphatically not for swimmers – the undertow will suck you straight down – but with its long lagoon behind is very interesting for beach-combers and nature-lovers. Swans nest on the great lagoon, which was used for trying out the World War II dam-busting bouncing bomb; now a peaceful spot, with lots of other birds too. The vicinity's pleasant walks are especially interesting if you've read J M Faulkner's *Moonfleet*. The Elm Tree at Langton Herring is handy for lunch.

EAST LULWORTH SY8280
Lulworth Castle 🏛 Restored 17th-c hunting lodge with splendid views over the wooded park from its SE tower; the formal gardens are a nice spot for a picnic. The Roman Catholic chapel was the first to be built in England after the Reformation, and an Anglican church was built in part by Thomas Hardy (there's an exhibition about him inside); also children's summer farm and play area. Snacks, shop, limited disabled access; cl Sat and 24 Dec to mid-Feb; (01929) 400352; £5.50.

EDMONDSHAM SU0611
Dorset Heavy Horse Centre (well signed from Verwood) Cheery place with five different breeds of huge heavy horse, and miniature shetland ponies at the other extreme as well as llamas, miniature donkeys and pygmy goats. Snacks, shop, disabled access; cl Oct–Easter; (01202) 824040; £4.95. Dogs welcome.

EGGARDON HILL SY5494
On the summit, this prehistoric hill fort has wonderful views and – still after thousands of years – impressive earthen ramparts. The Spyway at Askerswell is a pleasant food stop, also with good views.

HAMBLEDON HILL ST8412
In a commanding position just above Child Okeford (where the Saxon has reasonably priced food), this hill fort has a winning view, and still gives a

strong sense of how formidable it must have been thousands of years ago.

HINTON ST MARY ST7816
This attractive village has a superb manor house and a striking medieval tithe barn. The White Horse is a useful food stop.

HURN SZ1296
Bournemouth Aviation Museum
⊞ Well worth a visit if you're interested in aviation, with an increasing collection of aircraft inc vintage planes and helicopters, a large display of aircraft models, and occasional flying. Snacks, shop, disabled access; (01202) 580858; cl over Christmas and New Year, phone to check; £5.
Alice in Wonderland Family Park
See separate family panel on p.
The Avon Causeway Hotel does decent food.

KIMMERIDGE BAY SY9179
A lovely spot with intriguing rock strata, kept quieter than it might be by the toll. The New Inn up at Church Knowle is good for lunch. On the E side of the bay, the **Marine Centre** has displays on the rich marine life of the rocky ledges that run across the bay; also a live underwater camera, re-created rockpool, interactive computer, and microscope close-ups of what you find on the beach; free but donations welcome.

KINGSTON SY9579
From here there's an easy level path to Hounstout Cliff; fortify yourself beforehand at the Scott Arms, a good family pub with superb views of Corfe Castle. Turn left at the end and you are into Dorset fossil country, presided over by the primitive hermitage chapel on St Aldhelm's Head, with an excellent picnic place in the quarried ledge just below, looking down the undercliff; the path here is of the switchback sort (decidedly vertiginous), and the sticky mud can make it tough going in wet seasons. The walk down to Chapman's Pool is steep and exciting; some of the paths have disappeared through landslips, and you can scramble down to the beach.

KINGSTON MAURWARD SY7191
Kingston Maurward Park Well liked by readers, this feels like the heart of the countryside despite its proximity to Dorchester, with peaceful woodland and lakeside walks, visitor centre, farm park (children can feed the animals), and plenty of garden variety inc Elizabethan and Edwardian gardens, penstemon and salvia national collections. The agricultural college, based in an elegant mansion built for George Pitt in 1720, holds some good special events. Meals, snacks, shop, plant sales, some disabled access; usually cl end Dec–beginning Jan; (01305) 215003; £4.

LAMBERTS CASTLE SY3799
This unspoiled hill fort above Marshwood (B3165) is charming for strolls, especially in late summer when the heather is out; it's quite hard to spot the turning from the road.

LANGTON MATRAVERS SZ0078
Putlake Adventure Farm ⊞
Children are encouraged to join in the lively activities at this friendly unspoilt farm; they can help hand-milk the cows, collect eggs from the chickens, or bottle-feed the lambs and goats. They do pony and tractor rides, and there are plenty of delightful small animals to fuss over; a more novel feature is the daily ferret racing. Plenty of things to play on, from miniature or full-sized tractors to scramble over, to an adventure playground and indoor play area; they've recently added a walk-through aviary and a little children's maze. On wet days most of the attractions move under cover. Meals, snacks, indoor and outdoor picnic areas, shop (look out for the colourful sand art), disabled access; open daily Apr–Oct, plus maybe wknds in Nov, Dec and Mar, phone to check; (01929) 422917; *£4.20.

LULWORTH COVE SY8279
One of the great natural sights on the south coast, this is a gigantic scoop, with rock strata exposed and displaying all manner of rock types and contortions. Best appreciated out of season, this beauty spot, a magnet for summer visitors and geologists (especially now that it's been designated a World Heritage site), has a classic mini-walk W along the cliffs to Durdle Door, a natural arch eroded by the sea; the unusually shaped rocks are surrounded by particularly good beaches. Exhibitions on smuggling and country

wines, and a new bronze age display in the Lulworth Heritage Centre (cl 24–25 Dec; nearby parking £2.50 for two hours). E of Lulworth Cove is army training land, which means high-security fences and dire warning notices, but you are allowed in most wknds and daily July–Aug and during Easter (keep to the paths; firing times are published in local papers). Information boards by road junctions off the A351 and A352 nr Wareham give opening times; or ring (01929) 462721 ext 4824 and ask for the Guardroom. The coast walk between Lulworth Cove and Kimmeridge Bay is very strenuous but excellent, heading to Mupe Bay past the surreal 'fossil forest' (formed of petrified algae that once clung to tree-trunks; turn right after passing into the ranges from Lulworth Cove, and take steps down on to the undercliff). Another path ascends Bindon Hill, looking down over the semi-circular cove. Inland, at West Lulworth the thatched Castle Inn is useful for lunch; the Lulworth Equestrian Centre can arrange **horse-riding**; (01929) 400396; £14 an hour.

LYME REGIS SY3492
Enchanting old seaside town, with rather an elegant, steep main street and interesting side streets; the esplanade is pretty, and there's a lively little fishing and yacht harbour. A coast path snakes W through an intriguing nature-reserve undercliff, still subject to landfalls; this is a celebrated area for fossils and flora (several shops sell fossils, with show collections too). There are pleasant walks in the valley. The Pilot Boat on the front is popular for lunch; the Royal Standard has a suntrap terrace (lit at night) right by the broadest part of the beach. The town gets very busy in summer, but it is worth braving the crowds. The Jane Austen cliffside gardens have peaceful sea views, and the cleaned-up sea here now tempts some quite varied creatures to make the occasional visit.

Dinosaurland (Coombe St) An excellent collection of fossils, and they can tell you about any you may have at home. They do two-hour fossil walks along the beach. Shop; cl 25–26 Dec; (01297) 443541; £3.50, guided beach walks £4.50 (booking recommended).

MILTON ABBAS ST8001
Lovely thatched estate village, all white walls and grass verges, built in the 18th c to replace an earlier one which had spoilt the view from the big house; the 17th-c almshouses were moved here at the same time. For the best views, drive in from Hilton. Pleasant stroll past the lake through the Capability Brown park to the fine 15th-c **abbey church** of a former Benedictine monastery (it now serves the public school in the nearby house). There's an attractive signed walk over the lane to a former chapel in the wood. Another pleasant walk through the abbey estate leads into Green Hill Down Nature Reserve, and a longer walk continues NW to Bulbarrow Hill. The road through the Winterbornes to Okeford Fitzpaine has good downland views.

MINTERNE MAGNA ST6604
Minterne Gardens (Minterne House, A352) Beautiful landscaped gardens, with lakes, cascades, streams, rare trees and impressive spring shows of azaleas, rhododendrons and bulbs; the autumn colours can be quite spectacular. Open Mar to mid-Nov; (01300) 341370; £3. The road W up Gore Hill and Batcombe Hill to Holywell has memorable views.

NETTLECOMBE SY5295
This sleepy village is in charming walking country, little touched by agricultural improvement – delectable downland and valley landscapes, with a reasonably good path network. The Marquis of Lorne does enjoyable food.

ORGANFORD SY9392
Farmer Palmers (Organford, between A35 and A351 W of Poole) This well organised place appeals to under-9s, who enjoy the hands-on animal barn (the staff show them how to handle and feed a range of animals), straw mountain, indoor and outdoor play areas, and summer bouncy castles and pedal carts; daily milking demo, tractor trailer rides (50p), and a woodland walk (not in wet weather). Meals, snacks, shop, disabled access, cl Jan to mid-Feb and wkdys in winter term-time, phone to check; (01202) 622022; £4.25. The St Peters Finger (B3067 E) has good value food.

OWERMOIGNE SY7685
Mill House Cider Museum and Dorset Clock Collection Cider museum with fully restored 18th- and 19th-c equipment, and video demonstrating the process. Also collection of locally made 18th- and 19th-c clocks. Shop with local ciders, some disabled access; usually cl 25 Dec–2 Jan; (01305) 852220; £1.50 cider museum, £2 clocks, £2.90 both. The beautifully placed Sailors Return at East Chaldon is good value for lunch.

POOLE SZ0190
Merging indistinguishably into Bournemouth on the edges, its centre is wholly distinct, with a more lively feel, especially around the Quay (special events in summer, and a good pottery shop). The broad natural harbour is still busy with the comings and goings of boats and small ships (several decent pubs to watch them from – the nautical Portsmouth Hoy is best for lunch); launch ferries around the harbour, and out to Brownsea Island. There are interesting old buildings along here; the streets behind, some pedestrianised, are well worth strolling through; contrasting Dolphin Quays, a new luxury apartment development with shops and restaurants, is due to open in the summer. The town is well served for cyclists, with plenty of signed routes; the tourist information centre has leaflets on the town trail. The Guildhall Tavern (Market St) has good local fish, and the Crown (Market St) and Shah of Persia (A35) are also useful for lunch.

Brownsea Island In the middle of Poole's huge natural harbour, this unspoilt 500-acre island is famous as the site of the first scout camp in 1907. It's a splendid place to explore, with uncrowded beaches, heath and woodland, and the whole island is good for spotting birds and wildlife; they have a burgeoning population of red squirrels, as well as a neat little bird-watching hide, and a large heronry. The nature reserve at the northern end is run separately by the Dorset Wildlife Trust and is well worth a look; it costs £2 extra, and there are self-guided tours in Apr, May, Jun and Sept, with guided walks (2–3.45pm daily) in July–Aug; (01202) 709445. The visitor centre has a video, and in summer holidays activities like painting and clay making. Free walking trails and occasional special events for children. In summer there's an open-air theatre with Shakespeare or opera; tickets go fast, so apply well in advance; (01202) 251987. Ferries go from Poole Quay (twice hourly, takes around 20 minutes, £5 return fare for adults; (01202) 669955, Sandbanks (twice hourly, takes 10 minutes, £3 return for adults; (01929) 462383), Bournemouth Pier (three a day, takes 25 minutes (only Mon, Weds, and Fri outside summer), £6 return adults; (01202) 558550), and, less often, from Swanage; (01929) 424152. Decent restaurant and shop, and some disabled access; open Apr–Oct (cl 15 mins before last boat leaves); (01202) 707744; the landing fee (free to NT members) is £3.70 adults, £1.70 children 5–17. No dogs or bikes. There's a holiday cottage – the island's very quiet indeed after the last boat leaves. Brownsea is open to the public 22 Mar–2 Nov.

Chain ferry This runs from Sandbanks, by the harbour mouth, to the Studland side – a spectacular entrance to Dorset proper; it's quickest to go as a foot passenger or by bus (they have priority); (01929) 450203; car £2.20, foot 90p. The beach at Sandbanks is lauded as one of the best in Britain.

Compton Acres Gardens (Canford Cliffs) Perhaps Poole's outstanding attraction and a favourite with readers, with lovely statuary among fine plants landscaped in an eclectic variety of styles – the Japanese garden is the foremost in Europe, and there's a wildlife walk with models of Canadian animals. Good views of the hills and Poole Harbour. Sat is the least busy day to visit. Meals, snacks, shop and plant sales, disabled access; cl 25 Dec; (01202) 700778; £5.95. The Inn in the Park (Pinewood Rd, off B3065 E) has good value food.

Splashdown (Tower Park, 2m NE on A3049) Fun for children, a water park with 11 rides and slides (indoor and out), inc a near-vertical drop in total darkness. Snacks; cl ams outside school hols (in peak periods they may have limits on how long you can stay), best to phone; (01202) 716123; £6.50.

Waterfront Museum (High St) Four floors of well laid out local history; disabled access; (01202) 262600; cl Sun am, 25–26 Dec (reduced hours in winter); free. In Aug, you can go next door to **Scaplen's Court**, a well restored medieval merchant's home with exhibitions upstairs.

PORTESHAM SY6086
The high heathland above here is good walking territory, with a view covering the entire sweep of the West Dorset coast.

Hardy Monument As hideous as it is prominent, this commemorates Nelson's admiral, not the Dorset author; it has tremendous views. A track along Bronkham Hill SE from the car park feels truly ancient, with prehistoric burial mounds flanking it. If you don't feel like leaving the car, the Black Down rd passing the Monument towards Martinstown also gives fine views.

PORTLAND SY6973
This odd, much-quarried promontory with its narrow neck and long naval connections gives tremendous views from its peak. Nearer at hand, the remarkable sea defences of Portland Harbour laid out below are a fine sight – and you may glimpse Britain's first prison ship for generations moored off here. The George (not Weds), Pulpit, and the Lobster Pot (open Easter to mid-Nov – good crab sandwiches) are useful for lunch, and handy for a stroll to the cliffs and lighthouse, which is open Sun–Fri in summer, and on winter Suns; (01305) 861233.

Climbing With over 900 climbs, the Isle of Portland is the main centre for sports climbing in the south of England, with bolted climbs from easy to hard. Restrictions for nesting birds on some crags Mar–July, phone the Portland Ranger to check (01305) 266920; for equipment or information Rockies Sports Shop (Fortuneswell) is useful; (01305) 823100.

Portland Castle You can try on armour and soak in the views at this fortress, built under Henry VIII to defend the south coast; in 2003 they hope to open a new garden, based on the concept of a community square. Audio tour, snacks, shop, disabled access; cl Mon–Thurs Nov–Mar, 24–26 Dec and 1 Jan; (01305) 820539; £3.50; EH.

Portland Museum (Wakeham) A cottage used by Hardy in The Well-Beloved is now a local history **museum** which was founded by Dr Marie Stopes, the birth control pioneer. Shop, disabled access to ground floor; cl 1–1.30pm, Weds and Thurs (exc Aug), and all Nov–Easter; (01305) 821804; £2.

SANDFORD ORCAS ST6221
Manor House Interesting lived-in Tudor manor house, largely unaltered since 16th c, with fine furnishings and family portraits, and pleasant gardens, at their best May and Jun. Open Easter Mon, then pm Sun–Mon May–Sept (exc Jun); (01963) 220206; £3. The Mitre has decent food.

SEATOWN SY4291
This seaside hamlet has some charming stone cottages and a perfectly placed seaside pub, the Anchor. There's a steep walk up to the **Golden Cap**, the highest point on the county's coast, and another good walk along to the New Inn at Eype. Just inland, the village of Chideock is pretty – or would be, if it weren't sadly ripped in half by the busy A35.

SHAFTESBURY ST8623
Hilltop town with good views from Castle Hill and Park Walk; there are several craft shops and workshops. The most famous street is Gold Hill – thatched cottages stepped down a steep cobbled street, familiar from those old Hovis TV advertisements. At the bottom, St James (where the Two Brewers is the town's best family food pub) is attractive.

Shaftesbury Abbey Museum & Garden You can see some of England's most ancient graves at this abbey founded by Alfred the Great in 888AD (for 700 years the Benedictine community for women here was the most important in the country). An adjacent museum has excavated remains, and there's an Anglo-Saxon herb garden; a good audio tour sets the abbey's history in a national context. Shop, disabled access and facilities; cl Nov–Mar; (01747) 852910; £1.50.

Shaftesbury Town Museum At the top of Gold Hill, the local history museum includes an 18th-c fire engine and a collection of old farm implements. Limited disabled access to ground floor only; cl Oct–Easter; (01747) 852157; £1.

SHERBORNE ST6316
An attractive town to wander through, given a feeling of unchanging solidity by the handsome stone medieval abbey buildings that mix in with later ones of the public school here, and by many other fine old buildings in and nr the main st. The **abbey** itself is a glorious golden stone building with a beautifully vaulted nave; at the Dissolution the townspeople raised the money to buy it, and it's been the parish church ever since. The West Window is beautiful, as is the Laurence Whistler engraved glass reredos in the Lady Chapel, and for 20p you can illuminate the fan vaulting of the roof; (01935) 815191; free. The unspoilt Digby Tap (handy for the abbey but no food Sun), cheery Cross Keys (Cheap St – where the market is) and very foody Skippers (Horsecastles) are useful for lunch. Several craft shops include a working saddlery (Cheap St).

Sherborne Castle (just E of town) This striking old house, which has been in the same family for almost 400 years, was built by Sir Walter Raleigh in 1594. Its wonderful period furnishings are the highlight, though there are also interesting paintings and porcelain. Outside are gardens designed by Capability Brown, and beautiful parkland with an enormous lake. Meals, snacks, shop, limited disabled access; open Apr–Oct exc Mon (exc bank hols) and Fri; castle cl Sat am; (01935) 813182; £6 castle and gardens, £3.20 grounds only.

Sherborne Museum (Abbeygate House, Church Lane) An eclectic collection includes a reconstruction of the old castle in its heyday, as well as a Victorian doll's house and Roman remains. Shop, disabled access to ground floor only; cl Sun am, Mon (exc bank hols), and Nov–Easter; (01935) 812252; £1.

Sherborne Old Castle (Castleton) Facing Sherborne Castle across the lake is the original 12th-c castle, now a beautifully evocative ruin. Good for a picnic, and especially appealing in Apr when the dry ditch is full of wild primroses. Shop; cl 1–2pm, and Mon and Tues Nov–Mar, 24–26 Dec, and 1 Jan; (01935) 812730; £1.80.

STAPEHILL SU0500
Stapehill Abbey 🅰 Just right for a relaxed afternoon, a 19th-c Cistercian abbey (the nuns moved out in 1989, although the chapel has been preserved) now houses craft workshops and exhibitions on monastic life; acres of park and landscaped grounds inc a Japanese garden, with waterfalls and woodland walk, a play area, and farm animals for children. Snacks, shop, disabled access to ground floor only; cl Mon and Tues Oct–Easter, Christmas hols–Jan; (01202) 861686; £7.50. The Barley Mow at Colehill is a good food pub.

STOKE ABBOTT ST4500
With thatched houses, a good deal of charm, and a good pub (the New Inn), this offers walkers attractive undisturbed surrounding countryside, with a reasonably good path network.

STONEBARROW HILL SY3893
Reached by a steep narrow road just E of Charmouth, this has good easy walking, fine sea and inland views, and a disabled WC.

STUBHAMPTON ST9214
In good weather the bridleway from here along Ashmore Bottom to Ashmore is well worth exploring; but it can be muddy in a wet spring.

STUDLAND SZ0482
The scattered village has an interesting Norman church (more french than english), and is the start point for the one of most varied short walks on the south coast. In a couple of hours you can take in the Agglestone (a rock standing solitary on Dorset's largest surviving heath), Ballard Down (huge views over Poole Harbour) and Old Harry Rocks (tooth-like chalk pinnacles detached from the cliff), before ending by the coloured sands on the miniature cliffs at the lovely South Beach, which has two areas set aside for dog owners – and a summer parking charge (expensive exc for NT members, less after 2pm). Decent food at the Manor House Hotel (where Churchill and Eisenhower watched D Day rehearsals). Next to the

Sandbanks ferry, the simple Shell Bay is good for seafood.

STURMINSTER MARSHALL ST9500

White Mill Rebuilt in 1776 and restored over 200 years later, this waterside corn mill still has its original wooden machinery (too fragile to operate); delightfully set on the banks of the River Stour, it's a very pleasant spot for a picnic (or you could treat yourself indoors, over at the Anchor at Shapwick). Disabled access; open pm wknds and bank hols 29 Mar–26 Oct; (01258) 858051; £2.60; NT.

SUTTON POYNTZ SY7083

This attractive thatched village, with a decent pub, has a good path to the nearby village of Osmington (also thatched, pretty and with a nice pub). The path gives views of the **White Horse** – an equestrian portrait of George III etched into the hillside. You can walk back along the Dorset coast path, which here leads along the top of the downs rather than along the coast itself.

SWANAGE SZ0278

Fairly quiet 19th-c resort, with a clean, sandy beach; the seaview Mowlem Theatre restaurant (Shire Rd) is good. On Church Hill, the **Tithe Barn Museum & Art Centre** has local history displays inc an exhibition on quarrying (the town was once very important to the stone trade), a re-created 1930s chemist, dinosaur footprints and a huge ammonite; there's also a little summer art and craft gallery. Shop, mostly disabled access; cl 12.30–2, am wknds, and end Sept–end May (exc Easter wk); (01929) 423174; may be a small charge. This is a popular area for diving; the Pier Diving School does a 3-hr course for beginners (£40) and for more experienced divers there are boat trips to nearby wrecks (£15); (01929) 423565.

Durlston Country Park On the edge of Swanage, this has spectacular clifftop scenery and unspoilt countryside, with good views from the headland, the **Great Globe** (a 40-ton global representation in portland stone), and good spots to watch seabirds, butterflies or deer (let staff know if you see dolphins, seals or whales). Meals, snacks, shop, some disabled access; information centre cl wkdys Nov–Mar, park open all year; (01929) 424443; free, though there's a parking charge of £3 in summer (£1 in winter).

Swanage Railway Steam trains run along six miles of track to Corfe Castle (a joint ticket is available): a nice way of approaching the ruins – or you could walk there via Ballard Down and Nine Barrow Down (far-ranging views on all sides) and ride back. Corfe Castle station has an exhibition of old railway memorabilia, while a travel agency in Swanage station helps towards the railway's upkeep. Parking is easier at the Norden end of the line. Snacks, shop, disabled access; cl 25 Dec, and wkdys Nov–Apr; (01929) 425800 for train times and prices.

THORNCOMBE ST3504

Forde Abbey 🆓 The extensive gardens here really are special, with glorious trees and shrubs, a fine collection of Asiatic primulas, many other interesting plants, and sweeping lawns, as well as a visitor centre and Ionic-style temple. The striking abbey buildings still retain many of the features of the original 12th-c Cistercian monastery, but it was modernised in 1520 by Abbot Chard, and his great hall and tower remain. Cromwell's Attorney-General later turned the abbey into a house, and the interior has changed little since, with magnificently furnished rooms, unusual plaster ceilings and a set of Raphael tapestries. Meals and snacks (in 12th-c undercroft), shop, disabled access to gardens and ground floor only; house open pm Tues–Fri, Sun and bank hols Apr–Oct, garden and nursery all year; (01460) 220231; £5.40, £4.75 garden only. Thorncombe Wood is awash with bluebells in spring.

TOLPUDDLE SY7894

Famous for the agricultural workers who were transported to Australia after they united to improve their working conditions and terms of employment. The Martyrs' Tree under which they supposedly met still remains, and more of their story is explained in interactive displays in a little museum between the six cottages built by the TUC as a memorial. Shop, disabled access; cl Mon (exc bank hols),

and 21 Dec–2 Jan; (01305) 848237;
free. The Martyrs pub (open all day) has
good food.

TYNEHAM SY8880
On the army's Purbeck firing ranges
(open holidays and most wknds; see
Lulworth Cove for details), this
abandoned village is quite poignant;
there's an explanatory exhibition in the
former church. The army presence has
meant the landscape has been
preserved remarkably well; this is the
best starting point for walks through
the Lulworth Ranges – taking in
Kimmeridge and Lulworth Cove,
through some of the wildest coastal
scenery in southern England. It's quite
relentlessly tough-going, with nearly
1,000 metres (about 3,000 ft) of ascent
if you do the whole thing, but makes a
marvellous day's walking.

WAREHAM SY9287
This largely modern town has a few
striking old buildings, inc the church of
St Martin, with a finely carved memorial
to Lawrence of Arabia (a little local
history museum in East St has a display
of his photographs; usually open
Mon–Sat; (01929) 553448; free). The
church of Lady St Mary not far from the
Quay has the coffin of Edward the
Martyr, murdered at nearby Corfe
Castle in 978. Still surrounding the old
town, massive grassy banks mark the
Anglo-Saxon town wall. Two very
traditional old inns, the Black Bear and
Kings Arms; another, the Quay Inn, is in
a fine position. The attractive road over
the West Creech Hills may sometimes
be closed for army firing practice.

Blue Pool 🔳 (Furzebrook, 3m S)
Bluest on an overcast day, the water in
this former claypit changes colour with
the weather, depending on how the
light strikes diffracting particles in it; the
surrounding 25 acres of heathland in
this beauty spot are peaceful. There's a
small play area and museum. Cream
teas and snacks, shop, plant sales, some
disabled access; site open Mar–Nov;
(01929) 551408; £3.20.

WEYMOUTH SY6878
Elegant 18th- and 19th-c terraces along
its curving esplanade, and some older
buildings in the narrower partly
pedestrianised streets behind. The
harbour is lively, with big ferries leaving

from the outer quay, and the town's
inner ring road running one-way
around the inner harbour. There`s
decent cheap food in the lively Red Lion
(opposite Brewers Quay, with lots of
tables outside) and seafront Dorothy
(all day in summer), and readers
recommend the Café Royal (Esplanade)
as good value. On the far side of the
harbour the narrow streets of the old
town are worth exploring; you can go
on a guided tour of one of the town's
few remaining Tudor buildings (Trinity
St), furnished as the home of an early
17th-c middle-class family; Tues–Fri
pms Jun–end Sept, 1st Sun of month
Oct–May (exc Jan); (01305) 779711; £2.
The resort has a good beach, and lots of
lively family attractions.

Brewers Quay In the heart of the Old
Harbour, this is a skilful conversion of a
harbourside Victorian brewery into
shopping and leisure complex, with
plenty of good year-round activities.
Timewalk imaginatively re-creates
scenes from the town's history, and a
interactive gallery takes an interesting
look at its brewing heritage (£4.25, and
a good value family ticket, 2 adults and
up to 4 children, £12). There's also a
craft market, ten-pin bowling,
microbrewery, and lively hands-on
science centre. Several places to eat,
and good specialist shops, disabled
access (exc to Timewalk); cl 25–27 Dec,
and last two weeks in Jan; (01305)
777622; free admission to centre.
Deep Sea Adventure 🔳 (Custom
House Quay) Fascinating look at
underwater exploration, shipwrecks,
and the search for buried treasure, with
lots of interactive displays. Meals,
snacks, shop, disabled access; cl 25–26
Dec and 1 Jan; (01305) 760690; £3.75.
There's also an exemplary exhibition on
the *Titanic* (though they may change this
in 2003). Also here **Sharkies** is the
biggest indoor play area in the county
(£2 extra).
Model World (Lodmoor Country
Park, Preston Rd) In landscaped
gardens, this miniature world includes a
model airport, funfair, space centre,
zoo and 0 gauge railway (runs daily,
weather permitting); also plenty of
models to operate yourself, and an
aviary. Snacks, shop, disabled access; cl

Oct–May; (01305) 781797; £3.50.
Nothe Fort (Barrack Rd) Interesting Victorian fort on three levels, with displays spread over a staggering 70 rooms. Children can clamber over some of the vehicles and guns, and there are fine views of the harbour and coast. Snacks, shop, limited disabled access; open daily May–Sept, Easter hols and Oct half-term, plus Sun rest of year; (01305) 766626; £3.50. Good views too from the garden of the Nothe Tavern (with tasty fresh fish), and from the pleasant nearby Nothe Gardens.
Sea Life Park (Lodmoor Country Park) One of the most elaborate in the excellent Sea Life Centres chain. As well as the stunning marine displays and touch pools, features include a Shark Academy, with fun interactive games and quizzes leading to a Scholarship, a seal sanctuary, and a splendid outdoor play area. Meals, snacks, shop, disabled access; cl 25 Dec (reduced hours in winter); (01305) 788255; £8.95.
WIMBORNE MINSTER SZ0199 Georgian houses (and decent antiques shops and auctions) in the narrow central streets around the Minster – a fine, well preserved, largely Norman church with contrasting red and grey masonry, twin towers, and a brightly coloured jack striking the clock bell every quarter. Inside, an interesting Norman crypt, a distinctive astronomical clock and the original chained library. The low-beamed White Hart nr the Minster, Dormers (Hanham Rd) and the Cross Keys (Victoria Rd, W) are all useful for lunch. Just W of town at Pamphill is a good big farm shop, and just E there are pleasant country walks around the Fox & Hounds at Little Canford.
Iron Age hill fort The once formidable hill fort of **Badbury Rings**, just off B3082 NW of Wimborne, is associated by some with King Arthur. It's a good strolling ground with an impressive range of wild flowers – and if you feel more energetic, a **Roman road** lets you strike out for miles N.
Kingston Lacy House (B3082 NW) Impressive 17th-c mansion later remodelled by Charles Barry, with grand Italian marble staircase and superb venetian ceilings; outstanding

paintings such as the 'Judgement of Solomon' by Sebastiano del Piombo, and others by Titian, Rubens and Van Dyck. The enormous grounds have landscaped gardens and a herd of Red Devon cattle in the park. Lovely snowdrops in Feb and early Mar. There's easily enough here to fill a good day out. Meals, snacks, shop, disabled access to park and gardens; open Apr–Oct, house cl am and Mon–Tues; (01202) 883402; £6.80, £3.50 grounds only; NT. The Anchor at Shapwick is fairly handy for a good lunch (not Mon).
Knoll Gardens 🏛 (Stapehill Rd) Rare and exotic plants in various colourfully themed well developed gardens, with over 6,000 different well labelled species, many of which can be bought in the expanding nursery (which specialises in grasses and hardy perennials). They maintain a good working relationship with the Dorset Wildlife Trust. Snacks, disabled access; cl Fri–Sat Oct–Mar, and Christmas week, and perhaps at other times; (01202) 873931; £3.50. Adjacent Trehane Nurseries have a great range of camellias.
Priest's House Museum (High St) Historic townhouse with carefully researched period rooms, a gallery on local villages, and a charming walled garden. Summer teas, shop, disabled access to ground floor; cl Sun (exc July–Aug and bank hol wknds), and Nov–Mar (exc special 2-wk exhibition from 27 Dec); (01202) 882533; £2.50.
Walford Mill (Stone Lane) Former 18th-c flour mill with exhibitions and crafts. Meals, snacks, shop, disabled access; cl Sun am, 25–26 Dec, 1 Jan, and Mons Jan–Mar; (01202) 841400; free.
Wimborne Model Town & Gardens (King St) This entertaining 1950s model town is so accurate that it's used to assess the impact of planning applications here. Also well maintained gardens with some interesting plants, and an indoor miniature railway; young children like it here, there's a little play area with a Wendy house, and a children's trail. Good value café and picnic area, plant sales, disabled access; cl end Sept–Easter; (01202) 881924; (01202) 881924; £3.
WOOL SY8589

Monkey World (off A35 towards Bere Regis) As enjoyable as it is worthwhile, this enthusiastic rescue centre for apes and monkeys delights visitors of all ages. The centre looks after all kinds of primates that are gradually reintroduced to natural surroundings. As well as the biggest group of chimpanzees you'll see outside africa, residents include ring-tailed and ruffed lemurs, Barbary macaques, capuchins and woolly monkeys, orang-utans and gibbons, all roaming and climbing in decent-sized open enclosures. Keepers give useful talks, and you can see baby chimps playing in their nursery. A range of play areas includes a 15–stage obstacle course, plus a pets' corner – it's a very satisfying fine weather half-day out for families; usually special events most bank hols. Meals, snacks (and picnic area), shop, disabled access (a few steep paths); cl 25 Dec; (0800) 456600; £6.25. The attractive village was used by Thomas Hardy as the ancient seat of the D`Urbevilles; the Ship is a pleasant family pub with generous food all day.

WORTH MATRAVERS SY9677 In this prettily set coastal hamlet the unpretentious Square & Compass has lovely views, and is a good base for coast walks. Near here, the rock pool at Dancing Ledge is said to have been cut by a local schoolmaster.

Other attractive villages with decent pubs include Buckhorn Weston ST7524, Burton Bradstock SY4889, Chedington ST4805, Church Knowle SY9481, Evershot ST5704, Farnham ST9515, Fiddleford ST8013, Kingston SY9579, Langton Herring SY6182, Litton Cheyney SY5590, Loders SY4994, Okeford Fitzpaine ST8011, Powerstock SY5196, Puncknowle SY5388 (pronounced Punnel), Shapwick ST9302, Sydling St Nicholas SY6399, Symondsbury SY4493, Tarrant Monkton ST9408, West Knighton SY7387 and Whitchurch Canonicorum (fine church).

Where to eat

BOURNEMOUTH SZ1391 **Grove Seafood Restaurant** *79 Southbourne Grove (01202) 566 660* Bright, airy no smoking seafood restaurant with green and cream colours, wooden dining chairs and tables on the stripped oak floor, fresh flowers and potted plants, and a bustling, chatty atmosphere; delicious and interesting fresh fish dishes (as well as the occasional meat or vegetarian dish), a carefully chosen wine list, and friendly, helpful service; cl Sun pm, Mon. 3-course set dinner £15/2-course lunch |**£5.95**

CHIDEOCK SY4292 **Betchworth House** *(01297) 489478* Welcoming no smoking 17th-c house with attractive tearoom and pretty cottagey garden, with morning coffee and home-made clotted cream teas; bdrms; best to check weekday opening hours in mid-winter.|**£3.50**

CHRISTCHURCH SZ1592 **Splinters** *12 Church St (01202) 483454* Fine old building nr priory with three attractively decorated rooms, international modern cooking, lovely puddings, a fine British cheese choice, good value wines, and friendly helpful owners; also run Pommery's (next door) with delicatessen and lively upstairs café-bar; cl Sun, Mon. £30.50|**£8**

CORSCOMBE ST5205 **Fox** *(01935) 891330* Popular thatched and cottagey dining pub with Aga, Welsh dresser, lovely polished copper pots and pans, scrubbed pine tables, candles in champagne bottles, open fires in one room and woodburner in another, particularly good imaginative food, a super wine list, well kept real ales and local cider; nice surrounding walks; bdrms; cl 25 Dec; children must be well behaved; disabled access. £30|**£5.75**

DORCHESTER SY6990 **Oak Room** *Antelope Walk (01305) 250760* Genteel tea shop in a 1930s time warp and once the courtroom where Judge Jeffreys tried the Monmouth rebels in the Bloddy Assize; excellent sandwiches with interesting fillings, light hot meals and super clotted cream teas.|**£4.50**

DORCHESTER SY6990 **Potter In** *19 Durngate St (01305) 260312* All-day food inc English breakfast, enjoyable lunchtime meals and snacks, and afternoon teas;

walled garden for summer, open fire and fresh flowers, and a friendly welcome; cl 25–26 Dec; disabled access. £12.95|**£3.90**

EAST MORDEN SY9194 **Cock & Bottle** *(01929) 459238* Popular dining pub with several beamed communicating areas, a nice mix of old furnishings, good log fire, enjoyable food inc interesting daily specials with plenty of fish and seasonal game, well kept beers and good wines; cl 25–26 Dec; disabled access. £27.95|**£5.50**

EVERSHOT ST5704 **Acorn** *28 Fore St (01935) 83228* Well run old coaching inn with a comfortable L-shaped bar, two fine old fireplaces and copies of the inn's deeds going back to the 17th c; imaginative daily specials, well kept ales, home-made damson vodka and sloe gin, and a thoughtful wine list; nice village and good nearby walks; bdrms; disabled access. £30|**£6**

FARNHAM ST9514 **Museum Inn** *(01725) 516261* Odd-looking thatched building with various effortlessly civilised areas – flagstoned bar with big inglenook fireplace, light beams and good comfortably cushioned furnishings, dining room with a cosy hunt-theme, and what feels rather like a contemporary version of a baronial hall, soaring up to a high glass ceiling, with dozens of antlers and a stag's head looking down on to a long wooden table and church-style pews; excellent food, three real ales, a fine choice of wines, and very good attentive service; lovely bdrms in back stable block; children over 8; disabled access. £30|**£6.95**

MAIDEN NEWTON SY6097 **Petit Canard** *Dorchester Rd (01300) 320536* Welcoming little restaurant (they prefer you not to smoke) with simple furnishings, good very interesting food inc fine puddings, and a well chosen wine list; they do Sun lunch every 3rd Sun of month; cl am, Sun and Mon pm; children over 12. £32.50

PLUSH ST7102 **Brace of Pheasants** *(01300) 348357* Long low 16th-c thatched cottage with a civilised but relaxed atmosphere, good solid furnishings, fresh flowers and a good log fire in the airy beamed bar; interesting food, well kept real ales; swings and an aviary in the garden; children in the family room; cl winter Mon. £23|**£8.25**

STURMINSTER NEWTON ST8814 **Red Rose** *Market Cross (01258) 472460* Long-standing and very popular family-run lunchtime restaurant with proper English cooking using their own lamb and local produce, and with a very relaxed and happy atmosphere; cl most evenings (open Fri and Sat), cl Sun; disabled access. £16|**£6.75**

SWANAGE SZ0278 **Galley** *9 High St (01929) 427299* Enjoyable little evening restaurant not far from the seafront with emphasis on fresh local fish and game, good reasonably priced wines, and helpful service; cl Mon–Weds in winter, all Jan/Feb. £28.25

TARRANT MONKTON ST9408 **Langton Arms** *(01258) 830225* Charmingly set and welcoming 17th-c thatched pub with beams and an inglenook fireplace, no smoking bistro restaurant in an attractively reworked barn, no smoking family room with play area in skittle alley, well kept interesting real ales, popular enjoyable bar food, and garden with another play area; good nearby walks; bdrms; disabled access. £25|**£6.50**

UPWEY SY6684 **Wishing Well** *Church St (01305) 814470* Nice little restaurant, popular locally, with good interesting lunchtime food and afternoon teas, and friendly service; bring your own wine; cl Mon–Tues Mar, cl mid-Dec–beginning Mar; disabled access. £14

WIMBORNE MINSTER SZ0199 **Cloisters** *40 East St (01202) 880593* Friendly restaurant with pleasant décor and enjoyable food inc breakfast with home-made marmalade, lunchtime snacks and meals, and afternoon tea; cl bank hol Mon; disabled access. £18|**£4.75**

WORTH MATRAVERS SY9776 **Worth Café & Craft Centre** *(01929) 439360* Welcoming converted barn with enthusiastic staff, good home-made lunches (lots for vegetarians) and cakes, and good locally made crafts; walkers welcome; cl Tues, 2 wks Jan; disabled access. £25|**£7.50**

Special thanks to B and K Hypher, M G Hart, Mr and Mrs Hooper-Immins

ESSEX

**Pleasantly unassuming, with some nice surprises,
from quirky museums to ancient forests**

Interesting museums with hands-on displays for children (the one at the castle is the best), and a good zoo (well thought-out play areas and activities as well as animals) make Colchester an appealing place for families. For traditional seaside fun Southend-on-Sea is a popular choice; children really enjoy the Central Museum and Planetarium and Sea Life Adventure, and the museums here are worth a stop, too.

Saffron Walden is the finest small town in the region, lovely to potter around, with the bonus of magnificent Audley End House. Of the many beautiful villages in Essex, especially worth picking out are Finchingfield, Thaxted and Great Bardfield (all of which have windmills). Coggeshall has some fine medieval buildings, and waterside Burnham-on-Crouch (friendly railway museum) is fresh and lively in summer. Many of the churches are well worth a look.

Driving through North Essex, you pass lots of attractive houses right by the road, often with fine old timbering and distinctive colour-washed plasterwork – the intricate patterning is known as pargeting. Constable's Stour Valley still enchants, with its unspoilt landscapes still very much as millions of us know them from prints of his paintings. (They have managed to survive the impact of a good many visitors on footpaths and in small boats, but are now gravely threatened by a scheme to upgrade navigation on the river, bringing in big power boats and likely commercialisation.) The Blackwater/Crouch coast has a surprisingly remote feel, given the closeness of densely urban South Essex. Further north, there are good coastal walks at Walton-on-the-Naze, and Brightlingsea has the best beach.

Not only home is Waltham Abbey home to our Essex Family Attraction of the Year, the Royal Gunpowder Mills, it also has a friendly farm park; for other animal-based attractions we recommend the farm museum at Billericay and, new to the *Guide* this year, Marsh Farm Country Park at South Woodham Ferrers. In South Woodham Ferrers you'll also find one of the largest tropical houses in the country, while Mole Hill Wildlife Park at Widdington has animals and a butterfly house. Stansted has the double attraction of the House on the Hill Toy Museum (lots of the displays are aimed at children), and Mountfitchet Castle (an enthusiastic introduction to life 1,000 years ago); in fine weather, Layer Marney Tower has enough to occupy a peaceful afternoon.

The charming gardens at Little Easton, the RHS Garden at Rettendon, Beth Chatto Gardens at Elmstead Market and the Gibberd Garden in Harlow will all please gardeners, and Paradise Centre in Lamarsh keeps children as well as their plant-minded parents happy. There's a good railway museum at Castle Hedingham, and the tours of nuclear bunker at Kelvedon are thought-provoking; Walton Hall Museum at Linford has an appealingly eclectic mix of memorabilia.

Where to stay

BROXTED TL5827 **Whitehall** *Church End, Broxted, Dunmow, Essex CM6 2BZ (01279)* 850603 **£125**, plus special breaks; 26 pretty rms. Fine Elizabethan manor house in lovely walled gardens, with restful spacious lounge, a smaller cosier one with log fire, pleasant bar, good food in big, heavily timbered restaurant, and friendly service; cl 26–31 Dec

BURNHAM-ON-CROUCH TQ9595 **White Harte** *The Quay, Burnham-on-Crouch, Essex CM0 8AS (01621)* 782106 **£59**; 19 rms, 11 with own bthrm. Old-fashioned 17th-c yachting inn on quay overlooking the River Crouch with its own jetty; high ceilings, oak tables, polished parquet flooring, sea pictures, panelling, residents' lounge, and decent food in bar and restaurant; dogs welcome in bedrooms

DEDHAM TM0433 **Maison Talbooth** *Stratford Rd, Dedham, Colchester, Essex CO7 6HN (01206)* 322367 **£155***, plus special breaks; 10 luxuriously furnished rms. Tranquil Victorian country house in fine Constable country, with deeply comfortable seating and fresh flowers in elegant lounge, very good imaginative food in lovely timber-framed restaurant overlooking river and gardens, and marvellous breakfasts; restaurant cl winter Sun pm; disabled access

TOPPESFIELD TL7437 **Ollivers Farmhouse** *Yeldham Road, Toppesfield, Halstead, Essex CO9 4LS 01787* 237642 **£50**2 rms, 1 with own shower. Historic, no smoking 17th-c farmhouse in particularly pretty gardens with attached vineyard; lots of original beams and fireplaces, big sitting room with piano and large collection of modern paintings, and breakfasts with home-made brown bread and jam, free range eggs and locally cured bacon (and light suppers if ordered) in antique-filled dining room; children over 10

WIX TM1429 **Dairy House Farm** *Bradfield Road, Wix, Manningtree, Essex CO11 2SR (01255)* 870322 **£46**2 comfortable, no smoking bdrms. Victorian farmhouse on 700 acres of arable land with fine country views, many original features, a cosy sitting room, home-made cake on arrival, and enjoyable breakfasts with home-made preserves in elegant no smoking dining room (no evening meals); tennis and croquet; children over 12

We welcome reports from readers

This *Guide* depends on readers' reports. Do help us if you can – in return, we offer a discount on the next edition to people who've helped us with reports for it. Tell us what you think about places already in it, and anything extra you think we should say about them. And send us your ideas for inclusion in the next edition: places to visit, eat at or stay in, attractive drives or walks, maybe even unusual shops you know of. Use the card in the middle, the report forms at the end, or just write – no stamp needed: *The Good Britain Guide*, FREEPOST TN1569, Wadhurst, E Sussex TN5 7BR. Or log on to www.goodguides.com

To see and do

Essex Family Attraction of the Year

WALTHAM ABBEY TL3700 **Royal Gunpowder Mills** (Beaulieu Drive, off A121) Though a visit to these former gunpowder works can be absorbing enough at any time (with plenty for anyone not particularly interested in military history), it's the excellent programme of weekend events that really makes it a good choice for families. And what's particularly impressive is that none of the ones we've seen have involved an extra charge. One weekend a month they have costumed re-enactments, with demonstrations of weapons, manoeuvres and skirmishes from periods as diverse as the reign of Charles II, World War II and the American Civil War. The following weekend they have what they call Igniting Ideas, a series of workshops where children aged 7–14 can make models of radios, telephones and the like to find out how they work. The next week is a bit more specialist, with slideshows and a lecture on a particular theme, then the next weekend they have family activities aimed at children between 4 and 12: trails, games and some sort of art or craft. In the summer holidays they generally have extra activities one day every week – in 2002 that was Wednesday, when children were admitted free, and could take part in free activities such as quizzes, mask-making and nature trails; they may do this on more days next year. Their website, www.royalgunpowdermills. com, has full details of the schedule. The works were established in the 17th c and acquired by the Crown in 1787; they had an international reputation because of their superior production methods, and in World War I 5,000 people were employed here. Many of the restored old buildings around the site are open, and there are good displays on the evolution of explosives and development of the mills, with a film, and a nice mix of traditional and hands-on exhibits, with costumes to try on, and cogs and wheels to turn. Changing displays (not all of which are open every day) might look at fireworks, or small arms. It's a massive site, and even on a non-event day you'll need two or three hours to make the most of the 175 acres of surrounding parkland. Part of this is now a nature reserve, well laid out with boardwalks, bridges and footpaths, and now home to the area's largest colony of herons, as well as muntjac deer and otters. For £1 extra, they usually have guided tractor trailer rides throughout the day. If you're planning to explore properly, comfortable walking shoes are a must. A tower on the edge of the woodland offers good views of the area, with a mural showing the sort of animals you might be able to see. No dogs (except guide dogs). Meals, snacks, shop, disabled access; open late Mar–Oct, plus special events round Christmas; (01992) 707370; £5.90 adults, £3.25 children 5–16. The family ticket, for two adults and up to three children, is good value at £17. The Lee Valley Park attractions can make this a fuller day out.

ABRIDGE TQ4897
Crowther Nurseries (off A113 E) Working garden with decorative shrub beds, flower borders, a vegetable plot, greenhouses and over 400 varieties of clematis; also pets' corner inc goats, donkey and pony, and a Lego corner. Meals, snacks, plant sales, disabled access; cl 25–26 Dec; (01708) 688581; free. The Maltsters Arms in the village has bargain food.

BASILDON TQ6688
Langdon Nature Reserve (Lower Dunton Rd, Langdon) During the early 1900s little pieces of land, known as 'plotlands', were auctioned off mainly to East Enders who spent their free time here. The land gradually grew into a scattered settlement of some 200 homes, before being compulsorily purchased by the council after World War II. Almost all the homes have gone now, leaving 460 acres of ancient

woodland and meadows, lakes and ponds to wander through. One of the few surviving plotland homes, The Haven, has been restored in 1930/40s style, and you can learn more about the social history of the reserve in the museum. Visitor centre with displays, snacks, shop, disabled access; cl Mon (exc bank hols), and 25–26 Dec; (01268) 419103; free.

BATTLESBRIDGE TQ7894
Attractive village, with popular antiques

SUFFOLK

Essex

Lamarsh
Little Maplestead
Boxted
Dedham
Mistley
Harwich
A1124
Chappel
Colchester
Elmstead Market
Wix
A120
A133
TM
Coggeshall
Colchester Zoo
Feering
Copford
Rowhedge
Wivenhoe
Walton-on-the-Naze
Messing
Fingringhoe
Brightlingsea
Frinton-on-Sea
Layer de la Haye
Layer Marney
Peldon
St Osyth
Clacton-on-Sea
Wickham Bishops
Mersea Island
Tollesbury
Heybridge Basin
Maldon
River Blackwater
Bradwell-on-Sea
Purleigh
Burnham-on-Crouch
River Crouch
Paglesham
A13
Southend-on-Sea

0 Miles 10
0 Kilometres 16

and crafts centre, walks to head of Crouch estuary; the Barge and larger Hawk pubs both do food all day.
BILLERICAY TQ6991
Barleylands Farm Museum & Visitor Centre (A129 SE)

Expanding series of attractions, from farm animals and rural life displays to working glassworks, craft studios and miniature railway (summer Sun and daily (exc Sat) in Aug), also picnic and play areas. Meals, snacks, shop, disabled

access; cl Nov–Feb; (01268) 290229;
£4.50. The nearby Duke of York (South
Green) has good value food.

BOCKING TL7524

Windmills As well as the one here in
Churchstreet, good examples can be
found in Aythorpe Roding TL5815, and
Mountnessing TQ6397.

BOXTED TL9931

Carter's Vineyard 🖼 You can go on
a tour of this 7-acre vineyard, which is
powered by alternative energy (£3.50
inc samples), or just wander round
yourself. A few interactive displays on
alternative energy and a video, also
nature trail, picnic area and you can fish
for carp (£5, booking essential). Snacks,
shop, disabled access; cl end
Sept–Easter; (01206) 271136; free. The
Shepherd & Dog over at Langham is a
fine village pub.

BRADWELL-ON-SEA TL9907

Worth the long drive for the sense of
being right out on the edge of things –
the timeless emptiness if anything
exaggerated by distant views of vast
industrial installations. The walk E down
the old Roman rd across the marshes
takes you to a little restored **Saxon
chapel** of St Peter right on the sea wall,
the scene of an annual pilgrimage in July.
The Green Man is a good traditional
pub.

BRAINTREE TM6532

Original Great Maze 🖼 (A120
Dunmow–Braintree) Each year they try
to outgrow the previous year's crop
labyrinth with more than five miles of
pathways in around ten acres; children's
play area. Disabled access; open daily
mid-July to early Sept. **Blake End
Craft Centre** is also here; open
Tues–Sun and bank hols; (01245)
361411; £4.

BRIGHTLINGSEA TM0816

Surrounded on three sides by water,
this is a classic South-East seaside
resort; the beach here is probably the
county's best.

BURNHAM-ON-CROUCH
TQ9595

Attractively old-fashioned yachting
station, lively in summer (packed
around the Aug bank hol for its regatta),
but nice in winter too with rigging
clacking forlornly against the masts of
those yachts left to ride at anchor.

There is a local history museum on the
Quay; cl am, plus Mon, Tues, and Fri
(exc school hols); 50p, and pleasant
walks along the banks of the River
Crouch. The waterfront White Harte is
good for lunch.

Mangapps Farm Railway Museum
(B1021 towards Southminster) Friendly
and growing collection of vintage rolling
stock and railway memorabilia. They
have a station formed from railway
buildings from sites all over East Anglia,
and steam/diesel rides along fl mile of
track. Mostly under cover, snacks,
shop, limited disabled access; open pm
wknds, daily in Aug and Easter school
hols (cl Jan); (01621) 784898; £4 (£1
extra when the steam trains are running
– usually bank hols and special events,
and higher charges on other special
days). Further along, the Limes is a
decent **farm shop**, with nature trails
and **pick-your-own**; (01621) 782051.

CASTLE HEDINGHAM TL7736

🖼 The town, which has some
attractive buildings, is named for the
Norman **castle** which dominates it, the
magnificent four-storey keep towering
above the surrounding trees.
Exceptionally well preserved, it still has
its roof, banqueting hall and minstrels'
gallery. Teas, shop; cl Nov–week before
Easter; (01787) 460261; £4 (may be
more if there are special events on).
The **church** has grand Norman
masonry and interestingly carved choir
seats; the Bell is good for lunch. The
B1058 towards Sudbury then left
through Gestingthorpe and the
Belchamps is a pleasant excursion.

Colne Valley Railway and Museum
🖼 (A1017 N) Lovingly restored
Victorian railway buildings with
collection of vintage engines and
carriages; short steam-train trips Sun
pm mid-Mar to mid-Oct, and Weds pm
in hols; diesel rides Tues, and Thurs–Sat
pm in hols – best to ring for timetable.
Admission price includes train rides and
entry to rare breeds farm park. Meals
on Pullman coaches (you need to pre-
book these). Snacks, shop, limited
disabled access; cl Nov–Mar; (01787)
461174; £6, £3 when trains not running
(vouchers not valid for special events).

CHAPPEL TL8927

The prettily sited Swan has good food,

in sight of the Chappel Viaduct (reputedly the biggest brick structure in Europe), and there's a decent **railway museum**, and perhaps rides on a short demonstration line – best to ring for timetable. Wknd snacks, shop, some disabled access; cl 24–25 Dec; (01206) 242524; £6 (£3 non-steam days).

CHELMSFORD TL7007
A big busy city with little for visitors, but its 15th-c **cathedral**, consecrated as such only in 1914, has particularly harmonious Perpendicular architecture. The Alma (Arbour Lane) has good food in nice surroundings.
Chelmsford Museum (Oaklands Park, off Moulsham St) Local and social natural history museum in a Victorian mansion, with a live beehive, room reconstructions and changing exhibitions; the friendly staff will have a go at identifying any objects you bring in. Adjoining it is a museum devoted to the Essex Regiment; children's playground and picnic area in the park. Shop, disabled access to ground floor; cl am Sun, 25–26 Dec and Good Fri; (01245) 615100; free.

CLACTON-ON-SEA TM1714
Roomy family seaside resort, with long stretches of gently shelving sandy beach and all the usual amusements. The pier has an aquarium, reptile house and various rides (cl winter; (01225) 421115); and watching the fishing at its end has a curiously mesmerising charm; readers recommend the nearby shopping village. The Robin Hood (London Rd) is the best family dining pub in the area.

COGGESHALL TL8422
Attractive small town with a good few antiques shops, and a working **pottery** in Church St; (01376) 563600. The Woolpack out by the church is a magnificent timbered building.
Grange Barn (Grange Hill; B1024 S edge) 12th-c, one of the oldest surviving timber-framed barns in Europe, originally part of a Cistercian monastery. Disabled access; hours as Paycocke's (see entry below); (01376) 562226; £1.70, or joint ticket with Paycocke's £3.40; NT.
Marks Hall (B1024 N) Gradually being restored, this estate is pleasant for an undemanding stroll. There's a massive

13th-c oak and a developing arboretum, and work is well under way on re-creating a 17th-c walled garden. Meals, snacks and picnic area, shop, disabled access; cl Mon (exc bank hols), and wkdys Nov–Mar; (01376) 563796; £3.50 per car.
Paycocke's (West St) A fine timber-framed medieval merchant's home with unusual panelling and carvings, and pretty garden behind. Disabled access; open pms, Tues, Thurs, Sun and bank hols beginning Apr to mid-Oct; (01376) 561305; £2.30 (joint ticket with Grange Barn £3.40); NT. The Fleece next door has decent food.

COLCHESTER TL9925
Britain's oldest recorded town, the capital of Roman Britain. You can trace the Roman wall (the Hole in the Wall, Balkerne Gdns, is a decent pub built into the one surviving fragmentary gatehouse). The High St has handsome buildings, some extravagantly timbered, and plenty more historical buildings inc **St Botolph's**, the oldest Augustinian priory in the country. The good **Minories Art Gallery** at no 74 (01206) 577067), has recently been awarded a lottery grant; they plan to create a contemporary art space in the town, and work should start on the project this year. Town tours leave the Tourist Information Centre (Queen St) at 11am (Jun–Sept; £2.50), and they also do themed tours (6pm Sat; £3.50), with costumed guides. The Tudor Rose & Crown (East St) is good for lunch.
Bourne Mill (just off B1025 S) Delightfully quaint restored watermill by pretty millpond, worth a look from the outside even when it's not open. Usually open pm bank hol Sun and Mon, plus pm Sun and Tues Jun–Aug, but best to check; (01206) 572422; £2; NT.
Colchester Castle Museum 🖼 (Castle Park, off High St) Great for families: they let you try on Roman togas and helmets, or touch 2,000-year-old pottery excavated nearby; also splendid collection of Roman relics from jewellery to military tombstones. The castle itself has the biggest Norman keep in Europe, and stands on the site of a colossal Roman temple (you can still see the vaults). They go to some lengths to bring grisly moments in its

history to life: you can hear a dramatisation of one of the forced confessions of the suspect witches incarcerated here. For £1.20 extra a guided castle tour takes you up on the roof as well as to the vaults and chapel. Snacks, good shop, mostly disabled access (to castle museum but not to vaults or castle roof); cl 25–26 Dec and 1 Jan; (01206) 282939; £4.

Colchester Zoo ♿ (Maldon Rd, Stanway, 2m E by B1002) One of the country's most satisfying animal collections, with over 200 rare and endangered species kept in enclosures as close to their natural environments as possible. The zoo is particularly good on cats and primates, but one enclosure has shire horses, pigs, rabbits and other tame animals for children to get close to; they've recently opened new areas for warthogs and a vulture aviary. Several good play areas (our favourite is the Kalahari Capers under-cover complex), and an activity centre with changing animal-related or Native American crafts; activities such as face-painting and brass-rubbing included in the price. Meals, snacks, shops, indoor and outdoor picnic areas, mostly disabled access; cl 25 Dec; (01206) 331292; £9 (you can save up to £1.35 off the normal adult price by booking in advance on their website, www.colchester-zoo.co.uk); the tickets stay valid for a year.

Hollytrees Museum (High St) With hands-on and audio displays, this Georgian town house has displays on its history and famous local figures, as well as a collection of toys, costumes and curios from the last two centuries, inc a doll's house modelled on Hollytrees. Shop, disabled access; cl 25–26 Dec and 1 Jan; (01206) 282940; free.

Natural History Museum (All Saints church, High St) Lots of hands-on displays and a children's quiz, with an emphasis on man's impact on the environment; shop, disabled access; cl 25–26 Dec and 1 Jan; (01206) 282941; free.

Rollerworld ♿ (Eastgates) Children like this place, Britain's only international-standard roller-skating rink; open Weds–Fri eves (Weds adults only), wknds, and pms during school

hols – best to check; (01206) 868868; from £3.90; also Quasar and ten-pin bowling.

Tymperleys Clock Museum (Trinity St) A particularly unusual selection in a lovely 15th-c house; there's something very special about coming here and hearing all the ticking; also reconstructed Tudor herb garden. Shop, disabled access; cl Oct–Apr, best to check; (01206) 282931; free.

COPFORD TL9222
Copford church Worth a visit, particularly for its well restored 12th-c wall paintings.

CRESSING TL7918
Cressing Temple Barns (Witham Rd) Two impressively large medieval barns built by the Knights Templar, plus a Tudor walled garden; special events in summer. Meals, snacks, shop, disabled access; cl Mon–Tues, Sat and all Nov–Easter; (01376) 584903; £3.

DEDHAM TM0533
Several fine old buildings, especially the 15th-c flint **church**, its pinnacled tower familiar from so many Constable paintings. There's also the school Constable went to, and good walks through the protected riverside meadows to his father's mill at Flatford (across the river lock, so in Suffolk, and described in that chapter). The partly medieval Sun has decent food, and the handsome Marlborough Head, a wool merchant's house dating from 1475, is well worth a look. Worries about the hordes of visitors the Constable connection attracts have led local tourist boards to cut down on the publicity they give the village in their literature.

Dedham Art & Craft Centre (High St) A number of crafts in this converted church, such as floristry, glass engraving and wood turning, as well as a toy museum. Vegetarian meals, snacks, shop; cl 25 Dec, and Mon Jan–Mar; (01206) 322666; free.

Gnome Magic (Ipswich Rd) This attractive garden extends into woods where 500 gnomes live; picnic site; open Apr–Sept; (01206) 231390; £3.

Sir Alfred Munnings Art Museum (Castle House, Castle Hill) The house itself is a mix of Tudor and Georgian, and inside the artist's own furniture gives a real sense of how it would have looked when he and his wife lived here. His horsey paintings are hung throughout the house, and you can also view his studios and stroll through the pleasant gardens. Shop, disabled access to ground floor only; open pm Weds and Sun Easter–beginning Oct, plus Thurs and Sat in Aug; (01206) 322127; *£4.

ELMSTEAD MARKET TM0623
Beth Chatto Gardens A riot of colour in spring and summer, with lots of gardening ideas, and unusual varieties of plants for sale. It's hard to believe that these attractive gardens were once four acres of wasteland. Snacks during summer; cl Sun, bank hols, Sats Nov–Feb, and 2 wks over Christmas; (01206) 822007; £3.50. At Great Bromley the Old Black Boy has good value food.

EPPING FOREST TQ4197
A magnificent survival, an expansive tract of ancient hornbeam coppice, mainly tucked between the M25 and outer London. There are miles of leafy walks (and rides – you can hire horses locally), with some rough grazing and occasional distant views. There are so many woodland paths that getting lost is part of the experience; the long-distance Forest Way is however well marked. On the W side there's a pleasant diversion to High Beach, from where a few field paths lead SW; the Owl at Lippitts Hill is a useful refreshment stop.

FEERING TL8620
Feeringbury Manor (Coggeshall Rd) Fine big riverside garden with ponds, streams, a little waterwheel, bog gardens and a range of plants. Disabled access; open Thurs and Fri Apr–July; (01376) 561946; £2.50. The Sun towards Kelvedon has interesting food.

FINCHINGFIELD TL6734
The county's prettiest village, with charming houses spread generously around a sloping green that dips to a stream and pond; just off stands a pristine-looking small windmill. The Tudor Red Lion opposite the churchyard and the 15th-c guild-hall has sensibly priced food. There's a pleasant easily followed path along the Finchingfield Brook to nearby Great Bardfield.

FRINTON-ON-SEA TM2419
A pleasant, unspoilt family seaside resort, with long stretches of gently shelving sandy beach; it's a quieter place than its neighbour Clacton (it acquired its first pub ever, the Lock & Barrel, only in 2000). Beyond, the blowy open space of the Naze is pleasant for strolling, especially out of season when you're likely to have its 150 acres virtually to yourself.

GOSFIELD TL7729
Gosfield Hall Famous visitors to this Tudor house, built around a courtyard, include Elizabeth I, Louis XVIII of France and Horace Walpole; open pms Weds and Thurs early May–end Sept (tours 2.30 and 3.15pm); afternoon teas, disabled access; £3. The Green Man has good food.

GREAT BARDFIELD TL6730
Known as the Montmartre of Essex because of the group of artists who once lived here, this has several attractive pargeted houses, a village green, a church with a rare 14th-c carved stone screen, and a windmill.

GREAT SALING TL7025
Saling Hall Gardens 12 acres of tranquil gardens created over the last 50 years. There is a fine walled garden and water features, but the aboretum is the main draw here. Disabled access; open pm Weds May–Jul; (01371) 850243; £2.50 (which goes to charity). The ancient White Hart has decent food.

GREAT WALTHAM TL6913
Pleasant village, with an attractive and interesting church. The Dog & Gun in nearby Little Waltham is a good dining pub.

GREENSTED TL5302
St Andrew's church Tests have established that it was probably built around the time of the Norman Conquest – the oldest wooden church in the world; shop, disabled access. The nearby Green Man at Toot Hill has decent food (and fine wine).

HARLOW TL4611
A New Town, and not perhaps top of most itineraries, but has a couple of surprisingly good museums. A large part of the town around the town hall is currently being re-developed in order

to create new gallery space, a playhouse, and council buildings – work should be complete in 2004. The Marquis of Granby (Market St, Old Harlow) is an attractive old pub.

Gibberd Collection On the first floor of the town hall, this surprisingly fine collection of British modern art includes works by Graham Sutherland, Elizabeth Blackadder and John Nash. Disabled access; cl wknds and bank hols; (01279) 446763; free.

Gibberd Garden (Marsh Lane, Gilden Way) The master planner of Harlow New Town designed these gardens in the late 1950s and continued to develop them until his death in 1984. Planned as a series of individual 'rooms', the glades, groves, pools and allees provide settings for sculpture, architectural salvage, a gazebo and even a moated castle. Snacks, shop, disabled access; open wknd and bank hol pms Easter–Oct; (01279) 442112; £3.

Museum of Harlow (Muskham Rd) Newly re-opened here, the museum has an important Roman collection, a bicycle collection and period landscaped gardens, which include a Tudor herb garden and three walled gardens; shop, disabled access: museum cl 12.30-1.30pm Sat, and all Sun; (01279) 454959/439680; free.

HARWICH TM2430
The Redoubt here is a circular fort built in 1808 in case of invasion by Napoleon, with three small museums. Shop; cl Sept–Apr (exc Sun); (01255) 503429. Harwich's two lighthouses both have small museums, one a **Maritime Museum** (times as above; 50p), the other a collection of vintage radios and TVs (times as above; £1). Also a little lifeboat museum (times as above, 50p), and ferry rides. From the A120 W there's an unusual sight for this part of Essex – a tall narrow **windmill** (actually an interloper, as it was brought from Suffolk).

HATFIELD FOREST TL5320
(just S of Stansted Airport) This NT medieval Royal hunting forest is an unexpected survivor, with ancient mainly hornbeam woodland, not on quite the same scale as Epping Forest but still extensive enough, with nature trails, cycle paths, and a lake where you

can fish (mid-Jun to mid-Mar; around £4 – phone to check). Look out for the unusual shell grotto built in the 1750s by the family that once owned the forest; car park £3. Information centre and café; (01279) 870678.

INGATESTONE TQ6598
Ingatestone Hall 🏠 Interesting old house, not too grand and given life by enthusiastic tours guided by the family that live here, and lovely grounds. Teas, shop; open pm wknds, bank hols and Weds–Fri in school hols Easter-Sept; (01277) 353010; £4. The Cricketers out at Mill Green is a prettily set food pub.

KELVEDON HATCH TQ5599
Secret Nuclear Bunker (off A128) Who'd have thought that a three-storey Cold War underground complex lay beneath this innocuous 1950s bungalow? Knowledgeable tours take you through all parts of this clinically self-sufficient little world, and are done with real relish, so you can't help feeling relieved when you're back in the surrounding woodland. Audio tour, film shows (one showing what you needed to do in case of a nuclear bomb alert), wknd meals, snacks, shop; cl Mon–Weds Nov–Feb and 25 Dec, best to check; (01277) 364883; £5. The Black Horse in Pilgrims Hatch is a good handy dining pub.

LAMARSH TL8836
Paradise Centre (Twinstead Rd) Fascinating for gardeners, with a very wide variety of unusual plants beautifully laid out and for sale, particularly woodland ones; and plenty to keep kids amused, inc miniature goats, bantams and play area. Open wknds and bank hols Easter–Oct, or by appointment; (01787) 269449; free. The Lion is good for lunch, and the Bures–Henny Street road is a pretty drive.

LAYER DE LA HAYE TL9517
Abberton Reservoir Wildlife Centre (B1026, Layer de la Haye) Popular wetland stop for wildfowl; observation room and hides, nature trails, and events for families in summer. Snacks, shop, disabled access; cl Mon (exc bank hol) and 25–26 Dec; (01206) 738172; £1 suggested donation (more for special events). The Donkey &

Code GBG

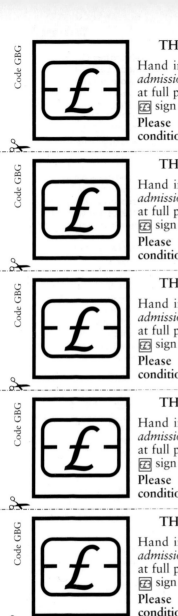

THE GOOD BRITAIN GUIDE 2003

Hand in this Discount Voucher to claim *free admission for one child* when you buy admission at full price for two adults at attractions with a ⏎ sign after their name.

Please see overleaf for further details and conditions.

Code GBG

THE GOOD BRITAIN GUIDE 2003

Hand in this Discount Voucher to claim *free admission for one child* when you buy admission at full price for two adults at attractions with a ⏎ sign after their name.

Please see overleaf for further details and conditions.

Code GBG

THE GOOD BRITAIN GUIDE 2003

Hand in this Discount Voucher to claim *free admission for one child* when you buy admission at full price for two adults at attractions with a ⏎ sign after their name.

Please see overleaf for further details and conditions.

Code GBG

THE GOOD BRITAIN GUIDE 2003

Hand in this Discount Voucher to claim *free admission for one child* when you buy admission at full price for two adults at attractions with a ⏎ sign after their name.

Please see overleaf for further details and conditions.

Code GBG

THE GOOD BRITAIN GUIDE 2003

Hand in this Discount Voucher to claim *free admission for one child* when you buy admission at full price for two adults at attractions with a ⏎ sign after their name.

Please see overleaf for further details and conditions.

Code GBG

THE GOOD BRITAIN GUIDE 2003

Hand in this Discount Voucher to claim *free admission for one child* when you buy admission at full price for two adults at attractions with a ⏎ sign after their name.

Please see overleaf for further details and conditions.

CONDITIONS

1. This discount offer cannot be used in conjunction with any other offer, and is not available as part of a group booking or for more than one child. The voucher is not transferable.
2. Free admission for one child is available only if two adults are paying the full normal tariff.
3. The offer may not be available on bank holidays, or on special event days – in this case our entry for that attraction notes this fact in brackets immediately after the ⛎ sign.
4. A very few attractions are offering some special variation on this offer – their entries spell this out in brackets immediately after the ⛎ sign.
5. This offer expires on 31 December 2003 (or at the close of the attraction's season if that is earlier).

CONDITIONS

1. This discount offer cannot be used in conjunction with any other offer, and is not available as part of a group booking or for more than one child. The voucher is not transferable.
2. Free admission for one child is available only if two adults are paying the full normal tariff.
3. The offer may not be available on bank holidays, or on special event days – in this case our entry for that attraction notes this fact in brackets immediately after the ⛎ sign.
4. A very few attractions are offering some special variation on this offer – their entries spell this out in brackets immediately after the ⛎ sign.
5. This offer expires on 31 December 2003 (or at the close of the attraction's season if that is earlier).

CONDITIONS

1. This discount offer cannot be used in conjunction with any other offer, and is not available as part of a group booking or for more than one child. The voucher is not transferable.
2. Free admission for one child is available only if two adults are paying the full normal tariff.
3. The offer may not be available on bank holidays, or on special event days – in this case our entry for that attraction notes this fact in brackets immediately after the ⛎ sign.
4. A very few attractions are offering some special variation on this offer – their entries spell this out in brackets immediately after the ⛎ sign.
5. This offer expires on 31 December 2003 (or at the close of the attraction's season if that is earlier).

CONDITIONS

1. This discount offer cannot be used in conjunction with any other offer, and is not available as part of a group booking or for more than one child. The voucher is not transferable.
2. Free admission for one child is available only if two adults are paying the full normal tariff.
3. The offer may not be available on bank holidays, or on special event days – in this case our entry for that attraction notes this fact in brackets immediately after the ⛎ sign.
4. A very few attractions are offering some special variation on this offer – their entries spell this out in brackets immediately after the ⛎ sign.
5. This offer expires on 31 December 2003 (or at the close of the attraction's season if that is earlier).

CONDITIONS

1. This discount offer cannot be used in conjunction with any other offer, and is not available as part of a group booking or for more than one child. The voucher is not transferable.
2. Free admission for one child is available only if two adults are paying the full normal tariff.
3. The offer may not be available on bank holidays, or on special event days – in this case our entry for that attraction notes this fact in brackets immediately after the ⛎ sign.
4. A very few attractions are offering some special variation on this offer – their entries spell this out in brackets immediately after the ⛎ sign.
5. This offer expires on 31 December 2003 (or at the close of the attraction's season if that is earlier).

CONDITIONS

1. This discount offer cannot be used in conjunction with any other offer, and is not available as part of a group booking or for more than one child. The voucher is not transferable.
2. Free admission for one child is available only if two adults are paying the full normal tariff.
3. The offer may not be available on bank holidays, or on special event days – in this case our entry for that attraction notes this fact in brackets immediately after the ⛎ sign.
4. A very few attractions are offering some special variation on this offer – their entries spell this out in brackets immediately after the ⛎ sign.
5. This offer expires on 31 December 2003 (or at the close of the attraction's season if that is earlier).

Buskins (B1026) is handy for a meal.
LAYER MARNEY TL9217
Layer Marney Tower 🏛 The
mansion here was never completed, but
its eight-storey Tudor gatehouse is very
impressive – one of the most striking
examples of 16th-c architecture in
Britain. Around it are formal gardens, a
rare breeds farm, medieval barn, farm
shop, parkland and a play area.
Tearoom, shop, disabled access to
grounds; cl am, all day Sat, and
Oct–Mar; (01206) 330784; £3.50.
LINFORD TQ6881
Walton Hall Museum 🏛 Private
collection of memorabilia in restored
farm buildings, with a bit of everything
from a decent collection of farm
machinery and engines, tricycles and a
19th-c gypsy caravan, to military items
and Victorian and Edwardian toys. Also
children's play area, picnic and barbecue
areas. On some summer days you can
watch blacksmiths, saddle-makers,
printers and wheelwrights, and they
sometimes bake bread. Snacks, shop,
disabled access; cl Mon–Weds (exc
school and bank hols), and Dec
24–Easter; (01375) 671874; *£3. The
Bell at Horndon-on-the-Hill is fairly
handy for lunch.
LITTLE BADDOW TL7707
Blakes Wood Ancient woodland of
hornbeam and chestnut coppice, with
lovely bluebells in spring. The Generals
Arms is useful for lunch.
LITTLE DUNMOW TL6521
Little Dunmow church Unusually
stately for such a relatively small village
– it's the surviving part of a priory
founded in 1106. The Flitch of Bacon is a
good pub.
LITTLE EASTON TL5924
Gardens of Easton Lodge 🏛 Queen
Elizabeth I once owned the 14th-c deer
park in which these charming gardens
are set. Handed down through
generations of the Maynard family who
lived in the apparently doomed Easton
Lodge (both the original and its
Jacobean wings were destroyed by
fires), the gardens were redeveloped by
the current owners in the mid-1990s,
and are a nice reflection of changing
tastes in gardening. Harold Peto
possibly left the biggest impression in
the early 1900s, with his sunken Italian

garden, unique courtyard and adults'
tree-house (now a ruin). They're
developing a flower bed with every
plant mentioned in Shakespeare's
works. Snacks and cream teas, shop,
disabled access (can be tricky in wet
weather); open pms Fri–Sun and bank
hols Feb–Oct (open daily when the
snowdrops are out, phone to check);
(01371) 876979; £3.80. The ancient
Green Man at Mill End Green NE of
here has good food.
Little Easton Manor Pleasant
summer gardens with topiary and lakes
– you can fish here (from £3). Snacks,
disabled access; open Thurs pm
Jun–Sept; (01371) 872857; £2 (inc a
deck chair). Little Easton church just
beside the manor is also worth a visit.
Nearby attractive Great Easton is good
for strolling through.
LITTLE MAPLESTEAD TL8234
Little Maplestead church Very
different from most in the area – an
unusual round building modelled on the
Holy Sepulchre in Jerusalem.
MALDON TL8506
🏛 The **Maeldune Centre** (junction
Market Hill/High St) houses a 13-metre
(42 ft) tapestry commemorating the
1,000th anniversary of the crucial Battle
of Maldon; Art gallery, shop, (01621)
851628. The **Millennium Gardens**
are named for the same event, and re-
create what a garden might have looked
like at the time of the battle. Also a
church with an unusual triangular
tower, some decent shops, a couple of
small museums, and a riverside stroll
past the golf course to the pretty weir
by Beeleigh Abbey. You can pick up
guided walk leaflets from the Tourist
Information Centre in Coach Lane, and
go on a tour of the Moot Hall (High St)
which has an interesting brick newel
staircase, courtroom and good views
from the roof; Sat 2 and 3.30pm
Mar–Oct or by appointment; (01621)
857373; £1.50.
Hythe Quay Full of life, and the best
chance to see one of the classic Thames
barges with its ox-blood sails in action.
At the quayside Jolly Sailor (Church St)
you can eat looking out over the water.
MERSEA ISLAND TM0012
Linked to the mainland by a little
causeway, which can get covered by the

tide; much of its coast is a National Nature Reserve for its shore life, and there's a bracing coastal walk from East Mersea along the sea dyke overlooking the Colne estuary. It does feel very much an island, and away from the extended village of West Mersea, popular for retirement homes, there are few people about out of season (in summer the caravan parks bring in lots of families). The Company Shed serves huge platters of shellfish in simple surroundings, and you can take your own wine and bread; the Willow Lodge has good food, and the Blackwater and Fox are good value too.

MISTLEY TM1031
Environmental & Animal Centre (New Rd) Very friendly animal rescue centre: Ping and Pong the white Vietnamese pot-bellied pigs may come to greet you as you go in. Snacks (wknds only in winter), shop, disabled access; cl Mon and in bad weather during winter – phone to check; (01206) 396483; £2.50. The village has the remains of a Robert Adam church (known locally as the Mistley Towers). If you come by train, don't miss the splendid station buffet at Manningtree.

MORETON TL5306
This is an attractive village, with an interesting circular walk from the White Hart (which has enjoyable food).

ONGAR TL5305
Blake Hall Gardens (Bobbingworth, off A414 W) A peaceful garden walk takes in an ornamental wood, ice house and bog garden, herbaceous borders, rose garden, sunken garden and large tropical house; in the south wing of the house is a little aviation museum. Snacks and picnic area, open Sat–Weds Easter-end Sept; £3. The White Hart at nearby Moreton has decent food.

PLESHEY TL6614
This attractive village has a ruined castle, charming churchyard, country walks – and a good pub, the White Horse.

PURLEIGH TL8302
New Hall Vineyards Covering 97 acres, this 30-year-old vineyard is the largest in East Anglia; free tastings, guided group tours (by arrangement May–Sept). They host an annual English wine festival (craft fair, live music, art

exhibitions) on the first wknd in Sept. Snacks, shop, disabled access; cl wknd pms, and 25 Dec ; (01621) 828343; free.

RETTENDON TQ7899
RHS Garden 🖼 (Hyde Hall) Twenty acres of year-round hillside colour, with woodland garden, big rose garden, a dry garden (this is one of the UK's driest areas), ornamental ponds, shrubs, trees, national viburnum collection, and a new millennium avenue with wildflower meadows. Meals and snacks in thatched barn, plant centre, visitor centre and shop, garden library, disabled access; cl Dec–Mar; (01245) 400256; *£4. The Windmill over at East Hanningfield has enjoyable food.

RIVER CROUCH WALKS TQ8596
The Ferry Boat Inn down nr the River Crouch at the end of the lane through North Fambridge is a good base for lonely waterside walks.

ROWHEDGE TM0221
The village itself is well worth a visit; and nearby is a nature reserve among former gravel workings at Fingringhoe, where the Whalebone (beside the county's oldest oak) has good inventive food. There's a pedestrian ferry to Wivenhoe – phone for times; (01206) 282920.

SAFFRON WALDEN TL5438
The finest small town in the region, with prime examples of warmly colour-washed pargeting throughout. Walking around looking at buildings, you'll find it difficult to avoid being tempted into one of the many antiques shops (or David Prue, the fine cabinet-maker in Radwinter Rd; cl Suns and am Sats; (01799) 522558). The grand airy **church** has a magnificent spire, the very ruined **castle** up on a grassy mound is worth prowling around, and children will enjoy the maze on the Common. The Eight Bells is an appealing food pub, and the Crown just N at Little Walden is very nice for lunch. The town has a goodish network of tracks for walks around it, extending into the parkland of nearby Audley End House. Longer rambles can take in Newport, where the houses have characteristic pargeted plaster walls, and Wendens Ambo. The B184 to Chipping Ongar is a pleasant country drive; about 4m along, Grace's Farm

Shop at Wimbish is good, with **pick-your-own** in summer; (01371) 830387. Another good drive is the B1053 to Braintree.

Audley End House (B1383, 1m W) Spectacular Jacobean mansion and former Royal palace remodelled by Robert Adam. This is serenely surrounded by splendid gardens landscaped by Capability Brown. Nothing inside can compete with the quite breathtaking façade, but it's not for want of trying – there are around 30 rooms to see, crammed with fine furnishings inc a magnificent doll's house, and art. There are also suitably grand concerts and other events in the grounds. Meals, snacks, shop, disabled access to gardens and ground floor; cl Mon (exc bank hols), Tues, and Oct–Mar; (01799) 522842; £6.95, £4 grounds only; EH.

Bridge End Gardens (Bridge St) These early Victorian gardens spread over 3fi acres, with rose garden, formal Dutch garden, kitchen garden and an atmospheric wilderness leading to a little grotto, are often closed, and they keep the yew maze locked anyway. So book ahead to collect a key from the tourist information centre (Market Pl). Limited disabled access; cl 25 Dec; (01799) 510444 to book; £10 refundable deposit.

Saffron Walden Museum (Museum St) Notable natural history section in the town museum, as well as social history, archaeology, ethnography and toys and dolls. Shop, good disabled access; cl Sun am and bank hols, 24–25 Dec; (01799) 510333; £1.

SOUTH WEALD TQ5992 Attractive village; the Tower Arms is an enjoyable food pub. **Old Macdonald's farm park** (Weald Rd) has a very extensive range of animals, with 30 breeds of sheep alone. Demonstrations, nature trails and craft displays, and plenty of opportunities to stroke the animals. Meals, snacks, shop, disabled access; cl 25 Dec and 1 Jan; (01277) 375177; £3.25. The nearby **country park** has a deer enclosure, lakes, woods, and visitor centre; (01277) 261343.

SOUTH WOODHAM FERRERS TQ8096

Marsh Farm Country Park You can get close to some of the animals at this working farm, and there play areas, tractor rides and a farm trail. Meals, snacks, shop, disabled access; open daily Feb half term-Oct half term then wkdys till middle of Dec, best to check; (01245) 321552; £5. Surrounded by the River Crouch on three sides, the 350-acre park also has a nature reserve attracting a variety of wild birds to its marshes and freshwater lakes.

Tropical Wings Butterfly and Birds (Wickford Rd) Lots of free-flying exotic butterflies and birds in this 560 sq metre (6,000 sq ft) tropical house, as well as a collection of creepy-crawlies; outdoor aviaries inc two walk-through ones, and a children's play area. Tearoom, good farm shop and plant centre, disabled access; cl wkdys Nov–Feb, 24–26 Dec, 1 Jan; £4.25.

SOUTHEND-ON-SEA TQ8885 Traditional seaside resort long favoured by East Londoners, with the attractions you'd expect. Most famous is the pier, the longest in the world, excellent for fishing, with a museum (open wknds, Tues–Weds and bank hols); (01702) 611214, and a restored train service – it's a long walk there and back. Like many such resorts, Southend in winter has a special appeal for people who wouldn't like it in summer – seafront shops by the endless promenade looking closed for ever, the sea itself a doleful muddy grey. Readers enjoy the Westcliff part of town, with its decent art gallery (cl 1–2pm; Sun and Mon, (01702) 347418; free), and on the Eastern Esplanade, Kursal, first opened in 1901, was the world's first theme park; (01702) 322322. The Victorian cliff gardens (Prittlewell Sq) are curently being restored with the help of a lottery grant. Summer **boat trips** include occasional runs on a vintage paddle-steamer; (01634) 827648 for dates (usually Jun–July, and Sept–Oct). The Last Post (Weston Rd) has decent food all day.

Central Museum & Planetarium (Victoria Ave) The only planetarium in the South-East outside London, with a local history museum and a hands-on discovery centre. Shop; cl Sun, Mon, inc bank hols (planetarium cl Sun–Tues);

(01702) 215131; planetarium £2.25, museum and discovery centre free.

Leigh-on-Sea Though attached to Southend, this has a quite distinct character, altogether more intimate, with wood-clad buildings and shrimp boats in the working harbour; Ivy Osborne's cockle stall here is justly famous, and the Crooked Billet overlooking the water has real old-fashioned character.

Prittlewell Priory Museum (Priory Park, slightly N of centre) 12th-c Cluniac priory in nice grounds, with eclectic collections of local and religious history. Shop, disabled access to ground floor only; usually cl 1–2pm, all day Sun, Mon and bank hols; (01702) 342878; free. Repairs to the museum will take place probably early 2003, so phone for information, or check their website www.southendmuseums.co.uk.

Sea Life Adventure 🗷 (Eastern Esplanade) The highlight is the walk-through tunnel along a reconstructed sea bed with sharks; you can watch shoals of piranhas being fed, and there are regular daily talks. Meals, snacks, shop, disabled access; cl 25 Dec; (01702) 442211; £4.95. Also here is a three-storey children's play centre (£3 or joint ticket £5.60).

Southchurch Hall Museum (Park Lane) An unexpected find, a medieval moated manor house in an attractive park, with period room settings, and fun talks on Tudor life; occasional lute demonstrations. Shop, limited disabled access; cl 1–2pm, all Sun and Mon and bank hols, plus a few days over Christmas; (01702) 467671; free (small charge for talks).

ST OSYTH TM1215
This pretty village is distinguished by the remarkable crenellated flint gateway leading to **St Osyth Priory**. Unfortunately, the lovely buildings and grounds behind are no longer open to the public. The White Hart towards Point Clear has good value food.

STANSTED TL5125
House on the Hill Toy Museum Home to what we think is the biggest privately owned toy collection in the world, with over 50,000 toys, games and playthings from Victorian times to the 1970s. Quite a few toy museums

attract parents more than children, but this one avoids that by making its very well thought out displays entertaining to look at; lots of them are animated, and it's great fun watching the soldiers, trains and Meccano in action. There are a few coin-operated slot machines and puppet shows, and a collection of celebrity memorabilia. All indoors, so good in any weather. Good shop, cl a few days over Christmas; (01279) 813237; £3.80 (you get 10% off if you visit the castle in the same day). The Three Willows over at Birchanger is a good food pub.

Mountfitchet Castle & 1066 Village Intriguing, an authentically reconstructed Norman castle and village, complete with thatched houses, and deer, sheep, goats and chickens wandering around between them. The castle includes a small chunk of the original, and dummies display gruesome tortures and punishments. Cheerful and enthusiastic rather than particularly sophisticated, it's a good introduction to life a thousand years ago, though you will need to visit on a dry day. Snacks (and space for picnics), shop, some disabled access; cl mid-Nov to mid-Mar; (01279) 813237; £5. It's under the same management as the toy museum five mins' walk up the hill.

Stansted Mountfitchet Windmill The well preserved 18th-c windmill still has much of its original equipment (though isn't working). Shop; open pm first Sun of month Apr–Oct, and pm bank hol Sun and Mons; 50p.

THAXTED TL6131
This engaging small town has a graceful, airy church (where Holst was organist) with a tremendous spire, several handsome buildings inc nearby almshouses, a fine 600-year old guild-hall (occasional craft markets), and a restored windmill. The Raven Armoury (B184 towards Dunmow) does hand-forged steel and weaponry. The 15th-c Swan has decent food.

TILBURY TQ6475
Tilbury Fort Well preserved 17th-c fort with unusual double moat, and good views of the Thames estuary. The most violent episode in its history was a 1776 cricket match that left three dead. Snacks, shop, some disabled access; cl

24–26 Dec and 1 Jan; (01375) 858489; £2.90; EH. For an extra £1.30 you can fire a 1943 anti-aircraft gun. There is a pleasant 3-mile walk along the Thames to **Coalhouse Fort** (off A1013 Orset–Stanford-le-Hope; usually open last Sun of month and bank hols Apr–Oct, but check on website for specific dates: www.coalhousefort.freeserve.co.uk; (01375) 858489; £2.50.

TOLLESBURY TL9510
This inland village is the ideal starting point for one of the best circular coastal walks in Essex, where linking paths head out to the sea wall skirting a breezy peninsula jutting into the Blackwater estuary; excellent for bird-watching, and lots of flora and insect life in the surrounding marshes. You can also start nr the marina and Edwardian sail lofts E of the village.

WALTHAM ABBEY TL3800
Despite the surrounding housing developments, the centre has some handsome buildings – especially the **Abbey church** with its famous peal of 14 bells (and a museum in the crypt). Shop, disabled access ground floor only; cl 26 Dec and during church services; (01992) 767897). There are claims that King Harold was buried here after the Battle of Hastings, and there's a memorial to him east of the church. Associated ruins include part of a Norman cloister, and the bridge dates back to the abbey's time.
Capel Manor College (Bullsmoor Lane, off A10 just S of M25) Plenty of useful tips for would-be gardeners, with over 30 acres of themed gardens, and lots of good special events; animal corner and holly maze; cl wkdys Oct–beginning Mar and over Christmas; (020) 8366 4442. Though officially in Enfield, this fits well with a Waltham Abbey visit. The nearby Pied Bull has well priced food.
Epping Forest District Museum (Sun St) Lively holiday activities for children, archaeological displays, Tudor room and Victorian gallery in two timber-framed old houses, and also a herb garden. Snacks, shop, limited disabled access; cl am (exc Sat), Weds–Thurs, and also Sun Oct–Mar; (01992) 716882; free.

Lee Valley Park Farms ▣ (B194, 2m N) Takes in Hayes Hill children's farm with plenty of traditional animals, a pet centre and play area, and Holyfield Hall working farm and dairy, with 150 cows milked every afternoon around 3pm, and seasonal events such as sheep-shearing and harvesting. Meals, snacks, shop, disabled access; (01992) 892781; *£3.15.
Royal Gunpowder Mills *See separate family panel on p.*

WALTON-ON-THE-NAZE TM2623
There's a nice walk N from this quiet seaside town, along the coast, round the tip of the Naze – with views of shipping entering and leaving Harwich and Felixstowe – to a nature trail through a nature reserve harbouring migrant birds. You can fish from the long pier (£5), and there are amusement arcades, various rides in summer, and a soft play area. Two-hour wildlife spotting boat trips (you'll see seals) leave from Foundry Slip (signposted from Hall Lane); (01255) 671852.

WETHERSFIELD TL7229
Boydells Dairy Farm ▣ Working dairy farm where you may be able to join in milking the goats and cows – or even the sheep. Also working beehive, various other animals, and ice lollies made from their own sheep yoghurt. Snacks, shop, disabled access; cl am, Mon–Thurs (exc school hols) and Oct–Easter; £3; (01371) 850481. The Bull over at Blackmore End is a popular dining pub welcoming children.

WIDDINGTON TL5431
Mole Hall Wildlife Park Family-run place with wide variety of animals around moated manor house. Otters a speciality, but also free-roaming wildfowl, deer paddock, a butterfly house, and a summer maize maze. Summer snacks, shop, some disabled access; park only cl 25 Dec, but butterfly house cl Nov to mid-Mar; (01799) 540400; £5, less in winter.

WRITTLE TL6700
Hylands House and Gardens ▣ (Hylands Park) Six rooms in this neo-classical villa have been restored, inc the gilded Victorian drawing room and Georgian entrance hall; they hope to

open the West Wing and basement by Easter. Outside are pleasure gardens and 500 acres of landscaped park; guided tours by arrangement; tearoom on Sun, shop, disabled access; open Sun and Mon (cl 25 Dec, and during its annual pop festival); (01245) 355455; £3 (free to park and garden). The Red Lion at Margaretting is a popular food pub **Other attractive villages**, all with decent pubs, include Arkesden TL4834, Blackmore TL6001 (big antiques/crafts shop), Fuller Street TL7416, Fyfield TL5606, Great Chesterford TL5143, Great Easton TL6126, Great Warley Street TQ5890, Knowl Green TL7841, Paglesham TQ9293, Roydon TL4109, Stebbing TL6624, Wickham Bishops TL8412, and (both waterside) Heybridge Basin TL8707 and Wivenhoe TM0321.

Where to eat

BRIGHTLINGSEA TM0816 **Coffee Pot** *Victoria Pl (01206) 305738* Spotless place with very good breakfast, lunch and tea – everything freshly made daily; helpful friendly staff; cl pm, Sun; disabled access.|**£3.55**

BURNHAM-ON-CROUCH TQ9595 **Contented Sole** *80 High St (01621) 782139* Long-standing, family-run evening restaurant (though they do Sun lunch), very popular for consistently good imaginative food with emphasis on fine seafood; popular wine tastings all year; cl Sun pm (open for lunch), Mon, Jan; disabled access. £27

CASTLE HEDINGHAM TL7835 **Bell** *St James's St (01787) 460350* Run by the same family for over 30 years, this interesting old coaching inn has a log fire in the beamed lounge bar, a traditionally furnished public bar, no smoking area, enjoyable traditional bar food, and lovely big walled garden behind; cl 25 Dec pm; disabled access. £20|**£5**

CHELMSFORD TL7107 **Alma** *37 Arbour Lane (01245) 256785* Attractively layed out place with a civilised country-pub feel, beamed bar, a comfortable mix of furniture and central brick fireplace, a nice collection of old advertising posters, well kept real ales and decent house wines; good friendly service, no smoking dining area and prettily decorated restaurant, and good, imaginative food; picnic-sets out on a crazy-paved front terrace and in a small back garden. £23.20/2–course lunch £5.

CLAVERING TL4832 **Cricketers** *(01799) 550442* Run by the parents of TV chef Jamie Oliver, this smart comfortably modernised 16th-c dining pub has an L-shaped beamed bar with standing timbers on new brickwork, gleaming copper, dried flowers in big fireplaces, and a wide choice of interesting and elaborate food inc super puddings; pretty bdrms; partial disabled access. £28.50|**£9**

COLCHESTER TL9925 **Clowns** *61–62 High St (01206) 578631* Huge helpings of good straightforward food in clean spacious restaurant; nice children's menu, too; they have another restaurant of the same name in Ipswich, Suffolk; cl 24–26 Dec; disabled access. £15|**£4**

COLCHESTER TL9925 **Warehouse Brasserie** *12 Chapel St N (01206) 765656* Bustling bistro with friendly relaxed atmosphere, pine settles and chairs, an upper gallery area, prints on warm red walls, real ales, enjoyable interesting food, and decent wines; cl Sun, Mon, last 2 wks Aug, first 2 wks Sept; disabled access. £23.50|**£5.95**

DEDHAM TM0433 **Milsom's** *Stratford Road (01206) 322795* Stylish place with ties linked to Le Talbooth and the Pier at Harwich; scrubbed wooden tables on wooden floors in two dining areas, contemporary bistro-style food, a good wine list, and smart, casual staff; open for morning coffee; disabled access. £25|**£6.50**

FINGRINGHOE TM0220 **Whalebone** *Chapel Rd (01206) 729307* Garden with a peaceful valley view, three opened-up room areas inside with a pleasant mix of chairs and cushioned settles around stripped tables on unsealed bare boards, a coal fire, and especially good changing daily specials cooked inventively and nicely presented; they do a good breakfast until 11.30am; good service, well kept real ales and decent house wines and coffee; partial disabled access. £20/2-course set menu £8.95

GOSFIELD TL7829 **Green Man** *The Street (01787) 472746* Smart dining pub with a relaxed chatty atmosphere, two little bars and no smoking dining room, good daily changing food inc marvellous lunchtime cold buffet and delicious puddings, well kept real ales and decent wines, many by the glass; no food Sun pm; partial disabled access. £19.50|**£6.95**

GREAT YELDHAM TL7637 **White Hart** *Poole St (01787) 237250* Striking black and white timbered building with beams, oak panelling, and stone or wooden floors, successfully ambitious food which can be eaten in bar or restaurant, a fine range of wines inc ten by the glass, real ales; best to book; seats in the attractive garden. £24.50|**£7.25**

HARWICH TM2532 **Pier at Harwich** *The Quay (01255) 241212* Attractive restaurant overlooking the Stour and Orwell estuaries, with particularly good fresh fish dishes (and lobsters from their salt-water tanks); more informal, brightly decorated Ha'penny Pier downstairs, and first-floor dining room with more ambitious dishes; thoughtful choice of wines; bdrms. £30|**£10**

HORNDON-ON-THE-HILL TQ6783 **Bell** *(01375) 673154* Flower-decked medieval inn with welcoming licensees, open-plan beamed bar with polished oak floorboards and flagstones, carefully prepared imaginative food that changes twice daily, five real ales, good choice of wines; restaurant cl 26 Dec, bank hol Mon; disabled access. £26|**£6.95**

LITTLE DUNMOW TL6521 **Flitch of Bacon** *(01371) 820323* Friendly pub with small attractively furnished timbered bar, decent reasonably priced food, several wines by the glass, and real ales; comfortable bdrms; children away from bar area; disabled access. £18|**£6.50**

MESSING TL8918 **Crispin's** *The Street (01621) 815868* Friendly Elizabethan restaurant with open fire in beamed lounge, candles on the walls and tables, good food inc fish and vegetarian choices, monthly themed evenings, a good wine list, helpful service, and quiet back garden; bdrms; cl Mon, Tues, Sun pms; children over 5. £29.50

PAGLESHAM TQ9492 **Plough & Sail** *East End (01702) 258242* Beautifully kept white weatherboarded 17th-c dining pub with pine tables and seats under its rather low beams, lots of brasses and pictures, big log fires, and pretty flower arrangements; consistently good imaginative food, well kept real ales, decent house wines, friendly attentive staff, and tables in an attractive neatly kept garden with an aviary. £20|**£7**

PELDON TM0015 **Rose** *Mersea Road (01206) 735248* Huge pastel-washed inn, recently gently smartened it up, with one or two standing timbers supporting the low ceiling, creaky close-set tables, some antique mahogany, brass and copper on the mantelpiece of the gothick-arched brick fireplace, and a very spacious airy no smoking conservatory; a very good wine list, with over 20 by the glass, well kept real ales, enjoyable food, and friendly, efficient staff; good teak seats in the spacious garden and a nice pond with white ducks. £21|**£6.95**

YOUNGS END TL7319 **Green Dragon** *London Rd (01245) 361030* Well run dining pub with attractive understated barn theme in no smoking restaurant area, extensive range of good interesting bar food inc lots of fish, well kept real ales, and plenty of seats in back garden. £20.50|**£6**

Please let us know what you think of places in the *Guide*. Use the report forms at the back of the book, write us a letter or log on to www.goodguides.com

GLOUCESTERSHIRE

Perfect Cotswold countryside, some of the prettiest villages in Britain, and a good mix of places to visit, from farm parks to elegant gardens

With their broad landscapes, charming stone-built villages and handsome towns, the Cotswolds help make Gloucestershire a very rewarding if rather grown-up place for a relaxing break. Chipping Campden, Cirencester, Northleach (with a very special mechanical music museum), Painswick (a cheery garden) and Stow-on-the-Wold are towns of real individuality, all crammed with sightseeing possibilities. Villages such as Lower and Upper Slaughter, Bibury and Eastleach are perfect for a lazy afternoon's wander, while at bustling Bourton-on-the-Water you can choose between a maze, a motor museum, two bird attractions and a collection of amazingly detailed models.

Two drawbacks to the Cotswolds are that they tend to be expensive, and that in season they can get very crowded. Also, away from the villages, the countryside (with long stretches of unchanging arable farmland) can be a bit monotonous for serious walkers – though great for cyclists. The long-distance Cotswold Way between Chipping Campden and Bath traces through much of the best scenery. Cheltenham, still with a considerable degree of Regency elegance, is a good base for exploring the area, and the TIC does a useful leaflet explaining how to get to most Cotswold attractions by public transport.

Much less well known, the Forest of Dean over by the Welsh border has a different type of time-warp charm. Flanked by a spectacular stretch of the Wye Valley, the hilly woodland is punctuated with all sorts of interesting features often connected with the living people have made here in past centuries, and there's plenty of space for children to run around and explore. High points here include the Dean Heritage Centre, Puzzle Wood and the Treasure Train, the spectacular Symonds Yat, tours of Hopewell Colliery, and the atmospheric caves at Clearwell – our Family Attraction for Gloucestershire this year.

Busy Gloucester has much to offer families, including the excellent National Waterways Museum in the docks.

The Wildfowl & Wetlands Trust at Slimbridge is another splendid outing for families. This is a good county for bird lovers, with an extensive collection of exotics at Bourton-on-the-Water, impressive flying displays at the Newent National Birds of Prey Centre, and at Prinknash Bird Park you'll find friendly animals too. Elsewhere we recommend the farm park at Kineton (lots under cover at this well organised place) and friendly Butts Farm in South Cerney; the country park at Tockington has good adventure play areas.

Favourite houses to visit are Snowshill Manor (an amazing collection of bric-a-brac), Sudeley Castle nr Winchcombe (splendid gardens here too),

Dyrham Park (hardly changed since the 17th c), Stanway House (a beautiful 16th-c manor), the well-preserved Roman villa at Yanworth and the never-finished Gothic mansion at Nympsfield. Attractive Tewkesbury with its outstanding abbey makes a nice objective for a peaceful day trip.

The magnificent arboretums at Moreton-in-Marsh and Westonbirt are unmissable if you like trees, and beautiful just for a walk. If you prefer roses you'll want to visit Kiftsgate Court (Mickleton) and Hunts Court (North Nibley). There are other fine gardens at Hidcote and Lydney Park, and good paintings inspired by nature at Twigworth.

Away from the Cotswolds, some less well known parts are delightful (and generally cheaper): the tortuously steep hills and valleys around Stroud, the quiet water-meadows of the upper Thames, the unspoilt orchard and farming countryside around the Severn Valley (so few river crossings that the little villages down by the W bank, with few people passing through, have a very secluded and unchanging feel). Most TICs keep copies of the Severn Way guide, detailing a walk through fine countryside from Mid Wales to Bristol (£6.95).

Where to stay

ASHLEWORTH SO8125 **Ashleworth Court** *Ashleworth, Gloucester, Gloucestershire GL19 4JA (01452) 700241* **£50***; 3 rms, shared bthrms. By a small elegant church and NT tithe barn, this striking ancient house is part of a working farm and has a homely kitchen with an Aga, a comfortable sitting room, enjoyable breakfasts served in what was originally part of the Great Hall, and chickens in the back garden; two good pubs in the village; cl Christmas; partial disabled access

BIBURY SP1106 **Bibury Court** *Bibury, Cirencester, Gloucestershire GL7 5NT (01285) 740337* **£125**, plus special breaks; 18 individual rms. Lovely peaceful mansion dating from Tudor times, in beautiful gardens, with an informal friendly atmosphere, panelled rooms, antiques, huge log fires, conservatory, a fine choice of breakfasts, and good interesting food; cl Christmas and New Year; disabled access; dogs welcome in bedrooms

BIBURY SP1106 **Swan** *Bibury, Cirencester, Gloucestershire GL7 5NW (01285) 740695* **£124**, plus special breaks; 20 very pretty individually decorated rms. Handsome creeper-covered hotel on the River Coln, with private fishing and attractive formal gardens; lovely flowers and log fires in carefully furnished comfortable lounges, a cosy no smoking parlour, good food in opulent dining room, nice breakfasts, and attentive staff; disabled access

BLOCKLEY SP1634 **Lower Brook House** *Lower Street, Blockley, Moreton-in-marsh, Gloucestershire GL56 9DS (01386) 700286* **£80*** ; 7 attractive rms with fresh fruit and chocolates. 17th-c Cotswold stone building with beams, flagstones and open fires, antique furniture and interesting bric-a-brac, good modern British cooking using home-grown produce and enjoyable breakfasts in cosy dining room, a comfortable drawing room, and helpful staff

BUCKLAND SP0835 **Buckland Manor** *Buckland, Broadway, Worcestershire WR12 7LY (01386) 852626* **£225***; 14 sumptuous rms. Really lovely 13th-c building in 10 acres of beautifully kept gardens, comfortable lounges with magnificent oak panelling, flowers and antiques, and elegant restaurant with fine food using home-grown produce; outdoor swimming pool, riding, tennis, croquet, putting; children over 12

CHARINGWORTH SP1939 **Charingworth Manor** *Charingworth, Chipping Campden, Gloucestershire GL55 6NS (01386) 593555* **£150**, plus special breaks; 26

SHIRE

WARWICKS

Mickleton

Chipping Campden

Ebrington

Willersey

Charingworth

Saintbury

Broad Campden

Buckland

Paxford

SP

Blockley

Todenham

Stanton

Snowshill

Toddington

A44

Alderton

Bourton-on-the-Hill

Moreton-in-Marsh

Greet

Stanway

M5

Broadwell

A435

Winchcombe

Kineton

Stow-on-the-Wold

Cleeve Common

Lower Swell

Lower Oddington

Belas Knap

Upper Slaughter

Oddington

Guiting Power

Bledington

Cheltenham

Lower Slaughter

Nether Westcote

Devil's Chimney

Bourton-on-the-Water

Brockhampton

Little Rissington

Hazleton

A429

River Windrush

Hampnett

Clapton

Great Rissington

Great Witcombe

Yanworth

A40

Great Barrington

Elkstone

Northleach

Little Barrington

Winstone

A417

COTSWOLDS

North Cerney

A429

R Leach

OXFORDSHIRE

Miserden

The Duntisbournes

Bibury

R Coln

Eastleach

Bisley

Daglingworth

Baunton

Coln St Aldwyns

Southrop

Frampton Mansell

Stratton

Sapperton

Thames & Severn Canal

Poulton

Fairford

Lechlade

A419

Cirencester

Meysey Hampton

A433

The Ampneys

Ewen

South Cerney

River Thames

Somerford Keynes

Shorncote

SU

Shipton Moyne

WILTSHIRE

0 Miles   10

0 Kilometres   16

lovely rms with thoughtful extras. Early 14th-c manor with Jacobean additions, mullioned windows, antiques, and log fires and heavy oak beams in relaxing sitting room; good modern cooking in charming restaurant, excellent breakfasts, friendly staff, fine grounds and leisure spa with indoor swimming pool, gym, and all-weather tennis court

CHELTENHAM SO9523 **Hotel on the Park** *Evesham Rd, Cheltenham, Gloucestershire GL52 2AH (01242) 518898* **£118.50**, plus special breaks; 12 lovely rms. Warmly welcoming and handsome Regency house with elegantly furnished drawing room and dining room, pretty flowers and antiques, and imaginative food in stylish restaurant – good breakfasts, too; children over 8; dogs by special arrangement

CHELTENHAM SO9421 **Kanninsky Hotel** *Bayshill Road, Cheltenham, Gloucestershire GL50 3AS (01242) 527788* **£110.90**48 large, stylish and well equipped rms. White-painted Regency hotel with an interesting mix of old and new furnishings, antiques and modern paintings, big pot plants, lots of mirrors, unusual collections on walls, tiled or wooden floors, and a relaxed, informal atmosphere; enjoyable modern food in bustling Café Paradiso, friendly bar, willing young staff, basement nightclub, and seats out on decked terrace; they are kind to families; dogs anywhere ☺

CHELTENHAM SO9421 **Lypiatt House** *Lypiatt Rd, Cheltenham, Gloucestershire GL50 2QW (01242) 224994* **£70**; 10 attractive rms. Carefully restored Victorian house in its own grounds, with an open fire, books amd fresh flowers in light, comfortable drawing room, attractive conservatory bar, and friendly personal service; cl Christmas/New Year

CHELTENHAM SO9421 **Wyastone Hotel** *Parabola Rd, Montpellier, Cheltenham, Gloucestershire GL50 3BG (01242) 245549* **£79.50***, plus special breaks; 13 pretty rms. Quietly set Victorian house with a panelled bar and cosy pink-coloured lounge, plenty of period features, warmly friendly owners, enjoyable breakfasts, and traditional French evening meals; charming little terraced garden; cl Christmas

CHIPPING CAMPDEN SP1539 **Badgers Hall** *High St, Chipping Campden, Gloucestershire GL55 6HB (01386) 840839* **£75**2 beamed rms. Opposite the historic market hall, this fine old stone and timber house has friendly helpful owners, a relaxed atmosphere, particularly good breakfasts plus a thriving teashop with home-made lunches and afternoon teas, and a display of local artists' work for sale; no smoking; plenty of pubs and restaurants nearby for evening meals; cl Christmas/New Year; children over 13

CHIPPING CAMPDEN SP1539 **Eight Bells** *Church St, Chipping Campden, Gloucestershire GL55 6JG (01386) 840371* **£70**, plus winter breaks; 6 rms. Neatly restored heavy-beamed 14th-c pub by church, with a newly refurbished bar, three log fires, interesting food with fresh local produce, friendly staff, decent wines and beers, a new terrace, and pleasant courtyard; cl 25 Dec; dogs anywhere

CLAPTON SP1617 **Clapton Manor** *Clapton, Cheltenham, Gloucestershire GL54 2LG (01451) 810202* **£70***; 2 charming rms. Fine 16th-c Cotswold stone house in lovely interestingly planted gardens with marvellous views across the Windrush Valley; large inglenook fireplaces, heavy beams, mullioned windows, antiques, and a relaxed, informal family atmosphere; log fire and TV in residents' sitting room, and good breakfasts with home-made jams and their own eggs served in the dining room or on the terrace; no smoking; several restaurants and pubs nearby for dinner; cl Christmas

CLEARWELL SO5708 **Tudor Farmhouse** *Clearwell, Coleford, Gloucestershire GL16 8JS (01594) 833046* **£70**, plus special breaks; 22 cottagey rms. Carefully restored Tudor farmhouse and stone cottages with landscaped gardens and surrounding fields; lots of beams, oak doors and sloping floors, delicious food in candlelit restaurant, and friendly staff; cl Christmas; disabled access; dogs welcome away from restaurant

CORSE LAWN SO8330 **Corse Lawn House** *Corse Lawn, Gloucester GL19 4LZ*

(01452) 780771 **£125**, plus special breaks; 19 pretty, individually furnished rms. Magnificent Queen Anne building with comfortable and attractive day rooms, a distinguished restaurant with imaginative food and excellent wines (there's a less pricey bistro-style operation too), warmly friendly staff, a relaxed atmosphere, and an indoor swimming pool, tennis court, croquet, and horses in 12 acres of surrounding gardens and fields; cl 24–26 Dec; disabled access; dogs welcome away from restaurant

GREAT RISSINGTON SP1917 **Lamb** *Great Rissington, Cheltenham, Gloucestershire GL54 2LP (01451) 820388* **£55***, plus special breaks; 14 pretty rms – several at higher price are suites with own lounge. Civilised 17th-c inn with a bustling and friendly atmosphere and nice mix of customers in the cosy bar, some interesting things to look at such as part of a propeller from a Wellington bomber that crashed in the garden in 1943, a residents' lounge with log fire, enjoyable bar food and a more extensive choice in no smoking restaurant, seats in the sheltered hillside garden, and good nearby walks; disabled access; dogs welcome in bedrooms

GREET SP0230 **Manor Farm** *Market Lane, Greet, Cheltenham, Gloucestershire GL54 5BJ (01242) 602423* **£50***; 3 rms. Carefully restored 16th-c manor house on mixed farm with nice breakfasts, fine views, and a big garden with a fish pond and croquet; steam train just 150 yards away; also, camp and caravan site

GUITING POWER SP0924 **Guiting Guest House** *Post Office Lane, Guiting Power, Cheltenham, Gloucestershire GL54 5TZ (01451) 850470* **£70**; 7 pretty rms with thoughtful extras. 16th-c Cotswold stone guest house with inglenook fireplaces, beams, and rugs on flagstones, two sitting rooms, enjoyable Aga-cooked food, attentive owners, and a very relaxed atmosphere; cl Christmas week; dogs in one rm

HAZLETON SP0818 **Windrush House** *Hazleton, Cheltenham, Gloucestershire GL54 4EB (01451) 860364* **£51**; 4 rms, 2 with own bthrm. Warmly friendly and neatly kept no smoking guest house, with exceptionally good imaginative food, lovely breakfasts, log fire, and traditional furnishings; cl mid-Dec to Feb; no children; dogs welcome

LEONARD STANLEY SO8003 **Grey Cottage** *Leonard Stanley, Stonehouse, Gloucestershire GL10 3LU (01453) 822515* **£60***; 3 rms overlooking garden or countryside, with flowers, fruit and biscuits. Carefully restored 170-year-old cottage with a pretty garden, really kind and thoughtful owner, interesting furnishings and fresh flowers, comfortable sitting room, marvellous breakfasts, and enjoyable meals by prior arrangement; children over 10

LITTLE RISSINGTON SP1919 **Touchstone** *Little Rissington, Cheltenham, Gloucestershire GL54 2ND (01451) 822481* **£40**; 3 rms with thoughtful extras. Attractive traditional Cotswold stone house with very friendly owners, good breakfasts in dining room with doors on to terrace, and lots of nearby walks; cl Jan; children over 7

LOWER SLAUGHTER SP1522 **Lower Slaughter Manor** *Lower Slaughter, Cheltenham, Gloucestershire GL54 2HP (01451) 820456* **£220**; 16 luxurious rms. Grand 17th-c manor house in four neatly kept acres, a 15th-c dovecot, all-weather tennis court, croquet, and indoor pool; lovely flower arrangements, log fires, fine plaster ceilings, antiques and paintings, excellent modern cooking and most enjoyable wines in the elegant restaurant, and attentive welcoming staff; children over 12; partial disabled access

MORETON-IN-MARSH SP2032 **White Hart Royal** *High St, Moreton-in-marsh, Gloucestershire GL56 0BA (01608) 650731* **£70**; 19 good rms. Busy and comfortable, partly 15th-c inn with interesting Civil War history, oak beams and stripped stone, big inglenook fire in lounge area just off main bar, friendly helpful staff, well kept real ales, and decent food in bar and pleasant restaurant; attractive courtyard; disabled access

NAILSWORTH ST8599 **Egypt Mill** *Stroud Rd, Nailsworth, Stroud, Gloucestershire GL6 0AE (01453) 833449* **£75**, plus special breaks; 17 comfortable airy rms. Carefully converted 16th-c watermill with original millstones and lifting equipment in the spacious lounge, a split-level restaurant, ground floor bar where two waterwheels can be seen, enjoyable food, friendly service, and seats in the waterside gardens; disabled access

NORTH CERNEY SP0107 **Bathurst Arms** *North Cerney, Cirencester, Gloucestershire GL7 7BZ* (01285) 831281 **£65**; 5 pleasant rms. Civilised and handsome old inn with lots of atmosphere, notably friendly staff, a nice mix of polished old furniture and a fireplace at each end of the beamed and panelled bar, small no smoking dining room, imaginative food, 11 well chosen wines by the glass (inc two champagnes), well kept real ales, and an attractive garden running down to the River Churn; lots of surrounding walks

PAINSWICK SO8609 **Painswick Hotel** *Kemps Lane, Painswick, Stroud, Gloucestershire GL6 6YB* (01452) 812160 **£125**, plus special breaks; 19 well equipped comfortable rms. 18th-c Palladian mansion – once a grand rectory – with fine views, antiques and paintings in the elegant rooms, open fires, good food using the best local produce, a thoughtful wine list, and a relaxed, friendly atmosphere; garden with croquet lawn; they are kind to families; dogs welcome in bedrooms ☺

PARKEND SO6108 **Edale House** *Folly Rd, Parkend, Lydney, Gloucestershire GL15 4JF* (01594) 562835 **£51**, plus special breaks; 5 rms. Georgian house opposite cricket green and backing on to Nagshead Nature Reserve; comfortable, homely sitting room, little bar, very good food in attractive no smoking dining room (overlooking the garden), and a relaxed atmosphere; cl New Year; children over 12; dogs welcome

ST BRIAVELS SO5504 **George** *St Briavels, Lydney, Gloucestershire GL15 6TA* (01594) 530228 **£55**; 4 rms. Pleasant old pub in particularly interesting village overlooking 12th-c castle, with three rambling rooms, big stone fireplace, a Celtic coffin lid dating from 1070 (found in a fireplace here and now mounted next to the bar counter), cosy dining room, real ales, and good food; outdoor chessboard; dogs may be accepted

STOW-ON-THE-WOLD SP1925 **Grapevine** *Sheep St, Stow-on-the-wold, Cheltenham, Gloucestershire GL54 1AU* (01451) 830344 **£130***, plus special breaks; 22 individually decorated, attractive, no smoking rms. Warm, friendly and very well run hotel with antiques, comfortable chairs and a relaxed atmosphere in the lounge, a beamed bar, and imaginative food in the attractive, sunny restaurant with its 70-year-old trailing vine

STOW-ON-THE-WOLD SP1925 **Old Stocks** *The Square, Stow-on-the-wold, Cheltenham, Gloucestershire GL54 1AF* (01451) 830666 **£80**, plus special breaks; 18 rms. Well run 16th/17th-c Cotswold stone hotel with cosy welcoming small bar, beams and open fire, comfortable residents' lounge, good food, friendly staff, and sheltered garden; cl 18–28 Dec; disabled access; dogs welcome away from restaurant

TETBURY ST8494 **Calcot Manor** *Calcot, Tetbury, Gloucestershire GL8 8YJ* (0666) 890391 **£145**, plus special breaks; 28 attractive rms inc 10 super family ones and suites in old Granary Barn. Charming former farmhouse with country house décor and log fires in comfortable lounges, extremely helpful friendly staff, imaginative food in conservatory restaurant and Gumstool brasserie, enjoyable breakfasts, and smallish outdoor swimming pool in enclosed courtyard; they are particularly kind to families, with a qualified nanny in the playroom (stuffed with toys and games), computers and Playstation, tasty high teas, two tennis courts, an outdoor play area with bikes and lots of equipment, and plenty to do nearby; disabled access ☺

THORNBURY ST6390 **Thornbury Castle** *Castle St, Thornbury, Bristol BS35 1HH* (01454) 281182 **£185**; 25 opulent rms, some with big Tudor fireplaces or fine oriel windows. Impressive and luxuriously renovated early 16th-c castle with antiques, tapestries, huge fireplaces and mullioned windows in the baronial public rooms, three dining rooms (one in the base of a tower), fine cooking, extensive wine list (inc wine from their own vineyard), thoughtful friendly service, and vast grounds inc the oldest Tudor gardens in England; cl 4 days Jan; partial disabled access; dogs allowed at discretion of manager

UPPER SLAUGHTER SP1523 **Lords of the Manor** *Upper Slaughter, Cheltenham, Glos GL54 2JD (01451) 820243* **£149**, plus special breaks; 27 rms carefully furnished with antiques, Victorian sketches and paintings. Warmly friendly hotel with mid 17th-c heart (though it's been carefully extended many times), lovely views over eight acres of grounds from very comfortable library and drawing room, log fires, and fresh flowers; fine modern English cooking in attractive candlelit restaurant overlooking the original rectory gardens, good breakfasts, and kind service; children over 7 in restaurant (high tea available); disabled access

WINCHCOMBE SP0327 **Sudeley Hill Farm** *Sudeley Rd, Winchcombe, Cheltenham, Gloucestershire GL54 5JB (01242) 602344* **£50***; 3 comfortable no smoking rms. Friendly 15th-c farmhouse on working mixed farm of 800 acres, with log fires, a guest sitting room, and dining room overlooking the large garden; cl Christmas

WINCHCOMBE SP0228 **Wesley House** *High St, Winchcombe, Cheltenham, Gloucestershire GL54 5LJ (01242) 602366* **£85**, plus special breaks; 6 pleasantly furnished rms with individual antiques and showers. Pretty, half-timbered 15th-c town house with quiet friendly atmosphere, log fire in comfortable front lounge, very good attractively presented food inc lovely puddings in beamed restaurant, enjoyable breakfasts, and friendly informal service; old-fashioned garden furniture on small back terrace with pretty view

WINSTONE SO9609 **Winstone Glebe** *Winstone, Cirencester, Gloucestershire GL7 7JU (01285) 821451* **£60**; 3 rms. Small Georgian rectory in quiet countryside with five acres of gardens and paddocks, tennis, and lots of surrounding walks; friendly hosts, traditional furnishings, and delicious food (by arrangement); cl Christmas; dogs by arrangement

---

To see and do

Gloucestershire Family Attraction of the Year

CLEARWELL SO5708 **Clearwell Caves** 🖼 (off B4228) A good way to spend an hour or so rather than a whole day, these atmospheric caverns are great for children who like to be spooked and don't mind going under ground. It's quite low-key, and not overly developed, so if you're after great facilities and dramatic effects it's not for you, but if you haven't toured many caves before and want to discover a bit about Britain's mining history, you should find it enthralling. You find your own way around nine caverns, reckoned to be some of the oldest underground workings in Britain. Generations of miners – many of them (like the owners) freeminers, with an ancient birthright allowing them to dig for minerals here – worked the site for iron ore, but today the very small-scale mining produces pigments used in allergy-free paints. In places, artificial pools make it seem as if you're in a natural cave, and the years of work down here have resulted in some unique shapes and colourful patterns. It's quite a labyrinth, so stout shoes are recommended, and, like most caves, it can feel dark and damp at times (you are 30 metres – 100 ft – below ground, after all), so wrap up well. If you can get a group together, very good guided tours take you down a little deeper. In the run-up to Christmas, young children will get more out of the caves than geologists, as they're transformed into a festive walk-through grotto. Other events might include subterranean Shakespeare performances. There are also displays of mining equipment and engines. Meals, snacks, shop; usually open Mar–Oct, plus the run-up to Christmas and wknds Jan/Feb; (01594) 832535; £3.80 adults, children 5–16 £2.40. A family ticket (two adults, two children) is £11 (discount voucher not valid for bank hols and end of Nov–Dec).

ASHLEWORTH SO8125
A **tithe barn** of some note, a good dining pub, the Queens Arms; and a splendidly traditional pub, the Boat, right on the River Severn – in the same family for centuries.

AUST ST5689
Saint Augustine's Vineyard You can go on a self-guided tour of this pretty two-ace landscaped vineyard (the old-fashioned roses are best in Jun, and there are olive and fig trees). Shop, disabled access (though you'll need a strong pusher); open pm Weds and Sat May–Oct; (01454) 632236; £2.50 (inc tasting).

BELAS KNAP SP0125
There's a pleasant walk up to Belas Knap, a massive 4,000-year-old barrow – one of England's best-preserved prehistoric burial sites, complete with original dry-stone walling enclosing four internal chambers. Great views from the Craven Arms in Brockhampton (a good pub, with a nice garden in a lovely setting); this could be tied in with a walk past some very surprising ruins of a Roman villa tucked away in the woods.

BERKELEY ST6899
Berkeley Castle (off A38) Excellently preserved castle, very much a family home, but still keeping a flavour of its days as a Norman fortress. Impressive paintings, furnishings and silver, fine old keep and Great Hall, terraced gardens, park, extensive butterfly farm – and the dungeon where Edward II was murdered in 1327. Snacks, shop, limited disabled access; open Weds–Sat and pm Sun Apr–Sept plus bank hol Mons; (01453) 810332; £6.25, £3 ground only, and £2 butterfly farm. The Pickwick at Lower Wick is a popular dining pub.

Cattle Country Adventure Park 🎟 (off B4066 E) Various cattle inc American bison, as well as birds of prey, miniature golf, willow maze, splash pool, and an aerial slide; they`ve also a farm trail and indoor and outdoor adventure playgrounds. Meals, snacks, shop, disabled access. Open daily Jun–Aug, Sun only rest of year (cl 25 Dec–1 Jan); (01453) 810510; £5.25 (less out of season).

Jenner Museum 🎟 (High St) Largely unchanged Georgian home of Edward Jenner, who discovered the principle of vaccination here, and after developing the smallpox vaccine gave free vaccinations from the thatched hut in the attractive grounds. Shop, some disabled access; cl am, all day Mon exc bank hols, Oct exc Sun, and all Nov–Mar; (01453) 810631; £3. The Berkeley Arms (Market Pl) is a pleasant country town hotel.

BIBURY SP1106
One of the most popular villages in the area (William Morris thought it the most beautiful in England), with lovely golden streamside houses (owned by the NT). Nowadays, summer crowds can rather blunt its appeal. The **River Coln** lets you approach Bibury more quietly and prettily, along the path from the toll-house just S of Coln St Aldwyns. This route takes you in by the mill and bridge over the Coln itself. The beautifully placed Swan Hotel has a reasonably priced brasserie.

Arlington Mill Museum The 18th-c machinery of this well restored watermill is demonstrated on some days, with guided tours by arrangement; at the back, a developing herb garden overlooks the river. Meals, snacks, shop, disabled access to tearoom; cl 25 Dec; (01285) 740368; £2.

Bibury Trout Farm 🎟 Long-established working farm breeding rainbow trout in 40 ponds and tanks. You can feed the fish, or try to catch your own (summer only). Summer snacks, good shop, limited disabled access; cl 25–26 Dec, (limited opening hours in winter); (01285) 740215; £2.

River Coln villages By the same trout-stream as over-visited Bibury, a pleasant drive links other villages that are just as engaging, but bypassed by most visitors, particularly Coln St Aldwyns (the New Inn is excellent) and Quenington (the Keepers Arms has decent food). On the far side of Bibury the back road tracking along the river passes through a string of pleasant little villages such as Coln Rogers, Coln St Dennis and Yanworth, eventually reaching the pretty village of Withington (the Mill Inn is delightfully set right on the stream).

BIRDWOOD SO7418
Old Ley Court (Chapel Lane) Working farm producing double and

single gloucester cheese – you can normally watch them make it on Tues and Thurs, 9.30–11am and 12.30–3pm. Ask about their home-cured bacon and sausages; some disabled access (but no facilities); (01452) 750225; £12.

BISLEY SO9106

Selsley Herb Nursery (Hayhedge Lane, E of centre) This friendly garden has a wide range of herbs and garden plants; cl am Sun; (01452) 770073; free. The ancient Bear has enjoyable food.

BLOCKLEY SP1635

Mill Dene Garden 🏛 Lovely 2fi-acre garden surrounding a Cotswold stone watermill with an orange stream (turned that colour by the rusted waterwheel), also shell grotto, water features and lots of scented plants; 78 species of bird have been seen in the garden, inc kingfishers and dippers. Meals, snacks; open wkdys Apr–Oct; £3. The village is attractive, and the Great Western Arms has good value food and nice views.

BOURTON-ON-THE-HILL SP1732

Bourton House Unusual plants inc tender ones in attractive garden around fine old house (not open). Teas in 16th-c tithe barn, shop; open Weds–Fri end May–Oct; *£4; (01386) 700754.

Sezincote House and Garden (off A424 about 1m S) Exotic onion-domed forerunner of Brighton Pavilion, stunning from the outside, less interesting inside. Also classic early 19th-c water garden, and a more recent Indian-style garden to match the building. Garden open pm Thurs, Fri and bank hols (cl Dec), house Thurs and Fri pm May–July and Sept; £5, £3.50 garden only. Children are not allowed in the house.

BOURTON-ON-THE-WATER SP1620

One of the best-known Cotswold villages, but submerged in sprawly crowds in summer unless you get there very early in the morning – when it's enchanting. There are all sorts of visitor attractions. The Mousetrap (Lansdown) and Old Manse (Victoria St – tables out by river) have decent food. The best walk out of the village heads out W past the church and school and over the old railway line, then following the lanes

and tracks S of Upper Slaughter to rejoin the River Windrush and back to Bourton.

Birdland 🏛 (Rissington Rd) A bird fanciers' favourite, with all its rarities and exotics on the banks of the meandering River Windrush, inc a large colony of penguins and over 50 aviaries. Also a play area, tropical and desert houses, and picnic areas. Snacks, shop, disabled access; cl 25 Dec; (01451) 820480; £4.60.

Cotswold Motor Museum and Toy Collection (Sherbourne St) In an old watermill, the collection here includes cars and motorcycles from vintage years to the 1950s, along with advertising signs, automobilia, a toy collection (inc Brum the children's TV character), and a new display showing how motorists got along before petrol stations and breakdown recovery. Shop, disabled access; cl Nov–Feb; (01451) 821255; £2.50.

Dragonfly Maze (Rissington Rd) Imaginative and stimulating for children and grown-ups. There's an interesting maze and puzzle to solve – if you find the dragonfly, the children get a little prize at the end. Shop, disabled access; usually open daily (exc 25–26 Dec, and in bad weather); (01451) 822251; £2.

Folly Farm Waterfowl 🏛 (A436 3m W) Lakes and pools with around 100 species of waterfowl at this unpretentious place, as well as friendly ducks, geese and poultry. Good for children, and a nice spot for a picnic. Snacks, shop, disabled access; cl 25 Dec; (01451) 820940; £3.50.

Miniature World (High St) Readers love this incredible collection of miniature scenes and figures made by over a hundred of England's leading model-makers. Detailed dioramas, full of life and drama, from a fruit and veg stall to a wartime Italian street – look out for the ghosts in the Victorian chemist's shop. Disabled access; open daily Mar–Oct, wknds only in winter; (01451) 810121; £2.95.

Model Village (High St) It won't take you long to look around this replica of the village, modelled from Cotswold stone in the 1930s to a scale of one-ninth. Good home-made food (and lovely river view) in adjacent welcoming

Old New Inn, snacks, shop; cl 25 Dec; (01451) 820467; £2.75.

Perfumery Exhibition ▣ (Victoria St) Includes the origins of perfume, a cinema with smells, and perfume quiz and garden. Shop, disabled access; cl 25–26 Dec; (01451) 820698; £2.

CHELTENHAM SO9523

Beautiful spa town useful for exploring Cotswolds, shopping, or admiring the elegant Regency architecture of its tree-lined avenues. These days Cheltenham is best known for its races, and the racecourse at Prestbury Park (N on A435) has an exhibition on Gold Cup winners; (01242) 513014; cl wknds; free. Lots of antiques shops, esp around the Montpellier area. Tailors (Cambray Pl), the Montpellier Wine Bar (Montpellier St), Mitres (Sandford St) and Belgian Monk (Clarence St) have decent food, and the well run café in the beautiful Imperial Gardens is good for families.

Art Gallery & Museum (Clarence St) Excellent Arts and Crafts collection inspired by William Morris, fine paintings inc 17th-c Dutch works, rare porcelain and ceramics, and special exhibitions. Meals, snacks, shop, disabled access; cl bank hols, and am Sun; (01242) 237431; free.

Holst Birthplace Museum ▣ (Clarence Rd) A 10-min walk from the Pump Room, this interesting Regency house is where the composer was born in 1874; you can see the piano on which he composed *The Planets*. Worthwhile even if you're not mad about Holst, as the rooms are all carefully furnished in period style. Shop; cl Sun, Mon and all Jan; (01242) 524846; £2.50.

Pittville Pump Room (Pittville Park) A short walk from the centre, this is the town's finest building, 19th-c Greek Revival with a colonnaded façade and balconied hall. It's easy to imagine the place's Regency heyday, especially strolling around the super park and gardens, or during concerts in the July music festival. On some summer Suns they may have teas accompanied by live music, also occasional art and craft exhibitions. You can still sample the spa water – rather salty. Meals, snacks, shop, disabled access to ground floor only; cl Tues; (01242) 523852; free.

CHIPPING CAMPDEN SP1539

Extremely attractive town, with interesting old buildings inc an ancient covered open-sided market hall, a grand Perpendicular church typical of the area's rich 'wool churches', enjoyable shops, and fine old inns. Many of our contributors would put it among the country's most delightful small towns, though until they get the cars out of the centre not all would agree. The Eight Bells, Volunteer, Kings Arms, Noel Arms and Lygon Arms are all good for lunch. The **Cotswold Way**, a 100-mile path from here all the way to Bath, carefully picks out some of the choicest Cotswold scenery – a worthwhile aid for those planning a shorter stroll.

CIRENCESTER SP0202

A busy country town, particularly on its Mon and Fri market days, with a succession of fine Cotswold stone streets off the long market place (there are plans to pedestrianise this). It has many attractive buildings, and interesting antiques and other shops inc traditional country saddlers, etc. Though one of the most handsome of all the Cotswold towns, it isn't too touristy. The **church** of St John the Baptist (Market Pl) is wonderfully grand, with a striking late Gothic tower (and an unusual medieval wall painting of the martyrdom of St Thomas à Becket). **Brewery Arts** has independent craft businesses and shops in former brewery (cl Sun and some bank hols), along with theatre, gallery and café. Also worth a look are the 12th-c remains of **St John's Hospital**, the **Norman arch**, and the various well preserved wool merchants' houses. Cecily Hill, one of the town's most attractive streets, gives on to **Cirencester Park** (open daily, free) a vast 3,000-acre forested country estate abutting the town. Nearby is the town's heated **open-air swimming pool** (May–Sept, £2.40; (01285) 653947), with the backdrop of the castle-like 19th-c former barracks. Decent places for lunch include the Corinium Court (Gloucester St), Somewhere Else (Castle St) and Twelve Bells (Lewis Lane).

Corinium Museum (Park St) Cirencester was one of the most important cities in Roman Britain, and this spacious museum has one of the finest collections of antiquities from the period (all clearly displayed and labelled). The museum will be closed for major refurbishments (inc larger gallery space and new education facilities) until around September; phone for opening times; (01285) 655611.

CLEARWELL SO5708

Clearwell Caves *See separate family panel on p.*

CLEEVE COMMON SO9924

The steep grassy slopes of the W escarpment of the Cotswolds make for some of the area's best walking. This, the highest point of the Cotswolds, has breezy, unkempt grassland on its open expanses and can either be reached from the nearby village of Cleeve Hill on the A46 (where the Rising Sun has decent food and lovely views to the Malvern Hills), or integrated into a circular walk past Belas Knap long barrow and through the Sudeley Castle estate into Winchcombe.

COTSWOLDS

COTSWOLDS SP0912

It's the countryside above all which delights here – especially the rolling hills themselves, with their traditional dry-stone-walled fields, occasional beechwoods, meandering streams, and beautiful villages of warm golden-tinted stone picturesquely roofed in heavy stone slabs. Many villages have handsome medieval churches, and their cottages and houses don't hide away behind gardens and high walls, but tend to be right by the road. Often, there's a strip of daffodil-planted grass between pavement and road (the area is particularly attractive in spring), and sometimes a little stream. *The Romantic Road*, a guide to the prettiest villages in the area, is available from Cheltenham Tourism (01242) 522878, or from TICs in the area. For cyclists, the Cotswolds are great – quiet village-to-village lanes with ever-changing views. Campus Holidays not only hire bikes (£12 per day) but can arrange your route and accommodation too; (01242) 250642.

DEERHURST SO8729

Ancient remains here include **Odda's Chapel**, a restored 11th-c chapel

discovered as part of a farmhouse, and the **Priory Church of St Mary**, a mainly Saxon church with a lovely atmosphere and some intriguing original carvings and features. The riverside Coal House at Apperley does substantial food.

DEVIL'S CHIMNEY SO9418

On the Cotswold Way, a viewpoint rock pinnacle amid old quarries on Leckhampton Hill, perched above Cheltenham.

DYRHAM ST7475

Dyrham Park In an ancient park grazed by fallow deer, this fine William and Mary house has hardly changed since the late 17th c. The interiors have Dutch-style furnishings, Delft ware, dutch bird paintings and a remarkable trompe l'oeil by Hoogstraten. Victorian domestic rooms inc a bakehouse, larders, kitchen and dairy are also open. Meals, snacks, shop, disabled access to ground floor; house cl am, Weds and Thurs, and all Nov–Mar, park open all year exc 25 Dec; (0117) 937 2501; £7.90, garden and deer park only £3; deer park only £2; NT. The Bull at Hinton Dyrham is an attractive nearby place for lunch.

EASTLEACH SP2005

Delightful Cotswold village; a lovely ancient clapper bridge links the two Norman churches, very photogenic when the daffodils are out. The Victoria, looking down on it all, has enjoyable food.

FAIRFORD SP1501

Pleasant riverside meadows, and a wonderful 15th-c Perpendicular **church**, which has Britain's only intact set of medieval stained glass windows (inc a fascinating depiction of Hell), and comical misericords. The Bull Hotel has decent food.

FOREST OF DEAN SO6212

The Forest of Dean has a unique landscape: hilly woodland that shows many traces of the way it has provided a livelihood for the people living around it. Its woodland colours are at their best in late May and autumn. Still largely ancient oak woodland despite encroaching pine plantations, the forest rolls over many miles of hilly countryside, giving plenty of space – even in summer you can often have much of the woods to yourself. There are ponds, streams with stepping stones, cattle and perhaps fallow deer. There are ancient iron workings, the tracks of abandoned railways and tramways, and still one or two of the freeminers, who've been digging coal by hand from surface seams for hundreds of years. The forest scenery has most impact on those prepared to delve into its past a bit – a good start is the **Heritage Centre** at Upper Soudley; the forest is well equipped with car parks, picnic sites and forest trails. The **Sculpture Trail** takes a four-mile route passing nearly 20 specially commissioned sculptures hidden deep in the forest (from picnic site nr the comfortable Speech House Hotel). The **Kidnalls Forest Trail** is a good way of tracking down some early industrial sites. The **Foundry Wood Trail** passes Soudley fish ponds and gains some fine views. The **Wench Ford Forest Walk** leads past a series of quite interesting rock outcrops. Signed paths ensure easy route-finding up to the open summit of May Hill, where on a clear day you can see the Cotswolds, Malverns, Welsh Marches and Severn estuary. Around the edges of the forest the scenery changes to a patchwork of steep pastures – also very attractive. It's well worth getting a forest map, either from the Dean Heritage Centre or direct from the Forestry Commission in Coleford (01594) 833057; these outline walks (inc the sculpture trail), and mark the best spots for views or picnics. The information centres can also provide details of canoeing, caving, cycling or fishing in the forest. The B4432 to Symonds Yat gives some good views, the B4228 down past St Briavels is a pleasant country road, and the little lanes around the edges of the forest are rewarding drives – but need a large-scale map.

Conifer arboretum SO6212 This makes an interesting change from the forest's predominantly broad-leaved trees; nr Speech House.

Dean Heritage Centre SO6513 (Camp Mill, Upper Soudley) Useful introduction to the Forest of Dean, set around an old watermill in pretty wooded valley. Plenty going on, inc a beam engine, a good collection of clocks all made by a local family, craft displays, adventure playground, and occasional traditional charcoal burning. A £½ million refurbishment of the museum should be complete by Apr, with better disabled access and facilities, and new displays (inc some good hands-on ones). The centre is also taking part in a lottery-funded project to preserve the ancient dialect of the Forest of Dean in a dialect dictionary and database. Meals, snacks, shop, disabled access; usually cl only 24–26 Dec and 1 Jan; (01594) 822170; *£4. The White Hart over in Cinderford (B4226/A4151) has good food.

Hopewell Colliery SO5911 (B4226 E of Broadwell) 45–min underground tours of the 'free' mine guided by ex-miners; the privilege of free mining dates back to the time when King Edward asked the miners to undermine a castle wall and blow it up, and freeminers must be born in the forest. You'll need sturdy shoes and warm clothing. Snacks, shop; cl Nov–Easter (exc wk leading up to Christmas for special events); (01594) 810706; £3.50.

Nagshead Nature Reserve SO5909 (off B4234 S of Parkend) A good place to see deer and other wildlife. The Swan Cheesehouse just S in Pillowell is an interesting cheese-and-beer shop-cum-pub, just right for light lunches (no children; cl Mon/Tues lunchtimes and winter Weds).

Puzzle Wood SO5808 (just off B4228 S of Coleford) Wooded paths arranged as a stroll-along puzzle, landscaped in the 19th c nr remains of Roman iron mines. Snacks, shop; cl Mon (exc bank hols), and Nov–Easter (maybe open Feb half-term); (01594) 833187; £3.25. Across the road is the [SCTreasure Train; steam trains run along a fl-mile stretch of narrow-gauge track, with children solving clues that lead to treasure along the way. There are four stops, with footpaths through the woods nearby. Snacks, disabled access; usually open various days Easter–Oct, phone for exact times; (01594) 834991; £3.50 for unlimited train journeys, plus £1.80 for the children's treasure trail. The Dog & Muffler at Joyford is a pretty place for lunch; good walks nearby.

Roman road SO6508 You can track the paving, still in good nick after nearly 2,000 years, just off the Cinderford–Nibley rd (B4431 on older maps) at Blackpool Bridge.

Symonds Yat Rock SO5615 Perhaps the Forest of Dean's most spectacular feature, where the River Wye rolls around a monumental wooded cliff barrier, a favourite spot with peregrine falcons; tremendous views in all directions from the top, and at the bottom a ferry runs between two inns (you can hail it from the opposite bank); (01600) 890435; 60p.

FRAMPTON ON SEVERN SO7407 **Frampton Court** Elegant lived-in Georgian house, with original furniture, porcelain, tapestry and paintings, and fascinating gardens. Disabled access to gardens; personal tours all year by appointment, (01452) 740267; £4.50. The village green is said to be the longest in the country, with the 18th-c orangery (now self-catering holiday accommodation) on one side, and the Bell (a comfortable dining pub, open all day) on another. Just outside the village the Gloucester & Sharpness Canal passes grand colonnaded lock keepers' houses by pretty swing bridges.

GLOUCESTER SO8318 A busy modern city despite its long history – you have to search out the old buildings among today's big shops (for instance the splendid timber-framed house tucked down a passageway off 26 Westgate St). Tours leave from the Tourist Office at St Michael's Tower (itself a fine ancient building at the central Cross) at 2.30pm Jun–Sept; £2.50; (01452) 421188. The Black Swan (Southgate St, close to docks) and – all handy for the cathedral – Fountain, 15th-c New Inn and Tailors House (Westgate St) are useful for a quick lunch.

City Museum and Art Gallery (Brunswick Rd) Local history (inc a very old backgammon set) and an art gallery. Shop, disabled access; open Tues–Sat; (01452) 396131; £2. Guided tours of the ancient **City East Gate** leave here on Sats May–Sept (10.15am, 11.15, 3.15, 4.15pm); free.

Docks The revitalised waterfront deserves much of the credit for the city's tourism renaissance; guided walks, summer boat trips along the canal or up the river as far as Tewkesbury (contact National Waterways Museum, see p.250). Attractions here include the unusually interesting **Soldiers of Gloucester Museum** which has life-size reconstructions inc a World War I trench; (cl winter Mon); (01452) 522682; £4.25), and a big **antiques centre**, with 110 varied antiques shops in Dickensian arcades (limited disabled access; cl am Sun; free wkdys, 50p wknds and bank hols); (01452) 311190.

Folk Museum (Westgate St) Social history in a group of Tudor and Jacobean timber-framed houses; Victorian classroom, reconstructed ironmonger's, wheelwright's and carpenter's shops, toy gallery, interactive displays and cottage garden. Shop, limited disabled access; open Tues–Sat; (01452) 396467; £2, children and Gloucester residents free.

Gloucester Cathedral Towering majestically over the city's more recent buildings, this has lovely fan-vaulted cloisters, the second-largest medieval stained-glass window in the country, and a fine collection of church plate in the Treasury. In 1330 the Abbot astutely purchased the remains of murdered Edward II, and the resulting stream of pilgrims paid for elaborate rebuilding, an early example of Perpendicular style. The cloisters' temporary transformation into parts of Harry Potter's Hogwarts school for wizards may persuade normally philistine younger visitors to spend some time here. Meals, snacks, shop, some disabled access; (01452) 508210; £2.50 recommended donation. Not far from here are what's left of 9th-c **St Oswald's Priory**, the city's oldest structure, and other ecclesiastical remains inc **Greyfriars** and **Blackfriars**, the latter pretty much unchanged since the 13th c, with a rare scissor-braced roof.

House of the Tailor of Gloucester (College Court) Inspiration for Beatrix Potter's story; exhibition and shop. Disabled access to ground floor only; cl Sun, 25–26 Dec and some other bank hols (phone to check); (01452) 422856; £1.

National Waterways Museum
(Llanthony Warehouse, Gloucester
Docks) Focusing on the history of
Britain's network of inland waterways,
there's quite an emphasis on hands-on
exhibits, with lots of touch-screen
activities ranging from building your
own canal, to an infuriating share
certificate game where you're allocated
a company and then follow its fortunes.
Elsewhere, a highlight is the miniature
lock chamber, where you can try
steering a narrow boat through the
locks. One gallery looks at the way
boats have been decorated from
ancient times. Most displays are under
cover, though there are some historic
boats outside, special events during the
school holidays, and Easter–Oct you
can take 45-min boat trips along the
canal (£3 extra). A traditional forge is
usually in full operation. Meals, snacks,
shop, disabled access (not to floating
exhibits); cl 25 Dec; (01452) 318228;
£5. They do family tickets that include
the boat trip as well: £22.50 for two
adults and three children.
Over farm shop (1m W) A good one,
with local produce and **pick-your-
own** in summer (plus, depending on the
harvest, a PYO pumpkin festival in Oct
half-term). Also farm animal centre with
ostriches, rare sheep, and a water
buffalo; disabled access; cl 25–26 Dec;
(01452) 521014.
Robinswood Hill Country Park (2m
S) A little outcrop of the Cotswolds,
with 250 acres of walks and trails, a
wildlife information centre (fun talks
and events), and wonderful views of the
city from the summit. Snacks, shop,
disabled access; (01452) 303206; free.
Not far away is a dry ski slope.
GREAT WITCOMBE SO9316
Crickley Hill Country Park (just N
of village) Has a few ancient sites, as
well as nature trails, lovely clearly
marked woodland walks, and fine
views. Some disabled access; visitor
centre cl winter; (01452) 863170; free.
The Air Balloon is a handy family dining
pub.
Roman villa The outlines of a
substantial Roman villa can still be
traced here, around a courtyard, with
several mosaics and evidence of an
underfloor heating system. The Golden

Heart at Brimpsfield nearby is good for
food.
GUIDED HORSE-RIDING SO8412
Ongers Farm at Brookthorpe run this,
(01452) 813344, from £10 an hour.
HARESFIELD BEACON SO8108
(3m NW of Stroud), 450 acres of NT
woodland and grassland on the
Cotswold escarpment, with spectacular
views; free, and just a short ascent from
the road.
KINETON SP0926
Cotswold Farm Park 🎟 (off B4077)
This friendly place, the original pioneer
in rare breeds, is full of delightfully odd-
looking species of sheep, cattle, pigs,
goats, horses and poultry. It's very
much a working farm rather than a
more developed leisure attraction, but
is particularly well organised as far as
children are concerned, and excellent
value too. Rabbits and guinea-pigs to
cuddle or feed, tractor and trailer rides,
battery-powered tractors for 3- to 12-
year-olds, good safe rustic-themed play
areas, and even a designated children's
shop. Audio tours are available for
adults; nature trails and woodland
walks, and plenty of space for a picnic.
Lots under cover, so still good when
the weather isn't perfect (best to wear
wellies then); seasonal demonstrations
inc lambing, shearing, and milking.
Meals, snacks, shop, disabled access;
open mid-Mar to Sept (ring for opening
times in Oct); (01451) 850307; £4.75.
LECHLADE SU2199
Graceful village with one or two decent
antiques shops, good traditional toy
shop, pleasant walks, and access to the
quiet reed-fringed Thames for footpath
walks – especially along to Kelmscot in
Oxfordshire. The New Inn, with a
Thames-side garden, is good value.
LITTLE LONDON SO6918
Angora Goat and Mohair Centre
(Blakemore Farm) Unusual goat farm fun
for children up to 10, with indoor and
outdoor play areas (inc one for
toddlers), farm animals, picnic areas and
trails; snacks, shop selling clothes made
from goat and other fleeces, and disabled
access; cl Mon–Tues during term time
and a few days over Christmas, best to
check in winter; (01452) 831137; £2.50,
£4 children. The Red Hart at Blaisdon is
attractive for lunch.

LONGHOPE SO6818
Harts Barn Craft Centre (A4136 W) Smart craft workshops inc furniture, jewellery and ceramics, in an attractive Norman hunting lodge with landscaped grounds and lake; there's also a play area and history trail. Courtyard tearoom, picnic area, disabled access; cl Mon exc bank hols and 25 Dec–2 Jan; (01452) 830954; free.

LOWER SLAUGHTER SP1622
With its sister village Upper Slaughter, this is perhaps the prettiest village in Britain – a perfect harmony of stone, water, grass and trees. It's not as overwhelmed by summer visitors as its nearby rival Bourton-on-the-Water, though it certainly gets its fair share. The riverside stroll from Lower to Upper Slaughter is a leisurely mile or so; to make a longer walk for a circuit of a couple of hours, you can follow the signposted Warden's Way.

LYDNEY SO6304
Dean Forest Railway (New Mills, slightly N) Lots of locomotives, waggons and equipment at the Norchard Railway Centre station (free parking), and steam trips run through here from Lydney Junction. An extension much deeper into the Forest to Parkend (where the Woodman has decent food and good nearby walks) should be finished by Jun. Snacks, shop, disabled access; static displays open Apr–Dec; best to ring for train times (01594) 843423; because of the engineering works fares are reduced to £5.

Lydney Park 🏚 Extensive sheltered spring garden rich with flowering shrubs, rhododendrons, azaleas and magnolias; also lakes and deer park. On an adjoining hilltop are the remains of a Roman temple; a museum has finds from the site, inc the astonishingly intricate Lydney dog. Snacks, shop, limited disabled access; plant sales; open Sun, Weds and bank hol Mons late Mar to mid-Jun, but best to check; (01594) 842844; £3 (£2 Weds).

MICKLETON SP1743
Hidcote Manor Garden (off B4081) Series of small gardens separated by walls and hedges of different species, with rare shrubs, trees and roses, and some interesting topiary. Very popular even mid-week. Meals, snacks, good shop, some disabled access; usually cl Thurs–Fri, but best to phone for opening times; (01386) 438333; £5.80; NT. The Kings Arms is good value for lunch.

Kiftsgate Court Garden (off B4081) Renowned for its old-fashioned roses (best Jun and July), inc reputedly the largest rose in England, this has many other rare plants, shrubs and trees, good views across the Vale of Evesham, and that special feel that comes from generations of care by a gifted gardening family. Snacks, rare plant sales; open pm Weds, Thurs, Sun and bank hols Apr–Sept, plus Mon and Sat pm Jun and July; (01386) 438777; £4.50.

MINCHINHAMPTON & RODBOROUGH COMMON ST8898
900 acres of open land with fine views and a wide range of wildlife; NT, free. The Halfway Inn at Box on the N edge has good food, and the steep lanes all around are interesting drives.

MISERDEN SO9308
Misarden Park Views over the wooded Golden Valley from handsome gardens of 17th-c manor house (not open), with Lutyens topiary, mature shrubs and trees, and colourful walled garden. Nursery, some disabled access; open Tues–Thurs Apr–Sept; (01285) 821303; £3.50. The quiet village is charming, with good food in the Carpenters Arms.

MORETON-IN-MARSH SP2032
Attractively bustling old place, former linen weaving centre and coaching town, with popular Tues market. For food, besides the good Marsh Goose, the Inn on the Marsh and Redesdale Arms are pleasant.

Batsford Arboretum 🏚 (Batsford Park, just NW) Well grown private collection of over 1,500 rare and beautiful species of tree and flowers spread over 55 acres; hundreds of maples, 90 different magnolias, and national collection of Japanese flowering cherries. Best in May and autumn, but relaxing any time. Meals, snacks, garden centre, limited disabled access; open daily Feb–early Nov, and wknds in winter; (01386) 701441; £4.

The park is home to many deer.
Cotswold Falconry Centre 🏛
(Batsford Park, just NW) Flying
demonstrations of eagles, hawks, owls
and falcons throughout the day, with a
chance to handle some of the birds.
Snacks, shop; open mid-Feb to mid-
Nov; (01386) 701043; £4.
Wellington Aviation Museum 🏛
(Broadway Rd) Collection of RAF
memorabilia, and local history displays.
Shop, disabled access; cl 12.30–2pm, all
day Mon, 25 Dec, and Jan–Feb; (01608)
650323; *£2.
NEWENT SO7225
Small country town with some
timbered buildings which have a bit of a
Worcestershire or Herefordshire look.
National Birds of Prey Centre 🏛
(Great Boulsdon, just S) Exceptional
collection of 81 species of birds of prey,
with flying displays and breeding
aviaries, also picnic and play areas.
Meals, snacks, shop, disabled access; cl
Nov–Jan (exc for special events); (0870)
990 1992; £5.95. Further S past
Clifford's Mesne the Glasshouse Inn is a
charming place for lunch.
**Shambles Museum of Victorian
Life** Enthusiastic re-creation of a
Victorian town, with shops, workshops
and furnished houses. Summer snacks,
shop, limited disabled access; cl Mon
(exc bank hols), wknds in Nov–Dec,
and Jan to mid-Mar; (01531) 822144;
£3.60. The George opposite is handy
for lunch.
St Annes Vineyard (Oxenhall, off
B4221 W) They grow and sell 100
varieties of vine, and make wines;
usually open pm Weds–Fri, and all day
wknds and bank hols mid-Mar to mid-
Oct, wknds only in winter; (01989)
720313; free.
Three Choirs Vineyard 🏛 (off
B4215 towards Dymock) One of the six
largest vineyards in England; meals,
shop, disabled access; cl 25 Dec and 1
Jan; tastings free, tour and exhibitions
£2.50; (01531) 890223. The Vineyard
Restaurant also has accommodation.
NORTH CERNEY SP0207
Cerney House Gardens 🏛
Expansive old garden behind 13th-c
church, with old roses, trees, shrubs,
walled and herb gardens, a few animals
(they make tasty goats cheese), and a

water garden. The surrounding woods
are lovely at bluebell time. Teas, plant
sales, some disabled access; open Tues,
Weds and Fri Easter–July; (01285)
831300; £3. The village is attractive, and
the Bathurst Arms is good for lunch.
NORTH NIBLEY ST7496
Hunts Court Informal gardens with
over 400 varieties of old roses, plus
unusual shrubs and other plants, and a
developing mini arboretum; fine views.
Plant sales, disabled access; cl Sun–Mon,
all Aug, Good Fri and 25 Dec–1 Jan;
(01453) 547440; £2. The walk up to the
Tyndale Monument gives even better
views, and the Black Horse is handy for
lunch.
NORTHLEACH SP1114
Fine example of an unspoilt small wool
town, with handsome stone-built
streets and a particularly interesting
church, renowned for its collection of
brasses.
Cotswold Heritage Centre (A429,
just outside) Decent collection of rural
bygones; snacks, shop, mostly disabled
access; cl Sun am exc bank hol, and all
Nov–Mar; £2.50.
World of Mechanical Music (Oak
House, High St) Readers are really
taken with this quite captivating
collection of clocks, musical boxes and
automata, demonstrated by
enthusiastic and knowledgeable guides
in period settings in an old wool
merchant's house. It's quite spooky
watching the instruments work
themselves. Snacks, shop, good disabled
and blind access; cl 25–26 Dec; (01451)
860181; £5. Don't miss it if you`re
nearby.
NYMPSFIELD SO8000
Woodchester Mansion (B4066)
Construction of this splendid unfinished
Gothic mansion was inexplicably
abandoned virtually overnight in 1870.
It's being repaired but not finished, and
you can usually see traditional building
techniques such as stonemasonry.
Readers have high praise for the guided
tours. Five species of bat have made this
their home, and infra-red CCTV in their
colonies (the only such installation in
Britain) let you can watch them. Snacks,
shop, disabled access to ground floor
only; open first wknd of month
Easter–Oct, plus bank hol wknds, Sun

July–Sept, plus Sat July–Aug, though best to check, park open all year; (01453) 750455; £4. The NT-owned 500-acre park is open all year (a herd of pigs, introduced to eat up brambles and nettles, made the news when they unearthed archaeological remains here). The walk up Coaley Peak gives tremendous views over the Severn Valley. In the village the Rose & Crown is a good value dining pub.

ODDINGTON SP2325
Charming Cotswold village; the 11th-c **church** has an interesting mural, and there are pleasant walks, especially from the Fox at Lower Oddington. This and the Horse & Groom at Upper Oddington both have good food.

OZLEWORTH BOTTOM ST7992
This valley, not far from Wotton-under-Edge, has a nostalgically forgotten quality about it, giving an interesting walk between Lasborough Manor and Ozleworth Park, with its unusual Norman church endowed with a hexagonal tower.

PAINSWICK SO8609
Readers really enjoy this delightful little town, sometimes referred to as 'Queen of the Cotswolds'. There's been a settlement here since Celtic times, and **Painswick Beacon** has the remains of the earliest structures; it's a short ascent from the road, with great views towards the Malvern hills. Plenty of old buildings to look at, such as the 15th-c **Post Office**, and several antiques shops and craft workshops. The **church of St Mary** has fine interesting tombs and a fascinating churchyard where 99 immaculately clipped yews form gateways and canopies. The Falcon opposite is good for lunch. **Rococo Garden** ⊞ (The Stables, Painswick House) Careful restoration of sizeable 18th-c garden to match a 1748 painting showing its fanciful mix of precisely trimmed hedging, paths and shrubs with unrestrained trees; also a maze and slightly zany garden buildings. Pleasant vistas, children's walks – a cheery-feeling place. Meals, snacks, shop, plant sales, disabled access; cl Nov–Dec; (01452) 813204; £3.60.

PRINKNASH SO8713
Prinknash Abbey Visitors Centre (off A46) Unusual 20th-c Benedictine monastery and earlier house, now home to the world-famous pottery; you can watch production from the viewing gallery. Shop, some disabled access; cl 25–26 Dec, Good Fri; (01452) 812066; £2 for pottery tours. The abbey buildings aren't to everyone's taste but the grounds are attractive, with good views over the Severn Vale. The Black Horse in the very steep village of Cranham has enjoyable food.
Prinknash Bird Park ⊞ (Prinknash Abbey) Exotic pheasants, peacocks and other birds, as well as deer, goats and waterfowl; most animals feed from your hand (the fallow deer are particularly friendly). Shop; cl 25 Dec, Good Fri; (01452) 812727; £3.70.

SELSLEY SO8203
Strung-out Cotswold village in the steep country just S of Stroud; William Morris, Maddox-Brown, Burne-Jones and Rossetti all worked on the **church windows**. The Bell has reasonably priced home cooking and is well placed for walks.

SEVERN BORE SO6904
Tidal wave surging upstream at high tide, which can sometimes reach up to two metres (6 ft) in height around the spring and autumn equinox. The Environment Agency produce a calendar listing the best times and places to catch the phenomenon, with a rating of how spectacular it's likely to be; (01684) 850951. A good quiet spot to get down to the river is from Purton.

SEVERN ESTUARY ST6196
This makes for some lonely walks along the sea wall, with power station cooling towers and the vast Severn bridges emphasising the emptiness of the tidal flats. The White Hart in Littleton-upon-Severn, Anchor in Oldbury-on-Severn and right by the embankment the Windbound at Shepperdine are useful starting points. Further upstream Arlingham is locked within a big bend of the Severn, about a mile from the river, with the river path looking across to the Forest of Dean; the Ship at Upper Framilode nearby is a good family dining pub.

SHEEPSCOMBE SO8910
Delightful Cotswold village, clinging to picturesque hillsides; the cricket ground's so steep that fielders can

scarcely see the bowler. The friendly Butchers Arms has good food.

SHORNCOTE SU0296

Cotswold Water Park 2,000 acres of lakes, country park and nature reserves, with facilities for fishing, windsurfing, sailing and other watersports, cycle hire and walks, and bird-watching; lots of activities for children in the summer hols. Meals and snacks at some lakes, shop, disabled access; some activities cl winter; (01285) 861459; car parking charge for some lakes. The Bakers Arms in pretty Somerford Keynes has decent food.

SLIMBRIDGE SO7204

Wildfowl & Wetlands Trust (off A38) The original and best of the Trust's nine centres, this enormous place is one of the most visitor-friendly bird reserves in the country. Showing off a comprehensive collection of geese, swans and ducks, this is the only place in Europe where you can see six species of flamingo, as well as plenty of other rare and wild birds, and a tropical house that re-creates the sights, sounds and smells of a rain forest. In the Pond Zone children can take part in pond-dipping and see the things they fish out of the water magnified on TV screens. Lots of touch-screen computers, video displays and games, and extra events and activities in the school holidays; there`s also a small play area. Other highlights include a discovery centre, a tower with a telescope (great views of the River Severn), and a wildlife art gallery. It's unusual in being somewhere that you might get more out of visiting in winter, when up to 30,000 wild birds fly in. Meals, snacks, shop, disabled access; cl 25 Dec; (01453) 891900; £6.30, free to WWT members. The Tudor Arms by the swing bridge across the canal is useful for food, and the village Post Office has details of pleasant little walks.

SNOWSHILL SP0933

Snowshill 🏛 It looks like an ordinary Cotswold manor house, but inside is one of those extraordinary collections of ephemera great eccentrics somehow amass. Each room is carefully themed, toys say in one, musical instruments in another, bikes hanging from a third's ceiling – and even 26 suits of Japanese samurai armour, spookily arranged to look like a group of warriors meeting in the gloom. There's a charming organic cottage garden, and you can stay in one of three cottages. Meals, snacks, shop and second-hand books by the entrance, disabled access to garden only; open Weds–Sun and bank hols Easter-Oct; (01386) 852410; £6; NT. This is one of the Trust's busier properties, and there's a timed ticket system; try to come midweek or out of season. The nearby Snowshill Arms is also popular for lunch (busiest 12–1.15), and the drive along the River Windrush to Ford, Kineton and Naunton is delightful.

SOUTH CERNEY SU0698

Butts Farm (1m NE, on A419) Unpretentious farm with a good range of animals for children to feed, and daily pony or cart rides and goat-milking. Hay play area and pets' corner with bunnies and chinchillas to cuddle. Snacks, shop, disabled access; cl Mon and Tues outside school hols and Nov–Easter (exc Feb half term); (01285) 862205; £3.75 The Eliot Arms in the prettily preserved 16th-c village has decent food.

SOUTHROP SP2003

Charming Cotswold village that really comes into its own when the daffodils appear, with a delightful riverside church. The Swan has good food.

ST BRIAVELS SO5504

Attractive and unusual small village focused on the ruins of its 13th-c castle (the inhabited part is a youth hostel), with a steeply grassy former moat and views from the ramparts of the curtain wall. The George is good for lunch, and there are various circular walks around the parish, devised by Mr McGubbin in the craft shop; (01594) 530201.

STANTON SP0734

One of the prettiest Cotswold villages, very small – and rarely overrun with visitors. The best views over it are from the Mount pub, up the steep no through road beyond the village centre. This is the start of a trio of timeless villages on the **Cotswold Way**, a well marked track that conveniently picks out some of the best scenery for walkers. The next two are Stanway and Buckland; field paths and farm track let you detour to Snowshill, and from there it's a pleasant 3-mile walk to Broadway just over the Worcs border.

STANWAY SP0632

Stanway Water Garden One of the most beautiful 16th-c manor houses in the country, a cluster of gabled buildings popping up unexpectedly from the countryside, with charming and clearly lived-in rooms. The early 18th-c grounds have fine trees, a restored canal and cascade, and interesting buildings inc a folly pyramid on a steeply wooded hill. Open Tues pm and Thurs July–Aug; (01386) 584469; £3.50. The Old Bakehouse in the charming village does teas.

STOW-ON-THE-WOLD SP1925

Handsome market town with fine stone buildings around its square and in the narrow lanes around, and a good few antiques shops, book shops and so forth – it`s a good place to buy presents. It's something of an antidote to the more sweetly pretty Cotswold villages, on quite a high plateau and altogether more austere in style – not for nothing was it known as 'Stow-on-the-Wold, where the wind blows cold', and the ancient stocks on the village green add a touch of quaint severity. The Queens Head and Talbot are both good for lunch.

STROUD SO8405

Museum in the Park (follow signs to Stratford Park Leisure Centre) Surrounded by parkland, this local history museum has a surprising amount for children, with interactive displays, various trails, and a play area for younger children, as well as the world's first lawnmower; an art gallery has changing exhibitions. Shop, disabled access; cl Mon (exc bank hols), ring for opening times in Dec; (01453) 763394; free; charge for some exhibitions.

TETBURY ST8993

A splendid raised **market house**, some interesting little lanes, quite a few antiques shops and craft workshops, and good food in the Snooty Fox (Market Pl). The old Court House (Long St) houses a little police museum with memorabilia inc handcuffs, uniforms, batons and photographs; you can peer into one of the old cells and look round the courtroom upstairs (partly disabled access; cl wkdys, bank

hols, 2 wks over Christmas and Easter; free)

Chavenage 🏛 (2m NW) Friendly unspoilt 16th-c manor house with entertaining tours by the owner. It's a popular location for TV programmes, providing a backdrop for characters from *Poirot* to *Casualty*. Shop, disabled access to ground floor only; open pm Easter Sun and Mon, then pm Thurs, Sun and bank hols May–Sept; (01666) 502329; £5. Out this way the Gumstool (A46/A4135) has very good food.

TEWKESBURY SO8832

Severnside town, site of the last battle in the Wars of the Roses in 1471, still full of attractive half-timbered medieval buildings in a maze of little alleyways. Most impressive is the **abbey**, its massively confident Norman tower one of the finest in existence. Also splendid vaulting, some 14th-c stained glass, and regular concerts. In Church St, the attractive **John Moore Countryside Museum** commemorates the work of the local naturalist/writer. Shop, open Tues–Sat (exc 1–2pm) Apr–Oct, Sats in winter; £1; (01684) 297174. The historic Bell Hotel and (simpler) ancient Black Bear are good for lunch.

THAMES & SEVERN CANAL SO9303

The rich, steeply sheltered valleys around Stroud make up a complicated landscape, seen to best advantage for example between Chalford and Sapperton. British Waterways plan to restore the atmospherically overgrown derelict canal here – its towpath forming an attractive wooded walkway. The Crown at Frampton Mansell, Butchers Arms at Oakridge Lynch or Daneway at Sapperton are useful jumping-off points.

THORNBURY ST6094

Oldbury Power Station As we went to press, tours of the power station had been suspended for security reasons, but the visitor centre is still open with hands-on displays and a multi-media show; there's also a nature trail. Snacks, shop, disabled access; cl Nov–Feb; (01454) 419899; free. The Anchor at Oldbury-on-Severn has good food.

TOCKINGTON ST6187

Oldown 🏛 (B4461) Lively country park with good adventure play areas for older children – lots of rope bridges, tube slides and climbing nets. Play area for younger children too, who'll probably get the most out of the animals and demonstrations at the farm. Miniature steam railway running through woodland and garden (£1), several picnic areas, pleasant walks, and summer **pick-your-own**. Snacks, shop, disabled access; cl Mon (exc in school hols), and Nov to mid-Feb; (01454) 413605; £4. The quiet village itself is attractive, with good value food in the Swan.

TODDINGTON SP0432

Gloucestershire—Warwickshire Railway Steam and some diesel train trips through some six miles of quiet countryside (though by May they hope to have opened the line all the way to Cheltenham), departing from restored GWR stations either here or in Winchcombe. Snacks, shop, good disabled access (though parts of the car park are uneven); phone for timetable (01242) 621405; from £7. The Pheasant is useful for lunch.

TWIGWORTH SO8223

Nature in Art 🖼 (Wallsworth Hall, A38) In an imposing Georgian mansion, a growing collection of well displayed paintings, sculpture, and mosaics inspired by nature; more interesting than you'd expect – besides David Shepherd, artists represented include Picasso, Henry Moore and Graham Sutherland. Good meals and snacks, shop, disabled access; cl Mon (exc bank hols), 24–26 Dec; (01452) 731422; £3.35.

ULEY ST7898

Attractive former weaving village with some 18th-c or older stone houses.
Uley Tumulus (off B4066 N) Quite daunting 55-metre (180-ft) long burial mound known as Hetty Pegler's Tump, with stone central passage and three burial chambers; key from nearby house.

Owlpen Manor (B4066, just E) Charming Tudor manor house, with lovely formal gardens and woodland. Restaurant; cl Mon (exc bank hol), ams and Oct–Mar; (01453) 860261; £4.50. Good views from this road.

WESTBURY-ON-SEVERN SO7114

Westbury Court Formal Dutch garden with canals, yew topiary, etc, restored to its 1700s layout using pre-1700 cultivars inc old fruit varieties. Disabled access; open Mon–Tues Mar–Jun, daily July–Aug, and Weds–Sun Sept–Oct, phone for winter opening; (01452) 760461; *£3; NT. The Red Lion has good generous food, by the **church** with its unusual detached tower. The village is a good spot for catching the Severn Bore.

WESTONBIRT ST8588

Westonbirt Arboretum Over 18,000 numbered trees and shrubs fill the 17 miles of pathways at this magnificent national collection, begun in 1829. Outstanding in spring and autumn, but interesting any time, with lots of wildlife hidden away among the trees; you'll need more than one visit to see it all. New restaurant, picnic areas, shop, disabled access; open all year, though visitor centre cl Christmas–New Year; (01666) 880220; £5. The Hare & Hounds is handy for food.

WINCHCOMBE SP0228

Very peaceful and photogenic – once the capital of Mercia, now worth a stop for a look at the **church** with its grotesque and sometimes rather rude gargoyles, or just to soak up the tranquil atmosphere. The White Hart (High St) has good food, and there are interesting craft and other shops here.

Folk & Police Museum 🖼 In the Victorian Town Hall, this has a sometimes surprising collection of British and international police uniforms as well as local history displays; shop; cl Sun, and Nov–Mar; (01242) 609151; £1.

Hailes Abbey (Hailes, B4632) Graceful ruins of 13th-c Cistercian abbey, once a centre for pilgrims who flocked to see a phial containing what they believed to be Christ's blood. Audio tour, snacks, shop, disabled access; cl Nov–Mar; (01242) 602398; £2.80; NT (EH members free too). Hayles Fruit Farm down the road is good for snacks, and has **pick-your-own**; (01242) 602123.

Sudeley Castle & Gardens (off B4632) Once home to Katherine Parr, the luckiest of Henry VIII's wives, the remains of the original medieval castle were skilfully blended into a 19th-c reconstruction. Rich furnishings, porcelain and tapestries, and notable paintings by Turner, Van Dyck and Rubens; dotted round the castle, you can also now see mannequins of Henry VIII's six wives and other important Tudor figures wearing sumptuous replica costumes. The ten gardens are splendid, and include a knot garden constructed using plants shown on a 16th-c tapestry on view in the library; displays in a former workshop show the life of Emma Dent, the woman responsible for the most attractive of the Victorian improvements, and an exhibition tracks the history of the garden; also adventure playground and picnic area. Snacks, shop and specialist plant centre, disabled access to garden; house open Apr–end Oct (gardens from Mar); (01242) 602308; £6.50, £5 grounds and exhibition only, audio tours £2. There's a working pottery nearby (cl winter Suns); (01242) 602462.

WOTTON-UNDER-EDGE ST7693
More small town than village, and full of charm, with a fine Schreider organ in its church, a little **heritage centre** (open Tues–Fri (exc 1–2pm), and am Sats; free) and some handsome old buildings; the Swan Hotel (Market St) has sensibly priced bar food, and the B4058 is a good drive.

WYE VALLEY SO5309
The lower Wye Valley on the W side of the Forest of Dean cuts through a gorge giving some very picturesque views. As there are few crossing points, and the scenery away from the gorge is relatively unspectacular, walks along it are generally of the there-and-back sort. The valley is tracked by the Offa's Dyke Path on the Gloucestershire side; the Wye Valley Walk takes in the western bank. S of Monmouth, the A466 threads through the valley below the paths.
Devil's Pulpit ST5499 A great viewpoint on the Offa's Dyke Path, where trees frame a perfect vista of Tintern Abbey far below on the opposite bank of the Wye (see South Wales section for Tintern).
The Kymin SO5212 Can be climbed

from May Hill just inside the England/Wales river border opposite Monmouth; at the summit is the Naval Temple, a quaint rustic conceit put up in 1800 to commemorate admirals of the Napoleonic Wars. A couple of miles S at Redbrook a footbridge from the A466 crosses the Wye to a beautifully set walkers' pub called the Boat.
Wintour's Leap ST5496 A highlight of the Offa's Dyke Path: a sheer cliff over the Wye N of Chepstow with dizzy views downwards.

YANWORTH SP0713
An attractive village, especially at daffodil time.
Chedworth Roman Villa ⊞ The best example of a 2nd-c Roman house in Britain, excavated in 1864 and nicely set in secluded woodland. Well preserved rooms, bath houses, 4th-c mosaics, and a water shrine, with smaller remains in the deliberately Victorian-feeling museum. Snacks, shop, some disabled access; cl Mon (exc bank hols), and mid Nov–Feb; (01242) 890256; £3.80; NT. The Mill at Withington and Seven Tuns in Upper Chedworth are quite handy for lunch, and the walk from each is very picturesque and unspoilt, with Chedworth Woods providing further scope for short walks.
Other attractive villages, all with decent pubs, include Alderton SP0033, Almondsbury ST6084, Amberley SO8401, Bisley SO9005, Bledington SP2422, Broad Campden SP1637, Broadwell SP2027, Brockhampton SP0322, the Duntisbournes SO9709, Eastington SO7805, Ebrington SP1840, Ewen SU0097, Frampton Mansell SO9102, Great Barrington SP2013 (good cheap bedrooms at the Fox, lovely walks), Great Rissington SP1917, Guiting Power SP0924, Kingswood ST4991, Lower Swell SP1725, Marshfield ST7773, Meysey Hampton SU1199, Nether Westcote SP2120, Poulton SP1001, Shipton Moyne ST8989, Slad SO8707 (the setting for Laurie Lee's Cider With Rosie), Somerford Keynes SU0195, South Woodchester (particularly for the views) SO8302, Todenham SP2436, Wick ST7072 (pleasant walks) and Willersey SP1039. Though there's no

pub to recommend there, Saintbury SP1139 is a winner when the daffodils are out. The B4060 N of Chipping Sodbury ST7282 and the side roads through Hawkesbury ST7786 and Hillesley ST7689 take you through attractive Cotswoldy scenery. Many villages have most attractive churches, few of them as yet locked. Cirencester is a good base for planning circuits of these. One such group E of the town consists of Ampney Crucis SP0602, Ampney St Peter SP0801, Ampney St Mary SP0802, Down Ampney SP1097 (Vaughan Williams was the vicar's son), Hampnett SP1015 and Northleach SP1114. Another group, NW of Cirencester, has Elkstone SO9612, Duntisbourne Abbots SO9707, Duntisbourne Rouse SO9806, Daglingworth SO9905 (with its finely preserved Saxon carving of Christ on the cross), Stratton SP0103, Baunton SP0204 and North Cerney SP0208.

Where to eat

BOURTON-ON-THE-WATER SP1620 **Vernes** *Riverside (01451)* 822005 Pretty 17th-c cottage with enjoyable lunch, early evening meals, and Sunday roasts, all-day savouries, and cream teas; cl winter Mon; disabled access. £16|**£4.75**

BOX SO8600 **Halfway Inn** *(01453) 832631* Extended tall house on edge of the Common with attractive open-plan bar, simple but sturdy chairs and tables, woodburner, fresh flowers and décor, and enjoyable imaginative food under a new licensee; well kept real ales, well chosen wines, and friendly helpful service. £25|**£6.25**

BROAD CAMPDEN SP1537 **Bakers Arms** *(01386) 840515* Atmospheric ex-granary in tranquil village with good value bar food (inc children's menu), a fine range of real ales, cosy beamed bar, log fires, friendly cats, pleasant service, and nice garden; open all day in summer; cl 25 Dec, pm 26 Dec. £16.15|**£5.95**

CHELTENHAM SO9421 **Champignon Sauvage** *24–26 Suffolk Rd (01242) 573449* Classic French cooking in quietly and simply decorated restaurant with a cheerful blue and yellow colour scheme, helpful service and good thoughtful wine list; cl Sun, Mon, 10 dys Christmas, 3 wks summer; partial disabled access. £26 lunch, £45.50 dinner

CHELTENHAM SO9421 **Petit Blanc** *The Promenade (01242) 266800* Bustling brasserie, part of Raymond Blanc's mini chain, with stylish modern décor of warm orange and terracotta in the two rooms, enjoyable contemporary English/French rustic cooking, several different menus (inc a good children's one), super puddings, a carefully chosen wine list, and helpful young staff; cl 25 Dec; partial disabled access. £40/2-course meal £12.50

CHIPPING CAMPDEN SP1539 **Hicks Brasserie Bar** *Cotswold House Hotel, The Square (01386) 840330* Fine 17th-c hotel, stylish and attractive brasserie with good interesting meals and light snacks, plus morning coffee and afternoon tea – more formal restaurant, too; pretty bdrms. £20|**£6.50**

CIRENCESTER SP0202 **Swan Yard Café** *6 Swan Yard, W Market Pl (01285) 641300* Popular with shoppers, this small simple family-run café has friendly service, and very good value totally home-made food (inc vegetarian choices); cl Sun Oct–Easter; disabled access. £11.30|**£5.25**

COLN ST ALDWYNS SP1405 **New Inn** *(01285) 750651* Civilised ivy-covered inn with beautifully presented restaurant-standard food served in a relaxed pubby atmosphere; attractively decorated rooms, a central log fire, well kept real ales and good wines, a no smoking restaurant, and split-level garden; nice surrounding countryside and walks; comfortable bdrms; children over 10 in eating area of bar. £35.25|**£8.50**

FRAMPTON MANSELL SO9201 **White Horse** *(01285) 760960* Excellent modern English cooking in this smart, friendly dining place with attractive furnishings in the main part, a cosy bar area with large sofa and comfortable chairs for those who want to pop in just for a relaxing drink; a well chosen wine list and well kept real ales. £24|**£5.75**

GUITING POWER SP0924 **Hollow Bottom** *(01451) 850392* Snug old cottage with a friendly homely atmosphere, comfortable beamed bar full of horse-racing memorabilia, winter log fire, flagstoned public bar, well kept ales, enjoyable food in bar and separate restaurant, and pleasant helpful service; good nearby walks; disabled access. £21.95|**£5.75**

KINGSCOTE ST8196 **Hunters Hall** *(01453) 860393* Civilised old creeper-covered inn with some fine furniture and big log fires in high-beamed connecting rooms, good bar and restaurant food, enjoyable breakfasts, and quite a few wines by the glass; big garden with play area; bdrms; disabled access. £20|**£5**

LITTLE BARRINGTON SP1913 **Inn For All Seasons** *(01451) 844324* Handsome and civilised old inn with an attractive, mellow lounge bar, low beams, stripped stone and flagstones, a big log fire, old prints, country magazines to read, particularly good fresh fish (from Brixham) and other food, well kept real ales and wines, lots of malt whiskies, and a pleasant garden surrounded by lots of walks; cl 1 wk Jan; disabled access. £23|**£7.50**

LOWER ODDINGTON SP2326 **Fox** *(01451) 870555* Carefully restored elegant inn with wine-related antiques in one room and fresh flowers, flagstones, hops, an inglenook fireplace, and daily papers in other spotless, simply furnished rooms, imaginative enjoyable food, neat helpful staff, well kept beers, and an excellent wine list; outside heaters under new awning for dining out in chillier weather; cl 25, pm 26 Dec, 31 Dec, 1 Jan. £22|**£5.50**

NAILSWORTH ST8699 **Weighbridge** *(01453) 832520* Bustling pub with particularly friendly, chatty licensees, a relaxed bar with three cosily old-fashioned rooms, black beams festooned with country bric-a-brac, raftered no smoking hayloft with an engaging mix of rustic tables; very popular 2-in-1 pies (half the bowl has the filling of your choice and the other is full of home-made cauliflower cheese), and other enjoyable food, 16 wines (and champagne) by the glass, well kept real ales, and a sheltered landscaped garden with picnic-sets under umbrellas; good disabled access. £20|**£4.75**

NORTHLEACH SP1114 **Wheatsheaf** *West End (01451) 860244* Handsome and civilised 16th-c stone-built dining pub on a quiet street of similarly attractive buildings, three light and airy big-windowed rooms, flagstones, bare boards and carpet matting, modern horse-racing oil paintings, and log fires; appealing choice of imaginative food, good interesting wines, well kept real ales, very friendly service; pretty back garden with picnic-sets on tiers of grass among flowering shrubs; bdrms. £23.50|**£7.95**

PAXFORD SP1837 **Churchill** *(01386) 594000* Busy yet friendly dining pub with restaurant extension off simply furnished flagstoned bar – low ceilings, assorted old tables and chairs, and a snug warmed by a good log fire in its big fireplace; well kept real ales, eight good wines by the glass, and constantly changing interesting food; in the best pub tradition, they don't take bookings, but your name goes on a chalked waiting list if all the tables are full; seats outside; bdrms; disabled access. £25.50|**£8.25**

SAPPERTON SO9403 **Bell** *(01285) 760298* Carefully renovated 250-year-old pub with a nice mix of wooden furniture in three separate cosy rooms, country prints on stripped stone walls, log fires and woodburners, fresh flowers, newspapers and guidebooks, imaginative bar food using local produce when possible, well kept real ales, up to ten wines (and champagne) by the glass, tables out on small front lawn and partly covered back courtyard; good surrounding walks, tether for horses; children over 10. £24|**£9.50**

TETBURY ST8494 **Gumstool** *Calcot (01666) 890391* Bustling pubby bistro (actually part of rambling Calcot Manor) with stripped pine, flagstones and neatly modern furnishings, a relaxed but civilised atmosphere, delicious interesting food, well kept real ales, a thoughtful choice of wines by the glass, and good service; comfortable bdrms; disabled access. £24|**£8**

TETBURY ST9195 **Trouble House** *(01666) 502206* (A433 2m NW) Popular newish dining pub in attractively reworked ancient building, lots of hops in line of three relaxed rooms, chesterfield by a good fire in one big stone fireplace, a mix of stripped pine or oak furniture, imaginative food, a nice choice of wines by the glass, well kept real ales, friendly service; smaller helpings for children, and they sell quite a few of their own preserves; one room is no smoking; picnic-sets on the gravel behind or in a back paddock. £27.50|£6.50

WOODCHESTER SO8402 **Ram** *Station Rd (01453) 873329* Bustling cheerful pub with spectacular valley views from terrace, attractive beamed bar, very enjoyable bar food inc interesting daily specials, prompt friendly service, and lots of real ales; children must be well behaved; partial disabled access. £17.60|£4.95

Special thanks to Michael and Jenny Back, Derek and Sylvia Stephenson, Michael Porter, Joyce and Geoff Robson, B Wells

HAMPSHIRE

Portsmouth's maritime bustle, plenty of enjoyable historic places to visit, and attractive countryside, especially the New Forest

Outstanding for naval history, Portsmouth (and nearby Gosport) has masses of attractions to suit all ages. The Historic Dockyard, which contains the Royal Naval Museum as well as a fantastic collection of old and modern ships, is an excellent place to spend a very full day or series of days, and the Royal Navy Submarine Museum (interesting tours bring it all to life), and Explosion! (children love the hands-on displays) have much to appeal to families too. Besides a beachfront amusement park, Southsea, Portsmouth's resort part, contains an excellent aquarium, a lively museum and a castle.

Military heritage is something Hampshire is very strong on and, out of a huge range of museums, we pick out Fareham's Fort Nelson (great fun – a bit like a huge adventure playground) and the Museum of Army Flying at Middle Wallop as especially worth noting. For museums with a more specialised appeal head to Aldershot. Hampshire County Council publish *Defence of the Realm*, a brochure detailing discounted entry to over 40 military-linked attractions; available from individual sites and most TICs. Another useful brochure has details on the Millennium Pilgrim's Trail, which passes through areas of historic and natural interest between Portsmouth and Winchester; phone (01962) 870500 to order, £2.99.

Marwell Zoo at Colden Common gains the title of Hampshire's Family Attraction this year, with all sorts of exotic species of animals in carefully thought-out surroundings. If you prefer your animals tame, you'll enjoy Finkley Down Farm Park, and the country park at Bursledon is based around a working farm; at Weyhill there's a splendid birds of prey centre. The energetic re-creations at Milestones Living History Museum in Basingstoke make for a first-class day out, and Paultons Park at Ower is a treat for younger members of the family. The Watercress Line steam railway has special events for children (there's a huge steam collection at Liphook). Good for a day trip, busy Southampton has quite a bit to keep families occupied too.

Mainly rolling heathland, the New Forest is great for free-form wandering among ponies and deer, and ideal for children to romp around in (the New Forest website has lots of useful information: www.thenewforest.co.uk). The coast close to it has sheltered yachting harbours, the pleasant waterside town of Lymington with warm Georgian buildings (the rest of Hampshire's coastline is largely built up), and the interesting Bucklers Hard. Excellent places to visit in and around the New Forest include Beaulieu with its great range of subsidiary attractions, farm and wildlife centres at Ashurst, and an owl sanctuary at Ringwood; the grounds of waterside Exbury are quite gorgeous in late spring, and there are more recent gardens at Boldre.

Hampshire

BERKSHIRE

Silchester Stratfield Saye Eversley

A339 A340 A33 A30 4

Burghclere
Old Burghclere
Sherborne St John Rotherwick
Watership Down Basing
Basingstoke 5 M3
6 Mapledurwell **Aldershot**
Overton Crondall
Whitchurch Steventon Upton Grey **SURREY**
North Waltham 7 M3
8 Dummer
Bedlam Bottom
Micheldever Lasham Binsted
East Stratton Alton
SU Beech
A31 Chawton Headley
Selborne Waggoners' Wells
Avington Alresford
Easton A32 Liphook
Winchester
10 Cheriton
Cheesefoot Head Froxfield Green
11 Hinton Ampner A272 Froxfield
M3 A272 Petersfield
Twyford
12 Colden Common A3
Exton East Meon Buriton
Old Winchester Hill
Meonstoke Queen Elizabeth Country Park
Bishop's Waltham Droxford
M27 Chalton
7 Botley A32 Hambledon
8 Wickham Rowland's Castle
Bursledon M27
9 Southwick Havant A27
Hamble 10 A3(M)
11 Fareham Langstone Emsworth
Titchfield 12 **WEST**
Portchester **SUSSEX**
Calshot Castle **Portsmouth**
Gosport Hayling Island
Lepe Country Park Southsea

SOLENT

SZ

OF WIGHT

A34 A33 A325 A32

0 Miles 5
0 Kilometres 8

Elsewhere fine houses and gardens include elegant Broadlands in Romsey, the Tudor mansion at Sherborne St John, Mottisfont Abbey (try and visit when their old-fashioned roses are in bloom), and peaceful Houghton Lodge at Stockbridge. You can get a taste of life below-stairs as well as upstairs at Stansted Park, new to our *Guide* this year. In contrast, the tranquil ruins of Basing House are very evocative, and the memorial chapel at Burghclere is moving. On a more humble scale, Jane Austen fans can visit her house in Chawton, and readers of Dickens will enjoy his birthplace in Portsmouth.

Central Hampshire has a broad belt of gentle countryside stretching from Andover, Stockbridge and Romsey along the Test Valley in the W, through Winchester (a lovely city for a relaxed trip) and Alresford, to Alton and Petersfield in the E. This is a quietly charming mix of rolling blowy chalk downland, a patchwork of hedged fields and clumps of steep beechwood, the rich valleys of the clear chalk streams, and attractive small villages often of brick and flint, with plenty of peaceful walking opportunities.

Where to stay

BEAULIEU SU3902 **Montagu Arms** *Palace Lane, Beaulieu, Brockenhurst, Hampshire SO42 7ZL (01590) 612324* **£130**, plus special breaks; 24 individually decorated pretty rms. Attractive creeper-clad hotel with lovely terraced garden, comfortable sitting room, conservatory lounge, very good food in beamed restaurant and more informal brasserie, and attentive staff; their health club is in the nearby village of Brockenhurst

CHERITON SU5828 **Flower Pots** *Cheriton, Alresford, Hampshire SO24 0QQ (01962) 771318* **£60**; 5 rms. Unspoilt and quietly comfortable village local run by very friendly family, with two pleasant little bars, log fire, decent bar food, super own-brew beers, and old-fashioned seats on the pretty lawns; no credit cards; cl Christmas and New Year; children over 12; dogs welcome

DROXFORD SU6018 **White Horse** *South Hill, Droxford, Southampton, Hampshire SO32 3PB (01489) 877490* **£50**; 3 rms, 1 with own bthrm. Rambling 16th-c inn with a relaxed atmosphere, small cosy lounge bars, log fires, a sizeable public bar, good reasonably priced bar food, no smoking restaurant areas, well kept real ales, and seats in a flower-filled courtyard; no accommodation over Christmas

HEADLEY SU8437 **Land of Nod** *Grayshott Rd, Headley Down, Borden, Hampshire GU35 8SJ (01428) 713609* ; 2 large rms with comfortable armchairs (no guests' sitting room). Handsome and substantial 1939 no smoking house built by the present owner's father; breakfasts in dining room decorated with hand-painted chinoiserie panels and a Japanese needlework picture, and lovely gardens inc an interesting Japanese one in 100-acre private estate with some very fine rare trees; tennis and croquet; cl Christmas; children over 12

HURSTBOURNE TARRANT SU3954 **Esseborne Manor** *Hurstbourne Tarrant, Andover, Hampshire SP11 0ER (01264) 736444* **£120***, plus special breaks; 15 individually decorated rms. Small stylish Victorian manor with a calm relaxed atmosphere, comfortable lounge and snug little bar, good modern cooking, log fires in elegant dining room, and friendly staff; neat gardens with tennis, and croquet; special arrangement with local golf club and health and leisure centre; disabled access; dogs welcome in bedrooms

LYMINGTON SZ3094 **Efford Cottage** *Milford Rd, Everton, Lymington, Hampshire SO41 0JD (01590) 642315* **£55**, plus winter breaks; 3 comfortable rms. Spacious Georgian cottage near New Forest, and in an acre of garden, with marvellous breakfasts inc home baked bread and home-made jams and preserves, enjoyable evening meals using home-grown produce (only as part of winter special breaks), and good parking; no children; dogs by arrangement and away from dining room

LYMINGTON SZ3295 **Stanwell House** *High St, Lymington, Hampshire SO41 9AA (01590) 677123* **£110***, plus special breaks; 29 pretty rms. Handsome town house with comfortable attractively furnished lounge, cosy little bar, good imaginative food, and pretty walled back garden; 50-ft yacht for charter; dogs welcome

LYNDHURST SU3107 **Poussin at Parkhill** *Beaulieu Rd, Lyndhurst, Hampshire SO43 7FZ (023) 8028 2944* **£110**, plus special breaks; 19 carefully furnished, spacious and comfortable rms. 18th-c former hunting lodge reached by a long drive through wood-flanked New Forest pastures; a nice, informal, family-run atmosphere, big welcoming peaceful lounge/hall with sofas, easy chairs, a writing desk, a good log fire and daily papers, and an inner hall with a grand piano and longcase clock; the pink-carpeted lounge has another big log fire, lots of sofas and deep easy chairs and low tables, and big windows looking over a narrow flagstoned terrace and pond-side lawn; a little library with lots of books, smallish cosy bar, and pretty, formal restaurant with conservatory-style extension; quite excellent, beautifully presented food, a good wine list with an exceptionally good choice of wines by the glass, and enjoyable breakfasts with home-preserved fruits and home-made jams and marmalade; dogs in one bedroom only

MIDDLE WALLOP SU2837 **Fifehead Manor** *Middle Wallop, Stockbridge, Hampshire SO20 8EG (01264) 781565* **£130**w, plus special breaks; 17 spacious rms, some in the garden wing. Friendly and comfortable old brick manor house in several acres of lovely gardens; a restful atmosphere, pleasant small lounge and bar, fine food in candlelit restaurant, enjoyable breakfasts, and friendly staff; croquet; disabled access; dogs in garden rooms

MILFORD ON SEA SZ2891 **Westover Hall** *Park Lane, Milford-on-sea, Lymington, Hampshire SO41 0PT (01590) 643044* **£145***, 12 individually furnished rms, 6 with fine views. Victorian mansion in marvellous spot nr peaceful beach, views of Christchurch Bay, Isle of Wight and the Needles rocks; impressive original features inc dramatic stained glass, magnificent oak panelling, and ornate ceilings, very good food using the best local produce in grand (but not stuffy) candlelit restaurant overlooking garden and sea, lighter lunches in lounge bar also with water views, sunny terrace, and helpful friendly staff; dogs welcome in bedrooms

NEW MILTON SZ2294 **Chewton Glen** *Christchurch Rd, New Milton, Hampshire BH25 6QS (01425) 275341* **£380**inc dinner; 59 really beautiful, individually designed rms. Luxurious hotel (a member of Relais & Chateaux) in immaculate grounds with fine antiques, paintings and an abundance of fresh flowers in sumptuous day rooms, the relaxing atmosphere of a large private house, excellent modern French cooking, and impeccable service; gardens inc nine-hole par 3 golf course, swimming pool, tennis (two indoor courts too) and croquet; also a new health club with gym, sauna, steam room, treatment rooms, and indoor swimming pool; children over 6; disabled access

NEW MILTON SZ2497 **Yew Tree Farm** *Bashley Common Rd, New Milton, Hampshire BH25 5SH (01425) 611041* **£70***; 2 lovely spacious rms. Marvellously warm and comfortable, well run traditional thatched smallholding on forest edge; small cosy hall, friendly welcome, extensive breakfasts (taken in bedroom on tables laid with fine china and crisp napery), and enjoyable home-made dinners (if required) using top-quality produce; riding nearby; no smoking and no children

OWER SU3318 **Ranvilles Farm House** *Pauncefoot Hill, Romsey, Hampshire SO51 6AA (023) 80 814481* *; 3 attractively decorated rms with antique furniture. Dating from the 13th c when Richard de Ranville came from Normandy and settled with his family, this Grade II* listed house is in five quiet acres of gardens and paddock, with warmly friendly owners and enjoyable breakfasts; no evening meals; cl 25 and 31 Dec, 1 Jan; disabled access.; dogs welcome in bedrooms

PORTSMOUTH SZ6299 **Fortitude Cottage** *51 Broad St, Portsmouth,*

Hampshire PO1 2JD (023) 9282 3748 **£55**; 3 neat and attractive rms. Comfortable B&B in cottage named after an old ship, with pretty beamed breakfast room overlooking fishing boats; no evening meals but places nearby; cl Christmas; children over 10

PORTSMOUTH SZ6399 **Sally Port** *High St, Portsmouth, Hampshire PO1 2LU (023) 9282 1860* **£65**, plus special breaks; 10 rms, most with own bthrm. Beautifully kept 16th-c inn in quiet spot, with good food and very friendly efficient service; said to have been a favourite of Nelson; disabled access

ROCKBOURNE SU1118 **Shearings** *Rockbourne, Fordingbridge, Hampshire SP6 3NA (01725) 518256* **£60**; 3 rms plus garden annexe. Beside a winter stream, this warmly welcoming and pretty 16th-c thatched cottage has inglenook fireplaces, ancient beams (some nearly 1,000 years old), and comfortable sitting room; good pub just up the road; cl mid-Dec to end Jan; children over 12

ROTHERWICK SU7155 **Tylney Hall** *Rotherwick, Basingstoke, Hampshire RG27 9AZ (01256) 764881* **£159**, plus special breaks; 110 comfortable well equipped rms. Grand Victorian mansion in 66 acres of lovely gardens and parkland; gracious rooms with oak panelling, oil paintings, log fires in big ornate fireplaces, fresh flowers, and fine ceilings, interesting modern cooking in candlelit restaurant, and good attentive service; tennis, golf, indoor and outdoor swimming pools, gym and sauna; disabled access

SPARSHOLT SU4431 **Lainston House** *Sparsholt, Winchester, Hampshire SO21 2LT (01962) 863588* **£150**, plus wknd breaks; 50 spacious, individually decorated rms. Close to Winchester, this elegant William and Mary hotel stands in 63 acres of fine parkland, with tennis court, croquet, fishing, archery, and clay pigeon shooting; fresh flowers and paintings in relaxing, elegant lounge, panelled bar and restaurant, a fine wine list, and good British cooking; gym; disabled access; dogs in some ground floor rms

THRUXTON SU2945 **May Cottage** *Thruxton, Andover, Hampshire SP11 8LZ (01264) 771241* **£60***; 3 rms. Creeper-clad early Georgian house in quiet village, with friendly owners, residents' sitting room, good breakfasts, and afternoon tea with home-made cake in pretty garden; no smoking; cl Christmas; children over 6

WICKHAM SU5711 **Old House** *The Square, Wickham, Fareham, Hampshire PO17 5JG (01329) 833049* **£85**, plus special breaks; 9 rms. Lovely ivy-clad early Georgian house fronting the village square, with beamed and panelled rooms, antiques, fresh flowers and open fires, reliably good French cooking in the restaurant (once the timber-framed outhouse and stables), and pretty back garden; cl 10 days over Christmas

WINCHESTER SU4729 **Hotel du Vin & Bistro** *14 Southgate St, Winchester, Hampshire SO23 9EF (01962) 841414* **£99**; 23 rms of real quality, each sponsored by a well known wine company with relevant paintings, labels and old photographs. An engaging early 18th-c town house with enthusiastic owners and hard-working staff, deeply comfortable sitting room, two relaxed and pretty eating areas with imaginative bistro-style cooking and an exceptional wine list, and a lovely walled garden for summer dining; disabled access

WINCHESTER SU4828 **Wykeham Arms** *75 Kingsgate St, Winchester, Hampshire SO23 9PE (01962) 853834* **£79.50**; 14 well equipped attractive rms. Very well run, smart old town inn, close to cathedral, with interestingly furnished bustling bars, two small dining rooms serving delicious daily-changing food (very good breakfasts, too), fine wines (lots by the glass), and prompt friendly service; several no smoking areas; cl 25 Dec; no children

---

Please let us know what you think of places in the *Guide*. Use the report forms at the back of the book, write us a letter or log on to www.goodguides.com

To see and do

Hampshire Family Attraction of the Year

COLDEN COMMON SU5121 **Marwell Zoo** (off A333 towards Bishop's Waltham) Undoubtedly one of Britain's best zoos, and one which doesn't just pay lip-service to its conservation message; the zoo's work has helped the survival of quite a few endangered species, several of which no longer exist in the wild, and they have an excellent breeding record. As we went to press they were celebrating the arrival of new zebra foals and red panda cubs. It's a beautifully laid out place, the attractive parkland featuring very well put together enclosures which in places quite rightly put the needs of the residents well before those of the visitors: the lemurs for instance enjoy plenty of space and freedom while you watch from covered walkways. Other well conceived viewing areas include a glass wall at the end of the tiger enclosure, and underwater windows into the big penguin world. Though many of the species aren't familiar names, children will see all the types of animal they'd want to, from giraffes and flamingoes to rhinos and bats. There's so much that's rewarding it's hard to single out highlights, but particularly impressive are the Into Africa house, the outstanding collection of primates, and the new Desert Carnivores house, where the four sweet-looking sand cats very much steal the show (and have quickly learned how to use the cat flaps between their enclosures). Children enjoy the nicely sheltered Encounters Village, where in summer holidays they might be able to handle a snake or ride a camel, and there's a good adventure playground. You'll need a whole day to do the place justice, and there's a fair amount of walking; luckily road and rail trains can whisk you between the different enclosures. Regular special events include fun days with costumed characters like Bob the Builder or Barney the Dinosaur, and toddler weeks with special rates and activities. Meals, snacks, shop, good disabled access; cl 25 Dec; (01962) 777407; £10 adults, £7 children 3–14. A family ticket (two adults, two children) is £32.50. Prices may be slightly lower between Oct and Mar, and as we went to press they were offering OAP tickets for £5 every Tuesday.

ALDERSHOT SU8651
Airborne Forces Museum
(Browning Barracks) One of the best of Aldershot's many military museums (most of which have been of rather specialist appeal), looking at the parachute forces. Lots to take in, with very traditional displays. Snacks, shop, some disabled access; cl Christmas and 1 Jan; (01252) 349619; £3.
Military Museum 🖾 (Queens Ave) Following a generous lottery-funded refurbishment, new galleries include one looking at early flying experiments and one with vehicles, with updated displays on the development of the local military camps and their impact on civilian and military life; quite a few hands-on activities inc the chance to try out a Victorian soldier's bed. Snacks, shop, disabled access; cl 24 Dec–2 Jan;

(01252) 314598; £2.
ALRESFORD
A charming little town, from the Roman ponds teeming with wildfowl in Old Alresford to the so-called New Alresford founded around 1200; good antiquarian bookshop here. The Globe overlooking the ponds does decent lunches, and the Café Cressdon is good. The Itchen road W through Ovington and Easton is pretty, the B3046 N shows high Hampshire farmland well, and the old road E past Ropley and Monkwood to Steep gives a fine downland impression.
Watercress Line One of the nicest steam railways in the country, with 10-mile trips between Alresford and Alton through wonderful countryside and its watercress beds. They try to create a pre-war feel, with stations decked out

accordingly. Their Thomas the Tank Engine weeks around Easter and in Aug are extraordinarily popular (the Thomas here is built to the design and proportions in the books). Properly called the Mid-Hants Railway, it runs special main-line monthly trips to places as far away as Brighton and Bristol. A visitor centre houses a museum and shop, meals, snacks, disabled access; phone for timetable; (01962) 734866, no trains Nov–Jan (exc Dec Santa specials); £9.

ALTON SU7139

Allen Gallery (Church St) Superb collection of pottery, and a little herb garden. Snacks, shop, disabled access to ground floor only; cl Sun–Mon and 2 wks over Christmas; (01420) 82802; free. The town is the other terminus of the Watercress steam line (see Alresford). Coors Brewery (Turk St – formerly Bass) offers wkdy tours inc snacks and beer tasting 11.30–3 and 7.30–10pm (not Fri), cl Sat–Sun, and all Aug; (01420) 520158; £10. The church bears scars from one of the last battles of the Civil War. The French Horn (The Butts) is a friendly food pub.

AMPFIELD SP3824

Sir Harold Hillier Gardens and Arboretum (Jermyns Lane, off A31) Impressive collection of trees and shrubs, the biggest of its kind in Britain, covering 180 beautifully landscaped acres. Full of colour and surprises all year, but particularly delightful in spring; good seasonal walks and events. A new visitor centre should be opening in the spring with a shop, exhibition centre and a larger restaurant. Nursery, disabled access; cl 25-26 Dec; (01794) 368787; £4.25. The White Horse nearby is a comfortable lunch break.

ANDOVER SU2744

Fast Helicopters (Thruxton Airport) The most exciting – and expensive – way to take in the local sights, with a chance to test your piloting potential; (01264) 772508; half-hour flight £139.

Finkley Down Farm Park (just NE) Well laid out working farm with wide range of animals and poultry inc rare breeds; they encourage you to touch the tamer animals, and there are varied activities every half-hour. Also countryside museum, adventure

playground and picnic site. Readers rate this very highly, and it has lots for children (inc space for them to run around). Meals, snacks, shop, disabled access; cl Nov to mid-Mar; (01264) 352195; £4.50. There are well stocked trout fishing lakes around Andover, inc Rooksbury Mill. Poplar Farm (A343 at Abbotts Ann) is a useful food stop, with an indoor play area.

Museum of the Iron Age Nr the church at the top of the impressive High St of this very extended country town, the museum looks particularly at finds from nearby Danebury Ring, giving a vivid impression of life for the pre-Roman Celts. Snacks, shop; cl Sun, Mon, and Christmas; (01264) 366283; free. The same building, has a more general local history museum (open same hours, free).

ASHMANSWORTH SU3758

Hampshire's high country There are fine views from many of the lanes around Ashmansworth and Linkenholt – best explored by car, though there are good walks too. The Plough does simple home cooking.

ASHURST SU3510

Longdown Dairy Farm (Deerleap Lane) This friendly place has plenty of animals to feed, and lots of hands-on activities; their herd of Friesian cows is milked from 2.30pm every day. There's an indoor and outdoor play area. Snacks, shop, disabled access; cl 22 Dec–Jan; (023) 8029 3326; £4.50. The Happy Cheese (A35) is a useful all-day dining pub.

New Forest Otter, Owl and Wildlife Park ⊞ (Longdown, off A35) Large collection of otters, owls and other indigenous or previously indigenous wildlife such as pine martens, polecats, wild boar and even lynx; woodland nature trails. Meals, snacks, shop, disabled access; cl wkdys in Jan; (023) 8029 2408; £6.25. The Pilgrim is an attractive thatched dining pub.

AVINGTON SU5332

Avington Park ⊞ Georgian mansion with Tudor origins, set in lovely parkland; the church too is worth a visit. Teas in the orangery; open pm Sun and bank hols May–Sept; (01962) 779260; £3.75. The Bush at Ovington is a good nicely placed pub.

BASING SU6652

Basing House Ruins Peaceful ruins of what was once the country's largest house, destroyed during a two-year siege during the Civil War. Also remnants of a Norman castle, a 16th-c barn, dovecotes, an exhibition explaining the eventful history of the site and a re-created 17th-c garden. Nice walks from here along the River Loddon. Shop, some disabled access; open pm only, Weds–Sun and bank hols Apr–Sept; (01256) 467294; £1.50. The Gamekeepers at pretty nearby Mapledurwell is handy for lunch.

BASINGSTOKE SU6252

Milestones Living History Museum (Leisure Park, off B3400, Churchill Way W) A network of streets and authentically assembled buildings has been constructed to re-create the sights and sounds of local life since Victorian times, with factories, a railway station, brewery (an attached pub will serve ales from Hampshire brewer Gales), fire station, and shops. Staff in period clothes will explain things. The whole thing is indoors, in a splendid very modern-looking glass building, and there's an interactive post office for under-5s, a big toy area where activity trucks compare today's toys and games with those from the past, and a hands-on history section for 7- to 11-year-olds, with a fun old-fashioned photographer's studio (you can have your picture taken on some wknds). There is some emphasis on local industries, with vehicles and collections inc steam engines, and early clothing from Burberrys, who first opened in Basingstoke in 1856. Good value meals and snacks, shop, disabled access; cl Mon (exc bank hols), 24–26 and 31 Dec, and 1 Jan; (01256) 477766; £6.50. The surrounding leisure park has ice-skating, cinemas and ten-pin bowling.

Viables Craft Centre (Harrow Way, off A30 and via Grove Rd off A339) Sixteen craft workshops on an old Victorian farm; ceramics studio, art and craft gallery, miniature railway, model car racing circuit, and various courses all year. Indian restaurant, disabled access; cl Sun and Mon; (01256) 473634; free.

BEAULIEU SU3802

Beaulieu Abbey A great day out, its centrepiece is the National Motor Museum, a collection that from humble beginnings has become one of the most comprehensive in the world; they've recently opened a new motorsport gallery. Other features have a motoring theme too: a hands-on gallery explains how cars work, and Wheels is probably the highlight for children – you sit in a pod-like vehicle and trundle through 100 years of motoring. For an extra charge a simulator ride gives you a more robust driving experience. A monorail whizzes round the grounds, and in summer you can ride on a replica 1912 London bus. Also go-kart style mini-bikes, and radio-controlled cars. Palace House is a fine old mansion based around the gatehouse of the huge Cistercian Abbey that stood here until the Reformation (still with what are thought to be the original monastic fan-vaulted ceilings). The surrounding lakeside parkland and gardens are rewarding to explore, with ruins of other abbey buildings, and an exhibition on the monks who lived here. Meals, snacks, shops, disabled access; cl 25 Dec; (01590) 612345; £11.95. In the village facing the Palace House gates, Montys is popular for lunch, and a marked trail leads from here down to Bucklers Hard.

BEAULIEU ROAD STATION SU3506

New Forest walks A good starting point, for its surrounding remote-feeling heaths.

BEDLAM BOTTOM SU6246

Pleasant partly wooded valley walks, particularly pretty in spring; just W of Ellisfield SU6345 (where the Fox has good food), with more downland walks above.

BEECH SU6838

Alton Abbey (signed off A339) The home of a community of Benedictine monks, in peaceful woodland so a relaxing place for a stroll. The grounds have mature specimen trees and shrubs, especially rhododendrons and azaleas. The traditional Sun at Bentworth does good food.

BINSTED SU7740

Binsted church Where Field Marshal

Montgomery is buried; after the war he lived a mile away at Islington Mill – a pretty spot. The Cedars has decent food.

BISHOP'S WALTHAM SU5517
Bishop's Waltham Palace 🏛️
Impressive ruins of Bishop of Winchester's majestic 12th-c palace, with the remains of state apartments round a cloister court, and William of Wykeham's great hall and tower. Snacks, shop, disabled access to ground floor and grounds; cl Nov–Easter; (01489) 892460; *£2.30; EH. The Barleycorn (Basingwell St) has good value home cooking, and the downs N of here between Owslebury, Beauworth and Warnford give scenic drives.

BOKERLEY DITCH SU0419
This acted as a bulwark from raiders into Dorset in the 4th c; still impressive to walk along, it marks the county boundary and can be reached by walking up from Martin. Towards Pentridge Hill is a nature reserve.

BOLDRE SZ3298
Spinners 🏛️ (School Lane) Wonderful gardens created since the 1960s. The nursery is famed for its rare trees (especially maples and magnolias), shrubs and woodland plants. Plant sales; gardens open Tues–Sat mid-Apr to mid-Sept, or by appointment, nursery open all year exc Sun and Mon; (01590) 673347; £2. The Red Lion (no children) is good for lunch.

BREAMORE SU1519
Breamore House Late Elizabethan manor house, with fine furnishings, tapestries and paintings (mainly 17th- and 18th-c Dutch School), and better than average countryside museum with displays of Roman artefacts found within the estate, and a rare 16th-c bavarian turret clock, currently being restored. Children aren't left out – there's a maze and adventure playground. Snacks, shop, disabled access; cl am, all Mon and Fri (exc Aug and bank hols), all Sept–Easter (may also be open Tues and Sun in Apr); (01725) 512468; £5. The village has many thatched houses, and is within a pleasant walk of Breamore House – and the mysterious Mizmaze, cut in the turf. The Cartwheel at Whitsbury has enjoyable food.

BROCKENHURST SU2902
New Forest trails The village is well placed for walks, or if you prefer you can hire bicycles at Country Lanes Cycle Hire (the Station); (01590) 622627; from £12 a day.

BUCKLERS HARD SZ4099
Bucklers Hard Maritime Museum
Very pretty little waterside village, with 18th-c cottage rows flanking a wide, grassed street leading to the Beaulieu River. It was once an important centre for shipbuilding, and the Maritime Museum tells the story of the industry, right up to the voyages of Sir Francis Chichester. You have to pay to come into the village, though admission includes entry to the museum and the various other exhibitions and reconstructions dotted around, inc the carefully restored 18th-c homes of a shipwright and labourer, and a typical inn scene complete with costumed figures, smells and conversation. Meals, snacks, shop; cl 25 Dec; (01590) 616203; £4. There are summer boat trips, and the Master Builders House is useful for lunch. A pleasant 2½-mile riverside walk takes you to Beaulieu, run by the same people.

BURGHCLERE SU4660
Sandham Memorial Chapel 🏛️ (Harts Lane) Stanley Spencer's moving masterpiece, dedicated to the memory of H W Sandham, killed in World War I. The final resurrection scene is especially dramatic, best on a bright day as there is no artificial lighting. Open Weds–Sun and bank hols Apr–Oct, wknds only Nov and Mar, best to check in winter; (01635) 278394; £2.80; NT. The Carpenters Arms opposite is pleasant for lunch, with superb views.

BURITON SU7320
Quiet village below the South Downs N-facing scarp slope nr Petersfield; enjoyable walks in all directions, and handy for the Queen Elizabeth Country Park and Butser Hill. With plenty of character and a relaxed atmosphere, the Five Bells is a good food stop.

BURLEY STREET SU1904
New Forest walks A good area, with a mix of wooded parts and more open country; the White Buck, and Burley Inn in busier nearby Burley, are both comfortable food pubs.

BURSLEDON SU4911
Manor Farm Country Park (Pylands Lane) Woodland and riverside walks based around traditional working farm, with lots of animals, crafts and activities inc a forge and a wheelwright. Lots of walks around the park (maps show the various paths; 80p). Meals, snacks, shop, mostly disabled access; park open all year, farm cl Nov–Apr exc Sun; (01489) 787055; £4.20, free entry to park, parking £1.40 (refundable against ticket to farm). There are **boat trips** in summer on Sat, Tues, and Thurs from here along the Hamble; £3. Bursledon also has a **windmill**; open Sun, plus Sats May–Sept; £1.20. The Jolly Sailor is a beautifully placed food pub.

CALSHOT CASTLE SU4802
Down past the oil refineries and power stations, this Tudor fort stands on the end of the spit of land out over the tidal mudflats at the end of Southampton Water; splendid views of the shipping and the Isle of Wight. The Jolly Sailor at Ashlett Creek nr Fawley is a pleasant waterside food pub.

CHALTON SU7117
Butser Ancient Farm 🆔 (Bascombe Copse) Using archaeological evidence, the farm aims to give you a feel of what life was really like in prehistoric and Roman times, with period crops, animals and crafts. There are hands-on activities for children, and they are currently working on a reconstruction of a Roman villa. Shop, disabled access; open last wknd in month Mar–Sept; (023) 9259 8838; £5. The ancient Red Lion is good for lunch. As there is hardly enough at the farm itself to justify a journey, you could tie this in with a visit to Butser Hill, a steep chalk hill that was once a large Iron Age fort (by the A3 towards Petersfield); it's a good place for kite flying and picnics, and you can walk from here to Queen Elizabeth Country Park.

CHAWTON SU7037
Jane Austen's House Enjoyable unpretentious 17th-c house where the author lived and worked 1809–17, still with some of her letters and possessions. Rooms are furnished in period style, and the pleasant garden is good for picnics. Good bookshop, disabled access to ground floor and garden; cl wkdys Dec–Feb, 25–26 Dec; (01420) 83262; *£4. The Greyfriar opposite has reasonably priced food, and there are good walks here. Just up the road, Chawton House, the former home of Jane Austen's brother Edward, is now the Centre for the Study of Early English Women's Writing.

CHEESEFOOT HEAD SU5327
(locally pronounced Chesford) Good for walks; a natural amphitheatre where Eisenhower and Montgomery addressed the troops before the Normandy invasion.

CHILBOLTON SU3940
An attractive village where the common is being carefully preserved; River Test and other walks. The Abbots Mitre (open all day Sun) is a decent pub.

COLDEN COMMON SU5121
Marwell Zoo See Separate family panel on p.267.
On the downs above, the Ship at Owslebury is good for a family lunch – quieter than nearby Fishers Pond.

DAMERHAM SU1016
Damerham churchyard Well worth a February visit, to see the carpet of snowdrops. The prettily set Compasses has good food, and there are downland walks nearby.

DANEBURY RING SU3237
Iron Age hill fort rich in (excavated) remains. The Peat Spade at Longstock to the E has worthwhile food.

EAST MEON SU6822
This appealing village has a splendid Norman church; the George is a good pub.
Snowdrop woods Many of the woodlands in this part of Hampshire fill with snowdrops in February.

EASTON SU5031
This attractive village is well placed for pleasant Itchen Valley walks; the Chestnut Horse is very good for lunch.

EXBURY SU4200
Exbury Gardens 🆔 Wonderful 200-acre landscaped woodland gardens on E bank of the River Beaulieu, with splendid rock garden, heather garden and river walk, and above all the Rothschild collection of rhododendrons, azaleas, magnolias and camellias – one of the world's finest, at its best Apr–May. A 12½ inch gauge steam railway runs through a new

summer garden (from £2). Meals, snacks, shop, disabled access; cl wkdys Nov–Dec, and all Jan–Feb; (023) 8089 1203; price varies with the season, from £3.50 in summer to £5 in spring. The Jolly Sailor at Ashlett Creek nr Fawley is quite handy.

FACCOMBE SU3957

Bright with daffodils in spring, this neatly attractive village in idyllic countryside has great views from Pilot Hill; the Jack Russell has enjoyable food.

FAREHAM SU6007

Fort Nelson (Downend Rd) You don't have to be interested in weaponry to enjoy a trip to this restored 19th-c fort, built in response to fears of an attack from France, and now part of the Royal Armouries Museum. It has been known as the noisiest museum in the world, thanks mainly to the roar of the two huge cannons fired twice a day, usually at 12 and 3pm, and the lingering smell of gunpowder adds to the atmosphere. Children aren't discouraged from clambering over the building and even some of the exhibits (which go back well beyond guns), and they've got the catapult used in the film *Gladiator*). With plenty of underground tunnels to investigate, it's not unlike an enormous adventure playground. Occasional battle re-enactment days (ring for dates), and regular guided tours. Good views of Portsmouth Harbour from the ramparts. Meals, snacks, shop, disabled access; cl 25–26 Dec; (01329) 233734; free. The Osborne View (Hill Head) has superb views, and is handy for the beach and walks in Titchfield Haven nature reserve.

FARLEY MOUNT SU4229

An attractive area of downland and woodland, with good views – good for walks.

FROXFIELD GREEN SU7124

Bluebells In May much of the woodland around Froxfield Green is carpeted with bluebells, as are woods elsewhere in the area – for example at East Tisted and Ropley.

GOSPORT SU6001

Several millennium grant-funded attractions have come to fruition here, inc a gigantic sundial by the harbour, and the Millennium Promenade (see also Portsmouth) which takes in some of the town's naval heritage.

Explosion! (Priddy's Hard, Priory Rd) Small boys of all ages will be particularly excited by this splendid museum of naval firepower, but it has a much wider appeal than that; the often lively displays offer a look at not just how weaponry has been made and used over the years, but also the effect it has on those who produce it – and the people on the receiving end. Housed in 18th-c naval stores, there's plenty to see from old muskets to the latest Exocet missiles. There are rooms devoted to small arms, mines, big guns, submarines and torpedoes; most have some kind of interactive feature or touch screen displays (from quizzes to explanations of how a rifle works), and children are able to handle lots of the hardware. A highlight is the well laid out and awesome Grand Magazine, where a number of films put the building and its history nicely in context. They've taken pains to make it relevant to girls as well, with displays on the lives of female munitions workers. There may be extra activities in school holidays. The best way to get there in fine weather is the three-minute ferry from Portsmouth, and stroll along the Millennium Promenade (if you show your Gosport ferry ticket you get a 10% discount). Waterside meals and snacks, shop, disabled access ; open Thurs, Sat, Sun and daily April–Sept and school hols; (023) 9250 5600; £5, £7.20 joint ticket with the Royal Naval Submarine Museum (free shuttlebus between the attractions).

Fort Brockhurst 🏛 A good overview exhibition of how the various forts protected Portsmouth. Shop; open wknds Apr–Oct; (023) 9258 1059; £2.20. The Dolphin (Fort Rd) has popular food, good views and a huge play area.

Gosport Museum (Walpole Rd) Imaginative geology and local history displays; snacks, shop, disabled access; cl Sun–Mon, and a few days over Christmas and New Year (best to phone then); (023) 9258 8035; free.

Royal Navy Submarine Museum (Haslar Jetty Rd) As well as *Holland 1*, a 100-year-old fully restored submarine (the Royal Navy's first, with an exhibiton on how she was recovered), other highlights include a tour (often by an ex-crewman) of beached World War II submarine HMS *Alliance*, still in full working order, and fascinating inside to boys of any age, with lots to fiddle with. More conventional features include an audio-visual show giving the flavour of diving into the depths, and you can look through two periscopes – one from the submarine that sunk the Belgrano. Snacks, shop, some disabled access; cl 24–25 Dec, and 1 Jan; (023) 9252 9217; £4. (£11 for a family ticket – two adults and four children). You can get a Waterbus across to Portsmouth (Apr–Oct), and the sea at Stokes Bay is probably Hampshire's cleanest for swimming in. The Clarence (A32) is a good pub brewing its own beer.

HAMBLE SU4806

This pleasant village in *Howards Way* country has interesting views of the yachts, and you can walk a long way up river or towards The Solent. There's a friendly little ferry to Warsash taking about 10 people at a time, with a wildfowl nature reserve just N. The Olde Whyte Harte is good for a pub lunch. Nearby Netley has a coastal **country park** and the extensive ruins of a 13th-c abbey.

HAVANT SU7208

Staunton Country Park 1,000 acres of landscaped parkland, created in the 1830s for botanist and explorer Sir George Staunton, containing the only remaining ornamental farm in England (you can buy animal feed, and there are children's trails and a play area). A walled garden has an impressive restored glasshouse; also a new maze and puzzle garden. Meals, snacks, shop, disabled access; cl 25–26 Dec; (023) 9245 3405; £4.10.

HAYLING ISLAND SU7201

Readers enjoy this holiday resort popular for water-sports. The Inn on the Beach (it is indeed right on the shingle) is good value.

HIGHCLERE SU4360

Highclere Castle (best approached from A34 rather than Highclere itself) Magnificent pastiche of a medieval castle, impressively grand inside and out. Elaborate saloon and main staircase, a desk that belonged to Napoleon, and a Van Dyck of Charles I. Exhibitions of Egyptian relics (the 5th Earl of Carnarvon discovered Tutankhamun's tomb with Howard Carter), and horse racing. The lovely gardens and grounds include a Victorian tropical conservatory and walled garden. Meals, snacks, shop and plant centre, disabled access; usually open Tues–Sun July–Sept, plus most bank hols wknds, but phone to check as they couldn't confirm this as we went to press; (01635) 253210; £6.50, £3 gardens only. The Yew Tree (A343 S of village) is a good value dining pub.

HINTON AMPNER SU5927

Attractive Georgian house, but it's the splendid grounds that impress most, with tranquil 20th-c shrub gardens. Teas, disabled access; gardens open Sat–Weds Apr–Sept, house open pm Tues–Weds Apr–Sept, plus wknds in Aug; (01962) 771305; £5 house and garden, £4 garden only; NT. The neighbouring Hinton Arms has good food.

HURST CASTLE SZ3189

Hurst Castle One of the most sophisticated fortresses when built by Henry VIII, on a long spit commanding the Solent, and best reached on foot or by summer ferry from Keyhaven (there's a pleasant walk from the 17th-c Gun pub – good value food). Fortified again in the 19th c, it still has two huge 38-ton guns. Summer snacks, shop, disabled access to ground floor; cl wkdys Nov–Mar, 25–26 Dec; (01590) 642344; £2.80.

LANGSTONE SU7104

Thatched cottages, an old tidal mill, and the nice Royal Oak looking out over the thousands of acres of silted harbour – winter sunsets are memorable. Swans float up at high tide, with oystercatchers and droves of darting dunlins on the low-tide mud flats. Interesting walks along the old sea wall.

LEPE COUNTRY PARK SZ4598

A pleasant spot for mild saunters along the coast.

LIPHOOK SU8330

Bohunt Manor Lovely woodland gardens owned by Worldwide Fund for Nature, with water garden, roses and herbaceous borders, lakeside walk, unusual trees and shrubs, and wildfowl. Disabled access; (01428) 727936; suggested donation £1.50. The nearby Links Hotel restaurant is handy for lunch.

Hollycombe Steam Collection (Midhurst Rd) Huge collection of steam-driven equipment, from paddle-steamer to an entire Edwardian fairground, inc the big wheel. Occasional open evenings when the fairground is delightfully lit. Traction engine rides, and woodland steam train trips. Snacks, shop, some disabled access; open pm Sun and bank hols Easter–mid Oct, and pms daily last wk July–Aug bank hol; (01428) 724900; £7.50. The nearest place for a good lunch is the Red Lion over at Fernhurst.

LYMINGTON SZ3295
Handsome and relaxed waterside town, very popular in summer with yachting people; it has quite a number of attractive Georgian buildings and some good shops. The 17th-c Kings Head (Quay Hill), Chequers (Ridgeway Lane, off A37 W) and Fishermans Rest (All Saints Rd) have good food. You can get ferries to the Isle of Wight from here (phone (0870) 5827744 for times), and the B3054 to Dibden Purlieu is a pretty road.

St Barbe Museum and Art Gallery Aimed at families, with quite a few hands-on exhibits (children can try on World War II uniforms, climb into a pilot boat, or weigh produce in the re-created shop), this local history museum has displays on subjects such as boat-building, smuggling, and salt-making. Two art galleries have changing exhibitions of arts, crafts, and local history. Shop, disabled access; cl Sun, 25–26 Dec, and 1 Jan; (01590) 676969; £3.

LYNDHURST SU2908
The tourist centre of the New Forest, as well as the main shopping town for people living here, so lots of tearooms, cafés etc. Traffic tends to bottle-neck here, so it's worth parking on the edge of town and walking in. The car park, with walks straight into the forest, has a good information centre for the area; (023) 8028 2269. The Crown Hotel (High St) has good value food and a cosy log-fire bar.

New Forest Museum (High St) This good museum (in the same building as the Tourist Information Centre) will reopen around Jun; they are redesigning some of their interesting themed displays which cover the forest's history and wildlife, and there'll be a new library and shop; there's also an audio-visual display and a 7½-metre (25-ft) embroidery. Disabled access; phone for opening times; (023) 8028 3914; £2.75.

MEONSTOKE SU6119
An attractive village, with decent food at the Bucks Head. The road from here down through Soberton runs by the River Meon, and is quiet enough to suit walkers; the old Meon Valley railway line nearby is now open as a walkway.

MICHELDEVER SU5138
Village of lovely thatched cottages and colourful gardens. There are fine walks in open countryside to the S, and up the River Dever valley to the E. The Half Moon & Spread Eagle has good food.

MIDDLE WALLOP SU3038
Museum of Army Flying 🏛 This exemplary military museum has plenty to interest, celebrating over 100 years of army aviation with kites, balloons, vintage aircraft, World War II gliders, helicopters, and an interactive science centre; frequent special events too. Snacks, shop, disabled access; cl Christmas wk; (01980) 674421; £5.

MINSTEAD SU2711
Furzey Gardens 🏛 Eight peaceful acres, with developing young arboretum, sensory garden and lake, around charming 16th-c thatched cottage and local craft gallery (cl Nov–Feb). Snacks, plant sales, limited disabled access; cl 25–26 Dec; (023) 8081 2464; £3.60 (£1.50 winter). The village is quiet and pretty, with a fine old church at the top of the hill; the Trusty Servant by the green has good food.

MOTTISFONT SU3227
Mottisfont Abbey 12th-c priory salvaged from the Reformation as a charming family house, in wonderful peaceful surroundings. The gardens are a delight, housing a national collection of old roses (largely scented). You can usually see a few of the rooms, inc one richly decorated by Rex Whistler. Meals, snacks, shop, good disabled access; open Sun–Weds Mar–Oct (plus

Thurs July–Aug), and daily during the rose season (9–29 Jun); (01794) 340757; *£6.50 rose season; NT. The Bear & Ragged Staff up on the A3057 does good value food all day, and the road along the Test through Houghton and on to the attractive village of Wherwell is pretty.

NETHER WALLOP SU2936
An attractive sleepy thatched village with an interesting Saxon church; surprisingly Leopold Stokowski died here, not in Hollywood. The Five Bells is a nice place for lunch. Just E of the village, you can look around **Danebury Vineyards**.

NEW FOREST SU2605
The New Forest countryside has great charm. Only parts of it are in fact wooded; the rest is unspoilt rolling heathland. Walkers can head off in virtually any direction without worrying about trespassing. Once away from the roads, it does give a great feeling of untrammelled space. Children like it: there are free-running ponies (and even the occasional pig), and plenty of scope for generally running riot without coming to grief. This unchanging blend of woodland and heath covers nearly 150 square miles, designated a Royal hunting preserve by William the Conqueror not long after the Battle of Hastings. The two best drives are the slow back rd from Brockenhurst N through Bolderwood and then round past Linwood to Rockford, and the rd from Brockenhurst to Burley; main rds can get very busy around the more popular areas, especially on summer wknds. Still with quite a medieval feel, the ancient woodlands are very atmospheric to stroll through, especially when you come across an unexpected sunlit leafy glade. It's most fun just to potter around, but you'll also get a lot out of a guided tour with people who've lived or worked in the forest all their lives; (023) 8028 3141 for details. Many of them have ancient forest rights and privileges, such as letting their pigs forage for acorns. The path network in the New Forest is remarkably comprehensive, and in most places there's no obligation to stick to rights of way (of which there are very few). The lack of major

objectives can be a problem for purists: there are no obviously defined hills, and long walks in the eastern woodlands, many of which are coniferous, can become monotonous. Further W, the scenery is more intricate and a touch more varied. It is often a good idea to use routes that have plenty of landmarks to guide the way; the heath and forest can be fiendishly disorienting. Besides the ponies, you may see fallow deer, especially at the Bolderwood Deer Sanctuary (and in the woods, very occasionally, the smaller, shyer roe deer; even in some places red deer). The best walks alternate mixed forest with heathland; isolated ponds and country pubs provide focal points. In summer you can usually go on guided badger watch evenings; (01425) 403412 (phone wkdys 9–10am). The Museum and Visitor Centre at Lyndhurst is a good place to start, and has details of watersports, riding and campsites (we recommend the Forestry Commission ones; (0131) 3146505). Handy pubs include the Royal Oak at Bank, Red Lion at Boldre (nr Roydon Woods nature reserve), White Buck at Bisterne Close just E of Burley, New Forest at Emery Down, Royal Oak at Fritham, Foresters Arms at Frogham, High Corner Inn or Red Shoot nr Linwood, Royal Oak at North Gorley, Alice Lisle at Rockford, Sir Walter Tyrell at Upper Canterton and Rockingham Arms at Canada nr West Wellow.

NEW MILTON SZ2396
Sammy Miller Museum 🏛 (Bashley Manor) Well regarded changing collection of 300 fully restored motor cycles, many the only surviving examples of their type in the world; farm animals too and a play area. Snacks, shop, disabled access; cl 25 Dec; (01425) 620777; £3.50. There's an adjacent craft shop.

OLD WINCHESTER HILL SU6420
This hill fort gives wide views of Hampshire, The Solent and Isle of Wight, with nature trails through natural downland that's never been ploughed and resown; fairly busy on fine wknds, wonderfully remote on a blustery spring or autumn weekday. The George & Falcon at Warnford is popular for food.

OVERTON SU5149

There's a charming **drive** along the B3400 to Hurstbourne Priors and B3048 to Wherwell; Overton though quite large is an attractive stop along the way, with a good pub – the Bush.

OWER SU3116

Paultons Park Agreeable family leisure park with over 40 attractions and rides, gardens, birds and wildfowl, as well as model dinosaurs in marshland, a 10-acre lake with working waterwheel, hedge maze, animated *Wind in the Willows* scenes, and unique Romany Experience with the sights, sounds and smells of traditional gypsy life. The mini log flume and digger ride for younger children join rides such as the Raging River log flume, swingboat, tea-cups, and go-karts (the only thing with an extra charge), bumper boats, roller-coaster and several good play areas, many ideal for toddlers. Meals, snacks, shop, disabled access; cl wkdys Nov and Dec (exc Christmas specials), and all Jan to mid-Mar; (023) 8081 4455; £11, various family tickets available.

PETERSFIELD SU7423

Bear Museum (Dragon St) The first of the various teddy museums, this good collection has bears, dolls and toys in a nursery setting. Children (or anyone else for that matter) can cuddle some exhibits; shop; cl Sun, Mon and bank hols; (01730) 265108; free. There's an interesting **church** on Market Sq, and the 16th-c Good Intent has decent food.

PORTCHESTER SU6204

Portchester Castle The imposing high walls and towers stretching right down to the waterfront were originally part of a 3rd-c Roman fort – they're the best example of their type in Europe, and from the top give good views across The Solent. Other remains include a 12th-c church and 14th-c great tower, and what's left of a palace built by Richard II. Audio tour, snacks, shop, disabled access to ground floor only; cl 24–26 Dec, and 1 Jan; (023) 9237 8291; £3.20 (inc audio tour); EH. The nearby Cormorant has good value food all day.

PORTSMOUTH SZ6299

The £85 million harbour redevelopment includes several interesting places to visit, and has opened up parts of the city which have been closed to the public for centuries. Portsmouth is at the heart of English naval history, and the city's rejuvenation focuses on this. The ongoing project, the **Millennium Promenade**, forms part of a trail linking the two parts most interesting to visitors: the Old Town and the Historic Dockyard, on either side of the ferry berths and well away from the traffic. Overlooking the narrow harbour neck, Georgian buildings on an old-fashioned cobbled hard give a good feel of the old days, and the little inner Camber Harbour still has fishing boats. The naval base has been revitalised in recent years, and now includes **Gunwharf Quays** – a huge waterfront factory outlet and leisure complex inc a cinema, bowling alley, bars and restaurants with tables on the waterfront, and occasional craft market. The landmark **Spinnaker Tower**, a graceful 165 metres (540 ft) tall, has lost its financial wind and will remain unfinished until more funding can be found. A lot of development is also happening across the harbour in Gosport (see separate entry), and a new Waterbus service links the two towns daily all year; £3.50. A passport ticket (ferry fare included) covers all the new attractions, £25 for a day. The Still & West and Spice Island family pubs have great harbourside positions, and the Dolphin's a nice old place in the old High St behind. The **cathedral**, dating from the 13th c to the present, is a delightful departure from the traditional layout. Portsmouth is an island city, with just two roads and the motorway bridging it and its residential/resort part Southsea to the mainland – traffic can be very slow indeed on the main approaches.

Blue Reef Aquarium ▣ (Clarence Esplanade, Southsea) Recently re-opened after a £1 million refurbishment, this is now even more enjoyable for families. The huge coral reef display is the centrepiece, and from an underwater walk-through tunnel you can spot black tip reef sharks among the colourful shoals of fish. A new freshwater display has Asian otters, and the hands-on rock pools are a big hit with children; there are regular talks and feeding demonstrations, and special events. Snacks, shop, disabled access; cl 25 Dec; (023) 9287 5222; £5.95 (they'll stamp your hand and let you come back later in the day). **Boat trips** round the harbour from nearby; Easter–Oct; (023) 9282 0564; £4.

City Museum (Museum Rd) Very good displays on the city's history, in an astonishing former barracks that looks rather like a French chateau. Also decorative art and crafts. Snacks, shop, disabled access; cl 25–26 Dec; (023) 9282 7261; free.

Cumberland House Natural History Museum (Eastern Parade, Southsea) As well as its good conventional natural history displays, this little museum has a butterfly enclosure, and an aquarium. Shop, very limited disabled access; cl 24–26 Dec; (023) 9282 7261; £2, £2.50 in butterfly season.

D-Day Museum (Clarence Esplanade, Southsea) The most notable of the museums devoted to Portsmouth's fighting history; it vividly recalls and explains the Normandy landings from the point of view of both sides. There's a remarkable 84-metre (272-ft) D-Day embroidery inspired by the Bayeux Tapestry. Snacks, shop, disabled access; cl 24-26 Dec; (023) 9282 7261; £5, free on 6 Jun.

Dickens' Birthplace Museum (Old Commercial Rd, in the main town) Restored to the modest middle-class style it had when the author was born here in 1812. Still various Dickens-related objects such as the couch on which he died. Shop; cl Nov–Mar (exc 7 Feb, his birthday); (023) 9282 7261; £2.50.

Guildhall (Guildhall Sq) Contains what's said to be the world's biggest glass mural; snacks, disabled access; free tours by appointment; (023) 9283 4560.

Portsmouth Historic Dockyard ⌖ The main stop for most visitors, with lots to see. It's home to **HMS *Victory*, the *Mary Rose*, HMS *Warrior***, and the **Royal Naval Museum**. The flagship is HMS *Victory*, which is still in commission; guided tours (not in school holidays) bring those Trafalgar days very close, and include the spot

where Nelson died. The raising of the *Mary Rose* from The Solent silt where it had sat for 437 years provided a wealth of material and information about the Tudor period. The discoveries are well shown in the Mary Rose Museum, while the great oak hull itself is in a separate hall, sprayed constantly to prevent the timbers from drying out (there are plans to build a new ship hall as part of the harbour redevelopment). HMS *Warrior* when launched 140 years ago was the most fearsome battleship in the world; she's been immaculately restored. A bit like a games arcade, **Action Stations** gives a new look at the modern Navy through a large format film and interactive displays; a big hit with children, there can be lengthy queues in the holidays. Housed in handsome 18th-c dockside buildings, the **Royal Naval Museum** has lively displays on the development and history of the Navy up to and beyond the Falklands War (or as it's called here the South Atlantic Campaign), with interactive galleries looking at Nelson, the sailing Navy, and HMS *Victory* (and its role in the Battle of Trafalgar). You can no longer buy separate cheaper tickets for individual ships, but have to pay for an inclusive ticket lumping in all the attractions for £13.75 (you don't have to see them all in one day); a family ticket (2 adults and up to 3 children) is £44. The site – which itself costs nothing to enter, after a security check – has a restaurant, caf≥s and shops, and there's limited disabled access to all the ships; cl 25 Dec; (023) 9272 7562.

Royal Garrison church (French St) Roofless now, this once-grand place was where Charles II was married in 1662; open wkdys Apr–Sept; (023) 9237 8291; free.

Royal Marines Museum ⌖ (Eastney Esplanade, Southsea) This vigorous place couldn't be more different from the usual military exhibitions – lively re-creations of major amphibious actions, a junior commando assault course, and a jungle room with a real snake and scorpion. Also lots of changing exhibitions and special events. Snacks, shop, disabled access; cl 24–26 Dec; (023) 9281 9385; £4.

Southsea Castle The fortifications in

defence of Portsmouth Harbour, here, around Gosport, and up on Portsdown, give a remarkably complete picture of the development of defensive strategy from Tudor times to the fears of french invasion in the 1860s, though they have more appeal to people interested in warfare than to those who like the romantic idea of a regular 'castle'. Southsea Castle and Museum is the best place to start, built in 1545 as part of Henry VIII's coastal defences. Good displays on Portsmouth's military history, and a time-tunnel experience of the history of the castle; special events (esp summer). Shop; cl Nov–Mar; (023) 9282 7261; £2.50. On the seaward side of Southsea are sturdy Tudor and later towers, bastions and batteries, alongside the resort's gardens and entertainments, giving interesting sea views. Good guided walks around the Tudor fortifications and the best parts of the Old Town leave the Square Tower at 2pm on Sun (mid-Apr to late Sept); (023) 9282 6722; £1.

Spitbank Fort Wind up an exploration of Portsmouth's naval past with the boat trip from the Naval Base to this granite, iron and brick fortress a mile out to sea. Its two floors are linked by a maze of passages, and there's a 130-metre (420-ft) deep well which still draws fresh water. The inner courtyard is now a sheltered terrace for summer refreshments from the caf≥ and bar. Open Suns in summer for day visits which include the boat trip (£6.95, ferries leave from the Histroric Dockyard and Gunwharf Quay in Portsmouth). They also do popular pub nights with – of course – a spit-roast (£15, ferries leave from Gosport ferry terminal and the Hard in Portsmouth); phone for more information; (023) 9250 4207.

QUEEN ELIZABETH COUNTRY PARK SU7117

Queen Elizabeth Country Park (Gravel Hill, NE of Clanfield) Lots going on all year, with woodland walks and rides (stables at the park), open downland, an adventure play trail, and events such as Easter egg rolling. You can arrange horse riding; (023) 9259 9669. Disabled access; park open all year, visitor centre, shop and café cl

wkdys Jan–Mar; (023) 9259 5040; £1.50 parking charge Sun and bank hols, £1 rest of wk. The good Five Bells at Buriton is not far.

RINGWOOD SU1604

New Forest Owl Sanctuary (Crow Lane, Crow – just S) A real mix of owls and hawks, not always easy to see as some enclosures are deliberately overgrown to resemble natural habitats. It can get a little congested when busy; daily flying displays. Snacks, shop, disabled access; cl Nov–early Feb (usually exc wknds and school hols, but phone to check); (01425) 476487; *£5.50. In the town the riverside Fish (open all day) has good food.

ROCKBOURNE SU1117

Rockbourne Roman Villa (off B3078) Remains of largest known Roman villa in the area, found by chance 50 years ago by a farmer digging out a ferret. Interesting mosaics in the museum. Shop, disabled access; cl Oct–Mar; (01725) 518541; £1.95. In the charming thatched village, the Rose & Thistle is pleasant for lunch.

ROMSEY SU3520

Broadlands 🅳 (just S) Elegant Palladian mansion on banks of the River Test, surrounded by beautiful landscaped grounds. Fine furnishings and paintings, and good exhibition on former resident Earl Mountbatten. Snacks, shop, limited disabled access; open pm early Jun–early Sept; (01794) 505010; £5.95. The nearby Dukes Head (A3057) is an attractive dining pub. Mountbatten is buried in the interesting 13th-c **abbey**, bought by the townspeople as their parish church at the Dissolution; it has some notable Saxon crosses and a 16th-c panel painting.

Romsey Heritage and Visitor Centre This includes King John's House, once the focus of a large 13th-c complex, with some interesting medieval graffiti and a rare bone floor, and period garden (open Mon–Sat Apr–Oct); the visitor centre has local history displays and recreations of a Victorian parlour and old gunshop. Snacks, shop, disabled access to visitor centre; cl Sun; (01794) 512200; £2.50 Apr–Sept, £1.50 Oct–Mar. Close by, the Abbey Hotel has an enterprising food choice.

ROWLAND'S CASTLE SU7610
Stansted Park (2m E) This fine
Caroline revival-style house was
actually built in 1903 (the original burnt
down a few years earlier). The bit most
people enjoy most is the re-created
Edwardian servants' quarters in the
basement – quite a contrast to the fine
furniture and paintings upstairs. The
surrounding parkland (no formal
gardens but ancient woodland, an
arboretum and a chapel) is pleasant for
a leisurely stroll. Tearoom in a restored
Victorian glasshouse, disabled access to
grounds only; house open pm Sun and
Mon Easter–end Sept, plus pm Tues and
Weds July–Aug, grounds open daily
(exc 25–26 and 31 Dec and 1 Jan); (023)
9241 2265; £5.50 house and grounds,
£1.80 grounds only. Also here, a
falconry centre (flying demonstrations
usually 1pm and 3pm; cl Thurs and
perhaps in winter; £3), craft workshops
inc a pottery and a glassblower, and a
popular garden centre set around a
walled garden; (023) 9241 3090. In the
village, the Castle Inn does good value
lunches.

SELBORNE SU7433
Gilbert White's House (The
Wakes) Impressive 18th-c home of
naturalist Gilbert White, furnished in
period style. The restoration of the
extensive gardens to their original form
is almost complete, and separate
galleries commemorate the explorers
Captain Oates and Frank Oates.
Impressive teas and 18th-c style snacks,
good shop, plant sales, disabled access
to ground floor and garden; cl 25–31
Dec; (01420) 511275; *£4.50. The
Queens Hotel is handy for lunch. There
are good pockets of scenery nearby –
the countryside White recorded in
such detail. The zigzag path he created
with his brother in 1753 still climbs
Selborne Hanger (the hangers
hereabouts are beechwoods which
cling to the abrupt escarpments). Noar
Hill close by has been designated a
nature reserve for its chalkland flora,
and from Selborne churchyard, a path
leads into the Lythe, a wooded hillside
that was another favourite haunt of
White's.

SHERBORNE ST JOHN SU6356
The Vyne Tudor mansion with

splendid 17th- and 18th-c
embellishments: see if you can spot the
stonemason's error which grafted a
parrot's beak on to an eagle. The
gardens include a 19th-c walled garden
and a summerhouse garden, and there
are pleasant woodland walks. Meals,
snacks, shop, disabled access; cl Thurs
and Fri, and all Nov–Mar (grounds open
wknds Feb–Mar); (01256) 881337;
£6.50, grounds only £3; NT. The Plough
over at Little London does good value
pub lunches.

SILCHESTER SU6262
Calleva Museum The site of Roman
town Calleva Atrebatum has been
excavated nearby; 1fi miles of city wall
to walk along (tricky in places), as well
as a 9,000-seat amphitheatre, 12th-c
church on the site of the Roman
temples, and a small **museum** giving a
pictorial account of the site; some
disabled access; cl 25 Dec; free. The
Calleva Arms (with a family dining
conservatory) does cheap lunches, and
sells a guide to the site. Over at Little
London the Plough (good snack
lunches) is handy for Pamber Forest
walks.

SOUTHAMPTON SU4111
Known early last century (through its
shipping importance) as the Gateway to
the World, this huge bustling city rather
unexpectedly has one of the three best-
preserved medieval town walls in the
country. The best stretch is along the
western side of the old core, around
from the magnificent partly Norman
Bargate; there are usually guided
walks along here at 10.30am Sun and
bank hol Mon (10.30 and 2.30 daily in
summer hols), (023) 8086 8401; or you
can walk it on your own at any time.
Lots of other old buildings are dotted
around the less appetising modern
townscape, though if you're short of
time it's best to concentrate your
efforts on the area around St Michael's
Sq, Bugle St and perhaps the old High St.
At the opposite end is the huge West
Quay shopping complex – serious
shopping, lots of cafés. You can take
trips from Southampton to the Isle of
Wight with Red Funnel Ferries (foot
and car ferries leave regularly all year);
(0870) 444 8898.
City Art Gallery (Civic Centre,

Commercial Rd) Extensive and distinguished collection of British and European paintings and sculptures from the last 600 years, with particular emphasis on the 20th c. Shop, disabled access; cl Mon, 24–26 Dec and Good Fri; (023) 8083 2277; free.

God's House Tower (Winkle St) An early 15th-c prototype gun battery, now housing an archaeology museum with displays on the city's Saxon forebear, Hamwic. Shop, usually cl 12–1pm, Sun am, all Mon, and some days over Christmas and New Year; (023) 8063 5904; free. The nearby bowling green is said to be the oldest in the world.

Hall of Aviation 🏛 (Albert Rd S) Various aircraft of local interest – inc prototype helicopters and the Spitfire. Snacks, shop, some disabled access; cl Sun am, all day Mon (exc bank and school hols), 25 Dec; (023) 8063 5830; £4.

Maritime Museum (Bugle St) A fine 14th-c warehouse with an impressive timber roof, and useful displays on the history of the port – especially good on the great liners, and there's a display on the Titanic. Shop, disabled access to ground floor only; cl 1–2pm, Sun am, Mon, and some days over Christmas and New Year; (023) 8022 3941; free. The ancient nearby Duke of Wellington has decent food.

Medieval Merchant's House 🏛 (French St) Fine timbered building ½m from city centre, splendidly refurbished with period furnishings which vividly re-create what life must have been like for a wealthy merchant's family; free audio tour. Shop; cl Nov–Mar; (023) 8022 1503; £2.30; EH.

SOUTHWICK SU6208
This attractive village, with a decent pub, is well placed for good walks on Portsdown Hill – fine views (where Eisenhower and Montgomery saw off the troops before D-Day).

SPARSHOLT SU4331
Attractive village very close to Farley Mount, with good woodland and downland walks, and good food at the Plough.

STEVENTON SU5447
Steventon church 12th-c, with a memorial to Jane Austen, who was born in the village.

STOCKBRIDGE SU3433
Houghton Lodge Gardens (just SW) Pretty and very peaceful gardens running down to River Test, with fine trees and lawns, a peacock statue made from recycled car metal, a herb garden, and a topiary dragon that breathes 'steam'. An intriguing hydroponicum demonstrates how to grow plants without soil, and there is a restored 18th-c shrubbery. Snacks, plant sales, disabled access; open all day wknds and bank hols and pm wkdys (exc Weds) Mar–Sept; (01264) 810912; £5 (children free). The Boot in Houghton has decent food; walks by this lovely stretch of the Test, or up on the Downs. The nearby town of Stockbridge has good art and antiques shops, with pleasant little waterways and ducks alongside its broad High St; the Greyhound and Three Cups facing each other across it both have good food.

STRATFIELD SAYE SU6962
Stratfield Saye House (off A33) Bought for the Duke of Wellington by a grateful nation after Waterloo, this 17th-c house should have re-opened by about Jun after essential restoration work. Perhaps surprisingly, the Duke had a taste for French furniture, lots of which is still here as is his splendid funeral carriage, and his hearing aid – needed after prolonged exposure to cannons. Snacks, shop, disabled access; phone for opening times and prices; (01256) 882882. The elegant Wellington Arms has good food. There are pleasant walks on Heckfield Heath E of the estate, and Wellington Country Park in Berks is nearby.

TITCHFIELD SU5406
Titchfield Abbey (Mill Lane) Ruined 13th-c abbey, almost overshadowed by the grand Tudor gatehouse built after the Dissolution. Some of Shakespeare's plays were reputedly first performed here. Disabled access; cl 25 Dec; free; EH. The Titchfield Mill, a nearby converted watermill, caters well for families, and there's a fine walk by the old canal to the coast at Meon Shore nr Hill Head.

TOTTON SU3612
Eling Tide Mill (Eling Toll Bridge) There's been a mill on this causeway for over 900 years, and the present one still

uses tidal energy to produce flour. Heritage centre (wknds only in winter; £1.30), snacks, shop, disabled access to ground floor only; cl Mon (exc bank hols), Tues, and 25–26 Dec – ring for milling times, which of course depend on the tide; (023) 8086 9575; £1.80 for mill, £2.90 for mill and heritage centre (tickets lasts for a year). In unpromising surroundings, the Anchor on Eling Quay is a good cheap place for something to eat.

TWYFORD SU4925

Waterworks Museum (Hazeley Rd) Worth a stop if you're at all interested in engines, this remarkably intact Edwardian waterworks was built to supply water to rural areas around Southampton (5m gallons of water are still extracted from here every day). Follow the evolution of water supply over the 20th c from steam engines (in steam 1st Sun in month in summer) to huge diesel engines to electric. You can still see the lime kilns (quick lime used to be added to the water to soften it), and the volunteers are enthusiastic and knowledgeable. Snacks, open Sun May–Oct; (01489) 784545.

WAGGONERS' WELLS SU8534 A series of hammer ponds, a legacy of the medieval Wealden iron industry, in a valley of charming heathy woodlands, perfect for a picnic. Paths skirt these NT-owned ponds, which are a haven for wildlife.

WATERSHIP DOWN SU4957 (just S of Kingsclere) The home of the rabbits in the novel by Richard Adams – their final adventure was down at Freefolk, where the eponymous pub often has live rabbits. Pleasant wooded walks through this area.

WEYHILL SU3046

Hawk Conservancy 🏷 One of the best birds of prey centres we've come across; you can handle some of the birds, and there are three daily flying displays (the best at 2pm). Wildflower meadow, ferret- and duck-racing in school hols, adventure playground and toddlers' play area. Snacks, shop, disabled access; cl Nov to mid-Feb; (01264) 772252; £6.25. The Weyhill Fair is handy for lunch, and the lanes N take you into a particularly unspoilt corner of Hants.

WHITCHURCH SU4648

Whitchurch Silk Mill (Winchester St) Interesting working silk mill, producing fabric for theatrical costumes, interior designers and historic houses using Victorian machinery and traditional processes. There's a self-guided audio tour, and visitors have a chance to work on a loom. Prettily set on an island in the River Test, where you can watch the trout or feed ducks. Helpful staff, good value snacks, shop; cl Mon exc bank hols, and 25 Dec–1 Jan; (01256) 892065; £3. The Red House (London St) is the best pub here, and you can get a good cup of coffee at the White Hart Hotel (The Square).

WICKHAM SU5711 An attractive village despite the traffic, notable for its huge village square, where the Kings Head and more upmarket Greens do enjoyable food.

WINCHESTER SU4829 The compact and fascinating medieval centre still has two city gates intact; it was England's capital in Saxon times. The most attractive part is the glorious and peaceful cathedral Close, surrounded by a very harmonious and distinguished collection of buildings; the handsome old Eclipse Inn nr the NE edge is a useful refreshment break. The Brooks Shopping Centre has a few jolly dioramas and displays on the city's history (free), with the chance for children to make their own Roman mosaic. Guided walks around the sights from the Tourist Information Centre at 11am Mon–Sat (plus 2.30pm Sat in Apr, 2.30pm Sat and Sun May–Jun, and 2.30pm Mon–Sun July–Oct, exc Sun in Oct), Sat only Nov–Mar; £3. There's a multi-storey car park at the top of the High St, or a Park & Ride nr the junction with the M3. There are pleasant walks up rounded St Catherine's Hill, which has a small medieval turf maze and traces of a hill fort.

City Mill (Bridge St) Restored and working 18th-c watermill, with timbered and raftered ceilings and a pretty little island garden. They are planning milling displays for this year (and to sell the flour they mill), but as we went to press they were unsure of times so phone to check. Shop, disabled access; open wknds in Mar, Weds–Sun Apr–Jun and Sept–Oct, daily July–Aug; (01962) 870057; £2; NT.

City Museum (The Square) This recently refurbished well organised museum is good for local history and archaeology, with a telling Roman mosaic. Shop, good disabled access; cl Sun am, Mon Nov–Mar, and 25–26 Dec; (01962) 848269; free.

Great Hall of Winchester Castle All that now remains is its huge 13th-c great hall, where Raleigh was tried and condemned to death; hanging on one wall is a round table they call King Arthur's (actually much the same date as the castle, and painted with its Arthurian scenes later). Restored roof, stone parapets and stained glass, and there's a small but interesting re-created medieval garden S of the hall. Shop, disabled access; cl 25–26 Dec; (01962) 846476; free.

Guildhall Gallery (Broadway) 19th-c building with changing exhibitions of fine art, crafts and photography. Snacks, shop, disabled access; cl Sun am, all Mon Nov–Mar, 25–26 Dec, and 1 Jan; (01962) 848289; free.

Gurkha Museum 🖼 Anyone interested in military history will enjoy the five military museums in Winchester, but of these only the Gurkha Museum (Romsey Rd) could be said to have a wider appeal. Shop, disabled access; cl Sun am, 25–26 Dec, and 1 Jan; (01962) 842832; £1.50.

Hospital of St Cross 🖼 Very attractively set around two quadrangles, the quaint 15th-c almshouses still provide bread and ale to travellers who ask at the massive gate (you have to ask for 'wayfarer's dole'). 19th-c scandals here inspired Trollope's *The Warden*. Summer snacks, shop, disabled access; cl Sun, Good Fri and 25 Dec; (01962) 851375; £2. The Bell here is useful for lunch, and the stroll out from the city centre, along the water-meadows by the River Itchen, is one of the nicest short walks in southern Britain.

Westgate Museum (High St) Local history above a formidable medieval city gate which was a debtors' prison for 150 years (the walls are still covered in prisoners' graffiti); brass rubbings here too, and an interesting Tudor ceilng. The panorama of the city and surrounding countryside is rewarding. Shop; cl Sun am, Mon in Oct and Feb, and all Nov–Jan; (01962) 848269; free.

Winchester Cathedral 🖼 Awesome and full of interest – one of Europe's finest, with the longest of all Gothic naves, and quite a mixture of architectural styles. Among many rare books and manuscripts in its library is a wonderful 12th-c illuminated Bible, while the sculpture gallery contains some outstanding late Gothic work. William of Wykeham paid for much of the rebuilding, so his tomb is appropriately the finest; also memorials and monuments to Jane Austen, King Canute and St Swithun. The cathedral hosts changing exhibitions of modern art through the summer, and a sculpture by Antony 'Angel of the North' Gormley beautifully exploits reflections in the winter flood waters of the crypt. Good guided tours, and first-rate visitor centre in 16th-c coach house, with very good meals and snacks (not cheap) and distinguished shop, disabled access; £3.50 suggested donation. The recently created Dean Garnier Garden between the deanery and the cathedral reflects the cathedral's architecture; open all day; free; for more info ring Sally Curtis (01962) 732246 or the cathedral office (01962) 857202. Close by are the appreciable remains of Wolvesey Castle, the original Bishop's Palace begun in the 12th c, and beside it (not open, but a handsome sight), the present Bishop's Palace of 1684. The best way out of the Close is through the medieval King's Gate, which includes the upper-floor church of St Swithun. This takes you into Kingsgate St, calm and old-fashioned, with an excellent dining pub, the Wykeham Arms. Down on the left a lovely riverside path takes you along to the City Mill and a mighty statue of King Alfred.

Winchester College 🖼 All along Kingsgate St are buildings connected with this, the oldest school in the country. Most of the original school buildings remain intact, especially around the grand 14th-c chapel and its calm, tilting cloisters with a delightful two-storey chantry in their centre, and a glimpse of the warden's garden through one gate. Good shop in former Tuck Shop, some disabled access; guided tours, cl Sun am, pm Tues and Thurs, 25 Dec and 1 Jan (but best to check then); (01962) 621209; £3. **Other attractive villages** with decent pubs include Abbots Ann SU3243, Amport SU2944, Bank SU2807, Botley SU5112, Brook SU2713, Cheriton SU5828, Crawley SU4234, Crondall SU7948, Dummer SU5846, East End SU4161 (the one nr Highclere), East Stratton SU5439, Exton SU6120, Hambledon SU6414 (Broadhalfpenny Down just E was the birthplace of cricket), Hurstbourne Tarrant SU3853, Lasham SU6742, Longparish SU4344, Mapledurwell SU6851, Monxton SU3144, North Waltham SU5645, Rowland's Castle SU7310, Upton Grey SU6948, Vernham Dean SU3456, Wherwell SU3840 and Woodgreen SU1717.

Where to eat

BISHOP'S WALTHAM SU5517 **Peppers** *The Square (01489) 891515* Ground-floor dining room and attractive bar, upstairs main dining room, friendly atmosphere, highly enjoyable and nicely presented bistro-style food with plenty of modern dishes as well as old favourites, suitably rich puddings, a thoughtful little wine list, and helpful service; cl Sun pm, Mon, Christmas, 2 wks Aug; disabled access. £37/2-course set lunch £12.95|£0

BOLDRE SZ3198 **Red Lion** *Boldre Lane (01590) 673177* Very busy, friendly pub with hard-working licensees, four black-beamed rooms, interesting bric-a-brac and bygones, impressive bar food, prompt service, a fine choice of wines by the glass, and well kept beer; worth getting there early; cl 25 Dec; no children; disabled access. £24.75|£8.90

BROCKENHURST SU2902 **Simply Poussin** *The Courtyard, Brookley Road (01590) 623063* Popular little simply furnished restaurant, run by the son of the former owners, with carefully cooked interesting food using the best local produce, good cheeses and puddings, a short wine list, and friendly service; cl Sun pm, Mon, 6-20 Jan; children over 7; disabled access. £22

BROCKENHURST SU3002 **Thatched Cottage** *16 Brookley Rd (01590) 623090* Charming 400-year-old thatched cottage with cosy beamed lounge, good dried and fresh flower arrangements, pretty no smoking restaurant, and enjoyable well presented imaginative food served by friendly staff; super cream teas in neat garden, morning coffee too; individually decorated bdrms; cl Sun pm, Mon, Jan; children over 12. £50

CRAWLEY SU4234 **Fox & Hounds** *(01962) 776006* Striking mock-Tudor building in a village of fine old houses, recently restored and reopened, with beamed rooms warmed by three log fires, a mix of attractive wooden tables and chairs, evening candlelight, a relaxed atmosphere, and helpful friendly staff; very good imaginative bar food using fresh local produce, interesting wines, well kept real ales; disabled access. £28|£7.25

EAST TYTHERLEY SU2927 **Star** *East Tytherley Rd (01794) 340225* 16th-c dining pub with stylish menu of imaginative food (you can eat the same menu in the bar or restaurant), well kept real ales, a thoughtful wine list with ten by the glass, pretty no smoking restaurant, and a mix of comfortable furnishings; log fires, horse brasses and saddlery, and skittle alley; seats on smartly furnished terrace, play area; comfortable cottage-style bdrms overlook the village cricket pitch. £23.70|£7.50

EASTON SU5132 **Chestnut Horse** *(01962) 779257* Smart but cosy 16th-c pub, candlelight even at lunchtime, dark comfortable furnishings, black beams and joists hung with all sorts of china, lots of attractive country pictures, some panelling, log fires in cottagey fireplaces; good generous creative food and Sunday brunch in no smoking restaurant areas, decent wines inc champagne by the glass, well kept real ales, nicely served coffee, a buoyant yet relaxed atmosphere, friendly efficient service; tables out on a smallish sheltered back terrace with pretty flower tubs and baskets; this sleepy village is handy for Itchen valley walks. £30|**£8.95**

EMSWORTH SU7405 **36 On The Quay** *47 South St (01243) 375592* Charming cheerfully decorated quayside restaurant with exceptional modern cooking, friendly helpful service and a sound wine list; cl Sat am and Mon am, all Sun, 3 wks Jan; disabled access. £44.45 dinner, £28.45 lunch|**£9**

EVERSLEY SU7861 **Golden Pot** *(0118) 973 2104* Little brick pub with a comfortable easy-going atmosphere in the different spreading areas, bowls of lilies, candles in bottles, fireside sofa; pretty no smoking restaurant, and good interesting food inc special Mon evening rπsti menu (landlady is Swiss) with lots of different toppings; well kept real ales and 12 wines (some from Switzerland) by the glass; picnic-sets out in front; disabled access. £33|**£7.50**

EVERSLEY SU7662 **New Mill Restaurant & Grill Room** *New Mill Rd (0118) 973 2277* 16th-c watermill by the Blackwater River with working waterwheel and grinding equipment; big windows overlooking the river and its wildlife, open fires and candlelit tables, a good range of interesting carefully cooked food, and a thoughtful wine list with many by the glass; the beamed Grill Room is more informal and cheaper; cl 24–29 Dec; partial disabled access. £28.50|**£6.95**

FROXFIELD SU7227 **Trooper** *(01730) 827293* NW of Steep) Interesting pub transformed by very jolly landlord, big windows looking across rolling countryside, airy feel, little Persian knick-knacks, lit candles all around, fresh flowers, and log fire; attractive raftered restaurant, good food, well kept real ales, and decent house wines; lots of picnic-sets on lawn and partly covered sunken terrace; the horse rail in the car park ('horses only before 8pm') does get used; bdrms; disabled access. £26|**£8.25**

LONGSTOCK SU3537 **Peat Spade** *(01264) 810612* Popular dining pub with airy attractive bar, toby jugs around the fire, an elegant little dining room, no smoking area, good interesting food, well kept real ales, and decent wines; bdrms; cl 25 Dec, 1 Jan; disabled access. £26|**£7.25**

LYMINGTON SZ2996 **Gordleton Mill** *Silver St, Hordle (01590) 682219* 300-year-old converted watermill in lovely romantic gardens, with attractive bars and restaurant, a relaxed bustling atmosphere, good modern English cooking, a carefully chosen wine list, friendly staff and tables on waterside terrace; comfortable bdrms. £28

MAPLEDURWELL SU6851 **Gamekeepers** *Tunworth Rd (01256) 322038* Neatly kept pub run by helpful welcoming licensees, with dark beams and timbers throughout, and a relaxed friendly atmosphere; country pictures, horse tack and fox masks, partly stripped brick walls, some flagstones, two-way log-effect gas fire and a large no smoking dining room with carp at the bottom of a glass-topped well; good popular food, well kept Badger ales, and a Lhasa Apso dog called Barney; picnic-sets on terrace and back grassy area; partial disabled access. £30|**£7.95**

MICHELDEVER SU5138 **Half Moon & Spread Eagle** *Winchester Rd (01962) 774339* Attractive country pub with a simply decorated beamed bar, woodburners each end, and solid furniture, generous helpings of interesting food inc lots of good daily specials, well kept real ales, and decent wines; seats on terrace and by cricket green; disabled access. £23|**£7.50**

OLD BURGHCLERE SU4658 **Dew Pond** *(01635) 278408* Beautiful 16th-c country house with log fires, friendly atmosphere, and imaginative attractively presented evening meals using fresh local produce on a frequently changing small menu – good game, fish and lovely puddings; no smoking; cl Sun, Mon, 2 wks Jan/Aug; no under-5s; disabled access. £34

ROMSEY SU3521 **Old Manor House** *21 Palmerston St (01794) 517353* Long-established Italian restaurant with comfortable lounge and tiny restaurant, consistently enjoyable, authentic food (inc home-shot game, home-smoked ham, and home-made salami) using the best local ingredients, classic puddings, and some interesting Italian wines; cl Sun pm, Mon, 1 wk over Christmas. £37.50

ROTHERWICK SU7156 **Falcon** *The Street (01256) 762586* Quietly placed and relaxed country pub with a light and fresh open-plan layout, informal mix of furnishings on varnished boards, sunny window seats, fresh décor, log fires; rather more formal no smoking back dining area, interesting, enjoyable food, well kept real ales, good coffee, and very friendly helpful service; tables and benches on front and back terraces, and picnic-sets in sizeable informal back garden with a pair of swings and pasture views; good easy walks nearby. £23.50|£6.95

SOUTHSEA SZ6598 **Tenth Hole** *Eastern Parade (023) 9283 0009* Bustling café by the pitch-and-putt with snacks, light lunches and generous teas served by friendly staff; cl 3 wks Jan; children over 10; disabled access.|£5.25

SPARSHOLT SU4331 **Plough** *(01962) 776353* Busy, neatly kept dining pub in attractive countryside, with a bustling atmosphere in the main bar, farm tools on the walls, winter log fire, friendly staff, enjoyable, popular and interesting food (best to book), well kept real ales, and thoughtful wine list; plenty of seats outside, children's play area; cl 25 Dec; disabled access. £27|£8.95

STOCKBRIDGE SU3535 **Three Cups** *High Street (01264) 810527* Enticing-looking 15th-c pub with little dormer windows in a very low tiled roof, low beams, soft lighting, an engaging mix of furnishings, dark red walls packed with old engravings, fishing gear and taxidermy, and a relaxed and easy-going atmosphere, with daily papers, logs blazing in the woodburner, and friendly staff; good interestingly cooked fresh bar food, several decent wines by the glass and well kept real ales; no smoking restaurant. £24|£5.50

STUCKTON SU1613 **Three Lions** *(01425) 652489* Warmly welcoming restaurant with informal atmosphere, a neat airy bar, fresh flowers, very imaginative food inc local fungi and lovely puddings, a fine wine list, superb breakfasts, and charming owners; good atmosphere and friendly efficient service; cl Sun pm, Mon, last 2 wks Jan, 1st wk Feb; disabled access; comfortable bdrms. £37/2-course lunch £14.50

SWAY SZ2798 **Nurses Cottage** *Station Rd (01590) 683402* Small, immaculately kept no smoking restaurant-with-rooms with emphasis on personal service by the resident chef/owner; outstanding breakfasts in Garden Room restaurant (which can be enjoyed by non-residents, as can afternoon tea), imaginative food using herbs and vegetables from the neat garden, and an exceptional wine list; booking essential; cl 2 wks Mar, 3 wks Nov; children over 10; disabled access. £25.65

WINCHESTER SU4829 **Cathedral Refectory** *Visitor Centre, Inner Close (01962) 853224* Excellent totally home-made food in bright airy modern conservatory, lovely breads and soups, afternoon cream teas, good children's menu, a friendly informal atmosphere, and nice staff; cl 25–26 Dec; disabled access. £17|£6.50

Special thanks to Mrs M Webster, Mrs C A Turner, Phyl and Jack Street, James Avery

HEREFORDSHIRE

The essence of traditional England, with classic unspoilt scenery, peaceful countryside, beautiful black and white villages, good food too – great for restorative short breaks

Herefordshire is smashing for a relaxing break: you can stay here in great comfort for a modest price, and there is an increasing range of pocket-friendly places for enjoyable meals out. It's a scenic county, and driving or walking here is especially rewarding. The well signposted Black and White Villages Trail (a 40-mile self-guided car tour) takes in five of the county's timeless villages – Eardisland, Pembridge, Lyonshall, Weobley and Dilwyn. As you head W the peaceful countryside becomes almost bewitchingly untouched. Not many tourists or second-homers have reached here, even at the height of summer, and yet the civilised small towns have an abundance of art galleries and bookshops.

Attractive towns ideal for an unhurried afternoon include Hereford (worthwhile little museums including one on cider, as well as the interesting cathedral), Ledbury, Kington, Leominster and Ross-on-Wye. In fine weather, scenic Symonds Yat is a popular place for pleasant walks.

Although overall it's adults who get the most out of this county, some places have been designed especially with children in mind. With lots of opportunities to get close to the animals and an enthusiastic approach, the Small Breeds Farm Park and Owl Centre in Kington is our Herefordshire Family Attraction winner. You'll find enjoyable farm parks too in Little Marcle and Pencombe, and this year we've added an appealing animal centre in Kentchurch to the *Guide*. On a different note, families enjoy visiting the Neo-Gothic castle at Ledbury (spacious grounds, a yew maze and good play area) and elegant 18th-c Berrington Hall (children's orienteering course, an adventure playground and fun trails).

Other splendid houses are Brockhampton in Lower Brockhampton, and Croft and Goodrich Castles. Fine gardens range from the recently planted gardens at Hope-under-Dinmore to the product of several generations in Kington, and from the spacious arboretum at Queenswood Country Park to a little cottage garden near Ross-on-Wye. This is a good county too for cider-lovers, who will appreciate the tours and tastings at Weston's Cider Farm (Much Marcle), or a visit to Dunkerton's Cider Mill (Pembridge); for other local produce, head for the expanding craft centre at Bishop's Frome.

Where to stay

BRIMFIELD SO5267 **Roebuck** *Brimfield, Ludlow, Herefordshire SY8 4NE (01584) 711230* **£70***; 3 rms. Smart country dining pub with an impressive inglenook fireplace in the quiet, old-fashioned locals' snug, two other civilised bars with small open fires, a cosy no smoking dining room, super stylish food, well kept real ales, carefully chosen wines, and caring staff; dogs welcome in bedrooms

BROMSBERROW HEATH SO7333 **Grove House** *Bromsberrow Heath, Ledbury, Herefordshire HR8 IPE (01531) 650584 £75**; 3 spacious rms with bowls of fruit and home-made biscuits, 2 with four-posters. Wisteria-clad 15th-c manor house with dark panelling, open fires, beams, fresh flowers and polished antiques, and good evening meals at huge dining table using home-grown produce; 13 acres of fields and garden, hard tennis court, and neighbour's outdoor swimming pool; cl Christmas

FOWNHOPE SO5734 **Green Man** *Fownhope, Hereford HR1 4PE (01432) 860243 £69.50**, plus special breaks; 20 rms. Attractive Tudor inn with impressive oak-beamed lounge (the residents' lounges are no smoking), log fire, and generously served popular bar food; adjoining leisure club with large swimming pool, solarium, spa, sauna and gym; partial disabled access; dogs in bdrms and bar area

GRAFTON SO4936 **Grafton Villa Farm** *Grafton, Hereford HR2 8ED (01432) 268689 £48**; 3 pretty rms. Beautifully kept early 18th-c farmhouse with an acre of lawns and garden, panoramic views, and lots of animals; an open fire in lounge, enjoyable hearty breakfasts in large dining room using their own free-range eggs and home-made bread, and friendly owners; nearby inn for evening meals; cl Christmas–New Year; self-catering; disabled access

HOARWITHY SO5429 **Old Mill** *Hoarwithy, Hereford, Herefordshire HR2 6QH (01432) 840602 £42*; 6 cottagey rms. Cream-painted 18th-c building with the mill-race flowing through the flower-filled garden; log fire and books in beamed sitting room, good breakfasts and enjoyable evening meals, friendly helpful owners, and lots to do nearby; no smoking; disabled access; dogs allowed if well behaved

KIMBOLTON SO5461 **Lower Bache House** *Kimbolton, Leominster, Herefordshire HR6 0ER (01568) 750304 £67*; 4 charming rms. Carefully renovated half-timbered 17th-c farmhouse surrounded by 14 acres of grounds, with antiques and flagstones in the sitting/dining room, lots of prints and interesting books, delicious food using organic produce, super breakfasts with home-made jams, marmalade and honey, home-baked bread, home-smoked fish, and free range eggs, and a relaxed atmosphere; no smoking; children over 8; lots to see nearby; limited disabled access

KINGTON SO3156 **Penrhos Court** *Lyonshall, Kington, Herefordshire HR5 3LH (01544) 230720 £95*, plus special breaks; 19 elegant rms. Beautifully restored 13th-c Hall in six acres, with fine beams and flagstones, a magnificent hall for dining, a huge wood fire, and very good carefully cooked food using seasonal organic home-grown herbs and vegetables; they run regular food and health courses; cl Jan; disabled access

KINNERSLEY SO3349 **Upper Newton Farmhouse** *Kinnersley, Hereford HR3 6QB (01544) 327727 £60**, plus special breaks; 3 prettily decorated rms with hand-crafted items and their own kitchen and sitting rm. Attractive 17th-c farmhouse in the middle of a working farm, with a particularly welcoming helpful landlady, log fires, beams, sloping floors, good food (inc vegetarian) using fresh farm veg, colourful garden, and lots of walks; no smoking; self-catering cottage; partial disabled access

LEDBURY SO7137 **Feathers** *25 High St, Ledbury, Herefordshire HR8 IDS (01531) 635266 £95*, plus special breaks; 19 carefully decorated rms making the most of the old beams and timbers. Very striking, mainly 16th c, black and white hotel with a relaxed atmosphere, log fires, comfortable lounge hall with country antiques, beams and timbers, particularly enjoyable food and friendly service in hop-decked Fuggles bar, a good wine list, and a fine mix of locals and visitors; health and leisure spa with indoor swimming pool; dogs welcome

LEYSTERS SO5762 **Old Vicarage** *Leysters, Leominster, Herefordshire HR6 0HS (01568) 750574 £70**; 2 rms. Comfortable and friendly 17th-c farmhouse with Victorian additions in 18 acres with a two-acre garden, all-weather tennis court, and surrounded by the unspoilt north Herefordshire hills; antiques, enjoyable dinner on request, often using home-grown produce, and eaten around a big dining table; cl Christmas and New Year; children over 12

LLANGARRON SO5321 **Trecilla Farm** *Llangarron, Ross-on-Wye, Herefordshire HR9 6NQ (01989) 770647* **£50***; 3 rms. Charming farmhouse in extensive pretty gardens with croquet lawn, fishing and riding, and free range chickens and geese; beams and an inglenook fireplace in snug, comfortable sitting room, good breakfasts and Aga-cooked evening meals, and friendly owners; no smoking; cl Christmas–New Year; children over 12

ROSS-ON-WYE SO6024 **Brookfield House** *Over Ross St, Ross-on-Wye, Herefordshire HR9 7AT (01989) 562188* **£45**, plus special breaks; 8 rms, some with own bthrm. Part Queen Anne and part Georgian house with sunny terrace and little garden, and a view over the town; welcoming owners, log fire in lounge, and super breakfasts in big airy room; cl Christmas; children over 8; dogs welcome

WEOBLEY SO4051 **Salutation** *Market Pitch, Weobley, Hereford HR4 8SJ (01544) 318443* **£72**; 4 pretty rms. Friendly 500-year-old inn with good bar food and elaborate restaurant meals using local produce, quiet lounge with standing timbers and log fires, and small public bar; the restaurant is no smoking; children over 6; partial disabled access

WOOLHOPE SO6135 **Butchers Arms** *Woolhope, Hereford HR1 4RF (01432) 860281* **£39**; 2 neat, attractive rms with fruit and chocolates (shared bthrm). Family-run 14th-c timbered building with low oak beams and log fires in bars, friendly staff, lots of flowers, and decent food inc good breakfasts; lovely surrounding walks

To see and do

Herefordshire Family Attraction of the Year

KINGTON SO3055 **Small Breeds Farm Park and Owl Centre** (Kingswood, off A4111 S) Plenty of opportunities to get close to the animals at this welcoming little park, very much the kind of place that people like to keep coming back to (the owners say they often spot parents returning without the children). It isn't huge, and even the keenest animal lovers probably won't need to stay much longer than half a day, but there's a genuine enthusiasm for both residents and visitors that you don't always find at bigger wildlife centres, and the atmosphere is particularly relaxed and friendly. What's especially nice for children is that many of the breeds are miniature ones, so there are lots of pygmy goats, and miniature horses and donkeys – most of whom can be fed by hand. Also, quite a few rabbits, guinea-pigs and chinchillas to pet, and you should be able to see chicks and ducklings hatching most days. There's a nicely laid out owl centre (the highlight for some visitors), with all the British species and a few from overseas, and an attractive waterfowl enclosure with ducks, geese and swans. It's still a good bet in poor weather, when most of the animals are shown under cover, and there's a heated barn for picnics (good outdoor picnic areas too). The views and setting are a bonus. No dogs around the park; if you have one you'll be cheerfully directed to well shaded parking areas. Father Christmas is usually here in December. Snacks, shop, disabled access; open daily Easter–end of October, and most winter wknds, but best to check first then; (01544) 231109; £3.50 adults, £2.50 children.

Please let us know what you think of places in the *Guide*. Use the report forms at the back of the book, write us a letter or log on to www.goodguides.com

ABBEY DORE SO3830

Primarily the impressive surviving part of a once-huge 12th/13th-c Cistercian abbey church, with Early English features and an awesome stone altar. **Abbey Dore Garden** are attractive riverside lawns and gardens, with good views across to the ruins. Snacks (in 17th-c stables), disabled access; cl Weds and Mon, and Oct–Mar; (01981) 240419; £3. The Neville Arms is a pleasant nearby stop.

ALMELEY SO3351

Early 18th-c half-timbered Quaker Meeting House, contemplative feel; key in porch

ASHTON SO5164

Berrington Hall ▣ (A49) This elegant 18th-c house has a few activities that make it a reliable bet for families. There are a good few quiz sheets and trails to follow going round the house (50p extra), some designed for under-7s, others for older children, as well as an I Spy sheet (10p) for the beautifully laid out grounds. The house itself has lots of interest; the finely painted ceilings and Regency furnishings are memorably elegant, and the main stairway is splendid. Many rooms are furnished in a way that lets you think they are still in use: there's a fully equipped Victorian nursery and a tiled dairy. Also a good adventure playground and a children's orienteering course, and plenty of walks and pathways. Capability Brown laid out the grounds (the house was built by his son-in-law); the most famous feature is the 14-acre lake with picturesque views, but there's also an attractive woodland garden, and rows of yew trees. The walled garden has some venerable apple trees. Snacks, shop, some disabled access; open pm Sat–Weds from Apr–Oct; (01568) 615721; £4.40.

BISHOP'S FROME SO6647

Hop Pocket Craft Centre Traditional hop farm, its hundred acres a hive of activity in the harvest season, with pretty gardens and a plant centre. The craft centre (which they plan to expand in 2003) includes wine, jewellery and delicatessen – you can also buy hop bines, hop confetti and their popular hop pillows for poor

sleepers. Restaurant, tearoom, disabled access; cl Sun am, Mons exc bank hols, plus Tues Jan–Feb; (01531) 640323; free.

BODENHAM SO5151

Queenswood Country Park 170 acres of woodland and arboretum with over 500 tree varieties; also wildlife displays and good views. Meals, snacks, shop and infomation centre, disabled access; cl 25–26 Dec; (01568) 798320; free. The Englands Gate has good food.

BROCKHAMPTON SO5931

Extraordinary turn-of-the-century Arts and Crafts church designed by Lethaby; note that this is in the little village between Hereford and Ross-on-Wye.

CAREY SO5630

Delightful tucked-away village, with a charming pub, the Cottage of Content.

CREDENHILL SO4443

Escargot Anglais (A480) Part of the National Snail Farming Centre, with snail trails showing various species (you may even see hairy ones) and exhibitions. You can buy snails here; open Thurs, Fri and wknds by appointment only; (01432) 760218; £2.70. The Bell at Tillington does more orthodox food.

CROFT SO4565

Croft Castle The walls and turrets date from the 14th and 15th c, but the inside is mostly 18th-c, with an interesting staircase and plastered ceilings. Attractive parklands with avenue of 350-year-old chestnuts. Tearoom, disabled access; open Weds–Sun and bank hols 29 Mar–Sept, plus Tues July–Aug, wknds only in Oct; (01568) 780246; £4.20, £3 gardens only; NT. The Bell at Yarpole is handy for lunch. The brackeny expanse of Leinthall Common, scattered with cottages, is a quiet corner of Herefordshire where you can walk around the Castle's estate, and scale the modest heights of Croft Ambrey, an Iron Age hill fort with a view into Shropshire.

EARDISLAND SO4158

A gorgeous riverside black and white village, with lovely views along the river. Outside the Cross Inn (which has decent food) is one of Britain's oldest AA boxes, restored as a landmark (though not in its original location), and

Herefordshire

SHROP

Leintwardine

Lingen

A4110

Richard's Castle

Croft

Brimfield

Ashton

Aymestrey

Yarpole

Leysters

Lucton

Kimbolton

Titley

Stockton Cross

Leominster

A44

Kington

Pembridge

Eardisland

Lyonshall

Almeley

Hope-under-Dinmore

Ullingswick

Weobley

Bodenham

A49

A417

Eardisley

A4112

Kinnersley

SO

Winforton

A438

Bredwardine

River Wye

Moccas

Credenhill

Merbach Hill

Swainshill

Hereford

Dorstone

Golden Valley

Tyberton

Eaton Bishop

Grafton

Fownhope

A465

Abbey Dore

Kilpeck

Carey

Olchon Valley

Hoarwithy

River Wye

Kings Caple

Sellack

A466

Walterstone

Kentchurch

Llangarron

A40

2

Goodrich

Symonds Yat

0 Miles 5

0 Kilometres 8

GWENT

M I D   W A L E S

you can peep inside; there's a display on it in the Georgian dovecote across the road (free). The well signposted Black and White Villages Trail takes you 40 miles round the lanes via Pembridge and Weobley.

Burton Court ⛾ (A44 just S) Interesting old house with 14th-c great hall, collections of ship models, costumes, natural history specimens and railway room; also working model fairground, and in season pick-your-own. Snacks, disabled access; open pm Weds, Thurs, wknds and bank hol Mons end May–Sept; (01544) 388231; *£3.50.

EARDISLEY SO3149

Eardisley church 12th-c font with wonderfully vivid carvings of sinner being wrested from clutches of evil.

GOLDEN VALLEY SO3141 The B4348/B4347 Golden Valley road is a pretty drive, with particularly satisfying walks in the surrounding hills; the tucked-away village of Dorstone has an impressive prehistoric burial mound nearby (and the county's oldest pub, the Pandy). The remoter roads parallel to this, to the W, are also well worth the drive, through Clodock (delightful church) and Michaelchurch Escley (another good pub down by the river), or passing Craswall, with its memorably good Bulls Head pub.

GOODRICH SO5719

Goodrich Castle ⛾ This proper-looking 12th-c castle (built using the same red sandstone rock it stands on so that it seems almost to grow out of the ground) appeals a lot to readers. Still plenty to see, with towers, passageways, dungeon and marvellous views of the surrounding countryside. Snacks (summer only), shop; cl 1–2pm, Mon–Tues in Nov–Mar, 24–26 Dec, and 1 Jan; (01600) 890538; £3.60. These formidable ruins are a feasible objective for stout-hearted walkers from Symonds Yat, or could be a start point for Wye Valley gorge walks. The partly Norman Mill Race at Walford has good value food.

HEREFORD SO5039 Grew as a regional market centre, and still has its livestock and general market every Weds. For the rest of the week it feels very quiet-paced and old-fashioned, its streets, some pedestrianised, lined with handsome Georgian and other buildings; Church St is almost wholly medieval. The local council, unhappy with the city's rather too peaceful reputation, want to rebrand Hereford 'City of Living Crafts': Church St and Capuchin Yard will be developed as a crafts quarter, and they'll be adding tree sculptures too. Guided walks leave the Tourist Information Centre every day mid-May to mid-Sept at 11am (2.30pm Sun); they also do a ghost walk (7.15pm Weds Jun–Sept; £2). Wye-side walks give a pleasing view of the city, its spires and towers. The Bay Horse (Kings Acre Rd), Gilbies (St Peters Cl), Green Dragon Hotel (Broad St) and Stagecoach (West St) are all useful for lunch.

Cider Museum and King Offa Distillery 🏆 (Pomana Rd, next to Sainsburys) Cider-making through the ages, with huge 17th-c French press, original champagne-cider cellars, and a working cider-brandy distillery – offering free samples. Snacks, shop, audio guides, disabled access to ground floor only; cl Mon Jan–Mar, 25–26 Dec, 1 Jan; (01432) 354207; *£2.70.

City Museum and Art Gallery (Broad St) Natural history and archaeology, interesting bee-keeping display, and changing art exhibitions. Disabled access; cl Mon (and winter Suns) 25–26 Dec, 1 Jan and Good Fri; (01432) 260692; free.

Hereford Cathedral Nicely placed on the bank of the Wye, this largely Norman building has a lovely 13th- and 15th-c chapel, as well as the country's biggest chained library (the second biggest is at All Saints church, at the opposite end of the main st), and the famous Mappa Mundi, the largest surviving 13th-c world map. There's a splendid interpretative exhibition, with some computer displays; the map itself is shown in a specially dimmed room to preserve it. Meals, snacks, shop, disabled access; cl winter Suns, most of Jan, Good Fri, 25 Dec (tower only open July–Aug); (01432) 374200; Mappa Mundi exhibition and chained library £4, suggested donation for cathedral £2. Guided tours at 11am and 2pm Mon–Sat Easter to end Sept (£2.50).

Old House (High Town) Glorious Jacobean house with period furnishings and paintings. Shop; open Tues–Sat, plus Sun and bank hols Apr–Sept; (01432) 260694; free.

St John Medieval Museum and Coningsby Hospital Little museum and chapel dating back to 13th c, with armour and relics relating to the Order of St John and the Crusades, and a display on the pensioners who lived at the hospital in the 17th c; in the rose garden you can see the ruins of Black Friars Monastery, and a rare preaching cross. They usually do guided tours, ask the friendly staff; disabled access; cl am, Mon, Fri and Sun, all Oct–Easter; (01432) 267821; £2.

Waterworks Museum (Broomy Hill) Restored Victorian pumping station, with giant steam pumping engines, and smaller handpumps; you can try working some. Snacks, shop, disabled access; open in steam pms 2nd and last Suns of month Apr–Oct (open not in steam Tues Apr–Oct, Easter wknd, Spring and Aug bank hol Mons) best to check; (01432) 344062; *£3.

HOARWITHY SO5429

Glenda Spooner Farm This friendly and caring place, former home of the jockeys Michael and Peter Scudamore, is now a centre for the International League for the Protection of Horses, offering care and rehabilitation for equine victims of maltreatment. Snacks, shop, some disabled access; open Sat and Weds 11–4pm or any time by appointment; (01432) 840253; free.

Hoarwithy church Remarkably Italianate, full of mosaics etc. The village, nr the River Wye, is attractive.

HOPE-UNDER-DINMORE SO5252

Hampton Court's Van Kampen Gardens (A417 S of Leominster) In the grounds of a romantic-looking castle (actually a grandly fortified medieval manor), these new gardens mix old-fashioned formal planted walks interspersed with bridges to little follies, with carefully contrived wilder areas (woods, waterfalls in rocky grottos), and a classic maze around a small tower. The surrounding parkland gives river walks. Meals, snacks, disabled access; cl 24 Dec–4 Jan;

(01568) 797777; £5 river walk and garden, £4 garden only. The 16th-c Englands Gate over at Bodenham has good food.

HOW CAPLE SO6130

How Caple Court Eleven acres of peaceful formal and woodland Edwardian gardens overlooking the river. Open daily Easter–Oct; (01989) 740626; *£2.50. Also interesting medieval church. The 15th-c Green Man at Fownhope is popular for food.

KENTCHURCH SO4126

Barton Hill Animal Centre Most of the animals here have been hand-reared so there are plenty of opportunities for getting close to the residents; also indoor and outdoor play and picnic areas. Snacks, shop, disabled access; open Weds–Mon Apr–Aug, wknds in Sept, and 1–23 Dec; (01981) 240749; £2.50.

KILPECK SO4430

Kilpeck church This small Norman church in a delightful little hamlet has amazing sandstone carving inside and out, beautifully preserved (except for the more uncomfortably pagan bits which prudish Victorians tried to remove).

KIMBOLTON SO5161

Stockton Bury Gardens (A4112 S) Attractive garden covering four acres, good for a gentle wander. No children or dogs allowed. Meals, snacks, plant sales, mostly disabled access; cl am, all Mon (exc bank hols) and Tues, plus mid-Oct–Mar; (01568) 613432; £3.50. The ancient Stockton Cross Inn is handy.

KINGTON SO2956

Attractive border town by the River Arrow, well placed for walks. Antiques and bric-a-brac are noticeably cheaper here than – say – in Gloucestershire; one shop specialises in cigarette cards, by the thousand. On Mill St there's a little local history museum (cl Sun, and Oct–Mar; (01544) 231486; free). The Queens Head has good value food. The long-distance Offa's Dyke Path passes through town, descending into it from Hergest Ridge, NW Herefordshire's answer to the Malverns; at the far end across the Welsh border the ridge tapers into horseback width above Gladestry, while N of Kington the path goes along one of the best-preserved stretches of Offa's Dyke.

Hergest Croft Gardens (just W, off A44) The splendid result of inspired work by several generations of keen gardeners; some of the centenarian rhododendrons in the woods are of incredible size. Famous kitchen garden with colourful flowerbeds, and the national collections of birches, maples and zelkovas. Snacks, shop, some disabled access; cl am, and all Nov–end Mar; (01544) 230160; £4, children under 16 free.

KINGTON SO3055

Small Breeds Farm Park and Owl Centre See separate family panel on p.288.

LEDBURY SO7137

The spaciously leisured High St has some fine buildings: the old Market House, the Feathers Hotel and Ledbury Park House are famous for their well balanced 15th- and 16th-c timbering, and there are plenty of similar structures. From the Market House an exceptional alley of ancient jettied buildings leads to the partly Norman church of St Michael and All Angels, with an unusual spire tower detached from the main building, and its carillon ringing out a well known hymn every third hour. The Old Grammar School along here has been restored as a **heritage centre** (cl Nov–Easter; (01531) 636147; free). The council offices (Church St) must be the only ones in the country decorated with medieval wall-paintings; you can see these any summer wkdy between 11am and 4pm; free. There are antiques shops and a decent book shop, and the Feathers has good food. The road N towards Mathon (where the pretty Cliffe Arms does good lunches) has some fine views.

Eastnor Castle (just E on A438) This splendid neo-Gothic structure is just what you want a castle to look like, with stirring battlements and exaggerated towers, and some breathtakingly extravagant rooms. Begun in 1812, it's still very much a family home. The house was designed by Pugin, and the richly furnished and decorated rooms are quite atmospheric – particularly the red hall with its masses of gleaming armour. The wonderfully over-the-top drawing room is another highlight, as is the great hall, done out like an Edwardian drawing room. You can get children's worksheets to keep up interest. The attractive grounds have an arboretum, 300-acre deer park, and plenty of space for a picnic, but what younger visitors enjoy most is the growing yew maze which has three trails to make it more fun (£1 extra). They also have a rope maze, and Nine Men's Morris. In mid-Aug they usually have a week with extra children's activities, and you can stay in the house for the full castle experience. The outside looks especially dramatic in autumn, when the virginia creeper that all but envelops the walls turns a fierce red. Dogs are welcome on a lead in the castle and grounds. Snacks, shop; open Sun and bank hols Easter-early Oct, daily (exc Sat) July and Aug; (01531) 633160; £5.50 adults, £3.50 garden only.

LEINTWARDINE SO4074
This appealing riverside village is notable partly for its church – much bigger than usual for this county. The Jolly Frog does imaginative food.

LEOMINSTER SO4958
An attractive centre, the medieval streets almost lined with black and white timbered houses. The red priory church still has many of its original Norman features. There's a little folk museum in Etnam St (cl Sat pm, Sun, and all Oct–Easter; (01568) 615186; free). The handsome old Talbot has decent food.

Herefordshire Cheesemaking 🖾
(A44, 2m W) You can watch cheese being made by hand using traditional methods. Meals, snacks (inc ploughman's with their own cheese), shop, disabled access; shop and caf≥ cl winter Sun and Mon (cheesemaking only Mon, Weds and Fri 10–2pm); (01568) 720307; £2.

LINGEN SO3667
Attractive village prettily set among hills, with Kim Davis's renowned alpine nursery and garden.

LITTLE MARCLE SO6637
Newbridge Farm Park (A4172 W of Ledbury) Friendly farm park with rare and traditional animals, large indoor and outdoor adventure play areas, and tractor and pony rides. Snacks and picnic areas, shop, mostly disabled access; open Mon–Sat Easter–end Sept; (01531) 670780; £3.50, £1.50 for pony rides.

LOWER BROCKHAMPTON SO7055
Brockhampton Idyllic moated and timber-framed 14th-c manor house in attractive secluded countryside. Particularly interesting 15th-c gatehouse, and the ruins of a 12th-c chapel. Tearooms, shop, disabled access to ground floor only; cl am and Mon (exc bank hols), Tues, and Nov–Feb; (01885) 488099; £3; NT. The Trust also own the surrounding 1,720-acre Brockhampton Estate, with splendid views from its park and woodlands, marked trails and a sculpture trail. The Talbot at Knightwick is an interesting place for lunch.

LUCTON SO4263
Mortimer's Cross Mill Charming watermill on banks of River Lugg, still in working order, with exhibition on the decisive Wars of the Roses battle fought here in 1461. Open Thurs pm Apr–Sept; (01568) 708820; *£2. The Riverside at Aymestrey has good food.

MERBACH HILL SO3143
Reached by driving up from Bredwardine, and then walking from the top of the lane, this gives a view right over the Black Mountains, Herefordshire and Radnorshire. A short stroll along the lane SE brings you to Arthur's Stone, a prehistoric burial chamber.

MUCH MARCLE SO6433
Hellens Unspoilt manor house dating from the 13th c, with a bedroom (said to be haunted) where Bloody Mary slept, the portrait of Catherine of Braganza that convinced Charles II to marry her, and a coach and carriage collection. Teas; tours at 2, 3 and 4pm, open pm Sat, Sun, Weds and bank hols Easter–Sept; (01531) 660504; £4 (£1 gardens only). The memorial monuments in the village church are unrivalled in the area.

Weston's Cider Farm 🖾 Still alongside the family house, this has an engaging combination of modern equipment and old-fashioned atmosphere. Enthusiastic guided tours, liberal tastings, interesting ciders and perries. Meals, snacks, good shop with wide range of ciders, tours by appointment; cl Sun, Sat pm and 25 Dec–1 Jan; (01531) 660108; £3. The nearby Slip has good dishes of the day and outstanding gardens.

OLCHON VALLEY SO3029
Perhaps the remotest place in Herefordshire, a magnificent dead-end valley beneath the E flank of the Black Mountains. From the well signed picnic site nr Longtown a path heads up the Black Hill, an exciting knife-edge ridge, its end-on aspect strikingly triangular – this bit is known as the Cat's Back; after the trig point you can make a circuit by dropping down from the very head of the Olchon Valley, or carrying on over peaty terrain to join the Offa's Dyke Path.

PEMBRIDGE SO3958
One of Herefordshire's most striking black and white villages, full of fine timbered buildings inc a medieval market hall, the ancient New Inn, an art gallery in a former chapel (East St); (01544) 388842, and a lovely church with an unusual detached belfry where you can watch the clock mechanism.

Dunkerton's Cider Mill 🔟 (Luntley, 1m S) Uses ancient traditional local cider-apple and pear cultivars, for distinctive organic ciders and perries; welcoming atmosphere, free tastings, and good restaurant; tours, shop, disabled access; cl Sun, and 25 Dec–1 Jan; £1.50 for tours.

PENCOMBE SO5951
Shortwood Family Farm Working organic farm ideal for children, with hands-on afternoon activities like milking Daisy or feeding the pigs and calves, usually sheep-shearing May bank hol. Good play area. Snacks, shop; cl Nov–Mar; (01885) 400205; £4.50. The Wheelwright Arms in the attractive village does bargain food (not Mon).

RICHARDS CASTLE SO4969
St Bartholomew There's little left of the Norman castle which gave this village its name. The nearby church, dedicated to St Bartholomew, is a magnificent medieval structure with a detached tower which probably doubled as a look-out for the castle; the

views from here stretch over three counties.

ROSS-ON-WYE SO5924
Picturesquely perched on a sandstone cliff by the river, with markets on Thurs and Sat at the striking 17th-c market hall; there's a little **heritage centre** in here too; cl Sun Nov–Mar; free. The lower riverside part has attractive waterside walks; the Hope & Anchor here is good value for family lunches, and on Broad St the Eagle does interesting bistro dishes and Oat Cuisine has substantial vegetarian food. There are woodland walks in Penyard Park, SE of the town.

Kingstone Cottages (Kingstone; off A40 E at Weston under Penyard, towards Rudhall) Charming, exuberant cottage garden, not to be missed at midsummer for its profusion of old-fashioned pinks and border carnations. Also fine views, and tucked-away little grotto – looking out it seems as though you're waist-high in water. Unusual plants for sale; open Sun–Fri 6 May–5 July, or by appointment; (01989) 565267; *£2.

SWAINSHILL SO4341
Weir Gardens Delightful riverside gardens at their best in spring, with displays of bulbs along woodland walks, and fine views from clifftop walks. Paths can be steep in places. Open Weds–Sun (and bank hols) 13 Feb–3 Nov; (01981) 590509; *£3; NT.

SYMONDS YAT SO5517
Shared with Gloucestershire on the other side of the river, this is a spectacular bend of the River Wye through a steep wooded rock gorge, where peregrine falcons nest (the RSPB have an information area with a telescope); splendid Wye views, nature trails. Two inns on either side of the river are linked by a hand-pulled ferry (see Symonds Yat entry, in Gloucestershire chapter for times and prices), and there's ample (walkers would say over-generous) parking. It's a big tourist draw. The gorge has potential for more ambitious walks, following an old railway line along the river; to the SW an entertainingly rickety wire-mesh suspension bridge at the Biblins gives access to the W bank.
Jubilee Park Centres on a hedge maze

created for the Queen's Silver Jubilee; a lively maze museum tells the history of similar labyrinthine creations. Meals, snacks, shop, disabled access; open daily Good Fri–Oct, wknds only in Mar and Oct; (01600) 890360; *£3.50.

Splendour of the Orient On the same site as Jubilee Park, this has oriental water gardens, and an indoor tropical garden area with a fairytale-themed adventure playground; £2 (summer treasure hunts; £1.50 extra, Christmas special events; £2 extra). Snacks, shop (specialising in cane furniture), disabled access; cl 25–27 Dec; (01600) 890668; free entry to gardens.

UPTON BISHOP SO6327
Wobage Farm Craft Workshops
Several potters, a furniture-maker, wood-carver and jeweller; open wknds all year plus Thurs–Fri Apr–Sept; (01989) 780233; free. The Moody Cow is a good individual lunch stop.

WEOBLEY SO4051
In the very top rank of the county's black and white villages, with its long sloping green, and idyllic stroll out past the bowling green to the church; the Olde Salutation is good for lunch.

WOOLHOPE SO6135
The elevated country around here has a good variety of scenery for walkers; the views from Ridge Hill E and the more densely wooded hills nr Mordiford (where the Moon has enjoyable food) are among the highlights.

YARPOLE SO4765
The church of this attractive streamside village has an uncommon free-standing medieval bell tower. The picturesque Bell Inn has good food.

Other attractive villages, all with decent pubs, include Bredenbury SO6516 (despite the main rd), Little Cowarne SO6051, Lyonshall SO3355, Walterstone SO3425 (peaceful walks) and Weston-under-Penyard SO6323. Quiet country drives can link several attractive **churches**, such as Bredwardine SO3344, Moccas SO3543, Tyberton SO3839 and Eaton Bishop SO4439; or perhaps Fownhope SO5834, Kings Caple SO5528 and even Foy SO5928 with Brockhampton and Hoarwithy.

Where to eat

AYMESTREY SO4265 **Riverside Inn** *(01568) 708440* Black and white timbered riverside inn (new licensees this year) with rambling beamed bar, some fine furniture, log fires and a relaxed atmosphere; enjoyable food, well kept beers, and decent wines; seats by the water and in steep garden; comfortable bdrms and fly-fishing for residents; does get very busy at peak times; cl 25 Dec. £25|**£7**

DORSTONE SO3141 **Pandy** *(01981) 550273* Ancient half-timbered pub (Herefordshire's oldest), with a good mix of customers in the heavily beamed and neatly kept main room, a no smoking area, side extension and chatty parrot called Oscar; enjoyable bar food, well kept real ales, and lots of malt whiskies; picnic-sets and a play area in the neat side garden, and pretty surrounding countryside; cl Mon am. £20.25|**£7.25**

HEREFORD SO5139 **Castle House** *Castle Street (01432) 356321* Smart hotel near the cathedral with elegant La Rive restaurant and terrace that overlooks the river and garden; beautifully presented imaginative food using first-class ingredients (delicious nibbles and canapés, and wonderful puddings, too), some produce from their own farm, an extensive wine list, and courteous formal service; fine bdrms; disabled access. £32.95

LEDBURY SO7137 **Market Place Restaurant** *1 The Homend (01531) 634250* Pleasant bustling restaurant open all day for morning coffee, lunch and afternoon tea with home-made cakes, flans and puddings; cl pm, 25–26 Dec, 1 Jan; partial disabled access. £10|**£3.75**

ROSS-ON-WYE SO5924 **Pheasants at Ross** *52 Edde Cross St (01989) 565751* Attractive little restaurant with hard-working owners, simple furnishings, particularly good food using the best local produce, an interesting wine list, and relaxed atmosphere; open Thurs–Sat evenings only; well behaved children welcome. £30

SELLACK SO5526 **Lough Pool** *(01989) 730236* Attractive black and white timbered cottage in lovely countryside, with a log fire at each end of the beamed central room, flagstones and bunches of dried flowers, other individually decorated rooms leading off, interesting food, well kept real ales, several malt whiskies, local farm ciders, and a well chosen wine list; cl pms 25 and 26 Dec; well behaved children in snug or restaurant only. £27|**£7.50**

STOCKTON CROSS SO5161 **Stockton Cross Inn** *(01568) 612509* Neatly kept black and white timbered pub with an old-fashioned atmosphere in its heavy-beamed long bar, a huge log fire and woodburner, solid furnishings, a wide choice of enjoyable food, well kept beer, and good welcoming service; seats in garden; cl Mon pm; children over 6. £24|**£6.95**

TITLEY SO3359 **Stagg** *(01544) 230221* Attractive old pub with main emphasis on the two dining rooms, one quite big, the other intimate; well kept real ales, up to ten wines by the glass from a carefully chosen list, a fine collection of malt whiskies, and particularly good, imaginative food inc a formidable cheese range; helpful service; tables out in the garden, and lovely surrounding countryside; bdrms; cl Mon (exc bank hols and then they cl Tues), first 2 wks Nov, 25–26 Dec, 1 Jan; disabled access. £30|**£7.50**

TRUMPET SO6639 **Verzons** *Hereford Road (01531) 670381* Charmingly reworked roadside country hotel with good interesting food in the linked rooms of its pleasantly informal restaurant, a nice mix of country pub furniture and log fire in its civilised bar, cheerful young staff, good house wines and well kept real ales; tables out in extensive neatly kept gardens with broad views to the Malvern Hills; bdrms. £24.75|**£5.50**

ULLINGSWICK SO5948 **Three Crowns** *(01432) 820279* As well as a place for local farmers to enjoy their well kept ales, this bustling pub is very popular for its good imaginative food from an extensive seasonally changing menu (the choice is smaller at lunchtime); charming, cosy traditional rooms with hops on low beams, open fires, some no smoking areas, and carefully chosen wines; tables outside; cl Mon, 2 wks from 24 Dec; children must be well behaved; disabled access. £28/2-course meal £10

UPTON BISHOP SO6326 **Moody Cow** *(01989) 780470* In a quiet village, this cheerful and friendly pub has several snug separate areas, a pleasant medley of stripped country furniture, a big log fire, no smoking rustic candlelit restaurant and second small dining room, a good choice of enjoyable food, and well kept beers; children must be well behaved; partial disabled access. £23|**£6.95**

WINFORTON SO2947 **Sun** *(01544) 327677* Very friendly and neatly kept little pub with beamed rooms, individual assortment of furniture, two woodburners, particularly good interesting food inc 10 different cheeses for their ploughman's (they also bake their own bread, make their own chutneys, and smoke their own meats), real ales, and a sheltered garden with its own 18-hole crazy golf course; good bdrms; cl Tues, last 2 wks Jan; disabled access. £23.50|**£7.50**

We welcome reports from readers

This *Guide* depends on readers' reports. Do help us if you can – in return, we offer a discount on the next edition to people who've helped us with reports for it. Tell us what you think about places already in it, and anything extra you think we should say about them. And send us your ideas for inclusion in the next edition: places to visit, eat at or stay in, attractive drives or walks, maybe even unusual shops you know of. Use the card in the middle, the report forms at the end, or just write – no stamp needed: *The Good Britain Guide*, FREEPOST TN1569, Wadhurst, E Sussex TN5 7BR. Or log on to www.goodguides.com

HERTFORDSHIRE

Unexpected finds from peaceful country escapes to some strange attractions, besides grand houses and cheery children's outings

Especially enjoyable in fine weather when children can make the most of the excellent adventure playground, lavish Knebworth House wins the title of Hertfordshire Family Attraction of the Year. The Paradise Wildlife Park in Broxbourne (lots going on throughout the day) and Standalone Farm in Letchworth (learning about animals here is fun) are highlights for younger children, and this year we've added the busy working farm at London Colney.

Ruined Berkhamsted Castle makes a nice spot for a picnic, and other sunny day excursions include Aldenham Country Park and the uncluttered expanses of the Ashridge Estate. Elsewhere, the fine Jacobean house in Hatfield holds the national collection of model soldiers, and Rye House Gatehouse in Hoddesdon is a fine example of early brickwork. The sculpture garden in Much Hadham is a favourite with readers, and Cheslyn Gardens are an oasis of tranquillity among the modern developments of Watford.

Some enjoyably quirky attractions include intriguing decorative caverns in Ware and Royston, the outstanding zoological museum at Tring and a cleverly preserved Roman bath near Welwyn.

An important Roman town, St Albans has enough variety to occupy families for a day. Although Hertfordshire is one of the victims of the seeping urbanisation from London, there are still some very pretty villages dotted about, and clearly waymarked footpaths allow good escapes into protected countryside.

Where to stay

CHIPPERFIELD TL0401 **Two Brewers** *Chipperfield, Kings Langley, Hertfordshire WD4 9BS (01923) 265266* **£69.50**w; 20 comfortable rms. Comfortable and very neatly kept country hotel with relaxing views of pretty village green, dark beams, bow windows, antique settles, sofas and easy chairs, log fires, and good bar and restaurant food; pleasant nearby walks; cl 24–26 Dec for accommodation; disabled access

ST ALBANS TL1407 **White Hart** *Holywell Hill, St Albans, Hertfordshire AL1 1EZ (01727) 853624* **£63**w; 11 rms, most with own bthrm. Civilised former coaching inn with two bar areas, antique panelling, handsome fireplaces and furnishings, residents' lounge reached by barley-twist staircase, courteous friendly service, and good restaurant; children over 5

Please let us know what you think of places in the *Guide*. Use the report forms at the back of the book, write us a letter or log on to www.goodguides.com

To see and do

Hertfordshire Family Attraction of the Year

KNEBWORTH TL2220 **Knebworth House** (Old Knebworth) One of very few historic estates that appeals to children just as much as it does to adults, thanks to its splendid adventure playground, big enough to keep most active boys and girls busy for quite some time. In addition to the usual wooden climbing equipment and so forth, there are quite a few exciting slides, including the fantastic monorail suspension slide (where you hang on to a rope and slide back down to the ground), and the twisting corkscrew. Younger children get their own enclosure, Fort Knebworth (you can just see it as you go past on the motorway). Best of all, as there's no extra charge for this area, you can keep coming back during your visit; you may find a vintage London bus runs you between the house and the playground. All the play equipment is outdoors, so it's not ideal in wet weather, when they may close some of the features. Children also enjoy the miniature railway (which has a nice little steam train on bank hols and event Suns), and the Victorian maze, and with lots of space in the park for a picnic, to run around or kick a ball about, there's enough here to occupy families for a good lump of the day. With its turrets, domes and gargoyles, the house is magnificent; it was originally a straightforward Tudor mansion, but was spectacularly embellished by Victorian author Edward Bulwer-Lytton (best known today for coining the phrase 'the pen is mightier than the sword'), who wanted it to be a castle fit for the romantic characters in his novels. The same family have lived here for 500 years, so the guided tours take in rooms and exhibits from a variety of periods; highlights include the marvellous Jacobean great hall, an exhibition on the glory days of the Raj, and mementoes of former guests like Dickens and Churchill. A huge draw in themselves, the well restored gardens were designed by Lutyens, and include a herb garden laid out to plans by Gertrude Jekyll, and a delightful rose garden. An intriguing pet cemetery has memorials dating back to the mid 19th c. Lots of special events such as craft fairs and even jousting. The 250-acre park also has lovely woodland walks, and a church with a nave and chancel dating back to the 12th c. Dogs allowed in the park on a lead. Meals, snacks, limited disabled access; open wknds Easter–Sept, and daily in July, Aug, and spring and summer school hols – house open only in the afternoons; (01438) 812661; an all-in ticket is £7 for adults (£6.50 children), with a family ticket (two adults, two children) not bad value at £23.50. A grounds-only ticket (which includes the play areas and gardens) is £5.50, or £19 for families.

ALDBURY SP9612
A perfect village green, stocks etc, attractive houses, teas, two good pubs; good walks nearby (inc Ivinghoe Beacon – see Buckinghamshire chapter).

ALDENHAM COUNTRY PARK TQ1695
Plenty of space for children to run around in, with adventure play area, nature trails, and a rare breeds centre; open all year; (020) 8953 9602; free, parking charge £3. You can also go sailing here (020) 8207 3782; or fishing (020) 8953 4978; £5 for a day.

ARDELEY TL3027
Attractive thatched village with good food at the Jolly Waggoner, and a pleasant quiet drive along the lane down through Wood End, Haultwick and Dane End. This rolling countryside is very rural, with quite an East Anglian flavour – some of Hertfordshire's best walking territory.

Cromer Windmill 🏚 (just NW)
Partly 13th-c, lovingly restored, the last remaining post-mill in the county, its sails turning again after standing idle for nearly 80 years. Snacks, shop, disabled access ground floor only; open Sun pm,

Hertfordshire

BEDFORDSHIRE

Ashwell

A505

10

Letchworth

A507

Hexton

Pirton

6

Ravensburgh Castle

A505

8

A1M

Stevenage

St Paul's Walden

A602

Knebworth

Ayot St Lawrence

Watton-at- Stone

Welwyn

6

Ringshall

9

5

A414

Tring

A4146

Aldbury

Redbourn

4

Mill Green

Wigginton

Frithsden

8

St Albans

3

Hatfield

Essendon

Berkhamsted

Northchurch

7

M10

A414

2

Great Wood

SP

A41

21/
6A

M25

London Colney

Chipperfield

20

21A

22

23

24

Sarratt

19

6

Aldenham
Country Park

5

18

Watford

Letchmore
Heath

17

Bushey

M1

A4140

TQ

GREATER LONDON

M25

9

bank hols and the second and fourth Sats mid-May to mid-Sept; (01438) 861662; £1.50.

ASHWELL TL2639
Attractive village with some fine houses and an unusually tall church tower; the Bushel & Strike just beside it and the Three Tuns are both pleasant for lunch.

AYOT ST LAWRENCE TL1916
Delightful little backwater, with a very picturesque 12th-c ivy-covered ruined church nr the appealingly old-fashioned Brocket Arms; the existing church is an incongruously grand neo-Grecian affair. The village is conveniently close to link to a walk along the River Lea, which has been dammed at Brocket Hall to form a lake (in view from the public right of way). Shorter walks can start from Ayot Green, where the Waggoners has good enterprising food and an abandoned railway line is open to walkers and forms a useful link.

Shaw's Corner Much as it was when GBS lived here, 1906–1950; Shaw devotees will enjoy seeing his exercise machine, pen, spectacles, and even the soft homburg he wore for 60 years. The tiny writing shed at the bottom of the garden was designed to revolve and so maximise sunlight. Shop, ring to arrange disabled access; open pm Weds–Sun and bank hols Apr–Oct; (01438) 820307; *£3.60; NT.

BERKHAMSTED SP9908
Berkhamsted Castle (next to
railway station) The remains of this
Norman castle boast a proud history –
William the Conqueror acceded to the
English throne here in 1066, and it lays
claim to some of the finest earthworks
from that time, inc the only double
moat in Europe, quite striking when
flooded. When the sun is shining, it's a
pleasant spot for a picnic. Shop, disabled
access; cl 25 Dec, and 1 Jan; (01442)
871737; free; EH. The well run Old Mill
(A4251, Hemel end) has at least some
food all day.
BRAUGHING TL3924
(pronounced Braffing) Attractive village

with pretty 14th-c riverside church;
decent pub.
BROXBOURNE TL3306
Paradise Wildlife Park 🏞 (White
Stubbs Lane) Younger children should
find plenty to keep them amused at this
friendly little zoo and leisure park.
Residents include Brazilian tapirs, red
pandas, and long-nosed potoroos, and a
small woodland railway passes big
fibreglass dinosaurs. There's a busy
schedule of live shows and displays,
from their jolly themed parrot displays
to feeding the lions and cheetahs (a
highlight worth watching). Children can
feed the camels, zebra and other
creatures in the paddocks, and go right
up to the usual farmyard animals. A
good collection of bugs and creepy-
crawlies, falconry displays and
undemanding rides and amusements inc
a bouncy castle, slides, helter-skelter,
roundabouts, and a paddling pool.
Older children won't find it so exciting,
though there is crazy golf. Most is
outdoors, so better in fine weather.
Meals, snacks, shop, disabled access;
open every day, inc Christmas Day
(no shows then, and they don't charge
for entry); (01992) 468001;
£9 adults.
ESSENDON TL2708
The mildly hilly partly wooded country
around here is popular with wknd
walkers, with pleasantly varied village-
to-village paths. The Beehive over in
Epping Green is a good refuelling stop
for walkers.
GREAT AMWELL TL3612
Pretty conjunction of church, pre-
Norman Emma's Well and pool with
islets. The Waggon & Horses has
decent food.
Van Hage Garden Co (A1170) A
popular place with an excellent range of
plants, and animal gardens with
monkeys and owls. They have a
miniature railway most summer wknds,
and good special events at Christmas.
Meals, snacks, shops, disabled access;
cl Easter Sun, 25–26 Dec and 1 Jan;
(01920) 870811; free. The Waggon &
Horses just S has enjoyable food.
GREAT HORMEAD TL4029
An attractive village, plenty of thatch
and timbering. The old Three Tuns has
good imaginative food.

GREAT WOOD TL2704
(off B157 N of Northaw, where the
Two Brewers is a good stop, with a
view of the ancient church from its
garden) Pretty woodland walks.

HATFIELD TL2308

Hatfield House A great Jacobean
house built in 1611 on the site of a
childhood home of Elizabeth I; the
splendid State Rooms include portraits
of that Queen, and even her gloves.
Also the National Collection of Model
Soldiers, with over 3,000 exhibits. The
scented garden and knot garden
contain plants that were typical in the
15th and 16th c. Alongside is an
extensive park. Meals, snacks, shop,
disabled access; open Easter Sat–Sept,
house cl am, and sometimes during
special events. Guided tours wkdys
only; (01707) 287010; £7, park only £2.
The nearby church has a window by
Burne-Jones, and the attractive village
of Old Hatfield has a handsome old pub
(the Eight Bells). Beyond is the
extensive modern built-up area that has
now taken the Hatfield name.

HERTFORD TL3212

Some quiet older parts include the old
main Fore St, which has handsomely
pargeted buildings. There are several
antiques shops in St Andrew St (one in a
fine 15th-c house). So-called **Hertford
Castle** is in fact the 15th-c gatehouse
for Edward IV's original moated castle,
carefully restored and now occupied by
the council; open pm first Sun in month
May–Sept, for guided tours (and
throughout the year for private tours
and special events); (01992) 584322;
free. The partly Tudor White Horse
opposite is good value, and the
extensive riverside castle grounds (with
the massive flint walls of Henry II's
castle) are always open. McMullens
Brewery is a striking Victorian building
on the river. The Old Barge with tables
out by the Lee Navigation Canal has
decent food. Nearby Hertingfordbury
is an attractive village, between river
and beechwoods.

Hertford Museum (Bull Plain)
Cheery local history museum, in an
elegant 17th-c building; it has a graceful
Jacobean knot garden. Shop, disabled
access to ground floor and garden; cl
Sun, Mon, 25–26 Dec, 1 Jan and Good

Fri; (01992) 582686; free.

HODDESDON TL3809

Rye House Gatehouse 🏛 (Rye Rd)
The Gatehouse, a rare and fine example
of early English brickwork, is all that
remains of this 15th-c manor which, in
Victorian times, attracted so many
Londoners to the banquets held in its
malthouse that a station was built near
it. You can climb the steep spiral
staircase to the roof (there are new
displays inside for people who can't
manage them), and inside is an
exhibition on the Rye House Plot, an
attempt to assassinate Charles II.
Canalside picnic area, shop, disabled
access to ground floor; open Sun in
term-time, plus wkdys during school
hols Easter–Oct, best to check; (01992)
702200; £1.30. At the back of the car
park is the entrance to the **RSPB Rye
Meads Nature Rese**rve; new visitor
centre, shop, disabled access to five of
the six bird-watching hides; cl 25–26
Dec; (01992) 702200; £2.50.

KNEBWORTH TL2220

Knebworth House See *separate
family panel on p.*
Old Knebworth is a pretty cluster of
houses – and a good pub the Lytton
Arms.

LETCHWORTH TL2232

**First Garden City Heritage
Museum** The world's first garden city,
begun in 1903. The First Garden City
Heritage Museum (Norton Way S), in
the architects' charming Arts and
Crafts thatched building (Arts and
Crafts style furniture inside too), shows
the thinking behind this uniquely 20th-c
idea; temporary exhibitions too. Shop,
some disabled access; cl Sun, 25–26
Dec; (01462) 482710; £1 (50p
residents). The nearby Three Magnets
(Leys Ave) is a decent pub.

Standalone Farm (Wilbury Rd) This
farm has got something of an
educational bent, so it appeals most to
younger children with a genuine
interest in animals. Plenty of animals to
enjoy from shire horse and Shetland
ponies to rabbits, chipmunks and
guinea-pigs. Pigs and rare breeds of
poultry wander around the farmyard,
and two friendly Jersey cows take part
in milking demonstrations every day at
2.30pm (1.30 during school term). An

exhibition farm has a working beehive, model dinosaurs and various creepy-crawlies, and there's an outdoor play area next to a decent spot for picnics. Indoors picnic areas too, and most animals and displays are under cover on a wet day. There's a play tractor to clamber on, and around 170 acres of farmland to explore, with walks and an arboretum. In spring you'll find new-born calves, chicks and other animals, and can watch the lambs being bottle-fed. Snacks, shop, disabled access; open daily Mar–Sept, and Oct half-term; (01462) 686775; £3.50.

LONDON COLNEY TL1902

De Havilland Aircraft Heritage Centre ☒ (adjacent to Salisbury Hall, off B556) The Mosquito aircraft were developed here in secret from 1939, and the site houses a collection of 20 different De Havilland aircraft, as well as engines and other memorabilia, and a display outlining the history of the aircraft company. Snacks in verandah-style area in main hangar, shop, disabled access; open pm Tues, Thurs and Sat, all day Sun and bank hols early Mar–end Oct; (01727) 822051; £5. The Colney Fox (Barnet Rd) is a reliable dining pub, and there are pretty riverside gardens down by the bridge.

Willows Farm Village Best for children under 12, with enough at this working farm to fill a happy afternoon. Regular activities throughout the day (check the blackboard in the courtyard) from duck racing to animal handling and falconry displays, a good adventure play area and big guinea-pig village; also tractor rides and a boating lake, and you can have a go at panning for gold. In the summer there's a maize maze, trampolines and a bouncy haystack. Meals, snacks, shop; cl early Nov–Easter; (1727) 822444; £7.95.

MILL GREEN TL2309

Mill Green Museum and Mill Well restored working watermill with craft demonstrations most Suns Apr–Sept and Sats July and Aug, from straw-plaiting to love-spoon carving. Shop, disabled access to ground floor only; cl am wknds, all day Mon and 25–26 Dec; milling Sun pm, Tues and Weds; (01707) 271362; free.

MUCH HADHAM TL4219

Forge Museum and Cottage Garden ☒ (High St) Based around a working blacksmith, the story of such craftsmen through the ages, with an unusual bee shelter in the Victorian-style garden. Shop, some disabled access; open Fri–Sun and bank hols Apr to mid-Dec; (01279) 843301; *£1.

Henry Moore Foundation (Dane Tree House, Perry Green) The excellent sculpture garden here is much enjoyed by readers. Several works are displayed in the studios where they were made, while the larger ones are shown off against a backdrop of woodland, pasture and hedgerows. Snacks, shop, disabled access; open wkdys (exc bank hols) and Sun Apr–Sept for 90-min guided tour, must book; (01279) 843333; £3. The Hoops opposite has good food (all day on Sun). Much Hadham is attractive, with fine Tudor and Georgian houses, and a good specialist nursery (Hopleys); (01279) 842509.

NORTHCHURCH SP9609
Largely swallowed up in Berkhamsted, but notable for the ancient church where Peter the Wild Boy is buried; the George & Dragon is handy for lunch.

PIRTON TL1431
Attractive village; the village green is actually the remains of a Norman motte and bailey.

RAVENSBURGH CASTLE TL1029
Up in the woods above Hexton (where the Raven is a good family dining pub), this is an easily traced Iron Age hill fort – a pleasant stroll.

RINGSHALL SP9912

Ashridge Estate Right on the Buckinghamshire border and nr Whipsnade Zoo in Bedfordshire, 4,000 acres of unspoilt woodlands and open spaces. Plenty of deer and other wildlife (inc dormice, though you won't see them in daylight), and a monument to the Duke of Bridgewater. Teas summer pms, shop and information centre, disabled access; cl am, mid-Dec to Mar (monument also cl winter wkdys); (01442) 851227; monument £1.20; NT. The Greyhound and Valiant Trooper at Aldbury just below are good for lunch.

ROYSTON TL3540

Royston Cave (Melbourn St) Tucked beneath the pavement, this cave is thought to have been cut into the chalk which underlies the town by the Knights Templar in the 13th c; fascinating figures of saints and kings are carved into the walls. Shop; open wknd pms and bank hols Easter–Sept (otherwise by appointment); (01763) 245484; *£2.

SARRATT TQ0498
Long and attractive village green; the church is partly Saxon, and the Cock near it and Boot on the green are both good. There are pleasant unspoilt walks from here into the Chess Valley in Buckinghamshire.

SCALES WOOD TL4133
(nr Anstey) A pleasant strolling ground; the thatched Woodman at Nuthampstead (open all day Sat) has generous home cooking.

ST ALBANS TL1407
Though modern shops dominate your first impressions, corners of real antiquity are tucked away between and behind them. This was one of the most important Roman towns in northern Europe, and has some fine well excavated remains in peaceful surroundings. A stroll in search of other notable buildings (the Tourist Information Office in the Town Hall, Market Pl, has helpful guide maps) is rewarded by the surprisingly large number of decent pubs here. Down between abbey gate and park, the Fighting Cocks is based on an ancient building which had some connection with the abbey, and its interesting layout includes the clearly discernible shape of a cockpit. In the quietly attractive largely Georgian St Michael's St, the Rose & Crown is very civilised, and the Six Bells is on the site of a Roman bath house, though not visibly so. The Cock (Hatfield Rd) is worth looking out because of its bizarre history; its floors were found to rest on thick foundations of human bones. Worth a look if you're nearby are the **museum** (Hatfield Rd), covering the town's post-Roman history (shop, disabled access to ground floor; cl Sun am, 25–27 Dec, and 1 Jan; (01727) 819340; free), and **Grebe House** in the park nr Verulamium, a regional wildlife trust HQ with a woodland garden (cl wknds and bank hols; (01727)

858901; free). The B651 N towards Hitchin is quite a scenic country drive.
Clock Tower This handsome free-standing stone building has a bell, striking on the hour, even older than the tower itself. Exhibitions on the way up and fine views from the top; shop; open wknds and bank hols Good Fri to mid-Sept; (01727) 860984; 30p. Nearby, French Row is a narrow alley of timbered buildings jettied out over the street, right by a modern shopping centre. The Fleur de Lys pub here is a remarkable medieval building.
Gardens of the Rose (B4630 S) There has been some uncertainty about the future of these rose-filled showgrounds, the HQ of the Royal National Rose Society. If all is sorted out as we hope, they are well worth a summer visit, but you must ring to check before going, in case of closure. Snacks, shop, disabled access; usually cl end Sept–end May; (01727) 850461; £4, £2 when the roses aren't in bloom. The Holly Bush at nearby Potters Crouch has decent food (not Sun).
Gorhambury Two miles out (the other side of Verulamium's park) but peaceful enough to make you think it's the heart of the country, an 18th-c house with extensive assemblage of 17th-c family portraits, and some 16th-c enamelled glass. Open Thurs pm May–Sept; (01727) 855000; £6.
Kingsbury Watermill (St Michael's St) 16th-c watermill half a mile from the city on the banks of the River Ver, still with one working waterwheel and a museum. Good meals and snacks, shop, disabled access; cl over Christmas; (01727) 853502; £1.10.
Organ Museum (Camp Rd, 2m E of centre, off A1057/B691 junction) Tuneful collection of automatically operated dance organs and other musical instruments, inc Wurlitzer and Rutt theatre pipe organs. Commentary and recitals every Sun 2–4.30pm, and Sat evening concerts once a month. Snacks, shop, disabled access (but no facilities); open Sun pm only; (01727) 869693; £3.50.
Roman Theatre of Verulamium 🆓 Most impressive; not large by the standards of some others in England (room for over 2,000), but taking into

account its good state of preservation it's unique. Shop, limited disabled access; cl 25–26 Dec, 1 Jan; (01727) 835035; £1.50.

St Albans Cathedral Up on a mound, this has good views; its 11th-c reddish exterior uses bricks recycled from the Roman remains. Once the country's premier abbey, it suffered a little after the Reformation, and its fortunes didn't revive until Victorian times. It was touched up a lot then, but the majestic building does have many earlier features, inc 13th- and 14th-c wall paintings in the long nave, the Norman central tower, and some Saxon transept pillars. Meals, snacks, shop, disabled access; cl pm 25 Dec, and during services Sun am; cathedral free, around £1.50 for audio-visual show. The great 14th-c abbey gatehouse beyond leads down to a neat park, its lake and willow-edged stream packed with ducks.

Verulamium Museum This was the name of the Roman city; its remains are down in the SW corner of town, past the cathedral and attractive park (coming from outside, most easily reached by the A4147 off the Hemel Hempstead exit from M1 junction 7). The place to start is the excellent Verulamium Museum (St Michael's) with its lively interpretation of everyday Roman life, as well as jewellery, wall paintings and domestic items found nearby. Shop, disabled access; cl am Sun, 24–26 Dec; (01727) 751810; £3.30. Unfortunately the best site outside is closed (we hope temporarily) because of vandals, but signs take you to a well preserved section of the Roman town wall.

ST PAUL'S WALDEN TL1922
A quiet village which, with the rolling rather East Anglian feeling surrounding countryside, offers some of Hertfordshire's most pleasant walking. The Queen Mother was born at **St Paul's Walden Bury**, and a few times a year you can visit the Grade 1 landscaped gardens there. Snacks, disabled access; phone for dates; (01438) 871218; £2.50.

STANDON TL3822
Has some good timbered buildings in its curving High St. The Nags Head over in

Wellpond Green does nice fresh food.

TRING SP9211
Walter Rothschild Zoological Museum (Akeman St, off High St) Part of the Natural History Museum, this is made up primarily of the remarkably eclectic collections of the second Lord Rothschild, started when he was a little boy; thousands of preserved mammals, insects, birds, fish and reptiles. Snacks, shop, limited disabled access; cl Sun am, and 24–26 Dec; (020) 7942 6171; free (under-5s might find the displays slightly startling). The olde-worlde Robin Hood (Brook St, B486) has good food. Tring has a choice of canal towpath walks from nr the Grand Junction Arms pub (B488 at Bulbourne), where the Grand Union Canal branches into a part-abandoned offshoot, the Wendover Arm, and the still-operational Aylesbury Arm. (There's also canal access from the Boat down Ravens Lane in Berkhamsted, and the Fisheries at Boxmoor). For more ambitious walkers, the nearby Ridgeway long-distance path, heads off W right across southern England.

WALKING IN HERTFORDSHIRE TL3206
Large areas of this county are taken up by the northwards spread of London with continuous swathes of development, and also by the first early 20th-c New Towns, the garden cities of Letchworth and Welwyn, and their more modern successors Hatfield, Hemel Hempstead and Stevenage. But between and beyond these are good green windows of carefully preserved farmland and some more wooded countryside. These yield pockets of good walking terrain, though there is little that is really outstanding. A good point is that even in the prairie-like arable farmland that characterises large chunks of the county, the field paths are often in remarkably good condition and very adequately waymarked. Pubs handy for walks include the Crown & Sceptre at Bridens Camp TL0411 above Hemel Hempstead, Clarendon Arms at Chandlers Cross TQ0698, Two Brewers on Chipperfield Common TL0401, Black Horse at Chorleywood TQ0295, John Bunyan at Coleman Green TL1812, Fish & Eels at Dobbs

Weir TL3808 nr Hoddesdon, Three Blackbirds at Flamstead TL0714, Bricklayers Arms and Green Dragon at Flaunden TL0100, Alford Arms at Frithsden TL0110, Huntsman at Goose Green TL3509 (for Hertford Heath), Plough between Great Munden and Dane End TL3523, Cross Keys at Gustard Wood nr Wheathampstead TL1716, Five Horseshoes at Little Berkhamsted TL2908, Bridgewater Arms at Little Gaddesden SP9913, Crown at Newgate Street TL3005 (for Northaw Great Wood), Cabinet at Reed TL3636, at Thorley TL4718 and Half Moon at Wilstone SP9014.

WARE TL3513
Scott's Grotto (Scotts Rd) Built in the 1760s by the poet John Scott, this is one of the finest bits of romantic gothickry in the world, extending 20 metres (67 ft) into the hillside under a modern housing development, with underground passages and chambers decorated with flints, shells, stones and minerals. Wear flat shoes and bring a torch. Open Sat and bank hol pms Apr–Sept, or by appointment; (01920) 464131; suggested donation £1. Several private gardens running down to the quiet River Lea have antique gazebos over the water, neatly restored with crisp white paintwork. The A10 N of here is quite a pleasant road, with decent food at the Sow & Pigs.

WATFORD TQ1097
Cheslyn Gardens An unexpected pleasure in this largely modern urban area, with 3fi acres of woodland and formal gardens, a pond and an aviary; cl 25 Dec; free. The local museum (High

St) has a display on the Watford Home Guard, the basis for the old TV series *Dad's Army*. Shop, disabled access; usually cl Sat 1–2pm, all day Sun, bank hols; (01923) 232297; free.

WELWYN TL2315
Welwyn Roman Baths (just off A1(M) junction 6 – towards Welwyn on A1000, and counting M-way slip roundabout as 1st roundabout go nearly all way round 2nd roundabout – car park through two five-barred gates) Excavated before the construction of the A1 and since then rather ingeniously preserved within the motorway embankment, this Roman bath house is all that remains of a 3rd-c villa. Very good condition, with explanatory displays. Shop, disabled access (but no facilities); open pm wknds and bank hols Jan–Nov, and pms daily during school hols (exc Dec); (01707) 271362; *£1.

WESTMILL TL3627
A happy combination of neat green-tiled cottages and fine old church; there are pleasant walks nearby.

WIGGINTON SP9310
The landlord of the Greyhound here is very helpful with suggestions for walks; the 18th-c summerhouse in the woods is an odd find.

Other attractive villages, all with decent pubs, include partly thatched Barley TL3938, Cottered TL3129, Hexton TL1230, Letchmore Heath TQ1597, Redbourn TL1012 (despite motorway noise Church End with its workhouse and Norman church is pretty) and Rushden TL3031.

Where to eat

ARDELEY TL3027 **Jolly Waggoner** (01438) 861350 Cream-washed dining inn in pretty, tucked-away village, with lots of woodwork, beams and an open fire, a restaurant extended into what was the cottage next door, a relaxed and civilised atmosphere, well presented food using local produce, a good range of wines, well kept Greene King ales, and attractive garden; cl Mon; children over 7. £32|£7.50
BUSHEY TQ1395 **St James** 30 High Street (020)8950 2480 Modern, airy bistro with parish church nearby, and church-themed decorations, helpful young staff, enjoyable contemporary food inc popular daily specials, and reasonably priced wines; cl Sun; disabled access. £35|£10.95
FRITHSDEN TL0109 **Alford Arms** (01442) 864480 Fashionably refurbished and secluded country pub with imaginative changing food, well kept real ales, and good wines; airy interior, simple prints on pale cream walls with dark green or deep red areas, and an appealing mix of good furniture from Georgian chairs to old

commodes on bare boards and patterned tiles. £28.75|£9

LITTLE HADHAM TL4321 **Nags Head** *The Ford (01279) 771555* Sociable 16th-c country dining pub with a fine choice of around 20 fresh fish dishes every day, plus plenty of meaty or vegetarian dishes too; cosy linked heavily black-beamed rooms with old local photographs, guns and copper pans in the small bar on the right, well kept real ales, decent house wines, a relaxed atmosphere, and friendly efficient staff; no smoking restaurant (best to book for the popular Sun lunch), and tables in pleasant garden area. Hopleys nursery specialising in unusual hardy perennials is just down the road; cl pms 25–26 Dec. £20|£5.50

REED TL3636 **Cabinet** *High St (01763) 848366* Tiled and weatherboarded 16th-c village house, now a civilised dining pub with new licensees, with a small cosy main bar, snug, restaurant with stripped floors, winter log fire and simple mix of wooden tables and chairs, enjoyable seasonally bar food, real ales, and decent wines; disabled access. £20.35|£5.95

SARRATT TQ0398 **Cock** *Church Lane (01923) 282908* Cosy white 17th-c country pub, with a carpeted snug, oak-panelled lounge, and inglenook fireplaces; no smoking restaurant in a nicely restored thatched barn, generous helpings of well liked food (esp the daily specials), and real ales; benches in front, and seats on a pretty back lawn with country views; disabled access. £25.25|£7.95

ST ALBANS TL1307 **Rose & Crown** *10 St Michaels St (01727) 851903* Relaxed and civilised pub with traditional beamed bars, unevenly timbered walls, old-fashioned wall benches, and black cauldrons in a deep fireplace (big fires in winter); a huge choice of interesting and enjoyable speciality sandwiches with a few more substantial dishes, well kept real ales; lots of tables outside and behind in pretty ivy-hung yard with shrubs and roses, flowerbeds and attractive hanging baskets – a haven from the town's bustle, and the walk down Fishpool St is pretty; disabled access. £20|£5

WATTON-AT-STONE TL2919 **George & Dragon** *82 High St (01920) 830285* Civilised pub first licensed in 1603, with a smart but relaxed atmosphere, antiques, open fires, and daily papers, friendly efficient service, first-class imaginative food in bar (good value daily specials) and no smoking restaurant, and good house wines; cl Sun pm; children must be well behaved. £22.85|£7.25

ISLE OF WIGHT

Great family holiday island: good beaches, better than average weather, plenty of entertaining visits, attractive prices, and appealing countryside including dramatic coastal scenery

The most attractive scenery is in the W, the largest concentration of things to do in the E. It's worth coming just for the coastal walks – the finest in SE England. Inland are long curving chalk ridges (tracks often follow the crests) and forestry plantations with many signposted woodland trails. The island bus service is excellent; a week's bus pass is good value, as is a daily Rover road/rail ticket. Prices are quite low compared to the mainland, and for longer stays some hotels do good value package deals that include the ferry fare. In high summer the main resorts and places to visit get very busy. Even then, away from the main tourist haunts, much of the island is surprisingly unspoilt and little visited. Out of season the island feels fresh, uncrowded and leisurely. But many of the places on the island aimed at children close for six months over the winter.

A number of the island's family attractions have a good policy on return visits. A return visit within four days to Blackgang Chine and its Downend counterpart costs only £1, while to Brickfields Horse Country in Binstead it's free. Other enjoyable outings include Flamingo Park in Seaview (what's really special is the way that you can get close to the birds), Amazon World in Newchurch (an inviting taste of the jungle) and Sandown Zoo (lots of endangered species). The Rare Breeds & Waterfowl Park at St Lawrence is very prettily set, while ruined Appuldurcombe House is an atmospheric setting for the owl and falconry centre; we've added a new farm this year, too, in Porchfield. A nice variety of attractions at Fort Victoria Country Park in lively Yarmouth make it our island Family Attraction this year.

More adult-oriented places include Osborne House in East Cowes, the favourite residence of Queen Victoria (the enthusiastic guides are full of anecdotes), and the Dimbola Lodge arts centre at Freshwater Bay (interesting Victorian associations); there's an appealing 16th-c house at Brading. The dedicated dinosaur museum near Brighstone and Dinosaur Isle at Sandown are among the island's more specialised attractions. Ventnor has a smuggling museum, and good subtropical gardens.

To get here, the crossing takes about 30 mins – half that for the Portsmouth–Ryde catamaran, even less for the Southsea Hovercraft. The Lymington–Yarmouth trip is the most rewarding (you'll need to book in summer). Foot fares start at around £9.80 for a period return. A typical summer car return fare (inc up to six people) is around £95, with cheaper day trips, offers and bargains: (08705) 827744 for Portsmouth to Fishbourne or Ryde (passengers only), and Lymington to Yarmouth; (023) 8033 4010 for Southampton–Cowes; (023) 9281 1000 for Hovercraft Southsea–Ryde.

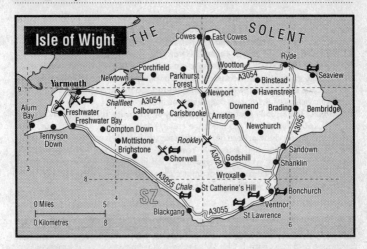

Where to stay

BONCHURCH SZ5777 **Lake Hotel** *Bonchurch, Ventnor, Isle Of Wight PO38 1RF* (01983) 852613 **£62.50***, plus special breaks; 20 rms. Early 19th-c country house in two acres of pretty gardens, 400 metres from beach; lots of flowers and plants in three light and airy lounges (one is an attractive conservatory), a well stocked bar, and enjoyable food in neat restaurant; cl Dec–Feb; children over 3; partial disabled access; dogs welcome in bedrooms

CHALE SZ4877 **Clarendon** *Chale, Ventnor, Isle Of Wight PO38 2HA* (01983) 730431 **£78***, plus winter breaks; 15 rms inc 3 suites. Warmly friendly hotel (and very well run Wight Mouse family pub, attached) with lots of charm and character, and good food, wines and real ales; excellent for families; disabled access ☺

SEAVIEW SZ6390 **Priory Bay Hotel** *Priory Croft, Priory Rd, Seaview, Isle Of Wight PO34 5BU* (01983) 613146 **£148**, plus special breaks; 18 individually furnished rms with 9 more in cottages. Former Tudor farmhouse with Georgian and more recent additions in grounds leading to a fine sandy private beach with a beach bar (good for lunch); lovely day rooms with comfortable sofas, books and magazines on coffee tables, pretty flower arrangements, imaginative food in restaurant with charming Georgian murals and elaborate plasterwork, and an informal, relaxed atmosphere; outdoor swimming pool, tennis, croquet, and a nine-hole par three golf course; disabled access; dogs in cottages in grounds ☺

SEAVIEW SZ6291 **Seaview Hotel** *High St, Seaview, Isle Of Wight PO34 5EX* (01983) 612711 **£80**, plus special breaks; 16 attractively decorated rms, some with sea views and private drawing rooms. Small, friendly and spotlessly kept hotel with fine ship photographs in the chatty and relaxed front dining bar, an interesting old-fashioned back bar, good imaginative bar food, and a highly regarded evening restaurant; cl 3 days over Christmas; proper high tea for children (must be over 5 in evening restaurant); partial disabled access; dogs welcome in bedrooms

SHORWELL SZ4582 **Westcourt Farm** *Shorwell, Newport, Isle Of Wight PO30 3LA* (01983) 740233 **£50**; 3 rms. Fine Elizabethan manor connected to a farm of 250 acres, with comfortable lounge/dining room, and a restful atmosphere; no smoking; lots of surrounding walks; children over 10

ST LAWRENCE SZ5476 **Lisle Combe** *Bank End Farm, Undercliffe Drive, Ventnor, Isle Of Wight PO38 1UW* (01983) 852582 **£40**; 3 rms, shared bthrm. Friendly, family-run Elizabethan-style farmhouse in five-acre coastal garden with sea views, and lovely paintings and furniture – it was once the home of poet Alfred Noyes and is still owned by the family; they keep their own rare breeds and waterfowl park, and are close to coves and beaches; must book months ahead (so popular with return customers); cl Nov–Mar ☺

VENTNOR SZ5577 **Royal Hotel** *Belgrave Rd, Ventnor, Isle Of Wight PO38 IJJ (01983) 852186* **£130**; 55 well equipped rms. Friendly Victorian hotel with fine sea views, neat gardens with heated outdoor pool, spacious and comfortable day rooms, cosy candlelit bar with open fire, good food in attractive restaurant, and helpful service; disabled access; dogs welcome in bedrooms

YARMOUTH SZ3589 **George Hotel** *Quay St, Yarmouth, Isle Of Wight PO41 0PE (01983) 760331* **£165**; 17 comfortable rms. 17th-c house by the harbour, with gardens leading to little private beach; a fine flagstoned hall, fresh flowers and open fires, a convivial bar and attractive residents' sitting room with marvellously relaxing atmosphere, imaginative enjoyable food in informal brasserie and smart restaurant, hearty breakfasts, and prompt courteous service; motor yacht for hire; children over 10; dogs welcome in bedrooms

To see and do

Isle of Wight Family Attraction of the Year

YARMOUTH SZ3589 **Fort Victoria Country Park** 🏛 (Westhill, Norton) The various attractions in the grounds of this 19th-c fort make a nice, traditional seaside family day out, very much in keeping with the old-fashioned holiday appeal of the island. The park itself is the big draw, best reached on foot with lovely sea views along the way. There are occasional guided walks, but at any time strolling along the seashore is enjoyable, with its fine views of The Solent. There's a mile or so of pebbly beach, good for running around but not ideal for swimming, thanks to strong currents. The 50 acres of adjacent woodland are also fun to explore, and there's plenty of space for picnics. Of the attractions – each of which you'll need to pay for individually (though after visiting one you'll usually save 10% on entry to another) – the one with the widest appeal is perhaps the aquarium, specialising in local marine life. Don't expect showpiece walk-through tanks, but the displays are just as absorbing; children like best its small sharks and starfish. Disabled access; (01983) 760238; £1.50 adults, 75p children. Next door's model railway will be the favourite with train buffs: the layout here is one of the biggest we've seen, and very highly regarded by devotees. Unusually, it's all digitally controlled. Good shop; disabled access; (01983) 761553; £3.50 adults, £2.50 children. Another highlight is the entertaining planetarium, with half-hour multimedia shows throughout the day; (01983) 761555; £2.40 adults, £1.60 children. If you're staying nearby, it's worth booking seats for one of their presentations on Tues–Thurs evenings at 8.45, when the planetarium's director does a longer, more individual show (£4.50), followed on clear nights by the chance to stargaze through the centre's telescopes (£3). There's also a maritime heritage exhibition, a bit like a local history museum, with plenty to read and look at, but interesting enough for anyone with at least a passing interest in the topic. Lots on local wrecks, and a replica of one of the 'First Fleet' ships that carried convicts to Australia. Disabled access; £1.50 adults, 75p children, £4 two adults and two children. The attractions are usually open only Easter–Oct, but the park itself is open free of charge all year round; like most seaside spots, in winter it has a certain wistful charm.

ALUM BAY SZ3085

The beach here is famous for its multi-coloured sands from the different rock strata in the cliff that runs down to it; 20 shades of pinks, greys and ochres, showing up most vividly after rain. The High Down Hotel towards Totland has decent food.

Needles Old Battery From Needles Park it's just under a mile's walk to this 19th-c Palmerstonian fort (you can't go by car but there's a half-hourly bus (01983) 532373); the parade-ground shows off two 12-ton gun barrels salvaged from the sea, and there's a World War I exhibition. A 60-metre (200-ft) tunnel leads to a look-out spot that gives stunning views of the Needles themselves, a group of wave-battered chalk pinnacles, and their lighthouse. Good views too from the 1940s-style tearoom; disabled access; cl Fri and Sat (exc July–Aug and Good Fri), all Nov–Mar, and in gale force winds; (01983) 754772; *£3.50; NT.

Needles Park Clifftop park with spectacular chairlift down to the beach, with wonderful views along the way; also crazy golf, a simulator ride, and you can create your own geological work of art by carefully layering differently coloured local sands in a glass tube. Meals, snacks, shop, disabled access; cl Nov–Easter; (01983) 752401; park entry free (though car parking is £3), then individual charges for attractions (£7 for saver ticket covering main attractions). Glass-blowing demonstrations at adjacent Alum Bay Glass, and tours of the Sweet Manufactory (cl over Christmas; 90p each); both have good factory shops.

ARRETON SZ5386

A pleasant place with a delightful 13th-c **church** (which has a brass-rubbing centre (01983) 527553). The lovely mellow stone Elizabethan manor house here is no longer open to the public, but nearby, the Country Craft Village has craft workshops, pub, and restaurant with home baking. The White Lion is good for lunch, and the cross-island Wootton Bridge–Niton back rd through here has quietly attractive views.

BEMBRIDGE SZ6488

Even in summer this is quiet for a coastal place, though with plenty going on in its yachting harbour, and a lifeboat station nearby. Though most of Wight's E coast is heavily developed, with the coastal path sometimes following roads and skirting large residential areas, Bembridge has the best opportunities for walks. Out on the Foreland the magnificent rock pools would keep any beachcomber happy for hours. The clifftop Crab & Lobster (Forelands), an easy walk up from the beach, has good food and fabulous views. There's also a good walk S to Culver Cliff, for more views.

Shipwreck Centre Maritime Museum (Sherbourne St) Six galleries of salvage and shipwreck items, and tales of pirates and mermen. Shop, disabled access ground floor only; cl Nov–Easter; (01983) 872223; £2.75.

Windmill Built in 1700 and used until 1913, this is the only surviving windmill on the island – much of its wooden machinery is intact. Shop; cl Sat (exc Easter Sat) and all Nov–Mar; (01983) 873945; £1.70; NT.

BINSTEAD SZ5792

Brickfields Horse Country 🏷️ Daily parades of horses in the summer, shire-powered waggon rides, tractor and pony rides, carriage and museum tours, porkers' paradise with the Lester Piglet Derby three times a day (Jun–Sept), and a farm corner. Informal show-jumping on summer Weds evenings (car boot sales Mon evenings). Picnic area, meals, snacks, bar, saddlery, shop, disabled access; cl 25 Dec; (01983) 566801; £4.95 (free return visit within four days). You can book country rides or riding lessons at next-door Upton Riding Stables here. The old White Hart at Havenstreet is handy for lunch.

BLACKGANG SZ4876

Blackgang Chine Fantasy Park This 40-acre family leisure park has an excellent policy on return visits: each ticket allows £1 entry for a second visit within four days. The liveliest attraction is an enjoyable high-speed water chute and Wild West town, and there are plenty more gentle rides to suit younger children, inc a badger-themed fairground. The most interesting parts are the maritime museum at the restored quayside, and the complete replica of a Victorian sawmill, inc working steam and oil engines. Lots of models of dinosaurs, goblins, and nursery rhyme scenes dotted around the gardens (pretty on summer evenings when they're illuminated). Also fossils and gemstones, a hedge maze, and several play areas, inc one for toddlers. Meals, snacks, shop, disabled access (some steep hills); open late Mar–Oct; (01983) 730330; £6.50 (children 3–13 £5.50). The Wight Mouse at Chale is an excellent family pub, and the A3055 in both directions gives fine sea and coast views.

BONCHURCH SZ5778
Much quieter than nearby Ventnor, with leafy lanes hugging the slopes and passing an unexpected tree-shaded pond; steep steps connect the different levels, and there's a quiet cove down below the cliff. The small 13th-c church has a lovely peaceful graveyard, and above the cliff St Boniface Down has tremendous views. The Bonchurch Inn is rather unusual, with its Italian landlord and food. For several miles along this section of coast, the cliffs have been and to some extent still are subject to massive landslides.

BRADING SZ6086
▣ Busy and attractive, with interesting monuments in its Norman church, and a pretty graveyard. The Bugle food pub is very well organised for families. The remains of a **Roman villa** has good mosaics (shop; cl Nov–Mar; (01983) 406223; £2.95). The road out over Bembridge Down to Culver Cliff gives fine views, especially from the Culver Haven pub at the end, nr the Yarborough Monument.

Isle of Wight Waxworks In the partly 11th-c Ancient Rectory Mansion, this is largely what you'd expect from a wax museum, with an adjacent natural history museum. Candle-carving demonstrations and shop open Easter–Sept. Open till 10pm summer hols; (01983) 407286; £5.25.

Lilliput Doll and Toy Museum Excellent private collection, with over 2,000 exhibits dating from as far back as 2000BC, and examples of almost every seriously collectable doll in Britain. Shop, some disabled access; cl 25 Dec; (01983) 407231; £1.95.

Morton Manor (off A3055 S) Friendly partly 13th-c manor house, in lovely landscaped gardens with ornamental ponds and Elizabethan turf maze. The little vineyard has an exhibition of wine-making relics. Tearooms, shop, some disabled access; cl Sat, and Nov–Mar; (01983) 406168; £4.50.

Nunwell House and Gardens ▣ (Church Lane, off A3055 NW) Lovely lived-in 16th-c house with later additions, interesting furniture and military and family memorabilia, and five acres of charming gardens. Charles I spent his last night of freedom here. Shop; open 25–26 May, Mon–Weds pm July–Aug; (01983) 407240; £4 (inc guide book), £2.50 garden only.

BRIGHSTONE SZ4490
Dinosaur Farm (A3055 SE) An enthusiastic working museum where you can watch and chat to the experts as they prepare dinosaur bones for scientific research and display. One of the most important dinosaur skeletons to be found in the UK was discovered in this area in 1992. Snacks, shop, disabled access; open Tues, Thurs and Sun Easter–Oct and every day July–Aug; (01983) 740401; £2.30. The Three Bishops has decent food.

Inland walks Inland, the island is characterised by long curving chalk ridges (tracks often follow the crests) and forestry plantations (with many signposted woodland trails). The hills N of Brighstone represent some of the pick of the scenery. The Countryman on Limerstone Rd is a good refreshment break, with fine views down to the sea.

CALBOURNE SZ4186
Attractive village with photogenic streamside thatched cottages and 13th-c **church**. It's worth getting here early to avoid the coach tours. Fine views from the Blacksmiths Arms, a good family pub on the Carisbrooke rd.

Watermill and Rural Museum ▣ (B3401) A six-metre (20-ft) waterwheel still powers this 17th-c mill, and the grounds have tame peacocks, a fire station, mini working water mill, bouncy castle, home-baked snacks, shop with stone-ground flour and so forth; some disabled access; cl Nov–Mar; (01983) 531227; *£4.

CARISBROOKE SZ4888
Carisbrooke Castle Ruins of the only medieval castle on the island, between 1647 and 1648 home to the imprisoned Charles I (his daughter died here in 1650). Some later buildings behind the imposing gatehouse and walls, and entertaining demonstrations of how donkeys drew water from one of the medieval wells. Shop, summer café, disabled access to ground floor; cl 24–26 Dec, 1 Jan; (01983) 522107; £4.50; EH. The Eight Bells above the waterfowl lake has decent food and good Solent views.

COMPTON DOWN SZ3785
Another good place for walks on this S coast, a hogsback grassy hill E of Freshwater Bay; circular walks can take in the coast path along Compton Bay – one of the island's best beaches, not touristy, with impressive cliff views (NT car park).

COWES SZ4995
Stylish and lively, very much centred on its yachting connections, with interesting buildings and shops inc fascinating ships' chandlers in the long narrow High St, and the battery of over 20 brass cannons used to start the yacht races down by the harbour. The Duke of York (Mill Hill Rd) and Globe (The Parade) have enjoyable food inc lots of seafood. Seafaring collections at the small Maritime Museum in the public library on Beckford Rd (cl Thurs, Sun and bank hols; (01983) 823847; free), and at the pretty Sir Max Aitken Museum (open Tues–Sat May–Sept; (01983) 292191; £1).

DOWNEND SZ5387
Robin Hill Country Park A very useful retreat for families, particularly those with younger children who want to run around. Like its stablemate Blackgang Chine, it has a few rather dated-looking representations of trolls and the like, but scores more highly for rides such as the pirate ship, the 400-metre toboggan run (best for older children, £1 extra) and the motion-platform cinema. Boasting good play areas, with underground tunnels and assault course equipment, the park also has a pitch and putt course, look-out tower, wooden maze, and plenty of space for football and basketball. An interactive wildlife area has recently been added. Paths and trails wind through the woodland. Meals, snacks, shop, disabled access but rather hilly in parts; cl 2 Nov–31 Mar; (01983) 527352; £5.95 if you're over 1.1 metre, £4.50 if under; (good value £1 return ticket allows a second visit within four days). The nearby Hare & Hounds is a useful family dining pub, open all day.

EAST COWES SZ5194
Osborne House (1m SE) Queen Victoria's favourite residence, where she died in 1901; the state and private apartments haven't changed much since. Designed to resemble an Italian villa, by Prince Albert with professional help from Thomas Cubitt, it's a striking place. Albert and his wife were also responsible for the original layout of the fine formal gardens, which seem filled with every conceivable English tree, masses of roses and clematis. The refurbished Durbar Wing is filled with opulent gifts to Victoria from the people of India. Swiss Cottage is where the Royal children learnt cooking and gardening. The house featured in the film *Mrs Brown*. Snacks, shop, some disabled access; cl 25–26 Dec, Jan 1; (01983) 200022; *£7.50; EH. Down on the River Medina, the beautifully placed Folly Inn has an appropriately nautical atmosphere.

Whippingham church Said to have been another of Prince Albert's designs, and a good deal more eccentric than Osborne House: a bizarre mix of different styles.

FRESHWATER SZ3386
A very extended rather sprawling village, with a charming quiet core. The picturesque 20th-c thatched church includes quite a few Tennyson family memorials, and beyond it a causeway crosses the head of the Yar estuary. The Red Lion has good food, and the Vine has a pleasant terrace for warm days. There are fine walks nearby, and Hill Farm has riding.

FRESHWATER BAY SZ3485
Dimbola Lodge (Terrace Lane) When the photography pioneer Julia Cameron lived here in the 1860/70s regular guests (and sitters) included Edward Lear, Lewis Carroll, Ellen Terry and her next-door neighbour Alfred

Lord Tennyson. Vacant for years (and very nearly demolished), the restored house now proudly displays her ground-breaking portraits, with changing exhibitions by contemporary artists; summer music recitals. Restaurant (good vegetarian meals), shop, disabled access; cl Mon (exc bank hols and summer hols), and five days over Christmas and New Year; (01983) 756814; *£3.50.

GODSHILL SZ5281
Best appreciated in winter, when the coach parties that descend on the tearooms and quaint little streets have gone home. Plenty of famously pretty thatched cottages, and a good 15th-c church, with interesting 15th-c wall painting. (Shanklin Rd). The Old Smith and Gardens is a little gift centre based around a former blacksmith's forge with an aviary of exotic birds, and a garden in the shape of the island itself (meals, snacks, disabled access; (01983) 840364; cl 25–26 Dec, gardens cl Oct–Mar; free). The Griffin is a decent family pub with a good play area (and maze), and the village is an inland starting point for a good walk via the Worsley Trail on to Stenbury Down (radio masts, but redeemed by wide views), then back via the atmospherically ruinous Appuldurcombe House and passing through a huge estate gateway.
Model Village (High St) Painstakingly re-creates old Shanklin, its Chine Valley, and Godshill in miniature (there's even a model model village). Shop, disabled access; cl Nov–Feb; (01983) 840270; £2.75.
Natural History Centre 🏛 (High St) Decent collection of fossils and minerals, and lots and lots of different sea shells; jewellery shop, disabled access; cl Jan and first 2 wks Feb; (01983) 840333; *£1.50.
Nostalgia Toy Museum (High St) Lots of post-war toys and die-cast model cars; fans of Dinky, Corgi and Matchbox toy cars will be happy here; cl Nov–Easter; (01983) 840181, £1.50.

HAVENSTREET SZ5589
Isle of Wight Steam Railway Well restored railway with very pleasant 10-mile trip from Wootton to Smallbrook

Junction nr Ryde (where you can change directly on to the main line). Vintage engines and rolling stock, and related memorabilia displayed in the old gasworks at Havenstreet Station. Meals, snacks, shop; open Apr–Oct (daily Jun–Sept); phone for timetable, (01983) 882204; £7.50. The Island Liner day ticket (£9) includes the steam railway and travel on all regular trains on the island. The White Hart (with lots of loco prints) does good generous food.

MOTTISTONE SZ4083
Charming old village with a well in the centre of the green; even the bus shelter is stone-built. The Bluebell Wood opposite the church is lovely in spring, and the picture-book thatched Sun over at Hulverstone has imaginative food.
Mottistone Manor The fine gardens with sea views are open pm only Sun and bank hols and all day Tues and Weds Apr–Oct; Teas, shop, some disabled access; (01983) 741302; £2.60; NT. The manor house, medieval with Elizabethan additions, is open Aug bank hol only.

NEWCHURCH SZ5685
Amazon World (Watery Lane, A3056) Among the 200 species are everything from anteaters to marmosets, tree porcupines, and crocodiles, through toucans and flamingos, to tarantulas and terrapins, and this year there's a new penguin pool. Some of the bigger animals are outdoors, but as most of the exhibition is under cover, it's enjoyable in any weather. Divided into several areas, it starts with the story of the rain forests, then goes on to look at how man lives and works in them, the damage that's been done to rain forests, and a look at the campaigns to reverse that. As well as twice-daily falconry displays (weather permitting) at 12.30 and 3.30pm, they have meet the animal sessions every day at 2pm, where keepers show off three animals at a time. There's an adventure playground, with a separate area for under-5s. Meals, snacks, picnic areas, shop, disabled access; cl 25 Dec and first week in Jan; (01983) 867122; £5.50 (£4.25 children 3–14).

NEWPORT SZ5089
The island's capital, with a good deal of character, some fine old Georgian houses, and warm red brick 18th-c buildings down by the quay. It's the main place on the island for antiques shops. The parish church of St Thomas is worth a look – it has an interestingly carved Jacobean pulpit and a 19th-c memorial to Charles I's daughter. The 17th-c Wheatsheaf nearby is good for lunch. The Quay Arts Centre (Sea St) has changing exhibitions and craft fairs monthly on Sat; (01983) 822490. The back road to Brading has pleasant views.
Classic Boat Museum 🎫 (The Quay) Vintage motor and sailing boats inc the oldest lifeboat in the country, and a 1910 wooden launch used for Thames cruises; you can watch some of the boats being restored; shop; disabled access; cl Mon, and Nov–Apr exc Tues and Sat ams; (01983) 533493; *£3.
Roman Villa (Cypress Rd) Well preserved baths and reconstructed rooms on the site of 3rd-c Roman villa, with an informative museum; also Roman garden. Shop, limited disabled access; cl Nov–Feb and am Sun; (01983) 529720; £2.
NEWTOWN SZ4290
For a while this was the island's capital, but it began a slow decline after a disastrous fire in 1377, and eventually faded out altogether – what used to be rich merchants' streets are now just grassy tracks. The Old Town Hall, rebuilt in 1699 but now left stranded and unusually isolated from any houses, is all that's left to mark the once thriving town; open pm Mon, Weds and Sun Apr–Oct, plus pm Tues and Thurs in July and Aug, Good Fri and Easter Sat; (01983) 531785; *£1.60; NT. Rewarding walks for bird-watchers at the nearby nature reserve. The New Inn at Shalfleet has good seafood.
Newtown Nature Reserve On the N coast, this has walks around the tranquil Norfolk-like creeks of the Newtown/Clamerkin estuaries, but there are few circular routes; from the village a boardwalk leads out into the heart of the reserve within a few minutes.
PARKHURST FOREST SZ4891
Just W of the prison, this is a couple of miles across, with plenty of signposted paths and a good chance of seeing red squirrels.
PORCHFIELD SZ4590
Colemans Animal Farm Pet and farm animals to handle and feed, two big straw fun barns, adventure play area, mini farm with pedal tractors, milking demonstrations, tearoom and barbecue area in 16th-c courtyard. Disabled access to most areas; cl Mon exc bank hols and school hols; (01983) 522831; £3.
RYDE SZ5992
Now the biggest town here, with a long triple pier, good sandy beaches, and a full set of holiday-resort amusements – just right for a straightforward family holiday. English Heritage has restored some of the buildings in the Old High St as part of its nationwide 'humble heritage' scheme. Tours and tastings at Rosemary Vineyard on Smallbrook Lane; (01983) 811084; £2
National Wireless Museum (Puckpool Hill, off Seaview toll rd) This tells the story of broadcasting from 1922 onwards, inc demonstrations of how the first radio sets sounded. Snacks, shop, disabled access; usually open pm wknds Oct–Apr and pm daily in summer; (01983) 567665; free.
SANDOWN SZ6084
All the usual things for a family beach holiday – pier, boat trips, canoeing lake, discos – and a fine beach. The new Ocean Deck (Esplanade) has tasty food inc seafood from their own boat. You can tour the partly underground winery of **Adgestone Vineyard** on Upper Rd, (01983) 402503; may close one day a week in winter; £3.50 for self-guided tour.
Dinosaur Isle 🎫 (Culver Parade) Housed in a building shaped like a pterosaur, displays include dinosaur skeletons, models, experts at work on dinosaur bones in an open laboratory, hands-on activities, fossil and rock collections and guided fossil walks (must be booked). Shop, disabled access; cl Christmas and New Year; (01983) 404344; *£4.60.
Sandown Zoo Rare and endangered animals such as a white tiger, panthers and leopards, and primates. Meals, snacks, shop, disabled access; open daily

Apr–Oct; (01983) 403883; £5.95.

SEAVIEW SZ6291

A timelessly quiet retreat, with sedate streets of unassuming villas; the Seaview Hotel does very good lunches.

Flamingo Park Wildlife Encounter (B3330) Attractively laid out in spacious landscaped grounds, this friendly and nicely unspoilt place has far more than just flamingos. Events and demonstrations throughout the day include feeding penguins, pelicans, macaws and parrots; there's a free-flying display of brightly coloured exotic birds (some tame enough to feed from your hand), owls, and a penguin pool. As well as a new wallaby walkabout (as the name suggests you can walk with them), there are beavers and red squirrels, with hands-on opportunities at pets' corner. You can usually feed their koi and huge mirror carp. Good keepers' talks try to bring out the birds' individual characteristics, as well as passing on a conservation message. No dogs, snacks, shop, picnic areas, disabled access; cl Nov–Mar; (01983) 612153; £5.75

SHANKLIN SZ5881

Shanklin Chine 🖼 Walk along quite glorious verdant natural gorge, illuminated at dusk, with magnificent 14-metre (45-ft) waterfall. A heritage centre gives details of rare flora, nature trails and life in Victorian Shanklin. Snacks, shop; cl Nov–Mar; (01983) 866432; *£3.50. Down on the beach, the thatched Fishermans Cottage is charmingly placed for lunch (cl Nov–Mar), and up at the top the Chine Inn is a good family pub (no food Sun evening or Mon).

SHORWELL SZ4583

One of the few really pretty villages on the island to have escaped a flood of tourist interest, with charming streamside thatched cottages and a fine church; the attractive Crown is very good for lunch.

ST CATHERINE'S HILL SZ4978

Capped by the ruins of a 14th-c oratory, a short walk up from the coast path further E; you can walk on along a ridge to the prominent Hoy's Monument at the far end of St Catherine's Down. The coast path meanwhile skirts the undercliff of St Catherine's Point, the isle's S tip, which has a modern working lighthouse; there are several other paths through the undercliff here.

ST LAWRENCE SZ5276

Isle of Wight Glass (Old Park Rd) You can watch glass-making (not wknds), lovely displays, and shop. Disabled access; cl winter wknds and for 3 wks at Christmas; (01983) 853526; 70p. The nearby St Lawrence Inn has good food (and brews its own beer).

Rare Breeds & Waterfowl Park 🖼 (Undercliff Drive) Good rare breeds centre in a really lovely setting, covering 30 secluded coastal acres, with fine views out to sea. The range of animals takes in miniature horses, deer, pigs, otter, llamas, meerkats, owls, and delightful pygmy goats. There are 50 or so species of waterfowl and poultry, a temperate waterfall house with free-flying birds, a play area, and plenty of animals to pet; they've recently built a guinea-pig village. Meals, snacks (with lots of space for picnics), shop; cl Nov–Easter; (01983) 852649; £4.90. They do B&B in the attractive old house, and there's a bus stop just outside.

TENNYSON DOWN SZ3285

On Wight's W tip, the best place of all for walkers here: a friendly grassy ridge and cliff walk rolled into one, with views over most of the island and across to the mainland. You pass the monument to Alfred Lord Tennyson (who lived nearby and loved this place), and the walk culminates in spectacular fashion above the Needles. You can walk the entire ridge from Freshwater Bay (summer bus service from Alum Bay to bring you back: (01983) 532373), or make a round walk from Alum Bay car park, past the Needles Old Battery and along to the monument, then up on to Headon Warren before going down to Alum Bay. The High Down Hotel (B3322) is another start point.

VENTNOR SZ5476

Relatively untouristy little town up on the cliff, the fairly restrained and decorous seafront down below linked to it by a tortuously steep loop of road; between them perched on ledges among the trees are quite a number of

Victorian villas – many of them still private houses rather than guesthouses. Its great pride is the **Botanic Garden**, where an exceptional collection of sub-tropical plants make the most of the mild climate (visitor centre, meals, snacks; free). The Garden Tavern here has decent food and sea views. The **Heritage Museum** on Spring Hill is good for local history (limited disabled access; cl 12.30–2, Weds and Sat pm, all Sun, and Nov to mid-May; 75p). The Spyglass is an interesting pub with superb sea views, and the seafront Mill Bay is good too.

Bonchurch Down Above Ventnor, this has unsightly radar installations but gives walkers fine views.

Museum of Smuggling History In the Botanic Garden (or more correctly under it), this demonstrates the tricks smugglers past and present have used to sneak in wool, brandy, tobacco or drugs. Shop; cl Oct–Mar; (01983) 853677; £2.80.

Undercliff Formed from the irregular masses of earth which have come to rest below, with often rocky chasms between each other and the cliff itself. Sometimes planted and sometimes with profuse natural vegetation, the resulting scenery is unlike anything else on the island, with quite a sub-tropical aspect. Some of the attractions along here we've listed under St Lawrence.

WOOTTON SZ5290

A terminus for the steam railway (see Havenstreet entry). It has an attractive partly Norman church. The Sloop down overlooking the creek is a reliable food pub.

Butterfly World & Fountain World (Staplers Rd) Tropical butterfly house, and Small World with fairylit fairytale scenes and jumping-jet fountains, next to a five-acre garden centre with water gardens and more fountains. Snacks, shop, disabled access cl Nov–Easter; (01983) 883430; *£4.75.

WROXALL SZ5480

Appuldurcombe House 🏛 (off B3327 W) Intriguing shell of Palladian house, nestling among grounds beautifully landscaped by Capability Brown. You can still catch something of the atmosphere of the days when this was one of the grandest houses on the island. The stables have been converted into holiday cottages, and the old laundry and brewhouse into an owl and falconry centre (daily flying displays at 11am, 1pm and also 3pm in summer) – Henry VIII is said to have stayed here with his falconers. Snacks, shop, some disabled access, though gravel paths may prove difficult for wheelchairs; cl 15 Dec 2002–mid-Feb 2003; (01983) 852484; *£4.75 for house, grounds and falconry centre, £2 house, grounds only. The Four Seasons (B3327 S) has enjoyable food.

YARMOUTH SZ3589

A lively place, its old harbour busy with yachts in summer. The **castle** was built as part of Henry VIII's coastal defences; it's in an excellent state, and you can see the Master Gunner's surprisingly homely parlour and kitchen. Outside, the open gun platform has good views of the harbour. Shop, disabled access to ground floor; cl Nov–Mar; (01983) 760678; £2.30; EH. The Wheatsheaf serves popular food all day.

Fort Victoria Country Park See *separate family panel on p.310.*

Yar estuary The unspoilt reed-fringed estuary is skirted by a footpath along the former railway line S from Yarmouth.

Where to eat

CARISBROOKE SZ4888 **Blacksmiths Arms** *Calbourne Rd (01983)* 529263 Very neatly kept pub with fine views over The Solent from the simply built and furnished dining extension, and from tables in the smallish back garden; several bars, four real ales, varied and imaginative food cooked by the welcoming Bavarian landlord (Bavarian-sized helpings, too) inc enjoyable platters and various German dishes, and polite helpful service. £21|**£6.95**

FRESHWATER SZ3487 **Red Lion** *Church Pl (01983)* 754925 Civilised white-painted house with a comfortable open-plan bar, lots of local pictures and photographs, open fires, and extremely popular very imaginative food – best to book ahead; well kept real ales, a fine choice of 16 wines by the glass, and tables on a grassy back area (behind which is the kitchen's herb garden); walks nearby, especially around the River Yar; cl 25 Dec; children over 10; disabled access. £23|£5.75

ROOKLEY SZ5083 **Chequers** *Niton Rd (01983) 840314* Former customs and excise house that's marvellous for families, with a large no smoking family room, a large play area outside with toboggan run and bouncy castle, and mother and baby room; cottagey ornaments and log fire in comfortable carpeted lounge bar, lively locals' bar, well kept real ales, and generous helpings of interesting bar food; disabled access. £15|£6.50

SHALFLEET SZ4089 **New Inn** *(01983) 531314* Welcoming former fishermen's pub with a partly panelled flagstoned public bar, yachting photographs and pictures, scrubbed deal tables, Windsor chairs, and a roaring log fire in a big stone hearth, a carpeted beamed lounge bar with more boating pictures and a coal fire; up to 16 good fresh fish dishes (the fish is bought from the quay only a short walk away) plus other enjoyable food, well kept real ales, and a decent wine list. £30|£6

SHORWELL SZ4583 **Crown** *(01983) 740293* Friendly and very popular old pub in an attractive rural setting, with a traditional atmosphere in four bustling rooms, individual furnishings, winter log fires, lots of houseplants, and several no smoking areas; enjoyable food (nicely presented daily specials), well kept real ales, and efficient service; picnic-sets and white garden chairs in the peaceful tree-sheltered garden, and decent play area; disabled access. £17|£6

YARMOUTH SZ3589 **Jireh House** *The Square (01983) 760513* 17th-c guest house with friendly owners, a relaxed atmosphere, and a range of home-made meals, snacks and afternoon tea inc daily specials and fresh fish; bdrms; cl Nov–Easter; disabled access (restaurant only). £15.50/special afternoon tea £4

KENT

An excellent mix of family attractions, wonderful castles and gardens, seaside resorts with traditional appeal, some charming countryside

You're spoilt for choice here if you like fine houses and well preserved castles. What's more, some of even Kent's most stately homes are making a special effort to appeal to children. Top of the list are Hever Castle (children love the water maze), lively Leeds Castle (good special events), magnificent Penshurst Place (toy museum and adventure playground), and Dover Castle (atmospheric underground tunnels and a good exhibition). Also rewarding for adults are Knole in Sevenoaks (the calendar home of the Sackvilles), the medieval manor at Ightham, and Squerryes Court in Westerham. Also near Westerham, Churchill's Chartwell, and Darwin's Down House in Downe have lots of fascinating information on their former owners.

Kent also boasts a multitude of magnificent gardens. One even gains the title of Kent Family Attraction of the Year: Groombridge has plenty to keep young children as well as their parents enchanted. The gardens at Sissinghurst, Lamberhurst and Doddington are all beautiful, too. For a diverse range of trees and plants head for Bedgebury Pinetum, and the gardens at Hadlow. The huge Brogdale fruit tree collection near Faversham and the unusual organic gardens at Yalding are also quite out of the ordinary. Vineyards to visit include ones at Barham, Small Hythe and Penshurst.

Full day family outings include Chatham's Historic Dockyard (a lively working museum with lots going on) and Hop Farm Country Park in Beltring (well organised with plenty of variety); Maidstone's Museum of Kent Life has more than enough for a pleasant afternoon. Elsewhere, there are unique collections at Birchington's Powell-Cotton Museum and Quex House, and at Goudhurst's Finchcocks.

Kent's very enjoyable top wildlife parks all have a strong conservation message: the late John Aspinall's wildlife parks at Bekesbourne and Lympne, Wingham Wildlife Park, and Wildwood in Herne Bay are outstanding if you're interested in animals. The good value South of England Rare Breeds Centre at Woodchurch and friendly Farming World at Boughton are ideal if you prefer more domesticated animals.

A great magnet for visitors with some good museums, Canterbury has many fine buildings besides the cathedral, which (along with St Augustine's Abbey and St Martin's Church) has recently been declared a UNESCO World Heritage Site. Rochester with its dramatic castle is another worthwhile destination, especially if you like Dickens.

The NE seaside resorts date from pre-railway Victorian days, and have kept a certain dignified charm that gives them an unusual appeal. Broadstairs (Dickens connections here too) is a fine example.

Inland, the Weald (roughly W of the M20) has peaceful and intimate landscapes of little hills and valleys, small pasture fields and oak woods, timeless windmills and villages with attractive tile-hung and weatherboarded houses, early medieval stone-built churches, and a good smattering of antiques shops, tearooms and so forth – pleasant territory for roaming about by car. The North Downs between M20 and M2, also N of the M25/M26, are more open; the best parts are above Wye. The flatlands of Romney Marsh have a certain bypassed-by

Please let us know what you think of places in the *Guide*. Use the report forms at the back of the book, write us a letter or log on to www.goodguides.com

Where to stay

ASH TR2959 **Great Weddington** *Weddington, Ash, Canterbury, Kent CT3 2AR (01304) 813407* **£80**; 3 pretty bdrms. Regency country house surrounded by farmland and extensive gardens, with log fire in drawing room, enjoyable breakfasts and evening meals, and a relaxing atmosphere; no smoking; cl Christmas and New Year; children over 8

BOUGHTON LEES TR0147 **Eastwell Manor** *Eastwell Park, Boughton Lees, Ashford, Kent TN25 4HR (01233) 219955* **£200**, plus special breaks; 63 prettily decorated rmss in hotel and 19 courtyard cottages (some cottages have their own garden and can also be booked on self-catering basis). Fine Jacobean-style manor (actually rebuilt in the 1920s) in 62 acres with croquet lawn, tennis court, two boules pitches and putting green; grand oak-panelled rooms, open fires, comfortable leather seating, antiques and fresh flowers, courteous helpful service, and extremely good food; health and fitness spa with 20-metre indoor pool and 14 treatment rooms, and lots of walks; disabled access; dogs welcome in bedrooms ☺

CANTERBURY TR1557 **Cathedral Gate** *36 Burgate, Canterbury, Kent CT1 2HA (01227) 464381* **£88**, plus special breaks; 27 rms, 12 with own bthrm and some overlooking cathedral. 15th-c hotel that predates the adjoining sculpted cathedral gateway; bow windows, massive oak beams, sloping floors, antiques and fresh flowers, continental breakfast in little dining room or your own room, and a restful atmosphere; municipal car parks a few minutes away; dogs welcome but bring own bedding

CANTERBURY TR1457 **Thanington Hotel** *140 Wincheap, Canterbury, Kent CT1 3RY (01227) 453227* **£73***, plus winter breaks; 15 rms, 5 large ones in the original house, 10 purpose-built ones linked to main building by Georgian-style conservatory. Thoughtfully run and warmly welcoming hotel with elegant little rooms, enjoyable breakfasts, a games room, sun-trap walled garden, and indoor swimming pool; partial disabled access

CHARING TQ9247 **Barnfield** *Barnfield Rd, Charing, Ashford, Kent TN27 0BN (01233) 712421* **£46***; 6 beamed rms, shared big bthrm. Delightful early 15th-c farmhouse with fine beams, big open fires, comfortable sitting rooms, lots of books, antiques and homely knick-knacks, good breakfasts, friendly owners, and fine views over garden and lake; cl Christmas

CHIDDINGSTONE HOATH TQ4842 **Hoath House** *Penshurst Rd, Chiddingstone Hoath, Edenbridge, Kent TN8 7DB (01342) 850362* **£55**; 4 rms, 1 with own bthrm. Wonderful medieval house – added to over the years – with huge beams and plastered walls in the sitting room, family portraits, open fire in the library, heaps of interest and atmosphere, homely suppers, welcoming owners, and a big garden with fine views; they are kind to children; cl Christmas ☺

DOVER TR3241 **Churchill** *Waterloo Crescent, Dover, Kent CT17 9BP (01304) 203633* **£97**, plus special breaks; 66 comfortable rms, several with balconies. Above the harbour, this Regency terrace hotel has a congenial bar, sun lounge and terrace, friendly staff, and enjoyable food (lots of fresh fish) in brasserie-style restaurant overlooking the Channel; new health club; disabled access

EAST PECKHAM TQ6651 **Roydon Hall** *East Peckham, Tonbridge, Kent TN12 5NH (01622) 812121* **£50***; 14 rms, some with own bthrm. Fine Tudor manor with many original features inc fine panelling in many of the public rooms, a peaceful atmosphere, and 10 acres of woodland and garden; vegetarian lunch and light supper by arrangement, and regular meditation courses; no smoking; cl Christmas/New Year/Easter

FRITTENDEN TQ8041 **Maplehurst Mill** *Mill Lane, Frittenden, Cranbrook, Kent TN17 2DT (01580) 852203* **£90**; 3 rms with views over the water and surrounding countryside. Carefully restored 18th-c watermill attached to 15th-c mill house with original machinery, millstones and waterwheel; big comfortable drawing room, delicious imaginative food using home-grown organic produce in candlelit beamed dining room, and 11 acres of gardens and grounds with heated outdoor swimming pool; no smoking; cl Christmas and New Year; children over 12; disabled access

GOUDHURST TQ7237 **Star & Eagle** *High St, Goudhurst, Cranbrook, Kent TN17 1AL (01580) 211512* **£60***; 10 character rms, 9 with own bthrm. Striking medieval inn with comfortable Jacobean-style furnishings in heavy-beamed day rooms, pretty views, polite staff, good food, and well kept ales; cl pm 25 Dec

MARDEN TQ7341 **Tanner House** *Goudhurst Rd, Marden, Tonbridge, Kent TN12 9ND (01622) 831214* **£45***; 3 rms (showers). Quietly set Tudor farmhouse on 150-acre, family-run mixed farm, with residents' lounge, inglenook dining room, large garden, and walks and picnic areas around farm; they breed shire horses, and have a quiet, secluded touring caravan and camping park with small play areas, and a shop; cl Christmas; children over 12

PLAXTOL TQ6054 **Jordans** *Sheet Hill, Plaxtol, Sevenoaks, Kent TN15 0PU (01732) 810379* **£68**; 3 rms, 2 with own bthrm. 15th-c no smoking house with leaded windows, beams, and an inglenook fireplace, good breakfasts, and pretty garden;

the helpful owner is a qualified tourist guide, and can tell you about the many historic houses and lovely gardens nearby; cl mid-Dec to mid-Jan; children over 12

PLUCKLEY TQ9145 **Elvey Farm** *Pluckley, Ashford, Kent TN27 0SU* (01233) *840442* **£65.50***; 9 rms, some in the oast house roundel, some in original barn and stable block. 15th-c farmhouse in secluded spot on 75-acre working family farm, with timbered rooms, inglenook fireplace, and French windows from lounge on to sun terrace; ample play areas for children; cl Christmas; disabled access; dogs welcome in bedrooms

SANDGATE TR1935 **Sandgate Hotel** *Wellington Terrace, The Esplanade, Sandgate, Folkestone, Kent CT20 3DY* (01303) *220444* **£68**; 14 restful, elegant rms. Smart, impeccably kept Victorian hotel overlooking the beach, with huge picture windows, open fires, fresh flowers, and antique mirrors, exceptional French cooking in pretty restaurant, enjoyable breakfasts, and friendly mainly French staff; cl Jan, 1 wk Oct

SISSINGHURST TQ8037 **Sissinghurst Castle Farm** *Biddenden Rd, Sissinghurst, Cranbrook, Kent TN17 2AB* (01580) *712885* **£56**, plus winter breaks; 5 rms, some with own bthrm. Gabled Victorian farmhouse in the grounds of Sissinghurst Castle Garden, with an attractively furnished sitting room, and a pretty garden; winter house parties available; cl Christmas; children over 8

SMARDEN TQ8842 **Chequers** *The Street, Smarden, Ashford, Kent TN27 8QA* (01233) *770217* **£70**; 4 rms. Neatly kept 14th-c inn with friendly hard-working owners, a no smoking restaurant, lots of beams, flagstones and an enormous fireplace, a dining area with elegant reproduction tables and chairs, and a cosy, comfortable bar with a good relaxed atmosphere and plenty of chatty locals; enjoyable food, huge breakfasts, well kept real ales, and a decent wine list; this is a very attractive village.

ST MARGARET'S AT CLIFFE TR3444 **Wallett's Court** *Dover Rd, Westcliffe, Dover, Kent CT15 6EW* (01304) *852424* **£90**, plus special breaks; 16 rms, some in converted stable block with gentle views. Fine old manor house with 13th-c cellars, beams, antiques, comfortable seating and open fires, particularly friendly and helpful service, charming owners, and marvellous food; swimming pool and leisure facilities; they are kind to children; very close to ferries; cl 24–26 Dec; disabled access

TUNBRIDGE WELLS TQ5839 **Hotel Du Vin and Bistro** *Crescent Rd, Tunbridge Wells, Kent TN1 2LY* (01892) *526455* **£105**; 32 (shortly to have 36) very attractive individually decorated rms with CD players, satellite TV and power showers. Handsome sandstone building, extended in the 19th c, with a relaxed atmosphere in the two rooms of the bar, comfortable sofas and chairs in the lounge rooms, good modern cooking in the airy, high-ceilinged and informally French-feeling restaurant, and particularly good wines; seats on the terrace; disabled access

TUNBRIDGE WELLS TQ5739 **Spa Hotel** *Langton Rd, Tunbridge Wells, Kent TN4 8XJ* (01892) *520331* **£131.50**, plus wknd breaks; 71 individually decorated rms. Run by the same family for three generations, this Georgian hotel stands in 14 acres of landscaped gardens; comfortable and quietly decorated, partly no smoking lounge, a popular and attractive bar with equestrian paintings and photographs, good enjoyable food in Regency-style restaurant, a carefully chosen wine list, and friendly long-serving staff; leisure centre with indoor heated swimming pool and well equipped gym; tennis court and pony riding; disabled access

WEST MALLING TQ6857 **Scott House** *High St, West Malling, Kent ME19 6QH* (01732) *841380* **£79***; 5 pretty little rms. No smoking Georgian town house (from which the family also run an antiques and interior design business) with big comfortable lounge, good breakfasts in dining room, a friendly atmosphere, and helpful owners; cl Christmas/New Year; children over 10

To see and do

Kent Family Attraction of the Year

GROOMBRIDGE TQ5337 **Groombridge Place Gardens** (B2210) You might not initially think that the beautiful walled gardens here – among the country's most spectacular – would be a good choice for children, but in fact over the last couple of years Groombridge has developed into a first-class family day out. Particularly well liked by younger visitors (and increasingly popular with adults too) is the delightfully inventive Enchanted Forest, a series of quirky gardens designed by Ivan Hicks, with surprises around every corner: mirrors suspended from trees above ponds, a formidable raised walkway through the treetops with rope slides, bridges and giant swings, dinosaur footprints, and a Celtic Forest with hidden snakes and spiders. With its sandpit and swings, the Groms Village is ideal for younger children, and the colourful Romany Camp has face-painting at weekends and school holidays. These splendidly atmospheric gardens are great for stimulating children's imagination: the more they look, the more they discover. Another innovation has been the introduction of the rather more incongruous pig racing, which usually takes place twice a day, to the joy of all age-groups. There's also a burgeoning yew hedge maze (not yet big enough to confound any but the smallest visitors), a rabbit enclosure, and a well established birds of prey centre, with good, lengthy flying displays of its eagles, owls, falcons, and hawks every day (weather permitting), at 11.30am, 1, and 3.30pm. Some of the birds fly very close to the audience – and don't be surprised if a local crow joins in the fun. Die-hard gardeners needn't worry: the glorious formal gardens are still very much the main attraction, but it's nice to see so much effort put into making the site more appealing to a younger audience – you really get the feeling here that the gardens are meant to be enjoyed, and not simply gazed at in awe. Many of the gardens date back 300 years, as do the famous peacocks, these days most often found patrolling the paths of the oriental garden. Highlights include the Drunken Garden, named for the way the junipers and ewe trees once clipped into topiary shapes now lurch drunkenly around the sundial pool, the white rose garden (not just roses, but white lavender, tulips and primulas too), and the pretty little secret garden. As many of the gardens are walled, and built on to a south-facing slope, quite a few species flower earlier than they do elsewhere. Beautifully arranged around a 17th-c moated mansion (not open), the gardens have inspired generations of artists and writers: Sir Arthur Conan Doyle set a scene in his Sherlock Holmes novel *The Valley of Fear* here, and there's a re-creation of his study. For a small extra charge you can take a canal boat trip between the formal gardens and the Enchanted Forest. On some bank holidays and weekends you may find extra events such as classic car rallies, archery displays, and an outdoor theatre. Snacks, shop, some disabled access (to formal gardens, but not Enchanted Forest); open Easter-Oct; (01892) 863999; £8 adults, £6.50 children 3–2. The family ticket (two adults, two children) offers a decent saving, at £26. At weekends and school holidays (though not usually Mon or Tues), a particularly enjoyable way to get here is on the Spa Valley Railway, from Tunbridge Wells (see entry on p.343); a combined ticket is available.

AYLESFORD TQ7258

Friars These carefully restored 13th/14th-c buildings are once again home to a group of Carmelite friars. Fine cloisters and chapels, sculptures and ceramics by modern artists, working pottery, and beautiful grounds. Snacks, shop, disabled access; cl Good Fri (but grounds open); (01622) 717272; free. The Little Gem pub is very quaint and ancient.

Kits Coty House (towards A229) This massive Stone Age tomb chamber 'mightily impressed' Pepys; free.

BARHAM TR1947

Elham Valley Vineyards You can look around this friendly little vineyard, set in a pretty and sheltered valley, and run by the Vale of Elham Trust which aims to provide work for adults with learning disabilities. Pottery (demonstrations wkdys only), cream teas, wine sales, good craft shop; excellent disabled access; cl wknds (exc pm Mar–Oct), best to check; (01227) 831266. The B2065 through this valley is a pretty drive.

BEDGEBURY TQ7233

Bedgebury Pinetum Lakeside landscaped valley full of an expanding collection of magnificent conifers, with walks up through forest plots designed to try out the commercial possibilities of all sorts of little-known species. They're also carrying out a programme of heathland restoration, and work on a new visitor and education centre and a lake should be complete by 2004. Meals, snacks, shop; visitor centre cl 25 Dec and 1 Jan; (01580) 211044; *£3.

BEKESBOURNE TR1956

Howletts Zoo 🏛 (signed off A2) The first of the excellent wildlife parks founded by the late John Aspinall. Pleasantly spread over lovely grounds, it's well known (along with its bigger sister park at Lympne, see below) for its genuinely dedicated approach to looking after the rare or endangered animals and – more controversially, because of the danger – the bonds developed between the keepers and the animals. Highlights include the world's largest colony of breeding gorillas (over 100 have been been born here, and two have been successfully released into the wild), and a unique

herd of breeding elephants. Other animals include deer, antelope, leopards and gibbons. Meals, snacks, shop, disabled access; cl 25 Dec; (01227) 721286; *£11.95.

BELTRING TQ6746

Hop Farm Country Park 🏛 (off A228) The conical Victorian oast houses used for drying hops are a distinctive feature of Kent and East Sussex; this is the largest surviving group, now converted into a popular and very well organised family outing. A couple of the galleried barns have comprehensive exhibitions, one on the hop industry, bringing to life with sounds and smells the experience of working on a hop farm, and the other an entertaining social history collection. Another barn has a big under-cover play area, and there are plenty of animals, and a pets' corner (feeding sessions throughout the day). They also have an impressive collection of shire horses, stables tours and dray rides – a spiritualist comes every Weds to see the horses, and you can watch him at work. Other areas include an exhibition on water and a little aquarium, a collection of tanks and other military vehicles, and a working potter – you can have a go at making and painting your own creation (50p extra). Also an outdoor adventure playground, paddling pools, sandpits and a bouncy castle. Special events most summer wknds. Meals, snacks, picnic areas, some disabled access (not into oast houses); cl 25–26 Dec; (01622) 872068; £6.50 adults.

BEWL WATER TQ6733

Bewl Water The reservoir, dissected by the Kent/Sussex boundary, is skirted by a 14-mile path, and is surrounded by attractive partly wooded pasture. They have summer events, and it can be very busy on bank hols. Boat trips (Easter–Sept, wknds only in Oct; (01892) 890661; £3 wkdys, 50p more at wknds) and trout fishing ((01892) 890352; from £10), picnic areas, cycle hire (summer only; (01323) 870310; from £3.50 for an hour), and a great adventure play area. Interactive displays and videos about the reservoir, and their extensive dry garden is interesting, overlooked by a glazed walkway. Meals, snacks, shop, disabled access; £4.50 parking charge summer wknds and bank hols, £3.50 at other times.

BIDDENDEN TQ8538
Attractive village with several interesting old houses on the S side of the High St, and a handsome 13th-c **church** with a bold tower. The picturesque old Three Chimneys just W has good food.
Biddenden Vineyards and Cider Works (Benenden rd) Thriving wine- and cider-producing vineyard, reputedly Kent's oldest. All-year tastings, harvesting in late Sept and bottling in Mar. Snacks, shop, disabled access (but no facilities); cl Sun Jan–Feb and 24 Dec–1 Jan; (01580) 291726; free, guided tours from £3.20 (groups only, book in advance).

BIRCHINGTON TR3068
Powell-Cotton Museum and Quex House (off A28) Fascinating museum attached to fine Regency house with furnished period rooms. Eight galleries show the collections of the late Victorian explorer and naturalist Maj Powell-Cotton, with hundreds of well mounted African animals, ethnic artefacts and oriental art. The gardens include a Victorian walled garden with restored glasshouses, lawns, mature specimen trees, herbaceous borders and a woodland walk. Meals, snacks, shop, disabled access; open Tues–Thurs, Sun and bank hols Apr–Oct (house open pm only), plus gardens and museum open Suns only in Mar and Nov; (01843) 842168; £4, £3 in winter. The Mortons Fork inland at Minster does worthwhile lunches, and the Minnis Bay beach is good.

BLEAN TR1161
Druidstone Park & Art Park 🖼
(A290) Farmyard, woodland trails, sculpture park and a couple of adventure playgrounds (one for under-5s). Snacks, shop, disabled access; cl Nov–Easter; (01227) 765168; £3.90. Nearby Blean Woods are protected as a nature reserve, with well signed walks in the RSPB area.

BOROUGH GREEN TQ6356
Great Comp Garden (St Mary's Platt, 2m E) Interesting collection of trees, shrubs, herbaceous plants and heathers with fine lawns and paths. Snacks, plant shop, disabled access; cl Nov–Mar; (01732) 886154; *£4. The Plough at Ivy Hatch a few miles S is a good restaurant.

BOUGH BEECH TQ4846
Bough Beech Nature Reserve At the N end of the reservoir, with wildlife exhibitions in a 19th-c oast house. Snacks, limited disabled access; open Weds, wknds and bank hols Apr–Oct; (01732) 750624; free. The Wheatsheaf has good food, and there are pleasant walks around here.

BOUGHTON TR0459
Farming World 🖼 (Nash Court) Friendly farm with traditional and rare breeds and heavy horses, tractor and waggon rides, nature trails, adventure playgrounds, walled garden, and seasonal fruit and veg. A hawking centre with daily flying displays and bird handling (summer only), and an incubation and conservation room where you can see baby birds hatching. Meals, snacks, farm shop, disabled access (sensory garden specially designed for the disabled); cl Nov–Feb; (01227) 751144; *£4.50. The White Horse at Boughton Street has decent food all day.

BRENCHLEY TQ6840
Marle Place 🖼 Pretty garden around a fine 17th-c house (not open), with interesting plants, a walled scented garden, artists' studios and gallery, mosaic terrace, woodland walk, and ponds. Teas, picnic area; cl Oct–Mar; (01892) 722304; £4. The village has some attractive old houses.

BRIDGE TR1953
Higham Park It is claimed that this restored Palladian manor was the first house in the world to have a wireless radio. The friendly owners are more than willing to pore through albums celebrating the house's colourful history with their visitors. The restoration of the gardens is almost complete, and the grounds are pleasant to stroll around: a highlight is the yew-lined Italian water garden with water-lilies, secret garden, and extensive terraced rose garden. You can now also see a replica of the classical temple built here by Harold Peto, and by 2003 they should have finished restoring the

Victorian carnation house. Meals, snacks, shop, some disabled access; cl Fri and Sat, and all Oct–mid-Mar; (01227) 830830; £3.50 garden, £2.50 for tour of the house. In the attractive village, the White Horse and Red Lion have decent food.

BROADSTAIRS TR3967
The most attractive of the NE Kent seaside resorts, much of it dating from pre-railway Victorian days, when well-to-do Londoners came by boat. With its bathing huts, neat gardens and fishing boats, this is still tranquilly old-fashioned. There's a lively little harbour (where the Tartar Frigate has good views from its upstairs restaurant), plus seven small sandy bays (Joss Bay, slightly E from the centre, is excellent for families), refreshing clifftop walks (even to Ramsgate if you're feeling energetic), and lots of Dickens connections ('Our watering place', he called the town). Bandstand concerts usually 2.30 on summer Suns. A pleasant way of approaching the town is to start from Ramsgate and walk along the coast – an easy 20–30-minute stroll.

Bleak House Dickens Museum (Fort Rd) Dickens's favourite seaside residence, where he wrote *David Copperfield*, and which he used as the title for another novel. Lots of his belongings and related memorabilia, plus displays on local wrecks and smuggling. Shop, some disabled access; cl mid-Dec to mid-Feb exc wknds in Jan; (01843) 862224; £3.

Dickens House Museum (Victoria Parade) Former home of Miss Mary Strong, the basis for Betsey Trotwood in *David Copperfield* – the parlour is furnished as in the book. Also more of Dickens's letters and possessions. Shop; open Apr to mid-Oct, and during Dec for special Christmas events, phone to check; (01843) 863453; *£2.

BROOKLAND TQ9626
Fairfield church Standing quite alone in Romney Marsh NW of Brookland, this is a tent-roofed brick-and-timber building, remarkable for its utterly lonely surroundings – and attractive inside.
Philippine Village Craft Centre (A259 SW) Unique centre selling crafts from the Philippines, with some special

events. Meals, snacks, limited disabled access; open wknds Easter-Whitsun, then daily till end Sept, other times by arrangement; (01797) 344616; free. The Walland Marsh here is an extension of Romney Marsh; the sign off the A259 to the Woolpack leads you to a particularly good pub with the right sort of atmosphere for the area.

CANTERBURY TR1457
At its most atmospheric out of season, as its compact and easily walked historic centre does get almost unpleasantly packed in summer. The most rewarding area is in the cathedral precincts, and the admission charge brings a measure of peace to one of Britain's greatest religious sites; the choicest parts elsewhere need a bit of seeking out. Good guided walks leave from the helpful Visitor Information Centre, 12 Sun St (2pm Apr–Oct, plus 11.30am July–Aug; (01227) 459779; £3.75), and every Fri and Sat at 8pm there are Ghost Tours (meet opposite Alberrys Wine Bar, Margaret St; (01843) 299460; £5). Summer boat trips leave daily from Kings Bridge; (07790) 534744; £5. If you're making your own way, don't miss Palace St, Burgate with the Buttermarket Sq, and St Peter's St, all of which have fine buildings, and you can follow quite a lot of the ancient city wall on a walk passing the remains of the Norman castle (some info panels, usually open). The city's Roman and ecclesiastical heritage is well known, but there are other remains here too, notably a prehistoric tumulus in Dane John Garden. The Whitefriars area of town is currently being redeveloped to include a new shopping centre and library, and they hope to open up archaeological excavations of the site to the public by spring 2003. There are good car parks on the fringes of the old centre. Canterbury Tales (just off St Peter's St) is a useful central pub for lunch.

Canterbury Cathedral Dramatically floodlit at night, this spectacularly lives up to expectations. The earliest parts are Norman, with much added in the 12th and 15th c. Rewarding features are everywhere – an airily impressive nave, fascinating stained glass, the Bell Harry Tower, lovely cloisters, and the shrine of Thomas à Becket, murdered here in the 12th c. The crypt has some wonderfully grotesque carvings, full of strange animals and fantastic fighting monsters. The precincts are particularly rewarding, containing buildings connected to the cathedral, inc the ruins of the former monastery in Green Court, the impressive Norman Staircase and the medieval Kings School. Summer snacks, shop, disabled access; may be closed for services at certain times, limited opening Sun; (01227) 762862; £3.50 – note this isn't a donation, you'll be charged this just to enter the precincts. There are additional charges for guided tours, audio tours, audio-visuals, and photo permits. Entry to the services is free, and the choir's singing is then a bonus.

Canterbury Tales 🅰 (St Margaret's St) Well put together, Chaucer's characters brought enthusiastically to life with smells, sound effects and lively celebrity voices. Meals, snacks, very good unusual shop, disabled access (prior notice preferred); cl 25 Dec; (01227) 479227; £6.50. They also have special events during most school hols.

Museum of Canterbury (Stour St) In the medieval Poor Priests Hospital with its magnificent oak roof; a splendid interpretation of the city's history, told with the deft use of up-to-date display technology – particularly rewarding. There's also gallery devoted to Rupert Bear. Redevelopment and expansion of the museum should be complete by early 2003, giving more gallery space, lots of hands-on displays, and a new medieval discovery gallery. New café, shop, disabled access (there'll be a new lift); cl Sun Oct–May, Good Fri and Christmas wk; (01227) 452747; £2.60. Hidden away through an arch beside the building is the charming Greyfriars, above the River Stour.

Roman Museum (Longmarket) Splendid underground museum, incorporating the remains of a Roman town house; lively reconstructions of a market and kitchen, as well as lots of hands-on and hi-tech displays. The mosaic floor is very well displayed. Shop, disabled access; cl Sun (exc Jun–Oct), Good Fri and Christmas wk; (01227) 785575; £2.60.

Royal Museum and Art Gallery (High St) Fine porcelain, glass, and ceramics, the city's picture collection inc Victorian animal paintings by T S Cooper. Shop; cl Sun, Good Fri and Christmas wk; (01227) 452747; free.

St Augustine's Abbey (Longport) Founded at the end of the 6th c, but most of the remaining ruins date from the Benedictine rebuilding in the 11th c. A free audio tour takes you around the ruins and adjacent museum. Snacks, shop, disabled access; cl 24–26 Dec, 1 Jan; (01227) 767345; £3; EH.

St Martin's church (North Holmes Rd) The country's oldest church in continual use; the Venerable Bede says it was built by the Romans, and there are certainly Roman bricks in the walls.

West Gate Towers (where St Peter's St meets St Dunstan's St) The city's last remaining fortified gatehouse, built in the late 14th c, with interesting cells, and excellent views from the battlements. Children can do brass rubbing or try on replica armour. Shop; cl 12.30–1.30, all day Sun, Good Fri, Christmas wk; (01227) 452747; £1.

CHALLOCK TR0152

Beech Court Gardens 🅰 Peaceful gardens surrounding a medieval farmhouse, with lots of spring and autumn colour; the firs and pines reflect the designer's admiration for Inverewe in Scotland. There are also a few farm animals, and a children's trail. Teas and snacks in oast house, picnic areas, plant sales and craft shop, disabled access; cl Fri and wknd ams, and Nov–late Mar; (01233) 740735; *£3.75. The 17th-c Chequers by the pretty village green has good value food.

CHATHAM TQ7568

Fort Amherst (Dock Rd) Perhaps the finest surviving 18th-c fort in the country, with massive ditches, gun emplacements, a warren of tunnels and a firing gun battery. 18 acres of parkland, and occasional live re-enactments on Sun. Meals, snacks, shop; cl wkdys Nov–Easter, 25–26 Dec, and 1 Jan; (01634) 847747; £4.50. The Command House just below by the water does limited but decent food.

Historic Dockyard Excellent 80-acre working museum in the most complete Georgian dockyard in the world – a visit here can easily fill most of the day. Lots to see and do: the Wooden Walls exhibition uses sights, sounds and smells to show how 18th-c warships such as HMS *Victory* were built here. Guided tours of the restored 1944 destroyer HMS *Cavalier*. You can also look around the Cold War submarine *Ocelot*, and watch the restoration of the Victorian sloop *Gannet*, which should be completed sometime in 2003. An exhibition on the RNLI has 16 lifeboats. An exhibition centre in the Flagship Brewery even explores the role of beer in the Navy (disabled access; open most wkdys, with new naval-theme pub nearby in Harbourmaster's House; free), and a gallery charts Chathams's historic relationship with the Navy. Also restorations, rope-making demonstrations, craft workshops, interactive exhibitions, and lively events. Meals, snacks, shop, disabled access; open daily Apr–Oct, plus wknds and Weds in Nov, Feb and Mar; (01634) 823807; £9.50. You can get a ticket that includes **boat trips** on the paddle steamer *Kingswear Castle*. There's a new visitor centre, and you can now travel between attractions on heritage buses (it's a big place), that are similar to those that would have taken workers to and from the dockyard in the 1960s.

CHIDDINGSTONE TQ5045
A favourite Kentish village, an unspoilt cluster of Tudor houses and buildings owned by the NT, in lovely countryside. The church and the mysterious stone which one story claims gives the village its name are worth a look. The Castle Inn has decent food all day.

Chiddingstone Castle 17th-c house rebuilt in castle style at the start of the 19th-c; renowned paintings and antiquities from England, Egypt and the Orient, inc fine collections of Japanese swords and Buddhist art. Attractively restored landscaped grounds, and you can fish in the lake (£8 a day for two rods). Tearoom, shop, disabled access to ground floor only; open pm Weds–Fri and Sun Easter-Sept, Sun and public hols only at Easter and in spring; (01892) 870347; £4.

CHILHAM TR0653
The lovely village square is the prettiest in Kent, and several antiques shops

reflect its popularity with visitors – in summer, get there early to catch it at its most photogenic. The Woolpack just down the hill is useful for lunch.

Badgers Hill Farm (New Cut Rd – towards Selling) Cheerily unspoilt spot, with cider-making, local crafts, a barrel merchant, free-roaming pigs and other animals, play area, and **pick-your-own** apples (ten types, Aug–Oct). Snacks, farm shop, disabled access; cl 24 Dec–Mar; (01227) 730573; free. Further towards Selling, the Rose & Crown at Perry Wood is a nice pub, with woodland walks nearby.

CHISLET MARSHES TR2366
Thousands of geese and ducks; duck food by the bag from the nice little Gate Inn at Boyden Gate.

CLIFFE MARSHES TQ7279
N of Rochester, these are bounded by a long sea wall cum footpath which feels (and is) extraordinarily remote and not a little surreal – perhaps the best Thames Estuary walk in N Kent, an internationally important wildlife site and given added poignancy by the fact that it's under consideration for a new airport, with other compulsory purchase orders threatening other nearby wildlife-rich farmland.

COBHAM TQ6570
Another attractive village, with a good mix of unspoilt buildings from various centuries – an excellent place to walk round (as Dickens liked to do). The partly 13th-c church is worth examining, with its magnificent brasses and tombs, as is the 14th-c **New College**, like a miniature Oxford college but far less known to visitors (open daily, disabled access; (01474) 814280; free). The Leather Bottle has decent food, interesting Dickens memorabilia and a good garden.

Cobham Hall The Earls of Darnley once lived in this impressive place, now a girls' school. The décor is quite splendid in parts (some notable marble fireplaces), and there are lovely grounds. A heritage lottery grant is currently helping to restore the Repton landscape and park buildings around the hall. Snacks, shop; open pms on selected Weds and Suns in the school hols; (01474) 823371; £3.50.

CRANBROOK TQ7736

This attractive miniature town has largely unspoilt lanes of tile-hung and weatherboarded buildings; also a friendly local history museum (open pms Tues–Sat and bank hols; £1.50), and for picnics Perfect Partners (Stone St) is the best delicatessen for many miles. The field walk to Sissinghurst and back is a pleasant way of joining two interesting places.

Cranbrook Union Mill As we went to press, this working windmill was undergoing extensive refurbishments which included replacing its Dutch-style sails with traditional Kentish ones. The restored workshop has visual displays, while upstairs you can discover the history of the mill and its owners. Shop, usually open pm wknds and bank hols Apr–Sept but phone to check; (01580) 712256; donations.

DEAL TR3752

Once the busiest harbour in SE England, and Caesar's landing point in 55BC; now a pleasantly understated seaside resort, full of pretty little streets and alleys – but beware of vigilant traffic wardens. The seaview Kings Head (Beach St) has good value food (and bedrooms).

Deal Castle The biggest in Henry VIII's chain of coastal defences, uniquely shaped like a Tudor rose with every wall rounded to deflect shot. Snacks, good audio tour, shop, disabled access to ground floor only; cl Mon and Tues Sept–Mar, and 24 Dec–1 Jan; (01304) 372762; £3.20, EH.

Walmer Castle (just S) Another of Henry VIII's coastal defence fortresses, later the official residence of the Lord Warden of the Cinque Ports (one was the Duke of Wellington, who left behind his famous boot). It became more stately home than fortress, with rooms furnished in 18th-c style, and pretty gardens laid out mainly by a niece of William Pitt (one designed by Penelope Hobhouse is dedicated to the late Queen Mother). Snacks, shop, some disabled access; cl Mon and Tues Nov–Dec and Mar, wkdys Jan and Feb, 24–26 Dec, 1 Jan and whenever Lord Warden is in residence; (01304) 364288; £5; EH.

DODDINGTON TQ9357

Doddington Place Gardens Grand 10-acre garden with formal plantings, some massive topiary, Edwardian rock garden, rhododendron woodland, broad views, folly and delightfully peaceful atmosphere. Snacks, plant sales, disabled access; open pm 3rd Sun of month Apr–Sept (exc Jun – pm 1st and 2nd Suns of month) though best to check; (01795) 886101; *£3.50. The George at Newnham is nice for lunch, with good walks nearby.

DOVER TR3241

The busiest ferry port in Europe, Dover is not in itself an attractive town but has several extremely interesting places to visit, reflecting the fascinating history it owes to its strategic importance. Blakes (Castle St) is a pleasant wine bar.

Crabble Corn Mill (Lower Rd) Beautifully restored working 19th-c watermill. Fairs held year round. Meals, snacks (made with their own flour), shop, limited disabled access; usually open daily Jan–Sept, Sun Oct–Dec, but phone to check winter opening; (01304) 823292; £2, 50p extra for a tour guide.

Dover Castle Not to be missed, an excellently preserved magnificent Norman fortress with its original keep, 74-metre (242-ft) well, and massive walls and towers. There's a lot to see inc the atmospheric complex of underground tunnels that played a vital role in World War II, and an exhibition which dramatically re-creates an early 13th-c siege. Also included are the Pharos Tower (a Roman lighthouse using a 4th-floor flaring brazier as a guide-light), and a restored Saxon church. A walk round the battlements gives bird's-eye views of the comings and goings down in the harbour (something which captivates small children); the audioguide adds interest to your stroll. Meals, snacks, shop, disabled access; cl 25–26 Dec, 1 Jan; (01304) 211067; £7.50; EH.

Dover Transport Museum (Whitfield, just off A2) All different kinds of road vehicles from bikes to buses (you might see some being worked on), a 1930s garage, model railway and tramway, and some maritime history. Snacks, shop, disabled access; open pm Weds–Sat, all Sun and bank hols Apr–Oct; (01304) 822409; £2.

Grand Shaft An unusual spiral stone staircase which links top and bottom of Dover's famous cliffs; open Tues–Sun pms July–Aug; £1.25.

Roman Painted House (New St) Well preserved remains of Roman hotel with unique wall paintings and panels, and elaborate underfloor heating system. Brass rubbing, shop, disabled access (though no facilities); cl Mon (exc bank hols and July–Aug), and Oct–Mar; (01304) 203279; £2.

Samphire Hoe (W of Dover, off A20 via steep road tunnel) Created from the spoil from the Channel Tunnel, this is Britain's newest land. Wild flowers have been encouraged, and there's a short walk around the site, giving privileged views of the cliffs from beneath (something previously possible only from the sea); charge for car park.

White Cliffs of Dover These provide an exhilarating walk (and interesting views of the harbour – you can even see France on a clear day) from Dover Castle to St Margaret's at Cliffe, passing the Roman lighthouse above Dover, and a curious scaled-down windmill at St Margaret's. There's a bus back to Dover (no point making a circuit, as the inland scenery here is not worth while), or you can press on to Kingsdown (the Rising Sun is a handy stop) or to Deal.

DOWNE TQ4464
Surprisingly rural village on the North Downs, technically in Greater London but quite Kentish in character. Decent, though unspectacular, walking area, with very clearly marked paths inc the varied Cudham Circular Walk; a good starting point is High Elms, 1m NE, where from the car park you can stroll through the wooded High Elms estate. The Queens Head is a good pub.

Down House (Luxted Rd, out towards Westerham) Attractive restored house, former home of Charles Darwin who lived here with his family for 40 years, during which he wrote most of his major works inc *On the Origin of Species*. Filled with his personal belongings, notes and journals, the ground floor is much as it was when the Darwins were in residence, while upstairs is an interactive exhibition on

Darwin's life and work; the gardens have also been restored. Snacks, shop, disabled access; cl Mon (exc bank hols), Tues, and 24 Dec–1st Weds in Feb; best to pre-book in Aug; (01689) 859119; £6; EH.

DUNGENESS TR0817
Fascinatingly odd, a real curiosity and quite foreign-feeling, its acres of shingle colonised by fishing shacks and railway carriages converted into homes (Derek Jarman used to live here). There are more pebbles than you could ever imagine. It's a terminus for the little steam railway described under New Romney, and the Britannia has good local fish.

Dungeness Nature Reserve RSPB, on the shingle headland, interesting for its unusual plants and variety of nesting and migrating birds. Snacks, shop, disabled access; cl 25–26 Dec; (01797) 320588; £3, RSPB members free (guided walks from £2 extra).

Dungeness Visitor Centre and Power Stations Although tours of the power stations have been suspended, you can still pop into the visitor centre which has some interactive displays, and find out more about how electricity is made. Snacks, shop, disabled access (but must be booked well in advance); open Mon–Fri Mar–Oct (Nov–Feb by appointment only); no under-5s, as everyone has to wear a hard hat; (01797) 321815; free.

Old Lighthouse Fine views from the top of its 167 steps; shop; open daily May–Sept, wknds only Mar, Apr, and Oct (exc bank hols and school hols); (01797) 321300; £2.50.

ETCHINGHILL TR1638
Saxon Shore Way This long-distance path gives some good views and interesting walks. A section starting here crosses under an old railway line, heads up an unspoilt dry valley, and leads along the top of the slope for sightings of Dungeness and the French coast (Cap Gris Nez in Picardy).

EYNSFORD TQ5365
Eagle Heights Informative birds of prey centre, good in any weather as many displays are indoors (outdoor ones at 12 and 3.30). There's also a reptile house with some incredibly large pythons. You can handle snakes and

reptiles (1.45pm) and meet the owls (2.15pm). Snacks, shop, disabled access; cl wkdys Nov–Feb; (01322) 866466; £5.80.

Eynsford Castle Norman fortress with impressive 9-metre (30-ft) walls, and remains of the hall and ditch; cl 24–26 Dec, and 1 Jan; (01322) 863467; free. There are organised trails from the nearby countryside centre at Lullingstone Park, with various special events such as nature rambles, and bat evenings; phone to book; (01322) 865995; from £2. The Malt Shovel has good seafood.

Lullingstone Castle Historic family mansion with fine state rooms, great hall, staircase and library, and beautiful grounds. The 15th-c gate tower was one of the first buildings to be made entirely of brick. Shop, disabled access; open pm wknds and bank hols May–Aug; (01322) 862114; £5.

Lullingstone Roman Villa (just SE off A225) Remains of 1st- and 2nd-c family's villa, with exceptionally well preserved floor mosaics and an extensive bath complex. Also an early Christian chapel – the only one so far found in a private house. Snacks, shop, limited disabled access; cl 24–26 Dec and 1 Jan; (01322) 863467; £2.80.

FAVERSHAM TR0161
Delightfully photogenic small town ideal for a stroll: plenty of colour-washed timbered old buildings such as the Elizabethan grammar school and the Guild-hall (one of the few raised market halls still to shelter stallholders in the pillared market court beneath it – Tues/Fri/Sat). The Sun in picturesque West St does good value lunchtime food. The **Shepherd Neame Brewery** in Court St has guided tours and tastings (no children under 14, and wear comfortable shoes as there are some steep staircases; phone to book (01795) 542016; £5). Just N of the town, a track off the road to Oare leads to a remote waterside pub, the Shipwrights Arms: a charming setting on summer evenings.

Brogdale Orchard (Brogdale Rd, S of A2) This mammoth fruit farm, inc the National Fruit Collection, is beautiful but baffling to stroll through (guided walks available), its 40 acres of orchards housing hundreds of distinct varieties of every hardy fruit imaginable; there are 2,500 variants of apple alone. The shop sells trees, bushes and flowering plants, as well as crops from pears, plums and cherries to cobnuts, quinces and medlars. Meals, snacks, disabled access; cl 25 Dec and 1 Jan; (01795) 535286; free (exc for special events), £4 for a guided tour.

Chart Gunpowder Mills (Westbrook Walk) Well restored gunpowder mill, one of the last left in the world (for another, see Waltham Abbey in Essex chapter). Open pm wknds and bank hols Apr–Oct, by appointment at other times (01795) 534915; donations.

Fleur de Lis Heritage Centre ☒ (Preston St) Closed for expansion as we go to press, this enthusiastically run museum will be well worth a visit after reopening, with colourful displays, reconstructions and a working vintage-telephone exchange. Shop (good for books on Kent), disabled access; phone for museum opening times; (01795) 534542; £2. The Tourist Information Centre (limited hours Sun) is also here, and walking tours of Faversham leave at 10.30am every Sat Apr–Sept (£1).

FOLKESTONE TR2335
Despite much development of this major cross-Channel port, there is an intact pre-19th-c area called the Bayle around the interesting old church – very pretty and Kentish, with the British Lion a nice old pub. The part around the harbour, previously a picturesque warren, was badly bombed in World War II, but the fish stalls there contribute authentic local colour, the Old High St has a Cornish-type quaintness, and Carpenters (The Stade) has good fresh fish. They're currently smartening up the town centre with new street furniture and paving and better lighting; a new shopping centre and conference facilities are also being built. Just E of the harbour is the only sandy beach for miles (cramped at high tide but otherwise safe and popular). Particularly pleasant is a stroll along The Leas, a clifftop expanse of lawns and flower gardens with good views. For a longer walk carry on beyond The Leas down to Sandgate, an older village

beneath the cliffs, somewhat picturesquely faded and with a cluster of antique shops; the Clarendon, up a steep cobbled lane on the way, has enjoyable food. Return along the cycle path beneath the cliffs to a children's adventure playground, where you can zigzag back up through a mock grotto to the top. A water-balanced Victorain cliff-lift operates between The Leas and the seafront. You can usually watch sweet and rock making on summer afternoons (exc Weds and Sun) at Rowlands Confectionery on the Old High St; (01303) 254723; free. The Rotunda Amusement Park has traditional fairground rides, crazy golf and roller-coasters, with lots under cover. A controversial 265ft by 100ft Celtic-style white horse should have been cut into Cheriton Hill, by the beginning of 2003; it'll be the first and last thing that Channel Tunnel users will see of England.

Battle of Britain Memorial (just W on B2011) The huge stone figure looking out in contemplation across the Channel gives this an extraordinary air of calm solemnity. Conservatory and Memorial Wall engraved with Churchill's unforgettable tribute to the airmen. Snacks, shop, disabled access; cl Oct–Mar; (01303) 276697; free.

Folkestone Museum and Sassoon Art Gallery (Grace Hill) Brings the town's local and natural history to life through audio-visual displays and hands-on activities. A contemporary art gallery shows works by local and international artists. Snacks, shop, disabled access; cl Sun and bank hols; (01303) 850123; free.

Martello Tower Visitor Centre 🖳 (East Cliff) One of 74 towers built to defend the south coast from Napoleon's advances in the early 1800s, and later used as a command post during World War II; it has various local history displays inside, and rewarding views from the top. Shop; open daily May–end Sept, and wknds in Apr; (01303) 852277; £1.

Russian Submarine (South Quay) Built in 1967, and used to train foreign submariners – you can explore the claustrophobic cabins yourself; shop; cl Mon and Fri Jan–Feb and 25 Dec;

(01303) 240400; £3.95.

Warren This intriguingly jungly tumbledown undercliff is reached from the East Cliff by a walk out past the Martello Tower; once there you can cross a railway footbridge and reach the shore, or go up a flight of steps and on to the clifftop, to return along the cliffs past the Battle of Britain Memorial. The cliff path also makes for a good bracing walk all the way to Dover, for the train or bus back.

GILLINGHAM TQ7669
Royal Engineers Museum 🖳 (Brompton Barracks, Prince Arthur Rd) More appealing than you might think, with sound effects, art and oddities brought back from various countries, a Harrier jump jet, and Wellington's battle-map from Waterloo. Snacks, shop, disabled access; cl Fri, 25–26 Dec; (01634) 406397; *£3.50 The town has a partly Norman church. Off the A2 between here and Boughton Street village, any of the little lanes take you deep into orchard country, with foody pubs at Dargate, Selling and Eastling; blossom-time Apr and early May, many farm shops with local apples Sept onwards. Covering a big swathe of former farmland, **Capstone Farm Country Park** (Capstone Rd) is typical of the rolling landscape of the North Downs. Visitor centre, pet area, picnic and play areas, fishing permits; (01634) 812196; free.

GOODNESTONE TR2653
Goodnestone Park Old-fashioned roses in traditional walled garden recalling Jane Austen's stays in the fine 18th-c house (not open). Also woodland garden with good trees. Teas, nursery, disabled access; cl Tues, Sat, Sun am and Nov–Mar; (01304) 840107; £3.30. The Fitzwalter Arms has good value food.

GOUDHURST TQ7237
Charming Wealden village, with quite a few antiques shops and so forth, and spectacular views from the graveyard of the 14th-c hilltop church (but during the day too much traffic for comfort).

Finchcocks (off A262 W of Goudhurst) The early Georgian house and its lovely gardens are attractive, but the main draw is the important collection of working keyboard instruments from the 17th c onwards. Some of these are played whenever the house is open, the well organised recitals really adding to the atmosphere. Special events, meals (by arrangement), snacks, shop, some disabled access; open Weds and Thurs pm Aug, as well as Sun pm and some bank hols Easter-Sept (otherwise by appointment) – phone to check; (01580) 211702; £7. The Green Cross Inn up by the main road is good for fish.

GRAVESEND TQ6573
New Tavern Fort (Milton Ave) Originally built in the 1780s to defend the Thames against the threat of a naval attack from France, it was extensively rebuilt in Victorian times (the huge guns date from then); you can explore the underground magazine complex, and there's an exhibition on Gravesend during the Blitz. Open wknds and bank hols May–Sept (though best to check as they were closed for repairs when we went to press), gardens open all year; (01474) 337470; £2. Along by the Tilbury ferry pier, the New Falcon has decent food. Also in the gardens, a 14th-c Chantry now houses a local history musem; shop, limited disabled access; usually open pm Weds–Sun May–end Sept, pm wknds Oct–Dec, Mar and Apr; (01474) 365984; £1.

GROOMBRIDGE TQ5337
Groombridge Place Gardens See *separate family panel on p.324.* The Crown prettily placed round the corner does good food.

HADLOW TQ6249
Broadview Gardens A good mix of traditional and imaginatively themed gardens put together by students at Hadlow College; the atmospheric Heaven and Hell Garden is one of our favourites. National collections of hellebores and Japanese anemones, and a well stocked plant centre. Meals wkdys only, snacks, shop, disabled access; cl mid-Oct to Mar; (01732) 850551; £2; free car parking. Hadlow's church has an interesting memorial dedicated to the 30 hop pickers who one wet day in 1853 drowned on their way back from the fields; the enormously tall folly of Hadlow Tower is worth a look, and the Artichoke (Park Rd) has decent food.

HAWKINGE TR2039
Kent Battle of Britain Museum Plenty of aeroplanes, and extensive collection of relics and memorabilia of British and German aircraft involved in the fighting, inc relics of more than 600 crashed aircraft. Snacks, shop, disabled access but no facilities; cl Mon, and Nov–Easter; (01303) 893140; £3.50. The Valiant Sailor at Capel-le-Ferne (A20) saves you going into Folkestone for lunch.

HERNE BAY TR1868
Not terribly exciting, but a decorous and spaciously laid-out 19th-c resort. There's a decent art gallery on William St; shop, disabled access; open Mon–Sat, plus Sun pm July–Aug; (01227) 367368; free. The working windmill on Mill Lane is also worth a visit; shop; open pm Sun and bank hols Easter–Sept, plus Thurs July–Aug; (01227) 361326; £1. The Rose (Mortimer St) is useful for lunch. Mike Turner runs boat trips around the bay and out to see seals, May–Oct; best to book for the seal trip (01227) 366712.
Wildwood (Herne Common) Decent woodland wildlife park, strong on conservation, with the only breeding pack of European wolves in Britain; other animals to spot include deer, badgers, polecats, rabbits and hedgehogs. Costumed artists demonstrate ancient crafts in the developing re-created Saxon village, and there's an enjoyably varied programme of events throughout the year; also picnic and play areas. Meals, snacks, shop, disabled access; (01227) 712111; £6.25.

HERNHILL TR0659
Mount Ephraim Gardens 🔟 Eight acres of pleasant gardens, with Japanese-style rock garden, topiary garden, water garden, woodland walk, and new rose garden; good views. Teas, shop; cl am, Tues, Fri, and Oct–Easter; (01227) 751496; £3.50. There's a craft centre on Sun pms. By the church and small green of this charming village, the ancient Red Lion has decent food.

HEVER TQ4745
Hever Castle & Gardens In 30 beautiful acres, double-moated 13th-c castle little changed externally since Anne Boleyn lived here as a child. Inside

it's a different story, as the rooms were magnificently restored by the Astor family in the early 1900s. Antiques, furnishings and art mostly from 16th c, plus a room dedicated to Henry VIII's wives. Another building is home to an exceptional collection of astonishingly detailed miniature houses, furnished and decorated in authentic period styles. The council chambers in the gatehouse (the oldest part of the castle) have recently been reopened; various gruesome instruments of torture are on display, and new information boards cover the castle's history. The grounds are a draw in their own right, with a lake, Italianate garden with antique sculptures, walled rose garden and maze; also very popular summer splashing water maze, and adventure playground. There are frequent Tudor costume events in summer. Meals, snacks, shop, good disabled access to gardens, but to ground floor only of castle; cl Dec–Feb, castle cl am; (01732) 865224; £8.20, £6.50 gardens only. The Henry VIII is popular for lunch.

HYTHE TR1634

A hillside town full of attractive corners: above the narrow High St, steep paths and lanes lead up towards the church, and there are numerous pleasant old houses. A path from the junction of Station Rd (B2065) and Mill Lane enters parkland and continues up to Saltwood Castle (the late Alan Clarke's house; not open to the public), which still has its impressive medieval curtain wall. You can extend the walk W to Lympne Castle and the Royal Military Canal at West Hythe. On the seaward side, beyond the Royal Military Canal, Hythe is quite different in character, though still distinctly quiet, with a beach stretching to Sandgate, also pleasant to stroll through.

Romney, Hythe & Dymchurch Railway Well run and friendly, this is the world's smallest-scale public railway, with 13½ miles of 15in-gauge track between Hythe and Dungeness. The station has a toy and model museum with two magnificent model railways. Engines are often changed en route, and the carriages are comfortable. Meals, snacks, shop,

disabled access (they prefer notice); trains daily Apr–Sept, wknds Oct and Feb, Mar – phone for timetable; (01797) 362353; £9.40 full fare (but wide range of lower ones).

St Leonard's church The crypt houses an amazing collection of 2,000 skulls and 8,000 thigh bones, dating from before 1500 and all neatly arranged on shelves or carefully stacked in a large heap; Shop, disabled access (exc to crypt); cl Sun am (exc for services), and Oct–Apr; 50p.

IDE HILL TQ4851

With its pubs and picture-book green, this is on the scarp slope of the lower greensand escarpment, and on the Greensand Way: a good walking area. Views from the eponymous wooded rise, Ide Hill, reached from behind the church, just to the S.

Emmetts Garden (Toys Hill, 1m NW) Charming hillside shrub garden with magnificent views – it's one of the highest gardens in Kent. Full of bluebells in spring and a riot of colour in autumn. Snacks, shop, some disabled access; open wknds, Weds and bank hols Apr–Oct (Weds–Sun Apr–Jun); (01732) 868381; £3.50; NT.

IGHTHAM TQ5853

Ightham Mote (off A227, 2m S) Lovely medieval manor house, still with its surrounding moat, a unique survival that looks esp beautiful on a sunny day. Fascinating great hall (recently re-opened after restoration), Tudor chapel and 14th-c crypt, while the drawing room has a striking Jacobean fireplace, frieze and windows. You can now look around a Victorian housekeeper's room and, if there are enough staff, visit the tower; restoration of the West Quarter should be complete by the end of 2003. Pretty courtyard, garden and woodland walks. The National Trust will have opened a second restaurant here by the time we go to press, shop, disabled access; cl Tues, Sat, and late Nov–Mar; (01732) 810378; £5.40; NT. The early 16th-c George and Dragon in the village is a good all-day dining pub (just lunchtime on Sun).

ISLE OF SHEPPEY TR0469

Walkers may enjoy the E end, with a path along the sea dyke S from

Leysdown-on-Sea to Shell Ness, at the mouth of the Swale.

LAMBERHURST TQ6436

Bayham Abbey (2m W, just over Sussex border) Impressive ruins of 13th-c Premonstratensian abbey and gatehouse in pretty wooded valley. Occasional outdoor theatre and special events. Snacks, shop, disabled access; cl wkdys Nov–Mar, and 24–26 Dec, 1 Jan; (01892) 890381; £2.30. The Elephants Head at Hook Green is a useful nearby pub.

Lamberhurst Vineyard Park (Ridge Farm) One of the biggest vineyards in SE England, no tours but you can wander round, and there are free tastings; play area and garden centre. Meals (in the vineyard's pub), snacks, shop, limited disabled access; cl 25 Dec–2 Jan; (01892) 890412; free.

Owl House Gardens 💷 (off A21 NE) 16 acres of sweeping lawns, flowers, shrubs and fruit trees around timber-framed 16th-c wool smugglers' house; sunken water gardens and woodlands. Teas (exc Sept–Apr), shop, disabled access; cl 25 Dec, 1 Jan; (01892) 890230; £4 (free for wheelchair users).

Scotney Castle Garden (A21 just S) Beautiful 19th-c gardens surrounding the ruins of a small 14th-c moated castle, with impressive rhododendrons, azaleas and roses – a really romantic place. Shop, some disabled access (they recommend a strong pusher); open Weds–Sun and bank hols 22 Mar–9 Nov (exc Good Fri), castle open same hours May–mid Sept, but best to check; (01892) 891081; £4.40; NT. A public footpath strides through the estate's woods and pastures, which can form a basis for circular walks from Kilndown to Lamberhurst and back. The Brown Trout, on B2169 nearly opposite the present main entrance, has good fish. The attractive village got the go-ahead for a bypass back in 1992, but has faced endless delays, including (against vociferous local opposition) a costly redesign of the scheme to add a new £3 million bridge to the castle.

LEEDS TQ8353

Leeds Castle Long renowned as one of the loveliest castles in the country, perfectly placed on two little islands in the middle of a lake in 500 acres of landscaped parkland. It dates from the 9th c, and was converted into a Royal residence by Henry VIII. Lots of paintings, furniture and tapestries, and a unique dog-collar museum in the gatehouse. The enormous grounds have gardens (inc a Mediterranean one), a maze and grotto, duck enclosure and aviary (well liked by readers), and a golf course; as this suggests, it's a busy place, not quite as idyllic as it appears from a distance, but very satisfying for a day out. Special events from food and wine festivals to open-air concerts. Meals, snacks, shop, good disabled access; cl 28 Jun, 5 July, and 25 Dec; (01622) 765400; £11 Mar–Oct, otherwise £9.50. The Windmill at Eyhorne Street is good value for lunch.

LYMPNE TR0935

Port Lympne Wild Animal Park 💷 In wonderful ornamental parkland around a well restored house, Port Lympne and its sister park Howletts are well known for their genuinely dedicated approach to looking after the rare or endangered animals in their care; animals are kept in enclosures as close to their natural habitat as possible, with an aim to return them to the wild if they can. They believe the bonds developed between keepers and animals well worth even the rare casualties. There's a lot to see, paths can be steep, and there are 300 acres altogether – the free shuttle trailers between enclosures are welcome. The gorilla-breeding programme (shared with Howletts) of 65 lowland gorillas is the most successful of its kind in the world. The park is also home to the country's largest breeding herd of black rhino. Other animals include tigers, elephants, lions and tapirs, and they hold occasional special talks and events. The house has unusual features, inc the Hexagonal Library used to sign the Treaty of Paris after World War I, Rex Whistler's incredible Tent Room, and one room entirely covered by a mural showing south-east Asian animals and birds. Meals, snacks, shop, disabled access; cl 25 Dec; (01303) 264647; £11.95

Royal Military Canal Built along the N fringe of Romney Marsh as a defence against Napoleon, this forms a section of the Saxon Shore Way long-distance path. You can combine it with a path along the escarpment at Lympne Castle; the Botolphs Bridge Inn just S has decent home cooking.

MAIDSTONE TQ7555
Busy modern town, but worth penetrating for its good museums. The Muggleton (King St) is an exemplary pub converted from a very grand Victorian building in conjunction with English Heritage. There are daily boat trips between here and the Malta Inn at Allington, hourly from midday, Apr–Oct; (01622) 661064; £3.
Archbishop's Palace (Mill St) Striking edifice used by the Archbishops of Canterbury as a stopping-place on their way from London, but now mostly converted offices. If there are no functions on, you can visit the Great Hall; cl 25–26 Dec; (01622) 663006; free.
Maidstone Museum and Bentlif Art Gallery 🖼 (St Faiths St) Handsome Elizabethan manor house with original period room settings. Snacks, shop; cl 25–26 Dec; (01622) 754497; free.
Museum of Carriages Notable collection of horse-drawn vehicles housed in the palace stables. Shop, disabled access to ground floor only; cl 25–26 Dec; (01622) 754497; £2. The site also includes the old parish church of All Saints.
Museum of Kent Life 🖼 (Sandling) The story of the Kent countryside, entertainingly told over 27 acres, taking in farming tools, crafts, gardens, animals, and an oast house. A fair bit for children and lots of special events. There are also two historic cottages, rescued from the path of the Channel Tunnel rail link at Lenham Heath; Old Cottage tells the story of the rescue, while Waterstreet Cottage has been reconstructed in World War II style. Meals, snacks, shop, disabled access; cl Nov–Feb; (01622) 763936; £4.90. Nearby, the well restored 17th-c Tyland Barn on Bluebell Hill is the HQ of Kent Wildlife Trust, with information on the area's nature reserves; cl 22 Dec–beginning Feb; (01622) 662012; free. The 16th/17th-c Kings Arms in the pretty neighbouring village of Boxley

has decent food (all day Sun), with pleasant walks nearby.
MARDEN TQ7444
This attractive village has a 12th/14th-c ragstone church with a unique white weatherboarded tower, and other buildings going back to the 14th c.
Marden Meadow (Staplehurst Rd) A lovely unimproved hay meadow, alive with wild flowers and butterflies in late spring and early summer. The Wild Duck just S (Pagehurst Lane) has good food.
MARGATE TR3571
Often rather brash seaside resort, though there's plenty here for families inc excellent sandy beaches. Huge grants from the European Union are going some way towards restoring its glory days, and a new Turner gallery is planned for 2005 – the artist visited the town regularly, and it inspired more than 100 of his paintings. You can find out more about Turner and the regeneration of the Old Town (which they'd like to turn into an artists' quarter) at Droit House in the harbour; cl Mon, free. The Old Town Hall (Market Pl) has a local history museum (cl Mon Easter–Sept, plus Tues–Weds in winter, and usually 3 wks over Christmas, but phone to check; (01843) 231213; £1), and nearby is the well preserved Tudor House, open only on special occasions, but worth a look from outside. The Spread Eagle (Victoria Rd) has popular food. To the E of town on College Rd there's a working windmill (usually open Sun pm May–Sept and Thurs eve Aug, but best to check; (01843) 226227; £1).
Dreamland Theme Park Once through the inauspicious entrance, this is a very satisfactory and well laid out fairground with rides from dodgems to a log flume, as well as the oldest working roller-coaster in Britain – the first fairground ride to be given a Grade II listing. Meals, snacks, shop; cl Nov–Mar; (01843) 227011; £11.99 if you are over 1.37 metres (4 ft 6 in), otherwise £7.99.
Margate Caves 🖼 (Northdown Rd) These huge caverns are atmospheric – with wall-paintings and spooky shapes and shadows. Shop; open Easter–Oct; (01843) 220139; £2.

Shell Grotto 🏛 (Grotto Hill) An unexpected puzzle is this 185 sq metre (2,000 sq ft) of winding underground passages and exquisitely decorated tunnels leading to a mysterious ancient shell temple, thought to be the only one in the world. No-one knows its origins or what it was for, but a museum shows all the different theories, so that you can make up your own mind. Gallery with exhibitions, art workshops, craft fairs, and Santa's grotto wknds in Dec; snacks, shop; grotto cl wkdys Nov–Easter; (01843) 220008; *£2.

MEOPHAM TQ6365

Meopham windmill Unusual both for its six sides and for the fact that its base is a meeting place for the parish council. Shop; usually open pm Sun and bank hols May–Sept though as went to press it was closed for repairs so best to check; (01474) 812465; £1. The Cricketers prettily set on the green is a useful food pub.

MINSTER IN THANET TR3164

Minster Abbey Site of one of the earliest nunneries in the country, with ruins and cloisters of the 7th-c building. The present house is still run by Benedictine nuns. Shop, some disabled access and facilities; open 11am-noon, then 2.30–4 pm, am only Oct–Apr, cl Sun and Sat pm; (01843) 821254; free. The Mortons Fork has interesting wine bar and restaurant food.

ONE TREE HILL TQ5653

Reached from a NT car park S of Godden Green (where the old Bucks Head facing the duck pond is useful for lunch), this gives walkers a grand view over the Weald. From here the Greensand Way (look for GW markers) follows the very edge of the lower greensand escarpment which dips gently down to Ightham Mote, two miles E; Ivy Hatch and Stone Street have handily placed pubs to make this into a circuit.

OTFORD TQ5159

This charming village has a ruined archbishop's palace, and pleasant walks along an easy track to the attractive nearby village of **Shoreham**, which has a lovely church. There are decent pubs in both villages. The downlands to the E give scope for longer walks across Magpie Bottom and past Romney Street.

OTHAM TQ7953

Stoneacre Lovely half-timbered 15th-c manor house, restored in 1920s, with charming cottage garden. Open pm Weds and Sat mid-Mar to mid-Oct; (01622) 862157; £2.60; NT.

PENSHURST TQ5243

A pretty village, with antiques shops, teas and so forth. The Leicester Arms now has good food all day, and up on Smarts Hill the Spotted Dog has lovely views down over Penshurst Place. The Bottle House and the Rock out in this direction are also both well worth tracking down if you're walking in this attractive area, which has some of the Weald's most luscious lowlands, predominantly pasture, the cottages characteristically tile-hung, and the paths just elevated enough to gain charming views. As with much of the rest of the area, route-finding for walks is fiddly and patient map-reading is in order. One of the best circular routes, passing several good pubs, is Penshurst–Chiddingstone Hoath–Chiddingstone.

Penshurst Place A great medieval manor house, unchanged since the Sidney family first came here centuries ago. Interesting combination of architectural styles, huge chestnut-beamed baronial hall, extensive collections of portraits and furnishings, toy museum, and marvellous formal gardens with woodland trail and adventure playground; special events. Snacks, shop and plant centre, disabled access to grounds (inc a garden for the blind); house cl am, wkdys in Mar, all Nov–Feb; (01892) 870307; £6.50, grounds only £5.

Penshurst Vineyards (Grove Rd) Self-guided tours, tastings and various animals inc wallabies and exotic waterfowl. Cl 24 Dec–2 Jan, and wknds Jan and Feb; (01892) 870255; £1.50 to see the animals (children free).

PLAXTOL TQ6154

Old Soar Manor An ancient oak door at this 13th-c knight's dwelling has graffiti spanning the ages, and there's also a very well preserved chapel and barrel-vaulted undercroft; cl Fri, and Sept–early Apr; (01732) 810378; free; NT. This general area is attractive orchard country, not too hedged, with good value apples from the farm shops, from Sept onwards; many here also have fresh cobnuts in Sept. The Tudor Kentish Rifleman (Dunks Green) has good food and an appealing garden.

PLUCKLEY TQ9245
This attractive estate village saw the filming of *The Darling Buds of May*, and has good pubs for refreshment, pleasant if not well marked walks.

RAMSGATE TR3864
Quietly civilised seaside resort, with some elegantly colonnaded Georgian buildings and other fine houses up on the cliffs (Pugin, the architect of parts of the Houses of Parliament, designed the church – where he's buried – and the house next door), and a historic harbour (bustling now with its yacht marina). Down by it, the Ramsgate Royal Harbour is an unusual café-bar doing its own brewing and baking all day.

Maritime Museum (Pier Yard) Good collection of historic ships and boats in a handsome early 19th-c harbour clock-house. Shop; cl Mon Easter–Sept, phone for winter opening; (01843) 587765; £1.50.

Motor Museum (West Cliff Hall, The Paragon) Vintage cars, motorbikes and bicycles in cheerful period settings; shop, disabled access; open daily Apr–early Sept, and Sun only in winter; (01843) 581948; £3.50.

RECULVER TR2269
Reculver Towers & Roman Fort
Built in the 3rd c, this was well preserved until the early 19th c, when cliff erosion collapsed some of it into the sea; some parts remain, though it's the proud pair of tall Saxon towers of the former church on the mound above the beach that stay in the memory. Surrounding these remains is a **country park**, with a visitor centre. Meals, snacks, shop, disabled access; (cl Mon exc bank hols, plus Tues in Sept and Mon–Sat Oct–Mar, but best to check); (01227) 740676; free.

RICHBOROUGH TR3260
Richborough Castle In Roman times, this was Britain's port of entry, and a sizeable town grew up here. You can still see the base of a vast triumphal arch which started people on their Watling Street journey inland, and there are

appreciable relics of the Roman castle curtain wall and other foundations; plus a small museum. Snacks, shop, disabled access. Cl Mon and Tues Mar, all wkdys Nov–Feb, 25 Dec, and 1 Jan; (01304) 612013; £2.80 (inc audio tour); EH.

ROCHESTER TQ7468
This busy town is well worth walking round, with several attractive buildings besides those we mention; one of the quaintest is Kent's oldest pub, the Coopers Arms (St Margaret's St; cheap lunches), and many of those on the High St feature in Dickens's novels. Casa-Lina (High St) has nice Italian family cooking.

Charles Dickens Centre (High St) Late Tudor house used in both *Pickwick Papers* and *Edwin Drood*, with scenes and characters from the author's books brought vividly to life using impressive hi-tech effects. Shop; cl 24–26 Dec, and 1 Jan; (01634) 844176; £3.90.

Gad's Hill School (Higham, A226 NW) Dickens fans should also try to visit this, the only house the writer ever owned. He wrote many of his novels here, and his first sight of the house, many years before he lived there, is described in *A Christmas Carol*. Cream teas; open pm first Sun of month Easter-Dec, plus bank hol Suns, during Rochester's summer and Christmas Dickens festivals, and other times – out of school hours – by arrangement; (01474) 822366; £3.50.

Guildhall Museum (High St) The highlight is a three-tier life-size replica of a late 18th-c convict hulk which was once moored on the Medway. There are also re-created Victorian and Edwardian drawing rooms, lots of Victoriana, 18th-c portraits, local history, and hands-on exhibits for children. The decorated plaster ceilings are impressive; changing exhibitions. Shop, disabled access to ground floor only; cl 25–26 Dec; (01634) 848717; free.

Restoration House 🖼 (Crow Lane) From Tudor beginnings to recent conservation work, you can trace the development of this city mansion where Charles II stayed and Dickens reputedly found inspiration for the home of Miss Haversham in *Great Expectations*; fine furniture and pictures inc works by

Kneller, Reynolds and Gainsborough. Pepys kissed a shopkeeper's wife in the very English interlinked walled gardens. Open Thurs and Fri Jun–Sept, phone to check; (01634) 848520; £5 (inc a guidebook), £2 gardens only.

Rochester Castle One of the best examples of 12th-c military architecture – dramatic too; the great square keep is one of the tallest in England. Shop; cl a few days over Christmas; (01634) 402276; £3.90, audio tour 50p; EH.

Rochester Cathedral Spectacularly Norman, with original richly carved door, vaulted crypt, St Gundulf's tower, tombs and effigies, and huge 15th-c window. A new fresco to be finished by Easter is the first to be painted in an English cathedral for 800 years; by contrast the Gundulf Door now turns out to be England's oldest, with wood dating from 822. The choir sings Evensong at 5.30 wkdys, 3.15 wknds. Snacks, shop, good disabled access; (01634) 401301; £3 suggested donation.

ROLVENDEN TQ8331
Good walking territory, with consistently appealing Wealden scenery, a **windmill** (not open to the public) and oast houses gracing the landscape; the Star has enjoyable food.

C M Booth Collection of Vehicles ⊞ (High St) Some unusual features inc a unique collection of 3-wheeled Morgans and a 1930s caravan; also toy and model cars and other automobilia. Shop; cl Sun, 25–26 Dec; (01580) 241234; £1.50.

SANDHURST TQ7828
Sandhurst Vineyard (Hoads Farm, Crouch Lane) Tours of vineyard and hop gardens (£2 with guide, otherwise free); hop-picking in Sept. Tastings and shop; cl am, and Jan–Easter exc by arrangement; (01580) 850296; free. They do B&B in a 16th-c farmhouse. The village has a fine 14th-c **church** with good views from the graveyard.

Tile Barn Nursery (Standen Street, Iden Green) The only nursery in the world to specialise in wild cyclamen, with four greenhouses filled with over two dozen miniature species, most of them hardy, in flower Sept–Apr, also other rare bulbs. Cl Sun–Tues; (01580)

24022; free. The 17th-c Woodcock signed nearby has decent food.

Wealden walk E of the village (which has a fine 14th-c church with good views from the graveyard) a pleasant round walk runs from Burnt House Farm on the A268, via Cledge Wood and Marsh Quarter Farm to the Kent Ditch and the River Rother, to take you round to Bodiam Castle in Sussex, and back via Northlands Farm and Silverden.

SANDWICH TR3358
One of the best-preserved old towns in South-East England, and surprisingly untouristy: in many of the quiet old streets there's not a jarring note, with fine timbered buildings in Strand St and by the attractive former quay on the River Stour, nr the photogenic Bargate. You can go on a guided tour of the handsome Elizabethan *guildhall* in New St (11.30 and 2.30 Tues–Thurs exc 24 Dec–2 Jan, best to check; (01304) 617197; £1). The numerous medieval remains include some sections of the old town wall and three handsome medieval churches, one part-Norman. In its day it was one of England's main commercial ports; the sea's now left it far behind. The Admiral Owen (High St), Kings Arms (Strand St) and Red Cow (Moat Sole) all have decent food and long histories, and the St Crispin in the pretty village of Worth just S is also pleasant for lunch.

White Mill ⊞ (A257 just outside) A cheerful developing place set around an 18th-c smock mill, with a little rural history museum and a cottage furnished in pre-1939 style. Shop, mostly disabled access; open all year am Fri and Sun, plus pm Sun and bank hol Mon Easter to mid-Sept; (01304) 612076; £2.

SEVENOAKS TQ5453
Although there's little to see in this commuters' town apart from the handsome old buildings of Sevenoaks School, the area around it has more walk potential than a glance at the OS map might suggest. The terrain is complicated, the Wealden villages unspoilt to a remarkable degree, and the path network dense and very well kept. Orchards, hop gardens, tile-clad timber-framed cottages and oast houses set the Kentish theme.

Newcomers may be surprised to find such attractive and deeply rural countryside so close to London.

Knole (just E) Originally a simple medieval manor house, this was transformed into a palace by a 15th-c archbishop, Henry VIII, and several generations of the Sackville family. It's now a magnificent set piece, the largest – some would say the grandest – still lived-in private house in the country. It's a calendar house, with 365 rooms, 52 staircases and 7 courtyards. Wrap up well: some of the beautifully furnished rooms can get a little chilly. Outside are 26 acres of attractive grounds and a 1,000-acre deer park. Meals, snacks, shop, some disabled access; open pm Weds–Sun and bank hol Mon Apr–Oct (the garden is usually open only on the first Weds of each month May–Sept) – best to check, park open daily; (01732) 450608; £5.50, £2.50 car park; NT. The park is criss-crossed with public paths and tracks encompassing the deer park, as well as the great house itself; free.

Riverhill House Gardens (A225 S) Hillside gardens with rose and shrub terraces, woodland walks among fine trees, rhododendrons, bluebells in spring, and fine views. Teas, plant sales; open pm Weds, Sun and bank hol Sat and Mon Apr–Jun; (01732) 458802; £3.

Sevenoaks Wildfowl Reserve (Bradbourne Vale Rd) 135 acres of lakes, ponds, woodland and reedbeds, several viewing hides and a satisfying nature trail. Snacks, shop, disabled access; open Weds, wknds and bank hols (exc over Christmas, phone to check); (01732) 456407; £4.

SISSINGHURST TQ8037

Sissinghurst Garden Created by Vita Sackville-West and her husband Sir Harold Nicolson, these several charming gardens are themed according to season or colour, all offset by the lovely Elizabethan tower (not open). Meals, snacks, shop, disabled access; cl Weds, Thurs, and Nov–Mar, best to check; (01580) 710700; £6.50; NT. The Three Chimneys on the way to Biddenden is nice for lunch.

SMALL HYTHE TQ8930

Smallhythe Place 🏠 (B2082) Handsome half-timbered house, now a museum of the life of former resident, the actress Dame Ellen Terry; charming rose garden. Open Sat–Weds Apr–Oct; (01580) 762334; £3.40; NT.

Tenterden Vineyard Park Acres of vines, attractive lake ideal for picnics, winery, herb garden, agricultural museum and children's adventure trail; group guided tours £3.50; meals, snacks, shop, some disabled access; cl 24 Dec–2 Jan; (01580) 763033; free.

Wittersham windmill (B2082 S) The tallest post mill in Kent, with good views over Romney Marsh and the Isle of Oxney; shop; open Sun pm and bank hols May–Sept.

ST MARGARET'S BAY TR3844

Pines Garden (Beach Rd) Six acres of trees, shrubs, flowers, an ornamental lake and waterfall and a Romany caravan, with an interesting small local history museum; £1. Summer snacks, shop, disabled access; museum cl am, Mon and Tues and all Sept–end May, garden cl 25 Dec; (01304) 852764; £2. The spectacularly sited Coastguard is useful for refreshments.

South Foreland Lighthouse You can go on a guided tour of this 19th-c lighthouse, used by Marconi in his early radio experiments; this was the first lighthouse to have an electrically powered beam, and the views from the top are excellent. The nearest parking is 2m away at the Langdon Cliffs visitor centre. Shop; cl Tues, Weds, and all Nov–Feb; (01304) 852463; *£2; NT.

STAPLEHURST TQ7842

Iden Croft Herbs 🏠 (Frittenden Rd) Peaceful walled herb gardens, with national collections of thyme, mint and marjoram, and gardens designed for the blind and disabled. Snacks, plant sales, disabled access; cl winter wknds; (01580) 891432; £2 gardens. The Lord Raglan (Chart Hill Rd) has good food.

STELLING MINNIS TR1446

Stelling Minnis windmill Working mill with small museum; usually open pms; donations welcome. The Tiger over at Stowting has good food.

STODMARSH TR2260

National Nature Reserve Huge expanse of watery marshland, with water channels and reedy lakes; wellingtons advisable at wetter times, when the paths may be flooded.

Beautiful walking country at any time of year, and a prime site for bird life, inc wild ducks, kingfishers and migrants such as avocets and sandpipers; mammals inc weasels, stoats and occasionally otters. Free descriptive map from car park just N of Stodmarsh (where the Red Lion is a delightful place for a good lunch).

STROOD TQ7469

Diggerland 🔢 (Whitewall Rd, via Anthonys Way off A289 by Medway Tunnel) This unusual adventure park may be moving – so best to phone to check the address before setting off. Under close supervision, children over 5 can work real excavation equipment inc JCB diggers, dumpers and a fork-lift truck. Rides or drives last around five minutes, and there are various challenges such as fishing a duck from a pond. Also pedal-power diggers, computer games and a video, bouncy castle, and a play area for under-6s. Meals, snacks, shop, disabled access. Open wknds, bank hols and school hols (exc 25 Dec); (08700) 344437; £2.50 entrance fee, from £1.50 per ride or drive.

SWINGFIELD TR2142

Butterfly Centre (MacFarlane's Garden Centre) Family-run garden centre and butterfly house; snacks, plant sales, shop; open Apr–Sept; (01303) 844244; £2.

TENTERDEN TQ8833

Busy but attractive small town with lots of charming 17th- and 18th-c weather-boarded buildings ranged along its broad High St (which could almost be somewhere in New England). A few antiques and reproduction shops, and the White Lion and Eight Bells both have enjoyable food.

Kent & East Sussex Railway (A28 W) Steam trains now run right through to Bodiam Castle in Sussex; lovely Wealden views. Meals, snacks, shop, disabled access; cl Nov and Jan–Mar, phone (01580) 765155 for timetable; £7.50. Over the crossing, a Nissen hut houses a small museum looking at the history of the railway (open pms Tues–Thurs, wknds and bank hols Jun–Sept, pms wknds and bank hols only Apr–May, and Oct; £1). There's a small local history museum further up

the road (open wknd pms in Mar, Sat–Thurs pms Apr–Oct, and all day Sat–Thurs late July–Aug, though best to check; (01580) 764310; £1).

THROWLEY TQ9856

Belmont 🔢 Pleasant 18th-c mansion in well placed parkland, with a sizeable collection of unusual clocks, and a walled garden inc a restored period kitchen garden. Teas, shop, disabled access to gardens and ground floor only; open pm wknds and bank hols end Mar–Sept; (01795) 890202; £5.25, £2.75 garden only. The Alma in Painter's Forstal has good value home cooking.

TONBRIDGE TQ5946

Tonbridge Castle 🔢 (just off High St) Splendid Norman castle, with interactive displays, audio tours and re-created medieval scenes. Shop; open Jun–24 Dec (they're building a new roof for the castle though, so best to check); (01732) 770929; £4 (free to motte and bailey castle site). The Chequers nearby has good value food. The commuter town is perked up a bit by the distinguished buildings of Tonbridge School, there are several wine bars and small trendy shops, and with an outdoor area the swimming pool is a cut above the average municipal baths. In summer you can hire rowing boats on the river; (01732) 360630; £7.

TROTTISCLIFFE TQ6561 (pronounced Trosley) There's a good walk E to the **Coldrum Stones**, a 4,000-year-old burial chamber, with an extension on to the North Downs (Trosley Country Park), densely wooded exc on the steep slope itself. A problem for walkers elsewhere around here is that as you head E the farmland soon gets arable, with tedious slogs over ploughed fields.

TUNBRIDGE WELLS TQ5838 Very much a commuters' shopping centre nowadays (and popular with foreign language students in summer), but parts still show its former character as a genteel spa town. The allegedly health-restoring water still trickles through the Pantiles, the former centre of the town, full of elegant buildings and interesting shops. You can try the water at the Chalybeate Spring here, 40p a glass; cl end Oct–Mar. The **church** of

King Charles the Martyr is an interesting chapel built in the late 17th c for the gentry visiting the Pantiles; it has a remarkable plaster ceiling. Above the Pantiles the hillside Common is pleasant for strolls, with plenty of trees and rocks.

A Day at The Wells🔌 (The Pantiles) The town's Georgian heyday elaborately brought to life using up-to-date display technology and re-creations. Shop, disabled access (prior notice preferred); cl 25 Dec; (01892) 546545; £5.50.

High Rocks🔌 (off A264 just W) On the edge of town, this former Stone Age camp has acres of impressive sandstone formations interlinked with bridges which give woodland walks; no unaccompanied children, and take care when wet. Meals, snacks; cl 26 Dec and 1 Jan; (01892) 515532; £2. Nearby on Tea Garden Lane the Beacon has enjoyable bar food.

Spa Valley Railway (West Station, by Sainsburys, off A26 just S of centre) Runs steam train trips to Groombridge. Snacks, shop, disabled access; cl Nov, Jan and Feb, best to ring (01892) 537715 for timetable; £4 return.

Tunbridge Wells Museum and Art Gallery (Civic Centre, Mount Pleasant Rd) Examples of Tunbridge ware, the area's speciality small-scale woodware, as well as local and natural history, historic costume, toys and dolls, and frequently changing art exhibitions. Shop, disabled access; cl Sun and bank hols; (01892) 554171; free.

UPCHURCH TQ8467
Upchurch church 13th-c, with a unique 'candle snuffer' tower. An attractive village, with a decent pub.

UPNOR TQ7570
Upnor Castle Well preserved Elizabethan castle notorious for failing to protect the Medway from the Dutch in 1667; attractive turrets, gatehouse and windows. Snacks, shop; open Apr–Oct; (01634) 718742; £3.90. In this pretty sailing village, the Waterfront (Pier Place) has good seafood, and the Kings Arms has inexpensive pub food.

WEST KINGSDOWN TQ5763
Saxon church Largely Saxon, given great appeal by its unique tranquil

setting, secluded in the middle of a wood; notice the ancient yew tree by the W door.

WEST MALLING TQ6857
Attractive village, most of which is a conservation area thanks to its many old timbered houses and wells; lots of nice alleyways to explore. Particularly worth a look are the **abbey**, one of the country's oldest ecclesiastical buildings, and **St Leonards Tower**, a fine Norman tower from an 11th-c castle. The Swan has good modern food.

WESTERHAM TQ4454
This pleasant country town is perhaps best known to visitors for Chartwell nearby; there are pleasant walks in the surrounding countryside, notably through the Squerryes estate and SE towards Chartwell, French Street and Toys Hill. The Grasshopper is our current choice for lunch.

Chartwell (off B2026 S) The home of Winston Churchill until his death. Still much as he left them, the rooms are full of his possessions and reminders of his career, and the gardens are attractive, with the famous black swans on the lakes. Though this is one of the NT's most popular houses, and even more so after the screening of the BBC's Churchill film *The Gathering Storm* which was largely set here, you need at least a passing interest in the statesman really to enjoy it. Entry is by timed ticket. Meals, snacks, shop, disabled access; house and garden cl Mon and Tues (exc bank hols), and Nov–Mar; (01732) 866368; £5.80 house and garden, gardens and studio only £2.90; NT. This is good walking country.

Quebec House Gabled boyhood home of General Wolfe, with exhibitions on his life and the battle that made his name. Shop, disabled access; open pm Tues and Sun Apr–Oct; (01372) 453401; £2.60; NT.

Squerryes Court🔌 Overshadowed by its more famous neighbour Chartwell but for some people more satisfying, this fine 17th-c manor house overlooks attractive grounds and has excellent collections of paintings, china and furniture. The formal garden, first recorded in 1686, has being painstakingly restored to the design laid out in 1709. Teas, shop, limited disabled access; open pm Weds, wknds and bank hols Apr–Sept; (01959) 562345; £4.60, grounds only £3.

WHITSTABLE TR1066

The focus of the town is still very much the busy working harbour; and the **Museum and Art Gallery** (Oxford St) explores its maritime history and traditions. Shop, disabled access; cl Sun (exc July–Aug), Good Fri, and a few days over Christmas; (01227) 276998; free. The Native Oyster House (Sea Wall) and Crab & Winkle (Harbour) make the most of the famed local seafood.

WILLESBOROUGH TR0342

Willesborough windmill 🏠
Working mill and heritage museum, open pm wknds and bank hol Mon Apr–Sept, plus pm Weds Jun–Aug; snacks, shop, disabled access; (01233) 661866; £1.50. The Blacksmiths Arms has good value food.

WINGHAM TR2558

Wingham Wildlife Park 🏠
Endangered birds from all over the world, with the emphasis very much on breeding and conservation; they have a large walk-through aviary. Also meerkats, monkeys, wallabies and other animals, and a good adventure playground (made from recycled materials). Meals, snacks, shop, disabled access; cl 25–26 Dec; (01227) 720836; £4.90. The village is attractive, with decent food in the lovely medieval Red Lion.

WOODCHURCH TQ9534

South of England Rare Breeds Centre 🏠 (B2067) Particularly well organised and good value, this 90-acre working farm has a huge collection of rare farm breeds. Younger visitors may be able to cuddle baby pigs, meet the goats or get close to the animals in the children's barn. It's amazing seeing the different varieties of one species: the biggest type of rabbit is about 15 times as heavy as the smallest. Under-5s are well catered for, with paddling pool and sandpit; there's a good playground for older children nr a picnic area, and they've recently opened an indoor play area. Lots of walks and trails, and some fine views of the Kentish countryside; a Georgian farmstead has been rebuilt here too. Also trailer and tractor rides, and indoor play area. Disabled access is particularly good (they

do a lot of work with people with physical or learning disabilities). No dogs. Meals, snacks, shop, plant centre; cl 24–25 Dec and every Mon Oct–Mar; (01233) 861493; £4.

WYE DOWNS TR0746

Some of Kent's nicest walks are on the North Downs – not that high, but steep enough along the escarpment to give some great views. The Wye Downs, designated a nature reserve for their chalkland flora that includes a variety of orchids, look across the orchards below to both the Thames estuary and the Channel. The road above Wye through Hastingleigh, Bodsham Green, Sole Street (where the Compasses is a pleasant stop-off) and along the Crundale Downs is a nice drive.

YALDING TQ6949

Yalding Gardens (B2162 just S) Interesting series of gardens maintained by the Henry Doubleday Research Association, the organic farming and gardening organisation (see also Ryton Gardens in Warwickshire); each looks at how people have cultivated land in a given period, from medieval physick gardens to modern organic vegetable plots. Meals, snacks, shop, disabled access; open wknds Apr and Oct, Weds–Sun May–Sept, and Easter and bank hols; (01622) 814650; £3. In the attractive village, the Walnut Tree has good value food.

Other attractive villages, all with decent pubs, include Addington TQ6559, Alkham TR2542, Bishopsbourne TR1852, Bodsham TR1045, Boughton Lees TR0247, Boxley TQ7758, Chillenden TR2653, Egerton TQ9047, Elham TR1743, Harvel TQ6563, Ickham TR2257, Leigh TQ5446, Lenham TQ8952, Martin TR3346, Offham TQ6557, Sandling TQ7558, Shipbourne TQ5952, Smarden TQ8842, Speldhurst TQ5541, Stalisfield Green TQ9553, Sutton Valence TQ8149, West Peckham TQ6452, Wickhambreaux TR2158, Worth TR3356 and Wrotham TQ6158. **Pubs useful for walkers** include the Woolpack at Benover TQ7048, Pepper Box at Fairbourne Heath above Ulcombe TQ8550, Woodman on Goathurst Common TQ4952, Bucks Head at Godden Green TQ5555,

Ringlestone Inn TQ8755 N of
Harrietsham, Rock at Hoath Corner
TQ4943, Cock at Ide Hill TQ4851,
Cock at Henley Street nr Luddesdown
TQ6667, Kentish Horse at Markbeech

TQ4742, Horns and Bull at Otford
TQ5359, Fox & Hounds at Toys Hill
TQ4751, Harrow at Warren Street
TQ9253 and Rising Sun at Woodlands
TQ5560.

Where to eat

BIDDENDEN TQ8238 **Three Chimneys** *Hareplain Rd (01580)* 291472 Ochre-coloured country pub with rambling, low oak-beamed small rooms, interesting old furniture on flagstones and coir matting, some harness and sporting prints on exposed brick walls, and good winter log fires; well kept real ales, good wines, and enjoyable imaginative food; smart garden terrace area with seats by outdoor heaters; classic car meetings; Sissinghurst Gardens nearby. £24|£8.95

BOUGH BEECH TQ4846 **Wheatsheaf** *Hever Rd (01732)* 700254 Lovely old pub – thought to have started life as a hunting lodge belonging to Henry V – with oak timbers in unusually high ceilings, several bars and some interesting decorations, a massive stone fireplace, and piles of smart magazines to read; nice nibbles, chestnuts to roast and mulled wine in winter, summer Pimms, and popular interesting bar food (served all day); real ales, decent wines, and lovely gardens; children in Long Bar only; partial disabled access. £24|£5.95

CANTERBURY TR1556 **Bonne Cuisine** *Canterbury Hotel, 71 New Dover Rd (01227)* 450551 Run by the same family for over 20 years, this neat little hotel is warmly friendly and comfortable and serves beautifully presented very good French food in the cheerfully yellow dining room; attractive bdrms; children over 6. £35

DARGATE TR0861 **Dove** *Plum Pudding Lane (01227)* 751360 Tucked-away pub with charmingly unspoilt rambling rooms, plenty of seats on bar boards, a winter log fire, and interesting restaurant-style food; pretty sheltered garden. £30|£6

EDENBRIDGE TQ4446 **Honours Mill** *87 High St (01732)* 866757 Charmingly converted watermill with lots of beams in downstairs bar and upstairs restaurant, good interesting food (the wkdy set menus are popular and good value), and a mainly French wine list; cl Sat am, Sun pm, Mon, 2 wks Christmas. £40/2-courses £12.50

FAVERSHAM TR0260 **Read's** *Macknade Manor, Canterbury Rd (01795)* 535344 Restaurant-with-rooms in Georgian manor house with neat surrounding gardens that provide home-grown vegetables and herbs for the kitchen; exceptionally good innovative English cooking including fine fish dishes and lovely puddings, a marvellous wine list, and neat young staff; cl Sun, Mon. £51 dinner, £27.50 lunch

FINGLESHAM TR3353 **Crown** *The Street (01304)* 612555 Pleasant and attractively refurbished 16th-c country pub with a wide choice of reasonably priced bar food, popular old-world restaurant with inglenook fireplace and flagstones, and good friendly service; cl pm 25 Dec. £20|£5

FOLKESTONE TR2235 **Paul's** *2a Bouverie Rd (01303)* 259697 Popular, enjoyable restaurant run by the same owners for well over 20 years, with very imaginative food inc good fish, game and vegetarian options, and a decent wine list; cl Sun pm, 2 wks after Christmas; disabled access. £28.70|£5.95

LANGTON GREEN TQ5439 **Hare** *Langton Rd (01892)* 862419 Popular, civilised dining pub with light, airy knocked-through rooms, a chatty atmosphere, imaginative generously served food from a menu that changes twice daily, attentive waitress service, and decent wines and beers; outside terrace; children before 7pm; cl pm 25 Dec; partial disabled access. £23.50|£6.95

NEWNHAM TQ9557 **George** *44 The Street (01795)* 890237 Distinctive 16th-c pub with a spreading series of attractive and interesting rooms, open fires, friendly staff, nicely presented, imaginative food using fresh local produce, well kept beers, and good wines; cl 25 Dec. £23.50|£7.95

PENSHURST TQ5142 **Bottle House** *Coldharbour Lane, Smarts Hill (01892)* 870306 Relaxed and friendly 15th-c pub with huge beams, stone pillars, and big windows in the unpretentious bars, quite a collection of china pot lids and old paintings and photographs, very good popular food, efficient service, and well kept local ales; cl 25 Dec. £26|**£5.50**

PLUCKLEY TQ9243 **Dering Arms** *The Grove (01233) 840371* Striking old building, originally a hunting lodge, with a variety of good solid wooden furniture on stone floors and a roaring log fire in a huge fireplace in the stylishly plain high-ceilinged bar, and a smaller panelled bar with similar furnishings; particularly good imaginative fish dishes (and other things, too), well kept real ales, an extensive wine list, and quite a few malt whiskies; bdrms; monthly vintage-car rally; cl 26–27 Dec. £26|**£7.95**

SEASALTER TR0664 **Sportsman** *Faversham Road (01227) 273370* Popular dining pub by the sea wall, three connected airy rooms with a relaxed, chatty bistro-type atmosphere, a mix of pine tables on the stripped wood floor, large modern photographs and big chrome ceiling fans; interesting modern cooking including lots of fish dishes, good wine list, well kept real ales, friendly landlord. £27|**£6.95**

SELLING TR0455 **Rose & Crown** *Perry Wood (01227) 752214* Quietly civilised tucked-away woodland pub with stunning tubs, pots and window-boxes, and a pretty, cottagey garden; lots of beams, hops and interesting corn-dolly work, a huge fireplace, comfortably cushioned seats, a relaxed atmosphere and friendly helpful service, good generously served food, well kept real ales, and decent wines; nearby walks; no food pms Sun/Mon, cl 25 Dec pm; no children; limited disabled access. £22|**£6**

SISSINGHURST TQ7937 **Rankins** *The Street (01580) 713964* Interesting enjoyable food from a fixed evening and Sun lunch menu in pretty white clapboarded cottage inc lovely puddings and vegetarian choices; no smoking until food service has finished; cl Mon, Tues, bank hols; children by prior arrangement; partial disabled access. £28.50|**£12.50**

STAPLEHURST TQ7844 **Lord Raglan** *Chart Hill Rd (01622) 843747* Unpretentious yet quite civilised country inn with hops along low beams, comfortably worn dark wood furniture on nice parquet flooring, a coal fire, a pleasantly relaxed atmosphere, and charming licensees; very generous attractively presented food (the imaginative daily specials are the thing to choose), well kept real ales, and a good wine list; small French windows lead to an enticing little sheltered terrace; wooden picnic-sets in side orchard; cl Sun; disabled access. £23|**£5.50**

STODMARSH TR2160 **Red Lion** *(01227) 721339* Interesting food in delightful little pub with several idiosyncratic rooms full of bric-a-brac (often to do with cooking), friendly landlord, a big log fire, well kept real ales, good wine list with several by the glass; pretty little back garden with chickens. £26|**£4.95**

TUNBRIDGE WELLS TQ5739 **Mount Edgcumbe Hotel** *The Common (01892) 526823* Bustling tucked-away hotel on one of several large rocky outcrops; small cosy bar with lots of exposed brick and grotto-like rock, enjoyable very popular brasserie food in big-windowed restaurant looking over the Common, cheerful staff, well kept real ales and a good wine list; bdrms; book at wknds. £20|**£7**

TUNBRIDGE WELLS TQ5839 **Sankeys** *39 Mount Ephraim (01892) 511422* Excellent fresh fish and seafood cooked inventively, several cosy and relaxed rooms, very good wines, real ales and friendly service; cheaper lively candlelit cellar wine bar too (get there early for a seat), and tables out on the terrace; cl Sun, Christmas. £23|**£8.50**

ULCOMBE TQ8550 **Pepper Box** *Windmill Hill (01622) 842558* Cosy old country inn with timbers and low beams hung with hops in friendly homely bar, copper kettles and pans on window sills, two armchairs and a sofa by the splendid inglenook fireplace, several cats, and a snug little no smoking dining room; good food (esp the daily specials), well kept real ales, and courteous service; nice country views from terrace and garden with small pond, swing and tables among trees, shrubs and flower beds; no children. £22.50|**£6.50**

Special thanks to M A Dixon

LANCASHIRE
(including Greater
Manchester and Merseyside)

Two cities full of interest, vibrant seaside resorts, a wealth of places to visit – and a quiet side too, with marvellous unspoilt countryside and coast

Lancashire has something for everyone, and the advantage of being very good value for money. Manchester, and Liverpool close on its heels, combine grand Victorian cityscapes with striking visitor-friendly modern developments, alongside some world-class museums – many of which are free (we've made one our Lancashire Family Attraction of the Year). With a flow of new, improved or extended attractions, these two cities, within easy reach of each other, have plenty for families; both have good public transport, and lively nightlife too.

Even away from these big cities, there is an abundance of great family attractions. Our pick includes Wigan Pier (with its superb mix of museum and theatre) and the well thought-out theme park at Charnock Richard; Leighton Hall is a pleasant place to spend a relaxed afternoon, and for more action head to the warships at Birkenhead. Knowsley Safari Park in Prescot has the biggest herd of African elephants in Europe, and there are good farm parks at Fleetwood and Martin Mere (bird-lovers enjoy the nearby Wildfowl & Wetlands Trust, and Rockwater Bird Conservation Centre in Burnley).

Brassy Blackpool with its Pleasure Beach, Tower, Illuminations, zoo and aquarium (not to mention the lively discos and bars) is the classic seaside resort, with immense appeal for families and young adults. In complete contrast, out of season Lancashire's long stretches of beach and dune are empty, with a lonely charm for walkers; year-round, there's an element of fascination about the treacherous tidal sands of Morecambe Bay. Lancaster is an attractive town with quite a few enjoyable things to while away a day.

A range of good industrial heritage museums include Hat Works in Stockport and the World of Glass at St Helens (both more fun than you might think), and Port Sunlight, a precursor of garden cities, is enjoyable to stroll around. Other worthwhile excursions include attractive Bramall Hall, Hoghton Tower with its grand state rooms, and Astley Hall in Chorley. The National Football Museum in Preston pleases fans.

There's glorious countryside even just outside the big cities, where the moors have plenty of scope for exhilarating drives and walks, and witchy Pendle Hill still holds the imagination. Other areas of fine countryside include the great whaleback of Longridge Fell, the wooded Beacon Fell country park, the magnificent Pennine moorland of the Forest of Bowland, and the equally peaceful Silverdale/Arndale area.

Lancashire

NORTH YORKSHIRE

BOWLAND

● Slaidburn
● *Newton*
Holden ●
● Bolton by Bowland
● *Gisburn*
A59
Cow Ark
Grindleton *Sawley*
Waddington ●
A59
Downham ●
Barnoldswick ●
Clitheroe ●
Pendle Hill ●
A56
Barrowford ●
Colne
0
Hurst Green
Great Mitton
Wiswell
Sabden ●
13
14
Whalley ●
12
Wycoller Country Park
A59
Langho
A671
Padiham ●
11
M65
A677
6
7
8
9
10
Burnley
● Accrington
A56
WEST YORKSHIRE
Blackburn
Oswaldtwistle ●
A646
M65
A677
A671
● Roddlesworth Valley
Helmshore ●
A666
Turton Bottoms
Ramsbottom ●
A615
Bromley Cross
Ashworth Valley
M66
Bolton
Bury ●
A58
21
M62
1
Heywood
20
M61
5
A58
A666
2
18
M60
19
20
A62
● Uppermill
4
Ringley ●
17
M60
A635
3
15
16
21
A627
14
22
Astley Green ●
1/12
Manchester
Ashton-under-Lyne ●
DERBYSHIRE
M62
11
M602
23
A57
10
Salford ●
24
1
2
3
M67
9
25
8
7
Salford Quays
M60
6
26
5
A56
A560
3
4
2
Stockport ●
Marple ●
Mellor
5
M56
A6
A34
Altrincham ●
● Bramhall
0 Miles 5
0 Kilometres 8

CHESHIRE

Where to stay

ASHWORTH VALLEY SD8512 **Leaches Farm** *Ashworth Rd, Rochdale, Lancashire OL11 5UN* (01706) 41117 **£42***; 3 rms, shared bthrm. Creeper-clad 17th-c hill farm with really wonderful views, massive stone walls, beams and log fires; cl 22 Dec–2 Jan; children over 8; dogs by arrangement

BILSBORROW SD5039 **Guy's Thatched Hamlet** *St Michael's Rd, Bilsborrow, Preston, Lancashire PR3 0RS* (01995) 640010 **£42***, plus wknd breaks; 53 smartly modern rms. Bustling complex of thatched buildings by the canal, comprising a restaurant and pizzeria, a tavern, and the accommodation part, Guy's Lodgings; craft shops and outside entertainment, a play area, all-weather cricket pitch, and crown green bowling; a useful base for exploring the area; open all day; cl 25 Dec; disabled access; dogs welcome in bedrooms ☺

BLACKPOOL SD3037 **Imperial Hotel** *North Promenade, Blackpool, Lancashire FY1 2HB* (01253) 623971 **£110**, plus special breaks; 181 well equipped pretty rms, many with sea views. Fine Victorian hotel overlooking the sea, with spacious and comfortable day rooms, lots of period features, enjoyable food and fine wines, and a full health and fitness club with indoor swimming pool, gym, sauna and so forth; children's club during summer, Christmas and Easter; lots to do nearby; disabled access; dogs welcome in bedrooms ☺

BROMLEY CROSS SD7213 **Last Drop Village Hotel** *Hospital Rd, Bromley Cross, Bolton, Lancashire BL7 9PZ* (01204) 591131 **£105**; 128 rms. Big well equipped hotel complex cleverly integrated into olde-worlde pastiche village complete with stone-and-cobbles street of gift and teashops, bakery, etc, even a spacious creeper-covered pub with lots of beamery and timbering, popular one-price hot and cold buffet, and heavy tables out on attractive flagstoned terrace; disabled access; dogs welcome in bedrooms

CAPERNWRAY SD5371 **New Capernwray Farmhouse** *Capernwray, Carnforth, Lancashire LA6 1AD* (01524) 734284 **£66**; 3 comfortable rms. Pretty 300-year-old ex-farmhouse with helpful friendly owners, cosy lounge, stone walls and beams, and candlelit dinner in what was the dairy with an informal house-party atmosphere; cl Nov–Feb; children over 9; dogs welcome in bedrooms

CHIPPING SD6343 **Gibbon Bridge Hotel** *Green Lane, Chipping, Preston, Lancashire PR3 2TQ* (01995) 61456 **£100**, plus special breaks; 29 spacious individual rms, inc 22 split-level suites, most with views of the Bowland Hills. Country hotel on the edge of the Forest of Bowland, with beautiful landscaped gardens (plus a popular bandstand which can be used for civil weddings or for music events), and old-fashioned values of quality and personal service; attractively presented food using home-grown produce in airy restaurant and adjoining conservatory, a quiet relaxing atmosphere, and fine wines; health and gym area; a good base for walking and short driving trips; good disabled access; dogs in two restricted bedrooms

COLNE SD8741 **Higher Wanless Farm** *Red Lane, Colne, Lancashire BB8 7JP* (01282) 865301 **£48**; 3 rms, two with own bthrm. Warmly welcoming farmhouse with beams, log fires and lovely surrounding farmland used mainly for breeding of shire horses, as well as sheep; cl Christmas and New Year; children over 10

COWAN BRIDGE SD6475 **Hipping Hall** *Cowan Bridge, Kirkby Lonsdale, Carnforth, Lancashire LA6 2JJ* (01524) 271187 **£96**, plus special breaks; 7 pretty rms, 5 in main hotel, 2 cottage suites across courtyard (with self-catering facilities). Relaxed country-house atmosphere and delicious food in handsome small hotel with help-yourself drinks in conservatory, an open fire, a lovely beamed Great Hall with minstrels' gallery, and four acres of walled gardens; small antiques/curios shop, fine walks from front door; cl 22 Dec–14 Jan; dogs in cottage suites

HURST GREEN SD6938 **Shireburn Arms** *Whalley Rd, Hurst Green, Clitheroe, Lancashire BB7 9QJ* (01254) 826518 **£70**, plus special breaks; 18 rms, several refurbished this year. Lovely 17th-c country hotel with a refined but friendly atmosphere, an airy and newly redecorated modernised bar, comfortable lounge, open fires, well presented enjoyable food in newly refurbished restaurant, good service, and fine view of the Ribble Valley from the conservatory; disabled access; dogs welcome in bedrooms

LANGHO SD7034 **Northcote Manor** *Northcote Rd, Langho, Blackburn, Lancashire BB6 8BE (01254) 240555* **£130**, plus special breaks; 14 attractive rms with antiques and board games, reached up a fine stairway. In pretty countryside, this neatly kept red brick Victorian house is more of a restaurant-with-rooms, with beams and oak panelling, big log fires, and two comfortable lounges, wonderful breakfasts, and delicious food in the civilised dining room; cl 25 Dec and 1 Jan; partial disabled access

MANCHESTER SJ8498 **Malmaison** *Piccadilly, Manchester M1 3AQ (0161) 278 1000* **£141.50**; 167 chic rms with CD player, in-house movies, smart bthrms, and really good beds. Stylishly modern hotel with comfortable contemporary furniture, exotic flower arrangements, bright paintings, very efficient service, French brasserie, generous breakfasts, and free gym; other hotels in the same small chain in Edinburgh, Glasgow, Leeds, and Newcastle; good disabled access

MANCHESTER SJ8398 **Meridien Victoria & Albert** *Water St, Manchester M60 9EA (0161) 832 1188* **£95**w, plus special breaks; 158 rms, individually styled and named after TV programmes. Carefully converted Victorian warehouse opposite Granada TV studios; original iron pillars, oak beams and exposed brickwork, particularly good service, comfortable bar overlooking river, and good imaginative food in restaurant; disabled access

WADDINGTON SD7243 **Backfold Cottage** *The Square, Waddington, Clitheroe, Lancashire BB7 3JA (01200) 422367* **£50***; 3 rms. Tiny 17th-c cottage in cobbled street, attractive millennium clock on the front, beautiful antique furnishings (inc a doll's house in the lounge); very good service, all-day snacks, and candlelit evening meals (bring your own wines); nearby walks; children at owner's discretion; dogs welcome in bedrooms

WADDINGTON SD7144 **Peter Barn** *Cross Lane, Waddington, Clitheroe, Lancashire BB7 3JH (01200) 428585* **£52***; 3 lovely rms. Converted old stone tithe barn with beamed sitting room, antiques, lovely home cooking using local produce, home-made jams and marmalade, warmly welcoming owners and a gentle atmosphere; surrounded by a delightful garden in fine walking country; cl Christmas and New Year; children over 12

WHITEWELL SD6547 **Inn at Whitewell** *Whitewell, Clitheroe, Lancashire BB7 3AT (01200) 448222* **£92**; 17 rms, some with open peat fires. Civilised Forest of Bowland stone inn on the River Hodder, with seven miles of trout, salmon and sea trout fishing, and grounds with views down the valley; interesting period furnishings, plenty of room, highly praised food (as well as coffee and cream teas all day), fine wines (they house a wine merchant), courteous service, and an art gallery; dogs welcome

YEALAND CONYERS SD5074 **Bower** *Yealand Rd, Yealand Conyers, Carnforth, Lancashire LA5 9SF (01524) 734585* **£59**; 2 attractive rms. Charming no smoking Georgian house in big garden with views of Ingleborough and the surrounding hills; friendly owners (keen bridge players), open fire and piano in comfortable sitting room, and enjoyable food served around a large table in the kitchen or dining room; children over 12

Please let us know what you think of places in the *Guide*. Use the report forms at the back of the book, write us a letter or log on to www.goodguides.com

To see and do

Lancashire Family Attraction of the Year

LIVERPOOL SJ3490 **Liverpool Museum** (William Brown St) You don't have to go to London for top-class museums: this remarkable building is a treasure-trove of antiquities and oddities from all over the world, its permanent galleries made up of varied collections each worth a look in their own right. It's currently in the middle of a big expansion, so it might seem odd to highlight the museum before this is complete (it will be a couple of years before the new galleries are unveiled), but we've been very impressed with the way they're handling the transition, still working hard to organise activities for children, and making sure visitors leave feeling they've got the most out of the place. A couple of galleries are currently closed (their aquarium for example), but you can effortlessly spend half a day here – and most of it's free. The best bits for children are – as ever – the dinosaur gallery, and the excellent Natural History Centre, where you can handle specimens and use video microscopes to get a closer look at some of the exhibits; there are plenty of staff on hand in this section to answer questions. Another highlight is the Space and Time gallery, with its rockets, chunks of moon rock, and plenty of interactive displays; children can get a free activity booklet, and the collection of time-keeping devices is interesting, from ancient sundials to the latest gadgets. It's worth paying the small charge for the planetarium (£1 adults, 50p children), which has an excellent half-hour journey between the planets, with some stunning images from the Hubble telescope and robotic spacecraft; you need to get tickets for this at the museum entrance. Shows are usually at 3.15 Tues–Fri (no show Mon, exc in school hols), and hourly in the afternoon at weekends and school holidays. In the holidays you'll also find special childrens' events such as building sculptures from recycled materials. Snacks, shop, disabled access; cl am Sun, and all day 23–26 Dec, 1 Jan; (0151) 207 0001; free.

ACCRINGTON SD7627
Haworth Art Gallery (Haworth Park, Manchester Rd) Notable for its collection of Tiffany glass, the biggest in Europe (an Accrington man used to manage the Tiffany studios). New education facilities, café, shop, and they've recently improved disabled access; cl am Weds–Sun and all Mon–Tues (exc bank hols); (01254) 233782; free.

ALLERTON SJ4086
20 Forthlin Road The former home of the McCartney family, this 1950s terrace house was where the Beatles developed some of their first songs; early memorabilia and photographs, and an audio tour. No access by car: you have to catch a minibus from Speke Hall or the Albert Dock; some disabled access; open Weds–Sat late Mar–end Oct, plus Sat early Nov–early Dec; phone for details (0151) 427 7231; £6; NT.

ALTRINCHAM SJ7387
Dunham Massey Hall, Garden and Park (off B5160 W) Early Georgian manor house extensively remodelled in the early 20th c, with impressive silverware, paintings and furnishings, and restored kitchen, pantry and laundry. The largely unaltered grounds have plenty of deer, formal avenues of trees, and a working Elizabethan saw mill. Concerts and events even in winter when the house is closed. Meals, snacks, shop, disabled access to ground floor of hall; open Sat–Weds Apr–Oct, house cl am; (0161) 941 1025; £5.50 house and garden, £3.50 garden only; NT. The Axe & Cleaver (School Lane) is a roomy nearby family dining pub.

ASHTON-UNDER-LYNE SJ9399
Museum of the Manchester Regiment (Town Hall, Market Pl) This recently refurbished museum, tells the story of the Manchester Regiment, with displays inc a reconstructed World

War I trench with special effects and a World War II air-raid shelter, also interactive computers, Home Front exhibition and medal collection. Shop, disabled access; cl most Sun and bank hols; (0161) 343 2878; free.

Portland Basin Museum
Enthusiastic local history museum overlooking the Ashton Canal, with a re-created 1920s street and displays on Tameside's crafts and trades; quite a few hands-on displays for children. Good value snacks, shop, disabled access, baby-changing facilities; cl Mon (exc bank hol), 25–26 Dec and 1 Jan; (0161) 343 2878; free. There's a heritage trail around the town, and plenty of places for a picnic.

ASTLEY GREEN SJ7099
Astley Green Colliery Museum
(Higher Green, just off A580) The only visible reminder of Lancashire's mining heritage, with its 30-metre (100-ft) steel headgear still intact, plus the largest steam winding engine in Europe, a narrow-gauge railway, working stationary steam engines, and displays on coal mining inc an exhibition of photography from 1908 to 1970. Shop; museum open pm Sun, Tues and Thurs, engines in steam 1st Sun of month Mar–Oct; (01942) 828121; free (exc special events).

BARNOLDSWICK SD9046
Bancroft Mill Engine Museum 🔲
The last working steam mill in the area – not that long ago Barnoldswick had 13. Snacks, shop, disabled access; usually open Sats Apr–Oct, and various Sun pms in month for steaming, phone for dates; (01282) 865626; £2. The Fanny Grey (B6251 towards Colne) has decent food.

BARROWFORD SD8639
Pendle Heritage Centre Growing local history centre, with an 18th-c walled garden, woodland walks, and an unusual cruck barn with friendly farm animals. The museum has an exhibition on the Pendle witches, and there's also an art gallery (and the Tourist Information Centre). Meals, snacks, shop, limited disabled access; phone for opening times and prices, as the centre was closed for building work when we went to press; (01282) 661704. This is picturesque, evocative countryside; the

church at nearby unspoilt Newchurch has the witches' grave, and there's good food at the Forest Inn at Fence and Bay Horse at Roughlee – a stone's throw from Alice Nutter's home. A few miles upstream from here, just below Blacko, the Water Meetings is an ideal place for a picnic and a paddle.

BIRKENHEAD SJ3288
Waterfront views over to Liverpool, of course, but a surprise in **Birkenhead Priory** (Priory St), a ruined 12th-c Benedictine priory with notable visitor centre. Shop, mostly disabled access; open pm Tues–Sun, plus am summer school hols and Easter; (0151) 666 1249; free. Good views from the tower of the neighbouring church. The **local history museum** is housed in the impressive former Town Hall (snacks, shop, disabled access; cl Mon and a wk over Christmas and New Year; free). The rejuvenated Hamilton Quarter has various craft and art galleries. Laid out in 1853 and now being restored, Birkenhead Park was the world's first public park, and Europe's first tramway was built here in 1860 – today various restored trams, one from as far away as Hong Kong, still run (£1 return). The Shrewsbury Arms out in Claughton Firs is the best place for lunch.

Historic Warships 🔲 (Birkenhead Docks) HMS *Plymouth* and the Submarine *Onyx* both took part in the Falklands War. You can peep up the periscope on the *Onyx*, and there's plenty for children to fiddle with. A few ladders to negotiate, but don't be put off – readers find this a very satisfying afternoon out. Snacks, shop with interactive displays, disabled access to visitor centre only; cl 24–26 Dec, 1 Jan; (0151) 650 1573; £5.50 for both ships. Adults can look around a German U-boat alongside, which spent 50 years on the seabed (phone to book a tour).

Shore Road Pumping Station
(Woodside, nr ferry terminal) This unusual **steam pumping station** has an adjacent small transport museum with a working tram. Open pm wknds, and daily (exc Mon) in school hols; (0151) 650 1182; free.

Williamson Art Gallery & Museum (Slatey Rd) English watercolours and other art by the

Liverpool school, sculpture and ceramics, model ships, and a collection of cars and motorcycles in period garage setting. Shop, disabled access; cl Mon, 24 Dec–2 Jan; (0151) 652 4177; free. On summer Suns in Jun–July and Sept there are generally free concerts here, and in Aug at the priory.

BLACKBURN SD6828
Put firmly on the map by the Industrial Revolution, this has bustling shops and market, some fine buildings, and lots of beautiful unspoilt countryside around. The parish **church** (actually now a cathedral) is very handsome – grand yet elegant. The Royal Oak (B6233, nr A6119 ring rd) has popular home cooking.

Blackburn Museum & Art Gallery
£ (Museum St) Quite a mixture – English watercolours, Japanese woodblock prints, Greek and Russian icons, illuminated manuscripts, and a fantastic collection of beetles, some pretty scary; they also have some interesting temporary exhibitions. Shop, disabled access; cl Sun, Mon and bank hols; (01254) 667130; free.

Witton Country Park (off A674 W) 480 acres of attractive countryside to explore. Snacks, shop; (01254) 55423; visitor centre cl am Mon–Sat, plus all Mon–Weds Oct–Mar, 25–26 Dec, and 1 Jan; free.

BLACKPOOL SD3036
Britain's most loved and loathed (and most popular) seaside resort. The atmosphere in summer is unashamedly boisterous, especially at wknds when it's geared towards young adults. Most families love it too, with plenty to do from donkey rides (not Fri) along the beaches (Blackpool South and Bispham are the cleanest), to days at the **Sandcastle** leisure complex; open wknds and school hols (plus daily Jun–Oct); (01253) 343602; £5.20. The tramway here was the first permanent electric tramway in the world, and has regular summer historic tramcar rides; phone (01253) 473001 for information. A Hopper Pass (£42) allows you entrance to the Blackpool Tower and circus, zoo, and Sandcastle complex, and acts as a wristband at the Pleasure Beach. An ambitious £1 billion plan to turn the town into a gambling centre modelled on Atlantic City in New Jersey, with a showy strip of hotel casinos along the seafront, looks likely to go ahead if the gambling laws are altered. The civilised Bispham Hotel out on Red Bank Rd is good value.

Blackpool Model Village Created by a landscape gardener, so the gardens are as much an attraction as the models. Very well done: tableaux range from a cricket match in a Tudor village to a Scottish castle, there are two miniature railways, they've recently added model boats, and there's even a replica Blackpool tram. Snacks, shop, disabled access; cl Nov–Dec, and wkdys Jan–Easter; (01253) 763827; £2.75.

Blackpool Pleasure Beach Founded in 1896, this is still Britain's most popular free attraction. Altogether more than 145 rides and attractions are squeezed into the park's 42 acres, inc several roller-coasters that can whiz you through 360 degrees, backwards, or in the dark, bungee trampolines, ice-skating, and traditional rides such as ghost trains, River Caves and dodgems. They've recently added a £1 million roller-coaster called Spin Doctors where riders spin 360 degrees, 37 metres (120 ft) off the ground at up to 60 mph, and a £1 million hall of mirrors (or interactive exploratorium as they're calling it now). One of the best rides is the hi-tech water ride, Valhalla, full of drops and effects that include real fire. At six minutes, it's also currently the longest dark ride in the world. There's still nothing to top the Big One though, a monster roller-coaster that climbs to 72 metres (235 ft) at speeds of up to 85mph. Most of the more exciting rides have height restrictions, so smaller children have their own section of the park, which includes a fine miniature wooden roller-coaster, the Zipper Dipper. Meals and snacks, shops, disabled access; open daily Easter–early Nov, plus wknds in Nov, Dec and Mar; (0870) 444 5566. Free entry to the park, then tickets for rides range from £1.30 to £2.30, or you can get a wristband offering unlimited rides on everything for £25.

Blackpool Tower This outstanding landmark has several lively attractions geared towards families, inc a circus, laser shows, aquarium (rare giant sea turtles), science gallery, dinosaur dark ride, a lift to the top, and the Walk of Faith – a 5-cm thick glass floor 116 metres (380 ft) above the ground. Perhaps most fun at night (they're open till 11pm in summer). You can try old-fashioned ballroom dancing (they've an impressive new organ), and there's non-stop cabaret music. Meals, snacks, shop, limited disabled access; cl winter wkdys (exc during Feb half term), best to check; (01253) 292029; £11, £6 after 8pm. These famous autumn light displays are the best of their kind, and they're continually adding new features – though you'll have to travel at a snail's pace along the Golden Five Hundred Yards (or Mile as they call it here) if you decide to drive.

Blackpool Zoo (East Park Drive) Readers really like this continually improving zoo, which has over 400 animals in 32 acres of landscaped gardens, inc a walk-through lemur wood, free-flying bird hall, and gorilla island; they've recently gained rare red pandas too. The big cats are usually fed at 3.30pm (not Fri), the sea lions at 11am and 2.30pm, and there is an animal handling session at 4pm; plenty of animals to stroke in the children's zoo. A train chugs around the grounds, and there's a good playground; it's a pleasant place to take a picnic. Meals, snacks, shop, disabled access; cl 25 Dec; (01253) 830830; £6.75.

Grundy Art Gallery (Queen St) This decent gallery away from the crowds is proof that there's more to Blackpool than rollicking seasidery. Shop, disabled access but no facilities; cl Sun and bank hols; (01253) 478170; free.

Sea Life Centre (Golden Mile Centre) Broadly similar to others in the chain, but with a bonus: one of the biggest displays of tropical sharks in Europe, with a walk-through tunnel underneath so you feel you're in there with them. The touch-pools with crabs and starfish are another highlight, and experts are on hand to answer questions; they've recently added a new seahorse aquarium. Meals, snacks, shop, disabled access; cl 25 Dec; (01253) 622445; £7.

BOLTON SD7109
Quite a few places to visit here; the Kings Head (Junction Rd, Deane), with a bowling green behind, is useful for lunch, as is the restaurant of the Bolton Moat House (Higher Bridge St), an interesting church conversion.

Bolton Museum & Art Gallery (Le Mans Crescent) Quite good, with Egyptian mummies, lots of watercolours and 20th-c sculpture. Shop, disabled access; cl Sun and bank hols; (01204) 332211; free.

Hall i'th' Wood (Crompton Way) 15th-c, where Samuel Crompton developed his Spinning Mule in 1779; it was refurnished by the first Lord Leverhulme in 1902. Shop, disabled access to ground floor; cl Mon (exc bank hols), Tues, and all Nov–Mar; (01204) 332370; £3.

Smithills Hall 🏛 (Smithills, Dean Rd) Interesting (though much restored) old manor house with 14th-c Great Hall and splendid panelled drawing room. Snacks, shop, disabled access to ground floor only; cl Sun am, all day Mon (exc bank hols), and Oct–Easter, but best to check; (01204) 332377; £3.

BOLTON BY BOWLAND SD7849
Attractive streamside Forest of Bowland village, with a fine **church**, and quaint cottages leading off its two village greens. The Coach & Horses has good fresh food.

BRAMHALL SJ8886
Bramall Hall One of the finest houses in the area (particularly from the outside), a splendid timber-framed 14th-c hall with rare 16th-c wall paintings and furniture, and extensive parkland; attractively restored in the 19th c. Meals, snacks, shop, disabled access to ground floor; open pm Mon–Sat, and all day Sun and bank hols Good Fri–Sept, pm Tues–Sat, and all day Sun Oct–Dec (exc 25–26 Dec), and pm wknds the rest of the year; (0161) 485 3708; £3.95, small parking charge. The Davenport Arms at Woodford does decent lunches.

BROMLEY CROSS SD7213
Last Drop Village (N of Bolton) Pastiche of an 18th-c village, very rustic and quaint, with courtyard, shops, decent pub, tearoom, and specialist shops. The B6391 and old Roman road through Edgworth N of here are fine moorland roads, as are the A675 N of

Bolton itself (good detours off at Belmont), and A666 to Darwen.

BURNLEY SD8530

The **canal wharf** (Manchester Rd), which has a small museum (open pm Sat–Tues), allows short towpath walks along the Leeds & Liverpool Canal, giving a vivid impression of the towering old weaving mills; the raised canal embankment across the valley is a remarkable sight. The Ram (A646 S) is a useful food stop.

Queen Street Mill (Harle Syke, NE outskirts) When it closed in 1982, this was the last surviving steam-powered cotton textile mill; today you can still see a few of the 300 Lancashire looms in action. Snacks, shop, disabled access; cl Sun and Mon (exc bank hol) and Dec–Feb; (01282) 412555; £2.50.

Rockwater Bird Conservation Centre (Foxstones Lane, Cliviger – above Mereclough SE) Expanding collection taking in waterfowl, pheasants, foreign birds and owls, as well as rabbits and chipmunks. Children can feed some animals. Snacks, limited disabled access; cl Mon (exc bank hols), and all Oct–Mar; (01282) 415016; £3. Nearby **Cliviger Gorge** has pleasant walks, with stream, woodland and farmland; moors above. The Kettledrum at Mereclough has good home cooking, and the moorland roads around it are attractive – especially the old packhorse road from Mereclough up Stansfield Moor; good views from the back road angling off SE from the A52 to the junction of the A671 and B6238.

Towneley Hall (A646 S) Home of the Towneley family from the 14th c until 1902; you can look around an Elizabethan long gallery, Regency rooms, and a Victorian kitchen. There's also an art gallery and a craft museum, a natural history centre and an aquarium. Woodland trails and space for picnics in the park. Meals, snacks, shop, cl Sat, Sun am, and around 2 wks over Christmas and New Year; (01282) 424213; free.

BURY SD8010

East Lancs Railway ▣ (Bolton St Stn) Well regarded by enthusiasts, a scenic 17-mile steam journey along the pretty Irwell Valley; you can get on or off along the way. Meals, snacks, shop, disabled access; open wknds, bank hols, and maybe Fri in July and Aug; (0161) 764 7790 for timetable; £6.50 full return. The Lord Raglan up at Nangreaves (off A56/A666 N) has great moorland views, good food, and brews its own beer.

CARNFORTH SD4970

The dilapidated station (once voted the worst in England) at this otherwise unremarkable little town starred in *Brief Encounter* in 1945. A project to restore it to its cinematic heyday is almost complete (and the famous clock is working again), though the heritage centre won't open till late in 2003. Ask at the visitor centre about guided tours (usually Mon); meals, snacks, shops, disabled access (and facilities); (01524) 735450. A mile or so N are the ruins of a 14th-c manor house, **Warton Old Rectory**, and the County Hotel (A6) has reliable traditional food.

Warton Crag (just N) Fine views over Morecambe Bay and the coast, and enjoyable walking.

CATFORTH SD4735

Lancaster Canal Between Preston and Carnforth, this is ideal for boating – 40 miles without a single lock; often through quiet countryside, with herons and even occasional kingfishers – best in spring or early summer, with ducklings and cygnets bobbing about, and lambs in the fields alongside. This is also a good departure point for pleasant towpath walks, largely through quiet countryside.

CHARNOCK RICHARD SD5415

Camelot Theme Park ▣ They've really stuck with the Arthurian theme at this excellent imaginative theme park. There is a spectacularly dizzying ride in the shape of Excalibur, the monorail round the place looks like a tamed dragon, and even the animals in their farm aren't out of place – they live in thatched and cobbled enclosures. A highlight is the splendid half-hour jousting display – twice a day in peak periods, but only once at the start and end of the season; the seating is under cover. Dozens of other attractions include something for most age groups. You can bottle-feed lambs or help with milking at the farm, and there's a big indoor play area. Also log flume and other water rides, a magician and jester, and a quirky show. The go-karts, and the driving school have an extra charge, and there are lots of arcade games. A fair bit is under cover, but if it rains continuously for two hours you can get a half-price return ticket. Meals, snacks, shop, disabled access; open wknds and school hols Apr–Oct, daily Jun–Aug; (01257) 452100; £13.50.

CHIPPING SD6445

Bowland Wild Boar Park (Leagram, towards Dunsop Bridge) Deer, llamas, and longhorn cattle as well as wild boar at this good-value park; in summer children may be able to feed lambs and other small animals; woodland walks, picnic and play area. Shop with wild boar meat and dry cured bacon, disabled access; park open all year, shop and café (with good bacon sandwiches) open Easter–Oct; (01995) 61554; £2. The village is picturesque, with one of the oldest continuously trading shops in the country, the Chipping Craft Centre; and there's very good food in the Derby Arms at Thornley down towards Longridge.

CHORLEY SD5718

Astley Hall 🏛 (Astley Park) This unusual-looking timber-framed 16th-c house has particularly elaborate carvings and plasterwork, interesting pottery and paintings, and extensive gardens and woodland. It was used in the TV adaptation of *Moll Flanders*. Shop, disabled access to ground floor only; cl am, Mon (exc bank hols), and Mon–Thurs Nov–Mar; (01257) 515555; £2.95, free for Chorley residents. The Farmers Arms at Eccleston over towards Southport is a good value dining pub.

CLITHEROE SD7441

Bustling old market town: hundreds of poultry and small livestock enthusiasts normally come to the Weds evening auctions, some from as far away as Scotland. The High St is dominated by the **castle** perched on its limestone rock. One of the oldest buildings in Lancashire, it has one of the smallest Norman keeps in the country. The **Castle Museum** has an extensive geology exhibition, re-creations of a Victorian kitchen, cloggers' workshop, printing press, and good views of the

Ribble Valley. Shop, limited disabled access; cl Thurs and Fri Oct–Mar, and all Jan; (01200) 424635; £1.60. Cowmans on Castle St has a wide range of traditional and speciality sausages, and Byrne's on King St stocks a remarkable range of wines. The **Platform Gallery** (Station Rd) has good changing contemporary craft exhibitions; regular workshops and special events; shop, disabled access; cl Sun and bank hols; 01200 443071; free. The Swan & Royal (Castle St) is handy for lunch, and readers enjoy the sculpture trail in Bungerley Park. There's a lovely drive through Bashall Eaves, the Trough of Bowland and Quernmore.

COW ARK SD6845

Browsholme Hall 🏛 This unpretentious-looking Tudor house, on the edge of the Forest of Bowland, has a surprisingly rich range of contents and good guided tours. Shop, disabled access to ground floor only; open spring bank hol wknd, late Jun to mid-July (exc Mons), and mid-Aug to 1 Sept (exc Mons, but inc bank hol); (01254) 826719; £4. The Inn at Whitewell in one direction and Red Pump at Bashall Eaves in the other offer a choice of good places to eat.

CROSTON SD4918

A good village to visit, with a very old (and well preserved) church surrounded by cobbled paths. The Black Horse has hearty home cooking, and the Memory Lane tearoom (Town Rd) is a pleasant place for lunch.

DOWNHAM SD7844

Below Pendle Hill, carefully preserved by the Assheton estate and outstandingly pretty, on the side of a steep pasture valley with a stream winding along the bottom; the Assheton Arms is good.

FLEETWOOD SD3448

Behind some decay, you can easily trace the elegance of its original 19th-c resort development (there was even landscaping by Decimus Burton). It still has plenty of smart buildings, a lively harbour, excellent market, two elegant lighthouses (the one in the middle of the street did serve a practical purpose, believe it or not), Freeport factory shopping centre (indoor and outdoor play areas), and trams from Blackpool right through the town. Worth a look, **Fleetwood Museum** (Queens Terrace) has displays on the fishing industry, a reconstructed salt mine, some interactive displays and touch-screen computers; cl Sun am, and all late Mar–early Nov; (01253) 876621; £2. In Fish Dock (Fleetwood Marina) you can go on a guided tour (often led by an ex-fisherman) of **Jacinta** a restored Icelandic fishing vessel, in service till 1994. Open daily Easter–Oct but best to check; (01253) 885642; £2. The architecturally interesting North Euston Hotel by the terminus is a safe bet for food, and the Marine Hall exhibition centre on the front has a decent bar (the Wyre – no food) with excellent views of the harbour and Morecambe Bay.

Farmer Parr's Animal World (Wyrefield Farm, Rossall Lane) This 20-acre farm has over 200 animals inc llamas, wild boar, emus and owls; pony and tractor rides, children's play area, a pottery (run by the charity Autism Initiatives), and a rural heritage centre. Snacks, shop, disabled access; cl 25–26 Dec; (01253) 874 389; £3.25.

FOREST OF BOWLAND SD6650 Magnificent Pennine moorland, less visited than most areas of comparable scenery, as much of the moorland, privately owned, is closed to walkers. Only a few paths cross the impressive massif that forms some of the county's most significant scenery; Ramblers Association has often organised mass trespasses as demonstrations against denial of access, and hopes for big changes here from right-to-roam legislation. Development in some of the villages (also in private hands) is controlled too strictly for any significant expansion of holiday accommodation – let alone a proliferation of camp sites and so forth. These restrictions make the area particularly appealing for people who want peace and quiet, and it's not impossible to find good walks. There are some fine ones on rights of way – for instance, up Clougha Fell from Quernmore; above Tarnbrook Wyre; up Dunsop Fell from Slaidburn or Dunsop Bridge; up Fairsnape and Wolf

Fell from Chipping or Bleasdale. Beacon Fell Country Park is an atmospheric place to wander through, and there are some pleasant walks around the Coronation Arms at Horton. Don't be confused by road signs by the Rivers Ribble and Hodder claiming some of the territory for Yorkshire (as in the past indeed it was).

FORMBY DUNES SD2808 Reached from the NW edge of Formby, a large tract of sweeping sandy dunes which in some areas is being stabilised by pine plantations; broad beaches and good walks through the adjacent pinewoods, made interesting by the chance of seeing and even feeding red squirrels (you can buy nuts here); £2.90 per car, though you may be able to park free within comfortable reach. Best in spring and autumn – can be busy in summer; NT.

GARSTANG SD4945 Quite an attractive small market town with a good deal of canal activity, and a fine aqueduct crossing the River Wyre. The entertaining waterside Owd Tithebarn is fun for lunch (they boast one of the largest collection of farming implements in the country), and the **Discovery Centre** (High St) is a useful introduction to the area's natural history; cl 25–26 Dec; (01995) 602125; free. From here a wheelchair-accessible footpath to Scorton gives panoramic views over the River Wyre.

GLASSON DOCK SD4456 Once an important port for Lancaster, this still has the occasional coaster berthing, but is mainly a lively summer boating place now, in pleasant countryside. The Victoria on the dock (with lots of fresh fish) is a popular dining pub, as is the 17th-c Stork up on the A588.

GREAT MITTON SD7139 **Great Mitton church** Attractive, with an outstanding range of memorial tombs. This is a nice spot by the River Ribble, and the Aspinall Arms has enjoyable food.

HELMSHORE SD7821 **Helmshore Textile Museums** (Holcombe Rd) Two stone mills with a comprehensive collections of textile machinery, much still in working order, and a new gallery with interactive displays on the textile industry. One of the best textile museums in the country, but if social history and machinery leave you cold it's unlikely to convert you. Snacks, shop, disabled access; cl am, Sat, and Nov–Mar; (01706) 226459; £3. The Duke of Wellington on the B6232 W of Haslingden is a reliable family dining pub in fine surroundings, with more views further on.

HEYSHAM SD4160

A tremendous contrast with the power station here is the quaint squint-walled little village **church**, partly Saxon, with Norse-carved hogback tombstone inside. Look out too for the unusual weighing machine, and the nearby **Heritage Centre** is worth popping into, with local history displays and a new Viking-theme children's room; shop, limited disabled access; cl wkdys, and am wknds end Sept–Easter; (01524) 859517; free. You can also once again buy non-alcoholic nettle beer, the village's traditional drink. The waterside Golden Ball at Heaton with Oxcliffe off the Lancaster road (may be cut off by very high tides) is fun for lunch.

HEYWOOD SD8510

Corgi Heritage Centre (York St) Hundreds of die-cast model vehicles from pre-war cars to James Bond's Aston Martins – even a turning Magic Roundabout; of course it's all a huge plug for the company that makes them, but fascinating for collectors. Shop, limited disabled access; cl Sun and bank hols; (01706) 365812; free. The Egerton Arms off the B6222 Bury rd is a good moorland dining pub.

HILBRE SJ1887

The biggest of three tidal islands which you can reach on foot at low tide from West Kirby; Hilbre is a **nature reserve**, once popular with sunbathers, now visited mainly by birds and occasional seals. Make sure you know the tide times – (0151) 648 4371 – as it's easy to be stranded out here.

HOGHTON SD6226

Hoghton Tower 🏛 (A675) This splendid 16th-c fortified hilltop mansion has grand state rooms, a Royal bedchamber, and a collection of doll's houses. The gardens are lovely (particularly the rose garden), and the surrounding grounds offer wonderful views of the sea, moors, Lakeland hills and Welsh mountains. Tearoom, shop; open Mon–Thurs and Sun pm July–Sept, and bank hols rest of year (exc Good Fri, 25 Dec, and 1 Jan); (01254) 852986; £2 parking and grounds, £3 house, £5 guided tour. The Royal Oak at Riley Green, with a footpath to the tower, does reliable meals.

HOLDEN SD7749

Holden Clough Nursery Old-fashioned nursery with thoroughly up-to-date approach to raising interesting plants in Victorian kitchen garden of Holden Clough Hall; beds of alpines, trough gardens, herbaceous perennials, shrubs and rhododendrons and maybe RHS special events. Shop, disabled access; cl 12–1pm, Sun (exc pms Easter and May bank hols), Good Fri, and 25 Dec–1 Jan; (01200) 447615; free. The Copy Nook has good food, and is a useful stop for walkers.

HOYLAKE BEACH SJ2088

These sweeping sands are beautiful, with an unusual partly tidal **nature reserve** at Red Rocks N of the golf links. The reopened Hilbre Court Hotel (Banks Rd) has decent food.

HURST GREEN SD6939

Stonyhurst College Magnificent 16th-c manor house, now home to the famous Roman Catholic boarding school. You can see the library, chapel, other historic rooms and the extensive grounds. Tolkien wrote most of his *Rings* cycle while working here (and some like to believe that Hobbiton is based on Hurst Green). Shop, limited disabled access; open pm Aug exc Fri, gardens usually open July–Aug – phone to check; (01254) 826345; £4.50. The village is attractive, the Punch Bowl and Bayley Arms are handy for lunch, and there are fine Ribble Valley walks nearby.

LANCASTER SD4761

Friendly and relaxed despite the grandeur of many of its stone buildings; ambling down the cobbled streets and alleyways (much is pedestrianised), it's hard to believe this was once a major West Indies shipping port; these days the water traffic is more sedate. Riverside paths have been improved;

there's now a 10-mile footpath and cycle route that follows the river from Lancaster to Lune Valley at Caton – along the way are various sculptures and other art works. The Lancastrian (Scale Hall Farm, A589 Morecambe rd) has good food, and other places worth knowing for lunch include the Brown Cow (Penny St) and canalside White Cross.

Ashton Memorial & Butterfly Park ⊞ (Williamson Park) A magnificent folly clearly visible from the motorway (Pevsner rated it the best in Britain), in 54 acres of lovely landscaped parkland; splendid views from the upper galleries. The butterfly house has a good collection of plants and lepidoptera, as well as free-flying birds, various creepy-crawlies, and small mammals. Snacks, shop, disabled access; cl 25–26 Dec, 1 Jan; (01524) 33318; £3.50.

Judge's Lodging (Church St) Enjoyed by readers, this 17th-c house (the town's oldest) has well restored period rooms, lots of Gillow furniture, and museum of childhood. Shop; open pms wkdys mid-Mar to Jun and Oct, plus am wkdys July–Sept (cl lunchtime); (01524) 32808; £2. Other decent collections at the firmly traditional **City Museum** on Market Sq, in a very grand Georgian former town hall (shop, disabled access; cl Sun, 24 Dec–1 Jan; free), and at the **Cottage Museum** opposite the castle, furnished in the style of an early 19th-c artisan's house (open pm Easter–Sept; 75p).

Lancaster Castle Dramatic 12th-c Norman fortress famous for hangings and witch trials, owned by the Queen as Duke of Lancaster. Part of it is still used as a prison, but the dungeons, tower and 18th-c Gothic Revival Shire Hall can all be visited. Shop; cl 2 wks over Christmas and New Year; (01524) 64998; £4.

Lancaster Maritime Museum (St George's Quay) In an 18th-c Customs House, this is an up-to-date look at the local maritime trade and fishing industry; the audio-visual show is good fun. Snacks, shop, disabled access; usually only cl am Nov–Easter, and a few days over Christmas; (01524) 382264; £2 (free to local residents).

Lancaster Priory Dates back to before the Conquest, though the present hilltop building is mainly 14th- and 15th-c; very interesting medieval choir-stalls, needlework and Anglo-Saxon cross fragments. Refectory and book shop, some disabled access; priory cl winter lunchtimes, refectory and shop cl Oct–Easter; (01524) 65338; free. Nearby are the remains of a Roman bath house.

LEIGHTON HALL SD4874

Leighton Hall ⊞ A notably friendly welcome at this neo-Gothic mansion (more restrained inside), still the home of the Gillow family and with early examples of their furniture. The grounds have a collection of birds of prey, nature trails, and beautifully kept gardens. The setting is lovely, with Lakeland hills rising behind. Snacks, shop, disabled access; cl am, all day Sat and Mon (exc bank hols), and all Oct–Apr; (01524) 734474; £4.50. The nearby New Inn at Yealand Conyers has enjoyable food.

LEYLAND SD5422

British Commercial Vehicle Museum ⊞ (King St) Jazzed up with sound effects, this has over 90 perfectly restored British wagons, buses, trucks, vans, fire engines and even a Popemobile, shining so much you'd think they were new. Snacks, shop, disabled access; open Sun, Tues, Weds and bank hols Apr–Sept, Sun only Oct; (01772) 451011; £4. The Midge Hall (Midge Hall Lane, about 2m W of here) is a popular food pub.

South Ribble Museum (Church Rd) The sturdy 16th-c former school has changing local history displays; open am Tues and Fri; (01772) 422041; free.

Worden Park has art displays and nine varied craft workshops, walks, gardens, a maze, and miniature golf; cl 25 Dec; (01772) 421109; free. Leyland also has a pleasant little town trail, and the medieval church has some fine stained glass.

LIVERPOOL SJ3590

The many fine 19th-c buildings recall Liverpool's past as one of the world's great ports (it's got more listed buildings than any other city except London) inc the Philharmonic (Hope St), probably the country's grandest late Victorian pub; nearby the Everyman

Bistro has good value food. The city's trademark Liver Building is best viewed from one of the famous ferries across the Mersey, which leave regularly from Pier Head (50 minute cruises with a commentary are £3.75); the real commuter ferries operate half-hourly during rush-hours (£1.95 return). Very lively at night, Mathew Street is the place to head if you like the Beatles, and Concert Sq is a popular place for a drink in summer with lots of cafes and bars. Liverpool's Chinese community is one of the oldest in Europe, and the Arch in Chinatown is the largest outside China; nearby at the top of Bold Street look out for the remains of St Luke's church, bombed out in World War II, now with trees growing inside it.

Albert Dock Spectacular restoration of previously redundant warehouse buildings by the river, now a lively complex of shops, cafés and exhibitions, with regular events, boat trips and of course Fred's weather map. The Baltic Fleet, a majestically restored Victorian dockside pub, is handy for lunch, and the Hope on the Waterfront cybercafé is different for a drink. The next four attractions are housed in the complex – you can easily base a whole day around a visit here.

Beatles Story (Albert Dock) Bouncy tribute to the local boys made good and the sights and sounds of the 60s, inc a reconstruction of the Cavern Club. Shop, disabled access; cl 25–26 Dec; (0151) 709 1963; *£7.95. Devoted Beatles fans might want also to go on a 2-hour tour of related city sites; the bus leaves the Beatles Story daily at 3pm, plus 12.30pm in summer, best to book in advance (0151) 709 1963; £10.95.

Bluecoat Arts Centre 🔄 (School Lane) Attractive Queen Anne building housing changing art exhibitions and a programme of performances, plus art, craft and book shops. Meals, snacks, disabled access to ground floor only; gallery cl Sun and Mon, centre cl Sun and bank hols; box office (0151) 709 5297; free (exc for events).

Cathedrals Unusually, both Liverpool's cathedrals were built this century, in widely differing styles. Walk along Hope St (the heart of the city's 18th-c area, with many Georgian brick terraces) to the impressive and more obviously modern Metropolitan Roman Catholic cathedral, designed by Frederick Gibberd after a vast earlier scheme by Lutyens ran out of money; blue light from the 16-sided glass tower reflects evocatively on the marble inside. The Anglican cathedral looks much older, but was completed only in 1978. Britain's biggest, it's undeniably powerful, though its soaring proportions and cavernous scale make it impersonal. Both have good concerts.

Conservation Centre (Whitechapel) Intriguing glimpse of the world of museum and gallery conservation; interactive displays and demonstrations explain how various objects are preserved, and exhibits range from a mummified Egyptian crocodile to two Beatles' gold discs; good programme of events. Meals, snacks, shop, disabled access; cl Sun am, 23–26 Dec, 1 Jan; (0151) 478 4999; free.

Croxteth Hall & Country Park 🔄 (5m NE) Period displays in Edwardian house, and working farm, Victorian walled garden, miniature railway, and country walks in the grounds – a pleasant family trip out. Meals, snacks, shop, some disabled access; house cl end Sept–Easter, farm cl winter wkdys, and 25 Dec–1 Jan, park open all year; (0151) 228 5311; park free, hall farm and garden £4, hall or farm only £2, walled garden only £1.20.

Grand National Experience 🔄 (Aintree Race Course) Takes you behind the scenes of the world's most famous steeplechase. A visitor centre has memorabilia charting the history of the race from its origins in 1839, while in the weighing room you can try on the silks of past winners, test out the scales and experience a steward's enquiry. Perhaps the highlight is the simulator ride – find out what it's like to jump a National fence; guided tours of the course (11am and 2pm Tues–Fri) include a look around the stables. Shop, disabled access; cl Mon, end Oct–end May, and all race days; (0151) 522 2921; visitor centre £3 (with simulator ride and tour £7).

Joseph Williamson Tunnels (Smithdown Lane) Built by an eccentric local philanthropist to create work for unemployed soldiers returning from the Napoleonic Wars, a very small section of these intriguing underground tunnels will be open to the public by the time we go to press; you can find out more at the new heritage centre, and there are guided tours throughout the day; they plan to hold regular special events. Meals, snacks, shop, limited disabled access to tunnels; cl 24–26 Dec and 1 Jan; (0151) 709 6868; £3.50.

Liverpool Ducks A fun way of getting to know Liverpool is this hour-long city tour and river experience. Bright yellow amphibious vehicles, built in World War II to land troops and supplies, drive you along the waterfront and through the streets taking in the city's main sites, then splash down into the Mersey to continue the tour by water. Tickets are available from the Atlantic Pavillion (Albert Dock), hourly tours leave daily mid-Feb to end-Dec; (0151) 708 7799; £9.95.

Liverpool Football Club Museum ⊞ (Anfield Rd) The visitor centre and Anfield tours are a must for the faithful. There are cups, trophies, programmes and other treasured memorabilia as well as films of the club's finest hours. The tour takes in the grounds, dressing room and pitch – you can even sit on the manager's bench. Snacks, shop, disabled access; visitor centre cl a few days over Christmas, no tours on match days and booking essential (0151) 260 6677; £8.50 (museum only £5).

Liverpool Museum See separate family panel on p.352.

The McCartneys' former home (20 Forthlin Rd, Allerton) 1950s terraced council house, the former home of the McCartney family. John, Paul and George met, rehearsed and wrote many of their earliest songs here, inc 'Love Me Do' and 'I Saw Her Standing There'. Open Weds–Sat end Mar–end Oct, Sat only Nov–mid-Dec; (0151) 427 7231; access is by minibus only from Albert Dock (am) or Speke Hall (pm) – see Speke entry; £6 (NT £2.50 for bus).

Mendips (Menlove Avenue) The National Trust have recently been given this three-bedroom 1930s semi, John Lennon's boyhood home, by his widow Yoko Ono; as we went to press

opening times and prices had not been decided (though access will be by minibus only), so phone Speke Hall for details; (0151) 427 7231.

Merseyside Maritime Museum (Albert Dock) Huge (and growing) museum spread over six floors, with boats, ships, craft demonstrations and a lively interpretation of what it was like for the millions who travelled from here to the New World. The Museum of Liverpool Life vividly re-creates social history from the last century or so, and the Customs and Excise museum, Anything To Declare, is much more fun than it sounds. It takes an intriguing look at concealment techniques, with demonstrations by sniffer dogs, and there's an interesting assortment of items seized by customs inc a guitar made from a turtle, a tiger-skin waistcoat, and a host of illegal weapons. A gallery on transatlantic slavery has divided local historians, who disagree on Liverpool's true role in the slave trade. Also galleries on the *Titanic* and *Lusitania*, and an art gallery; in summer they display some of their larger exhibits outside, and you may be able to board one of the ships at the preserved dockside. Meals, snacks, shop, disabled access; cl 23–26 Dec, 1 Jan; (0151) 478 4499; free.

National Wildflower Centre ⊞ (off A5080, nr M62 junction 5) In 35-acre Court Hey Park, this conservation centre for endangered British wildflowers was formerly a home of the Gladstones. Made up of traditional stable buildings and a 150-metre (500-ft) 'working wall' with big display panels and a rooftop walkway, it has hands-on activities and exhibitions about conservation, demonstration areas, sculpture garden, and a play area. You can also see how wildflower seed is harvested and cleaned. Special events, art exhibitions and craft workshops. Snacks, shop, garden centre, disabled access; open Apr–Sept; (0151) 737 1819; £3.

Open Eye Gallery (Wood St) Good changing photography exhibitions; disabled access; cl Sun, Mon, and bank hols; (0151) 709 9460; free.

Princes Road Synagogue Consecrated in 1874, this is one of the finest examples of high Victorian Moorish Revival synagogue architecture in Europe; guided talks cover the Jewish community in Liverpool, the history and architecture of the building, and an introduction to Jewish traditions. Shop, limited disabled access; tours Thurs pm, phone in advance to book (0151) 709 3431; free, donations welcome.

Robert Cain Brewery (Stanhope St) Evening tours of red brick brewery, inc buffet and tastings; tours start at 6.30pm and must be booked in advance (over-18s only); shop; cl Fri–Sun; (0151) 709 8734; £3.75. The splendidly restored Brewery Tap pub is good.

Sefton Park Palm House Magnificent 25-metre (82-ft) high three-tiered domed glasshouse, built 1896 but derelict and then unglazed for years; now restored with help from a £3 million lottery grant, with palms, cycads, orchids and tree ferns; it's surrounded by life-size statues of explorers and naturalists. Cl for events and performances (usually Tues and Thurs); (0151) 726 2415; free.

Sudley House 🏛 (Mossley Hill Rd) Former home of Victorian ship builder George Holt, this interestingly unspoilt private Victorian house has good gardens, attractive furniture, and paintings by Turner and Pre-Raphaelites. Shop, disabled access to ground floor only; cl Sun am, 23–26 Dec, 1 Jan; (0151) 207 0001.

Tate Liverpool (Albert Dock) In a converted warehouse, this is the largest collection of contemporary art outside London – all very well presented with especially good use of natural light; they give interesting half-hour talks most afternoons. Meals, snacks, shop, disabled access (and audio and Braille guides); cl Mon (exc bank hols), Good Fri, 24–26 Dec, 1 Jan; (0151) 702 7400; free, though £4 for special exhibitions.

Walker Art Gallery 🏛 (William Brown St) One of the finest art collections outside London, this outstanding place now has two new galleries for temporary exhibitions (a new craft and design gallery should also be open by the end of 2003). Especially notable Italian, Dutch and Pre-Raphaelite works (a blockbuster Rossetti exhibition starts in October 2003), and, a highlight for many, W F Yeames's 'When Did You Last See Your Father?'. Meals, snacks, shop, disabled access; cl 23–26 Dec, and 1 Jan, but best to check as they'll also be closed occasional days for repairs to the roof; (0151) 478 4199; free (may be charge for special exhibitions).

Western Approaches (Rumford St) Evocatively restored underground command centre for the World War II Battle of the Atlantic; a labyrinth of rooms covering 4,650 sq metres (50,000 sq ft) under the city's streets. Shop; cl Fri, Sun, and Nov–Feb; (0151) 227 2008; £4.75.

LYTHAM ST ANNE'S SD3228 Decorous conjoined seaside towns that seem a world away from nearby Blackpool. Lytham has a splendidly restored **windmill** by the promenade in the centre of its breezy green (shop, limited disabled access; usually cl 1–2pm, Mon and Fri, and all Sept–Mar; donations), and a small **Lifeboat Museum** next door (open Tues, Thurs and wknds, plus Weds pm July–Aug (exc 1–2pm, and Oct–Mar); (01253) 730155; donations). St Anne's has traditional seaside activities inc Pleasure Island (a beachside family entertainment complex), and a café quarter on Wood St. The Taps is a good real ale pub.

MANCHESTER SJ8398 Manchester is packed with interesting places to visit, and exciting new central developments add to its considerable attraction for visitors, such as the newly opened architecturally stunning **Urbis**, the centrepiece for the hugely ambitious new city-centre Millennium Quarter. On a fine wknd or summer evening, strolling around the impressive buildings is a real pleasure; Albert Sq is one of the finest areas, with the great Albert Memorial (predating London's). The Town Hall is a massively impressive piece of Victoriana; guided tours leave from the visitor information centre most Sats, phone to check (0161) 9417620; £4. The very wide 15th-c **cathedral**, with notable choir stalls, lies at the heart of the Millennium Quarter. The small medieval centre around it is now protected by a park, and nearby the reconstructed 18th-c Sinclairs Oyster Bar (Cathedral Gates) is good value (not just oysters). In front is the new pedestrian Exchange Sq, a shopping centre in the former Corn Exchange, the Printworks entertainments complex (which has an IMAX cinema) – and a group of tall post-modern stainless steel windmills. The Castlefield area by the basin where the Bridgewater and Rochdale canals meet is interesting: restored warehouses, viaducts and the like, lots of lively redevelopment inc a tramway and wonderfully light and airy footbridge, and a visitor centre; Dukes 92 is a good pub (may be street theatre outside). Not far off, on the other side of the GMEX exhibition centre, is the very smart Bridgewater Hall (box office (0161) 907 9000). By contrast, the Rochdale canal towpath is a fascinating seamy-side walk. Chinatown here has lots of authentic restaurants, and there's a Chinese Arts Centre in Edge St. Afflecks Palace on Church St is good for antique clothing and records, and for more main-stream shopping, there's a huge shopping centre with a 20-screen cinema at Trafford Park to the S. Metrolink trams quickly cover the centre. The major revamp of Piccadilly Station should be completed by the end of 2002, and Piccadilly Gardens, the old heart of the city, has been redeveloped into a public square, dramatically lit at night, and spanned by a pedestrian bridge. See also separate entries for Salford and Prestwich.

Chetham's Library (Long Millgate) Nestled among the modern developments of the Millennium Quarter, this is the oldest public library in Britain, founded in 1653. The attractive building itself dates from the 15th c and was originally a college for priests. Many of the original features remain, inc fellows' dormitories and 17th-c reading tables (still used). Cl 12.30–1.30, wknds, bank hols, Sats in Jun, and 25 Dec–1 Jan; (0161) 8347961; free.

Gallery of Costume (Platt Hall, Rusholme) The best museum of its kind, a Georgian mansion with comprehensive displays of fashion over the last 400 years. Displays change regularly – though like the styles themselves eventually come back. Shop, disabled access to ground floor only, but there's a video of the other areas; (0161) 224 5217; cl Mon, 25 Dec, and 1 Jan; free.

Heaton Hall (Prestwich) Splendidly decorated 18th-c neo-Classical house in extensive well used public parkland; fine paintings, plasterwork and furniture, unusual circular Pompeiian room, and usually temporary exhibitions. Snacks, shop, disabled access; usually cl Mon (exc bank hols) Tues and Weds, and Oct–Mar; (0161) 773 1231; free. The handsomely Victorian Woodthorpe by the main gate has decent food.

John Rylands Library (Deansgate) One of the city's most remarkable buildings, magnificently neo-Gothic, small exhibitions and tours (Weds 12pm, £1); shop, cl Sat pm, all Sun and bank hols, Christmas and Easter hols; (0161) 834 5343; free.

Manchester Art Gallery (Mosley St) After a £35 million project which has doubled gallery space and refurbished the existing galleries, this is now an even more rewarding place to visit with a tremendous collection of fine and decorative art. Aside from outstanding Pre-Raphelites, and a very good 20th-c British gallery, there's now a new interactive gallery with multi-media displays and hands-on activities for children, the Manchester Gallery is another highlight, and a vast high-ceilinged room on the top floor houses the new arts and crafts gallery; three spaces are given over to temporary exhibitions. The staff are friendly, and you can pick up an audio-guide to help you round. New café, large shop, good disabled access; cl Mon (exc bank hols), Good Fri, 24–26 and 31 Dec, 1 Jan; (0161) 235 8888; free.

Manchester Jewish Museum (Cheetham Hill Rd, A665 1m N) In a former synagogue, the story of Manchester's Jewish community over the last 200 years, with fascinating recorded recollections of life early last century. Shop, disabled access to ground floor only; cl Fri, Sat and Jewish holidays; (0161) 834 9879; £3.65. The nearby Derby Brewery Arms is a classic Mancunian pub, good value snacks.

Manchester Museum (Oxford Rd) Various parts of this excellent family-friendly museum will be temporarily closed for refurbishment and expansion until April 2003, so best to check if there's something you particularly want to see. Displays include a good Japanese collection, an interactive science gallery, an Egyptian gallery, a dinosaur display, a natural history gallery, they've revamped the aquarium and vivarium (the poisonous frogs are fascinating), and there'll be new ethnology and archery galleries; they've also a lively programme of special events. New café, and shop. Disabled access; cl Good Fri, 25–26 Dec and 1 Jan, but best to phone; (0161) 275 2634; free.

Manchester United Museum (Old Trafford) Purpose-built football museum, covering the club's history from its foundation in 1878 to the more recent glory days. Hundreds of exhibits (changing almost as frequently as their strip) and tours of the ground (must book in advance, not match days, and limited on the days before). Meals, snacks, shop (not unjustifiably they call it a megastore), disabled access; cl Christmas; (0870) 442 1994; £8.50 tour and museum, £5.50 museum only.

Museum of Science & Industry in Manchester (Castlefield) One of Britain's most impressive and imaginative museums, built on the site of the oldest passenger railway station in the world. There are hours of things to do, and plenty to touch and fiddle with. The main galleries take a broad and accessible look at power, industry and transport (going right up to space travel), with highlights inc an exciting simulator in the air and space gallery, a big hands-on interactive science area, and a fascinating exhibition on sanitation. The vast power hall has working engines and railway locomotives, and there's an absorbing exhibition on the history of photography, and a comprehensive look at Manchester's development. The changing exhibitions are particularly good. Meals, snacks, shop, disabled access; cl Dec 24–26 (0161) 832 1830; free, charges for temporary exhibitions.

Museum of Transport 🚌 (Boyle St, Cheetham) Around 80 vintage local buses and other vehicles, as well as photographs, tickets and memorabilia – even historic bus stops. Snacks, shop, disabled access; open Weds, wknds and bank hols (exc over Christmas); (0161) 205 2122; £3.

Pankhurst Centre (62 Nelson St, Chorlton on Medlock) Emmeline Pankhurst launched the Suffragette movement from this Georgian semi, with period-furnished parlour and interestingly planted garden. Meals, snacks, shop, disabled access; cl Sun and bank hols; (0161) 273 5673; free.

People's History Museum 🚌 (Bridge St) Takes a comprehensive look at the way ordinary folk toiled and struggled to change society. Lots of well put together displays inc the largest collection of political banners in the world, plus quizzes and games to entertain children; an upstairs gallery hosts changing exhibitions. Meals, snacks, shops, disabled access; cl Good Fri, 24–26 Dec, and 1 Jan; (0161) 839 6061; £1 (free on Fri).

Royal Northern College of Music (Oxford Rd) Regular concerts, recitals and exhibitions. Meals, snacks, shop; cl Aug; box office (0161) 907 5278/9.

Urbis (Cathedral Gardens, Corporation St) Another ambitious new attraction for the city, housed in a futuristic glass structure (supposed to resemble a huge early 20th-c cruise-liner). This ultra-modern museum aims to explore life in different cities of the world, with interactive displays and audio-visuals, focusing especially on Manchester, Los Angeles, São Paolo, Singapore, Paris and Tokyo. A glass elevator (the only one in Europe which rises at 45 degrees) whisks visitors to the top and you work your way down the four themed floors. Restaurant, cafe (great views), shops, temporary exhibitions, disabled access; cl 25 Dec; (0161) 907 9099; £5.

Whitworth Art Gallery (Oxford Rd) British watercolours from Sandby to Turner, plus modern paintings and sculpture, and unusual collections of textiles and wallpaper. Meals, snacks, shop, disabled access; cl am Sun, Good Fri, and Christmas wk; (0161) 275 7450; free.

MARPLE SJ9688

Peak Forest Canal Reached from

Marple, the towpath soon leaves suburbia for green countryside; N is the famous set of Marple locks and aqueduct over the River Etherow. To the S, you can leave the canal at Strines and climb on to Mellor Moor.

MARTIN MERE SD4214
Wildfowl & Wetlands Trust (off A59) Thousands of wild geese, swans, ducks and flamingos regularly visit the re-created natural open water habitats at this important 376-acre centre. Some birds will feed straight from your hand. Good visitor centre, an adventure playground, well organised walks, lively activities for children, and plenty of instructive and entertaining events. There are also several special events such as watching the return of an increasing number of migratory swans; phone for details. Meals, snacks, shop, disabled access; cl 25 Dec; (01704) 895181; £5.50. The canalside Ship at Lathom is very popular for lunch.
Windmill Animal Farm (Fish Lane, Holmeswood; just N) This friendly 40-acre place has animals and their babies to feed (inc rare breeds), pedal tractors, miniature railway, indoor play area and an adventure playground. Snacks, shop, disabled access; cl wkdys mid-Sept to Easter; (01704) 892282; £3.50.

MORECAMBE SD4264
Five miles of promenade and more of beaches to stroll along at this cheery resort, with pretty sunsets over the bay, and enjoyable guided walks across the sands (Cedric Robinson, the Queen's official guide, has been doing the job for more than 30 years); phone (01539) 532165; free. A lovely seafront statue commemorates the town's funniest son, Eric Morecambe, who so loved the place, he adopted its name. The Dog & Partridge (Bare) has decent fresh food.
Morecambe Bay Sands Vast mudflats and sands, home to 200,000 wading birds. Walks over them are easiest from the Cumbrian side, though guided walks are also available from Hest Bank; phone (01539) 532165 or ask at local tourist information centres – the galloping tides and quicksand do make a guide essential. The pleasant Hest Bank Hotel does enjoyable food all day.

OSWALDTWISTLE SD7428
Oswaldtwistle Mills ⊞ (Moscow Mill, Colliers St) This popular shopping village is still expanding; they have just opened an extension. It has various craft workshops inc a sweet factory (£1), and a textile museum (£1); also gardens, wildfowl reserve, nature trail, indoor play area (£1), and outdoor play area, and summer events such as donkey rides. Meals, snacks, disabled access; cl 25–26 Dec and 1 Jan; (01254) 871025; free (discount voucher valid for textile museum).

PADIHAM SD8034
Gawthorpe Hall Early 17th-c country house with fine panelling and moulded ceilings, minstrels' gallery, Jacobean long gallery, and some mid-19th-c alterations. Important collections of costume, embroidery and lace, and paintings from the National Portrait Gallery. Snacks, shop, limited disabled access; house cl am, Mon (exc bank hols), Fri, and Nov–Mar, grounds open all year; (01282) 771004; £3; NT. The hilly cobbled alleys in the town's centre are now a conservation area. The Red Rock (Sabden Rd) has good value food, with fine views from its garden.

PENDLE HILL SD8240
An excellent network of paths lets you walk round and almost all over it. Although Pendle's witch-persecuting days are happily over, the place still has a haunting elemental appeal. The view that enraptured George Fox, the founder of the Quakers, is as good as ever. The quickest way up is from Barley village.

PORT SUNLIGHT SJ3384
Lady Lever Art Gallery Lord Leverhulme, who had built his Sunlight Soap factory here, donated this outstanding gallery to the village. It has interesting Victorian paintings inc Turners and Pre-Raphaelites – many adapted for use in soap ads, to the fury of the artists. Meals, snacks, shop, disabled access; cl Sun am, 23–26 Dec, 1 Jan; (0151) 478 4136; free.
Port Sunlight Heritage Centre Sets the scene for this most famous of the garden villages built by 19th-c philanthropists, contriving something better than the appalling squalor of northern England's factory towns.

Historically important as the precursor of garden cities, garden suburbs and New Towns, it's perfectly preserved, with groups of mock-Tudor cottages, swathes of greenery and parkland: no two groups of houses are alike. Useful village trail leaflets. Shop, good disabled access; cl Christmas wk; (0151) 644 6466; 70p. Nearby Thornton Hough was also built by Lord Leverhulme, as a mock-Tudor estate village – Port Sunlight on a much smaller scale; the Seven Stars there is useful for lunch.

POULTON-LE-FYLDE SD3439
Quite an attractive pedestrianised market square, with a lovely church (as others in Lancashire, looking a good deal older than in fact it is), and several useful places to eat – the Old Town Hall is particularly good value.

PRESCOT SJ4793
Knowsley Safari Park Five-mile drive through very natural-looking reserves of lions, tigers, rhinos, monkeys and other animals; they have the biggest herd of African elephants in Europe, in a new elephant enclosure. There's a roller-coaster and a pirate ship ride; also pets' corner, miniature railway, and an information centre. Meals, snacks, shop, disabled access; cl 25 Dec; (0151) 430 9009; £8 (£5 children). If you have to pass through the town, the **museum** (Church St) has an interesting collection relating to the area's former clock-making industry; cl 1–2, Sun am, Mon (inc bank hols), Good Fri, 25 Dec–1 Jan; (0151) 430 7787; free. The Clock Face (Derby St) is a pleasant old mansion-house pub here.

PRESTON SD5329
The city has some decent museums: the impressive if rather dour Greek revival **Harris Museum and Art Gallery** on Market Sq (cl Sun and bank hols; (01772) 258248; free), and the **Museum of Lancashire** on Stanley St (cl Sun, Thurs and bank hols; (01772) 264075; £2) are worth a visit, and Fulwood Barracks (B6241/B6242) has a military heritage centre. There's a good big market (the space is used for car-boot sales instead on Tues and Thurs); decent food at Wall Street (Fishergate) and the Black Horse (Friargate). Phone for information about visiting **Moor Park Observatory** (01772)

257181.On the W side of the city, Haslam Park (A5085/B6241) is nice for a stroll.

Church of St Mary (Penwortham) 14th-c chancel, and the scant remains of a motte and bailey castle in the churchyard; nearby the Fleece (A59) is useful for lunch.

Millennium Ribble Link The first new canal to be built for over a century, completing an ambitious scheme begun in the 18th c, this connects the Lancaster Canal to the national canal network. Nine new locks had to be built, inc a stairflight lock at Tom Benson Way (nr Preston Sports Arena) and a sea lock; this linear water park includes an arts trail, cycle paths, and picnic and play areas.

National Football Museum 🅰 (Sir Tom Finney Way, Deepdale) Fans will be fascinated by this museum, and even if you go just to keep company with an enthusiast you'll find lots to interest you. The 'first half', with an incredible collection of footballing memorabilia, covers the evolution of the game; it also places football in its wider social context showing what was happening in the world off the pitch. The 'second half', which examines different aspects of football such as rules, tactics and equipment, is more hands-on: you can play table football and then watch your game on screen, or have a go at commentating on *Match of the Day*. Meals, snacks, disabled access; cl Mon (exc bank hols), 25 Dec; (01772) 908442; £6.95.

RAMSBOTTOM SD8017
Lovely village with a Saturday market, overlooked by Holcombe Hill and crossed by the River Irwell. Down by the Twine Valley trout lakes, the Fishermans Retreat has interesting food served with proper chips.

RIBCHESTER SD6535
Attractive little town, many of its buildings incorporating masonry plundered from the former Roman town here: the White Bull pub, with decent food, has a couple of Tuscan pillars for its porch and an excavated Roman bath house behind. The 15th-c **church** stands on the site of the Roman fort, and looks as if it uses much salvaged material from it.

Ribchester Roman Museum 🖼

More visitor-friendly after lottery-funded improvements, this is on the site of a fort occupied between the 1st and 4th c. Lots of coins and pottery, weaponry, jewellery and leatherwork; they've also got some interactive exhibits, and various replicas. The Roman remains outside which inc a Roman granary have been made more accessible, too. Shop, disabled access; cl 25 Dec; (01254) 878261; £2.

Stydd Nursery (Stoneygate Lane) There are excavated Roman remains behind this nursery, which specialises in old-fashioned roses and perennials; some disabled access; cl am wkdys, all Mon and Tues, and 25 Dec–1 Jan; (01254) 878797; free.

RINGLEY SD7605

Unexpected corner so close to urban areas – village stocks and ancient bridge over the Irwell (and a decent pub).

RIVINGTON RESERVOIRS SD6215

These attractive waters just outside Horwich make good walking territory. Lower Rivington Reservoir has a waterside path along its eastern edge, and a curious mock-up of Liverpool castle built in 1912 as an adornment to the vast and atmospherically decayed gardens of Lever Park, which cover the hillside. A trail guides you around the undergrowth and up to the Pigeon Tower, within a few minutes of Rivington Pike, the summit. The Great House Barn is the place to start, with information centre, maps and guides; (01204) 691549. The Millstone (A673, Anderton) has good food.

RODDLESWORTH VALLEY SD6622

Good woodland walks from the Royal Arms at Tockholes, and maybe on to the ruins of Hollinshead Hall and its restored curative well.

RUFFORD SD4616

Rufford Old Hall Lovely timber-framed Tudor house built by the Hesketh family in the 16th c, with an intricate hammer-beam roof in the Great Hall, and impressive collections of 17th-c Lancashire oak furniture, and 16th-c arms, armour and tapestries. Some later rooms too; audio tour. Meals, snacks, shop, limited disabled

access (no facilities); house cl am, all day Thurs and Fri, and Nov–12 Apr, garden and tearoom cl Thurs and Fri, and 25 Dec–12 Apr; (01704) 821254; £4, £2 garden only; NT. The Red Lion over in Mawdesley has good food.

SABDEN SD7737

Attractive village, with a decent antiques centre, on the slopes of Pendle Hill; linked by a scenic drive to another charming Pendle Hill village, Pendleton, where the Swan With Two Necks is a handy stop.

SALFORD SJ8198

Merging almost imperceptibly into Manchester, this owes its distinct place in the popular consciousness mainly to the works of L S Lowry, though it's been in the news more recently because of the impressive new Imperial War Museum North.

Imperial War Museum North

(Trafford Wharf Rd) Housing the new branch of the Imperial War Museum, this stunning new aluminium building is designed to resemble three shards of a shattered globe – representing conflict on land, in the air and on water. Inside, carefully displayed objects (from a T34 Russian tank and the artillery piece that fired the first British shell in World War I, to clothing, dairies and art) portray experiences of war and its impact on us all from 1900 to now. Six display areas look at aspects such as the role of women, and scientific and medical advances as a result of war . Every hour, there's a 360-degree audio-visual presentation made using the sound and photography archives; also interactive displays (and you can ask to touch some of the exhibits), and a changing exhibitions gallery. The building is what makes this museum special, though: look out for touches such as the black curved floor meant to reflect the earth's curve, and a viewing platform in the air shard has spectacular views across the Manchester Ship Canal to the city centre. Café and waterfront restaurant, shop, disabled access; cl 25–26 Dec; (0161) 836 4000; free. It's linked by a new footbridge to the Lowry, over the canal.

Ordsall Hall Museum (Ordsall Lane) Timbered Tudor manor house with local history and Victorian farmhouse kitchen. Shop, some disabled access; cl Sun am, Sat, Good Fri, 25–26 Dec, 1 Jan; (0161) 872 0251; free.

Salford Museum and Art Gallery (Peel Park) Five temporary exhibition areas, a gallery of Victorian art, a reconstructed Victorian street, and a new gallery charting Salford's history from Victorian times to the present; you'll need to book for their school hol children's activities. Snacks, shop, disabled access; cl am wknds, 25–26 Dec, 1 Jan, Good Fri; free.

SALFORD QUAYS SJ8398

Lowry ⊞ (Salford Quays) This shimmering much-praised steel building houses the largest collection of works by the eponymous artist; other galleries have changing exhibitions, and Artworks is a creative interactive gallery; it also has two theatres, and a plaza with bars and restaurants. The touch of hubris which led this new gallery to call itself just the Lowry (when other places like the Courtauld, Tate or V&A have won their shortened popular names informally, from admiring visitors) is perhaps a bit of a shame. Disabled access; cl 25 Dec; box office (0161) 876 2000; free, Artworks £3.75.

SAMLESBURY SD6130

Samlesbury Hall (A677) Well restored half-timbered 14th-c manor house, with good changing exhibitions and craft demonstrations, and sales of antiques. Meals, snacks, disabled access to ground floor only; cl Mon and Sat exc bank hols, and mid Dec–mid Jan; (01254) 812010; £2.50. The New Hall Tavern (B6230) has enjoyable food.

SCORTON SD5048

This appealing village is the gateway to the Trough of Bowland, and has scenic walks through the Grizedale Valley and over Nicky Nook; the Barn (The Square) is a popular plant centre and gift shop. The Bay Horse off A6 N of here has good food.

SILVERDALE SD4875

A little-visited peaceful oasis, up beyond the attractive town of Lancaster: hilly countryside well suited both to walkers and to drivers, and a coastline that's particularly interesting to bird-watchers and naturalists. The small town looks out over the tidal sands to the Cumbrian hills, with streets of quiet houses and a church that looks 14th-c but was built barely a century ago. Various crafts are sold at the Georgian buildings of the **Wolf House Gallery** (Gibraltar), so named because a former occupant of the house was reputed to have killed the last wolf in England. It also has an adventure playground and a courtyard garden; café, some disabled access (with notice); cl Mon Apr–Dec, and all wkdys Jan–Mar; (01524) 701405; free. There are good woodland walks behind the town; readers recommend the Waterslack tearooms (past the station), and the Silverdale Hotel on Shore Rd is worth knowing.

Leighton Moss Nature Reserve ⊞ (off Yealand Redmayne Rd) RSPB reserve with several roomy hides looking out on to reedbeds where bitterns, bearded tits and marsh harriers breed; good walks and views and a visitor centre. Events and guided walks throughout the year. Meals, snacks, shop, disabled access; cl 25 Dec; (01524) 701601; £4.50 (RSPB members free). The Moss is also crossed by a (free) public footpath.

Yealand Conyers Friends' Meeting House Unobtrusively charming, in a quiet and pleasant village; the New Inn here is a popular dining pub.

SKIPPOOL SD3540

Lots of yachting activity in an attractive boating area.

SLAIDBURN SD7152

A perfectly preserved Forest of Bowland village: charming stone cottages, a green with the River Hodder running by, and at the opposite end an early 18th-c schoolhouse and a church with a very 18th-c feel inside. The Hark to Bounty (named after a former squire's dog) is pleasant for lunch and has comfortable bedrooms. The B6478, and the narrow road N past Stocks Reservoir, have appealing views. This second road passes **Gisburn Forest**, the county's largest, with picnic areas and cycle paths.

SOUTHPORT SD3217

Smartish Victorian seaside resort, long famed as the most pleasant shopping town in the area, and as the place where the sea doesn't come in. In fact it comes in as often as anywhere else, but doesn't stay quite as long; they've recently made an effort to clean up the beach, and there are new walkways for visitors and other improvements to the seafront. The promenade is set back quite a way from the sea, and looks over a man-made lake with boat; they've recently restored the pier. Lord St is the elegant main shopping street; the Bold Hotel here has bargain food all day, and there's an excellent antiquarian bookshop down the Wayfarers Arcade just off it. **Pleasureland** is a typical fairground, adding new attractions every year, its wooden roller-coaster and gut-wrenching Traumatiser ride well regarded by connoisseurs; cl Nov–Feb, and wkdys in Mar; (08702) 200204; £16 wristband for all rides.

Atkinson Art Gallery (Lord St) Specialises in 19th- and 20th-c watercolours, oil paintings, prints and sculpture. Meals, snacks, shop, disabled access; cl Sun and bank hols; (0151) 9342110; free.

British Lawnmower Museum ⌸ (Shakespeare St) Over 300 fully restored and often bizarre machines from the 1890s to the present, inc racing lawnmowers, and celebrity lawnmowers; you can book a guided tour. Shop; cl Sun and bank hols; (01704) 501336; £1.

Churchtown Southport's villagey oldest part, with a number of pretty thatched cottages, and the lakeside **Botanic Gardens**, which are very attractive as well as being interesting to plantsmen; boating lake, fernery, pets' corner, and local history **museum** (open 11–3 Tues–Fri and wknd and bank hol pms; (01704) 227547; free). Just opposite, **Meols Hall** is worth a look for its paintings, inc works by Ramsey, Reynolds, Romney and Poussin. Disabled access; open pm mid-Aug to mid-Sept; (01704) 228326; £3. The Hesketh Arms across from the main gate is handy for lunch.

Southport Zoo ⌸ (Princes Park) Expanding family-owned zoo, with wild creatures from lions, porcupines and monkeys to pigs and owls; there's also a reptile house and aquarium, aviaries, a small cat enclosure, and a natural history museum. The pets' corner gives children the chance to get close to some of the animals, and there are play and picnic areas. Snacks, shop, some disabled access; cl 25 Dec; (01704) 548894; £4.

SPEKE SJ4282

Speke Hall Built around a square courtyard, this is one of the most beautiful and richly timbered black and white houses in the country; the inside is mainly Victorian, though there's a vast Tudor Great Hall. Restored Victorian garden. Hard to believe the centre of Liverpool is just six miles away. Meals, snacks, shop, disabled access; house open pm exc Mon and Tues 22 Mar–Oct, plus wknds Nov–8 Dec, garden open exc Mon all year (house and garden open bank hols); (0151) 427 7231; £6, £3 grounds only; NT.

ST HELENS SJ5195

World of Glass (Chalon Way E) This brings a lot of sparkle to the world of glass, through a wide range of informative and entertaining displays. The stylish modern building is fronted by a reconstructed traditional conical glasshouse, and includes several themed areas. Children enjoy the hands-on displays and crazy mirror maze in Glass Magic, while the Glass Revolution show takes a lively look at the importance of glass today. Earth Into Light includes a re-created glassmaker's parlour, and the evolution of glass from ancient times to the present day is studied in Glass Roots. An unexpected highlight is the labyrinth of tunnels to explore beneath the oldest Victorian furnace in Europe. Plenty of activities and demonstrations inc glass-blowers in action. Meals, snacks, shop, disabled access; cl Mon, 25–26 Dec, and 1 Jan; (08707) 444777; £5. The Carr Mill (E Lancs Rd) is a good value family dining pub.

STANAH SD3542

Out on the Wyre estuary, this has a stretch of waterside country with reedbeds, birds and views, attractive despite the chemical works in the background. On the opposite bank, over the toll bridge past Poulton, the Shard Bridge Inn at Hambleton is nicely placed for lunch.

STOCKPORT SJ8990

Hat Works ⌸ (Wellington Mill,

Wellington Rd S) Fun look at the town's hat-making heritage, with lots of millinery exhibits from early 19th-c fur hats to fully restored machines. There's quite a lot aimed at children, inc occasional story-telling in a mock-up of a felt tent (recalling the town's trading links with central Asia), and a milliner and textile designer sometimes give demonstrations. Meals, snacks, shop, disabled access; cl 25–26 Dec, and 1 Jan; (0161) 355 7770; £3.95.

Stockport Air Raid Shelters (Chestergate) Displays include a reconstructed canteen, tool stores and first aid post, re-creating a wartime atmosphere in this labyrinth of tunnels which protected thousands of people during World War II; guided tours around the more remote tunnels first Weds of month at 7pm (£4.50). Shop, disabled access; cl Sun am, 25–26 Dec and 1 Jan; (0161) 474 1940; £4. The Arden Arms (Millgate St) has good value food – and a great collection of working grandfather clocks.

SUNDERLAND POINT SD4255
This unique hamlet is cut off by the tide twice a day; the local legend of Sambo the slave recalls how he was brought to the point by his master who then went away for such a length of time that Sambo died of a broken heart. He died at Upsteps cottage, and a short path leads to his grave on the other side of the peninsula, which has become a shrine that is still tended to this day. The route passes a cottage which sells a publication about the area. The Globe at Overton, with a popular carvery, is handy for a family lunch.

THORNTON-CLEVELEYS SD3342
Marsh windmill (B5412) One of the largest in Europe, this working windmill has tours to the top (£1.25, no under-5s), demonstrations, a good range of craft shops alongside, and wknd entertainment in summer. Shop, disabled access to ground floor; cl 25–26 Dec; (01253) 860765; free to ground floor, 65p to 1st floor. Twelve (an imaginative conversion of a former dance studio here) has good inventive food; cl Mon. The nearby Burnside Garden Centre (New Lane) is worth a visit, with a nice café.

TURTON BOTTOMS SD7315
Turton Tower 15th-c Renaissance house with Elizabethan buildings and earlier peel tower; mostly a museum inside, but there are a couple of period rooms, and a major collection of carved wood furniture. It was interestingly extended by followers of the Romantic and later Arts and Crafts movements in the 19th c. Victorian woodland gardens. Tearoom, shop; open daily (exc Fri) May–Sept (cl am wknds), pm Sat–Weds in Mar, Apr and Oct, and just pm Sun Nov and Feb; (01204) 852203; £3. The Black Bull (Bolton Rd) has good value food, all day wknds.

UPPERMILL SD9905
This whole area of mill settlements in steep valleys cut through the moors is full of interest, and Uppermill itself is one of the most attractive places. Up above the town is a lonely moorland church, with good walks around it and an ancient pub opposite. Fine drives around here include the A635 over Saddleworth Moor, and B6197 Delph–Grains Bar then A672 or A640 over the moors.

Saddleworth Museum and Art Gallery (High St) Based around an old mill, and volunteers occasionally dress up in appropriate garb. Shop, limited disabled access, cl am Nov–Mar, 24–25 and 31 Dec and 1 Jan; (01457) 874093; £2.

WADDINGTON SD7243
Forest of Bowland village, with a fine **church**, attractive memorial gardens, and a lovely drive from Longridge. The Lower Buck has popular home cooking.

WHALLEY SD7336
Whalley Abbey 🔲 Striking remains of 14th-c Cistercian abbey – the monks' quarters, rather than the church which has virtually disappeared – in grounds of 16th-c manor house used as a religious retreat (they do B&B). Two gatehouses are intact, and there's a visitor centre. Good snacks, shop, disabled access; cl 24–25 Dec; (01254) 828400; £2. The separate 13th-c parish **church** has interesting woodwork and three ancient Celtic-Scandinavian crosses. In the Freemasons Arms at Wiswell just NE, the landlady's cooking is good.

WIGAN SD5908
Haigh Hall Country Park (N of

Wigan) 250-acre country park with guided walks, nature trails, beautifully set golf course, craft centre, walled gardens, play area, crazy golf, model village and miniature railway. Occasional tours of house – phone for dates, and a good programme of events. Meals, snacks, shops (one good for golfers), some disabled access; (01942) 832985; park free, charges for parking and attractions. The Boars Head over at Standish (A5106) has bargain food.

Wigan Pier £ (Wallgate) Rather different from when Orwell knew it, this is now a dynamic and entertaining wharfside centre demonstrating local life in the early 1900s, with actors performing in a reconstructed mine, pub, school, music hall, houses and even seaside. An ingenious mix of museum and theatre, it's an enormously enjoyable family day out, and you really do get a tangible impression of what life was really like at the turn of the century. A museum takes a nostalgic look at each decade of the 20th c; you can see a Victorian schoolroom, mill steam engine and textile machinery hall, and take a canal boat trip. Meals, snacks, shop, disabled access; cl Fri (exc Good Fri), 25–26 Dec, and 1 Jan; (01942) 323666; £7.50.

WIRRAL SJ2484
Its Merseyside parts aren't on the whole that appealing to visitors, especially on the built-up E side (with the notable exception of Port Sunlight). The NW corner can be rather more attractive, particularly along the edges of the Dee, looking across to the mountains of N Wales. The more interesting bits, inc unusual National Trust heathland, are linked by a 12-mile footpath, best joined at the **Wirral Country Park** at Thurstaston, and running down to the Cheshire parts of the Wirral. The Fox & Hounds at Barnsby has good value food.

WRAY SD6067
Charming small backwater with venerable cottages, and an increasingly popular annual Scarecrow Festival (events for the week leading up to the May bank hol). The welcoming George

& Dragon, with an attractive garden, has decent food. From here a spectacular drive over Tatham Fells leads to Slaidburn.

WYCOLLER COUNTRY PARK
SD9339
Lancashire Bront' country (the ruined hall at Wycoller may have been the base for Ferndean Manor in *Jane Eyre*), with walks along a beck to Clam Bridge, an Iron Age slab, and up to Foster's Leap, a finely placed crag. The Herders has hearty home cooking.

Other attractive villages, all with decent pubs and great surrounding scenery, include Goosnargh SD5537, Hurst Green SD6838, Tunstall SD6173 (Bront' church) and Wiswell SD7437. Particularly pretty ones in or on the edges of the Forest of Bowland are Gisburn SD8248, Grindleton SD7545 and Newton SD6950.

Pubs well placed for walks include the Hare & Hounds at Abbey Village SD6422, Pack Horse at Affetside SD7513, Bay Horse at Arkholme SD5872, Black Dog at Belmont SD6716, Dog at Belthorn SD7224, White House on Blackstone Edge SD9716, Owd Betts at Cheesden on Ashworth Moor SD8316, Edisford Bridge on the B6243 W of Clitheroe SD7241, Rams Head nr Denshaw SD9710, Diggle Hotel at Diglea Hamlet above Diggle itself SE0008, Wright Arms at Egerton SD7114, Strawbury Duck by Entwistle Station SD7217, Bulls Head on Grains Bar SD9608, Duke of Wellington on the B6232 W of Haslingden SD7522, Egerton Arms off the narrow Ashworth Rd above Heywood SD8513, Green Man at Inglewhite (nr Beacon Fell) SD5440, New Drop on Longridge Fell SD6439, Romper at Ridge End above Marple SJ9686, Kettledrum at Mereclough SD8632, Highwayman at Nether Burrow SD6275 (pretty stretch of the Lune Valley), Old Rosins at Pickup Bank, Old Hoddlesden SD6922, Roebuck on Roebuck Low SD9606 and Railway at White Coppice SD6118. Up on the moors, many of these are closed during lunchtime Mon–Thurs.

Where to eat

BISPHAM GREEN SD4813 **Eagle & Child** *Maltkiln Lane (01257) 462297*
Striking 3-storey dark brick pub with civilised mainly open-plan bar, fine old stone
fireplaces, oriental rugs and some coir on the flagstones, handsome oak settles,
imaginative food, well kept real ales, and friendly service; bowling green and croquet
behind; open all day Sun; disabled access. £21.50|**£6.90**

BLACKPOOL SD3036 **September Brasserie** *15–17 Queen St (01253)
623282* Not far from the seafront and above a hairdresser's, this busy little airy
restaurant's open-view kitchen does particularly good inventive food from a short
menu with ideas from all over the world (inc lovely puddings), and a thoughtful wine
list; cl Sun, Mon, 2 wks summer, 2 wks winter. £28|**£6.50**

CHIPPING SD6241 **Dog & Partridge** *Hesketh Lane (01995) 61201* Spotlessly
kept and relaxed dining pub with comfortable main lounge, winter log fire, good
choice of enjoyable food (inc fine home-made chips), real ales, and quite a few wines
and malt whiskies; disabled access. £21.50/3-course lunch £13.50

DOWNHAM SD7844 **Assheton Arms** *(01200) 441227* Charmingly set dining
pub in prettily preserved village, with rambling beamed bar, a massive stone
fireplace, no smoking area, popular bar food (lots of good fresh fish dishes), well
kept real ales, and decent wines; disabled access. £20.95|**£6.95**

KIRKHAM SD4232 **Cromwellian** *16 Poulton St (01772) 685680* Tiny evening
restaurant in 17th-c house with consistently good interesting food from a fixed-
price menu – thoughtful wine list, too; cl Sun, Mon, 1 wk May, 2 wks Oct. £25

LIVERPOOL SJ3589 **60 Hope Street** *60 Hope St (0151) 707n6060* Listed
Georgian double-fronted house with basement café bar and ground floor
restaurant, relaxed modern décor, interesting contemporary European cooking,
good puddings (try the popular deep-fried jam sandwich with Carnation ice-cream),
friendly knowledgeable service, and a decent wine list; cl Sun, bank hols. £35/2-
course set lunch £10.95

LIVERPOOL SJ3490 **Simply Heathcotes** *Beetham Plaza, 25 The Strand (0151)
236 3536* Chic modern restaurant with a curved plate-glass frontage, smart simple
furnishings, contemporary British brasserie-style food, a varied wine list, and
helpful, suited young staff; other branches in Manchester, Preston and Longridge; cl
bank hol Mon, 25–26 Dec, 1 Jan; disabled access. £31.90|**£10**

LONGRIDGE SD6137 **Paul Heathcotes** *104 Higher Rd (01772) 784969* Pretty
restaurant with flowers, beams and candlelit tables in little interconnected rooms,
exceptional modern British cooking, marvellous puddings, and exemplary service;
cl Mon, Tues, 1 Jan. £48/3-course lunch £16.50

MANCHESTER SJ8398 **Petit Blanc** *55 King Street (0161) 8321000* Stylishly
renovated former bank, with smartly presented brasserie-style food from a diverse
menu, helpful service, a good short wine list, and lovely flower arrangements; they
offer set children's menus with proper food; other branches in Birmingham,
Cheltenham, and Oxford; cl 25 Dec; disabled access. £21|**£5.25**

MANCHESTER SJ8096 **Rhodes & Co** *Quality Hotel, Waters Reach (0161) 868
1900* Popular brasserie in a new hotel with unfussy modern décor, an open kitchen,
Rhodes-style contemporary British cooking, attractive presentation, friendly
helpful staff, a relaxed atmosphere, and decent wines; cl Sat and Sun am; disabled
access. £32/2-course lunch £12.50

MANCHESTER SJ8398 **Simply Heathcotes** *Jackson Row, Deansgate (0161)
835 3536* Stylish modern restaurant with high ceilings, polished wood floors, bright
paintings on coloured walls, and contemporary furniture, up-to-the-minute
brasserie-style cooking inc very good value set lunches, thoughtful wine list, and
efficient service; cl bank hol Mon, 25–26 Dec; disabled access. £34.10/2-course
menu £13.50

MANCHESTER SJ8497 **Yang Sing** *34 Princess St (0161) 236 2200* Exceptionally
good sophisticated Chinese food using the best fresh ingredients (tanks of live fish,
too), wonderful dim-sum (the widest choice in Europe), some unusual dishes

among traditional Cantonese specialities, good value set meals, a bustling atmosphere, and efficient service; must book ahead; cl 25 Dec; disabled access. £21|**£8.50**

MAWDESLEY SD4914 **Red Lion** *New St (01704) 822208* Busily traditional village local with splendid very popular food prepared with real flair in brightly painted conservatory (best to book wknds); the colourful dining room décor is quite a shock after the far more conventional bar, which has a good chatty atmosphere; separate public bar, particularly helpful friendly service, well kept real ale, and well chosen wines by the glass; tables in a courtyard behind, and more among flowers in front. £26/£2-course lunch £9

MELLOR SJ9888 **Oddfellows Arms** *73 Moor End Rd (0161) 449 7826* Fine old building with low ceilings, open fires and a chatty atmosphere in two flagstoned rooms, no smoking restaurant, and a wide range of interesting food inc lots of different types of fresh fish; cl 4 days over Christmas; children must be well behaved; disabled access. £23|**£7**

SAWLEY SD7746 **Spread Eagle** *(01220) 441202* Quiet upmarket 16th-c dining pub with comfortably sophisticated feel in light and airy lounge bar, coal fire, smart no smoking restaurant with big picture windows overlooking a pretty stretch of the River Ribble, new chef doing splendid food inc good value wkdy set lunches and bargain early suppers (may be cl Sun evening), and occasional themed evenings and dinner dances; well kept real ales, several dozen malt whiskies, expanded list of well chosen wines, and friendly efficient service; cl Sun pm, Mon; disabled access. £23.75|**£5.50**

TUNSTALL SD6073 **Lunesdale Arms** *(01524) 274203* Civilised and brightly opened-up dining pub with enjoyable interesting food using home-baked bread, meat from local farms, and a lot of local organic produce; big unframed oil paintings (some for sale and often of bluebells) on yellow walls, cheerful bustling atmosphere, a couple of woodburners; well kept real ales, sensibly priced wines by the glass (in a choice of sizes), and good cafetière coffee; pretty Lune Valley village. £21.25|**£7**

WHALLEY SD7335 **Toby Jug Tea Shop** *20 King St (01254) 823298* 300-year-old listed building with oak beams, old stone fireplaces, and wooden panelling on the upstairs walls, afternoon tea with cream and scones, cakes and cucumber sandwiches (all home-made), lots of teas and coffees, and light lunches with a fine choice of filled sandwiches and rolls; cl Sun, Mon, end Jun, Christmas; children over 8; disabled access.|**£5**

YEALAND CONYERS SD5074 **New Inn** *(01524) 732938* Ivy-covered stone dining pub with log fire in little beamed bar, two communicating cottage dining rooms, novel daily specials, fine salads served with meals, friendly professional service, decent wines, well kept ales, and a sheltered side lawn. £20|**£5.50**

Special thanks to Margaret Dickinson, Steve Chambers, Helen Wharton, Mr and Mrs P A Stallard

LEICESTERSHIRE AND RUTLAND

A get-away secret – not that many visitors, but some surprising attractions, stately houses and castles, and sweeping country views

With the outstanding National Space Centre and a variety of things to visit (from Roman remains to an unusual public health museum), Leicester is a rewarding city for family days out. If it's sunny, developing Conkers at Moira is another good bet – it's Leicestershire's Family Attraction of the Year. Rutland Water is pleasant for walks, with quite a lot of varied things to see and do around it.

Families will find plenty to keep them happy at the lively Snibston Discovery Park in Coalville (lots of interactive exhibits, and a huge play area). For animal-oriented attractions there's Twycross Zoo (a popular place specialising in primates), and the friendly farm parks at Tilton on the Hill and East Leake; bird-lovers will enjoy the walk-through aviaries at Desford.

In Mountsorrel you'll find vintage cars as well as animals, and another good motor-related outing is the great collection of single-seat racing cars at Donington Park (summer motor sport meetings at Mallory Park too). Swinford has the twin attractions of a good motorcycle museum and a charming 17th-c house, and there's another interesting house at Donington le Heath. Cottesmore, Loughborough and Market Bosworth all have something for the steam railway enthusiast. Among the county's several castles, Belvoir is the grandest.

The sweeping countryside particularly suits scenic drives or cycle rides, especially in the east: graceful patches of woodland, plenty of charming stone-built villages to potter through, delightful churches. Many of the less busy roads stride along old coach routes, with broad views. There are quite a few good walks, too – and you get out into unspoilt countryside very quickly from the built-up areas.

Where to stay

EMPINGHAM SK9408 **White Horse** *Main St, Empingham, Oakham, Rutland LE15 8PR* (01780) 460221 **£65***, plus special breaks; 13 pretty rms, some in a delightfully converted stable block. Attractive, bustling old inn, handy for Rutland Water; a relaxed and comfortable atmosphere, a big log fire and fresh flowers in open-plan lounge, big helpings of very enjoyable food inc fine breakfasts, coffee and croissants from 8am, and cream teas all year; attractive no smoking restaurant, well kept real ales, and efficient friendly service; cots/high chairs; cl 25 Dec; good disabled access; dogs welcome in bedrooms

MARKET HARBOROUGH SP7387 **Three Swans** *21 High St, Market Harborough, Leicestershire LE16 7NJ* (01858) 466644 **£84**w, plus special breaks; 60 rms. Fine old coaching inn with plush lounge bar, attractive conservatory and glorious courtyard, very friendly helpful staff, and decent food in bar and restaurant; may cl 1–3 Jan; disabled access

Leicestershire & Rutland

NOTTINGHAMSHIRE

DERBYSHIRE

SK

Castle Donington
Donington Park
Kegworth
East Leake
Breedon on the Hill
A6006
Staunton Harold
A42
Belton
Loughborough
Ashby-de-la-Zouch
Shepshed
Walton on the Wolds
Swannington
Whitwick
A6
Moira
Charnwood Forest
Woodhouse Eaves
Packington
Coalville
A46
Mountsorrel
Gaddesby
A511
Swithland Reservoir
Donington le Heath
Newtown Linford
Rothley
Appleby Magna
M1
Barkby
Ashby Canal
A444
A47
Kirby Muxloe
Leicester
Twycross
Desford
Market Bosworth
Oadby
Mallory Park
Wigston
A6
Stoke Golding
Wistow
A5199
M69
SP
Hinckley
Peatling Magna
Arnesby
M1
Bruntingthorpe
Peatling Parva
A426
SP
A4304
Swinford

WARWICKSHIRE

LINCOLNSHIRE

TF

CAMBS

NORTHAMPTONSHIRE

Bottesford

Belvoir

Harby Knipton

Hose Branston

Grimston

A606

A607

Melton Mowbray

A607

Stapleford

Wymondham

Market Overton

Clipsham

Stretton

A606

Cottesmore

A1

A6121

Belmesthorpe

Ashby Folville

Burrough on the Hill

Exton

South Croxton Somerby

Oakham

Empingham

A606

Knossington

Upper Hambleton

Tilton on the Hill

Braunston

Rutland Water

Ketton

A47

Wing

A47

Billesdon

South Luffenham

King's Norton

Barrowden

Uppingham

Welland Viaduct

Lyddington

Kibworth Harcourt

Hallaton

Stoke Dry

Tur Langton

East Langton

Eyebrook Reservoir

Foxton

Thorpe Langton

Medbourne

Market Harborough

0 Miles 5

0 Kilometres 8

MEDBOURNE SP7992 **Nevill Arms** *Waterfall Way, Medbourne, Market Harborough, Leicestershire LE16 8EE (01858) 565288 wkdys* **£55**; 8 rms, 6 in separate cottage and barn conversion. Bright and busy old mullion-windowed inn just across footbridge over stream, with excellent food, friendly prompt service, and an inglenook log fire; cl pm 25 Dec

OAKHAM SK8608 **Whipper-In** *Market Pl, Oakham, Rutland LE15 6DT (01572) 756971* **£84**, plus special breaks; 24 rms. Attractive and well run 17th-c stone coaching inn with oak-beamed and panelled lounge opening into cosy eating area, log fires, good food in cosy restaurant, and well kept ales; disabled access; dogs welcome in bedrooms

PACKINGTON SK3514 **Springs Health Farm** *Measham Rd, Packington, Ashby-de-la-Zouch, Leicestershire NE65 1TJ (01530) 273873* **£150**inc full use of all facilities, plus special breaks; 89 rms. Britain's first purpose-built health farm with all the amenities, good healthy food, and friendly staff; cl 20–27 Dec; no children; disabled access

ROTHLEY SK5712 **Rothley Court** *Westfield Lane, Rothley, Leicester LE7 7LG (0116) 237 4141* **£105**; 32 rms (the ones in the main house have more character). Mentioned in the Domesday Book, this carefully run manor house with its beautifully preserved 13th-c chapel has some fine oak panelling, open fires, a comfortable bar, conservatory, and courteous staff; seats out on the terrace and in the garden; disabled access; dogs welcome in bedrooms

STAPLEFORD SK8118 **Stapleford Park** *Stapleford, Melton Mowbray, Leicestershire LE14 2EF (01572) 787522* **£246.75***; 51 individually designed rms, plus cottage. Luxurious country house, extravagantly restored, in lovely large grounds with riding and stabling, tennis, croquet, putting green, 18-hole championship golf course, trout fishing, falconry, and clay-pigeon shooting; lots of mahogany, opulent furnishings, fine oil paintings and an impressive library, delicious restaurant food, enthusiastic American owner, and warmly welcoming staff; health spa and indoor swimming pool; cots/babysitting; disabled access; dogs welcome away from restaurant

STRETTON SK9415 **Ram Jam Inn** *Great North Rd, Stretton, Oakham, Rutland LE15 7QX (01780) 410776* **£68.90**; 7 comfortable and well equipped rms. Actually on the A1, this civilised place has a comfortable airily modern lounge bar, a café bar and bistro, good interesting food quickly served all day from open-plan kitchen, and useful small wine list; large garden and orchard; cl 25 Dec

UPPINGHAM SP8699 **Lake Isle** *16 High St East, Uppingham, Oakham, Rutland LE15 9PZ (01572) 822951* **£108**, plus special breaks; 12 rms with home-made biscuits, sherry and fresh fruit, and three cottage suites. In a charming market town, this 18th-c restaurant-with-rooms has an open fire in the attractive lounge, a redecorated bar (once a barber's where the schoolboys had their hair cut), good, imaginative food in refurbished restaurant (enjoyable breakfasts, too), a carefully chosen wine list, and a small and pretty garden; dogs welcome in bedrooms

To see and do

Leicestershire and Rutland Family Attraction of the Year

MOIRA SK3115 **Conkers** (B586) Great fun, this busily developing site grew out of the former visitor centre for the embryonic National Forest – it's rapidly become a huge mix of indoor and outdoor activities ideal for finding out about trees and the creatures that live in them. Children get a lot out of coming here, and particularly enjoy the indoor Discovery Zones, where natural history is made spectacularly real with imaginatively conceived displays: you can crawl through a living leaf, see the world through the eyes of a spider, and dodge the nasties spat at you by a man-sized ant. If you remember the craze for virtual pets you'll love the virtual plant cell, which you keep alive by adjusting its water, light and sugar intake; sounds and colours let you know how you're getting on. Multimedia shows have speeded-up footage of the seasons, so a year in the forest flies by in an instant, and seeds swiftly grow into trees. You can even take charge of global warming – though be prepared for blasts of hot or cold air when you get it wrong. Outside are 120 acres with lakeside walks, nature and sculpture trails, mazes, play areas, bird hides, and a good assault course (aimed at adults); a steam train takes you round, or you can hire bikes. There's a very full programme of special events and lively activities at weekends and school or bank holidays; they may have pond-dipping, live music, or kite and mask making (£1 extra); you can find the schedule at www.visitconkers.com/events. Some activities can be messy. It's been put together very well, with lots of thought put into how best to attract people to woodland that's not yet fully grown. As we went to press they were already putting in place several additions, some of which – like the soft play area – were suggested by regular visitors. It's easy to spend a good chunk of the day here, though you'll like it best in dry weather. No dogs (exc guide dogs). Meals and snacks in two lakeside restaurants, craft workshops, shops, good disabled access; cl 25 Dec; (01283) 216633; £5.25 adults, £3.25 children 3–15; a family ticket (two adults, two children) is £14.95 – good value, considering how much you can do.

ARNESBY SP6192
Arnesby windmill Handsomely preserved, well worth a look. The Chandlers Arms over in Shearsby has interesting food.

ASHBY CANAL SK3707
The towpath has good countryside walking, with green fields and stone-arched bridges, as well as coots, moorhens, herons and perhaps even the flash of a kingfisher. The best parts run from the tunnel under Snarestone past Gopsall Park, and then on through Shackerstone and Congerstone to pass Shenton Park on an embankment, before heading into Warwickshire and its junction with the Coventry Canal. It also makes an ideal walking link between Bosworth battlefield and the steam railway to the N.

ASHBY-DE-LA-ZOUCH SK3516
Ashby-de-la-Zouch Castle The

Norman core and its 15th-c extension were largely destroyed in the Civil War, but the ruins are impressive (inc an underground passage, now illuminated), and the adjoining fields were the setting for Sir Walter Scott's *Ivanhoe*. Snacks, shop, limited disabled access; cl 24–26 Dec, 1 Jan, and Mon, Tues Nov–Mar; (01530) 413343; £3; EH. There's a little **museum** with local history displays (cl 1–2 and Oct–Easter (01530) 560090, free admission if you've been to the castle first, otherwise 50p), next to the Tourist Information Centre on North St. The Thirsty Millers (Mill Lane Mews) has fresh local food – and a reputed tunnel to the castle.

BELVOIR SK8133
Belvoir Castle 🏰 Pronounced Beaver, this has some impressive rooms, but is even better from the

outside, a glorious fantasy of turrets and battlements, pinnacles and towers, surrounded by terraced gardens peopled with sculptures. Meals, snacks, shop; open May–Sept; (01476) 871002; £7. The Chequers at Woolsthorpe has good food. Good drives on fine old coach roads centre on Belvoir: for instance, from Long Benington (Lincs) through Bottesford, Harby and Hose, or via Knipton down through Eastwell and past Grimston all the way to Barrow upon Soar, where the canalside Navigation (Mill Lane) has good value food.

BOTTESFORD SK8139
Bottesford church Packed with elaborate monuments to the Earls and Dukes of Rutland, two by Grinling Gibbons; they had to raise the roof to fit them all in. The welcoming church has informative displays. The Muston Gap in nearby Muston is a useful family food pub.

BREEDON ON THE HILL SK4023
Breedon on the Hill church On an interesting partly quarried Iron Age hill fort, this is unrivalled in Britain or abroad for its Anglo-Saxon carvings, over 1,100 years old.

BURROUGH ON THE HILL SK7510
Burrough Hill has an enjoyable path along its escarpment. The summit has splendid views, and an imposing Iron Age hill fort, its ramparts still largely intact (£1.50 parking for three hours). The Stag & Hounds has good value food.

CHARNWOOD FOREST SK4515
Charnwood Forest views The friendly Bulls Head (former B587 Whitwick–Copt Oak), with a big garden and lots of animals, has fine views over surviving remnants of this former hunting park, popular for walks; the Copt Oak pub itself, over on the B591, is also a useful base for walks.

CLIPSHAM SK9716
Yew Tree Avenue (just E, off Castle Bytham Rd) Delightfully quirky avenue of 150 yew trees, clipped in sometimes bizarre shapes to represent animals, characters and events; free. The surrounding woods are full of deer (not to mention bluebells in spring). In the attractive village, the Olive Branch has very good food.

COALVILLE SK4114
Snibston Discovery Park (Ashby Rd) Busy 100-acre site based around a former colliery (the first shaft was sunk by George and Robert Stephenson), with a huge outdoor science play area, a nature reserve, and historic mine buildings. At its centre an exhibition hall houses five interactive galleries – children like the Science Alive gallery best, with plenty of experiments and hands-on activities, even the illusion of cycling with a skeleton. Similarly organised galleries look at transport, mining and fashion. For an extra 50p, an incredible virtual reality experience puts you on an exploding oil rig, making a dash for the helicopter pad. The landscaped grounds include a sculpture trail and picnic areas, with extra charges for fishing. Evocative tours of the old colliery are taken by former pitmen. Until June, a temporary exhibition on life in Tudor times includes weaponry, life on the *Mary Rose*, and costumes. Meals, snacks, shop, disabled access; cl 24–25 Dec, 1 Jan and a week in Jan; (01530) 278444; £5.25. The charming old New Inn over at Peggs Green (off A512 Ashby—Shepshed) has lots of interesting old local photographs, inc colliery ones.

COTTESMORE SK8913
Rutland Railway Museum Nearly 40 industrial steam and diesel locomotives, and 60 other wagons and vehicles used in the ironstone quarries and industry. Occasional steam rides, and quite a nice lineside walk to the old Oakham Canal. Snacks, shop, disabled access; open most wknds – best to phone (01572) 813203 for dates of steam days; free (£3 on steam days). In the attractive village, the thatched Sun is good for lunch.

DESFORD SK4704
Tropical Bird Gardens 🐦
(Lindridge Lane) This pleasant five-acre woodland garden has over 50 different species, many in walk-through aviaries; the free-flying macaws are particularly spectacular – they may even perch on your shoulder. Meals, snacks, shop, disabled access; cl Nov–Jan and any inclement weather days till Mar (01455) 824603; £4. The Old Lancaster Inn (Station Rd) has decent food.

DONINGTON LE HEATH SK4212
Donington le Heath Manor House Except for some 17th-c refurbishment,

this medieval house has remained practically untouched since it was built in the 13th c. The developing 17th-c style gardens include a decorative maze and orchards with traditional trees and ornamental beehives. Meals and snacks (Sat–Weds), shop; disabled access to tearoom and ground floor only, cl 25–26 Dec; (01530) 831259; free.

DONINGTON PARK SK4225

Donington Grand Prix Collection Largest private collection of single-seat racing cars in the world, with vehicles driven by all the greats, and related memorabilia; the price means it's never too crowded, and enthusiasts find it all fascinating. Meals, snacks, shop, some disabled access; cl 24–26, 31 Dec, and 1 Jan; (01332) 811027; £7. The Nags Head is a good dining pub.

EAST LEAKE SK5525

Manor Farm Animal Centre and Donkey Sanctuary You can pet and feed some of the animals or walk a goat; an interactive nature trail leads to a lake where you can try dipping, and there are rides to a play fort. Also adventure playground, indoor activity centre, straw maze and pony rides (£1). Usually cl Mon, and over Christmas and New Year; snacks and picnic areas, shop, disabled access; (01509) 852525; £4. The Star at West Leake is good value for lunch.

EXTON SK9211

Handsome collection of thatched houses around a tree-studded green, with pleasant walks around; the attractive **church** is beautifully placed in a park, and the Fox & Hounds has decent home cooking.

Barnsdale Gardens (The Avenue, SW of village) Familiar to viewers of *Gardeners' World*: they were developed on the programme by the late Geoff Hamilton. The interesting plants are grown using peat-free compost, and there are plenty of useful ideas and techniques. Coffee shop, nursery, disabled access; cl 23, 25 Dec; (01572) 813200; *£5. S of here towards the A606 the Barnsdale Lodge Hotel has good food, comfortable bedrooms.

Rutland Falconry & Owl Centre (W of village) Small woodland centre with 100 or so birds of prey, with the chance to handle some of the birds;

daily flying displays (depending on weather). Picnic area, snacks, shop, disabled access; (07778) 152814; £3.50.

EYEBROOK RESERVOIR SP8595

Rewarding for bird-watchers and fishermen, although as it has no hides or facilities it will appeal mainly to true enthusiasts.

FOXTON SP6989

Foxton Canal Museum Next to an interesting staircase flight of locks, and based around the extraordinary Victorian steam-powered boat lift built to avoid using the lock and so save water – now being restored, but it will take years. Shop, some disabled access; usually cl Thurs–Fri in winter; (0116) 279 2657; site free, museum £2. Bridge 61 at the bottom of the locks has basic food and welcomes children (lots of ducks – take plenty of bread). The locks are a good focus for Grand Union Canal towpath walks. The reservoir over at Saddington is also a pretty spot.

GADDESBY SK6812

Gaddesby church Notable for its elaborate 13th-c external workmanship (and see the squire's heroic Waterloo statue inside). The Golden Fleece over at South Croxton has good value fresh food.

HALLATON SP7896

Picturesque village, with an Easter Monday tradition of bottle kicking and hare pie scambling; you can find out more about these curious ancient customs at the little award-winning local history **museum** in Hogg Lane; open pm wknds and bank hols May–Oct; (01858) 555416; free. The Bewicke Arms has decent food.

HINCKLEY SP4594

Burbage Common & Woods (off A47 just E) Ancient woodland with lots of footpaths (some accessible by wheelchair), observation hides, and spectacular ground flora. Visitor centre usually open Sun, pm only Sat, Tues and Weds Apr–Nov, plus Mon and Fri pms Jun–Aug, but phone to check; (01455) 633712; free. The Chequers (Lutterworth Rd) has home-cooked lunches (not Sun/Mon) and a nice family garden.

KEGWORTH SK4826

Country drive The Cap & Stocking in Kegworth is an interesting old tavern,

at the start of a pleasant drive through the Leakes, Wysall, Widmerpool, Kinoulton, Colston Bassett (just over the Notts border – the Martins Arms is the best lunch stop of all, though by no means cheap), Granby and Orston.
KIBWORTH HARCOURT SP6894
Kibworth Harcourt windmill The county's only remaining post mill, a fine example from the early 18th c. The Horseshoes is a decent restaurant, and the old coach road through Kibworth from Uppingham and on to Kilby, Counteshorpe and Cosby is a fine long-striding drive.
KING'S NORTON SK6800
King's Norton church A graceful Gothic Revival building; the thatched Queens Head over in pretty Billesdon has enjoyable home-made food.
KIRBY MUXLOE SK5204
Kirby Muxloe Castle 15th-c ruins (peaceful despite the sight of the M1 just under fi mile away); the castle was barely used by its original owner before he was executed. Shop, disabled access; open pms Sat, Sun and bank hols Apr–Oct; (01162) 386886; £2.10. The Royal Oak has enjoyable food.
LEICESTER SK5804
In this busy city's mix of ancient and modern, it's the modern which makes the most immediate impression. But a bit of digging around among the shops, office blocks and traffic schemes does turn up reminders of its long and varied past. Most notable among some fine old buildings is the 14th-c Guildhall; (0116) 253 2569; cl Sun am; free. The strikingly modern new National Space Centre at Abbey Meadows is a vivid contrast. Besides the museums described individually, several others are worth a look. **Newarke Houses** (The Newarke), in two historic houses with a quiet period garden, includes a Victorian street scene and the clothes of Daniel Lambert, Britain's heaviest man; cl Sun am and Christmas-New Year; (0116) 225 4980; free. The **City Gallery** (Granby St) has temporary exhibitions of contemporary visual arts and crafts; cl Mon–Sun and bank hols; (0116) 255 4100; free. **New Walk Museum and Art Gallery** (New Walk) includes an Ancient Egypt gallery with mummies, a natural history

section, an art gallery with a notable collection of Expressionist and European art from the 15th c to the present day, and a discovery room where children can try on replica clothes. The Royal Tigers exhibition covers the story of the Royal Leicestershire Regiment; (0116) 255 4100; cl Sun am; free. The **Jain Centre** (Oxford St) has some fantastic examples of traditional Indian architecture; disabled access; open pm wkdys; (0116) 254 3091; donations suggested. The Hindu temple on Narborough Rd is reckoned to be one of the finest outside India. Towpath walks along both the Grand Union Canal and the River Soar give a relatively tranquil back view of the city's industrial life, and Gorse Hill City Farm is a friendly little community farm in Anstey Lane; (0116) 2537582. Useful refreshment places include Café Bruxelles (High St), r/bar (Granby St) and Croques (Loseby Lane).
Abbey Pumping Station (Corporation Rd) With the largest working steam beam engines in the country, and now a museum of public health, these former sewage pumping works have some bizarre displays inc the Flush With Pride exhibition, where you flush imitation faeces down a see-through loo and follow their movements through the drains. Shop, mostly disabled access; cl Sun am, 24–26 Dec and 1 Jan; (0116) 299 5111; free (£3 when beam engines in steam).
Belgrave Hall (Church Rd, Leicester's N edge) A fine example of 18th-c Queen Anne architecture, furnished with Victorian and Edwardian pieces; charming gardens. Shop, disabled access to ground floor and gardens; cl 24 Dec–2 Jan; (0116) 266 6590; free.
Eco House (Western Park, Hinckley Rd) This extended 1920s house is a showcase for environmentally friendly living, with interactive displays in every room, and an organic garden. Snacks, shop, disabled access; cl ams, all Mon and Tues and 25 Dec–1 Jan; (0116) 254 5489; free (donations).
Jewry Wall Museum and Site (St Nicholas Circle) Site of 2nd-c Roman baths; the courtyard has been excavated to reveal porticoes and

shops sheltered by the remains of a massive stone wall (the largest free-standing Roman structure in the country). Excellent collections of mosaic pavements and painted wall plaster. Shop, disabled access; cl Sun am, 25 Dec, 1 Jan; (0116) 2254971; free.

National Gas Museum Trust (Aylestone Rd) Housed under a Victorian clock tower in what used to be the gatehouse to the gas works, this comprehensive study of the industry includes one of the largest collections of gas and gas-related artefacts in the world, from cookers and washing machines to a gas radio, hairdryers and magic lanterns. Disabled access to ground floor only; open Tues–Thurs pm (exc 24 Dec–1 Jan); (0116) 250 3190; free.

National Space Centre (Exploration Drive, off Corporation Rd) £52 million centre with everything in space, from stars and planets to rockets and satellites, with the latest museum technology and hundreds of interactive and hands-on displays. A striking 41-metre (135-ft) tower visible for miles around houses their biggest rockets, Blue Steak and Thor Able, and has good views of the city from the top. The glass lifts give a dramatic look at the rockets. An outstanding planetarium has better shows than you'll see elsewhere inc a film exploring the size of the universe, and one for under-5s (though in general it's older children who like the centre best). You'll get a timed ticket when you go into the main centre. The first of the four main galleries, Into Space, looks at astronauts. Exploring the Universe concentrates on how things began and the possibility of extra-terrestrials. The Planets examines our own solar system, and Orbiting Earth looks at how space technology affects our everyday lives. Along the way you can feel what it's like to be blasted into space, launch your own rocket, design your own alien, see pieces of the moon or Mars, and try forecasting the weather. A final section looks at the latest space happenings (any launches can be shown live), with staff to answer questions. Meals and snacks (with rockets suspended above you), shop, good disabled access; cl Mon in term-time, Dec 25–26 and Jan 1;

(0870) 607 7223; £7.95. You can book in advance by phone, though there is a booking fee.

LOUGHBOROUGH SK5419
Bell Foundry Museum (Freehold St) Part of the largest working bell foundry in the world (bell-casting Thurs pm – you must book ahead if you want to watch), with a quite remarkable array of bells in the tuning room. Best not to wear light colours (they coat the moulds with graphite). Shop; open Tues–Sat 10–12.30, 1.30–4.30, cl Christmas–New Year; (01509) 233414; £1.50. The Swan in the Rushes (A6) has good home cooking.

Great Central Railway 🆓 (Great Central Rd) Main line steam railway to Leicester, with a museum and engine sheds this end. Meals, snacks, shop;, disabled access is better at other stations on this line; no trains wkdys Oct–May (exc Easter and bank hols) – best to phone; (01509) 230726; £10, museum only £3.

Queen's Park With well organised local history, the little **Charnwood Museum** here has a couple of interactive displays inc a computer game about Loughborough. Snacks, shop, disabled access; usually only cl am Sun, and 25 Dec; (01509) 233754; free. The Carillon Tower here reflects the town's importance as a bell-founding town; carillon recitals Thurs 1pm and Sun 3.30pm; inside is a small war museum, and you can climb the spiral staircase to the top of the 46-metre (151-ft) tower; cl am Sun–Weds and Fri; (01509) 263370; 50p.

LYDDINGTON SP8796
Bede House This handsome 15th-c house was until the Reformation a residence of the Bishops of Lincoln. Notable carved ceilings, 15th-c glass, and tranquil garden. Snacks, shop, disabled access to ground floor only; cl Nov–Mar; (01572) 822438; £3. The stone-built village is attractive, and the Old White Hart is good for lunch.

MALLORY PARK SK4500
Mallory Park Circuit Motor sport meetings each wknd Mar–Oct; meals, snacks, shop, disabled access; (01455) 842931; from £9. The Windmill over at Brascote, Newbold Verdon, has good value food.

MARKET BOSWORTH SK3706

Battlefield Steam Railway Line 🖼 Runs from Shackerstone through Market Bosworth to Shenton by Bosworth Battlefield, a rather nice return trip of just over nine miles. There's a Victorian tearoom (open when trains run) and some displays at the Shackerstone end; the Belper Arms at nearby Newton Burgoland is a very interesting old pub. Trains usually run wknds and bank hols Mar–Oct, plus Weds pm July–Aug; (01827) 880754 for timetable; *£6 return.

Bosworth Battlefield Site of the deciding action in the War of the Roses, when Henry VII's 1485 victory over Richard III led to the Tudors' seizing the English throne. The visitor centre has explanatory films and exhibitions, as well as a detailed trail through the country park, following the sites of the fighting (now thought to be ever so slightly out). Meals, snacks, shop, disabled access; cl Mon–Sat Nov–Dec, all Jan–Feb, Mon–Fri in Mar; (01455) 290429; £3 entry, plus £1 for parking. The Royal Arms at nearby Sutton Cheney has good food. Market Bosworth village itself is interesting to walk through, and the Black Horse (by the Market Pl alms houses) has good value food.

MARKET HARBOROUGH SP7387

An attractive market town which used to specialise in the production of corsets; bizarre, florid and even agonising examples of which can be seen alongside many other aspects of the town's history in the **museum** (shop, disabled access with notice; cl Sun am, Good Fri and 24–26 Dec, and last full wk in Jan; (01858) 821085; free). The centre has some fine old Georgian buildings (don't miss the Old Grammar School, built on stilts), and above them the gracefully soaring 14th-c spire of the church. The Three Swans Hotel is useful for lunch. You can walk a mile along the river to nearby Welland Park.

Little Bowden church (outskirts, nr Sainsburys) Handsome 12th-c church, set off charmingly by its fine old rectory. The adjacent thatched Cherry Tree has good value food.

MELTON MOWBRAY SK7519

This little town is the home of Stilton cheese and pork pies; Dickinson & Morris (Nottingham St) still make the pies to a traditional recipe. **St Mary's church** (Burton St) is handsome, and the Anne of Cleves nearby has popular food.

Melton Carnegie Museum (Thorpe End) Recently refurbished, with local history inc a look at Melton Mowbray's fashionable 19th-c days, and interactive displays; shop, disabled access; cl Good Fri and 25–26 Dec; free (01664) 569946.

Websters Dairy (Saxelbye) A good place to buy Stilton cheese (01664) 812223. The Black Horse in nearby Grimston is pleasant for lunch.

MOIRA SK3115

Conkers See separate family panel on p.379.

Moira Furnace and Craft Workshops 🖼 Along the same road as Conkers above; guided tours take you around this 19th-c blast furnace, which has interactive displays about how it worked, a few craft workshops, woodland walks, and a children's play area. Meals, snacks, shop, disabled access; cl Mon, plus Tues in winter, 25–26 Dec and 1 Jan; (01283) 224667; £3. The towpath beside the canal (the first stretch of the Ashby Canal to be reopened in the county) links the furnace to the attractions listed under Market Bosworth, and the museum runs boat trips through the new Moira Lock (£2 one-way).

MOUNTSORREL SK5715

Stonehurst Family Farm & Motor Museum (Bond Lane) Traditional farm with animals to handle, pony rides, play barn, trailer rides, nature trail, and a small collection of vintage cars with a re-created 1920s garage. Meals, snacks, farm shop, disabled access to farmyard and tearoom; cl 25–26 Dec; (01509) 413216; £3.45. The waterside Swan (Loughborough Rd) does good lunches.

NEWTOWN LINFORD SK5210

Bradgate Country Park This extensive tract of the former Charnwood Forest hunting park is little changed over the last 750 years. At its heart are the ruins of the 15th-c home of Lady Jane Grey, and a visitor centre tells her sad story. Shop, limited disabled access; visitor centre cl early am, Mon (except bank hols), and Dec–Feb; (0116) 236 2713; parking from £1.50, visitor centre £1.20. Fallow and even red deer still roam these heathy slopes among the rock outcrops, and there's general access, plenty of waymarked paths, and lots of opportunities for picnics. Nearby Cropston Reservoir has waterfowl. The Pear Tree in Woodhouse Eaves has a wide choice of food.

OADBY SK6101

University Botanic Gardens (Stoughton Drive S) Set around student halls of residence, these university gardens are 16 acres filled with a wide variety of plants in different and delightful settings, inc a national hardy fuchsia collection. Some disabled access; cl wknds and bank hols mid-Nov to Mar, 25–26 Dec and 1 Jan; (0116) 271 7725; free.

OAKHAM SK8608

Rutland's pint-sized county town is attractive, with a good sense of country bustle about it, and one or two interesting shops. The Whipper In (Market Pl) has enjoyable food, and there's a handsome drive through Ashwell, Wymondham and Waltham on the Wolds to Harby.

Oakham Castle The magnificent Norman great hall is all that's left of the building, but earthworks, walls and the remains of a motte give a good idea of what it must have been like. The hall itself is decorated with a quirky collection of extraordinary horseshoes, some grossly opulent, some enormously oversized. Shop, disabled access; cl 1–1.30pm, Sun am, Good Fri and 25–26 Dec; (01572) 758440; free.

Rutland County Museum (Catmose St) In a late 18th-c riding school, this puts the emphasis on rural life, though there are some Roman and Saxon finds, and an exhibition on local military regiments. Snacks, shop, disabled access; cl Sun am, Good Fri and over Christmas; (01572) 758440; free.

RUTLAND WATER SK8707

Europe's biggest man-made lake, oddly shaped, with a number of attractions. On the N side are nature trails, an unusual drought garden created by the late Geoff Hamilton, places to hire bikes (01780) 460705 or 720888, and hourly

boat trips; Apr–Oct; (01572) 787630. You can fish in various parts of the water, and a visitor centre down at Normanton has a small **museum** in a church modelled on London's St John's, Smith Sq; open Apr–Oct. The refreshingly informal Normanton Park Hotel here has good food, as do the White Horse at Empingham and – with great water views – the Finches Arms at Upper Hambleton (what was Lower Hambleton is now under water).

Butterfly & Aquatic Centre 🖼 (off A606 Empingham–Whitwell) Next to the main Rutland Water information centre, a huge butterfly house with a good water feature, and various other insects and reptiles; also a video on the reservoir's construction in the 1970s. Snacks, shop, disabled access; cl Nov–Mar; (01780) 460515; £3.50.

Egleton Reserve and Birdwatching Centre 🖼 This part of the nine-mile reserve includes 14 hides and an interactive interpretation and observation centre, with something for beginners and more serious bird-watchers. Varied talks, walks and events; (01572) 770651; snacks, shop, excellent disabled access; cl 25–26 Dec; £4.

Lyndon Reserve (off Lyndon–Manton rd) Plenty of birds and wildlife, gentle trails through mixed habitat; Disabled access to some hides; reserve usually open all year, useful visitor centre cl Nov–Easter exc wknds, and Mon exc bank hols; (01572) 737378; £3.

SHEPSHED SK4618

Shepshed windmill Handsomely preserved, well worth a look.

STAUNTON HAROLD SK3720

Ferrers Centre for Arts and Crafts (off B587 N of Ashby) Seventeen workshops from contemporary furniture to Victorian models, in a striking Georgian courtyard; meals, snacks, shop, mostly disabled access; cl till 10.30 am, Mon exc bank hols, 25–26 Dec, and 1 Jan; (01332) 865408; free. In attractive parkland, the **church** out here, owned by the NT, was one of the few built during the 1649–60 Commonwealth (its builder died in the Tower of London for his defiance); open pm only Weds–Sun and bank hols Apr–Sept, plus wknds in Oct; (01332)

863822; £1 donation suggested. The Saracens Head over at Heath End by the reservoir visitor centre is an old-fashioned farm pub with good value snacks.

SWANNINGTON SK4117

Hough windmill Recently refurbished windmill; picnic area and nature trail; (01530 832704); open pm Sun Apr–Sept; free.

SWINFORD SP5879

Stanford Hall and Motorcycle Museum 5,000 books line the library of this handsome 17th-c house, an elegant place that still keeps a cosy lived-in atmosphere. Highlights are the painted ceiling in the ballroom, the portraits that accompany the winding grand staircase, and a good costume collection. The excellent motorcycle museum (open pms most Suns and bank hol Mon; £1 extra) is in the grounds, which also have a lovely 14th-c church with splendid stained glass, walled rose garden, Sun craft centre, and a replica of the country's first successful flying machine – well, it flew, but crashed fatally. Snacks, shop, limited disabled access; open pm only wknds, bank hol Mons Easter–Sept; (01788) 860250; house and grounds £4.50, grounds only £2.50. The Chequers (Swinford High St) is useful for lunch.

SWITHLAND RESERVOIR SK5713

Picturesque reservoir in natural woody surroundings, with the embankment of the Great Central Railway framing it along one side; you can feed the ducks and swans from the quiet Rothley–Swithland lane which crosses the water. The Griffin has decent food.

TILTON ON THE HILL SK7505

Halstead House Farm 🖼 (Oakham Rd) Farm animals inc some rare breeds, tractor rides, a local history museum with displays of old farming implements, fishing lake, gardens, a nature trail along a disused railway, and play areas. Snacks, well stocked farm shop, disabled access; cl Mon (exc bank hols), and Oct–Mar; (0116) 259 7239; £3. The village church is notable, and the Rose & Crown has good value food.

TWYCROSS SK3305

Twycross Zoo Park 🖼 (A444) Specialises in primates, with an

enormous range of apes, gibbons, orang-utans, and chimpanzees – every shape, size and species. Plenty of other animals too, inc giraffes, sealions, elephants and penguins, (the reptile house is 20p extra); readers tell us the keepers are friendly. Can get crowded on summer afternoons. Meals, snacks, shop, disabled access; cl 25 Dec; (01827) 880250; £6.50. The newly rethatched Bird in Hand over in Austrey is handy for lunch.

UPPINGHAM SP8699

Charming small town with an interesting square (Fri market) and curving 18th/19th-c High St. The Falcon Hotel does nice light lunches and teas. On most Weds lunchtimes in term-time, musicians from the famous local school (tours by arrangement (01572) 821264) give free concerts in the parish church; the Vaults next to it does decent food.

WELLAND VIADUCT SP9197

One of the county's most striking sights: nearly a mile long, swooping across the pastures of the valley, it is the country's longest viaduct. In the unspoilt nearby village of Seaton the George & Dragon has good value food (and viaduct views).

WIGSTON SP6099

Framework Knitters Museum (Bushloe End) A restored 18th-c knitters' house and workshop, with original hand frames. Open Sun pm and pm first Sat in month, plus most bank hols; (0116) 288 3396; £1. The Royal Oak has cheap food.

WOODHOUSE EAVES SK5114

Beacon Hill Country Park This is a good surviving chunk of the former vast Charnwood Forest hunting park. The hill itself (above Woodhouse Eaves and the site of a Bronze Age fort) is one of the best viewpoints in the area – an intriguing mix of the industrial and the very rural; it's a popular local beauty-spot, rising almost like a volcano above its lower woodland slopes. From the 245-metre (800-ft) summit, a Jubilee Walk heads N and E through partly wooded country. A trail S makes a small circuit around Broombriggs Farm, with boards along the way explaining farming methods. Recently over 30,000 trees have been planted on the West Beacon

Fields area, with paths, a woodland craft trail, viewing platform and straw shelter; £1 car park charge. The Wheatsheaf is handy for lunch.

Long Close Garden 🅰 (Main St) Hidden behind a high wall, these gardens have been lovingly restored and extended since 1925; many rare plants thrive unexpectedly so far north, and the wildflower meadow contains hedges thought to be 700 years old. Open Mar–July and autumn, cl Sun; (01509) 890616; get tickets from Pene Crafts Gift Shop opp at No 53 (cl 1–2); *£2.50.

WYMONDHAM SK8518

Wymondham windmill One of only four six-sailed mills in the country, with tearoom, craft shops and children's play area. Disabled access; cl Nov–Easter and Mon exc bank hols; free; (01572) 787304; for sale as we went to press, so best to check. The attractive old Berkeley Arms does enjoyable fresh food.

There are many **charming villages** here. Ones with decent pubs include Appleby Magna SK3109, Ashby Folville SK7011, streamside Barkby SK6309, Barrowden SK9400, Belton SK4420, Billesdon SK7202, Branston SK8129, Braunston SK8306, Bruntingthorpe SP6089, East Langton SP7292, Grimston SK6821, Harby SK7531, Hose SK7329, Ketton SK9704 (good walks), Knipton SK8231, Knossington SK8008, Market Overton SK8816, Medbourne SP7993 (interesting church too), Peatling Magna SP5992 and Parva SP5889, Somerby SK7710, South Croxton SK6810, South Luffenham SK9402, Stoke Golding SP3997, Tur Langton SP7194, Walton on the Wolds SK5919, Whitwick SK4316, and Wing SK8902, notable for its small medieval turf maze. Stoke Dry SP8596 and Wistow SP6496 have fine churches.

Pubs useful for walks here include the Saracens Head at Heath End SK3621, Bricklayers Arms in Thornton SK4607 (reservoir walks) and Pear Tree and Bulls Head in Woodhouse Eaves SK5214; and, all handy for canals, the Navigation or Soar Bridge in Barrow upon Soar SK5717, Griffin at Congerstone SK3605, Dog & Hedgehog at Dadlington SP4097, Navigation at Kilby Bridge SP6097, Rising Sun at Shackerstone SK3706 and George & Dragon at Stoke Golding SP3997.

Where to eat

BARROWDEN SK9400 **Exeter Arms** *28 Main Street (01572) 747247* Tranquil 17th-c coaching inn with a cheery yellow open-plan bar, straightforward furnishings on bare boards or carpet, own-brewed beers, enjoyable, generously served good food inc interesting daily specials, and picnic-sets on a narrow terrace in front overlooking the pretty village green, ducks on the pond, and broader views stretching away beyond; boules in back garden. £20|**£7.50**

BELMESTHORPE TF0410 **Blue Bell** *Shepherd's Walk (01780) 763859* Homely atmosphere in village pub, particularly in the first little beamed cottagey room with its open fire in huge stone inglenook and fresh flowers; originally three cottages, so it's on two levels: peer down into the bar counter, and a slope winds down round the counter to another area with similar cottagey furniture; well kept real ales, a good choice of wines by the glass, winter mulled wine and summer sangria, and imaginative bar food. £23.35|**£5.75**

CASTLE DONINGTON SK4326 **Nags Head** *Hill Top (01332) 850652* Civilised low-beamed no smoking dining pub with a simple little bar area, an intimate room with three chunky old pine candlelit tables on seagrass and a pretty slate art deco fireplace, and a much bigger similarly decorated yellow-washed dining area; through an opening to the kitchen you can watch the chefs preparing the beautifully presented imaginative food; very attentive staff and conscientious landlord, well kept ales, 20–30 malt whiskies, and quite a few wines by the glass; handy for Donington Race Track; cl 26 Dec–1 Jan; no children; disabled access. £28|**£4.95**

COTTESMORE SK9013 **Sun** *25 Main St (01572) 812321* 17th-c stone-built thatched village pub with a few tables in the rooms off the bar (best to get there early, or even book), a warm fire in the stone inglenook, sunny yellow walls with some nice sporting prints and other pictures, and stripped pine furnishings; imaginative food, real ales, decent wines, and friendly helpful service; tables and boules in garden, and a new terrace. £18.50|£6.50

EAST LANGTON SP7292 **Bell** *Main St (01858) 545278* Pretty creeper-covered inn with a warm inviting atmosphere, a log fire and plain wooden tables in the long stripped stone bar, imaginative food from a seasonally changing menu, OAP wkdy lunches, and a no smoking dining room; own-brewed beers, decent wines, and friendly efficient service; cl 25 Dec; children must be well behaved; partial disabled access. £22.50|£7.50

HALLATON SP7896 **Bewicke Arms** *I Eastgate (01858) 555217* Thatched cottage by village green with warm welcome and traditional feel in its two beamed bar rooms, some gentle refurbishments, a collection of memorabilia and some old photographs, generous helpings of good popular food inc fine puddings, well kept real ales, and friendly service; tearoom and gift shop in the converted stables (disabled access here), and there's a small farm park walk; cl 25 Dec; bdrms; children must be well behaved; disabled access. £19.95|£4.25

LYDDINGTON SP8796 **Old White Hart** *Main St (01572) 821703* Warmly welcoming 17th-c village inn with just three tables in front of the log fire, heavy bowed beams, and dried flowers in the cosy softly lit bar; an attractive no smoking restaurant with corn dollies and a big oak dresser, and a tiled-floor room with some stripped stone, cushioned wall seats and mate's chairs, and woodburner; very popular imaginative bar food, well kept ales, and picnic-sets and boules in the pretty walled garden; good nearby walks, and handy for the Bede House; no food Sun pm, cl 25 Dec; disabled access. £23.75|£5.95

THORPE LANGTON SP7492 **Bakers Arms** *Main St (01858) 545201* Extended thatched pub with a warm friendly welcome, simple country furnishings, well presented interesting food changing daily (need to book well ahead), helpful service, well kept beer, an extensive wine list, and no smoking snug; cl wkdy lunchtimes, Sun and Mon pm, New Year; children over 12. £28

UPPER HAMBLETON SK8907 **Finches Arms** *Oakham Rd (01572) 756575* Delightfully placed pub looking over Rutland Water, with stylish cane furniture and paintings (for sale) in both the bar and more modern no smoking restaurant, super imaginative upmarket food, and real ales; bdrms. £23.25|£7.25

Special thanks to Jenny and Michael Back, Bob and Maggie Atherton

LINCOLNSHIRE

Famous seaside resorts, and some little-known good value holiday prospects elsewhere – grand country houses, interesting towns, a good mix of wildlife attractions

The string of traditional resorts along Lincolnshire's sandy coasts are great for families, and there are lively seaside fairgrounds at Cleethorpes (children also enjoy Jungle, the Humber Estuary Discovery Centre and Pleasure Island) and Ingoldmells (Fantasy Island is an outstanding day out). Skegness and Mablethorpe both have good seal sanctuaries.

Away from the coast this is more of a county for adults than children, but there are some good family attractions. Lincolnshire's Family Attraction of the Year is the Butterfly & Wildlife Park at Long Sutton (birds of prey, play area and animals as well as a huge tropical house), and there are plenty of activities for children to join in with at the heavy horse centre in Great Steeping. This year we've added new farm parks in Rand and Louth, and a falconry centre in Langworth. Besides animals (and fish), Elsham Hall Country & Wildlife Park has craft demonstrations and a good playground.

Lincoln is an interesting city with plenty to see (good museums as well as the cathedral and castle), and Stamford (with the bonus of grand Burghley House) is an attractive town; Boston too is a pleasant place to spend a leisurely afternoon.

N and E of Lincoln, the rolling Wolds countryside makes for enjoyable drives on uncrowded roads, punctuated by attractive villages and charming small towns, and by soaring church spires. The huge fields can be rather tedious for walkers – and around The Wash and up the coast towards Wainfleet and Coningsby it's very flat. The flatness made this prime country for bomber airfields in World War II: for venerable aircraft head to Coningsby and East Kirkby (and there's a vintage vehicle collection at North Hykeham). It's also classic windmill territory. Claythorpe Watermill & Wildfowl Gardens is a picturesque place, the windmill at Heckington is the only one in Britain with eight sails, and in Boston is Britain's tallest working windmill.

Among the lovely houses and castles here, we pick out Belton, Tattershall Castle and Normanby Hall as especially worth a visit; Grimsthorpe Castle is an interesting mix of styles, and Isaac Newton's former home, Woolsthorpe Manor, has an interactive discovery centre. The Old Hall in Gainsborough has a good Walkman tour, and the ruins at Thornton Curtis are atmospheric.

Prices here compare favourably with other counties, and this is a corner of England that is largely off the tourist trail.

Where to stay

BUSLINGTHORPE TF0985 **East Farm House** *Middle Rasen Rd, Buslingthorpe, Lincoln LN3 5AQ* (01673) 842283 **£50***, plus special breaks; 2 rms. 18th-c farmhouse surrounded by family farm, with beams, stripped pine, log fires, relaxed atmosphere, and good breakfasts (evening meals by arrangement); tennis and lots of walks; self-catering cottage; cl Christmas and New Year

DYKE TF1022 **Wishing Well** *Main St, Dyke, Bourne, Lincolnshire PE10 0AF* (01778) 422970 **£65**; 12 rms with showers. The wishing well is at the dining end of the long rambling bar – heavy beams, dark stone, brassware, candlelight and a big fireplace; good value food, a newly refurbished no smoking restaurant, helpful service, friendly atmosphere; gardens and grounds with play area; disabled access

EAST BARKWITH TF1581 **Bodkin Lodge** *Grange Farm, Torrington Lane, East Barkwith, Lincoln, Lincolnshire LN8 5RY* (01673) 858249 **£52**; 2 pretty ground floor rms. Run by the same warmly friendly family as the farm, this carefully extended bungalow has a comfortable sitting room with books, fresh flowers, open fire and baby grand piano, good breakfasts in big dining room with home-made bread and jams (light suppers by arrangement), award-winning wildlife farmland trails from the door, and marvellous country views; mid-Dec–1 Jan; children over 10

EAST BARKWITH TF1581 **Grange** *Torrington Lane, East Barkwith, Lincoln, Lincolnshire LN8 5RY* (01673) 858670 **£47***; 2 attractive, airy rms. A friendly welcome in Georgian farmhouse on immaculate family-run farm with views of Lincoln Cathedral and the Wolds; good cooking using local produce, guest sitting room, and mature gardens with grass tennis court, farm trail, trout lake, and conservation areas; cl Christmas and New Year

HOLBEACH TF3426 **Pipwell Manor** *Washway Rd, Saracens Head, Holbeach, Spalding, Lincolnshire PE12 8AL* (01406) 423119 **£46***; 3 rms. Handsome 18th-c farmhouse, welcoming and spotless, with log fire in comfortable sitting room, pretty panelled dining room, afternoon tea with home-made cakes on arrival, good breakfasts with their own eggs and home-made preserves, and a conservatory; miniature railway in large gardens, and free bikes; no smoking; cl 24 Dec–1 Jan; children over 10

LINCOLN SK9771 **Carline** *1–3 Carline Rd, Lincoln LN1 1HL* (01522) 530422 **£46***, plus special breaks; 8 well equipped rms. Spotlessly kept and comfortable double-fronted no smoking Edwardian guest house 5 mins from the cathedral, with helpful and cheerful owners, quiet dining/sitting rooms, and fine breakfasts; cl Christmas and New Year; children over 2

LINCOLN SK9871 **D'Isney Place** *Eastgate, Lincoln LN2 4AA* (01522) 538881 **£86***, plus special breaks; 17 charming rms. Friendly 18th-c hotel with lovely gardens (one wall of the cathedral close forms its southern boundary), a relaxed and homely atmosphere, good breakfasts using free-range eggs served on bone china in your room (there are no public rooms), and friendly owners; partial disabled access; dogs welcome

STAMFORD TF0306 **George** *71 St Martins, Stamford, Lincolnshire PE9 2LB* (01780) 750700 **£105**, plus special breaks; 47 individually decorated rms. Ancient former coaching inn with a quietly civilised atmosphere, sturdy timbers, broad flagstones, heavy beams and massive stonework, and open log fires; good food in Garden Lounge, restaurant and courtyard (in summer), an excellent range of drinks inc very good value Italian wines, and welcoming staff; well kept walled garden and sunken croquet lawn; disabled access; dogs welcome in bedrooms

WINTERINGHAM SE9322 **Winteringham Fields** *1 Silver St, Winteringham, Scunthorpe, Lincolnshire DN15 9ND* (01724) 733096 **£105**; 10 pretty, chintzy rms with period furniture (3 off courtyard). Thoughtfully run restaurant-with-rooms in 16th-c manor house with comfortable and very attractive Victorian furnishings, beams and open fires, really excellent, inventive and beautifully presented food (inc a marvellous cheesboard) in no smoking dining room, fine breakfasts, exemplary service, and an admirable wine list; cl 2 wks Christmas, last wk Mar, 1st wk Aug, last wk Oct; disabled access; babes in arms and children over 8; dogs welcome in bedrooms

To see and do

Lincolnshire Family Attraction of the Year

LONG SUTTON TF4324 **Butterfly & Wildlife Park** 🏫 (Little London) Much more at this well organised place than simply the butterflies: they have everything from goats and pigs through llamas and wallabies to snakes and crocodiles. But if you've come for the lepidoptera you won't be disappointed: the walk-through tropical house is one of the country's biggest, with hundreds of butterflies flying free. If you're lucky, one may even land on you. Outside are lots of pretty wildflower walks to attract native species – very relaxing for a summer stroll. The Reptile House is fun, as is the splendid collection of insects and creepy-crawlies: the ant room is fascinating. They have the only UK colony of breeding possums, and there's a birds of prey centre with twice-daily flying displays (usually noon and 3pm, weather permitting). Many of the farmyard animals can be stroked. There's a decent adventure playground, and a separate area for toddlers; you can lengthen your visit by a round on the nine-hole mini golf course (extra charge). They have a couple of good events: the exotic pet handling day is fun, with the chance to get close to the sort of creatures you'd normally run a mile from. Lots under cover (including a picnic area), but best in fine weather, when it's a reliable bet for a couple of hours or more. No dogs (except guide dogs). Tearoom, shop, disabled access; open Easter–Oct; (01406) 363883; £5 adults, £3.60 children 3–16. A family ticket for two adults and two children is £16; two adults and three children is £18. This small town is pleasant to potter around, especially on market day (Fri).

ABY TF4179
Claythorpe Watermill & Wildfowl Gardens 🏫 Pretty spot around 18th-c watermill (where they've reconstructed an early 1900s bread shop), the grounds full of ornamental birds, and animals such as wallabies and otters. Fun to wander through the picturesque woods. Meals, snacks, shop, mostly disabled access; cl Nov–mid-Mar; (01507) 450687; £3.95. The Vine at South Thoresby is a civilised place for lunch.

ALFORD TF4575
Pleasant town with some attractive brick and thatch buildings, and a summer craft market (Tues and Fri). The White Horse Hotel and the Half Moon (both West St) are useful for lunch. W of here, just N of the A16/A1104 junction, the Bluestone Heath hill rd past S Ormsby and on to the A157 W of Louth is a splendid scenic drive.
Five-sailed windmill 🏫 Tall mid-19th-c restored five-sailed **windmill** on the A1104 towards Mablethorpe, now with Edwardian and Victorian antiques in an old engine house.

Tearoom, shop, disabled access; open every Tues, and wknd, plus Fri Apr–Oct, and daily July–Sept (cl 24 Dec–1 Jan); £2.50.

ALKBOROUGH SE8821
Overlooks the confluence of the Trent and Humber from a high (for this area) scarp called The Cliff; walks along it on a path leading S to the attractive village of Burton upon Stather.

ASWARBY TF0639
Aswarby church Delightfully set in a well tended park, by a pretty hamlet. Off the A15 just N, past Culverthorpe is a pleasant summer lakeside picnic spot.

BARTON-UPON-HUMBER TA0321
Baysgarth House Museum (Caistor Rd) This handsome 18th-c house has well displayed local history, especially good on rural crafts. Disabled access to ground floor only; cl Mon (exc bank hols), 25–26 Dec, 1 Jan; (01652) 632318; free.

BELTON SK8844
Belton House 🏫 Splendid Restoration-period mansion with wonderful carvings, ornate plasterwork, and sumptuous

furnishings, paintings and ceramics, as well as a 1,000-acre deer park (picturesque public road through here on the E side), orangery and formal Italian garden. Meals, snacks, shop, limited disabled access to house (best to phone); open Weds–Sun and bank hol Mons Apr–Oct; (01476) 566116; £5.60; NT. The Brownlow Arms in picturesque Hough-on-the-Hill is a good restaurant.

BOSTON TF3243

Once the country's second-largest seaport, this little town has a number of pretty spots and handsome historic buildings. Most famous is the **Boston Stump**, the graceful tower of the magnificent 14th-c church St Botolph's. Climb to the top for far views over this flat landscape – it's the second-tallest parish church in the country (the tallest is in Louth); the inside is spectacular too. Another prominent feature of the skyline is the waterside **Maud Foster Mill**, the tallest working windmill in the country, and one of the most photogenic; the shop sells organic flour; (01205) 352188. Goodbarns Yard (Wormgate) is a popular central pub/restaurant, and the Eagle (West St) has good value food. The surroundings (and the Lincolnshire coast generally) are too flat for driving to be very interesting around here, and side roads which look clear on a map can turn out to be tryingly slow in practice, with muddy agricultural vehicles trundling along; the B1183 and B1192 aren't bad.

BOURNE WOOD TF0721

(A151 just outside Bourne) Sheltered woodland good for a gentle stroll, esp welcome as so much of the country here is flat, treeless fens. Plenty of bird life, busy at wknds with locals exercising their dogs; parking charge. In the town's market place, there's decent food in the Angel Hotel, opposite an interesting antiques shop.

BRANDY WHARF TF0197

Cider Centre (B1205 SE of Scunthorpe) Pleasingly zany 18th-c riverside cider house with many different varieties of cider and fruit wines; also orchard and small museum. The enthusiastic owner really knows his stuff. Meals and snacks (not Tues lunchtime), shop, disabled access; open

Lincolnshire

YORKSHIRE

TA

Winteringham
Barton-upon-Humber
A1077
A15
Thornton Curtis
River Humber
A180
Elsham
5
Grimsby
4
Wrawby
Waltham
Cleethorpes
A46
Barnoldby le Beck
Covenham
St Bartholomew
Brandy Wharf
A16
Tealby
Hemswell
THE WOLDS
A631
Buslingthorpe
Louth
A46
Rand
East Barkwith
Mablethorpe
Nettleham
Langworth
A158
Viking Way
Aby
Lincoln
Horncastle
Alford
Ingoldmells
Snipe Dales
Candlesby
North Hykeham
Halton Holegate
Gunby
Burgh le Marsh
Coleby
A155
Great
Steeping
Skegness
A15
East Kirkby
Navenby
Tattershall
Coningsby
Wainfleet
A153
A16
Fulbeck
South Kyme
Sibsey
A52
Kirkby la Thorpe
A17
Boston
TF
Barkston
Heckington
THE
WASH
Aswarby
A52
Freiston Shore
A52
Newton
Frampton
Folkingham
Billingborough
A16
A15
Gedney Drove End
Surfleet
A17
Weston
Gedney Dyke
Grimsthorpe
Dyke
Spalding
Guys Head
Castle Bytham
Bourne Wood
Holbeach
Long Sutton
Witham on the Hill
A16
NORFOLK
Deeping
St James
Crowland
Stamford
CAMBRIDGESHIRE
A1

licensing hrs, though cl Mon Nov–Easter and 25 Dec–1 Jan; no children under 14; (01652) 678364; free.

BRANT BROUGHTON SK9154
Brant Broughton church spire Elegant and very tall, a landmark for miles around.

BURGH LE MARSH TF4965
Has a notable **church**, and a working **windmill** nearby has unusual left-handed sails.

CANDLESBY TF4567
Candlesby Herbs (Cross Keys Cottage) Good range of herb plants and products for sale and on display in the garden; cl Mon and 25 Dec; (01754) 890211; free. There's a specialist cactus grower at nearby Candlesby House, and the Blacksmiths Arms over at Skendleby has good food.

CLEETHORPES TA3108
Big traditional seaside resort with extensive gently shelving tidal sands, and a surprisingly ancient **church** among some attractive older houses in its original core. Some of the seafront buildings are being restored to their Victorian/Edwardian elegance, thanks to a generous English Heritage scheme. The newish road in from the A16 is a big help. Willys (which brews its own beer) is useful for lunch.

Cleethorpes Coast Light Railway (Kings Rd) Gentle mile through local scenery between Kingsway and Lakeside. Snacks, shop, disabled coach; cl wkdys Oct–Easter (01472) 604657; £2.20.

Humber Estuary Discovery Centre (Kings Rd) Unusual spiral-shaped building inspired by seashells, with an interactive journey through time (Cleethorpes lies on the Prime Meridian) looking at local natural and social history; also aquarium and telescopes for bird- and ship-spotting on the Humber estuary. Snacks, shop, disabled access; cl 25–26 Dec, 1 Jan; (01472) 323232; £1.95.

Jungle 🖼 (Lakeside, Kings Rd) Tropical wildlife from giant snakes and iguanas to meerkats and parrots, also llamas, raccoons and an alligator, plus a guinea-pig village. Shop, disabled access; cl Dec–Jan; (01472) 291998; *£3.

Pleasure Island (Kings Rd) Enough to keep a family entertained for the day,

this theme park has lots of suitably scary rides; the terrifying Hyper Blaster shoots you up and down a 27-metre (90-ft) tower. Also children's rides, cabaret and various animal shows. Meals, snacks, shop, disabled access; cl early Sept–Mar (exc autumn half term)r; (01472) 211511; £10.50.

CONINGSBY TF2257
Battle of Britain Visitor Centre (A153) Subject to operational commitments you can see the aircraft of the Battle of Britain Memorial Flight, inc the only flying Lancaster in Europe (no flights Jun–Oct in 2003, but you can still see the areoplanes, and the visitor centre will still be open with exhibitions). Snacks, shop, disabled access; cl wknds, bank hols, and 2 wks at Christmas; (01526) 344041 – check first if you hope to see a particular aircraft; £3.50. The **church** has what's said to be the biggest dial of any clock with just a single hand. Just out of town, the interesting old Lea Gate Inn (B1192 NW) is good for lunch.

CROWLAND TF2410
Crowland church The imposing remains of a once-great abbey, part still used as the parish church – the village also has a three-legged bridge.

DODDINGTON SK9070
Doddington Hall (B1190) Striking lived-in Elizabethan mansion, unchanged externally since it was built, and still with its original walled gardens, gatehouse and family church. The elegant rooms are mostly Georgian. Regular concerts in the Long Gallery. Teas, shop, disabled access to ground floor and gardens; open pm Weds and Sun May–Sept; (01522) 694308; *£4.60, garden only *£3.10. The Stones Arms prettily placed in nearby Skellingthorpe has good value food.

EAST KIRKBY TF3563
Lincolnshire Aviation Heritage Centre (A155) Enthusiastic World War II collection on a wartime airfield. The highlight is *Just Jane*, the famous Avro Lancaster NX611 lovingly restored by two brothers as a memorial to their brother who died during the Nuremberg Raid in 1944. They hope that one day it will fly again but for the moment are content with taxiing it around the airfield in summer. There is

also an original bouncing bomb on display. Meals, snacks, shop, disabled access; cl Sun and Christmas wk; (01790) 763207; *£5. The Red Lion, handy for lunch, has quite a collection of bric-a-brac itself (some interesting tools for sale behind).

ELSHAM TA0311

Elsham Hall Country & Wildlife Park 🖼 As well as the sheep, goats and donkeys you might expect, there are llamas, snakes and spiders, some of which you can stroke or feed. Especially unusual is the carp-feeding jetty, where monster-sized fish will feed straight from your hand. They have a talk and demonstration of some of their mini-beasts every day at 1 o'clock; at 2, weather permitting, they show off some of the owls. Most things are outside, so it's best on a dry day. A craft centre has demonstrations by a potter, woodturner and blacksmith (wknds); there's an arboretum, barn theatre, woodland garden, and plenty of space to let off steam. An adventure playground has sections for different age groups. Special events include lambing days in spring. Meals and snacks (good Sun lunch), picnic area, shops, garden centre, disabled access; cl Mon and Tues (exc bank and school hols), and all mid-Sept to Mar; (01652) 688698; £4.50.

EPWORTH SE7803

Old Rectory 🖼 (Rectory St) The childhood home of John and Charles Wesley, built in 1709 by their father. Restored in 1957, with rooms furnished in period style. Shop, disabled access to ground floor; cl Nov–Feb and 12–2pm Mar, April, Oct; (01427) 872268; £3. Thanks to the Wesley connection, the whole of this pleasant village which is the centre of the Isle of Axholme, with Georgian houses around the market place, has become something of a Methodist centre.

FOLKINGHAM TF0733

Picturesque village with a fine market place – where the Greyhound Inn, crammed with antiques and collectables for sale, is good for lunch.

FRAMPTON TF3239

Perhaps the prettiest fenland village. The Moores Arms has good traditional food.

FREISTON SHORE TF3942

(off A52 via Freiston) Good paths to the sea wall, with desolate views of myriad birds and even seals on the marshes and banks beyond – don't be tempted out among them, the tides are lethal.

GAINSBOROUGH SK8189

Old Hall (Parnell St) Restored medieval manor house with interesting Great Hall and original kitchen; good Walkman tour. Snacks, shop, disabled access to ground floor only; cl Sun Nov–Easter and am Sun all year, 25–26 Dec, 1 Jan; (01427) 612669; £2.50. The Elm Cottage (Church St) has good cheap food, and the lane N along the Trent embankment gives views of the flood plain of this powerful brooding river; the Jenny Wren along at Susworth has good seafood and some tables out by the water. Delicious ice-creams at nearby Blyton Dairy (Old Hall Farm, off A159) include Turkish delight and marshmallow dream.

GEDNEY DROVE END TF4828

Sea walk A good way of seeing the Wash is by following the dyke forming the sea wall; access is from a car park nr Gedney Drove End, from which you can follow the dyke to the mouth of the Nene, with its twin lighthouses either side. When the red flag is flying walks on part of the sea wall are banned.

GRANTHAM SK9136

Two rarities The unusually tall spire of the splendid parish church is commemorated in an early 19th-c jingle: 'Grantham, now two rarities are thine, A lofty steeple and a living sign'. The living sign is the hive with living bees – descended from those of that time – still used as an inn sign by the good value Beehive pub on Castlegate here.

GRANTHAM CANAL SK8435

Though largely derelict, its towpath is kept in very good condition throughout, and makes for easy interesting walks, with plenty of wildlife. Strolls or longer walks can be based at Woolsthorpe (for instance from the Rutland Arms, known locally as the Dirty Duck), or from several other villages along the canal in this and neighbouring counties, all of which have pubs with food; examples are Redmile SK7935, Plungar SK7633, Hose SK7329, Hickling SK6929 (the basin here is very popular, with its waterfowl) and Kinoulton SK6730.

GREAT STEEPING TF4364
Northcote Heavy Horse Centre
Supervised by friendly staff, a full programme of activities and demonstrations throughout the day could include grooming, harnessing and wagon rides. Snacks, shop, disabled access; usually open Sun–Weds Apr–Sept also daily (exc Sat) July–Aug, but times may differ in 2003 so best to phone before setting out; (01754) 830286; £6.50, wagon rides £2.50 extra. The Bell at Halton Holegate has good home cooking.

GRIMSBY TA2609
With nearby Immingham, this is Britain's busiest port, with a flourishing chemicals industry, and despite the decline of its own trawler fleet still the main English fish trading and processing centre. It's also making considerable strides towards attracting visitors, with improved road access. The Abbeygate Centre has reasonably priced antiques shops, also upstairs craft workshops inc lace-making and a café. Alfred Enderby's smoked fish house (Fish Docks Rd) demonstrates traditional methods of smoking salmon, haddock and cod (usually between 10am and 12pm not wknds). Cyclists are well catered for by routes both here and in adjoining Cleethorpes.

National Fishing Heritage Centre
(Alexandra Dock) Displays recalling the experiences of a trawlerman of the mid-1950s take you from the back streets of Grimsby to the fishing grounds of the Arctic Circle and back. Everything in the main centre is under cover, but outside there are enjoyable guided tours of a real trawler, the *Ross Tiger*, led by a former trawlerman. Meals, snacks, shop, disabled access (not to *Ross Tiger*); cl Oct–Mar; (01472) 323345; £4.95. There's good value food on the *Lincoln Castle*, a former Humber paddle steamer moored nearby at Fishermans Wharf.

Time Trap
In the prison cells of the Town Hall the town's social history gets a lively treatment; displays cover the building of the docks and the struggle for women's suffrage – and you can see what it's like to be locked in a prison cell; cl Fri–Sun and bank hols; (01472) 324109; free (donation recommended).

GRIMSTHORPE TF0422
Grimsthorpe Castle ⊞ A
patchwork of styles from its medieval tower and Tudor quadrangle to the baroque N front by Vanbrugh; the state rooms and galleries have especially fine furnishings. Outside are formal gardens and parkland with lake (you can take a tour with the ranger in his Land Rover), and red deer tame enough for children to feed, also play and picnic areas. Meals, snacks, shop, some disabled access; open Sun and Thurs Apr–Sept, plus Thurs–Sun in Aug, castle cl am; (01778) 591205; £6.50 all-in, £3 park only. The Black Horse is a good dining pub.

GUNBY TF4666
Gunby Hall (off A158 nr Spilsby)
Interesting neat red brick William III house, with fine oak staircase and clock collection; especially worth visiting for the nine acres of splendid gardens, said to be Tennyson's 'haunt of ancient peace'. Disabled access to garden only; open pm Weds, garden only open pm Thurs Apr–Sept; (01909) 486411; £3.70, £2.60 garden only. The Willoughby Arms over in the quiet village of Willoughby does pleasant lunches.

GUYS HEAD TF4925
Peter Scott Walk
A 10-mile walk E from the mouth of the Nene, with its twin lighthouses either side. Scott used to come here to study and paint wildfowl. It leads along the dyke into Norfolk, with access from a car park on the Nene's E bank.

HECKINGTON TF1443
Windmill ⊞
In an understated but pleasant village, this well restored windmill is the only one in Britain with eight sails; shop (selling their flour and locally made bread and ginger cake); open pm Thurs–Sun and bank hols Easter to mid-July, then pm daily until mid-Sept, and then Sun pm only until Easter (cl 25 Dec, and 1 Jan); (01529) 461919; £1.50. Nearby the Pearoom is a decent **craft centre** (cl pm Sun). The **church** still has many of its original 14th-c fittings, and is a delight.

HEMSWELL SK9590
Antiques, Craft & Design Centre

(signed off A631) One of the largest craft centres in Britain, with thousands of antiques and bric-a-brac crammed into 270 shops; also a small aircraft museum (wknds only; donations). Good meals and snacks, disabled access; cl 25–26 Dec; (01427) 667066; free.

HORNCASTLE TF2569
Attractive market town popular for antiques, with around 30 shops in the Bridge St Antiques Centre. You can still see parts of the town's **Roman wall**. The Admiral Rodney (North St) has a decent carvery, and the Fighting Cocks (West St) is also good value. Some 3m N the 'High Street' forking off the A158 is a good drive, following an Iron Age trackway up to Caistor. The A153 to Louth gives some good rolling Wolds views. Another good drive here includes Scrivelsby and its vast deer park, Belchford, Fulletby (perhaps a stroll on the footpaths here), Somersby (Tennyson's birthplace – his bust is in the church), Old Bolingbroke (castle ruins, and the Black Horse is a useful food stop), Spilsby, and, if you've made good time, Wainfleet and Boston.

INGOLDMELLS TF5666
Fantasy Island 🎢 (Sea Lane – beach just opposite) More elaborate than your average fairground and, unusually, most of the rides and other features are inside, with thatched buildings and palm trees nestling under a giant pyramid, though a number of rides are springing up outside too. The most exciting ride is the Millennium roller-coaster, which goes through 360-degree loops around the outside of the pyramid, at heights of 46 metres (150 ft) and a speed of around 100 mph. A huge new £28 million suspended roller-coaster Odyssey has the longest drop in Europe, and a new windmill-type ride called G-Force spins you round on giant sails; other highlights include an IMAX simulator and water-rides. Plenty for younger children, inc a train ride through the world of the Jellikins, and live shows with TV characters. Outside are a big play area for the under-5s, and a huge market, with around 780 stalls. Lots of places to eat, shops, disabled access; open daily Mar–Oct; (01754) 872030; free admission to park, rides

charged separately, and tokens are 60p. Here our discount offer is a special one – if you buy £10 worth of ride tokens, on production of the voucher you'll receive a further £12 worth free (this offer excludes Odyssey, G-Force and Millennium). It's open very late in the main season – till 11pm Fri and Sat.

LANGWORTH TF0875
Woodside Falconry and Conservation Centre (off A158 towards Appley) Pleasant for a sunny afternoon, with flying demonstrations at 12pm and 3pm (in summer they also have pig and ferret racing). There's a children's play area and woodland trail (they usually do guided walks), and the fun fishing lake is a hit with budding young anglers (£2, plus £2.50 per fish). Snacks, shop, some disabled access; open Mar–Oct; (01522) 754280; £3.75.

LINCOLN SK9771
The cathedral and castle, both very striking, share the central hilltop, with enough old buildings around them to keep a sense of unity. There's a lot to appeal up here, and in Steep Hill and Strait St ancient buildings run steeply down to the 15th-c Stonebow Gate at the top of the High St. This lower part of the town is a more normal bustling shopping and working centre, though even here there are a good few interesting old buildings – inc several Saxon churches and the Norman guildhall. The Time Travel Pass (from participating attractions, or the Tourist Information Centre on Castle Hill, giving unlimited access for a week) lets you visit the cathedral, castle, Museum of Lincolnshire Life, Ellis Mill, medieval Bishop's Palace and the Usher Gallery for £20. Guided tours leave from the tourist information in Castle Sq (11, 2.15 wknds (daily July–Aug); phone (01522) 873213; £3. The **Greyfriars Exhibition Centre** (Broadgate) is in a lovely 13th-c Franciscan building (open Weds–Sat (exc 1–2pm) and Tues July–Aug; (01522) 530401; free). The Wig & Mitre and Browns Pie Shop, both on Steep Hill, and Lincolnshire Poacher (Bunkers Hill) are good for lunch, and behind the castle the unpretentious Victoria (Union Rd) is good value. Brayford Pool, the heart of the Waterfront Quarter, has boat trips, a

multi-screen cinema, and lots of places to eat (bargain food at the riverside Royal William IV, for instance). There are some good views from the A607 to Grantham.

Ellis' Mill (Mill Rd, just NW of centre) Guided tours by volunteer millers take you right to the top of this 18th-c four-sailed mill, and when there's enough wind, you can see it working. Shop (inc their own wholemeal flour); open pm Sun, plus pm Sat May–Sept; (01522) 523870; 70p.

Incredibly Fantastic Old Toy Show (Westgate) Changing collection of old toys and end-of-pier amusements, close to both cathedral and castle, so a good treat for unwilling culture buffs. Shop, disabled access; open Tues–Sat and Sun and bank hol pms in school hols, and Thurs–Sat and Sun pms in term-time; (01522) 520534; £2.20.

Lincoln Castle ☒ In beautiful surroundings on a formidable earthwork, this was originally built in 1068 for William the Conqueror, but only two towers and two impressive gateways date from then. One of only four remaining originals of Magna Carta is on display, and there are super views from the ramparts. A 19th-c prison has suitably gruesome exhibits; its chapel is unusually designed so that none of the congregation could see each other. Special events such as medieval re-enactments, and open air theatre (phone for details), and they do free guided tours. Meals, snacks, shop, limited disabled access; cl 24–26 and 31 Dec, 1 Jan; (01522) 511068; £2.50.

Lincoln Cathedral Many people reckon that this is England's finest. The original building was largely destroyed in an 1185 earthquake, but the magnificent W front survived, and after nearly a century of rebuilding it was complete by 1280. The triple towers rise spectacularly above the nearby rooftops, and are beautifully lit at night. Inside, the carvings and stained glass are stupendous, and the architecture gracefully harmonious. Meals, snacks, shop, disabled access; (01522) 544544; £3.50. The impressive ruins of the once formidable medieval Bishop's Palace are close by, with a visitor centre containing displays, and two videos on its history; audio tour, snacks, shop; cl

wkdys Nov–Mar (exc for a few days at the beginning of Dec for the Lincoln market festival); (01522) 527468; *£3. There are also heritage gardens (their design was influenced by the cathedral), and there's even a small vineyard – supposedly one of the most northerly in Europe.

Museum of Lincolnshire Life ☒ (Burton Rd) County life over the last couple of centuries, well illustrated in big former barracks, inc galleries on the Royal Lincolnshire Regiment, and a new community gallery. Shop, mostly disabled access; cl am Sun Nov–Apr, 24–26 and 31 Dec, 1 Jan; (01522) 528448; £2. A lawn in the courtyard makes a good picnic area.

Roman remains These include the high wall along Westgate, and the largely reconstructed Newport Arch N of the cathedral (it had survived intact until a 1964 disagreement with a lorry); the Fossdyke canal between Lincoln and the River Trent is also Roman – you can walk out into the country along it from the city, and the Pyewipe Inn out by the Saxilby road there makes a good destination.

The Lawn (Union Rd) In 1820 this was the county's first lunatic asylum; now its landscaped grounds include hands-on history and archaeology, an aquarium and exotic glasshouse, and a restaurant, coffee shop and bar. Kite shop, disabled access; cl 25–26 Dec, 1 Jan; (01522) 873622; free.

Usher Gallery ☒ (Lindum Rd) Attractive gallery with fine watches, porcelain and miniatures, Tennyson memorabilia, and Peter de Wint watercolours. Snacks, shop, disabled access; cl Mon (exc bank hol), 25–26 Dec, 1 Jan; (01522) 527980; £2.

LITTLE REEDNESS SE8022 Attractive village with 14th-c **church**, Ouse walks; RSPB **nature reserve** just E at Blacktoft Sands marshes.

LONG SUTTON TF4324 **Butterfly & Wildlife Park** See *separate family panel on p.391.*

LOUTH TF3186 **Hubbard's Hill** A walk SW; not in fact a hill, but a river valley – surprisingly deep for the Wolds.

Louth church Elegant 16th-c building with the tallest spire of any parish church in Britain. The tower can be climbed on summer afternoons; hundreds of steps for a fabulous view. The market town is a pleasant stop, with lots of bustle on Weds, and some interesting shops; besides Chuzzlewits, the Masons Arms (Cornmarket) has enjoyable food.

Rushmoor Country Park (NE, towards N Cockerington) Around 40 different kinds of poultry inc rare breeds in the grounds of an attractive farmhouse. Friendly, strokeable animals inc rabbits, chinchillas, ponies and lambs, and there are play and picnic areas (phone to book the barbecue), a herb garden and wildlife pond; regular special events. Snacks, shop, disabled access; usually cl wkdys Nov–Easter; (01507) 327184; *£1.95.

MABLETHORPE TF4987

Seal Sanctuary (North End) Rescued seals and seabirds unable to return to the wild find a permanent home here, along with lynx, wildcats and many other animals. It's right by the beach. Snacks, shop, disabled access; cl Fri Oct–Easter; (01507) 473346; £4.

NAVENBY SK9957

Mrs Smith's Cottage (East Rd) Built in the mid-19th c, this simple brick cottage has remained almost unchanged for the last 100 years; a ladder is the only way to get to the first-floor bedrooms, the range was used for cooking until the 1990s, and there's an outdoor lavatory and washroom. Starting at the little visitor centre, volunteers show you around the house, and you can learn more about its unusual owner, Hilda Smith, who lived here till she was 102, and first married at the age of 64. Nearby tearoom, shop; open Sun and bank hol Mon pm mid-Mar to Nov, plus pm Fri–Sun Jun–July and Sept, plus Weds and Thurs in school hols; pre-booking is recommended as only five people allowed in at a time; (01529) 414294; £1. The Bell over at Coleby is a friendly dining pub.

NORMANBY SE8816

Normanby Hall Country Park (B1430) Pleasant spot with grazing deer, lots of wildfowl, nature trails, some interesting sculptures, colourfully and imaginatively restored entirely

organic Victorian kitchen garden, other Victorian-style plantings, and a farm museum in its 350 busy acres. Period rooms in the Regency mansion. Meals, snacks, shop, disabled access to ground floor only; house and museum open pm Apr–Sept, park open all year; (01724) 720588; £3.50. The Sheffield Arms at Burton upon Stather has decent food.

NORTH HYKEHAM SK9368

Road Transport Museum (Whisby Rd, off A46 bypass) Over 45 well restored vintage cars, buses and commercial vehicles; free classic bus rides on special open days – best to phone. Disabled access; open all day Sun and wkdy pms May–Oct, and Sun pm Nov–Apr; (01522) 500566; free (donations welcomed). The nearby Pride of Lincoln is a useful family food pub.

RAND TF1078

Rand Farm Park They encourage you to get close to the animals at this working farm, best for younger children who may even be able to help with feeding. Mostly under cover, so useful in wet weather, with a good heated play area; also go-karts, tractor rides and an outdoor play area. Snacks, shop, disabled access; cl 25–26 Dec and 1 Jan; (01673) 858904; £3.75.

SIBSEY TF3551

Trader Mill (A16 N of Boston) A splendidly restored six-sailed tower windmill with fine views from the top. Refurbished tearooms, shop, some disabled access; usually open 2nd and 4th wknds and bank hol Mons Apr–Sept; (01205) 750036; *£2. EH. The village's second windmill is now a private house.

SKEGNESS TF5663

Archetypal 19th-c holiday resort, with the first Butlin's Holiday Camp just up the coast; the beach has clean bathing water (and there's also an outdoor swimming pool). It's a very popular holiday spot, so traffic can be very slow in summer. The comfortable old Vine Hotel on the southern edge of the town was here long before the resort, welcoming Tennyson among others; it's pleasant for lunch.

Church Farm Museum 🖼 (Church Rd S) Cluster of restored farmyard buildings and cottage provide a good re-creation of daily farm life at the end of the 19th c, also craft demonstrations and special events. Snacks, shop, limited disabled access; cl Nov–Mar; (01754) 766658; £1.

Gibraltar Point Nature Reserve (Gibraltar Rd) 1,000 acres of sandy and muddy seashore stretching 3m S to the mouth of The Wash. The impressive complex of sand dunes and saltmarsh is good for bird-watching, and home to a wide variety of wildlife; guided walks and events in summer. Summer and bank hol snacks, shop, disabled access to visitor centre and some hides; reserve open all year, visitor centre cl wkdys Nov–May; (01754) 762677; free (parking £2 in high season).

Natureland Seal Sanctuary 🔲 (North Parade) Opposite the beach, this rewarding place is renowned for its seal-rescuing activities. It's fascinating to watch the seals being fed (they like showing off), and times are announced over the public address system. Other animals inc penguins, crocodiles, snakes, insects, tropical birds and free-flying butterflies May–Sept; also pets' corner, tropical aquarium and farmyard animals. You can see almost everything from covered walkways if it rains. Snacks, shop, disabled access; cl 25–26 Dec, 1 Jan; (01754) 764345; £4.50.

SNIPE DALES TF3368 Country park and nature reserve, managed by the county council, covering 210 acres rich in bird and plant life; the country park is a 90-acre area of pine woods, while the adjacent nature reserve has a trail leading through two valleys and to a viewpoint over the Wolds.

SOUTH KYME TF1650 A fine 14th-c battlemented tower stands alone in a meadow quite nr the road.

SPALDING TF2515 This is the centre of England's bulb – growing industry; on the May bank hol wknd there's a spectacular flower parade through the town. A remarkable fenland drive runs S from Spalding: turn left off B1172 in Little London, keeping alongside the Welland New River. Lagoons and reclaimed land on the right have water birds, with more on the river – perhaps even a seal, and on the

pastures great percheron horses. At the B1116 a short diversion left takes you to Crowland with a memorable landlocked triangular medieval bridge and what's left of a great abbey. Back towards Deeping the road has more river views, and passes the Exotic Pet Refuge (occasional open days; (01778) 345923).

Ayscoughfee Hall Museum (Church Gate) Spooky-looking medieval manor, housing a local history museum (and the Tourist Information Centre). The five acres of walled garden are peaceful; also aviaries, and a bowling green. Summer meals and snacks, shop, disabled access to ground floor only; museum cl wknds Nov–Mar, gardens open all year; (01775) 725468; free.

Tropical Forest (Rose Cottage Water Garden Centre, Pinchbeck, just N) One of the biggest displays of tropical and subtropical plants in the country. Snacks (summer Tues–Sun), shop, water garden centre, disabled access; cl 25 Dec–2 Jan; (01775) 710882; £2.45.

STAMFORD TF0307 Many would support John Betjeman's verdict that this is England's most attractive town. Within the medieval walls are no less than 500 listed buildings, inc a good number of attractive medieval **churches** – particularly All Saints in the centre, St George's with excellent 15th-c stained glass, and St Mary's nearby. There are riverside strolls and quite a few craft and antiques shops. The George, one of the town's grandest buildings with some parts going back to Saxon times, is excellent for lunch (and has food all day), and the much more modest Daniel Lambert (St Leonard's St) is also good.

Burghley House A 20-min walk from Stamford's centre leads to this splendid mansion, built by William Cecil and still the home of his family. The exterior is Tudor at its most solidly showy, but the state rooms inside are largely baroque, with wonderful frescoes by Antonio Verrio – the Heaven Room is astonishing. The peaceful grounds, where the Burghley Horse Trials are held, were landscaped by Capability Brown; there's a sculpture garden, and readers enjoy strolls in the deer park. Meals, snacks, shop, disabled access; cl Nov–Mar; (01780) 752451; £7.10.

Stamford Museum (Broad St) Local history inc Stamfordware pottery and life-size figures dressed in replica clothes of Tom Thumb (only one metre – 3 ft 4 in – tall) and Daniel Lambert, a portly visitor to the town who weighed 218 kg (50 stone) when he died on a racing outing here. Shop, disabled access to ground floor only; cl Sun am Apr–Sept, all day Sun Oct–Mar, 24–26, 31 Dec and 1 Jan; (01780) 766317; free.

Tolethorpe Hall (off A6121 N) Home to the Stamford Shakespeare company, this has Europe's finest **open-air theatre** in its grounds, with a covered auditorium and a good Shakespeare season of three plays Jun–Aug. Meals, snacks, shop, disabled access; cl Sun, and Oct–May; box office (01780) 756133; £10–£15. The Blue Bell nearby at Belmesthorpe has good food.

STOW SK8881
Stow church Notable for its fantastic Saxon arches, with plenty more of interest in this imposing building inc Viking ship graffiti; the attractive village has a decent food pub, the Cross Keys.

SURFLEET TF2528
Leaning spire The tower and spire of Surfleet **church** lean alarmingly. The riverside Mermaid has good food.

TATTERSHALL TF2056
Tattershall Castle 15th-c red brick castle with magnificent 30-metre (100-ft) turreted keep, with fine heraldic chimneypieces and stained-glass windows on each of the four storeys; there's a double moat, waterfowl and peacocks, and children can try on medieval costumes. Snacks, shop, disabled access to ground floor; cl Jan–Feb, Thurs, Fri Apr–Oct and Mon–Fri Nov–Dec, and Mar; (01526) 342543; £3.20; NT. The airy 15th-c church is also attractive, and just off the A153 towards Sleaford, on the left before you reach Tattershall Bridge, is a preserved steam engine which worked at keeping this area of fens drained for nearly a century. The Abbey Lodge Hotel (B1192 towards Woodhall) has good food.

TEALBY TF1590
The best example of that Lincolnshire

speciality – colourful **village cottage gardens**, easily seen from the road. Here, a great variety of neat and charmingly planted gardens front the stone-built cottages, some thatched, on the main street running down from the 12th-c **church** to a watersplash nr a watermill, and there is more colour in the quaintly named side lanes. The 14th-c Kings Head has popular food.

THORNTON CURTIS TA1118
Thornton Abbey (E Halton rd) Ruins of 12th-c Augustinian abbey, very atmospheric with its worn spiral stone stairs and dark corridors, well worth a visit. Also small exhibition in magnificent 14th-c gatehouse. Disabled access (not into gatehouse); grounds open daily, gatehouse open only pm third Sun in month, plus pm first Sun too Apr–Sept; (0191) 261 1585; free. EH

VIKING WAY TF3072
Long-distance path helping village-to-village walks, with 'Tennyson country' a popular focus (Tennyson was born at the rectory in Somersby, when his father was rector at Bag Enderby); the Black Horse at Donington on Bain TF2382, Bell at Coleby SK9760 and the Kings Head at Tealby are handy stops.

WAINFLEET TF4958
Batemans Brewery Displays, models and an audio-guide take you through the brewing process, and there's a collection of thousands of beer bottles from all around the world. You can also go on a guided tour of this classic family-run traditional brewery (2pm daily, no disabled access). A games room has traditional pub games such as quoits, ring the bull, and skittles, while outdoors you can have a go at croquet, giant draughts, and Connect Four. Meals, snacks, shop, disabled access to visitor centre; cl 25 Dec; (01754) 880317; £2 visitor centre and games room (£8 with brewery tour).

WALTHAM TA2503
Waltham windmill This late 19th-c six-sail tower mill with its traditional Lincolnshire ogree (onion-shaped cap) has displays on the different types of mills, and occasional milling demonstrations. Also here, in a Nissen hut, is a museum with exhibits mostly from the 1930s/40s, and various special

events such as RAF displays and classic car rallies (usually open pm wknds). Meals, snacks, shops (inc herb and old-fashioned sweet shops), some disabled access; open wknds (and perhaps other times during the week, phone to check) Oct–Easter; (01472) 752122; £1. The Ship at nearby Barnoldby le Beck has good food in very interesting surroundings.

WESTON TF2924

Baytree Owl Centre (A151) Good value expanding collection of around 70 owls and other birds of prey such as the snake-killing secretary bird, with displays in a big arena (11.30 and 1.30 Mar–Oct – depending on weather and breeding season); some birds can be handled, and everything's well labelled. Good meals and snacks, shop, disabled access (and parking); cl 25–26 Dec, and Easter Sun; (01406) 372840; £2. It's part of a busy little complex, with ducks and rabbits in a landscaped glasshouse, meerkats, good garden centre, and play area.

WOOLSTHORPE SK9224

Woolsthorpe Manor 🏛 (the Woolsthorpe nr Colsterworth) Birthplace of Isaac Newton, who conducted some of his more important experiments here: geometry workings said to be in his handwriting are scratched into the plasterwork – and of course the garden has a venerable apple tree. An interactive discovery centre exhibits his work. Snacks, shop, disabled access to ground floor; cl am, Mon (exc bank hol), Tues, and Nov–Feb, but open for events in Dec; (01476) 860338; £3.50; NT.

WRAWBY TA0208

Wrawby post mill Working windmill with snacks and a shop; open bank hols and some Suns Apr–Aug – phone Mrs Day to check; (01652) 653699; £1.

Other attractive villages, all with decent pubs, include Allington SK8540 (despite the nearby A1), Barkston SK9341, Barnoldby le Beck TA2303, Billingborough TF1134, Brant Broughton SK9154, Carlton-le-Moorland SK9058, Castle Bytham SK9819, Coleby SK9760, Deeping St James TF1609, Denton SK8632, Fulbeck SK9450, Halton Holegate TF4165, Kirkby la Thorpe TF0945, Nettleham SK9975, Newton TF0436, Witham on the Hill TF0516 and Woolsthorpe SK8435 (the one nr Belvoir). The woods at Stapleford SK8857 are pleasant for picnics (especially when the rhododendrons are in bloom). Langton by Partney TF3970 has an attractive church, and stone-built streamside Easton SK9226 is also pretty.

Where to eat

ASWARBY TF0639 **Tally Ho** *(01529) 455205* Handsome 17th-c stone inn with beams and open fire in country-style bar, a gently civilised atmosphere, and newspapers to read; good enjoyable food inc fine puddings, well kept real ales, decent house wines, and an attractive pine-panelled restaurant (best to book); bdrms; cl 26 Dec. £22|**£6.95**

BARNOLDBY LE BECK TA2303 **Ship** *Main Rd (01472) 822308* Carefully run home with charming Edwardian and Victorian bric-a-brac – stand-up telephones, violins, a horn gramophone, bowler and top hats, old rackets, crops and hockey sticks, stuffed birds and animals, and grandmotherly plants in ornate china bowls; a truly tempting choice of very reasonably priced fresh fish from Grimsby, plus meaty dishes and lovely puddings, too; well kept ales, an extensive wine list with plenty by the glass, tables outside; disabled access. £23|**£6.95**

GEDNEY DYKE TF4126 **Chequers** *Main St (01406) 362666* Stylishly unassuming but friendly fenland pub with beautifully presented food (super fresh fish and seafood), an open fire, and elegant dining conservatory; well kept beer, decent wines, and helpful service; cl winter Mon. £25|**£5.95**

GRIMSTHORPE TF0423 **Black Horse** *(01778) 591247* 18th-c coaching inn with log fires, beams, exposed stone and plenty of brass, excellent, beautifully presented food, an intimate candlelit dining room, real ales, an impressive wine list with helpful notes, and friendly staff; pretty bdrms. £25.25|**£8.50**

HORNCASTLE TF2669 **Magpies** *73–75 East St (01507) 527004* Popular well run restaurant with a relaxed atmosphere and good, enjoyable food using top-quality fresh local ingredients; cl Sun pm, Mon and Tues, 3 wks Aug; disabled access. £30

LINCOLN SK9771 **Browns Pie Shop** *33 Steep Hill (01522) 527330* Spectacular, really interesting pies (and lots of other good food), helpful staff, comfortable seats and pleasant traditional atmosphere; cl 25 Dec. £21.50|**£5.50**

LINCOLN SK9771 **Wig & Mitre** *30/32 Steep Hill (01522) 535190* Ancient, attractive pub with plenty of period features; simpler beamed downstairs bar with exposed stone walls and Gothic furniture on oak floor boards, with sofas in a back area, and a civilised upstairs dining room, light and airy, with views of the castle walls and cathedral; shelves of old books, an open fire, antique prints and more modern caricatures of lawyers and clerics, plenty of newspapers and periodicals; enjoyable food served all day, starting with full breakfast menu; well kept real ales, an excellent choice of wines, and proper espresso machine. £26|**£8.25**

LOUTH TF3287 **Chuzzlewits** *26 Upgate (01507) 611171* Family-run no smoking tearoom with a civilised atmosphere, little glass chandeliers, dining chairs around pretty print glass-covered table-clothed tables, potted palms, and big shop-front windows; wide choice of speciality teas and coffees, home-made cakes, pastries and biscuits, a good range of interesting snacks and light meals, and young waitresses in long black dresses with white frilly aprons and little lacy white caps; cl Sun, Mon and Tues; disabled access. £16|**£4.95**

Special thanks to Michael and Jenny Back

NORFOLK

Rewarding holiday territory, with interesting excursions, historic towns and villages, Broads boating, timeless unspoilt north coast, and a good range of beach resorts

Rich in attractions to suit all ages and tastes, Norfolk is an especially rewarding place for families. Besides our Family Attraction of the Year, the excellent Country World in Fritton, some outstanding animal-oriented days out include the Norfolk Wildlife Centre in Great Witchingham (lots of European wildlife and a birds of prey centre), Banham Zoo & Appleyard Craft Court (a well organised place in pretty parkland), and Pettitts Animal Adventure Park in Reedham (lots here to fill a day). Thrigby Hall Wildlife Gardens at Filby is also popular, and there's a working farm in Snettisham. You'll find good aquariums in Hunstanton and Great Yarmouth (Amazonia too is useful in wet weather), or you can go on a seal-spotting trip from Blakeney. Lenwade's Dinosaur Park is tremendous fun for younger children, and Burgh St Margaret restores all sorts of old-fashioned pleasures.

A nice choice of fine houses includes the magnificent 17th-c ones at Blickling and Felbrigg, and the equally impressive Palladian mansions at Holkham and Houghton. Sandringham is a must for royalists. In contrast to all this grandeur are the ruins at Baconsthorpe, Castle Rising and Castle Acre. There are the pleasant wooded water gardens at the Fairhaven Garden Trust (listed under the Broads), and Mannington Gardens in Saxthorpe are good for roses.

At Bressingham you'll find steam engines as well as glorious gardens (Aylsham, Sheringham, Wells-next-the-Sea, Forncett St Mary and Thursford Green are other options for steam enthusiasts).

The best of many bird sanctuaries and reserves here is the excellent Wildfowl & Wetlands Trust in Welney. For something a bit different you can explore Grimes Graves, where neolithic people mined their flint. The shell museum in Glandford is unusual, and in Heacham you can go round the UK's largest lavender-growing and distilling operation.

Bustling Norwich is not too touristy, with inviting museums and a smart new heritage centre. King's Lynn, too, has much to offer day-tripping families.

North Norfolk has a charmingly traditional feel, with a real sense of place from its Dutch-gabled buildings, flint walls, broad sweeps of sea, saltings and sky, and the odd windmill. A path runs the length of the coast, with often hundreds of sizeable and colourful birds in sight at a time. In summer the twisty coastal A149 is a bumper-to-bumper crawl, but it's a pleasant drive out of season, with a real get-away-from-it-all feel. Inland too, this part has the same sort of untouristy appeal (though the weather is often kinder on the coast). Hunstanton and Cromer are civilised seaside resorts, and there are many attractive smaller places. Further down, the coast is dotted with beach resorts, some large and full of life (most obviously, Great Yarmouth), some relaxed and more individual.

Much of the countryside is flat and repetitive – better for cyclists than walkers, with quiet lanes, attractive villages and country churches, and fair views. We've found some good bits of the Norfolk Broads for land-lubbers, but these winding rivers and reed-fringed meres are of course best seen from a boat – and for many people that's what Norfolk's all about.

There are some smashing places to stay in here (and we've added to the list this year), with plenty of good food too.

Where to stay

BLAKENEY TG0243 **Blakeney Hotel** *Blakeney, Holt, Norfolk NR25 7NE (01263) 740797* **£144**, plus special breaks; 59 very comfortable rms, many with views over the salt marshes and some with own little terrace. Overlooking the harbour with fine views, this friendly hotel has comfortable and appealing public rooms, good food, very pleasant staff, indoor swimming pool, saunas, spa bath, billiard room, and safe garden; very well organised for families, with plenty to do for them nearby; good disabled access; dogs welcome in bedrooms ☺

BURNHAM MARKET TF8342 **Hoste Arms** *Market Pl, Burnham Market, King's Lynn, Norfolk PE31 8HD (01328) 738777* **£96**, plus special breaks; 36 comfortable rms. Handsome inn on green of lovely Georgian village, with a smartly civilised atmosphere, attractive bars (the main bar has been renovated this year), some interesting period features, big log fires, conservatory lounge, stylish food (plus morning coffee and afternoon tea), well kept real ales and good wines, and professional friendly staff; big new awning covering a sizeable eating area in the garden; partial disabled access; dogs welcome

GRIMSTON TF7022 **Congham Hall** *Lynn Rd, Grimston, King's Lynn, Norfolk PE32 1AH (01485) 600250* **£150**, plus special breaks; 14 individually decorated rms. Warmly welcoming and handsome Georgian manor in 30 acres inc herb, vegetable and flower gardens (herbs for sale and garden open to public), outdoor swimming pool, tennis court, paddock and orchards – also, walks leaflets; lovely drawing room, a pretty orangery formal restaurant with excellent modern cooking (lighter lunches in bar), and exemplary service; children over 7

HOLKHAM TF8943 **Victoria** *Park Road, Holkham, Wells-next-the-Sea, Norfolk NR23 1RG* **£140**;11 rms decorated in colonial style or with a more Victorian theme. Transformed recently into a stylish hotel, beautifully and individually decorated throughout; engagingly cosmopolitan bar with eclectic mix of furnishings and décor – sprawling sofas, chunky candles, flowers and fruit, colourful wall hangings, nice fireplace; dining room with plenty of contemporary art and piped jazz; enjoyable food with emphasis on game or seafood, good range of wines with plenty by the glass, well kept real ales; friendly hard-working young staff; tables on the terrace and lawn, and a play area

MORSTON TG0043 **Morston Hall** *The Street, Morston, Holt, Norfolk NR25 7AA (01263) 741041* **£190** inc dinner, plus special breaks; 6 comfortable rms with country views. Attractive 17th-c flint-walled house in tidal village, with lovely quiet gardens, two small lounges, one with an antique fireplace, a conservatory, and hard-working friendly young owners; particularly fine modern English cooking (they also run cookery demonstrations and hold wine and food events), a thoughtful small wine list, and super breakfasts; croquet; cl Jan; dogs welcome away from public rooms; they are kind to families; cl 1 Jan–1 Feb; partial disabled access; dogs welcome in bedrooms ☺

MUNDFORD TL8093 **Crown** *Crown St, Mundford, Thetford, Norfolk IP26 5HQ* (01842) 878233 **£55**; 14 good rms. Friendly small village pub, originally a hunting inn and rebuilt in the 18th c, with an attractive choice of reasonably priced straightforward food, very welcoming staff, a happy atmosphere, and well kept real ales; disabled access; dogs welcome

NORWICH TG2208 **Beeches** *4–6 Earlham Rd, Norwich, Norfolk NR2 3DB* (01603) 621167 **£82**, plus special breaks; 36 quiet rms. Three separate listed Victorian mansions and an extension only 10-min stroll from city centre but with access to three acres of English Heritage Victorian gardens; relaxed informal atmosphere, friendly resident owners, enjoyable food in bistro-style restaurant, and good breakfasts; cl Christmas; no children; disabled access

NORWICH TG2308 **By Appointment** *25–29 St Georges St, Norwich, Norfolk NR3 1AB* (01603) 630730 **£95***; 4 exotically decorated comfortable rms. 15th-c merchant's house, very much a restaurant-with-rooms (you enter through the kitchen), in fine central location; there's a warren of rooms crammed with Victoriana and theatrical furnishings, beautiful dining rooms, delicious meals, excellent breakfasts, and particularly helpful, charming owners; cl 1st 2 wks Aug; no children

PULHAM MARKET TM1986 **Old Bakery** *Church Walk, Pulham Market, Diss, Norfolk IP21 4SL* (01379) 676492 **£58**; 3 large rms. No smoking 16th-c house with lots of beams and timbers, an inglenook with a fine log fire in lounge, good breakfasts, enjoyable evening meal using local produce, and friendly atmosphere; cl Christmas and New Year; no children

SOUTH LOPHAM TM0381 **Malting Farm** *Blo' Norton Rd, South Lopham, Diss, Norfolk IP22 2HT* (01379) 687201 **£50**; 3 well furnished rms, 1 with own bthrm. Welcoming no smoking Elizabethan farmhouse on working dairy farm, with inglenook woodburners in sitting and dining rooms, big breakfasts with home-baked bread and preserves around a large table, and a small play area with toys; the owner's passion is embroidery, patchwork, spinning and quilting and she holds winter classes; cl Christmas and New Year

SPROWSTON TG2612 **Marriott Sprowston Manor** *Wroxham Rd, Norwich, Norfolk NR7 8RP* (01603) 410871 **£150**, plus special breaks; 94 individually decorated spacious rms. Extended 16th-c manor house in 10 acres of parkland surrounded by its own 18-hole golf course; comfortable day rooms, good food in elegant no smoking restaurant, and extensive leisure facilities – indoor pool, sauna, steam room, gym and health spa; disabled access

STOKE HOLY CROSS TG2302 **Salamanca Farm** *Norwich Rd, Stoke Holy Cross, Norwich, Norfolk NR14 8QJ* (01508) 492322 **£48***; 4 rms. Mainly Victorian farmhouse (parts are much older) just a short stroll from the River Tas, with guest lounge, spacious dining room, garden for cut flowers, and farm shop; no smoking; cl 15 Dec–15 Jan; children over 6

SWAFFHAM TF8109 **Strattons** *Ash Close, Swaffham, Norfolk PE37 7NH* (01760) 723845 **£100***, plus special breaks; 7 interesting, pretty rms. No smoking and environment-friendly Palladian-style villa run by charming warmly friendly owners with comfortable individually decorated drawing rooms, family photographs, paintings, lots of china cats (and several live ones), antiques, patchwork throws, fresh and dried flowers, and open fires; delicious highly imaginative food using local (and home-grown) organic produce, a carefully chosen wine list illustrated with Mrs Scott's own watercolours, and super breakfasts; big cupboard full of toys and games for children; garden with croquet; cl Christmas; dogs welcome ☺

THORNHAM TF7343 **Lifeboat** *Ship Lane, Thornham, Hunstanton, Norfolk PE36 6LT* (01485) 512236 **£84**, plus special breaks; 13 pretty rms, most with sea view. Rambling old white-painted stone pub, well placed by coastal flats, with lots of character in the main bar – open fires, antique oil lamps, low settles and pews around carved oak tables, big oak beams hung with traps and yokes, and masses of guns, swords and antique farm tools; several rooms lead off; enjoyable popular food in bar and elegant restaurant and well kept real ales; sunny conservatory with steps up to terrace with seats and playground; marvellous surrounding walks; children welcomed rather than tolerated; partial disabled access; dogs welcome away from eating areas ☺

THORPE MARKET TG2434 **Elderton Lodge** *Cromer Rd, Thorpe Market, Norwich NR11 8TZ (01263) 833547* **£115**, plus special breaks; 11 rms. 18th-c shooting lodge for adjacent Gunton Hall, with lots of original features, fine panelling, a relaxing lounge bar with log fire, an airy conservatory where breakfast and lunch are served, and Langtry Restaurant with good food using fresh fish and game; six acres of mature grounds overlooking herds of deer; children over 6 or under a year; partial disabled access; dogs welcome away from restaurant

TITCHWELL TF7543 **Titchwell Manor Hotel** *Main Rd, Titchwell, King's Lynn, Norfolk PE31 8BB (01485) 210221* **£70**, plus special breaks; 16 light, pretty rms. Comfortable hotel, handy for nearby RSPB reserve, with an open fire, magazines and good naturalists' records of the wildlife, a cheerful bar, attractive no smoking brasserie restaurant (lots of seafood) with French windows on to sheltered neatly kept walled garden, and particularly helpful licensees and staff; lots of walks and footpaths nearby; high tea for younger children; disabled access; dogs welcome

WARHAM TF9441 **Three Horseshoes** *The Street, Warham, Wells-next-the-Sea, Norfolk NR23 1NL (01328) 710547* **£52**; 5 rms, one with own bthrm. Basic but cheerful local with marvellously unspoilt traditional atmosphere in its three friendly gaslit rooms, simple furnishings, a log fire, very tasty generous bar food, decent wines, home-made lemonade, and very well kept real ales; bdrms are in the Old Post Office adjoining the pub, with lots of beams and a residents' lounge dominated by an inglenook fireplace; cl 25–26 Dec; no children; dogs welcome

WELLINGHAM TF8722 **Manor House Farm** *Wellingham, King's Lynn, Norfolk PE32 2TH (01328) 838227* **£60***; 3 rms. Attractively converted self-contained annexe in old stables attached to a lovely farmhouse, with log fire in big sitting room and small kitchen area; good breakfasts served in the main house using home-produced or local ingredients, and charming helpful owners; immaculate gardens with a well stocked carp pond; places to eat nearby; children over 10 by arrangement; stabling for horses available; disabled access

WINTERTON-ON-SEA TG4919 **Fishermans Return** *The Lane, Winterton-on-Sea, Great Yarmouth, Norfolk NR29 4BN (01493) 393305* **£70***; 3 rms. Traditional 300-year-old pub in quiet village, close to the beach, with warmly welcoming owners, a relaxed lounge bar, open fire, good home-made food inc fresh fish (fine crabs in season), enjoyable breakfasts, and sheltered garden with children's play equipment; dogs welcome

To see and do

Norfolk Family Attraction of the Year

FRITTON TG4700 **Country World** (Church Lane) Families should find plenty to keep them amused for most of the day at this assortment of activities based around an attractive big lake. Younger visitors usually head first for the children's farm, which has the usual opportunities to get close to rabbits, chickens, ducks, ponies, sheep and pigs. More impressive are the adjacent heavy horses stables, with splendid-looking Suffolk punches and shires; they have regular harnessing displays, and (for an extra charge) pony and waggon rides. A falconry centre has twice daily flying displays, at 12 and 3; unusually, it's under cover, so not affected by the weather. You can go out on the water, in guided tours with a commentary on the local history and wildlife, or on pedaloes, and there are plenty of gentle walks around the edges and surrounding woodland, or in the formal Victorian gardens. Plenty of space for children to let off steam, with decent play areas including an assault course and aerial slides for older ones, and a separate area for under-7s. They've recently added several trails for children, including one for mountain bikes (you can hire bikes on site). A few features have extra charges: mini tractors (£1), a miniature railway (80p), and miniature golf. They generally have basket-making demonstrations. You can fish on the lake. Special events include the an annual Dogs Day Out, with competitions for dogs and their owners; at other times they don't allow dogs around the site, but have reserved parking spaces and an exercise area by the car park. Meals, snacks, shp, disabled access; open daily Apr–Sept, then wknds and half-term in Oct; (01493) 488208; £5.60 adults, £3.90 children. As we went to press you could save 50p per ticket by printing off a coupon from their website, www.frittonlake.co.uk.

ACLE TG3910
Acle windmill A fine example; the Kings Head has good generous home cooking.

ATTLEBOROUGH TM0292
Peter Beales Rose Nursery Specialist in old-fashioned roses that you won't find for sale elsewhere; you can wander around the three acres of gardens; snacks, disabled access; cl 21 Dec–5 Jan; (01953) 454707; free. The 15th-c **church** is interesting, its screen decorated with the coats-of-arms of the 24 bishoprics in England when it was built. The White Lodge next door has decent food.

AYLSHAM TG1926
Bure Valley Railway ⊞ Steam train trips along nine miles of narrow-gauge track between here and Wroxham; you can combine the journey with a 1½-hour Broads cruise. The stock isn't very old, but the people are friendly. Meals, snacks, shop, disabled access; cl Nov–Mar, best to ring for timetable; (01263) 733858; £7.50 return,

£12 inc Broads cruise.

BACONSTHORPE TG1336
Baconsthorpe Castle The gatehouses, curtain walls and towers are all that's left of this moated and semi-fortified 15th-c house, but displays show what it looked like in its glory. A very pretty peaceful spot, with swans on the lake adding to its charm; free; EH. Light lunches and teas are served in Margaret's Tearooms (cl Mon, and wkdys Nov–Mar), and the reopened Hare & Hounds over towards Hempstead has enjoyable food.

BANHAM TM0587
Banham Zoo & Appleyard Craft Court (B1113) This well established and splendidly organised zoo is beautifully laid out, with hundreds of animals spread over 35 acres of parkland. There's everything from kangaroos to colobus monkeys (who've recently gained a new enclosure with an overhead tunnel), with particularly good enclosures for their Siberian tigers and ring-tailed lemurs, and an

underwater viewing window into Penguin World. Talks and feeding sessions throughout the day, taking in fur seals, meerkats, tigers, and, in summer, bird of prey displays. Children can wander among the guinea-pigs, miniature donkeys, goats and sheep in the Farm Barn, and there's an adventure play area. Meals, snacks, shops, disabled access; cl 25–26 Dec; (01953) 887771; £8.50, less out of season. It's run by the same people as Suffolk Wildlife Park at Kessingland (see Suffolk chapter). Across the road are a few shops in converted barns, as well as a working cider mill; there's an adjacent campsite.

BLAKENEY TG0443

Crabbing is fun from here, and surprisingly successful. Also a (free) collection of waterfowl down by the harbour, long breezy walks, unspoilt flint cottages, broad sky and sea vistas, perhaps even a seal pup on the beach in spring. There's a good dyke walk to Cley-next-the-Sea, with the birds on the mudflats for company. Besides the Blakeney Hotel, the Manor, White Horse and Kings Arms are all good. In summer it gets packed.

Blakeney Point This NT-owned **nature reserve** is edged by a good stretch of the North Norfolk Coast Path, which gets better as you walk along it, although the shingle bank needs patience and is hard on the ankles; pleasant dunes await at the far end.

Seal boat trips Boats leave from Morston Quay slightly W on the A149 coast rd once or twice a day Mar–Oct (times depend on the tide), and on most winter wknds; when the tide allows you'll also find trips wending their way down the creek from the little harbour at Blakeney itself. Most last two hours, which takes in an hour or so exploring the NT-owned bird reserve at **Blakeney Point**. The highlight comes just before that, when the boat goes past the sandbanks at the end of the Point, where dozens of grey and common seals lie basking happily in the sun. Several different operators run boats, with the smaller ones owned by the Beans our favourites. Booking a few days in advance is recommended (esp in summer, when crowds of visitors wait

on the quay; in winter they usually run only at wknds or in good weather), on (01263) 740038. £5.50. Local information centres have full details of operators and times.

BLICKLING TG1728

Blickling Hall (B1354) Magnificent house dating mainly from early 17th c, though the hedges that flank it may be older. Dramatic carved oak staircase and splendid paintings (inc a famous Canaletto), but best of all is the 38-metre (125-ft) Long Gallery with its ornate Jacobean plaster ceiling, and the Chinese bedroom, still lined with 18th-c hand-painted wallpaper – all luckily unaffected by the water leak which damaged hundreds of antique books here in summer 2002. The gardens and grounds are lovely, with several miles of footpaths. Meals, snacks, shop, plant centre, good disabled access (a lift in the house); house open Weds–Sun pm Apr–Oct, garden also open am, Tues–Sun in Aug and winter wknds; (01263) 738030; £6.90, £3.90 garden only; NT. There's a pleasant walk from the Buckinghamshire Arms (useful for lunch), and free public access to the **parkland** on the W side of the pike-filled lake with its water birds, with large tracts of woodland and pasture, as well as a disused railway line, perhaps even kingfishers on the River Bure. There are circular walks within the park.

BRANCASTER TF7944

Scolt Head Miles of dunes, flat coastal saltings, broad tidal beaches: a fine lonely place, largely National Trust and full of birds – Scolt Head island is an important breeding ground, and in good weather a boat takes people across from Brancaster Staithe; (01328) 711866. Incidentally all along this coast the wading birds, surprisingly approachable, are best seen on a falling tide. The Jolly Sailors is good for lunch.

BRECKLAND TL9496

Pingo Trail Starting from Stow Bedon, this is an 8-mile path through the unforested part of the adjacent Breckland grasslands, largely army training ground. It passes through several Sites of Special Scientific Interest (inc Cranberry Rough, an alder swampland), taking you along a disused railway line before joining the Peddars Way at Hockham Heath. The picturesque 15th-c thatched Chequers at Thompson has good food.

Thetford Forest Park (off A1075 NE of Thetford) This shows how the region of poor flat sandy heathland around Thetford looked originally, with scattered shallow meres and scrubby mixed woodland. There are plenty of wild flowers, nature trails, a bat hibernaculum and hides for watching birds and four types of deer. Though there are picnic sites and car parks across the forest, a good starting point is **High Lodge** – you can pick up maps and

hire cycles, there's an adventure playground (and a giant play sculpture trail), and an unusual maze formed by young pine trees. Meals, snacks, shop, mostly disabled access; visitor centre cl 25 Dec; (01842) 815434; car park from around £3–£3.50. Great for the adventurous, **Go Ape** nearby is an unusual tree-top assault course – it takes around 2½ hours to complete with rope swings and bridges, zip slides and so forth; open in summer, phone to book (07736) 774818; £12 (no under-10s, and you need to be at least 4' 7"). Elsewhere Breckland is extensively planted now, with pines (though they are currently

re-creating 300-hectares of heathland);
there are forest walks, for example from
car parks on the A134 NW of Thetford,
where you may disturb roe deer. The
Crown at Mundford is the best nearby
lunch place.

BRESSINGHAM TM0880
**Bressingham Steam Museum &
Gardens** (A1066) The founder, Alan
Bloom, has effectively combined his
two interests at this rewarding site. The
six acres of informal gardens are
planted with 5,000 species and cultivars
of alpines and perennials in island beds,
with lots of the dwarf conifers Bloom
has done so much to popularise. Then

there's the excellent steam collection,
inc 50 road and rail engines, some
restored to working order, and a
charming fairground carousel. Three
steam-hauled trains run through the
countryside and parts of the garden (all
may not be in steam out of high season).
An exhibition is dedicated to that
enduring TV favourite, *Dad's Army*.
Meals, snacks, shop, disabled access; cl
Nov–Easter, phone for train times;
(01379) 687386; £7 (£10 on full steam
days). The Old Garden House is handy
for lunch.

BROADS TG3017
Norfolk's network of linking waterways

(formed in the Middle Ages when peat was dug for fuel) is not easy to visit on foot or by car; few paths get close enough to the Broads themselves, often tantalisingly out of sight, and once away from the waterside and fenny woodlands you are immediately into the flat, humdrum agricultural landscapes found in much of the rest of the area. There is some scope for strolling along rivers, with pumping-mills, birdlife and the boating scene being the principal features. The best way to see the Broads is undoubtedly by boat. Wroxham with its neighbour Hoveton is a main centre for boat hire, and like the other main centre Horning is probably better thought of as a base for longer spells afloat than short breaks or day trips. If you want a boat for just the day, the quieter reaches of the more northern Broads would probably suit you better – say, from Barton Turf, Hickling, Stalham or Wayford Bridge. Or for a quick taste you can combine a boat trip with the trains on the **Bure Valley railway** at Aylsham.

Berney Arms windmill TG4605 Across the water from Burgh Castle and amazingly remote, this and its nearby pub can be reached not by road but by either boat or train from Great Yarmouth, or as a worthwhile objective for a long walk with a real sense of adventure, across the marshes from Wickhampton or Halvergate, passing other former windpumps. The seven-storey mill dates from the 19th c, when it was used to drain water from the marshes. Cl 1–2 pm and all Nov–Mar; (01493) 700605; £1.60. There's also scope for walking by reedy Breydon Water, the estuarine channel of the River Yare between here and Great Yarmouth.

Boat cruising Broads cruising is generally a week-long affair, but could be worked into a short-stay holiday; the boats nowadays have every mod con and are easy for even a novice to handle, but it's a chilly pastime until summer's well established. Wroxham is the main centre for this, with several boat hire firms. So it's a good place to watch the boating activities from dry land, or to use as the start of a longer

cruising holiday. It can be very congested in summer.

Day boating The quieter reaches of the more northern Broads are probably more suited to this than the busier parts around Wroxham and Horning. Stalham TG3724, Barton Turf TG3522 and Wayford Bridge TG3424 are possible bases.

Fairhaven Garden Trust TG3713 Charming wooded water gardens beside the private South Walsham Inner Broad, the waterways linked by little bridges. Rare plants, masses of rhododendrons among the flowers, and a tree – the King Oak – said to be 950 years old. It's an extensive place, running to some 180 acres, inc a big **wildlife sanctuary** – to visit this part you need to get a key (£1 extra charge). Boat trips every half-hour (May–Aug; £2.50). Tearoom, shop, disabled access – but paths are quite uneven; open daily exc 25 Dec; (01603) 270449; £3.50. The Ship (B1140) has good home cooking.

Hickling TG4122 It's normally possible to hire a boat for just the day or perhaps an even shorter period here. And walkers have a pleasant path along the N shore; the Pleasure Boat (building, not boat) up at the quiet end has a fair-sized dining room, with good parking and lots of birds to watch.

Horning TG3417 One of the main centres for Broads boat hire, chiefly for longer spells afloat; there are also paddle-boat cruises. So it's a good place to watch the boating activity, perhaps from the Swan or the Ferry, busy dining pubs. There's also some scope for walking along the canalised parts of the River Bure.

Neatishead TG3520 This attractive village gives access to the **Barton Broad** nature reserve, and a little museum at RAF Neatishead traces the development and operational use of air defence radar; usually open 2nd Sat of month, bank hol Mon, plus Tues and Thurs early Apr–end Sept; (01692) 633309; £3. The White Horse has popular food (and lots of pictures of old Broads boats).

Ranworth Broad TG3514 One of the few Broads the cruise boats can't get to. The **conservation centre** here has interpretations of local and natural history; snacks, shop, disabled access; cl Nov–Mar; (01603) 270479; free. The village **church** has the best painted rood screen in the county, and a tower giving fantastic views over the Broads. **River Thurne** TG4117 The towpath by the canalised parts gives one of the relatively few opportunities for waterside walks in Broadland.

Strumpshaw Fen ▣ TG3306 (off Low Rd, Brundall) Partly drained water meadows and fen between woodland and River Yare, with RSPB hides for watching marsh birds inc harriers and bearded tits, winter geese, and perhaps swallowtail butterflies in June; disabled access to one viewing platform (and facilities); cl 25 Dec; (01603) 715191; £2.50 (RSPB members free). The Yare pub in Brundall is popular for food. **Watching the boats** There aren't a great many places where it's easy to get down to the water by car. Among them are the attractive village of **Coltishall** TG2719, where the Rising Sun pub overlooks a pretty bend of the River Bure; **Ormesby St Michael** TG4715 (attractive waterside lawns at the Eels Foot pub); **Sutton Staithe** TG3823, a lovely quiet spot, with a useful pub; **Surlingham** TG3006, which has a rowing-boat ferry alongside the Ferry House pub, and lovely riverside lawns at the Coldham Hall pub; **Stokesby** TG4310, with another Ferry House pub overlooking quite a busy stretch of the River Bure; and **Bramerton** TG2905 (the Woods End pub is useful), and **Dilham** TG3325 (the Crown is a handy refreshment place here). **Geldeston** TM3891 is at the navigable head of the River Waveney; down a long track from the road, the Lock, a remote candlelit pub, gives a flavour of how the Broads were 40 years ago – at least out of high season.

BURGH CASTLE TG4705
You can still see sections of the massive walls of this coastal Roman fortress, built in the 3rd c to guard against Saxon marauders; free. The Church Farm Inn overlooking the Yare and Waveney has decent food.

BURGH ST MARGARET TG4513
Village (A1064) Restoration and making old rides work again is a theme

of this rosy look at the past, set in over 30 acres. Expect to find restored fairground rides (inc traditional Victorian gallopers) and a working cinema organ collection. There's also a narrow-gauge railway, working sawmill, bear collection, swinging chairs, woodland walks, and decent indoor and outdoor adventure play areas. Meals, snacks, shops, mostly disabled access; cl Oct–Apr, phone for Christmas opening; (01493) 369770; £5.95.

BURNHAM MARKET TF8342
Handsomely opulent village with a fine green, gatehouse and 13th-c priory remains; the Hoste Arms is a good dining pub.

BURNHAM THORPE TF8541
This hamlet's strong Lord Nelson connections include a good pub named after him, with interesting related memorabilia. The lectern in the village church uses wood from HMS *Victory*, and the church has other Nelson mementoes.

CAISTER-ON-SEA TG5012
Caister Castle This moated ruin is set back from the town, a little way inland. Falstaff (the original behind Shakespeare's creation) built it on returning from Agincourt; its walls surround a 30-metre (98-ft) tower. The grounds contain a **motor museum** with a good collection of vehicles from 1893 onwards. Snacks, some disabled access; open late May–last Fri in Sept, cl Sat; (01572) 787251; £5.50. The Ship (Victoria St, off Tan Lane) has a remarkably colourful pub garden, and the beaches are wide and sandy.

CASTLE ACRE TF8115
A delightful village, with an 18th-c feel along the tree-shaded walk of Stocks Green. The sparse ruins of a great **Norman Castle** are still awe-inspiring. The site is on the Peddars Way, a Roman road following the track of an earlier herding way. West Acre, just W, has a few further priory remains, and (like Castle Acre itself) picturesque fords over the River Nar.
Castle Acre Priory Extensive ruins of a Cluniac building by William the Conqueror's son-in-law include the fine arcaded W front of the 11th/12th-c church, and a chapel and 15th-c gatehouse; good interpreter tour, some

special events. Well laid out, and very picturesque. Snacks, shop, some disabled access; cl Mon, Tues and 1–2pm from Nov–Mar; (01760) 755394; £3.70; EH.

CASTLE RISING TF6624

Castle Rising Castle 🏰 Massive earthworks surround this fine 12th-c keep. Shop, limited disabled access; cl Mon and Tues Nov–Mar, 24–26 Dec; (01553) 631330; £3.75. By the church and almshouse in the attractive village, the Black Horse is a reliable family dining pub.

CLEY NEXT THE SEA TG0443

Handy for the bird-sanctuary marshes towards the Blakeney Point sandspit, with excellent hides and plenty of avocets. The pleasant village has an imposing **church** with a fine tower, and the Three Swallows next door is a decent food stop. The neatly restored **windmill** is an even more obvious landmark, and has great views from the top (open pm Easter–Oct; (01263) 740209; £1.50), as well as very good accommodation. There's a long pebbly beach.

COCKLEY CLEY TF8004

🏰 Lots of interesting historical things to see around this village (pronounced to rhyme with 'sly'). There's a **museum** in a 17th-c cottage, nature reserve, carriage collection, and 7th-c Saxon church, but most unusual is the **Iceni Village**, built as and where it was believed to have existed 2,000 years ago. Snacks, shop, disabled access; open Apr–Oct; (01760) 724588; £4 covers all attractions. The Twenty Churchwardens is good for lunch.

CROMER TG2242

Popular seaside resort since Victorian times, with lovely sandy beaches, more sun than the average, bustling markets, golf courses, interesting shops and galleries, and lots of entertainments. The pier is one of the last in the country to have an end-of-pier theatre – very popular, so worth booking early. The tower of the imposing **church** on Church St – Norfolk's tallest – gives spectacular views of the surrounding countryside. A good local history **museum** next door is spread over five 19th-c fishermen's cottages (shop; cl Mon lunch, Sun am, Good Fri, 23–26

Dec, 1 Jan; (01263) 513543; £1.80), and on the prom a small **Lifeboat Museum** looks at local lifeboatman Henry Blogg, who over 53 years saved 873 lives (shop, disabled access; (01263) 512503; cl Oct–Apr; free). Nearby you often find dressed crabs for sale; the crab boats still work from here, and Cromer crabs are the best on England's east coast. The restaurant of the comfortable Victorian seafront Red Lion Hotel has a good choice of fresh seafood.

Beacon Hill The only place of any height on the north Norfolk coast (a humble 90 metres, 300 ft); the Coast Path here detours over the sandy heath and through woodlands.

DENVER TF5800

Denver Sluice (S of Downham Market) These towering hydraulic sluice gates control water levels in these parts – quite a sight. The riverside Jenyns Arms is a pleasant lunch stop nearby.

Windmill (Sluice Rd) Daily guided tours go right to the top of this fully restored windmill, and you can regularly see flour being made in the traditional way; their visitor centre has displays and a video on milling. Craft workshops, teashop and bakery (with cakes made using their own flour); cl am Sun, and around a wk over Christmas and New Year; (01366) 384009; £3.

DOWNHAM MARKET TF5903

Collectors World & Magical Dickens Experience 🏰 (Bridge Farm, A1122 just W) Based around an old chapel used by pilgrims on their way to Walsingham, the eclectic displays include mementoes of local boy Nelson (letters, birth certificate and death mask), re-creations of Dickensian scenes, a pink room devoted to Barbara Cartland, and a car museum; they've also a new replica of the 1st-c shrine at Ephesus. There's a wild-life sanctuary, riverside walk and picnic area. Tearoom, shop, disabled access; cl 25 Dec; (01366) 383185; £3.50. In town, the Crown (Bridge St) has good value food.

EARSHAM TM3188

Otter Trust (off A143) Charitable trust devoted to reintroducing otters to rivers from which they've disappeared. The information centre has an exhibition on their work, but it's obviously seeing the friendly little creatures themselves that children enjoy most, and there are plenty of them, in big semi-natural enclosures prettily set on the banks of the River Waveney. The British ones tend to be fairly shy, so watching the slightly more extrovert Asian short-clawed otters can be more rewarding; the best time to see them is around one of the feeding displays, at 12 and 3. Other wildlife inc lots of deer, and free-roaming wallabies, and their three lakes attract plenty of waterfowl. Nature trails and walks and a decent children's playground. Snacks, shop, disabled access; open Apr–Oct; (01986) 893470; £5 adults.

ERPINGHAM TG2032
Alby Crafts & Gardens 4½ acres of interesting shrubs, plants and bulbs, with a museum devoted to bottles (over 2,000 of them, mainly from regional brewers), and eight working craftsmen inc sculpture, wood-turning and cane work. Crafts gallery, tearoom, shop, some disabled access; cl Mon (exc bank hols), plus wkdys mid-Dec to mid-Mar; (01263) 761590; free, gardens £2, bottle museum 30p. The Ark, and the Saracens Head out at Wolterton, are both very good for lunch.

FAKENHAM TF9429
A pleasant market town; the comfortable Wensum Lodge Hotel has decent food (as does the prettily set Sculthorpe Mill off the A148 just W), and the roads N pass through attractive villages.

FELBRIGG TG1939
Felbrigg Hall ⊞ Magnificent 17th-c house in splendid grounds, inc an orangery with fine collection of camellias, and a colourfully restored walled garden overlooked by a dovecot. The house is decorated with paintings and furnishings from the 18th c, and has a wonderful Gothic library. Meals, snacks, shop, second-hand bookshop, disabled access to ground floor; hall and gardens cl Thurs, Fri, and Nov–Mar; (01263) 837444; £5.90, garden only £2.30; NT. There's public access all year to the 1,700-acre wooded grounds with their fine mature trees and lake.

FILBY TG4612
Thrigby Hall Wildlife Gardens
Popular 18th-c park filled with asian animals and birds, with tropical and bird houses, tree walk, willow pattern garden, and ornamental wildfowl on the lake. Also a huge jungly swamp hall where crocodiles doze under water. Snacks, shop, disabled access; (01493) 369477; £5.90.

FORNCETT ST MARY TM1694
Industrial Steam Museum Unusual collection of eight giant stationary steam engines and over 20 smaller ones rescued from all over the country, inc one that used to open Tower Bridge. Snacks, shop, disabled access; open first Sun of month May–Nov, with engines in steam; (01508) 488277; £4 (two children free with each adult). The Bird in Hand over at Wreningham is a good value dining pub.

FOXLEY WOOD TG0522
(signed from Foxley village) A big block of ancient woodland, mainly deciduous and grown naturally for many centuries; lovely woodland spring flowers.

FRITTON TG4700
Country World See separate family panel on p.408.

GLANDFORD TG0441
Shell Museum ⊞ Curious little museum built by Sir Alfred Jodrell (who lived in nearby Bayfield Hall), housing his collection of often very beautiful sea shells and other interesting objects such as a sugar bowl used by Elizabeth I, and a 4¼-metre (14-ft) tapestry of the north Norfolk coast. Shop, disabled access; cl 12.30–2pm, all Sun and Mon (exc bank hols) and end Oct–Easter Sat; (01263) 740081; £1.50. The Three Swallows at Cley next the Sea is handy for lunch.

GOODERSTONE TF7602
Attractive village with decent pub, ancient church and nearby watergardens.

GREAT BIRCHAM TF7632
Windmill ⊞ Not far from Houghton Hall, this striking mill is on that Norfolk rarity, a hill – so one of the few places with views. They sell bread baked at the mill's own bakery. Tearooms, shop, some disabled access; open Easter–Aug; (01485) 578393; £2.75. You can hire bikes. The village is attractive and the Kings Head Hotel (unpretentious despite being a

favourite with Sandringham shooting parties) is handy for lunch.

GREAT WITCHINGHAM TG0818
Norfolk Wildlife Centre 🏛
(A1067) In attractive parkland, this dedicated centre (with a big focus on conservation) has a good range of mostly British and European wildlife, with everything from lynxes and otters to tortoises, iguanas and snakes. There's a walk-through subtropical parakeet aviary, and birds of prey centre with twice-daily flying displays, and a farm and pets' pavilion, with animals that younger children can fuss and stroke. Good play areas include an adventure playground and monkey slide for older children, and a toddlers' play area in a fenced-off section next to the tearoom. A nice place to spend a couple of hours – perhaps longer with a picnic, Snacks, shop; open daily Apr–Oct, wknds and school hols Nov, Feb–Mar; (01603) 872274; £5.50 adults.

GREAT YARMOUTH TG5307
A cross between working town and resort, this still has a busy fishing harbour – used too as a port of call by the Broads cruising boats. There are lots of holiday entertainments, particularly good for families, a decent summer fairground, and some attractions that might well tempt older visitors into the town if they were nearby. The 14th-c church of St Nicholas at the top end of the market place has an exceptionally wide nave, and an impressive W front. The smart quay-view Star Hotel has good value bar food, and the backstreet Red Herring (Havelock Rd) is also worth knowing. On nearby Middle Scroby Sands construction is now starting on Britain's largest offshore wind farm.

Amazonia (Seafront) Indoor tropical paradise with reptiles, insects, butterflies and birds; they have a 4-metre (13-ft) alligator, and a python well over 5 metres (16ft long). Shop, disabled access; cl Nov–Feb; (01493) 842202; £4.50

Elizabethan House Museum (South Quay) This is a patchwork of historical detail – built in 1596, it has a Georgian façade, 16th-c panelled rooms and, among features from later periods, some rooms decorated and furnished in

19th-c style, and a functional Victorian kitchen. Shop; open wkdys and pms wknds Apr–Oct; £2.60. The 13th-c **Tolhouse Museum** (Tolhouse St) used to be the town's gaol and courthouse (you can still see the dungeons). It now has local history, and a brass-rubbing centre; open same times as above; (01493) 745526 (for both attractions); £2.60.

Merrivale Model Village 🏛
(Wellington Pier Gardens) Attractive landscaped gardens with the exceptionally detailed village – featuring a railway, radio-controlled boats and cars, and over 200 other models. Meals, snacks, shop, disabled access; cl Nov–Easter; (01493) 842097; £3.40.

Old Merchant's House (South Quay) 17th-c house among the narrow lanes or Rows nr the waterfront, with some well restored rooms. Close by and open with it is a group of the original 17th-c houses (Row 111). And admission includes the nearby ruin of 13th-c Greyfriars Cloisters. Shop; cl 1–2, and all Nov–Mar; (01493) 857900; tours on the hour £2.50; EH.

Sea Life Centre (Marine Parade) Displays of the kinds of marine life found on the Norfolk coast, as well as underwater tunnels through shark-infested oceans and colourful tropical fish. They've also touch-pools, and tanks with seahorses (they're very strong on breeding, and you may see baby ones), rays, and now octopuses too; talks throughout the day. Meals, snacks, shop, disabled access; cl 25 Dec; (01493) 330631; £6 (keep your recepit and you can go in and out).

GRESSENHALL TF9716
Norfolk Rural Life Museum 🏛
There's more than enough for a pleasant afternoon at this good museum of local and rural life, housed in a former workhouse (children enjoy the exhibition on life in the workhouse, with games and hands-on activities). The 50 acres also contain a 1920s working farm with rare breeds and Suffolk punch horses, gardens, trails, picnic areas and an adventure playground. There's a re-created 1930s post office, grocer and forge, steam engines (and the oldest car in Norfolk), special events and demonstrations.

Meals, snacks, shop, disabled access; open Tues–Sun, (plus Mon in school hols and bank hols) Mar–Oct, Sun only in Nov though best to check; (01362) 860563; £4.70. Darbys over at Swanton Morley is a good family food pub.

GRIMES GRAVES TL8189
You can climb into one of the 300 pits and vertical shafts which lead down into the galleries – some around 10 metres (33 ft) deep – where the neolithic people mined their flint; the landscape around is pitted by their efforts, and 2002 excavations in the area showed that much earlier, in the last Ice Age, Neanderthal men were using flint tools to butcher woolly mammoths around here. No lavatories at the site, but there are some within a mile. Snacks, shop, disabled access; cl 1–2pm, all day Mon and Tues Nov–Mar, 24–26 Dec, 1 Jan; (01842) 810656; £2.30; EH.

GRIMSTON TF7022
Congham Hall Herb Garden In summer this has around 500 different herbs, in traditional layouts, with many unusual varieties for sale; meals, snacks; (01485) 600250; free.

HEACHAM TF6837
Norfolk Lavender (Caley Mill) The largest lavender-growing and distilling operation in the country, along with a national collection of lavender species and cultivars. The guided tour (daily spring bank hol–Sept) really adds interest – it's best to go at harvest time (mid-July to mid-Aug) when they may drive visitors out to the fields. Also fragrant meadow and herb gardens. Meals and snacks (inc their lavender scones), shop, disabled access; cl 25–26 Dec, 1 Jan; (01485) 570384; tours £1.75, £3.95 at harvest time. The Gin Trap at Ringstead (with a decent nearby art gallery) and Rose & Crown at Snettisham both have good food.

HEYDON TG1127
Delightfully unspoilt tucked-away village, with a green that time seems to have passed by.

HOLKHAM TF9143
Holkham Hall Splendid Palladian mansion in delightful and very extensive tree-filled grounds with an ornamental lake and 18th-c walled garden. Sumptuously furnished state rooms, with fine paintings by Claude, Rubens, Van Dyck and Gainsborough. An ancestor of the present owner was Thomas Coke, whose revolutionary farming techniques are described in an exhibition in the porter's lodge; there's also a pottery. Meals, snacks, shop, limited disabled access; open pm only Sun–Thurs 26 May–Sept, plus bank hol wknds; (01328) 710806; £8 for everything, £5 hall or museum only. Walkers have free access to this coastal estate's driveways; the parkland is a bit sombre, but impressively landscaped with the lake, a temple and obelisk. The estate's Victoria Hotel is great for lunch. The beach has a bird reserve (and a nudist section). There is a car park quite close to the beach, where pine trees meet the sands; this coastal section of the North Norfolk Coast Path is good for lonely walks – westwards any summer crowds rapidly thin out.

North Norfolk Coast Path From Overy Staithe
a particularly fine stretch of the path follows a zigzag dyke – saltmarsh on one side, neat farmland on the other – to the dunes and sandy beach, which never quite looks the same from one day to the next.

HOLME NEXT THE SEA TF6943
From the sandy beach a two-mile walk passes a rewarding **bird sanctuary** and saltings to Thornham – another good bird-watching place. Another more serious walking possibility is the **Peddars Way** which starts here – an inland link from the Coast Path, running from Holme down through Castle Acre and then in a strikingly straight bee-line right across the county to Knettishall Heath nr Thetford, following ancient-feeling green ways and quiet lanes. Earnest walkers may find there is a little too much road-walking to sustain interest.

HOLT TG0738
Pleasant little town with some handsome Georgian buildings. Nicholsons in the High St sells anything from clothes to antiques, and has a useful continental-style licensed café; the friendly market-place Feathers Hotel has good value food and decent bedrooms. The terminus of the **North Norfolk Steam Railway** from Sheringham.

HORSEY TG4622

A quiet corner of the coast, below sea level – among the places most at risk of flooding if the sea defences are breached. There's a good path to the dunes and the sea from the lane past the Nelson Head (enjoyable homely food here). On the other side of the main road, **Horsey windpump** is a restored drainage windmill, now in full working order. Teas, small shop; cl Nov–Mar; (01493) 393904; £1.50; NT. There's a good varied round walk, along quiet reed-fringed Horsey Mere (NT, with wildfowl and otters) and the New Cut to another former drainage windmill – the marshes on the far side of the cut seem alive with birds. Then you can either walk straight back to the village, or for a total contrast join the beach for sea views nr Horsey Corner.

HORSHAM ST FAITH TG2114

Norwich Aviation Museum 🖭 (Old Norwich Rd) Enthusiastic displays of local aeronautical history, with aircraft (inc Vulcan bomber), engines, and other paraphernalia; on the edge of Norwich Airport, so a good view of the live article too. Snacks, shop; open Tues–Sat, pm Sun and bank hols Apr–Oct, Weds, Sat and pm Sun Nov–Mar, cl 20 Dec–5 Jan; (01603) 893080; £2.50. The thatched Chequers prettily placed at Hainford has popular food.

HOUGHTON TF7928

Houghton Hall Built for Robert Walpole and obviously designed to impress, this is a spectacularly grand Palladian mansion set in charming parkland. The state rooms were decorated and furnished by William Kent, and house an important collection of 20,000 model soldiers and other militaria. They occasionally have Shetland ponies and a llama. Snacks, shop, disabled access; open Weds, Thurs, Sun and bank hol pms Easter–Sept; (01485) 528569; £6. Driving along the C road nr North Pole farm you may spot white deer. The 17th-c Dukes Head at West Rudham has good home cooking (and good disabled access).

HOVETON TG3120

Hoveton Hall Gardens 🖭 Large attractive woodland garden with daffodils and rhododendrons, lakeside walk, kitchen garden and old-fashioned herbaceous walled 'spider garden'. You can stay in a wing of the house. Teas, plant sales, disabled access; open Weds, Fri, Sun and bank hol Mon (plus Thurs in May) Easter–mid-Sept; (01603) 782798; £3.50. The Black Horse is useful for lunch.

Wroxham Barns Craft Centre (Tunstead Rd) Good for families, with craft workshops in 18th-c restored farm buildings, as well as a children's farm and traditional fair. Meals, snacks, shop, play area, disabled access; cl 25–26 Dec, 1 Jan; (01603) 783762; £2.25 for farm, otherwise free.

HUNSTANTON TF6740

An East Coast resort which actually faces west, this is a clean, fresh and well kept place with gently shelving tidal sands (summer pony rides and boat trips), and pleasant dune walks past the golf course up to the **bird reserve** on Gore Point. On a clear day you can see Boston's Stump across The Wash. The low cliffs around the town are quite colourful, with different rock strata. The Le Strange Barns (Golf Course Rd) is an interesting craft gallery, and the bar of the Marine Hotel (St Edmunds Terr) has decent food all day.

Oasis Standing out among the typical resort entertainments is this giant leisure park on the prom, with tropically heated indoor and outdoor pools, and both towering and toddler aquaslides. Meals, snacks, disabled access; cl am in term-time and all Dec; (01485) 534227; £3.60.

Sea Life Aquarium (Southern Promenade) An ocean tunnel at this excellent place brings you face to face with deep-water creatures as well as octopuses and toothy conger eels; there are hands-on displays, and you can touch some of the inhabitants. Also seals, otters, penguins, and marine birds in their marine sanctuary. Meals, snacks, shop, disabled access; cl 25 Dec; (01485) 533576; £6.

KING'S LYNN TF6120

Once England's fourth-largest town, it's quieter now, with pleasant corners, some attractive Georgian brick buildings, and a few much older places such as the 17th-c Custom House on

the quay by the River Purfleet (now home to the town's Tourist Information Centre), the 15th-c church of St Nicholas (Chapel Lane; attractive for Festival concerts), the South Gates, Red Mount Chapel and the two medieval guildhalls. The first of these, the 15th-c **St George's Guildhall** (King St), is now the town's theatre, and home of the King's Lynn Festival (usually open 10–2pm Mon–Fri, cl bank hols and on concert days so best to ring (01553) 764864). Guided walks leave from the Old Gaol House; usually Weds and Sat 2pm and Sun at 2.30pm May–July, plus Mon and Fri at 2pm Aug–Sept, though best to check; (01553) 763044; £3. On Tues the main market-place has some good crafts stalls; the Olde Maydens Heade there does popular lunches inc OAP bargains. **Green Quay** ⊞ (South Quay) Housed in the Tudor Marriott's Warehouse, this discovery centre provides a solid introduction to The Wash, with interactive displays explaining how it was formed, and other exhibits on the wildlife that lives in and around it today, inc an aquarium and bird-watching gallery. There's a fair bit to interest children, inc the chance to make rubbings of animal footprints in the floor, and the Mussel Game, based around the mollusc's daily struggles with local currents. Meals, snacks, shop, disabled access; cl 25 Dec–1 Jan; (01553) 818500; £2.50.
Lynn Museum (Old Market St) Local history, archaeology and natural history inc a skeleton of a Saxon warrior, a surprisingly interesting collection of medieval pilgrim badges, and Victorian fairground gallopers. Shop, disabled access; usually cl Sun, Mon, bank hols, and a few days over Christmas and New Year; (01553) 775001; £1.
Tales of the Old Gaol House ⊞ (Saturday Market Pl) Lively journey through the town's rich history; with spirited models, and spooky sights, sounds and smells, this is particularly good for children. Shop, disabled access; cl Weds and Thurs end Oct–Easter, 25–26 Dec and 1 Jan; (01553) 774297; £2.40 (inc audio tour). The tour includes the 14th-c King John Cup and other fabulous examples of

civic paraphernalia housed in the Undercroft of the handsome medieval Trinity Guildhall.
Town House Museum (Queen St) Social history told through reconstructed room settings from the Middle Ages to the 1950s, inc Victorian kitchen, nursery and town garden. Shop; cl Sun Oct–Apr, bank hols, 25–27 Dec and 1 Jan; (01553) 773450; £1.80.
Trues Yard ⊞ (North St/St Anns St) Restored old fishermen's cottages giving a good picture of life here in the last century, when families of up to 11 were often squeezed into two little rooms. Snacks, shop, disabled access; cl Sun Nov–Apr, and around 25 Dec–1 Jan; (01553) 770479; £2.25.
LENWADE TG1017
Dinosaur Park (Weston Park, off A1067) A splendidly silly treat for small children (and some parents), this is a good value day out, with life-size reconstructions of dinosaurs (they've recently added a 16-ft tyrannosaurus made out of bicycle frames) hidden in 300 acres of nicely kept woodland – good for children to see how big some of these beasts really were. Themed play areas (one specially for under-5s) include the ingenious Climb-a-Saurus, a 23-metre (75-ft) brontosaurus replica with slides, ladders, and so on tucked away inside. Also woodland maze, go-karts, animals to handle, and other activities inc a deer safari, and crazy golf; the staff are very friendly. Meals, snacks, shop, disabled access; open Fri–Sun last 2 wks in Mar and Sept–Oct, daily Apr–Aug and Oct half-term, though best to check; (01603) 870245; £6.50.
LETHERINGSETT TG0638
The **church** has an unusual round tower. A restored **watermill** in a pretty setting still mills flour from local wheat. Cl Sat pm and all Sun (exc summer bank hols), with demonstrations pm Tues–Fri (less in winter); (01263) 713153; £3 during demonstrations, otherwise £2. The Kings Head is a great place for families.
LITTLE CRESSINGHAM TF8600
Little Cressingham windmill A fine example.
LITTLE WALSINGHAM TF9336
Once as popular a centre of pilgrimage as Canterbury, thanks to a replica of the

Virgin Mary's home in Nazareth. Things tailed off when Henry VIII destroyed the priory and its shrine in 1538, but have picked up again in the last few decades. The Bull Inn is a good place (with masses of clerical visiting cards). The village is the terminus of the **Wells & Walsingham Light Railway**, described under Wells-next-the-Sea.

Shirehall Museum Displays on pilgrimages and the history of Walsingham, in an almost perfect Georgian courtroom complete with original fittings. Shop, limited disabled access; cl wkdys Nov–Dec and all Jan; (01328) 820510; £3 (includes entry to abbey).

Walsingham Abbey Grounds Remains of the Augustinian Priory, inc the Abbey Gates, Great Arch, part of the refectory, and the Holy Wells. Pleasant gardens and woodland walks, with masses of snowdrops in early spring. Open via the Shirehall Museum and Tourist Information Centre in summer, or the estate office in winter (office hours only), shop, limited disabled access, open daily Feb, and Apr–Oct, plus wknds Mar and Nov–24 Dec, best to check; (01328) 820259; £3 (inc the Shirehall Museum).

LODDON TM3695

Reads Nursery 🖼 (Hales Hall, off A146 SE) Specialising for over a century in unusual conservatory plants, inc a good range of lemon, orange and other citrus fruits, also nut trees, etc. Disabled access; cl Mon (exc bank hols) and 24 Dec–5 Jan; (01508) 548395; nursery free, barn and garden £2. The village is attractive, and the 17th-c Swan has home-made food.

MUNDESLEY TG3136 Peaceful seaside resort with a clean sandy beach, a well preserved windmill, a church without a tower, and a tiny local history museum housed in the old coastguard lookout point. The Ship and the Seaview House Hotel both have decent food.

NEW BUCKENHAM TM0890 A fine village, largely medieval, with a decent pub.

NORTH CREAKE TF8539 **Creake Abbey** All that remains of this early 13th-c Augustinian priory is the crossing and E arm, but it's still worth a

passing look, and the village is charming. Cartwrights at South Creake has good food.

NORTH ELMHAM TF9821 **North Elmham church** An attractive 13th-c building, odd in that there's a step down into it; a little further N are the interesting ruins of a **Saxon cathedral**, and there are pleasant walks. The Kings Head has decent food.

NORWICH TG2308 Busy but civilised, the old centre has quite a concentration of attractive streets and buildings, with all sorts of surprises in the narrow streets and lanes that still follow its medieval layout. One such surprise is the **Forum**, a sleek horseshoe-shaped, glass-covered building between Bethel St and Theatre St; as well as one of Britain's most advanced public libraries, this has Origins, a good heritage centre with interactive displays on local history, several cafés, and a new Tourist Information Centre; cl 25 Dec; (01603) 727290; £4.95. Elm Hill is especially handsome, and there are plenty of antiques shops and so forth. Even the more commercial/industrial centre N of the River Wensum has fine patches (such as Colegate), and the main shopping areas are closed to traffic. Fortunately the visually disappointing university is hidden away out on the W edge, though in term-time its students do bring a good bit of life into the centre. Norwich is the home of Colmans Mustard, and the Mustard Shop (Royal Arcade) has some varieties you may not have come across before. There's a lively spring arts festival (first half of May). The ancient Adam & Eve (Bishopgate) is good for lunch, the Gardeners Arms (Timber Hill – also known as the Murderers) is interesting, and two pleasant riverside pubs are the Gibraltar Gardens (Heigham St) and Ribs of Beef (Wensum St).

Assembly House (Theatre St) Across the road from the new library, this is one of the few so-called Assemby Houses that actually still houses assemblies. In its time it's been much more, too: founded as a hospice in 1248, it has served as priests' college, family home, 18th-c cards house, girls' school and wartime camouflage school.

Although the chapel was completely destroyed in 1548, and, more recently, a fire ravaged the building in 1995, all the 18th-c buildings have now been restored, and a brick-vaulted medieval cellar still lies beneath the restaurant. Meals, snacks, shop, disabled access; cl Sun; (01603) 626402; free.

Boat trips From the River Wensum you can clearly see how some of the city's older buildings were designed for water-borne traffic, rather than road transport.

Bridewell Museum (Bridewell Alley) 14th-c building used as a prison from 1583 to 1828, with exhibits on the town's trade and industries, and reconstructed late 19th-c shops. Cl Sun, and Feb–Oct; (01603) 493625; £2.

Dragon Hall 🏠 (King St) Well preserved medieval merchant's hall, with splendid timber-framed roof, intricate carvings, cellars, vaulted undercroft, and some finely painted roundels. Shop, limited disabled access; cl wknds Nov–Mar, around 10 days over Christmas and New Year, and bank hols; (01603) 663922; £2.50.

Inspire Hands-on Science Centre 🏠 (Coslany St) In medieval St Michael's church (hence the punning name) this lively centre aims to encourage enjoyment of science with over 40 hands-on displays; there's an under-5s play area, and they have science shows during school hols. Snacks, shop, disabled access; cl 24 Dec–1 Jan; (01603) 612612; *£4.20.

Norwich Castle & Museum (Castle Meadow) This impressive four-square Norman fortress dominates the city from the hill. Built as a Royal palace, it now houses an art gallery and museum. As well as displays of art (with particular emphasis on the Norwich school), silverware (for which the town was famous), and ceramics (inc a huge collection of teapots), a gallery traces the history of Boudica and the Iceni-Roman conflict, while another has displays on Egyptian mummies; there are regular exhibitions from the Tate. Hands-on exhibits, interactives and a model give an idea of what life was like in Norman times. Snacks, shop, disabled access, cl am Sun, and 23–26 Dec; (01603) 493625, *£4.70.

Norwich Cathedral The modern city is firmly shut out by the great medieval gateways of the close. Basically Norman/Romanesque, the church has some fine features from later periods – the flying buttresses for example, and the late 15th-c vaulted roof, spire and west window with Victorian glass. The Norman cloisters are the largest in the country, rebuilt after a serious riot between city and cathedral in 1272, and remarkable for the 400 bosses carved with scenes of medieval life; there are hundreds more in the cathedral itself (you can see close-up pictures of the ones on the roof on touch-screen computers). Meals, snacks and shop (not Sun), disabled access; (01603) 218321; suggested donation £3. Free guided tours leave the Welcome Desk at 10.45am and 2.15pm Mon–Sat Jun–Sept, with additional tours in July–Aug, but there's often someone available who will be happy to show you around; they have children's activities too. The extensive precincts make an awe-inspiring impression: medieval alleys and secluded gardens, with all sorts of varied buildings from the cottages of Hooks Walk through the finer houses in the Upper Close to the buildings of Norwich School. The best view of the cathedral is from the river by Pulls Ferry; it's not easy to see from other parts of the town.

Norwich Puppet Theatre 🏠 (St James's Church, Whitefriars) Useful diversion for families, with performances and puppet-making workshops; phone for details. Shop, snacks, disabled access; cl Sun; (01603) 629921; £5.50.

Plantation Garden In an abandoned chalk quarry, this peaceful Victorian garden is enjoyable for a stroll, with some interesting detail; snacks Sun pm in summer, some disabled access; usually open daily; (01603) 621868; £2.

Sainsbury Centre for Visual Arts 🏠 (University of East Anglia, off B1108 W) Striking Norman Foster building with notable 19th- and 20th-c European art and a fascinating range of ethnographic art, inc African tribal sculpture, and Egyptian and Asian antiquities. Meals, snacks, shop, disabled access; cl Mon (inc bank hols),

2 wks over Christmas and New Year; (01603) 593199; £2.

Stranger's Hall Classic example of a wealthy merchant's house, and one of the oldest buildings in Norwich; room re-creations show how the occupants would have lived from Tudor to Victorian times, and highlights include a Tudor Hall and Georgian dining room. Tours leave Weds and Sat, phone to book, or ask at the castle or Bridewell Museum; (01603) 493636; £2.50.

OXBOROUGH TF7401

Oxburgh Hall [£] Henry VIII stayed in this pretty moated manor house in 1487, which shows hangings worked by Mary, Queen of Scots. Most of the house was thoroughly refurbished during Victorian times, but the gatehouse remains as an awe-inspiring example of 15th-c building work, 24 metres (80 ft) high. The garden has a colourfully restored French parterre, and there are pleasant woodland walks. Meals, snacks, shop, disabled access to ground floor only; cl Thurs, Fri, and early Nov–Mar, garden also open some wknds Mar, house cl am (exc bank hols), best to check; (01366) 328258; £5.50, £2.80 garden only; NT. The Bedingfeld Arms opp has decent food.

PASTON TG3135

Stow windmill A fine example.

PENSTHORPE TF9429

Pensthorpe Waterfowl Trust [£] (A1067) Good-sized collection of wild and exotic waterfowl; the visitor centre has wildlife art and photography. Also woodland, meadow, lakeside and riverside nature trails, adventure playground, and talks and events. Meals, snacks, shop, disabled access; cl wkdys Jan–Mar, 25–26 Dec; (01328) 851465; £5.40.

RAVENINGHAM TM3996

Raveningham Gardens This plantsman's garden has interesting herbaceous borders, shrub roses, a traditional walled kitchen garden, arboretum, Victorian conservatory, and herb garden; the 14th-c St Andrew's church is worth a look too. Teas; open pms Weds, Sun and bank hol Mon Apr–Sept; (01508) 548222; £2.50. The **Raveningham Centre** (Beccles Rd) is a set of Victorian farm buildings with furniture-making, piano

workshop, antiques and other craft workshops; teas; free. Loddon's the best nearby place for a meal.

REEDHAM TG4202

Pettitts Animal Adventure Park [£] (Church Rd) A good variety of attractions here, inc aviaries and a reptile house, gnome village, miniature railway, tractor rides, big adventure playground (and an indoor play area for toddlers). Also a roller-coaster and pirate ship, crazy golf, a miniature horse stud, and an animal petting area; daily children's entertainment. Meals, snacks and picnic area, shop, some disabled access; cl end Oct–Mar; (01493) 701403; £7.75. The Ferry Inn by the little car ferry here has good food.

REEPHAM TG0922

Attractive large village or small town with some worthwhile shops and a fine old inn (the Old Brewery House); the unusual churchyard with two churches (and a fragment of a third) is worth a look.

SANDRINGHAM TF6928

Sandringham House Many people come to this part of the county for its connection with the Royal Family. The house and 20,000-acre estate was bought by Queen Victoria for her son Edward in 1862, and has become famous as the family's Christmas residence; the 19th-c building is filled with their portraits and those of their continental counterparts, and has various gifts presented to the family over the years. Unlike at their other homes, you can see most of the rooms they actually use, so there's a much more intimate feel than you'd get at Windsor or Buckingham Palace, and the staff are particularly pleasant; expect queues though. The grounds and surrounding country park are lovely, with lakes, streamside flowers, handsome trees, sweeping lawns, and the colourful North Garden (the late Queen Mother's favourite); also nature trails, adventure playground, and the parish Church of St Mary Magdalene. Lovely rhododendrons in the woods May/Jun. Meals, snacks, shop, very good disabled access (a train runs between the grounds' entrance and the house); open Easter–Oct, exc during summer Royal visit (mid-July to early Aug);

(01553) 772675; £6.50, £5.50 grounds and museum only. There's free access to **Sandringham Country Park** with its majestic trees and glades, a notable parkland walking area (readers recommend coming when the daffodils are in season). The Feathers towards Dersingham is useful for lunch.

SAXTHORPE TG1332

Mannington Gardens The most beautiful feature of these gardens is the summer rose display, but 20 miles of footpaths around the hall and woodland are open all year (£1 parking), and there's a children's playground. Snacks, shop, disabled access; gardens usually open pm Suns May–Sept, plus Weds–Fri Jun–Aug; (01263) 584175; £3. Paths lead to the pleasant grounds of Wolterton Park. The Walpole Arms in the pretty nearby village of Itteringham has good food.

SHERINGHAM TG1543

The working fishing harbour has some old buildings around it, though there's a lot of more modern building up behind. The beach is nice, the Robin Hood (Station Rd) is a useful family food pub, and the Lobster (High St) is strong on seafood.

North Norfolk Railway Full-size steam railway, chugging through over five miles of lovely coastal scenery to Holt. Plenty of railway memorabilia at the Sheringham station, and a collection of steam engines and vintage rolling stock. Meals, snacks, shop, disabled access; (01263) 820800 for timetable; £7.50 all day ticket.

Sheringham Park Extensive parkland, gloriously landscaped by Humphry Repton (it was his favourite work), with excellent coastal views from its waymarked walks and viewing towers. Also mature trees and fine azaleas and rhododendrons (best late May/Jun), and good walks to the coast. Snacks, disabled access; (01263) 823778; free, but parking £2.70; NT.

Upper Sheringham The 14th-c **church** in this quiet flintstone village is very attractive, and the Red Lion is a pleasant stop. Footpaths from here lead to Sheringham Park.

SHOULDHAM TF6709

Just N of this attractive unspoilt village, which has a decent pub, are **nature trails** in pleasant woods; as well as lots of rabbits, you may be lucky enough to spot red deer.

SNETTISHAM TF6833

Park Farm 🔲 Working farm offering good insight into seasonal farming operations – lambing, shearing, and red deer calving. Lots of animals, plus impressive adventure playground, and a small craft centre. Snacks, shop, disabled access; open daily Mar–Oct, phone for winter opening times; (01485) 542425; £4.50 for either farm or 45-min guided ride around deer park, £7.95 for both. Pretty walks nearby, as well as a nature reserve along the beach (which is a couple of miles from the village). The Rose & Crown (Old Church Rd) is a good dining pub.

ST OLAVES TM4599

St Olaves Priory Ruins of 13th-c Augustinian priory; you can still see the fine brick undercroft in the cloister – a remarkable early use of this material; free. Priory Farm is very handy for lunch, and the riverside Bell is worth a look – very old indeed, though much modernised.

SUTTON TG3923

Sutton windmill The most striking mill in Norfolk and the tallest in Britain, nine floors high. Shop, limited disabled access; cl Oct–Mar; (01692) 581195; £3.50.

SWAFFHAM TF8109

EcoTech This discovery centre is full of fuel for environmentalists, with lots of tips on how you can care for the environment inc an organic demonstration garden; there's also an emphasis on children, with plenty of hi-tech interactive displays and games showing man's role in the history of the natural world. Besides the energy-effcent Eco Tech building, they've one of the largest wind turbines in the world. Weather and stamina permitting, visitors over 1.2 metres tall can climb the 300 steps to a glass-walled viewing platform giving magnificent views over East Anglia (booking advisable). Meals, snacks, shop, disabled access exc to wind turbine; cl wknds Oct–Easter, 24 Dec–2 Jan; (01760) 726100; £4.50 (£2.50 extra for wind turbine, £7 joint ticket). The comfortably old-fashioned George

Hotel (Station Rd) has decent food.

TERRINGTON ST CLEMENTS
TF5519

African Violet Centre Wide range of plants besides the African violets it's developed so successfully as house plants; play area and visitor centre. Good tearoom, shop, disabled access; cl 25–26 Dec, 1 Jan; (01553) 828374.

THETFORD TL8683

Ancient House Museum Early Tudor house with fine oak ceilings, now a local history museum with small period herb garden behind. Shop; cl 12.30–1pm, Sun Sept–May (exc pm Jun–Aug); (01842) 752599; free, exc July and Aug £1. At **Thetford Priory**, the ruins of a 12th-c Cluniac monastery, you can easily make out the full ground plan of the cloisters, and the 14th-c gatehouse still stands; disabled access; free. **Warren Lodge**, a 15th-c flint former hunting lodge, is also worth a look. The Bell, Dolphin and Thomas Paine are civilised places for lunch.

THORNHAM TF7243

Walks along the coastline here give marvellous views, and this is good bird-watching terrain, with wading birds, the occasional marsh harrier and maybe even seals. The Lifeboat is a favourite place for lunch. Beware of tides if parking on the seafront, as the lower road can be flooded.

THURSFORD GREEN TF9734

Thursford Collection Bouncy collection of barrel, street and fairground musical organs and a Wurlitzer cinema organ, most demonstrated every day. Also showmen's steam engines, adventure playground, and Venetian Gondola switchback ride. Meals, snacks, shop, disabled access; cl am, Sats, and Jan–Mar; (01328) 878477; *£5.

TITCHWELL TF7544

Bird-watching Pleasant coastal village with good RSPB reserve nearby; besides the Manor Hotel, the Briarfields has good value food and comfortable bedrooms.

WEAVERS WAY TG1531

This long-distance path can be used as part of a link from the parkland of Blickling Hall to take in walks through and around the **Wolterton Park** and **Mannington Hall** estates, both owned by the Walpoles, who have opened up a network of paths in the area extending NW to **Holt Country Park**. The Saracens Head on the edge of Wolterton Park is a very civilised dining pub.

WELLS-NEXT-THE-SEA TF9142

Pleasant rather gracious little village-sized town; don't be fooled by the name – the sea is a mile away these days, though there's a particularly good stretch of the North Norfolk Coast Path from here to **Overy Staithe**, where the sandy beach never looks quite the same from one day to the next.

Wells & Walsingham Light Railway Passing through quietly attractive scenery, this railway is remarkable for being the longest in the world to use a 10¼-inch gauge track, with a steam locomotive built specially for it. Snacks, shop; cl Nov–Good Fri; (01328) 711630 for times; £6 return.

WELNEY TL5393

Wildfowl & Wetlands Trust (Hundred Foot Bank) Excellent 1,000-acre wild bird reserve, with numerous hides, spacious observatory, and floodlit lagoon. During the summer there's a nature trail, while in winter the sights include 4,000 migratory Bewick's swans and all sorts of ducks; it can be busy then, and you'll need to wrap up well. When the marshes are flooded (quite a striking sight) so are the paths to the other hides – readers recommend relaxing in the comfortable chairs in the observatory and watching what flies in; you can hire binoculars. Snacks, shop, part disabled access; cl 25 Dec; (01353) 860711; £3.65, less when the marshes are flooded. In wet winters some local roads can be flooded, and then you can approach it only from the E.

WEST RUNTON TG2042

Norfolk Shire Horse Centre Extensive collection of draught horses with working demonstrations. You can hire riding horses by the hour, and there's a children's farm and rural museum. Meals, snacks, shop, disabled access; cl Sat (exc bank hol wknds and during Aug), and Nov–Easter; (01263) 837339; £4.95. The seaside village itself is attractive.

WEST WALTON TF4713
West Walton church A textbook example of early Gothic architecture; just about all of it dates from the mid-13th c, and there's a cool elegance throughout. Get the key from the next-door King of Hearts (which does good lunches, inc OAP bargains).

WEYBOURNE TG1043
Muckleburgh Collection (A149) Around 3,000 military items inc World War II fighting vehicles, on the site of a former military camp, once the lynch-pin of defences on this coast. You can ride in a Gama Goat (a six-wheel US personnel carrier), and there are usually tank demonstrations pm every Sun, plus pm bank hols and wkdys during school hols. Meals and snacks (in NAAFI-style café), shop, disabled access; open daily Feb half-term, then Sun only until Easter, then daily until 2 Nov; (01263) 588210; *£4.95. The Dun Cow overlooking the Salthouse marshes has decent food all day, with a nearby shack selling very fresh shellfish and samphire. Salthouse and Kelling back heathy hinterlands, allowing walkers a mix between this and the unvaryingly straight coast.

WIGHTON TF9439
Pleasant village in attractive coastal area, once home to the sculptor Henry Moore. The Old School House is a good art gallery, and the Wells & Walsingham Light Railway stops here. The Three Horseshoes over at Warham is the best pub in these parts.

WINTERTON-ON-SEA TG4919
One of the quieter seaside resorts on this coast, with a gentle villagey feel, and a particularly good beach over the dunes – nice for a wander by the sea; the 17th-c Fishermans Return is very pleasant for lunch.

WOODBASTWICK TG3215
Picturesque thatched estate village, home to Woodfordes Brewery, one of Britain's best microbreweries; the Fur & Feather dining pub is the brewery tap.

WROXHAM TG3017
Barton House Railway (Hartwell Rd) Miniature railway through a big riverside garden; snacks, shop; open pm third Sun of month Apr–Oct; (01603) 782470; 50p. Boats leave for here from Wroxham Bridge.

WYMONDHAM TG1001
Mid Norfolk Railway Heritage diesel trains run from here through 11 miles of countryside to the market town of Dereham (where there's a little railway museum; snacks, shop, disabled access); it stops at some pretty villages on the way. Special events throughout the year, phone for timetable (01362) 851723; £5 return.

Wymondham Abbey The parish church is all that's left of this once majestic abbey, but its twin towers dominate the countryside for miles around, and there's plenty to interest inside, with helpful guides on hand to talk you round the features. Originally founded as a priory in 1107, it became an abbey less than a century before the monastic buildings were destroyed as part of the Dissolution. The nave is a scaled-down version of that of Norwich cathedral, and its 15th-c roof is dotted with over 70 carved angels. Other things to spot include the delicate golden altar screen begun in 1919, and a 1904 Arts and Crafts triptych behind the Lady Chapel. Shop, disabled access; cl Sun during services; (01953) 605671; free (donations welcome). The picturesque 14th-c Green Dragon nearby has good food. At the other end of the small town, housed in a former prison, a lively **Heritage Museum** has plenty of well shown bygones of the area, and interactive displays on prison life in the old days; cl am Sun, and end Nov–beginning Mar; (01953) 600205; £2.

Attractive villages here, all with decent pubs, include Aldborough TG1834, Binham TF9839, Colkirk TF9126, Covenham St Bartholomew TF3395, Harpley TF7825, Mundford TL8093, South Wootton TF6422, Stiffkey (pronounced Stewkie) TF9743, Swanton Morley TG0116, Wiveton TG0342 and Worstead TG3025.

Where to eat

BAWBURGH TG1508 **Kings Head** *Harts Lane (01603) 744977* Bustling old pub with friendly licensees, four linked rooms with low beams and standing timbers, a big log fire and a woodburner, imaginative attractively presented food (the weekly specials are much liked), a no smoking restaurant, 12 wines by the glass, and well kept real ales; cl 25 Dec pm; disabled access. **£22|£7.50**

BLAKENEY TG0243 **White Horse** *4 High St (01263) 740574* Small friendly hotel nr harbour (if that's not too grand a word), with a good mix of chatty customers in the attractively decorated long bar, enjoyable food inc local fish, real ales, up to 11 wines by the glass, a small no smoking area and conservatory restaurant, and efficient friendly service; bdrms; cl 2 wks Jan. **£30|£7.50**

BRANCASTER STAITHE TF7944 **Jolly Sailors** *Main Rd (01485) 210314* On the edge of thousands of acres of National Trust dunes and salt flats, this stylish old-fashioned pub (open all day) has a diary of recent sightings of rare bird species; a log fire and good mix of seats in three small rooms, enjoyable often imaginative bar food, prompt friendly service, well kept real ales, decent wines, and an attractive no smoking restaurant; nice garden with a terrace and enclosed play area. **£22.20|£6.95**

CAWSTON TG1422 **Ratcatchers** *Easton Way, Eastgate (01603) 871430* Bustling, warmly welcoming dining pub with open fire and nice mix of wooden tables and chairs in L-shaped beamed bar, quiet and cosy no smoking candlelit dining room and no smoking conservatory, huge choice of good freshly prepared food inc interesting fresh fish dishes, real ales, and a nice wine list; cl 26 Dec; disabled access. **£25|£6.50**

ERPINGHAM TG1932 **Ark** *The Street (01263) 761535* Lovely individual food inc home-made bread and home-grown vegetables in simple relaxed cottage (restaurant is no smoking); log fire and courteous service; bdrms; cl Mon–Thurs, Oct, 25 Dec–1 Jan; partial disabled access. **£32/3-course Sun lunch £16.50**

ERPINGHAM TG1732 **Saracens Head** *Wolterton (01263) 768909* Comfortably civilised inn with simple but stylish two-room bar, a nice mix of seats, log fires and fresh flowers, excellent inventive food inc good value 2-course Sun supper and 3-course monthly feasts, very well kept real ales, interesting wines, and a charming old-fashioned gravel stableyard; good bdrms; cl 25 Dec; limited disabled access. **£22/2-course wkdy lunch £5.50**

HOLT TG0738 **Owl Tea Rooms** *White Lion St (01263) 713232* Georgian building with bakery and tearooms behind, serving home-made bread, scones, quiches and pies on plates made by the owners; organic local veg, daily specials and vegetarian choices, home-made preserves, and good cream teas; cl Sun, bank hols; disabled access. **£15|£3.85**

LITTLE WALSINGHAM TF9336 **Old Bakehouse** *33 High St (01328) 820454* In an attractive medieval village, this Georgian-fronted house has high beams in the main restaurant, a smaller dining room with a brick oven dating from 1550, and downstairs bar; enjoyable cooking every evening for residents (open to non-residents Fri and Sat evenings only) with plenty of choice, and reasonably priced French wines; bdrms; cl 2 wks Jan, 1 wk Jun, 1 wk Nov. **£31/3 courses £14.45**

NORWICH TG2208 **Adlards** *79 Upper St Giles St (01603) 633522* Warmly friendly and quietly decorated restaurant serving delicious carefully thought-out food from a menu that changes daily, lovely puddings, fine service, and good wine list; cl Sun, Mon am, 1 wk after Christmas; disabled access. **£50/2-course wkdy lunch £5.50**

REEDHAM TG4001 **Ferry** *Ferry Rd (01493) 700429* Perfectly placed pub beside River Yare with plenty of tables to watch boats or swans (good moorings); a secluded back bar with fine log fire, long front bar with big picture windows, no smoking restaurant, and very popular good food; partial disabled access. **£20|£4.50**

SNETTISHAM TF6834 **Rose & Crown** *Old Church Rd (01485) 541382* Pretty white cottage with boldly decorated no smoking Cellar Bar, cheerfully painted

Garden Room, and unchanging back bar; log fires, several real ales, around 20 wines by the glass, and very good imaginative food (super puddings); lovely walled garden with wooden play fort, guinea-pigs and chipmunks; lovely bdrms; well behaved dogs welcome. £30|£7

ST OLAVES TM4599 **Priory Farm** *Beccles Rd (01493) 488432* Good interesting food inc fresh fish and children's menu; right by St Olaves Priory; open all day Jun–Sept (normal hours the rest of the year); disabled access. £15|**£6.95**

STOW BARDOLPH TF6205 **Hare Arms** *Lynn Rd (01366) 382229* Pretty, creeper-covered pub with old advertising signs, fresh flowers, plenty of tables around its central servery, and a good log fire in welcoming bar; maybe two friendly ginger cats and a sort of tabby; spacious, heated and well planted no smoking conservatory, good interesting food, well kept real ales, a decent range of wines, and quite a few malt whiskies; pretty garden with picnic-sets and wandering peacocks and chickens; cl 25–26 Dec; children in conservatory and family room only. £30|**£8.50**

SWANTON MORLEY TG0217 **Darbys** *Elsing Rd (01362) 637647* Cosy beamed country pub decorated with lots of farm tools and so forth, very well kept real ales, and good, generously served, often interesting bar food (their beef comes from their own farm); log fire, friendly staff, children's room and adventure playground; also bdrms, self-catering, camping, caravan site, horse facilities, country trails; cl pm 25 Dec; disabled access. £22.45|**£6.75**

UPPER SHERINGHAM TG1542 **Red Lion** *The Street (01263) 825408* Relaxing little flint cottage with two quiet small bars, simple furnishings, a big woodburner, newspapers to read, and no smoking snug; good enjoyable food under new licensees and well kept real ales; disabled access. £22|**£5**

WELLS-NEXT-THE-SEA TF9143 **Crown** *The Butlands (01328) 710209* Completely refurbished 16th-c coaching inn now run by the owners of the well known Rococo restaurant (which was previously in King's Lynn); boldly decorated rooms of olive green, mustard, and red, stylish modern furnishings on stripped wooden or tiled floors, and paintings by the owner on the walls; exceptional food in no smoking Jewel brasserie and more formal evening restaurant, well kept real ales, a good wine list, and welcoming service; bdrms; £23|**£7.25**

Special thanks to Ben Dyson, Michael and Jenny Back, Stephen, Julie and Hayley Brown

NORTHAMPTONSHIRE

Classic English countryside, dotted with grand houses, graceful churches, and charming gold stone villages; not so much for families

The countryside of this archetypal shire is very relaxing, with gently appealing partly wooded landscapes, villages built of red or honey-coloured stone, and the fine churches of the Nene Valley.

Grand houses in beautiful surroundings are something that Northamptonshire excels in. Ones that appeal to children as well as their parents are Sulgrave Manor (outstanding special events), Holdenby House (birds of prey and activities for children), and richly furnished Boughton House (an adventure playground, and a fascinating collection of armoury). Other splendid houses include Althorp, Canons Ashby House, Cottesbrooke Hall, Coton Manor and Lamport Hall. Prebendal Manor House in Nassington is the oldest dwelling in the county, and Lyveden New Bield near Oundle and Rushton's Triangular Lodge (designed by the same man) are unique. There are interesting ruins at Kirby Hall. So there are plenty of ingredients for a very civilised if grown-up weekend here – say, staying at the Talbot in Oundle, perhaps sauntering around Boughton House and Rockingham Castle, taking a stroll in Rockingham Forest, and having a meal at the Falcon in Fotheringhay.

A splendid treat for children, Wicksteed Park in Kettering is Northamptonshire's top Family Attraction this year. The Old Dairy Farm Centre in Upper Stowe and West Lodge Rural Centre in Desborough are handy for families who like animals, and Stoke Bruerne with its canal museum is the place to head for boat trips.

Where to stay

ASHBY ST LEDGERS SP5768 **Olde Coach House** *Ashby St Ledgers, Rugby, Warwickshire CV23 8UN (01788) 890349* **£65***, plus special breaks; 6 rms. In an attractive thatched stone village, this handsome creeper-covered inn has several comfortable, rambling and cheerfully atmospheric rooms, a winter log fire, enjoyable food from an extensive menu, well kept beer, and big gardens with children's activity centre

BADBY SP5558 **Windmill** *Main St, Badby, Daventry, Northamptonshire NN11 3AN (01327) 702363* **£72**, plus special breaks; 8 rms. Carefully modernised and warmly welcoming thatched stone inn with beams, flagstones and huge inglenook fireplace in front bar, a cosy comfortable lounge, a relaxed and civilised atmosphere, good generously served bar and restaurant food, and decent wines; fine views of the pretty village from car park; disabled access; dogs welcome in bedrooms

CRANFORD SP9277 **Dairy Farm** *12 St. Andrews Lane, Cranford, Kettering, Northamptonshire NN14 4AQ 01536 330273* **£50**; 4 comfortable rms. Charming 17th-c manor house of great character on an arable and sheep farm, with oak beams and inglenook fireplaces, antiques and family paintings, good homely cooking using home-grown fruit and vegetables, kind, attentive owners, and garden with charming summer house; no smoking; dogs by arrangement ☺

EAST HADDON SP6668 **Red Lion** *Main St, East Haddon, Northampton NN6 8BU (01604) 770223* **£75**; 5 rms. Rather elegant and substantial golden stone hotel with a smart, well heeled feel in the neat lounge bar, a nice mix of furniture, recessed china cabinets, old prints and pewter, and small public bar with well kept real ales and decent wines; pretty restaurant, high quality daily-changing food, and enjoyable breakfasts; attractive walled garden; 25 Dec

OLD SP7873 **Wold Farm** *Harrington Rd, Old, Northampton, Northamptonshire NN6 9RJ (01604) 781258* **£50**; 5 rms. No smoking 18th-c farmhouse in a quiet village, with spacious interesting rooms, antiques and fine china, hearty breakfasts in the beamed dining room, attentive welcoming owners, snooker table, and two pretty gardens; dogs welcome in bedrooms

OUNDLE TL0488 **Talbot** *New St, Oundle, Peterborough, Cambridgeshire PE8 4EA (01832) 273621* **£95**, plus special breaks; 39 most attractive rms. Mary, Queen of Scots walked to her execution down a staircase that's now in this carefully refurbished 17th-c hotel; attractive cosy lounge, big log fire, good food in timbered restaurant, and garden; dogs welcome in bedrooms

PAULERSPURY SP7245 **Vine House** *100 High St, Paulerspury, Towcester, Northamptonshire NN12 7NA (01327) 811267* **£79***; 6 individually decorated rms. 300-year-old building with carefully preserved original features, a relaxed welcoming atmosphere, cosy bar with open fire, and very good modern English cooking (inc home-made bread and petits fours) in attractive restaurant; pretty cottage garden; cl 1 wk over Christmas; partial disabled access

To see and do

Northamptonshire Family Attraction of the Year

KETTERING SP8777 **Wicksteed Park** (off A6, S outskirts) This big amusement park stands out not just because it's one of very few family-based attractions in an area much more geared up for adults, but also for its rather sensible admissions policy: entry to the park is free, so if you're not going to go on any of the rides, you don't have to pay. They've recently added a good big playground for younger children, with lots of swings, see-saws, climbing frames and so forth, and that's free as well. You can wander round and see which ticket will suit you best before shelling out any money, which means that – unlike at some theme parks – you're unlikely to leave feeling shortchanged. Wicksteed was one of the first of its type, set up in 1921 when they introduced boating on the lake. That's still one of the attractions, and while several other original features still remain (an antique roundabout for example), in recent years they've put a lot of effort and money into jazzing up the facilities, bringing the park a little more up to date without spoiling its character. That said, it's still relatively low-key compared to some leisure parks: though they have gyroscopes and a roller-coaster, thrill rides here are mainly of the dodgems, ferris wheel and pirate ship type – and for many visitors that's precisely the appeal. Lots of good rides for under 12s (some have height restrictions), including a jolly little ladybird roller-coaster. The grounds are very pleasant for a stroll, with a pitch and putt course, various well laid out gardens, an aviary, and paddling pools. Special events range from marching bands to Civil War re-enactments from the Sealed Knot. Dogs are welcome on a lead. Meals, snacks, shop, disabled access; open Easter–Oct, and for special events at Bonfire Night and Christmas; (01536) 512475; £5 parking charge (less out of season, or after 3pm), then you buy vouchers for the rides (from 90p each), or a wristband for a day's unlimited rides for £12 adults, £8 children. (Discount voucher not valid bank hols).

Northamptonshire

ALTHORP SP6864

The home of the Spencer family since 1508, remodelled several times, especially in the 17th and 18th c, with a splendid collection of furnishings and porcelain, paintings by Rubens, Van Dyck and Lely. The staff are particularly pleasant and helpful. It is of course the resting place of Diana, Princess of Wales. You can't see the grave itself (it's on an islet in the Oval Lake in a small arboretum just NE of the house), but you can view the lake, and the former stable block is now a museum/memorial filled with her personal possessions, favourite clothes inc bridal gown, and audio-visual displays. Snacks, shop, good disabled access in many parts; open daily July, Aug and Sept (cl 31 Aug) but advance booking recommended; (0870) 167 9000; £10.50. The attractive **church** is on the edge of the park; its graveyard has fine views. On the far side of the estate there's public access to a sandy-floored area of wildlife-filled pine woods and heathland known as Harlestone Firs, pleasant for walking. The village of Great Brington is charming, and the Fox & Hounds here has decent food, and lots of character.

ASHBY ST LEDGERS SP5768

This village is quite a gem: fine manor house, Lutyens almshouses, and a remarkable church with wall paintings, pre-Reformation pews and triple-decker pulpit (few signs of interference by the Reformers, Cromwell or even the Victorians). The Olde Coach House is a good interesting food pub.

BADBY SP5559

Knightley Way This path takes a pleasant 12-mile course from the attractive village of Badby, through an area where gorgeous orange-coloured stone adds to the charm of buildings; it's well waymarked to Greens Norton. The finest part is between Badby Wood and Fawsley Park, where the path drops to landscaped lakes by the hall and estate church. In May the Badby Wood bluebells are lovely. The Windmill and Maltsters Arms are good food stops.

BLISWORTH SP7253

Grand Union Canal The towpath is popular for country walks, with access among other places from the thatched

Royal Oak here and the New Inn at Buckby Wharf SP6065.

BOROUGH HILL SP5962

This gives the best views in the region, from above the golf course; an Iron Age hill fort shares the top with a formidable array of television and telecommunications masts, but on a clear day the views are tremendous.

BOUGHTON SP8981

Boughton House ▣ (SE of Geddington) Impressively grand old place, sometimes compared to Versailles (some of its treasures were in fact made for there). Richly furnished and decorated, with gorgeous mythical scenes painted on the ceilings, and works by El Greco, Van Dyck, Murillo and Caracci lining the walls. Excellent armoury, beautiful parklands, and adventure playground and plant shop. Snacks, shop, disabled access; grounds open pm Sat–Thurs May–July, (daily pm Aug), house pm Aug only; (01536) 515731; £6, grounds only £1.50.

BRIGSTOCK SP9485

The **church** has a Saxon tower, and a bell that used to be rung three times a day to help anyone lost in the woods; the Green Dragon is useful for food. The recently renamed **Fermyn Wood Country Park** is good for a wander, especially around the wildlife-filled woods on the edge; it can be a little muddy; (01536) 373625; £1 parking charge.

BRIXWORTH SP7471

Brixworth church Particularly fine Anglo-Saxon church, one of England's oldest – mostly 7th c with much reused Roman material. It's an attractive village, and the Coach & Horses has enjoyable food.

Pitsford Water (just E) Praised for bird-watching, esp in winter when wildfowl flock to the N part of the lake; the S part is popular for fishing. The partly thatched White Swan at Holcot has decent food.

CANONS ASHBY SP5750

Canons Ashby House ▣ (B4525) Exceptional little manor house, more northern-looking than Midlands, beautifully restored with Elizabethan wall paintings and glorious Jacobean plasterwork. The formal gardens have also been carefully restored over the

last 20 years, and now closely reflect the layout of the early 18th c. A reasonably sized park has a hilltop 12th/14th-c priory church. Cottage garden tearoom, shop; open pm Sat–Weds Apr–Oct; (01327) 860044; £5.20; NT. The Royal Oak at Eydon is handy for lunch.

CASTLE ASHBY SP8659

Castle Ashby House Only the gardens can be visited, but the house is well worth seeing from outside – a splendidly palatial Elizabethan building at the end of a magnificent mile-long avenue planted nearly 300 years ago. The gardens include grand Victorian terraces, sweeping lawns, Italianate gardens with an orangery, and lakeside parkland that counts among Capability Brown's finest achievements. Plant centre; cl 25 Dec; (01604) 696187; £2.50. The **church**, within the park, is very attractive; there's a public path to it. Restored farm buildings nearby house a **Craft Centre and Rural Shopping Yard** (cl Mon exc bank hols). The Falcon in the handsomely preserved estate village has nice food, and the drive through Cogenhoe, Whiston, Grendon and Easton Maudit is pleasant.

CHAPEL BRAMPTON SP7366

Northampton & Lamport Railway ▣ (Pitsford Rd) Enthusiastic little railway, static viewing pms, and short train rides Sun and bank hols (not Jan–Feb); (01604) 820327. Snacks in a restored buffet car, shop; £3.20, £6 inc train ride. Its name is a proud commitment to growth northwards, but for the time being the 14-mile walk and cycle way through pretty countryside by the line is a very pleasant foretaste. The Brampton Halt here has decent food.

COTON SP6771

Coton Manor (off A428) Attractive views from charming gardens around 17th-c stone-built manor house (not open); interesting plantings, and water gardens with flamingos, cranes and ornamental waterfowl wandering freely. The wood is lovely at bluebell time. Grooms Cottage in the converted stables is good for a light lunch, there are interesting plant sales, and disabled access; open pm Tues–Sat Apr–Sept;

(01604) 740219; £4.

COTTESBROOKE SP7174
Cottesbrooke Hall Very attractive
Queen Anne house, reputedly the
model for Jane Austen's Mansfield Park,
with a renowned collection of mainly
sporting and equestrian paintings. The
lovely garden has formal borders,
venerable cedars, a statue walk and
extensive wild gardens. Teas, unusual
plant sales, disabled access to gardens
only; open pm Weds, Thurs 5 May–Jun,
pm Thurs July–Sept, and bank hol Mons;
(01604) 505808; *£6, garden only *£4.

CROUGHTON SP5433
Croughton church Handsome
church well worth a visit for its unusual
murals, dating from the 14th and 15th c.
The Cartwright Arms over in the
pleasant village of Aynho does good
food.

DEENE SP9592
Deene Park (off A43) Lord Cardigan
who led the Charge of the Light Brigade
used to live in this beautifully kept partly
Tudor house; there's a high-spirited
contemporary portrait of him in full
attack gallop, and other memorabilia
from the Crimean war. Rooms shown
are used by family and friends. Extensive
parklands with woodside and lakeside
walks, and gardens reflecting continuing
interest by the owners over the
generations. Cream teas, shop, disabled
access to ground floor and garden;
open Sun pm Jun–Aug, plus Sun and
Mon of bank hol wknds Easter–Aug;
(01780) 450278/450223; £5.50,
gardens only, £3. The Queens Head
opp the church in the pretty village of
Bulwick has good food.
Kirby Hall (W) Used in the film of
Mansfield Park, this splendid ruined
Elizabethan mansion has a bizarre mix
of styles and design; from some angles it
still looks intact – even close up. The
17th-c garden was restored fairly
recently, and it's a tranquil spot for a
picnic. Shop, disabled access; cl wkdys
Nov–Mar; (01536) 203230; £3.30 (inc
audio tour); EH.

DENFORD SP9976
Denford church Charming in any
event (like so many other churches
along this river valley); doubly worth a
visit for its nature-reserve churchyard
by the River Nene, with waterside

walks from here. The Cock is an
attractive place for lunch.

DESBOROUGH SP8184
West Lodge Rural Centre Based
around a working farm (so you can
watch them at work) with a pets
corner, indoor and outdoor play areas,
tractor rides and a little museum; the
nature trail inc a few interactive
sculptures for children. Meals, snacks,
shop, disabled access; cl 25 Dec and 1
Jan; (01536) 760552; *£3.25.

FOTHERINGHAY TL0793
Lovely village with interesting historical
displays in the charming if slightly out-
of-proportion 14th-c **church** across a
watermeadow from the River Nene. It
was part of a small pre-Reformation
college and doubles as a memorial to
the House of York, with some
interesting heraldry. There's only a
fragment left of the **castle** where
Richard III was born, and 135 years later
Mary, Queen of Scots was executed.
The Falcon is excellent for lunch.

GEDDINGTON SP8982
The very well preserved elaborate
13th-c cross was erected by Edward I
where Queen Eleanor's funeral cortège
rested on its way to Westminster. The
photogenic packhorse bridge is even
older, and there's a 12th-c church.
There are some pretty buildings made
of the brown ironstone once quarried
extensively in the area – look out for
tracks of old railway lines.

GRAFTON UNDERWOOD
SP9280
Pretty street of old stone buildings,
roadside stream with seats for watching
(or feeding) its ducks; pleasant drive
from here to Oundle, via Brigstock and
then the woods and open parkland of
Fermyn Woods around the ancient Hall.

HARRINGWORTH SP9197
This attractive village is famous for its
82-arch **railway viaduct**. The White
Swan has good food and comfortable
bedrooms.

HOLDENBY SP6967
**Holdenby House, Gardens &
Falconry Centre** 🅵 This fine-looking
house was originally eight times the size
it is now, and the largest house in
Elizabethan England. It was a Royal
palace for part of the 17th c, and
subsequently a prison, holding the

captured King Charles I at the end of the Civil War. The family that live here now (the Lowthers) have had more MPs than any other clan. In the afternoon on Easter, spring and summer bank hol Mons, you can look around the house with its collection of rare and unusual pianos, and there are very good special events and extra activities for children. The 20-acre gardens are lovely, with an Elizabethan-style garden laid out by Rosemary Verey that includes only plants that would have been grown in 1580. They've a splendid collection of birds of prey, with regular flying displays of buzzards, owls and kestrels. Teas and shop; (01604) 770074. The gardens are open Sun pm Easter–end Sept, and pm daily (exc Sat) 14 July–Aug. On event days admission is £5, other times £4. The civilised Red Lion over in East Haddon has good food.

IRCHESTER SP9265
Irchester Country Park (Gypsy Lane, Little Irchester) 200 acres of lovely woodland with nature trails, picnic sites, children's play area and even a railway museum (Sun only). The visitor centre has snacks, shop, disabled access and is open school hols and wknds; (01933) 276866; £1 parking.

KELMARSH SP7379
Kelmarsh Hall (A508) James Gibbs designed this splendid Palladian-style house in the early 18th c; the most interesting features are the Chinese room and double storey entrance hall. In the charming grounds the lake and triangular kitchen garden walls date from the 18th c, with other formal features (inc an 18th-c orangery that was moved here in the 50s) added in the 20th c. A former owner bred the famous British White cattle, whose descendants still graze the parkland. Tearoom; house and gardens open Sun pm 20 Apr–7 Sept, Thurs in Aug and bank hol Mons; *£4, gardens open Mon–Thurs pm 20 Apr–30 Sept £3.

KETTERING SP8678
Manor House Museum (Sheep St). Worth a look if passing, with free monthly family event days, children's activities in school hols, and a famous mummified cat. Meals and snacks, shop and disabled access; cl Sun and bank

hols; (01536) 534219; free. The adjacent **Alfred East Gallery** has a private collection and works for sale; cl Sun and bank hols; (01536) 534274.
Wicksteed Park See separate family panel on p.429.

KINEWELL LAKE SP9979
Well managed local **nature reserve** around former gravel-pit lakes by the River Nene; pleasant walks. The Elizabethan Cock over at Denford has good value food.

LAMPORT SP7574
Lamport Hall (A508) Mainly 17th- and 18th-c house in spacious park, with tranquil gardens containing a remarkable alpine rockery – the home of the first garden gnomes, only one of which now survives. Frequent antiques fairs, concerts and other events. Snacks, shop, disabled access to ground floor and gardens; open pm Sun Easter–Oct, plus daily guided tours at 2.30pm in Aug, and on bank hols; (01604) 686272; £4.30. The Swan, with great views, has good value food.

NASEBY SP6877
Battle of Naseby Model Model of the crucial Civil War battle set out by the owner of Purlieu Farm, using many hundreds of model soldiers, with a 10-minute commentary; open bank hol Sun and Mon pms and by appointment, (01604) 740241; £2. The nearby Fitzgerald Arms is a good value dining pub. One battle monument (Sibbertoft Rd) marks the position of Cromwell's New Model Army before his devastating counter-attack; there's another on the B4036 towards Clipston (this road from W Haddon and on to Market Harborough in Leics gives a good feel of rural Northants).

NASSINGTON TL0696
Prebendal Manor House The oldest surviving dwelling in the county, dating from the early 13th c, the manor forms the focus of a group of stone buildings inc a dovecote and tithe barn. Standing on the site of one of King Cnut's Saxon halls, it was used as a residence for influential prebends of Lincoln Cathedral. The six-acre re-created medieval garden has herbers, turf seats, arbours, fishponds, a vineyard and a nut walk; also medieval vegetable and pleasure gardens. Good views of the

village and River Nene. Snacks, some disabled access; open pms Weds and Sun May–Sept and bank hols; (01780) 782575; *£4.50. The Black Horse is a civilised dining pub.

NORTHAMPTON SP7560

This prosperous town these days owes much more to service industries such as Barclaycard, and the transport firms whose huge warehouses now ring it, than the declining shoemaking industry for which it has been famous. There are several fine **churches**, most notably the 12th-c Holy Sepulchre (one of only four remaining round churches in the country), the very grand central All Saints, and the ornate Norman St Peter's in Marefair right by the dual carriageway. The Welsh House and Hazelrigg House also recall the long-gone time when Daniel Defoe was able to call this one of the most handsome towns in England. A social history museum in Abington Park is set in the 15th-c home of Shakespeare's granddaughter; cl ams and Mon; (01604) 631454; free. The Malt Shovel (Bridge St) has good value food, though its forte is beer.

Central Museum (Guildhall Rd) Home to a remarkable collection of boots and shoes, inc an elephant's boot, Margot Fonteyn's ballet shoes, Roman sandals, and Queen Victoria's wedding slippers. Also local history and arts. Shop, disabled access; cl Sun am, 25–26 Dec, 1 Jan; (01604) 238548; free.

OUNDLE TL0488

Charming and elegant stone-built town with a graceful church, several antiques shops, a fine old public school, and a busy Thurs market day. The comfortable Rose & Crown (Market Pl) has imaginative food.

Barnwell Country Park (just S) A good spot for a walk, with a variety of birds; disabled access on gravel paths; parking £1 for 12 hours (free for disabled drivers, who can drive right up to the lake). The waterside Mill is a pleasant place for lunch.

Lyveden New Bield 🏛 (out towards Brigstock) This ruined Elizabethan garden lodge was abandoned in 1605 after the owner, Sir Thomas Tresham, died in debt. Intriguing and unusual, it was intended to celebrate the Passion of Christ, and is shaped like a Greek cross. The moated Elizabethan garden (thought to be one of Britain's oldest) now includes a young orchard which has been replanted with period varieties following the details of a letter written by Sir Thomas Tresham from prison. Snacks, shop; cl Mon (exc bank hols), and Tues; (01832) 205358; *£2.50; NT. It's a half-mile walk from the car park, but has disabled parking next to the house.

ROCKINGHAM SP8691

Rockingham Castle (A6003) Henry VIII granted the fortress to Edward Watson (ancestor of the present owner), who converted it into a comfortable Tudor house. This lovely old house is tucked away behind the original Norman curtain wall – obviously quite an effective defence, as the castle was able to resist repeated assaults in the Civil War. The outline of the two baileys and the drum towers survive, and the later building has a good range of furnishings and art inc 20th-c pictures. With fine views of five counties, the ramparts enclose 12 acres of lawns, formal and informal gardens, a circular rose garden on the site of the old keep, and a wild garden in the ravine below containing over 200 species of trees and shrubs, many rare. Meals, snacks, shop, limited disabled access; open pm Sun and bank hols Apr–Sept, plus Tues and Thurs July–Aug; (01536) 770240; £5.50, garden only £3.50.

ROCKINGHAM FOREST SP9892

Pleasant back roads through the former Forest of Rockingham give quiet views of a particularly attractive part of the county. This part is good for walks, too, with enough country houses scattered around it to spice interest, the odd red kite now, and grey-stone cottages – a local feature. If you follow the yellow signs you'll get the best kite views, and come to a centre with CCTV viewing. Forest Enterprise is gradually re-creating what the forest would have looked like when it was a Royal hunting forest by taking out the conifers and putting back indigenous trees. Around the edges we'd recommend the Queens Head in attractive Bulwick (interesting church), thatched Shuckburgh Arms at Southwick, and

White Swan at Woodnewton, for their food.

RUSHDEN SP9567

Rushden Station Transport Museum Steam trains run along the 400 yards of track on occasional special event wknds from Jun–Sept, and there's a little museum (summer Suns 10–3; donations). If you ask nicely they may sign you into the charming member's bar which is authentically lit by gas lamps and full of Victorian memorabilia – look out for Ginger, the station cat. (01933) 318988.

RUSHTON SP8388

East Carlton Country Park 100 acres with pleasant strolls, children's play area and café (01536) 770977.

Triangular Lodge (1m W) One of England's most unusual buildings, this 16th-c oddity was designed and built by Sir Thomas Tresham (also responsible for Lyveden New Bield nr Oundle), and lived in by his rabbit-breeder. Purposely intriguing and infuriating, it's covered in the symbolism of Tresham's Roman Catholic beliefs – notably three levels, three walls, three windows, three triangular gables and a three-sided chimney, to represent the Holy Trinity. Shop, limited disabled access; cl Nov–Mar; (01536) 710761; £1.95; EH. In the attractive village, opposite the cricket green, the Thornhill Arms has good value food inc OAP bargains.

SALCEY FOREST SP8051

A couple of miles of ancient forest, largely oak, now managed for nature conservation, with well marked trails inc one good for wheelchairs. The thatched White Hart in nearby Stoke Goldington has good value food, and more walks from just over the road.

STOKE BRUERNE SP7449

Canal Museum Close to a flight of locks on the Grand Union Canal, with fine old canal buildings (inc a popular pub, the Boat), and lots happening on the water, this is a handsome former corn mill housing a good collection of canal memorabilia, inc a reconstructed traditional narrowboat cabin complete with immaculately packed-in colourful furniture and crockery. Shop; cl winter Mon; (01604) 862229; £3. Boat trips run from the museum to a nearby tunnel; (01604) 862107. Good towpath

walks from here.

SULGRAVE SP5545

Sulgrave Manor ⊞ (off B4525) The ancestral home of George Washington's family, this modest manor is exceptional for families during their regular living history events, when the whole place returns to how it would have been during a particular period – Viking or Stuart, say. People in period costume go about their daily business, and children can take part in a wide range of activities from wassailing or helping in the kitchen at Christmas, to joining in the harvest during their Apple Day Festival. Worth a visit too on non-event days, when they do guided tours. As well as elegant rooms and well kept gardens, there are several relics of Washington, though he never lived here – it was his great-great-grandfather who emigrated to America; outdoor theatre in late July. Snacks, shop, some disabled access; open pm Apr–Oct and wknds Dec, cl Mon and Fri (exc bank hols or during events); (01295) 760205; around £6 on event days, otherwise *£5. Just down the road, the Star is enjoyable for lunch (now allowing children in its restaurant).

SYWELL COUNTRY PARK

SP8365 (off A4500) Woodland and lakeside walks, play areas, and a little wildlife display; you can fish on the lake – in fact a reservoir – with tickets in advance (01904) 479797. An information foyer (open all year) leads into a small visitor centre (open pm wknds and school hols) with snacks and shop; (01604) 810970. The Griffins Head on the edge of attractive thatched Mears Ashby has bargain food.

TOWCESTER SP6948

This small town (pronounced Toaster), despite some light industry on the edge, has quite a pleasantly villagey feel, and some attractive Georgian and Victorian buildings.

UPPER STOWE SP6456

Old Dairy Farm Centre Pigs, peacocks, ducks and donkeys, as well as craft workshops, galleries, antiques, plant nursery, gift and farm shop, and wool collection. Well organised, and decent views – though be prepared for it to be muddy. Restaurant, snacks, shop, disabled access; cl two wks from

25 Dec; (01327) 340525; free, exc special wknds. There are towpath walks on the Grand Union Canal not far off; the Narrow Boat at Weedon, with a big canalside garden and boat hire next door, has decent food.

Other attractive villages, all with decent pubs, include Apethorpe TL0295, Barnwell TL0484, canalside Bugbrooke SP6757, Bulwick SP9694 (interesting church), Denton SP8358, Duddington SK9800, Ecton SP8263, Evenley SP5834, Farthingstone SP6155 (Knightley Way walks), Gayton SP7054, thatched Grafton Regis SP7546, Great Houghton SP7958, Greens Norton SP6649 (Grafton Way walks), Grendon SP8760, Harlestone SP7064, Harrington SP7779, Hellidon SP5158 (pleasant walks nearby), Kilsby SP5671, Kings Sutton SP4936, Litchborough SP6353, Little Harrowden SP8671, Marston Trussell SP6985, Mears Ashby SP8466 (narrow lanes of thatched cottages), Nassington TL0696, Newnham SP5859, Sudborough SP9682, Thorpe Mandeville SP5344, riverside Wadenhoe TL0383, Welford SP6480 and Yardley Hastings SP8656. We'd also recommend rather Cotswoldy Kings Cliffe TL0097, and two lovely mellow orange ironstone villages, Preston Capes SP5754 and Everdon SP5957.

Where to eat

CHACOMBE SP4943 **George & Dragon** *1 Silver St (01295) 711500* Handy for the M40, this charming village pub has a tidy spacious bar with comfortable seats, beams, flagstones, and logs burning in a massive fireplace, real ales, a wide range of good imaginative food from a changing blackboard (also, afternoon snacks and teas), and friendly and attentive service; bdrms; disabled access. £24|**£7.75**

FARTHINGSTONE SP6155 **Kings Arms** *Main St (01327) 361604* In a pretty village, this handsome 18th-c stone building has homely comfortable sofas and armchairs, a huge log fire in the small bar, lots of decorative plates and pictures, spacious dining area, a good choice of cheeses (the only food they serve apart from winter soup), well kept real ales, decent wines and friendly licensees; nearby walks; cl wkdy lunchtimes; disabled access.|**£5.50**

FOTHERINGHAY TL0793 **Falcon** *(01832) 226254* Stylish but relaxed old country dining pub with a good mix of customers, comfortable lounge with fresh flowers and fireplaces at each end, no smoking conservatory and dining room, and little tap bar for locals; excellent food from a varied interesting menu, well kept real ales, and a fine wine list; neat garden; disabled access. £29|**£6.50**

GREAT OXENDON SP7383 **George** *Harborough Rd (01858) 465205* Though rather gaunt-looking on its bank high over the main road, inside, this carefully decorated dining pub is really cosy and convivial; two opened-together rooms of the main beamed bar have attractive prints and engravings, and there's a no smoking conservatory overlooking the shrub-sheltered garden; very good popular food (well liked by older lunchers especially), well kept real ales, decent wines, and daily papers. £22|**£8.25**

HARRINGWORTH SP9197 **White Swan** *Seaton Rd (01572) 747543* Neatly kept stone-built Tudor pub with generous helpings of enjoyable food, a comfortable lounge/dining area, a quieter dining room, and friendly licensees; bdrms; cl 25–26 Dec pm; disabled access. £19.65|**£7.95**

ROADE SP7551 **Roade House** *16 High St (01604) 863372* Smart and popular restaurant-with-rooms with long-serving owners, comfortable surroundings, courteous service, reliably enjoyable food using first class ingredients, and reasonably priced wines; cl pm Sun, Mon and Sat am; disabled access. £38

SULGRAVE SP5545 **Star** *Manor Rd (01295) 760389* Hospitable, small creeper-covered pub with small pews, cushioned window seats and wall benches on polished flagstones, a big inglenook fireplace, good seasonal food, friendly staff, lots to look at, well kept real ales, and no smoking restaurant; bdrms; cl 25 Dec. £22.50

Special thanks to Michael and Jenny Back, Rona Murdoch

NORTHUMBRIA

**Great holiday opportunities, excellent value: magnificent
untouched scenery, Hadrian's Roman legacy, and some
outstanding family attractions**

Northumbria is a great part of the world for anyone interested in the
visible past. The most striking feature is Hadrian's Wall; the Roman forts
and attractions (Segedunum and the full-scale reconstructions at
Vindolanda provide a good introduction for families) along its 73½ miles
make this amazing 2,000-year-old wall even more rewarding to visit. For
more recent history, the ever-expanding Historic Quay at Hartlepool
(our top Family Attraction here this year), and at Beamish the awesome
reconstruction of North of England life a century or two ago, are both
worth travelling for.

You're in the right place if you like castles. The most impressive are
Alnwick (the second-largest inhabited castle in the country), huge
Bamburgh (the stately home comes as a surprise after the forbidding
exterior), Raby in Staindrop (restored to its Victorian splendour), Bishop
Auckland (the main residence of the mighty Prince Bishops of Durham),
and striking Chillingham. The massive ruins in Embleton are memorable,
and Warkworth Castle is picturesque. Fine houses include magnificent
Cragside in Rothbury with its pleasant landscaped grounds and splendid
rooms; there's a fine house and gardens in Belsay, and Washington Old
Hall is well restored. At Barnard Castle the Bowes Museum houses its
dazzling display of fine arts in a beautiful French-style château, and elegant
Rokeby Park is nearby (staying at the Morritt Arms in Greta Bridge makes
it easy to visit both).

Vibrant Newcastle (with some excellent child-friendly museums
including the Centre for Life and Discovery Museum), and across the
water Gateshead (rejuvenation projects are greatly adding to its pull) are
increasingly rewarding destinations for families. The beautiful ancient city
of Durham has lots of sightseeing possibilities.

Fun outings for children include the friendly farm parks at Stannington
and Berwick-upon-Tweed, and for wilder creatures head to the Otter
Trust near Bowes. The National Glass Centre and Mowbray Gardens
make Sunderland worth visiting for an afternoon.

Other attractions include the profusion of railway centres scattered
around the homeland of George Stephenson. If Britain's emergence from
the Dark Ages has any fascination for you, tracing Christianity's early steps
through this area will lead you to lots of interesting and beautiful places;
the island of Lindisfarne and Bede's World in Jarrow are ideal places to
start.

The coast has majestic stretches, with a path along the finest sections. If
beaches as fine as these had Mediterranean sunshine, you'd never be able
to drag yourself away from them. And now the miles of extraordinary

black sand beaches in the south of the area have been cleaned up, and graced with sculptures and new visitor facilities, this coast is cleaner than it's been for centuries. Inland are great sweeps of largely unspoilt upland scenery, quiet and uncrowded even in summer. Peaceful lower landscapes are enlivened by streams and woodland, solid stone country buildings, and unhurried small market towns. The area is very good both for walking and for driving, with the least traffic in England (outside the Tyneside/Teesside industrial areas).

People up here are among Britain's friendliest, and low prices are helped along by welcome saver schemes such as the Power Pass, jointly developed by the Northumbrian Tourist Board and Northern Electric (available from their electrical shops and Tourist Information Centres throughout the area, £1). May and June are the best months to visit, with long evenings (stay away from inland waters in later summer, unless you're midge-proof). September can be delightful, but autumn tends to set in quite fiercely in October.

Where to stay

ALNMOUTH NU2410 **Marine House Hotel** *1 Marine Rd, Alnmouth, Alnwick, Northumberland NE66 2RW (01665) 830349* **£78**, plus special breaks; 11 rms. 17th-c stone hotel by golf links, with fine sea views; log fire and plenty of books in traditional upstairs residents' lounge, cosy bar, and enjoyable freshly prepared food in cheerfully decorated no smoking dining room; self-catering also; cl Jan; children over 7; dogs welcome

CAMBO NZ0584 **Shieldhall** *Wallington, Morpeth, Northumberland NE61 4AQ (01830) 540387* **£60**; 4 well equipped suites, each with its own entrance. 18th-c stone house and carefully converted farm buildings around a courtyard, with antiques and other interesting furnishings (Mr Robinson-Gay is a fine cabinet-maker), a library, bar, and cosy lounge with French windows opening on to the neatly kept big garden; enjoyable freshly produced food in candlelit beamed dining room; cl Christmas and New Year; children over 12

CHOLLERFORD NY9170 **George** *Chollerford, Hexham, Northumberland NE46 4EW (01434) 681611* **£125**, plus special breaks; 47 well equipped rms. Quiet hotel with fine gardens sloping down to the river, and the 17th-c bridge over North Tyne visible from the candlelit restaurant; thoughtful attentive service; swimming pool and leisure club; fishing, putting green, and mountain bike hire; limited disabled access; dogs welcome in bedrooms

CORNHILL-ON-TWEED NT8842 **Tillmouth Park** *Cornhill-on-Tweed, Northumberland TD12 4UU (01890) 882255* **£130**, plus special breaks; 14 spacious, pretty rms with period furniture. Solid stone-built country house in 15 acres of parkland, with comfortable relaxing lounges, open fires, a galleried hall, good food in bistro or restaurant, and a carefully chosen wine list; fishing, nearby golf, and shooting; lots to do nearby; dogs welcome in bedrooms

CROOKHAM NT9138 **Coach House** *Crookham, Cornhill-on-Tweed, Northumberland TD12 4TD (01890) 820293* **£54***; 9 individual rms with fresh flowers and nice views, 7 with own bthrm. 17th-c farm buildings around a sunny courtyard, with helpful and friendly long-serving owner, an airy beamed lounge with comfortable sofas and big arched windows, good breakfasts with home-made preserves (which you can also take home), afternoon tea, and enjoyable dinners using own-grown vegetables; lots to do nearby; cl 31 Oct–Easter; good disabled access; dogs welcome in bedrooms

DURHAM NZ2742 **Durham Marriott Royal County** *Old Elvet, Durham, County Durham DH1 3JN (0191) 386 6821* **£125**, plus special breaks; 150 attractive well equipped rms. In city centre with views of castle and cathedral, this extended and newly refurbished hotel has original Tudor beams, panelling and an unusual stained-glass ceiling, a convivial lounge area, airy conservatory, two restaurants, and good leisure facilities; disabled access; dogs welcome in bedrooms

GATESHEAD NZ2560 **Eslington Villa** *8 Station Rd, Low Fell, Gateshead, Tyne & Wear NE9 6DR (0191) 487 6017* **£69.50**, plus wknd breaks; 18 rms. Comfortable, extended Edwardian house in quiet residential area with some original features, a lounge with comfortably modern furniture and bay windows overlooking garden, good food in conservatory restaurant, and a friendly atmosphere; cl bank hols and Christmas; disabled access; dogs welcome in bedrooms

GREENHEAD NY6667 **Holmhead** *Greenhead, Carlisle, Cumbria CA8 7HY (01697) 747402* **£60**, plus special breaks; 4 cosy rms with showers. Family home, built of Wall stones, once a farmhouse but now a comfortable B&B with moorland, wildlife, Hadrian's Wall and Roman castles all nearby; airy lounge with TV at one end, small bar at the other, games and children's toys, good freshly prepared food using organic farm and local produce eaten family-style around candlelit oak table at 7.30pm, and pretty garden with a stream and games (table tennis and snooker in garage); Mrs Staff is a Hadrian's Wall tour guide, and there's a clue trail for children and special learning tour ; cl 18 Dec–18 Jan ☺

GRETA BRIDGE NZ0813 **Morritt Arms** *Greta Bridge, Barnard Castle, County Durham DL12 9SE (01833) 627232* **£83.50**, plus special breaks; 23 rms. Smartly old-fashioned coaching inn where Dickens stayed in 1838 to research for *Nicholas Nickleby* – one of the interesting bars has a colourful Dickensian mural; comfortable lounges, fresh flowers, good open fires, and pleasant garden; coarse fishing; pets allowed; attractive garden with children's play area; disabled access; dogs welcome away from bistro and restaurant

HEADLAM NZ1818 **Headlam Hall** *Headlam, Darlington, County Durham DL2 3HA (01325) 730238* **£87**, plus special breaks; 36 pretty rms in the main house and adjacent coach house, plus 2-bedroom cottage in village. Peaceful Jacobean mansion in four acres of carefully kept gardens with a little trout lake, tennis court, and croquet lawn; elegant rooms, a fine carved oak fireplace in the main hall, stylish food in the four individually decorated rooms of the restaurant, and courteous staff; indoor swimming pool, snooker and sauna, and gym; cl 25 Dec; disabled access; dogs welcome in bedrooms

KIRKWHELPINGTON NY9684 **Cornhills** *Kirkwhelpington, Newcastle upon Tyne, Tyne & Wear NE19 2RE (01830) 540232* **£45***; 3 rms. Big no smoking Victorian farmhouse on large stock-rearing farm, with marvellous views towards the coast and Tyne Valley; lots of original features, a comfortable lounge, good breakfasts (local pubs for evening meals), and indoor and outdoor games for children; self-catering also; cl Apr

LONGFRAMLINGTON NU1301 **Embleton Hall** *Longframlington, Morpeth, Northumberland NE65 8DT (01665) 570249* **£85**; 13 comfortable, pretty and individually decorated rms. Charming hotel in lovely grounds surrounded by fine countryside, with a particularly friendly relaxed atmosphere and courteous staff; neat little bar, elegant lounge, log fires, excellent value bar meals, and very good food in the attractive dining room; disabled access; dogs welcome in bedrooms

LONGHORSLEY NZ1596 **Linden Hall** *Longhorsley, Morpeth, Northumberland NE65 8XF (01670) 516611* **£128**, plus special breaks; 50 individually decorated rms. Georgian hotel in 450 acres of landscaped park with clay pigeon shooting, mountain biking (bike hire available), 18-hole golf course, pitch and putt, croquet, lots of leisure facilities inc a big swimming pool, and health and beauty treatments; pubby bar, elegant drawing room, and good food in attractive restaurant; children in main restaurant early evening only; disabled access; dogs welcome in bedrooms

NEWCASTLE UPON TYNE NZ2564 **Malmaison** *Quayside, Newcastle upon Tyne, Tyne & Wear NE1 3DX (0191) 245 5000* **£141.50**; 116 individually decorated and well equipped rms. In a former Co-op warehouse and overlooking the river, this stylish hotel (part of a small chain with others in Birmingham, Edinburgh, Glasgow, Leeds, London and Manchester) is boldly decorated throughout, with contemporary furniture and artwork, genuinely friendly staff, modern cooking in fashionable brasserie, and decent breakfasts; disabled access

ROMALDKIRK NY9922 **Rose & Crown** *Romaldkirk, Barnard Castle, County Durham DL12 9EB* (01833) 650213 **£90**, plus special breaks; 12 rms – those in the main house have lots of character. Smart and interesting old coaching inn by green of delightful Teesdale village, with Jacobean oak settle, log fire, old black and white photographs, and lots of brass in the beamed traditional bar; cosy residents' lounge, very good imaginative food in bar and fine oak-panelled restaurant, and well kept real ales and wines; cl Christmas; disabled access; dogs welcome in bedrooms

SEAHOUSES NU2232 **Olde Ship** *Main St, Seahouses, Northumberland NE68 7RD* (01665) 720200 **£82**, plus special breaks; 18 rms, inc 4 apartments. Thriving harbourside inn with small rooms full of nautical items and fishing memorabilia, windows looking out towards the Farne Islands, comfortable residents' lounge and sun lounge, popular bar food, five real ales, and good service; ideal for coastal walks; cl Dec–Jan; children over 10

STANNERSBURN NY7286 **Pheasant** *Stannersburn, Hexham, Northumberland NE48 1DD* (01434) 240382 **£65***, plus special breaks; 8 rms. Beautifully located unpretentious 17th-c stone inn close to Kielder Water and its quiet forests; traditional, comfortable lounge, simple public bar, a happy mix of customers, good food inc excellent fresh veg and enjoyable Sun lunch, well kept real ales, a fine choice of malts, good welcoming service, and nice breakfasts; picnic-sets in streamside garden; cl 25–26 Dec; disabled access; dogs welcome in bedrooms

SWINBURNE NY9374 **Hermitage** *Swinburne, Hexham, Northumbria NE48 4DG* (01434) 681248 **£70**; 3 large rms with big baths, overlooking the garden or vegetable patch. Lovely 17th-c country house reached through a grand arch and down a long drive with woodland on either side; graceful rooms with family portraits, prints and antiques, warm and friendly owners, and generous breakfasts; no smoking upstairs; several nearby pubs for meals; cl Oct–Feb; babes in arms or children over 10

WOLSINGHAM NZ1037 **Greenwell Farm** *Tow Law, Bishop Auckland, County Durham DL13 4PH* (01388) 527248 **£50***, plus special breaks; 6 rms in comfortably converted stone barn. Old farmhouse in peaceful spot with fine views, sitting and dining rooms, good food using naturally reared meats and locally grown produce, and spring lambs, calves and chicks, a nature trail, and conservation areas; can bring own horse or mountain bike; self-catering cottage; cl Christmas; disabled access; dogs by arrangement

---

We welcome reports from readers

This *Guide* depends on readers' reports. Do help us if you can – in return, we offer a discount on the next edition to people who've helped us with reports for it. Tell us what you think about places already in it, and anything extra you think we should say about them. And send us your ideas for inclusion in the next edition: places to visit, eat at or stay in, attractive drives or walks, maybe even unusual shops you know of. Use the card in the middle, the report forms at the end, or just write – no stamp needed: *The Good Britain Guide*, FREEPOST TN1569, Wadhurst, E Sussex TN5 7BR. Or log on to www.goodguides.com

Northumbria Family Attraction of the Year

HARTLEPOOL NZ5132 **Historic Quay** 🖼 Easily one of the best of its type, this is a vivid full-scale re-creation of an 18th-c port, with ships in the harbour, costumed characters going about their business, and painstakingly reconstructed furnished houses, market, prison, and well stocked shops. It's very well done, and so realistic that it's often used as a location for period dramas. They suggest allowing at least two hours to see it properly, but it's easy to spend much longer, and there's lots to entertain children for a full morning or afternoon. Behind some of the shop fronts are several well put together exhibitions and films: best (and certainly noisiest) is the one on Fighting Ships, and there's an eye-opening explanation of the press gangs who so dubiously drummed up volunteers to earn their sea legs. The highlight for most younger visitors is the big, interactive Maritime Adventure Centre, still fairly new, with themed areas exploring life at sea. You can plot a ship's course using the stars, take a turn at wiping out rats, or design you own seaman's tattoo. Elsewhere there's a good-sized adventure playship with a mast to climb up, and a splendid area where children are taught how to play historic games like skittles, shove ha'penny, or fishing for 'Frenchies'. At weekends and school holidays you may find more going on in the reconstructed port: staff usually fire rifles or demonstrate fencing then. Hartlepool's other great naval attraction, HMS *Trincomalee*, is moored here, though run separately (see main listings, below); there's a splendid view of it from the nicely placed picnic area. Quite a lot here is under cover, so though the open-air bits are best in dry weather, you won't be stuck if the weather turns sour. Meals, snacks, shop, disabled access; (01429) 860888; *£5.50 adults, *£2.75 children 5–16. The family ticket is good value: £14.50 for two adults and three children.

ALLENDALE NY8352
The B6305/B6295 is a great scenic drive; lots of walks up there, and the Kings Head in Allendale Town (really a village) is a good stop.
Allenheads Heritage Centre (Allenheads) The history of this former lead-mining village, the highest in England, is told in its heritage centre, blacksmith's shop and engine house; also nature trails. Meals and snacks in the Hemmel café, shop, disabled access; open Easter–Oct; (01434) 685395; £1. The Allenheads Inn is an entertaining stop.

ALNMOUTH NU2410
A pleasant town with attractive beaches, good coastal walks, and a lot for summer visitors. The Saddle has decent food.

ALNWICK NU1813
Busy town at the heart of prosperous farming country, with some attractive old streets nr the market square – it was used in the film *Elizabeth*. The

hillside **church** of St Michael and All Angels above the river is a perfect example of a complete Late Gothic building. An impressive number of second-hand books are on sale in the converted Victorian station, and the Market Tavern has bargain food.
Alnwick Castle The 'Windsor of the North' dates back to the 11th c, and is the second-largest inhabited castle in the country. Stone soldiers stand guard on the battlements, and inside all is Renaissance grandeur, with a magnificent art collection taking in works by Titian, Van Dyck and Canaletto, and an outstanding Claude. Also a famous collection of Meissen china, Roman remains, refurbished museum with displays on the Duke of Northumberland's own private army and local archaeology, and children's playground. Meals, snacks, shop, some disabled access; open Apr–late Oct; £6.95, joint ticket with garden £9.50.
Alnwick Garden Exciting for

gardeners, this 12-acre sloping walled garden is being reworked as a magnificent new partnership of water, topiary, and precision plantings, at a cost of £14 million to a design by the Wirtz family of Belgium. Water displays, ornamental garden, water tower walk, rose garden, and woodland walks. Meals, snacks, shop; disabled access; cl 25 Dec; (01665) 511133; £4, joint ticket with castle; £9.50.

Hulne Park Excellent for gentle parkland walks; dogs not allowed. Don't miss the whimsical Brizlee Tower and hermit's cave, also some abbey and priory remains.

AMBLE NU2604

This attractive small town has a solid old fishing harbour, and modern yacht marina; there are **boat trips** around nearby RSPB nature reserve, Coquet Island, with its colourful eider ducks and puffins; (01665) 711975.

AYDON NZ0066

Aydon Castle (just N of Corbridge) 13th c, and remarkably well preserved, in a lovely setting. Snacks, shop, some disabled access; cl Nov–Mar; (01434) 632450; £2.20; EH.

BAMBURGH NU1835

Bamburgh Castle Stunning huge square Norman castle on a cliff above the sea, its clock serving as timekeeper for the cricket green in the attractive village below. Despite the forbidding exterior, and a collection of armour from the Tower of London, the inside is very much a lived-in stately home. Snacks, shop; cl Nov to mid-Mar; (01668) 214515; *£5. There's a neo-Gothic shrine to Grace Darling the local shipwreck heroine in the yard of the interesting 13th-c **church**. The Lord Crewe Arms is well placed for lunch.

Grace Darling Museum (Radcliffe Rd) Pictures and mementoes of the local heroine, inc the boat in which Grace and her father rescued nine survivors from the wrecked SS *Forfarshire*. Shop, disabled access; cl am Sun, and Nov–Easter; (01668) 214465; free (donations to RNLI).

BARNARD CASTLE NZ0416

Pleasant market town, still coming to life on Weds market day, with several attractive buildings. In the centre, the Old Well, with a terrace over the town walls, has good value food. There's charming gorge scenery nearby, here wooded, romantic and unmistakably lowland in character – making for good walks. The valley path W eventually climbs above the river and follows field routes as it leads towards Cotherstone.

Bowes Museum A beautiful French-style chateau in 20 acres of meticulously kept formal grounds. The 40 rooms are filled with sumptuous fine arts and an outstanding display of paintings of national importance; also local history section, small display of 1950s toys; they hold concerts, events and temporary exhibitons throughout the year. Relatively few people find their way to this knock-out treasure-house, though it's one of the most worthwhile places to visit in the entire country – those readers who do get there love it. Meals, snacks, shop, disabled access; cl 25–26 Dec, 1 Jan; (01833) 690606; £5.

Castle These dramatically set 12th-c ruins include the original keep and the 14th-c hall. Shop, disabled facilities; cl 1–2pm, Mon and Tues Nov–Mar, 24–26 Dec, and 1 Jan; (01833) 638212; £2.40 (inc audio tour); EH.

Eggleston Abbey Downstream from Barnard Castle, this is reached by a couple of miles of enjoyable riverside walk – or by car. Substantial remains inc gracefully arched windows, and some remnants of the monastic buildings; disabled access; free. Nearby, there's a fine medieval packhorse bridge.

Rokeby Park (just SE) Elegant 18th-c villa in a fine setting, most famous for its Rokeby Venus by Velasquez (though the original is now in the National Gallery). The best of the other pictures is probably Pellegrini's *Venus Disarming Cupid*. Open May bank hols and the following Tues, then pm only Mon and Tues Jun to 1st Tues in Sept, but best to check; (01833) 637334; £5. The Morritt Arms nearby does good meals. The B6278 to Stanhope and Edmundbyers is a fine drive.

BEADNELL NU2329

On Northumberland's underpopulated coast, this attractive village has boats on the beach, and an interestingly restored waterside lime kiln; nearby Benthall is also a pleasant place to visit.

BEAMISH NZ2154
North of England Open-Air Museum (A693) An amazingly ambitious 300-acre museum exhaustively re-creating life in the North of England in the early 1800s and 1900s. There are five main sections: a town with streets, shops, houses and businesses (and a new horse-drawn vehicle collection), a colliery village with mine, chapel, cottages and school, a manor house with formal gardens, orchard and heavy horses, a railway station, and a home farm with animals and exhibitions (ducks and geese wander around for extra authenticity, and local Teeswater sheep graze on the ridge-and-furrow corrugations which were the rule in the English landscape before steam ploughs). Costumed staff really bring the place to life, answering questions and showing off period crafts and skills. What's nice for children is that they can wander around touching everything and joining in most of the activities – learning how to play hoops and hopscotch for example, or taking part in lessons in the schoolroom. The sweet factory and the dentist offer demonstrations, and a Victorian fairground has rides and a proper Hall of Mirrors (the only bit that has a small extra charge). A re-created engine shed has a magnificent 1822 locomotive, and a full-scale replica of Stephenson's *Locomotion No. 1*, which carries visitors down a ½-mile track (they've now also a full-size replica of another early locomotive, the *Steam Elephant*). Extra activities most wknds, from vintage car rallies to Meccano-building or whippet racing, and in summer there may be brass bands or choirs. Working trams and buses link the different areas, and there's plenty of space for picnics (dogs are allowed on a lead). Meals and snacks (some in a period pub), good shops, some disabled access; cl Mon and Fri Nov–Mar, and 16 Dec–1 Jan; (0191) 3704000; £12, £4 in winter, when only the town and tramway are open. The Shepherd & Shepherdess not far from the gate is useful for lunch, as is the more individual Beamish Mary (the sign to follow from A693 is a lovely one – 'No Place & Cooperative Villas'). which serves generous bar food.

Northumbria

Berwick-upon-Tweed
Horncliffe
Norham
LINDISFARNE
Cornhill-on-Tweed
Etal
Lowick
Ross Back Sands
NU
Crookham
Ford
Bamburgh
Seahouses
Warenford
Beadnell
Chillingham
Chathill
Low Newton
Embleton
Craster
Rennington
Boulmer
Windy Gyle
Alnwick
Ainmouth
CHEVIOT HILLS
Clennel Street
Newton-on-the-Moor
Warkworth
Rothbury
Amble
Longframlington
Longhorsley
Woodhorn
Kirkwhelpington
Cambo
Morpeth
Bomarsund
Bellingham
Whalton
Stannington
Seaton Sluice
Swinburne
Belsay
Whitley Bay
WALL
Chollerford
Ponteland
North Shields
Tynemouth
Matfen
Haydon Bridge
Great Whittington
Stamfordham
Newcastle upon Tyne
South Shields
Marsden
Hexham
Aydon
Corbridge
Stocksfield
Prudhoe
Gateshead
Jarrow
Whitburn
Riding Mill
Hedley on the Hill
Allendale
Rowlands Gill
Springwell
Washington
Sunderland
Carterway Heads
Burnopfield
Tanfield
Blanchland
Beamish
WEARDALE
Chester-le-Street
Lanchester
Durham
NZ
Wolsingham
Langley Park
Shincliffe
Peterlee
Newfield
Witton-le-Wear
Binchester
Hamsterley
Hartlepool
Bishop Auckland
TEESDALE
Shildon
High Force
Eggleston
Bishopton
Romaldkirk
Cotherstone
Staindrop
Stockton-on-Tees
Barnard Castle
Headlam
Darlington
Bowes
Greta Bridge
NORTH YORKSHIRE

BELLINGHAM NY8383
(pronounced Bellingjum) A small
country town with an attractive 13th-c
church, stone-roofed to protect it
against arson-minded Border raiders;
Black Middens Bastle House, a 16th-c
stone-built defensive farmhouse which
is 180 metres' walk from the road, is
open to the public at all reasonable
times; free; EH. There's a pretty walk
just N of the town, to the 9-metre (30-
ft) cascade of Hareshaw Linn. The
Riverdale Hall Hotel does interesting
bar food. This is the main town in
North Tynedale, one of the least known
and most unspoilt parts of
Northumberland, with good scenic
drives. Between the Pennines and the
Cheviots, it's a peaceful river valley
surrounded by wild moorland.

BELSAY NZ1078
Belsay Hall and Gardens (A696)
The same family lived here for nearly
600 years, first in a medieval castle, then
a Jacobean manor house, and finally a
grand mansion designed to look like a
Greek temple. All can still be seen, but
the mansion is strangely eerie: there's
no furniture, and in some rooms no
floors either. The 30 acres of grounds
and parkland, not just landscaped but
partly quarried into the underlying
rock, are spectacular, with
rhododendron garden, formal terraces
and woodland walks. Meals, snacks,
shop, disabled access; cl 24–26 Dec, and
1 Jan; (01661) 881636; £4; EH. The
Highlander is a good dining pub.

BERWICK-UPON-TWEED
NT9953
Captured or sacked 13 times before it
finally came under English rule for good
in 1482, the town is largely unspoilt,
with some handsome 18th-c buildings
and a fine 17th-c church. In Marygate,
the handsome Georgian town hall with
its 150-ft spire houses the **Cell Block
Museum**; unusual in being upstairs, the
gaol here was used between 1761 and
1849. Hour-long guided tours leave
10.30 and 2pm Easter–end Sept;
(01289) 330900; £1.50. Most people
who come here seem to while away at
least a bit of time watching the swans on
the River Tweed, or alternatively, look
out over the sea from the Rob Roy
(Spittal Rd), which has good local fish.

Other places we can recommend for
food are Barrels (Bridge St) and
Foxtons (Hide Hill). The town has an
impressive track record for hospitality:
in the early 19th c it boasted a
formidable total of 59 pubs and three
coaching inns. Today, a more striking
feature is its extraordinary trio of
bridges, best appreciated by walking
along the Tweed: there are paths on
both banks, starting from the East Ord
picnic site by the A1 road bridge. The
town ramparts, impressively intact,
were a masterpiece of 16th-c military
planning. Partly grassed over and easy
to walk, they give good views.
Berwick Barracks (The Parade)
Britain's oldest surviving purpose-built
barracks, now a local history museum
and gallery, with an interesting
exhibition on the British soldier,
another on early maps, and a
contemporary art gallery. Snacks, shop,
disabled access; cl Mon and Tues
Nov–Mar, 24–26 Dec, 1 Jan; (01289)
304493; £2.80; EH.
Conundrum Farm (just off A1 N)
The last farm in England (it reaches right
up to the Scottish border). A trail takes
you through various animal paddocks
with traditional farm animals inc rare
breeds to a pond where you can feed
the trout; there's a pets' corner, and
you can usually see chicks hatching in
the summer, and lambing at Easter and
in May. Also fly-fishing, pedal tractors,
playbarn, and play area. New café, shop,
disabled access; cl 24 Dec–Feb, but best
to check in winter; £2.95.

BINCHESTER NZ2332
Binchester Roman Fort Quite a lot
left of this 1st-c 10-acre fort, inc the
best-preserved military baths in the
country, with an exceptional hypocaust
system. Interesting events include days
when you may be able to sample Roman
food. Shop, disabled access; open cl
Oct–Easter; (01388) 663089; £1.60.
Nearby Escomb church is interesting,
built in the 7th c from stone from the
fort. A 3rd-c fort can be seen a few
miles S at Piercebridge (where the
riverside George, with its famous
grandfather clock which stopped when
the old man died, is useful for lunch),
and finds from both sites are shown at
the Bowes Museum in Barnard Castle.

BISHOP AUCKLAND NZ2130
Auckland Castle (N outskirts) The main country residence of the Bishops of Durham, a grand series of buildings entered through a splendid Gothic gatehouse in the town's market place. Some rooms are relatively stark, but a highlight is the chapel, splendidly transformed from a 12th-c aisled hall by Bishop John Cosin in the 17th c. The attractive grounds have an unusual 18th-c deercote. Shop, limited disabled access; open pms Mon, Thurs, and Sun Apr–Sept; (01388) 601627; £3.50. 2 or 3m N of here, the Fox & Hounds in Newfield does a good lunch (not Mon).

BLANCHLAND NY9650
The archetypal border village, every house looking a stronghold, alone in a great bowl of magnificent scenery; the Lord Crewe Arms here is an interesting hotel, in parts very ancient indeed.

BOMARSUND NZ2784
Earth Balance (signposted off A189 N of Bedlington) Enjoyable place spread over 260 acres, showcasing environmentally friendly living, with organic food and drink made on the premises, a green garden centre, and Re-Dress, where new clothes and textiles are made out of recycled products. A trail takes you around eco-buildings, a willow maze, a nature reserve, and a fishing lake that provides power for the complex. Café and shop (good choice of locally made food and crafts); disabled access difficult in some parts of the trail; cl around 20 Dec–6 Jan; (01670) 821000; free.

BOULMER NU2613
One of several attractive villages and small towns dotted down Northumberland's scenic and underpopulated coast, this has active fishing boats.

BOWES NY9913
Bowes Castle Within the earthworks of a Roman fort, these remains include the great Norman keep, three storeys high; free; EH. The comfortable Ancient Unicorn, with *Nicholas Nickleby* connections, has good food.

Otter Trust North Pennine Reserve (off A66 W) As well as having British otters (bred for release into the wild) in large semi-natural enclosures along the River Greta (feeding times 12

and 3), this appealingly wild upland reserve is rich in birds. Two shallow lakes have hides for watching wildfowl; in spring there are five species of breeding waders. There's a rabbit and guinea-pig village for childen, a nature trail, model farm with Asian otters, picnic area, and a visitor centre explaining the work of the Trust. Snacks, shop, disabled access; open Apr–Oct; (01833) 628339; £4.50.

BURNOPFIELD NZ1857
Gibside Chapel and Grounds Marvellous Palladian mausoleum for the Bowes family in 18th-c landscaped park, with the rather sad ruins of a hall and other estate buildings dotted around. Miles of pleasant walks. Snacks, shop, disabled access; cl Mon (exc bank hols), chapel open by appointment only Nov–Mar; (01207) 542255; £3.50; NT. The Harperley Hotel in Harperley Country Park, down past Tantobie, has good home cooking (and more nice walks).

BYRNESS NT7702
Chew Green Roman Camps Little-visited spectacular earthworks alone in wild country, well repaying the stiff walk up the Pennine Way through the Redesdale Forest. The Pennines up here contain a great many more unspoilt prehistoric and other archaeological remains – useful goals for walkers in these magnificent hills, often yielding remarkable views. Some areas N of the A68 (which as it approaches the Scottish border is a remarkably dramatic drive) and W of the B6341 may temporarily be put out of bounds by army training. The welcoming Redesdale Arms at Rochester has enjoyable food and comfortable bedrooms.

CAMBO NZ0283
Wallington House Although the 17th-c house will be closed for 2003, you can still visit the gardens: over 100 acres of lawns, terraces, lakes and woodland (there's a woodland walk and wildlife hide) landscaped by Capability Brown. Also showpiece fuchsias in the conservatory and an adventure playground. Meals, snacks, shop, plant centre, some disabled access; (01670) 773600; £4.10; NT. There is free access to the huge surrounding estate, which is

laced with footpaths and includes prehistoric sites and more parkland.

CAULDRON SNOUT NY8128 Beyond High Force, the Pennine Way rewards walkers with some truly wild landscape as the Tees rushes along a gorge beneath Cronkley Scar and tumbles down Cauldron Snout, a 60-metre (200-ft) cascade which can be reached from the dam at Cow Green Reservoir (where there is also a nature trail). The pleasant Langdon Beck Hotel is a short drive or walk below the dam.

CHATHILL NU1825 **Preston Tower** (Preston) Built by the Sheriff of Northumberland as a tower house during the Border raids of the late 14th c; half of the building was later pulled down to provide stone for surrounding cottages and farm buildings. A scale model shows what it would have looked like originally, and furnishings in the remaining quarters give an idea of what it must have been like to live there in the 15th c; open daily; (01665) 589227; £1.50.

CHESTER-LE-STREET NZ2751 **St Mary & St Cuthbert and Ankers House Museum** One of the oldest in the North, this church is on the site of a cathedral established in 883 by the monks of Lindisfarne, and this was where the Gospels were first translated into English. Adjoining the church is a little anchorite museum with a sobering re-creation of an anchorite's living quarters. Cl Sun, and Nov–Easter; (0191) 388 3295; free. The Chester Moor Inn (A167 S) has good value food.

CHEVIOT HILLS NT9716 Part of the Northumberland National Park, the Cheviots are strikingly empty and solitary, with only hardy upland sheep for company in most places – an area that suits walkers who really want to get away from other people.

CHILLINGHAM NU0525 **Chillingham Castle** Striking old castle dating back to 12th c, full of antiques, tapestries, arms and armour. Formal gardens, woodland walks, lake, and splendid views of the surrounding countryside; occasional concerts and special events. Brave souls can rent one of their haunted apartments (self-catering). Snacks, shop; cl am, Sat, and Oct–Apr; (01668) 215359; £4.50. The

Percy Arms at Chatton is good for lunch.

Chillingham Wild White Cattle Park ⊞ The famous large-horned white cattle have been here for the last 700 years, the only animals of their kind still pure and uncrossed with domestic breeds. As they're potentially aggressive, tours are led by a warden. Bring binoculars for a closer view. Shop; open Apr–Oct (exc 12–2, Sun am and Tues); (01668) 215250; £3. Above the park, Ross Castle hill fort has great views.

CHOLLERFORD NY9070 **Chesters Walled Garden (Hexham Herbs)** (B6318, nr Chesters) Over 800 varieties of herbs beautifully laid out in attractive walled gardens; also old-fashioned roses, many other plants, and woodland walk. Shop, plant sales, some disabled access; phone for winter opening times; (01434) 681483; £2.

CLENNEL STREET NT9207 This ancient drove road leading from Coquetdale is a good walking route into the Cheviots – lonely grassy moors (boggy in parts when it's wet), dry stone walls, sheep, dark conifer plantations. You can pick up the route nr Alwinton, and there's a pretty way back, along a track by the River Alwin.

CRASTER NU2519 A pleasant place to visit, with its tidal fishing harbour, good kippering factory, nice pub (the Jolly Fisherman), and magnificent clifftop walk to Dunstanburgh Castle. Just down the coast at Howick, the gardens of **Howick Hall** (former home of Earl Grey, not open) will interest gardeners; open Apr–Sept; (01665) 577285; £3.

DARLINGTON NZ2815 **Railway Centre & Museum** ⊞ Interesting museum in carefully restored North Rd Station, part of which is still used for train services. Exhibits inc Stephenson's *Locomotion* built in 1825, which pulled the first passenger steam train on a public railway. Snacks, shop, disabled access; cl 25–26 Dec and 1 Jan; (01325) 460532; £2.10. An extraordinary £760,000 **brickwork locomotive**, a 40-metre (130-ft) approximation of the pre-war record-breaking *Mallard* complete with clouds of bricky steam, lies beside Morrisons supermarket (Morton Park Way). In the centre, St Cuthbert's (Church Row) is an interesting Early English church, and Old Yard Tapas Bar (Bondgate) has decent food.

DURHAM NZ2742

The ancient core of the town stands on a crag defended by an almost complete loop of the River Wear, with a rewarding riverside path going from Prebends Bridge up to South St (with some of the best views of the cathedral's magnificent pinnacled towers), recrossing the river by Framwellgate bridge. The old part of town, already largely pedestrianised, is becoming even more pedestrian-friendly, with a new £2 charge on vehicles entering its citadel core (daytime exc Sun). It has attractive cobbled alleys and narrow medieval lanes, and fine medieval buildings among the Georgian and later ones, particularly around the 12th-c pedestrians-only Elvet Bridge (comfortably overlooked by the big-windowed Swan & Three Cygnets). There are several medieval churches, and interesting little shops. You can hire rowing boats nr Elvet Bridge, which is also the departure point for launches; (0191) 386 9525. The Millennium City, a £29 million development at the bottom of Claypath, includes a theatre, visitor and tourist information centre, craft workshops, and an IMAX-style giant-screen rundown on the city's past, plus a large public square. Work is starting on redeveloping the adjacent Walkergate area into a new leisure quarter (inc multiplex cinema, lots of bars, cafés and restaurants). Ghostly guided walks leave from outside the tourist information centre at various times throughout the summer – phone to check (0191) 386 1500. The bus service linking station, coach and car parks to the cathedral now runs more frequently. Bistro 21 out at Aykley Heads (off B6532 N) and the Seven Stars just out at Shincliffe are our firm food recommendations (see *Where to eat*), and the Court Inn and Cathedral's cafés (both Court Lane) are also useful for decent food all day exc Sun.

Crook Hall & Gardens 🏛

(Frankland Lane, Sidegate) Medieval manor surrounded by delightful themed gardens, with fine views of the castle and cathedral; you can look into their eerie Jacobean room, and they've a summer maze. Special events such as Easter egg hunts and ghost tours. Teas in the pretty courtyard; open pm Sun–Fri Easter–Sept; (0191) 384 8028; £3.80.

DLI Museum & Durham Art Gallery (Aykley Heads, just off B6532) This incorporates a museum with imaginative displays on Durham's illustrious light infantry regiment, as well as a gallery with unusual changing exhibitions. Snacks, shop, disabled access; cl 25 Dec; (0191) 384 2214; £2.50.

Durham Castle Developed from an early Norman motte and bailey. Still a proud building, with original chapel and 13th-c great hall, it's now used for university accommodation, and you can stay here. Shop; guided tours daily (usually every 30 mins in summer, less frequently in winter) – phone to check; (0191) 374 3800; £3.

Durham Cathedral Huge, and probably England's finest, a fiercely beautiful and unusually well preserved Norman building, breathtaking and very masculine inside; it was the first in Britain to use pointed arches. St Cuthbert's shrine is here, and they say that the Lady Chapel owes its odd position at the W end to his hatred of women; every time they tried to build it in the right place his spirit apparently caused the foundations to collapse. Try to spot the unique bronze knocker that seems to have a cheery grin. Rare books and manuscripts in the 15th-c monks' dormitory, and an exhibition on the cathedral's 900-year history. Meals, snacks, shop, disabled access; monks' dormitory open Mon–Sat, Sun pm Apr–Sept (80p), Treasury cl Sun am (£2), tower cl Sun, during services and inclement weather (£2); entry to the cathedral is free, but a donation of £3.50 is suggested. The close behind the cathedral has some handsome old houses (a shame about the cars).

Finchale Priory (3m NE, minor rd off A167) St Godric chose this site in 1110 as a place to meditate, and it's still a pleasant spot for contemplation, beside the graceful ruins of the 13th-c church. Snacks, shop, mostly disabled access; cl Oct–Mar; (0191) 386 3828; £1.40.

Houghall College Gardens (Shincliffe Rd) The county's main horticultural training centre, with ten acres of hardy plants, a water garden, woodland garden, alpine rock garden, parterre and arboretum. This area records some of the lowest temperatures in the country, so if it grows here, it'll grow anywhere. Snacks (some days), plant sales, disabled access; cl 25–26 Dec, but best to check; (0191) 386 1351; free.

Oriental Museum 🖼 (Elvet Hill) Exceptional collections of everything from ceramics, carvings, and paintings to costumes and mummies; also an activity room and Chinese gallery. Snacks, shop, disabled access; cl over Christmas and New Year; (0191) 374 7911; £1.50.

St Mary le Bow Church (The Bailey) The heritage centre here has exhibitions on the city's history, and you can have a go at brass rubbing. Shop, some disabled access; cl am (exc July–Aug), wkdys (exc bank hols) in Apr, May, and Oct and all Nov–Mar; (0191) 384 5589; £1 charge for brass rubbing.

University Botanic Garden (Hollingside Lane) Hugely enjoyable 18-acre garden in mature woodland with exotic trees from America and the Himalayas, tropical house, cactus house and visitor centre, and unusual sculpture garden. Snacks, plant sales, disabled access; cl over Christmas and New Year; (0191) 374 2671; £1.50.

University Museum of Archaeology On the river bank below the cathedral's SW corner, a former fulling mill with finds from the city and surrounding area. Snacks, shop; cl Tues–Thurs Nov–Mar, and 2 wks over Christmas; (0191) 374 3623; £1.

EGGLESTON NY9923

Eggleston Hall Gardens 🖼 A good example of an updated 19th-c country-house garden, with rare and unusual trees, shrubs, perennials and other plants. You can look around the early 17th-c chapel ruins, with photographs showing what it used to look like – a most tranquil place. They sell plants,

organically grown herbs, and fruit and vegetables from the walled kitchen garden. Summer meals, snacks, shop, some disabled access; (01833) 650115; £1. The sloping moorside village is attractive; the Rose & Crown at Romaldkirk is the best nearby place for lunch.

EMBLETON NU2522

Dunstanburgh Castle Screeching gulls add to the atmosphere at these huge ruins, standing imposingly on the cliff above the North Sea. Turner painted the scene three times. Snacks, small shop; cl 1–2pm, and Mon and Tues Nov–Mar, 24–26 Dec, 1 Jan; (01665) 576231; £2; EH (NT members also free). The Dunstanburgh Castle Hotel does good meals. The NT owns much of this stretch of coastline, inc the pleasantly bracing walk to Craster – one of the finest sections of the Northumbrian coast path.

ETAL NT9239

Pretty row of white cottages running down to a ford across the river, with a working forge and pleasant thatched pub, the Black Bull.

Etal Castle Good Walkman tours guide you round these evocative 14th-c ruins; also exhibition on Border history. Shop, disabled access to exhibition area; cl Nov–Mar; (01890) 820332; £2.80; EH.

FORD NT9338

Built as an estate-workers' model village, for Ford Castle; very attractive, with one or two craft workshops, a well restored working corn mill (cl Oct–Mar; (01890) 820338; £2.50), and the friendly Heatherslaw Bakery making good use of the resulting corn.

Heatherslaw Light Railway Steam journeys on narrow-gauge railway to Etal, along pretty valley of the River Till. Snacks, shop, disabled access; cl Nov–Mar; (01890) 820244 for times; £5 return.

Lady Waterford Hall Well worth a look: used till 1957 as the village school, with murals showing the village children and their families as characters from well known Bible stories; cl 12.30–1.30pm, and Nov–Mar (exc by appointment); (01890) 820503; £1.75.

GATESHEAD NZ2162

This previously much-maligned town is

getting a boost from the exciting regeneration projects currently taking shape on its quayside; a good new visitor centre in 13th-c St Mary's church (Oakwellgate) will tell you more about the development and history of the quay, and there's also a craft gallery. The monumental **Baltic Centre for Contemporary Arts** is now open, and work on the Norman Foster-designed £60 million music centre, the Stage, is set to be completed in 2003. The graceful curved steel and aluminium **Millennium Bridge**, working like a giant eyelid blinking up to form an arch under which ships pass, links Gateshead with Newcastle. The **Metro Centre** (A1 just W) is a useful rainy-day outing, a vast modern shopping and leisure complex with several different themed covered areas, all sorts of fairground attractions (better for younger children than teenage thrill seekers), even a Roman Catholic church. Don't forget where you put your car – there are 12,000 parking spaces. In the town itself, the **Shipley Art Gallery** (Prince Consort Rd) is worth a look (cl am Sun; free), the Keelmans riverside walk (off South Shore Rd) is quite pleasant.

Angel of the North (towering over the A1) With a 54-metre (177-ft) wing span and 20 metres high, it is the tallest sculpture in the country, and is seen by around 90,000 motorists each day. For a more peaceful view, use the Angel View Hotel (A167, Low Eighton).

Baltic Centre for Contemporary Arts (Quayside) In the gargantuan frame of a derelict 1940s grain warehouse (Rank Hovis who built it named their mills after various seas), this major contemporary arts centre – the biggest of its kind outside the capital – is one of the focal points of Gateshead's quayside regeneration. It aims to be not so much another art gallery, but a place for artists to work in, with various exhibitions inc the cavernous 'high art gallery', lit naturally from above. It houses a range of changing exhibitions (see their website www.balticmill.com) from giant sculpture to performance art. The centre also has lecture theatres, workshops, and a library, a café,

bookshop and rooftop restaurant. Open daily; (0191) 478 1810; free (exc special exhibitions).

HADRIAN'S WALL NY7868
An amazing sight, if you've never seen it before. It's extraordinary to imagine those Roman military engineers, so far from their warm homeland, building this remarkable construction through such inhospitable surroundings. Many of its 73½ miles run along the natural hard rock ridge of the great craggy Whin Sill, making it that much more formidable; the overall sense of grandeur is a definite part of the appeal. The stone Wall itself, with its turret watchtowers, milecastles and more sporadic forts, defines the N side of a narrow frontier zone, bounded on its S side by an equally remarkable ditch between turf ramparts; a military road runs between wall and ditch. It was this whole installation rather than just the Wall which the Romans used to control trade and cross-border travel. The B6318 following the military road is a fine drive, with some of the best views of the Wall. This road also gives walkers easy access to the line of the Wall, with numerous car parks on the way. There's not a lot of point trying to make walks into circuits: all the interest is along the Wall itself, although in places you may prefer to drop down beneath the switchback Whin Sill, which itself can be quite tiring. The views are bleak and exhilarating. Even in fine summer weather the wind can be chilly on the Wall, so go well wrapped up. English Heritage have been cutting back on the publicity for some sites – thousands of marauding tourists have caused more damage than centuries of harsh weather and unstable politics ever managed. However, an environmentally friendly path will let you follow the Wall from beginning to end. In summer a tourist bus runs between Hexham and several of the main sites (and even as far as Carlisle), and you can get on or off at any of the stages along the way; check with the information centre on (01434) 652220 for times. See also the elaborate Segedunum, in Wallsend. The best place to eat nr the main sites is the Milecastle Inn on the B6318 NE of Haltwhistle.

Birdoswald Roman Fort 🖪
NY6166 (Gilsland) Overlooking the
Irthing Gorge (and in fact just over the
Cumbrian border), this is one of the
most impressive sites on Hadrian's
Wall, partly because it has so many
features in such a small area, and partly
for its grand views; good visitor centre.
Snacks, shop, some disabled access;
visitor centre cl Nov–Feb; (01697)
747602; £3.

Carrawbrough Mithraic Temple
NY8571 Three 3rd-c altars to Mithras
were found here, on the line of the
Roman wall nr the fort of Brocolitia.
They're now in Newcastle's Museum of
Antiquities, but you can see replicas in
their original setting.

Cawfield Crags NY7166 One of the
best-preserved sections of the Wall.

Chesters Roman Fort NY9170
(B6318, slightly W of Chollerford) The
best-preserved example of a Roman
cavalry fort in Britain, in an attractive
riverside setting. In the bath house you
can see exactly how the underfloor
heating system worked, and a museum
has sculptures and inscriptions from
here and other sites. Summer snacks,
shop, some disabled access; cl 24–26
Dec, 1 Jan; (01434) 681379; £3; EH. The
Hadrian Hotel at Wall (A6076 S) has
good value food.

Corbridge Roman Site NY9864
(slightly NW) Granaries, portico
columns and what may be the legionary
HQ survive among these 3rd-c remains.
The adjacent museum has the
magnificent Corbridge Lion. Shop,
limited disabled access; cl 1–2 pm and
Mon and Tues Nov–Mar; (01434)
632349; £2.70; EH. The village, above
the Tyne, is attractive; the Angel, Black
Bull (popular all-day Sun lunch) and
Wheatsheaf are all good for lunch, and
Brocksbushes Farm (2m E) has **pick-
your-own** fruit and a farm shop;
(01434) 633400.

Cuddys Crag NY7567 Perhaps the
most beautiful section of the Wall, very
photogenic and giving glorious views.

Greenhead Roman Army Museum
NY6767 (Carvoran) Entertaining and
informative intrepretation of what it
was like to be a Roman soldier, with
everything you could possibly want to
know about his training, pay, and off-

duty hobbies. Snacks, shop, disabled
access; cl mid-Nov to mid-Feb; (01697)
747485; £3.10.

Housesteads Roman Fort and
Museum NY7969 (B6318) The best-
known and most visited section of the
Wall (and also one of the best
preserved), pretty much slap bang in
the middle. It owes its fine state of
preservation partly to the fact that
while other stretches were being used
as a handy source of free recycled
quality masonry, this fort was base
camp for a powerful group of Border
bandits; woe betide anyone who tried
to use their fortifications as material for
cowsheds or churches. A museum has
altars, inscriptions and models, and
there are good walks in either
direction. Snacks, shop; cl 24–26 Dec, 1
Jan; (01434) 344363; £3; EH.

Once Brewed National Park
Centre NY7567 Very useful
Northumberland National Park
Information Centre, handy for
Housesteads and Vindolanda, with
exhibitions and audio-visual
presentations. Guided walks leave from
here (though not every day). Snacks,
shop, disabled access; cl wkdys Nov to
mid-Mar; (01434) 344396; free; EH. The
walk from here to Housesteads offers
some of the best views of the Wall; it's
only 3 miles but its ups and downs can
take up to 2⅓ hours.

Segedunum NZ3066 (Buddle
St/Station Rd, Wallsend) A lot bigger
than any of the other museums along
Hadrian's Wall, these well put together
displays give an excellent idea of
everyday life in the fort that once stood
here, and take an intriguing look at how
the site developed over the centuries
that followed. The remains of this great
terminal fort lay buried under Victorian
housing until the 1970s, after which
they were excavated more thoroughly
than just about any other site in the
Empire: you can see plenty of the finds.
The most striking feature of the
complex is the spectacular 35-metre
(115-ft) viewing tower, which
superimposes virtual reality
reconstructions on the actual
excavations. Another unique feature is
a completely functional reconstructed
Roman bath house. Elsewhere are

videos, more reconstructions, and plenty of hands-on and touch-screen activities. There are also galleries on mining (there was once a colliery here) and shipbuilding (Swan Hunter are based next door). Children under 6 aren't going to be engaged for long, but older ones can be happily distracted for an hour or two, particularly if they learned about the Romans at school. Snacks, shop, disabled access; cl 25–26 Dec, 1 Jan; (0191) 295 5757; £3.50.

Vindolanda NY7766 Started well before the Wall itself, this Roman fort and frontier town soon became a base for 500 soldiers. Full-scale reconstructions, lots of well preserved remains, and further excavations in progress (weather permitting Sun–Fri Apr–Aug). The adjacent museum has a fascinating selection of hand-written letters and documents found on the site, inc party invitations, shopping lists and a note that could have been written by many a modern mother: 'I have sent you socks and two pairs of underpants'. Meals, snacks, shop, disabled access to museum but not site; cl Tues–Thurs mid-Nov to mid-Feb; (01434) 344277; £4.

Walltown Crags NY6766 One of the best-preserved sections of the Wall.

HAMSTERLEY NZ1231

Hamsterley Forest 5,000-acre fellside forest with good walks, cycle routes, four-mile forest drive, and visitor centre with local wildlife exhibitions and a tearoom. Meals, snacks, shop, disabled access; cl Nov–Mar; (01388) 488312; forest drive around £2 a car. The Cross Keys at Hamsterley is a useful base.

HARTLEPOOL NZ5132

The re-created 18th-c **Historic Quay** (see *separate family panel on p.442*) and stylish next-door Jacksons Landing factory shopping mall (The Marina, with decent food in its Highlight pub) are tourist landmarks in the town's wholesale regeneration – half a billion pounds spent since 1993. The historic Headland area with its medieval town wall remains and Abbey Church is benefiting from careful restoration thanks to lottery funding (the Harbour of Refuge up here, with great coast views, does nice lunches inc local fish).

The town centre is becoming much more a place to visit, with plenty of bars, restaurants and some interesting shops around Church St. Just S, there are miles of clean sandy beaches backed by dunes around the low-key resort of Seaton Carew.

HMS *Trincomalee* (Jackson Dock) This well restored frigate is the oldest ship afloat in Britain; you can climb aboard, and the re-created rooms (watch out for the low ceilings) give a good idea of what life must have been like almost two centuries ago; there's an audio-guide, a children's trail, and they do guided tours. Shop, mostly disabled access (not to the hold); cl 25–26 Dec, 1 Jan; (01429) 223193; £3.70.

Museum of Hartlepool & PSS *Wingfield Castle* (The Marina) Excellent local history, with something of a maritime emphasis; the well restored 1934 paddle steamer *Wingfield Castle* is used in part as a café. Shop, disabled access; cl 25–26 Dec, 1 Jan; (01429) 222255; free.

HEXHAM NY9364

A pleasant market town, not too big, with some attractive stone buildings. The Tap & Spile (Eastgate) does filling lunchtime food.

Border History Museum Formerly the country's first purpose-built prison; colourfully charts the chequered contacts between the English and Scots. Shop; open daily Apr–Oct, then Mon–Tues and Sat only Nov, Feb–Mar; (01434) 652349; £2.

Hexham Abbey Founded around 674 by St Wilfrid, once the largest church N of the Alps. The bulk of what is seen today dates from the 12th c, though there are two splendid Saxon survivals – the superbly atmospheric crypt, and the throne of the Bishop (St Wilfrid's Chair or Frith stool). The choir still descend the unique Night Stairs for services. Summer snacks, shop, disabled access; cl Good Fri; free, but £3 suggested donation.

Warden church (just N) Down a lane by the Tyne, this is a fine example of the sturdy northern churches that had to do double duty as holy places and watch-towers to warn of Border raiders.

HIGH FORCE NY8828

High Force waterfall England's most powerful waterfall, this drops into a craggy cauldron at the end of a striking wooded gorge – though you'll have to pay (on top of parking) for the short path from the B6277 for the best view. From Bowlees Visitor Centre you can make more of a walk of it, first detouring N to Gibson's Cave, a pretty waterfall at the top of a gorge, and then heading S to cross the Tees for an easy two miles upriver, passing Low Force on the way. The nearby High Force Hotel has decent food (and the highest brewery in England).

HORNCLIFFE NT9450

Chain Bridge Honey Farm Over 1,000 colonies of bees, a good visitor centre, and honey-based products for sale. Limited disabled access with notice; cl am Sun, wknds Nov–Mar, and around 2 wks over Christmas; (01289) 386362; free.

JARROW NZ3365

Bede's World The Venerable Bede lived here for most of his 7th/8th-c life, producing the 37 books that encompass much of what is known of life in early Christian England. Along with the other half of the monastery, St Peter's, at nearby Monkwearmouth, the site is still a major Christian shrine. Very little remains of the original monastery, but there's Saxon stained glass in the church, and the chancel incorporates one of the earlier chapels. A museum in adjacent Georgian Jarrow Hall has finely carved Anglo-Saxon stones, more stained glass, and excavated relics. There's an authentically re-created 11-acre period farm, and a herb garden too. Meals, snacks, shop, some disabled access; cl Sun am and Good Fri, phone for Christmas opening; (0191) 489 2106; £4.50.

KIELDER WATER NY6293

This huge reservoir has done a lot to open up a remote part of the Borders; an attractive drive from Bellingham. It's an interesting shape, modelled by the steep folds of the land, and already looks as if it's always been tucked away in these pine-blanketed hills. You can hire rowing boats for around £8 an hour (01434) 250217. Visitor centres supply fishing permits for the lake, and

you can rent **log cabins** around it by the week; (01502) 500500.

Bakethin Conservation Area Up at the top of the Water, this is particularly rewarding for wildlife.

Kielder Castle Visitor Centre This 18th-c hunting lodge built for the Duke of Northumberland is now a very good Forest Enterprise visitor centre, with exhibitions, closed-circuit TV bird-watching, a sculpture trail and a play area. Meals, shop, disabled access; cl wkdys Nov–Christmas, then daily till Easter; (01434) 250209; free. Regular guided walks from here into the great surrounding tract of Kielder Forest – miles of pine trees with a chance of seeing red squirrels, as well as deer. There are also self-guided walks (easy to follow) from half a dozen or more points along the road through, and from the remote 12-mile toll drive right across to the Redesdale Forest. The Pheasant at Stannersburn has good food.

Kielder cycling The forest surrounding Kielder Water has been well developed for cycling – the very friendly Kielder Bikes Company [bike] hire bikes from Kielder Castle (not Fri out of season), and are good for repairs too; cl Christmas and at other times for staff holidays; (01434) 250392; a good mountain bike costs £17.50 a day.

Leaplish Waterside Park (slightly round to the W) Another good starting point for Kielder Water, with lots to do in summer, inc plenty of walks and cycle trails, mini golf and a swimming pool. Restaurant and bar, shop, disabled access; (01434) 250312; park free, charges for some activities.

Tower Knowe Visitor Centre Down at the foot of the Water, with an exhibition and useful information about the area and its wildlife. Meals, snacks, shop, disabled access; cl Nov–Mar; (01434) 240398; free. **Cruises** start from here too, and call all around the lake (takes about 90 mins); £5.

LANCHESTER NZ1244

Hall Hill Farm (B6296 SW) Friendly working farm with lots of animals, riverside walk and trailer rides. Snacks, shop; usually cl wkdys Sept–Oct and all Nov–Mar exc Santa wknds in Dec – though best to check; (01388) 730300; £3.50. The Queens Head is good for food.

LANGLEY PARK NZ2145
Diggerland 🏛 (Riverside Industrial Estate) Another in this unusual chain of adventure parks where children from 5 up can operate and drive real excavation equipment. Meals, snacks, shop, disabled access; open daily during school hols and wknds and bank hols only in term time (cl 25 Dec); (08700) 344437; £2.50 to enter, from £1.50 per ride or drive.

LINDISFARNE NU1242
Otherwise known as Holy Island, this important centre for Christian pilgrims is linked to the mainland by a causeway which you can drive (or walk) over at low tide. Tide tables are posted at each end, or phone (01289) 330733; it really is worth checking these carefully – the causeway is impassable for around two hours before high tide and four hours after. If you want to visit a particular attraction, make sure that the tide and the opening times match on the day you want to go. There are nature-reserve dunes, fishermen's huts made of upturned former boats, old lime-kilns, a small extended village with tourist cafés and pubs (the Ship has good value food inc local seafood), and good views from the close-grazed grassy crags. The 3-mile walk around the island's shores is easy but fascinating.

Lindisfarne Castle The rather lonely and austere exterior belies what's within; the 16th-c fortress was restored by Lutyens for the editor of *Country Life* in a suitably monolithic quasi-medieval style. Sumptuous furnishings include a fine collection of antique oak furniture, and there's a walled garden designed by Gertrude Jekyll to protect against the North Sea winds. Cl Fri (exc Good Fri), and Nov–Mar, but varies according to tides; (01289) 389244; £4.20; NT. It's a mile's walk fom the car park.

Lindisfarne Priory From here St Aidan and monks from Iona replanted the seeds of Christianity in 7th-c England. These early monks were driven out by Vikings, so it's the extensive remains of a later 12th-c church you can see today; a very peaceful and romantic spot, with graceful red sandstone arches bordered by incongruously neat lawns. Shop, disabled access to visitor centre; cl

24–26 Dec, and 1 Jan; (01289) 389200; £3.

St Aidan's Winery Home of Lindisfarne Mead, a fortified wine made from grapes, honey, herbs, and water from an artesian well. They make preserves too, and the shop has British beers, ciders and cheeses, as well as local pottery and jewellery. Snacks, shop; cl 25 Dec–1 Jan, and other times according to tide – best to phone; (01289) 389230; free.

LONGFRAMLINGTON NZ1199
Brinkburn Priory Well preserved 12th-c church (thanks to unusually restrained Victorian restoration), still with medieval grave slabs, font and double piscina; occasional services and concerts. Shop, some disabled access; open Apr–Oct; (01665) 570628; £1.70; EH. The Granby has good food.

LOW NEWTON NU2325
A charming seaside village on a fine stretch of little-visited coast, with a sloping square of old cottages facing a spectacular seascape above the beach and its off-shore seal rocks, and a **bird reserve** nearby. The Ship has good snacks.

MARSDEN NZ3964
Grotto (A183) The Grotto here is unique: a lift (or 100 or so steps) down to a pub cut into the seaside cliffs.

MATFEN NZ0370
One of the prettiest inland villages in Northumbria, carefully laid out in the 18th c around a riverside village green.

MORPETH NZ2086
The clock tower here is one of only eight non-church bell towers in Britain, and still rings the curfew some nights. The Tap & Spile (Eastgate), open all day, has good value food.

Morpeth Chantry Bagpipe Museum 🏛 (Bridge St) Harmonious collection of small pipes and bagpipes from around the world. Headphones explain the difference between a rant and a reel. Shop; usually cl Sun (exc in Dec), Easter Sun and Mon, and 25–26 Dec; (01670) 519466; free. Good craft centre next door with occasional demonstrations (open same as museum).

NEWCASTLE UPON TYNE NZ2563
This big industrial conurbation is far from being conventionally pretty, but

has a strong personality and lively, heady atmosphere – and several excellent free museums. Its best parts are grouped very compactly high above the River Tyne with its seven great bridges – the city's trademark is the majestic arch of the Tyne bridge, the largest bridge of its kind when it opened in 1928. The Metro system makes it quick and straightforward to get around, and to the attractions noted under North and South Shields, Tynemouth and Whitley Bay; a one-day Day Rover ticket (available from stations or the Tourist Information Centre) costs £3.90 and is good for all Metro trips and the ferry between North and South Shields). You can still trace some stretches of the medieval **city wall**, especially from St Andrew's Church along the cobbled lane W of Stowell St – the city's Chinatown – and past the Heber Tower along Bath Lane. Steep alleys and steps lead from the centre down to The Quay, the oldest part of town, with several unexpected and quaintly attractive timber-framed medieval buildings; one of the oldest, the Cooperage, is a decent pub, and a good warehouse conversion here is the Quayside. Downstream, E of the Tyne Bridge, an area of refurbished warehouses provides an enjoyable stroll, with a traditional market on Sun, and a useful pub for food – the Bonded Warehouse. This quayside area has been rejuvenated, with impressive developments taking shape on the other side of the river, too. Another stylish quayside warehouse conversion, the Waterline (by New Law Courts) has good food, as does the Fog on the Tyne overlooking St Peter's Basin marina. Besides the pubs mentioned above, the handsome Crown Posada (The Side, off Dean St), the Duke of Wellington (High Bridge) and the imposing Union Rooms (Westgate Rd) are pleasantly civilised, and the Free Trade (St Lawrence Rd, off A186) has awesome river views.
Bessie Surtees House (Sandhill) Well renovated timbered Jacobean house, with elaborate plaster ceilings and carved panelling. Cl wknds, bank hols, 24–26 Dec, and 1 Jan; (0191) 269 1200; free; EH.

Centre for Life 🈯 (Times Sq) In a dramatic building beside the city's main railway station, this innovative visitor centre explores the origins of life. You'd think anywhere setting out to explain DNA in an accessible way would be on to a loser, but the main exhibition areas put across serious science in a surprisingly entertaining way. A visit starts with the River of Life, a trip back through billions of years of evolution, tracing how mankind has got to where we are today. One highlight is the Crazy Motion ride, a simulator ride designed to make you feel you're surfing, roller-blading, and even bungee-jumping, and among numerous other interactive attractions is the chance to score against a virtual goalie. A live show in the Secret of Life explains what we have in common with everything from dinosaurs to daffodils, and a multi-media spectacle (shown in a theatre resembling a giant brain) aims to illustrate the range of emotions and activities going on in our heads. Meals, snacks, shop, disabled access; cl 25 Dec and 1 Jan; (0191) 243 8223; *£6.95.
Discovery Museum (Blandford Sq) Thriving complex with galleries and interactive features on subjects likely to appeal to the whole family – it's the biggest and busiest museum in the area. A highlight is the interactive Science Maze with plenty to push, press and poke: TV effects create the illusion of flying down the Tyne, there's a soft play area for very young children, and lots of mirrors, magnets and microscopes to fiddle with. Other galleries offer a similarly hands-on look at the history of the city, with displays on fashion, shipbuilding, and local inventors. Don`t miss the remarkable 30-metre (100-ft) *Turbinia*, once the fastest ship afloat. A £12 million project to refurbish galleries and add new exhibitions should be completed in 2004 (parts might be closed till then). Family fun days every Sun, and during the Easter and summer hols. Meals, snacks, shop, disabled access; cl am Sun, Good Fri, 25–26 Dec, 1 Jan; (0191) 232 6789; free.
Hancock Museum (Barras Bridge) Very good natural history museum, with magnificent traditional collections of stuffed birds and mammals, as well as

Egyptology displays, fossils and minerals; lively temporary exhibitions, and plenty for children. Snacks, shop, disabled access; cl am Sun, 25–26 Dec, and 1 Jan; (0191) 222 7418; £2.50.

Laing Art Gallery (New Bridge St) Notable temporary exhibitions, and excellent children's gallery, the activities well designed to encourage young children to think about shapes, texture and patterns. Free guided tours of the main galleries 11.30 Sat. Meals, snacks, shop, disabled access; cl Sun am, Good Fri, 25–26 Dec, and 1 Jan; (0191) 232 7734; free.

Military Vehicle Museum 🖼 (Exhibition Park Pavilion, just off B6388 by A167(M)/B1318 interchange) Around 50 military vehicles mostly dating from before 1945, plus a World War I trench and Anderson air raid shelter, dioramas and lots of World War I and World War II memorabilia. It's in the only remaining pavilion of the 1929 North-East Coast Exhibition, erected using the principles used in shipbuilding at the time; an interesting structure – designed to stand for six months, it's lasted for over 70 years. Shop, disabled access; cl wkdys Nov–Mar, and Aug bank hol Sun and Mon; (0191) 281 7222; £2.

Museum of Antiquities (The University) Particularly good on Roman remains, with reconstructions of various points along Hadrian's Wall. The displays are organised in a very user-friendly fashion. Shop, disabled access with notice; cl Sun, Good Fri, 24–26 Dec, 1 Jan; (0191) 222 7846; free.

Newcastle Castle This is the building which gave the city its name; much still remains – it's one of the finest surviving examples of a Norman keep and chapel in Britain. Panoramic views from the roof, and there's a small museum inside. Shop; usually cl 24–26 Dec, and 1 Jan; (0191) 232 7938; £1.50.

Newcastle Cathedral This 14th/15th-c cathedral, dedicated to St Nicholas, is worth a look; a dramatic stone sculpture occupies the Chapel of the Incarnation. Refectory open wkdy lunchtimes only, shop (cl Sun), disabled access; cl pm Sun; free.

NORHAM NT9148
Norham Castle A key fortress commanding a ford over the Tweed, this has some interesting Tudor masonry, and was used by Scott as the setting for *Marmion*; the ruins high over the river dominate this pleasant border village, whose church was founded by a bishop of Lindisfarne in 830. Snacks, shop; open Apr–Oct; (01289) 382329; £1.90; EH.

NORTH SHIELDS NZ3568
Wet 'n' Wild (Royal Quays) Children like this well heated indoor water park, with exciting flumes and slides (one has a very steep drop). Meals, snacks, disabled access; cl 25–27 Dec and 1 Jan; (0191) 296 1333; £7.25.

NORTHUMBERLAND COAST NU2615
This has much to interest walkers along its sandy and rocky shores, but the hinterland is rather dull, so it's better for pottering and for there-and-back walks than for round ones. A coast path covers the finest sections, which we pick out individually on the map.

PETERLEE NZ4338
Castle Eden Dene Nature Reserve The biggest of Durham's wooded coastal ravines, now a picturesque nature reserve with 12 miles of footpaths over 550 acres; free.

PONTELAND NZ1577
Kirkley Hall Gardens (2m N towards Morpeth) Attractive and thoughtfully maintained, with big collection of herbaceous perennials, Victorian walled garden, pretty sunken garden, woodland garden and unusual trees and shrubs. Plant sales, disabled access; phone for opening times over Christmas; (01661) 860808; free. On the other side of Ponteland, the Badger (A696 SE) has decent food all day, with good disabled access (and a next-door garden centre).

PRUDHOE NZ0963
Prudhoe Castle 12th/14th-c ruined castle on an impressive mound (the name means 'proud hill') overlooking the Tyne, once the stronghold of the powerful Percy family. Remarkable restored gatehouse, and exhibition in nearby 19th-c manor house. Snacks, shop, disabled access; (01661) 833459; cl Nov–Mar; £1.90; EH. The Feathers at Hedley on the Hill does good wknd and evening food.

Stephenson's Birthplace (Wylam)
The single room open here is the NT's
least visited property; tearoom; open
Thurs, Sat, Sun, Good Fri and bank hol
Mon pms Apr–Oct; (01661) 853457;
80p. The Fox & Hounds (a short walk
along the old railway track) and
Boathouse (open all day, impromptu Sat
afternoon music sessions) have good
value food.

ROSS BACK SANDS NU1339
One of the finest sections of the
Northumbrian coast path – splendid
windswept solitude, looking out to
Holy Island.

ROTHBURY NY9799
Coquetdale Northumberland's most
scenic drive is the B6344 following the
river past Brinkburn Priory to
Rothbury, then W on the B6341 past
Hepple, then turning right on the
unclassified road past Holystone and
Alwinton. Picturesque walks around
Holystone (where the Salmon is a useful
stop), increasingly desolate up towards
Blindburn.
Cragside Opulent Victorian mansion
of Lord Armstrong, the armaments
king, with spectacular rooms and some
of the amazing gadgets he designed.
Best of all are the miles of well wooded
landscaped grounds, with lakes,
rhododendrons (glorious in Jun), showy
formal garden, and a walk illustrating
the various elements of the hydro-
electric scheme he devised to light the
house; there's also a children's play
area. Meals, snacks, shop, some
disabled access; house open pm
Tues–Sun and bank hols Apr–2 Nov,
estate and gardens open all day
Tues–Sun and bank hol Apr–2 Nov, and
Weds–Sun 5 Nov–21 Dec; (01669)
620333; £7.20, £4.80 grounds only; NT.
The Newcastle Hotel (open all day) has
good value food inc Apr–Oct high teas.
Nearby the Rothbury Terraces are
excellent for gentle parkland walks.

ROWLANDS GILL NZ1456
Derwentcote Steel Furnace (A694
towards Hamsterley, where the Cross
Keys does good value food) The
earliest and most complete steel-
making furnace to have survived, with
an exhibition on steel production. Shop,
disabled access; open Suns Apr–Sept;
(01207) 562573; free. There are good

nearby forest walks.
SEAHOUSES NU2232
An unpretentious seaside resort, with
amusement arcades and so forth – and a
busy fishing harbour, overlooked by a
good interesting pub, the Olde Ship.
Farne Islands From Apr to Sept,
weather permitting, boat trips from
Seahouses let you see the eider ducks,
thousands of other seabirds, and grey
seals. Breeding season for the birds is
usually around May–July, though
perhaps a little later for the seals,
whose plaintive-voiced pups stay on
shore for only a few weeks. Most boats
cost £9. Landing on the NT-owned
islands is extra (from £3.20, £4.20
breeding times); there is a shrine to St
Cuthbert, who came here to die in 687.
The NT has a shop with information
about the islands on Main St, cl winter
Mon and Tues, and 25 Dec–Mar;
(01665) 721099.
**Marine Life Centre & Fishing
Museum** (Main St) This enthusiastic
museum looks at various aspects of the
fishing trade, with re-created scenes
from a fisherman's kitchen and cooper's
workshop to a smokehouse. You can
compare early and modern methods of
fishing, and follow the fortunes of the
Joan Dixon, a 9-metre (30-ft) local fishing
vessel; there's also a seawater
aquarium, a video, and an atmospheric
new gallery, the **Haunted Kingdom**,
which has some gruesome
reconstructions. Shop; open daily
Easter–end Oct; (01665) 721257; £3
museum or Haunted Kingdom, £5 both.
SEATON SLUICE NZ3276
Seaton Delaval 🔁 Vanbrugh's
Palladian masterpiece, a splendid design
of central porticoed main block and
massive outer wings. Not all the
interior has survived unscathed, and
much of the original park and grounds
has been submerged by surrounding
developments. Snacks; shop; open pm
Weds, Sun and bank hols May–Sept;
(0191) 237 1493; £3. The buildings
around the Norman **church** are
attractive, and the Waterford Arms nr
the low-key seafront does generous
fresh fish.
SHILDON NZ2326
**Timothy Hackworth Railway
Museum** (Hackworth Cl, just SE)

Restored home of early railway pioneer, with working steam locomotive in goods yard, and occasional passenger rides along 400 yds of original Stockton & Darlington track bed. Snacks, shop, limited disabled access; cl Mon (exc bank hols), Tues, and Nov–Easter; (01388) 777999; £2. The Flag & Whistle (Strand St) has enjoyable food.

SOUTH SHIELDS NZ3667

Arbeia Roman Fort (Baring St) Huge variety of remains and reconstructions of a fort gateway, a barrack block, and part of the commanding officer's house; there's also a museum with excellently displayed finds, and plenty for children to enjoy. Snacks, shop, some disabled access; cl Sun (exc pm Easter–Sept), 25–26 Dec, 1 Jan and Good Fri, phone to check; (0191) 456 1369; free, £1.50 for Time Quest (splendid hands-on archaeology exhibition). In a great beach-edge spot, the Littlehaven Hotel (River Dr) does good bar meals in its conservatory, and the Marsden Rattler (South Foreshore) is an enjoyable seafront bar complete with two original railway carriages.

Marsden Bay The **nature reserve** here gives one of the few good coastal walks in industrial Tyneside. The spectacular coast stretches 2½miles from Trow Rocks to Lizard Point; Marsden Rock's birds include colonies of kittiwakes and cormorants.

SPRINGWELL NZ2858

Bowes Railway On certain days throughout the summer, well restored steam trains tow passengers in brake vans as far as Blackham's Hill, where you can see two working electric-powered inclines designed by George Stephenson. The railway was developed to carry coal between local mines and on to Jarrow for shipment, and the centre itself houses many of these locomotives and coal waggons, in use until the last colliery closures in 1974. Snacks and shop when staff available; centre open Mon–Fri, trains in steam monthly Suns and some bank hol Mons in summer, phone to check; (0191) 416 1847; free (£2 on steam days). The Waggon (Galloping Green Rd, Eighton Banks), with a conservatory overlooking the old railway, has decent food.

STAINDROP NZ1221

Raby Castle Imposing fortress with Saxon origins; vast medieval hall, 14th-c kitchen, and dazzling octagonal drawing room, restored to its Victorian splendour. From the outside, where there are walled gardens and a deer park, it looks just as a castle ought to. Guided tours (wkdy ams; £7.50 inc tea). Meals, snacks, shop (selling oven-ready game and venison from the estate), disabled access to grounds only; open bank hol wknds Sat to following Weds, Weds and Sun only May and Sept, and Sun–Fri Jun–Aug, though best to check (castle open pm only); (01833) 660202; £5, £3 park and gardens only. The village is pretty. Up at Butterknowle the Malt Shovel has good value food, evenings and wknd lunchtimes.

STANNINGTON NZ1981

Whitehouse Farm Centre (2m N, towards Tranwell) Bustling place with a good variety of animals from chinchillas, snakes and mice to llamas, 15 different breeds of sheep, and a shire horse. In an under-cover area, children can touch lots of the smaller animals (often piglets, lambs and other baby animals here). Also soft play area, adventure playground, pedal tractors (50p for proper tractor rides), and activities such as candle-making and face-painting. A few craft stalls inc a blacksmith, candle-maker and embroiderer. Meals, snacks, shop, disabled access; cl Mon in term-time, wkdys Nov and Jan; (01670) 789998; £3.95. The Ridley Arms has good value family food all day.

STAWARD GORGE NY8063

Part of the Allen Banks estate (NT), with year-round access to the paths along the wooded River Allen – frequented by roe deer – and a ruined peel tower. The moorland Carts Bog Inn (A686E) has good food.

STOCKSFIELD NZ0762

Cherryburn (slightly E at Mickley) Well preserved 18th-c farm, the birthplace of artist and naturalist Thomas Bewick, with an exhibition on his life. A nice spot, with farm animals running about the yard, occasional craft demonstrations, and good valley views. Annual special event 1st May bank hol, traditional music or dance Sun pms.

Shop, some disabled access; cl am, all day Tues and Weds, and Nov–Mar; (01661) 843276; £3; NT. The Blue Bell (Mount Pleasant) has popular food.

STOCKTON-ON-TEES NZ4419
Green Dragon Museum (Theatre Yard) Local history displays, and a photograph gallery with changing exhibitions. Shop, some disabled access; cl Sun, bank hols, 25–26 Dec and 1 Jan; (01642) 393938; free. There's a railway heritage trail around town. Slightly E along the river, the surprisingly graceful Tees Barrage keeps polluted tidal water from mixing with water from the hills, moors and valleys, which it's hoped will stimulate water-sports in the area.

HM Bark *Endeavour* (Castlegate Quay) Full-size replica of Captain Cook's famous vessel with re-created cabins and exhibits from surgeons' knives to telescopes. Shop, disabled access to main exhibition area; usually cl Thurs–Sat Nov–Mar, but phone to check; (01642) 676844; £3.

Preston Hall Museum (A135 Stockton—Yarm) Very well constructed Victorian high st and various period rooms, plus working craftsmen, aviary, and woodland and riverside walks. Snacks, shop, disabled access to ground floor only; cl Sun am Oct–Mar, Good Fri, 25–26 Dec, and 1 Jan; (01642) 781184; £1.20. On the same site **Butterfly World** has a re-created jungle environment with hundreds of exotic butterflies flitting between the trees, rocks and waterfalls. Shop, disabled access; open Mar–Sept; (01642) 791414; £3.30. **Riverside cruises** on the Teeside *Princess* sail from here to Yarm; they take 3½ hours return and there's a bar and café on board (no cruises Mon all year, or Tues, Thurs, Fri Oct–Apr); £3.50 single, £6 return.

SUNDERLAND NZ3957
Monkwearmouth Station Museum (North Bridge St) As well as trains, the chance to play in a bus and explore a Victorian station. Snacks, shop, disabled access; cl Sun am, 25–26 Dec, and 1 Jan; (0191) 567 7075; free.

Mowbray Gardens ⊞ This Victorian park has a children's play area with giant chess pieces, sculpture trail and duck house. The **Sunderland Museum and Art Gallery** takes a lively look at the city's history. Themes range from shipbuilding to geology, and, not for the squeamish, in the natural history section you can find out about all the tiny creatures that live on our bodies and in our homes. Lots of interactive and hands-on displays; children can crawl down a mine shaft, touch fossils, and try on Victorian clothes. The art gallery contains quite a few works by Lowry, who often visited the town. The nearby **Winter Gardens** feature around 1,500 plants from different climate zones. Meals, snacks, shop, disabled access; cl 25 Dec and 1 Jan; (0191) 5532323; free. For good food in a welcoming contemporary setting, we'd recommend 11 Tavistock Place.

National Glass Centre ⊞ (Liberty Way) This dazzling place is a fascinating cross between gallery and factory visit. In a striking glass structure on a sloping site alongside the River Wear (you can walk along the glass roof, looking down on the exhibitions below), it focuses on how glass is made and used all around the world. You can watch glass-blowing demonstrations. The Kaleidoscope Gallery explores the more imaginative ways glass is used, from time-lapse photography to a hall of mirrors. Several exhibits are interactive, with computer displays, and there's a changing exhibition programme. Meals, snacks, good shop, disabled access; cl 25 Dec, 1 Jan; (0191) 515 5555; £5.

Roker church The interesting church was designed by leading members of the Arts and Crafts movement.

St Peter's church Sister church of St Paul's at Jarrow, its early years equally well documented by the Venerable Bede. Much of the original Saxon church still remains, inc the west wall and tower. A striking Colin Wilbourn sculpture outside commemorates the church's 7th-c founder Benedict Biscop.

TANFIELD NZ2057
Tanfield Railway (A6076) The world's oldest surviving railway, built in 1725 to carry coal to the Tyne. Steam trains still chuff along the route through a picturesque wooded valley, and you can get off by a wooden gorge spanned

by **Causey Arch**, the earliest railway bridge. There's a collection of locomotives, and they often have a blacksmith forging new parts for restoration work. Summer snacks, shop, disabled access; trains usually run every Sun and bank hol Mon, plus Weds and Thurs in summer hols; (0191) 388 7545 for timetable; fares from £4 (unlimited journeys). The friendly Peacock (Tanfield Lea) has decent food.

TEESDALE NY9425

The best of County Durham's scenery; the B6277 below its moors and on to Alston in Cumbria is one of the finest drives in England. Upper Teesdale has much of the best walking in the Durham Pennines, and is famous for its limestone flora, inc rare arctic alpine species and the unique Teesdale violet; Widdybank Fell is a National Nature Reserve. The attractive villages of Middleton-in-Teesdale, Romaldkirk (there's an esp distinguished church here), Eggleston and Cotherstone all have good pubs and inns. A side track with a reward at its end is to the cosy Strathmore Arms in Holwick (open all day, at least in season). There's good fishing on the river or the reservoirs above it, and fine landscapes all the way along.

TYNEMOUTH NZ3670

Blue Reef Aquarium (Grand Parade, Beaconsfield) The best bit of this enjoyable place is the spectacular coral reef – you can see sharks, stingrays and shoals of brightly coloured fish from the underwater tunnel; also hands-on rock pools, daily talks and feeding demonstrations, and regular special events. Meals, snacks, shop, disabled access; cl 25 Dec; (0191) 258 1031; £4.95.

Castle and Priory (Priors Park, Pier Rd) Evocative clifftop ruins, high above the Tyne estuary. Little remains of the once-rich 11th-c Benedictine priory beyond its stirring nave and chancel, and the spooky gravestones outside. Even less is left of the 11th/14th-c castle, but it's unusual to find two such ruins next to each other, and it's a great spot for picnics. Shop, disabled access; cl 1–2pm and Mon and Tues Nov–Mar, 24–26 Dec, 1 Jan; (0191) 257 1090; £2.20; EH. The Salutation (Front St) is

comfortable for lunch.

WARKWORTH NU2305

Hermitage Prettily placed a short way upstream, this 14th-c cell of retreat is cut into the sandstone cliff, with some crude wall carvings and a tiny vaulted chapel; usually on Weds, Sun and bank hols Apr–Sept a boat can take you; (01665) 711423; £1.70.

Warkworth Castle The main st of this quietly picturesque small town rises attractively from the riverside 12th-c Norman church with its finely vaulted chancel to the striking **castle** on its hill above the River Coquet. It's virtually complete, so wandering around the crooked passageways and dark staircases is wonderfully atmospheric. Events here were immortalised in Shakespeare's *Henry IV*. Shop, limited disabled access; cl 1–2pm and Mon and Tues Nov–Mar, plus 24–26 Dec, 1 Jan; (01665) 711423; £2.50; EH. The Masons Arms and Hermitage Hotel are good for lunch, there are one or two antiques shops, and this stretch of coast has some beautiful clean beaches.

WASHINGTON NZ3156

Washington Old Hall 🏛 (The Avenue) Well restored stone-built manor dating from the 12th c, for several hundred years the home of George Washington's family, though his ancestors had been established elsewhere (notably Sulgrave Manor in Northants) for quite a while by the time his great-grandfather emigrated to America. Re-created Jacobean rooms and garden, and an exhibition on the hall's spell as a tenement in the 19th c. Snacks, shop, disabled access to ground floor only; open Sun–Weds Apr–Oct; (0191) 416 6879; £3; NT. The unspoilt old village comes as a real surprise when you've penetrated the surrounding New Town. The Washington Arms is good value for lunch.

Wildfowl & Wetlands Trust (District 15, off A1231 E) 100 acres with hides, well laid out walks, adventure play area, and very good visitor centre. Some birds will feed from your hand (you can buy birdseed). Meals, snacks, shop, disabled access; cl 25 Dec; (0191) 416 5454; £5.20.

WEARDALE NY8242

This gave much of County Durham's

wealth, with lead- and iron-mining along its length and in the moors above. There's little reminder of those days now (the last big quarry, a cement works, has just closed), but the A689 is a memorable drive. A **riding centre** at Low Cornriggs Farm has lessons, guided rides along scenic former packhorse routes; (01388) 537089; also farmhouse B&B (01388) 537600. Along the dale is a string of attractive villages such as Wolsingham (good value food at the Black Bull), as well as pleasant waterside and moorland walks. The Golden Lion at St John's Chapel, open all day in summer, is a useful stop.

North of England Lead Mining Centre ⛏ Probably the best-preserved lead-mining site in Britain, and unmissable if you're at all interested in industrial history. Equipped with hard hat and lamps, you're led through the mine's dark, chilly passageways to a huge underground waterwheel; there's also a new woodland walk, and play area for the under-7s. Meals, snacks, shop, some disabled access; open daily Apr–Sept, wknds and half-term only in Oct; (01388) 537505; £3.40 for surface exhibitions, £5 inc mine trip.

Rookhope This diversion is worthwhile: fine alpine plants nursery, small craft centre, decent pub, more good walks.

Weardale Museum (Ireshopeburn) Nr the source of the river, this re-creates life in this high valley's heady lead-mining days, and has an exhibition on John Wesley, who often preached in the adjacent chapel. Shop; cl am, Mon, Tues, and all Oct–Apr; (01388) 537417; £1.

WHITBURN NZ4064

Souter Lighthouse When built in 1870, this was the most advanced lighthouse of the day, and the first to be powered by electricity; it still has period rooms and equipment. Meals, snacks, shop, disabled access (but not to tower); cl Fri (exc Good Fri), and all Nov–Mar, phone to check; (0191) 529 3161; £3; NT. The Trust also own the Leas, the spectacular stretch of coastline around here, leading to Marsden Rock with its seabird colonies. The Jolly Sailor has decent food.

WHITLEY BAY NZ3575

St Mary's Lighthouse Out on St Mary's Island, reached by a causeway at low tide. Good views from the top – for those unable to climb the 137 steps, a camera at the top relays the image to a colour TV at the bottom. Snacks, shop; cl wkdys Nov–Mar (exc school hols and occasional days in Feb), and possibly other times depending on the tide; (0191) 200 8650; £2. When the lighthouse is closed the island is worth a visit for the rock pools alone, and is visited all through the year by a wide range of birds. The Shiremoor House Farm up on Middle Engine Lane, New York (handy too for North Shields and Tynemouth), has some of the best food in this area – good value.

WINDY GYLE NT8515

High summit by a fine ridge section of the Pennine Way, along the Scottish border – the best of the Way's long, lonely plod over the Cheviots' grassy moors. You have to walk some way from the road to reach this main ridge: start from Barrowburn in Coquetdale and walk along The Street, an ancient drovers' track. Gradients are mild but the peaty ground can get boggy after rain; not all routes are defined on the ground, but stone boundary walls and forest plantations are useful guides.

WITTON-LE-WEAR NZ1631

Low Barns Nature Reserve ⛏ 100-acre reserve with nature trails, woodland, grassland, lake and lots of interesting wildlife. Snacks, shop, good disabled access; cl 25–26 Dec, 1 Jan; (01388) 488728; free. The village is attractive, with a tree-lined sloping green. The Red Lion over in North Bitchburn has good food.

WOODHORN NZ2889

Woodhorn Colliery Museum (Queen Elizabeth II Country Park) Former colliery buildings re-creating life in the pit and the communities around it. Also short trips on narrow-gauge railway, displays of art by local miners, interactive exhibition on the Lindisfarne Gospels, and woodland walks. Meals, snacks, shop, some disabled access; cl Mon (exc bank hols), Tues, and around 10 days over Christmas and New Year; (01670) 856968; free, though charge for railway.

Attractive or beautifully placed villages, with decent pubs for something to eat, include Bishopton NZ3621, Cotherstone NZ0119, Eggleston NY9924, Lowick NU0139, Rennington NU2118, riverside Riding Mill NZ0161, Romaldkirk NY9922, Stamfordham NZ0772 and Whalton NZ1382.

Where to eat

AMBLE NU2604 **Charlie's Chip Shop** *Amble St (01665) 710206* Popular family-run restaurant serving good chips with fish, chicken, and pies, vegetarian options and children's dishes, plus a take-away service; cl Sun–Weds am (opening 4.30 then); disabled access|**£4.15**

BAMBURGH NU1835 **Copper Kettle Tearooms** *21 Front St (01668) 214315* 18th-c cottage nr castle, with beams, panelling, and copper implements; light lunches, home-made scones and cakes, more substantial suppers, a fine range of teas inc many fruit and herb ones, and a good choice of other drinks; no smoking; cl winter Mon, Dec to mid-Feb; limited disabled access. **£10|£3.20**

BARNARD CASTLE NZ0516 **Market Place Teashop** *29 Market Pl (01833) 690110* Long-standing tearoom in 17th-c building with flagstones and an open fire, smart uniformed waitresses, home-made cakes, light lunches, a good choice of teas, and a friendly relaxed atmosphere; cl Sun am, all day winter Sun, Christmas–New Year; disabled access|**£3.50**

CARTERWAY HEADS NZ0452 **Manor House Inn** *Kiln Pit Hill (01207) 255268* Popular slate-roofed stone house with fine southerly views over moorland pastures; interesting food from a wide changing menu, a partly no smoking restaurant (with a huge collection of jugs), and a friendly atmosphere; comfortable bdrms, nice breakfasts; cl pm 25 Dec. £20.20|**£7.50**

CORBRIDGE NY9864 **Valley** *Old Station House, Station Rd (01434) 633434* Extremely friendly Indian restaurant in attractively reworked sandstone station house with wide choice of very good Indian food and kind service; also, a special train service for parties from Tyneside with uniformed escort and free travel, and your order is phoned ahead to be ready on arrival – good fun; cl lunchtimes, cl Sun, 25 Dec, 1 Jan. £20

CRASTER NU2519 **Craster Restaurant** *(01665) 576230* Upstairs restaurant overlooking the harbour with candles on the tables, exceedingly welcoming staff, and huge helpings of fairly priced really fresh fish from the owners' fish depot – they have their own smoking yard, too; cl Mon, Oct–Apr; well behaved younger children lunchtime only, over 12 in evening. £16.50|**£6.50**

DURHAM NZ2643 **Bistro 21** *Aykley Heads House (0191) 384 4354* Light and airy Mediterranean-style restaurant in former 17th-c farmhouse, with pine dining chairs on wooden or flagstoned floors, a good choice of very enjoyable interesting modern cooking, a thoughtful wine list, and professional but relaxed service; cl Sun and all public hols; disabled access. £30

GREAT WHITTINGTON NZ0071 **Queens Head** *(01434) 672267* Simple but civilised stone inn with two beamed, comfortable and neatly furnished rooms, a wide choice of good interesting food, a no smoking restaurant, log fires, well kept real ales, decent wines, and quite a few malt whiskies; cl Mon exc bank hols; disabled access. £26|**£8.95**

HAYDON BRIDGE NY8364 **General Havelock** *(01434) 684283* Very civilised old stone terraced house with smart stripped-stone back dining room overlooking the Tyne, good interesting bar lunches and stylish restaurant meals from a monthly changing menu, well kept real ales, good wines by the glass, pleasant service, and a friendly local atmosphere; cl Sun pm, Mon; disabled access. £27|**£6**

HEDLEY ON THE HILL NZ0759 **Feathers** *(01661) 843607* Little stone local with three neatly kept traditional bars, woodburners, straightforward furnishings, a charming, relaxed and welcoming atmosphere, imaginative meals from a twice-weekly changing menu, and well kept real ales; cl wkdy lunchtimes exc bank hols; disabled access. £18.75|**£6.75**

NEWCASTLE UPON TYNE NZ2563 **Café 21** *19–21 Queen St (0191) 222 0755* Very popular quayside restaurant with a bustling informal atmosphere, helpful staff, especially good modern European cooking attractively presented, and a carefully chosen wine list with good value house wines; no smoking area; cl Christmas and bank hols; £30/£2-course lunch £12

NEWCASTLE UPON TYNE NZ2666 **Fisherman's Lodge** *Jesmond Dene (0191) 281 3281* In a pretty spot down a long leafy lane, this popular restaurant has an attractive bar and elegant dining room, and specialises in delicious fresh seafood – though the local meat and lovely puddings are quite a draw too; professional service and reasonably priced wines; cl Sat am, Sun pm. £34.50 dinner/3-course set lunch £19.50

NEWFIELD NZ2033 **Fox & Hounds** *Stonebank Terrace (01388) 662787* Comfortable and gently lit, mainly no smoking, with candles and flowers, big brass platters on dark pink timbered walls, and big windows looking over steeply rolling countryside; good winter fires, appealing attractively priced food (more elaborate in the evening), good house wines, and friendly, thoughtful service; Sat night fully booked well ahead. £24.70|**£5.50**

NEWTON-ON-THE-MOOR NU1705 **Cook & Barker Arms** *(01665) 575234* Beautifully prepared imaginative food in bustling stone pub's unfussy, long beamed bar, with partly panelled walls, paintings by local artists, a coal fire and coal-effect gas one, and a no smoking area; changing real ales, decent whiskies and 12 wines by the glass; bdrms; cl 25 Dec pm; disabled access. £16|**£8**

RENNINGTON NU2119 **Masons Arms** *(01665) 577275* Friendly, well run old coaching inn with good value quickly served bar food inc nice daily specials, a comfortably modernised beamed lounge bar, friendly helpful staff, real ales, and decent breakfasts; comfortable bdrms; no children. £18.95|**£6.50**

SHINCLIFFE NZ2940 **Seven Stars** *High St N (0191) 384 8454* Just ten minutes' or so drive from central Durham, this early 18th-c village inn with its pretty window-boxes and creepers has a civilised but largely unspoilt and welcoming atmosphere; the lounge has a coal fire in a handsome Victorian fireplace, copper kettles hanging from the beams, real ales, enjoyable and imaginative bar food from a changing menu (the candlelit dining room is no smoking), and quite a few malt whiskies; parking can be tricky. £24|**£7.50**

WARENFORD NU1328 **Warenford Lodge** *(01668) 213453* Very individual old (though rather modern-feeling) dining pub with stripped stonework, a big stone fireplace, comfortable extension with woodburner, really good attractively presented imaginative food, and decent wines; children in evening dining room only; cl Mon, Tues–Fri am, 2 wks Jan; children in restaurant (not bar); limited disabled access. £19.70|**£6.90**

Special thanks to Michael Doswell, Les Duncan, Bernice Saltzer

NOTTINGHAMSHIRE

Varied family excursions, some attractive countryside, low prices

Our top Nottinghamshire Family Attraction this Year, the Making It! Discovery Centre, joins a satisfying range of places to visit in lively Nottingham. Besides the good museums (children like best the Galleries of Justice), there's an unusual science centre, and for something completely different you can go on a tour of Nottingham's caves (there are ancient caves too at Creswell).

Enjoyable excursions for younger children include the fairytale-themed Sundown Adventureland in Rampton and the White Post Modern Farm Centre in Farnsfield. Sherwood Forest is great for sunny days (the visitor centre in Edwinstowe is a good place to start, and there's an enjoyable farm park and a little amusement park there too).

Fans of D H Lawrence will find a visit to Eastwood rewarding, and splendid Newstead Abbey was the home of Lord Byron. In Worksop, Mr Straw's house is a remarkable 1920s time capsule; there's a huge doll collection in Cromwell, while in Upton you'll find antique clocks.

The county has some charming and interesting villages, and one or two attractive old towns such as Southwell (the newly opened Workhouse here is fascinating) and Newark (with its castle and nearby air museum). The mansions and families which gave the name of the Dukeries to the countryside in the north are long gone, but broad tracts of landscaped wooded parkland remain, such as Clumber.

Our recommended places to stay include a couple of nice new entries this year.

Where to stay

BLIDWORTH SK5555 **Holly Lodge** *Rickett Lane, Blidworth, Mansfield, Nottinghamshire NG21 0NQ 01623 793853* **£54***; 4 neat, comfortable rms in converted stables. Victorian hunting lodge in 15 acres with fine country views, a woodland walk, and tennis; log fire in sitting room, a relaxed and friendly atmosphere, light suppers if ordered (local restaurants and pubs close by), good breakfasts, and helpful owners; no smoking; children at owner's discretion

LANGAR SK7234 **Langar Hall** *Church Lane, Langar, Nottingham, Nottinghamshire NG13 9HG (01949) 860559* **£130***, plus special breaks; 10 lovely rms, some in wing and courtyard as well. Fine country house in spacious grounds with beautifully furnished elegant rooms, pillared dining hall with paintings for sale, antiques and fresh flowers, a relaxed informal atmosphere, a lively and friendly owner, and very good food; quite a few facilities for children; disabled access; dogs welcome in bedrooms ☺

NOTTINGHAM SK5739 **Lace Market** *29–31 High Pavement, Nottingham, Nottinghamshire NG1 1HE (0115) 852 3232* **£120.90**; 29 modern, comfortable rms. Next to a lovely church, this Georgian town house has a relaxed atmosphere, friendly young staff, a convivial bar with daily papers, wood-strip floors and strong but subtle colours, good brasserie-style food in contemporary restaurant, and enjoyable breakfasts; dogs welcome in bedrooms

SOUTHWELL SK7053 **Old Forge** *Burgage Lane, Southwell, Nottinghamshire NG25 0ER (01636) 812809* **£70**, plus special breaks; 4 rms. 200-year-old former blacksmith's house with welcoming owner, interesting furnishings, super breakfasts in conservatory overlooking the Minster, and pretty terrace; disabled access

To see and do

Nottinghamshire Family Attraction of the Year

LITTLEWORTH SK5361 **Making It! Discovery Centre** (Littleworth) Hugely enjoyable, whatever your age, this is one of those cunning places where children learn lots while having a great time. In the former Mansfield Brewery, it sets out to show the process of making a new product, from having the initial idea, through testing and producing it, to marketing the finished result. It's all interactive, with lots of touch screens, hands-on activities and practical things to do; you can test materials to destruction, press buttons to make a fizzy drink, look through goggles into a virtual factory, and use touch screens to work a chocolate assembly line. And in the marketing section, you end up on the front page of a newspaper, launching your product. Along the way you'll learn about bar codes, circuits and all sorts of manufacturing processes, but the education side never gets in the way of the fun. For many visitors the highlight is the final part, where you make something yourself; you can choose between eight different kits, included in the price, and put together a buggy, boat, rocket, or even a clock – which of course you can take home with you afterwards. Staff are on hand to help if necessary. Adults seem to enjoy this bit even more than children – though aren't necessarily quite as skilled. Further kits are on sale in the shop. You'll need to allow three hours to enjoy the place properly: expect to spend half of that on the displays, and half building your kit. It's still very new, but is already deservedly doing very well; under-12s love it, but there's lots to stimulate older visitors too. Internet café, shop, disabled access; cl 25 Dec; (01623) 473273; *£5.95 adults, *£5.50 children. The family tickets offer decent savings: £19 for two adults and two children, £24 for two adults and three children. There are some fun (and instructive) interactive games on their website, at www.makingit.org.uk/games.

BEACON HILL SK7490
Above the Chesterfield Canal at Gringley on the Hill, this gives magnificent views in all directions; you can make out the towers of Lincoln Cathedral on a clear day.

BLYTH SK6185
An attractive small town, with interesting wall paintings in the **church**; the cheerful old Angel is useful for lunch.
Hodsock Priory Gardens (off B6045 S) Especially lovely at snowdrop time; open 1 Feb– 8 Mar; (01909) 591204; plant sales; *£3.50.

CHESTERFIELD CANAL SK7283
This has scope for towpath walks; one attractive stretch is by the Gate Inn at Clarborough (good value food),

another by the Chequers at Ranby SK6580 (wknd boat trips, food all day then).

CLUMBER PARK SK6275
One of the great former Dukeries estates, nearly 4,000 acres of farmland, parks, lake and woodland and the longest lime avenue in Europe, almost 2 miles long. Other surviving features include a Victorian Gothic chapel, stable yard and garages, and ornate entrance lodges. The superb 19th-c glasshouses incorporate a palm house, vineries and working bee colonies, and overlook the walled kitchen garden. The estate is outstanding for its walks (120 different types of tree here offer year-round colour), enough for a full-day excursion. You can also hire bikes.

Meals, snacks, shop, disabled access; cl 25 Dec and concert days; (01909) 544917; £3.50 per vehicle; NT.

COSSALL SK4842

Attractive village in D H Lawrence country: he was once engaged to the girl who lived in Church Cottage (Church Lane). The Gate Inn over in Awsworth pleasantly keeps up the Lawrence mood, and is handy for strolls in Rushcliffe Country Park.

CRESWELL SK5474

Creswell Crags Visitor Centre
Stone Age man lived in the caves and rock shelters of this limestone gorge right by the Derbyshire border (the village is actually across the border). Even on days when there aren't cave tours it's an intriguing prehistoric site, with a good visitor centre, reconstructions of Ice Age family life, and other displays and activities. In summer and school holidays a tour for children leaves at 11.30, best to check for other cave tour dates. You can't go into the caves wearing sandals or open shoes. Picnic area, shop, disabled access; cl Nov–Jan exc Sun; (01909) 720378; site free, cave tours £2.75. The Mallet & Chisel in nearby Whitwell (Hillside) has cheap food.

CROMWELL SK7961

Vina Cooke Museum of Dolls (Old Rectory) Thousands of toys and objects related to childhood, in an imposing 17th-c rectory. Especially lively on Easter Mon, with morris dancers, crafts and the like. Shop, limited disabled access; cl 12–2 pm, all day Fri and Nov–Feb; (01636) 821364; £2.50.

EASTWOOD SK4647

D H Lawrence Birthplace Museum (8a Victoria St) The writer was born in this typical working-class house in 1885; it's been carefully restored to how he knew it. Shop (where you can buy all his works), limited disabled access; cl 23 Dec–2 Jan; (01773) 763312; free till Sept 2003, best to check after that. Craft workshops next door (usually cl Weds pm and Sun). Two rooms in Lawrence's early boyhood home on Garden Rd are furnished as he described them in *Sons and Lovers*; open by appointment with John Elliott (01773) 712132; donations. The chatty Foresters Arms (Newthorpe) is appealing.

Durban House Heritage Centre
Decent centre housing an exhibition on D H Lawrence, with original manuscripts and changing displays such as the copy of *Lady Chatterley's Lover* used as evidence in the notorious obscenity trial; also changing local history displays, and a Tourist Information Centre. Meals and snacks, disabled access; cl 23 Dec–2 Jan; (01773) 717353; free till Sept 2003, best to check after that.

EDWINSTOWE SK5865

Sherwood Forest Farm Park (Lamb Pens Farm, off A6075) Unusual breeds of traditional farm animals, water buffalo and wallabies, pets' corner, and colourful waterfowl on a sizeable lake. Also an owl garden, adventure playground (with a separate section for the under-5s), and picnic area. They usually have some activities in a barn, but it's very much a place for fine weather. Special events may include an Easter treasure hunt. Home-baked teas and snacks, shop, mostly disabled access (can be tricky around the lakes); open daily Easter to mid-Oct; (01623) 823558; £4.50.

Sherwood Forest Visitor Centre
With an exhibition on Robin Hood, the visitor centre is a good springboard for the forest itself, only a fraction of what it once was (it used to cover a fifth of the county) but still miles across, though the heathland that Robin himself would have known has largely been swallowed up either by farmland or by forestry plantation. Good waymarked paths and footpaths, the most popular being to the Major Oak (a huge tree in the heart of the forest). Meals, snacks, shop, disabled access; (01623) 823202; car park £1.50. A couple of minutes' walk away **Sherwood Forest Amusement Park** has a few fairground rides and attractions; usually open Mar–Oct but may close in very bad weather; (01623) 823536; free, charges for rides. Nearby too **Sherwood Forest Art and Craft Centre** has 16 craft studios housed in a purpose-built centre; cl Mon and Tues Oct–Mar; (01623) 825786. The best drive is the B6034 N towards Worksop, then the right turn to Carburton and Clumber Park.

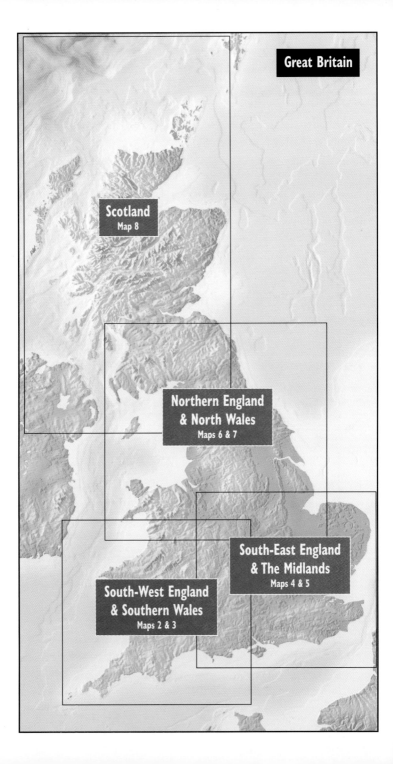

Great Britain

Scotland
Map 8

Northern England
& North Wales
Maps 6 & 7

South-East England
& The Midlands
Maps 4 & 5

South-West England
& Southern Wales
Maps 2 & 3

South-West England & Southern Wales

CARDIGAN BAY

Tywyn
Aberdyfi
Aberystwyth
Aberaeron
A487
A485
Tregaron
Cardigan
Lampeter
PRESCELLI HILLS
A485
CAMBRIAN
Fishguard
WEST WALES
Llandeilo
St David's
Carmarthen
A40
Haverfordwest
A40
Narberth
Pembroke
Tenby
Burry Port
CARMARTHEN BAY
Llanelli
GOWER
Swansea

BRISTOL
Lundy
Ilfracombe
Lynton
A39
Barnstaple
EXMO
Bideford
A377
A39
Bude
A386
Hatherleigh
Okehampton
Camelford
A39
Launceston
DARTM
Wadebridge
BODMIN MOOR
Tavistock
A30
A386
Bodmin
Liskeard
Yelverton
Newquay
A38
Plymouth
CORNWALL
St Austell
Redruth
A390
Fowey
Looe
St Ives
Truro
Camborne
Burgh Island
Penzance
Falmouth
Land's End
Helston
MOUNT'S BAY
Lizard Point

Family Attractions of the Year

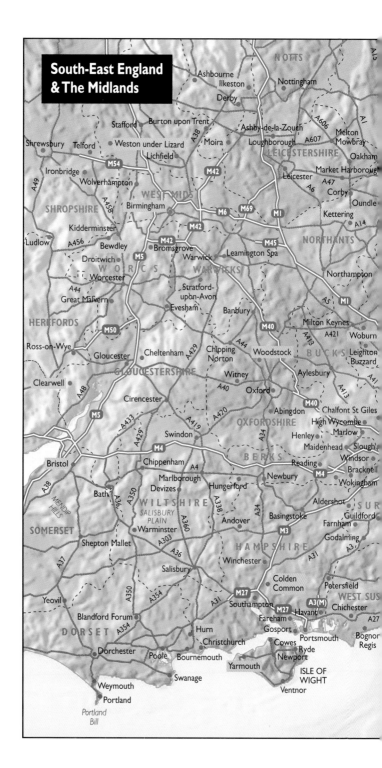

South-East England & The Midlands

| Hurn | Family Attractions of the Year |

Northern England & North Wales

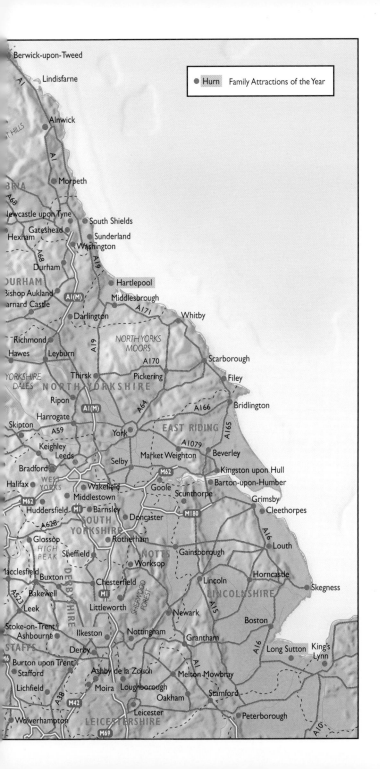

Hurn Family Attractions of the Year

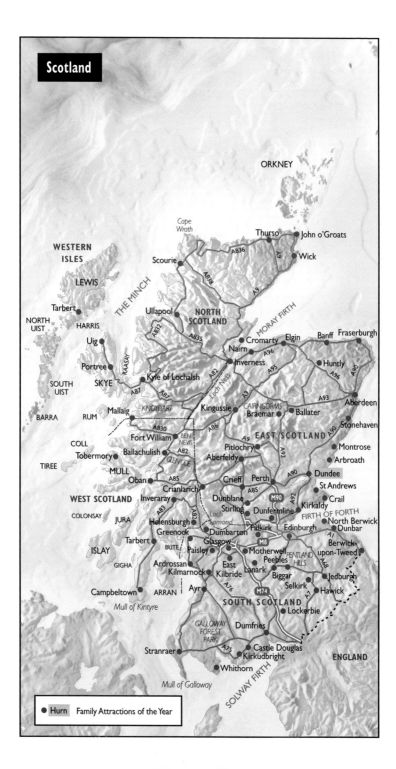

Scotland

ORKNEY

Cape
Wrath

Thurso · · John o'Groats
Scourie · A836 A9 · Wick

**WESTERN
ISLES**

LEWIS

THE MINCH

Tarbert · Ullapool · **NORTH
SCOTLAND**

NORTH
UIST

HARRIS

RAASAY

Uig · A832 A835 MORAY FIRTH

Cromarty · Elgin · Banff · Fraserburgh

Portree · Nairn A96 A90

SKYE · Kyle of Lochalsh · Inverness · Huntly

SOUTH
UIST

A87 A82 A95 A96

Loch Ness A93 · Aberdeen

BARRA · Mallaig · KNOYDART A9 CAIRNGORMS · Stonehaven

RUM

A830 · Kingussie · Braemar · Ballater

Fort William · BEN NEVIS A86 **EAST SCOTLAND** A90

COLL

Tobermory · Ballachulish A82 GLENCOE · Pitlochry · Montrose

TIREE

MULL · Oban · A85 · Aberfeldy A93 · Arbroath

Crianlarich · Crieff · Perth A90 · Dundee

WEST SCOTLAND · Inveraray · A85 M90 · St Andrews

Dunblane A92 · Crail

COLONSAY · JURA · Helensburgh · Loch Lomond · Stirling · Dunfermline · Kirkaldy FIRTH OF FORTH

Greenock · Dumbarton · Falkirk · Edinburgh · North Berwick

Tarbert · A83 A82 M8 · Dunbar

ISLAY · BUTE · Paisley · Glasgow · Motherwell · Peebles · Berwick-upon-Tweed

GIGHA · Ardrossan · East Kilbride · Lanark PENTLAND HILLS A68

Kilmarnock · Biggar · Selkirk · Jedburgh

Campbeltown · ARRAN · Ayr A76 M74 · Hawick

Mull of Kintyre · **SOUTH SCOTLAND** A7

Lockerbie

GALLOWAY FOREST PARK · Dumfries · **ENGLAND**

Stranraer · A75 · Castle Douglas

Kirkudbright

Whithorn · SOLWAY FIRTH

Mull of Galloway

● **Hurn** Family Attractions of the Year

Sherwood Forest has one of England's three **Center Parcs**, a rewarding place to stay with excellent leisure facilities; (0870) 520 0300.

FARNSFIELD SK6257

White Post Modern Farm Centre (A614, 1m W) One of the better of its kind, this bustling modern working farm has everything from a mouse town to llamas, quails, snakes and fish, and a goat mountain. In the summer holidays (ring for times) an enjoyable show talks you through a farmer's year, with the help of pigs, rabbits, ducks and rats. You can buy food for many of the animals, and pet some of them. They're particularly strong on pigs, and may have hatching eggs in their huge incubator. Most displays and animals move indoors if the weather is bad (and there's an indoor sand pit). Lots of activities in the field, and along with farm trails and pony rides there's also a bat house and aviary. They sell various insects and reptiles, and have reptile handling sessions. They have attended kennels if you want to take your dog. Meals, snacks, heated picnic area, good farm shop, disabled access; (01623) 882977; £5.50. The Plough in the village has decent food. **Wonderland** 🏠 (1m W) Useful for families. As well as a bar for the grown-ups there's lots for kiddies inc junior roller-coaster, train rides, woodland walk, tropical house with free-flying butterflies, a maze, indoor play area, pets and farm animals, crazy golf, scented garden and more. Meals, snacks, shop, disabled access; cl 24–26 Dec and Jan; (01623) 882773; *£4.80. Combs Farm Shop nearby is a good one.

HOLME PIERREPONT SK6339

Holme Pierrepont Hall Early Tudor manor house with interesting early 15th-c timbers, and an elaborate parterre in the formal courtyard garden. Several rooms inc the ballroom and billiard room have been restored. Teas, shop, disabled access to gardens only; open Thurs Jun, Weds–Thurs July, Tues–Thurs Aug, and Sun–Mon pm on Easter, spring and summer bank hols – but best to check; (0115) 933 2371; *£4, £2 garden only. The Black Lion in Radcliffe on Trent has decent food.

LAXTON SK7267

Unique for having kept the pattern of its **medieval farming**, with different villagers each owning strips of the three great fields. You can walk the grass paths, or sykes, which divide groups of these strips – the visitor centre behind the Dovecote (a good village pub) explains it all. The church has a fine 15th-c screen.

LITTLEWORTH SK5361

Making It! Discovery Centre See *separate family panel on p.467*.

MANSFIELD SK5361

Mansfield Museum and Art Gallery (Leeming St) Very good for local history, with displays of 18th-c porcelain, local watercolours, stuffed birds in the natural history gallery, and a thorough look at Mansfield's industrial heritage. Shop, snacks, disabled access; cl Sun and bank hols; (01623) 463088; free. Hidden away behind shop fronts **White Lion Yard** (Church St) was recently discovered after a rock fall and has been re-created through the restoration of two historic buildings (Tudor House is one of the town's oldest houses) and four adjoining man made 18th-c caves. Once used as store rooms and workshops (you can still see a bread oven's flue), the caves now house a restaurant, and a visitor centre covering the history of the Yard and Mansfield's development; (01623) 463088.

MAPLEBECK SK6961

Delightfully rustic village; the Beehive's a classic country tavern, and nearby Woodborough and Lambley are also worth a look.

NEWARK SK7953

Attractive old market town with some interesting buildings in its side streets, a fine church, and walks by the River Trent, with summer boat trips from the Castle. Useful museums include the **Millgate Folk Museum** on Millgate (cl am wknds, bank hols, cl 25–26 Dec; (01636) 655730; free; lunchtime food at the nearby riverside Navigation Waterfront); and the local history collection at **Newark Museum** on Appletongate (cl 1–2, Thurs, bank hol ams, and Sun exc summer pms; (01636) 655740; free; decent fresh food in the nearby Fox & Crown).

Newark Air Museum (Winthorpe, NE) Just under 60 aircraft and cockpit sections from across the history of aviation inc transport, training and reconnaissance aircraft, helicopters, and diverse jet fighters and bombers inc two russian MiGs; half the exhibits are under cover, so fine all year round. Snacks, shop, disabled access; cl 24–26 Dec; (01636) 707170; £4.25.

Newark Castle ⊞ The ruins date from the 12th c, and there's still a fair bit to see; it was partly destroyed during the Civil War, then later had periods as a cattle market and a bowling green. The gardens have been relandscaped as they were in Victorian times. Good explanatory displays at the **Castle Story Exhibition** in the grounds; Meals, snacks, shop, disabled access to gardens only; gardens cl 25–26 Dec, 1 Jan; (01636) 655765; free (castle tour £2, 10, 12, 3 Weds and Fri–Sat, but less frequently in winter when it's best to phone for times).

NEWSTEAD ABBEY SK5454 (off A60) Splendid former home of Lord Byron, in gorgeously romantic grounds; many of his possessions can still be seen. Rooms are decorated in a variety of styles from medieval through to Victorian, and there are substantial remains of the original priory. Adventure playground, and dressing up for children. Meals, snacks, summer shop, limited disabled access; house cl am and Oct–Mar; grounds cl last Fri in Nov only; (01623) 455900; house and gardens £4, gardens only £2. The Horse & Groom in the attractive nearby village of Linby is a useful stop, as is the Griffins Head at Papplewick (B683/B6011).

NORTH CLIFTON SK8272
Pureland Meditation Centre & Japanese Garden ⊞ (Trent Lane) Japanese meditation garden reflecting the harmony of nature and inner peace of man, and a meditation centre (open all year). Snacks, shop, some disabled access; garden cl Mon, and Nov–Mar; (01777) 228567; £4.

NOTTINGHAM SK5739
During the industrialisation of the 18th and 19th c, Nottingham developed its international reputation for lace-making to become one of the biggest lace-producing cities in the world. A few places still produce lace. You can see how it was made at the Museum of Costume and Textiles, examples at the Lace Museum Centre and for sale at the Lace Market Centre (3–5 High Pavement). These days, although Nottingham is a big city it does have a pleasantly personal feel in its vibrant centre, and with traffic discouraged in the central strolling streets they are nice for a wander, with plenty of trendy clothes shops and the like. Throughout most of 2003 they will be testing a new tram system that will run from the station to the North and will open to the public in November. The city also boasts the only Olympic-size ice rink in Britain. The parts around the parish church (which has some interesting carvings) and the Lace Market are particularly attractive. In the evenings and wknds there's almost a festival feel, with lots of young people around. Perhaps because of its enormous and growing student population, the town has an amazing number of decent bars and pubs. The Via Fossa (Canal St) and Pit & Pendulum (Victoria St) are fun to look around, and other useful lunch places are Fellows Morton & Clayton (Canal St; brews its own beer), the quaint old Bell (Angel Row), Limelight (attached to the Playhouse) and Lincolnshire Poacher (Mansfield Rd).

Attenborough Nature Reserve Unusual reserve with good bird-watching down by Beeston at the extensive partly wooded Attenborough lakes; on the far side a path takes you along the narrow spit of land dividing them from the mighty River Trent. The Manor at Toton is a useful nearby dining pub.

Brewhouse Yard Museum (Castle Boulevard) Museum of Nottingham life spread over five 17th-c houses with period rooms, schoolroom and reconstruction of a shopping street and caves. Lovely historic roses and plants descended from original Victorian plants in the cottage garden. Shop, some disabled access; cl 25, 26 Dec, 1 Jan; (0115) 9153600; £1.50 wknds and bank hols, otherwise free.

Castle Museum and Art Gallery Up on the summit, this dates from the 17th c, but the gateway is from an earlier 13th-c fortress. It now houses an appealing museum, with a history of the site and the underground passages. Meals, snacks, shop, disabled access; cl 24–26 Dec and 1 Jan; (0115) 915 3700; £2 wknds and bank hols.

Cave tours The rock on which old Nottingham stood is honeycombed with hundreds of galleries, cellars and passageways. Tours (which are quite strenuous) usually leave the castle at 11, 2 and 3 Mon–Thurs and Sat, and 2 and 3 Fri, there may be additional tours in the summer, and in case of occasional rock falls it's best to call (0115) 915 3700 first; £2. The attractive Olde Trip to Jerusalem (Brewhouse Yard) has a fascinating bar tunnelled many centuries ago right into the rock face.

Caves of Nottingham 🖼 (Upper Level, Broadmarsh Centre) Tour with taped commentary of 750-year-old man-made caverns beneath a busy modern shopping centre. Rambling interiors have been reconstructed in their earlier guises as an underground medieval tannery, Victorian slum, air raid shelter, and pub cellar. Shop; cl 24–26 Dec, 1 Jan and Easter Sun; (0115) 924 1424; *£3.75.

Djanogly Art Gallery (University Arts Centre, University Park, SW of centre) Good temporary exhibitions; Meals, snacks, shop, disabled access; cl am Sun, am bank hols, 24–26 Dec, 1 Jan; (0115) 951 3189; free.

Galleries of Justice 🖼 (Shire Hall, High Pavement) The grim realities of a 19th-c trial and prison life are re-enacted with verve at this first-rate centre, set around two Victorian courtrooms in use through to 1986. On arrival children are given a criminal identity number and sent for trial in the Criminal Court. 'Prisoners' are then led down to the cells, where warders, gaolers and a fellow prisoner prepare them for their fate, lock them in a cell or put them to the treadmill. The other highlight is a police station experience, where you can try your hand at cracking a murder case. Traditional displays about justice through the ages, prisons and legal issues, the world's largest collection of handcuffs and other restraints, and temporary exhibitions about anything from the great train

robbery to Judge Dredd.. Snacks, shop, some disabled access; cl Mon (exc school hols); (0115) 952 0555; *£6.95.

Green's Mill and Science Centre (Windmill Lane) Once home to the 19th-c mathematical genius and miller George Green, this is Britain's only inner city working windmill: the restored tower mill still produces flour, and you can try grinding corn on part of an old millstone. Among the exhibits at the hands-on Science Centre next door is a weather satellite receiver showing pictures live from space. Shop, limited disabled access; cl Mon (exc bank hols) and Tues – best to phone to check if the mill is working; (0115) 915 6878; free.

Lace Museum Centre (Castle Rd) This pretty 15th-c house has lace hanging from almost every beam, much of it for sale. Lace-making demonstrations pm summer Thurs. Shop, some disabled access; (0115) 941 3539; free.

Museum of Costume and Textiles (Castle Gate) Period rooms in a row of 17th/18th-c houses (originally owned by the Sheriff of Nottinghamshire) cover over 200 years of costume with emphasis on Nottingham's extensive lace-making industry: early examples of lace-making machinery, along with clothing featuring the world-famous lace, and a fine collection of 16th-c hand-made lace too. Shop, disabled access to ground floor; cl Mon–Tues (exc bank hols), 24–26 Dec, 1 Jan (0115) 915 3500; free.

National Ice Centre (Lower Parliament St) With two ice rinks (one Olympic size), it covers the full range of related sports from ice-hockey to speed skating; also regular concerts and events, and courses in the school hols. Snacks, shop, disabled access; centre open daily, but best to phone for skating times; (0115) 853 3000; skating from £3.10 (£1.30 extra skate hire).

Tales of Robin Hood (Maid Marian Way) Robin, his men and their tales are brought to life as you travel in cars through the sights, sounds and smells of a re-created medieval Sherwood Forest. A film looks at the truth behind the stories, there's an interactive quiz and wknd displays such as falconry or historical weaponry. Meals, snacks, shop, disabled access; cl 25–26 Dec; (0115) 948 3284; £6.50.

Wollaton Hall (Wollaton Park, 3m W) Splendidly ornate Tudor house with the city's natural history collection. The delightful 500-acre grounds have two adventure playgrounds, a sensory garden, and picnic areas. Snacks, shop, disabled access to the ground floor only; cl 24–26 and 1 Jan; (0115) 915 3900; £2 wknds and bank hols, free at other times, car parking £2 for the day. The **Yard Gallery** has changing exhibitions and sales that explore art and the environment (cl 24–26 and 1 Jan). The adjacent **Industrial Museum** (Courtyard Buildings) looks at lace-making and other local industries, and has working steam-powered machines (steamings last Sun of month); cl Nov–Mar; (0115) 915 3910; £1.50 wknds, £2 joint ticket with Wollaton Hall, also free wkdys).

OLLERTON SK6567

Ollerton Mill 🏛 (Market Pl) The only working watermill in the county, still working as it did in the early 18th c, in a pleasant setting on the edge of Sherwood Forest. The good tearoom has a viewing panel of the mill race, and river views (open March-Nov Tues–Sun and bank hols), shop; mill open Sun Apr–Sept; (01623) 822469; *£1.50. The White Hart opposite the church in this pretty market place has good value food.

Rufford Country Park (off A614 S) Pleasant woodland, arboretum, 18th-c lake, park and formal gardens on edge of Sherwood Forest. At the centre are the ruins of a 12th-c Cistercian abbey, with an exhibition on Cistercian life in the vaulted undercroft, also craft centre in former stable block, gallery in former orangery, shops and family activities some wknds. Meals, snacks, disabled access; cl 25 Dec; (01623) 822944; free; parking £1.50.

OXTON SK6251

Attractive village; the lane up hill N below the power lines leads to an Iron Age hill fort.

RAMPTON SK7978

Sundown Adventureland (Treswell Rd; N of A57) This cheerful little leisure park is best for children up to 10. It's full of decent life-size representations and

tableaux of stories and fairy-tales, from the Wild West to the Three Little Pigs. There are gentle rides and several themed play areas, one under cover (height restrictions apply in here). Good Christmas displays, when Santa gives every child a present. Snacks (mostly fast food), shop, some disabled access; cl 25–26 Dec, wkdys Jan to mid-Feb; (01777) 248274; £5.50.

RAVENSHEAD SK5753

Longdale Craft Centre 🏛 (Longdale Lane) Very good craft centre, partly set out as a Victorian village street, with rows of period workshops and a small museum. Decent restaurant, snacks, shop, disabled access; (01623) 794858; cl 25–26 Dec; *£2.

Papplewick Pumping Station (Longdale Lane) Working Victorian waterworks in fine building with two beam engines; best to ring for steam days (when they have miniature steam train rides around the landscaped gardens), though open for static displays pm most Suns Easter–Oct. Club members sail model boats, yachts and steam boats on the cooling pond on most Sundays; (0115) 963 2938; £1.50 (£3 steam days). The Burnstump in the Country Park is a good value family dining pub.

RUDDINGTON SK5732

Framework Knitters Museum (Chapel St) Housed in restored 19th-c workshops, cottages and frameshop, this museum explores the industry for which Nottinghamshire was once famous. Besides reconstructed cottages you can see the machinery working, inc the bizarre circular sock-knitting machines. Snacks, shop; open Weds–Sat Easter–Dec and Sun Easter–Sept; (0115) 984 6914; £1.50.

Nottingham Transport Heritage Centre (Loughborough Rd) Steam trains usually leave every hour from here between 11.30 and 4.30 on Suns and bank hol Mons Apr to mid-Oct, but phone to check; the train runs as far as Gotham Moor (they hope to extend to Rushcliffe Halt in 2003), and the 8m round-trip lasts 50 mins. Meals, snacks, shop, mostly disabled access; open Sun, bank hols and some Sats Easter–Oct and Dec (0115) 940 5705; £4.50.

Village Museum (Church St) Reconstructed Edwardian shops; open pm Weds–Thurs and bank hol Mons Easter–Sept; (0115) 914 6645; £1.

SOUTHWELL SK7053

Southwell Minster Magnificent 12th-c cathedral, a fine sight from miles around (especially when it's floodlit), and glorious to walk through. Fine leaf carvings in the chapter house, and lovely choir screen; Evensong is sung daily during term-time, and it's worth catching one of the regular concerts. There's also a smart visitor centre. This attractive old town, small and quiet, is the home of the bramley apple, developed by Henry Merryweather in the 19th c. The original tree survives in a private garden at 75 Church St, and another prospers at his descendant's garden centre on Halam Rd, where there's a small exhibition on the subject. The Bramley Apple just down from the cathedral has decent food.

Workhouse The National Trust's only workhouse, and one of the best preserved, it has rapidly become a hit since opening in 2002 (booking strongly recommended at peak times). Vividly conjuring up the stern gloom of how the 19th-c poor were treated, it's laid out in three wings, for men, women and children: the long rows of closely placed beds allowed no privacy, and death was often the only release from disease and punishment. Shop, limited disabled access; open pm daily exc Tues and Weds 2 Apr–2 Nov; (01636) 817250; *£4.20.

SUTTON BONINGTON SK5025 Pleasant village to saunter through.

SUTTON-CUM-LOUND SK6985

Wetlands Waterfowl Reserve (off Loundlow Rd) Lagoons full of ducks and swans, and many more wild birds inc parrots and emus in the surrounding countryside. Also owls, deer, monkeys, llamas, wallabies, prairie dogs, and a children's farm. Snacks, shop, disabled access; cl 25 Dec; (01777) 818099; £2.50. The canalside Gate at Clarborough has good value food.

UNDERWOOD SK4851

Felley Priory Garden (A608, just off M1 junction 27) Developed over the last 25 years or so around a romantic old house (not open) dating back over 400 years, these richly planted hillside gardens have several areas nicely broken up by thick hedges, rose and clematis pergolas, and old masonry. They span styles from medieval to high Victorian and later, and are filled with mainly old-fashioned plants, often rare. Plants sales (all grown here), tearoom, disabled access; open Tues, Weds and Fri ams, plus 2nd and 4th Weds and 3rd Sun Mar–Oct; (01773) 810230; £2. The Red Lion (Church Lane) has good value family food.

UPTON SK7254

British Horological Institute 🖾 Includes a museum of clocks and timepieces from marine chronometers to the first telephone speaking clock. Some exhibits are over 300 years old, so don't expect them to keep perfect time. Tearoom, shop, disabled access to first floor; cl Sun am, Mon, ams and Sat Nov–Mar; (01636) 813795; £3.50. The nearby Cross Keys is a useful lunch stop.

WELLOW SK6665

An attractive village, unusual for its permanent maypole – which used to be the trunk of a Sherwood Forest tree, but is now metal. It stands on the only genuine village green in the county, kept that way since the village was founded in the 12th c (all the others were just open spaces used by the villagers and itinerant traders for buying and selling, which have been grassed over since all that stopped). The 16th-c Olde Red Lion has good value fresh food.

WINKBURN SK7158

Attractive village; unusually, its simple 12th-c village church was formerly a temple of the Knights Hospitaller.

WORKSOP SK5880

Mr Straw's House (7 Blyth Grove) One of the NT's most unusual properties, an ordinary 1920s semi, left untouched by two brothers who inherited it when their parents died. Even the calendar remains unturned. A fascinating time-capsule, it's open for prebooked timed tickets only – by limiting numbers the National Trust ensure that you can get a really good feeling of what it was like to live here; cl Nov–Mar and Sat, Sun; (01909) 482380; £4.20. The Mallard at the station ½ mile away) is an apt refreshment stop. The town museum has a display on the Pilgrim Fathers (cl Sun and pm Thurs and Sat; free), and the priory church is worth a look for the elaborate scrollwork on its 12th-c yew door. **Other attractive villages** with decent pubs include Collingham SK8663, East Bridgford SK6943 (the Reindeer has good fresh fish), Elkesley SK6875, Epperstone SK6548, Sutton Bonington SK5025, and, with their more Leicestershire-like character, Colston Bassett SK7033 (the Haby Lane dairy makes good stilton), Linby SK5351, Normanton on the Wolds SK6232 and Staunton in the Vale SK8043.

The **River Trent** gives a tremendous sense of power even when it's on its best behaviour, sliding swiftly and massively along; its occasional floods are devastating, and most years it claims lives. Villages giving pleasant access to it include Laneham SK8076 and Thrumpton SK5031.
Decent pubs and inns in good riverside spots include the Hazleford Ferry at Bleasby SK7149, Lazy Otter in Wyke Lane, Farndon SK7651, Bromley Arms at Fiskerton SK7351, Unicorn Hotel at Gunthorpe SK6844, Ferry Boat at Stoke Bardolph SK6441, Waterfront at West Stockwith SK7995 and Ferry at Wilford SK5637.

Where to eat

BEESTON SK5336 **Victoria** *Dovecote Lane (0115) 925 4049* Carefully converted from an almost derelict railway hotel, this friendly pub is popular for its imaginative food (half the menu is vegetarian), excellent choice of a dozen changing real ales, half a dozen wines by the glass, and over 100 malt whiskies; the lounge and bar back on to the railway station, and picnic-sets in a pleasant area outside (with new heaters) overlook the platform where trains pass just feet below; a good chatty atmosphere, newspapers to read, simple solid traditional furnishings, very unfussy décor, and stained-glass windows. £18.75|£6.50

CAUNTON SK7459 **Caunton Beck** *(01636) 636793* Built in 1820, this civilised, roomy and welcoming place was carefully restored using reclaimed oak and Elizabethan timbers, and has an open fire, daily papers and magazines, and under the new licensees, a wide choice of imaginative food, served all day from breakfast onwards; good house wines, real ales, and pleasant staff; disabled access. £22|£7.50

COLSTON BASSETT SK6933 **Martins Arms** *School Lane (01949) 81361* Civilised, rather smart pub with particularly good imaginative food in bar and restaurant (lovely puddings), well kept real ales, a fine choice of malt whiskies, quite a few wines by the glass, an open fire, and smart uniformed staff; disabled access. £39|£9.50

NOTTINGHAM SK5639 **Harts Restaurant** *Standard Court, Park Row (0115) 911 0666* Lively, popular brasserie with cheerful modern décor, friendly polite staff, dynamic British cooking with Mediterranean influences (super fish and interesting vegetarian dishes), delicious puddings, and short, thoughtful wine list; theatres nearby; cl 25 Dec; disabled access. £37/2-course lunch £11.95

NOTTINGHAM SK5740 **Lincolnshire Poacher** *161 Mansfield Rd (0115) 941 1584* Cheerful town pub with really tasty, good value, home-made food using fresh local produce (inc lots of vegetarian dishes); interesting real ales on 13 handpumps, lots of whiskies, decent wines, pleasant service, a big wood-floored bar with breweriana, a lively smaller bar, and chatty back snug; popular with young people in the evening. £17|£5.25

NOTTINGHAM SK5739 **Sonny's** *3 Carlton St (0115) 947 3041* Large, airy modern brasserie with pale-painted walls hung with lots of artwork, a relaxed friendly atmosphere, knowledgeable staff, consistently interesting and enjoyable food from a sensibly short menu, and a thoughtful wine list; cl bank hols; disabled access. £27

NOTTINGHAM SK5739 **World Service** *Newdigate House, Castle Gate (0115) 8475587* Fine Georgian house, lavishly decorated, with indonesian masks, panelled walls, polished tables on tiled floors, and staff in Indonesian-style dress; most attractively presented French/Pacific rim-influenced food, and a good choice of wines at all prices; no smoking in dining room. £35/2-course lunch £9.50

PLUMTREE SK6132 **Perkins Restaurant and Bar** *Old Railway Station, Station Rd* (0115) 937 3695 Delightfully converted old railway station with very popular fresh and delicious modern dishes, excellent friendly service, and good wines; cl Sun pm, Mon; children must be well behaved; disabled access. £28.50|£5.50

SIBTHORPE HILL SK7273 **Mussel & Crab** *Sibthorpe Hill* (01777) 870491 Friendly, well run dining pub with spacious lounge bar, a Mediterranean-style restaurant leading off, most enjoyable food with a strong emphasis on fish, a thoughtful wine list (quite a few inc champagne by the glass) with helpful notes, and two outside terraces; good disabled access. £22|£6.50

WALKERINGHAM SK7792 **Three Horse Shoes** *High St* (01427) 890959 Warmly welcoming distinctive pub, rather like a French logis, with quite amazing flowers and hanging baskets (using 9,000 plants); a wide choice of often inventive food, and well kept real ales; disabled access. £19|£5.50

Special thanks to Michael and Jenny Back

OXFORDSHIRE

Richly varied scenery, and lots to delight older visitors, from the dreaming spires of Oxford to the antiques shops and markets of charming country towns; some good family places, too

A rich academic history, splendid buildings, unique museums (including England's oldest, the Ashmolean, and the charmingly old-fashioned Pitt Rivers) make Oxford immensely attractive – a very popular place to visit. Just outside the city in Woodstock our Oxfordshire Family Attraction, Blenheim Palace, has much to appeal to children, even though it's one of England's grandest stately homes.

Other enjoyable family outings are topped by the Victorian recreations and animals at Cogges Farm Museum in Witney, and the Cotswold Wildlife Park near Burford (hundreds of different creatures, a children's farmyard and an adventure playground). There are animals and birds too in Ipsden and Wigginton Heath.

Riverside Henley (with its famous summer regatta) and Abingdon are pleasant to potter around, as is the delightful Cotswolds mini-town of Burford. Oxfordshire has lots of other rewarding villages and small towns to explore, with picturesque stone houses (in the NW corner many glow with golden stone), and antiques and craft shops. The scenery has considerable variety, from the edge of the Cotswolds in the W and some sweeping downland in the S to the lush fringes of the Chilterns in the E, with some of the finest Thames scenery. There are very good hotels and places to eat in – at a price.

Oxfordshire's great houses range from 18th-c Buscot Park (with its amazing art collection) and handsome Jacobean Chastleton House to Nuffield Place with its original 1930s furnishings. Admirers of William Morris enjoy his house at Kelmscot, and there's a 15th-c watermill in the grounds of Mapledurham House; Dorchester Abbey is impressive. If you're interested in transport, you can choose between the Didcot Railway Centre and the Oxford Bus Museum in Long Hanborough, and there's a detailed model railway in Long Wittenham.

Where to stay

BURFORD SP2512 **Burford House** *High St, Burford, Oxfordshire OX18 4QA* (01993) 823151 **£95**, plus winter breaks; 8 cosy individually decorated rms. Attractive partly stone and partly timbered 14th-c building, with two comfortable lounges (one for residents only), log fires, super breakfasts, and lots of plants in pretty stone courtyard; cl 2 wks Jan/Feb

BURFORD SP2412 **Lamb** *Sheep St, Burford, Oxfordshire OX18 4LR* (01993) 823155 **£120**, plus special breaks; 15 rms. Very attractive 500-year-old Cotswold inn with lovely restful atmosphere, spacious beamed, flagstoned and elegantly furnished lounge, classic civilised public bar, bunches of flowers on good oak and elm tables, three winter log fires, antiques, imaginative food in airy restaurant, and pretty little walled garden; cl 25–26 Dec; dogs welcome away from dining room

CHURCH ENSTONE SP3725 **Crown** *Mill Lane, Church Enstone, Chipping Norton, Oxfordshire OX7 4NN (01608) 677262* **£50**; 2 well appointed rms. Cotswold stone inn in pretty village, with attractive horseshoe bar, conservatory, friendly atmosphere, imaginative food in bar and restaurant, and enjoyable breakfasts; Heritage barn nearby can be viewed by appointment

CLIFTON SP4931 **Duke of Cumberlands Head** *Clifton, Banbury, Oxfordshire OX15 0PE (01869) 338534* **£70**; 6 rms in sympathetic extension. Pretty thatched 17th-c stone inn with a friendly atmosphere, very good food in bar and no smoking back restaurant, enjoyable breakfasts, log fire, well kept beers and wines, and helpful service; tables in garden; dogs welcome

GREAT MILTON SO7874 **Manoir aux Quat' Saisons** *Church St, Great Milton, Oxford OX9 7PD (01844) 278881* **£245***, plus winter breaks; 32 opulent rms. Luxurious Jacobean manor in 27 acres of parkland and lovely gardens with an impeccable kitchen garden; sumptuous lounges with fine furniture, beautiful flowers and open fires, conservatory, exquisitely presented superb food (at a price), and exemplary service; residential cookery courses; disabled access ☺

HENLEY SU7682 **Red Lion** *Hart St, Henley-on-Thames, Oxfordshire RG9 2AR (01491) 572161* **£170**, plus special breaks; 26 rms, some with river views. Handsome family-run 16th-c riverside hotel with comfortable public rooms, very good interesting food in elegant Regency-style restaurant, and particularly helpful warmly friendly staff

HORTON-CUM-STUDLEY SP5912 **Studley Priory** *Horton-cum-Studley, Oxford OX33 1AZ (01865) 351203* **£165**, plus special breaks; 18 rather luxurious rms. Once a Benedictine nunnery, this lovely Elizabethan manor stands in 13 wooded acres; fine panelling, 16th- and 17th-c stained-glass windows, antiques, big log fires, and good sofas and armchairs in the elegant drawing room and cosy bar, smartly uniformed friendly service, and seasonally changing menus in attractive high-beamed restaurant, hung with lots of landscape prints; grass tennis court and croquet; dogs welcome in bedrooms

KINGHAM SP2523 **Mill House** *Station Rd, Kingham, Chipping Norton, Oxfordshire OX7 6UH (01608) 658188* **£110**, plus special breaks; 23 good rms with country views. Carefully renovated 17th-c flour mill in seven acres with trout stream; comfortable spacious lounge, open log fire in lounge bar, original features such as two bread ovens, a cosy popular restaurant, and very good interesting food; disabled access; dogs welcome in bedrooms

KINGSTON BAGPUIZE SU3997 **Fallowfields** *Southmoor, Kingston Bagpuize, Abingdon, Oxfordshire OX13 5BH (01865) 820416* **£150***, plus special breaks; 10 rms. Delightful Gothic-style manor house with elegant, relaxing sitting rooms, open fires, good imaginative food using home-grown produce in attractive conservatory dining room, courteous helpful service, and 12 acres of pretty gardens and paddocks; tennis court; no smoking; lots to see nearby; cl 24–25 Dec; dogs welcome in bedrooms

LONG HANBOROUGH SP4214 **Old Farmhouse** *Station Hill, Long Hanborough, Witney, Oxfordshire OX29 8JZ (01993) 882097* **£44***; 2 rms, 1 with own bthrm. Former farmhouse dating back to 1670, plenty of character inc beams, flagstones and inglenook fireplace; quality breakfasts with home-made preserves, charming cottage garden with conservatory filled with geraniums; Oxford only 10-minute train ride away, and Blenheim Palace and Woodstock are nearby; cl Christmas; children over 12

MOULSFORD SU5983 **Beetle & Wedge** *Ferry Lane, Moulsford, Wallingford, Oxfordshire OX10 9JF (01491) 651381* **£175**, plus special breaks; 10 pretty rms, most with a lovely river view. Civilised riverside hotel where Jerome K Jerome wrote *Three Men in a Boat* and where H G Wells lived for a time (it was the Potwell in *The History of Mr Polly*); informal old beamed Boathouse Bar and lovely conservatory dining room (both with wonderful food – but must book), a carefully chosen wine list, open fires, fresh flowers, a riverside terrace and waterside lawn with moorings; nice walks; they are kind to families; disabled access; dogs welcome in bedrooms

OXFORD SP5009 **Cotswold House** *363 Banbury Rd, Oxford OX2 7PL (01865) 310558* **£78**; 7 comfortable rms with showers. Beautifully kept modern no smoking Cotswold stone house with particularly helpful owners, residents' lounge, very good breakfasts, pretty flowers throughout, and neat back garden; children over 6

OXFORD SP5106 **Old Bank Hotel** *92–94 High St, Oxford, OX1 4BJ (01865) 799599* **£171**; 42 distinctive, luxurious rms, with lovely bthrms. Stylish hotel with a Georgian façade masking a partly Elizabethan building; an impressive collection of 20th-c British art, excellent modern food with an Italian slant in contemporary Quod restaurant and bar with zinc-topped counter, leather seating and stone floors, a carefully chosen wine list, courteous helpful staff, and seats out on the terrace, overlooking the garden; cl 24–27 Dec; disabled access

OXFORD SP5107 **Old Parsonage** *1 Banbury Rd, Oxford OX2 6NN (01865) 310210* **£170**; 30 lovely rms. Handsome and civilised 17th-c parsonage, fairly central, with very courteous staff, good breakfasts and excellent light meals in cosy bar/restaurant; small lounge, open fires and fine paintings, and pretty little garden; they provide picnics; cl 24–27 Dec

OXFORD SP5106 **Randolph** *Beaumont St, Oxford OX1 2LN (01865) 247481* **£170**, plus special breaks; 114 rms. Fine neo-Gothick Victorian hotel facing the Ashmolean Museum; elegant comfortable day rooms, grand foyer, graceful restaurant with lovely plasterwork ceiling, and cellar wine bar; disabled access; dogs welcome in bedrooms

SHILLINGFORD SU5991 **Shillingford Bridge Hotel** *Shillingford Rd, Shillingford, Wallingford, Oxfordshire OX10 8LZ (01865) 858567* **£110**, plus special breaks; 42 rms. Riverside hotel with own river frontage, fishing and moorings, spacious comfortable bars and attractive airy restaurant (all with fine views), squash, outdoor heated swimming pool, and Sat dinner-dance; disabled access; dogs welcome away from restaurant

SHIPTON-UNDER-WYCHWOOD SP2717 **Shaven Crown** *High St, Shipton-under-Wychwood, Chipping Norton, Oxfordshire OX7 6BA (01993) 830330* **£95**, plus special breaks; 8 comfortable rms. Densely beamed, ancient stone hospice built around striking medieval courtyard with old-fashioned seats on cobbles, lily pool and roses; impressive medieval hall with a magnificent lofty ceiling, sweeping stairway and old stone walls, log fire in comfortable bar, intimate candlelit restaurant, well chosen wine list, good friendly service, warm relaxed atmosphere, and bowling green; children over 5 in evening dining room; disabled access; dogs welcome away from restaurant

SHIPTON-UNDER-WYCHWOOD SP2717 **Shipton Grange House** *High St, Shipton-under-Wychwood, Chipping Norton, Oxfordshire OX7 6DG (01993) 831298* **£62**; 3 rms. Carefully converted no smoking Georgian coach house and stabling, with elegantly furnished sitting rooms, good breakfasts, a friendly welcome, and attractive walled garden; cl Christmas; children over 12

STONOR SU7488 **Stonor Hotel** *Stonor, Henley-on-Thames, Oxfordshire RG9 6HE (01491) 638345* **£145***, plus special breaks; 11 individually decorated rms looking over intimate walled garden. Elegantly restored 18th-c coaching inn, with good imaginative food in charming conservatory restaurant and flagstoned Blades Bar; friendly staff; disabled access; dogs welcome in bedrooms

UFFINGTON SU3098 **Craven** *Fernham Rd, Uffington, Faringdon, Oxfordshire SN7 7RD (01367) 820449* **£70***, plus special breaks; 5 pretty rms, most with own bthrm. Very attractive and recently refurbished 17th-c thatched house with beamed sitting room, log fire in inglenook fireplace, antiques, a friendly relaxed atmosphere, and good food in beamed farmhouse kitchen; lots of nearby walks; disabled access

WOODSTOCK SP4416 **Feathers** *Market St, Woodstock, Oxfordshire OX20 1SX (01993) 812291* **£135**, plus special breaks; 20 individually decorated rms. Lovely old building with a fine relaxing drawing room and study, open fires, first-class friendly staff, a gentle atmosphere, daily-changing imaginative food inc lovely puddings, and a sunny courtyard with attractive tables and chairs; dogs welcome in bedrooms

To see and do

Oxfordshire Family Attraction of the Year

WOODSTOCK SP4416 **Blenheim Palace** 🖼 (A44) Few stately homes can rival this extraordinary estate for its range of things to see, splendidly opulent grandeur, or just its sheer scale: the house itself covers 14 acres, and the grounds stretch for well over 2,000 (that's nearly four square miles). As well as being one of Britain's most impressive historic houses, it's also one of the best organised for visitors, which is just as well: thousands flock through the gates in summer, and most people stay all day. The land was given to the Duke of Marlborough by Queen Anne as a reward for his victory over the forces of Louis XIV; the Queen promised to pay for the house's construction, but, thanks to the politics of the court, the Duke eventually stumped up most of the cash himself. It's quite astonishingly grand: highlights include the sumptuous State Rooms, 56-metre (183-ft) Long Library, and elaborate ceiling in the Great Hall, along with plenty of luxurious furnishings and sculpture. You can walk around on your own, or half-hour guided tours leave every 5–10 minutes. The very extensive parkland, landscaped by Capability Brown, is no less majestic, though not stuffily so: you can picnic just about anywhere, saving you venturing into the slightly expensive restaurants. Various monuments and statues are dotted around the grounds, and the formal gardens are magnificent, particularly the water terraces and italian garden. Included in the price are a miniature railway, and butterfly house with free-flying butterflies and other insects, but there's a small extra charge to cover the rest of the family activities: the Maze (a good big one, its design inspired by some of Grinling Gibbons's carvings in the palace), a model village based on Woodstock and its surroundings, and play areas with swings, ropes and slides. There's enough space to absorb the crowds (Sunday is busiest, while Wednesday is popular with overseas students), but you'll find the house usually gets quieter after about 3pm. And you can avoid queuing for tickets by arriving early: though most parts are closed till 10.30am, the gates and ticket office open at 9. Churchill was born here in 1874, and there's a straightforward exhibition on his life. You can hire rowing boats or, with notice, arrange coarse fishing on the lake. Dogs on a lead are welcome in the park, which is just as pleasant out of season, though the house is closed then, and there isn't so much for families. Meals and snacks (three different restaurants), several shops and plant centre, some disabled access; house and most attractions open mid-Mar to Oct, park open all year; (01993) 811325; a full ticket is £10 adults (£5 children 5–15), with an extra £1.50 (£1 children) for the maze, play areas and model village. Entry to just the park is £6.50 a carload – or £2 (£1 children) for pedestrians. For a brief taste of the estate, a public right of way runs through it, with pleasant walks (for example from the attractive village of Combe).

ABINGDON SU4997
Attractive Thames-side town, until 1974 the county town of Berkshire. Much expanded around its old partly pedestrianised core, which still has a fine old gatehouse, medieval bridge, and several handsome old buildings and almshouses around the impressive 15th/16th-c Church of St Helen (its steeple is 13th c), unusually wider than it's long, at the junction of East and

West St. A good museum in the 17th-c former county hall (free) has changing exhibitions. Remains of the partly Norman Benedictine abbey, once the second most powerful in England, have been restored, with part now housing a local theatre. The riverside Old Anchor is prettily placed for lunch.
ARDINGTON SU4388
Attractive small village, with several craft workshops in the Home Farm

buildings, and an upmarket dining pub.

BANBURY SP4540

The busy shopping town was actually without its famous cross for 250 years, between the Puritans destroying it in 1602 and the construction of its replacement in 1859. In the church graveyard is the tomb from which Jonathan Swift borrowed the name Gulliver for his traveller. The Tourist Information Centre is now in the new canalside shopping complex, and there is also a decent local history **museum**; free. The interesting old Reindeer in Parsons St is good for lunch. The B4035 towards Sibford Ferris runs through attractive hilly farmland; the loop N through North Newington, Shutford and Epwell is good too.

BENSON SU6292

Benson Veteran Cycle Museum
Private collection of over 500 bicycles from between 1818 and 1930; open am (exc Sun) Easter–early Sept by appointment with Mr Passey, on (01491) 838414; free. Down by the river at the Cruiser station you can hire boats; (01491) 838304; Apr–Oct; from £25 per hour. The footpath beyond the weir bridge leads to Wallingford. The Home Sweet Home at Roke is a charming dining pub.

BIX BOTTOM SU7285

Oxfordshire Way This long-distance path gives one short walk with a palpable sense of peace, from the lane out past Bix Hall to Valley End Farm.

Warburg Reserve Extensive wildflower-rich rough grassland and ancient beechwood, good for wild orchids and butterflies, besides birds and maybe deer.

BROUGHTON SP4138

Broughton Castle 🏰 (B4035 SW of Banbury) Striking early 14th/16th-c house with proper moat and gatehouse, originally owned by William of Wykeham. Exceptional oak panelling, period furniture, and Civil War relics. Some rooms have bare stone walls under elaborately plastered ceilings, an unusual combination that works rather well. *Shakespeare in Love* was partly filmed here. Snacks, shop, disabled access to ground floor only; open pm Weds, Sun (plus Thurs July–Aug) and bank hol pms mid-May to mid-Sept;

NORTHAMPTONSHIRE

A423
A361
M40
Cropredy
Upper Wardington
Wroxton
Banbury
11
Broughton
A361
Bloxham
Adderbury
Swerford
Clifton
Deddington
Souldern
Great Tew
Duns Tew
Hethe
SP
10
A421
Stratton Audley
Lower Heyford
Church Enstone
Rousham
M40
A4260
Wootton
Oxford Canal
A4095
A34
9
Woodstock
Weston-on-the-Green
Combe
Otmoor
Long Hanborough
Horton-cum-Studley
Wytham
Forest Hill
A40
M40
Waterperry
Farmoor
Oxford
Upper Thames
Wheatley
Rycote
Thame
A420
Cumnor
Cuddesdon
8
Sydenham
7
Great Milton
Chinnor
Kingston Bagpuize
Nuneham Courtenay
Chalgrove
A34
Abingdon
Marsh Baldon
Lewknor
A40
Garford
Frilford
Clifton Hampden
Cuxham
6
Cowleaze Wood
Sutton Courtenay
Dorchester
Brightwell Baldwin
Watlington
Milton
Benson
Watlington Woods
A338
Long Wittenham
Shillingford
Ewelme
Christmas Common
Wantage
Didcot
A4130
Stonor
Ardington
East Hendred
SU
Wallingford
Maidensgrove
A417
Nuffield
A4130
Bix Bottom
Blewbury
Ipsden
Moulsford
Checkendon
Stoke Row
Henley
A4155
Goring
A4074
Sonning Common
Whitchurch
Mapledurham
THAMES VALLEY

B E R K S H I R E

BUCKINGHAMSHIRE

(01295) 276070; £5. The Joiners Arms over in Bloxham has enjoyable food.

BURFORD SP2512

Lovely small Cotswold town with interesting shops and teashops along its pretty main street. The church is particularly intriguing, with a super graveyard, and 17th-c graffiti by some of the 400 Leveller mutineers imprisoned here by Cromwell. The town also has an interesting little museum (open pm Tues–Fri, and Sun and bank hol Mon, plus all day Sat Apr–Oct; (01367) 823196; 72p), and is full of attractive pubs: the best for food and atmosphere is the Lamb, and the Mermaid serves food all day at wknds. Burford does get very busy indeed with visitors, and it's worth noting that several smaller and altogether quieter nearby villages are, in their way, as pretty: Taynton, the Barringtons (just over the Gloucs border), Fulbrook, Swinbrook and Asthall. All except the first have the additional attraction of a decent pub. There are attractive walks between these, along the River Windrush for much of the way – the back roads along the Windrush Valley give pleasant drives, too.

Cotswold Wildlife Park (Bradwell Grove, A361, 2m S of junction with A40) One of the things that makes this place so enjoyable is the way it's been attractively laid out in the grounds of a 'gothick' manor house. It's spread over 160 acres of the estate's gardens and parkland, and even parts of the house have been nicely adapted: the former stables and outbuildings are now a reptile house and Bat Belfry, and the old dining room is an animal-themed brass-rubbing centre. Hundreds of different animals range from flamingos and ostriches through zebras and the delightful red panda, to lions, and rhinos, all in spacious re-creations of their natural environments. Everything's well signposted and labelled. They have various animal encounters and feeding displays throughout the day. A children's farmyard has the usual petting opportunities, and there's a good adventure playground (with an old-fashioned carousel in summer). A narrow-gauge railway operates

Apr–Oct (£1 extra). As well as the animals outside, there's a tropical house (plenty of interesting plants, as well as colourfully exotic birds), insect and butterfly house, and a 49-metre (160-ft) walk-through aviary. Plenty of space for picnics: several shelters are under cover. Some summer wknds they may have birds of prey displays, and there's a grotto in the run-up to Christmas. Dogs on a lead allowed in some areas. Meals and snacks, shops (one specially for children), disabled access; cl 25 Dec; (01993) 823006; £7.50.

BUSCOT SU2496

Buscot Park (A417) What makes this 18th-c house really special is the amazing collection of art and furnishings amassed by its owners; paintings by Reynolds, Gainsborough, Rembrandt, Murillo and several of the Pre-Raphaelites (inc a splendid series by Burne-Jones), with some more recent pictures too. The attractive grounds have formal water gardens and a walled kitchen garden, and perhaps pick-your-own in summer. Teas (when house is open); open pm Weds–Fri and bank hols (plus pm Mon–Tues garden only) and pms every 2nd and 4th wknd in the month Apr–Sept (plus 3rd wknd in Apr, and 1st wknd in May and July), best to check; (01367) 240786; £5, £4 grounds only; NT. The Thames-side Trout (A417 towards Lechlade) is popular for lunch.

CHALGROVE SU6396

Attractive small village, with notable medieval wall paintings in the 11th-c **church** – which owns the village pub, the good Red Lion.

CHASTLETON SP2429

Chastleton House (off A44 NW of Chipping Norton) This handsome restored Jacobean manor house was little changed by the family who lived in it 1605–1991, really feeling like a well worn in family house of that period, and not oversmartened despite the lovely plasterwork, beautiful oak and walnut furnishings, embroideries, Jacobite glassware, even the Bible Charles I took to the scaffold. Peaceful Jacobean gardens inc topiary, and the first-ever standard croquet lawn. Car park up hill from house. Open pm Weds–Sat Apr–Oct; (01608) 674355; £5.40, they advise you to have a prebooked timed ticket; NT. There's pleasant walking in the area between this village, Cornwell and (just over the Gloucs border) Adlestrop. The Red Lion in nearby Little Compton has good food.

CHECKENDON SU6682

Wall painting (Church of St Peter and St Paul) It wasn't until the church organ was taken away to be repaired in 1999 that this almost perfectly preserved fragment was discovered. Covering 18 sq ft and dating from the 1330s, it depicts a gesturing figure and three knights on horseback, and is thought to belong to a much larger series of paintings destroyed in Victorian times. The subject is still unclear, but it may be of 'Christ in the Cornfield'. The Black Horse here is a classic village local. Other churches with fine wall paintings are those of Shorthampton SP3220, South Leigh SP3908 and South Newington SP4033.

CHINNOR SP7500

Chinnor & Princes Risborough Railway Four-mile train trips up into Buckinghamshire; trains most wknds Apr–Sept, some steam-hauled – (01844) 353535 for timetable and prices (you may need to book for special events).

CHIPPING NORTON SP3127

Chipping Norton Museum of Local History Local history in the Co-op Hall of this pleasant old stone-built wool town; shop, cl am, all day Sun and Mon exc bank hols, Nov–Easter; (01608) 645402; £1. The market place is unusually wide, there's a pretty church, fine 17th-c almshouses, and a good few antiques and book shops; the Chequers and Blue Boar do nice lunches. The roads to Hook Norton, or B4026/B4022 to Witney, are good Cotswoldy drives.

COLESHILL SU2393

This attractive village is owned by the NT; lots of good walks nearby, and the Radnor Arms has decent food.

COWLEAZE WOOD SU7295

Between the M40 and Christmas Common, this has forest art exhibits scattered around as part of a sculpture trail. You may see red kites soaring overhead, and the Fox & Hounds on Christmas Common is now an attractive dining pub.

CROPREDY SP4646

An attractive village, where you may find sheep grazing the raised churchyard. The thatched Red Lion has decent food.

CUXHAM SU6695

Pretty thatched houses by the stream which runs along beside the road – and a good village pub, the Half Moon, recovering from a bad thatch fire in 2002.

DEDDINGTON SP4631

Deddington Castle 12th-c fortress remains; there are attractive stone buildings around the village square, inc several antiques shops, and the Deddington Arms and Unicorn (useful for lunch; the Unicorn has a nice garden).

DIDCOT SU5290

Didcot Railway Centre ▣ The biggest collection anywhere of Great Western Railway stock, housed in the original engine shed, inc 20 steam locomotives, a diesel railcar and lots of passenger and freight rolling stock. Meals, snacks, shop, disabled access; open wknds all year and wkdys Easter–Sept, best to ring for steam dates, which usually include every Sun and Weds in summer hols; (01235) 817200; £4–£7 depending on event. The town itself more or less sprang up around the railway. The Fleur de Lys out at East Hagbourne has good value food.

DORCHESTER SU5894

Dorchester Abbey Impressive and well preserved abbey, with 12th-c nave and rare lead font. The tower was rebuilt in 1605 and has a 14th-c spiral staircase, as well as a sanctuary with an exceptional Jesse window from the same period, and some mosaic-like 12th-c glass in other windows. Refurbishments are under way to make the abbey more comfortable, and allow more concerts, so parts might occasionally be closed; (01865) 340007. The adjacent former guesthouse now houses a little museum. In summer they do very individual ever-so-English teas (pm Weds–Sun (exc Fri) and bank hols), all home-made and quite addictive. Shop, disabled access; museum cl Mon, wkdys in Oct and all Nov–Apr; free.

The Fleur de Lys opposite does good lunches. The whole village is a lovely place to explore, with interesting antiques shops. The River Thames has pleasant walks starting and finishing here; you can cross at Day's Lock, and a short walk brings you to Wittenham Clumps (alternative access from adjacent car park), a pair of hillocks which look across the Chilterns and Berkshire Downs.

EWELME SU6491
One of Oxfordshire's prettiest and most unspoilt villages; the cheerful Shepherds Hut is popular for food.

FARMOOR SP4405
Farmoor Reservoir Trout fishing, sailing, bird-watching, and other activities, though you'll need a permit; (01865) 863033 for details and prices.

FILKINS SP2207
Cotswold Woollen Weavers Friendly working woollen mill, with demonstrations of traditional production methods in 18th-c buildings. Snacks, well stocked shop, some disabled access; (01367) 860491; cl am Sun, 25–31 Dec; free. It's a nice village, and the Five Alls has good food and bedrooms.

FOREST HILL SP5807
Above Oxford, this gives several pleasant walks from the White Horse pub.

FRILFORD SU4397
Millets Farm Centre Pick-your-own fruit and veg and a garden centre, animals, walks, and an unusually extensive farm shop which takes in a bakery, delicatessen, butcher's and fishmonger; a maize maze is usually open daily throughout the school summer hols (£3.50); cl 25 Dec; (01865) 391555. In nearby Fyfield, the ancient White Hart, owned by an Oxford college for 400 years, is well worth a visit.

GARFORD SU4394
Venn Mill ⊞ (A338 N of Wantage) The area's regularly used working water-powered corn mill; you can buy their own wholemeal flour; open 2nd Sun in month Apr–Oct; (01367) 718888; £1. The Black Horse in nearby East Hanney has good food.

GREAT COXWELL SU2693
Great Coxwell Barn As noble as a cathedral according to William Morris, a 13th-c stone-built tithe barn 46 by 13 metres (152 ft long, 44 ft wide), with beautifully crafted timbers supporting the roof; free (donations). In charming thatched Little Coxwell the Eagle is pleasant for lunch.

GREAT TEW SP3929
The most charming village in the area (some would say in all England). It's an outstanding series of golden stone 17th- and 18th-c cottages, some thatched and others with stone-slabbed roofs, around an attractive sloping green and among ancient trees, with wooded slopes above. The Falkland Arms is good.

HENLEY SU7781
Agreeable, well heeled Thames-side town famed for its summer regatta. You can usually see other rowing races or practices on the river throughout the year, or hire your own boat on (01491) 572035; from £7.50 an hour. The informal Anchor (Friday St) is a good value pub nr the river, and the civilised Three Tuns (Market Pl) is pleasant for lunch; just over the bridge in Remenham, the Little Angel is a good dining pub.

Greys Court ⊞ (Rotherfield Greys, 3m W) Attractive gabled Tudor house with interesting ruins of its medieval predecessor; the gardens are even more alluring, with white and rose gardens, ancient wisterias, a kitchen garden, wheelhouse, icehouse and brick maze. Teas, bookstall, some disabled access; house and gardens open pm Tues–Fri (house cl Tues) and bank hols Mon Apr–Sept; (01491) 628529; £4.80, £3.40 gardens only; NT. The village **church** is delightful, and the Maltsters Arms dining pub has lovely country views, and good nearby walks. The B480 to Watlington is a pleasant Chilterns drive.

River and Rowing Museum (Mill Meadows) In a stunning modern building, this has comprehensive displays on the sport inc the Regatta, and the history and life of the river itself; also special events. Meals, snacks, shop, disabled access; cl 24–26, 31 Dec, 1 Jan; (01491) 415600; £4.95.

HOOK NORTON SP3433
Hook Norton Brewery Visitor

centre and little museum charting the history of this charming 150-year-old brewery; tours are 10am Mon–Fri, and occasional evenings Apr–Sept (other times too) phone to book (01608) 730384; £6.95 inc samples and a glass. As well as the 25 horsepower steam engine which has provided nearly all the brewery's power since it first opened, you can also usually see the shire horses at work (they're still used to carry out some local deliveries); cl Sat (exc in Dec) 25–26 Dec, 1 Jan, and over Easter; £2 for museum. The stone-built village is attractive, and the Sun has good food. (See *Where to eat*).

IPSDEN SU6386
Wellplace Zoo Mainly a bird park, but also animals such as lambs, goats, otters, donkeys and monkeys. You can feed several of them, so good for children. Snacks, shop, disabled access; cl wkdys Oct–Mar; (01491) 680473; £2. The charming King William IV at Hailey has good food (and great views). Ian Smith can arrange **horse-drawn waggon rides** through these pretty Chilterns fringes; most fine summer days he runs two-horse wagons from Darkwood Farm, Park Corner on a local pub tour; (01491) 641324. Even by car, these are pleasant Chilterns drives – for instance the loop S of Nettlebed through Highmoor Cross, Stoke Row and Nuffield.

KELMSCOT SU2599
Kelmscott Manor The summer home of William Morris until his death in 1896, now with one of the best assemblages of Morris memorabilia, standing out all the more for its domestic setting. Works by other Pre-Raphaelite artists inc splendid paintings by Rossetti, who initially shared the lease. Meals, snacks, shop, disabled access; open Weds (exc 1–2 pm), and pm third Sat of month Apr–Sept, plus pm first and third Sats July–Aug; (01367) 252486; £7. There's a nice Thames-side walk of 1½ miles E to the Swan at Radcot Bridge.

KINGSTON BAGPUIZE SU4098
Kingston House (off A415) Charming 17th-c manor house, remodelled in the early 18th c, with lovely panelling, attractive furnishings and friendly unstuffy feel; peaceful garden with mature flowering shrubs, woodland walks, and Georgian gazebo. Shop, disabled access to garden; open various Sun and bank hol Mon pms 16 Feb–12 Oct, phone for dates; (01865) 820259; £4, £2 garden only. The Hinds Head has enjoyable food.

LITTLE ROLLRIGHT SP2931
Rollright Stones Dramatic and mysterious Bronze Age stones, chiefly in a circle about 30 metres (100 ft) across, now thought to date from between 1500 and 2000 BC; legend has it that the stones are a king and his men tricked by a witch into falling under her spell, and petrified. It's supposed to be impossible to count them as you can never tell where you started. The Gate Hangs High nr here is very good for lunch.

LONG HANBOROUGH SP4314
Oxford Bus Museum 📷 (Old Station Yard) Around 45 vehicles, from Oxford horse trams to rather more modern machines (up to the 1960s), some roadworthy, others being restored. Snacks, shop, disabled access; open pm Sat Easter–Oct, and all Sun and bank hols; (01993) 883617; £2. The Hand & Shears at Church Hanborough is a very good dining pub.

LONG WITTENHAM SU5493
Pendon Museum of Miniature Landscape and Transport 📷 Charming exhibition showing a highly detailed model railway and meticulously researched model 1930s village scenes; you can often see modellers working on the exhibits, and they're always happy to chat. Snacks, shop; open pm wknds and bank hols, plus pm Weds July–Aug; (01865) 407365; £4.50. The Plough (long garden by the Thames) is handy for lunch.

MAPLEDURHAM SU6776
Very attractive little community with lovely beechwoods full of birds; the nicest way to reach it is by boat from the Caversham Promenade at Reading (summer only); (0118) 948 1088.
Mapledurham House Impressive Elizabethan mansion in pretty Thames-side parkland, with paintings and family portraits, great oak staircases, and moulded Elizabethan ceilings. In the grounds is the last **watermill** on the Thames to use wooden machinery;

dating from 1423, it still produces flour, bran and semolina. Also riverside walks and island with picnic area. Teas, shop, disabled access to ground floor only; open pm wknds and bank hols Easter–end Sept; (0118) 972 3350; £6 house and watermill, £4 house only, £3 watermill only. You can stay in one of the lovely cottages on the estate (some thatched).

MILTON SU4892

Milton Manor Elegant 17th-c manor house with splendid Strawberry Hill Gothic library, interesting chapel, walled garden, and unusual collections of teapots and fine china. Phone for opening times and prices; (01235) 862321. The cherry orchards around Milton Hill are a fine sight when the white blossom is out in spring, and around July roadside stalls sell plump red-black fresh cherries – the Grove Farm Shop (A4130) is especially friendly. The Cherry Tree pub in nearby Steventon is a useful food stop.

MINSTER LOVELL SP3211

One of the prettiest and most unspoilt old villages in the area; there's an attractive 15th-c church, village green, and 15th-c bridge over the River Windrush narrow enough for the Welsh drovers to use for counting the sheep in the flocks they brought this way each year. The smart Old Swan does light lunches.

Minster Lovell Hall Imposing and attractively set, this was being used as ramshackle farm buildings until its 'restoration' as neat ruins in the 1930s. Macabre stories about the 15th-c Hall usually involve people being shut up in various places and forgotten about until their skeletons are discovered much later. Open every day, free. There's a well restored medieval dovecot nearby.

NORTH LEIGH SP3813

Roman Villa Occupied between the 2nd and 4th c, when it was a very grand place with several dozen rooms, it's now just a few neat but poignant traces, in a very pleasant wooded setting; free. The medieval village church, with a Saxon tower, is lovely inside, and the Woodman is popular for lunch.

NUFFIELD SU6787

Nuffield Place ⊞ The home of Lord and Lady Nuffield 1933–1963, with the original 30s furnishings. Good gardens with mature trees and shrubs inc rhododendrons, lawns, pond and rockery, as well as Lady Nuffield's own Wolseley and a display of vintage cars. Teas, small shop, disabled access to ground floor only; open pm 2nd and 4th Suns of month Apr–Sept; (01491) 641224; £3.50. The Crown pub here has decent food.

NUNEHAM COURTENAY SU5599

Harcourt Arboretum (A4074) Part of the Oxford University botanic department, with a good collection of conifers introduced in 1835, a 13-acre bluebell wood, traditional English meadow and lots of rhododendrons. Disabled access; cl wknds Nov–Apr, 22 Dec–3 Jan and Good Fri–Easter Mon; free, car park £2.

OTMOOR SP5614

Several square miles of flatland, so poorly drained that in very wet weather its river actually flows backwards, and interesting to walk through (there are several paths). Because serious farming is virtually out of the question, it does have more natural wildlife than most places in the county, and having purchased some of the land from local farmers, the RSPB (backed by local authorities) is working on making it an even more outstanding refuge. The Abingdon Arms at Beckley, with a pretty garden, is one good starting point; the Nut Tree at Murcott is a good dining pub (not Mon).

OXFORD SP5105

On first impression this can seem quite a frenetic city: the ancient university buildings with their medieval lanes and scholarly corners are surrounded by a bustling largely industrialised town, with a formidable amount of traffic. Some of the major city centre thoroughfares have been pedestrianised in a bid to relieve the nightmarish congestion problems (you can't drive your car through the centre between 7am and 6.30pm). If you don't come by train or coach, it's certainly a good idea to leave your car at one of the Park and Rides around the ring road; £1 parking, and £1.60 return on the buses. Guided walks around the city (£6.50) usually leave from the tourist information centre (Old School pub, Gloucester Green) at 11 and 2 daily (more often in the summer) exc 25–26 Dec. For first-time visitors, hop-on-and-off **tour buses** take in all the best sites and last about an hour (£8.50). Many of the city's oldest or most interesting buildings are grouped around the Bodleian Library, the Sheldonian Theatre and the splendid domed Radcliffe Camera (also a library). This partly cobbled central university area is most attractive, but does sometimes overfill with visitors. In the streets and lanes leading off, the honey-coloured stone makes for a harmony that unites different styles and different centuries. There are a few good shops dotted about; Blackwells is the main bookseller, with several branches around the Broad St area, and the Tourist Information Centre on Broad St has a leaflet on the best antiquarian book shops here.

Colleges Most allow visitors into at least some of their quads, and do have a wonderful timeless appeal. One of the few they failed to impress was William Cobbett, who wrote in his *Rural Rides* that he 'could not help reflecting on the drones that they contain, and the wasps they send forth'. Newcomers are often surprised to discover that the colleges are all separate bodies with little in common, each firmly maintaining its own dons, rules and traditions; the university itself is little more than an administrative umbrella. Several now charge admission, notably Christ Church, New, Magdalen, Trinity and Brasenose. Access may be more limited in term-time. A few may let you in only with a guide; ideally though, it's worth trying to explore at your own pace away from the crowds – afternoons are best, with more colleges open then. Besides colleges we pick out individually, more are tucked down some of the town's prettiest streets, such as charming Exeter, Jesus and Lincoln down Turl St, and Corpus Christi and Oriel around Merton Lane and Oriel Sq. This last college has a very attractive and unusual entrance to its dining hall. Trinity on Broad St though not large is very grand. Around Radcliffe Sq, Brasenose is quaint (and has good

views of the surrounding skyline from its quads), and Hertford has its Bridge of Sighs over New College St, in itself worth exploring for some more unusual and less busy views and a good look at the gargoyles on the backs of some of the buildings. Worcester has particularly nice gardens, and many of the other colleges' private Fellows' Gardens not usually open to visitors can be seen under the National Gardens Scheme.

Christ Church (St Aldates) The best known college, a magnificently stately place begun by Cardinal Wolsey in the 16th c, but soon taken over by Henry VIII. The main entrance is through Tom Tower, designed by Christopher Wren and named after its famous bell that rings out 101 times at nine o'clock every night – in less liberal times the hour when students were due back in their rooms. The hall is worth a look, with its remarkable hammerbeam roof, paintings of alumni and benefactors by all the most expensive portrait-painters of the period, and the long tables laid out with silver for meals. The elaborate little cathedral is England's smallest, and doubles as the college chapel. It has some excellent stained glass by Burne-Jones, fantastic pendent vaulting in the choir, and some of the original Norman priory work. Entry into the college may be limited on Suns. A hidden treasure unnoticed by most visitors is the college's Picture Gallery (Canterbury Quad), with an important collection of Old Master paintings and drawings, and various temporary exhibitions. Shop; cl 1–2pm, am Sun, and end Mar, guided tours by arrangement; (01865) 276172; £2 (free on Mons).

Keble College (Parks Rd) Brightly Victorian and very red brick, with perhaps the most famous Pre-Raphaelite painting of all, Holman Hunt's *Light of the World*, in its chapel.

Magdalen College (High St) The most beautiful college, its tower a dramatic sight for visitors entering the city from the S. The quads and cloisters are very pleasant to stroll through, but the chief attraction is the deer park, an unexpected haven in the heart of the bustling city. There's a circular path around this meadow (you can't go in) called Addison's Walk; in spring it's a mass of snowdrops and daffodils, then has hundreds of thousands of fritillaries in later spring, and after that the deer. Over a small bridge is the Fellows' Garden with a small ornamental lake – a very peaceful, sheltered spot.

Merton College (Merton St) The most ancient buildings, with the country's oldest library.

New College (Holywell St) Impressive chapel, atmospheric wisteria-covered cloisters, and remains of the city wall. Nearby, the tucked-away Turf Tavern is a splendid ancient place.

St Edmund Hall (Queens Lane) The only surviving medieval college, complete with Norman crypt.

University College (High St) Harmonious buildings – and an interesting monument to Shelley despite having thrown him out.

Ashmolean Museum (Beaumont St) The country's first museum, and still one of its finest, opened in 1683 and rehoused in this imposing building from 1845. The well arranged galleries include marvellous European paintings from the Renaissance to the 20th c, and antiquities from ancient Egypt, Greece and Rome; they've also a collection of Asian art inc a gallery of modern Chinese paintings. Meals, snacks, shop, disabled access; cl Mon (exc bank hol pms), 3 days for St Giles Fair (early Sept), and a few days over Christmas and Easter; (01865) 278000; free.

Bate Collection of Musical Instruments (St Aldates) Outstanding constantly developing collection of early keyboards, woodwind, brass, percussion and other instruments, and very friendly staff. Shop, some disabled access; cl am, wknds (exc Sat am during term time), and a few days at Christmas and Easter, but phone to check; (01865) 276139; free.

Bodleian Library (Broad St) One of the oldest in Europe, its splendidly grand quad dominated by the Tower of the Five Orders. Most of it is closed to the public, but guided tours take in the beautifully vaulted 15th-c Divinity School, which shows some of the library's treasures inc the Chancellor's Court, Convocation House and Duke Humfrey's Library, the oldest reading room. (Tours usually leave at 10.30, 11.30, 2 and 3 mid-Mar–Oct; 2 and 3 only wkdys in winter); (01865) 277224; no under-14s, excellent shop, limited disabled access (with notice); cl Sat pm and all Sun; £3.50. Altogether the library houses over 6,500,000 books, going down six storeys under the centre of the city.

Carfax Tower Right at the traditional centre of Oxford, all that remains of a 14th-c church; good views from the top, and the bells in the tower are interestingly designed. Shop; cl 25 Dec–1 Jan; (01865) 792653; £1.50.

Castle Mound There isn't much of the Norman castle left save a tower and crypt of the castle church, and an underground well chamber, but the Mound gives quite good views over the city and its surroundings.

Christchurch Meadow A lovely unspoilt expanse of green astonishingly close to the busy city streets. You can gaze across the fields of grazing longhorn cattle to the spires in the distance, or walk under overhanging trees along the banks of the river to the boathouses; college eights row from here all year, in just about any weather.

Covered market (High St) A maze of stalls with something different at every turn; speciality shops, cafés, delicatessen and old-fashioned butchers and poultry merchants. The Oxford Sandwich Co do excellent take-away sandwiches here, and Ben's Cookies are a favourite with students.

Curioxity 🎟 (Gloucester Green) The Old Fire Station complex houses a theatre and a nightclub as well as this interactive science gallery, which has enough to keep children captivated for an hour; visitors can experiment with the exhibits, and the staff are helpful. Shop; open wknds, and daily during school hols (phone to check over Christmas and Easter); (01865) 247004; £2.50. This area, interestingly rejuvenated with trendy shops, cafés and bustling markets on Weds and Thurs, was once one of the less desirable parts of town. Not far from here among the fashionable shops and boutiques of Little Clarendon St, George & Davies is a good ice-cream parlour.

Iffley Meadows These are conserved for wildlife, and in late spring are a sea of purple snake's-head fritillaries. The towpath walk by pretty Iffley Lock is pleasant, passing the Isis Tavern, which has food all day and can't be reached by road.

Museum of Modern Art (Pembroke St) Recently reopened after refurbishments to increase gallery space, this modern art museum has the sort of exhibitions and displays not often found in galleries outside London. They open till 8pm on Thurs. Meals, snacks, disabled access; cl Mon, and bank hols – worth checking; (01865) 722733; free.

Museum of Oxford (St Aldates) Interesting little local history museum, with re-created rooms, maps, and period music. Shop; cl Mon, Sun am, Good Fri, 24–26 Dec and 1 Jan; (01865) 252761; £2.

Museum of the History of Science (Broad St) Excellent collection of national importance, in one of the city's nicest old buildings; recent refurbishments have created more gallery space, and a new temporary exhibition gallery. Shop, some disabled access; usually cl am, Sun, Mon and bank hols, and 25 Dec–1 Jan; (01865) 277280; free.

Oxford Story 🎫 (Broad St) One of Europe's longest dark rides, with cars designed as desks taking you through a cheerful and well researched re-creation of university history, complete with sights, sounds and smells. A useful introduction to the city (esp for families), though no substitute for the real thing; special events during most school hols. Good shop (you can just visit here, using the entrance on Ship St), disabled access; cl 25 Dec; (01865) 728822; £6.50.

Oxford University Museum of Natural History (Parks Rd) Victorian Gothic structure specialising in natural history – outstanding if solidly earnest collection, enlivened by a working beehive in summer. Shop, disabled access to ground floor; cl am, and a few days over Easter and Christmas; free.

Pitt Rivers Museum (entrance via University Museum, Parks Rd) This fascinating close-packed ethnographic museum is off the tourist track. Shrunken heads, totem poles and fertility rites, along with art and ingenuity from all cultures and periods. The half-million or so artefacts in the collections range from Captain Cook's Pacific Islands collection and 18th-c ship models to severed fingertips and an Inuit coat made from seal intestines. Displays are still in firmly traditional cases or drawers, with neatly handwritten labels, so it has kept something of the Victorian atmosphere that's part of its charm. Objects Talk, an exhibition on the personal connections people make with objects, runs until the summer. Shop, disabled access to ground floor only; cl am and a few days over Christmas and Easter; (01865) 270927; free.

Port Meadow This is the best outlying area for Oxford walks, an expanse of waterside common land with grazing horses and flocks of geese, which extends N from Jericho and can be reached on the far side of the Oxford canal via Walton Well Rd, crossing the Thames and turning right along the W bank. Just beyond the far end of Port Meadow is the ruin of 12th-c Godstow Nunnery, where Fair Rosamund the mistress of Henry II is buried; nearby, the riverside medieval Trout pub is touristy but very attractive, and there are often peacocks around here. A second well sited riverside pub, the thatched Perch at Binsey, is another popular walking objective in this direction.

Punting and boat trips Good fun in sunny weather; once you've got the knack it's a very nice way of spending a lazy afternoon. You can hire boats from Magdalen Bridge or Folly Bridge; from around £10/£12 an hour – you'll have to put down a big deposit. Salters run steamer trips from Folly Bridge to Abingdon; May–Sept; (01865) 243421; from £4.60 for a 40-minute trip.

Ruskin walk From the big garden of the Fishes pub at North Hinksey, a footpath towards Oxford partly follows a causeway built originally by John Ruskin to give students experience of healthy outdoor labour.

Sheldonian Theatre (Broad St) A grand classical building, with a lovely painted ceiling. In its time it's been used for parliaments, and nowadays university ceremonies are held here; you may see gowned students heading for these on some wknds, though the theatre is closed to the public then. Nearby, the Kings Arms is a famous university haunt.

St Mary's (High St) Interesting university church with fine views from the tower, and a nice – if busy – café in the Congregation House (the oldest university building); usually cl Sun am, Good Fri and 24–26 Dec (tower cl Sept–May); (01865) 279111; £1.60.

St Michael at the North Gate 🔳 (Cornmarket St) Oxford's oldest building, this Saxon church has displays of silver, clocks and bells; great views from the tower. Shop, disabled access to church; cl Sun am, 25 Dec and Good Fri; £1.50.

University Botanic Garden (High St) Britain's oldest botanic garden, founded in 1621, with 8,000 species of plant from all over the world. It's a lovely place to sit for a while, or wander through on the way to the river. Disabled access; cl Good Fri and 25 Dec; (01865) 286690; £2.50 Apr–Oct, otherwise free. They also administer the Harcourt Arboretum at Nuneham Courtenay.

University Parks There are countrified walks almost from Oxford's city centre. The Parks (primarily playing fields) are the closest place for a good stroll – and in summer you can watch first-class cricket matches for free.

Waterside walks The rivers Thames and Cherwell cut strikingly rural corridors through the city, though walks along the Cherwell may be impeded by closed college gates. They are most likely to be open in mid-afternoon.

OXFORD CANAL SP4816
For towpath walks, there's access from the Boat pub at Thrupp SP4816. The towpath is shadowed by the railway, so you can walk by the canal from one village to another, for example from Lower Heyford SP4824 to Nethercott SP4820, and return by train.

RIDGEWAY SU2885
Near the N crest of the downs, the Ridgeway tracks right across from Wiltshire to Berkshire. This broad grassy trackway was used as a herding highway for some 2,000 years before the Romans came, and after the break-up of the Roman empire came back into use for the same purpose, well into medieval times. It's now part of the long-distance path network, and gives good walking with fine views. The particularly atmospheric short stretch nr Compton Beauchamp takes in the ancient sites of Waylands Smithy, the White Horse and Uffington Castle.

ROUSHAM SP4823
Rousham House Nicely unspoilt 17th-c house embellished by court artists and architects, and remodelled in the 18th c by William Kent to give the external appearance of a Gothic Tudor mansion. It still has Civil War shooting holes in the door. Excellent 18th-c classically landscaped garden with buildings, cascades, statues and vistas in 30 acres of hanging woods above the River Cherwell, and walled flower and vegetable gardens. No children under 15. Some disabled access to grounds; house open pm Weds, Sun and bank hols Apr–Sept, gardens open daily all year; (01869) 347110; £3 house, £3 garden. There's a 12th-c church, and the Bell in a pretty square of thatched cottages at Lower Heyford has enjoyable food, and canal walks nearby.

RYCOTE SP6604
Rycote Chapel (off A329) Peaceful little 15th-c private chapel, later visited by both Elizabeth I and Charles I. Shop, disabled access; open pm Fri–Sun and bank hols Apr–Sept; £2; EH.

SEGSBURY CAMP SU3883
Extensive Iron Age hill fort, later used by the Romans, with good views; reached by the dead-end lane up past the Sparrow in Letcombe Regis.

SHIPTON-UNDER-WYCHWOOD SP2717
Old houses around a lovely big sloping green; the Shaven Crown is a fine ancient inn.

SIBFORD GOWER SP3537
There are pleasant walks in the countryside around the quiet village of Sibford Gower, which has a handsome manor house; the 17th-c Bishop Blaize pub has lovely views from its attractive garden.

SONNING COMMON SU7079
Herb Farm (Peppard Rd) Extensive range of herb plants and products, with over 200 different species in the display garden, and a Saxon-design maze (summer only; £1.50). Snacks, shop, disabled access; cl 25–26 Dec, and 1 Jan; (0118) 972 4220; free. The Greyhound (Gallowstree Common Rd) has good food.

STONOR SU7489
Stonor House Even older than the stately Tudor façade suggests, with beautiful furnishings, paintings, sculptures and tapestries, and mementoes of Jesuit scholar Edward Campion, one of the many Catholic recusants who found refuge here during the Reformation. There are lovely gardens, a medieval chapel, and a wooded deer park. Snacks, shop; open Sun pm and bank hols Apr–Sept, plus Weds pm July–Aug, and pm May and Aug bank hol Mon; (01491) 638587; £5.50, chapel and garden only £3.50. The smart Stonor Arms is useful for lunch. The deer park is skirted by an attractive right of way from the village, and you can link this with the famous and unusual Maharajah's Well in the charming village of Stoke Row; or for a longer Chilterns walk you can continue E to Turville in Buckinghamshire.

SUTTON COURTENAY SU5093
An attractive village to stroll through, with things to look out for – like Asquith and Orwell, unlikely bedfellows in their final rest in the graveyard. The Fish is a good dining pub.

SWALCLIFFE SP3737
Swalcliffe Barn (B4035) A very well preserved tithe barn, with much of its medieval half-cruck timber roof intact; there's a display of agricultural and trade vehicles, and a local history exhibition. Shop, disabled access; open pm Sun and bank hols Easter–Oct; (01295) 788278; free. The village is pretty, and the picturesque thatched Stags Head has good food.

SYDENHAM SP7301
A charming village, with a lovely church; the low-beamed Crown's new licensees are doing good value home cooking.

THAME SP7006
Well worth a look for its splendid range of unspoilt architecture. The very wide main street has escaped any significant development this last century, and has medieval timber-framed buildings next to stately Georgian houses; the 13th-c **church** is attractive. The 15th-c Bird Cage Inn used to be the town lock-up, and the interesting old Swan has good bar food.

THAMES VALLEY SU7678
Shared with Berks and Bucks, this has a classic, very English sort of beauty, with boating scenes, superb trees and riverside architecture. Riverside walks on the Oxfordshire side are possible only in places, notably between Henley and Sonning – for instance to Shiplake Lock from the Plowden Arms at Shiplake; you can also get down to the Thames from the Perch & Pike dining pub at South Stoke SU5983.

UFFINGTON SU3089
Charming village, with decent food at the Fox & Hounds. Opposite here is John Betjeman's former home Garrard Farm, which you can rent in summer, (01328) 851155; as warden of the magnificent 13th-c St Mary's church, he made sure even its oil lamps were preserved.
Tom Brown's School Museum [£]
(Broad St) Young Mr Brown's schooldays were based on those the author Thomas Hughes passed here; there's an exhibition on his life and work. Shop; open pm wknds Easter–Oct; (01367) 820259; 60p.
Uffington Castle High above the village, this Iron Age fort covered eight acres but had only one gateway; great views over the vale below. On the hillside a 115-metre (375-ft) **white horse** carved into the chalk is now thought to be around 3,000 years old; it's a striking design, very Celtic (local hunt supporters who in 2002 added a huntsman and hounds used biodergradable colours which have quickly faded). If you stand in the centre of the eye and turn around three times with your eyes closed, any reasonable wish will be granted. This is one good setting-off point for the Ridgeway. The flat-topped little hill below is said to be where George killed the dragon. A bit over a mile E, off the B4507, the turning off up towards the downs opp the

Kingston Lisle road almost immediately passes a cottage on the left which has outside a huge pitted flint rock, locally known as the blowing stone: if you blow in the right hole and in the right way you can produce a splendid deep blast of sound. A popular nearby pub/restaurant is named after it.

UPPER THAMES SP4001
W of Oxford, the Thames flows through low-lying country, giving the sort of walk you enjoy more for the people you're with than the scenery itself. The Maybush dining pub on the A415 at Newbridge is a useful focus for pleasant if undramatic riverside strolls through low-lying country, and the Rose Revived here is worth knowing for its big Thames-side lawn. Other pubs handy for quiet Thames walks which also have decent food are the Ferryman off the B4449 S of Stanton Harcourt at Bablock Hythe SP4304 (it runs a ferry for walkers and cyclists), the Talbot on the B4044 nr the Swinford toll bridge SP4409, and the Trout at Tadpole Bridge SP3300 on the unclassified road between Bampton and Buckland.

WALLINGFORD SU6089
Wallingford Museum (High St) Very good sight-and-sound history of the area, complete with reconstructed Victorian street. Shop; cl am (exc Sat), all Mon (exc bank hols), winter Suns, and all Dec–Feb; (01491) 835065; £2.50. The George, an old coaching inn nearby, has decent food. There are the ruins of a Norman castle on a hill, and you can hire boats from Benson just a little way upstream.

WANTAGE SU3987
Historic town where King Alfred was reputedly born; recently much expanded, though there's an attractive quiet corner by the 13th/15th-c church with its raised graveyard, and in Newbury St (where the Royal Oak does decent lunches Fri/Sat) 17th-c almshouses have a courtyard cobbled with bones. The downland roads S into Berks have fine views.
Vale and Downland Museum Centre (Church St) Nicely diverse, from well displayed local history to a Formula 1 Williams racing car; a children's gallery has good hands-on

activities such as brass rubbing, also films and touch-screen computers. The Tourist Information Centre is here as well. Good home-made lunches and cakes, shop, disabled access; cl Sun am, Good Fri, a few days over Christmas and New Year and some bank hols, phone to check; (01235) 771447; £1.50 (unlimited visits for a year).

WATERPERRY SP6206
Waterperry Gardens (nr Wheatley) Colourful 100-year-old gardens with herbaceous borders, formal rose garden with new and old roses, medieval knot and alpine gardens, and a pleasant river walk; there's a Saxon church with original windows, a little agricultural museum (cl am, and Mon), and a craft gallery with changing exhibitions (cl Mon). Meals, snacks, garden shop with interesting plants, disabled access; cl 25 Dec–1 Jan, and around 17–20 July for an arts and crafts festival; (01844) 339226; £3.50. The little Sun in Wheatley has enjoyable food.

WATLINGTON WOODS SU7093
A mass of bluebells in spring, these give great views over Oxfordshire from this steep edge of the Chiltern Hills.

WAYLAND'S SMITHY SU2885
Midway along the Ridgeway between the Uffington White Horse and the B4000 above pretty thatched Ashbury (where the Rose & Crown is ideally placed for walkers), this was even in Saxon times reputed to be the forge of a magic blacksmith, who would invisibly shoe your horse overnight if you left it there with a silver coin – and exact horrid penalties if you tried to slip by without paying. It's an impressive place, alone on the downs, an excavated neolithic burial chamber rather over 5,000 years old, made with massive sarsen stones each weighing several tons; free.

WESTON-ON-THE-GREEN SP5318
Godwin's Icecream Farm You can get around 50 different flavours of ice-cream at this developing family-run farm (and from a window in the café you may be able to see them milking the cows). They have a mini driving school for children over 4 (wknds only, best to check), pleasant farm trails, and they plan to add a pets' corner and tractor

rides in 2003. Snacks, shop, disabled access; 01869 350354; cl 25–26 Dec and all Jan; free.

WHEATLEY SP5805

A place of bizarre-shaped buildings: the unusual octagonal windmill is open by appointment, and some Suns May–Sept; (01865) 874610; free; while the village lock-up is shaped like a pyramid. The Sun (Church Rd) has good bar food. Garsington has decidely smart open-air operas.

WHITCHURCH SU6377

An attractive little village, with nice walks nearby. Just over the toll bridge, the riverside Swan has a good range of food all day.

Boze Down Vineyard (B471 N) Free tastings pm wknds, and guided tours by appointment, cl Jan–Feb; (0118) 984 4031.

WIDFORD SP2712

Widford church and lost village (just outside Burford) The church is very simple, but notable for three things – its medieval wall paintings, the remains of a Roman pavement at the west end of the chancel, and its surroundings, a former village that save one solitary house has now virtually disappeared.

WIGGINTON HEATH SP3834

Waterfowl Sanctuary & Children's Animal Centre £ Set up especially with children in mind, this pleasantly undeveloped place has plenty of baby animals to cuddle, as well as rare breeds, uncommon aviary birds, and 12 well set out waterfowl ponds, awash with ducks. Wear wellies in wet weather. Summer snacks, shop, disabled access; cl 25 Dec; (01608) 730252; £3. The little White Swan in Wigginton has decent food.

WITNEY SP3609

Saxon kings used to hold their meetings, or witans, here – hence the name. It was a prosperous town in the Middle Ages, and is still well known for its blankets, made here ever since. Quiet and relaxed, with picturesque stone buildings, market square still with its ancient butter cross and 17th-c clock, and quite a few interesting old buildings such as the 13th-c church and 18th-c blanket hall. Just off Church Green you can see the excavated

foundations of a 12th-c palace of the Bishops of Winchester (pm wknds Easter–mid-Sept; (01993) 772602; free). The Three Horseshoes (Corn St) has good food.

Cogges Farm Museum £ (Church Lane) This charming old place gives a vivid illustration of Victorian rural life. Most popular with children are the demonstrations of cooking in the Victorian kitchen, and younger visitors can usually try on period clothes. The striking manor house dates back seven centuries in parts; there are taped tours of the upstairs rooms, and an activity room with Victorian toys and games. Outside are the sorts of animals you'd have found on the farm 100 years ago: shire horses, pigs, cows, chickens and turkeys, with regular feeding displays, and hand-milking in the old dairy. On some days they have weaving, spinning, lace-making or butter-making demonstrations, and they hold regular special events. The grounds are attractive, with walled gardens, a riverside walk and a peaceful orchard. Meals, snacks, shop, mostly disabled access; cl Mon, and Dec–Mar; (01993) 772602; £4.20.

WOODSTOCK SP4416

Civilised and prosperous small town, with good antiques shops and fine stone buildings. The Black Prince (riverside garden), Star (food all day) and grander Feathers Hotel are all good. The graveyard of nearby Bladon church, where Churchill is buried, has views over Blenheim Park.

Blenheim Palace See *separate family panel on p.479.*

Oxfordshire County Museum (Fletcher's House) Elegant town house with pleasant gardens and good displays. Snacks, shop, disabled access; cl Sun am, Mon, Good Fri, and 25–26 Dec; (01993) 811456; *£2.50.

WOOLSTONE SU2987

An attractive village in the Vale of the White Horse; Thomas Hughes reputedly wrote *Tom Brown's Schooldays* in the bar of the friendly White Horse inn here (good value bedrooms).

WYTHAM SP4708

Charming unspoilt village, all houses owned and preserved by Oxford University.

Other charming small towns and villages, all with decent pubs, include Adderbury SP4635, Ashbury SU2685, Bampton SP3103, Blewbury SU5385, Bloxham SP4235 (splendid church spire), Brightwell Baldwin SU6595, Buckland SU3497, Chadlington SP3222, Church Enstone SP3724, Clifton Hampden SU5495, Combe SP4115, Crawley SP3412, Cuddesdon SP5903, Cumnor SP4603, Denchworth SU3791, Duns Tew SP4528, East Hendred SU4588 (interesting church), Epwell SP3540, Faringdon SU2895, Goring SU6080, Hethe SP5929, Kingston Lisle SU3287, Lewknor SU7198, Little Coxwell SU2893, Lower Heyford SP4824, Marsh Baldon SU5699, Milton-under-Wychwood SP2618, Shenington SP3742, Shilton SP2608, Souldern SP5131, Sparsholt SU3487, Stratton Audley SP6026, Upper Wardington SP4945, Wootton SP4320 and Wroxton SP4142.

Where to eat

BLEWBURY SU5285 **Blewbury Inn** *London Rd (01235) 850496* Small downland village inn with a charming mix of stylishly simple furnishings and log fire in the left-hand bar, separate dining room, a warmly friendly atmosphere, good imaginative food cooked by the French landlord/chef, nice house wines, and well kept real ales; monthly themed dinners; bdrms. £25/2-course option £18.50

BUCKLAND SU3498 **Lamb** *(01367) 870484* Rather smart 18th-c stone dining pub in a tiny village, with a civilised little bar, newspapers to read, and examples of their own chutneys and jams; popular imaginative food changing seasonally, good value house wines from a strongly French wine list, real ales, and smart helpful service; comfortable bdrms; good walks nearby. £28.90|£8

BURFORD SP2512 **Jonathan's at the Angel** *14 Witney St (01993) 822714* Pretty 16th-c coaching inn with three brasserie-style rooms, beams, white walls and chunky pine furniture, an informal atmosphere, very good modern European cooking from a short but wide-ranging menu, and helpful service; pretty walled garden for summer dining; attractive bdrms; cl Sun pm, Mon, Tues–Weds am, 19 Jan–7 Feb; children over 9. £29.40|£7.95

BURFORD SP2512 **Mermaid** *78 High St (01993) 822193* Busy pub with handsome Tudor frontage, an attractive long narrow bar with flagstones, stonework and some panelling, pretty dried flowers, a no smoking dining conservatory, and an upstairs restaurant; a wide choice of interesting food (all day wknds), well kept real ales, and courteous efficient staff; cl 25 Dec; children over 5. £25.30|£7

CHALGROVE SU6397 **Red Lion** *High St (01865) 890625* Appealing old traditional pub with a smartly contemporary twist to its décor, a log fire and old woodburner, carefully collected prints and period cartoons, and fresh flowers; well kept ales, decent wines, imaginative well presented food, a helpful landlord, and no smoking back dining room; no food Sun pm; cl 25 Dec; children must be well behaved; disabled access. £21.50|£8.95

CHRISTMAS COMMON SU7193 **Fox & Hounds** *(01491) 612599* Extended dining pub with new barn restaurant and a couple of new bars plus unchanged original rooms with beams, big inglenook fireplace, and wooden tables and chairs, good interesting food (they also sell free range eggs and honey), well kept real ales, and decent wines; lovely Chilterns countryside all round with enjoyable walks – especially during the bluebell season. £27|£6.50

HOOK NORTON SP3533 **Sun** *High St (01608) 737570* Facing the church in a pretty village, this bustling, friendly pub has a flagstoned front bar with a huge log fire and hop-strung beams, a snug carpeted room with comfortable banquettes, and an attractive partly no smoking green-walled restaurant; a wide choice of imaginative popular food (inc very good filled baguettes), real ales, good value wines, and efficient service; bdrms; good disabled facilities. £24.70|£6.95

MAIDENSGROVE SU6990 **Five Horseshoes** *(01491) 641282* High in the Chilterns beechwoods, this little 17th-c brick house has fine views from several tables in its extended restaurant, and from the sheltered back garden; rambling bar with log fire and lots of banknotes from around the world, good imaginative food, a decent wine list, well kept real ales, and separate walkers' bar; cl pm 25 Dec, 26 Dec, 1 Jan; children in top bar; partial disabled access. £24.20|£7.95

OXFORD SP5106 **Browns** *5–11 Woodstock Road* (01865) 511995 Cheerful bustling brasserie with lots of plants, mirrors, wooden tables and chairs, helpful friendly staff, and a good choice of enjoyable fresh food; half the restaurant is no smoking, and they are kind to children; cl 25–26 Dec; disabled access. £24|£6.50 ☺

OXFORD SP5107 **Gees** *61a Banbury Rd* (01865) 553540 Relaxed, airy atmosphere, fresh herbs and spices to enliven interesting vegetarian pastas, wild mushrooms and so forth as well as good meat and fish dishes, good unusual wines; in genuine old conservatory; no smoking (except in bar); cl 25–26 Dec; disabled access. £30/2-course lunch £9.75

OXFORD SP5009 **Gousse d'Ail** *268 Woodstock Rd* (01865) 311936 Big 1930s villa, recently refurbished and now a sophisticated restaurant with an elegant feel and modern art on the walls; beautifully presented modern French cooking using luxurious ingredients, lovely puddings, a fairly priced wine list, and efficient formal service; cl Sun pm, Mon. £45/3-course set lunch £24

OXFORD SP5007 **Petit Blanc** *71–72 Walton St* (01865) 510999 Very popular, stylish and airy two-room brasserie, open all day for breakfast, lunch, afternoon tea and dinner; from the smarter room you can see into the kitchen and watch the preparation of the extremely good Mediterranean food; friendly service and helpful notes against each wine listed; children very welcome; cl 25 Dec; disabled access. £30/2-course set menu £12.50

STOKE ROW SU6884 **Crooked Billet** *Nottwood Lane* (01491) 681048 Open-plan beamed dining pub with a relaxed homely atmosphere (rather like a French country restaurant), log fires, a wide choice of good interesting food inc vegetarian menu, decent wines and real ales, and big garden by Chilterns beech woods; children must be well behaved. £28/2-course lunch £11.95

SWERFORD SP3830 **Masons Arms** *Banbury Rd* (01608) 683212 Stylish contemporary food in smartly refurbished and very popular dining pub with a neat and brightly modern bar, rugs on light wooden floors, carefully lit stone fireplace, and comfortable blue armchairs around big round tables; roomy dining room with fine views (and candles at night), well kept real ales, decent wine list, and hard-working staff; tables outside to enjoy the country surroundings. £26|£8

WALLINGFORD SU6089 **Annie's Tearooms** *79 High St* (01491) 836308 Prettily decorated and friendly no smoking 17th-c house serving morning coffee, lunches with a home-made daily dish, and afternoon tea inc a fine choice of home-made cakes and quite a few teas; cl Weds, Sun; partial disabled access|£4.20

WATLINGTON SU6894 **Chequers** *Love Lane* (01491) 612874 Cheerful, cosy old pub with low beams, candlelight, nice old chairs and antique tables, a conservatory, a wide choice of good popular food, real ales, and a pretty garden; no food Sun pm, 25–26 Dec; no children. £25|£7.50

WOOTTON SP4319 **Kings Head** *Chapel Hill* (01993) 811340 Pretty beamed 17th-c Cotswold stone pub with civilised no smoking lounge, a nice mix of furniture, open log fire, very good imaginative food inc lovely puddings, well kept real ales, and decent wines; cl Sun pm, Christmas; children over 12. £29.50|£8.95

Please let us know what you think of places in the *Guide*. Use the report forms at the back of the book, write us a letter or log on to www.goodguides.com

SHROPSHIRE

England at its most unspoilt, with lovely untouched countryside and medieval market towns; several entertaining family destinations, with plenty of farmyard fun

Shropshire's outstanding family attraction is the energetic re-creation of the county's industrial past at the Ironbridge Gorge Museum. Elsewhere it's country and farm-related places that Shropshire is particularly strong on – not surprising given that it's such a rural county. There's enough in busy Hoo Farm Animal Kingdom (Preston-on-the-Weald) to fill a good chunk of the day, while Oswestry's Park Hall (handy in bad weather) and Acton Scott Historic Working Farm (just as enjoyable for adults as for children) are also well worth a family visit. There's a nicely traditional farm in Billingsley, and at Onisbury you'll find an eye-opening collection of rare poultry. On a fine day Hawkstone Park Follies is enchanting, and Secret Hills Discovery Centre at Craven Arms has good interactive exhibitions on the history of the countryside.

Places to visit with more of an adult appeal include the fine medieval manor at Stokesay, grand Attingham Park at Atcham, and Boscobel House (famous for its connection with King Charles II); readers also like Elizabethan Benthall Hall near Broseley, and this year we've added a Victorian villa in Wellington. Elsewhere, there's a first-class aviation museum in Cosford, and a railway (and bicycle) museum in Oswestry.

Beautiful Ludlow is worth a visit, with more than 500 listed buildings including its splendidly craggy castle. Bridgnorth and Much Wenlock are both pleasant for a relaxed afternoon, and Wroxeter is the place to head for if you're interested in the Romans. Shrewsbury has quite a lot to discover among its more workaday trappings.

Shropshire, particularly in its southern parts, has very attractive unspoilt countryside, with charming places to stay in. Drives and walks pass attractive buildings in stone or black and white timbering, haunting ruins, and a set of uncommonly distinctive hills give sleepy views. The splendid Severn Valley Railway passes through beautiful scenery in the south of the county, as does the Severn Way – a riverside walk from mid-Wales to Bristol, guides £6.95 from Tourist Information Centres. In general Shropshire holiday prices are good value.

Where to stay

ALL STRETTON SO4595 **Jinlye** *Castle Hill, All Stretton, Church Stretton, Shropshire SY6 6JP (01694) 723243* **£54**, plus special breaks; 8 spacious comfortable rms with lovely views. Charming 16th-c house in large grounds surrounded by National Trust land; log fires in the comfortable lounges (one has an inglenook fireplace, lots of heavy beams, and a mix of interesting furniture), good home cooking in big no smoking dining room, enjoyable breakfasts, and friendly owners; self-catering also; children over 12; disabled access

BISHOP'S CASTLE SO3288 **Castle Hotel** *Market Sq, Bishop's Castle, Shropshire SY9 5BN (01588)* 638403 **£70**; 6 spacious rms with fine views. On the site of the old castle keep, this enjoyable 17th/18th-c hotel has good fires, a relaxed and friendly atmosphere, lovely home-made food, well kept beers, and welcoming owners; crown bowling green at top of garden (available for residents); cl 24–26 Dec; disabled access

CLUN SO2882 **New House Farm** *Clun, Craven Arms, Shropshire SY7 8NJ (01588)* 638314 **£55***; 2 rms. Remote 18th-c farmhouse nr the Welsh border with plenty of surrounding hillside walks; no smoking homely rooms, packed lunches, good breakfasts, plenty of books, a country garden and peaceful farmland (which includes an Iron Age hill fort), and helpful friendly owner; cl end Oct–Easter; children over 10; dogs welcome in bedrooms

DIDDLEBURY SO5085 **Delbury Hall** *Diddlebury, Craven Arms, Shropshire SY7 9DH (01584)* 841267 **£120**; 4 rms. Beautiful stately Georgian house in 80 acres of landscaped parkland with ornamental duck on the lake, trout fishing, flower-filled gardens, and hard tennis court; large hall with fine oak staircase, spacious drawing room, and sitting room, enjoyable food using their own vegetables and eggs, a good wine list, and hearty breakfasts; cl Christmas; children by arrangement

HANWOOD SJ4409 **White House** *Hanwood, Shrewsbury, Shropshire SY5 8LP (01743)* 860414 **£65***, plus special breaks; 6 rms, 3 with own bthrm. Charming 16th-c black and white half-timbered house with two sitting rooms, breakfasts using their own eggs, and two acres of garden; no smoking; children over 12

HOPESAY SO3883 **Old Rectory** *Hopesay, Craven Arms, Shropshire SY7 8HD (01588)* 660245 **£80***; 3 comfortable rms, one with own sitting room. 17th-c rectory with lovely two-acre garden overlooking Hopesay Hill (NT); comfortable drawing room with log fire and baby grand piano, attractive recently redecorated dining room with excellent home cooking, and hearty breakfasts with home-baked bread; no smoking; super walks from the house; cl Christmas and New Year; no children

HOPTON WAFERS SO6376 **Crown** *Hopton Wafers, Kidderminster, Worcestershire DY14 0NB (01299)* 270372 **£75**, plus special breaks; 7 rms. Attractive creeper-covered stone inn in pleasant countryside, with interestingly furnished bar, inglenook fireplace, enjoyable food, decent house wines, beers and malt whiskies, friendly efficient service, and streamside garden; children over 12; dogs welcome in bedrooms

IRONBRIDGE SJ6603 **Valley Hotel** *20 Buildwas Rd, Ironbridge, Telford, Shropshire TF8 7DW (01952)* 432247 **£120**; 35 rms, some in renovated stables and servants' quarters. Carefully refurbished 18th-c country house in secluded grounds close to the famous iron bridge; friendly, pleasant and helpful staff, good food from a varied menu using top quality ingredients in no smoking restaurant

KNOCKIN SJ3321 **Top Farmhouse** *Knockin, Oswestry, Shropshire SY10 8HN (01691)* 682582 **£48***; 3 pretty rms. Most attractive Grade I listed black and white timbered house dating back to the 16th c, with friendly owners, lots of timbers and beams, a log fire in the restful comfortable drawing room, good breakfasts in the large dining room, and an appealing garden; grand piano; children over 12; dogs welcome away from dining room

LONGVILLE SO5393 **Longville Arms** *Longville, Much Wenlock, Shropshire TF13 6DT (01694)* 771206 **£48***; 4 comfortable rms in converted stables, with showers. Warmly friendly inn with two spacious bars, well kept real ales, a wide range of enjoyable food in the new dining room, superb breakfasts, and a large terrace overlooking the big children's play area; disabled access; dogs welcome

LUDLOW SO5174 **Wheatsheaf** *Lower Broad St, Ludlow, Shropshire SY8 1PQ (01584)* 872980 **£45**, plus special breaks; 5 comfortable oak-beamed rms with showers. Attractively furnished small 17th-c pub built into medieval town gate; traditional atmosphere, two log fires, lots of hops, timbers, and exposed stone walls, wide range of good food in bar and no smoking restaurant (super steaks), and real ales; dogs welcome away from restaurant

MUCH WENLOCK SO6299 **Talbot** *High St, Much Wenlock, Shropshire TF13 6AA (01952) 727077* **£70**, plus special breaks; 6 rms. Dating from 1360 and once part of Wenlock Abbey, this converted 18th-c malthouse is very civilised, with pretty flowers, log fires, prints, pleasant staff, good food in no smoking restaurant and bar, and well kept real ales; cl 25 Dec

NORTON SJ7200 **Hundred House** *Bridgnorth Rd, Norton, Shifnal, Shropshire TF11 9EE (01952) 730353* **£99**, plus special breaks; 10 cottagey rms with swing and lavender-scented sheets. Carefully refurbished mainly Georgian inn with quite a sophisticated feel, neatly kept bar with old quarry-tiled floors, beamed ceilings, oak panelling and handsome fireplaces, elaborate evening meals using inn's own herbs, friendly service, good bar food, and excellent breakfasts; delightful garden; dogs welcome in bedrooms

RHYDYCROESAU SJ2430 **Pen-y-Dyffryn Hall** *Rhydycroesau, Oswestry, Shropshire SY10 7JD (01691) 653700* **£90**, plus special breaks; 10 rms with really helpful information packs about where to go. Handsome Georgian stone-built rectory in five acres with lovely views of the Shropshire and Welsh hills, and trout fishing, hill-walking and riding (shooting can be arranged); log fires in both comfortable lounges, good food using the best local ingredients, helpful staff, and a relaxed friendly atmosphere; cl Jan; dogs welcome

SHREWSBURY SJ4417 **Fitz Manor** *Fitz, Bowmere Heath, Shrewsbury, Shropshire SY4 3AS (01743) 850295* **£60***; 3 rms, shared bthrm. Lovely black and white timbered 15th-c manor house with oak panelling and log fire in comfortable sitting room, a big dining room with antiques, paintings and parquet flooring, good evening meals, big breakfasts, and friendly owners; outdoor heated swimming pool

STREFFORD SO4485 **Strefford Hall Farm** *Strefford, Craven Arms, Shropshire SY7 8DE (01588) 672383* **£46***; 3 rms. No smoking Victorian stone-built farmhouse surrounded by 360 acres of working farm; woodburner in sitting room, good breakfasts, and lots of walks; cl Christmas and New Year; disabled access; dogs welcome in bedrooms

WESTON SJ5828 **Citadel** *Weston, Shrewsbury, Shropshire SY4 5JY (01630) 685204* **£90**; 3 rms in twin turrets. Fine castellated house overlooking Hawkstone Park, with country-house atmosphere, baby grand piano and unusual strapwork ceiling in the elegant sitting room, full-sized table in snooker room, enjoyable food (bring your own wine) in no smoking dining room, and welcoming owners; cl Christmas and Easter; children over 12

WORFIELD SO7595 **Old Vicarage** *Hallon, Worfield, Bridgnorth, Shropshire WV15 5JZ (01746) 716497* **£130**, plus special breaks; 14 pretty rms. Restful and carefully restored Edwardian rectory in two acres; two airy conservatory-style lounges, very good interesting food in no smoking restaurant, a fine wine list, a cosseting atmosphere, and warmly friendly, helpful service; good disabled access; dogs welcome in bedrooms

WREKIN SJ6309 **Buckatree Hall** *Wrekin, Telford, Shropshire TF6 5AL (01952) 641821* **£85**, plus special breaks; 62 rms, several with own balconies and many with lake views. Comfortable former hunting lodge dating from 1820, in large wooded estate at the foot of the Wrekin; extended and modernised with comfortable day rooms, enjoyable food in the Terrace Restaurant, and helpful attentive service; dogs welcome in bedrooms

WROCKWARDINE SJ6212 **Church Farm** *Wrockwardine, Telford, Shropshire TF6 5DG (01952) 244917* **£58**; 6 individual well equipped rms, most with own bthrm. Friendly Georgian farmhouse on very ancient site overlooking the attractive garden and church; a relaxed atmosphere, particularly good caring service, beams and log fire in lounge, and good daily changing food in traditionally furnished dining room; children over 10; dogs welcome in bedrooms

To see and do

Shropshire Family Attraction of the Year

IRONBRIDGE SJ6703 **Ironbridge Gorge Museum** As if there wasn't already enough to see at this outstanding collection of linked attractions – one of the most satisfying places to visit in the entire country – they've recently opened an interactive design and technology centre, Enginuity, with lots of fun experiments and games to help children learn about engines and power. They can pull a locomotive, control the flow of water to make electricity, and work in a team to operate the Crazy Boiler – and easily spend a couple of hours in just this part alone. It's fair to say there's now no way you could ever hope to see all ten of Ironbridge's varied museums in one day, but luckily you don't need to: the all-in Passport ticket (one of the best value admission deals we've come across, offering a single visit to each) lasts indefinitely, so it's easy to spread them over several visits, which can be hours, days or even years apart. If you want to see Enginuity but bought your part-used Passport before it opened, don't worry: you can upgrade your old ticket to cut the cost of entry. The other museums – not in one place, but scattered over six miles along the gorge – are based around the sites that give this area its claim to be birthplace of the Industrial Revolution. For most visitors the undoubted highlight is still the reconstructed Victorian village at Blists Hill, a fascinating 50-acre site that's the biggest, and many would say best, open-air museum of its kind. Every aspect of 19th-c life is here, from shops, houses, bank, and steam-operated pit, to the school, pub, pig sties and summer fairground. Costumed staff add authenticity, and there are lots of extra activities at weekends and in the holidays – including the occasional period wedding. They nicely illustrate seasonal events, from May Day to Hallowe'en and Christmas, but at any time there's lots for children here. Dogs on a lead are allowed in this part of the museum only. Not all the sites have the same appeal to young children as Enginuity or Blists Hill, but several turn up unexpected surprises: the echoes in the remarkable brick kilns at Coalport for example, or the bitumen still oozing from the walls of the Tar Tunnel. The China and Tile Museums usually have activity workshops in the summer holidays (the first also has a soft play area, and a few interactive displays). On bank holiday Sun and Mons the various museums are usually linked by a bus, otherwise it's best to drive (or walk if you're keen); you'll need to use Pay and Display car parks at the Museum of the Gorge and the Iron Bridge itself. Useful leaflets (and the website, www.ironbridge.org.uk) have suggested itineraries for visits of three hours, a day and longer. You can buy individual tickets for the parts you're most interested in (Blists Hill is £8, Enginuity £4.95), but it really does make sense to get the Passport. Meals, snacks, shop, disabled access; cl 24–25 Dec, 1 Jan, and some parts cl Nov–Mar – best to ring first then; (01952) 432166; a full Passport ticket, including Enginuity, is £12.95 for adults, £8.25 for children over 5; a family ticket, covering two adults and up to five children, is excellent value at £40 (remember it's valid as long as it takes you to use it). You can get a Passport ticket that leaves out Enginuity, which may suit older visitors better: £10.50 adults, £6.50 children (£32.50 for families). See main listings below for other activities around the town.

Please let us know what you think of places in the *Guide*. Use the report forms at the back of the book, write us a letter or log on to www.goodguides.com

ACTON BURNELL SJ5301

Acton Burnell Castle Ruined red
sandstone manor house built in the
13th c, but almost abandoned by 1420;
disabled access; free; EH. The Plume of
Feathers at Harley is fairly handy for
lunch. The Swan at nearby Frodesley
has good interesting food.

ACTON SCOTT SO4589

**Acton Scott Historic Working
Farm** (off A49) Vivid introduction to
traditional rural life, with plenty of rare
breeds, and crops cultivated using old
rotation methods; all the work is done
by hand or horse power, with period
farm machinery. Lots of craft
demonstrations, and daily butter-
making. There's a willow maze for
children; unusually, this is a farm aimed
just as much at adults. Meals, snacks,
shop, disabled access; cl Mon (exc bank
hols), and Nov–Mar; (01694) 781306;
£3.95. The Station Hotel at
Marshbrook does decent food.

ASTLEY ABBOTS SO7096

Astley Abbots Lavender Farm (off
B4373 N of Bridgnorth) You can pick
your own lavender at this friendly farm;
also five acres of gardens, and an
intriguing look (through an infra-red
viewing screen) at bumblebees busy at
work, and honey bees too in
observation hives. Tearoom, shop,
disabled access; open July–Aug; (01746)
763122; farm free, gardens £2.50 (inc
tea and biscuits).

ATCHAM SJ5409

Attingham Park Splendidly grand late
18th-c house on the site of an old
Roman town, with an imposing three-
storey colonnaded portico. The
extensive picture gallery was designed
by Nash, who made imaginative use of
early curved cast iron and glass for the
ceiling. A new visitor room has
interactive activities; attractive mature
gardens, deer park and children's
adventure playground in the walled
garden. Snacks, shop, disabled access by
prior arrangement; grounds open daily
(exc 25 Dec), house open pms, cl
Weds/Thurs and Oct–late Mar; (01743)
708123; house and grounds £4.60,
£2.20 grounds only; NT. The Mytton &
Mermaid opposite the entrance is a
useful food stop.

Home Farm 🖼 Rare breeds and

traditional farm machinery; you can watch the milking of the Jersey cows (3.30pm), and play with the pets. Interactive activities in the new discovery barn. Farmhouse teas, shop, limited disabled access; cl am (till 11 in school hols), all day Thurs and Fri (exc school hols), and Oct–Mar; (01743) 709243; £3.25.

BILLINGSLEY SO7183

Rays Farm Country Matters
Traditional farm in pleasant countryside, with sheep, horses, cattle and llamas, a good collection of owls, and plenty of red, fallow, axis and sika deer; they also have otters. Pleasant woodland walks, myth and legend sculpture trail, play barn and indoor and outdoor picnic areas. They have seasonal activities in the run-up to Christmas. Snacks, shop, disabled access; cl Jan–Feb; (01299) 841255; *£4.50. For longer walks, you can try a section of bridleway starting at the farm, meandering eventually into Wales.

BISHOP'S CASTLE SO3288
Historic little market town with some fine Elizabethan and Georgian buildings, art, antiques and New Age shops, a little railway and transport museum (open pm wknds Easter–Oct (01588) 638446), and a local history museum housed in the curious House on Crutches (open Easter–Oct pms wknds and bank hols; (01588) 63000; free). It's handy for exploring Offa's Dyke.

Three Tuns Brewery Sadly ale is no longer brewed in the four-storey Victorian tower brewhouse across the yard from the friendly pub, but you can still arrange a tour of the unusual Grade I listed building, which now houses a little beer museum; (01588) 638797; £1.

BOSCOBEL SJ8308
Boscobel House Interesting old house renowned for sheltering Charles II after the Battle of Worcester, with an unusually well preserved 17th-c garden and cobbled courtyard, and 19th-c décor giving a romanticised view of his escape. Good guided tour. Meals, snacks, shop, disabled access to gardens only; cl Dec–Mar and wkdys during Dec; (01902) 850244; £4.40. The **Royal oak** here is said by some to have been the hiding place of the king, by

others to be a descendant, and by still others to be just a fine old tree. The Bell in Tong has decent food, and Weston Park at Weston under Lizard (Staffs) is nearby.

White Ladies Priory (just SW) Ruins of Augustinian nunnery destroyed in the Civil War; free; EH.

BRIDGES SO3996
Pleasant quiet village, with a good pub (the Horseshoe) and nearby walks.

BRIDGNORTH SO7193
On the Severn, this old market town is picturesque without being touristy. It's divided into the High Town and Low Town, with steps between the two – though it's easier (and more fun) to take the hair-raising **Cliff Railway** (70p return). At the bottom of the cliff are some small caves that people lived in till 1856 (they're not open, but labelled). As well as some handsome red brick, High Town has lots of fine timbered buildings, such as the odd town hall built on a sandstone-arched base that straddles the road in the High St. The **castle** was largely destroyed in the Civil War, but part of the keep remains, left at a scary tilt by the constant bombardment; the grounds are now a park with good views – the best are from Castle Esplanade. The unusual **church** on nearby East Castle St was designed by Thomas Telford. **North Gate Museum** looks at local history (open Fri–Sun Easter–Oct, bank hols and school hols exc Thurs). The best pubs for food here are the Bear (Northgate) and Punch Bowl (B4364 W; good carvery, great views).

Costume & Childhood Museum (Newmarket Building) Lots of old costumes, dolls, and a Victorian nursery; usually cl Tues and Sun am, perhaps other times; (01746) 764636; £1.25.

Daniels Mill (B4555, 1m S) Working cornmill still powered by its big waterwheel; a picturesque old place, run by the same family for 200 years. Snacks, shop; open pm Weds and wknds, Easter–Sept; (01746) 762753; £2.50.

Severn Valley Railway The leading standard-gauge steam railway, with a great collection of locomotives, a splendidly lively atmosphere, and trips through beautiful scenery; for details see entry under Bewdley, in Worcestershire. The Railwaymans Arms in the station fits in perfectly, good for a snack.

BROSELEY SJ6701

Benthall Hall 🏛 (just NW of Broseley) Well liked by readers, an Elizabethan sandstone house with fine oak woodwork and panelling, decorative plasterwork, interesting garden, and 17th-c church (services 3.15pm 3rd Sun in month). Some disabled access; open pms Weds, Sun and bank hols, cl Oct–Mar; (01952) 882159; £3.60, £2.30 garden only; NT. The Pheasant (Church St) is a good country dining pub.

Broseley Clay Tobacco Pipe Museum (Duke St) Part of the Ironbridge Gorge Museum (and included in its Passport ticket); see how they made those long clay pipes that are a trademark of olde-worlde pictures. Shop; open pms Apr–Oct; (01952) 433522; £2.90. The Pheasant here is a smart dining pub.

BROWN CLEE HILL SO5986

Aptly named, this is Shropshire's highest point at nearly 550 metres (1,800 ft). It has a disappointingly flat top but offers walkers a certain solitary grandeur. The Boyne Arms below its wooded E side at Burwarton has good value food.

BUILDWAS SJ6404

Buildwas Abbey (B4378) Beautiful remains of 12th-c Cistercian abbey – apart from the roof it's practically all still here. Snacks, shop, reasonable disabled access; cl Oct–Mar; £2.20. It's right next to the gigantic cooling towers of a power station, which this close seem to have a geometrical beauty of their own. The Meadow coming out from Ironbridge has decent food.

BURY DITCHES SO3283

Iron Age ring fort, high on a hill, with superb views of south Shropshire and north Herefordshire.

CAER CARADOC SO4794

(E of Church Stretton) This hill has a pleasingly compact summit, and the pick of the local views. The best start for walks is Hope Bowdler, not far from Shropshire's oldest pub, the Royal Oak at Cardington.

CHIRBURY SO2698

An attractive village, with a famously haunted graveyard.

CLAVERLEY SO7993

An attractive village of black and white timbered houses. The church has impressive medieval wall paintings.

CLEOBURY MORTIMER SO6775

Civilised small town, most notable perhaps for its church's **crooked spire**, though timbered Tudor buildings among its more elegant Georgian ones are picturesque. There's a delightful churchyard at nearby Hopton Wafers, and good food at the Crown there.

CLUN SO3080

Attractive stone-built village on the edge of the **Clun Forest**, a peaceful pastoral area of rolling partly wooded hills. The ruined Norman **castle** gives fine views from the castle mound; free. Down by the River Clun, the 16th-c stone bridge is very picturesque. The Sun and White Horse are both good for lunch.

COSFORD SJ7805

Royal Air Force Museum (A41) One of the country's best aviation museums, housing a spectacular collection of carefully arranged aircraft inc the Victor and Vulcan bombers, Hastings, York and British Airways airliners inc the last airworthy Britannia, as well as lots of missiles and a display of engines. Visitors can view the restoration process from a gallery in a new conservation centre. A large modern extension houses an art gallery, hands-on exhibits and a display on the history of military photography. Annual Jun airshow (phone for date). Meals, snacks, shop, disabled access; cl 24–26 Dec, 1 Jan; (01902) 376200; now free. The Bell at Tong is a reliable family dining pub.

CRAVEN ARMS SO4282

Secret Hills Discovery Centre 🏛 (A49 just S) Another of the Millennium Commission's projects, this grass-roofed structure in 25 acres of meadows takes a fresh look at the natural and cultural history of the surrounding countryside. Various galleries house interactive exhibitions on topics as diverse as the geology of landscape, and the art and music it has inspired. A simulated balloon ride over the hills should amuse children, and other attractions include a full-size model of a mammoth skeleton, and craft gallery. Restaurant, shop, good disabled access; cl Mon Oct–Mar; (01588) 676040; £4.25.

ELLESMERE WALKS SJ4035
There are several meres or lakes around here – the Mere (with a visitor centre and plenty of geese and ducks) by Ellesmere itself, Blake Mere, and Cole Mere, which has a country park around it. This is close enough to the Shropshire Union Canal to include a walk along the towpath, with Colemere village a suitable starting place.

GRINSHILL HILL SJ5223
(between Grinshill and Clive) This gives walkers much wider views than you'd expect from its modest height, and quite an atmospheric summit, where woods open out by sheer quarried rock-faces.

HAUGHMOND ABBEY SJ5214
Haughmond Abbey (off B5062 E of Shrewsbury) Extensive ruins of Augustinian abbey, inc a fine Norman doorway in the chapter house, some interesting sculpture, and well preserved lodgings and kitchens. Good for picnics. In the grounds are some plants unique to the area. Shop, some disabled access; cl Oct–Mar; (01743) 709661; £2.10 ; EH.

HAWKSTONE PARK SJ5628
Hawkstone Park Follies 🏛 Created in the 18th c, this remarkable steeply wooded parkland has been restored, giving spectacular views from the monuments dotted around its 100 acres. Highlights include the ruins of a medieval red castle, intricate arches and pathways, and a fantastic underground grotto with tales told by an eerily convincing laser-powered animatron. The full circuit can easily take up to three hours and the path isn't always easy going, so sensible shoes are recommended (and you may need a torch for some of the caves and tunnels). Readers really like this place, and recommend their children's Easter egg hunt. The BBC filmed their *Chronicles of Narnia* here. Meals, snacks, shop, limited disabled access; open daily Jun–Aug, cl Mon/Tues Mar–May and Sept–Oct, cl wkdys Jan–Feb; (01939)

200611; £5.50. The Caspian Bar of the Hawkstone Park Hotel has good value food.

HODNET SJ6128
Several attractive half-timbered houses here, and some interesting old books in the church. At the **Rocking Horse Workshop** (Drayton Rd) you can watch the production and restoration of traditional rocking horses; cl Sun, 21 Dec–6 Jan; (01630) 685888; free.
Hodnet Hall Gardens Sixty acres of lovely landscaped gardens with spacious lawns, lush pools, plants and trees; the astonishingly decorated tearoom is full of big-game trophies. Meals, snacks, shop, disabled access; cl ams, Mon, and Oct–Mar; (01630) 685202; *£3.50 The Bear Hotel opposite is good for lunch.

IRONBRIDGE SJ6703
This steep town, with intriguing hillside paths and narrow lanes, was the birthplace of the Industrial Revolution: it was Abraham Darby's use here of coke instead of charcoal for smelting which made mass-production of iron possible. Well set among the woods and grassy slopes of the Severn Gorge, it was known as Coalbrookdale until the Darbys built the restored **iron bridge** across the river that today gives the town its name. As their industry took off they produced the world's first iron rails, boats, trains and wheels, and for quite some while the valley, so quiet now, was the biggest iron-making area in the world. Attractively placed by the riverside, the Meadow, Robin Hood and particularly the Malthouse are all good lunch stops. The Boat at Jackfield and Shakespeare at Coalport are handy for Maws Craft Centre and the Coalport Museum. There's a pleasant terraced walk between the river and the Golden Ball (Wesley Rd, off Madeley Hill). For a fuller restaurant meal, the Coracle in the square is nice.
Ironbridge Gorge Museum *See separate family panel on p.499.*
Maws Craft Centre Across a footbridge from the Coalport tile museum, big centre with 20 workshops selling things as diverse as pottery, puzzles and pictures. Snacks, disabled access to ground floor; cl 25 Dec; (01952) 883030; free.
Merrythought Teddy Bear Shop

Next to the Ironbridge Gorge Museum, there's a small vintage teddy and toy display in the famous shop that has been making bears here since the 1930s; disabled access; (01952) 433029; cl 25 Dec and 1 Jan; free.

Museum of Steel Sculpture (Cherry Tree Hill) Dramatic sculptures inspired by the industrial heritage, in ten attractive acres. Disabled access; cl Mon exc bank hols, and Dec–Feb; (01952) 433152; £2. The Coalbrookdale Inn is a good lunch stop (not Sun).

Severn Gorge This has such fascinating and picturesque (though not always exactly pretty) scenery that its industrial monuments cry out for a tour on foot. Steep lanes and paths connect Ironbridge and Coalbrookdale, and an old railway track and a path along the base of Benthall Edge Wood assist walking routes along the gorge. A fine linear walk can be taken from Broseley, descending NW into the gorge via Corbett's Dingle to Coalport. From Coalport, you can even follow the river all the way S to Bridgnorth.

LILLESHALL SJ7314
Lilleshall Abbey Impressive ruins of 12th-c abbey in pleasant setting surrounded by yew trees – it's a nice spot for a picnic, peaceful and undisturbed; open daily Apr–Oct; free; EH.

LLANYBLODWEL SJ2422
This attractive village, with its ancient riverside Horseshoe pub, has an exuberantly decorated church, full of bright colours and Victorian lettering.

LONG MYND SO4294
The partly heather-covered Long Mynd, England's southernmost grouse moor, has great character, with the much smaller but very striking Caer Caradoc facing it across the valley. For walks, it's best reached from Church Stretton. The bracken-and-bilberry-clad massif has a flat plateau-like top, crossed by the Port Way, an ancient track dating from neolithic times. Its sides are cut into by a series of narrow, remote-feeling valleys, of which Cardingmill Valley (NT) is best known because of its relative accessibility. The Green Dragon in Little Stretton is a good food stop.

LUDLOW SO5174
Beautiful 12th-c town, its original grid plan still obvious today. The best road in is via Wigmore and Leinthall Starkes – lovely views as you approach. Dotted around are 500 listed buildings, with particularly good examples down Broad St, a charming mixture of Tudor and Georgian architecture. Book well in advance if you're planning to visit during the Festival in the last wk Jun/first wk July. The most famous building is the lavishly carved and timbered Feathers Hotel on the Bull Ring; some parts inside are almost as striking. The Broadgate, the only one of the town's 13th-c gates to have survived, is interesting. Quite a few antiques shops, and no shortage of good restaurants; the Unicorn is the nicest pub for lunch. The town is overlooked by the rather volcanic-looking Titterstone Clee to the NE.

Castle Lodge (Castle Sq) Tucked up by the castle walls, this is reputed to have more wood panelling than any other house in England, and was once home to Elizabeth I's Master of Requests. Still inhabited today, it was originally built in the 13th c, rebuilt in 1580, and was finally re-opened to the public in 1999. The sparsely decorated rooms with lovely doors and fine ceilings are spread over three floors, and have plenty of atmosphere; privately funded restoration work continues. The Persian carpets displayed throughout the house are for sale. Some disabled access; open daily; (01584) 878098; £3.

Ludlow Castle Dating from around 1086, this splendid fortress has lots of original parts inc the Norman keep, and the chapel with its unusual circular nave. The towers and battlements on their wooded crag over the River Teme have wonderful views, and a properly 'castle-ish' feel. Shakespeare plays are performed here during the end Jun/beginning July festival, also various events throughout the year; shop, cl 25 Dec, and wkdys Jan; (01584) 873355; *£3.50.

Ludlow Museum (Castle St) Good local history museum with lots of hands-on activities. Shop; cl 1–2pm, all day Sun exc Jun–Aug, and all Nov–Mar; (01584) 875384; free.

St Laurence church (off King St) Ludlow's parish church dominates the town almost as much as the castle, with its magnificent pinnacled tower; it's in an attractive tranquil enclave behind the old buttermarket, and has a wonderful sense of timeless peace inside. Magnificently intricate carvings, especially on the ceiling and the choir stalls. Oct–Mar it's open 11–3 only, other times you can visit all day (exc am Sun unless you want to attend the service); (01584) 872073; £1 suggested donation.

LYDBURY NORTH SO3485
Walcot Hall 🖼 Big walled garden, 30-acre arboretum with rhododendrons, azaleas, specimen trees, and a mile-long lake in front of fine Georgian house (open only pms 25–26 May or by appointment) built for Clive of India; free-standing ballroom, stable yard with matching clock towers. Mostly disabled access; gardens cl ams, also Tues–Thurs and Nov–Apr; (01568) 610693; *£3. You can stay in various wings of the house, and fishing can be arranged.

MARKET DRAYTON SJ6734
The traditional home of gingerbread; the unique local recipe is locked in a bank, but you can still find plenty of toothsome samples in the shops. The Gingerbread Man (Adderley Rd) is a decent family dining pub.
Wollerton Old Hall Garden Full of colour and interest, this lovely three-acre garden with formal and more relaxed room designs has been developed around a 16th-c house (not open). Meals, snacks; open pms Fri, Sun and bank hols Easter–Sept; (01630) 685760; £3.50.

MELVERLEY SJ3316
Craft Centre and Church The stables of the Old Rectory have a craft centre (snacks; open Fri–Sun Apr–Sept and by appointment; (01691) 682455). The beautiful black and white St Peter's church was rebuilt in 1406 after Owain Glyndwr burned the previous one; it has a fine Jacobean pulpit and chain Bible. The Old Three Pigeons over at Nesscliffe has decent food, with Kynaston Cave and good cliff walks nearby.

MORETON CORBET SJ5623
Moreton Corbet Castle Destroyed by Parliament in 1644, but you can still

see a small 13th-c keep and the substantial ruins of the once-grand Elizabethan house; free. There are some elaborate tombs and a beautiful chancel in the adjacent **church**; the 18th-c Raven at Tilley up towards Wem is a good dining pub.

MUCH WENLOCK SJ6200
Lovely little medieval market town, with lots of timbered and jettied buildings. The Talbot, George & Dragon, Gaskell Arms and Wheatland Fox all have enjoyable food.
Much Wenlock Museum Local history in the Old Market Hall, with displays on geology, natural history and local doctor William Penny Brookes, founder of the modern Olympic Games – the town still holds its own version of the games every summer. (01952) 727679; cl 1–3pm, Sun exc Jun–Aug, and all Oct–Mar; free.
Much Wenlock Priory 🖼 Has its origins in the 7th c, but it's the magnificent remains of the 11th-c building and later additions you can see today, all set off well by striking clipped topiary. The chapter house has remarkably patterned interlaced arches. Snacks, shop; disabled access; cl Mon–Tues Nov–Mar, 24–26 Dec and 1 Jan; (01952) 727466; *£3 (inc audio tour); EH.
Wenlock Edge This very long smooth hill is wooded (and much quarried) along its flanks, but has possibilities for walks. The B4371 along Wenlock Edge has good views.

NEWCASTLE SO2482
An attractive village, with good local walks, and a decent pub, the Crown.

NORTON IN HALES SJ7038
Attractive village with a 13th-c church and a mysterious brading stone on its green. The Hinds Head has good food and attentive service; good nearby walks.

ONIBURY SO4378
Wernlas Collection of Rare Poultry (Green Lane, W of A49) Huge collection of large fowl and bantams with some really unusual ones (they've around 220 breeds of rare chicken), plus donkeys. About 15,000 chicks are hatched each year, so usually some for children to handle. Summer snacks, shop (they can give you advice on keeping chickens); cl Mon (exc bank

hols and mid-July to mid-Sept); (01584) 856318; £3.

OSWESTRY SJ2929

Cambrian Railway Museum (Oswald Rd) Joint museum with Oswestry Cycle Museum, so lots of old bicycles, as well as steam engines and railway memorabilia; one locomotive may be in steam bank hols and last Sun of month. They are negotiating to buy a nine-mile branch of the line nearby, so their displays may change. Snacks on operating days, shop; cl 25 Dec; (01691) 671749; *£1. In the bustling town itself, the Butchers Arms (Willow St) has good value food, and out at Candy to the W the Old Mill does inventive meals.

Old Oswestry (just N) Impressive Iron Age hill fort covering 68 acres. The elaborate western defensive entrance and five ramparts remain; free; EH.

Park Hall (Park Hall, Burma Rd – off A495 NE) Looks at past, present and future farming techniques and countryside activities, in restored Victorian farm buildings, with vintage farm machinery inc a working gas engine. Much is under cover: a play barn houses a bouncy castle and pedal tractor circuit, and there's a soft play area and computer centre; also a collection of rare cars and bikes. A few animals include shire horses, rare breeds of cattle, pigs, sheep and poultry, and more cuddly creatures in the pets corner. There's also a woodland area with unusual tree carvings and adventure playground, children's driving school (chances to test drive electric vehicles), new quad bikes, and a summer maize maze. With milking demonstrations (by hand or machine) at 1pm, and tractor-drawn carriage rides, it's a good half-day's fun for families with smaller children. Meals, snacks, shop, good disabled access; cl 25–26 Dec and Mon–Thurs in winter term times; (01691) 671123; £4.50.

PICKLESCOTT SO4399

Attractive tucked-away village, with good value food in the delightfully placed ancient Bottle & Glass, and good walking nearby.

PRESTON-ON-THE-WEALD SJ6814

Hoo Farm Animal Kingdom 🖼 Plenty to do at this enthusiastically run farm. Highlights include a sheep steeplechase Easter–Sept afternoons (exc Fri) at 3pm with a Tiny Tote for bets, an air rifle range and quad biking for children over 6. Play barns house a miniature tractor circuit, an area where children can bottle-feed lambs and collect eggs, a display of creepy-crawlies and reptiles, and plenty of games. Outside are ride-on electric tractors, lots of animals inc llamas and ostriches, as well as milking demonstrations, a nature trail, a big walk-in beehive with glass window, a craft centre and an evergreen maze, with a trail for toddlers to follow. Quite a few seasonal displays and activities in Dec, inc Father Christmas. Snacks, picnic areas, shop, disabled access; cl 24 Dec–22 Mar, and perhaps Mon Sept–Nov; (01952) 677917; £3.95, children get a free return visit. Entry to the site is free in the run-up to Christmas, though there's a charge for the special displays.

QUATT SO7487

Dudmaston (off A442) 17th-c house with the old flower-painting collection of Francis Darby of Coalbrookdale, modern art, and lakeside and woodland walks in the extensive parkland. Snacks, shop, disabled access; open pms, cl Thurs–Sat and Oct–Mar, house also cl Mon exc bank hols; (01746) 780866; *£4.10; garden only *£3; NT. Parts of the estate are open for public access all year.

River Severn The charming 16th-c Lion at Hampton Loade (cl Mon) is a good jumping-off point for riverside walks, inc the pleasant 1½m to Dudmaston. You can also meet the Severn Valley Railway here (see Bridgnorth).

SHIFNAL SJ7407

Much expanded under the influence of nearby Telford, but still with a villagey heart and attractive buildings, inc an interesting church and some worthwhile food pubs such as Oddfellows (Market Pl) and the White Hart (High St).

SHREWSBURY SJ4912

Though your first impression is of a workaday town of modern shops and offices, the central street layout is still largely medieval, with oddly named streets (Shoplatch, Murivance, Wyle Cop), and plenty of quiet corners tucked away up narrow alleys and courtyards. It's rich in striking architecture, both Tudor timbering and Georgian brick. Around The Square numerous buildings reflect the medieval wool fortunes, inc the old market hall; in the adjacent High St, Owens Mansion and Irelands Mansion are fine half-timbered houses worth looking at from outside. Even McDonalds is in a medieval building. The walk up Castle St is worth while, passing the original Grammar School building and the half-timbered Council House Court. Nearby the church of **St Mary** has one of the tallest spires in England and is known for its beautiful stained glass, some dating back to the 14th c. The unusual Greek Revival St Chad's church (St Chad's Terrace) caused great controversy when it was built in 1792 because of its round nave (even the pews are circular). Shrewsbury Abbey (Abbey Foregate) is well known through the novels of Ellis Peters. Besides the church (partly 11th-c) very little of the abbey buildings survive. A guided walk of the town leaves the Tourist Information Centre daily at 2.30 May–Oct exc Sun in Oct and Sat only Nov–April (£2.50) , or you can pick up a trail leaflet (99p) which will take you round some of the more interesting buildings. The original town is almost entirely ringed by a loop of the Severn which has quiet waterside paths and parks, and you can hire boats along some stretches or take a river cruise (hourly in summer from Victoria Quay by the Welsh Bridge). Our two main food recommendations are the Armoury (Victoria Quay) and Poppy's (Milk St), and other useful stops are the no smoking Three Fishes (Fish St), riverside Boat House (New St/Quarry Park), Coach & Horses (Swan Hill; brews its own beer) and Cromwells (Dogpole). The restaurant in 12th-c St Julian's church (St Alkmunds Sq) is nice, especially for vegetarians.

Scenic drive Heading SW from Shrewsbury, the old coach road through Longden and Pulverbatch is an attractive drive – great views the further you go.

Shrewsbury Castle and Shropshire Regimental Museum 12th-c, castle guarding the narrow neck of land between the river's loop. It was refurbished by Thomas Telford in 1790 when the romantic Laura's Tower was built, though still has parts of the earlier building. It includes the **Shropshire Regimental Museum**, with military displays from the American War of Independence to the present day. Shop, some disabled access; cl late Dec to mid-Feb, Sun–Tues Oct–late Dec and mid-Feb to Apr, and Mon–Tues (exc bank hols) in May; (01743) 358516; £2. The attractive grounds (cl late Dec–early Jan) are free.

Shrewsbury Museum & Art Gallery (Barker St) Impressive timber-framed building with social and natural history, and some Roman remains; the art gallery has changing exhibitions. Shop; cl Sun/Mon Oct–May; (01743) 361196; free.

Shropshire Wildlife Trust 18th-c HQ of the Trust, with displays covering their nature reserves, a wildlife garden, and small shop with bird food, feeders and gifts; cl Sat, Sun; (01743) 284280.

STIPERSTONES SO3799 The rather eery Stiperstones are outcrops of harder quartzy rock leaving strange-shaped boulders, tors and crests on the skyline – and strange tales among the people living nearby. The ridge is crowned by dramatic rocks and has a splendid view; a short walk from a nearby car park (you can make an interesting 8½-mile circuit with a stop at the More Arms at Shelve), or you can take the longish walk up from the former lead-mining village of Snailbeach, where the friendly Stiperstones Inn has enjoyable fresh food all day (inc local whinberry pie).

STOKESAY SO4381 **Stokesay Castle** (off A49) One of the finest examples of a medieval manor house, in a notably charming setting. The hall with its cruck-framed roof and Early English windows is just as it was 700 years ago, and there's a timbered Tudor gatehouse. Good views from the top of the tower, and excellent Walkman tour. Summer snacks, shop; cl 1–2, Mon–Tues Nov–Mar, 24–26 Dec and 1 Jan; (01588) 672544; £4.40.

The Plough up at Wistanstow has good home cooking.

TELFORD SJ7008

Wonderland The attractions at this 450-acre park are a useful enough distraction for younger children if you happen to be in the area, with some re-creations of fairy tales, a maze, indoor and outdoor play and picnic areas, road train rides (£1), pedalo boat hire (£3 for 20 mins), and crazy golf (£1). Snacks, shop, disabled access; cl wkdys Oct–Mar; (01952) 591633; £2.95.

WELLINGTON SJ6510

Sunnycroft Surviving virtually unaltered, this typical late Victorian gentleman's suburban villa still contains much of its original contents; the grounds, like a mini estate, are interesting too. Open pms Sun, Mon Apr–Oct; (01952) 242884; £4.20. The owner probably knew the well run nearby Cock in its days as a coaching inn.

WEM SJ5128

Mythstories (Morgan Library, Aston St) Exploring myths, legends and stories from all around the world, this unusual attraction is rated very highly by us for its ability to catch and hold the interest of children of most ages. Everyone will hear a story, and there are lots of innovative activities; Shop, disabled access; open pm, cl Fri/Sat and Nov–Mar exc by appointment; (01939) 235500; £3.50.

WHITTINGTON SJ3131

(off A5) Handsome remains of 13th-c **Whittington Castle**; the Olde Boot alongside does food.

WREKIN SJ6108

(just W of Telford – and towering boldly over it) The Wrekin is no Everest (an easily attained 407 metres, 1,334 ft), but because it's so isolated on the edge of the Shropshire uplands it offers walkers a huge panorama, spanning places over 100 miles apart;

just below, the Huntsman in Little Wenlock is handy for refreshment.

WROXETER SJ5608

Roman Vineyard Friendly little place producing several wines; also lavender farm, rare breeds, and some interesting glacial stones – not to mention a Roman wall. Teas, farmshop (with various lavender-based products), disabled access; usually open daily (exc 25 Dec) but there's not much to see in winter; (01743) 761888; free.

Wroxeter Roman City One of the country's most important Roman sites, though most of the remains are buried under fields. There's a well preserved colonnade and municipal bath, with useful explanatory boards, and the museum has a good range of finds from the town (then Britain's fourth biggest) and the earlier fortress. Snacks, shop; some disabled access; cl 24–26 Dec, 1 Jan; (01743) 761330; £3.60 inc audio guide; EH. The Horseshoes at Uckington is a decent family dining pub.

Other attractive villages, all with decent pubs or other eating places, include Aston on Clun SO3982, Leighton SJ6105, Little Stretton SO4392, Loppington SJ4729, Lydbury North SO3586, Munslow SO5287, Neen Sollars SO6672, Neenton SO6488, Norbury SO3692 (good walks), Selattyn SJ2633 (unusual church), Tilley SJ5027, Tong SJ7907, Wentnor SO3893 and Worfield SO7595.

Local Tourist Information Centres have details of **imaginative trails** around the region, centring on the work of Thomas Telford, haunted villages, the novels of Ellis Peters, and sites connected with King Arthur (recent theories suggest the mythical king was a 5th-c warlord ruling from a post-Roman city here – possibly Wroxeter). They also have balloon trip details.

Where to eat

BROMFIELD SO8477 **Cookhouse** *(01584) 856565* Once the home of Clive of India, this handsome brick house looks from the outside like an immaculately maintained Georgian home, but inside is smartly contemporary and brightly modernised: fresh flowers on the sleek space-age bar counter, newspapers to read, and light wooden tables, and a cosier high-ceilinged back room with huge brick fireplace, exposed stonework, and soaring beams and rafters; very good well presented food in the café-bar style dining room, and a big open kitchen behind a stainless steel counter at one end; some areas are no smoking; seats on secluded terrace outside; cl pm 25 Dec; disabled access. £26|**£7.95**

BURLTON SJ4526 **Burlton Inn** *(01939) 270284* Attractively restored pub with three cottagey connecting rooms, fresh flowers, magazines to read, winter open fires, very attractively presented interesting food from a seasonal menu, well kept real ales, and neatly uniformed helpful staff; bdrms; cl 25–26 Dec, bank hol Mon am; disabled access. £25|**£7.50**

CHURCH STRETTON SO4593 **Acorn Wholefood** *26 Sandford Ave (01694) 722495* Simple, unpretentious family-run restaurant with friendly service in several no smoking rooms, good filling food (mostly vegetarian) changing daily, delicious puddings and soups, and cream teas with a choice of 25 teas; cl Tues, Weds (but open during school hols), 2 wks Feb, 2 wks Nov; children must be well behaved. £10|**£3.50**

DORRINGTON SJ4702 **Country Friends** *(01743) 718707* Cosy half-timbered no smoking restaurant with consistently enjoyable interesting food, inc lovely puddings and British cheeses with home-made bread; super breakfasts; bdrms; cl Sun, Mon, Tues, two wks mid-July, 1 wk Oct. £38.50|**£9.90**

IRONBRIDGE SJ6603 **Malthouse** *Wharfage (01952) 433712* Nicely decorated large pub with a laid-back feel (despite the buzz and lively bustle), opposite the river; spacious and spotless bar with lots of scrubbed light wooden tables, candlelight, local artists' work, good interesting food using local produce plus fresh fish from Brixham, real ales, several wines by the glass, and helpful staff; no smoking restaurant; live music Weds–Sun evenings; bdrms. £19.25|**£6.95**

LUDLOW SO5175 **Merchant House** *Lower Corve St (01584) 875438* Two simply furnished rooms in friendly and relaxed Jacobean house with exceptionally good food from set 3-course menu, good value interesting wines, and competent service; cl Sun, Mon, am Tues–Thurs, 1 wk Christmas, 1 wk spring. £40

LUDLOW SO5174 **Olive Branch** *2/4 Old St (01584) 874314* Cheery wholefood restaurant in 17th-c former inn, with a changing range of tasty lunchtime meals and snacks inc often inventive vegetarian meals (and meaty ones, too), super puddings, and teas with home-made cakes and scones; cl 25–26 Dec; disabled access. £12.95|**£6.10**

PORTH-Y-WAEN SJ2623 **Lime Kiln** *(01691) 831550* Good inventive blackboard food using lots of local produce in cheerful attractively opened-up pub with stripped pine woodwork and furniture on quarry tiles, warm coal fires, interesting photographs, no smoking corner; friendly helpful staff, well kept real ales, good value wines, and picnic-sets in side garden with boules pitch; cl Mon, 1 wk Jan. £21.70|**£8.95**

SHREWSBURY SJ4912 **Armoury** *Victoria Quay, Victoria Ave (01743) 340525* Smartly converted warehouse with big arched windows overlooking river, lots of old prints and documents, cabinets with shells and explosives, corks and bottle openers, interesting bistro-style food, eight well kept real ales, 25 wines by the glass, 70 malt whiskies; cl 25 Dec, 1 Jan; no children after 9pm. £22.50|**£5.95**

SHREWSBURY SJ4912 **Poppy's Restaurant and Tearooms** *8 Milk St (01743) 232307* Lovely 17th-c building with really fine timbers in upstairs room, plenty of space for shoppers on ground floor and in courtyard, a little room for smokers, enjoyable lunches with interesting daily-changing salad garnish, and popular morning coffee and afternoon tea; cl Sun; good disabled access.|**£4.95**

SHREWSBURY SJ4912 **Sol** *82 Wyle Cop (01743) 340560* Welcoming and relaxed split-level restaurant decorated in cheerful Mediterranean colours with imaginative enjoyable food (super Cornish fish dishes and attractively presented puddings), a reasonably priced wine list, and helpful service; cl Sun, Mon, 1 wk winter, 1 wk summer; children over 8. £36|£13

WENTNOR SO3892 **Crown** *(01588) 650613* 16th-c inn in quiet village with beams, standing timbers, good log fire, collection of china and glass, and mix of tables set for eating in the main area; snug end with comfortable sofas, a good choice of enjoyable food, and a cosy beamed no smoking restaurant; well kept real ales, decent wines, helpful friendly staff, and fine views of the Long Mynd from seats on the neat back lawn; children must be well behaved; cl 25 Dec; disabled access. £21|£6.50

Special thanks to Michael and Jenny Back, Mrs June Pritchard, M A Dixon

SOMERSET

Lots for families, with an excellent mix of attractions from first-class city museums to country farms and wildlife centres; also beautiful Bath, charming towns and villages, traditional seaside resorts and some interesting scenery; good value

Elegant Bath has a fine range of things to see and do from boating and ballooning to enjoyable museums (ask about their money-saving multi-pass). By tradition, we also include Bristol in this chapter. Though it's less obviously a place to enjoy wandering around, it too has a profusion of excellent attractions, including our top Somerset Family Attraction this year, the exceptional Bristol Zoo. Popular @Bristol, the British Empire & Commonwealth Museum, and a medley of maritime and industrial heritage around the docks are just some of the city's other high points.

Pretty Dunster and the charming miniature city of Wells make good day trips, and there are some pleasant walks on the brooding Mendips. On the coast, Minehead is a pleasant traditional resort, and Weston-super-Mare (we've added a the helicopter museum, aquarium and good local history museum here) and Clevedon have some appeal. At Cheddar, Wookey Hole showcaves are spectacular, and the Cheddar Gorge is a big draw too (Ebbor Gorge is a better bet if you hate crowds).

A good number of enjoyable animal attractions include Horse World at Whitchurch (not just horses), Washford's Tropiquaria (the indoor jungle is quite an eye-opener), Cricket St Thomas Park (with a walk-through lemur wood), Keynsham's Avon Valley Country Park (excellent playground as well as animals), and the unspoilt animal park at Highbridge.

Among the county's many museums, our top picks are the American Museum in Britain at Claverton (a fascinating look at America's past, with splendid re-created rooms), the Fleet Air Arm Museum in Yeovilton (a huge place with lots to see), and Haynes Sparkford Motor Museum at Sparkford (great if you like classic cars and motorcycles). There are decent local museums in Glastonbury, Taunton, Chard and Bridgwater.

As well as the fine 16th-c house, Barrington Court has splendid gardens, and there are other noteworthy gardens at Cheddon Fitzpaine, East Lambrook, Greenham, Cannington College and Castle Cary. It's a good county for cider drinkers, who can indulge themselves at Dowlish Wake (best in the autumn when you can see it being made), Bradford-on-Tone (made by the same family for over 200 years) and the cider distillery at Kingsbury Episcopi.

The countryside is dotted with landmark church towers, pinnacled, turreted and gargoyled. Many churches, particularly in the W, have intriguingly carved 15th- and 16th-c bench ends, also fine oak wagon roofs, brass candelabras and carved screens. In the hillier parts, buildings are generally of stone, varying in colour and character from the Cotswold style of the NE, through the pale limestones of the Mendips and the golden warmth of south Somerset's Ham stone, to the rugged and stolid greys of the hamlets tucked into the green folds of the Quantocks.

Over in the W the countryside feels very secluded and self-contained, with each small valley of the Quantocks seeming a private world, and the Blackdown Hills are charmingly untouristy, too – classic quiet English countryside with some lovely villages, some with delightfully eccentric names. The Somerset Levels are an interesting contrast – vivid green marshy pastures, rewarding for wildlife and for traditional crafts such as basket-making. Towards the E, richer more rolling farmland with small valleys and wooded hillsides offers some gentle country drives.

Exmoor (including its Somerset part) is covered as a separate section in the Devon chapter.

Where to stay

BARWICK ST5613 **Little Barwick House** *Barwick, Yeovil, Somerset BA22 9TD* *(01935) 423902* **£110**, plus special breaks; 6 attractive rms. Carefully run listed Georgian dower house in 3½ acres 2m S of Yeovil, and thought of as a restaurant-with-rooms; completely refurbished throughout this year but still with a lovely relaxed atmosphere, log fire in cosy lounge, excellent food using local produce, a thoughtful wine list, super breakfasts, nice afternoon tea, and particularly good service; cl Christmas, 2 wks Jan; dogs welcome in bedrooms

BATH ST7464 **Badminton Villa** *10 Upper Oldfield Park, Bath BA2 3JZ (01225) 426347* **£68***, plus special breaks; 5 rms. Big no smoking Victorian house with marvellous city views, comfortable lounge, good breakfasts, and helpful friendly owners; cl 22 Dec–30 Jan; children over 8

BATH ST7565 **Old Boathouse** *Bath Boating Station, Forester Rd, Bath BA2 6QE* *(01225) 466407* **£65**; 5 rms. Edwardian boating station with black and white timbered verandah overlooking river, free launch to Bath centre, punting and rowing boats for hire, sitting room with river views, new conservatory, and separate restaurant; no smoking; children in cottage only; partial disabled access

BATH ST7464 **Paradise House** *86–88 Holloway, Bath BA2 4PX (01225) 317723* **£65***, plus special breaks; 11 rms (room 5 has a super view). Classically elegant early 18th-c hotel, lovingly restored, with marvellous views over the city; pretty breakfast room, restful drawing room, log fire, and spacious walled gardens; peaceful, though only 7 mins' walk to centre; cl 3 days Christmas

BATH ST7465 **Queensberry** *Russel St, Bath BA1 2QF (01225) 447928* **£120***, plus winter breaks; 29 lovely rms. Four beautifully decorated Georgian town houses in quiet residential street, with comfortable, restful drawing room, open fire, attractive modern restaurant (Olive Tree, see *Where to eat*) and professional service; seats in the courtyard garden; cl 4 days over Christmas; disabled access

BATH ST7465 **Royal Crescent Hotel** *16 Royal Crescent, Bath BA1 2LS (01225) 823333* **£230**, plus special breaks; 45 luxurious rms. Elegant Georgian hotel in glorious curved terrace, with comfortable antique-filled drawing rooms, open fires and lovely flowers; imaginative modern cooking in Pimpernel Restaurant (in summer you can eat in the delightful garden), and impeccable service; plunge pool and croquet; they are kind to children; disabled access; dogs welcome

BATH ST7565 **Villa Magdala** *Henrietta Rd, Bath BA2 6LX (01225) 466329* **£85***, plus winter breaks; 18 comfortable rms. Overlooking Henrietta Park, this elegant, quietly set Victorian house is only 5 mins' walk to the centre; good breakfasts in attractive dining room, a spacious comfortable lounge, and friendly helpful staff; no smoking; cl Christmas week; children over 7

BECKINGTON ST7952 **Pickford House** *Bath Road, Beckington, Frome, Somerset*

BA11 6SJ (01373) 830329 **£38**; 5 rms with river view, some with balcony. Honey-coloured hilltop stone house, with open fire in sitting room, bar, delicious evening meals (by arrangement) and breakfasts, a relaxed friendly atmosphere, and helpful courteous owners; big garden with swimming pool; you can take over the house with a group of friends for a gourmet wknd; cl Christmas; partial disabled access; dogs welcome in bedrooms

BEERCROCOMBE ST3020 **Frog Street Farm** *Hatch Beauchamp, Taunton, Somerset TA3 6AF (01823) 480430* **£60**, plus special breaks; 3 rms. Peaceful 15th-c listed farmhouse deep in the countryside on a big working farm; beams, fine Jacobean panelling, inglenook fireplaces, a warmly friendly owner, delicious food (much produce from the farm, local game and fish; bring your own wine), and traditional breakfasts; cl Nov–Mar; children by arrangement

BRISTOL ST5873 **Hotel du Vin & Bistro** *Narrow Lewins Mead, Bristol BS1 2NU (0117) 925 5577* **£115**; 40 loft-style rms with spacious bthrms. The third in this small chain (others in Birmingham, Tunbridge Wells and Winchester); attractively converted former Sugar House with big pillars and arched cellars, wine prints, posters and empty bottles, comfortable armchairs on stripped wooden floors, and a bustling but relaxed dining room with white napery; particularly good imaginative Mediterranean-style cooking, helpful efficient staff, and an interesting wine list; disabled access

CANNINGTON ST2538 **Blackmore Farm** *Blackmore Lane, Cannington, Bridgwater, Somerset TA5 2NE (01278) 653442* **£50***; 4 rms. Grade I listed manor house dating from 15th c, with garderobes, beams and stone archways, good breakfasts around a huge table in the Great Hall, and log fire in comfortable sitting room; no evening meals; large garden with croquet, and animals to see (this is a working farm); self-catering, too; good disabled access

GLASTONBURY ST4938 **Number Three Hotel** *3 Magdalene Street, Glastonbury, Somerset BA6 9EW (01458) 832129* **£85***; 5 individually furnished pretty rms, 3 in the Garden House. Lovely Georgian house (once home to Winston Churchill and his mother) by Glastonbury Abbey, with antiques and fresh flowers, enjoyable breakfasts in attractive dining room, and a fine floodlit walled garden; cl Dec–part Jan

HATCH BEAUCHAMP ST3020 **Farthings** *Hatch Beauchamp, Taunton, Somerset TA3 6SG (01823) 480664* **£99**, plus special breaks; 10 spacious rms (inc a cottage suite) with thoughtful extras. Charming little Georgian house in three acres of gardens with helpful and hard-working long-serving owners, open fires in quiet lounge and convivial bar, and good varied food using fresh local produce; can arrange golf and other activities; children must be well behaved; dogs welcome in bedrooms

HINTON CHARTERHOUSE ST7759 **Homewood Park** *Hinton Charterhouse, Bath BA3 6BB (01225) 723731* **£139**, plus winter breaks; 19 lovely rms. Charming Victorian hotel on the edge of Hinton Priory and in ten acres of gardens and woodlands; flowers, oil paintings and fine furniture in graceful relaxing day rooms, and an elegant restaurant with very good imaginative food (honey from their own bees – you can help them collect it); tennis, croquet, and outdoor swimming pool; disabled access

HOLFORD ST1541 **Combe House** *Holford, Bridgwater, Somerset TA5 1RZ (01278) 741382* **£82**, plus special breaks; 16 rms. Warmly friendly former tannery (still has waterwheel) in a pretty spot, with comfortable rooms, log fires, good home-made food, and a relaxed atmosphere; heated indoor swimming pool and tennis court; cl mid-Nov–mid-Feb (but open Christmas and New Year); dogs welcome in bedrooms

HUNSTRETE ST6461 **Hunstrete House** *Hunstrete, Pensford, Bristol BS39 4NS (01761) 490490* **£195**, plus special breaks; 25 individually decorated rms. Classically handsome, mainly 18th-c country-house hotel on the edge of the Mendips, in 92 acres inc lovely walled garden and deer park; comfortable and elegantly furnished day rooms with antiques, paintings, log fires, fresh garden flowers, a tranquil atmosphere, excellent service, and very good food using home-grown produce when possible; popular special events (wine tastings, jazz bands, champagne and horse racing); new fitness room, croquet lawn, heated swimming pool, all-weather tennis court, and nearby riding; limited disabled access; dogs welcome in bedrooms

LUXBOROUGH SS9738 **Royal Oak** *Luxborough, Watchet, Somerset TA23 0SH (01984) 640319* **£65**; 12 rms. Unspoilt and interesting old pub in idyllic spot, marvellous for exploring Exmoor; bar rooms with log fires in inglenook fireplaces, beams, flagstones, character furnishings and a thriving feel, three distinctive dining rooms (two no smoking), good food, and well liked breakfasts; dogs welcome away from dining rooms

NORTH PERROTT ST4709 **Manor Arms** *Middle St, North Perrott, Crewkerne, Somerset TA18 7SG (01460) 72901* **£54***, plus special breaks; 9 rms in restored coach house inc a fine panelled and beamed one. Comfortable and attractive 16th-c inn with friendly helpful licensees, beams, exposed stone, and inglenook fireplace, and good home-made food in small restaurant and bar; garden with play area; disabled access

NORTH WOOTTON ST5641 **Riverside Grange** *Tanyard Lane, North Wootton, Wells, Somerset BA4 4AE (01749) 890761* **£45**; 2 well equipped rms. Quietly set converted tannery on river edge and overlooking a cider orchard; charming, welcoming owner and enjoyable breakfasts (places in nearby village for evening meals); no smoking; cl Christmas and New Year; no children

NORTON ST PHILIP ST7755 **George** *High St, Norton St Philip, Bath BA3 6LH (01373) 834224* **£80**; 8 comfortable rms of real character in galleried wing.

Carefully restored, exceptional building that has been offering hospitality to travellers for nearly 700 years; individual bars with trusses and timbering, fine old stone fireplaces, really heavy beams, 18th-c pictures, oak dressers and settles and so forth, a marvellous restaurant, good food, real ales, decent wines, and organised, friendly service; a stroll over the meadow behind the pub (past the picnic-sets on the narrow grass pub garden) leads to an attractive churchyard around the medieval church whose bells struck Pepys (here on 12 June 1668) as 'mighty tuneable'.

POLSHAM ST5142 **Southway Farm** *Polsham, Wells, Somerset BA5 1RW (01749)* 673396 **£48***; 3 rms. Friendly creeper-covered Georgian farmhouse on a working farm between Wells and Glastonbury, open fire in comfortable sitting room, attractive dining room, good breakfasts, and pretty garden; cl Christmas wk

ROADWATER ST0337 **Wood Advent Farm** *Roadwater, Watchet, Somerset TA23 0RR (01984)* 640920 **£50**, plus special breaks; 5 rms. Relaxed, spacious farmhouse on 340 acres of working farm within Exmoor National Park, great walks; log fire in comfortable lounge, good country cooking using their own produce in attractive dining room with woodburner, grass tennis court, outdoor heated swimming pool, and fishing, clay pigeon and pheasant shooting; children over 12

SHEPTON MALLET ST6342 **Charlton House** *Charlton Rd, Shepton Mallet, Somerset BA4 4PR (01749)* 342008 **£155**; 16 attractive and stylish rooms with nice extras, and large bthrms. Substantial Georgian hotel in landscaped grounds; bare-boarded rooms with oriental rugs, dark red walls with lots of old photographs and posters, and show-casing the owners' style of new-but-used look informal furnishings; smart dining room and 3-bay conservatory with lots of interesting plants and lovely flowers on the tables, exceptionally good modern cooking, beautifully presented, interesting wines, and helpful, efficient uniformed staff; seats on the back terrace overlooking a big lawn, unusual miniature moated castle as a water feature on the front lawn, and croquet; they are kind to children; dogs welcome in bedrooms

SOMERTON ST4828 **Lynch Country House** *4 Behind Berry, Somerton, Somerset TA11 7PD (01458)* 272316 **£49**; 8 prettily decorated rms, plus 3 extra in summer cottage. Carefully restored and homely Georgian house, with books in comfortable lounge, and good breakfasts (no evening meals) in airy room overlooking tranquil grounds and lake with black swans and exotic ducks; cl Christmas and New Year; dogs welcome in bedrooms

STANTON WICK ST6162 **Carpenters Arms** *Stanton Wick, Pensford, Bristol BS39 4BX (01761)* 490202 **£84.50**; 12 rms. Warm and attractively furnished tile-roofed inn, converted from a row of miners' cottages, in peaceful countryside; big log fire and woodburner, stripped stone and beams, fresh flowers, a wide choice of good food inc generous breakfasts, well kept beers, and friendly efficient staff; pianist Fri/Sat pm

STOGUMBER ST1037 **Hall Farm** *Station Rd, Stogumber, Taunton, Somerset TA4 3TQ (01984)* 656321 **£40**; 6 rms. Old-fashioned B&B with optional evening meals (bring your own wine) – wonderfully unpretentious, with warmly friendly staff; cl Christmas and New Year; well behaved dogs welcome; cl Christmas and Jan; disabled access; dogs welcome in bedrooms

STOKE ST GREGORY ST3527 **Rose & Crown** *Woodhill, Stoke St Gregory, Taunton, Somerset TA3 6EW (01823)* 490296 **£50**; 6 rms, some with own bthrm and 2 in annexe. Very friendly 17th-c cottagey inn with a cosy and pleasantly romanticised stable theme, generous helpings of particularly good value food in no smoking dining room, excellent breakfasts, a decent wine list, and efficient service from hard-working family in charge; seats out on enclosed terrace; self-catering nearby; partial disabled access; dogs welcome in bedrooms

STON EASTON ST6254 **Ston Easton Park** *Ston Easton, Bath BA3 4DF (01761)* 241631 **£185**, plus special breaks; 21 really lovely rms. Majestic Palladian mansion of Bath stone with beautifully landscaped 18th-c gardens and 26 acres of parkland; elegant day rooms with antiques and flowers, an attractive no smoking restaurant with good food, fine afternoon teas, library and billiard room, and extremely helpful, friendly and unstuffy service; children over 7 in dining room

TAUNTON ST2224 **Castle** *Castle Green, Taunton, Somerset TA1 1NF (01823) 272671* **£180***, plus special breaks; 44 lovely rms. Appealingly modernised partly Norman castle, its front almost smothered in wisteria, with fine old oak furniture, tapestries and paintings in comfortably elegant lounges, really excellent modern English cooking, good breakfasts, a range of good value wines from a thoughtful list, and efficient friendly service; pretty garden; disabled access; dogs welcome in bedrooms

WELLS ST5445 **Infield House** *36 Portway, Wells, Somerset BA5 2BN (01749) 670989* **£49**, plus winter breaks; 3 comfortable rms (best view from back one). Carefully restored no smoking Victorian townhouse with period furnishings and family portraits, elegant lounge (with lots of local guidebooks), good breakfasts in dining room with Adam-style fireplace, evening meals by arrangement, and friendly personal service; cl 1 wk early Dec, 1 wk Jan; children over 12; dogs welcome in bedrooms

WOOKEY HOLE ST5347 **Glencot House** *Glencot Lane, Wookey Hole, Wells, Somerset BA5 1BH (01749) 677160* **£88**; 13 rms, many with four-posters. In 18 acres of gardens and parkland (with own cricket pitch), this Jacobean-style Victorian mansion has some fine panelling, carved ceilings, antiques and flowers in the public rooms and hallways, a friendly atmosphere, and good food in the restaurant; fishing, table tennis, snooker, and small indoor jet stream pool; two friendly dogs and pet pig, lots to do nearby; cl 31 Dec for several days; they are kind to children; dogs welcome in bedrooms ☺

To see and do

Somerset Family Attraction of the Year

BRISTOL ST5673 **Bristol Zoo Gardens** (Clifton Downs; easily reached by buses 8, 9, 508 and 509 from the centre) A big new enclosure full of birds and animals from Brazil is the latest addition to this busy place, already one of the most enjoyable zoos in the country. Designed to highlight threatened species in the coastal rain forests (the zoo is heavily involved in conservation overseas), it has a winding wooden walkway that takes you through a re-created rain forest area, with tapirs, parrots, and other creatures, including the world's biggest rodent, the capybara. They already have several first-rate displays, notably the spectacular Seal and Penguin Coasts, where a transparent underwater walkway lets you watch penguins and seals from almost every conceivable angle. More long-standing favourites include the interactive Twilight World, with its nocturnal desert, forest and walk-through bat enclosure, and Bug World, showing off inhabitants as diverse as flat-tailed scorpions and moon jellyfish. The zoo is particularly good for monkeys and gorillas, and there's a big open-air aviary, with free-flying birds, as well as a reptile house and aquarium. Regular visitors look forward to seeing Wendy the Asian elephant, one of the most popular, long-standing residents. There are feeding time talks throughout the day (more in summer), and a good adventure playground, with separate areas for toddlers and younger children. The Zoolympics trail is fun, encouraging children to measure their skills against some of the animals: seeing how their speed compares with a cheetah's, or trying to flap their arms as often as a hummingbird does its wings. You'll find plenty of extra activities in the summer holidays, but at any time it's not hard to spend most of a very full day here; a fair bit is under cover, including some picnic areas. An added bonus is that everything is spread over beautifully laid-out gardens, with spacious lawns and colourful borders. Meals, snacks, shop, good disabled access; cl 25 Dec; (0117) 973 8951; £8.60 adults, £5 children 3–14.

AXBRIDGE ST4354

Pleasant small town with an appealing largely medieval square and narrow winding High St, unusual in this part of the world for its jettied timber-framed buildings. The rambling old Lamb on the corner of the tranquil market square is good for lunch.

King John's Hunting Lodge (The Square) Actually built around 1500 so having no connection with King John (nor in fact with hunting) – but no less attractive for that. It houses a local history museum. Shop, disabled access to grounds; open pm only Easter–Sept (open all day Sats in summer); (01934) 732012; free; NT.

BANWELL ST3860

Court Farm (Wolvershill Rd, off A371 N) Much of this lively farm park (the county's biggest) is under cover, so it's good even in the wet. Friendly animals from shire horses to ferrets, with feeding sessions throughout the day, and summer pony rides; also play barns and an adventure fort, as well as tractor rides, and a themed summer children's maze. Snacks and picnic areas, shop, disabled access; cl Mon Nov–Feb and a few days over Christmas; 01934 822383; £4.95.

BARRINGTON ST3918

Barrington Court In the grounds of a splendid 16th-c house, a magnificent series of gardens influenced by Gertrude Jekyll, inc rose garden, and traditional walled kitchen garden, the produce from which is on sale in the shop. The house shows off the reproduction furniture of Stuart Interiors. Meals, snacks, plant centre, disabled access to garden and ground floor; house and grounds open Thurs–Sun Mar and Oct, plus Mon–Tues Apr–Sept; (01460) 241938; £5.20; NT. The village itself is attractive, and the Royal Oak does good lunches.

BATH ST7564

For many this is England's most rewarding old town, though its throngs of summer visitors tend to mask its charms a bit then. Many places enjoyably recall the days of Beau Nash and the building of Bath as a fashionable resort; other draws go back to the Roman Baths, and come right up to date with the city's interesting and unusual shops. The new Bath Spa complex, opening in February, will bring taking the spa waters into the 21st century. In the meantime our favourite places to visit are the Roman Baths, Museum of Costume at the Assembly Rooms (these attractions offer a good value joint ticket), Pump Room, Building of Bath Museum, Industrial Heritage Centre, No 1 Royal Crescent, and Bath Abbey. The American Museum on the edge of the city at Claverton is very special. Parts not to be missed include the great showpieces of 18th-c town planning, Queen Sq, the Circus and the Royal Crescent; the quieter Abbey Green and cobbled Abbey St and Queen St; and the great Pulteney Bridge (there's a fine view of it from the bridge at the end of North Parade, or the riverside Parade Gardens, where brass bands play in summer). The narrow little lanes between the main streets can be fascinating. In summer lots of informal eating places have tables outside. The Old Green Tree (Green St) is a good pub with decent food. Walcot St has a good flea market (Sat am), and every Sat a farmers' market by Green Park Station has lots of fresh fruit and vegetables. The beautifully restored historic **Theatre Royal** presents more pre-West End productions than anywhere else in the country. Don't try to drive around the city: Bath's streets were laid out for travel by sedan chair, not car, and a tortuous one-way system seems designed to deter drivers rather than to make traffic flow more easily. It's better to leave your car at one of the city's four park-and-ride sites and take the shuttle bus in. Walking around Bath is a delight; there are flat parts, though to make the most of it you have to be prepared to slog up some of the steeper streets. Readers particularly enjoy the somewhat irreverent **Bizarre Bath** walking tours that leave the Huntsman Inn on North Parade Passage at 8pm daily, Apr–Sept (£5) – more street theatre than a typical tour; or you can go on one of the free daily walking tours which leave from outside the Roman Baths at 10.30am and 2pm (10.30 only on Sats). The rush of a day trip doesn't do justice to the host of things worth seeing; it is best to stay, preferably out of season. On summer days crowds of trippers and school parties tend to spoil the best-known parts, and if you want to visit during Bath's early summer Music Festival, book accommodation well ahead. The Bath Pass, giving entry to several places here, plus bike hire and canoeing, for £19 (£29 for a 2-day pass), is worth considering if you want to pack lots into a visit; details from Tourist Information Centre, (01225) 477101.

Balloon trips Hot-air balloons give a good view of the city as it's shown in the great architectural drawings. They take off, subject to weather, from the Royal Victoria Park; (01225) 466888; from £135.

Bath Abbey & Abbey Heritage Vaults Particularly renowned for its fan vaulting, the current building is the third great church to be built on this site, begun in 1499. The Elizabethans called it the Lantern of the West because of its profusion of stained glass. Most impressive is the great E window, depicting 56 scenes from the life of Christ. On one side of this is a finely carved memorial to Bartholomew Barnes (1608), and on the other the beautiful medieval carving of the Prior Birde chantry. Restoration has returned the interior's gradually blackened Bath stone to its more appealing honey colour. Bookshop, disabled access; cl Good Fri, 24–26 Dec, 1 Jan, and during private services (usually Sun); £2 suggested donation. The carefully restored 18th-c vaults have a very good exhibition on the abbey's history. Disabled access; cl Sun; (01225) 422462; £2.

Bath Postal Museum 🖭 (Broad St) First-class exploration of the development of the postal system since the 16th c, inc a full-scale replica Victorian post office; it was from here that the world's first postage stamp was sent in 1840. Snacks, shop, disabled access to ground floor only; cl Sun and 1 week in Jan; (01225) 460333; £2.90.

Bath Spa By February, people should be able to bathe in the city's natural thermal spa waters (a luxury denied since 1978 when the baths were closed by doubts over the purity of the

source). Just 100 metres from the famous Roman Baths (see below), this stunning Millennium Commission project will comprise one purpose-built and two restored bath houses, with a little interpretation centre in a former pump room. The focal point is the new spa complex, designed by the architect of Waterloo's Eurostar terminal and crafted from Bath stone and glass. The building, crowned with a roof-top pool and terrace, is a 'centre for well-being', a health-minded pleasure-seeker's paradise replete with whirlpool, steam room, massage rooms, and other restorative perks; also restaurant, gym and visitor centre. Open daily exc 25, 31 Dec, and 1 Jan; bathing prices will start from around £17, phone for details; (01225) 780308.

Beckford's Tower (Lansdown Rd) Italianate tower with fine views from the top, and a little museum commemorating the well travelled collector William Beckford. Shop; open wknds and bank hols Easter–end Oct; (01225) 460705; £2.50.

Boating 🖭 Cruises leave Pulteney Bridge landing stage at a quarter to and a quarter past the hour (not Oct–Easter). Boats and punts can be hired Apr–Oct from the Boating Station on the River Avon, Forester Rd, Bathwick; (01225) 466407; £5 for an hour. The revivified **Kennet & Avon Canal** is one of Bath's pleasures, with quiet towpath walks along to Bathampton (where the George I is popular for lunch) and beyond; it has quite a few colourful narrow-boats in summer. You can cycle right into the centre along the Avon Cycleway, cycle tracks converted from the old Bath and Bristol railway.

Building of Bath Museum (The Vineyard, Paragon) Fascinating displays on how John Wood and others transformed the town and its architecture, with full-scale reconstructions, original tools, and a fabulous model of the entire city, lighting up when you press the buttons. Shop; cl Mon (exc bank hols), and Dec to mid-Feb; (01225) 333895; £4. The nearby Star is an appropriately antiquated pub.

Envolve (Green Park Rd) Visitor

centre for the exemplary charity which promotes environmental awareness among the local community. Disabled access; cl Sat pm, all Sun and bank hol wknds; (01225) 787910; free.

Georgian Garden (Gravel Walk) Nr Queen Sq, another striking reminder of the period, this re-creates the original layout and the kind of plants that would have been used in a small town garden in the 1760s. Cl wknds and all Nov–Apr; (01225) 477752; free.

Holburne Museum of Art 🔒 (Gt Pulteney St) Fine old building displaying art and objects collected in the 19th c by Sir Thomas William Holburne, inc Old Master paintings, portrait miniatures and Italian bronzes. Meals, snacks, shop, disabled access; cl Sun am, Mon and all mid-Dec to mid-Feb; (01225) 466669; £3.50.

Jane Austen Centre 🔒 (Gay St) Jane Austen lived in this street 1801–6, and this enjoyable centre takes a comprehensive look at the novelist's life, as well as the ways in which the city influenced her writing. Displays include re-creations of a Georgian shop-front and town garden, exhibitions on places mentioned in her novels, and elegant costumes; also news on Austen-related events and walking tours (£3.50 extra). Shop (selling every Austen-related book in print), disabled access; cl 24–26 Dec; (01225) 443000; £3.95.

Museum of Bath at Work 🔒 (Julian Rd) The highlight here is the engaging **Mr Bowler's Business**, an elaborate re-creation of a factory first established in 1872, providing various services from plumbing and engineering to gas-fitting and bell-hanging. Everything is just as it was then, inc the antique soda fountain that turned out such intriguingly named drinks as Cherry Ciderette. Snacks, shop; cl wkdys Nov–Mar; (01225) 318348; £3.50.

Museum of Costume & Assembly Rooms (Bennett St) Dazzling – more than 150 figures in original costumes from the late 16th c to the present, one of the most impressive displays of fashion and fashion accessories in the world. It's housed in the Assembly Rooms built in 1771 by John Wood the Younger, where the audio-guide has a particularly entertaining commentary –

listen out for the bun fight. Shop, disabled access; cl 25–26 Dec, and Assembly Rooms may be closed other dates for functions; (01225) 477785; *£5. Along the same street is a small **Museum of East Asian Art**.

No 1 Royal Crescent The most splendid example of the architecture that sprang up in the town's Georgian heyday. In 1768 it was the first house built in Bath's most regal terrace, and now has two floors restored and beautifully furnished in the style of that time. Shop; cl Mon (exc bank hols), and end Nov to mid-Feb; (01225) 428126; £4. The Crescent is closed to traffic at one end, with the hope of reducing damage inflicted by tour buses.

Prior Park Landscape Garden 🔒 (Ralph Allen Drive, off A3062 S) In a sweeping valley, this striking 18th-c landscaped garden is being comprehensively restored by the National Trust. Capability Brown and Alexander Pope originally helped with the design, and there are plenty of unique ornamental features (inc 18th-c graffiti on the Palladian bridge). Woodland walks offer unusual views over Bath (ring for details of events). Note you can't drive all the way here: there's no car parking on site or nearby (though there are some spaces for disabled visitors, phone to book). You can walk from town, but the hill is very steep, so best to take the number 2 or 4 bus. Cl Tues Feb–end Nov, Mon–Thurs Dec–Jan, 25–26 Dec, 1 Jan; (01225) 833422; £4 (£1 off if show bus or train ticket or cycle); NT. There's decent food at the Cross Keys on Midford Rd.

Pump Room This stylish 18th-c mecca for the fashionable was built directly above the Roman temple courtyard; you can catch a glimpse of the baths next door. It now houses a restaurant serving morning coffee, lunches and teas to the strains of the Pump Room Trio. You can sample the hot spa water, which always comes out at 46°C (116°F).

Roman Baths Founded by AD 75, and undoubtedly one of Britain's most remarkable Roman sites. They were built to service pilgrims visiting a temple to Sulis Minerva, which had been constructed around a sacred hot spring.

After this the spring played a dual role – as both a focus for worship, and a reservoir supplying the baths with spa water. The temple and baths were all but forgotten until the 18th c, when workmen chanced upon a bust of Minerva, and it was not until 1878 that most of what you see today was uncovered. The main baths are pretty much intact, though the columns are 19th-c reconstructions. In July and Aug they're open at night and quite beautifully floodlit. A **museum** shows finds made during excavations, inc the bust of Minerva, a remarkable Gorgon's Head pediment, and lead tablets inscribed with messages and thrown into the spring by pilgrims; also models and an audio-guide. Meals, snacks, shop, some disabled access (though not to baths themselves); cl 25–26 Dec; (01225) 477785; £8, inc an audio-guide.
Sally Lunn's Refreshment House & Museum (North Parade Passage) Reputedly the oldest house in Bath, a charming partly timbered medieval structure, still preserving in its cellars the original kitchen of the legendary Sally Lunn, who in the 17th c created her famous brioche bread buns here. Meals and snacks (inc of course the buns, made to a secret recipe), shop; cl 25–26 Dec; (01225) 461634; 30p. They have a sister shop in Windsor.
Victoria Art Gallery (Bridge St) European Old Masters and 18th- to 20th-c British paintings and drawings, as well as decorative arts inc porcelain, glass and watches. Disabled access to ground floor only; cl Sun am, all day Mon, 25–26 Dec; (01225) 477233; free.
William Herschel Museum & Star Vault ⬚ (New King St) Interesting Georgian home and workplace of William Herschel, the astronomer (and composer), with period rooms, models of his telescopes, and other scientific equipment. He discovered the planet Uranus from the back garden. Bookshop; cl am (exc wknds), and wkdys Nov–Feb; (01225) 311342; *£3.50.
BISHOPS LYDEARD ST1729
Attractive village, interesting church with handsome carving. The Lethbridge Arms has enjoyable food.
BITTON SD6769
Avon Valley Railway ⬚ (Bitton

Station) Friendly little railway extending lines along the old Midland Railway towards Bath and North Somerset (hence its inclusion in this chapter, though Bitton itself is actually just over the Gloucestershire border). As we went to press they were building a platform to link the railway to Avon Valley Country Park. Snacks, shop, disabled access; open Sun and bank hols May–Sept plus Easter, Weds in Aug, and wknds in Dec; (0117) 932 7296 for timetable; £3.50.
BRADFORD-ON-TONE ST1722
Sheppy's Cider ⬚ (Three Bridges) The Sheppy family has been making cider here since the early 19th c, and you can follow the process through a video. Tastings in the shop, and a small museum. Tearoom (late Jun–Sept), shop, disabled access to shop and museum; cl Sun Christmas–Easter; (01823) 461233; farm free, museum *£2. The White Horse has enjoyable food.
BREAN DOWN ST2958
Protruding into the Bristol Channel between Weston-Super-Mare and acres of holiday camps, this gives the best coastal walk in east Somerset.
BRENDON HILLS SS9738
These give breezy walks with long views; the Royal Oak at Luxborough is a good base.
BRENT KNOLL ST3450
The attractive village has a church with remarkable carved bench-ends; the Red Cow is a popular dining pub. A path leads up to the prominent summit giving the village its name.
BRIDGWATER ST3036
Once you're through the industrial outskirts, some central bits are worth seeing: Castle St is the finest early 18th-c street in the county. Cross Rifles (Bath Rd) has good value food.
Blake Museum (Blake St) Now the local history museum, this picturesque house was probably Robert Blake's 1598 birthplace, and you can still see some of his personal possessions (inc his sea chest) and a diorama of his great victory over the Spaniards at Santa Cruz; also displays on the Monmouth rebellion, and a maritime gallery. Shop; cl Sun, Mon, Good Fri, 25 Dec, and 1 Jan; (01278) 456127; free.

BRISTOL ST5873
A busy industrial city with the usual big-city problems (it's one of the UK's Crime Priority Areas), this nevertheless has all sorts of things to fill a lively day visit. There are parts with handsome buildings, great waterfront panoramas, hilly parts with interesting alleys and sudden leafy quarters, and plenty of cafes, pubs and bars; with a lively university, it has a vivid nightlife. One excellent initiative here is free entry to five of the city's best museums: City Museum & Art Gallery, Industrial Museum, Georgian House, Red Lodge and Blaise Castle Museum (see separate entries). It's easily reached from Bath or from one of the cosseting nearby country-house hotels we list, and day visits are made easy by good rail connections, and the motorway that plunges right into the city's heart. The city's prosperity still stems from its port, though aerospace now predominates among many other manufacturing interests. There are some striking buildings around the centre, notably the Corn Exchange and the Old Council House on Corn St, and on Broad St the Grand Hotel (1869), the Guild Hall (1843) and the art nouveau façade of the former Edward Everard printing house. The Theatre Royal, opened in 1766, is one of the oldest working theatres in the country. A good part for leisurely strolls is the elegant suburb of Clifton, with handsome Georgian terraces (it's got more Georgian buildings than Bath) and its famous suspension bridge. Useful central places for a cheapish lunchtime bite are the Commercial Rooms (Corn St), Cottage (Cumberland Rd), Llandoger Trow (King St), Old Fish Market (Broad St) and Horts City Tavern (Broad St). A 250-mile cycle way runs from here to Padstow in Cornwall, keeping off roads as much as possible.

@Bristol (Harbourside) Explore is the part to head for if your time is limited: full of interactive and hands-on features, it lets you star in your own TV show, play virtual volleyball, or get an idea of how it feels to be in the eye of a tornado. The latest technology gives a new spin to time-honoured activities like generating electricity or making things fly, and there are novelties like the virtual sperm journey and the walk-in womb. Especially good is the Imaginarium, a next-generation planetarium that looks like a metal sphere and takes you into a 3-D virtual universe, and the interactive exhibition Dinomites explores the prehistoric world with authentic models, jungle settings, and fossil displays. There are also workshops, such as on how chocolate is made. Wildwalk is a well put together walk-through journey around evolution, particularly strong on insects, with lots of videos and multi-media bits; its best part is the re-created tropical rain forest, with free-flying birds and butterflies. These sections, and a huge IMAX cinema with a screen four storeys high, are linked by appealingly landscaped squares and avenues, dotted with trees, sculptures, shops and restaurants. New café, shop, disabled access; cl 25 Dec; (0845) 345 1235; £6.50 IMAX or Wildwalk, £7.50 Explore, the All-Star ticket (everything exc Imaginarium) is £16.50.

Blaise Castle House Museum (Henbury, 4m NW, off B4047) A spacious and locally popular undulating park with some woodland, and a new adventure play area. The late 18th-c house contains displays of everyday objects from toys and dolls to Victorian water closets and baths. The castle itself is a Gothic folly built in 1766 within the now scarcely discernible ramparts of an Iron Age hill fort. Shop, disabled access to ground floor only; museum cl Thurs and Fri, and all Nov–Mar, park open daily; (0117) 903 9818; free. Nearby Blaise Hamlet is a NT-owned estate village designed by John Nash.

Bristol Cathedral On the other side of the water, this was originally an Augustinian monastery, founded on what's supposedly the spot where St Augustine met the Celtic Christians in the early 7th c. It's a real mix of architectural styles, and perhaps the country's most splendid example of a hall church, where the nave, choir and aisles are all the same height. Highlights include the Chapter House (one of the finest Norman rooms in Britain), and the candlesticks given in thanks by the privateers who rescued Alexander Selkirk (whose adventures inspired Daniel Defoe to write *Robinson Crusoe*). Snacks, shop; (0117) 926 4879; free (donations welcomed).

Bristol Industrial Museum (Princes Wharf) In a converted dockside transit shed, and especially good on transport, with locally built steam locomotives and aircraft (inc a mock-up of Concorde's flight deck), and a good look at the development of the port. Shop, disabled access; open Sat–Weds Apr–Oct, wknds only Nov–Mar; (0117) 925 1470; free. Steam trains run along the docks between here and the SS *Great Britain* every ¼hr 12–5pm on selected days Mar–Oct; £1.

Bristol Zoo Gardens See *separate family panel on p.518*.

British Empire & Commonwealth Museum (Clock Tower Yard, Temple Meads) This enterprising museum – in a former railway station designed by Brunel – tells the story of the rise and fall of the British Empire and the emergence of the modern Commonwealth, from John Cabot's departure from Bristol in 1497 to the present day. Exhibits include rare film, historic photographs, sound recordings, and costumes. Meals and snacks, shop, disabled access; cl 25 Dec; (0117) 925 4980; *£4.95.

Cabot Tower The attractive park at the end of Great George St is an urban nature reserve, and its tower rewards those willing to climb the hundreds of steps with probably the best views of the city. Snacks, cl 25 Dec; free. Nearby **St George's** has good Fri lunchtime concerts, usually with seats available on the day, but best to check on (0117) 923 0359.

Christmas Steps This famously old-fashioned alley is quaintly lined by steep buildings. At the top is the tiny late 15th-c **Chapel of the Three Kings of Cologne** (the 'three kings' are the three wise men whose shrines are in Cologne Cathedral); the warden of the nearby almshouses can let you in. And at the bottom is the lodge of **St Bartholomew's** – all that remains of the 13th-c hospital and almshouse which once stood on this site. This is a good area for shops selling antiques, stamps and old books.

City Museum & Art Gallery (Queens Rd) Good collections of fine and applied art, archaeology, geology, and history – well worth a look. Meals, snacks, shop, mostly disabled access; cl 25–26 Dec; (0117) 922 3571; free. The neo-Gothic Wills Memorial tower next door is a distinctive landmark.

Create Centre (Smeaton Rd, Spike Island) Lively environmental centre with hands-on displays about recycling, some intriguing exhibits inc a column made from 6½ million cans, and an ecohome (pms only) showcasing methods for greener everyday living. Also changing exhibitions of local art. Shop, café, disabled access; cl wknds; (0117) 925 0505; free.

Docks Now largely restored, with distinctive blue and yellow ferries (Apr–Sept) linking several points. The old part around King St, between the waterfront and the Bristol Old Vic, has quiet cobbled streets of Georgian buildings, pleasant to wander through, and elsewhere some of the bigger warehouses (and even the boats) have been pressed into service as museums, café-bars and the like. The Arnolfini, a big former tea warehouse, is now a contemporary arts complex with bar, restaurant, exhibitions, cinema, theatre and so forth.

Historic Boat Trips (from Princes Wharf) The 1860s steam-tug *Mayflower*, the 1930s fireboat *Pyronaut* and the tug *John King* give interesting trips round the dock in the summer – best to check times with the Industrial Museum; (0117) 925 1470; £3. From Apr to Oct the **pleasure steamers** *Waverley* and *Balmoral* run fairly frequent day cruises from here, along the Avon and Severn or to Devon, Wales or Lundy; (0141) 221 8152 for timetable. The *Balmoral* has well kept real ale in its bar.

Lord Mayor's Chapel (College Green) Rare civic church, with glorious 16th-c stained-glass windows, floor tiles and fan-vaulted ceiling; tours by appointment only; (0117) 929 4350.

New Room – John Wesley's Chapel (Horsefair) Incongruously set in a shopping centre, but much as it was when Wesley preached here (from his famous double-decked pulpit, as well as a less-known predecessor, returned here from Anglesey in 1999); the oldest Methodist chapel in the world, built in 1739 and rebuilt in 1748. Guided tours by arrangement. Shop, disabled access to ground floor only; cl Sun, Good Fri, and 25–26 Dec; (0117) 926 4740; free (£2.80 tour).

Red Lodge (Park St) The house was altered in the 18th c, but on its first floor still has the last surviving suite of 16th-c rooms in Bristol, as well as a wonderful carved stone chimney-piece, plasterwork ceilings and fine oak panelling. They occasionally open the reconstructed Tudor-style garden. Open Sat–Weds and most bank hols Jun–Oct; (0117) 921 1360; free. There are several elegant Georgian streets round here, notably Great George St, where the **Georgian House**, built in 1790 for a wealthy sugar merchant, is a fine illustration of a typical townhouse of the day. Three floors are decorated in period style, inc the below-stairs area with kitchen, laundry and housekeeper's room. Times as for Red Lodge; (0117) 921 1362; free.

SS *Great Britain* On the dockside, on some summer wknds a small steam railway will whisk you along the old cargo route to and from this ship, designed by Brunel as the first iron, screw-propelled, ocean-going vessel, and a real departure from what had gone before. A £10m restoration project over the next three years will preserve and restore the ship; you can go behind the scenes to see some of the work being done. Meals, snacks, shop; cl 24–25 Dec; (0117) 926 0680; £6.25. This includes entry to the **Maritime Heritage Centre**, with reconstructions and original machinery illustrating the city's long history of ship-building. The nearby diesel-powered firefloat *Pyronaut* (1934) and Fairbairn steam-crane (1876) operate occasional summer wknds.

St Mary Redcliffe (Redcliffe Hill) Elizabeth I described this as 'the goodliest, fairest and most famous parish church in England'. Most of the current building dates from the late 13th c, inc the wonderful hexagonal outer porch. Notable features include the tomb of Admiral Sir William Penn, the father of Pennsylvania's founder, and the Handel Window, where eight passages of the *Messiah* commemorate the great composer's ties with this church. Wkdy meals and snacks, shop, disabled access but no facilities. May be free organ recitals Thurs lunchtimes during term-time; (0117) 929 1487.

St Werburgh's City Farm (Watercress Rd) Half an hour's walk from the centre, this working urban farm is kept going largely by volunteers who look after the animals and tend the various gardens (inc a scented one); also adventure playground and wildlife pond. Meals and snacks (not Mon or Tues), farm shop, disabled access; open daily; (0117) 942 8241; free.

University Botanic Gardens (Bracken Hill, North Rd, Leigh Woods) Attractive gardens with several rock and water features, set around students' halls of residence. All the plants are excellently labelled, and the grounds include the TV *Gardener's World* microclimate gardens; some disabled access; cl wknds and bank hols, guided tours by appointment; (0117) 973 3682; free.

BRUTON ST6834
Fascinating little town; worth looking out for are the Bartons, narrow alleys leading down from the High St to the river (which you can cross either by footbridge or by using stepping stones). **St Mary's church** is on the site of a medieval Augustinian priory and abbey – the old abbey wall with its buttresses still stands in Silver St. The church has a spectacular altar-piece, and in the chancel is a fine effigy of Sir Maurice Berkely, a great survivor who was standard-bearer to Henry VIII, Edward VI and Elizabeth I. Interesting and individual shops – antiques, books and prints. The Castle Inn is good for lunch, and the delicatessen on High St has a good range of local and French cheeses. The drive up towards Alfred's Tower gives some open views; the Bull up there at Hardway is a reliable dining pub.

Gants Mill and Garden 🖳 There's been milling on the site since 1290, and this is now one of the last working watermills in the county; in the past it's been a fulling mill, silk mill and grist mill, and today it's used to grind barley. The attractive colour-themed garden has water features, sculptures on display, and a bog garden. Snacks, shop, disabled access to garden; open pms Sun, Thurs and bank hol Mon mid-May to end Sept; (01749) 8132393; £3.50.

BURNHAM-ON-SEA ST3050
In summer a bustling inexpensive family seaside resort, with wide beaches, sandy dunes, and the usual holiday facilities. Its plain-looking **church** surprises with its collection of Grinling Gibbons carvings from the long-demolished Palace of Whitehall in London. The Lighthouse (Highbridge Rd) has cheap generous family food.

Animal Farm Adventure Park 🖼
(Red Rd, N of Berrow) Good fun for children, with animals and conservation trails, trampolines, huge slides and play areas (inc one for the under-7s and one under cover). Meals, snacks, shop, disabled access; cl 24–26 Dec; (01278) 751628; £4.20. There's a small **nature reserve** in the nearby sand dunes.

BURRINGTON COMBE ST4858
An easy walk by the B3134 (the best drive through the Mendips), this great steeply wooded limestone gorge on the N flank of the Mendips can be combined with walks up on to Black Down for memorable views in all directions, and over the heather and cranberry tops to Dolebury Warren, where the site of an Iron Age hill fort marks a splendid Mendip viewpoint. Other good starting points for Mendips walks include the Crown at Churchill, Swan at Rowberrow, and Ring o' Bells at Compton Martin.

BURROWBRIDGE ST3428
Somerset Levels Basket Centre
(Lyng Rd) Sells baskets made from local materials cut on the surrounding Levels as well as other crafts. Shop, disabled access; cl Sun, Tues, some bank hols, plus 2 wks for hols so best to check; (01823) 698688; free. The Rose & Crown at East Lyng has good food.

CADBURY CAMP ST4572
This Iron Age hill fort makes a good destination for a walk from the engaging Black Horse in Clapton-in-Gordano, by a lane past the church, which leads to a footbridge high over the M5. Don't

confuse this with the more famous Cadbury Castle down towards Yeovil.

CANNINGTON ST2539
Cannington College Heritage Gardens Extensive gardens inc over 10,000 different types of plant, display and ornamental beds. Meals, snacks, disabled access; open daily Apr–Oct; (01278) 655000; £1. The Malt Shovel at Bradley Green has well liked food, and there's a nice drive to Nether Stowey via Combwich and Stogursey.

CASTLE CARY ST6432
Very attractive – basically a medieval market town, now with a useful range of traditional family-run shops and crafts and antiques shops. The 18th-c **Roundhouse** is Britain's smallest prison, and the George, a comfortable old thatched coaching inn, has decent food.

Castle Cary Vineyard and Winery
🖼 (Honeywick, just E) Produces award-winning wines and welcomes visits; shop, disabled access; cl 24 Dec–2 Jan; (01963) 351507; free.

Hadspen Garden (off A371 2m SE) Beautiful five-acre gardens surrounding fine 18th-c house; many old favourite plants, but also lots of exotics. The unique D-shaped walled garden provides a rare micro-climate and has all sorts of herbaceous plants and old-fashioned roses, and there's a lily pond and ancient flower meadow. Teas and snacks, nursery, some disabled access; open Thurs–Sun and bank hols Mar–Sept; (01749) 813707; £3.

CASTLE NEROCHE ST2715
This isolated ruined Norman fortification, with more the aspect now of a hill fort than a castle, is the central feature of well marked woodland walks down towards the Blackdown Hills S of Taunton; fine views at the top.

CHAPEL ALLERTON ST4150
Ashton Windmill The only complete mill left in Somerset, built in the 18th c, with splendid views over the Cheddar Gorge and Somerset Levels. Shop, open pm Sun and bank hols Easter–Sept, phone to check; (01278) 435399; free.

CHARD ST3108
Chard Museum 🖼 The local history museum (High St) has good displays inc one on John Stringfellow, who flew a powered flying-machine in 1848, local

industries such as lace-making, and there's a collection of early artificial limbs. Shop, disabled access to ground floor only; cl pm Sat, Sun (exc July–Aug), and Nov–Apr; (01460) 65091; £2. The attractive 16th-c Choughs nearby has cheap food. There are a couple of places to hire bikes; the local tourist board do good cycle routes. **Forde Abbey**, just over the border in Dorset, is particularly worth visiting.

CHEDDAR ST4553
In its older part, this extended village has a very fine market cross, with some interesting shops and a tall-towered 14th/15th-c **church**. The Gardeners Arms and thatched Kings Head (both 16th-c, in Silver St) have enjoyable food, and this area has roadside strawberry stalls and pick-your-own in summer. Cheddar gets astonishingly busy in summer, when every building seems to be either a tearoom or a shop selling cheese or cider.

Cheddar Gorge The area's big attraction, a magnificent limestone gorge with picturesque cliffs, formed when a cavern roof collapsed. Further up the dramatic B3135 road through the gorge, it rapidly loses its commercialised trappings. When you reach the far end two worthwhile paths leave the road. On the E side is a quiet dale with two nature reserves, Black Rock and Velvet Bottom. On the S side, the West Mendip Way climbs through woods and gives access to another path which skirts the top of the gorge (the views into it are hair-raising). The look-out tower up at the top has views of the Somerset Levels and Glastonbury Tor. You can also get up to this via the 274 steps of Jacob's Ladder from the road at the W entrance to the gorge, and to make things easier on the feet, a cable-car system should open within the next few years.

Cheddar Gorge Cheese Co Village (The Cliffs) Shops and traditional crafts based around a factory that thanks to its location claims to make the only genuine Cheddar cheese in the world. You can watch each stage of the seven-hour process, and of course taste the matured product. Also fudge-making, scrumpy sampling, and less flavoursome crafts inc lace- and candle-making.

Snacks, shops, disabled access; cl Christmas and New Year; (01934) 742810; £1.50, free in the winter when there's less going on.

Cheddar Showcaves Well worth a look, this busy spot boasts two quite remarkable showcaves, and it's efficiently organised for families. The highlight for adults is probably Gough's Cave, named after the retired sea captain who stumbled across it in 1890; this series of stunning underground caverns goes on for around a quarter of a mile, each area seeming more dramatic than the last, with spectacular stalactites and stalagmites joining to form columns (they've an audio tour for this part). Nearby Cox's Cave is smaller, and more beautifully coloured; it has several very narrow passageways. Children may prefer the Crystal Quest, a cave entertainingly fitted out with goblins, wizards, and a smoke-filled dragon; a story and challenge lead you through. There's also an exhibition devoted to Cheddar Man, Britain's oldest complete skeleton, with a re-creation of what his world was like, 9,000 years ago. The ticket also includes a Mar–Oct tour bus through some of the narrow roads of the gorge, with a decent commentary. Meals, snacks, unusual shops; cl 24–25 Dec; (01934) 742343; £8, £24 for a family ticket. You can arrange introductory sessions of caving, climbing and abseiling for children over 11 (you have to book in advance, and there are height restrictions; £12.50).

CHEDDON FITZPAINE ST2428
Hestercombe Gardens Raised walks, sunken lawns and a water garden are all part of the grand design which Lutyens and Gertrude Jekyll created for this beautifully restored garden around what is now Somerset Fire Brigade HQ; also intriguing landscaped secret gardens and restored Georgian garden with woodland walks and classical temples, pleasant even on a gloomy day. Tearoom, shop (inc plant sales), limited disabled access; cl 25 Dec; (01823) 413923; £4.50.

CHEW VALLEY LAKES ST5760
The Chew Valley Lake itself and Blagdon Lake are more popular as breathing places for people living

nearby than as places for visitors from afar; both are pleasant large stretches of water, with managed fishing, and the B3130 and B3114 have pleasant views. The New Inn at Blagdon has good food.

CLAVERTON ST7864

American Museum in Britain (Claverton Manor, just SE of the city) Quite a contrast to the rest of Bath's attractions, a fascinating illustration of American history and life, in lovely gracious surroundings. Eighteen rooms are fully furnished and decorated to re-create the style of transatlantic homes from the 17th to the 19th c, while the grounds include a replica of part of George Washington's garden at Mount Vernon, and an arboretum. Collections of folk art and patchwork quilts with sections on Native Americans and Shakers, and good special events. It's the only museum in the country completely devoted to our colonial cousins. Snacks, shop, some disabled access; cl am, all day Mon (exc bank hols), and Dec–late Mar; (01225) 460503; £6.

CLEVEDON ST4071

After partly collapsing in 1970, the Victorian **pier** was lovingly restored, and finally re-opened in 1998. It is pleasant for a stroll, and there are sailings and fishings from the pier itself (shop, disabled access; cl Weds Oct–Mar; £1). Above the tollhouse, a gallery sells paintings; shop, disabled access; cl Weds Oct–Mar, and 25 Dec; (01275) 878846. Round the corner in Waterloo House is a **Heritage Centre** (open same times as above); donations. Good views from Church Hill, and in Moor Lane the **Clevedon Craft Centre** has 15 varied workshops and a tearoom; most parts cl am Sun, Mon, and Tues; (01275) 872149. Hill Rd is a Victorian shopping street with some antiques shops (and decent food in the Regent). The Little Harp and Moon & Sixpence are seafront family dining pubs with views to Wales.

Clevedon Court (B3130 just E) Much of the original structure of this manor house, built in 1320, is still intact, though it has interesting later additions inc a charming 18th-c garden. Open pm Sun, Weds, Thurs and bank hols

Apr–Sept; (01275) 872257; £4.50; NT.

CLIFTON ST5673

The quiet side of Bristol, with some fine late 18th- and 19th-c terraces, an antiques market (Victorian Arcade, cl Sun, Mon), a big park right on the spectacular Avon gorge facing the NT woodlands on the crags opposite, and the remarkably modern-looking Suspension Bridge, based on an 1836 design by Brunel and finished in 1864. The Hope & Anchor (Jacobs Well Rd) does cheap substantial food.

COMBE FLOREY ST1531

Combe Florey church Charming church with attractive carvings; Evelyn Waugh lies buried outside.

COMBE HAY ST7359

This charming steep village has a good pub, the Wheatsheaf, and the road to Monkton Combe gives good views.

CRANMORE ST6643

East Somerset Railway 🎫 Steam trips along what's known as the Strawberry Line, as well as engine shed and workshops, with nine steam locomotives and rolling stock, and art gallery with wildlife paintings by David Shepherd, who founded the railway. Meals and snacks (on steam days), shop, disabled access; open daily (exc 24–25 Dec), though trains don't run every day – best to ring for timetable; (01749) 880417; £5.75, less when no trains running. The village is quiet and pleasant, and the Strode Arms is handy for lunch.

CREWKERNE ST4409

Thriving town with some decent antiques shops and a number of inexpensive tearooms, restaurants and hotels; we like the White Hart (East St/Market Sq).

CRICKET ST THOMAS ST3708

Cricket St Thomas Park 🎫 In the lovely parkland of a great estate (still remembered by fans of *To The Manor Born*), this wildlife centre with a good emphasis on conservation is home to over 600 animals, many endangered in the wild. A highlight is a walk through the lemur woods – you can watch them swinging happily from the trees above. There's plenty more to amuse children, inc a pets' corner, miniature railway, crazy golf and safari jeep rides. Meals, snacks, shop, disabled access; cl 25 Dec;

(01460) 30111; *£6.50.

CROSCOMBE ST5844

Croscombe is an attractive village, with great 17th-c woodwork in its 15th-c church. The long walk from here to Wells (you'll need a map) gives unforgettable views of the cathedral.

CUCKLINGTON ST7527

Cucklington church 13th-c, with small side chapel dedicated to St Barbara, whose sacred well lies further down in the village.

DOWLISH WAKE ST3712

Perry's Cider Mills They've been making cider here for centuries, and between Oct and Nov you can watch it being produced (phone first to check). The cider mill is in a group of thatched 16th-c buildings around a yard with brightly painted old farm wagons and so forth. Enthusiastically run, with a video on cider-making, liberal tastings and half a dozen different ciders for sale, in old-fashioned earthenware flagons if you want. Shop, disabled access; cl Sun pm, 25–26 Dec, 1 Jan; (01460) 52681; free. The nearby New Inn is good for lunch.

DUNDRY HILL ST5666

Just S of Bristol's suburbs, this gives walkers views over the city, Chew Magna and Blagdon lakes and the Mendips.

DUNSTER SS9943

Well worth a day of anybody's time, with fine medieval houses along the wide main street below the wooded castle hill, as well as a handsome octagonal former yarn market and market cross, a lovely 15th-c priory **church** with particularly tuneful bells, and a well established **doll museum** in the Memorial Hall (cl Oct–Mar; (01643) 821220; £1). If you plan to visit Exmoor the National Park Information Centre is a useful first stop. The Dunster Castle Hotel has enjoyable food, and there's a wealth of tearooms.

Dunster Castle Dramatically set in a 28-acre park rich with exotic flora and even subtropical plants, the castle was largely rebuilt in the 19th c, but has older features inside such as the 17th-c oak staircase and gallery with its brightly painted wall hangings. Excellent views. Shop in 17th-c stables, disabled access (a buggy avoids the steep climb up the hill); castle cl Thurs, Fri, and 2

Nov–22 Mar (gardens open all year); (01643) 821314; £6.40, £3.50 garden and park only; NT.

Old Dovecote (St Georges St) In summer you can go right up this 12th-c dovecote, special for still having its potence, or revolving ladder, used for harvesting the plump squabs from the nesting boxes.

Watermill 🅱 Well restored 18th-c mill still grinding and selling flour; teas in a pleasant riverside garden. Cl Fri, and all Nov–Mar; (01643) 821759; £2.20.

EAST COKER ST5412

Charming quiet village; T S Eliot's ashes are buried here, and there's information about his ancestors in the church. The Helyar Arms has good food and comfortable bedrooms.

EAST LAMBROOK ST4318

East Lambrook Manor Garden 🅱 Well loved cottage garden around a 15th-c house (not open), started by Walter and Margery Fish in 1937, and described by Mrs Fish in her immensely popular book, *We Made A Garden*. There's a national collection of geraniums here, the original plant nursery area has been restored, and art exhibitions are held in the converted 17th-c malthouse. Meals, snacks, plant sales, shop, some disabled access; cl Nov–Jan; (01460) 240328; £2.95.

EAST QUANTOXHEAD ST1343

Delightful village with archetypal duckpond, tiny church with fine oak carvings, and walks to the coast. The Hood Arms at Kilve does good meals.

EBBOR GORGE ST5248

If you like Cheddar Gorge but don't like the souvenir stall, coach parties and all, then Ebbor Gorge is for you. It's the same sort of thing, above Wookey Hole, but altogether quieter and more unspoilt. It has an attractive nature trail, and a good walk runs from Wookey Hole through the Gorge to Pen Hill for panoramic views. The Hunters Lodge and New Inn up around Priddy have sensibly priced food.

FARLEIGH HUNGERFORD ST8057

Farleigh Hungerford Castle Extensive ruins of 14th-c castle, with monuments in the chapel to the Hungerford family, who once owned the land from here to Salisbury. Picnics welcome, snacks, shop, limited disabled access; cl 1–2pm and Mon–Tues Nov–Mar, 24–26 Dec and 1 Jan; (01225) 754026; £2.30 inc audio tour; EH. The Hungerford Arms has a family dining room overlooking it.

GLASTONBURY ST4938
Tales of King Arthur can be found all over the country, but are especially prominent here; they like to say that bones reinterred in the abbey in 1191 were those of Arthur and Guinevere. The best approach is by the B3151, showing the town below the famous Tor. The NT has begun work on improving access to the Tor; you can walk there (it takes about 25 mins) or catch a park-and-ride bus from the abbey car park (Magdalene St, Easter–Sept; £1), as there is no parking at the Tor. Glastonbury has quite a New Age feel, probably due to all the legends and the famous annual rock festival. The brasserie of the Hawthorns Hotel (Northload St) is good for lunch, and the medieval carved façade of the George & Pilgrims is one of the sights of the town, which the bypass has made much more pleasurable.

Chalice Well (Chilkwell St) Legend has it that the Holy Grail was hidden here; the spring, now set in a colourful 2½-acre garden, has apparently had healing powers ever since. True or not, it's a nice peaceful spot. Shop, disabled access; (01458) 831154; *£2.40.

Glastonbury Abbey 🖼 These noble ruins are said to mark the location of the birth of Christianity in this country. The story goes that Joseph of Arimathaea struck his staff into Wearyall Hill, where it took root. Offshoots of the tree, the famous Glastonbury Thorn, have flourished to this day, with a fine specimen here. The remains of the church date mainly from 1539, though the Lady Chapel is much older. An interpretation area has a good range of stories connected with the site, and in the summer, a monk actor will tell you more about how the monks used to live. Snacks July–Aug, shop, disabled access; cl 25 Dec; (01458) 832267; *£3.50.

Glastonbury Tribunal (High St) Glastonbury was formerly an island rising from a vast inland lake, and you can almost see this from the top of the Tor, the highest point of the hills and ridges among which the little town nestles, with fantastic views. Excavations here have revealed a prehistoric **lake village** covering three or four acres below it, consisting of nearly a hundred mounds surrounded by a wooden palisade. Lots of items and timbers from the village have been unusually well preserved thanks to the waterlogged state of the site, and some of the finds, giving a fascinating insight into the life of the settlement, are shown in this fine 15th-c merchant's house. The Tourist Information Centre is here too, and there's some notable plasterwork in the lower back room. Shop, cl 25–26 Dec; (01458) 832954; £2; EH.

Somerset Rural Life Museum (Chilkwell St) The Abbey Barn and outbuildings have displays of traditional regional skills such as cider-making, peat-cutting and basket-weaving. Also orchard, rare breeds, and bee garden with hives. Summer snacks, shop, some disabled access; cl Mon, plus Suns Nov–Mar, 25–26 Dec, Easter and Good Fri; (01458) 831197; £2.50.

GRABBIST HILL SS9843
Not as famous as Dunkery Hill (and less frequented even in summer), but recommended to walkers in search of rewarding views; it can be climbed from nearby Dunster.

GREENHAM ST0821
Cothay Manor and Gardens 🖼
Picturesque 7-acre plantsman's garden surrounding a fine classic medieval manor. Laid out in the 1920s and redesigned and replanted over the last nine years, a series of small formal gardens (inc colour-themed gardens, and bog and cottage gardens) lead off a 200-yard yew walk. Teas, plant sales, disabled access; open pms Weds, Thurs, Sun and bank hols May–Sept; (01823) 672283; £3.50, under-12s free. Go via the Globe over at Appley, for a good lunch first.

HIGHBRIDGE ST3146
Alstone Wildlife Park Unspoilt family-run animal park with various animals to feed inc red deer, llamas, wallabies, and a hand-reared Mongolian

camel, also rare breeds and owls, peacocks and waterfowl; space for picnics (dogs on leads welcome). Snacks, disabled access; open Easter–Oct; (01278) 782405; £3. The Crossways at West Huntspill is a useful food stop.

ILCHESTER ST5222

Charming, with a useful range of well stocked little shops. Used to be a Roman town, and one of the houses has a piece of Roman paving. The whole of the green fronting the Town Hall is said to be the burial ground of Plague victims. The comfortable Ilchester Arms has good food.

ILMINSTER ST3614

Ilminster church Magnificent 15th-c tower, all turrets, pinnacles and gargoyles.

KENNET & AVON CANAL ST6470

Attractively restored, with a good footpath alongside, it runs from Bristol through Hanham (where the Lock & Weir is a charmingly placed pub), Keynsham (the Lock-Keeper is another good pub here), Saltford and Bath to the spectacular aqueduct at Avoncliff (and beyond, across Wiltshire and into Berkshire).

KEYNSHAM ST6768

Avon Valley Country Park (Pixash Lane) Lots of animals from rare breed pigs to wallabies, deer park, riverside trails (inc plenty of places to fish), an excellent adventure playground, and free boating on the pond. There's also a soft play area, quad bikes, falconry displays, and land-train rides. Meals, snacks, shop, disabled access; cl Mon (exc school hols and bank hols), and Nov–2 wks before Easter; (0117) 986 4929; £4. The waterside Lock-Keeper (Keynsham Rd) has enjoyable food.

KINGSBURY EPISCOPI ST4321

Somerset Cider Brandy Co
Somerset's only cider distillery, with huge copper stills, oak vats and wooden presses, traditional cider orchards to stroll through, and tastings of their cider brandy. Shop; cl Sun, 25 Dec; (01460) 240782; free. The village green has an ancient lock-up, and the Wyndham Arms is useful for lunch. Anyone with a serious interest in cider shouldn't miss the Rose & Crown at Huish Episcopi N of here (A372 E of Langport) – a classic old-fashioned Somerset cider pub.

KINGSDON ST5226

Lytes Cary Manor Most of the surviving building dates from the 16th c, though there are interesting earlier features inc the 14th-c chapel, and the Tudor Great Hall. The attractive garden was designed and stocked by Henry Lyte, a notable Elizabethan horticulturist, and otters have returned to the grounds following improvements to the river banks. Plant sales, disabled access to garden only; open pm Mon, Weds, Fri, and Sat Apr–Oct (perhaps plus Fri pm Jun–Aug); (01485) 224471; £4.60; NT. The Kingsdon Inn (charming thatched cottage with lots of atmosphere) does good home cooking.

KINGSTON ST MARY ST2229

Pretty village, with attractive church.

LIMINGTON ST5422

Limington church Interesting for its effigies of the Giverney family, dating back to the 1300s.

LONG ASHTON ST5571

Ashton Court Estate 850 acres of historic woods and grassland, with two deer parks, pitch and putt golf, and views across Clifton and Bristol to the hills beyond. The large manor house (not open) is mostly 19th c, although some parts date from medieval times. Part of the stables is now a visitor centre (open wknds Apr–Sept, most wkdys July–Aug, and Sun in winter; (0117) 963 9174. Café, shop, disabled access; park open all year; free. The Angel has imaginative food.

MARTOCK ST4619

The magnificent **church** has a splendid roof; also look out for the old Court House turned into a Grammar School by William Strode in 1661, with the inscription above the door 'Martock neglect not your opportunities' in English, Latin, Hebrew and Greek. The Fleur de Lis in Stoke sub Hamdon is useful for lunch.

Somerset Guild of Craftsmen (B3165 S) A big, multi-roomed display of Guild members' work inc jewellery, paintings and furniture. Good coffee shop, disabled access to ground floor only; cl 25–26 Dec and 1 Jan; (01935) 825891; free.

MELLS ST7249
Delightful and venerable stone-built village, with marvellous church and graveyard, charming ancient inn (the Talbot), pleasant walks nearby.

MERRIOTT ST4412
Scotts of Merriott Perhaps the last of the big general retail nurseries to raise and grow most of their own trees and shrubs, on 90 acres – well worth a visit by gardening folk. Shop, disabled access; cl 25 Dec, Good Fri; (01460) 72306; free. In the village **D B Pottery** (Highway Cottage, Church St) make a range of items at good prices using a variety of glazing techniques; (01460) 75655; free.

MILVERTON ST1225
The parish church has some fine carving, and the High St is charming.

MINEHEAD SS9646
There's an easily missed area of sloping streets and thatched cottages around the church, with Church Steps a quaint steep back lane. Around this original fishing village is a spacious resort, its beach and promenade sheltered by the wooded hills to the NE. It has the usual attractions, a lively harbour, a sizeable holiday camp, a modern shopping area, and a lovely cedar-fenced seafront walkway. The Old Ship Aground has good value food and pleasant harbour views. There's an unusual **pottery shop** (cl 1–2pm, Sat pm and all day Sun) on Park St. From the harbour you may be able to catch the *Waverley* (paddle steamer) or *Balmoral*, along the Bristol Channel or to Lundy Island. The clifftop Blue Anchor at the end of the B3191 E has decent food, great views.
West Somerset Railway Steam trains run from the Minehead terminus along the coast to Watchet and then inland to Bishops Lydeard – a splendid long run stopping at several little stations. Snacks, shop, very good disabled access, with a specially adapted coach; station open daily but no trains Mon (exc bank hols) or Fri in Apr, May and Oct, and none exc Santa specials in Dec, Nov–Feb, best to phone (01643) 704996 for timetable; £9.80 full return fare.

MONKSILVER ST0737
Combe Sydenham Country Park (B3188) Over 500 acres of Exmoor-edge woodland, with walks and trails, and play areas; the 16th-c house is open only to groups; (0800) 7838572; £5 car park. The Notley Arms is excellent for lunch.

MONTACUTE ST4917
Montacute House ⌨ Magnificent 16th-c honeyed stone house in beautiful little village, with interesting tapestries, furniture, paintings and ceramics, in rooms with decorated ceilings, ornate fireplaces and fine panelling. A highlight is the collection of Tudor and Jacobean paintings from the National Portrait Gallery, and the formal gardens are impressive. Enjoyable meals and snacks, shop, disabled access to grounds only; cl Tues and Nov–Mar; (01935) 823289; £6.20, £3.40 garden only; NT. The park is open to walkers. In the village, parts worth seeing include the Borough (a quite charming square of two-storey houses), and Abbey Farm and the Monk's House – all that remains of a Norman priory destroyed during the Dissolution. The Phelips Arms and Kings Arms are both good for lunch.

MUCHELNEY ST4224
Muchelney Abbey The abbey was founded in the 9th c (perhaps earlier), but the well preserved ruins date from the 15th, inc part of the cloister, and the abbot's lodging with its splendidly carved fireplace. Shop, limited disabled access; cl Nov–Mar; (01458) 250664; £2; EH. The tiny 14th-c priest's house opposite is worth a quick look; open Tues–Sat and Sun pm Mar–Oct; (01326) 270526; £2.60. The **John Leach Pottery** has a few items on display in the abbey, with the main showroom a couple of minutes' drive S (cl lunchtime, and most Suns).

NETHER STOWEY ST1939
An appealing large village with winding streets, handy for both Exmoor and the Quantocks, with good views over the Levels from the mound of the former Norman castle. The Rose & Crown (open all day) is a useful food stop, and the road up wooded Cockercombe gives a lovely sense of the Quantocks' feeling of peace and timelessness. Follow it down to the pretty village of Crowcombe on the W side, which has a delightful church and archetypal old Quantocks pub, the Carew Arms; it is generally the roads on this W side that

give the best views.

Coleridge Cottage (Lime St) The poet moved here in 1796; he lived here with a pig or two, and his friends the Wordsworths resided in considerably more style not far away – the two families were regarded with suspicion by the local population. Open pm Tues–Thurs and Sun Apr–Sept; (01278) 732662; £3; NT.

NORTON ST PHILIP ST7756
Norwood Rare Breeds Farm (B3110 N; this road has some steep intricate views) Friendly organic farm on high open land with plenty of traditional and rare breeds, nature trails, and good views. You can go right up to the animals, and watch the pigs being fed. Meals, snacks, good farm shop, disabled access; open end Mar–mid-Sept; (01373) 834356; £4.50. In the village, the George is a splendid ancient building, and across the meadow behind is an attractively set medieval church with bells which struck Pepys as 'mighty tuneable'.

NUNNEY ST7345
Nunney Castle This 14th-c fort was reduced to ruins in the Civil War, but has one of the deepest moats in the country; it and its feeder stream running through the green of this quaint and quiet village are jostling with ducks. The castle's layout and round towers were supposedly modelled on France's Bastille; free. There's a small covered market place just above the stream, and nearby are 18th-c weavers' cottages. The **church**, as usual in so many Somerset villages, is well worth a look, and the George has decent food.

PEAT MOORS ST4241
Peat Moors Visitor Centre (Shapwick Rd, Westhay) In the heart of the peat-cutting area of the Levels, with an excellent exhibition on the topic, and a reconstructed Iron Age village. Craft demonstrations some summer wknds. Snacks, shop, disabled access; cl Nov–Mar; (01458) 860697; £2.50. The Olde Burtle Inn over past Catcott Burtle has enjoyable food.

QUANTOCK TOPS ST1537
The moorland tops of these hills are quite a different world, where ancient trackways lead past prehistoric cairns and burial mounds; Exmoor, the Bristol

Channel, South Wales and the Mendips are in sight. Walkers have easy access to the moor from the tiny road crossing the ridge between Nether Stowey and Crowcombe.

QUANTOCK WALKS ST1540
The Quantock Hills have the most for walkers in W Somerset (short of Exmoor). Their secretive quality is illustrated by the dense broad-leafed woodlands on the N side, where shady combes display splendid spring and autumn colours. The village of Holford is a good starting point: the paths begin with helpful signposts, though you may soon get bemused by the complexity of the path junctions. Holford Combe is reasonably easy to find, and a map will get you to the ancient hill fort site capping Dowsborough, from where a moorland track leads gently N to Holford. Another good approach is from Kilve, from where you can take a path to and along the coast, then through East Quantoxhead to the north Quantock slopes for a remarkably varied circuit.

QUANTOCKS – WESTERN SLOPES ST1139
The west slopes of the Quantock Hills, less wooded than the NE side, have some charming valleys enclosed by plunging slopes, with tracks along the bottom: Bicknoller with its fine church (good carvings) is an attractive start for walks, and the Blue Ball at Triscombe is an excellent port of call.

RADSTOCK ST6854
Radstock Museum 🏛 (Waterloo Rd) Local history museum, with mining displays, a reconstructed Victorian classroom and Co-op shop. Temporary exhibitions throughout the year; snacks, shop, disabled access; cl am, Mon, and all Dec–Jan; (01761) 437722; £3.

SOMERTON ST4928
Built in light grey stone, this market town has a 17th-c market cross and fine old Georgian buildings in the quiet main square, where the Globe has good food. **St Michael's church** is stupendous, its roof supposedly created by monks of Muchelney from 7,000 fetter pieces, among which is a beer barrel – apparently a reference to Abbot Bere.

SOUTH CADBURY ST6325
An attractive scatter of golden cottages huddle around the church with its striking gargoyled tower; Waterloo Crescent is a distinctive row of farm workers' cottages built in 1815.
Cadbury Castle Its Arthurian connection is the main draw. The legendary king and his knights are still said to sleep below the turf of this huge hill fort, waking on Christmas Eve to ride down the hill, along what's long been known as King Arthur's Hunting Causeway, and through the village on their pilgrimage to Glastonbury. The castle, covering about 18 acres, is in fact a massive Iron Age camp: many relics have been found there – especially Roman artefacts. It's quite a steep climb, and can be muddy; stout walking shoes recommended. Compton Pauncefoot just E is pretty.
SOUTH PETHERTON ST4317
The **church** has the second-highest octagonal tower in the country. The thatched Royal Oak at Over Stratton is a good family dining pub.
SPARKFORD ST6127
Haynes Sparkford Motor Museum (A359) Huge collection of gleamingly restored vintage and classic cars and motorcycles; you should be able to see some being test-driven outside on their event and family fun days (usually only a few days each year). Meals, snacks, shop, disabled access; cl 25–26 Dec, 1 Jan; (01963) 440804; £6. The Sparkford Inn is a nice place for lunch.
STAPLE FITZPAINE ST2618
Pretty village with a fine pub, the Greyhound; a quiet drive with good views loops along the S edge of Staple Hill then crosses the B3170 to run over Culmhead (where the Holman Clavel is another good stop), along the Blackdown Hills, passing the Merry Harriers (an excellent dining pub), and then the Wellington Monument.
STAPLEGROVE ST2027
Staplecombe Vineyards Friendly little vineyard, with self-guided tours of the fields, then back at the house a cheery couple happy to chat. Shop, disabled access; cl Sun am, but phone first; (01823) 451217; free. Avoiding Taunton, the Lethbridge Arms at

Bishops Lydeard does decent lunches.
STEEP HOLM ST2260
A small island a few miles off shore, its 50 acres a nature reserve teeming with rare plants, wildlife and historic remains. Terrific views from the rugged cliffs. You can get snacks out here, and there's a shop in former Victorian barracks, but it's not really suitable for the disabled. Boat trips to the island run from Knightstone Causeway, Weston, Apr–Oct – Mrs Rendell has dates and times on (01934) 632307 (booking essential); all-day trip £14.
STOGUMBER ST0937
Charming village with cottage gardens, an unblemished main street, and an interesting **church**; the White Horse has good food.
STOGURSEY ST2042
Stogursey church Exceptional Norman church with charming carved 15th- and 16th-c pew ends – fascinating figures, faces and grotesques.
STOKE ST GREGORY ST3326
Willow & Wetlands Visitor Centre (Meare Green Court, towards N Curry) How the area – the most important wetland region in England – developed from marsh and swamp, showing its wildlife (complete with birdsong), and the rise and decline of its willow-growing and basket-making industries, inc a good 15-min video, and a museum of products from bath chairs and prams to hot-air balloon baskets (willow is still really the only thing that will do for these). This is a working willow-weaving firm; tour of willow yards and workshop £2.50. Tearoom, shop, some disabled access; cl Sun, and 25–26 Dec; (01823) 490249; free. The Rose & Crown at Woodhill is good for lunch.
STOKE SUB HAMDON ST4716
Ham Hill Country Park 140 acres of grassland and woodland, full of wildlife and plants. The hill has provided the stone for many of the villages in the area, producing that distinctive warm honey-coloured look. The elevated area of old stone quarries gives walkers splendid views; you can go E from here on paths past St Michael's Hill, topped by an 18th-c pepperpot tower, to Montacute.
Stoke sub Hamdon Priory The

former 14th- and 15th-c priory manor house has long since vanished, but its fine thatched barn and the screens, passage and Great Hall of the chantry can still be seen; free. The village is charming, and the Fleur de Lis is good for lunch. Between here and Montacute is a striking folly, St Michael's Tower; it's one of three, all built by neighbouring friends in the 18th c – whenever one had a flag up it was an invitation for the others to go round for a hearty evening.

STRATTON-ON-THE-FOSSE ST6550

Notable for the spectacular modern (though not modern-looking) Downside Abbey. The White Post Inn, open all day, has good value food.

STREET ST4836

Shoe Museum (High St) Examples of footwear from Roman times to the present, along with machinery and advertising material. Shop, disabled access wkdys only; usually cl 10 days over Christmas; (01458) 842169; free. Behind here **Clarks Village** is an attractively laid out factory shopping centre, with well known names from Jaeger to Black & Decker (and of course Clarks Shoes); some real bargains, plenty of snacks.

TAUNTON ST2224

Busy and prosperous shopping country town, with a lively Sat cattle market, and a farmers' market on the last Thurs of the month in summer. It's not of great visual distinction; the best bit is Hammet St, a short street of 18th-c red brick terraces leading to the county's biggest **church**, which has an exceptionally ornate roof, lofty Perpendicular chancel and lovely pinnacled tower. The Tudor House on Fore St is attractive. Just behind Riverside Pl the **Shakespeare Glassworks** may have demonstrations of glass-blowing, (01823) 333422; and in Bath Pl **Makers** is a decent craft shop selling local hand-made crafts (cl Sun). Besides the good Castle Hotel, the Masons Arms in Magdalene St is good for lunch (not Sun).

Somerset County Museum Fine museum in part of the former castle (whose 13th-c portcullised gate-tower is absorbed into the County Hotel), with a rare Bronze Age shield. The biggest hoard of Roman silver coins ever found in Britain is on show here; thousands of them, dating from the 3rd c. Shop, disabled access to ground floor only; cl Sun, Mon (exc bank hols), Good Fri, 25 Dec–2 Jan; (01823) 320201; £2.50.

Somerset Cricket Museum 🖼 (Priory Avenue) Old building, thought to have been the gatehouse for the priory that once stood by this cricket ground: bats, balls and blazers, cards, cuttings and caps, and a cricketing reference library too. Some disabled access; open wkdys Apr–Oct; (01823) 275893; £1.

TEMPLECOMBE ST7022

Ancient village with stocks still in place; the name comes from the medieval order of Knights Templar, dedicated to the protection of the Holy Sepulchre and pilgrims to it. The church, supposedly founded by King Alfred's daughter, houses a 13th-c painting of Christ, found by accident in an outhouse 30 years ago; possibly an early copy of the Turin Shroud, which the Knights Templar may have had in their possession for a while.

TINTINHULL ST5020

Tintinhull House Garden Colourful and attractive 1930s formal garden sheltered by walls and hedges, around 17th-c house with Queen Anne façade (not open). Teas; open pm Weds–Sun Apr–Sept; (01935) 822545; £3.80; NT. The nearby Lamb has bargain lunches.

TOLLAND ST1131

Gaulden Manor Gardens 🖼 (B3224) The gardens of this nicely tucked-away medieval manor house are pleasant, with a rose garden and bog garden. Shop, plant sales, disabled access; garden open pm Sun, Thurs and bank hols early Jun–Aug; (01984) 667213; *£3.50.

TYNTESFIELD ST5071

As we went to press the National Trust hoped that this stunning 127-year-old stately home would be open to the public (at least to small groups) in 2003. It's the first stately home that they've bought for more than a decade, and is probably the country's finest Gothic-Revival country house; unlike other properties of this period, which have been divided and stripped of their original features, Tyntesfield has kept its original furnishings and contents. Also wonderfully unspoilt, the 539-acre estate contains a sumptuous chapel, home farm, gardens and parkland. Phone for details (01985) 843600; or look at their website www.nationaltrust.org.uk.

WAMBROOK ST2908
Attractive village, in quiet countryside suiting both walkers and cyclists; the Cotley Inn here is useful.

WASHFORD ST0440
Cleeve Abbey (signed S) Remarkably well preserved 12th-c Cistercian abbey, the gatehouse, dormitory and refectory all in good condition. Fine timbered roof, detailed wall paintings and traceried windows, and an exhibition on monastic life. Snacks, shop, some disabled access; cl 1–2pm Nov–Mar, 24–26 Dec, 1 Jan; (01984) 640377; £2.80; EH. The Notley Arms at Monksilver is fairly handy, for a good meal.

Tropiquaria Animal and Adventure Park ⬛ (A39 – easy to spot by tall radio masts) This enjoyable place is an amazing transformation of a 1930s BBC transmitting station into an indoor jungle with high waterfall, tropical plants, free-flying birds and weird and wonderful animals. You can touch all sorts of creatures: plenty of snakes and lizards, perhaps a tarantula. There's an aquarium beneath the hall, while out in the landscaped gardens are birds, lemurs, chipmunks, guinea-pigs and wallabies, as well as a couple of good play areas inc two pirate adventure ships and a new indoor play castle. A delightful puppet theatre (for many, the highlight) has 20-min marionette and shadow puppet shows (usually hourly in summer, but at other times much less frequent – so worth checking first). Also an intriguing collection of vintage radios and televisions. Meals, snacks, shop, disabled access (not to aquarium); open daily Easter–Oct, then wknds and school hols Nov–Mar; (01984) 640688; £5.50. The nearby station on the steam line from Minehead has a little **railway museum** devoted to the old Somerset & Dorset Railway; open most days (when West Somerset Railway is

running – see earlier entry) May–Sept, phone for winter opening; (01984) 640869; £1.

WATCHET ST0743
This small working port has a new marina (the only one on the S side of the Bristol Channel), a tidal harbour with fishing boats and coasters, and enough industry to keep it from being too touristy – and it's by no means unattractive. In Harbour Rd a dedicated **Working Boat Museum** has hands-on activities for children inc a boat they can clamber around in and a trail; usually open pms Tues–Thurs and wknds Easter–end Oct; shop, mostly disabled access; (01984) 634242; free. The friendly little **Market House Museum** in Market St has local history displays; cl 12.30–2.30, and end Oct–Easter; donations welcome. The Bell (Market St) has good value simple food.

WELLS ST5546
With a population of only 9,500 this delightful place wouldn't normally even qualify as a big town, but in fact it's England's smallest city. The **Vicars Close** is said to be one of the oldest complete medieval streets in Europe; the cathedral's Vicars Choral still live here, passing the 15th-c Chain Gate to the cathedral itself. The Fountain, a good nearby dining pub, is popular with the choir – you may even be served by a Vicar Choral. There are a good few other attractive old buildings, many now used as offices and shops (inc several antiques shops), and several grouped around the Market Pl; the City Arms is a pleasant place for lunch. The High St and Saddler St have recently been made more pedestrian friendly. The B3139 through Wedmore and side roads off it give a good feel of the dead flatness of the Somerset Levels.
Bishop's Palace Moated and fortified, approached through a 14th-c gatehouse; it's quite dramatic going across the drawbridge. The beautiful series of buildings still has some original 13th-c parts, notably the banqueting hall and undercroft, as well as several state rooms and a long gallery hung with portraits of former bishops. The grounds are the site of the wells that give the city its name, producing on

average 150 litres (40 gallons) of water a second. Also lovely gardens, decent arboretum, and a pair of swans trained to ring a little bell under the gatehouse window when they're hungry (so many people feed them in summer that this isn't terribly often). Meals (May–Sept), snacks, shop, disabled access to ground floor; open Tues–Fri plus bank hols and pm Sun Apr–Oct, most days in Aug; (01749) 678691; £3.50, perhaps more for special exhibitions.

Wells Cathedral Stunning structure right in the centre, its three towers stretching up against the Mendip foothills. The spectacular W front is reckoned by many to be the finest cathedral façade in the country; dating from the 13th c, it carries 293 pieces of medieval sculpture. Unmissable oddities inside include the wonderful scissors-shaped inverted arches, the north transept's 14th-c clock where horsemen still joust every ½ hour, and the fine carvings in the south transept, inc various victims of toothache and four graphic scenes of an old man stealing fruit and getting what for. The embroidered stallbacks in the choir (1937–1948) are a riot of colour, and the library, with documents dating back to the 10th c, is at 51 metres (168 ft) the longest medieval library building in England. Evensong is at 5.15 wkdys (not Weds), 3pm Sun. Meals, snacks, shop, disabled access; £4.50 suggested donation.

Wells Museum ☒ (Cathedral Green) Tudor building with good local history museum inc notable embroidery samplers, and stone figures originally on the W front of the cathedral, but now too fragile to be returned there. Shop, some disabled access; cl Tues Oct–Apr, 25 Dec; (01749) 673477; £2.50.

WEST BAGBOROUGH ST1733 Tiny village well placed below the Quantocks, with a traditional working **pottery**, and fresh generous food (and comfortable bedrooms) at the Rising Sun.

WEST MENDIP WAY ST3956 This long-distance footpath, all the way between Wells and Weston-super-Mare, crosses the Mendip plateau, poor windswept sheep pasture on top,

pocked with unseen caverns used by potholers, and more visible Bronze Age funeral barrows; there are some stunning views from the section along Crook Peak, Compton Hill and Wavering Down. A path up from Compton Bishop ST3955 gives good access.

WESTON-SUPER-MARE ST3161 Friendly family seaside resort, its Latin epithet added in the 19th c in an attempt to be one up on the fashionable French resorts. An ambitious seafront development comprising a state-of-the-art leisure complex (inc an indoor swimming pool, cinema, cafés, and plenty of parking) should be completed by summer 2004. The quietest beaches are to the N, around Sand Bay. The Claremont Vaults, with good views from the N end of the seafront, is a popular dining pub, the olde-worlde Woolpack out at St Georges has good food, and there are pleasant walks (and a toll road) through the woods around the Iron Age fort above the town.

Helicopter Museum ☒ (B3146, was A370) An unexpected find, with over 60 helicopters and autogyros on show. Usually on the second Sun each month (Mar–Oct), they have an open cockpit day, when some helicopters are opened up for visitors to inspect, and others even offer flights. Snacks, shop, disabled access; cl Mon and Tues (exc summer and Easter hols) and 25–26 Dec, 1 Jan; (01934) 635227; £3.95.

Heritage Centre (Wadham St) Displays on local history; meals, snacks, shop, disabled access to ground floor only; cl Sun and bank hols; (01934) 412144; £1.

North Somerset Museum ☒ (Burlington St) Local history museum, focusing mainly on Victorian domestic life, with reconstructed shops and lots of seaside displays; it includes adjacent Clara's Cottage, a typical Westonian home of the 1900s with period kitchen, parlour and bedroom. Snacks, shop, disabled access to ground floor only; cl Sun, 25–26 Dec, 1 Jan; (01934) 621028; £3.50.

Seaquarium (Marine Parade) Right by the beach, with walk-through underwater tunnel, and plenty of sharks, rays and seahorses; talks and feeding sessions throughout the day. Meals, snacks, shop, disabled access; cl 25 Dec; (01934) 641603; £4.75 (they stamp your hand so you can come back).

WESTONZOYLAND ST3534
Steam museum 🔳 Pretty village with a **steam pumping station**; snacks, shop, disabled access; open Sun pm; in steam 1st Sun of month Apr–Oct, plus Sun and Mon bank hol wknds; (01823) 275795; £2.50 (£3 steam days). The Sedgemoor Inn (a Royalist base before the Battle of Sedgemoor, with interesting memorabilia) has decent food.

WHITCHURCH ST6167
HorseWorld 🔳 (Staunton Lane, off A37 S edge of Bristol) Home to over 220 rescued and retired horses, ponies and donkeys; what makes it special is the range of other attractions on offer, with plenty to fill a busy half day. Pleasantly restored farm buildings house an interactive museum examining the origins of the horse and its influence on the human world, a video theatre, and an extensive collection of tack and harnesses. There's a twice-daily horse parade (11.30 and 2.30), a nature trail around the paddocks, a horse-themed play area, plenty of space for picnics, and other animals to meet such as goats, lambs, chickens and rabbits. Meals, snacks, shop, disabled access; cl 22 Dec–1 Jan; (01275) 540173. Free, but a self-guided tour (taking in all the areas mentioned above) costs £4.50.

WILLITON ST0740
Bakelite Museum Incongruously but charmingly housed in an 18th-c watermill, this unusual and surprisingly interesting museum is devoted to vintage plastics from the Victorian age to World War II. Exhibits range from jelly moulds and ashtrays to a Bakelite plastic coffin, and incredibly small 1930s 'pod' caravans; other items include early refrigerators, lots of radios, and a horrific-looking hair perming machine. Cream teas, shop, disabled access to ground floor; open Thurs–Sun Easter–Oct, daily in school hols; (01984) 632133; £3, free for wheelchair users. The Notley Arms at Monksilver is in easy reach, for a good lunch.

WINCANTON ST7128

Fine Georgian houses and many of the multitude of inns and hotels survive from the coaching era; lots still have old coach-entry gates. The **church porch** has a medieval relief of St Eligius. The cheerful Nog (South St) has decent food.

WOOKEY HOLE ST5347
Wookey Hole Caves & Papermill 🔳 Guided tours of half a mile of dramatic subterranean tunnels and caverns, using remote-controlled lighting and special effects to spotlight the geological features and bring to life associated history and myths (young children may find it all a bit frightening). Just along the river the paper mill demonstrates paper production (visitors can have a go too Mon–Thurs), and also houses a Magical Mirror Maze and Old Penny Arcade. A bustling place, all under cover, so ideal when the sun's not shining. Meals and snacks, shop, disabled access exc to caves; cl 17–25 Dec; (01749) 672243; £8. The Burcott Inn nearby is a good choice for lunch.

WRINGTON ST4862
Barley Wood Walled Gardens This small Victorian walled garden has views over Wrington Vale, craft workshops and a good farm shop. Meals, snacks and a picnic area; cl over Christmas; (01934) 863713); £2. In the village the Plough (open all day) has good value food.

YENSTON ST7121
Gartell Light Railway The friendly staff who run this 2-ft gauge railway through attractive Blackmore Vale countryside succeed in making it really enjoyable, even though the line's under a mile long. The trains leave every 15 mins, along the track of the defunct Somerset & Dorset Railway; there's a little railway museum, a picnic area by a lake, and a visitor centre. Snacks, shop; open bank hol Mons and some Suns May–Oct, plus two Santa wknds in Dec – phone for dates; (01963) 370752; £4 for a day's unlimited travel.

YEOVIL ST5515
Little in the town to interest visitors, but the **Museum of South Somerset** (Hendford) is worth a look if passing, with a good range of local history and reconstructed Roman and Georgian rooms. Shop, disabled access; usually cl

Sun, Mon and bank hols, plus Sats Oct–Mar, and around a wk over Christmas and New Year; (01935) 424774; free. There's also a partly 14th-c **church** (and a dry-ski centre).

YEOVILTON ST5423

Fleet Air Arm Museum 🏛 (Royal Naval Air Station, off A359) Big place concentrating on the story of aviation at sea from 1908, and the history of the Royal Naval Air Service. Lively displays on the WRENS, the Falklands and Gulf Wars, jets and helicopters, as well as around 40 historic aircraft, and lots of models, paintings, weapons and photographs, plus an exhibition on supersonic flight. A highlight is the carrier hall, which leads you through various parts of the aircraft carrier while it is involved in an assignment: lots of flashing lights and dialogue as you follow the tour of the bridge, the operations room, and best (and noisiest) of all the flight deck. Viewing galleries look out over the aircraft using this busy base. Also adventure playground, and hi-tech flight simulator. You could easily spend a good few hours here. Meals, snacks, shop, disabled access; cl 24–26 Dec; (01935) 840565; £8.50. The Kingsdon Inn is the best nearby place for lunch.

Other attractive villages, all with decent pubs, include Batcombe ST6838, Brompton Regis SS9531, Compton Dando ST6464, Crowcombe ST1336, Evercreech ST6438, Faulkland ST7354, Hinton St George ST4212, Huish Episcopi ST4226, Litton ST5954, Luxborough SS9837, North Perrott ST4709, Norton sub Hamdon ST4615, South Stoke ST7641 (picturesque views from the steep nearby lanes), Waterrow ST0425, Wellow ST7458, Winscombe ST4157 and Winsley ST7961. High Ham ST4320, Pilton ST5940 and Stowell ST6822 and are also well worth a visit.

Where to eat

APPLEY ST0621 **Globe** *Appley (01823) 672327* Cheerfully run and unspoilt 15th-c pub with a relaxed chatty atmosphere, consistently enjoyable food inc adventurous specials and vegetarian meals, and super puddings; no smoking dining room; cl Mon lunch exc bank hols. £25|**£6**

BATCOMBE ST6838 **Three Horseshoes** *(01749) 850359* Honey stone, slate-roofed pub serving good, imaginative food under new licensees in bustling main room decorated with pretty ivy stencils and artificial ivy, fruit and flower decorations, and a few naive farm animal paintings on the lightly ragged dark pink walls; a woodburner and big open fire, attractive stripped stone dining room, well kept real ales, a good choice of wines, and big well equipped play area in garden. £25|**£4.95**

BATH ST7464 **Moody Goose** *7a Kingsmead Sq (01225) 466688* Stylish basement restaurant with large namesake pottery goose, paintings on whitewashed walls, fresh flowers on crisp white tablecloths, deft modern English cooking, and a thoughtful wine list; cl Sun, bank hols, 2 wks spring; children over 8; disabled access. £40/2 courses £12

BATH ST7464 **Old Green Tree** *12 Green St (01225) 338259* Genuinely unspoilt pub with enjoyable lunchtime food, a bustling cheerful atmosphere in its three oak-panelled little rooms, a no smoking back bar, several well kept real ales, lots of malt whiskies, and a nice little wine list with a dozen by the glass; they do not take bookings; cl 25 Dec, 1 Jan; no children.|**£5**

BATH ST7465 **Olive Tree** *Russel St (01225) 447928* Light and airy no smoking basement restaurant in the Queensberry Hotel; stylishly simple modern decor, friendly helpful service, super Mediterranean cooking (delicious fish and tempting puddings), and good value wines; cl Sun, 4 days over Christmas. £40/2 courses £13.50

BATH ST7564 **Rajpoot** *4 Argyle St (01225) 466833* Exceptionally good carefully cooked Indian food in attractively decorated restaurant, particularly good service (you are met at the door by a colourfully uniformed doorman), and used by stars of screen and stage; cl 25–26 Dec; disabled access (by arrangement). £20|**£6.95**

BRISTOL ST5774 **Fishworks Seafood Café** *128 Whiteladies Road (0117) 974 4433* Bustling, lively restaurant where you choose your fish or seafood from the absolutely fresh produce (they have a fishing boat in Newlyn, Cornwall) that is then simply cooked and presented – though there are some interesting dishes; helpful efficient staff, and a short, good value, mainly white wine list; cl Sun pm, Mon. £32|£11

BRISTOL ST5872 **Harveys Wine Cellars** *12 Denmark St (0117) 927 5034* Attractive restaurant in 13th-c wine cellars with lots of interesting memorabilia (old sherry casks, wine bottles, and old silver and glassware), very good imaginative food, an exceptional cheese board, friendly knowledgeable staff, and a wonderful wine list; guided tours and tastings (for groups of over 20) and wine merchants and wine shop; cl Sun, bank hols, 1 wk Feb, 2 wks Aug; children over 5. £50 dinner, £28 lunch

BRISTOL ST5873 **Markwicks** *43 Corn St (0117) 926 2658* Elegant restaurant in the vaults of an old bank building, delicious daily changing classic French cooking (first-class fish, lovely puddings), a carefully chosen wine list, and good friendly service; cl am Sat, Sun, 1 wk Christmas, 1 wk Easter, 2 wks Aug. £42|£12.50

BRISTOL ST5872 **Riverstation** *The Grove (0117) 914 4434* Converted ex-River Police HQ on waterfront with informal downstairs café and deli, airy first-floor restaurant, contemporary furnishings, enjoyable popular modern British cooking with Mediterranean slant, and a fine choice of wines by the glass; regular art exhibitions; cl 25–26 Dec; disabled access downstairs only. £35|£5.50

COMBE HAY ST7359 **Wheatsheaf** *(01225) 833504* Popular country pub in a pretty setting, with pleasantly old-fashioned rooms, a big log fire, shuttered windows, reliably good food (plenty of game and fish), well kept real ales, decent wines, and friendly staff; cl 25–26 Dec, 1 Jan; seats outside with nice views; disabled access. £21.95|£6.50

DOULTING ST6545 **Waggon & Horses** *Beacon (01749) 880302* 18th-c inn with stone-mullioned latticed windows, a rambling bar with interesting pictures for sale, two no smoking rooms, a choice of enjoyable robustly flavoured food, decent house wines, cocktails, real ales, and a lovely big walled garden with some remarkable fancy fowl (they sell the eggs), a goat and horses; big raftered gallery for art shows and classical music; cl 25 Dec; children must be very well behaved; disabled access. £24.75|£7.50

HOLCOMBE ST6649 **Ring o' Roses** *Stratton Road (01761) 232478* Quietly placed and extensively modernised open-plan country pub, relaxed and comfortably civilised, with consistently good modern cooking using only local suppliers, afternoon teas, decent wines, local ciders and ales, and helpfully efficient service; no smoking restaurant side, modern prints, gently lit parlourish area with sofas and cushioned chairs, pleasant panelled lounge, daily papers; peaceful farmland views from picnic-sets on terrace and lawns; bdrms. £28.20|£7.50

LANGLEY MARSH ST0729 **Three Horseshoes** *(01984) 623763* Unpretentious red sandstone pub with short changing choice of enjoyable food using some produce from their own garden (no chips or fried food), a wide choice of often unusual real ales, farm ciders, no fruit machines or pool tables, skittle alley, tables outside, and sloping back garden with play area and farmland views; good nearby walks; cl winter Mon; children must be well behaved. £18|£4.50

LOVINGTON ST5931 **Pilgrims Rest** *(01963) 240597* Quietly placed and civilised country bar/bistro with good interesting food cooked by the landlord, using all fresh ingredients; chatty and relaxed, with sunny modern prints, settees and easy chair by cosy inner area's big fireplace, snug heavy-beamed eating area with candles on its American-clothed tables, and no smoking dining room; nice wines by the glass, well kept ales from the nearby brewery, daily papers, some tables outside. £28|£8

MONKSILVER ST0737 **Notley Arms** *(01984) 56217* Immensely well liked, friendly pub with beamed L-shaped bar, candles and fresh flowers, woodburners, reasonably priced very good food (they don't take bookings, so must get there early), well kept beers, especially nice licensees, and neatly kept cottagey garden running down to a swift clear stream; pub games, skittle alley, and table tennis; cl 25 Dec, 2 wks Feb; limited disabled access. £20.40|**£5.95**

RUDGE ST8251 **Full Moon** *(01373) 830936* Attractive country pub with friendly licensees, a lot of character in the different rooms, a gently upmarket atmosphere, small flagstoned dining room (and separate plush restaurant), generous helpings of imaginative bar food inc a bargain 3-course set lunchtime and early evening meal, and well kept real ales; comfortable bdrms plus new village cottages and indoor pool. £25|**£5.95**

SHEPTON MALLET ST6144 **Blostins** *29 Waterloo Rd (01749) 343648* Friendly little candlelit evening bistro with consistently good interesting food inc lovely puddings, and fairly priced wines; cl Sun, Mon, 2 wks Jan, 1 wk Easter, 2 wks Aug. £22

SHEPTON MONTAGUE ST6731 **Montague Inn** *(01749) 813213* Tastefully furnished country pub (new licensees this year) with stripped wooden tables, kitchen chairs and a log fire in the attractive inglenook fireplace, a gently upmarket atmosphere, particularly good food using as much organic produce as possible, well kept real ales, fine wines, and elegant candlelit dining rooms (one is no smoking); pretty back garden and terrace with nice views. £21.50|**£6**

TAUNTON ST2224 **Brazz** *Castle Bow (01823) 252000* Stylish, lively brasserie (there's another in Exeter) with fun décor inc an interesting aquarium, good interesting bistro-type food, and reasonably priced wines (ten by the glass); partial disabled access. £34|**£8**

TRISCOMBE ST1535 **Blue Ball** *(01984) 618242* On the first floor of a lovely 15th-c thatched stone-built former coaching stables: three levels with carefully crafted oak partitions, interesting, tasty food, 400 wines (they will open any bottle under £20 for just a glass), well kept real ales and old cognacs; the decking at the top of the terraced garden makes the most of the peaceful views. £22.90|**£7.95**

WESTON-SUPER-MARE ST3261 **Reflections** *22 Boulevard (01934) 622454* Informal family-run restaurant, a good but ordinary café at lunchtimes (exc Sun, when decent set lunch), but transformed Thurs, Fri and Sat evenings with elaborate and well presented high quality meals; cl Sun–Weds pms, 1 Jan for 10 days. £23.50|**£4.25**

WILLITON ST0741 **White House** *11 Long St (01984) 632777* Charming shuttered Georgian hotel under the same friendly owners for over 30 years, with antiques and more modern furnishings, paintings and ceramics, very good enjoyable carefully cooked food using the best local produce, and a fine choice of reasonably priced wines; good breakfasts; bdrms; cl Nov–May; partial disabled access. £40

WOOKEY ST5245 **Burcott Inn** *Wookey Rd (01749) 673874* Little roadside pub, neatly kept and friendly, with two simply furnished small front bars, an open fire, a roomy attractive back restaurant (shut Sun/Mon pms), nice bar food, well kept real ales, and a sizeable garden; cl pms 25 Dec and 1 Jan; children must be well behaved; disabled access. £16|**£6.50**

We welcome reports from readers

This *Guide* depends on readers' reports. Do help us if you can – in return, we offer a discount on the next edition to people who've helped us with reports for it. Tell us what you think about places already in it, and anything extra you think we should say about them. And send us your ideas for inclusion in the next edition: places to visit, eat at or stay in, attractive drives or walks, maybe even unusual shops you know of. Use the card in the middle, the report forms at the end, or just write – no stamp needed: *The Good Britain Guide*, FREEPOST TN1569, Wadhurst, E Sussex TN5 7BR. Or log on to www.goodguides.com

STAFFORDSHIRE

An outstanding theme park, other family draws, Potteries porcelain, and some lovely countryside with fine walking opportunities

Alton Towers can hardly be beaten as a theme park; with an entirely different type of appeal, Weston Park this year gains our title of Staffordshire Family Attraction. Tamworth is another rewarding place for families, with the twin draw of Drayton Manor (a little zoo as well as heaps of fun rides), and the castle. Among other attractions, magnificent Shugborough Hall has a working rare breeds farm and puppet collection, and Winkhill, Eccleshall and Stowe-by-Chartley all have something to offer families too.

Many of the cluster of museums and showrooms around Stoke-on-Trent celebrate the area's pottery industry; the Wedgwood and Royal Doulton visitor centres are especially popular. In Burton upon Trent the Bass Museum and Burton Bridge Brewery take a look at the town's brewing industry from opposite ends of the scale. Izaak Walton's Cottage in Shallowford will interest fly-fishermen, while readers of Samuel Johnson will enjoy visiting his birthplace in attractive Lichfield.

The Peak District limestone country (NE of county) is a beautiful area for walking and driving (for Dove Dale see Derbyshire chapter). In the more industrial S of the county, Cannock Chase has miles of fine landscape, and the extensive canal network provides some unexpectedly attractive walks.

Places to stay at and eat in here are good value.

Where to stay

BETLEY SJ7847 **Adderley Green Farm** *Heighley Castle Lane, Betley, Crewe, Cheshire CW3 9BA (01270) 820203* **£45***; 3 rms. Georgian farmhouse on big dairy farm, with good breakfasts in homely dining room, and large garden; cl Christmas and New Year; dogs allowed by prior arrangement

CHEADLE SK0044 **Ley Fields Farm** *Leek Rd, Cheadle, Stoke-on-Trent, Staffordshire ST10 2EF (01538) 752875* **£44**; 3 rms. Listed Georgian farmhouse on working dairy farm in lovely countryside with lots of walks; traditional furnishings in lounge and dining room, good home cooking, and friendly welcome; cl Christmas and New Year

CHEDDLETON SJ9651 **Choir Cottage** *Ostlers Lane, Cheddleton, Leek, Staffordshire ST13 7HS (01538) 360561* **£57***, plus special breaks; 3 pretty rms with four-posters in 17th-c cottage next to owners' home, one with private entrance. No smoking cottage with comfortable lounges, attractive dining room with country views, and good breakfasts; cl 25 Dec; children over 5

HOPWAS SK1704 **Oak Tree Farm** *Hints Rd, Hopwas, Tamworth, Staffordshire B78 3AA (01827) 56807* **£75**; 8 comfortable, spacious and pretty rms. Carefully restored no smoking farmhouse with elegant little lounge, fresh flowers, an attractive breakfast room, a friendly atmosphere, enjoyable breakfasts, gardens overlooking the River Tame, and an indoor swimming pool and steam room; cl Christmas–New Year; no children; disabled access; dogs welcome in bedrooms

OAKAMOOR SK0544 **Bank House** *Farley Lane, Oakamoor, Stoke-on-Trent, Staffordshire ST10 3BD (01538) 702810* **£80**, plus special breaks; 3 lovely big rms. Carefully restored no smoking country home in neat gardens on the edge of the Peak National Park, with lovely views; log fire in comfortable drawing room, library, piano in the inner hall, and most enjoyable food (by prior arrangement using home-grown and local produce) – super home-made breads, brioches, pastries and jams and marmalade at marvellous breakfast; friendly dog and cats; lots to do nearby; cl Christmas wk; dogs welcome by prior arrangement only

ROLLESTON ON DOVE SK2327 **Brookhouse Hotel** *Station Rd, Rolleston on Dove, Burton upon Trent, Staffordshire DE13 9AA (01283) 814188* **£105***, plus wknd breaks; 19 comfortable rms with Victorian brass or four-poster beds. Handsome ivy-covered William & Mary brick building in five acres of lovely gardens with comfortable antiques-filled rooms, and good food using seasonal local produce in elegant little dining room; children over 12; disabled access; dogs welcome in bedrooms

WARSLOW SK0858 **Greyhound** *Warslow, Buxton, Derbyshire SK17 0JN (01298) 84249 £35*; 4 clean and comfortable rms with shared bthrm. Warm, welcoming atmosphere in comfortably refurbished slated stone inn handy for Peak District, with generous helpings of home-made food inc hearty breakfasts, live Sat evening entertainment; cl Christmas and New Year; children over 12

WETTON SK1055 **Olde Royal Oak** *Wetton, Ashbourne, Staffordshire DE6 2AF (01335) 310287 £45*, plus wknd breaks; 4 rms. Shuttered old stone village inn in lovely NT walking country, with a warmly cheerful welcome; an attractive older part leads into a more modern-feeling area, with open fires, country furniture, a sun lounge overlooking a small garden, decent food, and nice breakfasts; no children; cl wknds during school term

To see and do

Staffordshire Family Attraction of the Year

WESTON UNDER LIZARD SJ8010 **Weston Park** (A5) Nowhere in Staffordshire compares with Alton Towers as far as children are concerned, but if you're after something completely different, this striking 17th-c house has a good range of features for all age groups, and the family ticket is quite exceptional value: five people can spend a day here and still have change from a tenner. Run by an educational charity, it's very well organised, and the staff are knowledgeable and friendly. Each of the richly decorated rooms has its own dedicated guide, as good with the family gossip as they are with the facts about the furnishings and art. You generally get to see nine of the main rooms, of which the highlight is the very elegant dining room, with its excellent collection of works by Van Dyck. The library, home to over 3,000 books, also impresses, and there are plenty of other notable paintings, including works by Rubens, Gainsborough and Constable. They've recently started showing off the family silver, and may in summer open a few of the first-floor bedrooms. There's a small toy museum, and letters and mementoes of Disraeli, who was a frequent 19th-c visitor; he claimed to detest country houses, but described Weston as 'a place that always pleased me'. One of the gifts he brought was a yellow parrot, which for years was thought to be male, until it suddenly produced two eggs, and promptly died; parrot and eggs are still proudly on display. Landscaped by Capability Brown, the grounds are huge, with a deer park, restored 18th-c terrace garden, brightly planted broderie garden, and interesting trees and shrubs; in the last century it took 37 gardeners to look after it all. The best way to explore is with one of their fairly detailed walking trails, which you can pick up free from the visitor centre. Children are well catered for: there's a good adventure playground in the woodland, and a pets' corner with the usual animals to fuss. The miniature railway has a small extra charge. The inspiration for P G Wodehouse's Blandings Castle, the estate still maintains a tradition for hosting influential events, in recent months providing the setting for an international peace conference, and the music festival V2002. During events like this it may be closed to visitors, so best to ring before visiting. Meals, snacks, shop, disabled access; usually open weekends Easter–early September, and daily in July and August, though see above; (01952) 852100; entry to the park and gardens is £2.50 (£1.50 children), with the house a further £2 (£1 children), but you'll very quickly make savings with the family ticket, £7.50 for two adults and up to three children.

ABBOTS BROMLEY SK0824
Half-timbered houses and red-brick Georgian buildings, as well as a 17th-c butter cross, in a village famed for its ancient Horn Dance which is held annually in early Sept; (01283) 840224; pleasant countryside around. The Royal Oak is popular for food.

ALTON SK0743
Alton Towers (off B5032) 200-acre giant theme parks with lots of features, rides and a very broad appeal (height limits on some attractions). You need a full day to fit everything in and many features have queues; the average wait is 10 mins, but can be longer. You can book timed rides in advance on two attractions and save a couple of pounds on the admission price. A new futuristic ice show featuring the magician Wayne Dobson runs several times a day in the Big Top, and Air (a stomach stalling roller-coaster) is the latest new ride. Other famous rides include Oblivion (a vertical drop ride) and Nemesis (whisks you through unfeasible angles at a greater G-force than experienced by astronauts in a rocket launch). Several areas are geared for younger children, inc an indoor play area. Dozens of other attractions include log flumes and lovely extensive gardens. Staying at their splendidly zany hotel gets you into the park half an hour before the main gates open. This is by no means a cheap day out, but the presentation and facilities are excellent. Meals, snacks, shop, disabled access (on most rides too); open mid-Mar–early Nov; (01538) 702200; full price entry is £23.50 for adults, and £19.50 children aged 4–12; parking £2 (wkdys off-peak tickets £5 cheaper). You can usually buy a good value second day's entry from any of the information points around the park.

BIDDULPH SJ8858
Biddulph Grange Garden (Grange Rd) Notable and really quite charming high Victorian garden, extensively restored; divided by its founder into a number of smaller themed gardens to house specimens from all over the world. The recently restored ice house and new rose garden are now open. Snacks, shop; cl am, all day Mon (exc bank hols), Tues, Good Fri and Nov–Mar (exc wknds mid-Nov to mid-Dec, when it's free); (01782) 517999; £4.50; NT. You can get a voucher for a reduced ticket for Little Moreton Hall in Cheshire, 7m away past the prettily placed Egerton Arms in Astbury (good value lunches); what a shame neither place opens in the mornings, to make a more sensible day of it.

BLYTHE BRIDGE SJ9441
Foxfield Steam Railway Five-mile return trip through scenic countryside: ticket gives unlimited travel for the whole day (not during special events). Staff are particularly friendly, and there's a museum (Tues–Sun in season) and collection of locomotives and rolling stock. Steam trains run Sun and bank hols Jun–Sept (and occasional days in winter) but best to check; (01782) 396210; £4.50. The Red Lion at Dilhorne, overlooking the wooded Cheadle Hills with plenty of country walks, has good value food.

BREWOOD SJ8808
Charming small town, with many attractive Georgian and older buildings. The Victorianised Admiral Rodney has good value food.

BURTON UPON TRENT SK2523
⊞ The town is dominated by its connections with what used to be the British brewing industry (now largely foreign-owned), and the **Bass Museum** (Horninglow St) with a virtual historic tour and audio guide explores this topic in some detail – with an emphasis on Bass and the company's famous shire horses. You can tour the brewery (no under-13s); also indoor and outdoor play areas, and special events. Meals, snacks, shop, disabled access; cl 25–26 Dec, 1 Jan; 0845 600 0598; £5.50.

Burton Bridge Brewery A complete contrast to the giant breweries that dominate the town, this shows brewing at the very opposite end of the scale; (01283) 510573. There's an attached pub; or the Queens Hotel is a comfortable place for lunch, as is the Marquis Suite carvery at the New Talbot Hotel on Anglesey Rd.

CALDON CANAL SK0348
The towpath gives many miles of good interesting walks. There's usually something happening at the Froghall Wharf canal terminus (inc narrow-boat

trips twice a week mid-May to Aug (01538) 266486), with an interesting walk along the canal to remote Consallforge, where the traditional Black Lion has enjoyable food. The nearby Nature Park continues this strange lost-valley scenery. There's also good access to this, the most attractive of Staffordshire's canals, from the good Boat pub at Cheddleton, and from Denford nr Leek.

CANNOCK CHASE SK0215
Miles of lovely woodland and rolling heath, threaded with quiet side roads – the breathing space for the more industrial part of Staffordshire, and appreciated all the more if you read up on the area's industrial heritage. Dotted around the 17,000 acres are Iron Age hill forts, nature trails, streams, pools and springs, and lovely spots for picnics or dramatic views; fallow deer are often seen. There's an information centre at Marquis Drive, and decent campsites. The canalside Moat House at Acton Trussell is popular for food.
Castle Ring This large hill fort has fine views over the forests of Cannock Chase to the Trent Valley.

CAULDON SK0749
Notable for its pub, the **Yew Tree**; a very unpretentious place packed with an extraordinary and delightfully higgledy-piggledy collection of remarkable bygones, esp mechanical music.

CHARTLEY SK0228
Chartley Castle (just over 6 miles W of Uttoxeter) A fine old ruin, with good views.

CHEDDLETON SJ9752
Cheddleton Flint Mill (Cheadle Rd) Fully preserved 17th- and 18th-c water mills, with a little museum. Shop; cl Nov–Mar and am; (01782) 502907; free. The Boat does decent lunches, with pleasant canal walks from it.
Churnet Valley Railway (Station Rd) Small steam locomotive museum in Victorian station building, complete with signal box and engine sheds. Ten-mile round trip steam and diesel runs in attractive surroundings. Snacks, shop; open wknds Mar–Oct with steam rides on Sun, also on Weds and Sat in Aug and at other times for special events; ring to check train times; (01538)

360522; train trip £7, donations for museum only.
CHURNET VALLEY SK0545
Very pretty walks from Alton or Oakamoor; the best goes through Hawksmoor and Greendale to pass the broad fishponds in wooded Dimmings Dale and comes back down to the river past an old smelting mill – and a good café called the Ramblers Retreat. Hawksmoor Wood is itself an attractive nature reserve, and the Talbot by Alton Bridge is useful for lunch.
CLIFTON CAMPVILLE SK2510
Clifton Campville church One of those rare country churches that seems practically perfect in every way.
CODSALL SJ8604
Notable in summer for its profusion of lupins. Moors Farm has a good farm shop and small country restaurant. The listed Codsall Station buildings have been interestingly redeveloped as a pub.
CROXDEN ABBEY SK0639
Ruins in quiet surroundings, with some towering arches surviving; EH. The Raddle at Hollington is a good family country pub.
ECCLESHALL SJ8329
Fletchers Garden Centre (Bridge Farm, Stone Rd) Plenty to amuse children, inc adventure playground, a miniature railway (wknds, bank hols and school hols Easter–Oct), crazy golf (£1.50) and about 20 enclosures in a little wildlife centre (£2.50). Restaurant, shop; cl 25–26 Dec, 1 Jan; (01785) 851057. The George (Castle St) does food all day wknds, and on the other side of town the Star out at Copmere End is prettily set overlooking the lake, with pleasant walks.
ENVILLE SO8287
Staffordshire Way This way-marked footpath offers scope for walking; the 17th-c Cat, with generous food, is a useful place to join it.
FRADLEY JUNCTION SK1513
Trent & Mersey Canal Generally less opportunity for towpath walks than with other Staffordshire canals, but this junction, with a waterside pub and lots happening on the water, is an attractive place for a stroll.
GREAT HAYWOOD SJ9923
There are interesting **canal walks**

from here, and the longest **packhorse bridge** in the country is nearby.

HANBURY SK1728
The Cock pub at Hanbury is a start for several attractive walks, inc a poignant one to the vast crater left by the 1944 Fauld bomb dump explosion, a tragedy understandably not much publicised at the time.

ILAM SK1350
Attractive estate village in the Manifold Valley (nr its junction with Dove Dale), surrounded by a NT-owned country park which runs on both banks of the River Manifold and was formerly the parkland for 19th-c Gothic Ilam Hall; free access to the park but pay and display parking; NT tearoom, shop and information centre.

INGESTRE SJ9824
Ingestre church Designed by or under Christopher Wren, and reckoned by some to be the finest small 17th-c church outside London.

KINVER SO8582
(the one right over in the W) Interesting village, with some of Britain's only rock houses nearby, still lived in 30 years ago; the nearby country park gives good views from the Iron Age fort on the ridge above. The rambling old White Hart is a useful stop.

LEEK SJ9856
Coombe Valley Bird Reserve This nearby RSPB reserve has a shop, and disabled access; cl 25 Dec; (01538) 384017; free. The A53 high moorland road N has good views, and E of here the B5053 gives an excellent impression of the dales country (the Jervis Arms at Onecote is a good family stop).

LICHFIELD SK1109
The attractive centre is largely pedestrianised, with many 18th-c and older buildings among the more modern shops (and antiques shops). The **cathedral**, with its three graceful spires and close with lovely half-timbered buildings around it, is magnificent inside, and its W front is memorable, esp at dusk or in the dark when shadows seem to bring the profusion of statues to life. Wonderful illuminated 8th-c gospels in the chapter house; cl during services and concerts; (01543) 306240; suggested donation

£3. On Sat May–Sept you can see two bleak 16th-c cells under the Guildhall (Bore St); (01543) 264972; 40p. The Queens Head (Queen St) does good value lunches.

Heritage Exhibition and Treasury (Market Sq) Worth a look, in a sympathetically restored chapel site; cl 25–26 Dec and 1 Jan; £3.50. Sometimes (not for under-12s) you can go up to the viewing platform in the spire, which has splendid views of the surrounding countryside (£1).

Samuel Johnson Birthplace Museum (Breadmarket St) Dr Johnson was born here in 1709; the house is now furnished in period, with many mementoes of him. Shop; cl ams Oct–Mar, 25–26 Dec, 1 Jan; (01543) 264972; *£2.20 – and a nice celebratory gesture, free entry on Sat nearest to Dr Johnson's birthday, 18 Sept.

LONGNOR SK0865
Finely sited in quiet, rolling limestone country this former market town, now pleasantly villagey in feel, has a cobbled market place, a good craft centre, and several pubs; the interesting 14th-c Olde Cheshire Cheese has good food.

LONGSDON SJ9655
Deep Hayes Country Park (Sutherland Rd; village off A53, 2m SW of Leek) Pleasant mixture of two freshwater pools, stepping stones, waterfalls, woods and meadows redeveloped from a reservoir built in the mid-19th c by the Potteries Waterworks. A wknd visitor centre has details of ranger-led and self-guided walks, as well as a shop and disabled facilities – one path is suitable for wheelchairs; (01538) 387655; free (inc parking). Readers recommend a walk around the park then through farmland, stopping for a snack in the Holly Bush nr Denford, and returning along the canal.

MANIFOLD VALLEY SK1350
The surfaced Manifold Track takes in the most scenic section of this limestone dale, from the B5054 (W of Hartington) S to the A523 nr Waterhouses. This has fewer of the sensational rock features that abound in Dove Dale, but plenty of charm – more or less steep riverside pastures, ancient woodland in the narrower steeper gorges, waterside caves; there's good

access to the hills above it, such as Wetton Hill, which have attractive views. The best viewpoint of all, not to be missed, is Thor's Cave, high above the dale. The branch off up Hamps Dale is extremely pretty. There are good pubs nearby at Warslow, Wetton and Hulme End.

MEERBROOK SJ9959

Tittesworth reservoir Large reservoir with visitor centre and restaurant, nature trails and bird hides, adventure playground and a sensory garden for the partially sighted; restaurant, shop; cl 25 Dec; (01538) 300224; £1 parking. The Three Horseshoes on nearby Blackshaw Moor is a reliable food stop.

ROACHES SJ9963

These form an impressive western barrier at the edge of the Dark Peak; this is perhaps the most exhilarating of several moorland walks from the side roads off the A53 N of Leek. A walk here can be combined with the path through the unspoilt Dane Valley to Danebridge on the Cheshire border; hidden in the woods above the Dane is Lud's Church – not a church, but a miniature chasm reputed to have been a hiding place for religious dissenters.

RUDYARD LAKE SJ9459

Though man-made it's perhaps one of Staffordshire's prettiest sights (Kipling owed his given name to his father's delight in it); you can hire a boat (£5 an hour), and the muddy marshland provides a haven for wading birds. The meadows and forested slopes above are pleasant for walks and picnics.

RUGELEY SK0418

Quite a few attractive old buildings, inc a beautiful 12th-c **church**.

SHALLOWFORD SJ8729

Izaak Walton Cottage (Worston Lane) Smartly rethatched home of the author of *The Compleat Angler*, with displays on the development of angling, period herb garden and picnic orchard. Snacks, shop, limited disabled access; cl ams, Mon–Tues (exc bank hols), and Nov–Mar; (01785) 760278; free. The Worston Mill at Little Bridgeford is attractive for lunch.

SHUGBOROUGH SJ9921

Shugborough Hall & County Museum 🖾 (A513) Imposing ancestral home of the Earls of Lichfield, begun in the late 17th c and enlarged in the 18th; magnificent state rooms, restored working kitchens, interesting puppet collection, and exhibition of the present Earl's photography. The park has a variety of unusual neo-classical monuments, working rare breeds farm, and restored corn mill. Meals, snacks, shop, disabled access; grounds cl Christmas–Mar, everything else cl Mon and Oct–Feb (exc Suns in Oct and special events); (01889) 881388; entry to estate £2, house and museum £6, house £4.50, farm £4.50; NT. Their all-in ticket £8 is best value on one of their special event days, when there are more activities (such as hands-on Victorian cookery displays) for no extra cost. The canalside Wolseley Arms towards Rugeley is a handy food stop.

STAFFORD SJ9223

The Great British Kitchen, a national centre for the culinary arts, is planned for autumn 2003. It will be housed in the old St George's hospital off Corporation St, to be a showplace for kitchen wizardry as well as a training ground for chefs. Greengate St has what's said to be the biggest timber-framed house in the country, built with local oak in 1595; period room settings; cl Sun; (01785) 619130; free. The Picture House (Bridge St/Lichfield St) has decent food all day.

Shire Hall Gallery (Market Sq) Handsome former county hall and crown court used until 1991; you can look round one courtroom. Also art, craft and photography exhibitions, and good craft shop. Snacks, shop, limited disabled access; cl Sun, during exhibition changes, and bank hols; (01785) 278345; free.

Stafford Castle (A518 SW) Norman remains, rebuilt in Gothic Revival style in the early 19th c, then allowed to fall into disrepair. Interactive displays in good visitor centre, and a medieval herb garden. Snacks, shop, disabled access to visitor centre; grounds open all year, visitor centre and castle cl Mon (exc bank hols), 25 Dec–2 Jan; (01785) 257698; free.

STOKE-ON-TRENT SJ8745

The Potteries The five linked towns within the Stoke-on-Trent conurbation still produce some of the finest china and pottery in the country; it's a strange, disjointed urban landscape, nothing like as grimy as it once was. You can tour several of the factories, and most have museums or a visitor centre. Three of the best sights are close to rail stations: Etruria Industrial Museum (Etruria station), Spode (Stoke) and Gladstone Pottery Museum (Longton).

Etruria Industrial Museum (Lower Bedford St, Etruria) This well restored and enjoyable museum sandwiched between two canals and based around the only surviving steam-powered potter's mill in the country (grinding flint for the ceramics industry right up to 1972; the modern factory that succeeded it is adjacent) includes an exhibition hall and also working blacksmith. Museum cl Thurs–Sun, also cl wknds Jan, Feb, Mar, engine in steam one wknd each month May–Nov, usually the first, but best to check; (01782) 233144; £2. The Plough (off A53 opposite Festival site in Etruria) is our current lunch recommendation for the Potteries.

Ford Green Hall ⌨ (Smallthorne) An interesting little 17th-c house and garden with special events. Snacks, shop, disabled access to ground floor, cl am and Fri and Sat; (01782) 233195; £1.50.

Gladstone Pottery Museum ⌨ (Uttoxeter Rd, Longton) Particularly engrossing, a complete Victorian pottery very appealing to families with lively demonstrations and interpretation, the story of the loo, historic tile gallery and 19th-c doctor's surgery. The museum's very much hands-on, and even hands-in – they're quite keen to get your fingers round the clay, and children love throwing pots (though it can work out expensive as all 'makes' have to be bought). It's quite possible to spend up to half a day here. Meals, snacks, shop, mostly disabled access; cl Christmas week; (01782) 319232; *£4.95.

Penkhull Despite the development of the Potteries on the slopes below and all around, this hilltop enclave somehow preserves an undisturbed village feel. The Greyhound up here has good value snacks.

Potteries Museum & Art Gallery (Bethesda St, Hanley) With around 5,000 ceramic items on show this is the best place to see the full range of ceramics produced locally over the centuries. There are also displays on the history of the Potteries, and even a Spitfire, produced by local son R J Mitchell. Meals, snacks, shop, disabled access; cl Sun am and 25 Dec–1 Jan; (01782) 232323; free.

Royal Doulton Visitor Centre ⌨ (Nile St, Burslem) Potted history of the famous fine china company, with craft demonstrations, and a well displayed collection of Royal Doulton. Factory tours wkdys (exc factory hols) at 10.30am and 2pm (1.30 Fri), booking recommended; no under-10s on factory tour. Meals, snacks, good shop, disabled access to visitor centre only; cl Christmas–New Year; (01782) 292434; visitor centre £3, visitor centre and tour £6.50.

Spode ⌨ (Church St) The birthplace of fine bone china, this is the oldest manufacturing ceramics factory in the Potteries, and still the most atmospheric. A museum has rare and precious pieces, esp in the beautifully laid-out Blue Room, and you can watch craft demonstrations, and have a go at painting a piece yourself. Meals, snacks, mixed outlet factory shop, disabled access; no tours wknds though shop and visitor centre open daily, cl 25–26 Dec, 1 Jan; tours by appointment; (01782) 744011; visitor centre and museum £2.75, factory tour £5.50, 2½-hour connoisseur's tour £7.50.

Wedgwood Story Visitor Centre ⌨ (Barlaston) Tells the story of this famous pottery, through a range of interactive and audio-visual displays. A self-guided audio tour leads you round various exhibitions on the history of the pottery, and the factory itself. There's a demonstration area where you can throw your own pot and paint your own plate. Restaurant and bistro, good shop, disabled access; cl Christmas–New Year; (01782) 204218; *£7.95.

STOWE-BY-CHARTLEY SJ9927

Amerton Farm Well liked by readers, with a farm shop, trails, garden centre, craft workshops, pottery, wildlife rescue centre (£2), and little steam railway (Sun and bank hols Apr–Oct, diesel summer Sats; £1.40). Meals and snacks (with delicious ice-cream made here), shop, disabled access; cl 25–26 Dec and 1 Jan; (01889) 270294; free. The Plough opposite is handy for lunch.

STRETTON SK2624

Claymills Pumping Station 🖼 Well preserved pumping station with Victorian steam-driven workshop, blacksmith's forge, and Britain's oldest working electricity generator. One of the four beam engines is restored and working, as is one of their five Lancashire boilers. Snacks, shop, disabled access; open Thurs and Sat, phone for dates of their eight steaming wknds; (01283) 509929; donations (£3 on steam days). The Spread Eagle over in the nice village of Rolleston on Dove does good value food all day.

TAMWORTH SK2003

A worthwhile town trail links a number of historic buildings; St Editha's church has windows by William Morris. The Moat House, a former manor house in Lichfield St, has decent bar food.

Drayton Manor Family Theme Park 🖼 (off A4091 S of Tamworth) Popular theme park, with white knuckle rides inc a new million-pound tower drop and Europe's only stand-up roller-coaster, as well as tamer rides for small children, mini golf, circus, a small zoo and nature trail. Meals, snacks, shop, disabled access; cl Mon–Tues in Oct and all Nov–Mar; (01827) 287979; £16.50. The good Twycross zoo is a few miles E, just over the Leics border.

Snowdome (River Drive) Try your luck at skiing, snowboarding, tobogganing, sledging and tubing on real snow at this indoor centre, the first of its kind in Europe. Competent skiers can take to the pistes as they wish, but novices need a lesson first (must book in advance); various regular events. Bar and restaurant overlooking the slope, mountain sports shop, disabled access (and lessons); cl 25 Dec; (08705) 000011; hourly ski or snowboard sessions start from £10 (inc ski/board hire), tobogganing £6 for 30 mins.

Tamworth Castle (off Market St) Glorious mixture of architectural styles, from the original Norman motte and bailey walls through the furnished Elizabethan timbered hall to the fine Jacobean state apartments. Perhaps more museum than historic home, but plenty to see, with a fair amount to please children, inc interactive gallery and high-tech talking heads. Shop, disabled access to ground floor; cl am and Mon; (01827) 709626, £4.35.

TUTBURY SK2129

Pleasant village where cut glass has been manufactured for many years; you can still see glass-cutting and -blowing and buy glass at Georgian Crystal (01283) 814534, and Tutbury Crystal (01283) 813281. An attractive ruined **castle** has good views, a Great Hall dressed as a 1570s State Room, a Tudor garden, and birds of prey; snacks; cl Mon–Tues and Nov–Mar; (01283) 812129; *£3.50. The Norman church has a notable W doorway and elaborate carvings. A **museum** covers local history; cl Sun and Oct–Good Fri; (01283) 815920; free. The Olde Dog & Partridge has popular food.

WALL SK0806

Wall Roman Site (Watling St) An important military base from around AD50; excavations began in the 19th c and revealed one of the most complete Roman bath houses in the country. Good audio tour, and finds from the area. Snacks, shop; cl Nov–Mar; (01543) 480768; £2.50. The nearby Trooper has good bar food.

WESTON UNDER LIZARD SJ8010

Weston Park See *separate family panel on p.544.*

WETTON SK1055

Peak District School of Hang Gliding Adventurous souls can learn to hang glide here; (01335) 310257; 2-day courses start at £130.

WILLOUGHBRIDGE SJ7539

Dorothy Clive Garden (A51) Woodland gardens created by the late Col Harry Clive in memory of his wife; at their best perhaps in spring and early summer, but lovely all year. Rhododendrons, azaleas, old roses, water garden, rock garden and stunning views of the surrounding countryside. Tearoom with good home-made cakes, disabled access; cl mid-Nov to mid-Mar; (01630) 647237; *£3.50. The Falcon in

Woore does good lunches.
WINKHILL SK0551
Blackbrook Zoological Park
Unusual species and aviaries, as well as waterfowl, insects and reptiles, under-5s' playroom and children's farm – all much enjoyed by readers. Tearooms, shop, good disabled access; cl 25–26; (01538) 308293; £5.95. At pretty Waterhouses nearby you can hire bikes from the Old Station Car Park; (01538) 308609; around £8 for three hours. The attractively set Cross there has decent food – or treat yourself at the Old Beams.
Other attractive villages, with decent pubs, include Alstonefield

SK1355, Butterton SK0756, Coven SJ9006, Longdon SK0714, Rolleston on Dove SK2427, Salt SJ9527, Stourton SO8585, Swynnerton SJ8535 and Whitmore SJ8141.
There's good *canal access* from the *pleasant pubs* at Acton Trussell SJ9318, Amington SK2304 (the Gate), Armitage SK0816, Gnosall SJ8220, Hardings Wood SJ8354, High Offley (Anchor, in Peggs Lane) SJ7725, Norbury Junction SJ7922, Filiance Bridge in Penkridge SJ9214, Forton SJ7521, Shebden SJ7626 (great echoes under the aqueduct) and Wheaton Aston SJ8412.
Moseley Old Hall nr Wolverhampton is listed in the Warwickshire chapter.

Where to eat

BUTTERTON SK0756 **Black Lion** *(01538) 304232* Friendly and unspoilt 18th-c stone inn with neat rambling rooms, lots of brassware and china, a good log fire and fine kitchen range, generous popular bar food, well kept real ales, games room, seats on prettily planted terrace, and pleasant Peak District views; bdrms; cl Mon am. £18.50|£5

CHEADLE SK0342 **Queens at Freehay** *Counslow Road (01538) 722383* Thriving atmosphere in well run popular pub with an attractively decorated comfortable lounge bar that opens through an arch into a light and airy dining area, with neatly spaced tables; nicely presented, carefully cooked good food with interesting daily specials, well kept real ales, and quick attentive service; disabled access. £27|£7.95

SALT SJ9627 **Holly Bush** *(01889) 508234* Thatched house dating in part from 14th c, with pretty hanging baskets and a big back lawn, some ancient beams in several cosy spreading areas, a more modern back extension, coal fires, extremely good popular food (the daily specials are the thing to go for), Sun roasts, and well kept ales; children in eating area until 8.30; disabled access. £17.75|£6.50

TEANFORD SK0040 **Ship** *(01538) 722253* Busy little local with generous choice of good home-made food inc weekly changing specials, good value Sun lunch, and friendly staff; cl Mon am; disabled access. £14.42|£5

TUTBURY SK2129 **Olde Dog & Partridge** *High St (01283) 813030* Handsome, well managed Tudor timbered inn, largely given over to big and attractively laid out carvery (popular and with an impressive pudding range), good choice of wines, well kept beers, and friendly helpful service; nice bdrms; brasserie cl Sat am, Sun pm, Mon; disabled access. Brasserie £27, carvery £21|£4.95

We welcome reports from readers

This *Guide* depends on readers' reports. Do help us if you can – in return, we offer a discount on the next edition to people who've helped us with reports for it. Tell us what you think about places already in it, and anything extra you think we should say about them. And send us your ideas for inclusion in the next edition: places to visit, eat at or stay in, attractive drives or walks, maybe even unusual shops you know of. Use the card in the middle, the report forms at the end, or just write – no stamp needed: *The Good Britain Guide*, FREEPOST TN1569, Wadhurst, E Sussex TN5 7BR. Or log on to www.goodguides.com

SUFFOLK

Sleepy villages, attractive medieval market towns, rewarding country houses, and lonely beaches – ideal for getting away from it all

A good place to take it easy, Suffolk is a fine area for eating out (fresh local fish is a speciality), and prices are quite appealing, both for things to do and places to stay. For a pleasant seaside break in quiet surroundings Southwold, Walberswick, Aldeburgh and Orford are all fine choices. Even at the height of summer you can walk for miles along empty beaches and coastal bird land. The attractive drowning village of Dunwich and the Shotley peninsula are two other suggestions for walkers.

Inland, Clare, Lavenham and Long Melford head a crop of delightfully strollable villages with colour-washed timbered buildings, glorious churches, attractively restored windmills – and lots of antiques shops. There's plenty to enjoy in Bury St Edmunds, and Newmarket is fascinating for anyone with even a passing interest in horseracing. Suffolk is excellent for cycling – quiet back roads, lots of villages, gentle gradients, and a very low accident rate; for an especially safe route, try the one at Alton Water near Stutton.

The Suffolk Wildlife Park in Kessingland is our top Suffolk Family Attraction, and at Easton Farm Park children enjoy the chance to get really close to the animals (there's also an owl sanctuary at Stonham Aspal, and a good equestrian centre in Wickham Market). Stately homes that make a special effort to appeal to the whole family are the beautiful Kentwell Hall in Long Melford (rare breeds farm and lively re-creations), and Ickworth House at Horringer (quizzes, trails, a play area and activities, along with fine collections of art and Georgian silver). Other great houses include elegant Euston Hall (excellent art collection), unusual Somerleyton Hall (there's a maze), and the turreted Tudor hall in Long Melford.

The archaeological site at Sutton Hoo is unmissable if you're interested in the Anglo-Saxons (they've recently dramatically improved visitor facilities), and at West Stow you can see a reconstructed Anglo-Saxon village. In Stowmarket the Museum of East Anglian Life has plenty for a pleasant family outing. There's an interesting transport museum in Lowestoft, and an air museum at Flixton. Elsewhere are a good collection of instruments and music-related items in Cotton, and keen birdwatchers will enjoy Minsmere Reserve near Westleton.

This is territory which has hardly changed since it inspired some unforgettable paintings. Constable country (around East Bergholt by the border with Essex) is very pretty; visitors can combine visits to Flatford Mill (*The Haywain*), the great collection of paintings at Christchurch Mansion in Ipswich (free), and Gainsborough's House in Sudbury. There are lovely gardens at Helmingham, Stanton and Coddenham.

Where to stay

BEYTON TL9363 **Manorhouse** *The Green, Beyton, Bury St Edmunds, Suffolk IP30 9AF* (01359) 270960) **£58**; 4 pretty rms, 2 in house, 2 in barn conversion. Overlooking the village green, this charming no smoking 15th-c longhouse has lots of beams and panelling in the sitting/dining room, fresh flowers, antiques and paintings by the friendly owner's mother, super breakfasts, enjoyable dinners (by arrangement), and large garden; cl Christmas; no children

BILDESTON TL9949 **Crown** *High St, Bildeston, Ipswich, Suffolk IP7 7EB* (01449) 740510 **£65**, plus special breaks; 13 individually furnished rms. Lovely timber-framed Tudor inn with a comfortable well furnished beamed lounge (refurbished under the new licensees), open fires, good food in popular restaurant, welcoming courteous service, an attractive two-acre informal garden – and resident ghost; self-catering apartment; disabled access; dogs welcome

BURSTALL TM0944 **Mulberry Hall** *Burstall, Ipswich, Suffolk IP8 3DP* (01473) 652348 **£50***; 2 comfortable rms. Once owned by Cardinal Wolsey, this lovely old farmhouse has a fine garden, an inglenook fireplace in the big beamed sitting room, excellent food (ordered in advance) in pretty dining room, very good breakfasts with home-baked bread and preserves, and helpful friendly owners; tennis and croquet; cl Christmas week

BURY ST EDMUNDS TL8564 **Angel** *3 Angel Hill, Bury St Edmunds, Suffolk IP33 1LT* (01284) 753926 **£113**, plus special breaks; 65 individually decorated rms. Thriving creeper-clad 15th-c country-town hotel with particularly friendly staff, comfortable lounge and relaxed bar, log fires and fresh flowers, and good food in elegant restaurant and downstairs medieval vaulted room (Mr Pickwick enjoyed a roast dinner here); disabled access; dogs welcome in bedrooms

CAMPSEY ASH TM3255 **Old Rectory** *Station Rd, Campsey Ash, Woodbridge, Suffolk IP13 0PU* (01728) 746524 **£65**, plus special breaks; 7 comfortable, pretty rms. Very relaxed and welcoming no smoking Georgian house by church, with charming owner and staff, log fire in comfortable and restful drawing room, quite a few Victorian prints, first class food from a set menu in summer conservatory or two other dining rooms with more log fires, a good honesty bar, a sensational wine list with very modest mark-ups on its finest wines, and sizeable homely gardens; cl Christmas, 3 wks Feb/Mar; dogs welcome in bedrooms

HADLEIGH TM0242 **Edgehall** *2 High St, Hadleigh, Ipswich, Suffolk IP7 5AP* (01473) 822458 **£65***, plus special breaks; 8 pretty rms. Friendly family-run Tudor house with Georgian façade, comfortable carefully restored rooms, personal service, traditional English cooking using home-grown produce in no smoking dining room, and attractive walled garden with croquet; self-catering also; dogs welcome in bedrooms

HARTEST TL8453 **Hatch** *Cross Green, Hartest, Bury St Edmunds, Suffolk IP29 4ED* (01284) 830226 **£60**; 2 comfortable, pretty rms. Charming 15th-c thatched cottage with warmly welcoming owners, a lovely beamed drawing room with antiques, separate dining room for enjoyable breakfasts, afternoon tea, log fires, conservatory, seats out on terrace, and peaceful garden; occasional evening meals, and the nearby Crown does enjoyable food; no smoking; cl Christmas; children over 9 (though babies welcome); limited disabled access; dogs welcome in bedrooms

HIGHAM TM0335 **Old Vicarage** *Higham Rd, Higham, Colchester, Essex CO7 6JY* (01206) 337248 **£58**, plus special breaks; 3 rms, 2 with own bthrm. Charming Tudor house nr quiet village with very friendly owners, pretty sitting room with fresh flowers, log fire and antiques, and enjoyable breakfasts in attractive breakfast room; play room with toys for children, grounds and fine gardens with river views (they have boats), tennis court, trampoline, and heated swimming pool; dogs welcome ☺

HINTLESHAM TM0743 **College Farm** *Hintlesham, Ipswich, Suffolk IP8 3NT* (01473) 652253 **£45***; 4 spacious rms, 2 with own bthrm and one self-contained rm

Suffolk

in newly converted stable. Late 15th-c farmhouse on 600-acre farm with neat garden, guests' lounge with TV and log fire in inglenook fireplace, hearty Aga-cooked breakfasts in separate dining room, and friendly owners; walks around the farm, and riding and golf nearby; no smoking; cl Christmas and New Year; children over 12

HINTLESHAM TM0843 **Hintlesham Hall** *Hintlesham, Ipswich, Suffolk IP8 3NS (01473) 652334 £110**, plus special breaks; 33 lovely rms. Magnificent mansion, mainly Georgian but dating from Elizabethan times, in 175 acres with big walled gardens, 18-hole golf course, outdoor heated swimming pool, croquet, and tennis; restful and comfortable day rooms with books, antiques and open fires, fine modern cooking in several restaurants, a marvellous wine list, and exemplary service; snooker, sauna, steam room, gym, and beauty salon; well behaved children over 10 in evening restaurant; dogs welcome in bedrooms

LAVENHAM TL9149 **Angel** *Market Pl, Lavenham, Sudbury, Suffolk CO10 9QZ* (01787) 247388 **£75***, plus special breaks; 8 comfortable rms. 15th-c inn with original cellar and pargeted ceiling in attractive residents' lounge, several Tudor features such as a rare shuttered shop window front, civilised atmosphere, good food in bar and restaurant (they smoke their own meat and fish), decent wines, several malt whiskies, well kept real ales, thoughtful service, and maybe live classical piano Fri pm; cl 25–26 Dec; disabled access; dogs welcome in bedrooms

LAVENHAM TL9149 **Lavenham Priory** *Water St, Lavenham, Sudbury, Suffolk CO10 9RW* **£78**; 6 big rms with sloping beamed ceilings, antiques, fresh flowers, and pretty bthrms. Dating back to the 13th c, this is a lovely Grade I listed house once owned by Benedictine monks: Elizabethan wall paintings, beams and oak floors, a huge flagstoned Great Hall, inglenook fireplaces, and all lavishly restored; lovely civilised breakfasts, evening meals by arrangement, and helpful, friendly owners; a charming garden with herb beds, kitchen garden and some fine trees; cl 25 Dec–1Jan; children over 10

LAVENHAM TL9149 **Swan** *High St, Lavenham, Sudbury, Suffolk CO10 9QA* (01787) 247477 **£140**; 51 smart rms. Handsome and comfortable Elizabethan hotel that incorporates several fine half-timbered buildings inc an Elizabethan house and the former wool hall; lots of cosy seating areas, interesting historic prints and alcoves with beams, timbers, armchairs and settees, good food in lavishly timbered no smoking restaurant with a minstrels' gallery (actually built only in 1965), afternoon teas, intriguing little bar, and friendly helpful staff; disabled access; dogs welcome

LONG MELFORD TL8645 **Bull** *Hall St, Long Melford, Sudbury, Suffolk CO10 9JG* (01787) 378494 **£120***, plus special breaks; 25 rms, ancient or comfortably modern. An inn since 1580, this fine black and white hotel was originally a medieval manorial hall, and has handsome and interesting carved woodwork and timbering, and an old weavers' gallery overlooking the courtyard; a large log fire, old-fashioned and antique furnishings, enjoyable food, and friendly service; dogs by prior arrangement

NEEDHAM MARKET TM1053 **Pipps Ford** *Norwich Rd, Needham Market, Ipswich, Suffolk IP6 8LJ* (01449) 760208 **£77**, plus winter breaks; 8 pretty rms with antiques and fine old beds, 4 in converted Stables Cottage. Lovely 16th-c farmhouse in quiet garden surrounded by farmland alongside attractive river; log fires in big inglenook fireplaces, good imaginative food using home-baked bread, locally produced meats, honey, eggs, and preserves, and organic local veg and herbs, and conservatory with subtropical plants (some meals can be communal); cl 2 wks over Christmas; children over 5; disabled access

ROUGHAM TL9063 **Ravenwood Hall** *Rougham, Bury St Edmunds, Suffolk IP30 9JA* (01359) 270345 **£96***, plus special breaks; 14 comfortable rms with antiques, some rms in mews. Tranquil Tudor country house in seven acres of carefully tended gardens and woodland; log fire in comfortable lounge, cosy bar, good food in timbered restaurant with big inglenook fireplace (home-preserved fruits and veg, home-smoked meats and fish), a good wine list, and helpful service; croquet and heated swimming pool; they are kind to children and have themed occasions for them and lots of animals; disabled access; dogs welcome away from restaurant ☺

SOUTHWOLD TM5076 **Crown** *High St, Southwold, Suffolk IP18 6DP* (01502) 722275 **£92**; 14 rms, 11 with own bthrm. Outstanding old inn with excellent imaginative food in no smoking restaurant and smart but relaxed main bar, inventive breakfasts, lots of interesting properly kept and fairly priced wines by the glass, well kept real ales, and friendly helpful staff; cl 2 wks Jan

SOUTHWOLD TM5076 **Swan** *Market Pl, Southwold, Suffolk IP18 6EG* (01502) 722186 **£110**, plus winter breaks; 41 clean, well equipped rms with boxes of chocolates and newspapers. 17th-c hotel with comfortable and restful drawing room, upstairs reading room, a convivial bar, interesting enjoyable food in elegant no smoking dining room, fine wines, well kept real ales (the hotel backs on to Adnams Brewery), and polite helpful staff; no dogs in main hotel; children must be over 5 in evening dining room; limited disabled access

STOKE-BY-NAYLAND TL9836 **Angel** *Polstead St, Stoke-by-Nayland, Colchester, Essex CO6 4SA* (01206) 263245 **£69.50**; 6 comfortable rms. Civilised and elegant dining pub in Stour Valley with Tudor beams in cosy bar, stripped brickwork and timbers, fine furniture, huge log fire and woodburner, decent wines, and particularly good, imaginative and reasonably priced bar food; cl 25–26 Dec, 1 Jan; children over 8

WESTLETON TM4469 **Crown** *The Street, Westleton, Saxmundham, Suffolk IP17 3AD* (01728) 648777 plus freephone **£74.50**; 19 quiet, comfortable rms. Smart, extended country inn in lovely setting with good nearby walks; comfortable bar, no smoking dining conservatory, more formal restaurant, a wide range of enjoyable attractively presented food (nice breakfasts, too), log fires, several well kept real ales, decent wines, and a pretty garden with outside heaters and a pets' corner; cl Christmas; disabled access

WOODBRIDGE TM2548 **Seckford Hall** *Seckford Hall Rd, Great Bealings, Woodbridge, Suffolk IP13 6NU* (01394) 385678 **£120**, plus special breaks; 32 comfortable rms. Handsome Tudor mansion in 34 acres of gardens and parkland with carp-filled lake, putting, and leisure club with indoor heated pool, beauty salon, and gym in lovely tithe barn; fine linenfold panelling, huge fireplaces, heavy beams, plush furnishings and antiques in comfortable day rooms, good food (inc lovely teas with home-made cakes), and helpful service; cl 25 Dec; dogs welcome in bedrooms

WORLINGTON TL6973 **Worlington Hall** *Mildenhall Rd, Worlington, Bury St Edmunds, Suffolk IP28 8RX* (01638) 712237 **£75**, plus special breaks; 9 comfortable rms with decanter of sherry and fruit. 16th-c former manor house in five acres with a 9-hole pitch and putt course, comfortable panelled lounge bar with log fire, good food in relaxed candlelit bistro, and friendly staff; dogs welcome

To see and do

Suffolk Family Attraction of the Year

KESSINGLAND TM5286 **Suffolk Wildlife Park** (A12) Attractively set in almost 100 acres of coastal parkland, this very committed place looks after mainly animals from Africa, many of which you won't be able to see anywhere else in the country. Some of the residents are from critically endangered species, so they're justifiably proud of their success in breeding, and of being able to reintroduce some of them to the wild, as they've done with lemurs in Madagascar. Everything children most like to see is here: from lions, cheetah and giraffes, to snakes, flamingoes and meerkats. Current stars of the show are their very rare white rhinos, shown off to great effect in their spectacular new rhino house, with elevated indoor viewing areas. They share it with an intriguing family of hyrax, the closest living relative to the elephant. Younger visitors enjoy following the progress of Sprout, their latest baby giraffe, rapidly growing towards the size of his parents. Other highlights include a unique family of aardvarks, and one of the largest lemur collections in Europe, who live on an appealing series of islands. There are plenty of feeding displays and talks spread throughout the day (the giraffes are usually fed at 12.30, the rhinos at 3, and Reggie the lion at 3.15), so it's easy for animal-minded youngsters to happily spend most of the day here, particularly in fine weather. The play areas have a separate section for under-5s, and there may be extra activities in the summer holidays. A train makes it easier to get round the site. Future plans include new stables for the zebra and ostrich, and the development of an expansive outdoor area for rhinos, giraffes and antelopes to roam freely together as if in their natural habitat. Meals, snacks, shop, disabled access; cl 25–26 Dec; (01502) 740291; prices vary throughout the year, from £5.95 for adults (£4.50 children 3–14) in January and February, to £7.95 (£5.95 children) from June–September.

ALDEBURGH TM4656
Fishing village, once an important port, with quaint little streets running down to the shingle beach where the fishermen still haul in and sell their catch, and a much loved boating pond; touristy, but in a quiet way. Benjamin Britten, founder of the town's annual music festival, and his companion the singer Peter Pears are now buried side by side in the churchyard. The Avocet Gallery (High St) has tin toys and automata to play with; cl Sun pm, and pms and wknds in winter; (01728)

452928. The bustling beach-side Cross Keys does enjoyable bar lunches, as does the Mill (summer cream teas too). There's an RSPB reserve just N at North Warren, and the Landmark Trust offer self-catering accommodation (at a price) in the Martello Tower, the largest and most northerly of the east coast's defences.

Moot Hall Museum 16th-c brick and timber, with outside staircase; scene of the trial in Britten's *Peter Grimes*. It has displays on maritime history and coastal erosion, and finds from the Anglo-Saxon ship burial at Snape. Shop; open pm wknds Apr–May, Sept–Oct, plus daily pm Jun, and all day July–Aug (exc lunchtimes) though best to check; (01728) 452730; £1.

ALDRINGHAM TM4461
Aldringham Craft Market Three extensively stocked galleries of crafts and art. Snacks, disabled access; cl Sun am, 25–28 Dec, 1–2 Jan; (01728) 830397; free. The Parrot & Punchbowl has good wines and decent food.

ASHBOCKING TM1855
James White/Big Tom Company (Helmingham Rd) Spicy tomato- and apple-juice making and tasting, with pick-your-own apples in season. Farm shop, snacks; phone to book a tour wkdys Sept–Mar; (01473) 890202; free. The Moon & Mushroom over at Swilland has good food.

BARDWELL TL9473
Bardwell windmill Carefully restored and now an attractive sight; usually open daily; (01359) 251331; donations. The village green, with ancient church opposite 16th-c pub, is attractive, too.

BAYLHAM TM1152
Baylham House Rare Breeds Farm (Mill Lane) Working farm with rare breeds of cattle, sheep, pigs, goats and poultry; also riverside walk and picnic area; a visitor centre has information about the Roman site underlying the farm. Snacks, shop, disabled access; cl 25–26 Dec; (01473) 830264; £3.50. The Highwayman at Creeting St Mary does good value lunches.

BECCLES TM4290
Beccles and District Museum (Ballygate) Decent local history

museum housed in a 17th-c school. Shop, disabled access, open pm Tues–Sun and bank hols Apr–Oct; (01502) 715722; free.

William Clowes Print Museum (Newgate) Interesting look at the development of printing from 1800 onwards, with wide range of machinery, woodcuts and books. Open wkdys Whit Mon–Sept, or by appointment; (01502) 712884; free.

BLYTHBURGH TM4575
Blythburgh church Magnificent building in a lovely setting above the marshes; there's a little working pottery nearby, and the White Hart is a good family dining pub.

BRAMFIELD TM4073
Bramfield church Interesting building, with an unusual detached round tower. The Queens Head has good food.

BRANDON TL7884
Brandon Country Park Largely pine woods, and pleasant to stroll around; for a car-borne impression of Thetford Heath, the best road is the B1106.

Brandon Heritage Centre (George St) Brandon used to be the centre of the Stone Age flint industry, so among the local history here is a reconstructed flint-knappers' workshop; also displays on the fur industry and Thetford Forest. Shop, disabled access; open Sun pm, Sat, and bank hols Apr–Oct; (01842) 813707; 50p.

BRUISYARD TM3266
Bruisyard Vineyard 🏷 (signed off B1119 Framlingham rd) Picturesque 10-acre vineyard producing decent wine, with herb garden, water gardens, woodland picnic area, Walkman tours and tastings. Snacks, shop, some disabled access; cl Mon (exc bank hols), 24 Dec to mid-Jan; (01728) 638281; free, tours £4.50.

BUNGAY TM3389
Right in the centre of this historic little market town are the ruins of its Norman **castle**, with twin towers and massive flint walls; there's a visitor centre; cl 25–26 Dec; (01986) 896156; £1. Bungay straddles the county border.

BURY ST EDMUNDS TL8464
This busy shopping town has a good deal of character, with quite a few

attractive Georgian and earlier houses, and several antiques shops. The **cathedral** gained that status only in 1913; parts are 15th-c, but the hammer-beamed ceiling is 19th-c, and work on building the tower continues. The nearby Queens Head (Churchgate St) has good food. Another fine old church, **St Mary's** (Crown St), contains the tomb of Mary Tudor. Walking tours usually leave the Tourist Information Centre at 2.30 every day Jun–Sept; (01284) 764667; £2.50. The Linden Tree (Out Northgate St), Old Cannon (Cannon St) and Cupola House (Traverse) are other useful food places. **Art Gallery** (Market Cross) A fine Robert Adam building with changing exhibitions and a decent craft shop. Shop; cl Sun, Mon, and between exhibitions, Christmas; (01284) 762081; £1.

Greene King Brewery Visitor Centre (Westgate St) You can go on an hour's tour of this highly successful brewery, where Greene King has made beer for over 200 years (11am Mon–Fri and 11 and 2pm Sat, plus 7pm wkdys, phone to book; £5, evening £6); lots of samples, which after all the stairs (wear comfortable shoes) you'll probably feel you deserve. A museum follows the history of brewing, and the fortunes of families Greene and King. Shop, disabled access to museum only; cl am wkdys, all Sun; £2.

Manor House Museum 🏛 (Honey Hill) Georgian mansion with a marvellous collection of watches, clocks and other timepieces, as well as period costumes, quite a few hands-on displays, and even a ghost and mouse hunt. Meals, snacks, shop, disabled access; cl Mon, Tues, Good Fri, and 25 Dec; (01284) 757072; £2.50, free for locals.

Moyses Hall Museum 🏛 (Cornhill) As well as a good range of redisplayed Suffolk history (inc gruesome relics of the 'Murder in the Red Barn' – the murderer's account of his trial is bound in his own skin), there's a new gallery on the Suffolk Regiment, and an interactive gallery. Shop, disabled access; cl Good Fri, and 25–26 Dec; (01284) 706183; £2.50, free for locals.

Theatre Royal (Westgate St) Britain's third-oldest working theatre, and very handsome – built in 1819 by William Wilkins, the designer of London's National Gallery. It's owned by the NT, and you can look round or go behind the wings on a guided tour (11.30 and 2.30 Mon and Weds, 11.30 Sat); open Mon, Weds and Sat (exc 1–2) Apr–Sept; (01284) 769505; free entry (guided tour £2.50).

BUTLEY TM3751
Butley Pottery (Butley Barns, Mill Lane) Working pottery, with café, restaurant and disabled access; cl Mon–Weds (exc Jun–Aug when open daily, and Apr–Jun when open Tues–Sun), and all Jan, best to phone for winter opening; (01394) 450785; free. The Oyster pub is good for lunch. The B1084 Woodbridge–Orford is a quietly attractive drive, and the even quieter back road S to Capel St Andrew passes the remains of a medieval abbey gatehouse.

CLARE TL7645
One of the area's very special timber-and-plaster villages, with a huge and beautiful **church**, the sketchy ruins of a **castle** on an Iron Age earthwork above the River Stour, some remains of a 13th-c Augustinian priory, and little modern intrusion; nature trails around the castle. There's a three-storey antiques warehouse (Maltings Lane), and the Bell and Swan (which does not allow children) have decent food. The A1092 to Long Melford, with a back road on to Lavenham, links this trio of lovely villages, and passes Cavendish, also pretty, with an attractive medieval church, and good value food at the 16th-c Bull. The back roads N of here are also pleasant drives, with plenty of colour-washed old houses.

Clare Ancient House Museum (High St) Local history in an attractive listed 15th-c building. Shop; open pm Thurs–Fri and all day Sun and bank hols May–Sept, and over Easter; (01787) 277662; £1.

CODDENHAM TM1252
Shrubland Hall Gardens 🏛
Stunning Victorian gardens inc formal terrace and a wild woodland garden; there's a magnificent conservatory (not open) and enchanting follies inc a Swiss chalet. Limited disabled access; open

pm Sun and bank hol Mon Apr–Sept, best to check; (01473) 830221; £3.

COTTON TM0667
Mechanical Music Museum & Bygones 🔖 Large collection of instruments and musical items taking in not just the expected organs, street pianos, polyphons and gramophones, but dolls, fruit bowls and even a musical chair. Their pride and joy is the Wurlitzer theatre pipe organ in the reconstructed cinema. Teas, shop, disabled access; open Sun pm Jun–Sept, plus first Sun in Oct (a fair organ enthusiasts' day); (01449) 613876; *£4. The Trowel & Hammer is good for lunch.

COVEHITHE TM5281
Covehithe church Attractive building; just down the lane this stretch of coast is good for nature walks, especially out of season. The Five Bells at South Cove has good value food.

DEBENHAM TM1763
This attractive village has a fine partly Saxon **church**; the pottery in Low Rd specialises in unusual teapots.

DENNINGTON TM2866
Dennington church Interesting and attractive church – with excellent sermons – in pleasant surroundings. The Queens Head next door is good.

DUNWICH TM4770
Once quite a sizeable town, but it's slipping slowly under the sea – most is now submerged. Some say that on quiet nights, when there's a swell running after a storm, they can hear the bells of a submerged church tolling. **Dunwich Museum** (St James St) has interesting exhibitions on the village's erosion; shop, disabled access; cl Nov–Feb; (01728) 648796; free. There are some fragmentary ruins of a friary up on the cliffs. Excellent coastal walks along the cliffs, beaches and heathland of Dunwich Heath, which has a NT tearoom.

EAST BERGHOLT TM0733
Bridge Cottage, Flatford 17th-c cottage near the mill immortalised by Constable, with a good interpretative centre for his paintings. Good teas, shop, disabled access; cl Mon and Tues (exc May–Sept), wkdys Jan–Feb, and Christmas–New Year, limited opening times in winter so best to phone;

(01206) 298260; free; NT. Guided walks through areas that inspired his work leave here several times a day Apr–Sept, but fill up quickly (£2). You can hire rowing boats for trips along the River Stour. The mill itself and its famous partner **Willy Lott's Cottage** are both owned by the NT and leased by them to the Field Studies Council. You can see inside only by taking part in one of their many courses, such as art and photography, or popular wildlife watching wknds; (01206) 298283. The church with its uncompleted tower has a unique 16th-c timber-framed bell cage, and the Kings Head (with a haywain out in front) has good value food. From the village the walk along the water-meadows by the Stour is East Anglia's most famous walk – picturesque views immortalised by Constable, and well worth while. This ties in with the more elevated Essex Way to make a very worthwhile circular walk, from Dedham to Lawford church, then via Manningtree Station (extraordinarily good station buffet) to join the Stour itself.

EASTON TM2758
Easton Farm Park In 35 acres of attractive countryside, there are plenty of opportunities for children to get close to the animals at this delightful working farm, and as well as poultry, Suffolk punch horses, pigs and goats, there are usually some young animals (you can watch chicks hatching and help collect eggs). Daily pony rides (no extra charge) and animal handling sessions. There are indoor and outdoor play areas, as well as token-operated battery-powered tractors, and a full-size one to scramble over. Other attractions include a working blacksmith, face-painting, environmental trail and vintage farm machinery. Dogs on leads are welcome. Snacks, picnic areas, shop; cl Oct to mid-Mar exc Feb and Oct half-terms; (01728) 746475; £5. The quaint White Horse has decent food, and the Wickham Market–Debenham road through here via Brandeston and Cretingham has some attractive views.

EUSTON TL8978
Euston Hall (A1088) Elegant house built by Charles II's Secretary of State

Lord Arlington. The highlight is probably the excellent art collection, with several portraits of the king, his family and court, inc works by Lely and Van Dyck. The grounds were laid out by John Evelyn, William Kent and Capability Brown, so reflect centuries of development, with stately terraced lawns, fine trees, a lake, lovely rose garden and classical temple. Teas in former kitchen, shop, disabled access to grounds and tearoom; open Thurs pm Jun–Sept, 29 Jun, and 7 Sept; (01842) 766366; *£4.

EYE TM1473

Eye church Beautiful stonework and rood screen.

FELIXSTOWE TM2832

Quite a busy port, with a ferry (passengers, not cars) across to Harwich, and further afield to Zeebrugge. Thanks to its beaches and relatively dry climate it's developed into a popular low-price family resort. The White Horse (Church Rd) has inexpensive food and a play area. Along the coast N, past a Martello Tower, golf course and quiet sand dunes, is the gently attractive and altogether quieter little settlement of Felixstowe Ferry, with another foot-ferry across the estuary of the River Deben (going to Bawdsey), and good value food inc local seafood in the Ferry Boat and Victoria, both very family-friendly.

Landguard Fort 🏛 18th-c, and well worth a look; open daily Apr–Nov; (01394) 277767; *£2.50. Displays on local history in adjacent museum; usually open pm Sun and bank hol Mon Apr–end Oct, plus pm Weds Jun–Sept; £1.

FLIXTON TM3288

Norfolk & Suffolk Aviation Museum (Homersfield Rd) Aircraft and related items from the Wright Brothers to the present day, with aeroplanes displayed outside and in the blister hangar. Snacks, shop, disabled access; cl Fri and Sat (plus Thurs and Mon Nov–Mar), and all mid-Dec to mid-Jan; (01986) 896644; donations. The Buck nearby has good food (inc a Sun carvery).

FRAMLINGHAM TM2863

The sloping market square is attractive, and the **church** has an excellent hammer-beam roof. The Station Hotel has interesting food, and the B1116 to Fressingfield is quite a pleasant drive.

Framlingham Castle (B1116) 12th c, where Mary I heard that she had become queen. Unusually the entire curtain wall has survived (you can walk all the way along it), and there are 13 towers, some 17th-c almshouses, and an array of Tudor chimneys. Good views, interesting local history museum. Snacks, shop, disabled access to ground floor only; cl 24–26 Dec, and 1 Jan; (01728) 724189; £3.90; EH.

GREAT LIVERMERE TL8871

There's a charming shortish walk from the church here, past the Ampton Water lake, to Ampton church. A longer path leads through farmland from Great Livermere to Ixworth.

HADLEIGH TM0242

Old market town with some striking buildings (inc the church, famously painted by Gainsborough); there's a nearby woodland RSPB reserve. The Ram has bargain food.

HARTEST TL8352

The village green is attractive; at the end by the church, the Crown is pleasant for lunch.

Giffords Hall 🏛 (Shimpling, just SE) 33 acres with vineyard and winery, wildflower meadows, rare breeds of sheep, cattle, pigs, goats, wallabies, and domestic fowl, and a rose garden. It's perhaps best known among gardeners for its sweet peas, and they have a rose and sweet pea festival the last wknd in Jun. Meals, snacks, shop, disabled access; cl Oct–Easter; (01284) 830464; *£3.50. They do B&B.

HELMINGHAM TM1857

Helmingham Hall Gardens (B1077) Beautiful gardens pretty much as they were in Tudor times. The grand battlemented house they stand around (not open) is ringed by a moat, over which the drawbridge is still raised each night. Extensive deer park with hundreds of red and fallow deer, as well as Highland cattle and Soay sheep, and magnificent old oak trees. Constable painted several views of the woodlands. Teas, shop (inc Helmingham produce), disabled access; open Sun pm 4 May–14 Sept; (01473) 890363; £3.75. The welcoming Dobermann at Framsden has good food.

HERRINGFLEET TM4797
Herringfleet windmill An attractive sight above the river (open occasionally when it's working; (01473) 583352).

HORHAM TM2172
St Mary's churchyard The churchyard here has for generations been conserved as natural grassland around its older graves, cut only after the flowers have seeded; so from spring onwards it's a mass of wild flowers, with plenty of butterflies (and beehives). The White Hart in the quiet village of Stradbroke has decent simple food.

HORRINGER TL8261
A serenely attractive village with well spaced colour-washed buildings, and a good dining pub (the Beehive).
Ickworth House, Park and Gardens Very untypical stately home, an oval rotunda 30 metres (98 ft) high, with two curved corridors filled with a fascinating art collection inc pictures by Gainsborough, and an exceptional array of Georgian silver. They try hard to make sure children enjoy their visit, with quizzes, trails, handling boxes and a free touch tour, introduced primarily for partially sighted visitors. Outside are formal Italianate gardens, and 1,800 acres of attractive parkland with woodland walks and cycle routes. There's a decent-sized play area, special events and activities for children, and themed events in the run-up to Christmas. Meals, snacks, shop, plant centre, good disabled access; house cl am, also Weds/Thurs and 3 Nov–21 Mar; garden cl 22 Dec–1 Jan, park open all year; (01284) 735270; £6.10 house, park and garden; £2.80 park and gardens only; NT.

IPSWICH TM1644
After King John granted a charter in the 13th c, this flourished as a port sending cloth to the continent; the port is still quite active. The busy town has quite a few things to look at on day visits, and a pedestrianised centre (traffic schemes make getting in and out by car rather slow). Cardinal Wolsey set up a college here, but all that remains is the 16th-c gatehouse in College St. The Ancient House in the Butter Market (now a kitchenware shop) has some 15th-c carvings, exceptionally neat pargeting (decoratively patterned external plasterwork) and even a priest's hiding hole – if it's not too busy, ask the staff to show you. Dotted about the town are several attractive **medieval churches**, nicely floodlit at night. The finest is the 15th-c St Margaret's (Soane St); St Mary at the Elms (Elm Rd) has the town's oldest cottages behind it. The Golden Lion (Cornhill), County (opposite County Hall) and Old Rep (Tower St) have decent food.
Christchurch Mansion (Soane St) Perhaps the town's highlight; the original 16th-c house was altered in the following century after a fire, but since then it's escaped any further redevelopment. The rooms are furnished in period style, with a Victorian wing inc servants' quarters, and the Suffolk Artists' Gallery has the best collection of works by Constable and Gainsborough outside London. Snacks, shop, disabled access to ground floor only; cl am Sun, Mon (exc most bank hols), 24–26 Dec, 1 Jan, Good Fri, but best to check; (01473) 433554; free. The **Wolsey Art Gallery** next door has frequently changing exhibitions, and the surrounding park has play areas and a bird reserve.
Ipswich Museum (High St) The natural history section has been painstakingly restored to how it was in its Victorian heyday, and includes the first gorillas brought to Europe in the mid-19th c. Other parts have quite an emphasis on Roman Suffolk. Snacks, shop, disabled access to ground floor only; cl Mon, 25 Dec, 1 Jan; (01473) 433550; free.
Tolly Cobbold Brewery (Cliff Rd) Striking waterside Victorian brewery, with tours. Some particularly interesting old equipment, inc a Victorian steam engine, and tastings in the Brewery Tap (which functions as a separate pub, with decent food all day). Shop; tours Fri and Mon July–Aug 2.30pm, best to check for other times; (01473) 261112; £4.50 (inc drink).
Transport Museum (Lupin Rd) In an old trolley-bus depot, a developing collection of around 100 ancient commercial and engineering vehicles built or used in the area, from fire engines to buses and milk floats. Snacks, shop, disabled access; open Sun and

bank hols Apr–end Nov, and pm wkdys during school hols; (01473) 715666; £3.

KEDINGTON TL7046
Kedington church One of Suffolk's many attractive churches, this is unusual for its Saxon crucifix.

KERSEY TM0044
A very pretty one-street village, full of timbering and attractive and colourful plasterwork. It runs from a fine 14th-c church down to a ford with ducks, and up the other side; several craft and antiques shops.

KESSINGLAND TM5286
Suffolk Wildlife Park *See separate family panel on p.557.*

KNETTISHALL HEATH TL9480
This Country Park has some pleasant strolls – and if you're overflowing with energy (and several days' supplies), you may even be tempted northwards on the Peddars Way, waymarked from here all the way to Norfolk's N coast. For more sedentary souls, the Mill (B1111, over towards Market Weston) has good food.

LAKENHEATH TL7182
Lakenheath church One of Suffolk's elegant and charming churches, though now a bit hidden away among the sprawl edging the nearby huge air base.

LAVENHAM TL9149
One of the finest surviving examples of a small medieval town, this lovely little place has delightfully rickety-looking 14th- and 15th-c timbered buildings wherever you look; many now house tearooms or antiques shops. The old wool hall has been incorporated into the ancient timbered Swan Hotel, well worth a look despite its prices. The Angel opposite the Guildhall is good for lunch. Self-guided audio tours of the town are available from the pharmacy, 98 High St (01787) 247284; £3. The A1141 through Monks Eleigh and then the B1115 to Hitcham, through Chelsworth (where the prettily set Peacock has enjoyable food), is a pretty drive.
Guildhall (Market Pl) Picturesque 16th-c timbered building, at various stages in its life a town hall, prison, workhouse and wool store; its beamed interior has interesting local history displays. Disabled access to tearoom (cl Mon) and shop; cl Dec–Feb, plus

Mon/Tues Mar–May and Oct–Nov; (01787) 247646; £3; NT.
Little Hall (Market Pl) Delightful 14th-c house, attractively presented, showcasing the Gayer-Anderson collection of books, pictures and antiques, with a pleasant enclosed garden. Open pm Weds, Thurs, wknds and bank hols Easter–Oct; (01787) 247179; £1.50. There's a good wildlife art gallery nearby.

LAXFIELD TM2972
Laxfield church Well worth a visit, in tucked-away quiet surroundings; nearby is a charmingly preserved very old-fashioned pub, and a small museum (open pm wknds and bank hols mid-May to Sept; (01986) 798460; free).

LEISTON TM4462
Long Shop Steam Museum 🏛
(Main St) Big industrial museum in preserved buildings of Garrett Engineering Co, with steam engines, steam rollers, traction engines, and memorabilia from the nearby World War II air base. Snacks and picnic garden, shop, disabled access; cl Nov–Mar; (01728) 832189; *£3.50. The Engineers Arms opposite has so much memorabilia it seems almost an extension. The sizeable shopping town has the fragmentary remains of a 14th-c abbey off the B1122 just N.

LETHERINGHAM TM2858
Letheringham watermill Pretty, and surrounded by nice gardens; occasional open days in summer.

LEVINGTON TM2338
A pleasant spot, with ancient almshouses, a marina below, and the Ship is a good pub (no children) with estuary views.

LINDSEY TL9744
St James's chapel A charming little thatched flint and stone chapel, built during the 13th c but inc some earlier work too.

LITTLE BLAKENHAM TM1048
Blakenham Woodland Garden Woodland garden richly planted with camellias, rhododendrons, magnolias and the like; lovely in May when the bluebells are out. Lots of rare trees and shrubs. Open pm Sun–Fri Mar–Jun; (01473) 833249; £1. The 16th-c Duke of Marlborough at Somersham now does good food.

LONG MELFORD TL8645

A very nice old place to stroll around: the fine green and exceptionally long main Hall St are lined with buildings from various eras, many with lovely timbering. Lots are now antiques shops (not cheap, but interesting). The **church** of Holy Trinity is glorious, with ornate carvings and dozens of spectacular windows; very attractive when floodlit at night. The Bull Hotel, one of the finer old buildings here, does good light lunches; the Crown, Cock & Bell and George & Dragon are also useful for food.

Kentwell Hall ⊞ Beautiful Tudor mansion with genuinely friendly lived-in feel, best during their enthusiastic re-creations of Elizabethan and 1940s life (several wknds Apr–Sept), when everything is done as closely as possible to the way it would have been done then – even the speech. It's surrounded by a broad carp-filled moat, and there's a rare breeds farm in the grounds. Meals, snacks and picnic area, shop, disabled access; house cl am, plus late Sept–mid-July (exc Sun Apr–Oct and Easter week); (01787) 310207; most re-creations cost around £9, though the Great Annual one is £12. On non-event days entry is £6.50, or £4.50 garden and farm only.

Melford Hall Turreted Tudor house mostly unchanged externally since Elizabeth I with hundreds of servants and courtiers stayed here in 1578; it also still has the original panelled banqueting hall. Fine collection of Chinese porcelain and Beatrix Potter memorabilia; the gardens have a Tudor banqueting house. Some disabled access; cl am, also Mon/Tues exc bank hols, wkdys Mar and Oct, and all Nov–Feb; (01787) 880286; £4.50; NT.

LOWESTOFT TM5492

Britain's most easterly town, this is the area's main fishing port, so the harbour always has lots to see. It's developed as a resort thanks to its beaches (South Beach has the best bathing water) and proximity to the Broads. Cobbled streets of old buildings survive in the part known as The Scores, and the early medieval **parish church** is imposing and attractive. The last surviving steam drifter, the *Lydia Eva*, in dry dock here,

was being restored when we went to press but should be open in 2003. The seaview Jolly Sailors near the quaint Pakefield church is good value for lunch, and has an all-day Sun carvery. Plans are now going ahead for the world's tallest wind turbine, just N at Ness Point.

East Anglia Transport Museum (Carlton Colville; B1384 SW of Lowestoft) Lots of lovingly restored vehicles around three acres of woodland. The best part is the reconstructed 1930s street scene used as a setting for working trams, trains and trolley-buses. Snacks, shop, some disabled access; open Easter, then Suns May–Sept, plus Sat pms Jun–Sept, and wkdy pms in summer hols and half-terms; (01502) 518459; £4.50. The nearby Crown (A146) does good cheap lunches.

Maritime Museum ⊞ (Whapload Rd) Housed under the lighthouse on Whapload Rd; shop, disabled access; cl Oct–Easter; (01502) 561963; 75p. There's a small **Royal Naval Museum** nearby; usually cl 12–2pm, Tues, Sat, and all mid-Oct to Easter; (01502) 564344; free.

Mayhem Adventure Play (East Point Pavilion, Royal Plain) Lively children's play area themed as an underwater world. Meals, snacks, shop, disabled access; cl 25–26 Dec and 1 Jan; adults free, children from £2.50 an hour (£2.95 in school hols); (01502) 533600. It shares the rather grand old pavilion with the Tourist Information Office and good local history displays.

Pleasurewood Hills Theme Park ⊞ (off A12) Lots of rides and family attractions to occupy a good bit of the day, inc a spinning roller-coaster; trains and chairlifts speed up travel around the grounds. Meals, snacks, shop, disabled access; cl mid-Sept to mid-May (exc wknds, bank hols and school hols Easter–Oct); (01502) 508200; £12.99 (voucher not valid with any other offer, for special events or at Christmas).

MICKFIELD TM1461

Mickfield Water Garden Centre Two acres of ornamental water gardens and working nursery, with displays of freshwater fish, secret garden and lily pond. Garden centre, disabled access; cl 25 Dec; (01449) 711336; free.

NAYLAND TL9734

Well rewards a stroll – its fine **church** has an altar painting by Constable; the old White Hart is now a smart restaurant.

NEEDHAM MARKET TM0854

Needham Market church The marvellous hammer-beam roof has been described as 'a whole church seemingly in the air'.

NEWMARKET TL6463

Newmarket has been the centre of horseracing since 1605, when James I used to slope off here, and in the early morning people driving through are quite likely to have to give way to a string of racehorses. The Tourist Information Centre (occasional exhibitions, when you can go upstairs) is housed in the remains of Charles II's 17th-c palace; cl Sat pm and Sun; (01638) 667200; free. The Rutland Arms (High St) and Bedford Lodge Hotel (Bury Rd) are useful for lunch.

National Horseracing Museum 🏛 (High St) The stories and scandals of the sport's development through the centuries, with trophies, videos of classic races, a display on the history of betting, and racing relics from saddles to skeletons. You don't have to be interested in racing to get something out of it. Meals, snacks, shop, disabled access; cl Mon (exc bank hols and July–Aug), and Nov–Easter; (01638) 667333; £4.50. They also organise informative tours of the local breeding and racing scene, with a look at horses at work on the gallops, and visits to a training yard, stud and to the handsome Georgian Jockey Club itself; booking essential on (01638) 560622; prices start at around £16.50.

National Stud (A1304 W) Tours of this mecca of horse breeding by arrangement; (01638) 663464. Snacks, shop, disabled access; guided tours are at 11.15am and 2.30pm Mon–Sat (2.30 pm only Sun), cl Oct–Feb (exc race days); £5. The Kings Head at Dullingham is a good nearby lunch spot.

ORFORD TM4249

Dunwich Underwater Exhibition 🏛 (Front St) The process of coastal erosion is well illustrated; Meals, snacks, shop; cl 25–26 Dec; 50p.

Havergate Island Bird-watchers can arrange whole-day trips to this marshy RSPB reserve by writing to the warden, Mr Partridge, at 30 Mundays Lane, Orford, Woodbridge IP12 2LX (with SAE); permits usually available every Thurs and 1st and 3rd Sats of month Apr–Aug, then in winter just the first Sat of the month; around £5 inc boat trip from Orford quay. A sea wall walk S from the quay lets you look across to the island.

Orford Castle When Henry II commissioned this castle it was right on the shore, but since then the river has silted so much that it's now slightly inland. It has an amazing 18-sided keep rising to 27 metres (90 ft), supported by three extra towers. Good views from the top (as usual, at the end of a spiral staircase). Shop; cl Mon–Tues Nov–Mar, 24–26 Dec, 1 Jan; (01394) 450472; £3.20; EH. The **church** has the ruined chancel arches of a Norman predecessor in the graveyard. There's a long lane down to the shore with its quay and old smugglers' inn, the good Jolly Sailor. The road through Iken Heath to Snape is a pleasant drive through quiet pinewoods.

Orford Ness After years of belonging to the Ministry of Defence (who barred access to anyone who wasn't in uniform), this magnificently desolate spit just opposite the quay is now owned by the NT and open to the public, though it's more for serious wildlife fans than day trippers. Ferries leave the quay roughly every 15 mins 10am–2pm Tues–Sat Easter–end Sept and Sat only in Oct – phone to check; (01394) 450057; £5.60. There are also longer boat trips from the quay.

PAKENHAM TL9369

Pakenham watermill 🏛 (Mill Rd) 18th-c watermill (with a pretty pond) restored to working order by preservation society; they hope to restore the Tudor mill house too. There's a picnic area and a pleasant riverside walk. Snacks, shop (selling their own flour); open pm Weds, wknds and bank hols (and often am Thurs) Easter–Sept; (01359) 270570; £2.

Pakenham Windmill (Thurston Rd) Carefully restored and now an attractive sight; it may open for visits Sun Apr–Sept; donations.

PIN MILL TM2037
A nice spot below the wooded slopes by the River Orwell, with Thames barges on tidal moorings, and much favoured by artists; the Butt & Oyster here is attractively placed for a bite to eat.

RIVER DEBEN TM3041
Broad winding river close to the coast, with good walks best reached from side roads off B1083 S of Shottisham, where the thatched Sorrel Horse is a useful stop. On the opposite bank, the Maybush at Waldringfield has enjoyable food and lots of tables out by the water; and there may be river cruises from the quay.

SAXMUNDHAM TM3863
This pleasant bypassed village has yet another fine **church**. Nearby Yoxford has good food at the Griffin.

SHOTLEY GATE TM2434
At the meeting of the Stour and Orwell estuaries, this is at the hub of a rewarding walk with good views across to Harwich and its shipping. Start inland at Shotley and cross the fields either N to the Orwell or S to the Stour, then follow the waterside. The Bristol Arms, with great estuary views, has good fresh fish (and various things for sale), and up the hill, the colossal mast of HMS *Ganges* (now a police training centre) is a dizzying sight.

SIZEWELL BEACH TL4761
Generally virtually deserted out of season, and pleasurable walking ground despite the rather graceless Sizewell nuclear power plant in the distance. Agate and other semi-precious stones are common among the pebbles, even sometimes amber after stormy E winds, and heathland, an old railway track walk and The Meare (Thorpeness's lake) justify detours inland.

SNAPE MALTINGS TM3957
The converted and expanded 19th-c **maltings** are home of the Aldeburgh Music Festival begun by Benjamin Britten, with other concerts throughout the year. The centre is pleasant to wander around, with unusual shops and galleries. The Plough & Sail just outside is good for lunch; up in the village, the Crown (with a bar re-created in Britten's *Peter Grimes*) and Golden Key are both good, too.

SOMERLEYTON TM4997
Somerleyton Hall 🏛 (B1074) This interesting Jacobean house was rebuilt in the Anglo-Italian style in the 1840s, and today is still very much lived-in, with period furnishings and paintings. The lovely gardens have a maze, and there is occasional live music. Snacks, shop, disabled access; open pm Sun, Thurs and bank hols Easter–Oct, plus pm Tues and Weds July–Aug and perhaps other times, best to check; (01502) 730224; £5.50. The Plough at Blundeston, home of Barkis ('is willing') in *David Copperfield*, is useful for lunch. A couple of miles N of here, wooded **Fritton Lake** attracts numerous wildfowl, particularly in autumn and winter.

SOUTH ELMHAM TM3385
St Peter's Brewery 🏛 Medieval St Peter's Hall, in a pretty spot by a moat with black swans, has in its outhouses this more modern small brewery, whose excellent bitters, porters and fruit beers are made with water from their own source. Good tours take in the whole brewing process, as well as parts of the hall. Good meals and snacks, shop, some disabled access; open Fri–Sun and bank hols, tours every hour 12–4pm; (01986) 782322; free entry to site, £3.50 tour.

SOUTHWOLD TM5076
Once an important fishing port, now a quite enchanting and civilised little resort, with its recently restored pier joining the distinctive lighthouse as a second landmark. The pier has an exhibition on the history of piers and seaside holidays, with old amusement machines; £1. They hope to introduce lighthouse tours, phone the Tourist Information Centre for information; (01502) 724729). The Denes is the best beach. Southwold Jack in the nave of the interesting **church** is worth a look. Across the golf course or along the breezy sea wall you come to the harbour, a tidal inlet, with its cheerful mix of beached fishing boats, multitudes of sailing boats, and tall black fishing shacks; the Harbour Inn here is full of character. There's no end of other good pubs and inns supplied by the local Adnams brewery (their wholesale wine shop has interesting stock). For food,

the Crown is outstanding, and the smart Swan Hotel is good; the Kings Head is popular with families, and the Lord Nelson has the most atmosphere. The rowing-boat ferry (cl end Oct–Easter) goes over to **Walberswick** on the other side of the water – an attractively decorous seaside village, popular with artists ever since Wilson Steer's days there in the 1890s. The Bell here is a striking old inn, and the 15th-c church, parts now destroyed and other bits looking shaky, is attractive. The circular walk from Southwold, along the sea wall and over the river by ferry to Walberswick, returning along the course of the former railway line over the footbridge into Southwold, makes a very pleasant stroll and allows exploration of both. The drive round by car between Southwold and Walberswick is several miles.

Amber shop and museum (Market Pl) The longest-standing retailer of amber in Britain, with an impressive collection of related ornaments from 19th-c chinese scent bottles to fossilised insects. Shop, disabled access; cl 25–26 Dec; (01502) 723394; free.

River Blyth Broad river winding close to the coast, with delightful waterside paths, and marshy and heathy expanses to explore around its mouth.

Southwold Museum (Bartholomew Green) Decent town collections, in a 17th-c Dutch-gabled cottage; shop, disabled access (but no facilities); usually open pms Easter–Oct, plus ams in Aug; free.

STANTON TL9671

Wyken Hall Gardens 🏚 Formal herb, knot and woodland gardens, walled old-fashioned rose garden, copper beech maze, pond, and woodland walk to 7-acre vineyard. A very nice unspoilt estate, just right for exploring. Good restaurant and snacks in medieval barn (open all year), unusual country shop, disabled access; cl am, also cl Sat and all Oct–Mar; (01359) 250287; £2.50.

STONHAM ASPAL TM1459

Suffolk Owl Sanctuary 🏚 (Stonham Barns, A1120) Flying displays Apr–Oct, and every species of British owl plus hawks, falcons, vultures and eagle; also

woodland trails with red squirrel enclosure, pond-dipping and songbird viewing hide. Shop, disabled access; cl around ten days at Christmas; (01449) 711425; £4.75. Around 30 small businesses share the site, inc various craft workshops, crazy golf and garden centre. You can get something to eat here, or the Ten Bells does bargain home-made food.

STOUR ESTUARY WALKS TM1534

Stutton gives access to a fine stretch of the broad Stour estuary just S, with good bird-spotting opportunities. The Kings Head does bargain lunches.

STOWMARKET TM0458

Museum of East Anglian Life (Iliffe Way, opposite Asda) Excellent 70-acre open-air museum. Children look at the reconstructed buildings with a genuine sense of astonishment, and even the 1950s domestic room settings seem prehistoric to fresher eyes. Most of the buildings have been removed from their original settings and rebuilt here; the oldest is a splendid 13th-c timber barn, now housing a collection of horse-drawn vehicles. Among the rest are an old schoolroom, a smithy, chapel, windpump, and a very pretty watermill. They're quite spread out, so a fair bit of walking is involved. Also wandering around are various traditional farm animals, and on some Suns they often have demonstrations of local crafts and skills like wood-turning and basket-making; their occasional event days with extra children's activities are usually around the spring and summer bank hols. There's a decent rustic-style adventure play area, and it's great for a picnic; dogs are welcome on a lead. They have a big fireworks display near Guy Fawkes night (1 Nov this year). Snacks, shop, disabled access; cl end Oct–Mar; (01449) 612229; £5.

STUTTON TM1534

Alton Water Reservoir Attractive man-made lake circumscribed by a cycle track which takes in some interesting features on the way, inc the Tattingstone Wonder, a folly built for a local squire with pious pretensions who wanted to look across the valley and see a church – the ecclesiastic façade hides a row of almshouses (not open to public); cycle hire is £5.80 for 3 hours; (01473) 328873. Also bird reserve (several hides), fishing (permits available from visitor centre), and watersports; (01473) 328408. Café, some disabled access (though gravel paths might prove tricky for wheelchairs); reservoir open all year, facilities cl wkdys Nov–Easter; (01473) 328268; a day's parking, £2. In the village itself, the Kings Head has good value food.

SUDBURY TL8741

Gainsborough's House 🔢 (Gainsborough St) The painter was born here in 1727, and the house has an excellent collection of his work. Plenty of period furniture and china too, and contemporary arts and crafts. Shop, disabled access to ground floor only; cl Sun am, Mon (exc pm bank hols), over Christmas and New Year, Good Fri; (01787) 372958; £3. This market town is pleasant, with useful market stalls on Thurs and Sat; the nearby Waggon & Horses (Acton Sq) has enjoyable fresh food.

SUTTON HOO TM2849

One of the most famous archaeological sites in the country, where in 1939 the discovery of an Anglo-Saxon ship burial and burial ground of an early 7th-c ruler made historians completely reinterpret the Dark Ages. £5 million has recently been spent on improving access to the site and new visitor facilities. A modern-looking reinterpretation of an Anglo-Saxon Hall houses a permanent exhibition on the site's history, inc a full-size reconstruction of part of the ship, complete with replica treasures. Another houses changing exhibitions (which should run from Mar–Oct), with finds from the site on loan from the British Museum; also new restaurant, visitor centre and shop. Guided tours at wknds for an extra charge (they advise you to book). Excellent disabled access; facilities cl Nov–21 Mar exc wknds, also cl wkdys Mar–May and Oct exc half-terms; (01394) 389700; *£4. The site is open every day throughout the year; £2.50 car parking when facilities are closed. A turn off the B1083 S takes you to the Ramsholt Arms at Ramsholt for lunch among waterside pinewoods, with quiet walks along the Deben estuary.

TANGHAM NATURE TRAIL
TM3548

A short walk among the plantations off the B1084 towards Woodbridge specially designed for disabled people; there are also longer walks through the pinewoods here, where red squirrels often show themselves.

THORPENESS TM4759

At the S end of Sizewell beach, this curious place was built as a holiday village in a deliberately fanciful olde-worlde style, with quite a few attractive mock-Tudor houses (one even masking a water-tower), a sizeable picturesque lake, and a windmill (brought over from Aldringham). The Dolphin has enjoyable food.

North Warren Miles of RSPB nature reserves stretching along the coast between Thorpeness and Aldeburgh; nature trails, many different birds (esp good for wildfowl in winter), butterflies and dragonflies; (01728) 688481; free.

WENHASTON TM4275

Wenhaston church Attractive building, with a 15th-c wall painting (in excellent condition) full of lovely devils; it's a nice peaceful village, too.

WEST STOW TL7971

West Stow Country Park 🔢 Attractive, with 125 acres of heath and woodlands bordered by the River Lark. There's a nature trail, bird hides and bird-feeding, but the most interesting feature is the reconstructed **Anglo-Saxon Village**, its buildings erected using the same methods and tools as in the 5th c. A visitor centre houses original finds from the Anglo-Saxon site; occasional costumed days, and special events. Snacks, shop, disabled access; cl 25–26 Dec; (01284) 728718; park free, village £5. The Red Lion at Icklingham has good food.

WESTLETON TM4369

A pleasant village with an attractive green; the smart Crown has good food. **Minsmere Reserve** Big RSPB reserve with over 200 species of bird recorded every year among the heath, woods, marshes and lagoons – good observation hides, and enjoyable walks at any time of year. The heathlands around here are also home to red deer, and are spectacularly carpeted with heather in summer. Lunches, snacks, well stocked shop, disabled access (can be difficult in places (readers recommend getting in touch with the warden for details); cl Tues, and 25–26 Dec; (01728) 648281; £5 for non-RSPB members. The reserve is skirted by public paths, and one hide is available free for public use, but you need an entry sticker for the rest of the reserve. Approach points are Dunwich and the pretty village of Eastbridge. Mount Pleasant Farm at Dunwich, which borders the reserve, has recently been bought by the RSPB and NT, who intend to turn it back into heathland to link the existing Minsmere and Dunwich heathlands.

WICKHAM MARKET TM2956
Valley Farm Riding & Driving Centre 🏛 (½m W on B1078) Family-run equestrian centre offering a wide range of activities from all-day pony treks to carriage driving, and even stunt riding. They also have a collection of animals inc Suffolk punches, donkeys, goats, a camel, and a breeding herd of Camargue horses. Snacks, shop, disabled access; cl 25–26 Dec; (01728) 746916; site free, riding lessons start from £18 for 30 mins. The comfortable Three Tuns at Pettistree has civilised food (and bedrooms now).

WINGFIELD TM2276
Wingfield College and Gardens 🏛 Quite a surprise to find a splendid medieval timber-framed building behind the Georgian façade. One of its 18th-c owners constructed the Palladian exterior to make his home more fashionable, using false ceilings, floors and windows so skilfully that for 200 years the house's early origins were forgotten. Striking great hall and period interiors, topiary, walled gardens, and garden sculptures; art displays in new visitor centre. Snacks, shop, disabled access; open pm Weds, wknds and bank hols Apr–Sept; (01379) 384505; £3.90. It's also the home of Wingfield Arts, a varied programme of events across the region; phone for a programme. The De La Pole Arms has good food.

WOODBRIDGE TM2749
Quietly attractive and rather dignified market town, with many fine buildings and interesting book and antiques shops, and a **church** of great style and interest. The Anchor (Quay St), Bull and Kings Head (Market Hill) and Old Mariner and Olde Bell & Steelyard (New St) all do decent bar lunches. The B1079 and then B1077 up to Eye is a pleasant drive on an old coach road.
Buttrums Mill 🏛 (Burkitt Rd) Six-storey tower mill, fully restored, with displays of its history. Shop; open pm Sun and bank hols Easter–Sept, plus pm Sat May–Aug; *£1.50.
Tide Mill Restored 18th-c mill on busy quayside, its wheel usually working when tides allow. Shop, disabled access to ground floor only; cl Oct–Apr exc wknds Oct and Apr; £1.50. The Wilford Bridge Hotel nearby at Melton is a good lunch stop – and well placed for river walks.
Woodbridge Museum 🏛 (Market Hill) Tells the story of Woodbridge from its Anglo-Saxon roots to the present. Shop, disabled access (but no facilities); cl Sun am, all day Mon and Tues (exc bank and school hols), Weds, and Nov–Easter; (01394) 380502; £1.

WOOLPIT TL9762
The **church** here has a hammer-beam roof, and a translation of the village tale that in the 12th c two slightly strange-looking green-skinned children were found by a pit that was suddenly blasted in the earth one night; the boy soon died, but the girl lived, and grew up to marry a local lad and have children. She never said more about her origins than that she'd come from a land far far away. The drive to Buxhall (where the Crown is a good pub) is pretty.
Woolpit & District Museum (The Institute) Small but interesting, with annually changing local history displays (and more on the 12th-c children). Shop, disabled access; open pm wknds and bank hols Easter–Sept; (01359) 240822; donations.
Other attractive villages, all with decent pubs, include Bentley TM1138, Bildeston TL9949, Blaxhall TM3657, Blyford TM4277 (and nearby Holton windmill is pretty), Boxford TL9640, Chelsworth TL9848, Dalham TL7261, Eastbridge TM4566, Fressingfield TM2677, Groton TL9541, Grundisburgh TM2250, Haughley TM0262 (Jacobean manor house in lovely grounds), Hoxne TM1777,

Huntingfield TM3374, Ixworth TL9370, Middleton TM4367, Polstead TL9938, Risby TL8066 (with a decent antiques centre), Ufford TM2953 and Shimpling Street TL8752.

Where to eat

ALDEBURGH TM4656 **Regatta** *171–173 High St* (01728) 452011 Bustling seaside restaurant decorated with pennants and seaside murals, and specialising in fresh local seafood – though they also offer interesting meat dishes and fine puddings; a relaxed atmosphere, friendly service, and no smoking area; cl winter Mon, Tues, Weds, Sun pm; disabled access. £19.50

BRAMFIELD TM3974 **Queens Head** *The Street* (01986) 784214 Popular pub with pleasantly relaxed high-raftered lounge bar, a good log fire in impressive fireplace, no smoking side bar, family room, and wide choice of very good interesting food inc organic dishes (super puddings also); well kept real ales, good wines, and maybe home-made elderflower cordial; cl 26 Dec. £18|£5.95

BROME TM1376 **Cornwallis** *Rectory Rd* (01379) 870326 Very civilised largely 19th-c country hotel grandly approached down a tree-lined drive through its 20-acre grounds, with imaginative choice of excellent food in elegant restaurant, nicely planted Victorian-style side conservatory, and beamed and timbered 16th-c bar – stylish and comfortable, with a good mix of old and antique tables, oak settles and cushioned library chairs, and a handsome woodburner; well kept real ales, an extensive, carefully chosen wine list with 20 by the glass, and warm friendly service from attentive young staff; bdrms. £23.75|£8

BURY ST EDMUNDS TL8564 **Maison Bleue** *31 Churchgate St* (01284) 760623 Airy French seafood restaurant with big seaside mural, super fish dishes (and some meaty ones too), a thoughtful wine list, and helpful friendly staff; cl Sun, Mon, Jan; disabled access. £25|£7.95

BUXHALL TL9957 **Crown** *Mill Road* (01449) 736521 Welcoming 17th-c timbered country pub with carefully cooked individually prepared enjoyable food emphasising fresh seasonal ingredients, well kept real ales, decent wines, and quick friendly service; intimate little candlelit bar, open fire in big inglenook, low hop-hung beams and standing timbers, a further light and airy room; seats on heated terrace and in pretty garden; cl Sun pm. £21.95|£6.95

CAVENDISH TL8046 **Bull** *High St* (01787) 280245 Cheerful pub hiding an attractive 16th-c beamed interior behind a Victorian frontage; big standing timbers and attractive fireplaces in open-plan rooms, a thriving atmosphere, wide range of enjoyable good food (fresh fish delivered daily), well kept real ales, and a decent choice of wines by the glass; cl Mon. £21|£6.95

COTTON TM0667 **Trowel & Hammer** *Mill Rd* (01449) 781234 Civilised wisteria-covered pub with a spreading series of quiet rooms, fresh flowers, lots of beamery and timber baulks, a big log fire, good interesting food, and a large pretty back garden with swimming pool; cl 25 Dec; no small children in Cotton Club restaurant; disabled access. £21.65|£7.50

DUNWICH TM4770 **Flora Tearooms** *Fore St* (01728) 648433 Extended former fisherman's hut right on the beach, with great views of the sea and fishing boats, famous for very good fish and chips but also other snacks, teas and home-made cakes; cl Dec–Feb; disabled access.|£5.95

DUNWICH TM4770 **Ship** *St James's St* (01728) 648219 Pleasant old pub by the sea, with a good bustling atmosphere, friendly helpful staff who cope cheerfully with the crowds, wonderfully fresh fish off the boats on the beach, traditionally furnished bar, conservatory, sunny back terrace, and well kept garden; bdrms; the RSPB reserve at Minsmere is close by; cl 25 Dec pm. £17|£5.95

ERWARTON TM2134 **Queens Head** *The Street* (01473) 787550 Remote and unspoilt little pub with lovely views, a welcoming unpretentious atmosphere, a cosy coal fire in beamed bar, good well priced bar food inc fresh fish and game in season and decent value Sun lunch, well kept real ales, and friendly service; cl 25 Dec;

children in restaurant only; disabled access. £24.95|£4.75

FRAMSDEN TM1959 **Dobermann** *The Street (01473) 890461* Charmingly restored thatched pub with twin-facing fireplace separating the friendly spotlessly kept bars, good popular food, and a decent choice of beers and spirits; cl Mon; disabled access; no children. £20|£6

HORRINGER TL8261 **Beehive** *The Street (01284) 735260* Particularly well run and pretty ivy-covered pub with extremely helpful service, friendly atmosphere, excellent imaginative food with lots of daily specials and a puddings board, attractively furnished little rambling rooms, woodburner, well kept real ales and decent wines; no food Sun pm. £25|£7.95

ICKLINGHAM TL7872 **Red Lion** *The Street (01638) 717802* Civilised and rather smart thatched pub with a nice mix of wooden chairs, candlelit tables, fresh flowers, inglenook fireplace and heavy beams, very good food inc lots of fresh fish dishes and season game choices, well kept real ales, and country wines; disabled access. £25|£7.95

IPSWICH TM1644 **Mortimers Seafood Restaurant** *1 Duke Street (01473) 230225* This is the place for really fresh daily changing fish and shellfish, simply cooked; a thoughtful French wine list and relaxed atmosphere; cl Sat am, Sun, bank hols, 24 Dec–5 Jan; disabled access. £23|£4.95

IXWORTH TL9370 **Theobalds** *68 High St (01359) 231707* Consistently good imaginative food in 17th-c restaurant with log fires, beams and standing timbers in cosy rooms, very good wine list, and kind service; cl Sat am, Sun pm, Mon; children in evening over 6 only. £27/2-course menu £12.95

LAVENHAM TL9149 **Great House** *Market Place (01787) 247431* Restaurant-with-rooms in ancient house behind a handsome Georgian façade; bare boards, antiques, open fires (inc an inglenook in the restaurant itself), very good French cooking plus lighter lunches and a super French cheeseboard, friendly staff, mainly French wines, and attractive flower-filled courtyard for outside eating; charming beamed bdrms; cl Sun pm, Mon, Jan. £27.90|£8.50

LIDGATE TL7257 **Star** *The Street (01638) 500275* Quaint old place with interesting small bar, big log fire, handsomely moulded heavy beams and polished oak and pine tables, big helpings of hugely enjoyable food, good wines and ales, a cosy simple dining room, and tables in front and in the little rustic back garden; cl Sun pm. £28.60|£6.50

LONG MELFORD TL8645 **Chimneys** *Hall St (01787) 379806* Lovely beamed 16th-c building with very good carefully prepared interesting food, a thoughtful wine list, and helpful staff; paintings for sale; cl Sun, bank hols (exc Easter); partial disabled access. £42/2-course lunch £15

NAYLAND TL9734 **White Hart** *High St (01206) 263382* Smart 15th-c restaurant-with-rooms in lovely countryside, with tiny bar, rather formal dining room, particularly good French-influenced cooking, a wide choice of wines, and polite willing service; cl Mon (apart from bank hols), 26 Dec–9 Jan; disabled access. £34.31/2-course lunch £9.95

ORFORD TM4249 **Butley Orford Oysterage** *(01394) 450277* Simple restaurant with its own oyster beds, fishing boat and smokehouse; very popular locally and with yachtsmen for its wonderfully fresh fish, decent wines, and brisk friendly service; disabled access. £23|£5.75

RATTLESDEN TL9758 **Brewers Arms** *Lower Rd (01449) 736377* 16th-c village pub with pleasantly simple beamed lounge and small lively public bar, very welcoming friendly service, imaginative food, decent wines, well kept ales, and magnificent old bread oven in main eating area; children must be well behaved; cl Mon; disabled access. £21.70|£7.95

REDE TL8055 **Plough** *The Green (01284) 789208* Welcoming partly thatched cottage in lovely spot, with particularly helpful owners, lots of well presented fresh fish and game in season, imaginative daily specials, good evening restaurant, decent wine, and lovely sheltered cottagey garden; cl Sun pm; disabled access. £22|£8.95

SNAPE TM3958 **Crown** *Bridge Rd (01728) 688324* Unspoilt smugglers' inn with a relaxed and warmly friendly atmosphere, old brick floors, beams, big brick inglenook and nice old furnishings; particularly good interesting well presented food served by smiling staff, pre- and post-concert suppers, a thoughtful wine list (16 by the glass inc champagne), well kept real ales, and tables in pretty garden; bdrms; cl 25 Dec, pm 26 Dec; no children; partial disabled access. £20|£6.95

STOWMARKET TM0360 **Tot Hill House** *Tot Hill (01449) 673375* Although beside a busy road, once inside this friendly and charming family restaurant, the atmosphere is welcoming and peaceful; comfortable furnishings, smart, helpful staff, highly enjoyable and interesting modern cooking, and a varied wine list; no smoking in dining room; cl Mon, Tues, Sat am, Sun pm, 2 wks Jan, last wk July; no children Sat pm and over 7 on Sat; disabled access. £30.25

WINGFIELD TM2276 **De La Pole Arms** *Church Rd (01379) 384545* Beautifully restored village inn, tucked away in lovely countryside; deliberately simple yet elegant décor, interesting bric-a-brac, comfortable traditional seating, a pleasantly civilised feel, courteous friendly staff, and very good popular bar food; no smoking restaurant and well kept real ales. £21.65|£7.95

WOODBRIDGE TM2748 **Captain's Table** *3 Quay St (01394) 383145* 16th-c cottage with three interlinked beamed rooms, cheerful décor, enjoyable interesting food inc plenty of fresh fish, helpful service, and a thoughtful wine list; cl Sun pm, Mon (open bank hols), 1st 2 wks Jan; disabled access. £23|£6.95

Special thanks to Michael and Jenny Back

We welcome reports from readers

This *Guide* depends on readers' reports. Do help us if you can – in return, we offer a discount on the next edition to people who've helped us with reports for it. Tell us what you think about places already in it, and anything extra you think we should say about them. And send us your ideas for inclusion in the next edition: places to visit, eat at or stay in, attractive drives or walks, maybe even unusual shops you know of. Use the card in the middle, the report forms at the end, or just write – no stamp needed: *The Good Britain Guide*, FREEPOST TN1569, Wadhurst, E Sussex TN5 7BR. Or log on to www.goodguides.com

SURREY

Unexpectedly rural, with some special gardens, peaceful commons, heaths and perfect walking territory; some very lively family outings, too

Despite its commuter-belt image, Surrey is England's most wooded county, and away from the urban corridors much of the countryside is beautifully preserved, and quite hilly. The National Trust owns vast tracts of the finest scenery, and walkers have an excellent choice, with relatively free access. There are some lovely villages, too.

Leith Hill and Box Hill are walkers' favourites. Other country outings gain a bit of family appeal from special features, such as the colourful ornamental birds at Busbridge Lakes near Godalming, Britain's oldest working windmill by the pretty bluebell woods around Outwood, and the splendid views from the semaphore tower on Ockham Common, with its surrounding heath and woodland. A boat trip along the River Wey & Godalming Navigation or a cycle ride along the Downs Link Path are other fine-weather suggestions.

The theme parks at Chessington and particularly Thorpe Park (our Surrey Family Attraction) are terrific for an action-packed day out. Farnham's bustling Birdworld & Underwater World (plenty to do even on wet days) is another popular choice, and there are several enjoyable farm parks.

Horseracing fans are well served, with several racecourses even aside from Epsom, and for motor-racing there's the Brooklands Museum in Weybridge (now with a hands-on science gallery for children). Two little-known treats for art lovers are Watts Picture Gallery at Compton, and the Hannah Peschar Sculpture Garden in Ockley. The Rural Life Centre at Tilford is interesting. There are vineyards to visit in Godstone and Dorking, and if beer is more your drink, head for the Hogs Back Brewery at Tongham.

Some superb gardens include England's oldest landscape garden in Esher, and the instructive mix of styles at Wisley. There's lots to see at Painshill Landscape Garden in Cobham, and Winkworth Arboretum is enchanting in autumn. Great houses include Polesden Lacey at Great Bookham (once the centre of Edwardian high society), Elizabethan Loseley Park near Guildford, grand Clandon Park (West Clandon), and Hatchlands (East Clandon). A complete contrast is the entertaining tour through the network of tunnels underneath Reigate.

Please let us know what you think of places in the *Guide*. Use the report forms at the back of the book, write us a letter or log on to www.goodguides.com.

Where to stay

BAGSHOT SU9062 **Pennyhill Park** *College Ride, Bagshot, Surrey GU19 5ET* (01276) 471774 **£228**, plus special breaks; 123 individually designed luxury rms and suites. Impressive Victorian country house in 120 acres of well kept gardens and parkland inc a 9-hole golf course, tennis courts, outdoor heated swimming pool, clay pigeon shooting, archery, fishing, and an international rugby pitch; friendly courteous staff, wood-panelled bar with resident pianist, comfortable two-level lounge and reading room, very good imaginative food in two restaurants, jazz Sun lunchtime, and terraces overlooking the golf course; disabled access; dogs welcome in bedrooms

CHERTSEY TQ0467 **Crown** *7 London St, Chertsey, Surrey KT16 8AP* (01932) 564657 **£65**w; 30 comfortable modern rms. Bustling, friendly place with some original features and open fire in large bar, conservatory extension, good food, attractive restaurant, and lovely big garden; disabled access; dogs welcome

EWHURST TQ0840 **High Edser** *Shere Rd, Ewhurst, Cranleigh, Surrey GU6 7PQ* (01483) 278214 **£55***; 3 charming rms, shared bthrm. 16th-c timber-framed farmhouse in lovely countryside, with comfortable residents' lounge, friendly owners, enjoyable food (by arrangement), and open fire in dining room; tennis court in grounds; cl Christmas

FARNHAM SU8145 **Farnham House** *Alton Rd, Farnham, Surrey GU10 5ER* (01252) 716908 **£69**w, plus special breaks; 25 comfortable rms. Attractive Victorian Gothick manor house with oak panelling and open fires in comfortable public rooms, split-level restaurant, and tennis court and outdoor heated swimming pool in five-acre gardens

HASLEMERE SU9228 **Deerfell** *Blackdown, Haslemere, Surrey GU27 3LA* (01428) 653409 **£48***; 3 comfortable rms. Comfortable no smoking stone coach house with wonderful views and good nearby walks; generous meals in handsome dining room (ordered in advance), open fire in sitting room, pictures, antiques and old rugs, a sun room, good breakfasts, and friendly owners; cl mid-Dec to mid-Jan; children over 6; dogs by prior arrangement

HASLEMERE SU9232 **Lythe Hill Hotel & Spa** *Petworth Rd, Haslemere, Surrey GU27 3BQ* (01428) 651251 **£153**, plus special breaks; 41 individually styled rms, a few in the original house. Lovely partly 15th-c building in 20 acres of parkland and bluebell woods (adjoining the NT hillside) with floodlit tennis court, croquet lawn, and jogging track; plush, comfortable and elegant lounges, a relaxed bar, two no smoking restaurants (one with French cooking, the other with traditional English), and good attentive service; new spa with swimming pool, sauna, steam and beauty rooms and gym; disabled access; dogs welcome in bedrooms

HOLMBURY ST MARY TQ1144 **Bulmer Farm** *Holmbury St Mary, Dorking, Surrey RH5 6LG* (01306) 730210 **£52***; 8 big comfortable rms, 5 in no smoking barn conversion with own showers. Attractive and welcoming 17th-c farmhouse on 30-acre beef farm in lovely countryside, with oak beams and inglenook fireplace in attractive sitting room, breakfasts with home-made preserves in neatly kept dining room, and large garden; self-catering also; children over 12; disabled access

HORLEY TQ2943 **Langshott Manor** *Langshott, Horley, Surrey RH6 9LN* (01293) 786680 **£175**, plus special breaks; 15 individually furnished rms. Elizabethan house in fine three-acre garden with roses and lakes; beams, oak panelling, fresh flowers and open fires in elegant rms, and enjoyable traditional cooking in no smoking restaurant; disabled access

NUTFIELD TQ2950 **Nutfield Priory** *Nutfield, Redhill, Surrey RH1 4EL* (01737) 822066 **£150**, plus special breaks; 60 rms. Impressive Victorian Gothick hotel in 40 acres of parkland with lovely elaborate carvings, stained-glass windows, gracious day rooms, a fine panelled library, cloistered restaurant, and even an organ in the galleried grand hall; extensive leisure club with indoor heated swimming pool; dogs welcome in bedrooms

To see and do

Surrey Family Attraction of the Year

CHERTSEY TQ0368 **Thorpe Park** (A320 N) In the last couple of years this 500-acre leisure park has been pulling out all the stops in a vigorous attempt to top their competitors, and there's no doubt that their spectacular new rides easily give the best at Alton Towers a run for their money. It's by no means a cheap day out (you'll need the whole day to make the ticket price worthwhile), but there's lots to do, with a fairly even balance between the rides for thrill-seekers, and gentler activities for younger children. Every recent season they've opened a new, multi-million pound ride, each more dramatic than the last; turning heads (and stomachs) in 2002 was Colossus, the world's first ten-looping roller-coaster. It's fast, furious, and terrifying, climbing 30 metres (100 ft) before repeatedly spinning through complete circles at up to 40mph. Connoisseurs rate it very highly, and you can get a taste with an online virtual version, at www.thorpepark.co.uk. Other recent additions include a fun spinning water rapids ride, Detonator (which winches you up to 30 metres and fires you back down to the ground at nearly 50mph), and Vortex, where, surprise, surprise, you're spun round at high speeds and then swung backwards and forwards. And they haven't finished yet: for 2003 they're adding what they promise will be the world's biggest roller-coaster, Nemesis: Inferno, themed around a volcano. You'll still find old favourites like Loggers Leap, the highest log flume in the country; the website has a thrillometer guide, so you can plan which rides to head for first. Younger children aren't left out: there are plenty of less frantic rides, particularly in the Octopus's garden area, several play areas, and still lots of water-based activities around Neptune's Kingdom. They have a man-made beach and pools, so it's worth bringing swimming costumes, and even a bucket and spade. Across the lake (reached by either a train or waterbus) is a decent-sized traditional working farm, with animals and craft centre. The visitor facilities throughout are excellent, but expect crowds and queues on busy summer days. Meals, snacks, shop, disabled access; open Easter–Oct, though they're usually closed some weekdays at either end of the season; (0870) 444 4466; on the door, prices at the height of the season are £23 adults, £18 children under 12, and £65 for a family – it's a fair bit cheaper to come on quieter days, or you can save money by booking in advance, either online (up to two days before you plan to visit), or on the phone (up to 5pm the day before).

ABINGER COMMON TQ1245
Charmingly set village with pretty church, ancient pub (the Abinger Hatch) and duckpond surrounded by woodland – popular for walks.
ALBURY TQ0547
Attractive village with pleasant walks nearby, and glimpses of the Victorian mansion Albury Park – or at least its famous chimneys. The Drummond Arms is a civilised place for lunch.
St Peter and St Paul church (Albury Park) This pleasantly set disused Saxon church has some interesting monuments.
BANSTEAD WOOD TQ2657
Popular strolling-ground, surprisingly

peaceful despite the proximity of Surrey's northern suburbia and heavily used trunk roads. In Banstead the Mint (Park Rd) is good value for lunch.
BETCHWORTH TQ2149
Attractive village, pleasant for strolls along an annotated trail from a church where *Four Weddings and a Funeral* was filmed. The Dolphin is a decent pub, the Red Lion more of a dining place, and there's a nice drive via Brockham and Newdigate to Rusper in Sussex.
BOX HILL TQ1751
Surrey's most popular viewpoint, with a summit car park and walks on its steep juniper and boxwood slopes: wild orchids and butterflies in early summer,

perhaps field mushrooms in early autumn; the attractively placed King William IV at Mickleham is excellent for lunch.

CHALDON TQ3155
Attractive church, particularly worth a visit for its unique wall-painting of the *Ladder of Salvation*.

CHERTSEY TQ0467
A good few Georgian buildings in its main streets, and pleasant walks by the Thames – for instance from the Kingfisher dining pub (Chertsey Bridge Rd).

Chertsey Abbey Medieval remains standing in Abbeyfields Park.

Surrey

GREATER LONDON

Esher • Chessington

Epsom

A24

9
9

A217

Banstead
Wood

Fetcham **Leatherhead** ✕ *Tadworth*

Great Bookham

Headley Heath

Chaldon

Tatsfield

M25

6 *Limpsfield*   A25

✕ *Mickleham*

• Box Hill

8   A25

7/8

Nutfield

Oxted

Dorking ✕

✕ *Betchworth*

Brockham

• *Wotton*

Holmwood
Common

A24 ✕

Blackbrook

Leigh

A217   A23

Reigate

Godstone

Bletchingley   Marden Park

*Limpsfield
Chart*

Tandridge

M23

• Outwood

A22

TQ

Horley

✕

Lingfield

Ockley

Charlwood

9A   9   • *Burstow*

• *Okewoodhill*

KENT

EAST
SUSSEX

0 Miles   5

0 Kilometres   8

S U S S E X

Chertsey Museum (Sainsbury Centre, Guildford St) In the summer this interesting museum will move back from here into its original Georgian building in Windsor St (where disabled access will have been greatly improved, also more display space and an improved shop and café). There are displays on the abbey, a good fashion collection, and temporary exhibitions and events. Cl am wkdys, all day Sun, Mon, Easter bank hols and 25–26 Dec, 1 Jan; (01932) 565764; free.
Great Cockcrow Railway (Hardwick Lane, Lyne, slightly NW) A notable miniature steam railway, with a

unique signalling system. Snacks, disabled access; open Sun pm Apr–Oct; (01932) 255500; £2. The Golden Grove on St Ann's Hill out towards here is a nice spot for lunch.

Thorpe Park *See separate family panel on p.575.*

CHESSINGTON TQ1762

Chessington World of Adventures (A243) This is the place to head for unadulterated fun. The big thrill ride is Rameses' Revenge, which spins you round 360 degrees at speeds of up to 60 mph, while plummeting towards a rock-lined water-blast pit. Though the more traditional-seeming Rattlesnake looks a little gentler it still packs quite a punch (all have height restrictions). There's plenty to amuse younger children, from the Dragon River log flume and Action Man Training HQ to the simpler rides around Toytown. They'll also get the most out of the once-famous zoo from which everything else developed, with sea lion and penguin displays at set times throughout the day, and a good reptile and insect house. A monorail gives bird's-eye views of the lions, tigers and meerkats, and from an African-style game lodge you can watch their large family of gorillas. Meals, snacks, shop, some disabled access; usually open Apr–Oct but phone to check as they are closed some days then; (0870) 4447777; £21, £17 off peak. The Star down towards the M25 is a good value food stop.

CHIDDINGFOLD SU9635

Exceptional village in fine countryside, with one window of its church made up from locally excavated fragments of 13th-c glass made here. The Rams Nest (A283 S) has good value food in charming surroundings.

Ramster (A283 S) Splendid Edwardian woodland garden, bog garden and millennium garden. Teas, plant sales, disabled access; usually open May–Jun though best to check; (01428) 654167; £3.

COBHAM TQ1159

Quite a busy shopping town, with some fine older buildings around the church and in Church St; just SW, Downside Common is a classic cricket green, with cottages scattered around it, and an attractive pub – the Cricketers.

Cobham mill (Mill Rd) Prettily set working watermill, authentically restored by enthusiastic locals. Shop, disabled access; open pm 2nd Sun of month Apr–Oct; (01932) 867387; free.

Painshill Landscape Garden (A425 slightly W) These beautiful 18th-c landscaped gardens, currently being restored, are a continual surprise, with a lake with seemingly endless bays and inlets, a Chinese bridge, waterwheel, grotto, Gothic temple, even a Turkish tent, and other follies at every turn. Lots of unusual trees and shrubs. Snacks and picnic area, shop, disabled access (best to ring); cl Fri, plus Mon Nov–Mar; (01932) 868113; *£4.50. Almost opposite the gates, the Little White Lion has enjoyable food.

COMPTON SU9547

Watts Picture Gallery (Down Lane) Memorial gallery in tranquil rural setting to Victorian Symbolist painter and sculptor G F Watts (in his time one of the most celebrated artists in the world), with over 250 of his works. Shop, disabled access to main gallery; cl Thurs, and am Mon, Tues, Fri and Sun, plus 24–25 Dec and Good Fri; (01483) 810235; free. Just down the road the unique circular Watts Chapel in the village cemetery is covered in Celtic and art nouveau decoration, and was designed and built by his wife Mary Watts and villagers. The village church is attractive, and the tearoom nearby serves up to 24 different teas.

DEVIL'S PUNCHBOWL SU8936

A spectacular fold of the downs, with nature trails through mixed woodlands, quiet valleys and sandy heaths with scattered ponds. The area is quite developed but the woods and intricacy of the landscape give it a wholesome country feel, and the footpath network is dense. **Gibbet Hill** above the A3 gets a view over most of it.

DORKING TQ1649

Pleasant market town with lots of antiques shops, and a local museum in West St (open pms Weds and Thurs and all day Sat; (01306) 743821; £1). The roads S of the A25 W of here are the county's most pleasant drives, and the steep road up Box Hill N opens a great panorama. The 16th-c Kings Arms in West St has decent food.

Denbies Wine Estate 🎫 (A24 just N) Britain's biggest vineyard, and at 265 acres bigger than most in Europe. The tour is unique and you don't have to be a wine buff to enjoy it. Beginning with a 20-minute film in their unusual 360-degree cinema, you are then taken through the winery on a road train to the cellars where you can try out some of their produce. A train tour takes you round the vineyard (Apr–Oct, £4). Meals and snacks (in conservatory restaurant) and B&B, big shop, good disabled access; cl 25 Dec, 1 Jan; (01306) 876616; £7.25, combined ticket for outdoor and indoor tours £10.25. Fine views and walks nearby, and the Stepping Stones at Westhumble has enjoyable food.

DOWNS LINK PATH TQ0735
Follows a disused railway track through pleasant countryside – popular for walks and family cycling. The Thurlow Arms at the former Baynards Station nr Cox Green is handy for access.

DUNSFOLD TQ0036
One of Surrey's most picturesque village greens; the Sun overlooking it has decent food.

EAST CLANDON TQ0651
Hatchlands (A246) Handsome 18th-c brick house with more floors than are visible from the outside, thanks to an ingenious use of false windows. The grand rooms are especially notable for their ceilings and fireplaces, early examples of the work of Robert Adam. A fine collection of historic keyboard instruments includes a piano once owned by Marie Antoinette. The formal garden was designed by Gertrude Jekyll. Meals, snacks, shop, disabled access; cl Nov–Mar, house and garden also cl am plus Mon, Fri (exc Aug) and Sat exc bank hols; park walks daily from 11; (01483) 222482; £6, £2.50 park walk; NT. A visit here is easily combined with Clandon Park at West Clandon (joint ticket; £9). The Wishing Well is a welcoming dining pub.

EPSOM TQ2158
The Derby held here, and first run in 1780, is one of the oldest flat races in the world – and a grand social event; (01372) 726311 for dates. The nearby Derby Arms is a reliable food pub. Other famous racecourses in this area

include Sandown Park (01372) 463072; Kempton Park (01932) 782292; and Lingfield (01342) 834800; all have good facilities.

Horton Park Children's Farm (B280 W) Plenty of animals to feed and cuddle, tractor rides (50p), an adventure playground and indoor play area. Meals, snacks and picnic area, shop, disabled access; cl 25–26 Dec; (01372) 743984; £4.30 each child (one accompanying adult free).

ESHER TQ1464
Claremont Landscape Garden (off A307) The oldest surviving landscaped garden in the country, laid out by Vanbrugh and Bridgeman before 1715 and extended and naturalised by William Kent; 49 enchanting acres with lakes, turf amphitheatre, grotto, island, guided walks in summer, children's trail and Braille guide. Meals, snacks, shop, disabled access; cl Mon Nov–Mar, 25 Dec; (01372) 467806; £4; NT. Marneys (Alma Rd) and the Prince of Wales (West End Lane) have enjoyable food.

FARNHAM SU8346
Handsome town that owed its Georgian heyday to the importance of local corn and hops. Many elegant buildings from this period remain, and there are some even older ones such as the early 17th-c Spinning Wheel. The area around Castle St is especially nice to stroll round, and in Lower Bourne there's good food at the Fox and Spotted Cow.

Birdworld & Underwater World 🎫 (Holt Pound, off A325 3m SW – actually just over the Hampshire border) This popular place has masses of birds from tiny tanagers to rheas, emus and ostriches, spread over 26 acres of thoughtfully laid out gardens and parkland. Children can go right up to some of the birds, and to the animals in the farmyard (some of which they can feed), and there's always a section with baby birds. They have a good programme of shows, feeding sessions and display, and children's activities in the school hols. Other highlights include the parrots flying around their aviary, and the decent aquarium with tropical and other freshwater and marine fish, and a few alligators in a jungly swamp. There are several decent play areas, and many features are under cover. Interesting talks on their birds of prey, though the feeding of these is not for the squeamish. The woodland trail leads round to a very good, extensive garden centre. Meals, snacks, shop, disabled access; usually cl wkdys Nov to mid-Feb (exc Christmas school hols), and 25–26 Dec; (01420) 22140; £9.25. The 16th-c Cherry Tree in nearby Rowledge has good food.

Castle For 800 years a residence of the Bishops of Winchester. Most of the buildings have been adapted to suit the briefing organisation based here, but the major rooms, inc the great hall, can be seen on a guided tour Weds 2–4 pm; snacks, shop; cl 25 Dec–1 Jan; (01252) 721194; £2.50.

Castle Keep Administered separately; includes the massive foundations and entrance of a Norman tower. Shop; open Apr–Oct; (01252) 713393; £2.30, inc Walkman tour; EH.

Foyer and James Hockey Galleries (Surrey Institute of Art & Design, Falkner Road) Balanced programmes of exhibitions inc art, craft, design and multi-media, housed in two galleries, one a swish modern extension. Disabled access; cl Sun; (01252) 892668; free.

Maltings Gallery (Bridge Sq) Diverse arts and crafts. Meals, snacks, limited disabled access; cl Mon, Sun, am Sat, over Christmas, and Easter; (01252) 713637; free, may be a small charge for national exhibitions.

Museum of Farnham (West St) Excellent local history museum; some William Cobbett memorabilia (his picturesque birthplace in Bridge Sq is now a pub named after him), and a pleasant walled garden. Shop, disabled access to ground floor; cl Sun and Mon, around a wk at Christmas, and Good Fri; (01252) 715094; free.

FETCHAM TQ1555

Bocketts Farm Park ▣ Working farm in a pretty, historic setting, with traditional and rare breeds, tractor rides, play areas, goat milking, pig racing, and a huge new four-lane slide. Meals, snacks, shop, disabled access; cl 25–26 Dec and 1 Jan; (01372) 363764; £3.95.

FOREST GREEN TQ1241

Forge & Dragon Gallery (Ewhurst Rd) Picturesque working forge dating from the 16th c, and prettily set by the village green (where the Parrot has good food). A gallery shows the resourceful work of resident artist/ironworker James Davies – usually on hand to discuss any personal requests. Some disabled access; cl 1–2pm, Sun, and 24 Dec–2 Jan; (01306) 621222; free.

FRENSHAM COMMON SU8540 Popular for walks, with heather and woodland around a lake formed in the 13th c for fish breeding. The Holly Bush does good value food.

GODALMING SU9643 Attractive town with a good few interesting buildings and, because of its narrow streets (part cobbled and pedestrianised), a more old-fashioned feel than most in Surrey. The 18th-c Kings Arms & Royal (High St) is a nice place for a bar lunch, and its Tsar's Lounge is worth seeing.

Busbridge Lakes (Hambledon Rd, off B2130) Very pretty spot with three lakes in fine parkland – exotic waterfowl, peacocks, ornamental pheasants and many other kinds of bird, as well as follies and grottoes throughout the grounds. Snacks, shop; only open 13–21 Apr, 4–5 and 25–26 May, and 17–25 Aug; (01483) 421955; *£4.

Godalming Museum (High St) 15th-c house with local history, interactive displays, Gertrude Jekyll gallery and Jekyll-style walled garden. Snacks, shop, some disabled access; cl Mon, Sun and Christmas–New Year (01483) 426510; free. The town hall opposite is known affectionately by the locals as the Pepper Pot.

GODSTONE TQ3551 Attractive despite its main roads, spread around a broad green with a duck pond, and a pretty group of houses around the imposing **church**, 14th/15th c with a Norman tower. The White Hart is a sound beamed and timbered dining pub.

Godstone Farm ▣ (Tilburstow Hill) Friendly 40-acre working farm; children are encouraged to touch the animals (and even climb in with some of them); very good play areas. Meals, snacks, shop, disabled access; cl 25 Dec;

(01883) 742546; £4.10 per child (accompanied adults free).

Godstone Vineyard 🔲 (Quarry Rd, just off A22 N) Looking up to the downs, this friendly vineyard produces a range of ciders and apple juice as well as its wines; free tastings, shop, disabled access; cl 25–26 Dec, and 1 Jan; (01883) 744590. Quarry Rd winds on down into Flower Lane, where the same people own Flower Farm, with **pick-your-own** produce; cl Oct–Apr; (01883) 743636; free.

GOMSHALL TQ0846

Gomshall Gallery (A25) Contemporary arts and crafts for sale; also French wine wholesaler. Cl Sun, Mon, and bank hols; (01483) 203795. The Compasses (with a streamside garden) does good value lunches, and wooded Netley Heath above the village has strolling opportunities.

GREAT BOOKHAM TQ1352

Polesden Lacey (off A246 S) Attractive Regency house once at the centre of Edwardian high society, now with photographs of some of the notable guests, as well as splendid tapestries, porcelain, Old Masters and other art. The spacious grounds have a walled rose garden and open-air theatre. Meals, snacks, shop, disabled access; house cl Mon/Tues exc bank hols, and all Nov–Mar, grounds open all year; (01372) 458203; £3 house only, £4 grounds only; NT. On the other side of the extended commuter village, the Bookham Commons, with a mixture of thorny scrub (full of birds), small lakes, marshy bits and oak woods, are well wooded and attractive. In Effingham nearby, the Plough has honest home cooking.

GUILDFORD SU9949

The biggest town (despite having a cathedral – it's not a city) in the area, Guildford is older than you might at first think; although many of the buildings are Georgian-fronted, what's behind often dates back much further. The sloping High St has attractive parts as well as its briskly modern shops, with interesting buildings inc the **Abbots Hospital** and the **Grammar School**. Tunsgate Arch is the start for free guided walks of the town – 2.30pm every Sun, Mon and Weds May–Sept, also 7.30 Thurs till end Aug.

Grange Air Champagne Balloon Flights (Bannisters Field) If you're brave enough (and you don't get the champagne till afterwards), hot-air balloons give a good view of the area, flights most days (exc winter), weather permitting; phone for information (01420) 520717; £135.

Guildford Boat House (Millbrook) Old-established boat house where you can hire narrow and rowing boats for the Wey Navigation (see below); phone for information; (01483) 504494. Nearby the Weyside does enjoyable up-to-date food in a lovely riverside setting.

Guildford Castle The hill of the ruined 12th-c **castle** has fine views of the town, and a garden in the former castle ditch. As we went to press the castle itself was closed for restoration, and it wasn't clear when this would be complete; (01483) 444702.

Guildford Cathedral The cathedral which was begun in 1936 is one of only two entirely 20th-c Anglican cathedrals in the country; it's quite austere, but has a cool elegance inside; meals, snacks, shop, disabled access; (01483) 565287; donations.

Guildford Museum (Quarry St) Local history from prehistoric man to the Victorians, with a display on Lewis Carroll, who died here in 1898. Shop; cl Sun, Good Fri, 25 Dec and some bank hols; (01483) 444751; free. Carroll is buried in the cemetery on the Mount, the continuation of the High St.

Guildhall (High St) Mainly Tudor, with one of the few surviving sets of Elizabethan standard measures. Disabled access to ground floor only; usually open only for guided tours at 2, 3 and 4pm Tues and Thurs; (01483) 444035; free.

Loseley Park (off B3000, 3 miles SW) Most people are familiar with the name from the yoghurts and ice-cream produced here (try the white chocolate and butterscotch). The stately Elizabethan stately home was built in 1562, and has fine panelling, paintings and tapestries. The walled gardens include an amazing rose garden with over 1,000 bushes, and a fountain garden. Meals, snacks, shop and plant sales, limited disabled access; cl Mon exc bank hols, Tues, house open pm Jun–Aug, gardens open May–Sept; (01483) 304440; £6 house and gardens, £3 gardens only.

River Wey & Godalming Navigation This 17th-c canal, passing through some fine scenery, by 1763 linked Godalming (where the wharf has some handsome Georgian buildings) with the Thames. A visitor centre at **Dapdune Wharf** here has interactive exhibitions on the waterway and the people who lived and worked on it, housed in a restored Wey barge. There's a new hands-on activity area in an old gunpowder store; they also have children's trails, guided nature walks and various special events, and you can take a 40-min boat trip from here (£2, best to phone for dates). Snacks and picnic areas, shop, disabled access; cl Tues, Weds and Nov–21 Mar; (01483) 561389; *£3. The locks and towpath have been restored by the NT, and you can walk all the way from Godalming to Weybridge, some 20 miles, or hire boats from Farncombe Boat House; Mar–Nov; (01483) 421306.

HAMBLEDON SU9639
You can climb inside what's said to be a witch's tree in front of the church here; walk round the tree three times and the witch may well appear. Restore your poise in the Merry Harriers; pleasant walks nearby. Open by appointment, 16th-c timber-framed **Oakhurst Cottage** (Cricket Green) has been restored and furnished as a simple labourer's dwelling; (01428) 684090; cl ams, plus Fri, Mon, Tues, and all Nov–Mar; £3; NT.

HASCOMBE SU9940
Lovely village with an interesting **church**; the White Horse is good for lunch (with a great garden), and the B2130 S and then the Dunsfold–Chiddingfold back road is a pleasant drive.

Winkworth Arboretum (B2130 just NW) Nearly 100 acres of lovely hillside woodland, with fine views over the North Downs – esp nice in spring, and with unusual flaring colours in the autumn; dogs welcome on leads. Snacks, shop spring–autumn, limited disabled access; (01483) 208477; £3.50; NT.

HEADLEY HEATH TQ2053
Sandy walks and rides through heather, birch woods – and as summer wears on rather too much bracken.

HOLMWOOD COMMON TQ1845
Popular for walks, with undulating oak and birch woods and lots of good paths; the Plough at Blackbrook is good for lunch.

HORSELL COMMON TQ0060
A touch of interest for walkers in the sandpits which inspired and saw the start of H G Wells's *War of the Worlds*; the Cricketers at Horsell Birch has decent food (all day Sun and bank hols).

HURT WOOD TQ0943
Large areas of private broadleafed forest around here are open to walkers; relatively unfrequented, so it's a good place to spot birds and wild animals.

HYDON'S BALL SU9739
There's unspoilt walking terrain off the road between Loxhill and Hydestile S of Godalming, with Hydon's Ball a fine viewpoint, though rather hard to find.

JACOBS WELL TQ0053
Burpham Court Farm Park The bit children like best is the help-the-farmer session (around 3pm in winter, 4pm in summer) where they get the chance to join in activities such as feeding the pigs, collecting eggs or bringing in the goats. They've llamas and an aviary as well as rare breeds; play and picnic areas, seasonal activities, and you can buy a day ticket to fish here. Snacks, shop, some disabled access (but no facilities); cl 25 and 26 Dec, though best to check in winter; (01483) 576089; £3.95.

LEATHERHEAD TQ1658
Fire & Iron Gallery (Oxshott Rd, A244 N) Unusual exhibitions of ornamental metalwork. Shop; limited disabled access; cl Sun, bank hols, 25–26 Dec, 1 Jan; (01372) 386453; free.

Museum of Local History (Church St) In a pretty timber-framed 17th-c building, and well worth a visit. Shop, disabled access to ground floor; open Sat, pm Thurs–Fri Apr–Christmas; (01372) 386348; free. The Dukes Head in the pedestrianised High St is pleasant for lunch, and there are riverside walks nearby.

LEITH HILL TQ1343
Perhaps the best stretch of country for

walkers in Surrey, with heather, sandy walks, steep pine woods and tremendous views. An 18th-c tower on top of the hill, the highest point in SE England, is the best viewpoint of all, with an unexpected view of S London – which feels 100 miles away (snacks; open wknds and bank hols, plus Weds pm Easter–Sept; (01306) 711777; £1.50). Friday Street, with a lake and a useful pub (the Stephan Langton, open all day in summer), is one starting point for switchback routes S through a series of brackeny summits to the tower. Leith Hill can also be approached through attractive farmland from the S, from Ockley, or from the Parrot (also normally open all day) at Forest Green.

LIGHTWATER SU9262

Lightwater Country Park Visitor centre with heathland exhibition and plenty of nature trails. Snacks, shop, disabled access; park open all year, visitor centre usually open pm Sun plus pm Tues–Fri in school hols; (01276) 479582; free. The Inn at West End is handy for a good lunch.

MARDEN PARK TQ3653

A peaceful spot for strolls – surprising, as it's so near suburbia and even the M25.

MYTCHETT SU8955

Basingstoke Canal Now fully rehabilitated; in its Surrey section it does not pass through such fine scenery as the Wey Navigation, but its towpath has been well restored. The **Canal Visitor Centre** (Mytchett Place Rd) has displays on the canal, and good access to its towpath, with boat trips (usually wknds and bank hols Apr–Sept, and daily in school hols Easter–Oct). Snacks, shop, disabled access; cl Mon (exc bank hols), wknds Oct–Easter; (01252) 370073; free.

OCKHAM COMMON TQ0858

Chatley Heath Semaphore Tower (Old Lane, off A3 to Effingham) Unique tower rather like a lighthouse, the only surviving member of a chain that sent messages by visible signals between the Admiralty in London and Portsmouth, long before telephones or telegraph; excellent views from the top of the 88 steps. Surrounding it are 700 acres of heath and woodland, with a nature trail

and good walks (inc the 20-minute trek from the car park to the tower). Shop; open pm wknds and bank hols Apr–Sept, plus Weds in school hols, 1st Sun of month only during winter; (01932) 862762; £2. The extraordinary 'gothick' Hautboy (Ockham Lane), under new management, has good food.

OCKLEY TQ1439

Some attractive old houses along the Roman road here, with the 15th-c Cricketers, and the Kings Arms and Old School House, all doing good value food.

Hannah Peschar Sculpture Garden 🏠 (Black and White Cottage, Standon Lane) Lush garden filled with contemporary sculpture: the water garden is now more like a tropical rainforest than the cottage garden it started as, and the sculptures and ceramics blend perfectly with its unusual design. Mostly disabled access but no facilities; open Fri–Sat, and pm Sun and bank hols (Tues–Thurs by appointment) May–Oct; (01306) 627269; *£8.

OUTWOOD TQ3245

Spread around an attractive common, with an antiques shop, and adjacent NT woodlands which are ideal for a picnic. The Bell near the common is a good value dining pub.

Outwood post mill Very well preserved, Britain's oldest working windmill, built in 1665. It's a lovely spot, 120 metres (400 ft) up, with ducks, goats and geese wandering freely in the grounds. The adjacent woods look lovely in Apr when the bluebells are out. Shop, disabled access to ground floor only; open pm Sun and bank hols Easter–Oct; (01342) 843644; £2.

OXTED TQ4055

Titsey Place and Gardens Below the North Downs in parkland that's peaceful despite the nearby M25, this is one of Surrey's largest surviving great estates. Although parts date back to the 16th c, most of the rooms inside are 19th-c (though there is an early Georgian bedroom). The grounds include ten acres of formal gardens with a walled kitchen garden. The picturesque hamlet has an ancient yew tree reputed to be a thousand years old. Shop; open pm Weds and Sun mid-May to Sept; (01273) 407077; £4.50 house and gardens, £2 gardens only. On the B269 the Botley Hill Farmhouse is a popular dining pub, and over in Tatsfield the Old Ship prettily set opposite the duckpond on Westmore Green has enjoyable food.

PITCH HILL TQ0842

Though largely wooded, this is good country for walkers, with pleasant views on the relatively open approach from Ewhurst; above the village, the Windmill pub has glorious views from its garden.

RANMORE COMMON TQ1551

Chalk downland with sheep, wild orchids and dense woodlands, within close range of Polesden Lacey. You can walk on the well marked North Downs Way, which emerges on to unspoilt downland on Denbies Hillside (car park nearby), a rich site for butterflies; here you look over Dorking and The Weald. The main landmark hereabouts is St Barnabas church by Gilbert Scott, the so-called 'Church on the North Downs' of 1859, hinting at the grandeur of his other projects such as the Albert Memorial.

REIGATE TQ2548

Barons Cave tours Below the peaceful castle grounds is a network of old tunnels, prime among them this splendid cavernous passageway with all sorts of myths and stories attached. The tours are enthusiastic and entertaining; for an appointment ring the Wealden Cave and Mine Society (Malcolm Tadd) on (01737) 823456, for full details and dates; around £1.50. Among the few surviving original buildings in this mainly modern town are one or two timber-framed houses around the High St, where the beamed Red Cross has decent food.

Windmill church (off A25 W) The 250-year-old former windmill on Reigate Heath was converted into a church in 1880. They still have services on the 3rd Sun each month in summer and perhaps at Christmas. Disabled access; open all year – if cl, key at golf club clubhouse. There are pleasant walks out here, and the Skimmington Castle is a classic country pub.

RUNNYMEDE TQ0071

A field by a main road; not worth visiting unless you are fascinated by Magna Carta, though up the hill beyond the trees, the nearby memorials to John F Kennedy and the named aircrew who died during World War II are dignified and touching.

SHEPPERTON TQ0766

One of the best places to watch the comings and goings on the **River Thames**, with the **Wey Navigation** joining the river here; the Thames Court (Ferry Lane), with a good waterside terrace, has decent food all day, and there's a quiet and attractive 18th-c village square with a pleasant church.

SHERE TQ0747

Very picturesque village, with 17th-c timber-framed cottages, a grassy-banked stream with ducks and ford, and lots of interesting corners. In the partly Norman **church** a quatrefoil blocked hole in the chancel wall marks the spot where a 14th-c anchorite had herself walled in, being fed through another hole outside. The Malt House is a decent local history museum, and the ancient White Horse is a good place for lunch. The village is within reach of both the North Downs around Ranmore Common and the greensand hills to the S; the view from the Ewhurst road is particularly memorable.

ST MARTHA'S HILL TQ0348

(E of Guildford) The church on its summit can be reached only on foot, and by starting from the attractive village of Chilworth, you can see the long-abandoned gunpowder mills by the Tilling Bourne.

STOKE D'ABERNON TQ1259

Stoke d'Abernon church Notable for the earliest surviving memorial brass in Britain, dating from the 13th c; set in the floor of the chancel, it's very well preserved.

THURSLEY COMMON SU9040

Mainly pleasant sandy walking country, with heather and quite often unusual birds, also boggy patches with shallow ponds where dragonflies breed.

TILFORD SU8543

Rural Life Centre (Reeds Rd, just W) Carefully displayed collection of historic farm machinery, tools and crafts, spread over ten acres of field and woodland, with an arboretum, playground, narrow gauge railway on Suns, and 19th-c cricket pavilion, chapel and village hall. Meals, snacks, shop, disabled access; cl Mon/Tues (exc bank hols) and mid-Oct to Mar exc Weds; (01252) 795571; £5. The village has a massive oak tree, thought to be 800 years old; the Barley Mow between the river and the goose-cropped cricket green is a pleasant spot for lunch, there are nice walks in the area, and it's not far from here to the remains of Waverley Abbey.

TONGHAM SU8848

Hogs Back Brewery (Manor Farm, The Street) Tours of friendly little brewery, using traditional methods to produce its nine distinctive regular ales, and sometimes seasonal ones too. The shop has over 500 different British, Belgian and German beers (as well as their own), alongside English wines and farm ciders. Tours 6.30pm Weds, Thurs and Fri, 11 and 2.30 Sat, 2.30 Sun, other times by arrangement, shop open daily (exc 25 Dec and 1 Jan), disabled access; (01252) 783000; tour £6.50 (inc tastings and commemorative glass). The Barley Mow up at The Sands just past Seale does enjoyable lunches.

WALLISWOOD TQ1138

Attractive village, with delightful woodland walk from the old-fashioned Scarlett Arms to the 13th-c church.

WEST CLANDON TQ0451

Clandon Park (A247) Grand 18th-c house with unusual collection of porcelain birds, Meissen figurines, and fine furnishings and paintings. Regular concerts in the grand two-storeyed Marble Hall. Also the Queen's Royal Surrey regimental museum. The gardens have a Maori house brought over from New Zealand in 1892, a grotto and a sunken Dutch garden. Meals, snacks, shop, disabled access to ground floor; cl Fri, Sat and Mon exc bank hols, and all 3 Nov–Mar; (01483) 222482; £6, joint ticket with Hatchlands £9; NT. The smart Onslow Arms is good for lunch, and the 16th-c Bulls Head is popular too.

WEYBRIDGE TQ0862

Brooklands Museum (B374) Exhaustive museum re-creating the racing circuit's 1920s and 30s heyday, with a growing collection of racing cars, motorbikes and bicycles displayed in the restored clubhouse. Also a restored Wellington bomber and a comprehensive collection of vintage Vickers and Hawker planes. This was the site of the first British Grand Prix (an exhibition telling the history of the race is housed in the converted motoring sheds) and first 100 mph motor ride – just walking round the original banked racetrack is surprisingly enjoyable. Demonstrations and events some wknds. Children really enjoy the lively new hands-on science gallery (moved from what was the Guildford Science Discovery Centre). The range of activities includes the chance to build your own suspension bridge, see how a plane flies, and send messages across the room using light; perhaps science shows and experiments in the school hols. Snacks, shop, good disabled access; cl Mon (exc bank hols), Good Fri, Christmas wk; (01932) 857381; £7. In the town the Badgers Rest (Oatlands Chase) and waterside Old Crown and Minnows (both Thames St) do good value food.

WISLEY TQ0658

Wisley Garden (A3) These 240-acre gardens have come a long way since they were developed in 1904 as experimental gardens for the Royal Horticultural Society; it's a mix of grand landscaped gardens with all sorts of model and trial gardens, orchard, woodland and alpine meadow. There are exemplary glasshouses. The gardens get very busy (esp at wknds) but are big enough to cope; special events and demonstrations. Good meals and snacks (though you may have to wait), good shop and garden centre, disabled access; cl 25 Dec; (01483) 224234; £6.

Other attractive villages, all with decent pubs, include Alfold TQ0334, Bletchingley TQ3250 (Norman church), Brockham TQ1949 (lovely green and church), Englefield Green SU9970 (handy for Savill Garden in Berkshire), Friday Street TQ1245 (good walks), Holmbury St Mary TQ1144, Hurtwood TQ0845, Leigh TQ2246, Limpsfield TQ4148 (church where Delius is buried), Limpsfield Chart TQ4251 (good walks), Ripley

TQ0556, Shackleford SU9345, Thorpe TQ0268 and Wood Street SU9550. Besides those mentioned, other **churches** worth a look include Burstow TQ3140, Okewoodhill TQ1337, Tandridge TQ3750, Tatsfield TQ4156 and Wotton TQ1247. You'll usually have to get the key from a local keyholder.

Popular starts or finishes for **walks** include the William IV at Little London TQ0646, Sportsman at Mogador TQ2452, Donkey at Charleshill SU8944, Plough high on its hill at Coldharbour TQ1543 and Surrey Oaks at Newdigate TQ1942.

Besides places already mentioned for the **River Thames**, the Swan in Staines TQ0471 (The Hythe), the Magpie in Sunbury TQ1068 (Thames St), and the Anglers Tavern (off Manor Rd) and Weir (Sunbury Lane) in Walton-on-Thames TQ1066 all have good views and access to the river. The county council has guided walks all year, exploring historical or more usually natural history themes; a typical Sun might have eight or more to choose from. For the current programme ring (08456) 009009.

You can book **balloon trips** on (01252) 844222.

Where to eat

BETCHWORTH TQ2149 **Dolphin** *The Street* (01737) 842288 Bustling, genuinely friendly village local with homely front room, panelled back bar, three open fires and some 400-year-old flagstones, real ales and 18 wines by the glass, popular good value food, and seats on the front courtyard and on lawn; no children inside; disabled access. £17.55|**£6.55**

BETCHWORTH TQ2150 **Red Lion** *Old Rd, Buckland* (01737) 843336 Civilised dining pub – indeed, almost more a restaurant-with-rooms – with a light, airy bar, log-effect gas fire, plenty of tables, steps down to a long stylish new flagstoned room, and no smoking candlelit dining room; good interesting food, nice puddings, and enjoyable Sun lunch, well chosen house wines, well kept real ales, and helpful service; plenty of picnic-sets on lawn with play area, and in good weather tables set for dining on a rose-trellised terrace; bdrms. £25.70|**£6.95**

BLACKBROOK TQ1846 **Plough** (01306) 886603 Popular pub with award-winning hanging baskets and window-boxes, a no smoking red saloon bar and public bar with a formidable collection of ties, old saws on the ceiling, and flat irons and bottles, and generous helpings of good imaginative food inc popular curry evenings; very friendly service from smart staff, 16 wines by the glass, and well kept real ales; pretty cottagey garden with Swiss play house for children; cl 25–26 Dec, 1 Jan; limited disabled access. £18.85|**£6.95**

COMPTON SU9547 **Teashop** *Down Lane* (01483) 811030 Well liked cottagey teashop doing morning coffee, light lunches and afternoon tea, home-made cakes, scones and jams, free range eggs, a wide range of drinks inc interesting juices, seltzers, and fruity mineral waters, lots of Indian, Chinese, herbal and fruit teas, and different coffees; cl 24 Dec–6 Jan; partial disabled access|**£3.50**

DORKING TQ1649 **Partners & Sons Restaurant** *2–4 West St* (01306) 882826 Heavily beamed 16th-c building with dining rooms on two floors, very good imaginative modern cooking, and a thoughtful wine list; delicatessen and cookery school, too; cl Sun, Mon, Sat am; disabled access. £42

ELSTEAD SU9043 **Woolpack** *Milford Rd* (01252) 703106 Cheerfully old-fashioned pub, bustling and friendly, with generous helpings of good interesting, regularly changing bar food, a fair amount of wool trade memorabilia, open fires, well kept real ales, and play area in garden; cl 25–26 Dec; children in family room or dining room only. £18.50|**£5.75**

LINGFIELD Hare & Hounds *Lingfield Common Road* (01342) 832351 Homely country local with a light, airy open-plan smallish bar (soft lighting and nightlights in the evening), bare boards and flagstones, an informal variety of scatter-cushioned dining chairs and other seats around a mix of tables, lots of chatty, happy customers, black and white pictures of jazz musicians, and piped jazz; quieter dining area with big abstract-expressionist paintings, a wide range of good imaginative food using local produce, well kept real ales, decent wines, and quick, friendly service; tables out in a pleasant split-level garden, some on decking, and nice surrounding walks. £21.95|£7.95

MICKLEHAM TQ1753 **King William IV** *Byttom Hill (01372) 372590* Relaxed and unpretentious pub cut into the hillside with fine views from the snug front bar, a spacious back bar with log fires and fresh flowers, wide range of interesting daily specials inc good vegetarian choice, well kept ales, lovely terraced garden, and nice walks; cl 25 Dec, pm 31 Dec; children over 12. £22.35|£7.50

RIPLEY TQ0556 **Michels** *The Clock House (01483) 224777* Charming Georgian house with carefully cooked seasonal food (inc some unusual dishes), a good range of wines, and courteous, helpful service; cl Sat am, Sun pm, Mon; 2 wks Jan, 10 days Aug; children welcome Sun am. £50/£21 lunch

SHERE TQ0747 **Kinghams** *Gomshall Lane (01483) 202168* Beamed 17th-c cottage with a relaxed atmosphere, unpretentious surroundings, cheerful service, good sound cooking from a shortish menu inc daily fish dishes and vegetarian choices, and nice puddings; cl 25 Dec–3 Jan; Mon, Sun pm; disabled access. £35|£9.95

TADWORTH TQ2356 **Gemini** *28 Station Approach Rd (01737) 812179* Bustling and popular local restaurant with very good modern cooking using influences from all over the world, super puddings, a mainly French wine list, and courteous service; cl Sat am, Sun pm, Mon, 2 wks Christmas; children under 12 lunchtime only; disabled access. £39

WEST END SU9460 **Inn at West End** *42 Guildford Rd (01276) 858652* Open-plan roadside dining pub with constantly changing, consistently good food inc lots of fresh fish, and friendly efficient service; smart line of dining tables, crisp linen, attractive modern prints on canary yellow walls, also chatty bar area with plenty of pale woodwork and woodburner, tiled garden room and pleasant garden; good drinks inc espresso machine and good value champagne by the glass (landlord is a wine merchant, and can also supply by the case), daily papers. £30|£6.75

Special thanks to Michael and Jenny Back, B and K Hypher

SUSSEX

All the ingredients for a rewarding holiday, from the buzz of Bohemian Brighton and some great family days out to quieter pleasures – stunning gardens, noble houses, attractive scenery

Top of a tremendously varied list of things to do and see, Bodiam Castle is our Sussex Family Attraction this year. Other castles include splendid Arundel and ruinous Pevensey, while Newhaven Fort is brilliant for children to explore, with underground displays and re-creations. Historic houses with more of a grown-up appeal are beautiful Glynde Place, unusual Goodwood House, and the more intimate St Mary's House in Bramber. Readers of Kipling can look around his handsome home in Burwash, while fans of the Bloomsbury set will be keen to visit Charleston Farmhouse in Firle and Rodmell's Monks House. Fishbourne Roman Palace and the Roman Villa & Museum in Bignor are fascinating for anyone interested in Roman Britain, and for rather more recent history, head to pretty Battle.

The Weald & Downland Open-Air Museum in Singleton is ideal for a whole family day out (there's an open-air museum in Amberley as well). Drusillas Park zoo in pretty Alfriston and the friendly Seven Sisters Sheep Centre in East Dean are superb for children (other farm parks at Wisborough Green and Coombes). Halland, Earnley, Herstmonceux and Newhaven all have an entertaining mix of ingredients for family outings.

Sussex is home to some of Britain's finest gardens. Outstanding Wakehurst Place (administered by the Royal Botanic Gardens, with something to see all year round), Pashley Manor Gardens near Ticehurst (guaranteed to banish stress and strain), Leonardslee at Lower Beeding (wallaby and deer, and a collection of Victorian motorcars as well as beautiful gardens), romantic Nymans at Handcross, Borde Hill near Haywards Heath (lovely woodland walks), Great Dixter at Northiam (you can look round the house too) and Sheffield Park (especially lovely in autumn). Also in Sheffield Park is the beautiful Bluebell Line, the earliest preserved steam railway in Britain.

Top of a list of coastal resorts in Sussex is Brighton. With a lively, young feel, good museums, and interesting shops and cafés, there's a whole host of things to keep you busy even on a wet Sunday afternoon. Though more restrained, Eastbourne in summer (and Worthing too) is a popular choice for families. Picturesque Rye is ideal for a civilised afternoon; nearby Camber Sands is one of the best beaches in the area (Bognor Regis also has the draw of a sandy beach). Hastings has quite a bit to offer the day-tripper.

The Sussex countryside has very varied yet characteristic scenery: the South Downs, with attractive flint buildings and expansive views, culminating in Beachy Head and its nearby cliffs; the sparsely wooded high sandy heathland of the Ashdown Forest; and the intricate landscapes of

The Weald. Much of the coast is developed, but the great sea inlet of Chichester Harbour has some very attractive places along its shore. Chichester itself has plenty to see in and around it.

Sussex has a good network of country walks; trails along the Saxon Shore and a 1066 Country Walk are noted in a free brochure, *Walk South East England*, available from most Tourist Information Centres here (and also in Kent and Surrey). A 90-mile High Weald Landscape Trail, running from Horsham to Rye and crossing four counties, includes both trailside accommodation and transport links for day-walkers. A booklet (£8) is available from bookshops and Tourist Information Centres, or phone (01622) 221526.

Quite a few of the places we recommend to stay at here are fine buildings in their own right.

Where to stay

ALFRISTON TQ5203 **George** *High St, Alfriston, Polegate, East Sussex BN26 5SY* *(01323) 870319* **£60**; 7 rms. 14th-c timbered inn opposite the intriguing façade of the Red Lion, with massive low beams hung with hops, appropriately soft lighting, a log fire (or summer flower arrangement) in a huge stone inglenook, lots of copper and brass, plenty of sturdy stripped tables, and a thriving atmosphere; popular home-made food, a cosy candlelit restaurant, nice breakfasts, well kept real ales, and a jovial landlord; seats out in the charming flint-walled garden behind; dogs welcome in bedrooms

AMBERLEY TQ0213 **Amberley Castle** *Church St, Amberley, Arundel, West Sussex BN18 9ND (01798) 831992* **£155**; 19 very well equipped charming rms. Magnificent 900-year-old castle with suits of armour and weapons in the day rooms – as well as antiques, roaring fires and panelling; friendly service, imaginative food in no smoking 13th-c dining room, and exceptionally pretty gardens; children over 12

ARLINGTON TQ5507 **Bates Green** *Tye Hill Rd, Arlington, Polegate, East Sussex BN26 6SH (01323) 482039* **£65**; 3 rms. Originally an 18th-c gamekeeper's cottage, now a no smoking farmhouse on a 123-acre sheep farm; beams and log fire in oak-panelled sitting room, tea and home-made cake on arrival, and big breakfasts with home-made preserves; sizeable plantsman's garden (open under the National Gardens Scheme), and a fine wood with lovely May bluebells and plenty of wildlife; cl Christmas; children over 10

BATTLE TQ7714 **Little Hemingfold Hotel** *189 Hastings Rd, Battle, East Sussex TN33 0TT (01424) 774338* **£88***, plus special breaks; 12 rms. Partly 17th-c, partly early Victorian farmhouse in 40 acres of woodland, with trout lake, tennis, gardens, and lots of walks (the two Labradors may come with you); comfortable sitting rooms, open fires, restful atmosphere and very good food using home-grown produce at own candlelit table; tennis court; children over 7; cl 2 Jan–13 Feb; dogs welcome in bedrooms

BATTLE TQ7414 **Powder Mills** *Powdermill Lane, Battle, East Sussex TN33 0SP (01424) 775511* **£105**, plus special breaks; 40 rms, some in annexe. Attractive 18th-c creeper-clad manor house in 150 acres of park and woodland with four lakes and outdoor swimming pool, and next to the 1066 Battlefield; country-house atmosphere, log fires and antiques in elegant day rooms, attentive service, and good modern cooking in Orangery restaurant; children over 10 in evening restaurant; well behaved dogs by prior arrangement; disabled access; dogs welcome

BOSHAM SU8004 **Millstream** *Bosham Lane, Bosham, Chichester, West Sussex PO18 8HL (01243) 573234* **£130**; 35 rms. Warmly friendly hotel in charming waterside village, with attractive bar and sitting room, open fire and fresh flowers, very good food using fresh local produce, good wine list, streamside garden; disabled access; dogs welcome in bedrooms

BRAMBER TQ1810 **Old Tollgate** *The Street, Bramber, Steyning, West Sussex BN44 3WE (01903) 879494* **£90.90**, plus special breaks; 31 spacious, smart rms. In a quiet village at the foot of the South Downs, this neatly kept hotel has comfortable public rooms, a popular carvery-style restaurant, tasty breakfasts, and helpful staff; no dogs; disabled access

BRIGHTON TQ3004 **Grand** *97–99 Kings Rd, Brighton, East Sussex BN1 2FW (01273) 321188* **£230**, plus special breaks; 200 handsome rms, many with sea view. Famous Victorian hotel with marble columns and floors and fine moulded plasterwork in the luxurious and elegant day rooms; good service, very good food and fine wines, popular afternoon tea in sunny conservatory, a bustling nightclub, and health spa with indoor swimming pool; disabled access; dogs welcome in bedrooms ☺

BRIGHTON TQ3004 **Topps** *16–17 Regency Sq, Brighton, East Sussex BN1 2FG (01273) 729334* **£84**; 15 lovely comfortable rms, 11 with gas-effect coal fires and many with sea view. Carefully furnished and immaculately kept Regency town house nr seafront with thoughtful, attentive service, good breakfasts in attractive basement room, and a library/reception room; disabled access

CHARLTON SU8812 **Woodstock House** *Charlton, Chichester, East Sussex PO18 0HU (01243) 811666* **£76**; 12 rms. 18th-c country house close to Goodwood with a relaxed atmosphere, log fire in homely sitting room, cocktail bar, imaginative food in attractive dining room (also open to non-residents), and sun-trap courtyard garden; lots to see nearby and plenty of downland walks

CHICHESTER SU8604 **Suffolk House** *East Row, Chichester, West Sussex PO19 1PD (01243) 778899* **£95**, plus winter breaks; 11 rms, some overlooking garden. Friendly Georgian house in centre and close to the cathedral, with homely comfortable lounge, little bar, traditional cooking in no smoking restaurant, good breakfasts, and small walled garden; disabled access; dogs by arrangement

CLIMPING TQ0000 **Bailiffscourt** *Climping St, Climping, Littlehampton, East Sussex BN17 5RW (01903) 723511* **£160**, plus special breaks; 32 rms, many with four-poster beds and winter log fires, and with super views. Mock 13th-c manor built only 60 years ago but with tremendous character – fine old iron-studded doors, huge fireplaces, heavy beams and so forth – in 30 acres of coastal pastures and walled gardens: elegant furnishings, enjoyable modern English and French food, fine wines, a relaxed atmosphere, and outdoor swimming pool, tennis and croquet; children over 7 in restaurant; disabled access; dogs welcome away from restaurant

CUCKFIELD TQ3024 **Ockenden Manor** *Ockenden Lane, Cuckfield, Haywards Heath, West Sussex RH17 5LD (01444) 416111* **£150**, plus special breaks; 22 individually decorated, pretty rms. Dating from 1520, this carefully extended manor house has antiques, fresh flowers and an open fire in the comfortable sitting room, good modern cooking in fine panelled restaurant, cosy bar, and super views of the South Downs from the neatly kept garden (in nine acres)

EAST GRINSTEAD TQ3634 **Gravetye Manor** *Gravetye Manor Vowels Lane, East Grinstead, West Sussex RH19 4LJ (01342) 810567* **£222**; 18 lovely rms. Elizabethan manor house in magnificent grounds and gardens and run for four decades by the Herbert family; antiques, fine paintings, and lovely flower arrangements in spacious panelled public rooms, an excellent restaurant offering superb food using home-grown produce (inc spring water and free-range eggs) and their own home-smoked fish and meats, an exceptional wine list, exemplary service, and a relaxed, almost old-fashioned atmosphere; children over 7 (but babies welcome); restaurant cl pm 25 Dec to non-residents

EAST HOATHLY TQ5116 **Old Whyly** *Halland Rd, East Hoathly, Lewes, East Sussex BN8 6EL (01825) 840216* **£110**; 3 rms. Handsome 17th-c manor house in lovely garden with tennis court and swimming pool and very close to Glyndebourne (hampers can be provided), fine antiques and paintings, delicious food inc super breakfasts with their own honey and eggs; plenty of walks nearby; children must be well behaved

EASTBOURNE TV6198 **Grand** *King Edward's Parade, Eastbourne, East Sussex BN21 4EQ (01323) 412345* **£165**, plus special breaks; 152 rms, many with sea views. Gracious and very well run Victorian hotel, with spacious, comfortable lounges, lots of fine original features, lovely flower arrangements, imaginative food in elegant restaurants, and courteous helpful service; leisure club and outdoor pool and terraces; disabled access ☺

ETCHINGHAM TQ6828 **King John's Lodge** *Sheepstreet Lane, Etchingham, East Sussex TN19 7AZ (01580) 819232* **£70***; 4 rms. Jacobean house in lovely 4-acre gardens – wonderful views, romantic and secret gardens, a wild garden with rose walk, white garden, and lily pond – plants and statuary for sale; guests' private sitting room, stone-mullioned windows, heavy beams and inglenook fireplaces, breakfasts served in Elizabethan dining room (on terrace in fine weather), and evening meals by arrangement; swimming pool, tennis court and croquet; cl Christmas and New Year; children over 7

FAIRLIGHT TQ8611 **Fairlight Cottage** *Warren Rd, Fairlight, Hastings, East Sussex TN35 4AG (01424) 812545* **£50**, plus winter breaks; 3 rms, one with four-poster. Comfortable and very friendly no smoking house in fine countryside with views over Rye Bay and plenty of rural and clifftop walks; big comfortable lounge (nice views), good breakfasts in elegant dining room or on new balcony, and generous carefully prepared food (by prior arrangement, but not at Christmas); children over 7; dogs welcome

FITTLEWORTH TQ0118 **Swan** *Lower St, Fittleworth, Pulborough, West Sussex RH20 1EL (01798) 865429* **£60**; 15 rms. Attractive 14th-c inn with big inglenook log fire in comfortable lounge, friendly service, enjoyable food in beamed restaurant, attractive panelled side room, and sheltered back lawn; good nearby walks; cl 25–26 Dec

FRANT TQ5935 **Old Parsonage** *Church Lane, Frant, Tunbridge Wells, Kent TN3 9DX (01892) 750773* **£84***, plus special breaks; 4 very pretty rms, 2 with four-posters. Just two miles from Tunbridge Wells, this carefully restored imposing former Georgian rectory has antiques, watercolours and plants in elegant sitting rooms, a spacious Victorian conservatory, good food in candlelit dining room, and balustraded terrace overlooking quiet 3-acre garden; several nearby walks; children over 7; dogs welcome in bedrooms

HARTFIELD TQ4837 **Bolebroke Mill** *Perry Hill, Edenbridge Rd, Hartfield, East Sussex TN7 4JP (01892) 770425* **£66**, plus special breaks; 5 rms, some in the mill and some in adjoining Elizabethan miller's barn. A working mill until 1948, this ancient place was mentioned in Domesday Book, and is surrounded by mill streams and woodland; the internal machinery has been kept intact and steep narrow stairs lead to bedrooms that were once big corn bins; both this and the barn have their own sitting room, breakfasts are marvellous (good nearby pubs and restaurants for other meals), and the owners very friendly; no smoking; cl 20 Dec–12 Feb; children over 8

LEWES TQ4109 **Shelleys** *High St, Lewes, East Sussex BN7 1XS (01273) 472361* **£180**, plus special breaks; 19 pretty rms. Once owned by relatives of the poet, this stylish and spacious 17th-c town house is warm and friendly, with good food, nice breakfasts and bar lunches in elegant dining room, and seats in the quiet back garden; limited disabled access

MAYFIELD TQ5826 **Middle House** *High St, Mayfield, East Sussex TN20 6AB (01435) 872146* **£65**; 6 spacious rms, 4 have been extensively refurbished this year. Old-world Elizabethan hotel nr church, with lovely panelled restaurant, red leather chesterfields and armchairs by cosy log fire, chatty locals' bar with big open fire (maybe spit roasts), a wide choice of good interesting bar food, an attractive back garden, and pleasant views; cl 24–26 Dec

PEASMARSH TQ8823 **Flackley Ash** *Peasmarsh, Rye, East Sussex TN31 6YH*

(01797) 230651 **£124**; 45 rooms. Attractive and extended Georgian house in 5 acres of landscaped gardens with croquet and putting; good, nicely presented food using local produce in the conservatory or dining room, log fire in lounge bar, and indoor heated pool and leisure centre; dogs welcome in bedrooms

PETWORTH SU9719 **Old Railway Station** *Station Rd, Petworth, West Sussex GU28 0JF (01798)* 342346 **£120***, plus special breaks; 6 rms, some in Pullman railway cars. Petworth's former railway station, carefully restored, with large lounge and dining area (the former waiting room with original ticket office windows), fine breakfasts, friendly owners, and terrace (once the platform) and garden; children over 10; disabled access

ROGATE SU8022 **Mizzards** *Rogate, Petersfield, Hampshire GU31 5HS (01730)* 821656 **£62**; 3 rms. 16th-c house in quiet country setting with a comfortable and elegant sitting room, enjoyable breakfasts in vaulted dining room, outside swimming pool, attractive landscaped gardens and lake, and fine farmland views; no evening meals; no smoking; cl Christmas; children over 9

RUSHLAKE GREEN TQ6218 **Stone House** *Rushlake Green, Heathfield, East Sussex TN21 9QJ (01435)* 830553 **£145**; 7 rms, some with four-posters. In a thousand acres of pretty countryside (with plenty of walks and country sports) and surrounded by an 18th-c walled garden, this lovely house was built at the end of the 15th c and extended in Georgian times; there are open log fires, antiques and family heirlooms in the drawing room, a quiet library, an antique full-sized table in the mahogany-panelled billiard room, wonderful food in the panelled dining room, fine breakfasts, and a cosseting atmosphere; cl 24 Dec–1 Jan; children over 9; dogs welcome in bedrooms

RYE TQ9120 **Jeakes House** *Mermaid St, Rye, East Sussex TN31 7ET (01797)* 222828 **£84**; 12 rms overlooking the rooftops of this medieval town or across the marsh to the sea, 10 with own bthrm. Fine 16th-c building, well run and friendly, with good breakfasts, lots of well worn books, comfortable furnishings, linen and lace, a warm fire, and lovely peaceful atmosphere; children over 11; dogs welcome in bedrooms

RYE TQ9220 **Little Orchard House** *West St, Rye, East Sussex TN31 7ES (01797)* 223831 **£70**; 2 four-poster rms. Beautifully furnished fine old house with antiques and personal prints and paintings, Georgian panelling, big open fireplace in study, good generous breakfasts (the friendly owners will make evening reservations at any of the many nearby restaurants), and an unexpectedly wonderful secluded garden; children over 12

RYE TQ9220 **Old Vicarage** *66 Church Sq, Rye, East Sussex TN31 7HF (01797)* 222119 **£84**, plus bargain breaks; 4 pretty rms with newspaper and glass of sherry, and two rooms carefully redecorated this year. Charming quietly placed mainly 18th-c house with helpful friendly owners, comfortable sitting room or small library, log fire in elegant dining room, and marvellous breakfasts with freshly baked breads, free-range eggs, and home-made jams, jellies and ketchups; no smoking; cl 23–27 Dec; children over 8

SHIPLEY TQ1523 **Goffsland Farm** *Shipley Rd, Southwater, Horsham, West Sussex RH13 7BQ (01403)* 730434 **£44**; 2 rms, 1 family rm with own sitting/dining rm and own access. 17th-c Wealden farmhouse on 260-acre family farm with good breakfasts, afternoon tea and evening meals by arrangement, and a friendly welcome; horse-riding and plenty of surrounding walks; dogs welcome

SLINFOLD TQ1131 **Random Hall** *Stane St, Slinfold, Horsham, West Sussex RH13 7QX (01403)* 790558 **£86**, plus special breaks; 13 comfortable rms. Restored 16th-c farmhouse with lots of beams, flagstones, copper and brass in lounge, a friendly relaxed atmosphere, good breakfasts, and cocktail bar; cl 24 Dec–8 Jan; disabled access

TILLINGTON SU9622 **Horse Guards** *Tillington, Petworth, West Sussex GU28 9AF (01798)* 342332 **£75**; 3 spacious clean rms. Prettily set 18th-c dining pub in lovely village setting with neatly kept and cosy beamed front bar, imaginative restaurant-style food, 10 wines by the glass, and real ales; children must be over 7 in evening restaurant; dogs allowed if well behaved

UCKFIELD TQ4718 **Horsted Place** *Little Horsted, Uckfield, East Sussex TN22 5TS (01825) 750581* **£145**, plus special breaks; 20 individually decorated spacious rms. Stately Victorian country house on extensive estate, with antiques, flowers and log fires in luxurious drawing rooms, delicious food and good wine list in no smoking dining room, and croquet and tennis; reduced green fees at East Sussex National Golf Club; cl early Jan; children over 7; disabled access

WISBOROUGH GREEN TQ0625 **Old Wharf** *Wharf Farm, Wisborough Green, Billingshurst, West Sussex RH14 0JG (01403) 784096* **£75**; 3 rms with views over farmland and canal. Carefully restored no smoking canal warehouse with fine old hoist wheel, comfortable sitting room with log fire, breakfasts using free-range eggs from the farm, walled canalside garden, and friendly atmosphere; cl Christmas and New Year; children over 12

To see and do

Sussex Family Attraction of the Year

BODIAM TQ7825 **Bodiam Castle** Children love coming to Bodiam, a proper picture-book castle, with its exterior still virtually complete. It's a classic example of 14th-c fortification at its peak, with massive walls rising sheer from the romantic moat, and round drum towers steadfastly guarding each corner. You can rush through in an hour, but some families stretch it out much longer, a visit's length bound only by the limits of the imagination. Built to withstand attack from the French, it was only ever besieged by other Englishmen, and on both occasions was rather weedily handed over without a fight. The interior was destroyed around the time of the Civil War, and wasn't repaired until Lord Curzon bought it in 1916; he left the castle to the National Trust in 1925. It's great fun climbing the spiral staircases up to the battlements (splendid view from the top), and there are plenty of mysterious nooks and crannies along the way. Also, a couple of short films on medieval castle life, and lots of space for picnics. You can buy various quiz sheets for children. They have several enjoyable special events, and you'll find extra activities in the summer holidays (including costumed interpreters at weekends), but it can get busy then; visiting out of season can be more gripping as well as less crowded. It's worth reading the leaflet and map they give you on arrival at the car park, otherwise you won't realise that the lavatories are at this end and not near the castle itself, so you'll have to trudge the quarter of a mile back again. Dogs are welcome on a lead in the grounds, though not in the castle itself. Meals, snacks, shop, limited disabled access (the ground is uneven); cl wkdys Nov to mid-Feb; (01580) 830436; £2 car park charge, then the castle is £3.90 for adults, and £1.95 children; National Trust members free. The family ticket is good value: £9.75 for two adults and three children. In summer you can put together a very enjoyable full day out by taking the 45-minute boat trip to the castle through peaceful countryside from Newenden (they don't run in bad weather); (01797) 280363 for times. And the **Kent & East Sussex Railway** (see Tenterden entry in our Kent chapter) now runs steam trains to Bodiam's restored station.

ALFRISTON TQ5102
In a sheltered spot below the downs, and with inviting paths along the Cuckmere River, this is one of the south-east's showcase villages – at quieter times of year (in high summer the ice-cream eaters, teashops and curio shops somewhat blunt its appeal). It has thatched, tiled and timbered houses, and a fine **church** built on a Saxon funeral barrow, by a large green just off the single main street. One of the most engaging buildings in the village is the Star Inn, with its Old Bill, a

bright red figurehead lion on one corner taken as a trophy from a 17th-c Dutch ship, and some intricate painted 15th-c carvings among its handsome timbering. The George and Market Cross are good for lunch. All alone just E of the village is **Lullington church**, a tiny fragment of a building with scarcely enough space for a congregation of 15. Just over a mile S of Alfriston, the road gives good views of the famous Cuckmere meanders.

Clergy House (The Tye) This thatched, half-timbered 14th-c cottage was in 1896 the first building to be taken over by the National Trust. Carefully restored, it now tells a story of medieval life and building methods; charming cottage garden. Shop; cl Tues, also Fri (Mon instead 12 Nov–21 Dec), wkdys till mid-Mar, and all 22 Dec–Feb; (01323) 870001; £2.80; NT.

Drusillas Park (up towards A27) They keep only animals that they can provide with everything they'd have in the wild, so no lions, tigers or elephants, but plenty of smaller and arguably more entertaining creatures. You watch the meerkats through a little dome, there's a walk-through fruit bat enclosure, and Penguin Bay has underwater viewpoints. Elsewhere is everything from snakes and other creepy-crawlies to a splendid range of monkeys. There's a farmyard area, and Pet World gives younger visitors a chance to get close to rabbits, chinchillas and perhaps even snakes. The play areas are excellent, a jolly little railway chuffs its way around the park, and they have recently added a paddling pool and sand play area. Some of the extras have an additional charge: an activity centre open at wknds and in school holidays costs from £1 an activity; also £2 for face-painting, £2 for miniature golf, £1.50 to pan for gold, and 50p for the bouncy castle. Good meals and snacks, picnic areas, shops, excellent disabled access (there's also a sensory trail); cl 24–26 Dec; (01323) 874100; £8.99.

English Wine Centre (up by A27) Good cross-section of wines made in this country, as well as regional foods and crafts. Shop, disabled access; cl 23 Dec–2 Jan; (01323) 870164; free, tours (of vineyard and beyond) and tastings from £5.75.

AMBERLEY TQ0212
Tucked beneath the South Downs, an enchantingly peaceful thatched village, facing the **Wild Brooks**, a large expanse of watermeadows which form an important habitat for wetland plants and birds. Its imposing castle is now a good hotel, not that easy to see, though you can peer into it from the churchyard. There's enjoyable food in the unspoilt Black Horse, and the Sportsman (lovely downs views).

Amberley Working Museum (by Amberley Stn) A carefully thought-out open-air museum covering 36 acres of former chalk quarry and limeworks, with plenty of traditional crafts and re-created workshops. Lots going on, from pottery and cobbling to a working village telephone exchange. Meals, snacks, shop, disabled access; cl Mon and Tues (exc school or bank hols), and mid-Nov to mid-Mar; (01798) 831370; £6.75. The riverside Bridge Inn at nearby Houghton Bridge is great in summer; the B2139 is a pleasant drive.

ARDINGLY TQ3431
Wakehurst Place Garden (B2028 towards Turners Hill) The 'Kew in the Country', administered by the Royal Botanic Gardens and the most visited National Trust site, with a tremendous variety of interesting trees and shrubs inc many tender rarities. Lakes and water gardens, steep Himalayan glade, woodland walks and fine rhododendron species. Plenty to see throughout the year, and all very peaceful. The building of the Millennium Seed Bank houses one of the largest international conservation projects ever undertaken, to safeguard over 24,000 plant species from around the world against extinction, and to secure the future of Britain's flowering plants; an interactive exhibition tells you more about the scheme. Meals, snacks, plant and book sales, disabled access; cl 25 Dec, 1 Jan; (01444) 894004; £6.50 (free to NT members). Guided walks usually start in front of the mansion at 11.30am and 2.30pm (2pm in winter) most days; (01444) 894004 to check; £1 extra. The Gardeners Arms (children in garden only), Oak and Ardingly Inn do good

lunches. Nearby **Ardingly Reservoir** offers pleasant strolls by its shores, or you can seek out the restored **Ouse Valley Viaduct**, an astonishing railway-age span carrying the London to Brighton line, best appreciated from below (access by path nr road SE of Balcombe).

ARUNDEL TQ0107
Decidedly French-looking from a distance, with its spikily Gothic revival Roman Catholic **cathedral** and vast **castle** dominating the hilltop town. A fine range of historic buildings line the steep High St and side streets, with antiques shops to browse around, and a local history museum (High St; cl Sun am, and Oct–Mar; £1). The Swan has decent food. There's scope for walking straight out of town into some choice countryside within a few minutes – along the canalised River Arun, or past the lakes in Arundel Park and up on to the South Downs. Or you can take a boat trip from the town quay with Skylark River Cruises; (01903) 717337.
Arundel Castle ⊞ Seat and home of the Dukes of Norfolk and their ancestors for nearly a thousand years – a magnificent sight, a great spread of well kept towers and battlements soaring above the village and the trees around it. The keep and the curtain wall are the oldest parts; the rest dates mainly from the 19th c. Excellent art collection, inc portraits by Van Dyck, Gainsborough and Canaletto, as well as 16th-c furniture, and personal possessions of Mary, Queen of Scots; the library is a highlight, and there are Victorian flower and vegetable gardens. Snacks, shop, limited disabled access; cl am, Sat, Good Fri and all Nov–Mar; (01903) 883136; £8.50.
Wildfowl & Wetlands Trust ⊞ (Mill Rd) Over 60 acres of well landscaped pens, lake, and paddocks, home to over a thousand ducks, geese and swans from all over the world inc rare species; hides overlook the various habitats. They've recently added a children's discovery trail, reed bed boardwalk, and a wildlife art gallery; children's activities in school hols. Meals, snacks, shop, disabled access; cl 25 Dec; (01903) 883355; £5.50. The lane past the Trust ends at a little

cluster of houses by an isolated church and former watermill. On the way to the Trust, the Black Rabbit has a superb location and does food.

ASHDOWN FOREST TQ4832
A surprisingly wild place for Sussex: partly wooded, but predominantly hilly, rolling heathland punctuated by clumps of Scots pines – instantly familiar from the E H Sheppard drawings for A A Milne's *Winnie the Pooh* stories. Five Hundred Acre Wood is the Hundred Acre Wood of Pooh's world, and with a little searching you can find, SW of Hartfield, the reconstructed Poohsticks Bridge made from locally grown oak and, by the B2026, Gills Lap (the 'enchanted place' at the top of the forest, near Piglet's house), where a memorial to Milne has been placed near the triangulation point. There's free access for walkers to all the paths (far more exist than are shown on OS maps); the useful 1:30,000 scale walkers' map issued by the Ashdown Forest Centre shows all the paths and rides as well as naming the car parks – extremely helpful given the forest's lack of other landmarks, though for longer walks you may need a compass. Handy pubs for forest walks include the Foresters Arms at Fairwarp and Hatch at Colemans Hatch. To the N, the attractive village of **Hartfield** has Pooh Corner (a shop with the world's widest range of Pooh-related items), an unusual station conversion (now the village play group) and a good food pub, the Anchor. On the W side of the Forest, **Nutley windmill** was saved by enthusiastic locals; usually open pm last Sun of month Mar–Sept, 2nd Sat and Sun in May (also most Weds); (01825) 762341; free.

BARCOMBE MILLS TQ4316
One of Sussex's secrets, with lazy riverside walks (or rowing boat hire) from the tucked-away Anchor pub here.

BATTLE TQ7515
Takes its name from certainly the most celebrated and perhaps the most disorganised skirmish in English history, thrashed out here in 1066. The main street (carrying a fair bit of traffic, so not exactly peaceful) has a lot of attractive old buildings, several housing

antiques shops and cafés; beyond them the town extends into spreading new estates. The **church** of St Mary has some 13th-c wall paintings, and the Squirrel (A269) has generous cheap home cooking and a big family garden.
Battle Abbey The **battlefield** has a mile-long walk around it with a good audio tour explaining what happened. Four years after the bloodshed William built an abbey on the site as penance, the altar reputedly on the very spot where Harold fell. Not much is left of the original building, but later remains include the monks' dormitory and common room, and the great 14th-c gatehouse which looms over the small market square. Snacks, shop, mostly disabled access; cl 24–26 Dec, 1 Jan; (01424) 773792; £4.50; EH.
Battle Museum of Local History (High St) From spring 2003, this good local history museum will have been rehoused in this ancient Almonry; displays include a diorama of the Battle of Hastings and a reproduction of the Bayeux Tapestry. Shop, disabled access; usually cl am Sun and all Nov–Mar, but best to check; (01424) 772210; £1. The little garden here is pretty.
Weald views The B2096 Heathfield road gives views S to Beachy Head from its highest points, near Netherfield and just before Dallington. Off this road any of the narrow side roads N into the countryside between Burwash and Dallington take you into the most unspoilt part of the steep Wealden woods and pastures.
Yesterday's World (High St) Carefully reconstructed period shops, railway station and the like; lots of hands-on activities, and mini golf. Snacks inc home-made fudge (summer only), shop; cl 25–26 Dec; (01424) 774269; £4.75.
BEACHY HEAD TV5997
Part of the county's best coastline, stretching W to the Seven Sisters and Cuckmere Haven; dizzying views from this towering, crumbly 163-metre (534-ft) sheer chalk cliff that constitutes the end of the South Downs, with the lighthouse dwarfed far below. It's easily reached from Eastbourne, and the eponymous hotel, open all day, has decent food.

BEXHILL TQ7407
A low-key seaside town with a pebble beach interrupted by cumbersome groins – an unlikely setting for a gem of Bauhaus architecture, the shoreside De La Warr Pavilion designed by Mendelsohn and Chermayeff. It's now an arts and social centre with changing exhibitions, events in the main hall, theatre, restaurant and pleasant sea-view café-bar upstairs. Usually open daily (free) though parts may be closed for refurbishments, which are due to finish summer 2004. The Italian-run café opposite is good value, and the town's junk shops are always worth a browse.
Bexhill Museum of Costume Set in the delightful grounds of the Old Manor House up towards the tiny 'Old Town', a good look at 18th- to 20th-c fashions, with accessories and other domestic items as well as the clothes. Shop, disabled access; cl am wknds, Weds, and all Nov–Mar; (01424) 210045; £2.
BIGNOR SU9814
Roman Villa & Museum One of the largest villas discovered so far, with marvellous mosaics housed in quaint thatched buildings erected by the farmer on whose land the site was found in 1811. One mosaic, 25 metres (82 ft) long and still in its original position, is the longest in Britain. Snacks, shop, some disabled access, and largely under cover; cl Mon (exc bank hols and May–Sept), and all Nov–Feb; (01798) 869259; £3.65. The White Horse at nearby Sutton has good food (and good value bedrooms), and the top of Bignor Hill (just S of the Villa; not signed) is excellent for picnics and views. Here you can follow Stane St, a highly evocative Roman road (now a path with some of the original ditch and surface in evidence), taking a strikingly straight course SW through attractive landscapes.
BIRDHAM SU8401
Sussex Falconry Centre (Lockacre Aquatic Nursery, Wophams Lane) Originally set up as a breeding and rescue centre, then opened to the public with birds such as falcons, hawks, eagles and owls flown throughout the day at 11.30, 1.30, and 3.30. Shop, disabled access; cl Mon (exc bank hols), and Oct–Easter; (01243) 512472; £4.

This area S of Chichester is flat country, full of nurseries and huge glasshouses; the Lamb towards West Wittering is a popular dining pub.

BODIAM TQ7825

Bodiam Castle See *separate family panel on p.594.*

The Curlew (B2244 just W) now has good food.

BOGNOR REGIS SZ9398

An old-fashioned seaside family resort, popular above all for its sandy beaches (they've recently added seafront showers). Its pier, one of the oldest, was originally 305 metres (1,000 ft) long, but has been shrinking – the pavilion end sank in 1965, and a 20-metre mid-section was swept away in a 1999 storm. Two museums share the same building on the High St: one has a wireless display of 40 years of valve radio, and the other contains local history inc some hands-on displays, and re-created street shops. Shop, disabled access; usually both cl Mon (exc bank hols), and Nov–end Mar; (01243) 865636; free. The Alex (London Rd) has good value food.

BOSHAM SU8004

The Saxon **church** here figures in the Bayeux Tapestry, and the village is a lovely cluster of old cottages around it, the green, and a broad, almost landlocked, inlet of Chichester harbour, busy with boating in the summer. Don't be tempted to park on the shore – the incoming tide is well known for its trick of lapping around parked cars. Very pleasant to stroll around, with good antique shops and craft galleries, esp on Bosham Lane. The White Swan up by the A259 roundabout has decent food.

BOXGROVE SU9007

Boxgrove Priory Now the parish church, this 12th-c building is one of the most outstanding Early English churches in the region, with a surprising 16th-c painted ceiling, free-standing chantry chapel, and the haunting remains of various monastic buildings outside. The Anglesey Arms at Halnaker has decent food.

BRAMBER TQ1810

St Mary's House Striking medieval house, with fine panelling, and an unusual Elizabethan painted room; there's a pretty garden with topiary.

Concerts in spring and autumn. Teas, shop; open pm Sun, and bank hols May–Sept; (01903) 816205; *£5. The Bramber Castle, named after the nearby castle ruin (free access, EH), has decent food. Adjacent Steyning has some of the best village streetscapes in Sussex, with particularly choice timber-framed and Georgian buildings, a museum, a pleasant Tudor pub (the Chequer), and a grand Norman church.

BRIGHTON TQ3104

A thriving resort as well as a big shopping town, Brighton owes some of its lively feel to two vigorous nearby universities and several language schools for foreign students; on hot days the seafront between the two piers becomes one huge open-air bar, thick with rollerbladers, drummers, beach volleyball players and hair-braiders. There's also a booming gay scene, and things really liven up during the massive three-week Brighton Festival in May. The city still has plenty of glistening white Regency buildings dating from its fashionable days in the 18th c, when the idea that sea-bathing was good for you sent London's finest scurrying to the coast. The oldest part is the (mostly pedestrianised) Lanes – 17th-c fishermen's cottages squeezed together in narrow twisting byways, now crammed with jewellery and antiques shops, restaurants and bars. English's here is entertaining for lunch. The North Laine area (SE of the station) is slightly more trendy, with good buskers, funky shops and cool cafés. Lots of money has been invested in regeneration projects: the Brighton Dome concert hall has recently reopened after a £30 million restoration, the Theatre Royal is being refurbished, and even the station has been smartened up. Throughout, there's no shortage of simple places to eat (notably in the Lanes, Preston St near the West Pier, and St James's St), inc the Cricketers (Black Lion St), Greys (Southover St, Kemp Town), and Basketmakers Arms (E end of Gloucester Rd). The George (Trafalgar St) is popular for its all-day organic vegetarian and vegan food, and the trendy Freemasons (Western Rd, Hove) has good contemporary food upstairs. The council are keen to improve access to the South Downs, and a new bus service may run to Devil's Dyke, and Ditchling Beacon; phone for information (01273) 292480.

Barlow Collection (University of Sussex, Falmer; off A27 N) Reckoned to be one of Europe's finest collections of Chinese ceramics. It's usually open 11.30–2.30 Tues and Thurs (exc Dec–Jan, Apr and Aug); (01273) 606755; free.

Booth Museum of Natural History (Dyke Rd) Wide-ranging collection of animal skeletons (inc some dinosaur bones), as well as the Victorian collection of birds the museum was first built to house. Shop, disabled access; cl Thurs, 25–26 Dec, 1 Jan and Good Fri; (01273) 292777; free.

Brighton Fishing Museum (Kings Rd) The seafront Arches across from the Old Ship Hotel used to be occupied by local fishermen. Though a couple still are, the rest are now given over to little craftshops and artists. One houses this collection of local boats, nets, models and pictures. Shellfish stall and fish smokery, shop, disabled access; cl 25–26 Dec, and any day Nov–Apr when the weather is poor; (01273) 723064; free.

Brighton Marina (E of centre) This modern place is lively in summer, with lots of boutiques, bars, tables out by the water and so forth. A waterfront entertainment centre includes a factory shopping outlet, bars and restaurants and a celebrity walk of fame, and there's a new casino here too. An electric train runs to here from Apr–Sept along the beach from the pier.

Brighton market On Sun mornings there's a good market in the station car park; do get there well before breakfast for the bargains, as it's become a major source of supply for the countless Brighton antiques dealers. Near here **St Bartholomew's church** (Anne St) is a strange Grade I listed building, like a huge brick barn, but supremely impressive inside. Film buffs will be well satisfied with the Duke of York's cinema at nearby Preston Circus, which shows the kind of movies not always found outside London.

Brighton Museum and Art Gallery (Church St) Reopened after a £10 million redevelopment, this outstanding museum (in the Prince Regent's stables, and riding school) now has new galleries on fashion, 20th-c design, and world art, as well as extensive art nouveau and art deco collections; also costume gallery, local history and interactive displays. A new entrance through the Pavilion gardens is a convenient link between museum and palace. Café, shop, disabled access; cl Mon (exc bank hols), am Sun, 24–26 Dec, and 1 Jan; (01273) 290900; free.

Brighton Toy and Model Museum ⊞ (Trafalgar St) Over 10,000 objects, from Victorian dolls to Meccano. Shop, disabled access; cl Sun, Mon (exc bank hols), phone for opening times over Christmas; (01273) 749494; £3.50.

British Engineerium ⊞ (Nevill Rd, Hove) All sorts of road, locomotive and marine steam engines, as well as tools and models in a restored Victorian water-pumping station. Shop, limited disabled access; cl wk before Christmas–26 Dec, engines in steam first Sun in month and bank hol Sun and Mon; (01273) 559583; £4.

Foredown Tower (Foredown Rd, Portslade) Very well done, with a **camera obscura** (best on bright days, shown on the hour) as well as astronomy displays, and splendid views. They can arrange visits to Portslade Old Manor, a ruined medieval house a short stroll away. Snacks, shop; cl Mon–Weds; (01273) 292092; £2.30.

Hove Museum and Art Gallery (New Church Rd) After extensive redevelopment (and now much more family-friendly) this grand Victorian villa is due to reopen early in 2003. There are new galleries for the collections of toys (the split child's bedroom, one half Victorian and the other contemporary, is thought-provoking), fine art, local history, there's an interactive early film gallery (with working optical toys, magic lanterns, cameras, and they'll be showing early films) and a contemporary craft gallery. Meals, snacks, shop, disabled access; cl Mon but best to phone; (01273) 290200; free.

Museum of Penny Slot Machines ⊞ (250C Kings Rd Arches) Nostalgic collection of over 50 vintage seaside amusements from penny slot-machines to strength-testers and fortune-tellers. Shop, disabled access; usually open wknd and school hol pms Easter–Aug, plus fine weather Sun pm in winter; free (charge for individual games – they change your money into old coins).

Palace Pier The hub of the seafront, Palace Pier is packed with the usual amusements, but also sports palmists' booths and the like; it looks magnificent at night. The sadly ruinous older West Pier, to the W, is Britain's only Grade 1 listed seaside pier, and is at last being restored.

Preston Manor (A23) Entertaining and vivid illustration of life in Edwardian times, with fully furnished period rooms; restored walled gardens with fish pond and a pets' cemetery. Shop; cl ams Sun and Mon, 25–26 Dec, Good Fri; (01273) 292770; £3.40.

Regency Town House Hove, the quieter half of the resort, is just W of Brighton proper. On the way you may be able to visit this Regency house in Brunswick Square – being restored, but they have regular open days – see their website www.rth.org.uk or phone for dates (01273) 206306; £2.50, £3 tours.

Royal Pavilion Nash's flamboyant Indian-style confection should be top of anyone's itinerary: the most eccentric of all Royal palaces, a riot of chinoiserie inside. Queen Victoria was the last monarch to own it, but was hardly its greatest fan; if the town council hadn't bought it from her she might well have demolished it. The interior has been restored to its full overblown glory, and the gardens have been returned to their original Regency layout. The whole building is beautifully floodlit at night. It's less busy after 3 o'clock – and better still out of season, when you may find more going on. Delightful upstairs tearoom overlooking garden, shop, disabled access to ground floor only; cl 25–26 Dec; (01273) 290900; £5.35.

Sea Life Centre (Marine Parade) Lively displays of British and tropical creatures inc rays, eels, seahorses, and even turtles (they plan to add an exhibition devoted to creatures with claws); also touch pools and a soft play area. Meals, snacks, shop, disabled access; cl 25 Dec; (01273) 604234; £6.99.

West Blatchington windmill (Holmes Ave, Hove) With local history displays; shop, disabled access, open pm Sun and bank hols May–Sept; (01273) 776017; 70p.

BURPHAM TQ0309
Great views from this attractive hill village (which sometimes surprises with the sight of buffalo), with pleasant walks from here along the river or through hilly Arundel Park into Arundel. The George & Dragon has good food.

BURWASH TQ6724
The single main street of this ridge village has many attractively restored tile-hung cottages, inc an antiques centre with a teashop, with lime trees along its brick pavement. The graveyard of the Norman-towered church gives fine views over the Dudwell Valley, and the flower-decked Bell is useful for lunch. Around here the intricate landscapes of the Sussex Weald show steep slopes and valleys, ancient woods and hedgerows punctuated by great oaks, pretty villages, tile-hung or weatherboarded oast houses and wood-and-tile barns with their long cats'-slide roofs.

Batemans (off A265) Handsome early 17th-c stone-built ironmaster's house, home to Rudyard Kipling 1902–1936. His study is kept much as it was then, as is the hefty pipework he installed for a pioneer hydro-electric lighting plant. The attractive gardens have a quaint operating watermill, grinding flour every Sat at 2pm (though as we went to press it and the millpond were awaiting overhaul, so phone to check it's open). Dog crèche, snacks, shop, disabled access to ground floor only; cl Thurs, Fri (exc Good Fri), and Oct–Feb; (01435) 882302; *£5.20 (*£2.60 1–23 Mar as only Wild Garden open then); NT. Good little-used walks up the wholly unspoilt valley from here, where you can look for Kipling landmarks such as Pook's Hill and Willingford Bridge (aka Weland's Ford).

CHANCTONBURY RING TQ1312
One of the great South Downs landmarks, a Romano-British temple site within an Iron Age earthwork, now

a prominent hilltop clump of trees: a bracing walk, best reached from Steyning (the Tudor Chequer has generous food) or Washington, or from Cissbury Ring.

CHICHESTER SU8504
Partly pedestrianised and easy to get around, this handsome former Roman city is one of the country's finest examples of Georgian town planning and architecture. The **South Downs Planetarium** (signposted from Kingsham Rd) has regular shows based around themes such as the northern lights; phone for times; (01243) 774400; £5. Useful central pubs for food are the Fountain (Southgate), Nags (St Pancras), Dolphin & Anchor (West St), and lively Toad (redundant church, West St).

Centurion Way This short stretch of disused railway track has been converted to an easy route for cyclists (and walkers) W of Chichester to Mid Lavant, where the Earl of March Arms has cheap generous food.

Chichester Cathedral Mostly Norman, and unusual for rising straight out of the town's streets rather than a secluded close. The spire collapsed in 1861 (the latest in a long line of structural problems), and was rebuilt, but even now the scaffolding always seems to be up as restoration work continues. Highlights include the 14th-c choir stalls, John Piper's Aubusson tapestry, and the window by Chagall. Guided tours (not Sun) at 11.15am and 2.30pm Easter–end Oct. Meals, snacks, shop in the medieval bell tower, disabled access; cl only for special services and events; (01243) 782595; £2 suggested donation. The Bishops Palace gardens are very pleasant.

Chichester District Museum (Little London) Enthusiastic local history museum in an 18th-c corn store, with some hands-on activities for children, changing exhibitions and regular events; cl Sun, Mon and bank hols; free.

Guildhall (Priory Park) began life as a 13th-c Greyfriars church, and later the poet William Blake was brought to trial here (1804); it now houses more local history items. Shop, disabled access; open pm Sat 7 Jun–13 Sept; (01243) 784683; free. The Park Tavern opposite has decent food.

Mechanical Music & Doll Collection (Church Rd, Portfield) A multitude of barrel, fair and Dutch street organs, music boxes and phonographs – all restored and ready to play. Shop, disabled access; open pm Weds Jun–Sept; (01243) 372646; £2.50.

Pagham Harbour (off B2145 S) Peaceful nature reserve, largely silted marshy tidal flats, full of wading birds and wildfowl, particularly in spring and autumn. Depending which side you approach from, the Lamb at Pagham and Crab & Lobster at Paglesham are both handy lunch stops.

Pallant House Gallery (North Pallant) Interesting Queen Anne town house with Edwardian kitchen and fine furnishings. The gallery has fine Bow porcelain, and an excellent range of carefully chosen 20th-c art – Sutherland, Moore, Piper, Nicholson and the like. Shop; cl Sun am, all day Mon (exc bank hols), 25–26 Dec; (01243) 774557; £4, children free.

St Mary's Hospital (St Martin's Sq) 13th-c hospital with a splendid tiled roof, unique misericords in its chapel, and a pretty walled garden; disabled access; open wkdys by appointment; (01243) 783377; donations.

CHICHESTER HARBOUR SU7702
The most attractive views for walkers are from the shoreside path which skirts the quiet unspoilt peninsulas of Thorney Island and Chidham.

Boat trips Peter Adams runs these around Chichester Harbour, full of yachts and dinghies in summer. They leave from Itchenor (where the Ship has good food) and are best at high tide; (01243) 786418; £5. There's also an hourly passenger ferry between here and the landing at the end of the lane S from Bosham (usually daily Jun–Aug, wknds only Apr, May and Sept).

East Head A NT-owned promontory on the E entrance of Chichester Harbour, a sandy spit with dunes overlooking the marshes and mudflats of the estuary.

CISSBURY RING TQ1308
Another of the great downland landmarks, a huge ramparted Iron Age hill peppered with much earlier flint mines, and good views over to the Isle of Wight (looking surprisingly near). It's

quite close to Findon, where the Gun is good for lunch. There's a pleasant walk from here to Chanctonbury Ring.

CLIMPING BEACH TQ0000
This allows an attractive few miles' walk; this bit of coast between Middleton-on-Sea and Littlehampton is the only appreciable undeveloped seaside stretch in W Sussex, apart from Chichester Harbour.

COOMBES TQ1908
Church Farm 🖾 Trailer rides over farmland and through conservation areas – you have to book, but it's great fun, especially in the lambing season. Snacks, shop, and they hope to improve disabled access; usually open daily Mar to mid-Apr, and Tues, Thurs and Sun at 2.30 in Aug, but best to check; (01273) 452028; *£4. They also have a coarse fishing lake.

DANEHILL TQ4026
Heaven Farm 🖾 (Furners Green, A275 S) A handy place for a relaxing easy-on-the-pocket afternoon, with an interesting 1½-mile nature trail (look out for the wallabies), and a farming museum spread over various 19th-c farm buildings. There's also an aviary, and lots of free-roaming poultry and game, plenty of space for picnics, and a caravan and camping site; fine views. Snacks, craft shop, mostly disabled access; usually open pm Tues–Thurs, Sun and bank hols Apr–Nov, nature trail open daily; (01825) 790226; £2.50 nature trail, £1 museum. The Coach & Horses in Danehill has good food.

DELL QUAY SU8303
Attractive waterside hamlet with remains of a Roman quay.

DITCHLING TQ3313
Ditchling Beacon Right by the road, with superb views all around, especially out over the villages and towns to the N; a nice walking area of preserved sheep-cropped unimproved downland, with chalk hill blue butterflies in summer. The village below is pleasant, with a tearoom, the 14th-c Bull, and a decent **museum** – inc displays on artist/typographer Eric Gill and other local craftsmen (shop, disabled access; usually cl Mon (exc bank hols) and mid-Dec to mid-Feb; £2.50). Developing **Stonywish Country Park** (East End Lane) has a little nature reserve with

some farm animals (and a new goat mountain), woodland walks, good play area; tearoom, shop, disabled access; open daily Mar–Oct, and most days in winter; (01273) 843498; £3. The B2116 to Offham has views of the South Downs, and off it the Jolly Sportsman at East Chiltington has very good food.

EARNLEY SZ8297
Earnley Gardens 🖾 (Almodington Lane) This five-acre site is quite a busy day out; as well as the 17 long-established themed gardens, exotic birds and free-flying butterflies, there's a shipwreck display, small animal farm, and a refreshingly informal nostalgia museum, Rejectamenta. This takes in thousands of everyday objects from the last 100 years, collected over 30 years by a former art student who says she just can't stop. Meals, snacks, shop, disabled access; open Mar–Oct; (01243) 512637; around £6 everything, £3.85 just gardens and butterflies or just nostalgia museum, £1.50 crazy golf.

EAST DEAN TV5597
Seven Sisters Sheep Centre 🖾 (Gilberts Drive) A particularly enjoyable and genuine place to visit, with 47 different types of sheep, some tame enough to touch and feed. There's a good commentary when the sheep are milked, demonstrations of yoghurt- and cheese-making, and daily shearing and wool handling displays. Other animals include pigs, horses, goats, chickens and ducks, with a barn where children can fuss rabbits, chinchillas and so on; a tractor/trailer ride across the farm is 50p extra. The best time of all is the Mar–May lambing season, when children can bottle feed the lambs. Snacks, shop (with products made from ewe's milk), good disabled access; usually open wkdy pms and all day wknds Mar to mid-May, then July to mid-Sept (all day in school hols), best to check; (01323) 423302; *£3.25. The village itself is prettily set around a sloping green, with an attractive pub, the Tiger. A lane past the farm continues to the **Birling Gap**, a cleft in the coastal cliffs famous since smuggling days, with walks up to Belle Tout, a former coastguard station and lighthouse moved back 17 metres (55 ft) in 1999 to save it from coastal

erosion, and on to Beachy Head.

EAST GRINSTEAD TQ3835

Standen (off B2110 W) A fine example of the many talents of the 19th-c Arts and Crafts Movement. Designed by Philip Webb (even down to the unusual light fittings), a friend of William Morris, and little changed since, the inside is decorated with several different William Morris wallpapers, and many of the furnishings are of the period. Meals, snacks, shop, limited disabled access; cl Mon (exc bank hols), Tues and Nov–Mar; (01342) 323029; £5.50, £3 garden only; NT.

EASTBOURNE TV6198

The Duke of Devonshire still owns much of this civilised seaside resort; as he prohibits seaside tat the place has a more dignified and solid feel than many of its livelier rivals – appealing to people who appreciate old-fashioned virtues. It's perfect for seafront strolling, and a promenade links the smart marina with the long shingle beach; there are good bandstand concerts in summer, and you can take a boat trip to Beachy Head. The **church** in the Old Town is lavish; next to it the Lamb is a nice old pub. The **Lifeboat Museum** (King Edward's Parade) makes up in enthusiasm what it lacks in size; (01323) 730717; shop, disabled access, cl Jan–Easter; free.

How We Lived Then 🖼 (Cornfield Terrace) One of the most comprehensive museum of shops we've come across, with 20 reconstructed shops and rooms on four floors, full of interest (they've over 100,000 exhibits), inc an old seafarers' tavern. Shop, disabled access to ground floor only; cl 24–26 Dec; (01323) 737143; £3.

Redoubt Fortress (Royal Parade) A splendid fort, housing a more interesting than average military museum. Open-air concerts (every Weds and Fri late Jun–early Sept) always end in a firework display. Shop; cl early Nov–Easter; (01323) 410300; £2.50.

Sovereign Park Shingle Nature Reserve Paths around an attractive stretch of shingle coastline, best between Easter and Jun, when most plants are in flower; Easter–autumn, a train connects this with the rest of the seafront. Some disabled access; open all year; (01323) 411400; free. There's a grassy picnic site at the W end.

Towner Art Gallery & Museum (High St, Old Town) Handsome 18th-c building, with mainly 19th- and 20th-c British art; also contemporary art, good temporary exhibitions and local history displays. Shop, disabled access; cl am, and all day Mon (exc some bank hols), 25–27 Dec, 1 Jan and Good Fri; (01323) 411688; free entry, charges for some exhibitions.

Wish Tower (King Edward's Parade) One of the 103 Martello Towers built in case of French invasion; there's a fascinating collection of puppets, some centuries old. Shop; usually open wknds Easter–Oct, plus wkdys mid-July to Aug; (01323) 411620; £1.80.

ETCHINGHAM TQ7126

Etchingham church Lovely sturdy ancient semi-fortified building in honey-coloured stone – quaintly, the station is built to match.

FERNHURST SU8928

Nicely varied surrounding countryside for walkers; much is densely wooded, but there are some chances to get out on to the open hillsides – as on Woolbeding Common and the S tip of Black Down. The prettily tucked-away Red Lion has good value food.

FIRLE TQ4707

A classic example of a living estate village (belongs to Firle Place), in a hidden corner off the A27, with a decent pub (the Ram). Firle Beacon, a South Downs landmark, is a lovely walk above the village (car park nearby, at top of hill), or you can walk along an easy track at the foot of the downs.

Berwick church 1940s murals by the Bloomsbury Group; the Cricketers Arms here is a good lunch place.

Charleston Farmhouse 🖼 (A27 Firle–Selmeston) Delightful 17th/18th-c house which was the home of Duncan Grant and Clive and Vanessa Bell; decorated by them, it and its magical garden still evoke the atmosphere of those Bloomsbury days. Teas, shop; cl am (exc July/Aug), Mon/Tues exc bank hols, and Nov–Easter, no guided tours Sun or bank hols; (01323) 811265; £6. Nr here at Alciston, the Rose Cottage has very good home cooking.

Firle Place 🖼 (off A27) Beautiful house, essentially Tudor but remodelled in the 18th c, with some real treasures of European and English painting, and wonderful furnishings. Meals, snacks, shop, disabled access to ground floor; cl am, and Mon, Tues, Fri and Sat (exc bank hols), also all Oct–late May; (01273) 858335; £5. There are longer unguided tours the first Thurs in the month, when more rooms are open (and the price is higher).

Middle Farm (A27 E) You can sample ciders straight from the barrel before buying (they call this the national collection of cider and perry); also farmhouse cheeses, English wines, good sausages, organic meats, and other produce. A children's farmyard has sheep, goats and other small animals (daily milking demonstrations), and there's a play area; lots going on at apple harvest time. Restaurant, bakery, plant and crafts shops, disabled access; cl 25–26 Dec; (01323) 811411; site free, £2 for farmyard.

FISHBOURNE SU8304
Roman Palace 🖼 (Salthill Rd) This magnificent villa with its 100 or so rooms was occupied from the 1st to the 3rd c, and is the largest known residence from the period in Britain. Some archaeologists now think the Romans first landed here (and not in Kent as was originally supposed), to reinstate the recently evicted king. They probably built his successor this place. You can see 25 mosaic floors (some are quite remarkable, and it's a bigger collection than anywhere else in Britain), and a garden has been laid out according to its 1st-c plan. Much of the palace is buried beneath nearby housing. Snacks, shop, disabled access; cl wkdys mid-Dec to Jan; (01243) 785859; £4.70. The Bulls Head has good food.

FLETCHING TQ4223
Attractive village – often Sussex's Best-Kept Village; and it has a charming waymarked Millennium Walk; the Griffin is a very good food pub.

FONTWELL SU9406
Denmans Garden (off A27) Colourful series of vistas over 3½ acres, inc exuberantly oriental-feeling areas with a gravel stream, ornamental grasses, bamboos and flowering cherries, as well as a beautiful richly

planted walled garden. Meals, snacks, plant sales, disabled access; cl Nov–Feb; (01243) 542808; £2.95. In the pretty nearby village of Eartham there is a small but charming church; the George there, open all day summer wknds, is an enjoyable dining pub.

GATWICK AIRPORT TQ2740
Skyview (S Terminal) Visitor gallery, with a multi-media show demonstrating a typical airport day, a good explanation of cockpit controls, and splendid runway views. Shop, disabled access; cl 25 Dec; (01293) 502244; £1.50.

GLYNDE TQ4509
Glynde Place 🖼 Elizabethan manor house in beautiful setting, extensively remodelled inside in the 18th c, but outside left pretty much unchanged. Portraits and mementoes give a good grounding in the family history, while outside are pleasantly wild parklands and lawns. Snacks, shop; open pm Weds, Sun and bank hols Jun–Sept, plus Thurs July–Aug – may vary, so phone to check; (01273) 858224; £5. There's a neat neo-Palladian **church** nearby, and the Trevor Arms has decent food. The Glyndebourne Festival, with its decidedly smart operas and marvellous auditorium designed by Sir Michael Hopkins, takes place May–Aug; tickets are very scarce, but it's always worth ringing on the day for returns, and you have a better chance of getting into the Touring Opera during the shorter (and cheaper) October season; (01273) 813813.

GOODWOOD SU8808
Goodwood House Unusual-looking flint building in beautiful downland countryside, especially renowned for its paintings, inc works by Canaletto and Stubbs. There's quite a riding feel – it was acquired by the first Duke of Richmond in 1697 so that he could ride with the local hunt, and the stables added during 18th-c alterations seem grander even than the house. The restored drawing room contains 18th-c French furniture. Snacks, shop, disabled access; open most pms Sun and Mon Apr–Sept (plus Tues–Thurs in Aug), best to check; (01243) 755040; £6.50. The adjacent **racecourse** is the setting for Glorious Goodwood, and around 19 race days a year; also monthly

antiques markets; (01243) 755022 for dates. The Royal Oak at East Lavant is a good nearby dining pub.

Sculpture at Goodwood (Hat Hill Copse, towards East Dean) Excellent changing exhibitions of sculpture in 20 acres of beautiful wooded parkland; it's established an excellent reputation in the few years it's been open, so it's a shame the high admission price limits it to people with more than just a passing interest in the subject. Shop, some disabled access; cl Sun–Weds (exc bank hol) and Nov–Mar; (01243) 538449; £10. This is a good area for a country drive; the Anglesey Arms at Halnaker has enjoyable food.

HADLOW DOWN TQ5323
Cabbages and Kings ⓔ Made by garden designer Ryl Nowell to show potential clients and interested gardeners how she solves design problems; interlinked contemporary gardens show a huge variety of features, and renovated farm buildings house an exhibition on garden design. Garden shop (with plants grown in their own nursery), snacks which you can have in the garden; limited disabled access; cl 25–26 Dec; (01825) 830552; £4.

Wilderness Wood (A272) 62 acres of working woodland, good for learning about forests and their wildlife, or for a pleasant stroll. Several picnic areas and play area, occasional demonstrations of heavy horses and other traditional woodland working methods, and a discovery trail for children; their bluebell walk during end Apr–May is popular. Teas and snacks, shop (they make chestnut furniture and other goods), disabled access; (01825) 830509; £2.50. Nearby Buxted has enjoyable food in the White Hart.

HAILSHAM TQ5709
Knockhatch Adventure Park (A22, W of Hailsham) Plenty to do in this 80-acre park which has a children's farm and birds of prey centre, adventure playgrounds, and more unusual attractions such as a laser adventure game (£3.25), and karting (£3.50). Also crazy golf, boating lake, woodland trail and picnic area, and now a new ski centre. Snacks, shop, disabled access; cl term-time wkdys, and all Nov–Jan; (01323) 442051; £6.20.

HALLAND TQ4815
Bentley Wildfowl & Motor Museum ⓔ Busy estate centred around Tudor farmhouse converted into Palladian mansion, filled with fine furnishings and paintings, inc watercolours by local artist Phillip Rickman. The motor museum has gleaming veteran, Edwardian and vintage vehicles, while the lakes and ponds that surround it are home to countless varieties of rare and exotic wildfowl. There are also woodland trails, a little adventure playground, on-site craftsmen and artists, and miniature trains that steam through the grounds (wknds Easter–Oct plus Weds in Aug). Special events (may be a charge) run from veteran and vintage car and other transport rallies to fire brigade and birds of prey displays. Snacks, shop, disabled access; cl Nov–Mar, house also cl am (but rest open wknds in Nov and Feb/Mar, daily from mid-Mar); (01825) 840573; £5.20, less winter. The Black Lion (A22/B2192) has decent food.

HANDCROSS TQ2629
Nymans Garden (B2114) Perhaps the most romantic of all Wealden gardens, rewarding at any time. Rare trees inc magnificent southern beeches and eucryphias, as well as fine camellias, rhododendrons and magnolias, countless other interesting flowering shrubs, a secluded sunken garden, and an extensive artfully composed wilderness. Meals, snacks, plant sales, shop, disabled access; cl Mon (exc bank hols), Tues, and wkdys Nov–Feb; (01444) 400321; £6.20; NT. The Wheatsheaf (B2110 W) has good food.

HASTINGS TQ8209
The seaside town has a really dramatic setting in the cliffs, unique in the south-east, with the aptly named Old Town huddled below the ruins of the castle. The labyrinth of alleys and stepped paths threading through its former fishermen's quarter make for highly enjoyable wandering, and it's refreshingly not over-tidy. Down below, the fishermen still haul their boats up on to the beach and sell excellent fresh fish by the unusual tall black wooden net huts. At each end of the cliffs is a steep funicular railway down to sea level (90p). The First In

Last Out in the Old Town has interesting food and brews its own beer. The rest of the town is a busy shopping town, rather run-down in parts, with 19th-c resort buildings nearer the seafront, seaside hotels and B&Bs, a good prom (with miles of cycle path), and shingle beach.

Clambers Play Centre (White Rock Gdns) Well kept indoor and outdoor activities for under-12s inc climbing frames, ball ponds, huge sand pit, paddling pool, play houses, and a separate play area for younger children – handy for a rainy day. Snacks (baby food available), and picnic tables, cl 25–26 Dec, and 1 Jan; (01424) 423778; £4.75 for 2 hrs for children, adults free. For those with energy still left, Hastings Adventure Golf next door is open daily in summer; £2.50.

Fairlight Cove A good destination for walks from Hastings Old Town, by a path climbing on to the sandstone cliffs for a rugged couple of miles; the tumbled appearance of the coast here bears witness to the occasional cliff-falls. The Cove Continental does enjoyable lunches.

Fishermen's Museum (Rock-a-Nore Rd) Interestingly housed in a former fishermen's church, and crammed full of stuff; the centrepiece is a 29-ft sailing lugger, there's a new audio-visual presentation, and a huge stuffed albatross. Shop, disabled access, cl 25 Dec; (01424) 461446; donations.

Hastings Castle Bracingly set above crumbling cliffs and the tracked lift, the evocative Norman ruins (which encompass, unusually, a collegiate church) are close to the site of William the Conqueror's first English motte and bailey castle. There's a lively audio-visual exhibition on the Battle of Hastings. Shop, some disabled access; cl 24–26 Dec; (01424) 781112; £3.20.

Hastings Museum and Art Gallery (Johns Pl, Bohemia Rd) A little out of the centre, but worth a look for its Native American displays; children may prefer the dinosaur gallery. Shop, limited disabled access; cl 25–26 Dec and Good Fri; (01424) 781155; free.

Shipwreck Heritage Centre (Rock-a-Nore Rd) Find out more about local wrecks, with lots of items brought up from the sea bed from wine bottles and muskets to a cabin boy's leg bones; also an audio-visual show, a few hands-on activities, and you can see radar and live satellite weather pictures. Shop, disabled access; cl a few days over Christmas; (01424) 437452; donations.

Smugglers Adventure (Cobourg Pl) A labyrinth of deep caverns and passages, with models, museum and well done life-size tableaux illustrating life for an 18th-c smuggler; spooky lighting and sound effects in places. Shop; cl 25–26 Dec; (01424) 422964; £5.50.

Underwater World 🎫 (Rock-a-Nore Rd) With walk-through underwater tunnel and a tropical marine section with coral. Snacks, shop, mostly disabled access; cl 24–26 Dec; (01424) 718776; £5.50.

HAYWARDS HEATH TQ3226
Borde Hill Garden (Balcombe Rd, N) Lovely 40-acre gardens most noted for their rare trees and shrubs introduced a century ago from the Himalayas and Andes; woodland, lakeside and parkland walks, and a mix of informal and more formal areas – gorgeous rhododendrons and magnolias, flaming autumn maples, roses, herbaceous borders, Italian garden, restored Victorian greenhouses. Meals, snacks, plant sales, disabled access; (01444) 450326; *£5.50. The White Harte in Cuckfield does bargain lunches.

HERSTMONCEUX TQ6410
Herstmonceux Castle 🎫 (SE of village) Extensive Elizabethan gardens around handsome 15th-c moated castle, with nature trails, and guided tours Sun–Fri (extra charge). Tearoom, shop, disabled access; cl Nov–Apr; (01323) 833816; grounds and gardens £4. The site also includes a hands-on science centre, and astronomy displays in former Greenwich Royal Observatory buildings. Snacks, shop, disabled access; cl Nov–late Mar (exc perhaps Feb half-term, best to check); (01323) 832731; £4.95, joint ticket with castle £8. The Ash Tree over at Brownbread Street has good old-fashioned home cooking.

HIGH BEECHES TQ2730
High Beeches Gardens 🎫 (B2110, Handcross) Well worth a visit, 20 acres

of landscaped woodland and water gardens, lots of rare plants, and wildflower meadows. Restaurant, plant sales on event days; open pm daily (exc Weds) Easter–Jun and Sept–Oct, and pm Sun–Tues July–Aug, best to check; (01444) 400589; £4.50.

HIGH SALVINGTON TQ1206

High Salvington windmill An 18th-c post mill; open pm 1st and 3rd Sun of month Apr–Sept; (01903) 264045; £1.

HORSHAM TQ1730

Horsham Museum (The Causeway) Timber-framed Tudor house with well organised local history, and an extraordinary collection of early bicycles. The small but pretty garden has some unusual wild cyclamen. Shop, some disabled access; cl Sun and bank hols; (01403) 254959; free. The town's much developed, but this quiet corner by the church is particularly attractive. The Black Jug (North St) has good food.

HURST GREEN TQ7328

Merriments Garden (Hawkhurst Rd) Varied four-acre demonstration garden with lots of planting ideas, some unusual plants, and comprehensive nursery inc rare hardy plants. Tearoom, disabled access; garden open Good Fri–Sept, nursery all year; (01580) 860666; *£3.50.

KINGLEY VALE SU8210

An interesting walk though needing some stamina, whether you approach via the nature trail on the S side or from Stoughton to the N. This nature reserve is Europe's largest yew forest, a magical place where the trees create some eerie pools of darkness on the S slopes of the downs; above, you can look over Chichester Harbour from a pair of prehistoric burial mounds.

LEWES TQ4110

The administrative capital of East Sussex, this is a pleasantly unrushed country town below the quarried white edge of the South Downs. It has attractive old buildings, mainly with Georgian façades (often covering older structures) though with a few stone-built or timber-framed specimens, particularly along its steep High St and in the little narrow alleys and other streets alongside. This is where you'll see Sussex tile-hanging at its best; there's also quite a lot of 'mathematical

tiling' – sham bricks over timbered buildings to make them look more progressive. There are several decent antiques shops, a good regional auction house (Gorringes; (01273) 472503 for viewing days), and an attractive complex of **craft shops** in a former candlemaker's factory in Market Lane; café, cl Sun; (01273) 472322. The Brewers Arms (High St), Gardeners Arms and John Harvey (both Cliffe High St), interesting Lewes Arms (Mount Pl) and more Bohemian Snowdrop (South St) are all useful for lunch. Bill's by the river bridge in Cliffe High St is a greengrocer's with an in-house café, where you can eat things from the shop. From Bell Lane on the SW edge you can follow the old Juggs Road track, used by the Brighton fishwives, up past Kingston and the downland nature reserve by Newmarket Hill to the outskirts of Brighton itself. There are more public paths than the OS map suggests; from the town centre you can walk up Chapel Hill, through the golf course and on via an unspoilt dry valley to **Mount Caburn**, rather grandiosely named for its size but capped by an Iron Age fort and with views towards the coast; it's also popular with paragliders.

Anne of Cleves House 🏠 (Southover High St) Henry VIII's fourth wife got this fine 16th-c house as part of her divorce settlement. She probably never came here, but its rooms give a good idea of regional life over the following two centuries. Shop; cl Sun and Mon Nov–Feb; (01273) 474610; £2.80 (combined ticket with castle £5.80). Guided tours of the ruined Norman **priory** leave here in summer; phone David Edy (01323) 894199 for details.

Lewes Castle Unusual for being built on not one but two artificial mounds, more recently thought to be part of a prehistoric complex of mounds (Lincoln is the only other such place we know of). The roof of the keep gives the best view of the town, and there's a good museum of local history. Shop; cl Mon in Jan, and 24–26 Dec; (01273) 486290; £4.20, plus £1 for entertaining audio tour.

Southover Grange Gardens (Southover Rd) Diarist John Evelyn's handsome boyhood home is now the District Registry Office, but you can visit the attractive gardens; teas May–Sept weather permitting; cl 25 Dec; free.

LITTLEHAMPTON TQ0202

Little sign here of its age (it was an important port up to the 1500s), but its long sandy beaches make it a popular simple family resort. Towards the W, beyond the River Arun, there's quite an extensive area of unspoilt dunes between beach and golf course. The 18th-c Arun View right on the river does decent lunches.

Littlehampton Museum 🖼️ (Church St) This early 19th-c manor house has displays on local history and archaeology – and more than 200 model ships. Shop, disabled access; cl Sun and Mon, and 25 Dec–2 Jan; (01903) 738100; free.

LOWER BEEDING TQ2225

Leonardslee Enormous Grade I listed garden loved by our readers, in a 240-acre valley with seven beautiful lakes; marvellous rhododendrons, magnolias, oaks and unusual conifers, delightful rock garden, extensive alpine house, bonsai exhibition, Victorian motorcar collection, Behind the Doll's House (an interesting model of an early 20th-c country estate), and wallabies and deer. The gardens are on the edge of the ancient St Leonard's Forest. Meals, snacks, plant sales, some disabled access (ring to check); cl Nov–Mar; (01403) 891212; May £7 (£8 May bank hol wknd), other times £6.

LURGASHALL SU9327

Attractive small village, with an unusual loggia outside the largely Saxon **church** where parishioners walking in from a distance could eat their sandwiches. The Noahs Ark here is prettily placed for an enjoyable lunch. Lurgashall Winery (Windfallwood) produces a wide range of traditional country wines, meads and liqueurs; tastings and snacks.

MAYFIELD TQ5826

One of Sussex's prettiest villages, with interesting shops, and pleasant hilly terrain around it. A reasonable network of paths includes a short waymarked circular walk. The Middle House, a handsome 16th-c half-timbered inn, is a civilised place for lunch.

MIDHURST SU8821

Little market town with some attractive half-timbered buildings, and several antiques shops; H G Wells went to school here. The Bricklayers Arms and Wheatsheaf both have good value food, and the Tourist Information Centre is very helpful. On the outskirts lie the ruins of Cowdray House (the estate is known for its July polo competition).

NEWHAVEN TQ4500

Genuine fishing harbour (with fish for sale), outside the compact town centre, itself not really a tourist place; a long harbour wall attracts anglers, and there's a popular shingle beach on the W side. Ferries and Sea Cat service to Dieppe in France from here. The harbourside Hope has decent food.

Newhaven Fort (Fort Rd) Built 120 years ago in case of French attack, this is a big place to explore, with underground installations, period reconstructions and exhibits of life in World War II, a new display on World War I, tunnels burrowing into the cliffs, super views from its ramparts, and an assault course for children. Snacks, shop, disabled access to exhibitions only; cl wkdys in Mar, and all Nov–Feb; (01273) 517622; £4.75.

Paradise Park 🖼️ (Avis Rd) Garden centre with exhibition on the last few million years of evolution, complete with earthquake experience and life-size moving dinosaurs. Themed gardens inc an indoor oriental garden, Caribbean and seaside gardens, and there's also a model village with miniaturised Sussex landmarks, history trail, crazy golf and a miniature railway. Meals, snacks, shops, disabled access, cl 25–26 Dec; (01273) 512123; *£4.99, garden centre free.

NEWTIMBER TQ2614

Southdown Llama Trekking You don't actually ride on these friendly creatures – they carry your lunch; (01273) 835656; shop, £50 per person (or £75 if you share a llama) for a 5-mile trek.

NORTHIAM TQ8225

Great Dixter (turn off A28 at Post Office) Timbered 15th-c house, carefully restored and added to by Lutyens in the early part of this century. He designed the attractive gardens too;

originally arranged as a series of distinct areas, they have since been stocked more informally with interesting plants by the gardening writer Christopher Lloyd who lives here. Snacks, plant sales; cl am, all day Mon (exc bank hols) and all end Oct–Mar; (01797) 252878; £6, £4.50 gardens only. The White Hart at Newenden has decent food.

OLD HEATHFIELD TQ5920

Charming peaceful hamlet, with good food in the ancient Star by the interesting church; a different world from the sprawly small town of Heathfield nearby, which sprang up around a defunct railway (it now functions as the Cuckoo Trail for walkers and cyclists – see Polegate). The town does surprise with a growing cluster of good value bric-a-brac shops, an excellent delicatessen specialising in unusual cheeses, and first-rate farmer/butcher – Pomfrets.

PETWORTH SU9721

Petworth Cottage Museum 🏠

(High St) Convincing reconstruction of an estate worker's cottage in 1910; cl am, and Mon (exc bank hols), Tues and Nov–Mar; (01798) 342100; *£2.50.

Petworth House Splendid, its magnificent rooms filled with one of the most impressive art collections in the country, inc Dutch Old Masters and 20 pictures by Turner, a frequent visitor. Other highlights include the 13th-c chapel, grand staircase with frescoes, and the carved room, elegantly decorated by Grinling Gibbons. You can see extra rooms Mon–Weds. Meals, snacks, shop, disabled access; cl Thurs, Fri and Nov–Mar; (01798) 342207; £7; NT. The deer park, with stately trees and prospects still recognisable as those glorified by Turner, is open all year; free. The town (cruelly carved up by busy traffic) is now an antiques honey-pot, with dozens of antiques shops in its narrow streets of attractive old houses. The Angel Hotel fits in well, and has a good wknd carvery; the Well Diggers (A283 E – almost a museum of the rural 1920s) and stylish Badgers (A285 S) have good food too.

PEVENSEY TQ6505

Pevensey Castle Formidable castle based around huge 4th-c Roman fort,

with massive bastions and walls of Roman masonry still up to 9 metres (30 ft) high in places. The Norman keep was built by William the Conqueror, and you can see interesting interior details inc fireplaces, dungeons and an oubliette. Shop, some disabled access; cl Mon and Tues Nov–Mar, 24 Dec–1 Jan; (01323) 762604; £2.80; EH. The Castle Cottage restaurant does decent food, inc light summer lunches in the castle garden.

POLEGATE TQ5804

Cuckoo Trail Surfaced track following the route of a former railway to Heathfield, with links into Eastbourne; good for traffic-free walking or family cycling – the mileposts, crafted by local artists, each have a cuckoo hidden in their design.

Filching Manor Motor Museum (Jevington Rd, Wannock) Gleamingly restored vintage cars, shown to great effect in the grounds of a striking manor house. Unique panelling in the minstrels' gallery, acres of woodland, and Donald/Sir Malcolm Campbell connections. They also have a go-kart track (Weds–Sun and bank hols; £10 for 10 mins). Snacks, disabled access; some guided tours usually 11am and 2.30pm wknds and bank hols, but phone before to check; cl Nov to just before Easter; (01323) 487838; £5. The Eight Bells in Jevington is a good value food stop, with plenty of walks nearby.

PULBOROUGH TQ0518

The town has some attractive buildings down towards the river; the Waters Edge, with lake views, has a good choice of food. There's an RSPB Reserve just S, and the Citrus Centre (off A283 E, just past White Horse pub; cl Mon/Tues) has all sorts of orange, lemon and related trees.

Nutbourne Vineyards (Nutbourne Manor) 18-acre vineyard with tours and tastings, visitor centre in a former windmill, and a family of llamas. Shop; no tours wkdy ams (exc bank hols) and Oct–Apr, best to check; (01798) 815196; free. The Elephant & Castle in West Chiltington has good value food.

Parham House Charming Elizabethan house, still a family home, its panelled rooms full of notable portraits, furniture, oriental carpets and rare needlework. The surrounding grounds are really very special; a four-acre walled garden has a greenhouse, herbaceous borders, vegetable garden and an apple orchard, and the 18th-c pleasure grounds include a maze designed for children. Snacks in 15th-c kitchen, shop, plant sales, some disabled access; open pm Weds, Thurs, Sun and bank hol Mons Easter–Sept, and Suns only in Oct; (01903) 744888; £5.50, £4 garden only.

RODMELL TQ4206

Monks House Just a quiet lived-in house, in a pleasant village, but a beautifully kept place of pilgrimage for followers of the Bloomsbury Group, as Leonard and Virginia Woolf lived here from 1919; Virginia drowned herself in the river nearby in 1941, and Leonard died in 1969. Open Weds and Sat pm Apr–Oct; (01892) 890651; £2.60; NT.

ROTTINGDEAN TQ3602

Grange Museum and Kipling Gardens A pretty place, where enthusiastic local volunteers look after both the handsome Georgian grange, now a **museum** (usually cl Weds, Sun am and 23 Dec–2 Jan; (01273) 301004; free), and the pleasant two-acre **Kipling Gardens**, well restored Victorian gardens named after the author who lived here for five years from 1897. Burne-Jones was a resident for a while too, designing the windows made by William Morris for the Early English **church**.

RYE TQ9321

Enchanting, and still relatively unspoilt despite its many charms. Before the wind and sea currents did their work, the little town was virtually surrounded by sea, and as one of the Cinque Ports played an important part in providing men and ships for coastal defence. It's built on a hill crowned by the partly Norman **St Mary's church** (with a notable churchyard, and very early turret-clock, two quarter-jacks by it striking the quarter-hours); up here the largely cobbled streets still follow a 12th/13th-c narrow layout, with most of the houses lining them dating from the 16th c. The town is full of antiques shops, book shops, craft shops and an exceptional kitchenware shop; Rye Art Gallery (107 High St) is a non-profit

trust with several floors selling the best of local art and craft. The views are lovely, and steep Mermaid St with its handsome old Mermaid Inn is famously photogenic.

Camber Castle This massive Tudor fort had the sea lapping up to it when it was built, but is now stranded a mile or so inshore by the encroaching shingle (open wknd pms July–Sept; (01797) 226728; £2; EH). Beyond it the Ship on Winchelsea Beach is a welcoming refuge. **Camber Sands** on the other side of the river is the finest sandy beach in the SE, with plenty of room for walking (though it is massively popular in summer, when roads can be gridlocked; try taking a bike on the train and using the cycle path from Rye for a less congested journey).

Heritage Centre ⊞ (Strand Quay) A useful introduction, with a sound-and-light show based around an intricate town model, and a self-guided Walkman tour (£2.50). Snacks, shop, disabled access; cl 24–26 Dec; (01797) 226696; £2.50.

Lamb House ⊞ (West St) Built in 1723 for former mayor James Lamb, and chiefly devoted to mementoes of the author Henry James, who lived here 1898–1916; after his death E F Benson, who also became mayor, moved here. Open pm Weds and Sat Apr–Oct; (01892) 890651; *£2.60; NT.

Rye Castle Museum ⊞ (just below Church Sq) Lively local history museum now split between two sites: the main gallery is in East St, while other displays are housed in the striking 13th-c Ypres Tower (as in Wipers) – good views of the harbour from here too. Shop, disabled access to East St museum; cl 1–2pm, Tues, Weds Apr–Oct, and wkdys Nov–Mar; (01797) 226728; £1.90 per site or £2.90 joint ticket.

Rye Harbour Because of the build-up of shingle along this coast, it's now a mile or two from the town, though yachts and fishing boats do still come right up the river to the pretty quay. The Inkerman Arms has good fresh fish. Tony Easton will take you **sea fishing** for the day, phone for details; (01797) 252104. The expanse of shingle stretching around the river mouth is now preserved as a **nature reserve**,

with hides to watch the shore birds.
SALEHURST TQ7424
Attractive tucked-away village with
14th-c church and good pub, the
Salehurst Halt.
SEDLESCOMBE TQ7719
Attractive village, with an unusual
organic vineyard.
SELSEY BILL SZ8592
One of the nicest and cleanest
beaches along the S coast.
**SEVEN SISTERS COUNTRY
PARK** TV5199
(A259, Exceat) Part of a magnificent and
quite unspoilt sweep of coastline, with
the River Cuckmere meandering its
way through sheep-grazed meadows to
a vast shingle bank at Cuckmere Haven,
the only undeveloped estuary in Sussex
(no car access to sea; about a mile's
walk). From here you can walk up on to
the Seven Sisters (open access), a series
of vertical chalk headlands forming the
spectacular finale of the South Downs
Way (leading on to Beachy Head above
Eastbourne). Opposite the car parks is
an exhibition on the surrounding area
(the heritage coast); adjacent you can
hire bikes from the Cuckmere Cycle
Co at Granary Barn; (01323) 870310,
and eat at the Exceat Farmhouse. For an
interesting circular walk you can head
inland by Friston Forest, West Dean
and East Dean. The roomy Golden
Galleon just W does good food and
brews its own beer.
SHEFFIELD PARK TQ4124
Sheffield Park Wonderful 120-acre
garden partly landscaped by Capability
Brown, since then imaginatively planted
with many varieties of tree unknown to
him, especially chosen for their autumn
colours. Also marvellous
rhododendrons, azaleas and water-lilies
on the lakes. Snacks, shop, disabled
access; cl Mon (exc bank hols), all wkdys
Jan–Feb and 22 Dec–3 Jan; (01825)
790231; £5; NT. The Griffin at Fletching
nearby is very good for lunch.
SHEFFIELD PARK STATION
TQ4023
Bluebell Line (A275) Earliest
preserved standard gauge steam railway
in Britain, and one of the best; 9-mile
trips from Sheffield Park via Horsted
Keynes to Kingscote (where there are
wknd bus connections to East

Grinstead), with splendid stations
decked out with period advertisements
and wonderful genuine period carriages.
The journey passes woodlands that are
a mass of bluebells in late spring, usually
at their best in mid-May – hence the
name of the line. Part of the station
houses the region's largest railway
collection, inc some 30 locomotives.
The Revd W Awdry based his Fat
Controller on the man who organised
the railway's restoration in the late
1950s. Pullman dining specials, Santa
specials, shop, café, disabled access
(with notice); trains wknds all year, daily
May–Sept and school hols – (01825)
720800 for timetable; £8. Depending on
which direction you're coming from, the
Griffin at Fletching and Sloop at Scaynes
Hill are good for lunch.
SHOREHAM-BY-SEA TQ2106
Though not one of England's more
famous ports, this is quite a busy one,
with several attractive old buildings
around the harbour. Inland, in Old
Shoreham, the early Norman **church** is
accompanied by some handsome old
houses (among them the good 16th-c
Red Lion). The Norman building
(thought to have been a customs house)
called **Marlipins** contains an absorbing
local and maritime museum which will
probably be closed for refurbishment
until late summer, so phone for opening
times and prices; (01273) 462994. The
next-door pub of the same name does
tasty bar lunches. Cross the footbridge
over the estuary and turn right for a
wonderful array of house boats, some
converted from very ancient-looking
craft with all manner of subsequent home
improvements. Just W is striking
Lancing College Chapel, begun in
1868, with a soaringly handsome nave,
and elaborate stained-glass rose window.
Museum of D-Day Aviation 🖼
(Shoreham Airport) Uniforms, engines,
artefacts and a replica Spitfire. Shop,
disabled access; cl wkdys in Mar and
Nov, and all Dec–Easter; (01903)
851447; *£3.50. In England's oldest
airport, with an appealing 1930s art
deco terminal (tours available, £3.50),
which has uninterrupted views from its
good value Fly Inn bar/restaurant.
SINGLETON SU8713
Weald & Downland Open-Air

Museum (A286) Fascinating collection of over 40 historic buildings rescued from all over the south-east, dismantled and re-erected here. They're arranged to form an authentic-looking village, with outlying farm and agricultural buildings, Medieval farmstead and shops, blacksmith's forge, tollhouse and Victorian schoolroom. You can buy flour from the working watermill, and now you can also watch craftsmen preparing timber frames in the timber-built but impressively futuristic new gridshell building. Well organised children's activities might include brick-laying or basket-making. Snacks, shop, some disabled access, but the site is rather steep; cl Nov–Feb (exc wknds and Christmas week); (01243) 811348; £7. The 16th-c Fox & Hounds nearby is a good stop.

SOUTH DOWNS TQ2609
Open rolling downland, becoming more appealing to walkers, with increasing incentives for farming here to turn away from arable crops and intensive livestock production. The steep N slopes are the most impressive. **Devil's Dyke** above Brighton is one tremendous viewpoint within visible Iron Age ramparts, usually busy with kite-fliers. Although it's a bit crowded around the car park and modern pub there, things get better close by – head along the South Downs Way in either direction. The Dyke itself is a magnificent dry valley cutting deep into the downs, making a lovely route down to Poynings. The Shepherd & Dog at nearby Fulking has a pretty, informal garden huddled beneath the downs, and makes a good focal point for round walks. Other high points are Wolstonbury Hill, and the Jack and Jill windmills nr Clayton.

SOUTH HARTING SU7819
A pretty downland village, with good value food in the nicely set Ship. The chalk Harting Downs involve no more than a level stroll from the road above the village; with more good food, the Coach & Horses in the pleasant nearby village of Compton is another good base for walks in this area.

Downland drive The roads around here give attractive drives – the B2141 and B2146 S of South Harting, the Walderton–East Mardon back road between them, and the downs-foot road E through East Harting, Elsted, Treyford and Cocking.

Uppark (B2146 S) Splendid 17th-c house, extensively restored after a disastrous fire in 1989. Incredibly, most of the house's public treasures were rescued, even the wallpaper. The grounds, designed by Humphrey Repton, have a woodland walk and fine views towards The Solent. Meals, shop, disabled access; cl Fri, Sat and Nov–Mar, house also cl am; (01730) 825415; £5.50; NT. The Ship and White Hart are handy for pub lunches.

TANGMERE SU9106
Military Aviation Museum (off A27) Good collection of flying memorabilia based around the former RAF station where H E Bates finished writing *Fair Stood the Wind for France*. New displays include a Spitfire and an English Electric Lightning fighter. Meals, snacks, shop, disabled access; cl Dec–Jan; (01243) 775223; £4. The nearby Bader Arms has more memorabilia; and the 16th-c thatched Gribble at Oving is an attractive place for lunch.

TICEHURST TQ7029
Pashley Manor Gardens (B2099) Now one of the most charming gardens in the south-east, eight acres of beautifully restored mainly Victorian formal gardens around a handsome house once owned by the Boleyn family. Magnificent old trees, delightfully placed moat and walled garden, views, folly, fine shrubs, roses, herbaceous beds, and clever focal points; very relaxed and peaceful. Tulip festival in early May, and a summer flower festival in Jun. Snacks, plant sales, shop, limited disabled access; cl Sun, Mon and Fri exc bank hols, and all Nov–Mar; (01580) 200888; £6. The village is attractive; up a side road at Three Legged Cross, Maynards has good pick-your-own.

TURNERS HILL TQ3335
Tulleys Farm Huge range of pick-your-own soft fruit and vegetables throughout the season, as well as a tearoom, good farm shop. Big annual crop labyrinth (don't worry if you get stuck, from a watchtower an eagle-eyed guide will lead you to the centre) with other activities for younger children inc

tractor rides, straw mountain and mini mazes; mid-July to mid-Sept; £4.50. They have special events around Hallowe'en and Easter. PYO Jun–Oct, shop open all year; (01342) 718472. The Crown is an enjoyable dining pub.

UPPER DICKER TQ5509

Michelham Priory Part of a 13th-c Augustinian priory, with 14th-c gatehouse by the moat (which has plenty of waterfowl). Interesting furniture, tapestries and local ironwork, as well as crafts, working watermill, and rope museum. Meals, snacks, shop, disabled access to gardens and ground floor only; cl Mon (exc bank hols and Aug) and all Nov–Feb; (01323) 844224; £5; EH.

WARBLETON TQ6018

Right off the beaten track and as a result very unspoilt – the village has more pre-1750 Sussex barns than anywhere else in the county. The Warbil in Tun is a friendly dining pub.

WEIR WOOD RESERVOIR TQ3935

A pleasant waterside walk traces along its N shore, with paths leading up to Standen House.

WEST CHILTINGTON TQ0918

West Chiltington church Beautiful building in lovely downland countryside – this is windmill country, too. The village is pretty, and the Elephant & Castle has good value food and a good family garden.

WEST DEAN SU8612

West Dean Gardens Old roses, very long 1911 pergola, wild garden, walled kitchen garden with all sorts of espaliered fruit trees and impressive 19th-c glasshouses, and interesting collection of stately mature conifers in park and arboretum; a splendid downland setting, notably peaceful and relaxed. Meals, snacks and shop in new visitor centre, limited disabled access; cl Nov–Feb; (01243) 818210; *£5. The Fox Goes Free at Charlton is good for lunch.

WEST HOATHLY TQ3632

Attractive village tucked quietly away from the road, with tremendous views from the lane down past the ancient Cat dining pub. On a clear day you can see the whole sweep of the South Downs between Chanctonbury Ring

and the Long Man of Wilmington.

Priest House Near the 13th-c church, 15th-c timbered house, now a folk museum with a little cottage garden containing over 150 herbs. Shop, some disabled access; cl Sun am, and Nov–Feb; (01342) 810479; £2.60. They can arrange guided tours of the village.

WESTFIELD TQ8115

Carr Taylor Vineyard One of England's most successful commercial vineyards, producing sparkling wine as well as still; snacks. Shop, disabled access (but no facilities); cl 25 Dec–1 Jan; (01424) 752501; free, wine trail £1.50.

WILMINGTON TQ5403

Long Man of Wilmington Gigantic chalk-cut figure so far impossible to date – guesses hover anywhere between the early 18th c and the Bronze Age. You can take paths up to the top of the South Downs and carry on S over glorious downland towards **Lullington Heath** National Nature Reserve, which gives some idea of how the downs looked before large-scale agriculture; botanically unusual for its mixture of chalkland and heathland flora. The Giants Rest in Wilmington has good home cooking.

WINCHELSEA TQ9017

A rare example of a planned medieval town (now decidedly village-like in character), ranged around a grid of peaceful streets, and an interesting contrast in style to nearby Rye. Storms, French raids and the Black Death put paid to Winchelsea's commercial importance. Most of the buildings are post-medieval: there are fine 17th-c and 18th-c houses with much older vaulted cellars in their basements, while the tranquil church of St Thomas is elaborately decorated, with some fine old stained glass and medieval tombs. The New Inn is popular for lunch.

WISBOROUGH GREEN TQ0526

Fishers Farm Park (Newpound Lane) Friendly farm, well equipped for families, with animal show and petting areas, good indoor and outdoor play areas, trampolines, tractor-trailer and pony rides. Meals, snacks, shop, disabled access; cl 25–26 Dec; (01403) 700063; £7.75, less in winter. The Three Crowns (A272) has good value food.

WORTHING TQ1402
Restrained but rather charming town, with a pleasant seafront; in the same mould as Brighton but altogether quieter and less gaudy. There's an excellent **herb shop** on Field Row, opposite M&S. The formerly separate village of West Tarring has a folklore museum in a row of 15th-c cottages, and enjoyable food in two welcoming old pubs, the Vine and George & Dragon. At nearby Goring-on-Sea, the English Martyrs' Church (Compton Ave) has a unique nearly full-sized reproduction of the Sistine Chapel ceiling.

Worthing Museum and Art Gallery (Chapel Rd) Highlights are a rich archaeological collection, costume galleries, a Victorian nursery, and a sculpture garden; temporary exhibitions. Shop, disabled access; cl Sun and bank hols; (01903) 239999; free.

WYCH CROSS TQ4235
Ashdown Llama Park 🖾 Working farm with breeding herds of llamas and alpacas; they've a little museum, farm trail, and adventure playground. Snacks and picnic area, shop, disabled access; cl 25–26 Dec; (01825) 712040; £3.25. The Sussex Country Information Centre is now based here too (01825) 713812, and Barnsgate Manor Vineyard (a few miles down the road at Herons Ghyll) has great views from its attractive restaurant.

Other attractive villages, all with civilised pubs doing decent food, include Barns Green TQ1227, Brightling TQ6921 (the pub is at nearby Oxleys Green), Byworth SU9820, Chiddingly TQ5414, Easebourne SU8922, the other East Dean SU9013, Elsted SU8119, Findon TQ1208, Fittleworth TQ0118, Funtington SU7908, Hellingly TQ5812, Henley SU8925, Jevington TQ5601, Kirdford TQ0126, Lodsworth SU9223, Robertsbridge TQ7323, Rotherfield TQ5529, Rudgwick TQ0833, Rushlake Green TQ6218, woodland Selham SU9320 (partly pre-Norman church), Slaugham TQ2528, Stopham TQ0218, Sutton SU9715 and Waldron TQ5419 (ancient church).

Where to eat

ALCISTON TQ5005 **Rose Cottage** *(01323) 870377* In the same family for over 30 years, this small charming wisteria-covered cottage is full of harness, traps, ironware and bric-a-brac; Jasper is the talking parrot (mornings only); very good promptly served food (esp the simply cooked fresh fish) using organic vegetables and their own eggs, well kept real ales, decent wines and a good range of other drinks like kir and Pimms, a small no smoking evening restaurant, and seats outside; cl 25–26 Dec; children over 10. £27.50|**£6.50**

ASHURST TQ1816 **Fountain** *(01403) 710219* Welcoming 16th-c country pub with a carefully restored main dining room, charmingly rustic bar with flagstones, heavy beams and inglenook log fire, well kept real ales, freshly squeezed apple juice from their own press in Sept (proceeds to a children's charity), and decent wines; popular imaginative food using local produce, pleasant attentive service, a prettily planted garden (inc raised herb beds for the kitchen), and plenty of tables on the wooden decking; no children inside. £18.50|**£6.50**

BRIGHTON TQ3105 **Black Chapati** *12 Circus Parade (01273) 699011* Particularly good Eastern cooking with Anglo-Indian influences in starkly furnished restaurant with white walls and black tables and chairs, and Breton cider – wine does not always suit the style of food; cl Sun, Mon; disabled access. £28

BRIGHTON TQ3004 **Browns** *3–4 Duke St (01273) 323501* Relaxed and chatty restaurant with an airy spacious feel, bentwood chairs around wooden tables, lots of greenery, ceiling fans, and enjoyable reasonably priced English food with European influences; welcoming for families; disabled access. £23|**£7.50** ☺

BRIGHTON TQ3203 **One Paston Place** *(01273) 606933* Just off the seafront, this airy enjoyable restaurant has a big mural, very good modern British food inc super fish and game dishes, nice puddings, decent house wines, and a friendly atmosphere; cl Sun, Mon, first 2 weeks winter, 2 wks summer; children over 8 in evening. £48

BROAD OAK TQ8220 **Rainbow Trout** *Chitcombe Rd (01424) 882436* Well run olde-worlde pub with attractive low-beamed bar, big no smoking restaurant extension, a wide range of well cooked food (esp fish) served by friendly waitresses, and well kept real ales; cl pm 24 and pm 26 Dec; partial disabled access. £18|**£5.50**

BURPHAM TQ0308 **George & Dragon** *(01903) 883131* Smartly comfortable dining pub with splendid views down to Arundel Castle and river; good promptly served food with unusual specials inc good vegetarian dishes, elegant restaurant – worth booking; cl Sun pm during winter; children over 8; disabled access. £33|**£5.75**

CHICHESTER SU8606 **Comme Ça** *67 Broyle Rd (01243) 788724* Busy little restaurant close to Festival Theatre with good classic French cooking, popular Sun lunches and children's menu; cl Sun pm, Mon, bank hols; partial disabled access. £30/3-course set lunch £18.75

CHICHESTER SU8604 **St Martin's Tearoom** *3 St Martin's St (01243) 786715* Handsome brick Georgian-fronted house with pretty garden for summer eating, good lunchtime snacks and meals (mainly vegetarian but with some fish dishes) and afternoon teas using organic produce; cl Sun and bank hols; children must be well behaved; disabled access. £19|**£5.95**

DANEHILL TQ4128 **Coach & Horses** *(01825) 740369* Cottagey pub in attractive countryside with a really relaxed chatty atmosphere, well kept real ales, a lower part leading to dining area with flowers, candles, woodburner and hops on beams, enjoyable interesting bar food (the specials are well worth checking out), and good wines; big back garden with plenty of seats, with more out in front; no food Sun pm (exc bank hol wknds); cl pm 25 Dec, 26 Dec, pm 1 Jan; children must be well behaved; disabled access. £24.50|**£4.95**

DUNCTON SU9517 **Cricketers** *(01798) 342473* Pretty little white pub with enjoyable popular food, a friendly, chatty and relaxed mix of diners and drinkers, inglenook log fire, country chairs around scrubbed wooden tables, and no smoking area down steps; well kept real ales and decent wines; charming garden with plenty of seats and proper barbecue area. £22.50|**£7.95**

EAST CHILTINGTON TQ3615 **Jolly Sportsman** *Chapel Lane (01273) 890400* Tucked-away Victorian dining pub with stripped wooden floors, contemporary light wood furniture and modern landscapes on pale yellow-painted brick walls in the informally civilised restaurant, chatty little bar, imaginative cooking from a changing menu, remarkably good wine list and well kept real ales; rustic tables and benches under gnarled trees in a pretty cottagey front garden; cl Sun pm, Mon, 5 days Christmas; disabled access. £29|**£8.45**

EASTBOURNE TV6099 **Downland** *37 Lewes Rd (01323) 732689* Pretty candlelit evening restaurant in well run small hotel, with carefully prepared innovative food, good vegetables and lovely puddings, a relaxed atmosphere, and friendly service; bdrms; cl Sun; children over 10. £23

EASTBOURNE TV6199 **Pavilion Tearooms** *Royal Parade (01323) 410374* Bustling tearoom by the prom with neatly uniformed friendly staff, attractive bamboo furniture, and morning coffee, enjoyable light lunches, and afternoon teas; cl 25 Dec. £16.50|**£5.25**

EDBURTON TQ2111 **Tottington Manor** *Edburton Rd (01903) 815757* Cosy country house with particularly good food using fresh seasonal produce in bar and no smoking restaurant, winter log fire, friendly service and a relaxed atmosphere; bdrms; cl Sun pm, first 2 wks Jan; children over 5; disabled access. £34|**£7**

ELSTED SU8119 **Three Horseshoes** *(01730) 825746* Cosy Tudor pub in lovely setting with fine views of South Downs from the garden (and good nearby walks); snug rustic rooms with huge log fires, ancient beams and venerable furnishings, very good English country cooking inc lovely puddings, well kept real ales, decent wines by the glass; children tolerated. £25|**£6.95**

FLETCHING TQ4223 **Griffin** *(01825) 722890* Civilised old country inn with blazing log fires in quaintly panelled rooms, old photographs and hunting prints, very good innovative food, well kept beers, a good wine list with lots (inc champagne) by the glass, relaxed friendly atmosphere, and lovely garden; bdrms; cl 25 Dec; disabled access. £30|£7.50

HARTFIELD TQ4735 **Anchor** *Church St (01892) 770424* Relaxed and friendly pub on the edge of Ashdown Forest, with good bar food, quick service, a chatty heavily beamed bar, dining area, well kept real ales, and popular front verandah; cl pm 25 Dec; disabled access. £20|£5

HASTINGS TQ8209 **Harris** *58 High St (01424) 437221* Relaxed, informal and chatty, reasonably priced mainly Spanish food (enjoyable tapas), friendly staff in long white aprons, and decent wine; cl Sun, Mon. £22|£5.50

HORSHAM TQ1730 **Black Jug** *31 North St (01403) 253526* Most attractively refurbished Edwardian town pub with a relaxed atmosphere, a big airy bar around central servery, lots of old prints and photographs, a plant-filled conservatory, very popular interesting bar food, chilled flavoured vodkas, well kept real ales, 14 wines by the glass, and small back terrace; no children Sat/Sun pm; cl Sun pm. £24|£7.95

JEVINGTON TQ5601 **Hungry Monk** *(01323) 482178* Long-standing popular candlelit evening restaurant (also Sun lunch) with three beamed sitting rooms, bar, little dining room, open fires, a friendly dinner-partyish atmosphere, and good interesting food; cl Mon–Sat am, bank hols (exc Good Fri), 24–26 Dec; children over 4 in main dining room. £39

LITLINGTON TQ5201 **Litlington Tea Gardens** *(01323) 870222* Established 150 years ago, these tearooms still keep their quaint Victorian elegance, with seating on an attractive sheltered lawn under a copper beech or ginkgo, in renovated beach huts with open fronts, or indoors; colourful hanging baskets and flowering tubs, quick efficient service; morning coffee, light lunches, and cream teas; handy for Alfriston; cl end Oct–1 wk before Easter; disabled access.|£5.50

LODSWORTH SU9321 **Halfway Bridge** *Midhurst Rd (01798) 861281* Civilised family-run pub with big helpings of inventive home cooking in no smoking restaurant or attractively decorated comfortable bar rooms, log fires, well kept real ales, ciders and wines; bdrms; cl Sun pm in winter; children welcome over 10; disabled access. £29|£5.50

RYE TQ9220 **Flushing Inn** *4 Market St (01797) 223292* Fine old timber-framed inn serving particularly good local fish and seafood (local meat dishes, too) and staging various gastronomic events; note the fine 16th-c wall painting; bdrms; cl Mon pm, Tues, first 2wks Jan. £28|£7.50

RYE TQ9220 **Landgate Bistro** *5–6 Landgate (01797) 222829* Simply furnished beamed bistro (evenings only) with good accomplished English cooking, nice puddings, relaxed service, and a carefully chosen little wine list; cl Sun, Mon, 2 wks summer, 1 wk Christmas. £30

TROTTON SU8322 **Keepers Arms** *(01730) 813724* 18th-c beamed and timbered pub, sofas by big log fire, some unusual pictures and artefacts, interesting medley of old or antique furniture, pretty candelabra, and bowls of fruit and chillis; particularly good interesting food inc yummy puddings, friendly service, relaxed atmosphere, well kept real ales and decent wines; country views from the latticed windows, and tables out on a terrace in front; cl Sun pm, Mon (exc bank hols); disabled access. £22|£5

Special thanks to J A Snell, E G Parish, Gemma Warren, Mrs C Turner

WARWICKSHIRE
(with Birmingham and the West Midlands)

A lively mix of places to visit including some outstanding museums and art galleries; excellent family days out, too

Birmingham (becoming much more visitor-friendly after extensive regeneration) does well for family attractions, and this year, the city's excellent discovery centre, Thinktank, is winner of Warwickshire Family Attraction. Cadbury World (a must for chocolate lovers) and the National Sea Life Centre (the chain's flagship) are other first-class choices, and a bonus is that quite a few of the good museums and art galleries here (and in nearby Walsall) are free.

Warwick (with its splendid castle and some worthwhile museums) has the character and atmosphere to make a short stay enjoyable, while Stratford-upon-Avon is the obvious focus for theatre-goers and Shakespeare devotees (there's a money-saving all-in ticket for most Bard-related sites). Leamington Spa still has some of its heyday elegance.

The excellent re-creation of a Black Country village at Dudley has something to interest all ages (there's a zoo nearby), and children like the farm parks at Middleton and Bodymoor Heath. A big plus for the area are the outstanding transport museums in Coventry (a lively place, with a new gallery), Gaydon (a joy if you like classic cars) and Bickenhill (full of interest for the motorcycle enthusiast). Elsewhere, there are dazzling displays at the glass museum in Kingswinford, and interesting organic gardens at Ryton-on-Dunsmore.

Historic houses include grand Palladian Ragley Hall in Alcester (adventure playground, maze and woodland walks), Coughton Court (in the same family for more 600 years), Farnborough Hall (lots to look at inside) and Upton House (exceptional art collection). In and around Wolverhampton, striking Wightwick Manor, Bantock House and Moseley Old Hall are unexpected treats. Charlecote Park is a good fine-weather outing.

The countryside (which edges into the Cotswolds in the south) is quietly attractive, laced with canals and dotted with charming villages and appealing places to stay in (some of them of notable value).

Where to stay

AVON DASSETT SP4150 **Crandon House** *Avon Dassett, Leamington Spa, Warwickshire CV33 0AA (01295) 770652* **£42***, plus winter breaks; 5 no smoking rms, 2 in converted dairy. Welcoming farmhouse on small working farm with rare breeds livestock, fine views, big garden, comfortable sitting rooms (one with woodburner), and extensive breakfast menu with home-made marmalade and preserves and free-range eggs; cl Christmas; children over 8

BIRMINGHAM SP0687 **Hotel du Vin & Bistro** *25 Church St, Birmingham, Warwickshire B3 2NR (0121) 200 0600* **£147**; 66 stylish rms, named after wine producers. In the converted Birmingham eye hospital, this early Victorian building is right in the old city centre; basement bar with leather sofas, Bubbly Bar with a choice of 50 champagnes, imaginative modern cooking in wooden-floored bistro, an excellent wine list, super breakfasts, lovely flower arrangements, and friendly, professional staff

BISHOP'S TACHBROOK SP3262 **Mallory Court** *Harbury Lane, Bishop's Tachbrook, Leamington Spa, Warwickshire CV33 9QB (01926) 330214* **£195***, plus special breaks; 18 wonderfully comfortable and luxurious rms. Fine ancient-looking house – actually built around 1910 – with elegant antiques and flower-filled day rooms, attentive staff, and excellent food using home-grown produce in oak panelled restaurant; ten acres of lovely gardens with outdoor swimming pool, tennis, and croquet; children over 9; dogs welcome in bedrooms

BLACKWELL SP2343 **Blackwell Grange** *Blackwell, Shipston-on-Stour, Warwickshire CV36 4PF (01608) 682357* **£60***; 3 pretty rms. 17th-c Cotswold farmhouse with log fire in comfortable beamed sitting room, large inglenook fireplace in flagstoned dining room, good home cooking using own free-range eggs (evening meal by arrangement; bring your own wine), pretty garden, and nice country views; cl 24–25 Dec; children over 12, but parents with younger children stay in annexe; good disabled access; dogs by arrangement

HOCKLEY HEATH SP1571 **Nuthurst Grange** *Nuthurst Grange Road, Hockley Heath, Solihull, West Midlands B94 5NL (01564) 783972* **£155***, plus special breaks; 15 comfortable, spacious rms with lots of extras. Red brick, creeper-clad Edwardian house in landscaped gardens, with light, airy and prettily decorated public rooms, lovely fresh flowers, enjoyable modern British cooking using home-grown produce, good breakfasts, and pleasant helpful staff; cl 1 wk at Christmas; well behaved children welcome; disabled access; dogs welcome in bedrooms

ILMINGTON SP2143 **Howard Arms** *Ilmington, Shipston-on-Stour, Warwickshire CV36 4LT (01608) 682226* **£88***, plus special breaks; 3 country-style rms. Neatly kept golden stone 17th/18th-c inn opposite village green with pleasant sheltered garden and terrace; beamed and flagstoned dining bar with antiques and country furniture, open fires, friendly service, very good food, and decent wines; cl 25 Dec; children over 8

LITTLE COMPTON SP2630 **Red Lion** *Little Compton, Moreton-in-Marsh, Gloucestershire GL56 0RT (01608) 674397* **£45***; 3 rms, shared bthrm. Attractive 16th-c stone inn with low beams, log fires, separate dining area, extensive menu with tasty food, no smoking area, real ales, long wine list, and seats in the sizeable attractive garden; children over 8

LOXLEY SP2755 **Loxley Farm** *Stratford Rd, Loxley, Warwick, Warwickshire CV35 9JN (01789) 840265* **£64***; 2 suites with their own sitting rooms in attractive barn conversion. Not far from Stratford, this tucked-away, thatched and half-timbered partly 14th-c house has low beams, wonky walls and floors, antiques and dried flowers, open fire, helpful friendly owners, and good Aga-cooked breakfasts; peaceful garden, and fine old village church; cl Christmas and New Year; dogs welcome in bedrooms

SHERBOURNE SP2562 **Old Rectory** *Vicarage Lane, Sherbourne, Warwick, Warwickshire CV35 8AB (01926) 624562* **£85**; 7 rms with hand-carved four-posters. Charming 17th-c country house (new owners this year) with cosy sitting room, big log fire in inglenook fireplace, beams, flagstones and elm floors, and enjoyable breakfasts; cl Christmas and New Year; no children

STRATFORD-UPON-AVON SP1954 **Carlton** *22 Evesham Pl, Stratford-upon-Avon, Warwickshire CV37 6HT (01789) 293548* **£42***; 8 homely rms, some with own bthrm. Neatly kept and very welcoming no smoking Victorian house, close to theatre and restaurants, with helpful owners, very good breakfasts in airy dining room, and little garden; no children; disabled access to one room

STRATFORD-UPON-AVON SP1954 **Caterham House** *58–59 Rother St,*

Stratford-upon-Avon, Warwicks CV37 6LT (01789) 267309 **£85**, 10 individually decorated rms with antiques and fresh flowers. Popular Georgian house just ten mins from Royal Shakespeare Theatre, and run for nearly 20 years by charming helpful owners; interestingly furnished sitting room opening on to pretty terrace, French country-style furniture, and excellent breakfasts (plenty of restaurants nearby for evening meals); cl Christmas; self-catering flat and cottage also; dogs welcome in bedrooms

STRATFORD-UPON-AVON SP2054 **Melita** *37 Shipston Rd, Stratford-upon-Avon, Warwickshire CV37 7LN (01789) 292432* **£69***, plus special breaks; 12 well equipped, no smoking rms. Friendly family-run Victorian hotel with pretty, carefully laid-out garden, comfortable lounge with open fire, extensive breakfasts; close to town centre and theatre; cl Christmas and New Year; dogs welcome in bedrooms

STRATFORD-UPON-AVON SP2054 **Shakespeare** *Chapel St, Stratford-upon-Avon, Warwickshire CV37 6ER (0870) 400 8182* **£151**, plus wknd breaks; 74 comfortable well equipped rms. Smart hotel based on handsome lavishly modernised Tudor merchants' houses, with comfortable bar, good food, quick friendly service, and civilised tea or coffee in peaceful chintzy armchairs by blazing log fires; seats out in back courtyard; three mins' walk from theatre; disabled access; dogs welcome in bedrooms

STRATFORD-UPON-AVON SP2056 **Welcombe Hotel** *Warwick Rd, Stratford-upon-Avon, Warwickshire CV37 0NR (01789) 295252* **£185**, plus special breaks; 64 rms with antiques and luxurious bthrms. Jacobean-style mansion in parkland estate with 18-hole golf course, and two all-weather floodlit tennis courts; deeply comfortable day rooms inc fine panelled lounge, open fires and fresh flowers, elegant restaurant (children over 13 in evening), and good service; disabled access

SUTTON COLDFIELD SP1394 **New Hall** *New Hall Drive, Sutton Coldfield, West Midlands B76 1QX (0121) 378 2442* **£153**w, plus special breaks; 60 lovely rms (the ones in the manor house are the best). England's oldest moated manor house, in 26 beautiful acres, with luxurious day rooms, a graceful panelled restaurant with carefully cooked imaginative food using the freshest (often home-grown) produce, and excellent service; they can hold wedding ceremonies, and have a leisure club; children over 8; disabled access; dogs welcome in bedrooms

WALCOTE SP1258 **Walcote Farm** *Walcote, Alcester, Warwickshire B49 6LY (01789) 488264* **£42**; 3 newly decorated rms with fine views, 1 with a late 16th-c window. Attractive 16th-c farmhouse in pretty hamlet with plenty of surrounding walks; a warm welcome from friendly owners, log fires in inglenook fireplaces, beams and flagstones, good breakfasts (several local pubs for evening meals), and pretty garden; no smoking; cl Christmas–New Year

WARWICK SP2864 **Forth House** *44 High St, Warwick, Warwickshire CV34 4AX (01926) 401512* **£72***; 2 appealing and spacious suites – one almost a garden flat with its own kitchen. Prettily decorated no smoking house with a lovely, surprisingly big garden, and good breakfasts (supper trays by prior arrangement); self-catering flat; limited disabled access

WILMCOTE SP1658 **Pear Tree Cottage** *7 Church Rd, Wilmcote, Stratford-upon-Avon, Warwickshire CV37 9UX (01789) 205889* **£56***; 5 rms. Charming half-timbered Elizabethan house owned by the same family for three generations, with beams, flagstones, country antiques, a cosy atmosphere, good breakfasts, and sizeable shady garden; self-catering also; cl 24 Dec–2 Jan; children over 3

Please let us know what you think of places in the *Guide*. Use the report forms at the back of the book, write us a letter or log on to www.goodguides.com.

To see and do

Warwickshire Family Attraction of the Year

BIRMINGHAM SP0787 **Thinktank** (Millennium Point, Curzon St, Digbeth) Billed as a museum of science and discovery, this huge place is much more than that, its ten comprehensive galleries squeezing in dozens of interactives and well put together displays on everything from local industry and inventions to life in the future and how the body works. Children of all ages have lots to keep them intrigued and entertained; while younger ones have fun pushing buttons on the hands-on digestive system, older siblings are challenged by activities based around medical ethics. Most fun for under-7s is Kids in the City, full of games designed to show the range of jobs people do: children can mend pipes, make tea, be a postman delivering letters, or simply watch the changing seasons in the indoor park. Things About Me is a gallery that sensibly answers tricky questions about the body for children between 7 and 11, while Medical Matters (aimed at slightly older children) lets them try their hand as a surgeon in a virtual hip operation. Elsewhere, you can find out how everyday objects work, have a go at nurturing lettuce beds that cry out if you give them the wrong nutrients, explore Birmingham in the past, see a sweet-wrapping machine in action, and discover how animals communicate with each other. Adults aren't left out: it's hard not to be stimulated by the wealth of information here. The power gallery has a good collection of steam engines (including the oldest active one in the world, designed by James Watt in 1778), and there's a fascinating display on robotics. There's almost too much to take in, so it's worth allowing a good chunk of the day to get the most out of it. They may have extra activities in the holidays (when it can seem a bit noisy and crowded). There's also a huge IMAX cinema, the first in this area. Millennium Point is the biggest millennium project outside London, costing a whopping £114 million; looking at the amazing museum building it's easy to see where at least some of that went. Meals, snacks, shop, disabled access; cl every Friday (except in local school hols); (0121) 202 2222; £6.75 adults, £4.75 children aged 3–15. The family tickets stand out not just for their savings, but for being among the few to look after families of differing sizes: a ticket for one adult and one child is £9, two adults and two children, £18. You can get a ticket that also includes a film at the IMAX cinema (£10.50 adults, £7.50 children). If you're coming by train you may be able to get a combined train/museum ticket.

ALCESTER SP0755
Ragley Hall (B4088 SW – was A435) Privately owned family home of the Marquess and Marchioness of Hertford, this perfectly symmetrical Palladian house stands in nearly a mile of parkland and formal gardens; excellent baroque plasterwork in Great Hall, fine paintings (inc some modern art) and a mural by Graham Rust; adventure playground, maze and woodland walks in the grounds, many special events inc good outdoor concerts. Meals, snacks, shop, disabled access; cl Mon–Weds and Good Fri, all Oct–Easter; (01789) 762090; £6, grounds also open every day during main school hols £5. The nearby village of Arrow is attractive and

interesting to stroll around, despite some development. Fruit farming around here is much rarer than it used to be, but you can still find delicious fresh dessert plums for sale in Sept. The county's best drive (partly in Worcs) circles this area, via Wixford (the Three Horseshoes has good food), Radford, Inkberrow, Holberrow Green, New End, Kings Coughton, Walcote, Aston Cantlow, Wilmcote and Temple Grafton.

ARBURY SP3388
Arbury Hall (off B4102 just S of Nuneaton) Splendid-looking mansion, the original Elizabethan house elaborately spruced up in the 19th c to make it one of the best examples of the

Gothic Revival style. The writer George Eliot was born on the estate, and her *Mr Gilfil's Love Story* describes some of the rooms – not unreasonably comparing the dining room to a cathedral. Some work by Wren in the stables, and the gardens are a pleasure. Snacks, shop, limited disabled access; open pm Sun and Mon of bank hol wknds Easter–Sept; (024) 763 82804; *£6.50, *£4.50 gardens only.

ARMSCOTE SP2444
Picturesque Cotswold stone village; good imaginative food in the Fox & Goose.

ASHBY CANAL SP3688
Canal towpaths offer some of Warwickshire's nicest walks, and this canal has perhaps the prettiest of them, heading off into the Leics countryside from its junction with the Coventry Canal at Marston Junction on the edge of Bedworth.

ASHORNE SP3057
Nickelodeon (Ashorne Hall, off B4100) Unique collection of mechanically played musical instruments inc self-playing harps, drums and violins, and a vintage theatre, complete with organ rising from the floor (demonstrated Sun at 4.15pm). They show silent comedies and 1950s Pathé newsreels, and have various nostalgic tea concerts and events. A miniature railway in the grounds is £2.30 extra. Meals, snacks, shop, disabled access; phone for opening dates (usually pm 1st and last Sun mid-Mar to mid-Oct); (01926) 651444; £7.90. The Leopard over at Bishop's Tachbrook has enjoyable food.

AUSTREY SK2906
Attractive village with black and white timbered houses and cottages, some thatch. The Bird in Hand has decent food.

BADDESLEY CLINTON SP2072
Baddesley Clinton House ⊞
Romantic 15th-c moated manor house, mostly unchanged since the 17th c. Interesting portraits, priests' holes, chapel and garden with pretty walks. The family history is intriguing. Meals, snacks, shop, some disabled access; cl am, and Mon (exc bank hols), Tues and mid-Dec to mid-Feb (house cl Nov/Dec too; shop and restaurant open till

Christmas); (01564) 783294; £5.80 (timed ticket system); NT. The nearby **church** has a lovely E window, and the canalside Navigation at Lapworth and prettily set Cock Horse at Rowington do decent food.

BICKENHILL SP2083
National Motorcycle Museum ⊞ (Coventry Rd) Handy for the NEC, five halls displaying over 700 gleamingly restored motorcycles, all British. Incongruously, they also have the biggest theatre organ in Europe. Meals, snacks, shop, disabled access (not to restaurant); cl 25–26 Dec; (01675) 443311; £4.95.

BIRMINGHAM SP0786
The city has masses of things to see and do. It has a long heritage despite its mainly modern centre, and a rich and varied industrial history taking in everything from guns to chocolate buttons. Reputedly there are more canals here than in Venice, and the redevelopment of old canal buildings has brought a lively new focus of restaurants, bars, hotels and offices to the Gas St/Brindley Pl area, with plenty of crafts and entertainments too. Billions of pounds have been going into improving the city for shoppers, inc the luxury new Mailbox leisure and shopping complex, and by autumn 2003 the massive pedestrian-friendly redevelopment of the central Bullring shopping area should be finished. The stunning new **Millennium Point** with its excellent interactive discovery centre is also now open. In recent years the city has become more fun for nightlife, and there are enough pubs to keep visitors happy: the Fiddle & Bone (Sheepcote St), Old Joint Stock (Temple Row W) and Tap & Spile (Brindley Wharf) are our current recommendations.

Aston Hall (Aston, 2m NE of centre) Strikingly grand Jacobean mansion with panelled long gallery, balustraded staircase and magnificent plaster friezes and ceilings. Snacks, shop, disabled access to ground floor; cl am, all Mon, and Nov–Apr; (0121) 327 0062; free (and more satisfying than a good many houses you'd have to pay for). A few minutes' walk away on Witton Lane, a **transport museum** in a former tram

Warwickshire

LEICESTERSHIRE

Nuneaton

Ashby Canal

Monks Kirby

Easenhall

Ryton-on-Dunsmore

Rugby

Bubbenhall

Offchurch Bury

Napton on the Hill

Flecknoe

Priors Marston

Avon Dassett

Farnborough

Radway

Warmington

Ratley

Upton House

NORTHANTS

OXFORDSHIRE

depot is usually open wknds and bank hols; snacks, shop, disabled access; (0121) 322 2298; £1.

Barber Institute of Fine Arts (Birmingham University, E gate) Excellent collection of paintings and sculptures, well housed in a very attractive gallery and just the right size to be enjoyable without being overwhelming. Quite a lot of Impressionist works as well as European masters. Snacks, shop, disabled access; cl Sun am, 25–26 Dec, 1 Jan, Good Fri; (0121) 472 0961; free. The university (marked out by its huge clock tower) is on the outer fringes of Edgbaston, a couple of miles S of the city centre. This area developed as a smart residential part of town, where industry and commerce gave way to parks and greenery, much of which still remains.

Birmingham Museum and Art Gallery (Chamberlain Sq) Perhaps the best collection of Pre-Raphaelite paintings anywhere, plenty still looking as brilliantly, almost shockingly, fresh and detailed as when they were first painted. Other notable paintings too, and lots of coins and archaeology. The new Water Hall expansion houses the museum's modern and contemporary art collection. Meals, snacks, shop, disabled access; usually cl 24–26 Dec, and 1 Jan; (0121) 303 2834; free. Local boy Burne-Jones, a leading light in the Pre-Raphaelite movement, was responsible for four stunning windows in **St Philip's church** on Colmore Row nearby, since 1905 the city's cathedral. The Old Contemptibles (Edmund St) is a useful nearby Edwardian pub, quite striking in its own right.

Birmingham Nature Centre (Pershore Rd) British and European animals in indoor and outdoor enclosures designed to resemble natural habitats. Meals and snacks, shop, disabled access; cl wkdys Nov–1st wknd in Apr; (0121) 472 7775; £1.50.

Blakesley Hall (Blakesley Rd, Yardley, 6m E of centre) This timber-framed 16th/17th-c farmer's house, furnished according to an inventory of 1684, now has a new visitor centre (with a café and exhibitions), and a replanted 17th-c herb garden. Shop, disabled access to ground floor and garden; cl am, all Mon and Nov–Mar; (0121) 464 2193; free.

Botanical Gardens 🈯 (Westbourne Rd, Edgbaston) Outstanding: 15 acres featuring a tropical house (with lily pool, bananas and cocoa), subtropical house, Mediterranean house, national bonsai collection, and an arid house. The gardens themselves are filled with rhododendrons and azaleas and over 200 trees. Bands play on summer Sun and bank hol pms. Meals, snacks, shop, disabled access; cl 25 Dec; (0121) 454 1860; £5, £5.50 summer Suns and bank hols.

Cadbury World Not a factory tour, but a specially built centre with all you could feasibly want to know about how Cadbury's chocolates are made and marketed. The history of chocolate is given something of a corporate bias, but the exhibitions have been put together with a real sense of fun. Many of the major parts have been specially designed with younger visitors in mind. Highlights for them include an alternative view of chocolate-making offered in the Fantasy Factory, and Cadabra – a nicely silly ride through an imaginative themed world. What really sticks in the memory is the chance to sample fresh liquid chocolate, straight from the vat; you can have a go at dipping it into moulds. Older visitors may prefer the nostalgic Cadbury's TV adverts from the last 40 years, and there's a collection of period wrappers shown in a 1930s-style sweet shop. Also an exhibition on how they make the chocolate ads that start and end *Coronation Street*. The outdoor play area is good, and there are plenty of picnic-sets next to it. Meals, snacks, good shop, mostly disabled access; cl Nov–Feb (may open some days then), and perhaps some other days – phone to book; (0121) 451 4159; £8.75.

Ikon Gallery (Oozells Sq) Vibrant contemporary art in stunningly converted school building. Café (with tapas), shop, disabled access; cl Mon (exc bank hols), over Christmas and New Year and during installation of exhibitions so best to phone; (0121) 248 0708; free. The next-door Petit Blanc complements it well on the food side.

Museum of the Jewellery Quarter (Vyse St) Birmingham is still Britain's biggest producer of gold jewellery, if not as important to the jewellery trade as it used to be. This excellent centre is built around the perfectly preserved workshops of the Smith & Pepper company, still much as they were at the start of the century. There's a good overview of the industry, as well as tours of the factory and demonstrations of jewellery-making techniques. Snacks, shop, disabled access; cl Sun, 25–27 Dec, and 1 Jan; (0121) 554 3598; £3. Around 100 jewellery shops nearby, so useful for browsing or repairs. The Rosevilla has decent food.

National Sea Life Centre 🈯 (Waters Edge, Brindley Pl) The flagship of the excellent Sea Life Centre chain that we recommend in quite a few resorts around the country. The hi-tech displays are both fun and instructive, with around 3,000 British marine and freshwater creatures shown off in careful re-creations of their natural habitats, also themed soft play area, a reconstructed *Titanic* wreck, and a recently added otter sanctuary. The highlight is a walk-through tube designed to give the impression of walking above the sea bed, with sharks, rays and other creatures swimming above, alongside and beneath you. Norman Foster designed the building. Meals, snacks, shop, disabled access; cl 25 Dec; (0121) 643 6777; *£8.50.

Pen Room (Argent Centre, 60 Frederick St) Cheerfully run little museum in a handsome building, focusing on the city's past importance to the pen trade; you can try out lots of different pens, and there's even the chance to make your own nib. Shop, limited disabled access; cl am Sun, and a few days over Christmas; (0121) 236 9834; free.

Sarehole Mill (Hall Green, 3m SE of centre) Working 18th-c watermill, with displays explaining the milling process, and on Victorian farming; Tolkien often came here as a child. Cl am, Mon (exc bank hols) and Nov–Apr; (0121) 777 6612; free. Other local sites that influenced Tolkien are listed on a leaflet available at Tourist Information Centres, and a Tolkien Trail, following where the writer lived as a child, went to school, and might have dreamed up various characters, has been devised to catch interest generated by the *Lord of the Rings* films.

Selly Manor Museum (Maple Rd, A441 4m S) When the Cadbury family moved their factory out of the city centre in 1879, part of their plans for this new garden suburb involved uprooting timber-framed manor houses from elsewhere and re-erecting them here; two survive as this museum, with herb garden, crafts and various exhibitions. Shop, disabled access to ground floor only; cl Mon Apr–Sept, plus wknds in winter, and 2 wks at Christmas; (0121) 472 0199; £2.

Soho House Elegant former home of Matthew Boulton, famous for his development of the steam engine with James Watt, and possibly the first centrally heated house in England since Roman times. Furnished in 18th-c style with Boulton-related displays. Snacks, shop, disabled access; cl am Sun, and all day Mon (exc bank hols); (0121) 554 9122; £3.

Thinktank See *separate family panel on p.620.*

Tyseley Locomotive Works (Warwick Rd, Tyseley; A41 3m SE) Working railway museum with fully equipped workshop, steam locomotives, and several historic carriages and wagons. Shop, limited disabled access; open wknds and bank hol Mon; (0121) 707 4696; £2.50. On summer Suns the **Shakespeare Express** runs steam trips from Birmingham Snow Hill to Stratford-upon-Avon (£15 return – same phone number).

BODYMOOR HEATH SP2095
Kingsbury Water Park (Bodymoor Heath) 30 lakes and pools, created by gravel excavations, in 620 landscaped acres. Waterside and woodland walks, nature trails (maps and leaflets at the visitor centre), and two play areas. You can fish (from £1.90, under-16s fish for free at Mitchell's Pool), and there's jet bike hire. Meals, snacks, shop, good disabled access (mobility scooters available free); cl 25 Dec; (01827)

872660; free, £2.20 for parking. The park also contains **Broomey Croft Children's Farm**; all the usual farm animals for children to feed, plus tractor rides (wknds and school hols) and play and picnic areas. Snacks, shop, disabled access; cl Sept–Easter exc wknds and usually half-terms; (01827) 873844; £2.80. The canalside Dog & Doublet has decent food.

CASTLE BROMWICH SP1489
Castle Bromwich Hall Gardens 🏛 (Chester Rd) Restored 18th-c formal gardens, with authentic collection of period plants, inc historic vegetables and herbs, plus a holly maze. Snacks, plant sales, disabled access; cl am, Mon (exc bank hols) and Fri, and Nov–Mar; (0121) 749 4100; £3.50.

CHARLECOTE SP2656
Charlecote Park 🏛 250 acres of parkland, full of deer (Shakespeare is said to have poached here), along with the descendants of reputedly the country's first flock of Jacob sheep. Well furnished Great Hall and Victorian kitchen, an impressive Tudor gatehouse, and a garden designed by Sir Edmund Fairfax Lucy. Playground, meals, snacks, shop, disabled access; cl Weds, Thurs and Nov–8 Mar; (01789) 470277; £5.80; NT. By the park is a charming little 19th-c estate village of timbered cottages, and a show Victorian church. In nearby pretty Hampton Lucy, which has a lovely church, the Boars Head has decent food.

CLIFFORD CHAMBERS SP1952
Pretty black and white timbered houses and cottages, and a Tudor former rectory which has some claim to being the true birthplace of Shakespeare.

COUGHTON SP0860
Coughton Court (A435) Several priests' holes are hidden in this mainly Elizabethan house, renowned for its imposing gatehouse and beautiful courtyard; the Throckmortons have lived here since 1409. Notable furniture and porcelain, and an exhibition on the Gunpowder Plot; the grounds have a lake, two churches, pleasant walks, formal gardens, and a play area. Meals, snacks, shop, plant sales, limited disabled access; cl Mon exc bank hols, and Tues Sept–Jun, and all Oct–Mar

(exc wknds Oct and late Mar); *£9.45 house and gardens, *£6.95 grounds only, £2.50 walled garden only; NT. The Green Dragon on the fine old green at Sambourne and interesting Old Washford Mill at Studley are good for lunch.

COVENTRY SP3379

More a place to dip into than to fix on as your base for a short holiday, gaining appeal from well funded projects to open up new shopping and strolling areas, and to make the most of its landmarks, many now well floodlit. Its most interesting street is Spon St, with one or two ancient buildings that started their lives here and others that have been rescued from elsewhere and rebuilt here (the picturesque Old Windmill does cheap basic lunches). One of the town's most famous inhabitants was 11th-c Lady Godiva, commemorated best by the Coventry Clock – where she pops out in the pink every hour (and the statue in Broadgate). The earliest image of her, reconstructed from 14th-c stained glass fragments, is among other art and statuary excavated from the long-destroyed ruins of the city's first cathedral, now on show in a visitor centre at the Priory Gardens; shop, disabled access, cl Sun am, 25–26 Dec, 1 Jan; (024) 7655 2242; free. Browns (food all day, Earl St), medieval Whitefriars (Gosford St), Royal Court Hotel (Tamworth Rd, Keresley End), Flying Standard (Trinity St – food all day), Greyhound out at Sutton Stop (Aldermans Green/Hawkesbury – a new canal arts trail runs out to here) and Prince William Henry and William IV (both Foleshill Rd – authentic Indian) are all popular for lunch. On the edge of the city **Coombe Country Park** has 400 acres of historic parkland.

Coventry Cathedral (Priory Row) Bombed during the war, the old cathedral ruins have been carefully preserved, and parts of it such as the 14th-c tower remain intact. These have been joined by the new cathedral, and a new chapel has been added to commemorate the millennium. It is, perhaps quite rightly, in no way an orthodox church building, but is worth a look for unusual modern art (inc windows by John Piper, tapestry by Graham Sutherland, even holograms). Meals, snacks, shop, disabled access; cl for a few days for degree ceremonies; (024) 7622 7597; £3 suggested donation.

Herbert Art Gallery and Museum (Jordan Well) Lively interactive history of the city, with lots of events, and temporary exhibitions. Meals, snacks, shop, disabled access; cl am Sun, and a few days over Christmas; (024) 7683 2381; free.

Lunt Roman Fort (Coventry Rd) Fun reconstruction of 1st-c Roman fort, interesting to see such a site in all its glory. Good interpretative displays. Shop, picnic area, some disabled access; cl Weds, other wkdys Oct–Jun (exc bank hols and Jun half-term), and all Nov–Mar; (024) 7683 2381; £2.

Midland Air Museum (Coventry Airport) Displays of civil and military aircraft spanning more than 70 years. Snacks, shop, disabled access; cl 25–26 Dec; (024) 7630 1033; £4. The Old Mill is a smart nearby dining pub.

Museum of British Road Transport The largest collection of British road transport in the world, shown in the birthplace of the British motor industry, which developed here as an offshoot of sewing-machine production. They've over 500 cars, commercial vehicles and bicycles, together with thousands of die-cast models. Also the Blitz Experience, the new Landmarques gallery (telling the story of Coventry's transport industry from 1869–1948), and the fastest car on earth show (they've recently acquired ThrustSSC, the first car to break the sound barrier). Parts are undergoing substantial refurbishment till Jun 2003 (so there may be some additional temporary closures); the museum will gain a striking new front, lots more space for temporary exhibitions and interactive and other new displays, and better disabled access. Snacks, shop, disabled access; cl 24–26 Dec; (024) 76832425; free.

St Mary's Guildhall (Bayley Lane) Very well preserved medieval building, with its minstrels' gallery still, and some Flemish tapestries; it's usually open Easter–end Sept (exc Fri and Sat), provided there aren't any civic functions, but best to check; (024) 7683 2381; free.

Toy Museum (Much Park St) Toys from 1740 to 1990, in a 14th-c monastery gatehouse. Shop; cl am, bank hols, 25–26 Dec, and 1 Jan; (024) 7622 7560; *£1.50.

DUDLEY SO9591

Black Country Living Museum (Tipton Rd, 1m N of town centre) Good value, well thought out, open-air museum (with much under cover), giving a good feel of how things used to be in the Black Country, the heavily industrialised and proudly individual areas in the W part of the Birmingham conurbation. It's an authentically reconstructed turn-of-the-century village, complete with cottages, chapel, chemist, baker, pub, and trips into limestone caverns (summer only) or even down a mine, as well as black and white comedies from Laurel and Hardy or Harold Lloyd in the old cinema, school lessons in the school room, and an old-fashioned working fairground just outside the village (extra charges for rides). Staff in period costumes illustrate traditional crafts and test-drive old vehicles, and there are plenty of extra activities for children during school holidays. Meals and snacks (and space for picnics), shop, mostly disabled access; cl Mon and Tues Nov–Feb, and several days over Christmas, best to phone; (0121) 557 9643; £8.25.

Dudley Museum and Art Gallery (St James's Rd) Some fine paintings, well displayed geology, and appealing temporary exhibitions. Shop, disabled access to ground floor but no facilities; cl Sun and bank hols; (01384) 815575; free.

Dudley Zoo 🏰 (The Broadway) Based around an impressive **ruined castle** – a rather special place for a zoo. Meals, snacks, shop, disabled access; cl 25 Dec; (01384) 215313; £7.50.

Tunnel boat trips The Dudley Canal Trust do boat trips along part of a unique network of canal tunnels and limestone mines. Trips Mar–Nov, and some days in Dec – best to ring for times; (01384) 236275; £3.35.

EXHALL SP1055

Pretty black and white timbering, and

some pleasant gently hilly walks nearby; very quiet, as no through road. The Three Horseshoes at Wixford has good food.

FARNBOROUGH SP4349

Farnborough Hall Palladian villa filled with splendid sculptures, paintings and fine rococo plasterwork; the staircase, hall and two main rooms are on show. The 18th-c landscaped gardens have a couple of ornamental temples, and views from the terrace walk – less impressive than they were thanks to the arrival of the M40. Disabled access to ground floor only; open pms Weds and Sat Apr–Sept, terrace also open pm Thurs and Fri by special arrangement only; (01295) 690002; £3.50, £1 terrace walk; NT. The recently reopened Inn at Farnborough now has good imaginative food.

GAYDON SP3354

Heritage Motor Centre (Banbury Rd) Busy centre with the world's biggest collection of classic British cars – 300 in all, starting with an 1895 Wolseley. Also hundreds of drawings, photographs, trophies and models, hi-tech displays and video shows. There's a 4-wheel-drive demo circuit, quad bike track, and a nature reserve. The design of the building is incredible, esp inside. Meals, snacks (lunchtimes only), shop, disabled access; cl 24–26 Dec; (01926) 641188; £8. The Malt Shovel has good value food.

HARTSHILL HAYES SP3194

Country park with mixed woodland, opening out at the top for broad views towards the Peak District. The Coventry Canal below allows more extended rambles.

HENLEY-IN-ARDEN SP1565

More small town than village, but a pretty conservation area, with good churches, and a heritage centre in the High St. The Bird in Hand (A34) has good value food.

HONILEY SP2472

The village has virtually gone now, and there are only vestiges of the big house, but you can still sense the vanished settlement around the surviving 18th-c church.

HONINGTON SP2642

Attractive village, its church prettily set on the edge of the lawn of charming late

17th-c Honington Hall, open pms Weds and bank hol Mon Jun–Aug; (01608) 661434; £3.50. The Cherington Arms over at Cherington does good lunches, with pleasant nearby walks.

ILMINGTON SP2143
Quietly attractive village with peaceful path to partly Norman church, lovely inside; pleasant walks on hills above; Howard Arms good for lunch.

KENILWORTH SP2772
Kenilworth Castle 🏛 Dramatic castle transformed by John of Gaunt into a spectacular fortress, now one of the finest castle ruins in the country, with a still impressive keep and several other buildings within the sandstone walls. Also restored Tudor garden and an interactive castle model; various re-enactments, open-air plays and operas, and children's activities summer hol wknds. Meals, snacks, shop, disabled access (but no facilities); cl 24–26 Dec, 1 Jan; (01926) 852078; £4.40 inc audio tour; EH. The town itself has a Norman church and some pleasant strolls, especially around the castle area. The Clarendon House (High St) has good food.

KINGSWINFORD SO8888
Broadfield House Glass Museum (Barnett Lane) Excellent collection of glass from nearby Stourbridge, displayed to dazzling effect. Clever use of lighting shows off the exhibits quite spectacularly, and even the audio-visual shows create a sense of excitement. One of the area's least expected treasures. Snacks, shop, disabled access to ground floor; cl Mon (exc bank hols), phone for Christmas and Easter opening; (01384) 812745; free.

LEAMINGTON SPA SP2864
Elegant spa resort popularised by the rich who came to take the waters in the 18th and 19th c. Still many fine Regency buildings, though today the town is better seen as a civilised shopping centre, and perhaps as a base for sallies into the surrounding countryside – or into Warwick, across the River Avon. Recently restored and beautifully laid-out, **Jephson Gardens** (The Parade) are well worth strolling around, with wild ducks on the lake. The Benjamin Satchwell (The Parade) and Hogshead (Warwick St) have decent food.

Art Gallery & Museum 🏛 (Royal Pump Rooms, The Parade) Restored Regency bath house originally built in 1814 but later extended and remodelled to suit changing fashions. It's now home to the town's decent museum and art gallery, as well as its library and Tourist Information Centre. Meals, snacks, shop, good disabled access; cl Thurs am, all Mon, and a few days over Christmas; (01926) 742700; free.

LONG COMPTON SP2932
This pleasant Cotswoldy village of thatched stone houses has some antiques shops, and a pretty garden with a sundial; the Red Lion has good food.

LOWER BRAILES SP3139
Attractive Cotswold-edge village with lovely slender-spired church, pretty stone houses, good views, nice old inn – the George.

MERIDEN SP2482
A cross on the green marks what the village feels is the centre of England – one of the streams rising in the village pond ends up in the Severn and the other over in the Humber. The pub on the green used to be the manor house.

MIDDLE TYSOE SP3344
Charming village – with a very traditional cottage bakery.
Interesting walk The walk S from Upper Tysoe over Windmill Hill (which does have a windmill) takes you to the church on the edge of Compton Wynyates park, giving views of the attractive Tudor manor – a refreshing bit of brick building, in this Cotswold-edge stone country.

MIDDLETON SP1797
Ash End House Farm 🏛 (off A4091) Friendly farm set up specifically for children; animals from a shire horse to baby chicks and fluffy ducklings, as well as rare breeds of goats, pigs and sheep. A pony ride is included in the price, and there's plenty under cover for wet days. Snacks, shop, disabled access; cl 25–29 Dec, 1–2 Jan; (0121) 329 3240; £4 children, adults half-price (discount voucher valid for 1 adult free for every child paying full price, one voucher per family).
Middleton Hall (A4091) Varied architecture in the house, also nature reserve, walled gardens, and a play area.

There's a good craft centre in the stables. Meals, snacks, shop, some disabled access; house open Sun and bank hol pms Easter to mid-Sept (£2.50); craft centre open Weds–Sun all year; free (01827) 283095. The Green Man is a decent family dining pub.

NAPTON ON THE HILL SP4661
Attractive village on a rounded hill above a curve in the Oxford Canal – perhaps the prettiest canal in this part of the world, with pleasant towpath walks, and enjoyable food from the Folly and the Napton Bridge Inn. Great views of seven counties from the hill.

NUNEATON SP2792
Hoar Park Craft Centre & Granary Antiques (B4114, nr Ansley) Children's farm (£1.50), antiques and garden centres, and tearoom, as well as various craft shops housed in 18th-c farm buildings; some parts cl Mon (exc bank hols), phone for Christmas opening times; (024) 7639 4433; free.
Nuneaton Museum & Art Gallery (Coton Rd) Nicely set in colourful Riversley Park, with display on George Eliot. Meals, snacks, shop, disabled access; cl Sun am, all day Mon (exc bank hols), and 25 Dec; (024) 7635 0720; free. The central Felix Holt has decent food all day.

OFFCHURCH BURY SP3565
Attractive riverside parkland, with a pleasant walk winding through from the thatched Stags Head (good value food).

PACKWOOD SP1772
Packwood House 🖻 (off A34) Friendly old house with origins as a 16th-c farmhouse, carefully restored and not at all commercialised; interesting panelling, furniture and needlework, and in the garden unusual yew trees clipped to represent the Sermon on the Mount; look out for the 18th-c bee boles built into the S face of the garden terrace wall. Snacks, shop, some disabled access; cl Mon (exc bank hols), Tues and Nov–Mar; (01564) 782024; £5.20, garden only £2.60; NT. The Boot at Lapworth (B4439) is a fairly handy canalside dining pub.

PRIORS MARSTON SP4857
Attractive old houses around the village green, and unusual blue brick paths; the ancient Holly Bush has good food. There's a walk up Marston Hill behind,

and quite a good network of paths around nearby Priors Hardwick taking you down to the Oxford Canal. The old drovers' Welsh Rd through here via Southam to Cubbington is a pleasant drive; just before Offchurch it crosses the remarkable Fosse Way, a quiet Roman road running dead straight from Brinklow through Stretton-on-Dunsmore and Princethorpe down to Halford.

RIVER AVON SP0950
There is a pleasant riverside walk from the Cottage of Content at Barton.

RUGBY SP5075
Gilberts (St Matthew's St) The game the school invented is commemorated at this shop that's been making the standard rugby ball since 1842. You can watch them do it, and there are related displays (inc a film) and collections. Shop, some disabled access; cl Sun, bank hols and 25–26 Dec and 1 Jan; (01788) 333889; free. The friendly Three Horseshoes Hotel not far off in Sheep St has interesting food.
Rugby Art Gallery & Museum (Little Elborow St) Impressive centre housed in an attractive modern building, with a fine collection of modern and contemporary art inc works by L S Lowry and Freud (you can make an appointment to see paintings not on show) and changing exhibitions, as well as a display of Roman artefacts and a decent look at local social history; the building also houses the town's library. Disabled access; cl Sun and bank hol ams, all day Mon, and 25–26 Dec, 1 Jan; (01788) 533201; free.
Rugby School 🖻 Founded in 1567, moving to its current site in the mid-18th c. A museum on Little Church St looks at its history and former pupils, such as Rupert Brooke and Lewis Carroll. Shop, disabled access; cl lunchtimes, Sun am and 25 Dec–1 Jan; (01788) 556274; £1.50. Guided tours of the school buildings leave here at 2.30pm most days but ring to check; £4.

RYTON-ON-DUNSMORE SP3874
Ryton Gardens (Wolston rd, off A45) Even readers who describe themselves as dedicated gardeners learn a lot from this interesting place, home of the Henry Doubleday Research Association (the organic gardening and

farming organisation, which also champions tasty but endangered varieties of veg). It's landscaped with thousands of organically grown plants and trees; herb garden, rose garden, garden for the blind, and shrub borders among the displays, as well as a cooks' garden where all the plants are edible, and the Paradise Garden dedicated to the late Geoff Hamilton. A new interactive visitor centre, due to open spring 2003, is dedicated to vegetables. Very good meals and snacks in organic restaurant, shop, disabled access; cl 25 Dec–1 Jan; (024) 763 03517; £3.95.

SHIPSTON-ON-STOUR SP2540
Small town with quite a busy shopping centre, but also rewarding to stroll through, with a good church and quite a few handsome old stone buildings, antiques shops among them. The White Bear (High St) and Black Horse (Station Rd) are good for lunch.

SHOTTERY SP2055
Anne Hathaway's Cottage A substantial thatched Tudor farmhouse, the home of Anne Hathaway until her marriage to William Shakespeare. Displays of domestic life during the period, and colourful cottage garden. Snacks, shop, disabled access to ground floor and gardens only; cl 23–26 Dec; (01789) 292100; £5. The Bell is handy for something to eat away from the tourists.

STONELEIGH SP3271
Though primarily known as the showroom for the Royal Show, with an increasing number of permanent displays, the village itself has an attractive sandstone Norman church, timber-framed houses, and Stoneleigh Abbey; open Sun and Tues–Thurs from Apr–Oct; (01926) 858585; £5.

STRATFORD-UPON-AVON SP2055
Visitors who look at the town just as a town can be disappointed, but if you have a grounding in Shakespeare's plays the interesting buildings seem that bit more interesting – and not so outnumbered by the workaday ones, the high-priced antiques shops and the gift shops. The gardens by the River Avon make a memorable setting for the Royal Shakespeare Theatre. If you're looking forward to a good production at the theatre that evening, or, better

still, able to run through much of the verse in your head, then you'll love Stratford. But if you've always thought Shakespeare overrated, then you'll think the same about Stratford, too. The pub with the most thespian connections is the Mucky Duck (Southern Way); the Arden Hotel has the closest bar to the Memorial Theatre, with good snacks. Useful places for lunch include the quaint old Garrick (High St), Brasserie (Henley St), Vintner Wine Bar (Sheep St) and Slug & Lettuce (Guild St/Union St). Tea in the smart Shakespeare Hotel (Chapel St) is relaxing, and the White Swan Hotel (Rother St) has a pre-Shakespeare mural of Tobias, the angel and the fish. With lively re-creations and lots of bizarre facts, **Falstaffs Experience** on Sheep St is well worth a visit; cl 25–26 Dec and 1 Jan; (01789) 298070; £3.50.
Butterfly Farm ⊞ (Swans Nest Lane, off A3400 S side of bridge) Cascading waterfalls and tropical blossoms, with up to 1,500 exotic butterflies flying free in a rainforest habitat, also an incredible collection of spiders and insects. Snacks, shop, disabled access; cl 25 Dec; (01789) 299288; £4.25.
Hall's Croft (Old Town) Lovely gabled Tudor home of Dr John Hall, who married Shakespeare's daughter; good displays on the medicine of the time, Elizabethan and Jacobean furniture, and a walled garden. Meals, snacks, shop, disabled access to ground floor; cl 23–26 Dec; (01789) 292107; £3.50.
Harvard House (High St) Late 16th-c home of the mother of the man who founded Harvard University – no direct connection with Shakespeare, but a striking example of houses of his day with possibly the most ornately carved and timbered frontage in the town, and home to the Museum of British Pewter. Shop; cl Tues and Weds, plus Mon–Thurs Sept–Jun (exc bank hols), plus all Nov–Apr; (01789) 204507; £1.50.
Holy Trinity church (Waterside) 15th-c, where Shakespeare was baptised and buried; cl Sun am and for other services; £1 to enter the chancel where the grave is.
New Place/Nash's House (Chapel St) Shakespeare died here in 1616; the house was destroyed in the 18th c, but

the Elizabethan knot garden remains, and the adjacent house, former home of the writer's granddaughter, has a good collection of furniture and local history. Disabled access to ground floor and gardens only; cl 23–26 Dec; (01789) 292325; £3.50.

Ragdoll Shop (Chapel St) Ragdoll make lots of children's TV programmes inc *Teletubbies* and *Rosie and Jim*. The shop has plenty to amuse small children inc play areas and a replica of Teletubbies' Home Hill, and they can talk to their favourite characters on the phone. Shop, disabled access; cl 25–26 Dec, 1 Jan; free.

Royal Shakespeare Theatre 🖭 (Waterside) Shakespeare's plays are of course still performed here by the Royal Shakespeare Company. You can book guided tours of the Royal Shakespeare Theatre and their other theatre, the Swan (usually at 1.30, 5.30, and after evening performances; best to phone as they quickly get booked up); the gallery has temporary exhibitions. Meals, snacks, shop, disabled access for plays but not tours; phone for opening times as they depend on performances; (01789) 403405; £2 for gallery, theatre tours £4. The RSC productions themselves are performed in repertory, so if you're in the area for a few days it's quite possible to see several. Advance booking is recommended – (01789) 403403 – though some tickets are kept back for each performance and sold on the day from 9.30am; don't leave it much later, they go pretty fast. A two-hour guided walk around Shakespeare's Stratford leaves the RSC Thurs, Sat and every day during the Easter hol, plus Sun July–Sept; (01789) 403405; £6.

Shakespeare's Birthplace (Henley St) Though there's no guarantee the playwright really was born here, there are interesting period features, and good interpretative displays. Shop, disabled access to ground floor; cl 23–26 Dec; (01789) 204016; £6.50. If you want to see all the Shakespearian houses it makes sense to buy a joint ticket; this costs £12, and covers this, New Place, Hall's Croft, and the Shottery and Wilmcote sites. You can also buy tickets covering just the three in-town sites for £8.50. A tour bus with

commentary links the sites but costs another £7.50; (01789) 294466.

Teddy Bear Museum 🖭 (Greenhill St) Delightfully displayed, furry friends of all shapes and sizes – mechanical and musical ones, ones that belonged to famous people, and some that are famous themselves; children's quiz. Shop; cl 25–26 Dec; (01789) 293160; *£2.50.

STRATFORD-UPON-AVON CANAL SP1867
This gives some pleasant towpath walks; the Fleur de Lys at Lowsonford is a good start.

SUTTON-UNDER-BRAILES SP3037
Attractive stone-built village, with some pleasing Cotswold countryside around it – good walks.

UPTON HOUSE SP3645
🖭 (A422 nr Ratley) The exceptional art collection is the main draw here, an enormous range of paintings inc works by Bosch, El Greco, Bruegel and Hogarth, and an exhibition of posters commissioned by Shell all sensibly arranged and displayed. Also Brussels tapestries and Sèvres porcelain. The fine garden has terraces, herbaceous borders, a kitchen garden, 1930s bog garden and ornamental pools, as well as a national collection of asters. Meals, snacks, shop, some disabled access; open pm (all day wknds) Sat–Weds and Good Fri Apr–Oct; (01295) 670266; £6 house and garden, garden only £3; NT. There's a timed ticket system on bank hols. Ratley itself is a pretty village, with a lovely church and good home cooking in the Rose & Crown; and the Castle on Edge Hill is a very interesting place for lunch, with terrific views.

WALSALL SP0099
Birchills Canal Museum (Top Lock, Old Birchills) Small museum with a replica boat cabin; shop; open Tues, Weds am, Thurs–Sun pm, cl 25–27 Dec and 1 Jan; (01922) 645778; free.

Jerome K Jerome Birthplace Museum (Bradford St) Dedicated to the life and work of the author of *Three Men in a Boat*, with a reconstructed 1850s parlour; cl Sun, Mon and pm Weds, Fri, Sat open only 12–2; (01922) 653116; free. The good value Green Dragon (High St, a short walk away) fits in well with the period.

New Art Gallery (Gallery Sq) This imaginative building has collections of European art inc great paintings by Rembrandt, Goya, Constable, Manet, Degas and Freud. Lots has been done to make the gallery appeal to all ages and tastes, including an interactive children's gallery, plenty of seating, and sensibly low hanging heights so that you don't have to strain. Everything's very accessible. The centrepiece is the Garman Ryan collection – over 300 works donated to the local people by Kathleen Garman, Jacob Epstein's widow, in 1973, and shown in a sort of two-storey house within the building itself – this cleverly gives the feeling of looking at somebody's private collection. Also changing exhibitions, activity and conference rooms, and a rooftop terrace. Meals, snacks, shop, disabled access; cl Mon exc bank hols; (01922) 654400; free.

Walsall Leather Museum (Littleton St West) Well restored Victorian leather goods factory with tours of aromatic workshops and leather-making demonstrations (not Sun); also displays about the history of the local leather trade and a new trail of the town's historic leather quarter. Meals, snacks, shop (lots of local leather goods), disabled access; usually cl Sun am, Mon (exc some bank hols), Good Fri and a few days over Christmas; (01922) 721153; free.

WARMINGTON SP4047

National Herb Centre (Banbury Rd) Wide range of herbs in display gardens in an attractive valley; also walks, nature trails and a children's activity area. Bistro, herb and plant centre, disabled access; cl 25 Dec–1 Jan; (01295) 690999; free. In the charming sleepy village, the Plough has decent food.

WARWICK SP2864

Though many older buildings survived a major fire in 1694, today's centre is dominated by elegant Queen Anne rebuilding. Some of the oldest structures are to be found around Mill St, which is very attractive to stroll along; there are a good few antiques and other interesting shops. There is a Farmer's Market on the 3rd Fri of each month. The Tilted Wig (Market Pl – neat bedrooms too) and Zetland Arms (Church St) do good lunches; the Saxon Mill (Guy's Cliffe) is a prettily placed waterside family dining pub, and the Warwick Arms Hotel does good value teas.

Doll Museum (Castle St) Half-timbered Elizabethan house with comprehensive collection of antique dolls and toys. A fun video shows the exhibits come to life. Shop; cl Nov–Mar exc Sat; (01926) 495546; £1.

Lord Leycester Hospital (High St) Delightfully wonky half-timbered building built in 1383, still used as a home of rest for retired servicemen. Fine old guildhall, candlelit chapel, gatehouse and courtyard, and garden with Norman arch and a 2,000-year-old urn from the Nile. Meals, snacks, shop, disabled access to ground floor only; cl Mon, Good Fri, 25 Dec; (01926) 491422; £3.20.

Mill Garden Delightful series of plantings in a super setting on the river beside the castle – very nice to stroll through, with plenty of old things to look at along the way; some disabled access; cl Nov– Easter; (01926) 492877; £1.

St John's House (St John's) 17th-c house with exhibits from the county museum, a changing collection of costumes, several room reconstructions, and an under-5s discovery room. Shop, disabled access to ground floor only; cl all Mons (exc bank hols) and Sun ams, plus all Suns end Sept–Apr; (01926) 412132; free.

St Mary's church (Old Sq) Splendid medieval church on the town's highest point, with Norman crypt, chapter house and magnificent 15th-c Beauchamp chapel. In summer you can go up the tower (small charge), for excellent views.

Warwick Castle (Castle Hill) Well liked by readers, this lively place is one of the country's most splendid castles, with plenty for all ages, especially in summer; you can spend a happy day exploring every corner, though half a day is probably enough for most families. The influence of the Tussauds group, who own the site, shows in the flair for presentation, and of course the castle's waxwork inhabitants, done in careful and convincing life-size detail. Live castle-dwellers add to the fun: perhaps the jocular wandering rat-catcher, or an instructive bowman. The rooms are excellently preserved, and their fine furnishings and art well worth braving the crowds for; the armoury really kindles interest, instead of being a dry-as-dust collection . The marvellous grounds were designed by Capability Brown, and as well as the delightful gardens, have pleasant strolls along the banks of the River Avon; the views from the parklands are dramatic. They've recently restored the Mill and Engine House, which in Victorian times provided the castle with electricity. Good café, shop, disabled access to grounds only; cl 25 Dec; (0870) 4422000; £13, £10.75 in winter.

Warwickshire County Museum (Market Pl) In the 17th-c Market Hall, with lots of fossils, and a Sheldon tapestry map of the county. Shop, disabled access to ground floor; cl Sun exc May–Sept, Mon all year, and 25–26 Dec; (01926) 410410; free.

WELLESBOURNE SP2653

Wartime Museum 🖼 Partly housed in the underground HQ of a former RAF base, a collection of aeronautical archaeology, wartime memorabilia and several aircraft. Shop, some disabled access (not underground); open Sun and bank hol Mon (exc 25–26 Dec); (01789) 778816; £1.50. The Kings Head is a decent pub.

Wellesbourne watermill (B4086) Historic watermill still producing flour in secluded rural setting, with striking wooden wheel. Helpful staff, nature trails and traditional crafts. Meals, snacks, shop; cl Mon–Weds (exc bank hols) and Oct–Easter; (01789) 470237; £3.50.

WILMCOTE SP1658

Mary Arden's House & Shakespeare Countryside Museum Research has recently shown that picturesque Palmer's Farm, for the last 70 years treated as the home of Shakespeare's mother, wasn't even built until five years after she'd left the village. Her real home was the neighbouring early Tudor Glebe Farm, which you can also look around (it's furnished in Victorian style). The farm barns now re-create Elizabethan farm life, and there are country crafts, rare breeds and daily falconry displays; children's play area. Snacks, shop, disabled access to ground floor only; cl 23–26 Dec; (01789)

293455; £5.50. The Masons Arms has good generous home cooking.

WOLVERHAMPTON SJ9400 Continuing redevelopment and improvements are making the town more appealing to visitors. It has some points of interest, such as medieval St Peter's church, a reminder of the city's pre-industrial wool prosperity; it was also once the heartland of lock- and clock-making. The interesting art gallery in Lichfield St has been recently refurbished (good collection of contemporary and pop art, and a new sculpture gallery); snacks, shop, disabled access; cl Sun and bank hol 23–27 Dec and 1 Jan; (01902) 552055; free. The quaint Combermere Arms (Chapel Ash) is the nicest pub for lunch here. Wightwick Manor and Moseley Old Hall (see below) right out on the outskirts are splendid.

Bantock House and Park (1m SW of centre, off A454) The ground floor of this Edwardian family home has been restored, and upstairs are displays on the city's history inc some interactive ones; they have a decent collection of decorative art. In 43 acres of parkland, with re-created formal gardens and a Dutch garden, also a nature trail and play area. Meals, snacks, shop, disabled access; cl Mon, and Nov–Mar (exc pms Fri–Sun); (01902) 552195; free.

Moseley Old Hall 🖼 (Featherstone, off A460/A449 4m N, just over Staffs border) Tudor house famed as a hiding place for Charles II after the Battle of Worcester. The façade has altered since, but the furnishings and atmosphere in its panelled rooms don't seem to have changed much, and there's a 17th-c knot garden. Readers particularly enjoy the guided tours. Teas, shop, limited disabled access; cl am, also Mon/Tues (exc bank hols), Thurs/Fri, and all Nov–late Mar (exc tours Sun 9 Nov to mid-Dec); (01902) 782808; £4.20; NT.

Wightwick Manor (just off A454, 3m W) Only a century old, but beautifully and unusually designed by followers of William Morris, and a fine testimonial to the enduring qualities of his design principles. Flamboyant tiles, fittings, furnishings and glass, and lots of Pre-Raphaelite art. Also period garden with yew hedges and topiary. Snacks, shop, some disabled access; open pm Thurs, Sat and bank hol wknds Mar–Dec, garden also open Weds; (01902) 761108; £5.60, £2.50 garden only; NT. The Fieldhouse Inn is a useful food pub just below the car park.

Other attractive villages, almost all with decent pubs, include Avon Dassett SP4049, Barston SP2078, Barton-on-the-Heath SP2532 (no pub), Berkswell SP2479 (pretty Norman church), Bubbenhall SP3672, Easenhall SP4679, Flecknoe SP5164, Hampton in Arden SP2081, Hampton Lucy SP2557, upmarket Lighthorne SP3355, Lower Quinton SP1847, Monks Kirby SP4683 (huge church), Preston on Stour SP2049, Radway SP3748 (we've had no pub recommendation here yet), Ratley SP3847 (lovely church), Temple Grafton SP1255 (Shakespeare's

'Hungry Grafton'), Warmington SP4147, Welford-on-Avon SP1452 and Whichford SP3134.

Canals give some of the county's best walking opportunities. Besides places already mentioned, useful canalside pubs include the Rose & Castle at Ansty SP3983, Kings Head at Atherstone SP3097, Waterman at Hatton SP2467 (by a flight of locks), Black Boy and Herons Nest at Knowle SP1876, Navigation and Boot at Lapworth SP1670, Anchor at Leek Wootton SP2868, Two Boats at Long Itchington SP4164, Manor Arms at Rushall SK03001 (handy too for Park Lime Pits nature reserve), Boat at Stockton SP4365 (the flight of locks usually has plenty going on), Wharf Inn SP4352 (A423 Banbury–Southam), and Bulls Head at Wootton Wawen SP1563.

Where to eat

ALDERMINSTER SP2348 **Bell** *(01789) 450414* Popular and rather civilised dining pub nr Stratford, with excellent imaginative food using fresh local produce (and they hold regular food and music evenings), several neatly kept communicating areas with flagstones and wooden floors, fresh flowers, good wines, real ales, obliging service, and no smoking restaurant; conservatory and terrace overlooking garden; disabled access. £22|**£6.75**

ARMSCOTE SP2444 **Fox & Goose** *(01608) 682293* Pretty village pub with contemporary décor but quite a pubby feel, bright crushed velvet cushions and coverings on wooden pews and stools, big mirrors on the walls (a warm red colour in the bar, cream in the eating areas), polished floorboards, and lots of stylish black and white animal pictures; a stuffed fox and goose guard the dining room's woodburner, and there's a log fire in the flagstoned bar; friendly service, imaginative enjoyable food, well kept real ales, good wines, and lots of soft drinks; elegant new deck area out overlooking a big lawn with tables and fruit trees; bdrms; cl 25–26 Dec, 1 Jan; disabled access. £25|**£5**

ASTON CANTLOW SP1461 **Kings Head** *21 Bearley Rd (01789) 488242* Carefully restored and beautifully timbered Tudor pub with a massive inglenook fireplace and flagstones in comfortable village bar, an old-fashioned snug, a gently upmarket atmosphere, inventive food from a creative menu in the carpeted main room, cheerful service, well kept ales, and decent wines; disabled access. £27|**£8.50**

BERKSWELL SP2479 **Bear** *Spencers Lane (01676) 533202* Handsomely refurbished 16th-c timbered pub (a well run Chef & Brewer) with a relaxed atmosphere, comfortable snug low-beamed areas, nooks and crannies, beams and panelling, bric-a-brac, wide choice of food inc interesting daily specials, well kept ales and decent house wines; new games bar for drinkers only; seats on back lawn; children in restaurant. £20.65|**£7.50**

BIRMINGHAM SP0686 **Bank** *4 Brindley Pl (0121) 633 7001* Branch of the fashionable London restaurant, this busy place is bright and modern with lots of efficient staff, kitchen views through glass wall, huge varied choice of French-style dishes inc some fine fish and attractively presented puddings, and a good range of wines; next door to the National Sea Life Centre; cl Sat am, Sun, bank hols; disabled access. £33/2-course set meal £10

BIRMINGHAM SP0586 **Petit Blanc** *9 Brindley Place, 2–3 Oozells Sq (0121) 633 7333* Part of Raymond Blanc's small brasserie chain, this stylish and spacious restaurant is relaxed and friendly, with helpful staff, good modern cooking with a French bias, plenty of choice, lovely puddings, and a short, well chosen wine list; cl 25 Dec; they are kind to children; disabled access. £30/2-course fixed lunch £12.50

GREAT WOLFORD SP2434 **Fox & Hounds** *(01608) 674220* Inviting 16th-c stone inn with a good mix of locals and visitors in the cosy low-beamed old-fashioned bar; candlelit tables, flagstones and a roaring log fire, really enjoyable imaginative daily specials, and a little tap room with several changing real ales; bdrms; cl Mon; disabled access. £24|£6.95

HATTON SP2367 **Falcon** *Birmingham Rd (01926) 484737* Well reworked old pub with five calm, relaxing open-plan rooms working their way around a central island bar; lots of stripped brickwork, low beams, tiled and oak-planked floors, good prints and old photographs, pretty fresh flowers, big Turkey rugs and a nice mix of stripped and waxed country tables and various chairs; a big barn-style back dining area is no smoking; a wide choice of interesting food, well kept real ales, and decent wines; seats out on lawns. £21.40|£6.95

MONKS KIRBY SP4682 **Bell** *Bell Lane (01788) 832352* Busy pub with warmly chatty Spanish landlord, timbered and flagstoned rambling rooms, cheerful locals, good tapas and plenty of Spanish dishes as well as more usual bar food, an extensive wine list, well kept real ales, and quite a few whiskies; cl Mon am, 26 Dec; disabled access. £27.75|£4.95

SHIPSTON-ON-STOUR SP2540 **Chavignol** *8 Mill St (01608) 663888* Carefully renovated, charming old mill (the owners have moved here from Chipping Norton) with a no smoking dining room, conservatory, and new bedrooms; innovative, impressive cooking, a thoughtfully chosen wine list, and helpful friendly service; individually decorated bdrms; cl pm Sun, Mon; disabled access. £45

STRATFORD-UPON-AVON SP2055 **Benson's** *4 Bards Walk (01789) 261116* Close to Shakespeare's birthplace, this light and airy tearoom has lots of plants and flowers, neatly dressed staff, papers and magazines to read, a wonderful patisserie, a marvellous choice of teas and coffees (plus Pimms, buck's fizz and kir), and breakfasts, morning coffee, lunches, and afternoon tea; no smoking; cl Sun in winter; disabled access. £17.50|£5

STRATFORD-UPON-AVON SP2054 **Boathouse** *Swans Nest Lane (01789) 297733* Above a working boatyard right on the river, this popular restaurant has simple wooden tables on bare boards, lots of rope fancywork, and views of the RSC theatre; good interesting modern bistro dishes using influences from all over the world (enjoyable fish dishes), a short reasonably priced wine list, and friendly helpful service. £24

STRATFORD-UPON-AVON SP2054 **Garrick** *25 High St (01789) 292186* Attractive ancient pub with small, heavily timbered and often irregularly shaped rooms, some walls stripped back to bare stone and others heavily plastered with theatrical posters, and long upholstered settles and stools made from barrels on bare boards; small air-conditioned back dining room with an open fire, well kept real ales, generous enjoyable bar food (sandwiches served all day), and very friendly helpful staff. £20.40|£7.25

STRATFORD-UPON-AVON SP2054 **Opposition** *13 Sheep St (01789) 269980* Small bustling restaurant with friendly atmosphere, generous helpings of enjoyable food, and a good choice of drinks – handy for theatres and open for after-show meals; cl 25 Dec; disabled access. £23|£5.95

STRATFORD-UPON-AVON SP2054 **Russons** *8 Church St (01789) 268822* Cheerful and popular bistro in 17th-c malthouse with very good imaginative food (plenty of fresh fish) and good value simple wine list; pre-theatre meals, too; cl Sun, Mon, wk between Christmas and New Year, 1 wk Easter, 2 wks end Aug; children over 10. £25.80|£5.95

Special thanks to B and K Hypher, Mrs J Piercey, Mrs J M Preston, Mrs June Pritchard

WILTSHIRE

A charmingly sedate corner of England, with one or two great family outings and some pleasant surprises

The beautiful small city of Salisbury, with its lovely cathedral precinct, is ideal for a short quiet break, and there are several attractive little towns elsewhere in the county. Handsome Bradford-on-Avon (Westwood Manor and Iford Manor Garden are worth a look), Devizes (lots of grand buildings), Malmesbury (tranquil abbey) and attractive Marlborough particularly stand out, while Castle Combe and Lacock are exceptionally pretty villages.

Longleat, with a multitude of attractions, even aside from the famous safari park, has plenty to keep families entertained for the day. Steam in Swindon is good fun, with lots of appeal even if railways aren't usually something you're mad about: it's this year's top family attraction here. More for adults, Wilton House is a particularly satisfying stately home, Corsham Court has an outstanding art collection, Lacock Abbey is lovely (with an absorbing photography museum), and Lydiard Park is excellent value. Bowood at Calne and Stourhead in Stourton both have stunning landscaped gardens; you'll find other memorable gardens at Tollard Royal, Holt and Middle Woodford. Elsewhere, you can see the oldest beam engines in the world at work in Crofton, or watch carpet-making in Wilton.

A visit to Cholderton Rare Breeds Farm is a treat for younger children, for a taste of life on a dairy farm there's Farmer Giles Farmstead in Teffont Magna, and bustling Roves Farm in Sevenhampton is well liked by readers.

One of Wiltshire's claims to fame is its profusion of prehistoric sites. The best known is Stonehenge, and it's well worth going – though in some ways Avebury is even more of a surprise.

The most appealing countryside is along the valleys of the southern chalk streams – intimate scenery with stone or flint houses and sparkling rivers. The northern parts have some quietly attractive drives and walks, especially around Marlborough. Running across the county, the restored Kennet & Avon Canal has lots of scope for enjoyable boat trips or relaxing towpath walks. Wiltshire is also dissected by several cycleways; many Tourist Information Centres have routes and maps, and you can get free advice on cycling and walking here by phoning (01980) 623255.

Where to stay

BRADFORD-ON-AVON ST8261 **Bradford Old Windmill** *4 Masons Lane, Bradford-on-Avon, Wiltshire BA15 1QN (01225) 866842* **£79***; 3 rms, one suite, one with waterbed, another with round bed, and the third with a Gothic iron bed. Interesting and carefully converted windmill with log fire in attractive circular lounge (former grain store), lots of books, a friendly atmosphere; good vegetarian evening meals with dishes from Thailand, Nepal, Mexico and so forth (Mon, Thurs and Sat only), and fine breakfasts eaten around communal refectory table; pretty cottagey garden; no smoking; cl Jan–Feb; children over 6

BRADFORD-ON-AVON ST8359 **Widbrook Grange** *Trowbridge Rd, Widbrook, Bradford-on-Avon, Wiltshire BA15 1UH (01225) 864750* **£110**; 19 pretty rms, many in carefully converted courtyard cottages. Handsome stone former farmhouse in 11 acres, with comfortable drawing rooms, good food in elegant dining room, a sunny conservatory, and indoor swimming pool and exercise machines; disabled access

BRADFORD-ON-AVON ST8361 **Woolley Grange** *Woolley Green, Bradford-on-Avon, Wiltshire BA15 1TX (01225) 864705* **£165**, plus winter breaks; 23 rms, with fruit and home-made biscuits. Civilised Jacobean manor house with a relaxed informal atmosphere, lovely flowers, log fires and antiques in comfortable and beautifully decorated day rooms, and pretty conservatory; delicious food using local (or home-grown) produce, often organic, inc home-baked breads and muffins and home-made jams and marmalades for breakfast, marvellous staff, and swimming pool, tennis, badminton, and croquet; particularly well organised for families, with nannies and plenty of entertainment; disabled access; dogs welcome in bedrooms ☺

CALNE ST9871 **Chilvester Hill House** *Chilvester Hill, Calne, Wiltshire SN11 0LP (01249) 813981* **£80***; 3 charming spacious rms. Big Victorian house with neat gardens and grounds, particularly helpful friendly owners, comfortable sitting rooms with antiques, good breakfasts and honest no-choice dinners around large table in separate dining room (using home-grown produce), and plenty of local sights; cl 1 wk spring and/or autumn; children over 12 (babies allowed)

CASTLE COMBE ST8477 **Manor House** *Castle Combe, Chippenham, Wiltshire SN14 7HR (01249) 782206* **£177**, plus special breaks; 47 lovely rms, some in mews cottages just 50 yds from the house. 14th-c manor house in 360 acres of countryside inc an Italian garden and parkland; gracious day rooms with panelling, antiques, log fires and fresh flowers, a warm friendly atmosphere, and very good innovative food; 18-hole golf course, croquet, boules, and all-weather tennis court

CHICKSGROVE ST9730 **Compasses** *Lower Chicksgrove, Tisbury, Salisbury, Wiltshire SP3 6NB (01722) 714318* **£55**; 4 rms with showers. Lovely thatched house in delightful hamlet with old bottles and jugs hanging from the beams, good home-made food, well kept real ales, and peaceful farm courtyard and garden; dogs welcome in bedrooms

COLERNE ST8272 **Lucknam Park** *Colerne, Chippenham, Wiltshire SN14 8AZ (01225) 742777* **£205** exc breakfast, plus special breaks; 41 luxurious rms. Noble Georgian house reached by a long beech-lined drive through extensive grounds, with elegant carefully furnished day rooms, panelled library, lovely flowers, antiques and paintings, and excellent food and extremely good service in charming restaurant; snooker, hairdresser, leisure spa with indoor swimming pool, gym and beauty salon, and floodlit tennis courts; croquet; an all-weather equestrian centre; children over 12 in evening restaurant; limited disabled access

CROCKERTON ST8642 **Springfield House** *23 Crockerton, Warminster, Wiltshire BA12 8AU (01985) 213696* **£60***; 3 rms with garden views. Charming, welcoming 17th-c house on the edge of Longleat Estate, with a comfortable sitting room, breakfast room and terrace, lawn tennis, and an acre of south-facing garden; lots to do nearby; cl Christmas; children over 6

CRUDWELL ST9592 **Old Rectory Country House Hotel** *Crudwell, Malmesbury, Wiltshire SN16 9EP (01666) 577194* **£98**; 12 big homely rms. Elegant, welcoming country-house hotel, formerly the rectory to the Saxon church next door; three acres of lovely landscaped Victorian gardens, an airy drawing room, interesting and enjoyable food in panelled no smoking restaurant, a relaxed atmosphere, and unpretentious service

DEVIZES SU0061 **Bear** *Market Pl, Devizes, Wiltshire SN10 1HS (01380) 722444* **£75***, plus special breaks; 24 rms. Very much at the town's heart, this 16th-c inn has an old-fashioned feel, a wide choice of food from snacks to more elaborate meals in the oak-panelled Lawrence Room, two more formal restaurants, beams, and fresh flowers; cl 25–26 Dec; dogs welcome in bedrooms

EBBESBOURNE WAKE ST9924 **Horseshoe** *Ebbesbourne Wake, Salisbury, Wiltshire SP5 5JG (01722) 780474* **£60***; 2 rms. Particularly welcoming pub with beautifully kept little bar, open fire, fresh flowers and interesting bric-a-brac on beams, popular home-made food in bar or no smoking restaurant, big breakfasts and nice Sunday lunches, well kept real ales, pretty little garden, play area, and pets' corner in paddock; no children; cl 25 Dec; dogs welcome anywhere

FORD ST8476 **White Hart** *Ford, Chippenham, Wiltshire SN14 8RP (01249) 782213* **£84**; 11 spacious, well equipped rms. Very well run, popular and attractive ivy-covered inn in lovely spot by trout stream; an old-fashioned atmosphere, heavy black beams, big woodburner in ancient fireplace, particularly good imaginative food, well kept real ales, malt whiskies and fine wines, attentive cheerful service, and secluded small swimming pool

GASTARD ST8867 **Boyds Farm** *Chapel Knapp, Gastard, Corsham, Wiltshire SN13 9PT (01249) 713146* **£45***, plus special breaks; 3 rms. Friendly and handsome 16th-c house on family-run working farm with pedigree Herefords; homely lounge, woodburner, traditional breakfasts; no evening meals (local pubs nearby); cl Christmas–New Year

GRITTLETON ST8680 **Church House** *Grittleton, Chippenham, Wiltshire SN14 6AP (01249) 782562* **£68***, plus special breaks; 4 big comfortable rms. Large Georgian rectory on the edge of a lovely village, in 11 acres of gardens and pasture with a heated indoor swimming pool and croquet; relaxed and friendly house-party atmosphere, open fire, antiques and paintings in the drawing room, very good imaginative food using organic home-grown vegetables and fruit (advance notice needed), and breakfasts with their own eggs; children under 2 and over 12

HEYTESBURY ST9242 **Angel** *High St, Heytesbury, Warminster, Wiltshire BA12 0ED (01985) 840330* **£65***; 8 comfortable rms. 16th-c coaching inn with armchairs, sofas, and a good fire in cosy homely lounge, a long beamed bar with woodburner, quite a few prints, and good service from friendly staff; well kept real ales, decent wines, and a wide choice of consistently good food in charming back dining room that opens on to secluded garden; dogs welcome in bedrooms

LACOCK ST9168 **At the Sign of the Angel** *Church St, Lacock, Chippenham, Wiltshire SN15 2LB (01249) 730230* **£99**; 10 charming rms. This fine 15th-c house in a lovely NT village is full of character, with heavy oak furniture, beams and big fireplaces, a restful oak-panelled lounge, and good English cooking in three candlelit restaurants; cl Christmas wk; disabled access; dogs welcome in bedrooms

MALMESBURY ST9387 **Old Bell** *Abbey Row, Malmesbury, Wiltshire SN16 0BW (01666) 822344* **£130***, plus special breaks; 31 rms. With some claim to being one of England's oldest hotels and standing in the shadow of the Norman abbey, this fine wisteria-clad building has traditionally furnished rooms with Edwardian pictures, an early 13th-c hooded stone fireplace, two good fires and plenty of comfortable sofas, magazines and newspapers; cheerful helpful service, very good food, and attractively old-fashioned garden; particularly well organised for families; disabled access to ground floor bedroom; dogs welcome in bedrooms ☺

MILDENHALL SU2169 **Fisherman's House** *Mildenhall, Marlborough, Wiltshire SN8 2LZ (01672) 515390* **£60***; 5 lovely rms, most with own bthrm. Extremely pretty house with lawns running down to the River Kennet, fresh flowers and stylish furniture, friendly owners, and good breakfasts in airy conservatory; cl 25–26 Dec; children over 12

NETTLETON ST8378 **Fosse Farmhouse Hotel** *Nettleton, Chippenham, Wiltshire SN14 7NJ (01249) 782286* **£120***, plus special breaks (inc some interesting craft wknds); 5 rms. 18th-c Cotswold stone house extensively restored with decorative French antique furniture and pretty English chintzes; morning coffee, lunch and cream teas served on the lawns or in very attractive dining room; antiques shop with dried flowers and decorative items in former dairy behind the house; dogs welcome in bedrooms

PURTON SU0987 **Pear Tree** *Church End, Purton, Swindon, Wiltshire SN5 4ED (01793) 772100* **£110***; 17 very comfortable, pretty rms. Impeccably run former vicarage with elegant comfortable day rooms, fresh flowers, fine conservatory restaurant with good modern English cooking using home-grown herbs, helpful caring staff, and 7½ acres inc a traditional Victorian garden; cl 26–30 Dec; disabled access; dogs welcome in bedrooms

SALISBURY SU1430 **Farthings** *9 Swaynes Cl, Salisbury, Wiltshire SP1 3AE (01722) 330749* **£50***; 4 rms, most with own bthrm. Spotlessly kept no smoking house with friendly owners, good breakfasts, and pretty garden; nr cathedral; cl Christmas; children over 12

SALISBURY SU1428 **Rose & Crown** *Harnham Rd, Harnham, Salisbury, Wiltshire SP2 8JQ (01722) 399955* **£100***; 28 rms in the original building or smart modern extension. It's almost worth a visit just for the view – well nigh identical to that in the most famous Constable painting of Salisbury Cathedral; elegantly restored inn with friendly beamed and timbered bar, log fire, good bar and restaurant food, and charming Avonside garden; disabled access; dogs welcome in bedrooms

SALISBURY SU1431 **Stratford Lodge** *4 Park Lane, Salisbury, Wiltshire SP1 3NP (01722) 325177* **£70***, plus special breaks; 8 rms. Warmly friendly and relaxed Victorian house (redecorated last year), with antique furnishings, fresh flowers, generous helpings of very good carefully prepared evening food, super breakfasts in conservatory, and quiet garden; children over 5

WARMINSTER ST8944 **Bishopstrow House** *Bishopstrow, Warminster, Wiltshire BA12 9HH (01985) 212312* **£199***, plus special breaks; 32 sumptuous rms, some with jacuzzi. Charming ivy-clad Georgian house in 27 acres with heated indoor and outdoor swimming pools, indoor and outdoor tennis courts, fitness centre and beauty treatment rooms, and own fishing on River Wylye; very relaxed friendly atmosphere, log fires, lovely fresh flowers, antiques and fine paintings in boldly decorated day rooms, and really impressive food; disabled access; dogs anywhere except restaurant

WARMINSTER ST8745 **Old Bell** *42 Market Pl, Warminster, Wiltshire BA12 9AN (01985) 216611* **£55***, plus special breaks; 15 comfortable rms. 14th-c country-town hotel with traditional bar food, bistro and restaurant, good choice of wines, pretty central courtyard, and friendly service; maybe cl Christmas; lots to do nearby

WINSLEY ST7960 **Burghope Manor** *Winsley, Bradford-on-Avon, Wiltshire BA15 2LA (01225) 723557* **£85**; 8 rms. Lovely 13th-c family home in attractive countryside, with carefully preserved old rooms and an interesting fireplace engraved with Elizabethan writing, antiques in big drawing room, welcoming caring owners, nice breakfasts, and evening meals by arrangement; self-catering in Dower House in grounds; cl Christmas and New Year; children over 10

WOOTTON BASSETT SU0783 **Marsh Farm Hotel** *Wootton Bassett, Swindon, Wiltshire SN4 8ER (01793) 848044* **£70**w, plus special breaks; 38 rms. Handsome Victorian farmhouse in landscaped grounds with particularly warm and friendly atmosphere, comfortable lounge, convivial bar, and enjoyable food in conservatory restaurant; cl 25–31 Dec; disabled access

To see and do

Wiltshire Family Attraction of the Year

SWINDON SU1385 **Steam** 🖼 (Kemble Drive, next to the well signed Great Western Designer Outlet Centre) In the former works of the Great Western Railway, this brings to life the sights and sounds of the railway age, when 12,000 people used to work here to produce everything needed to keep it running. It has good reconstructions and up-to-date display techniques to get you really involved – as well, of course, as several of the locomotives built here. Particularly good fun is a simulator that re-creates the experience of riding on a steam train footplate, even down to the hisses, whistles, jolts and swaying as the countryside rushes by. There's as much emphasis on the people who worked and travelled on the railways as there is on the trains, and there may be lively talks by people who used to work here. Children have plenty to keep them amused, from the various touch-screen games and hands-on activities to a track layout where younger visitors have fun shunting the trucks. Other displays focus on Isambard Kingdom Brunel and the GWR's days as the 'holiday line', and you can watch restoration work on old engines and carriages. This has much wider appeal than many steam-themed collections, and all ages seem to get something out of it. There's a good programme of special events, particularly in the summer holidays, when actors re-create anything from real-life railway dramas to Victorian music-hall. Meals, snacks, shop, disabled access; cl 25–26 Dec, 1 Jan; (01793) 466646; £5.95 (£3.80 children). A family ticket, for two adults and two children, is £14.70. There are lots of bargains at the outlet shopping centre next door, and decent food in the Old Pattern Shop.

ALTON BARNES SU1061
Kennet & Avon Canal Here the canal lies close enough to Pewsey Down nature reserve for an afternoon's walk to incorporate both features; the spine of the downs here is followed by the Wansdyke, an ancient earthwork which runs across the downs for miles from Morgans Hill, near Calne, nearly as far as the Savernake Forest. The canalside Barge at Honeystreet is a good lunch stop.
ANSTY ST9526
Pleasant village, notable for England's tallest maypole.
AVEBURY SU1070
Avebury Stone Circle This spectacular 4,500-year-old henge monument encompasses the pretty village – where Stones does good vegetarian food. It's the largest stone circle in Europe, the 200 surviving stones enclosed in a massive earthen rampart nearly a mile in circumference. Originally, there were two smaller internal stone circles, too. The site was excavated in the 1920s and 1930s, in the most unusual way. A marmalade magnate bought the entire village, and

had the stones re-erected – many had become buried or dilapidated. The **Alexander Keiller Museum** named after him gives a succinct introduction to the archaeological wonders of the area, inc a new interactive barn gallery exhibition. Meals, snacks, shop, disabled access; cl 24–26 Dec; (01672) 539250; *£4; NT.
Avebury Manor (behind church) Much altered house, formerly a monastery. The present buildings date from the early 16th c, with Queen Anne alterations and then Edwardian renovations. The attractive topiary and flower gardens contain medieval walls and some ancient evergreens. Disabled access to most of garden (but not to house); cl am, all Mon (exc bank hols), Thurs–Sat and Nov–Mar; (01672) 539250; *£3.60, gardens only *£2.70; NT.
Fyfield Down SU1470 Primeval-feeling and unkempt, scattered with outcrops known as sarsen stones, the raw material of Avebury Stone Circle and of part of Stonehenge.
Silbury Hill SU1068 This towering prehistoric mound, purpose unknown,

is the largest man-made mound in Europe – it would have taken a thousand men about ten years to build. There's a parking and viewing area, or you can walk the short distance from Avebury car park; there's no access to the top of the hill (where a huge shaft, perhaps a relic of 1776 treasure-hunters, has suddenly opened up, threatening further collapses).

West Kennett Avenue Leading away from the circle is this 1½-mile avenue of stones, virtually destroyed by ploughing and mostly replaced by modern concrete posts. It leads to the site of the Sanctuary, a stone circle (on the site of an earlier wooden temple) that was similarly razed, then marked out with posts in modern times.

West Kennett Long Barrow The prehistoric remains of a 5,000-year-old chambered tomb and barrow (one of the largest in the country), where several dozen people were buried. Take a torch if you want to venture in behind the massive entrance stone: the chamber with two side chapels runs some 9 metres (30 ft) or more into the barrow. You have to park in either the car park next to Silbury Hill or the layby at the bottom of the field next to the A4, and then walk about half a mile up the track. The Waggon & Horses at Beckhampton (of *Pickwick Papers* fame) is quite handy.

Windmill Hill Reached by footpath NW, this, the earliest monument in the area, is a neolithic enclosure dating back some 5,000 years. There's not a great deal to see apart from mild lumps, but the site is quite evocative.

BARBURY CASTLE SU1476
One of Wiltshire's 4,500 recorded ancient sites. Many are scarcely a lump in the ground, but this Iron Age camp at the northernmost point of the Marlborough Downs, splendidly remote, still has formidable ramparts. There is a car park nearby, but you can also walk up to it from Ogbourne St George along Smeathe's Ridge, a preserved stretch of downland (gorse and all). The Castle is on the long-distance Ridgeway Path.

BISHOPS CANNINGS SU0364
Attractive village, with an outstanding **church**. The Crown has good value

food, and the Kennet & Avon Canal is a walk away.

BOX ST8268
An attractive up-and-down village, its interesting parts hidden down the steep valley below the A4, with cottages and houses using the same stone that's been quarried nearby since Roman times. There's a story that on 9 Apr, Brunel's birthday, the rising sun shines right through the great railway tunnel he quarried through the hill above here (you can see the restored grand entrance from the A4). The Quarrymans Arms up above has good food.

Hazelbury Manor (off B3109 just E) Richly varied landscaped gardens, with a medieval archery alley, stone and yew circles, fountain, waterfall, pond, large rockery, formal areas and laburnum walk, all laid out as a sort of giant maze. Open by appointment; (01225) 812952; £3. In Chapel Plaister on the way, look out for the 15th-c chapel for Glastonbury pilgrims on the little hilltop green.

BRADFORD-ON-AVON ST8260
Attractive hillside town given a distinguished air by the same sort of golden stone as was used in Bath; it's very steep, and has some handsome buildings reflecting its past wealth as a wool town – and quite a few serious antiques shops. Nr the Norman parish church is a tall narrow late **Saxon church**, unusual for having virtually no later additions. The Dandy Lion (Market St) is good for lunch. From here you can cycle around 11m E to Devizes or 10m W to Bath along the towpath of the Kennet & Avon Canal. Cycle hire from TF Cycles, at the Lock Inn (Frome Rd); £5 for 1st hour, then £1.10 an hour after that; canoe (£10 for 2 hours) and boat hire too; (01225) 867187.

Avoncliff A short walk along the canal, this quite steep gorge is shared by canal, river and railway, the canal disdainfully stepping over the river by way of a recently restored aqueduct. The Cross Guns has remarkable views over it, and is a good place for lunch.

Barton Farm Country Park (Pound Lane) Between the river and canal, a short walk from the town centre.

Lovely walks, bird-watching, riverside picnic area, also rowing, canoeing and fishing. The medieval **tithe barn** (its massive stone-slab roof supported by an impressive network of great beams and rafters) was built to store Shaftesbury Abbey's share of the farm's output. Some other medieval farm buildings have been converted into craft shops, workshops, galleries, and a tearoom.

Iford Manor Garden (just past Westwood) Notable for its stylish Edwardian Italianate riverside terraced garden, with romantic cloisters, colonnade and statues; house not open. Teas wknds and bank hols, May–Aug; cl am, Mon, Fri (exc bank hols), and Oct–Apr (exc Sun Apr and Oct and Apr bank hols); (01225) 863146; *£4

Westwood Manor (above Avoncliff, just SW) Fully furnished 15th-c stone manor house with its original Gothic and Jacobean windows, fine 17th-c plasterwork, and modern topiary garden. No facilities, cl am, and Mon, Thurs–Sat and Oct–Mar; (01225) 863374; £4.20; NT. The church in Westwood village has some interesting late medieval stained glass.

BROKERSWOOD ST8352

Country Park & Woodland Railway 80 acres of ancient woodland, with carp lake, adventure playground, play trail and indoor soft play area, picnic and barbecue areas, and a little woodland railway (wknds and school hols Easter–Oct). Meals (not Mon), snacks, shop, some disabled access; (01373) 822238; cl 25–26 Dec, 1 Jan; *£3. The Poplars over at Wingfield does good lunches.

CALNE SU0069

Atwell-Wilson Motor Museum About 90 vehicles, mostly vintage cars but also lorries, mopeds and classic motorbikes, plus lots of motoring memorabilia; there's a little play area and a 17th-c water meadow walk. Shop, disabled access; cl Fri–Sat (exc Good Fri); (01249) 813319; £2.50.

Bowood (off A4) The extensive Capability Brown parkland and colourful pleasure gardens are the glory of Bowood, with their temples, cascades and hermit's cave shielded from the outside world by further miles of partly wooded grounds; in May a woodland garden is open for rhododendron walks. Much of the main building was demolished in 1955, but there's plenty left, inc the impressive library designed by Robert Adam. Joseph Priestley discovered oxygen here in 1772 and it's home to an excellent collection of watercolours. There's an outstanding adventure playground and new soft play area. Meals, snacks, shop, limited disabled access; cl Nov–Mar; (01249) 812102; £6.05. The Lansdowne Arms at Derry Hill, near the house, is nice for lunch, and Calne also has a **motor museum**.

CASTLE COMBE ST8477

For many the prettiest village in Britain, this has a classic group of stone-tiled Cotswoldy cottages by the turreted church, at the bottom of a tree-clad hill running down to a trout stream and its ancient stone bridge. Preservation of the village is taken so seriously that you won't even see television aerials on the houses; several villagers occasionally open their beautifully kept gardens for charity. Best of all during the week out of season; at other times it does get a great many visitors, even though the car park is some way up the hill. The charming old Castle Inn has good food. The village has surroundings that are equally appealing, and attractive paths along deep peaceful valleys.

CASTLE EATON SU1495

Attractive village, by a quiet stretch of the upper Thames, pleasant for strolling. The Red Lion, with an impressive new conservatory, has decent food.

CHERHILL DOWN SU0469

This large NT area of ancient downland has free access for walkers. A range of man-made features of various periods adorn its slopes, inc an Iron Age hill fort (Oldbury Castle), an assortment of long barrows, tumuli and ancient field systems, a figure of a white horse, and the mid-19th-c Lansdowne Monument; the site is rich in chalkland flora such as orchids, and associated butterfly and bird life.

CHICKSGROVE ST9730

Charming tucked-away hamlet; peaceful walk to Sutton Mandeville church, and back by the Nadder Valley,

and good imaginative food at the Compasses.

CHILMARK ST9732

Attractive village, with a partly 13th-c church. The Black Dog, with links to early Massachusetts settlers, has enjoyable food.

CHOLDERTON SU2042

Cholderton Rare Breeds Farm (Amesbury Rd, just off A338) Fun, friendly and well laid out, good for families with young children. There are plenty of opportunities to get close to the animals, inc the youngest of the 50 or so breeds of rabbit they keep. Other friendly residents include Coco the donkey, Ebenezer the goat and some pygmy goats. Visitors really enjoy their National Grunt pig racing (twice a day at wknds and in school hols, usually around 12.30 and 3.30pm); also tractor and trailer rides, a couple of play areas inc one for under-7s, and trampolines. Nature trails lace through orchards and woodland, and there are tranquil water gardens in the attractive grounds. Meals, snacks (good cream teas), shop, disabled access; cl Nov–Mar; (01980) 629438; £4.25. The Malet Arms at Newton Tony does good lunches.

CLEY HILL ST8344

This steep-sided hill just W of Warminster involves a short, puffy stroll to the Iron Age hill fort at its summit, looking across Longleat Park.

CORSHAM ST8770

Corsham Court Fine house and park begun in 1582 but later added to and developed by those busy masters Capability Brown, John Nash, Robert Adam and Humphry Repton. The paintings are among the best in any stately home in Britain, inc works by Lippi, Reynolds, Dolci and Van Dyck. The extensive lawns and a Georgian bath house are patrolled by peacocks. Cl am, Mon (exc bank hols), wkdys Jan to mid-Mar, and all Dec (01249) 701610; £5, £2 garden only. Nearby are some attractive former weavers' cottages; the **church**, on the edge of the park, is largely 12th c, partly Saxon. The Methuen Arms is good for lunch.

CRANBORNE CHASE ST9319

Some of the finest walking in the S of Wiltshire is to be found here close to the Dorset border, where the county's abundant chalk downland shows at its best. A good example is Ashcombe Bottom N of Tollard Royal, a deep remote valley which plunges into the heart of the Chase. The Grove Arms at Ludwell has good food.

CRICKLADE SU1093

Small town quietly separated from the busy A419, with some attractive buildings and a glorious tower crowning the fine parish church. At the end of the High St, just N of the Thames, a path on the left off the slip road heading back towards the A419 leads to a broad riverside meadow kept unimproved for decades, and mown only in July after the numerous wild flowers have seeded. The Vale has up-to-date food.

CROFTON SU2662

Crofton Beam Engines 🔲 Still pumping water into the Kennet & Avon Canal, the oldest working beam engines in the world, an 1812 Boulton & Watt, and an 1845 Harveys of Hayle. Snacks, shop; cl Oct– Easter, engines usually static, but in steam bank hol wknds and last wknds of Jun, July and Sept; (01672) 870300; static *£2.50, steam wknds *£4. Nearby Wilton village is picturesque, with a windmill; the Swan there is good if not cheap for family lunches.

DEVIZES SU0061

Lots of grand old buildings in this interesting and friendly town, and a good town trail takes most of them in. There's still an active market square (with a statue of Ruth Pierce, who fell dead on the spot after telling a porky and calling God to witness it as true). The 29 locks of the Kennet & Avon Canal coming up Caen Hill from the W form one of the longest flights of locks in the country. The HQ of the Canal Trust on the Wharf has a museum and information centre; Cl 25 Dec–Feb; (01380) 729489; £1.50. The handsome Bear (Market Pl) and Moonraker (A342) are good for lunch. **Broadleas** (Potterne Rd) Rare plants in secluded dell among rhododendrons, magnolias and other fine flowering shrubs, unusual trees, particularly good in spring with sheets of bulbs under flowering trees. Teas Sun, unusual plant sales; open pms Sun, Weds and Thurs, Apr–Oct; (01380) 722035; *£3.

Wiltshire Heritage Museum (Long St) First-class local history, particularly good on finds from the area's ancient sites (the Bronze Age gallery is especially interesting); art gallery with John Piper window. Shop, some disabled access; usually open daily (exc most bank hols); (01380) 727369; £3 (free on Mons).

DINTON SU0031

Philipps House and Dinton Park Fine early 19th-c mansion with interesting Portland stone staircase and underfloor heating system. The surrounding parkland offers plenty of scope for a stroll. Some disabled access; house open Sat am and Mon pm Apr–Oct, park open all year; (01985) 843600; house £3, park free.

EBBLE VALLEY SU0024

The valley of the Ebble chalk stream winds prettily through a sleepy stream of villages from Odstock to Alvediston – a delightful drive.

FIGSBURY RING SU1833

Iron Age hill fort with good views over Salisbury.

FOVANT SU0128

Regimental Badges Huge chalk carvings on the escarpment, clearly seen from the road, cut by troops stationed here in World War I – a sight to rival England's various white horses. The Pembroke Arms, with touching memorabilia of the time, has good value food.

GREAT BEDWYN SU2764

Bedwyn Stone Museum Fascinating little open-air museum demonstrating the ancient art of stonemasonry (the nearby church has fine examples of the finished product). Disabled access but a bit bumpy in places; cl 25 Dec; (01672) 870234; free. The Three Tuns has good value food.

HAYDOWN HILL SU3156

Reached from the E by a walk up from Vernham Dean in Hampshire, this has the ramparts of a hill fort bounded by steep gradients on its S side; the three counties of Berkshire, Hampshire and Wiltshire meet close by at SU350590.

HOLT ST8663

Great Chalfield Manor (N of Holt) Beautiful medieval moated manor house, restored in 1905 and still with its original Great Hall. Large gardens.

Guided tours only, at 12.15, 2.15, 3, 3.45 and 4.30pm; cl Fri–Mon and Nov–Mar; (01225) 782239 to book; *£4; NT. Next door is a small 13th-c parish church.

The Courts Garden ⬛ (B3107) Weavers used to come here to settle their disputes; the 15th-c house isn't open, but the extensive formal gardens are lovely and full of yew hedges, pools and borders. Grounds beyond are given over to wild flowers among interesting trees, with a newly planted orchard and herb and vegetable gardens. Snacks, some disabled access; cl am, Sat, and mid-Oct to Mar; (01225) 782340; £4; NT. The Toll Gate (Ham Green) does good interesting food.

KENNET & AVON CANAL ST8559

This restored canal runs right across the county, and there are pleasant boat trips from several places, among them Bradford-on-Avon and Devizes, or you can hire a boat for the day in Hilperton (01225) 769847 or Semington (01380) 870654. In the canal's restoration, a great deal of attention has been paid to the natural environment, so it's attractive for walks alongside; in winter you may even see a kingfisher flashing along it. For a more sedentary view, try the Barge Inn at Seend Cleeve ST9361, French Horn at Pewsey Wharf SU1560, Barge at Honeystreet SU1061 or Bridge Inn at Horton SU0563. The Golden Swan at Wilcot SU1461, Crown at Bishops Cannings SU0363, Somerset Arms at Semington ST3960 and Hop Pole at Limpley Stoke ST7861 are also within a walk.

LACOCK ST9168

A favourite village of both visitors and film-makers (see for instance the first Harry Potter film), its grid of quiet and narrow streets a delightful harmony of mellow brickwork, lichened stone and timber-and-plaster. The church is 15th-c, and nothing in the village looks more recent than 18th c. It's remained so remarkably unspoilt because most of its buildings were owned for centuries by the Talbot family, until they left them to the NT in 1944. It gets very busy in summer, but the Trust has preserved it against a surfeit of antiques shops (you'll find all you want in the nearby old market town of Melksham). The village does on the other hand have a splendid collection of pubs – the George is the best.

Lackham Country Park ⬛ Plenty of family activities, inc farm museum, walled garden and glasshouses, animal farm, pleasant woodland walk. The 500-acre estate is the home of the Wiltshire College Lackham, and the old roses are worth catching from May to July. Snacks, shop, plant sales, disabled access; open Sun and bank hols Easter–Aug; (01249) 466847; *£2.

Lacock Abbey ⬛ Tranquil spread of mellow stone buildings around a central timber-gabled courtyard, based on the little-altered 13th-c abbey. Tudor additions include a romantic octagonal tower, and there was a successful 18th-c Gothicisation. Surrounded by meadows and trees, this was the setting for Fox Talbot's experiments which in 1835 led to the creation of the world's first photographic negative – a picture of part of the abbey itself. There's an interesting museum devoted to this in a 16th-c barn at the gates, and the gardens are evidence of Fox Talbot's skills in other fields. Limited disabled access; cl Good Fri, Tues and Nov–Mar, Abbey also cl ams; (01249) 730227; £6.20, museum, grounds and cloisters only £4; NT. The photography museum is also open winter wknds (exc Christmas–New Year).

LONGLEAT ST8043

(off A362 4m W of Warminster) Few places can boast such a range of activities for families, and the Passport Ticket allows you to spread the attractions over more than one visit. Children will probably get most excited about the safari park, which as well as the famous lions has rhinos, camels, elephants and a rare white tiger. Unusually, you can walk through some parts, and if you haven't got a car you can go by bus (it gets booked up very quickly, so go early in the day). A boat trip leads to Gorilla Island, where two gorillas live in a miniature stately home. Also displays of parrots and butterflies, a narrow-gauge railway, simulator ride, pets' corner, and an elaborate play area in a full-size mock castle. Older visitors may prefer the collection of dolls' houses or the peaceful formal gardens laid out by Capability Brown, and of course there's the handsome 16th-c house itself, much restored inside, but with impressively grand formal rooms, and the individual murals of the colourful current Marquis of Bath. He has had several mazes and labyrinths built around the grounds: the yew hedge maze is the world's longest, and one new maze is the prize design of a 12-year-old *Blue Peter* winner. Changing exhibitions, lots of extra events, and you can get coarse fishing permits. Meals, snacks, shop, disabled access; largely cl Nov–early Apr, phone to check; (01985) 844400. You can get individual tickets for the attractions, but it works out much cheaper to buy the all-in Passport Ticket, £15 adults, £11 Children.

LUDGERSHALL SU2651
Ludgershall Castle The ruins of a Royal castle and hunting palace, still with some of the original large Norman earthworks, as well as the later flint walling; free; EH. The church is also Norman; the Queens Head has cheap food. The nearby area is very pretty and unspoilt, the little villages of the Chutes, Tangley and Vernham Dean straddling the Hampshire border all worth a look (with the pubs over that way worth exploring too).

LYDIARD PARK SU1084
Lydiard Park (nr M4 junction 16, or A3102) Painstakingly restored grand Georgian house, with interesting early wallpaper, rare painted glass window, and elegant furnishings much as they would have been when first installed. Extensive lawns, lakes and well wooded parkland, with nature walks and adventure playgrounds. Snacks, shop, disabled access; cl Sun am, 24–26 Dec, 1 Jan, Good Fri and pm of second Sat in May; (01793) 770401; house £1.40 – quite a bargain. The adjacent parish **church** has interesting monuments to the St John family, who lived in the house for 500 years, and the Sun at Lydiard Millicent has enjoyable food.

MALMESBURY ST9387
Yet another charming old town, especially around the green facing its serene Norman abbey, from the tower of which a medieval monk called Elmer made one of the earliest semi-

successful attempts at flight – he covered a couple of hundred yards, but did break both legs when he crash-landed. The picturesque Old Bell is almost as old as the abbey beside it, and the Smoking Dog (High St) has good value interesting food. The B roads radiating from here are all quite pleasant drives.

MARLBOROUGH SU1868
One of the area's most attractive towns; its very pleasing wide High St has a market each Weds and Sat. The annual autumn Mop Fair (as in most market towns, formerly for the hiring of servants) has been revived here as a general celebration. Even the more modern additions don't look obtrusively out of place among the harmonious mix of Georgian and Tudor buildings. You can see renovations in progress and sometimes craftsmen in action at the 17th-c **Merchant's House** (High St) which has some completed and period furnished rooms; cl Mon–Thurs and all Oct–Easter; (01672) 511491; £3. The Bear and Castle & Ball are useful for lunch. The Broad Hinton road N gives a good feel of the downs' great open spaces, as does the Manton–Alton Priors road to the SW, passing one of the area's several white horses cut into the chalk, and leading into a pleasant valley drive through Allington and Horton to Devizes. To the E, the quiet road along the Kennet Valley has some attractive views, with pleasant walks and a good food stop at the Red Lion in Axford; there are also walks through the surviving miles of Savernake Forest woodland.

MERE ST8132
Attractive village, dominated by its 30-metre (100-ft) church tower, and with good views from Castle Hill. The interesting 16th-c Old Ship has good value food.

White Sheet Hill Easily reached from Mere (via a road bridge over the busy A303) or Stourton, this lofty chalk downland is studded with antiquities – among them a neolithic causewayed camp and Bronze Age barrows. It's a good site for cowslips, orchids and such butterflies as adonis and chalkhill blues.

MIDDLE WOODFORD SU1236
Heale Gardens & Plant Centre
Eight acres of lovely formal gardens

beside the Avon chalk stream, with lots of varied plants; the water garden is especially nice in spring and autumn. Snacks, shop, specialist plant sales with many rare types propagated from the main gardens, disabled access; gardens cl 25–26 Dec and Mon exc bank hols; (01722) 782504; £3.25. The Bridge Inn in nearby Upper Woodford has good food and a nice riverside garden, and this Salisbury road along the Avon's quieter bank is a pretty drive (as is the continuation N of Amesbury, through Fittleworth and East Chisenbury).

NOMANSLAND SU2517
Forest-edge walks There are some pleasant walks in countryside that's unusual for Wiltshire, around the good value Lamb down on the edge of the New Forest.

PEPPERBOX HILL SU2125
(5m SE of Salisbury) Named after the hexagonal 17th-c tower (built as a folly) on its summit. You can't get into the tower, but the site commands fine views over Salisbury itself, and S as far as Southampton. The White Hart over at Bishopstone has decent food.
Bentley Wood Beyond East Grimstead N of here, a nature reserve with good walks.

SALISBURY SU1429
A beautiful and gently relaxed city, with a good many fine old buildings, particularly around the lovely cathedral close. The most extensive close in the country, it's always been a distinct area of town, and the gates to it are still locked each night. The buildings cover a variety of architectural styles from the 13th c to the present, and while of course its great glory is the elegant cathedral itself, you can't help being struck by how impeccably mown the lawns are. Outside the close, there are some interesting antiques and other little independent shops, and the broad Market Sq still has a traditional market each Tues and Sat; parking in town can be tricky then, so it's a good idea to take advantage of the Park and Ride system (parking at Old Sarum to the N on the A345). The Haunch of Venison (Minster St) is an interesting old town tavern. Besides places we describe individually below, the close also includes striking St Anne's Gate, a regimental museum (cl

Mon Feb–Mar and Nov and all Dec–Jan; (01722) 414536; *£2.75).
Medieval Hall (West Walk, The Close) The regular 40-min sound and picture shows in this 13th-c hall give a colourful introduction to the city and its environs. Teas during the show, disabled access (but not facilities); cl Oct–Mar and for occasional special events; (01722) 412472; £1.50.
Mompesson House (The Close) Exquisite Queen Anne building, probably the most interesting in the close, with period furnishings, china and paintings, remarkable collection of 18th-c drinking glasses, and interestingly carved oak staircase. Tearoom with nice home-made cakes, disabled access to ground floor; cl Thurs–Fri and Oct–Mar; (01722) 335659; £3.90, 80p gardens only; NT. The NT shop is a couple of minutes' walk away on the High St.
Old Sarum (off A345 2m N) This substantial and easily defended Iron Age hill fort continued as a town right through the Roman occupation and Dark Ages into Norman times. In the early 13th c there was a general move to the much more fertile site of the present city, and the fort gradually fell into decline, becoming a quarry for the new centre; consequently there's not much left, but the views are splendid, and the foundations give interesting clues to ancient architecture and styles. Snacks, shop, limited disabled access; cl 24–26 Dec, 1 Jan; (01722) 335398; £2; EH.
Salisbury & South Wiltshire Museum 🖼 (Kings House, The Close) Local history and archaeology in lovely building, with excellent up-to-date Stonehenge gallery, collections of Wedgwood china, costume, lace and embroidery, and some beautiful local watercolours by Turner. One of its more obscure but intriguing exhibits is an aestel, an Anglo-Saxon jewel with links to King Alfred, found by a metal-detector enthusiast in a Wiltshire field. Meals, snacks, shop, disabled access; cl Sun exc July–Aug, 25–26 Dec; (01722) 332151; £3.50.
Salisbury Cathedral Begun in 1220 and completed in only 38 years – giving a rare uniformity of style. The magnificent spire (added in 1315 along

with the tower) is at 123 metres (404 ft) the tallest in the country, and many would say the finest in the world. 332 winding spiral steps take you to the top of the tower, giving spectacular views of the city and surrounding countryside – and you can peer up into the spire, with its internal medieval scaffolding. Also notable are a fascinating floor-mounted 14th-c clock (the oldest working mechanical clock in the world), and the tomb of the first Earl of Salisbury, who gave the church one of only four surviving editions of the Magna Carta; it's still on show in the Chapter House, alongside remarkable early silver. The cloisters stand out too. Meals and snacks (with good views of the spire), shop, disabled access; (01722) 555120; £3.50 suggested donation, tower tour £3. The guides are entertaining and knowledgeable. There's a classic view of the cathedral from across the water meadows, where the Old Mill has decent food.

St Thomas's church (St Thomas's Sq) Built for cathedral workers and in part slightly older than it; has a well preserved medieval Doom painting. Shop; (01722) 322537.

SALISBURY PLAIN ST9648
Better for driving over than walking – an almost unbroken expanse of rolling high ground, a mixture of pasture and broad unhedged arable fields intersected by tank-training tracks. The A360 gives a good feel of its emptiness. Tourist Information Centres in the area carry a leaflet that maps out clearly way-marked walks around the edges of the Army's Imber firing range, totalling some 30 miles for the complete circuit: generally peaceful countryside with large-scale arable farming, but some wide views and sometimes the sight of tank and infantry training. On the W edges, the Angel at Upton Scudamore is a good dining pub.

SANDY LANE ST9668
Attractive village; the road from here through Bowden Hill is the prettiest approach to Lacock.

SEMLEY ST8926
Attractive village, with an interesting church; the Benett Arms is good.

SEVENHAMPTON SU2188
Roves Farm 🔠 The eight-week

spring lambing season is one of the best times to come to this friendly farm, but it's lively at any time, with pig, sheep and goat racing, lots more animal action such as summer shearing, and a clever two-acre living willow maze. Also huge barns with craft sessions and play areas indoors as well as out, bouncy castle, long tractor trailer rides. Good café, shop, disabled access; cl Mon–Tues in term time and Nov–Mar; (01793) 763939; £4. The Saracens Head in Highworth has good value food.

STONEHENGE SU1142
Stonehenge (off A344) One of the most famous prehistoric monuments in the world; everyone knows what it looks like, and how they got the stones here has been pretty much sorted out (the larger ones local, the smaller ones all the way from South Wales), but nobody's really sure exactly what Stonehenge (with its careful astronomical alignments) was for. In the interests of conservation, you can't normally go right up to the stones (see below), but you can get pretty close, and the fact that people are kept back means that your photos won't be cluttered by the crowds. The best views are very early in the morning from the track from Larkhill, on the other side of the A344, or on a cold clear winter evening looking W past the monument towards the sunset; the ancient stones look very impressive silhouetted against the sky. Even in the crowded light of day the place never quite loses its power to inspire awe. The car park area and busy main roads nearby detract a little, but great improvements here and to the visitor centre are in the pipeline, and may be completed by 2006. Snacks, shop, disabled access (and a Braille guide); (01980) 624715 – but beware, it's a very long-winded answering machine; cl 24–26 Dec, 1 Jan; £4.40 (inc very good audio tour); EH. Private access outside normal hours (not Oct–Nov) can be booked in advance, phone (01980) 626267 (£10 for an hour visit); or Astral Travels (0870) 902 0908 organise day trips from London (£52). Good walks from here around associated ancient monuments (leaflet available in the car park). There's good pick-your-own

fruit late Jun–late July at Rolleston Manor Farm on the B3086 NW.

Woodhenge The scant traces of another prehistoric monument further E which consisted of six rings of timber posts in a ditch; the positions are now marked by concrete posts, and a cairn marks the central spot where the tomb of a little girl ceremoniously axed to death was found.

STOURTON ST7835

Stourhead (off B3092) Marvellous 18th-c landscape garden, laid out in Italian style by the banker Henry Hoare II following his return from the grand tour; a beautifully harmonious landscape of temples, lakes, bridges and splendid trees and other plants. Remarkable views into Somerset from King Alfred's Tower, the tall 18th-c folly at the far end, though there are 221 steps (cl am and Nov–Mar; £1.85). The early Georgian Palladian house has some good Chippendale furniture, and the church in the grounds is in a lovely hillside setting. Meals, snacks, shop, art gallery, disabled access; garden open all year, house cl Weds–Thurs and Nov–Mar; (01747) 841152; £8.90 for gardens and house, £5.10 for one or the other (£1.15 less for gardens Nov–Feb) – if you can do only one, make it the gardens; NT. The Spread Eagle at the entrance is good for lunch and does cold food all day.

SWINDON SU1484

Much older than you might think, this bustling market town and business centre was caught up with a vengeance in the railway age, and in the Railway Village had one of the earliest examples of a planned workers' estate. The Savoy (Regent Circus) has decent food in an interestingly converted cinema.

National Monuments Record Centre (Great Western Village, off Kemble Drive) The public archive of English Heritage, full of information on England's architecture and archaeology. Lots of photographs (inc some from the mid-19th c, and aerial shots of all of England), plus maps, plans and data about historical buildings and ancient sites. A gallery hosts interesting temporary exhibitions; there may be guided tours of the building (the former HQ of the Great Western Railway) on

the third Sat in the month – best to check on (01793) 414600. Meals, snacks, shop, disabled access; cl Christmas–New Year and bank hols, archive cl Sat–Mon, gallery cl Mon/Tues; (01793) 414700; free. Steam (see family panel, p.640) is in the same former railway complex.

Steam See separate family panel on p.640.

Swindon & Cricklade Railway (Blunsdon, off B4553 N) One of the only live steam projects in the area, gradually being restored, with trips through the countryside, and small museum. Snacks, shop, disabled access; open Sun and bank hols (exc 25–26 Dec and 1 Jan); (01793) 771615; £2 (more on special event days).

Swindon Museum & Art Gallery (Bath Rd) Includes works by great 20th-c artists such as Moore and Sutherland. Shop, disabled access to ground floor only; cl Sun am, bank hols; (01793) 466556; free.

TEFFONT MAGNA ST9832

Farmer Giles Farmstead Friendly working dairy farm, with 150 cows milked every afternoon; children can feed some of the animals, or simply sit and stroke them. Also tractor-trailor rides, indoor play area, outdoor play area with old tractors for clambering, old farming equipment, and small vineyard. Snacks, shop, disabled access; cl wkdys Nov–Mar; (01722) 716338; £3.95. The village is very attractive, full of charming stone-built cottages with neatly banked stone-walled gardens; the Black Horse has good food.

TISBURY ST9429

Charming small town, left behind by the main roads so largely unspoilt, with some fine old buildings, riverside church, and just outside to the E an immensely long medieval tithe barn. The lovely old Crown does decent food.

Old Wardour Castle (a couple of miles S) Remains of a substantial 14th-c lakeside castle. Though badly damaged in the Civil War, its walls still stand to their original 18 metres (60 ft), and you can walk almost to the top (signs indicate what life was like when the castle was still lived in). It's a lovely peaceful setting, landscaped in the

18th c, with country walks of varying lengths from the car park. Snacks, shop, disabled access to grounds only; cl lunchtimes and Mon–Tues Nov–Mar and 24–26 Dec, 1 Jan; (01747) 870487; £2.50; EH.

TOLLARD ROYAL ST9517
Larmer Tree Gardens (off A354) Attractive Victorian pleasure gardens in the heart of Cranborne Chase. Laid out by General Pitt Rivers, they were the first privately owned gardens open to the public but then closed for almost a century, opening again a few years back. Pheasants, macaws and peacocks may strut their stuff, you can play croquet (by arrangement), and the temples and grottoes are an appealing backdrop to the band concerts they have summer Suns; also adventure playground and special events. Teas, some disabled access; cl Sat, all July and Oct–Mar; (01725) 516228; £3.75.

WESTBURY ST8951
To the E you can see the huge Westbury white horse cut into the chalk of the downs; late 18th-c, it was an 'improvement' on an altogether older one which may have been Saxon, and which faced in the opposite direction. Above the white horse is an extensive Iron Age hill fort, with good views right down to the Mendips in Somerset.

WHITE SHEET HILL ST9424
The Harepath here is a high track giving sweeping views; you can branch off into a forest plantation. Below in the pretty thatched village of Berwick St John, the Talbot has decent food. Note that Wiltshire has a second hill with the same name, above Mere.

WILTON SU0931
Wilton Carpet Factory 🅴 (King St) Surprisingly interesting demonstrations of how they make Wilton weaves and Axminster carpets, as well as a museum and carpet-making exhibition. Tours four times a day between 11 and 5, best to book on (01772) 742733. Meals, snacks, shop, disabled access; cl Easter Sun and 10 days over Christmas and New Year; *£4. There is a shopping village next door.
Wilton House Particularly satisfying to visit, well organised and friendly, and usually free from too many crowds. The

original house was damaged by a fire in 1647, and superbly redesigned by John Webb and Inigo Jones, the latter responsible for the magnificent Double Cube room, considered by many to be one of the country's finest surviving rooms from this period; it's full of splendid works by Van Dyck. The Tudor kitchen and Victorian laundry have both been well restored to give a good impression of their original use. The furnishings and art are exquisite, and a lovely doll's house re-creates some parts of the house in miniature. For children the highlight of the 21-acre grounds is the bigger-than-average adventure playground; there's also plenty of space for picnics, as well as water and rose gardens, restful cloister garden, a striking Palladian bridge, and woodland walks. Meals, snacks, shop, disabled access; cl Nov–Mar; (01722) 746720; £9.25. The ornately Italianate 19th-c **church** incorporates all sorts of treasures, esp its magnificent medieval continental stained glass and 2,000-year-old marble pillars. Wiltons (Market Pl) is good for lunch, and the charming Victoria & Albert in nearby Netherhampton is nicely off the tourist track, with a pleasant riverside walk into Salisbury.

WILTON SU2861
Wilton windmill (off A338 E of Burbage) Wiltshire's only working windmill, built in 1821 after the construction of the Kennet & Avon Canal had diverted the water previously used to power mills. Now restored, it's beautifully floodlit most evenings. Shop (sells flour milled on site); open pm Sun and bank hols Easter–Sept; (01672) 870266; £2. This little village of Wilton (not to be confused with the larger town near Salisbury) is attractive; the Swan has good if not cheap food.

WROUGHTON AIRFIELD SU1379
Science Museum A storage facility for lots of the larger items from the National Museum of Science and Industry with national collections of aircraft, rockets, hovercraft, and road transport vehicles, and one of the best displays of tractors in the world. Not really aimed at entertaining the general

public, it's usually open around eight times a year at wknds, during the school summer holidays, and if you book for their tours on the first and third Weds of the month; disabled access; (01793) 814466; now free (it used to be £5).

WYLYE SU0037
Attractive village in delightful valley; one lane is called Teapot St, and the Bell is a good dining pub.

Other attractive villages, all with decent pubs, include Aldbourne ST2675, Alderbury SU1827, waterside Ashton Keynes SU0494, Axford SU2370, Berwick St John ST9323 (steep walks nearby), Biddestone ST8773, Bishopstone SU2483, Broughton Gifford ST8763, Chitterne ST9843 (good walks), Collingbourne Ducis SU2453, thatched Clyffe Pypard SU0777, Donhead St Andrew ST9124, Great Cheverell ST9754, Great Hinton ST9059, Great Wishford SU0735, Hannington SU1793, Heddington ST9966, Highworth SU2092, Kilmington ST7736, Kington Langley ST9277, Lockeridge SU1467 (good walks), Marston Meysey SU1297, Monkton Farleigh ST8065, Newton Toney SU2140, Oare SU1563, Pewsey SU1560, Pitton SU2131 (wood and downland walks), Potterne ST9938, Poulshot ST9559, Ramsbury ST2771, Sherston ST8585, Steeple Ashton ST9056, Stockton ST9738, The Green ST8731 (nr East Knoyle), Upton Lovell ST9440, West Dean SU2527, Winsley ST7961 and Wootton Rivers SU1963.

Where to eat

AXFORD SU2370 **Red Lion** *(01672) 520271* Welcoming brick and flint pub with fine views over valley from sheltered garden or bustling beamed and pine-panelled bar, good popular food in bar and no smoking restaurant (enjoyable daily specials and fresh fish and game), decent wines, and well kept real ales. £24.25|**£6.95**

BOX ST8369 **Quarrymans Arms** *Box Hill (01225) 743569* Unspoilt tucked-away hillside pub with fine views, two small interesting knocked-together rooms with quarrying memorabilia, a wide choice of enjoyable and popular home-cooked food, well kept real ales, and very friendly staff; bdrms. £20|**£5.25**

BRADFORD-ON-AVON ST8261 **Dandy Lion** *35 Market St (01225) 863433* Particularly relaxed and friendly, with an interesting mix of people, big windows on either side of the door with a table and chairs in each, high-backed farmhouse chairs and old-fashioned dining chairs on the stripped wood floor, newspapers to read, nostalgic pop, and a snug little back room; very well liked and reasonably priced food, real ales, good coffee, and candlelit upstairs restaurant; children in restaurant only. £22.50|**£5**

BRINKWORTH SU0184 **Three Crowns** *The Street (01666) 510366* Friendly atmosphere in villagey pub with imaginative food from a changing menu that covers an entire wall, ten wines by the glass, well kept real ales, elegant no smoking conservatory, and garden looking out towards church and rolling country; get there early as it is very busy; cl 25 Dec; disabled access. £26

CORTON ST9340 **Dove** *(01985) 850109* Charming cottage country pub with an attractively furnished main bar, huge winter log fire in big central fireplace, a mix of chairs, cushioned wall seats and dining tables in areas leading off, and no smoking conservatory; good inventive well presented food at sensible prices (though evening dishes are more expensive), real ales, several wines by the glass, attentive friendly staff, and daily papers; tables on the neatly kept back lawn; charming bdrms; disabled access. £21|**£7.50**

GREAT HINTON ST9059 **Linnet** *(01380) 870354* Attractive old brick pub with pretty summer-flowering tubs and window-boxes; little right-hand bar with lots of interest on the green walls, comfortable wall banquettes, a biggish rather smart dining room with pink ragged walls, bric-a-brac, plenty of dining chairs and tables, reliably good food inc enjoyable bar snacks and imaginative daily specials and evening choices, real ales, quite a few malts, and nice summer Pimms; cl Mon exc bank hols. £23|**£6.95**

HINDON ST9033 **Angel** *High St (01747) 820696* Attractively refurbished 18th-c coaching inn with Victorian prints and artefacts in the pubby red-painted traditional bar, flagstones, a lovely log fire, and candlelight, a civilised no smoking lounge, a smartened up long dining room with a huge window giving you a view of the busy kitchen, enjoyable popular food inc imaginative daily specials, well kept ales, a dozen wines by the glass, and daily papers; seats in flower-filled back courtyard; good bdrms; cl Sun pm. £27.50|£7.25

HOLT ST8561 **Toll Gate** Ham Green (01225) 782326 Popular dining pub furnished and decorated with flair – part with cosy settees and a log fire, the rest more adapted to eating; hunting prints on pinkish walls, black panelling, charming high-raftered restaurant (formerly a chapel for weavers working here) with attractive bric-a-brac; beautifully presented imaginative food inc good value set lunch, kind helpful service, eight or so wines by the glass, good coffee, farm cider, half a dozen well kept changing beers. £26.75/2-course set lunch £9.95

MARLBOROUGH SU1969 **Munchies** 8 The Parade (01672) 512649 Lovely beamed building with marvellous range of really interesting and delicious sandwiches with daily changing home-made fillings using the freshest ingredients; cl Sat–Sun; disabled access|£2.50

MARLBOROUGH SU1869 **Polly Tearooms** 26 High St (01672) 512146 In centre of pretty High St, well known for very good cream teas, with home-made bread, scones, jams and cakes; also light lunches and cooked breakfasts; cl evenings, and 25–26 Dec. £16|£5.50

NORTON ST8884 **Vine Tree** (01666) 837654 Civilised dining pub with a lively atmosphere in its three smallish rooms, sporting prints, lots of stripped pine, candles in bottles on the tables, and some old settles; a wide range of enjoyable food from a seasonally changing menu, well kept real ales, ten wines by the glass, and a no smoking dining area; picnic-sets in a two-acre garden, a good play area, and three boules pitches. £27.70|£10

PITTON SU2131 **Silver Plough** White Hill (01722) 712266 Stylish village inn with lots to look at in comfortable beamed front bar, good bar snacks and more elaborate meals with emphasis on fresh fish and seafood, well kept real ales, country wines, and efficient service; cl pms 25–26 Dec; children in snug and restaurant but must be well behaved. £30|£5

REDLYNCH SU2120 **Langley Wood** (01794) 390348 Very good innovative food and a carefully chosen wine list in homely and warmly friendly creeper-covered restaurant-with-rooms, in its own grounds; cl Sun pm, Mon, Tues; children must behave (small helpings but no special menu); disabled access. £30

ROWDE ST9762 **George & Dragon** High St (01380) 723053 Interesting old pub with log fire, a fine collection of brass keys, and plenty of dark wood, a simple no smoking dining room, exceptional imaginative food (esp delicious fresh fish and lovely puddings), a relaxed atmosphere, and well kept real ales; cl Mon, 25 Dec, 1 Jan; children must be well behaved. £25|£5

SHERSTON ST8586 **Rattlebone** Church St (01666) 840871 Lively 16th-c pub with low beams, country furnishings, lots of jugs and bottles and a pleasant relaxed atmosphere in several spotless rambling rooms; decent, well liked food plus more elaborate daily specials, partly no smoking restaurant, decent wines, well kept real ales, lots of malt whiskies, and a pretty little garden with boules; cl 25 Dec am; good disabled access. £21.10|£5.25

WHITLEY ST8866 **Pear Tree** Top Lane (01225) 709131 Attractive honey-coloured stone farmhouse with a civilised, friendly and chatty atmosphere, front bar with cushioned window seats, some stripped shutters, a mix of dining chairs around good solid tables, a variety of country pictures, and a little fireplace on the left, with a lovely old stripped stone one on the right; popular big back restaurant, enticing and delicious food beautifully presented and served by first-class staff, well kept real ales, a good wine list with ten by the glass, and seats on the terrace; boules; bdrms; cl 25 Dec, 1 Jan; disabled access. £29.75|£6

WOODBOROUGH SU1159 **Seven Stars** Bottlesford (01672) 851325 Civilised pub in seven riverside acres, with attractively moulded panelling in the main bar, a hot coal fire in a range at one end and a big log fire at the other, a pleasant mix of seats and tables, cosy nooks, and retired wine bottles on delft shelves; attractive back dining area, good daily changing Anglo/French cooking (inc marvellous veg, winter game and summer seafood), exemplary wine list with a dozen by the glass, and very friendly owners; cl Sun pm, Mon and Tues after bank hols; children must be well behaved. £22.95|£7.95

WOOTTON RIVERS SU1963 **Royal Oak** *(01672) 810322* Prettily thatched 16th-c pub with a relaxed atmosphere, L-shaped dining lounge with woodburner, comfortably furnished timbered bar, very popular food from a huge and interesting menu, well kept beer, decent wines and some interesting whiskies, and friendly service; bdrms. £23|£5

WYLYE SU0037 **Bell** *High St (01985) 248338* Cosy and civilised little 14th-c country pub, three log fires, neatly kept black-beamed and timbered rustic front bar, comfortably carpeted no smoking restaurant with pristine white linen and a more sophisticated feel; very well cooked bar food using fresh ingredients with interesting daily specials, four well kept real ales, seven wines by the glass, quite a few country wines, daily papers, and seats out on pleasant walled terrace and in back garden; children in restaurant only; fine downland walks nearby; disabled access. £30|£7.50

Special thanks to B and K Hypher, Mrs Y Champion, Jenny and Chris Wilson

WORCESTERSHIRE

Some great landscapes, classic black and white timbered villages, and a few entertaining outings

The Malvern Hills which dominate the county provide one of England's great ridge walks. On their flanks the elegant spa town, Great Malvern, is good to potter around and gives easy access to this wonderful hill scenery. The orchards make blossom time (usually April through early May) and harvest time (September) an appealing time to visit Worcestershire: local tourist board trails make it easy to see the best of this, especially in the Vale of Evesham. Prices are generally low, making the area good value for short breaks.

Busy Worcester has interesting places to visit (children like best the Commandery and Bennetts Farm Park), and some attractive medieval buildings. Beautiful Cotswolds-edge Broadway is also well worth a stop. The attractive little town of Bewdley is home to the West Midlands Safari Park, our top Family Attraction here this year (exotic animals plus fairground rides ensure a fun day out for youngsters), and splendid Severn Valley Railway steam trips leave from here too. The Avoncroft Museum of Historic Buildings in Bromsgrove is good for a relaxed afternoon.

The ruin of the Italianate palace in Great Witley is an awesome sight. Those who like their houses intact will prefer Hanbury Hall (with its outstanding painted ceilings), the state rooms at Hartlebury Castle, or a guided tour of Hagley Hall. The gardens at Burford and Croome Park are pleasant fine weather excursions. At Elgar's birthplace in Lower Broadheath, a museum celebrates his life and work (the Elgar Trail starts here too). Bird lovers enjoy the friendly Domestic Fowl Trust at Honeybourne, and the Falconry Centre in West Hagley.

Where to stay

ABBERLEY SO7367 **Elms** *Stockton Rd, Abberley, Worcestershire WR6 6AT (01299) 896666* **£120**, plus special breaks; 21 comfortable rms. Lovely Queen Anne mansion with fine views from the well kept grounds, elegant restful drawing room with antiques, log fires and flowers, other reception rooms with original ornate plasterwork and finely carved fireplaces, very good food and wines in airy restaurant, and friendly efficient staff

BROADWAY SP0937 **Broadway Hotel** *The Green, Broadway, Worcestershire WR12 7AA (01386) 852401* **£118**, plus special breaks; 20 well kept rms. Lovely 15th-c building, once a monastic guest house, with galleried and timbered lounge, cosy beamed bar, attractively presented food served by attentive staff in airy comfortable restaurant, and seats outside on terrace; disabled access; dogs welcome in bedrooms

BROADWAY SP0937 **Lygon Arms** *High St, Broadway, Worcestershire WR12 7DU (01386) 852255* **£229**, plus special breaks; 69 lovely period rms (some more modern, too). Handsome hotel where Oliver Cromwell and King Charles I once stayed; interesting beamed rooms, oak panelling, antiques, log fires, fine traditional food in the Great Hall with minstrels' gallery and heraldic frieze, excellent service, and charming garden; health spa; children over 8 in evening restaurant; disabled access; dogs welcome in bedrooms

CHADDESLEY CORBETT SO8873 **Brockencote Hall** *Brockencote, Chaddesley Corbett, Kidderminster, Worcestershire DY10 4PY (01562) 777876* **£135***, plus special breaks; 17 individually decorated rms. Grand country-house hotel in 70 acres with half-timbered dovecot and lake, and plenty of wildlife; large, airy and attractively furnished rooms, conservatory lounge with garden views, elegantly refurbished restaurant with enjoyable modern French and English cooking, and very good service; disabled access

EVESHAM SP0443 **Evesham Hotel** *Coopers Lane, Off Waterside, Evesham, Worcestershire WR11 1DA (01386) 765566* **£108***, plus special breaks; 40 spacious rms with games and jigsaws. Comfortably modernised and cheerful family-run hotel with a warmly friendly, relaxed and jokey atmosphere, popular restaurant with very good food (esp lunchtime buffet), huge wine and spirits list, and sitting room with games and toys; indoor swimming pool surrounded by table tennis and table football, and grounds with croquet, trampoline, swings and putting; particularly well organised for families (but they do not get overrun by children); cl 25–26 Dec; partial disabled access; dogs welcome in bedrooms ☺

HARVINGTON SP0548 **Mill** *Anchor Lane, Harvington, Evesham, Worcestershire WR11 5NR (01386) 870688* **£89***, plus special breaks; 21 comfortable rms overlooking grounds. Handsome Georgian hotel in eight acres of parkland with 180 metres (600 ft) of river, mooring for guests' boats, fishing, hard tennis court, and heated outdoor swimming pool; carefully furnished airy lounges with open fires, courteous helpful staff, fine imaginative food using fresh local produce, thoughtful wine list with helpful notes, and good breakfasts; cl New Year; children over 10

HIMBLETON SO9459 **Phepson Farm** *Phepson, Droitwich, Worcestershire WR9 7JZ (01905) 391205* **£50***, plus winter breaks; 6 rms, 4 in renovated farm buildings. Relaxed and friendly 17th-c farmhouse on small sheep farm with a fishing lake; a comfortable guests' lounge, good breakfasts in separate dining room; self-catering apartment; cl Christmas and New Year; partial disabled access; dogs welcome in bedrooms

KEMERTON SO9437 **Upper Court** *Kemerton, Tewkesbury, Gloucestershire GL20 7HY (01386) 725351* **£95**, plus special breaks; 6 rms, plus others in cottages. Lovely Georgian Cotswold manor with Domesday watermill, a lake (lots of wildfowl and free fly-fishing in season), and dovecote in 15 acres of fine gardens, outdoor heated swimming pool, tennis court, croquet, and boating; relaxed atmosphere and many antiques (the owners run an antiques business and there is always something for sale) in elegant rooms, very good food using home-grown produce (by prior arrangement) around candlelit communal table, and nice breakfasts; cl Christmas; good disabled access

MALVERN SO7647 **Cowleigh Park Farm** *Cowleigh Park, Cradley, Malvern, Worcestershire WR13 5HJ (01684) 566750* **£56***; 3 rms. Carefully restored and furnished black and white timbered 17th-c farmhouse in own grounds, surrounded by lovely countryside, with good breakfasts and light suppers or full evening meals (prior booking); self-catering also; cl Christmas; children over 7; dogs welcome in bedrooms

MALVERN WELLS SO7742 **Cottage in the Wood** *Holywell Rd, Malvern, Worcestershire WR14 4LG (01684) 575859* **£95***, plus special breaks; 20 compact but pretty rms, some in separate nearby cottages. Family-run Georgian dower house with quite splendid views across the Severn Valley and marvellous walks from the grounds; antiques, log fires, comfortable seats and magazines in public rooms, and modern English cooking and an extensive wine list in attractive no smoking restaurant; dogs welcome in bedrooms

WICKHAMFORD SP0642 **Wickhamford Manor** *Manor Rd, Wickhamford, Evesham, Worcestershire WR11 6SA (01386) 830296* **£75***; 3 rms. Striking 16th-c timbered manor, once owned by Queen Elizabeth I and first mentioned in the Domesday Book; set in 20 acres of woodland and pasture with a 12th-c dovecote and lake (created by monks when the abbot lived in a grange here); big log fire in beamed drawing room, good breakfasts in the flagstoned kitchen, and a really warm welcome from the friendly owners; tennis and coarse fishing; cl Christmas and New Year; children over 12 (or babies)

To see and do

Worcestershire Family Attraction of the Year

BEWDLEY SO8075 **West Midlands Safari Park** (Spring Grove, just E on A456) Readers rate this drive-through safari very highly – not least because you can feed some of the animals through the car window, with special feed available from the ticket office. And it's good for children because as well as the animals there's an adjacent leisure park, with around 30 rides; the two parts are kept sensibly separate, so you don't have to go into the leisure park if you don't want to. The animal reserves are home to over 40 rare and exotic species, so lions, tigers, monkeys, elephants, camels, giraffes and wolves have the run of the park while you sit in your car; you'll envy them their freedom if you come on a bank holiday, when the hour-long circuit takes much longer thanks to traffic jams. Bear in mind that though some animals may come right up to your car, others will watch nonchalantly from a distance; luckily you can go round as often as you like, so if you don't see what you want it's easy enough to give it another go, and a second circuit invariably turns up something different. The cost of admission includes an entertaining sea lion show, a seal aquarium with well positioned viewing platforms, hippo feeding displays, insect and reptile house, and Animal Encounter sessions showcasing anything from a sheep to an iguana (it's worth checking when these are when you arrive, so you can plan the safari around them). It costs extra to go into the leisure park – hardly Alton Towers, but with a good mix of children's rides from gentle carousels and dodgems to a log flume and a couple of decent roller-coasters. Dogs aren't allowed in the animal enclosures, but they have free kennels. Meals, snacks, shop, mostly disabled access; open mid-Mar to early Nov; (01299) 402114; the safari park costs £6.25 for adults and children, which includes a free return visit any time during the rest of the season. You can buy individual tickets for rides in the leisure park, but it's better value to buy an all-day wristband: £7.50 for anyone over 1.2 metres, otherwise £6 (some rides have height restrictions). Doing both parts isn't cheap, but you do get a very full day of activities.

ABBERLEY SO7567
Notable for its picturesque, steeply hump-backed packhorse bridge, looking more like a part of Devon or Derbys; ironically, cars have to use a more ancient crossing, the shallow ford beside it. The village was once owned by John of Gaunt. The Bell at Pensax is a good nearby food pub.
ABBERLEY HILLS SO7567
(nr Stourport) Little visited by walkers but rewarding for them: partly wooded, with good views and close to the extraordinary ruins of Witley Court.
ABBOTS MORTON SP0255
Charming village, with a lovely church.

The Boot over at Flyford Flavell is a popular food pub.
ASHTON UNDER HILL SO9938
Charming black and white timbered houses and a good Norman church; made all the more attractive by the brooding backdrop of Bredon Hill.
BEWDLEY SO7874
Attractive small town, with riverside walks and interesting side streets. The Little Pack Horse (old High St) is full of character.
Bewdley Museum (Load St) An 18th-c row of butchers' shops houses this local history museum, which has daily craft demonstrations. Shop, some

disabled access; cl Nov–Mar; (01299) 403573; £2.10.

Severn Valley Railway Britain's leading standard-gauge steam railway, with 16 miles of track from Kidderminster at this end to Bridgnorth in Shropshire. The route largely follows the Severn and as there aren't many roads in the valley this is the only way of seeing some parts of this delightful countryside. You'll cross a particularly dramatic single-span 60-metre (200-ft) bridge. A return journey takes around 2½ hours, but it's fun to base a day around it, getting off at stations on the way, and strolling around villages and surrounding countryside (there are plenty of well marked footpaths and riverside walks). Most trains have refreshment cars, and there are cafés in the stations at Bewdley, Kidderminster and Bridgnorth (which also has a notable collection of locomotives). You can usually watch work on some of the fine old carriages in the yard at Bewdley, which also has a good model railway, and the showpiece station here has been splendidly restored. Various special events include Santa Specials in the run-up to Christmas; you may find different fares and trains then. Trains run wknds all year, and daily May–Sept and in local school hols; (01299) 403816. A full return fare allows unlimited travel that day, getting on or off as you please; £10.

West Midlands Safari Park *See separate family panel on p.657.*

BREDON SO9236
Attractive village above River Avon with a magnificent medieval tithe barn. The two stone figures sitting astride the rectory roof are supposedly Charles II and Oliver Cromwell. The Fox & Hounds is a good food pub.

Bredon Hill The Vale of Evesham's one notable feature for walkers is an outlier of the Cotswolds, distinctively rounded and on cloudy days rather ominous. It's dotted with Bronze Age barrows, three Iron Age hill forts, a Norman castle, a folly and a holy well. Although easily reached from Overbury, the best walk over it is from Bredon's Norton to Elmley Castle.

BRETFORTON SP0944
One of the prettiest black and white

thatched villages, with an interesting church and a splendid medieval pub, the Fleece, left to the National Trust after being in the same family for several centuries; a proper pub, it's kept just as it was as a farmhouse pub, with a magnificent collection of Jacobean oak furniture and pewter.

BROADWAY SP0937
Exceptionally harmonious stone-built Cotswold village, with the golden stone and uneven stone-tiled roofs perfectly blending the grand houses and the

humbler cottages together, in a long, grass-lined main street. It's decidedly on the coach-tour trail, very busy indeed in summer. Fine things for sale in expensive antiques shops, and a very grand old inn, the Lygon Arms, with a useful side brasserie. The Broadway Hotel also does good bar lunches; a pleasant escape from the tourists is the Crown & Trumpet in Church St, an archetypal Cotswold pub, and the Buckland Manor does good teas.

Broadway Tower (off A44 SE) Above the village, this late 18th-c folly has marvellous views that on a clear day – with the help of the telescope – are said to stretch over 13 counties. There are exhibitions on the history of the tower and regular visitor William Morris, while the country park around it has farm animals and nature trails. Meals, snacks, shops, some disabled access; cl wkdys Nov–Mar; (01386) 852390; £3 tower only, £3 animal park.

Magic Experience 🔲 (High St) Museum with decent collection of old teddy bears, toys and magical animated scenes; cl 25–26 Dec and Jan; (01386) 858323; £2.50.

Vale of Evesham farm shops Good for all manner of local produce inc eggs, jams, pickles and trout as well as fruit and veg, but the highlights of the year are asparagus in May and apples and particularly plums in Sept. The A44 W almost always has good pickings.

BROMSGROVE SO9468

Avoncroft Museum of Historic Buildings 🖼 (2m S at Stoke Prior, by A38 bypass and B4091) An enjoyable place to spend a relaxing afternoon. Around 25 buildings from the last seven centuries have been saved from demolition and rebuilt here: there's a timber-framed merchant's house, a Victorian church and gaol, even a 1946 prefab. A lovely working windmill is particularly popular with children, and, more incongruously, there's a unique collection of telephone kiosks, from Tardis-style police boxes to unlovely modern hutches, with everything in between. Also a play area, and donkeys and chickens wander about. Several of the buildings are furnished inside, but it's very much a place to visit on a dry day, when children can make the most of the open space the museum stands on. Meals, snacks, picnic area, shop, disabled access; cl Dec–Mar, Mon Mar–Jun and Sept–Nov, also Fri Mar and Nov; (01527) 831363; £5.20. The nearby Country Girl has enjoyable food, and is handy for walks on Dodderhill Common.

BURFORD SO5968

Burford House Gardens 🖼 (off A456, W of Tenbury Wells) Delightfully set by the River Teme, these tranquil gardens are the home of a national collection of clematis. Lots of other colourful plants too, a wild flower garden, and on the ground floor of the Georgian house a contemporary art gallery (mid-Jun to Sept). Meals, snacks, plant sales, disabled access; cl 25–26 Dec and 1 Jan; (01584) 810777; *£3.50. The Ship in Tenbury has good imaginative food.

CHADDESLEY CORBETT SO8973

Despite the trunk road attractive village, with a fine partly Norman **church**.

CHILDSWICKHAM SP0738

This streamside village has some delightful timbered stone cottages (and enjoyable food in the Childswickham Inn).

CLENT SO9380

Clent Hills Country Park A fine high hillscape for walkers, open and exhilarating, with waymarked routes. The Fountain at Clent is a good dining pub (food all day, Sun).

CLIFTON UPON TEME SO7161

A pleasant village, with lots of quiet strolls above the orchards; the Lion is a civilised food stop.

DROITWICH SO8963

Droitwich Spa Brine Baths (St Andrews Rd) Just the thing after an exhausting morning's sightseeing – you don't drink the water of this famous spa town, but float in it. Meals, snacks, disabled access; cl Easter Sun and 25–26 Dec. The baths open from 11.30am; (01905) 794894; £7 (inc sauna). Interesting buildings in the town include the timbered houses around the High St, and the Sacred Heart church (Worcester Rd) with its fine stained-glass mosaics. The Old Cock (Friar St) is a useful food stop.

Heritage Centre (Victoria Sq) Exhibition on broadcasting inc items from the BBC Home Service radio station which was once based at nearby Wychbold, also brass rubbing and a look at Droitwich's past as a prehistoric salt town. Shop, disabled access; cl Sun and bank hols; (01905) 774312; free.

ELMLEY CASTLE SO9841

Very old-fashioned village below Bredon Hill, with attractive houses strung out between its lovely church and the millpond, where the Old Mill has good value food and comfortable bedrooms.

EVESHAM SP0343

The pedestrianised market square has some fine buildings around it, inc a 12th-c abbey gateway; the church's striking 16th-c bell tower is well preserved, and some altogether more ruined remnants in the town park beyond lead to riverside meadows. The Tourist Information Centre is in another attractive abbey building, the Almonry, a Tudor timbered house with a museum and nice gardens (cl

Christmas–New Year and Sun pm Nov–Jan; £2). The Green Dragon (Oat St), visibly brewing its own ales, has inexpensive food. In Apr or early May the orchard drive through Harvington, the Lenches, Badgers Hill, Fladbury Cross, Wood Norton and Chadbury is pretty.

FECKENHAM SP0061
Attractive green and some fine Georgian red brick; the Lygon Arms has good cooking.

FLADBURY SO9946
This appealing village offers walks by the River Avon, a 9th-c Saxon cross, and a handsome Georgian village green. The Anchor downstream at Wyre Piddle has enjoyable food (all day summer wknds).

GREAT MALVERN SO7745
Elegant hillside spa town with easy access to inspiring hill scenery; the B4232 from Upper Colwall to Wynds Point has some of the best high views, while the B4218 on the E side gives several good views of the hills themselves. A good few galleries and craft workshops inc Hibernian Violins (Players Ave); cl wknds. The Nags Head (Bank St) has interesting food.

Barnard's Green House On the E side of the Malvern Hills, this has an attractive garden with a wide range of plants and gardening ideas around a gracious 17th-c house (not open). The owner is an authority on dried flowers. Teas, plant sales, disabled access; open Thurs pm Apr–Sept; (01684) 574446; *£2.50. The nearby Bluebell is useful for lunch

Malvern Hills Forming a splendid backdrop to the Vale of Evesham, these offer good walking. From a distance they look a formidable mountain range, but seem to get milder and more welcoming as you approach. The gentle up-and-down path along their spine makes one of England's great ridge walks, with the Cotswolds and Midland plain on one side and wilder Wales on the other. The Herefordshire Beacon, capped by ramparts of an Iron Age hill fort, is easily reached from the car park on the A449 near Little Malvern. Great Malvern is well placed for the Worcestershire Beacon, the highest point of the range (425 metres, 1,395

ft), and for long circular walks. The Chase Inn at Upper Colwall and Malvern Hills Hotel by the British Camp car park on Wynds Point are also useful start or finish points. On their Herefordshire side, Ledbury and Eastnor are good bases for rambles into the attractive western slopes.

Malvern Museum (Abbey Rd) This splendid former gatehouse of a Benedictine monastery houses a museum with displays on local history, Malvern spring water, Morgan cars, radar, and Elgar's life. Shop; cl Weds in term time, all Nov–Mar; (01684) 567811; *£1. The beautifully symmetrical priory just along the road has a notable collection of medieval wall tiles.

Picton Garden (Old Court Nurseries, Walwyn Rd, Colwall) On the W side of the Malvern Hills, this has a nicely laid out cottagey collection of hardy plants and shrubs, and a rock garden. Best late Sept–early Oct when the national collection of asters are at their best. Plant sales, disabled access; open Weds–Sun Aug, daily Sept–19 Oct and by appointment to end Oct; (01684) 540416; £2.50. The nearby Crown has good food.

GREAT WITLEY SO7765
Witley Court Astonishing ruined shell of Jacobean house transformed into an Italianate palace by the Earl of Dudley, and partly destroyed by fire in 1937. It's an elaborate place, with an enormous Perseus fountain, evocative balustraded garden (very special to wander through), and an expanding wilderness sculpture trail. Overlooking the lake beside it, a gloriously baroque church is no less dramatic, and one of the county's great finds; it has splendid paintings and stained glass around the largely papier mâché interior. Snacks, visitor centre, shop, some disabled access; cl Mon–Tues Oct–Apr, 24–26 Dec, 1 Jan; (01299) 896636; *£4 inc audio tour; EH. The Hundred House (a former court) is handy for lunch.

HAGLEY SO9180
Hagley Hall Completed in 1760, this was the last of the great Palladian houses; guided tours take in the fine rococo plasterwork, 18th-c furniture and family portraits inc works by

Reynolds and Van Dyck, and then you can stroll around the picturesque deer park. Meals, snacks; phone for opening times; (01562) 882408; £3.50. The Fountain over at Clent is a good dining pub.

HANBURY SO9463

Hanbury Hall 🖼 18th-c country house with outstanding painted ceilings and staircase, fine porcelain, exhibition on the Vernon family, ice-house, a working mushroom house, and an orangery in the grounds; the formal gardens include a reconstructed 18th-c bowling green. You can book rooms in the N and S wings, or the lodge on the edge of the estate. Snacks, shop, some disabled access; cl am, Thurs–Sat, and Nov–Mar ; (01527) 821214; £4.60; NT. The church, high on a hill, has superb views over the countryside. The canalside Eagle & Sun has decent food.

Jinney Ring Craft Centre (B4091 Droitwich Rd) Twelve craft workshops in beautiful timbered barns and pretty gardens, from pottery to violin-making; craft gallery and some wknd courses. Meals, snacks, shop, some disabled access; cl Mon and three days at Christmas; (01527) 821272; free. The nearby Vernon Arms has good value food.

HANLEY CASTLE SO8342

Well worth a stop, a rustic little place around a great cedar tree, with an unusually unspoilt pub, the Three Kings.

HANLEY SWAN SO8142

An attractive village, with a good value traditional pub, the Swan, by the village green and large duck pond.

HARTLEBURY SO8371

Worcestershire County Museum and Hartlebury Castle State Rooms Victorian folk life inc costumes, room displays and gypsy caravans, housed in Hartlebury Castle. The castle, mainly 18th-c, is also the official residence of the Bishops of Worcester, and (Tues–Thurs only) you can visit some of the elegant state rooms. Snacks, shop, some disabled access; cl am Fri and Sun, all day Sat, Good Fri, and all Dec–Jan; (01299) 250416; £2.50. The White Hart has good value food.

HARVINGTON SP0549

One of the area's oldest villages, brilliantly black and white. The Golden Cross has nice food.

Harvington Hall 🖼 Moated Elizabethan manor house with secret chapels, the largest number of priest hides in England, and original wall paintings. Also herb garden and picnic area; restaurant, shop, ground floor disabled access; cl Mon, Tues, wkdys Mar and Oct, and all Nov–Feb; (01562) 777846; *£4.20.

HONEYBOURNE SP1147

Domestic Fowl Trust (Station Rd) Friendly place with rare breeds of sheep, hens, ducks, geese and turkeys (good signs on enclosures), plus young chicks for children to handle, adventure playground and an indoor play area. You'll need wellies on wet days. Summer snacks, shop, limited disabled access; cl 25 Dec; (01386) 833083; £3. The Kings Arms over at Cleeve Prior has good food.

KIDDERMINSTER SO8376

Not an alluring place to visit, but a terminus of the excellent Severn Valley steam railway (see Bewdley), with a cheerful and very good value replica of Edwardian station refreshment rooms.

Kingsford Forest Park (Blakeshall, 2m N) 200-acre park with pine woods, birch groves and plenty of walks and trails. Very nice unspoilt feel – even the signposts and picnic-sets are made at the saw mill here. The Live & Let Live at Wolverley has good value food.

KYRE SO6263

Kyre Park Gardens Restoration started in 1994 on this 29-acre garden and shrubbery of Kyre Park House has almost been completed, revealing much of their former romantic charm, and spectacular views. Some surviving Georgian features include waterfalls and rapids connecting five lakes, hermitage ruins, a restored thatched summer house, grotto, tunnel and a tower folly. A church in the grounds is linked to the house (not open) by a small timber cloister passage, and there's a medieval dovecote. A tithe barn houses a toy shop and play area. Plant sales, tearoom; cl 23 Dec–Jan; (01885) 410669; £2.50.

LICKEY HILLS COUNTRY PARK SO9975

A good example of the interesting topography W of Birmingham: high (rising to over 300 metres/1,000 ft), and densely wooded, a fragment of primeval forest, with the views suddenly opening out over the sprawling city; waymarking makes the maze of paths and tracks less confusing. There's a sculpture trail, wheelchair pathway and viewing platform, visitor centre ((0121) 447 7106) with leaflets and information on guided walks, tearoom, and large adventure playground. The Peacock at Forhill has good value food.

LOWER BROADHEATH SO8157
Elgar Birthplace Museum (Crown East Lane) Modest cottage where the composer was born in 1857; now, as he wanted, a museum of his life and work, with displays of photographs and letters, and the desk where he did his writing. A visitor centre concentrates on his music and inspirations, with audio and visual displays, manuscripts, musical scores, concert programmes and other memorabilia. Shop (with CDs), disabled access to centre, gardens, and ground floor of cottage; cl 23 Dec–end Jan; (01905) 333224; £3.75 (audio tour £1). You can pick up routes and information here about the Elgar Trail around the area. The Bear & Ragged Staff over at Bransford is a good dining pub.

MARTLEY SO7559
Martley church Notable for its 13th-c wall paintings. The Admiral Rodney (Berrow Green) has good food.

OFFENHAM SP0546
Still has its original gaily striped maypole in its wide black and white main street; a nice village.

OMBERSLEY SO8463
Attractive mix of handsome black and white timbered houses with elegant Georgian brick.

OVERBURY SO9537
Immaculate stone-built estate village, with older buildings and fine church. In adjacent Conderton the beamed and flagstoned Yew Tree has good value food, and scope for Bredon Hill walks.

PERSHORE SO9445
Very much a working town, this 'capital' of the fruit- and vegetable-growing area around it stages an annual plum festival (Aug bank hol Mon). It's a pleasant place, largely Georgian, with an impressive abbey, and River Avon

walks. The Brandy Cask (Bridge St) has a nice riverside garden, good value food and brews its own beer. Heading out along the A4104 SW, when you've passed the Oak in Defford keep your eyes skinned for a group of cottages on your right; the last, surrounded by farm animals and without an inn sign, is the Monkey House, a uniquely old-fashioned cider tavern. In the opposite direction, Charlton is a pretty thatched village.

REDDITCH SP0468
Forge Mill Needle Museum and Bordesley Abbey 🔾 Redditch was the centre of the needle-making industry, and this working 18th-c scouring mill (used to clean the needles before they were sold) shows how they were made; extraordinary variety of needles on show, temporary needlework exhibitions, special events throughout the year. The visitor centre explains the excavation of the 12th-c Cistercian abbey alongside, with its medieval watermill (thought to be one of the oldest in Britain), plus some hands-on activities for children. Snacks, shop, some disabled access; cl am wknds Easter–Sept, Fri–Sat and Sun am Feb–Easter and Oct–Nov, all Dec–Jan; (01527) 62509; £3.50. The surroundings are pretty, and there are picnic-sets. It's not far from here to the newish **Arrow Valley Countryside Centre**. With wildlife displays and exhibitions, a children's play area and an enjoyable lakeside walk (good for wheelchairs and buggies), this provides a useful introduction to the 900-acre landscaped park. Meals, snacks, shop, some disabled access; (01527) 464004; free (charges for watersports).

RIPPLE SO8737
Appealing village, with finely carved choir seats in its largely 13th-c church.

SEVERN STOKE SO8745
Croome Park Gradually being restored, this was Capability Brown's first complete landscape, helping make his reputation and establish a new style of parkland design; the elegant park buildings and other structures are mostly by Robert Adam and James Wyatt. Snacks; cl Tues–Thurs; (01905) 371006; £3.40; NT. The Rose & Crown (A38) has good value food.

SHATTERFORD SO7980
Wildlife Sanctuary and Fishery
Animals here include roaming goats and
sika deer, also red deer, llamas, sheep,
pigs, ponies, wallabies and rhea in
enclosures: you can feed them all;
fishing permits available too. Snacks,
picnic area, shop, disabled access; cl 25
Dec; (01299) 861597; £3. The smart
Bellmans Cross does good lunches.
SHRAWLEY SO7964
Eastgrove Cottage Garden 🖾
(Sankyns Green, off A443 E of Great
Witley) Cottage garden with
abundance of plants and arboretum
around half-timbered 17th-c farmhouse
(not open). Home-made ice-cream,
good plants for sale, disabled access; cl
am, also Mon–Weds (Sun too
Sept/Oct), and all Aug and mid-Oct to
Apr; (01299) 896389; £3 Jun and July,
otherwise £2.50.
STONE SO8675
Stone House Gardens 🖾 Unusual
walled garden with colourful plants,
especially climbers and tender
flowering shrubs; interesting plant sales.
Some disabled access; cl Sun–Tues and
Oct–end Feb; (01562) 69902; £2.50.
WEST HAGLEY SO8979
Falconry Centre 🖾 (Hurrans Garden
Centre, Kidderminster Rd S) Frequent
flying displays of hawks, owls and
falcons; day falconry courses (£80).
Shop, some disabled access; cl 25–26
Dec, and Easter Sun; (01562) 700014;
*£2.50. The Robin Hood over at
Drayton is an attractive dining pub
(open all day wknds).
WICHENFORD SO7759
Wichenford dovecote Unusually
constructed timber-framed wattle-and-
daub 17th-c dovecote with nearly 600
nesting boxes. Open daily Apr–Oct and
in winter by appointment, cl Good Fri;
(01684) 855300; £1; NT.
WICK SO9645
This riverside village has attractive
houses and a good church.
WOLVERLEY SO8279
Steeply gabled cottages below a brick-
built hilltop church, and the decent
cliffside Lock Inn by the quaint Staffs &
Worcs Canal.
WORCESTER SO8554
Though it's a busy commercial centre,
this has some splendid medieval

buildings dotted about, with lots of half-
timbered houses, particularly around
Friar St, where the Lemon Tree has
good food, and New St (the King
Charles here is a good restaurant).
Plenty of shops, inc some nice specialist
ones, and cafés in Hopmarket Yard, a
former coaching inn. You can visit
handsome Georgian Guildhall (usually
cl Sun); free.
Bennetts Farm Park 🖾 (Lower
Wick, SW of city) Working dairy farm
with animals, weekend milking parlour
and vintage machinery museum in
pretty 16th-c farm buildings. Walks and
fishing in season. Snacks (inc their own
ice-cream), shop; (01905) 748102; cl
Mon; *£2.
City Museum and Art Gallery
(Foregate St) Local and natural history,
contemporary art exhibitions, and
children's activities. Meals, snacks,
shop, disabled access; cl Sun, 25–26
Dec, 1 Jan and Good Fri and Easter
Mon; (01905) 25371; free.
Commandery (Sidbury) Lively
museum wholly devoted to the Civil
War, in striking timber-framed 15th-c
building. Lots of weaponry, spectacular
audio-visual shows and life-size talking
figures re-creating events from the war.
Unusual special events and historic
military displays. Snacks, shop; cl am
Sun, 25–26 Dec, 1 Jan; (01905) 361821;
£4.
Greyfriars (Friar St) Beautiful and
carefully restored medieval timber-
framed town house (still lived in), with
delightful walled garden. Cl am,
Fri–Tues and Nov–Mar; (01905) 23571;
£3; NT.
Museum of Local Life (Friar St) This
15th-c building houses an interesting
museum of local life, with events such as
children's workshops. Good shop; cl
Thurs, Sun, 25–26 Dec, 1 Jan, Good Fri;
(01905) 729423; free.
Museum of Worcester Porcelain
🖾 (Severn St) Home of Royal
Worcester, the country's oldest
continuous producer of porcelain, with
wkdy factory tours (no under-11s),
period room settings, and displays of
porcelain dating back to the 18th c.
Meals, snacks, shop, disabled access to
museum only; cl 25–26 Dec and Easter
Sun; (01905) 746000; factory tour £5,

tour of the museum and visitor centre £4.50, museum £3. The Potters Wheel opposite has decent food.

Worcester Cathedral Founded on the site of a Saxon monastery, in a calm and peaceful setting overlooking the river. It took from 1084 to 1375 to build, and has an attractive 14th-c tower, Norman crypt, and the tombs of Prince Arthur and King John, the latter topped by the oldest Royal effigy in the country. Lots of Victorian stained glass, and some monastic buildings. Guided tours, (book on (01905) 28854), snacks, shop, some disabled access; £3 suggested donation.

Worcester Woods Country Park ▣ (just E off A442) Ancient woodland and wildflower meadows with waymarked circular walks, trails and map-reading games, information displays in countryside centre, and play, picnic and barbecue areas. Meals,

snacks, shop, some disabled access; park open daily, centre cl 25–26 Dec, 1 Jan; (01905) 766493; free. The Swan at nearby Whittington has good value food.

WYCHBOLD SO9165

Webbs Garden Centre (A38 towards Bromsgrove) One of the best in the country, attractively laid out with terrace and riverside display gardens, a massive choice of things to buy, fine amusements for children. Extended thatched café, good disabled access; cl 25–26 Dec and Easter Sun; (01527) 860000; free.

WYRE FOREST SO7574

This major broadleaved woodland, on the Shropshire border, has numerous ready-made Forestry Authority trails (leaflets available from the Visitor Centre). The Royal Forester nearby, if open, is useful for lunch.

Where to eat

BRANSFORD SO8052 **Bear & Ragged Staff** *Station Rd (01886) 833399* Stylish dining pub with proper tablecloths, linen napkins, and fresh flowers, very good imaginative food inc super fresh fish dishes, fine views over rolling country from the relaxed and cheerful interconnecting rooms, open fire, no smoking restaurant, well kept beers, a fine choice of wines, lots of malt whiskies, and willing helpful service; children until 9pm; disabled access. £25|**£6.50**

BREDON SO9236 **Fox & Hounds** *Church St (01684) 772377* Pretty, thatched pub in an attractive setting next to a church down a lane leading to a river and bedecked with brightly coloured hanging baskets; comfortably modernised bar with a welcoming atmosphere, stripped timbers and dressed stone pillars, a central wood-burning stove, and dried grasses and flowers, a smaller side bar with an open fire at each end, and a no smoking restaurant; attractively presented bar food served by friendly, efficient staff, well kept real ales, and wines by the glass. £23.75|**£6.75**

CROWLE SO9256 **Old Chequers** *Crowle Green (01905) 381275* Handy for the motorway, this smoothly run much-modernised dining pub rambles extensively around an island bar, with pubby furniture, lots of pictures for sale at the back, and a coal-effect gas fire at one end; there's a big square extension on the right with more tables; popular generous food (all home-made) includes good value imaginative light lunches plus more substantial dishes, prompt, friendly service, well kept real ales, and picnic-sets on the grass behind; cl Sun pm; disabled access. £23|**£5.95**

KEMPSEY SO8548 **Walter de Cantelupe** *34 Main Rd (01905) 820572* Popular roadside pub with friendly relaxed bar, quite a mix of furniture, flowers and candles on tables, a good big fireplace, interesting food, well kept real ales, a good choice of wines by the glass, and hard-working landlord; bdrms; cl Mon exc bank hols; no children after 8.15pm. £21.75|**£6.75**

OMBERSLEY SO8463 **Kings Arms** *Main Rd (01905) 620142* Big black-beamed and timbered Tudor pub with comfortably informal rambling rooms, various nooks and crannies full of stuffed animals and birds, rustic bric-a-brac and four open fires, excellent varied bar food, well kept real ales, and seats in sheltered courtyard and terrace; cl 25 Dec; children must be well behaved; disabled access. £23.90|**£5.50**

WELLAND SO8039 **Anchor** *Drake St (01684) 592317* Pretty, fairy-lit Tudor cottage with a welcoming L-shaped bar, a spreading comfortably furnished dining area, nicely set with candles and pink tablecloths and napkins, attentive staff, an extensive choice of enjoyable, changing bar food, and well kept real ales; picnic-sets on lawn, and field for camping with tents or caravans; bdrms; handy for the Three Counties Showground. £21.55|£6.99

WORCESTER SO8454 **Browns** *24 Quay St (01905) 26263* Most attractive and spacious warehouse conversion with big windows overlooking river, excellent modern cooking inc fish and vegetarian dishes, and good wines; cl Sat am, Sun pm, Mon, 1 wk Christmas; well behaved children over 8; disabled access. £37 dinner, £27 lunch

WORCESTER SO8554 **King Charles House** *29 New St (01905) 22449* From where King Charles I made his escape through the back door, closely pursued by Cromwell's forces, and now a relaxed restaurant ; enjoyable food, open fires, and a relaxed atmosphere in downstairs restaurant and upstairs bar; cl Sun, bank hols, 25–26 Dec. £25|£8.95

WYRE PIDDLE SO9647 **Anchor** *Main Rd (01386) 552799* Relaxing 17th-c pub with lovely views over lawn, river and on over the Vale of Evesham; friendly, neatly kept little lounge with log fire in attractively restored inglenook, comfortable bar, and generous reasonably priced popular food; cl 26 Dec; disabled access. £18|£6.95

Special thanks to Ben Dyson, Jenny and Michael Back, Nathalie Soanes

---

YORKSHIRE

Very friendly, with prices to match, and a tremendous variety of things to see and do, this is a most rewarding place for holidays. The city of York itself is excellent for a short break. We have separate sections on the other three main areas, each of which has a great choice of places to visit. With the Dales, first-class walking country, we include Ripon, civilised Harrogate, and their surroundings (virtually all North Yorkshire W of the A19). The Moors and East Yorkshire (North Yorkshire E of the A19 along with the administrative county of East Yorkshire) also include memorable walks and drives, with plenty to keep children amused on the coast. West and South Yorkshire (particularly West Yorkshire) have an outstanding range of unusual visitor attractions, especially for families, often free.

York

A great place for a short break, full of life and atmosphere, with lots to see and do

York's centre, ringed by medieval city walls, has twisting alleys filled with lovely ancient buildings, interesting shops, and lively cafés, pubs and bars – and all this is virtually traffic-free, wonderful for carefree strolling. It has plenty of remarkably varied things well worth visiting – good for all ages. The magnificent Minster is one of Britain's great sights, the Castle Museum and National Railway Museum are first-class, and Jorvik Viking City is among the country's best heritage centres (though over rather quickly for the price). This is undeniably a tourist city, with crowds at the main attractions; but most people find that all the other visitors actually seem to add to the atmosphere, rather than detracting from it. You can do the circuit of the 13th-c city walls and their many towers in a couple of hours or so, mostly on top. One of the best stretches, with good views of the Minster, is between the Monk Bar and Bootham Bar. There's a good fun guided ghost walk at 7.30pm (exc 24–31 Dec) beginning at the Shambles; (01904) 608700; £3. Shaped like a bike wheel, the Millennium Bridge over the Ouse is part of a 23-mile walkway which takes in villages and choice countryside around the city. York's racecourse is a good one, with monthly meetings; the Ebor Festival in August is the biggest event in the northern racing calendar. The York Pass is worth considering if you plan to visit lots of sites in one go (£21 for a day, it covers more than 30 of the city's attractions), and there are Nov–Mar special offers on many of the major attractions, restaurants, and places to stay – phone the tourist information (01904) 621756 or take a look at their website www.visityork.org for more information.

Where to stay

YORK SE5952 **Arnot House** 17 Grosvenor Terrace, York YO30 7AG (01904) 641966 **£54***; 4 rms individually decorated and named after North Yorkshire abbeys. Friendly, very well run no smoking Victorian terraced house with lots of original features, antiques and paintings, good breakfasts in neat dining room, and a pleasant relaxed atmosphere; cl Jan; no children

YORK SE5849 **Curzon Lodge** 23 Tadcaster Rd, Dringhouses, York YO24 1QG (01904) 703157 **£65**, plus winter breaks; 10 rms, some in former old coach house and stables. Charming early 17th-c house in marvellous spot just S of city centre overlooking Knavesmire racecourse, with an attractive and comfortable drawing room, a sunny farmhouse dining room (enjoyable breakfasts), and parking in grounds; no smoking throughout; cl Christmas; children over 7

YORK SE6050 **Dairy Guesthouse** 3 Scarcroft Rd, York YO23 1ND (01904) 639367 **£55***; 5 attractive rms, most with own bthrm. Carefully restored no smoking Victorian house with lots of original features and attention to detail, enjoyable breakfasts with vegetarian and vegan dishes, warmly hospitable atmosphere, friendly, entertaining and knowledgeable owner, and charming little flower-filled courtyard; cl mid-Dec to end Jan; disabled access; dogs welcome in bedrooms

YORK SE6052 **Dean Court** Duncombe Pl, York YO1 7EF (01904) 625082 **£140***, plus special breaks; 39 attractive, quiet rms. Next to the Minster, this comfortable hotel has a country-house atmosphere and fresh flowers in restful lounge areas, very helpful efficient staff, enjoyable food in the elegant restaurant, and tearoom/conservatory serving late breakfasts, light lunches and so forth; good for families with thoughtful extras; children over 6 in evening restaurant ☺

YORK SE5952 **Grange Hotel** 1 Clifton, York YO30 6AA (01904) 644744 **£135**, plus special breaks; 30 individually decorated rms with antiques and chintz. Close to the Minster, this Regency town house has elegant public rooms, an open fire, newspapers, good breakfasts, excellent restaurant food (there's also a brasserie), and warmly friendly staff; car park; disabled access; dogs welcome in bedrooms

YORK SE6052 **Hazelwood** 24–25 Portland St, York YO31 7EH (01904) 626548 **£80***, plus winter breaks; 14 individually styled rms. Just 4 mins from Minster, this no smoking, neatly kept Victorian house has quite a few original features, a cosy newly refurbished lounge, attractive dining room, helpful owners, and a pretty little garden; off-street parking; children over 8

YORK SE5951 **Holmwood House** 112–114 Holgate Rd, York YO24 4BB (01904) 626183 **£75***, plus special breaks; 14 pretty rms, some with four-posters or spa baths, and 1 garden suite. Built as two 19th-c houses, this recently redecorated no smoking hotel is 7 mins from the city walls, with open fire in comfortable sitting room, and very good breakfasts; children over 8

YORK SE5947 **Middlethorpe Hall** Bishopthorpe Road, Middlethorpe, York YO23 2GB (01904) 641241 **£189**, plus special breaks; 30 elegant rms, most in the adjoining courtyard. Lovely, immaculately restored William III country house just S of the city, with fine gardens and parkland, antiques, paintings and fresh flowers in comfortable, quiet day rooms, and excellent food and service; indoor swimming pool and health and fitness spa; children over 8

YORK SE6052 **Palm Court Hotel** 17 Huntington Rd, York YO31 8RB (01904) 639387 **£50***; 8 rms. Quiet and spotlessly kept Victorian house 5 mins from Minster, with pleasant sitting room, very good breakfasts, and particularly helpful friendly owners; private car parking; cl Christmas

To see and do

ARC 🏛 (St Saviourgate) This refreshingly accessible archaeology centre aims to get you involved personally in a hands-on encounter with the past. With archaeologists on hand for advice, you're encouraged to probe the city's Viking history by yourself, using genuine period relics inc bones, tiles and pottery to piece together a personal impression of Viking-age York. Very much on the school-trips circuit, it's usually open to individuals only in school hols, so best to check out of term-time. It's in a beautifully restored medieval church, with a new sensory garden. Shop, disabled access; cl wknds during term-time, Sun only during school hols, last 2 wks Dec, 1st 2 wks Jan; (01904) 643211; £4. The Tudor Black Swan (Peaseholme Green) is handy for something to eat.

Barley Hall 🏛 (Swinegate) The Archaeological Trust that runs the ARC (and the Jorvik Centre) restored this medieval family home, complete with audio tour. Shop, partial disabled access to ground floor only; cl all Mons (exc bank hols), Tues Nov–Feb, and 25 Dec–1 Jan; (01904) 610275; *£3.50. The nearby Punch Bowl has good food.

Castle Museum (Tower St) In 18th-c prison buildings on the site of the former castle (part of the outer wall still stands), this is one of the best social history museums in the country, with a huge range of everyday objects from the past four centuries shown in convincingly reconstructed real-life settings, from Edwardian streets to prison cells and more contemporary living rooms. There's even a watermill, by the river outside. They have one of only three Anglo-Saxon helmets in the world. Again, best out of term-time. Shop, disabled access ground floor only; cl 25–26 Dec, 1 Jan; (01904) 653611; £5.95.

Churches Besides the Minster, the city has a good few other fine medieval churches, though many are no longer used for services. Most were built during the prosperous 15th and 16th c, and among the finest are Holy Trinity (Goodramgate, which also contains in Our Lady's Row the oldest houses in the city) and St Helen's (St Helen's Sq). All Saints (North St) has some fascinating windows illustrating the last 15 days of the world.

City Art Gallery (Exhibition Sq) Well displayed collections running from Old Masters to the lusciously romantic nudes of William Etty, with some very handsome stoneware pottery. Shop, disabled access; cl 25–26 Dec and 1 Jan; (01904) 551863; £2 (free for York residents). The nearby York Arms (High Petergate) has good value food.

Clifford's Tower (Tower St) This former castle keep is perhaps York's most interesting building after the Minster. You can walk around the top of the walls (children especially like this bit, and climbing the grassy slopes), and there are good views of the city. It gets its name from Roger Clifford, who was hanged from the tower in chains. There's an unusual Lowry painting of the tower in the City Art Gallery (see entry above). Shop, Braille guide; cl 24–26 Dec, 1 Jan; (01904) 646940; £2.10. EH. The Kings Arms down on King's Staithe by the river is a handy stop.

Fairfax House 🏛 (Castlegate) Magnificently restored mid-18th-c town house, probably one of the finest in England, its richly decorated rooms fully furnished in period style. Much of the impressive collection of paintings, pottery, clocks and Georgian furniture was donated by the great-grandson of the confectionery baron Joseph Terry, and there's a re-created mid-18th-c meal; changing exhibitions. Shop, some disabled access by arrangement (steps at front); cl Fri (exc guided tours, 11am and 2pm), am Sun, and 6 Jan–14 Feb; (01904) 655543; £4.50.

Guildhall (St Helen's Sq) Exact replica of the original building of 1446, destroyed in a 1940 air raid. The stone walls of the earlier building form the framework of the new one. Disabled access; usually cl wknds Nov–Apr, am Sun in summer, and bank hols; (01904) 613161; free. The nearby Lendal Cellars has good plain food all day.

Jorvik Viking City (below Coppergate Shopping Centre) A well researched and absorbing re-creation of Viking life: a time capsule carries you back to the year 975, then a viewing car floats you over a muddy road, past street scenes with workshops and alleys, and even up through a two-storey house, all enhanced (if that's the word) with smells from the polluted River Foss, a cess-pit, and the reek of newly tanned leather. A darkened futuristic gallery brings seemingly mounted artefacts slowly to life (using illuminations and mirrors) as they would have appeared in contemporary Jorvik. You're unlikely to spend as much as an hour here, so you have to reckon on the realism rather than the time you spend here making this worth while. It's best to book ahead, to cut the queue. Snacks, shop, disabled access; cl 25 Dec; (01904) 643211; £6.95.

Merchant Adventurers' Hall 🖼 (Piccadilly) The largest timber-framed building in the city, and one of the finest in Europe. Built for the powerful Merchant Adventurers' Company in the 1350s and hung with banners of medieval guilds, it has a chapel and undercroft as well as the great hall itself. Shop, phone for disabled access; cl Suns 29 Sept–23 Dec, plus all 24 Dec–2 Jan, but best to check as they may also be closed till end Mar 2003 for building work; (01904) 654818; *£2.

Micklegate Bar Museum Another of York's medieval gateways, now housing social history displays. Cl 25–26 Dec, 1 Jan, wkdys Nov–Jan, and possibly other times depending on the weather (also closed when the city walls are shut); (01904) 634436; £2.

Murton Park (Murton, just E; SE6552) Busy ten-acre park, excellent for children and best known for its Museum of Farming, with exhibitions of agricultural equipment, some animals and a Land Army display. Also here, the Derwent Valley Light Railway has trips along what was once known as the Blackberry Line, and there's a reconstructed Dark Age settlement and Roman fort (aimed mostly at children). Café and picnic area, shop, disabled access; cl 24 Dec–4 Jan, limited entry wkdys during term-time; (01904) 489966; £3.60. Further out this way, the Agar Arms at Warthill has good value food in pretty surroundings.

National Railway Museum (Leeman Rd) Somewhere to spend a whole day, celebrating the great railway age with lots of panache; the background sounds and smells of a steam-era station add to the atmosphere. The centrepiece is the spectacular great hall, in which tracks radiate from a central turntable with a display of two dozen great locomotives from the museum's huge collection. Children get the most out of the Interactive Learning Centre, where plenty of hands-on exhibits and activities vividly explain how trains and railways work, though they're also bound to relish the chance to build their own model train in the excellent Works wing, where you can also watch the engineers and craftsmen as they carry out conservation work. The Working Railway looks at the technology behind Britain's rail network, with a live link to York station's signal box. A miniature railway operates most wknds and school holidays, with steam train rides during school hols. You can usually get a road train from York Minster to the museum in summer. Meals, snacks (and picnic areas), shop, disabled access; cl 24–26 Dec; (01904) 621261; free. Their all-day car park costs £4.

Richard III Museum (Monk Bar, Goodramgate) The most striking and best preserved of York's four turreted medieval gateways houses this museum dedicated to the much-maligned monarch (or, depending on your point of view, evil hunchbacked murderer). Displays are themed as if he were on trial – you put your verdict in the appropriate Guilty or Innocent book on the way out. Shop; cl 25–26 Dec, perhaps 1 Jan; (01904) 634191; *£2. The nearby Royal Oak has good value food.

Treasurer's House (Chapter House St; next to the Minster) There's been a house here since Roman times – this one dates from the 17th c, and the basement has an exhibition on its history. The timbered hall is very fine, as is the period furniture and kitchen.

Good meals and snacks; cl Fri, all Nov–Mar; (01904) 624247; £3.70; NT.

York Brewery 🏛 (Toft Green) Tours and tastings daily pm Mon–Sat (not 25–26 Dec or 1 Jan). Shop; (01904) 621162; £4.25 – inc a pint of their beer. Just along the road from here, the Bar Convent has a museum looking at early Christianity (and decent accommodation); museum tours usually Mon–Fri (not bank hols, late-Dec–Jan, and around 2 wks over Easter – best to check) 10.30am and 2.30pm; (01904) 643238; £3.

York Dungeon 🏛 (Clifford St) Carefully researched exploration of 2,000 years of superstition, torture and various forms of death, full of grue and gore. There's an extensive Guy Fawkes Experience and Dick Turpin Story, an exhibition on the Plague, and a new feature, Gorvik, giving the low-down on the bloodthirsty Vikings. Snacks, shop, some disabled access; cl 25 Dec; (01904) 632599; *£7.50.

York Minster A glorious example of Gothic architecture, in soft-coloured York stone, this is Britain's largest medieval building, begun in 1220 and taking a staggering 250 years to build. The richly detailed interior contains more original medieval glass than any other church in England – and indeed is reckoned to house half of all that's known in the country. Look out for the great E window which shows Genesis and Revelations in 27 panels, the splendid five sisters window in the N transept, and the beautiful ceilings of the central tower and chapter house. The choir screen has 15 niches containing statues of the kings of England from William the Conqueror to Henry VI. There's a display on the church's turbulent history in the Undercroft, Treasury and crypt. Meals, snacks, shop, disabled access and facilities (touch and hearing centre, Braille guides, guide dogs welcome); cl Sun am, and occasionally for major

services; (01904) 557216; £3.50 suggested donation; Undercroft museum, Treasury and crypt £3. You can climb the tower for good views of the city (£3). Largely traffic free, the Close outside is fairly quiet, but not enclosed, and without the tranquil serenity of say Exeter, Salisbury or Winchester.

York Minster Conference & Banqueting Centre 🏛 (College St, opposite Minster) 15th-c St William's College, with three finely timbered rooms – and a good restaurant. Shop, meals, snacks; cl 25–26 Dec, Good Fri, and if they have conferences, so best to phone and check; (01904) 557233; *£1.

York Model Railway (York Railway Station) Lovingly re-created miniature town and country landscape, running as many as 20 trains at a time, also a Thomas the Tank Engine working display, with lots of buttons for children to press; a third smaller model shows a typical Germanic town at night. Shop, disabled access; cl 25–26 Dec; (01904) 630169; *£3.40.

Yorkshire Museum (Museum Gardens) A real treasure-trove, crammed with myriad archaeological finds and riches from Roman, Anglo-Saxon, Viking and medieval times, inc the fabulous medieval Middleham Jewel. All set out very sensibly, with the displays effectively put into context. Shop, snacks (summer only), disabled access; cl 25–26 Dec, 1 Jan; (01904) 551800; £3.95, less for York residents. Outside are ten acres of botanical gardens by the wall: peaceful and attractive, around a shapely group of ruins inc the Benedictine St Mary's abbey and the Multangular Tower (medieval, on a Roman base), as well as a working observatory.

There's a picturesque riverside walk out to the pleasant village of Bishopthorpe (handy for the racecourse), where the Marcia does good value lunches

---

Where to eat

YORK SE6051 **Betty's** *6–8 St Helen's Sq (01904) 659142* Famous tearooms opened in 1937 with fine teas and coffees (they import their own), good sandwiches, salads and hot specialities, delicious scones, tea breads and pastries, home-made milk shakes, Alsace wines, and evening pianist; cl 25, 26 Dec, 1 Jan|£5.45

YORK SE6050 **Meltons** *7 Scarcroft Rd (01904) 634341* Smart and friendly little restaurant with banquettes under the murals, lots of wood and mirrors, very good imaginative modern cooking using tip-top ingredients (plenty of vegetarian choice), lovely puddings, fairly priced wines, and a relaxed friendly atmosphere; no smoking on ground floor; they've opened another restaurant, Meltons Too at 25 Walmgate; cl Sun pm, Mon am, 3 wks Christmas, 1 wk Aug. £33/3-course set lunch £16.50

YORK SE6052 **St William's College Restaurant** *3 College St (01904) 634830* Lovely 15th-c buildings with enclosed courtyard for outside summer eating next to York Minster, with varied food, and candlelight in evening; cl 25, 26 Dec; disabled access. £23.75|**£6.95**

YORK SE6052 **Treasurer's House Tearoom** *Minster Yard (01904) 646757* Lovely National Trust property, once home to the medieval treasures of York Minster, with a tearoom in the converted cellars: traditional and herbal teas, good coffee, fruit wines, home-baked cakes and scones, savoury dishes and good puddings, all served by friendly staff; no smoking; cl Fri, Nov–end Mar. £14|**£4**

The Yorkshire Dales, Harrogate & Ripon

Dramatic scenery, great for walkers – family outings too, and castles, stately homes, and abbey ruins

With some of the most invigorating scenery in Britain, the magnificent landscape is the special draw here. The Dales' steep stone-walled pastures, majestic moors, wind-carved limestone crags and rushing streams give drivers and particularly walkers a succession of captivating, quickly varying views. There are plenty of appealing villages and colourful market towns, and each of the main dales or valleys has its own distinct character. The visitor centres at Malham (near particularly striking Dales scenery) and Aysgarth (by a romantic series of waterfalls) are handy places to start.

In easy reach of both Dales and Moors, civilised Harrogate (with fine botanical gardens) is a comfortable base to explore from. Ripon and Richmond are appealing, and Hawes too has quite a bit to offer day-trippers.

Fun for families are the theme park at North Stainley, and the enchanting Forbidden Corner at Coverham; there's a friendly farm in Aiskew, a birds of prey centre at Giggleswick, and you can fish at Kilnsey. Other enjoyable excursions include a scenic train journey over the Pennines from Settle to Carlisle, and a trip on the steam railway from Embsay to tranquil Bolton Abbey. There are brewery tours in Masham, and caves to explore in Clapham.

Stately Beningbrough Hall (fine paintings and regular special events),

Newby Hall (attractions for children in the grounds), and Edwardian Sion Hill Hall at Kirby Wiske all have much to offer visitors. There are well preserved castles at Skipton, Castle Bolton, and Ripley (splendid gardens too), and poetic Fountains Abbey is the largest monastic ruin in the country. There are fine terraced gardens near Leyburn, and rare trees and shrubs (and a falconry centre) in the arboretum just outside Bedale.

Where to stay

ALDBOROUGH SE4066 **Ship** *Low Rd, Aldborough, Boroughbridge, North Yorkshire YO51 9ER (01423) 322749* **£49***; 3 rms. Friendly and neatly kept 14th-c pub nr ancient church and Roman town, with coal fire in stone inglenook and old-fashioned seats in heavily beamed bar, ample food, separate restaurant, good breakfasts, well kept real ales, and seats on spacious lawn

BAINBRIDGE SD9390 **Rose & Crown** *Bainbridge, Leyburn, North Yorkshire DL8 3EE (01969) 650225* **£64***, plus special breaks; 12 comfortable rms. 15th-c coaching inn overlooking lovely green, with antique settles and other old furniture in beamed and panelled front bar, open log fires, cosy residents' lounge, big wine list, and home-made traditional food in bar and restaurant; pets welcome by prior arrangement; disabled access; dogs welcome

BOLTON ABBEY SE0753 **Devonshire Arms** *Bolton Abbey, Skipton, North Yorkshire BD23 6AJ (01756) 718111* **£195***, plus special breaks; 41 individually furnished rms with thoughtful extras. Close to the priory itself and in lovely countryside, this civilised former coaching inn owned by the Duke of Devonshire has been carefully furnished with fine antiques and paintings from Chatsworth; log fires, impeccable service, beautifully presented imaginative food in elegant restaurant, super breakfasts; health centre; children over 12 in restaurant; disabled access; dogs welcome in bedrooms

BRAFFERTON SE4370 **Laurel Manor Farm** *Brafferton, North Yorkshire YO61 2NZ (01423) 360436* **£60**; 3 big beamed rms. Tall Georgian house with lovely views, surrounded by 28 acres of farmland: rare breeds, horses, fishing in the River Swale, 1,500 trees, carefully planted landscaped gardens, and croquet and tennis; open fire in comfortable sitting room, antiques and family photographs, aircraft models and pictures, good breakfasts and enjoyable candlelit family dinners using home-grown produce (by arrangement), and friendly, attentive owners; horses and other pets welcome in stable room; dogs welcome in bedrooms

BUCKDEN SD9477 **Buck** *Buckden, Skipton, North Yorkshire BD23 5JA (01756) 760228* **£79***, plus special breaks; 14 comfortable rms. Busy pub, popular with walkers and surrounded by moorland views; snug original area and bustling extended open-plan bar, popular food served by smartly uniformed staff in attractive no smoking dining room, decent wines, and well kept real ales; cl 2nd/3rd wk Jan; children over 7 in restaurant; disabled access; dogs welcome in bedrooms

CRAY SD9479 **White Lion** *Cray, Skipton, North Yorkshire BD23 5JB (01756) 760262* **£55**, plus special breaks; 9 comfortable rms, most with showers. Welcoming little pub spectacularly isolated 335 metres (1,100 ft) up with super views, lots of walks, traditional feel with flagstones, beams and log fires, good bar food, and decent wines; dogs welcome

FEIZOR SD7967 **Scar Close Farm** *Feizor, Austwick, Lancaster, Lancashire LA2 8DF (01729) 823496* **£52***, plus special breaks; 4 clean well appointed rms. Friendly converted barn on working farm with big guest lounge, books, magazines and TV, and big breakfasts and homely evening meals – packed lunches, too; lovely quiet countryside; cl 25 Dec; disabled access

HARROGATE SE2955 **Alexa House** *26 Ripon Rd, Harrogate, North Yorkshire HG1 2JJ (01423) 501988* **£65***, plus special breaks; 13 rms, some in former stable block. Attractive Georgian house with friendly staff, comfortable lounge, good home cooking in no smoking dining room, and marvellous breakfasts; good disabled access; dogs welcome in bedrooms

KNARESBOROUGH SE3457 **Dower House** *Bond End, Knaresborough, North Yorkshire HG5 9AL (01423) 863302* **£89**, plus special breaks; 31 clean, comfortable rms. Creeper-clad 15th-c former dower house with attractively furnished public rooms of some character, good food in Terrace Restaurant, super breakfasts, helpful service, and leisure and health club; partial disabled access; dogs welcome in bedrooms

LONG PRESTON SD8355 **Maypole** *Main St, Long Preston, Skipton, North Yorkshire BD23 4PH (01729) 840219* **£49***, plus winter breaks; 6 comfortable rms. Neatly kept 17th-c pub with generous helpings of enjoyable traditional food (and

The Dales

nice breakfasts) in spacious beamed dining room, open fire in lounge bar, real ales, and helpful service; dogs welcome

MALHAM SD9062 **Miresfield Farm** *Malham, Skipton, North Yorkshire BD23 4DA (01729) 830414* **£50**, plus winter breaks; 11 rms. Spacious old farmhouse with good freshly prepared food in beamed dining room, pleasant conservatory and two lounges, and lovely garden by stream and village green; cl Jan; dogs welcome in bedrooms

MARKINGTON SE2764 **Hob Green** *Markington, Harrogate, North Yorkshire HG3 3PJ (01423) 770031* **£100***, plus special breaks; 12 well equipped pretty rms. Lovely gardens and over 800 acres of rolling countryside surround this charming 18th-c stone hotel; comfortable and pretty lounge and garden room, log fires, antique furniture, fresh flowers, relaxed atmosphere, good interesting food, decent choice of wines, and friendly service; dogs welcome in bedrooms

NEWTON-LE-WILLOWS SE2189 **Hall** *Newton-le-Willows, Bedale, North Yorkshire DL8 1SW (01677) 450210* **£90***; 3 spacious rms. Handsome Georgian house with quiet gardens and acres of paddocks; lots of fine antiques, paintings and wall hangings, tranquil drawing room with an open fire and French windows into the garden, cosy homely snug with another fire, honesty bar, good breakfasts in light breakfast room (home-made fruitcake, tea and coffee always available), enjoyable food in elegant dining room (by prior arrangement), and a helpful and hospitable owner; children over 13 (or by arrangement); dogs welcome in the stable block by arrangement

RAMSGILL SE1171 **Yorke Arms** *Ramsgill, Harrogate, North Yorkshire HG3 5RL (01423) 755243* **£170*** inc dinner, plus special breaks; 14 attractive rms inc a cottage on the village green. Enjoyable small former shooting lodge (now best thought of as a restaurant-with-rooms) with antique furnishings, log fires, exceptionally good imaginative cooking in comfortable dining rooms and new Beckside room, fine wines, real ales, courteous service, and lovely surrounding walks; cl last 2 wks Jan; children over 12 in dining room; dogs in cottage

RICHMOND NZ1700 **Millgate House** *Millgate, Richmond, North Yorkshire DL10 4JN (01748) 823571* **£70***; 3 rms, 2 overlooking the garden. Georgian town house with lots of interesting antiques and lovely plants, a peaceful drawing room, warm friendly owners offering meticulous attention to detail, and good breakfasts in charming dining room which also overlooks the garden; it is this award-winning small garden with views over the River Swale and the Cleveland Hills beyond, that is so special, filled with wonderful roses, ferns, clematis and hostas – they have a booklet listing the plants; children over 10; dogs welcome in bedrooms

RICHMOND NZ1404 **Whashton Springs Farm** *Whashton, Richmond, North Yorkshire DL11 7JS (01748) 822884* **£50***; 8 comfortable rms. Attractive stone-built Georgian farmhouse on 600-acre working mixed farm; log fire in comfortable sitting room, good country breakfasts in attractive dining room (no evening meals) and lovely surrounding countryside; cl Christmas and New Year; self-catering coach house also; children over 5

RIPLEY SE2860 **Boars Head** *Ripley, Harrogate, North Yorkshire HG3 3AY (01423) 771888* **£120***, plus special breaks; 25 charmingly decorated rms. In a delightful estate village, this fine old coaching inn has a relaxed, welcoming atmosphere, with comfortable sofas in attractively decorated lounges, long flagstone bar, notable wines by the glass, fine food in bar and restful dining room, and unobtrusive service; games, videos and special menus for children; disabled access; dogs welcome in bedrooms

RIPON SE3171 **Ripon Spa** *Park St, Ripon, North Yorkshire HG4 2BU (01765) 602172* **£95**, plus special breaks; 40 individually furnished rms, many overlooking the grounds. Neatly kept friendly and comfortable Edwardian hotel with seven acres of charming gardens, yet only a short walk from the centre; attractive public rooms, winter log fires, and good food in bar and restaurant; disabled access; dogs welcome away from eating areas

SEDBUSK SD8790 **Stone House** *Hawes, North Yorkshire DL8 3PT (01969) 667571* **£79**, plus special breaks; 22 rms, 5 with own conservatories. Small, warmly friendly Edwardian hotel in a stunning setting with magnificent views; country-house feel and appropriate furnishings, attractive oak-panelled drawing room, billiard room, log fires, and exemplary service offering good local information; pleasant extended dining room with excellent wholesome food (special needs catered for) inc super breakfasts, and reasonable choice of wines; tennis lawn in the grounds, wonderful walks; P G Wodehouse stayed here as a guest of the original owner who employed a butler called Jeeves – it was on him that Wodehouse based his famous character; cl mid-week Dec and Jan; good disabled access; dogs welcome in bedrooms

STUDLEY ROGER SE2970 **Lawrence House** *Studley Roger, Ripon, North*

Yorkshire HG4 3AY (01765) 600947 **£90***; 2 spacious, lovely rms. Attractive Georgian house with two acres of lovely garden on the edge of Studley Royal and Fountains Abbey; fine antiques and pictures, log fires, good breakfasts, and delicious evening meals; cl Christmas and New Year; children by arrangement; dogs welcome in bedrooms

THORNTON WATLASS SE2385 **Buck** *Thornton Watlass, Ripon, North Yorkshire HG4 4AH* (01677) 422461 **£70***, plus fishing, racing and special breaks; 7 rms, most with own bthrm. Cheerful country pub overlooking cricket green in very attractive village, with interesting beamed rooms, open fire, jazz Sun lunchtime twice a month, enjoyable food, and lots of nearby walks; cl pm 25 Dec; dogs welcome in bedrooms

WATH SE1467 **Sportsmans Arms** *Wath, Harrogate, North Yorkshire HG3 5PP* (01423) 711306 **£80***, plus special breaks; 13 lovely rms. Friendly, quietly placed 17th-c restaurant-with-rooms, with lovely views, an elegant bar, delicious food using the best local produce (fish from Whitby, game from the moors, and Nidderdale lamb, pork and beef) in no smoking evening restaurant, super lunchtime bar food, a carefully chosen wine list, and attentive service from the long-standing owner and his genuine staff; cl 25 Dec

WEST WITTON SE0688 **Wensleydale Heifer** *West Witton, Leyburn, North Yorkshire DL8 4LS* (01969) 622322 **£80***, plus special breaks; 9 rms. Friendly 17th-c coaching inn with comfortable furnishings, log fires and oak beams, and a cosy bar; good local game and fresh seafood in bistro or spacious restaurant; dogs welcome in bedrooms

WIGGLESWORTH SD8056 **Plough** *Wigglesworth, Skipton, North Yorkshire BD23 4RJ* (01729) 840243 **£66**, plus special breaks; 12 well equipped rms, some in newer extension. Friendly and well run early 18th-c country inn, redecorated outside last year, with popular food in conservatory restaurant, oak panelled dining room and bar, and lots of little rooms surrounding bar area – some smart and plush, others cosy and friendly; big breakfasts, packed lunches, and views of the Three Peaks; no smoking family room; seats in secluded garden; disabled access

To see and do

AISKEW SE2787
Big Sheep & Little Cow Farm
Small-scale dairy farm, with friendly sheep and Dexter cows (Britain's smallest), pigs and chicks, and an under-cover animal display – the family in charge love talking to visitors. Snacks, shop selling ewe's milk and ice-cream made here from it, some disabled access; open Apr–Oct; (01677) 422125; £4.

ALDBOROUGH SE4066
Aldborough Roman Town The northernmost civilian Roman town was here, its houses, courts, forum and temple surrounded by a massive 6-metre (20-ft) wall. All that's left is a couple of pavements, the position of the wall and, in the museum, some finds from the site. Shop; open Easter–Oct (cl 1–2pm); (01423) 322768; £1.80; EH. It's a pleasant village with an impressive church (check out the sundial); the Ship

opposite is good for lunch.
ARNCLIFFE SD9371
Charming tucked-away Dales village, well placed for walks. The road up Littondale is pretty, and that to Langcliffe in Ribblesdale runs through dramatic scenery. The Falcon is an archetypal Dales inn.
ASKRIGG SD9491
Elegant stone houses around neat streamside greens, walks to nearby waterfalls, fine 15th-c church, and two decent pubs.
AYSGARTH SE0188
Aysgarth Falls The Lower Fall is the most spectacular of this famously romantic series of waterfalls, via a path over the road from the car park. The falls are the National Park's chief visitor honeypot and do get crowded, particularly through Aug (when even parking can be a problem here). They're better in late spring or early autumn,

when there tends to be more water in the river and therefore a better show. In severely cold weather they can be stunning, with wonderful ice sculptures building up. There's generally a small charge to see the Upper Fall (it's on private land), but you can see it almost as well, without paying, from the bridge on the road. The main car park (£2 for the day) has a **National Park Centre**, with displays on the Dales, and useful walks, maps, and guides. Café, shop, disabled facilities; cl Mon–Thurs Nov–Mar, best to check over Christmas; (01969) 663424; free. The George & Dragon is a good place for lunch. Walking routes hereabouts don't join up that neatly, but you can follow paths to West Burton, an idyllic village with a long green, and good value food at the Fox & Hounds.

Yorkshire Carriage Museum (Yore Mill) A collection of Victorian coaches and carriages; they also hope to open a rare breed pig centre. Meals, snacks, large charity shop (free entry); usually only cl 25 Dec; (01969) 663399; £3. The George & Dragon is a good place for lunch.

BAINBRIDGE SD9390
Delightful, its broad sloping green still with the village stocks. The ancient Rose & Crown, open all day, has enjoyable food.

BEDALE SE2685
Thorp Perrow Arboretum (off B6268 S) Well laid-out 85-acre landscaped lakeside collection of rare trees and shrubs among some splendid mature specimens that have been growing here for over 400 years. Particularly strong on oaks, ornamental cherries, willows and hazels, and lovely for spring walks when the bulbs are out; also a falconry centre and tearoom (Nov–Mar). Shop, disabled access; (01677) 425323; £5.25. In the pretty streamside village of Snape nearby, the friendly Castle Arms has good food (and there is indeed a castle).

BENINGBROUGH SE5358
Beningbrough Hall Stately early 18th-c baroque mansion, with a good collection from the National Portrait Gallery, also marvellous staircase with balusters carved in imitation of wrought iron, fine carvings, and a big restored

Victorian dairy. Regular events for families, and lovely formal gardens. Meals, snacks, shop, disabled access to ground floor only; cl Thurs, and Fri (exc July–Aug, Good Fri and last 2 wks in Oct), and all Nov–Mar, house also closed am; (01904) 470666; *£5.50, garden only *£4; NT. The riverside Dawnay Arms at Newton-on-Ouse does decent bar lunches.

BISHOPDALE SD9885
One of Wensleydale's tributary dales, broader than the others but still quite dramatic for walkers.

BOLTON ABBEY SE0754
Beautiful spot in lovely rolling wooded parkland on a knoll above the River Wharfe. Most of the priory buildings, dating from the 12th to the 16th c, are in ruins, but the central core of the main church is still used for Sunday services. 19th-c additions such as stained glass (some by Pugin) and murals oddly don't strike a false note. The car park (£4) gets rather full in summer. The Devonshire Arms is very fine for lunch. Attractive walks lead off in most directions: the landscape has a lowland beauty, with the ruined abbey, the turf banks of the Wharfe and the oaks of the Strid Wood. A steep ascent from Howgill is rewarded by views from Simon's Seat, perched on the edge of moors.

BRIMHAM ROCKS SE2065
(off B6265) Spectacular and extraordinarily weathered gritstone pinnacles, tors and boulders facing the winds at a height of 290 metres (950 ft), conjuring up people, animal heads and other strange figures – a Victorian guidebook declared that they were 'grim and hideous forms defying all description and definition'. Children like them a lot – Henry Moore said that when he was a boy they strongly moulded his imagination. Exhibition room, shop and snacks; site open all year, centre cl wkdys (exc Jun–Sept and bank hols), all Nov–Easter (exc Sun Nov–Dec), and perhaps in bad weather; (01423) 780688; parking £2.50; NT. The Royal Oak down at Dacre Banks is a friendly food stop.

CASTLE BOLTON SE0095
Apedale Head This spectacular viewpoint is reached by a 3-mile plod up tracks NW; on fine days it feels like the

top of the world, with views encompassing both Wensleydale and Swaledale.

Bolton Castle (off A684) A massive 14th-c structure towering over the tiny single-street village built for it. Considering it was partly dismantled in 1645 and has been empty ever since, it's still in fine shape; great views from the 30-metre (100-ft) towers, dungeons and medieval gardens. Meals, snacks, shop, disabled access to grounds; cl 25 Dec; (01969) 623981; £4. The Kings Arms at Redmire has good food.

CHAPEL LE DALE SD7477
Nr the Hill Inn on the Ingleton–Ribblehead road, a tiny church in a pretty wooded setting has a memorial made from fossilised marble to the 100 or so men, women and children who died during the building of the Settle–Carlisle line; their bodies are buried in unmarked graves, and the railway's engineer is also buried here, separately.

CLAPHAM SD7469
Attractive village that has turned walking and caving into something of an industry. The riverside New Inn has good honest food (a good place for walkers to stay in).

Ingleborough (721 metres/2,365 ft) Best approached from Clapham, along the Reginald Farrer Trail, via Ingleborough Cave (see below) and Gaping Gill (a vast pot-hole); the panorama extends far across Lancashire and into Cumbria.

Ingleborough Cave One of the most easily visited of the vast network of caverns plunging into the limestone hills around here – and we think the only one that wheelchairs can go all the way through. It's in the grounds of the outdoors centre at Ingleborough Hall – formerly the family home of the great plantsman Reginald Farrer, who in his short life introduced and eulogised many notable plants from the Himalayas and China. The **Reginald Farrer nature trail** leads past Farrer's woods and small lake to the cave (40p); unusually, it's a place that looks better in wet weather. Snacks, shop, some disabled access; cl wkdys (unless by appointment) end Oct–Easter; (01524) 251242; £4.50.

COVERDALE SE0481
Wensleydale's major tributary valley, relatively very quiet; fairly gentle in its lower reaches (where the Foresters Arms in pretty Carlton is a great lunch stop – not Mon or Tues), climbing high into a wild and untamed-feeling world of lonely sheep farms.

COVERHAM SE0986
Forbidden Corner (Tupgill Park Estate) Enchantingly different, and really memorable: a labyrinth of tunnels, chambers, follies and surprises imaginatively laid out in an attractive four-acre walled garden. A clue-guide leads you over stepping stones, down dead ends, and through water walls to the centrepiece, a story-book underground grotto. Other features include a huge glass pyramid, a 6-metre (19-ft) giant, optical illusions (a normal-looking corridor shrinks to a mere burrow), and statues that range from picnicking bears to griffins (watch out for the ones that squirt water). You can buy food to feed the mirror carp, and there are panoramic Coverdale views. Snacks, shop; cl am wkdys, and 25 Dec–Mar, phone to book; (01969) 640638; £5.50.

CRAKEHALL SE2490
Crakehall watermill As we went to press, this restored 17th-c mill was changing hands, though you should still be able to buy flour here. Tearoom; usually open Weds–Sun and bank hol Mons Easter–end Sept, but phone to check; (01677) 423240; £1. The Bay Horse in a nice spot on the nearby green does good lunches.

CROFT-ON-TEES NZ2809
Right on the border with Co Durham is a pleasant church where Lewis Carroll's father was parson; there's a plaque in memory of the writer, complete with an enamelled White Rabbit, and an unusual family pew reached by a staircase. If the church is closed, the key is kept at the Croft Spa Hotel across the road. Nice river views.

DENTON MOOR SE1450
Above the pleasantly wood-flanked reservoirs at Fewston (where the 18th-c Sun has decent food inc summer afternoon teas), this offers scope for fairly stretching walks, though nothing to compare with the Dales themselves.

DRUIDS TEMPLE SE1879
Nr the hamlet of Ilton a no-through road leads up to woodlands where you can walk to this scaled-down Stonehenge, built by a landowner in the 1820s as work for local unemployed people.

EMBSAY SE0053
Embsay & Bolton Abbey Steam Railway Steam trips along a track prettily set beneath limestone crags, through to Bolton Abbey. Collection of old locomotives and carriages; the quaint cabman's shelter was brought over from Ilkley. Snacks, two shops (remarkable range of books), disabled access (notice preferred); usually open Sun all year, daily in summer, and other days – phone (01756) 710614; *£6. The Elm Tree has good hearty food (and comfortable bedrooms).

FOUNTAINS ABBEY SE2769
Fountains Abbey & Studley Royal Water Garden (off B6265) The largest monastic ruin in the country, this romantic place was founded in 1132 by Cistercian monks, in a delightful riverside setting. Most of the remains are 12th-c, but the proud main tower is 15th-c. Opposite are the lovely landscaped gardens begun by William Aislabie in the 1760s, which include ornamental temples and follies, formal water gardens, lakes aflutter with waterfowl, and 400 acres of deer park. The most beautiful approach is through the extraordinarily ornate Victorian church at the far end (may be restoration in progress, best to phone for opening), and this 'back-door' entrance is the most tranquil too; you can now also explore three floors of the 12th-c watermill that produced flour for the monks. A helpful modern visitor centre blends in and doesn't spoil the view. Free guided tours of abbey 11am, 2.30pm, 3.30pm Apr–Sept, and perhaps other times, phone to check. Meals, snacks, shop, good disabled access; cl Fri Nov–Jan, and 24–25 Dec; (01765) 608888; £4.80, deer park – an excellent strolling ground – free; NT. The very civilised Sawley Arms in Sawley just W does good food.

GIGGLESWICK SD7867
Falconry & Conservation Centre (top of Crows Nest, off A65 N of Settle) Well organised, with lots of vultures, eagles, hawks, falcons and owls, and regular flying displays (from noon). Meals, snacks, shop, disabled access; cl 25 Dec; (01729) 825164; £4.95. The village down by the Ribble below is peaceful and pretty, with good food in the 17th-c Black Horse near the church.

GLASSHOUSES SE1764
Yorkshire Country Wines (The Mill) Traditional country wines produced in 19th-c flax mill, with free tastings, antiques, and tearoom overlooking the River Nidd; limited disabled access. Cl Mon, Tues and Nov–Easter wkdys, winery tours (£2.50) Fri and Sat at 11.45; (01423) 711947.

GRASSINGTON SE0063
At the heart of Wharfedale, a pleasant small town or large village around a sloping cobbled square, depending a lot on walkers and other visitors, with some attractive shops and a few interesting old buildings; there's a National Park information centre. The Devonshire on the square has a good range of food. The B6160 gives lovely Wharfedale views, and the B6265 to Pateley Bridge also has memorable views (and passes the colourfully lit underground Stump Cross Caverns, well worth a look if you're passing).

GRINTON SE0498
Attractive riverside Wensleydale village with charming church known as the Cathedral of the Dales, and pleasant walks nearby. The waterside Bridge Inn (open all day) has decent food.

HARROGATE SE3054
This elegant and self-confident inland resort has kept its Victorian spa-town atmosphere despite now filling many of its handsome hotels with up-to-date conferences and so forth. The layout of the town is very gracious, and you couldn't ask for better shops (interesting antiques and some top-notch specialist shops). Almost every available space is filled with colourful plant displays, as if to shake off the gloom of the dark stone buildings. The first thing a visitor notices is the great sweep of The Stray, open parkland which runs right along and through the S side of the centre. The first sulphur well was discovered in the 16th c and

named the Tewit Well, **after the** local word for the lapwings which led a local sporting gent to ride into what was then a smelly bog. It's up on The Stray, grandly encased in what looks like an Italianate mausoleum. The elegant buildings of the compact central area run down from here to the pleasantly laid-out Valley Gardens, very Victorian, with a curlicued central tea house. The relaxed tempo of the place, and the clean bracing climate (it's quite high on the moors), have made it a popular retirement area. Besides the places mentioned in **Where to eat**, the Drum & Monkey (fish restaurant/wine bar, Montpellier Gardens) and Hedleys (wine bar, Montpellier Parade) are good for lunch or a snack; the café of the Theatre Royal is also pleasant, as is the Lascelles Arms out in Follifoot.

Harlow Carr (Crag Lane, off B6162 W) Ornamental and woodland gardens over 68 acres, being developed with new funds since a 2001 merger with the Royal Horticultural Society: streams, pools, rockeries, rhododendrons, spring bulbs and many interesting plants. Also a museum of gardening, model village and scented garden. A place of real peace and fresh moorland air, the finest strolling ground near Harrogate, and very quiet out of season, when the excellent collection of heathers comes into its own. Good meals and snacks, expanding plant centre, disabled access; (01423) 565418; £4.50. The New Inn on the B6162, and the adjacent Harrogate Arms, also have good value food.

Mercer Art Gallery (Swan Rd) An early spa building, with an excellent fine art collection, and an archaeology display with ancient Egyptian and Greek artefacts; temporary exhibitions and events. Cl Mon (exc bank hols), Sun am, 24–26 Dec and 1 Jan, free.

Royal Pump Room Museum (Crown Place) The central sulphur wells are housed here, enclosed by glass to contain the reek; you can still sample a glass of the water at the original spa counter, now the ticket counter for the museum. The Victorian pump room building contains displays on the town's spa history, and changing exhibitions; to celebrate the museum's 50th birthday,

from March there'll be a new exhibition on the 1950s. Shop, disabled access; cl Sun am, 24–26 Dec and 1 Jan; (01423) 556188; £2.

HAWES SD8789
Busy in summer with hikers and coach-parties exploring Wensleydale, but pretty, and a proper market town, its Tues mart full of livestock in late summer. The bustling White Hart has good value food, and occasional craft fairs upstairs.

Dales Countryside Museum (Station Yard) Interesting displays of local crafts and domestic and industrial life as well as hands-on exhibits, re-creations, a static steam locomotive and displays on transport; also changing exhibitions, demonstrations and special events. Shop, disabled access; cl a few days over Christmas and New Year; (01969) 667450; £3.

Hardraw Force (just N at Hardraw) England's tallest waterfall cascading over a 30-metre (100-ft) lip; it's best after rain (though the paths can be muddy then), and at dry times you may see barely a trickle; small fee at Green Dragon pub. A longer excursion follows the Pennine Way from Hawes and over the River Ure. The valley above the falls is attractive, and this can be a start for the long day's walk to Great Shunner Fell.

High-level drives The B6255 S to Ribblehead gives fine upland views, and the Buttertubs Pass northwards through High Shaw over into Swaledale is a spectacular drive (the Buttertubs are deep ferny holes near the summit where carriers used to cool their butter in hot weather).

Outhwaites Ropemakers (A684, Town Foot) They've been making rope for 200 years – see how it's done. Shop (not just great hawsers, useful things too like dog-leads), disabled access; cl wknds (exc Sats July–Oct), 10 days at Christmas, and Good Fri; (01969) 667487; free.

Wensleydale Creamery 🅔 (Gayle Lane) You can watch the cheese being made by the traditional method, all by hand, and there's a fascinating visitor centre, with a well set out dairying/cheese museum. The shop (busy in summer) has samples of their variously flavoured cheeses – our favourite was the one with blueberries. Very good café, disabled facilities; cl 25 Dec; (01969) 667664; £2.

HEBDEN SE0263

Hebden lead mines There's a rewarding walk up Hebden Beck with its legacy of old lead-mine workings; the route can be extended to take in Grassington and the path along the River Wharfe.

HUBBERHOLME SD9377

Beautifully placed riverside Dales hamlet at the meeting of Wharfedale and Langstrothdale with a good 13th-c church, built on an ancient burial site, with Norman tower, unusual rood loft and pews by Thompson of Kilburn – with their little carved mouse trademark. The charmingly set George, J B Priestley's favourite pub, has good food and bedrooms. A walk not to be missed is up to Scar House and along a level turfy terrace, which commands magnificent views down Wharfedale, to Cray (the White Lion's a good pub there). The walk can be expanded to include Buckden (then return to Hubberholme along the river) – in fact there are rewarding walks between all the Wharfedale/Littondale places flagged on our map, with pub food available in each of them.

INGLETON SD6973

Steep and pretty village, full of walkers. The Wheatsheaf, with hawks in its garden, has good value fresh food. On the edge, **Ingleton Glen** is a lovely wooded gorge walk up the River Twiss, not too strenuous, past a series of picturesque waterfalls; most people take it about a mile, as far as Thornton Force, a textbook example of geological faulting. It takes 2–4 hours to do a full circuit, over the moor and back past more falls on the River Doe. The B6255/B6479 is a very scenic long way round to Settle.

White Scar Cave (B6255 towards Hawes) The country's longest show cave and one of the most spectacular, with underground waterfalls and streams, and an Ice Age cavern. Wrap up well – the guided tour takes about 80 mins so gets chilly. Snacks, shop, some disabled access by arrangement; cl 25 Dec (and sometimes after heavy rain);

(01524) 241244; £6.50.

JERVAULX ABBEY SE1785

Less imposing than Fountains, Rievaulx and Bolton, but in some ways even more appealing – perhaps because the rough-cropped grass and wild flowers around the shattered walls emphasise the slightly melancholy atmosphere of a place of great worldly wealth and power that's come to nothing. Tearoom (cl end Oct–mid-Mar), shop, disabled access; abbey open all year; (01677) 460391; £2. The Blue Lion at East Witton nearby has superb food.

KETTLEWELL SD9672

Popular Wharfedale village for walkers, with three decent pubs; there are exhilarating views from the back roads from here up into Coverdale, and to Hawes via Hubberholme.

KILNSEY SD9767

Kilnsey Park & Trout Farm (B6160) Two lakes for fly-fishing, plus a fun-fishing area for children, adventure playground, and good estate shop with fish, oven-ready game and other local produce. There's an aquarium and craft shop in the visitor centre, and a sizeable collection of orchids. Look out for red squirrels – this is a conservation area for them. Good meals and snacks (inc tasty trout from their smokery, and local cheeses), disabled access; cl 25 Dec; (01756) 752150; £1, £3.85 for children's fishery (50p for spectators), and proper fishing from around £16 per day. The Tennants Arms has decent food, and views of memorably bulging Kilnsey Crags.

KIRBY WISKE SE3684

Sion Hill Hall Splendid Edwardian mansion, one of the last great country houses to be built, with period furnishings and an enormous collection of antiques. Shop (inc bric-a-brac), disabled access to ground floor only; open pms Easter Sun and bank hol Mons, plus pm Weds Jun–Aug, best to check; (01845) 587206; £4.50, £1.50 grounds only (guided tours by appointment). The Nags Head at Pickhill does good lunches.

KNARESBOROUGH SE3557

The little town above the steeply picturesque river gorge, with its spectacular railway viaduct, is pleasant and colourful (esp on Weds market day), with some attractive buildings. The chemist's shop on the square is said to be the oldest in the country; established in 1720, it still has all its original fittings. You can hire **rowing boats** down on the river, and there are pleasant riverside paths and walks: from Abbey Rd for example you should be able to see the intriguing **House in the Rock**, and a 15-min walk down here brings you to St Robert's Cave, the riverside home of a 12th-c hermit. The Mother Shipton has good value food.

Knaresborough Castle All that remains are the 14th-c keep, secret medieval sally port, and a 16th-c courthouse (now a museum) but it's easy to imagine what an imposing sight it must have made, glowering over the gorge of the River Nidd – a suitable spot to hide Thomas à Becket's murderers. Shop, limited disabled access; cl Oct–Easter; (01423) 503340; £2 inc a guided tour.

Mother Shipton's Cave and Well In the 19th c quite a little tourist industry was concocted for the toffs from Harrogate around the alleged 16th-c prophecies of Mother Shipton. The cave she lived in is pleasantly set in 12 acres of riverside parkland, along with this limestone spring, which quickly coats teddy-bears and other unlikely objects in rock; there are guided tours, and a local history museum. Snacks, shop; cl 25 Dec; (01423) 864600; *£4.95.

LANGTHWAITE NZ0002
Idyllic Dales hamlet, with good circular walks from the nice Red Lion – and this Arkengarthdale road up to the remote but very popular Tan Hill Inn is a very fine drive.

LEYBURN SE1190
Bustling little agricultural town with a proper country atmosphere and lively market (Fri): the Sandpiper's the nicest pub, and Tennants (Harmby Rd) is Europe's largest auction room for house clearances and antiques. At the **Teapottery** (Leyburn Business Park, A684), a walkway through the production area gives visitors the chance to see craftsmen at work on these imaginative teapots. Snacks, good shop, disabled access; cl 25–26 Dec and 1 Jan; (01969) 623839; free. Off the

A684 W are fine drives: up Coverdale to Kettlewell; up Bishopdale on the B6160 and on down past Cray into Wharfedale; up into the Eden Valley's Cumbrian headwaters on the B6269; and the Carperby–Castle Bolton–Reeth road.

Constable Burton Gardens (A684 E) A series of fine terraced gardens around a handsome Georgian house (not open); the cyclamen at the end of the short lime avenue flower beautifully in late Aug, and it's worth trying to catch their tulip festival (around May). Disabled access but no facilities; open end Mar to mid-Oct; (01677) 450428; £2.50. The nearby Wyvill Arms is good.

LINTON IN CRAVEN SD9962
A gem of a Dales village, with lovely stone buildings, set off by lawns running down to a duck-filled stream crossed by a delightful packhorse bridge. The Fountaine has food all day.

MALHAM SD9062
Justifiably touristy village on the Pennine Way, with a good National Park information centre; the Listers Arms is a good refuge.

Malhamdale Perhaps the most remarkable and certainly the most visited of all Dales landscapes, cut tortuously and deeply out of the limestone by the River Aire and its steep tributaries, leaving spectacular cliffs, extensive upland stretches of bare fissured rock (so-called limestone pavements), craggy bowls carved out of the overhanging hillsides, and sparkling waterfalls. The dale is compact enough to be explored on foot, with well beaten paths linking the natural sites. Just above the village, **Malham Cove** is a great craggy cliff; the Pennine Way climbs to a famous tract of limestone pavement on its top. You can keep on through a landscape of limestone scars, disappearing streams and green turf to the lake of **Malham Tarn**. E of Malham, a level path leads along the stream to **Janet's Foss** waterfall, and to the romantic severity of dramatic **Gordale Scar**, Malhamdale's most memorable natural feature, where a stream makes a spectacular leap from the rocks.

MASHAM SE2280
(pronounced Mazzum) Civilised small

market town, with an interesting church, and dignified Georgian houses around its broad market square – which comes to life on Weds and Sat. The Kings Head does enjoyable food.

Black Sheep Brewery (Wellgarth) Set up by a breakaway member of the Theakston family a few years back, its beers since proving very popular. The tours are fun and imaginative: best to book; (01765) 689227 – evening tours are best, with more time to enjoy samples at the end; disabled access (not on tour); £4.50. Good place for refreshments, too.

Theakston Brewery & Visitor Centre Next to the big Scottish & Newcastle brewery, this explains the brewing process behind Theakstons beer, inc their Old Peculier. Shop; usually open Fri–Mon Apr–end Oct, daily in school hols, but phone to check; (01765) 684333; visitor centre £1, enthusiastic tours of the brewery £4.50.

Uredale Glass (42 Market Pl) Hand-made glassware, with glass-blowing demonstrations (Mon–Fri); shop; cl 25–26 Dec and 1 Jan, best to phone for opening times in Jan; (01765) 689780; free.

MIDDLEHAM SE1287

Attractive and civilised stone-built village, largely Georgian, still with the style that came from its days as the country's top racehorse-training centre in the 18th and early 19th c. Even now there are times when it seems to have more horses than people: pick up breeding and gallops gossip in the White Swan and Black Swan, both good, on the sloping square. This is a great area for self-catering accommodation – and fine walking country.

Middleham Castle This 12th-c structure dwarfs the village. For a time it was the home of young King Richard III. Only the huge keep and some later buildings remain, but there are marvellous views from the top, and an informative exhibition centre. Snacks, shop, disabled access; cl 1–2pm and Mon and Tues Jan–Mar, 24–26 Dec, 1 Jan; (01969) 623899; £2.60; EH.

MUKER SD9197

Attractive Swaledale hamlet, with very good woollens shop, well liked tearooms, and decent food in the friendly Farmers Arms. Between here and Keld, the River Swale cuts through a deep valley and tumbles over waterfalls; there are paths on both sides of the river, or you can take a more upland route over neighbouring Kisdon.

NEWBY HALL SE3467

🏠 (off B6265 E of Ripon) In beautiful formal gardens covering 25 acres, this late 17th-c mansion with Robert Adam interiors has an important collection of classical sculpture and Gobelins tapestries, as well as a good range of Chippendale furniture. In the grounds are a miniature railway, children's adventure garden, paddling pool, woodland discovery walk and sculpture park. Meals, snacks, shop, some disabled access; house cl Mon (exc bank hols), and Oct–Easter; (01423) 322583; £7, £5.50.

NIDDERDALE SE1073

This quiet yet beautiful valley has an impressive solitary grandeur. Just outside the National Park, it and the hills above are less liberally laced with footpaths and open-access moorland than the other dales here, and attract far fewer visitors – but there are plenty of relatively unfrequented walks, often on good paved but untarred tracks. The Nidderdale Way allows a fine fairly gentle walk of a couple of hours or so, up on to the high pastures (see lambs being born in spring) and moorland at Glasshouses and back, with spectacular views almost all the way. It's well signed; start from the good Royal Oak in Dacre Banks and take the lane a couple of hundred yards past the church. The stretch between the attractive small town of Pateley Bridge and the little village of Lofthouse is dominated by the sheltered two-mile waters of Gouthwaite Reservoir, serenely set below the hills with some tall trees alongside. From Lofthouse a path runs beside the River Nidd, with picturesque tracks among small woods and ruined farmhouses, to Scar House Reservoir, quite exposed at the valley head (there's also a toll road up to it); high, exposed routes line the N side of the dale up here.

How Stean Gorge To the W of Lofthouse, this is a spectacular ravine pocked with pot-holes and caverns; a footpath snakes between miniature cliffs, with bridges giving views into the gorge; there's also a visitor centre.

NORTH STAINLEY SE2876
Lightwater Valley Theme Park
Family fun from the nostalgic pleasure of a steam train to the white-knuckle, green-faced thrills of one of the world's biggest roller-coasters; another roller-coaster is entirely underground. Meals, snacks, shop, disabled access; usually open wknds and school hols (not Christmas) Easter—Oct, and daily Jun—early Sept; (01765) 635321; £13.50. There's an adjacent factory shopping village, open all year. The Staveley Arms does decent food.

NORTON CONYERS SE3076
(3½ miles N of Ripon) The same family have lived in this late medieval house for almost 380 years, and the furniture and pictures reflect the fact that it's still very much a family home. Charlotte Brontë used the building as one of her models for Thornfield Hall. Look out for the hoofprint on the stairs. Attractively planted 18th-c walled garden. Seasonal pick-your-own fruit, shop (with unusual hardy plants), limited disabled access; house open pm Easter Sun and Mon, pm bank hol Sun and Mon 11 May—7 Sept, daily 7—12 July, garden open Thurs all year, phone to check; (01765) 640333; house £4, garden free. The Bull and Bruce Arms in West Tanfield are useful for lunch.

NUN MONKTON SE5057
This attractive village is in appearance almost more like France than Yorkshire, with its broad avenue, and the stately meeting of the rivers Nidd and Ouse.

PARCEVALL HALL SE0660
Parcevall Hall Gardens Surrounding an Elizabethan house, 16 acres of woodland gardens charmingly set on a hillside E of the main Wharfedale Valley. Superb views from the cliff walk; tearoom (usually open when garden open exc Mon, perhaps plus Tues in Sept), picnic area, plant sales; cl Nov—Easter exc by appointment; (01756) 720311; £3.

PEN-Y-GHENT SD8473
(694 metres/2,277 ft) Reached from Horton in Ribblesdale, where the Crown and Golden Lion are good value; its satisfyingly compact summit is the craggiest feature on the Pennine Way, which near here passes some pot-holes inc Hull Pot.

RAYDALE SD9187
(nr Bainbridge) The most interesting of Wensleydale's subsidiary valleys for walkers. Its lower neck is quite narrow, but it broadens out into quite a broad sheltered bowl of valley, with Semer Water, a sizeable glacial lake which legend has it was conjured up by a wandering beggar to drown a village that had spurned him. It's Yorkshire's third-largest natural lake, and has a path along its half-mile-long S side, but to make up circular routes you have to do some road walking. The walled track (a Roman road) just N has wide-ranging views as it descends to Bainbridge.

REETH SE0399
Attractive Swaledale village with a high, wide, sloping green (the local brass band plays out here on some summer wknds); the Kings Arms in Market Place is a popular family dining pub. The village is a centre for rambles ranging from pottering along the meadows by the Swale to walks over moors into adjacent Arkengarthdale (where the ascent on to Fremington Edge is memorable).

RIBBLESDALE SD7776
Climbing above Settle into severe and grand mountain scenery, this is craggy and remote, a strange landscape riddled with pot-holes, which you can see from some paths – inc some gaping chasms of sensational size. Two friendly refuges are the Hill Inn at Chapel le Dale (good food under its new owners), and the isolated Station Inn at Ribblehead (interesting view of the Settle–Carlisle railway). A major magnet for walkers is the **Three Peaks Walk**, 24 miles taking in the summits of Ingleborough, Pen-y-Ghent and Whernside. This is a tough undertaking in its entirety, but each of the peaks on its own is a manageable half-day excursion: choose a clear day – not just for the magnificent views but for your own safety. Below Settle, the valley is less interesting for walkers, and marred by some quarrying.

RICHMOND NZ1600

One of Britain's most satisfying small towns, on a spectacular hillside high above the Swale, with steep and pretty streets of old stone buildings, and a splendid broad sloping market square (still cobbled, and perhaps the biggest in the country; market day is Sat). Scollards Hall, built in 1080, is possibly the oldest domestic building in Britain. The very friendly **Richmondshire Museum** is worth a look, with some detailed re-creations inc the vet's surgery from the TV series *All Creatures Great and Small*. Shop, disabled access; cl Nov–Good Fri; (01748) 825611; £1.50. An attractive riverside walk beneath the towering bulk of its castle heads W through Hudswell Woods, with an extension to Whitcliffe Scar, a cliff above the Swale with an exciting path along its top. The army connection with the town is still strong; nearby Catterick Camp is the biggest in the north. The Black Lion in Finkle St is good value, as is the Coffee Bean Café (Market Pl).

Easby Abbey Extensive remains of a 12th-c Premonstratensian abbey, a pretty riverside walk SE; free; EH.

Green Howards Museum (Market Sq) In a converted 12th-c church, this includes among duller regimental history the blood-stained pistol holsters of the Grand Old Duke of York. Shop, mostly disabled access; usually cl wknds in Feb–Mar and Nov, Sun am late May to Sept, all day Sun in Apr and Oct, and all Dec–Jan; (01748) 822133; £2.

Richmond Castle These austere and intricate ruins dominate the town, and overlook the River Swale from a high rocky outcrop. Shop, some disabled access; cl 24–26 Dec and 1 Jan, and perhaps in bad weather; (01748) 822493; £2.90; EH.

Theatre Royal (Victoria Rd) Due to reopen around May, this is the country's oldest and most authentic working theatre still in its original form, and complete with gallery, boxes and pit. Built in 1788, it doesn't look much from the outside, but the immaculately restored interior is really special. New café, shop, museum and guided tours, phone for information; (01748) 823710.

RIPLEY SE2860

Ripley Castle (off A61) Beautifully picturesque castle, in the same family for an amazing 26 generations. Most of the current building dates from the 16th c, inc the tower housing a collection of Royalist armour. For some the main attraction is the splendid gardens, the setting for a national collection of hyacinths and (under glass) a fine tropical plant collection; also lakeside walk. Very good meals and snacks, shops inc a superb delicatessen, some disabled access; cl Sept–May exc Tues, Thurs and wknds; (01423) 770152; £5.50, £3 gardens only. The attractive village was rebuilt around a French theme in the 1820s, and consequently has a rather continental feel; the Boars Head Hotel is a fine old place for lunch.

RIPON SE3171

On Thurs colourful stalls fill the attractive and ancient market square; it's largely unspoilt, lined with specialist shops and old inns and hotels. At 9pm each night the Wakeman, a red-coated bugler, blows a buffalo horn here, as one has done for centuries. Going from here down one of the town's engagingly narrow old streets, you're rewarded by a magnificent view of the elegant Early English W front of the cathedral. The Golden Lion just off the market square has good value food. Fountains Abbey is within a walk from here, and Newby Hall and Norton Conyers are also quite close.

Ripon Cathedral Spectacularly floodlit at night, this is one of the largest half-dozen in the country, and has plenty to see, inc very fine carving indeed in both stone and wood, and a 7th-c crypt – probably the oldest surviving crypt outside Italy. Shop, disabled access; (01765) 603462; £3 suggested donation.

SETTLE SD8163

The town has wound down a bit in recent years, with many of the old shops gone, but market day (Tues) around the Shambles is still fun; look out to the right of here for the Folly, an extraordinary 17th-c townhouse. Mary Milnthorpe & Daughter is a good antique jewellery and silver shop, Poppies tearoom provides welcome relief from shopping, and the Golden

Lion has good food.

Settle–Carlisle Railway A magnificent 72-mile route carved up through Ribblesdale across the wild moors between here and Cumbria, and then dropping down through the lovely Eden Valley; (0845) 748 4950 for times and fares, £16.30 for a day return; the most scenic stretch is from Settle to Appleby. Throughout the year on wknds and occasional Weds there's a programme of walks connecting with the moorland stops; they start quite early, and dates and times are listed on the timetable, or take a look at their website www.settle-carlisle.org. Aside from the setting, it's an ordinary railway line. The B6479 is not quite comparable to the train, but a good drive.

SKIPTON SD9851

On Sat the High St has a colourful market (at least some stalls most other days too, exc Sun, Tues and Thurs); the bustling Red Lion here has decent food, and in Sheep St the 17th-c Woolly Sheep is good value. The 14th-c church has a 16th-c rood screen and interesting stained glass. A canal runs through the town.

Skipton Castle 12th-c, and properly romantic, with sturdy round towers, broad stone steps, and a lovely central flagstoned and cobbled courtyard with a seat around its 350-year-old focal yew tree. One of the best-preserved medieval castles in Europe, it really is remarkable how much is left, interior and all – very few other castles have kept their roofs and stayed habitable. The medieval arched gateway still stands – the word 'Desormais' meaning 'Henceforth' carved above it is the motto of the family who lived here 1310–1676. Meals, snacks, shop; cl Sun am, 25 Dec; (01756) 792442; £4.60. The Black Horse opposite is popular for lunch.

STAINBURN MOOR SE2452

The area E of the Dales really has nothing to compare with the Dales themselves for serious walking, but this moorland W of Harrogate has some possibilities for fairly stretching walks, for instance from the car park by the woods along the side road W from Beckwithshaw; it gets more scenic to the W around the reservoirs of the Washburn Valley.

STAINFORTH SD8167

There's a pleasant and gentle Ribblesdale walk from Stainforth Force to Langcliffe. A short walk west of the village itself, a packhorse bridge crosses the river at Knight Stainforth, a particularly lovely stretch of the Ribble.

STARBOTTON SD9574

Tiny but delightful Wharfedale village; a good base for walks, for example along the river to Kettlewell, then back up over the high land; or follow less obvious paths W to Arncliffe in Littondale – which is very similar to the Wharfedale parent valley, though with a flatter damper valley floor.

SWALEDALE SE0098

The northernmost of all the dales, and one of the least visited – giving more chance of getting away from it all at even peak times. Its bold hills, abundant stone barns and extreme tranquillity make it a walkers' favourite. It's grandly austere for the most part, though quite heavily wooded as it drops down towards Richmond. The steeper parts have some fine waterfalls. The upper slopes, especially towards the Durham and Cumbrian borders, are wild and empty, except for the huge scattered flocks of hardy clean-limbed swaledale sheep with their dark faces, grey muzzles, thick fleeces, and curly-horned rams. The meadowland down in the valleys of this dale and its broad tributary **Arkengarthdale** is largely unimproved, with slow-growing natural grasses and lots of wild flowers. Many of the area's 1,200 traditional stone hay barns which are such a distinctive feature here have been rehabilitated, with generous National Parks grant aid. **Gunnerside** still has around it many of the 'rushes' where lead-miners dammed streams to form torrents that could break up the lead-bearing rock strata below; this whole area was an important lead centre until Victorian times, and other visible mementoes are ruined mill buildings, tunnel entrances and spoil heaps.

WATH SE1467

Attractive Dales hamlet spreading up the valley, with pleasant walks along past the reservoir to Ramsgill – beyond there is a splendid moorland drive over to Masham. The Sportsmans Arms has good food.

WENSLEYDALE SD9889

More expansive in character and not quite as dramatic as Swaledale, but richly picturesque; its unspoilt villages and numerous waterfalls make for pleasurable walking. It used to be one of the richest dales, its broad pastures and countless sheep supporting the wealthy abbeys and castles whose ruins now add so much interest to its scenery. Wensleydale sheep are very distinctive, with long fleecy dreadlock curls. Upper Wensleydale (around and W of Hawes) is steep and wild; E of here the valley starts broadening out, with richer lower pastures, and more regular farmland below Middleham.

WHARFEDALE SD9769

With its tributary valley Littondale and its headwaters up in the steep conifer plantations at the top of Langstrothdale, this is one of England's most popular areas for walkers, and very beautiful indeed in parts. The Dales Way follows the River Wharfe for the length of the dale, except between Kettlewell and Grassington. Upper Wharfedale above Grassington has a level floor of sheltered well drained pastures with the river winding through, a few grey stone barns, and steep sides laced with dry-stone walls, gnarled woodland and occasional austere crags, climbing up to high fairly level tops some 365 metres (1,200 ft) above the valley floor. The smaller villages are delightfully private and unspoilt, their grey or whitewashed stonework blending perfectly with the long scars of the limestone terraces above them. Away from the valley floor, stone-walled grassy tracks are the easiest ways of gaining height. Below Grassington is an extremely pretty stretch where the valley winds more sinuously past Burnsall, Appletreewick, and Bolton Abbey, below hills which though less grand are more varied in shape, with rather sensitively laid-out conifer plantations adding a slightly subalpine feel to some of the views.

WHERNSIDE SD7381

(736 metres/2,415 ft) Sometimes criticised by keen walkers as the boring one of the Three Peaks, this is Yorkshire's highest point, and has an exhilarating ridge section; start from the magnificent Ribblehead Viaduct carrying the Settle–Carlisle railway over the head of the dale (the Station Hotel here is a comfortable halt).

WIDDALE SD8287

This steep-sided and dramatic tributary of Wensleydale has extensive conifer plantations above.

Other attractive villages include Aldbrough St John NZ2011, Appletreewick SE0560, Austwick SD7768, Bilbrough SE5346, Bishop Monkton SE3366, Boroughbridge SE3967, Brearton SE3261, Buckden SD9477, Burnsall SE0361, Cray SD9379, East Witton SE1586 (ancient houses, long wide green), Gargrave SD9354 (on the Pennine Way), Gilling West NZ1804, Grantley SE2369, Gunnerside SD9598, Hampsthwaite SE2659, Hudswell NZ1400, Kirkby Malham SD8961, Kirkby Overblow SE3249, Low Row DD9897 (popular with potholers), Middlesmoor SE0874, Newton-on-Ouse SE5160, Ogden SE0730, Ramsgill SE1271, Redmire SE0591, Roecliffe SE3765, Saxton SE4736 (magnificent church), Scorton NZ2500, Snape SE2784, Thornton in Lonsdale SD6873 (Conan Doyle was married in the charming church), Thornton Watlass SE2486 and Wigglesworth SD8157.

Where to eat

ASENBY SE3975 **Crab & Lobster** *Dishforth Rd* (01845) 577286 Thatched dining pub with nautical-theme dining pavilion, heavily beamed L-shaped bar with lots of bric-a-brac, a relaxed, informal but civilised atmosphere, delicious highly enjoyable food, a fine wine list with plenty by the glass, well kept real ales, and an interesting garden; opulent bdrms. £27|£7.25

ASKRIGG SD9491 **Rowan Tree** (01969) 650536 Cosy little candlelit stone barn run by Irish husband and German wife, just a few tables so booking advisable, good imaginative evening meals and reasonably priced wine list; cl Mon and Tues, cl

Jan–Feb; children over 12. £25.70/Sun lunch £14.50

BOROUGHBRIDGE SE3966 **Black Bull** *6 St James Sq (01432)* 322413 Attractive 13th-c inn with big stone fireplace and brown leather seats in main bar area (served through an old-fashioned hatch), a cosy, traditional snug, well liked interesting bar food, well kept real ales, enjoyable wines (with nine by the glass), and afternoon teas; friendly and attentive service; bdrms; disabled access. £22/£4.95|**£4.95**

BREARTON SE3261 **Malt Shovel** *(01423)* 862929 Popular village pub with friendly, helpful licensees, heavily beamed rooms with open fires and lively hunting prints, enjoyable bar food, well kept real ales, and a fine choice of malt whiskies and wines; no food Sun pm, cl Mon. £15.50|**£6.95**

BURNSALL SE0361 **Red Lion** *(01756)* 720204 Pretty 16th-c inn overlooking the River Wharfe with views from the back terrace and from seats on the front cobbles; bustling main bar with attractive panelling, beams and log fires, good food in bar and no smoking restaurant, a decent wine list with 11 by the glass, and well kept real ales; 75 yds of private fishing, permits for further seven miles; bdrms; disabled access. £35/£6.95|**£6.95**

CARLTON SE0684 **Foresters Arms** *(01969)* 640272 Friendly, carefully restored inn with log fires, low beams and a nice atmosphere, well kept real ales, a good choice of whiskies, imaginative food in bar and restaurant, and friendly helpful service; good bdrms; cl Mon; children over 12 in restaurant. £25 not inc wine|**£8**

CARTHORPE SE3083 **Fox & Hounds** *(01845)* 567433 Pretty little extended village house with two log fires and some evocative Victorian photographs of Whitby, an attractive high-raftered, no smoking restaurant with lots of farm and smithy tools, enjoyable interesting food (fine daily specials and puddings inc yummy home-made ice-creams), decent wines, and helpful, friendly service; cl Mon, first wk Jan; disabled access. £20|**£9**

EAST WITTON SE1486 **Blue Lion** *(01969)* 624273 Stylish and civilised dining pub with log fire, daily papers, bric-a-brac and rugs on flagstones in the distinctive old rooms, exceptionally good imaginative food, nice breakfasts, a carefully chosen wine list, real ales, and pretty garden; bdrms; cl 25 Dec; disabled access. £33|**£5.50**

FERRENSBY SE3660 **General Tarleton** *Boroughbridge Rd (01423)* 340284 Smart, bustling 18th-c dining pub with beams and open fires, relaxed atmosphere, delicious sophisticated food inc super puddings in bar/brasserie and more formal dining room, polite service, and plenty of wines by the glass from a good list; bdrms; cl 25 Dec; disabled access. £25 not inc wine|**£6**

HARROGATE SE3055 **Betty's** *1 Parliament St (01423)* 502746 Famous cake shop with special blends of teas and coffees, Alsace wines, wonderful light home-cooked meals, traditional afternoon tea, over 75 different delicious cakes and pastries; they also have two tearooms in York, one in Ilkley and one in Northallerton – same details apply to each; cl 25–26 Dec, 1 Jan. £15|**£5**

HARROGATE SE3055 **Tannin Level** *5 Raglan St (01423)* 560595 Very good basement wine bar with brick walls and country dining chairs, imaginative food inc lovely puddings, fine wine list, and early evening tapas Mon–Fri; children tolerated; cl Sun and bank hols. £25|**£6**

HARROGATE SE2954 **William & Victoria** *6 Cold Bath Rd (01423)* 521510 Busy wine bar with upstairs evening restaurant and hearty helpings of decent country cooking; cl Sat am, Sun; first 3 wks Jan; disabled access. £27.95|**£5.95**

HETTON SD9658 **Angel** *(01756)* 730263 Extremely popular and particularly well run dining pub with old-fashioned rambling rooms, consistently excellent imaginative food, very good service from hard-working friendly staff, well kept real ales, and over 300 wines; cl 2 wks Jan; children must be well behaved; disabled access. £24|**£8.50**

LANGTHWAITE NZ0002 **Charles Bathurst** *Arkengarthdale (01748)* 884567 In a lovely – if bleak – spot, with wonderful views and lots of surrounding walks, this solid-looking converted cottage has light pine tables, country chairs and benches on the stripped floors, a roaring fire, a no smoking dining room, popular, imaginative food using local ingredients, a short but interesting wine list, and well kept real ales; pretty bdrms. £22.80|£7

LITTON SD9074 **Queens Arms** (01756) 770208 Welcoming, quietly placed 17th-c inn with good popular food, big collection of cigarette lighters in main bar, another room with more of a family atmosphere, and two coal fires; cl Mon exc bank hols, Jan; pretty bdrms; disabled access. £15|£6

MASHAM SE2280 **Floodlit** 7 Silver St (01765) 689000 Bustling little candlelit restaurant with lots of bric-a-brac, particularly good sound cooking using top local ingredients with emphasis on fish and game, lovely puddings, and a sizeable fairly priced wine list; cl Mon, am Tues–Thurs. £22/2-course lunch £11.50

MOULTON NZ2303 **Black Bull** (01325) 377289 Decidedly civilised, well run pub with old-fashioned style and standards of service, memorable bar snacks (excellent smoked salmon), conservatory restaurant or one in the Brighton Belle Pullman dining car, and good wines; cl Sun, 24–27 Dec; children over 7; disabled access. £33|£35

PICKHILL SE3483 **Nags Head** (01845) 567391 Deservedly popular old inn run for nearly 30 years by two brothers, with a nice mix of customers, busy tap room, smarter lounge, no smoking restaurant, particularly good food inc interesting daily specials and lovely puddings, friendly efficient staff, a fine wine list and well kept real ales; bdrms; cl 25 Dec; disabled access. £27.50|7.95

North York Moors & East Yorkshire

Plenty of nicely varied outings, plus wild open countryside and interesting coastline – great for walking; Hull is increasingly worth a visit

North of genteel Scarborough (lots to see and do here), the cliffy coast is full of character, with some delightful little fishing villages. The traditional seaside town of Bridlington is also attractive (Sewerby Hall is a highlight), and there are excellent bird-watching opportunities at Bempton Cliffs and Flamborough Head, just N. Steep Whitby, with its dramatic abbey, is a working fishing port of real individuality, and the shoreline of Robin Hood's Bay is great for fossil hunting. Inland, Helmsley and Beverley are attractive small towns; the far N of the county makes the most of its Captain Cook connections.

A good pocket-friendly destination for families, Hull has some fascinating free museums, as well as the exceptional marine centre, The Deep. For traditional family entertainment, Staintondale's Shire Horse Farm, Cruckley Farm in Foston on the Wolds, and the developing centre at East Ayton are enjoyable places to spend an afternoon; in Middlesbrough, Newham Grange Leisure Farm and the Dorman Museum are other handy suggestions.

Awesome Castle Howard, the charming Elizabethan houses at Burton Agnes and Sproatley, and Sledmere House are worth visiting if historic houses are something you enjoy; there's a fascinating collection of miniature rooms at Nunnington Hall. Duncombe Park in Helmsley and Sutton Park in Sutton-on-the-Forest have lovely grounds. The area is also spread with haunting ruins – Rievaulx Abbey is the most dramatic.

The re-created World War II scenes at Eden Camp just outside Malton are superb (more good military history in Beverley and Elvington), and at Fort Paull they hold a good range of special events. There's a mining museum at Skinningrove, and an engaging folk museum at Hutton-le-Hole. In Coxwold you can see Laurence Sterne's Shandy Hall.

The North York Moors National Park is less visited than the Dales, but gives walkers (and drivers) broad and inspiring landscapes. Its valleys have rich pastures, with red-tiled stone farmhouses, twisting rivers, quiet roads, and few villages. The higher moorland is generally very grand and empty, mile after mile of heather scoured by breath-snatching winds, where the few walkers have for company scatterings of hardy sheep and the occasional harsh cry of a grouse. The North Yorkshire Moors Railway passes through wonderful countryside.

Where to stay

AMPLEFORTH SE5678 **Carr House Farm** *West End, Ampleforth, North Yorkshire YO62 4ED (01347) 868526* **£45***; 3 rms. In peaceful undulating farmland and with an acre of garden, this no smoking 16th-c stone farmhouse has beams and oak panelling, a flagstoned dining room with an inglenook, and separate lounge; good breakfasts using home-made preserves, local bacon, and fresh farm eggs; cl 24–25 Dec; children over 7

BLAKEY RIDGE SE6799 **Lion** *High Blakey, Kirkbymoorside, North Yorkshire YO62 7LQ (01751) 417320* **£58***, plus winter breaks; 10 good rms, most with own bthrm. The fourth-highest inn in England, this has spectacular moorland views, rambling beamed stripped stone bars, blazing fires, generous helpings of decent food served all day, good breakfasts, candlelit restaurant, quite a few real ales, and genuinely friendly licensees and staff; monthly live music nights; fine walking country; disabled access; dogs welcome in bedrooms

EGTON BRIDGE NZ8004 **Horse Shoe** *Egton Bridge, Whitby, North Yorkshire YO21 1XE (01947) 895245* **£50**, plus special breaks; 6 simple rms, most with own bthrm. Beautifully placed inn by River Esk (stepping stones big enough for children to sit on), with lots of friendly wild birds and a pleasant sheltered lawn; open fires, attractive traditionally furnished bars, well cooked food inc excellent breakfasts in cottagey dining room, and decent wines; no accommodation 25 Dec; dogs in bar only

ESCRICK SE6243 **Church Cottage** *York Rd, Escrick, North Yorkshire YO19 6EX (01904) 728462* **£75***; 5 comfortable, individually furnished rms. Friendly extended no smoking house next to church with a spacious dining room (which converts into a Thai restaurant in the evening) overlooking the landscaped gardens, a comfortable lounge, and enjoyable breakfasts; cl Jan; disabled access

FLAMBOROUGH TA2270 **Manor House** *Tower St, Flamborough, Bridlington, East Yorkshire YO15 1PD (01262) 850943* **£66**; 2 rms, the more expensive one has a 17th-c four-poster. Beautifully restored Georgian house with log fire and books in the guest' sitting room, lots of antiques (Mrs Berry is a dealer), good breakfasts, and a friendly atmosphere; the old stable block has antiques and intricate local hand-knitted fishermen's sweaters called ganseys for sale; cl Christmas; children over 8

HAROME SE6481 **Pheasant** *Mill St, Harome, Helmsley, North Yorkshire YO62 5JG (01439) 771241* **£92***, plus special breaks; 12 rms. Family-run hotel with a relaxed homely lounge, and traditional bar with beams, inglenook fireplace and flagstones, good very popular food, efficient service, and indoor heated swimming pool; cl Dec–Feb; children over 7; disabled access; dogs welcome in bedrooms

HAWNBY SE5690 **Laskill Grange** *Easterside, Helmsley, North Yorkshire YO62 5NB (01439) 798268* **£59***, plus special breaks; 6 rms, some in beamy converted outside building. Attractive and welcoming creeper-covered stone house on big sheep and cattle farm near Rievaulx Abbey; open fire, antiques and books in comfortable lounge, conservatory overlooking the garden, good food using home-grown produce, and own natural spring water; self-catering also, with a play area; cl 25 Dec; partial disabled access; dogs welcome

HELMSLEY SE6183 **Black Swan** *Market Pl, Helmsley, North Yorkshire YO62 5BJ (01439) 770466* **£150**, plus special breaks; 45 well equipped and comfortable rms. Striking Georgian house and adjoining Tudor rectory with beamed and panelled hotel bar, attractive carved oak settles and Windsor armchairs, cosy and comfortable lounges with lots of character, and a charming sheltered garden; dogs welcome in bedrooms

KILBURN SE5179 **Forresters Arms** *Kilburn, North Yorkshire YO61 4AH (01347) 868386* **£58***, plus special breaks; 10 clean, bright rms. Friendly old coaching inn opposite the pretty village gardens; sturdy but elegant furnishings made next door at Thompson mouse furniture workshop, big log fire in cosy lower bar, interesting Henry Dee bar in what was a stable with manger and stalls still visible, and enjoyable food in restaurant and beamed bar; disabled access; dogs welcome away from dining room

MIDDLETON SE7887 **Cottage Leas Country Hotel** *Nova Lane, Middleton, Pickering, North Yorkshire YO18 8PN (01751) 472129* **£83**, plus special breaks; 11 comfortable newly refurbished rms. Delightful, peaceful 18th-c farmhouse with extensive gardens, comfortable informal rooms, beamed ceilings, open log fire in cosy lounge, a well stocked bar, and enjoyable creative food; partial disabled access; dogs welcome in bedrooms

SCARBOROUGH TA0091 **Wrea Head Hotel** *Scalby, Scarborough, North Yorkshire YO13 0PB (01723) 378211* **£95***, plus special breaks; 20 individually decorated rms inc 2 new luxury four-poster rms. Victorian country house in 14 acres of parkland and gardens; friendly staff, minstrels' gallery in oak-panelled hall and lounge, open fires, a bow-windowed library, pretty flowers, and good food in airy restaurant.

WASS SE5579 **Wombwell Arms** *Wass, North Yorkshire YO61 4BE (01347) 868280* **£62***, plus winter breaks; 3 individually furnished rms. Attractive, warmly welcoming small inn with a spotless central bar, three low-beamed comfortable dining areas (one restaurant is no smoking), good imaginative food, enjoyable breakfasts, well kept real ales, and decent wines; cl Mon and Sun pm in winter

WILLERBY TA0230 **Willerby Manor** *Well Lane, Willerby, Hull, East Yorkshire HU10 6ER (01482) 652616* **£72**w; 51 individually decorated rms. Originally the home of an Edwardian shipping merchant, this carefully extended hotel is surrounded by three acres of gardens; airy and attractive conservatory, dining bar and more formal restaurant, good food, helpful service, and health club with swimming pool

To see and do

BECK HOLE NZ8202
Charming tucked-away village; Birch Hall here is a unique cross between country tavern and village store. The most rewarding way to get here is walking along the historic rail trail along the abandoned line that preceded the current North Yorkshire Moors Railway route, between Grosmont and Goathland.

BEMPTON TA1973
Bempton Cliffs The RSPB bird reserve here has the biggest colony of seabirds in the country, with up to a quarter of a million of them nesting in the cliffs. Best views of puffins Jun–July, but plenty of skuas and shearwaters later in summer, with wknd boat trips from Flamborough (North Landing) or Bridlington, though what you'll see

depends on the weather. Snacks, shop, some disabled access; visitor centre cl all Jan, wkdys Dec and Feb; (01262) 851179 – book well ahead for the boats; £3 car parking charge, RSPB members free

BEVERLEY TA0339

Attractive country town, in a way like a small-scale York, with much the same sort of appeal. It's partly pedestrianised, with many fine Georgian buildings, several antiques shops and the like, but unlike York is still very much an honest market town rather than a tourist place. There's a market on Sat (and a little one on Weds), and the racecourse is central to local life. The Corner House (Norwood) has good food. The B1248 N gives rolling Wolds views.

Art Gallery & Museum (Champney Rd) Includes lots of pieces by Fred Elwell the woodcarver, famous for his paintings of the town and its characters; cl 12.30–1.30pm wknds, all Mon and Tues, and a wk over Christmas; (01482) 392780; free.

Beverley Minster Wonderful 13th/14th-c building, considered by some to be one of the most architecturally interesting in Europe, with elegant buttressing and elaborately pinnacled towers. The W front is richly carved yet extraordinarily harmonious. Inside are several delights, inc the intricately carved Percy tomb canopy, the unusual Saxon *fridstol* (one of only two such seats in the country), and the biggest collection of misericords in Britain. Shop, disabled access; open daily exc 25 Dec and during weddings and funerals, guided tours in summer and by appointment in winter; (01482) 868540; £2 suggested donation.

Museum of Army Transport (Flamingate) Huge hangar with all sorts of military vehicles inc planes, tanks and cars, many displayed in realistic settings from World War II farm-building camouflage to desert scenes. Children can climb into some vehicles in an explore area, and there is a junior assault course. Meals, snacks, shop, disabled access; cl 24 Dec–2 Jan; (01482) 860445; £4.50.

St Mary's church (Hengate) The former wealth of the town can be guessed at from the magnificence of

another subsidiary church not far from the Minster (and originally intended to be a chapel for that marvellous building); the weather-vane on the SW turret is said to have been the last design by Pugin, who sketched it on the back of an envelope. Opposite is the White Horse, a quaint old gaslit bare-boarded tavern.

BLACKTOFT SE8424

Attractive Humber-side village; its pub the Hope & Anchor, with tables out by the waterside, is great for bird-watchers, right by the RSPB marsh reserve.

BOLTON PERCY SE5341

Behind its medieval gatehouse the 15th-c church has perhaps the most unusual **churchyard** in the country: local lecturer Roger Brook has transformed it into a splendidly colourful garden, with more than a thousand different types of plant creeping around and over the headstones. Rather like a semi-wild cottage garden, it houses part of the national collection of dicentras and is open all the time. The Crown has generous simple food (not Mon or Tues).

BRIDLINGTON TA1767

Famous for its bracing image in the heyday of the traditional seaside resort, and the way the scenery rolls down to the long sands of the shore still gives that feeling. The centre is a quay and small harbour, with the usual summer attractions, but the original core of the town is half a mile in from the sea, with some charming old houses among the more modern ones around the heavily restored priory church. A 14th-c gateway (the Baylegate) gives some idea of how imposing the priory must have been before the Dissolution. The cheerfully nautical Hook & Parrot (Esplanade) has decent lunchtime food. The coast to the S is generally much flatter.

Bondville Model Village (Rivierà Drive, Sewerby) Readers enjoy this; shop, disabled access; cl Oct–Apr; (01262) 401736; £2.50. A walk along the low cliff from here towards Flamborough Head soon brings you to a strip of woodland by a stream; if you follow the lane up from here past the

North York Moors & East Yorkshire

NORTH SEA

Filey

Bempton

Flamborough

Flamborough Head

Bridlington

Foston on the Wolds

TA

Hornsea

Sproatley

Hull

HOLDERNESS

A1033

Paull

Withernsea

Patrington

Spurn Head

SHIRE

car park and along the wood, you come to Iron Age earthworks which cut right across the head – making it a pretty impressive defensive position.

John Bull's World of Rock (Carnaby Industrial Estate, off A614 SW) See how they squeeze the words into the candy, and perhaps even personalise your own stick of the seaside favourite. Open Easter–Sept; (01262) 678525; *£1 factory and exhibition.

Park Rose Pottery (Carnaby Covert Lane, off A614 SW) Factory visits and a seconds shop, as well as 12 acres of strollable parkland with play areas; an owl and bird of prey sanctuary and bee exhibition is usually open Easter–Oct (best to check; (01262) 606800; £1.75). Meals, snacks, shop, disabled access; cl 25–26 Dec; (01262) 602823; site entry free.

Sewerby Hall (NE edge) In spacious parkland right on the coast, with a miniature zoo and aviary (good for children), and a charming garden. The elegant early 18th-c house includes some Amy Johnson memorabilia – the pioneer aviator lived nearby. A little land train links the gardens with central Bridlington in summer. Snacks, shop, disabled access (but not to the hall); grounds open daily all year, house usually cl Weds–Fri end Oct–end Mar, 24 Dec to mid-Feb; (01262) 673769; £3.10.

BUGTHORPE SE7757
Attractive village, especially in spring, with an interesting church; the Fleece at nearby Bishop Wilton is a good value dining pub.

BURTON AGNES TA1063
Richly decorated Elizabethan house, with fantastically carved Great Hall, 16th-c antiques, and some splendid Impressionist paintings. A fine walled garden has colourful borders, there's a pets' corner and topiary bushes. Meals, snacks, shop, disabled access to gardens and ground floor only; cl Nov–end Mar; (01262) 490324; £4.80. The earlier Norman manor house stands between here and the church. The attractive church at nearby Kilham has a Norman door; the 18th-c Bell in Driffield is pleasant for lunch.

BYLAND ABBEY SE5478
Byland Abbey The jagged ruins of this

abbey, built by the Cistercians, date from the 12th c. Enough detail survives to show how fine it must have been: look out for the well preserved floor tiles and carved stone. Good for picnics. Shop, disabled access; cl Nov–Mar; (01347) 868614; £1.70; EH. The nearby Abbey Inn is most enjoyable for lunch. The drive past here from Bagby (SE of Thirsk), Kilburn and Coxwold, and on via Wass and Ampleforth to Oswaldkirk, is very attractive.

CASTLE HOWARD SE7170
(off A64 W of Malton) Magnificent 18th-c palace designed by Sir John Vanbrugh, who up to then had no architectural experience whatsoever, but went on to create Blenheim Palace. The striking 90-metre (300-ft) long façade is topped with a marvellous painted and gilded dome, an unforgettable sight beyond the lake as you approach from the N. Splendid apartments, sculpture gallery and long gallery (58 metres/192 ft long to be exact), magnificent chapel with stained glass by Burne-Jones, and beautiful paintings inc a Holbein portrait of Henry VIII. The grounds are impressive but inviting, inc the domed Temple of the Four Winds by Vanbrugh, a beautiful rose garden with over 2,000 roses, a notable woodland garden, and the family mausoleum designed by Hawksmoor. There's a good unobtrusive adventure playground. Meals, snacks, shop, disabled access; cl Nov to mid-Mar; (01653) 648333; £8. A grand public road runs through the grounds, from Slingsby on the B1257; the vast estate is also threaded by a few public footpaths which gain glimpses of the great house and the landscaped parts of its grounds. The Bay Horse at nearby Terrington has good food.

CLEVELAND WAY NZ8215
One of the best ways of encountering the North York Moors is by this well marked long-distance path, which takes a 110-mile horseshoe course from Helmsley to Filey Brigg around the moorland escarpments of the Hambledon and Cleveland hills, before a coastal finale along the highest cliffs on the eastern seaboard. Highlights include Sutton Bank, Roseberry Topping and the coast around Staithes, Robin Hood's Bay, Ravenscar and Hayburn Wyke; a particularly fine section can be reached off the B1257 N of Chop Gate NZ5703 (where the Buck does good food). The path westwards on the N slopes of the moors takes in rock outcrops. The frequent bus service between Scarborough and Whitby is useful for getting you back if you're walking shorter coastal sections.

COXWOLD SE5377
Neat and very attractive little stone-built village, very harmonious.
Newburgh Priory 🏛 (just S) Charming old house, partly Norman with Tudor and Georgian additions. One of the family married Oliver Cromwell's daughter, who is supposed to have rescued her father's headless corpse and had it reburied here; the room with the tomb is on the tour. Outside is a 40-acre lakeside garden with a fine collection of dogwoods, splendid formal borders and lots of unusual plants. Snacks; open pms Weds and Sun Apr–Jun and perhaps bank hols, best to check; (01347) 868435; *£5 inc guided tour, *£2.50 grounds only.
Shandy Hall Laurence Sterne's quaint house has been well restored, the little study much as it must have been when he wrote the closing parts of *Tristram Shandy* here. This, his second living, was given to him by a local landowner after publication of the first two volumes. Outside is a lovely walled garden. Shop with unusual plant sales; open May–Sept, house pm Weds and Sun, gardens daily exc Sat; (01347) 868465; £4.50, £2.50 garden only. Close by is the attractive 15th-c church of which Sterne was parson – it still has the box pews it had in his day.

CROPTON SE7588
Cropton Brewery The small family-run brewery has guided tours (best to phone for times), and samples of their robustly flavoured beers, and the adjacent New Inn is good. Disabled access to ground floor; (01751) 417330; £2.95. They sell local walks leaflets.

DALBY FOREST SE8789
The E part of the North York Moors National Park has large forest plantations; this area has colour-coded trails. Varied walking is to be had by

taking in the moorland to the W (extending to the car park on A170 S of Saltergate Inn) and the mushroom-like rocks of Bridestones nature reserve.

DANBY NZ7108

Moors Centre (Lodge Lane) Helpful National Park information centre, with exhibitions, guided walks and events; terraced riverside and woodland grounds. Meals, snacks, shop, disabled access to ground floor only; cl wkdys Jan–Feb, and 25 Dec (reduced hours in winter); (01287) 660654; free, £1.50 charge for car park. This area has decent **horse riding centres**, good for experts and beginners alike; the Moors Centre has the full list, and can also provide numbers for the various cycle hire firms dotted about the region. The Fox & Hounds at Ainthorpe, a traditional moorland pub, has good fresh food.

EAST AYTON SE9985

Betton Farm and Visitor Centre Exhaustive exhibition on bees and honey-making, with sales of wax and honey-based products. Also children's farm, craft shops, play area, and by the time this edition comes out there should be a new birds of prey centre too. Tearoom, bakery, farm shop, some disabled access; cl 25–26 Dec; (01723) 863143; £2.95. The Cayley Arms in the pretty village of Brompton has good food, and the Forge Valley drive to Hackness runs through ancient woodlands.

EGTON BRIDGE NZ8005

Charming Eskdale village, pleasantly eccentric, twinned with a fictional French one; lovely Esk views; the riverside Horse Shoe is good.

ELVINGTON SE6748

Yorkshire Air Museum Part of a World War II airfield and base preserved as it was then, with fine aircraft, an old control tower and plenty of other memorabilia inc a Halifax Mk III, engines, models and photographs. Meals, snacks, shop, disabled access; cl 25 Dec; (01904) 608595; £4. The St Vincent Arms at Sutton upon Derwent is good for lunch.

ESTON NAB NZ5618

Outside the North York Moors National Park, this gives walkers a massive view over industrial Teesside.

FADMOOR SE6789

Attractive village on charming drive from Kirkbymoorside, on over Rudland Slack and past Cockayne to Helmsley. The Plough (cl Tues) has good food.

FARNDALE SE6697

The largest dale in the National Park, with characteristic North York Moors scenery – lush green fields and red-roofed yellow-stone houses beneath the brooding moorland plateau. It's famous for its miles of wild daffodils in Apr, introduced and naturalised here many centuries ago; worries that they may be declining have prompted an ambitious new research and conservation partnership between local farmers and the National Park's ecology department. They're at their best around Low Mill, and any walk to enjoy them gives the chance of coming back down the ancient green lane of Rudland Rigg, for spectacular views. The friendly Feversham Arms at Church Houses, right next to the daffodil reserve, does good value food.

FELIXKIRK SE4684

Attractive village, with prettily floodlit church and good drive to Kepwith and Nether Silton; the Carpenters Arms is a good dining pub.

FILEY TA1180

Much quieter resort than Scarborough, its neighbour up the coast, with the main road dropping down a steep little valley between the church and the old town (and under a footbridge linking the two) to the beach, where fishermen still beach their boats. Filey Brigg, the rocky headland N of the town beyond the sands, marks the end of the Cleveland Way; to the S are holiday camps, and the seafront Coble Landing Bar has decent food and great views. **Filey Museum** ▣ (Queen St) Small and attractively homely local museum in former medieval fishermen's cottages. Shop, disabled access to ground floor and garden (video of the upper floor), and good facilities for the blind; cl am Sat, and all end Oct–Easter; (01723) 515013; £1.50.

FLAMBOROUGH TA2270

A blowy place high on the headland, with some old houses in the core around the 15th-c church, and interesting for the nearby cliff scenery.

Down below past the holiday camp the natural rock harbour is well sheltered, with a lifeboat station, and there are fine views of coast and sea from the point of the headland, by the lighthouse. You may be able to buy a local version of guernseys, weatherproof 'ganseys', hand-knitted in the round. The Seabirds is good for lunch, and the B1259 and B1229 are the most interesting coast roads. There is some quite exciting walking, particularly around the N side of Flamborough Head, with the cacophony of thousands of kittiwakes sounding within the inlets; puffins can sometimes be seen on rock ledges. A level mile and a half from the lighthouse along clifftops leads to North Landing (café and car park). A longer walk making the Head the midway point starts from the village, skirting fields to join the coast path; to avoid anticlimax, walk the southern cliffs first and keep the real drama for later on. To the N the path follows the coast closely nearly all the way, and hilly country coming right to the coast makes for interest.

FOSTON ON THE WOLDS
TA0855

Cruckley Farm 🏛 Friendly working farm, with lots of animals to fuss over – inc some very strange-looking rare breeds. Daily milking displays (usually around 10.45). Snacks, shop, some disabled access; cl Oct–Apr; (01262) 488337; £3. The Trout at Wansford has decent food.

GARTON-ON-THE-WOLDS
SE9859

Garton-on-the-Wolds church 12th-c, and very High Church inside, with 19th-c mosaics and frescoes.

GOATHLAND NZ8301
In the heart of the moors, this was the picturesque setting for TV's *Heartbeat* (beware coach loads of fans). There are interesting walks from here, inc the short one from opposite the church to **Mallyan Spout**, a lovely waterfall which tumbles into the side of a fine wooded smooth-rocked gorge. The rambling Inn on the Moor (Mill Green Way) does good meals.

GREAT AYTON NZ5610
Captain Cook Schoolroom Museum 🏛 (High St) In two rooms of the Postgate School (built in 1704)

where James Cook got his early education, it features a reconstruction of an early 18th-c school, plus interactive displays about the explorer's early life and later achievements. Cl am exc July–Aug, and all Nov–Mar exc by appointment; (01642) 722208; *£2. The Royal Oak overlooking the elegant village green has good food.

GUISBOROUGH NZ6116
Gisborough Priory 🏛 12th-c ruined priory, one huge window rising dramatically from the rest of the more or less foundation-level ruins. The gatehouse is fairly well preserved, and it's a charming spot for a picnic. Shop; cl Mon (plus Tues Oct–Mar), phone for opening times over Christmas; £1.10; EH. The Fox nearby has decent food, and the market town is attractive.

HAWNBY SE5489
Attractive village, on the very scenic Rievaulx Abbey–Osmotherley road; the Hawnby Hotel is well set for walkers.

HAYBURN WYKE TA0096
From the Hayburn Wyke Hotel (a lively pub with popular food) steep Victorian woodland paths wind down to the cliff-sheltered cove; a clifftop path to the S gives fine views.

HELMSLEY SE6184
Lanes run straight up on to the moors from this attractive neatly kept small market town (the B1257 is one of the best moorland roads). There's a large cobbled square (busy Fri market), and enough antiques and craft shops to please a visitor without seeming too touristy. A lively and bustling place, with a lot of class. The Royal Oak (open all day) does substantial food. A rewarding and very varied drive is past Rievaulx Abbey, Old Byland and Cold Kirby to Sutton Bank, left along the A170 then next right turn to Kilburn, Coxwold, Byland Abbey and back via Ampleforth and Oswaldkirk.

Duncombe Park Beautifully restored early 18th-c house, rebuilt after a fire a hundred years ago. The landscaped gardens, with grand terracing, are magnificent, covering around a tenth of the 300 acres of memorable parkland. Meals, snacks, shop, some disabled access; cl Fri–Sat, and end Oct to mid-Apr; (01439) 770213; *£6, *£3 gardens only. You can wander through the estate, run as a nature reserve, for £2.

Helmsley Castle This 12th-c pile, ruined in 1644, stands within enormous earthworks and dominates the town; good for picnics. Shop; cl 1–2 pm, Mon and Tues Oct–Mar, 24–26 Dec; (01439) 770442; £2.50; EH.

Helmsley Walled Garden With a good variety of clematis and roses and a restored Victorian orchid house, this friendly place is continuing restoration started in 1994. Dating from 1756, it has an excellent choice of plants for sale, and a good café. Disabled access; cl Nov–Mar exc wknd pms; (01439) 771427; £3.

HOLDERNESS TA3029
The area between Wolds, Humber and coast is flat: rich farming country with huge fields and not many buildings, though the fine village churches often with soaring towers or spires reflect the wealth that this fertile land has put into them in the past. The long southern stretch of fast-eroding coast is flat country too, without a great deal of appeal for walkers – except for long lonely off-season walks above the crumbling cliffs.

HORNSEA TA2145
Sizeable resort; behind the town, Hornsea Mere, 2m long, is the biggest natural lake in this region, with herons and other birds.

Hornsea Freeport 🖭 (Rolston Rd) One of the area's most visited attractions, leisure centre based around a factory shopping village. Lots of well known brands and stores (some good bargains), and family features such as butterflies (£1), model village (£1), crazy golf (£1), and indoor and outdoor adventure playgrounds (from £1). Meals, snacks, shop, disabled access; attractions cl Nov–Easter, shops cl 25–26 Dec; (01964) 534211; site free.

Hornsea Museum 🖭 (Newbegin) Enthusiastic folk museum with re-created period rooms, craft demonstrations and large gardens. Shop, mostly disabled access; cl Mon, Sun am, and Oct–Easter; (01964) 533443; £2.

HOVINGHAM SE6675
Attractive estate village, with wonderfully conserved buildings, pretty gardens, and a pleasant drive S to Sheriff Hutton and Flaxton. The Malt Shovel has good value food.

HOWARDIAN HILLS SE6575
These gentle generously wooded hills have a path followed by the Ebor Way along their N flanks, giving intermittent views across the plain to the North York Moors.

HOWDEN SE7428
Unpretentiously attractive, with cobbled alleys, a fine market hall, a majestic **minster** with a tall tower, the ruins of a charming medieval chapter house, and a small marshland country park down the lane opposite the minster, with ponds and raised walkways. The White Horse is useful for lunch.

HUGGATE SE8855
Attractive Wolds village, with decent pub and easy walks nearby.

HULL TA1028
Kingston-upon-Hull is the full name of this big port, surprisingly pleasant for visitors now that the former docks have been so well tidied up. In the centre there's little sign of the decay and local government problems which in 2002 led to serious criticism from the Audit Commission, though parts have a strange but oddly intriguing mix of estuary views, abandoned warehouses awaiting trendification, spaces which seem to have been empty since World War II bombing, and cobbled streets partly inlaid with fragmentary tramlines. On the waterfront a developing esplanade lets you walk for miles along the Humber, though much is still rather desolate: one attractive enclave is the landing stage for the former Humber ferry, with some solid well restored Georgian buildings, an amazing Victorian public lavatory, and Humber views from the waterfront Minerva (which brews its own beer). Nearby, the original dock has become a vast and thriving yacht marina, with cheerfully buoyant modern buildings around it. Princes Quay is now a smart shopping centre (with good value food in the Mission, a converted seamen's mission over in Posterngate). Trunk roads to the modern container and ferry port separate this waterfront from the old town (an elevated walkway is planned

to link them). A core of ancient buildings has survived in the narrow streets around the old town's High St, notably around Holy Trinity church, cobbled Prince St, colourful Victorian Trinity Market and the adjoining arcade which leads to Silver St. A delightful old building nearby is the Olde Whyte Harte; it was in its heavily panelled upper room that the decision was made to lock the town's gate against King Charles in 1642, depriving him of the arsenal that might otherwise have swung the Civil War in his favour. Hull's good free museums are mostly concentrated in the old town, so it's easy to walk from one to another. Old warehouses and shops are turning into trendy new bars, restaurants and loft-style flats, and there's a growing clubbing scene. A free copy of the city's ale trail (a self-guided tour around the best pubs) is available from the Tourist Information Centre in Paragon St, and there's a fish trail for children (40p) with witty pavement brass rubbings and a certificate at the end.

Ferens Art Gallery Queen Victoria Sq) Enterprisingly run general collection, with lots of maritime paintings, Dutch Old Masters, and a good 20th-c British section (inc works by Stanley Spencer and Wyndham Lewis). There's also an interactive children's gallery. Snacks, shop, disabled access; cl Sun am, 24–26, 31 Dec and 1 Jan; (01482) 613902; free.

Hands-on History (South Church Side) In Hull's oldest secular building, originally a school dating from 1583, this has an expanding social history collection, also displays on the Victorians and the Egyptians. Shop, disabled access; cl am Sun, and term-time wkdys; (01482) 613902; free.

Hull & East Riding Museum (High St) Newly refurbished with new displays tracing the geology, archaeology and natural history of the region up to the medieval period; highlights include the prehistoric Hadholme boat, and a new walk-through Roman gallery has a re-creation of late 3rd-c Brough, a little local town. Shop, disabled access; cl Sun am, 24–27 Dec and 1 Jan; (01482) 613902; free.

Hull Maritime Museum (Queen Victoria Sq) This massive yet solidly stylish three-domed Victorian building has good (and pleasantly old-fashioned) displays on Hull's maritime history. There's a long-established section on whales and whaling, and the huge skeletons on display were mentioned in *Moby Dick*; also models of trawlers, figureheads and paintings. Shop, disabled access; cl am Sun, Good Fri, and a few days over Christmas and New Year; (01482) 613902; free.

Maister House (High St) Only the staircase and entrance hall are open in this mid-18th-c building (the rest is still used as offices), but the Palladian staircase is splendid, and the doors ornate and finely carved. Cl wknds, 24 Dec–2 Jan and all bank hols; (01482) 324114; free; NT.

Spurn Lightship (Princes Dock, Marina) Operating from the 1920s to the 1970s – interesting to go below decks and imagine being confined to this for weeks at a time, not going anywhere, tossed about in storms or blanketed in fog. Shop, cl Sun am and Oct–Mar; (01482) 613902; free.

Streetlife Museum (High St) Extensively refurbished last year, this good collection is devoted mainly to local public transport and bicycles, some weird and wonderful. Improvements include a new motor car gallery, a major extension of the carriage gallery (you can now go on a re-created mail coach ride – you may have to queue), a larger street-scene with several new shops, and a hands-on interactive exhibition area. Shop, disabled access; cl Sun am, and a few days over Christmas and New Year; (01482) 613902; free. From behind there's a great view of the old warehouses along the River Hull where it meets the Humber – the most evocative part of the waterfront.

The Deep (Tower St, Sammy's Point) This hi-tech new exhibition on the sea offers far more than your average aquarium. It's an astonishing building; all the walls are at an angle, and the main bit juts out 30 metres (100 ft) above the Humber estuary. The focus is on the world's oceans: how they were formed, how marine life has developed, and how they're affected by outer space, the equator, and by man; lots of interactives, and the latest lighting and effects bring it all to life. The Polar Galley has a pair of real ice walls, and they have around 500 species of fish from around the planet, some of which take their chances alongside the sharks in their showpiece aquarium, said to be the deepest in Europe. A futuristic centre has activities and experiments, inc the chance to pilot a submarine or work out a crew's diet. Meals, snacks, shop, disabled access; cl 24–25 Dec; (01482) 381000; £6 adults.

Wilberforce House (High St) William Wilberforce was born in this 17th-c house (the introductory video on this remarkable politician is interesting), and its Jacobean and Georgian rooms have a good exploration of the horrors of the slave trade and the struggle for its abolition. Shop, disabled access to ground floor; cl Sun am, and a few days over Christmas and New Year; (01482) 613921; free. The Olde Black Boy nearby was the site of slave auctions. On Wilberforce Quay you can see a restored 1960s fishing vessel; tours of the **Arctic Corsair** last about an hour – wear sensible shoes; open Weds, Sat and pm Sun Apr–end Oct; (01482) 658838; £2.

HUMBER BRIDGE TA0225
Humber Bridge Country Park At the N end of the second longest single-span suspension bridge in the world, nearly a mile between the towers, and a very impressive sweep of engineering (there's a footway across as well as the road). Plenty of woodland and clifftop walks, and an old windmill. There's a Tourist Information Centre and café at the bridge amenity area.

HUTTON-LE-HOLE SE7089
Neat and pretty streamside village at the mouth of Farndale; sheep wander the streets – though they won't be alone in the summer months. Its excellent **Ryedale Folk Museum** is practically a village itself, made up of various old buildings from the area re-erected in the 3-acre grounds, inc an Elizabethan manor house, gipsy caravan, and an Edwardian photographic studio; craft demonstrations most Sat–Weds. Shop, disabled access; cl Nov–Mar;

(01751) 417367; £3.25. The friendly Crown does generous food. There's a pleasant walk (an hour or so) over to Lastingham, and the Blakey Ridge road to Castleton is a great drive with classic moorland views.

KILBURN SE5179
Robert Thompson Furniture Workshop The quiet village is almost a place of pilgrimage to this workshop, famous for the unobtrusive little mouse carved as a trademark that you'll see all over North Yorkshire, on church pews and in the better inns and pubs. They make lovely, simple furniture – though not cheap; the oak they use can be seen all around. There's a workshop viewing gallery, and their refurbished visitor centre and museum is due to open at Easter; charge for entry. Cl 2 wks at Christmas, disabled access. Near the church (with a memorial to Thompson carved by his own craftsmen) the Singing Bird does refreshments, as does the Forresters Arms – full of Thompson work. Up above the village on Roulston Scar is a white horse cut in the turf in 1857 and unique in this part of the country.

KIRKDALE SE6686
Kirkdale church Saxon, with a unique original sundial, and 7th-c Celtic crosses and carved stones.

KIRKHAM SE7365
Kirkham Priory Remains of Augustinian priory in an attractive quiet spot by the River Derwent; finely sculpted lavatorium, graceful arcaded cloister, and handsome 13th-c gatehouse with some finely carved sculptures and shields. Snacks, shop, disabled access; cl Nov–Mar; (01653) 618768; £1.70. The Stone Trough overlooking the ruins has good food (not Mon exc bank hols), and a pleasant path meanders S by a placid stretch of the River Derwent, to Howsham Bridge and beyond.

KIRKLEATHAM NZ5921
Kirkleatham Owl Centre (In the grounds of Old Hall) Birds of prey centre with an emphasis on owls – they've one of the largest collections in the country; around 100 birds on show, inc falcons, buzzards, vultures and kites. There are daily flying displays in school holidays (Easter–end Oct, depending

on weather); around midday in the early summer, there's usually the chance to meet baby owls and vultures. Snacks, shop, disabled access; cl Mon (exc bank hols), limited opening hours in winter; (01642) 480512; £3. The early 18th-c former school, **Old Hall**, houses a local history museum. Snacks, shop, disabled access; cl Mon (exc bank hols), Good Fri and 25 Dec–1 Jan; (01642) 479500; free.

LASTINGHAM SE7290
Particularly attractive village, with church on a former abbey site, once one of the area's most sacred spots of pilgrimage, with an outstanding 11th-c crypt; the friendly 17th-c Blacksmiths Arms has enjoyable food. The hillside just S gives a classic North York Moors view, and there's a pleasant hour's walk over to Hutton-le-Hole.

LEVISHAM SE8390
A good spot for walkers, with open scenery around it, a track across the blustery moors, and an attractive valley giving separate routes to and from the Hole of Horcum, just below the A169. The Horseshoe has enjoyable food.

MALTON SE7871
Comfortable market town with some interesting side streets, in prosperous farming and racehorse-training country. Sat is a busy market day. The Crown, brewing its own beer, welcomes children in its conservatory courtyard. A scenic road towards York is the old coach road parallel to the A64, from Norton to Buttercrambe and Gate Helmsley.

Eden Camp (A64/A169 N)
Elaborately re-created wartime scenes in buildings of former prisoner-of-war camp, very well done with sound, smells and even smoke effects – it really brings back the feel of the 1940s. Covers a wide range of World War II experiences, from the rise of the Nazis to the Blitz and Bomber Command ops room. There's also a children's commando assault course. Meals and snacks in NAAFI, shop, disabled access; cl 23 Dec to mid-Jan; (01653) 697777; *£4.

MARGROVE PARK NZ6515
South Cleveland Heritage Centre
Right on the edge of the moors, with archaeology, history and wildlife exhibitions, and can organise walks, nature trails and activities. Snacks, shop, disabled access; cl Fri, Sat, and all Oct–Mar; (01287) 610368; free.

MARKET WEIGHTON SE8741
Neat and pleasant old market town with one or two useful antiques shops. Here the well signposted Wolds Way long-distance path briefly divides in two, allowing walkers a circuit taking in the old railway line, now the Hudson Way, and the villages of Goodmanham and Londesborough with its fine parkland.

MIDDLESBROUGH NZ5116
Captain Cook Birthplace Museum
🖼 (Stewart Park, Marton, 3m S) Lots that will appeal to children at this interesting museum, which looks at the life and voyages of Captain Cook with hands-on displays, computer interactives and films; the landscaped grounds are impressive too. Meals, snacks, shop, disabled access; cl Mon (exc bank hols, and Easter and summer school hols), 25–26 Dec, 1 Jan; (01642) 311211; £2.40. The stylish nearby Apple Tree has good food.

Dorman Museum (Linthorpe Rd)
Due to re-open in spring after major refurbishments, the eight themed galleries (four are new) house an extensive display of the town's social history; also a discovery centre for children, and interesting changing exhibitions. In summer, they run a programme of children's activities. New café, disabled access; usually only cl Mon, and a few days over Christmas, but best to check; (01642) 358101; free.

Nature's World 🖼 (Sandy Flatts Lane/Ladgate Lane – B1380) Thriving environmental demonstration centre, developing all the time, with organic gardens, nature trails, and a number of re-created natural habitats inc a model of the River Tees quarter of a mile long. An innovative earth-sheltered 'eco-structure' houses displays on the latest in environmental technology (solar and geothermal power and so forth), as well as a futuristic hydroponicum. They've also built up a seed bank for locally endangered wildflowers. Splendid home-cooked meals and snacks, shop, good disabled access; (01642) 594895; £4.

Newham Grange Leisure Farm ▣
(Coulby Newham, off A174) Rare
breeds and other animals (with a
petting area for children), an
agricultural museum with craft displays,
reconstructed vet's surgery, and play
and picnic areas. Snacks, shop, disabled
access; cl wkdys Oct–Mar; (01642)
300202; £2.

Transporter Bridge (A178) Unique,
with the central section serving as a
ferry, every 15 mins shuttling cars and
pedestrians across the Tees. A visitor
centre uses interactive displays to tell
the story of the town's industrial
heritage, as well as the history of the
bridge itself; centre open pm wknds
(plus pm Thurs–Fri during school hols)
and bank hol Mon; (01642) 246566;
50p. Bridge cl Sun am, 25–26 Dec, 1 Jan,
and maybe in bad weather; crossing 80p
cars, 30p pedestrians.

MILLINGTON SE8351
Wolds Way The village is a good base
for round walks based on this well
signed way, with the landscape here
rolling most attractively.

**NORTH YORK MOORS
NATIONAL PARK** SE6889
Classic views The graveyard of
Gillamoor church makes a picturesque
foreground for the interlocking moor
and valley landscapes which surround it;
in this pretty village the Royal Oak has
good food. The lane at SE6188 a bit
more than a mile N of Carlton, itself N
of Helmsley, gives another fine moors
view.

NUNNINGTON SE6679
Nunnington Hall Big 16th/17th-c
house nicely set on the banks of the
River Rye, with fine panelling and a
magnificent staircase. A family home for
nearly 400 years, with the intriguing
Carlisle Collection of miniature rooms,
each of them ⅛ life-size. Tearooms,
shop, limited disabled access; cl am, all
day Mon (exc bank hols) and Tues (exc
Jun–Aug), and all Nov–Mar; (01439)
748283; £4.50, garden only £2; NT. In
the attractive village the Royal Oak is a
good dining pub, and the church has a
fine effigy of a knight said to have rid the
district of a Loathly Worm.

ORMESBY NZ5317
Ormesby Hall Elegant 18th-c house
with elaborate plasterwork, Victorian
laundry and kitchen, model railway, and
pleasant gardens and grounds. Snacks,
shop, disabled access to ground floor
only; cl am, all day Mon (exc bank hols),
Fri, Sat, and Nov–Mar; (01642) 324188;
£3.70, garden and railway only £2.50;
NT.

OSMOTHERLEY SE4597
Perhaps more small town than village,
but quietly attractive; the Golden Lion,
welcoming to walkers, is good for a
meal, and the smart Three Tuns is a
popular bistro. A lonely stretch of the
Cleveland Way well signed long-
distance path runs up over the
Hambleton Hills from here, with some
road access along the way; and the 44-
mile Wyke Way path starts here.

Mount Grace Priory (A19 NW)
Carthusian monks not only took a vow
of silence but rarely emerged from their
own individual cells. One of those cells
at this ruined 14th-c priory has been
fully restored, giving a good illustration
of how the monks must have worked
and lived. The ruins are better
preserved than those of any other
Carthusian establishment in England; in
spring an impressive display of daffodils
makes it especially attractive, and there
are plenty of nice picnic spots in the
surrounding woodland. An adjacent
17th-c manor house has an exhibition,
and interesting Arts and Crafts
connections. Snacks, shop; cl 1–2pm,
plus Mon–Tues Nov–Mar, 24–26 Dec;
£3; EH.

**North York Moors Adventure
Centre** (Ingleby Cross) can organise
climbing, caving, abseiling, orienteering,
raft building, mountain biking and
canoeing. Snacks, shop; (01609)
882571.

PATRINGTON TA3122
Patrington church Glorious, with
lovely carving inside – its graceful spire
beckoning you from a long way off.

PAULL TA1625
Fort Paull Based around the only
Napoleonic fort left in Yorkshire, this
new family attraction is best in summer,
with frequent special events from
classic car rallies and battle
reconstructions to falconry days.
Underground labyrinths contain re-
creations from key moments in the
fort's development, from a coastal

defence originally built by Henry VIII in the mid-16th c to an anti-aircraft station during World War II. Also period military vehicles and guns (children can clamber over some of them), and you can have a go on a rifle range and archery field (each £1, ask a member of staff on wkdys). There's a children's assault course, nature trails and craft shops; good views over the Humber estuary. Meals, snacks, shop, mostly disabled access; cl 25–26 Dec, 1 Jan; (01482) 882655; £4.50.

PICKERING SE7984
Another attractive small town, usually very quiet (busier Mon market day), with vividly restored medieval murals in the splendid tall-spired church. The White Swan has good food; the A169 N has sweeping moorland views (up there the Saltergate Inn is a useful stop).

Beck Isle Museum Charmingly set 17th-c riverside house with a wonderful collection of local bygones and period shops. Shop, good disabled access; cl Nov–Mar; (01751) 473653; *£3.

North Yorkshire Moors Railway (Pickering Station) Steam trips through some lovely countryside and nostalgically restored stations, a distance of 18 miles; the line was originally built by George Stephenson. The Grosmont end has various locomotives and antique carriages, and you can stop off at Goathland. Meals, snacks, shop, disabled access; cl Nov–Mar (exc Nov and Dec wknds, and over New Year); (01751) 472508 for timetable; £10 full return journey. The nearby Station Hotel has decent food.

Pickering Castle Tall ruins of 12th-c keep and later curtain walls and towers, with fine views from its imposing castle mound above the town. Snacks, shop, some disabled access; cl 1–2, and Mon and Tues Nov–Mar; (01751) 474989; £2.50; EH.

POCKLINGTON SE8048
An open-faced market town below the Wolds, with a good few handsome buildings; the Feathers is popular for lunch (and has decent bedrooms). The B1246 Driffield road runs through some quite picturesque hills.

Burnby Hall (B1247 S) Famous for their water-lilies, with dozens of varieties in two lakes; also lots of koi carp, and an intriguing collection of all sorts of ethnic material and sporting trophies from across the world. Snacks, shop, disabled access; cl Oct–Mar; (01759) 302068; £2.50. From out here it's not far to the Plough at Allerthorpe (good for lunch).

RIEVAULX SE5785
Rievaulx Abbey Elegant and evocative ruins of magnificent and once highly prosperous abbey, among the wooded hills of Rye Dale (the most dramatic views are gained by walking down the dale from the N). The nave, dating from 1135, is one of the earliest built in England. Also among the spectacular three-tiered remains is a fine 13th-c choir; there's a visitor centre, and interesting museum with hands-on displays about the site's history. The graceful colonnades, arches and lancet windows are especially impressive without the crowds, early or late on a wkdy out of season. Snacks, shop, some disabled access; cl 24–26 Dec, 1 Jan; (01439) 798228; £3.60; EH. Besides the many places in Helmsley not far off, the Hare over in Scawton (a pleasant drive) is good for lunch.

Rievaulx Terrace & Temples This half-mile grass-covered 18th-c terrace overlooks the abbey, with dramatic views. Each end is adorned with a classical temple; one a small Tuscan rotunda built to while away the hours in peaceful contemplation, the other, an elaborate Ionic creation, for hunting parties. An ideal spot for a picnic, with good frescoes and an exhibition on landscape design. Snacks, shop; cl Nov to mid-Mar; (01439) 798340; £3.30; NT.

ROBIN HOOD'S BAY NZ9505
Picturesque fishing village, once popular with smugglers and still largely unspoilt (though there are quite a few shops and cafés for visitors now), its cottages clustered steeply above the rocky shore – a rich hunting-ground for fossil hunters at low tide, when a surprising expanse of sand is exposed beyond the fascinating rock pools. You can walk along a fine section of cliffs to Ravenscar, where a geological trail takes in old alum quarries; an

abandoned railway provides an easy walkway back. The Laurel down in the village is a charming fishermen's pub; the Victoria Hotel up on the cliff has a good choice of food. The village car park is also up at the top – quite a climb.

Music in Miniature Exhibition (Albion Rd church hall) This charming collection of highly detailed models illustrating English musical history should reopen around Easter with a new exhibition on Robin Hood's Bay. Shop, disabled access; usually cl Nov–Easter exc wknds till Christmas, but best to check times and prices; (01947) 880512.

ROSEBERRY TOPPING NZ5712 A memorable viewpoint on the extreme N edge of the moors, reached by a moorland walk from Gribdale Gate car park E of Great Ayton; a popular circuit goes by way of Airy Home Farm, the childhood home of Captain Cook. The Kings Head (Newton, A173) is a popular dining pub

ROSEDALE SE7296 With its lush fields and red-roofed yellow-stone houses sheltering warmly below the gaunt moorland, this now seems to typify the quiet pastoral countryside of the area. But until around 70 years ago it was a busy iron-working site: the old railway track that once served the quarries loops around the moor above, and makes an easily followed stroll. The Milburn Arms has good food. The hillside at the top of the dreadfully steep Rosedale Chimney road heading S over Spaunton Moor gives motorists too a classic view.

RUNSWICK BAY NZ8016 Very pretty harbourless fishing village, with fresh fish and great views from the Royal; an attractive stretch of the well signed Cleveland Way long-distance path runs from here to Staithes (or you can begin closer from tiny Port Mulgrave).

SALTBURN-BY-THE-SEA NZ6621 Originally a superior Victorian seaside resort, with traces of those days still in the Italianate valley garden and the water-balanced cliff lift by the pier. The Ship Inn, a good pub right by the boats pulled up on the beach, is probably the most ancient building. The beach is sheltered by the great headland of Warsett Hill to the S, and a grand section of the well signed Cleveland Way long-distance path takes walkers over this and beyond.

Saltburn Smugglers Heritage Centre ⬚ (Whitby Rd) Vivid interactive exhibition on the town's smuggling heritage, housed in old seaside cottages. Shop; cl Oct–Mar; (01287) 625252; £1.90.

SCARBOROUGH TA0488 All the usual seaside attractions in a place of some style, its two great curves of firm sandy beach separated by the small harbour below a high narrow headland. Between castle and cliff are the remains of a Roman signal station, one of five such structures built in the 4th c to warn of approaching raiders. To the S is the older part of the resort, with antique tracked cliff lifts between prom and the pleasant streets of the upper town; a house associated with Richard III here is now a restaurant. The train station has one of the longest benches in the world – 139 metres (456 ft) long, it can seat 228 people; the Steven Joseph theatre opposite is run by Alan Ayckbourn. Interesting churches include medieval St Mary's, where Anne Brontë is buried, and 19th-c St Martin's with elaborate work by William Morris, Burne-Jones and other Pre-Raphaelites. One unique and entertainingly quaint tradition is the summer staging of miniaturised sea battles with all sorts of special effects among the ducks on the lake of Peasholm Park in the less seasidey N part of town; phone the tourist information for dates and times; (01723) 373333. Good views of the bay from the top of Oliver's Mount (and harbour views from the Golden Ball on the front); good value food all day in the very grand Lord Rosebery (Westborough), and the stylish Raffels (Falsgrave Rd/Belgrave Cres), a former gentleman's club, has a plush restaurant.

Cleveland Way S of Scarborough to Filey is an agreeable few hours' walk along the well signed Cleveland Way, though of less scenic significance than the cliffs further N. Oddly, the Way stops just short of Filey, at the headland of Filey Brigg, although there is nothing to prevent you from walking on into town.

Rotunda Museum (Vernon Rd) Georgian local history museum, with a Bronze Age skeleton, displays on the resort's Victorian heyday, and a new display on seaside activities. Shop; cl Mon and Weds–Fri Oct–May; (01723) 374839; £2 joint ticket with Wood End Museum and Art Gallery.

Scarborough Art Gallery (The Crescent) Striking Italianate villa with good temporary exhibitions. Snacks, shop; cl Mon, also Sun–Weds Oct–May; (01723) 374753; £2 joint ticket with Rotunda and Wood End Museum.

Scarborough Castle Looking down over the town from the headland, this stands on the site of British and Roman encampments. It was a Royal palace of some importance until the reign of James I. Remains include the 13th-c barbican, medieval chapels and house, and the shell of the original 12th-c keep; great coastal views from the walls. Shop, snacks, disabled access; cl 24–26 Dec, 1 Jan; (01723) 372451; £2.80; EH.

Sea Life Centre 🆔 (Scalby Mills) Busy marine sanctuary with seal pups, otters, turtles and seahorses, as well as thousands of other sea creatures; feeding sessions and talks throughout the day, a touch-pool, and a soft play area for younger children. Meals, snacks, shop, disabled access; cl 25 Dec; (01723) 376125; £6.50.

Terror Tower (Martin Marine, Foreshore Rd) A diversion for children on wet days, with ghoulish reconstructions of horror film sets, and actors adding to the tension. Shop; cl Oct–Apr exc pm wknds; (01723) 501016; £2.50.

Wood End Museum (The Crescent) The Sitwells lived here for 60 years from 1870 (Edith was born here), and there are displays of their work and associated memorabilia. Also lots of fossils, and Victorian conservatory with tropical plants – though not the free-flying birds that once mingled with party-goers. Shop; cl Mon, and Oct–May exc Weds and wknds; (01723) 367326; *£2 joint ticket with Rotunda and Scarborough Art Gallery.

SHERIFF HUTTON SE6566
Attractive village, with a ruined castle and a 12th-c church with an effigy of a child, said to be Richard III's only son, Prince Edward; there are some interesting motte and bailey earthworks behind the church. The Highwayman has enjoyable food.

SKINNINGROVE NZ7119
Tom Leonard Mining Museum 🆔 Good mining museum well demonstrating the reality of work underground. You can see how the stone is drilled, charged with explosives and fired. Shop; cl ams, Sun (exc July and Aug) and Nov–Mar; (01287) 642877; *£3.50. The village is industrial, with a steel-rolling mill – far from picturesque, but it has strong local colour, with its odd shanty town of pigeon-fanciers' sheds spreading over the cliff. Walkers can join the well signed Cleveland Way southwards to ascend monumental Boulby Cliff, the highest point on the E coast, before re-entering the National Park.

SLEDMERE SE9365
Sledmere House Grand 18th-c mansion decorated and furnished in the style of the period, with one showpiece room done in Turkish tiling and a library bigger than many public ones. There's an 18th-c walled garden, and the extensive park was landscaped by Capability Brown. They usually play their pipe organ pm Weds, Fri and Sun. Meals, snacks, shop, disabled access. Cl before 11.30am, all day Mon (exc bank hols), Sat, and Oct–Easter; (01377) 236637; £4.50, garden only £2. The Triton nearby is a handy food stop.

SPROATLEY TA1836
Burton Constable Hall The wonderful exterior gives away this delightful house's Elizabethan origins, but the inside was extravagantly remodelled in the 18th c. Around 30 beautifully preserved rooms to see, with a sweeping long gallery and some intriguing collections. Capability Brown landscaped the 200 acres here too, and there's a riding centre in the stables. Study days and group visits by prior arrangement. Snacks, shop, mostly disabled access; cl am, all day Fri, and Nov–Easter Sat; (01964) 562400; £5. Camping, caravanning and seasonal fishing are available, and the Old Blue Bell in Old Ellerby is a cheerful

refreshment stop.

SPURN HEAD TA4010
This spit which curls like a claw round the mouth of the Humber estuary has a rough track open to cars almost to its end: a bleak place to some but a paradise for bird-watchers, who often wait here in spring and autumn for glimpses of rare migrant species. Thanks to the vagaries of nature the peninsula is gradually becoming an island, so best to check tide times carefully. The estuary itself is usually grey, solemn and grim. The Crown & Anchor at Kilnsea, open all day, has good value food.

STAINTONDALE SE9998
Llama trekking Bruce Wright organises this, across the moors or along the coast; the llamas hump your bags while you walk beside them. They can do specialist treks with guides, covering subjects such as the moors, geology, dinosaurs and smuggling. All treks inc home-made food; (01723) 871234; from £27 for three hours.
Shire Horse Farm (Staintondale) Friendly little farm with good demonstrations and talks; nature trails, and bracing clifftop walks along part of the Cleveland Way. Snacks, shop, limited disabled access; cl Mon exc bank hols, Thurs, Sat and mid-Sept to Apr; (01723) 870458; *£3.50. The Falcon (just off A171) has good value food.

STAITHES NZ7818
Steep fishing village, unspoilt down by the shore, where little cottages and the storm-battered Cod & Lobster pose fetchingly against the staggering background of a great red sandstone headland, a striking colour picture as the sun comes up.
Captain Cook & Staithes Heritage Centre (High St) This converted Methodist chapel in the village where the great explorer worked as a young man, in 1745, now houses a decent heritage centre, with a reconstructed street scene showing village life at the time; lots of Cook-related artefacts inc a collection of Webber's superb engravings from the voyages. Also displays looking at the importance of local industries such as fishing, mining and smuggling. Shop, disabled access to ground floor only; cl 25–26 Dec, and

wkdys Jan; (01947) 841454; £2.50.
SUTTON BANK SE5182
This steep escarpment gives an enthralling view, particularly from the very popular section of the Cleveland Way that runs S from the A170 along the level clifftop to the white horse cut into the hill. Immediately N of the A170 you can combine the path along the top of the slope with a venture down the nature trail into Garbutt Wood, a nature reserve abutting Gormire Lake, the only natural lake in the National Park.

SUTTON-ON-THE-FOREST SE5864
Sutton Park 🏠 The friendly 1730s manor house itself is open pms only Weds and Sun, bank hol Mons and Easter Fri and Sat, but the delightful grounds are open daily end Mar–Sept, with terraced gardens, a Georgian ice house, lily pond, pleasant woodland walks, nature trails and an adventure playground. Snacks, meals; (01347) 810249; £5, £2.50 gardens only. The village is pretty, and the smart Rose & Crown has good food.

THIRSK SE4281
World of James Herriot (23 Kirkgate) A lively look at the country's favourite vet as well as his profession, set in the Skeldale House of his novels; period rooms and hands-on exhibits. Shop, disabled access; cl 25 Dec; (01845) 524234; £4.50. The George in the handsome adjoining village of Sowerby has good food.

THORNTON DALE SE8383
Despite the main road, one of the most delightful villages in this part of Yorkshire – with an attractive forest toll road running NW to Langdale End. The New Inn has good food and nice bedrooms.

WADE'S CAUSEWAY SE8097
Also known as Wheeldale Roman road, this is a mile-long stretch of broad paved Roman road up over the moors, well restored and maintained. It's open to walkers only, but reached easily by the narrow moorland lane S from Egton Bridge (or a longish walk S from Goathland).

WELTON SE9627
Wolds Way Good area for round walks based on the well signed Wolds

Way, with fine views over the Humber in places. The Half Moon in Elloughton has enjoyable food.

WHARRAM PERCY SE8564
The most famous of the medieval abandoned villages of the Wolds, with lots of grassy humps and an evocative ruined church; EH, free access. From Thixendale (where the Cross Keys has sensibly priced food) a stretch of the well signed Wolds Way gives walkers a view of the village, and takes in a stretch of classic dry valley.

WHITBY NZ8911
Famous as the port at which Count Dracula came ashore; Bram Stoker got the idea for the book in the fishermen's graveyard of the partly Norman church, 199 steps up from the harbour, with lovely woodwork. Not too far from the abbey on Church St is a small but interesting workshop where you can watch jet being crafted into jewellery. Away from the bright waterfront the town is steep and quite attractive, with picturesque old buildings (now often rather smart shops and cafés) and some quaint cobbled alleys in its original core E of the busy harbour, where excellent fresh fish is sold straight from the catch in the early morning. Besides excellent fish and chips from the Magpie Café, the Duke of York (Church St, at the bottom of the 199 steps) does decent food all day, though sadly a new bye-law has banished its nice tables outside. In the two wks around the summer solstice the sun both rises and sets above the sea.

Captain Cook Memorial Museum (Grape Lane) In the house where the great explorer lived as an apprentice in the shipping trade from 1746; rooms are furnished in period style with models, letters and drawings from Cook's later voyages. Shop, disabled access; cl Nov–Feb; (01947) 601900; £2.80.

Dracula Experience (Marine Parade) Children probably won't be satisfied until they've visited this vividly spooky re-creation of scenes from the classic tale. Shop; cl wkdys Nov–Mar; (01947) 601923; *£1.95.

Whitby Abbey Impressive set of 13th-c ruins dramatically overlooking the harbour from their windswept clifftop setting. You can see the skeletal remains of the magnificent three-tiered choir and the N transept, and it's an evocative spot for a picnic. An earlier building had been the site of the Synod of Whitby, where the dating of Easter was thrashed out in 664. Also here are a Celtic Christian cemetery, and a recently restored 17th-c stone garden made by descendants of the family who bought the abbey after Henry VIII's dissolution of the monasteries. Though admission price has doubled, we think it's justified by recent improvements under a £5½ million English Heritage conservation and access project. An innovative new visitor centre, housed in the roofless shell of a 17th-c house, has well thought-out displays with plenty of interactive features, videos and an activity centre, and there's a good new audio tour. Snacks, shop, disabled access; cl 24–26 Dec, 1 Jan; (01947) 603568; £3.60; EH.

Whitby Museum (Pannett Park) Delightfully old-fashioned and crowded, with the only surviving part of Captain Cook's original journal, Queen Victoria's nightdress, some spectacular fossils and the hand of a murderer used as a candle-holder by superstitious burglars. Shop, disabled access; cl Sun am all year, plus Mon (exc most bank hols) and pm Tues Oct–Apr, plus 2 wks over Christmas and New Year; (01947) 602908; £2.50.

WITHERNSEA TA3327
Withernsea Lighthouse Towering above the houses of this little resort, with fantastic views for those keen enough to climb the 144 steps. Exhibits on local history, coastguard lifesaving and the RNLI. Teas, shop, disabled access to ground floor only; usually open pm wknds and bank hols (exc Good Fri) end Mar–Oct, plus wkdys mid-Jun to mid-Sept; (01964) 614834; *£2. The Commercial Hotel has cheap food.

YORKSHIRE WOLDS SE8461
Quiet agricultural chalk country dissected by dry valleys, with extensive views over huge corn fields. The bulk of the off-road walking is found on the well signposted 79-mile Wolds Way from Hessle Haven down on the Humber to Filey Brigg on the coast, where it meets

the Cleveland Way. Some of the lesser roads are a delight to walk on, with wide verges, good views and virtually no traffic.

Other attractive villages here, all with decent pubs, include Ainthorpe NZ7008, Ampleforth SE5879 (with its famous school and partly wooded moors), Bishop Burton SE9939, Brompton SE9582, Castleton NZ6908 high above the Esk Valley, Cloughton Newlands TA0196, Crayke SE5760,

Gillamoor SE6890, Great Ayton NZ5611, Horsehouse SE0481, Hovingham SE6775, Hutton Rudby NZ4706, Lealholm NZ7608, Lund SE9748, Nether Silton SE4692, North Dalton SE9352, Oldstead SE5380, Rosedale Abbey SE7395, Seamer TA0284, Sinnington SE7485, South Dalton SE9645, Thixendale SE8461, Thorganby SE6942, Thornton le Clay SE6865, Weaverthorpe SE9771 and Welburn SE7268.

Where to eat

BYLAND ABBEY SE5478 **Abbey Inn** *(01347) 868204* Beautifully placed dining pub opposite haunting abbey ruins, with an interesting series of rambling old rooms, big fireplaces, polished floorboards, and flagstones; very good varied food, decent wines and well kept beers, and big garden; charming bdrms; cl Sun pm, Mon am (exc bank hols); limited disabled access. £25.55|£7.50

CRAYKE SE5670 **Durham Ox** *West Way (01347) 821506* This is said to be the hill up which the Grand Old Duke of York marched his men; bustling, popular inn with venerable tables and antique seats and settles, flagstones, interestingly carved panelling, enormous inglenook fireplace with winter log fires (flowers in summer), bottom bar with illustrated local history (some of it gruesome) going back to the 12th c, good food inc imaginative daily specials, well kept real ales, seats outside and bdrms in converted farm buildings; cl 25 Dec; disabled access. £27.50|£9.95

FLAMBOROUGH TA2270 **Seabirds** *Tower St (01262) 850242* Friendly old pub full of shipping memorabilia and a few stuffed birds, with enjoyable food (some fresh fish dishes, too), quite a few wines, and cheerful hard-working staff; cl Sun and Mon pm in winter; children must be well behaved; partial disabled access. £18|£15

HAROME SE6482 **Star** *High St (01439) 770397* Pretty, thatched, 14th-c inn with a charming interior, plenty of bric-a-brac and interesting furniture, two big log fires, daily papers and magazines, and a no smoking dining room; excellent inventive food using the best local produce, well kept real ales, freshly squeezed juices, and quite a few wines by the glass from a fairly extensive wine list; seats and tables on a sheltered front terrace with more in the garden behind; lovely bdrms; cl Mon, 2 wks Jan; disabled access. £35|£7

KIRKHAM ABBEY SE7366 **Stone Trough** *(01653) 618713* Quaint beamed inn with small, cosy and interesting bars, log fires, enjoyable inventive food in bar and no smoking farmhouse-style restaurant, and seats outside with valley views; cl Mon (exc bank hols), 25 Dec. £27|£3.75

MIDDLESBROUGH NZ4920 **Purple Onion** *72–80 Corporation Rd (01642) 222250* Bustling Victorian building filled with bric-a-brac, ornate mirrors, and house plants, an informal atmosphere, downstairs cellar bar with live music, particularly good interesting food, friendly staff, and decent wine list; cl Sun pm; disabled access. £30|£6.95

NUNNINGTON SE6679 **Royal Oak** *Church St (01439) 748271* Attractive little dining pub nr Nunnington Hall with log fires, beams hung with copper jugs, antique keys and earthenware flagons, carefully chosen furniture, and enjoyable generous home-made bar food – super daily specials; cl Mon. £22.50|£4.95

PICKERING SE7984 **White Swan** *Market Pl (01751) 472288* Former coaching inn with very comfortable recently reworked bedrooms, a charming country atmosphere, panelling, and log fire in small and civilised front bar, another log fire in no smoking snug, an attractive no smoking dining room, and busy but comfortable family room; particularly good imaginative food using carefully sourced local produce (lunchtime dishes are simpler and breakfasts are enjoyable), well kept real

ales, and an impressive wine list. £30|£7

SCARBOROUGH TA0488 **Golden Grid Fish Restaurant** 4 Sandside (01723) 360922 Very long-standing and famous fish restaurant overlooking the harbour, serving snacks, lunches (super daily-fresh fish), vegetarian dishes, and afternoon teas; cl 20–25 Dec. £15|£3.99

STADDLEBRIDGE SE4499 **McCoys Bistro** Cleveland Tontine (01609) 882671 A rather special place with a friendly bustling atmosphere in ground-floor bistro, some eccentric furnishings, old-fashioned music, particularly good modern food, a thoughtful wine list, a quieter dining room open only Fri/Sat evenings, and good breakfasts; bdrms; cl 25–26 Dec. £42.50|£7.50

STAITHES NZ7818 **Endeavour** 1 High St (01947) 840825 Popular little quayside restaurant (lunch by prior booking only) at the bottom of a steep hill, with lovely fresh local fish (delicious meat and game, and vegetarian dishes, too), super puddings, decent good value wine list, and friendly service; bdrms; cl Sun, Mon; well behaved children only. £25|£5

SUTTON UPON DERWENT SE7047 **St Vincent Arms** Main St (01904) 608349 Family-run pub with a relaxed atmosphere in traditional panelled front parlour, a huge fire in the big stone fireplace, high-backed old settles, collections of plates and whisky jugs, very popular and enjoyable home-made food in spacious dining room, friendly staff, up to nine well kept beers, and good choice of wines; big garden. £21|£7.25

THORGANBY SE6841 **Jefferson Arms** Main St (01904) 448316 Handsome old village inn refurbished this year under its new licensees: a stylish and spacious main bar, delightful little beamed lounge with leather sofas and armchairs, open fire and fresh flowers, and narrow conservatory; quite a choice of interesting food, real ales, and a decent wine list; quiet bdrms; cl Mon, Tues am; children must be well behaved. £22.70|£7.95

WHITBY NZ9011 **Duke of York** 124 Church St (01947) 600324 Bustling, welcoming pub with fine outlook over harbour entrance and western cliff from the comfortable beamed bar (lots of fishing memorabilia), a wide choice of good value fresh local fish as well as other things, well kept real ales, decent wines, and quick, pleasant service; bdrms. £16|£5.95

WHITBY NZ8911 **Magpie Café** 14 Pier Rd (01947) 602058 Overlooks the town and river, with lots of wonderfully evocative sepia photographs of old Whitby, and much liked for its delicious fresh haddock served by cheerful staff; cl mid-Jan to early Feb. £20|£7

West & South Yorkshire

Lots of interesting family outings, first-class museums (many free) – great possibilities for unorthodox but really enjoyable short breaks

Energetic Leeds is full of things to interest visitors, with an abundance of good museums (our favourites are the Royal Armouries Museum, the Thackray Medical Museum and Abbey House), and other attractions from pleasant parks to a steam railway. Other cities are worth considering for a visit, too: Sheffield now has an increasing amount to offer families; Halifax is rewarding, with Eureka! (excellent for younger children) and the enjoyable Shibden Hall & Folk Museum; and Bradford despite its bad press has some great places to visit, topped by the National Museum of Photography, Film and Television and the lively Industrial Museum.

A striking feature here is the profusion of 'stately museums' (fine

houses, many of them free and often in attractive grounds filled with equally fine exhibits): beautiful Bagshaw Museum in Batley, Brodsworth Hall, and Cusworth Hall Museum are particularly noteworthy. Oakwell Hall (good value, with a children's discovery gallery), magnificent Harewood House (lots to see, from splendid furnishings to the famous bird garden), sumptuous Nostell Priory (outstanding collection of Chippendale furniture), and huge Conisbrough Castle are other appealing suggestions. The gallery in Saltaire has one of the country's largest private art collections, and Saltaire itself is well worth a look.

Magna puts the less-visited town of Rotherham on the tourist map. There are interesting flat-cap heritage centres in Elsecar and Golcar, and our Yorkshire Family Attraction of the Year in Middlestown gives a compelling taste of life as a coal miner. Aside from its obvious appeal to Brontë fans (who should also head to Gomersal and Thornton), Haworth has a classic steam railway. Cannon Hall Open Farm at Cawthorne (good play areas and some unusual animals), and the Tropical Butterfly House in North Anston (children are encouraged to touch some of the creatures) provide traditional family entertainment. The ambitious environmental centre at Denaby Main makes an unusual alternative day out.

In the W is a real Yorkshire mix of steep stone cottage terraces, remarkable mill buildings and some dramatic moorland coming right up to the towns, with plenty of exhilarating walking. Ilkley on the edge of the moors is attractive, and Hebden Bridge is also worth a trip, with the Hardcastle Crags above ideal for a peaceful picnic.

With the present counties of South and West Yorkshire, this chapter includes the bottom corner of North Yorkshire, below York itself and the A64.

Where to stay

BRADFORD SE1632 **Victoria Hotel** *Bridge St, Bradford, West Yorkshire BD1 1JX* (01274) 728706 **£60**w, plus special breaks; 60 well equipped rms with CD and video. Carefully renovated Victorian station hotel with many original features and lots of stylish character, bustling bar, popular and informal brasserie serving good modern food, and marvellous breakfasts, small private gym and sauna; disabled access; dogs welcome in bedrooms

HALIFAX SE0829 **Holdsworth House** *Holmfield, Halifax, West Yorkshire HX2 9TG* (01422) 240024 **£98**, plus wknd breaks; 40 traditional, individually decorated, quiet rms. Lovely, immaculately kept 17th-c house a few miles outside Halifax, with antiques, fresh flowers and fires in comfortable lounges, lots of sitting areas in the two bar rooms, friendly, particularly helpful staff, two carefully furnished dining rooms (one oak panelled) with enjoyable food and very good wine list, and garden; cl 26–30 Dec; dogs welcome in bedrooms

HAWORTH SE0237 **Old White Lion** *6–10 West Lane, Haworth, Keighley, West Yorkshire BD22 8DU* (01535) 642313 **£62***, plus special breaks; 14 rms, many with lovely views. Friendly, warm and comfortable 300-year-old inn with three bars, cosy restaurant with enjoyable food, and oak-panelled residents' lounge; nr Brontë museum and church, and Keighley & Worth Valley steam railway

LEEDS SE3033 **42 The Calls** *Leeds, West Yorkshire LS2 7EW* (0113) 244 0099 **£176.50**w, inc bottle of champagne, plus special breaks; 41 attractive rms using

West & South Yorkshire

Linton
Boston Spa
Bramham
Saxton
Lotherton Hall
Ledsham
Ledston
Monk Fryston
Wakefield
Heath
Nostell Priory
Monk Bretton
Brodsworth
Worsbrough
Elsecar
Denaby Main
Wentworth
Conisbrough
Doncaster
Cusworth
Rotherham
Maltby
Tickhill
Firbeck
Ulley
North Anston
Sheffield
Anston Brook

SE

LINCS

NOTTS

0 Miles 5
0 Kilometres 8

original features, with lots of extras, CD stereo with disc library, satellite TV and good views. Stylish modern hotel in converted riverside grain mill in peaceful spot overlooking the River Aire, with genuinely friendly staff, marvellous food in restaurant and next-door chic but informal Brasserie Forty-Four, and fine breakfasts; cl 4 days over Christmas; disabled access; dogs welcome in bedrooms

LEEDS SE3033 **Malmaison** *Sovereign Quay, Leeds, West Yorkshire LS1 1DQ (0113) 398 1000* **£141.50**, plus wknd breaks; 100 spacious rms with CDs and air conditioning. Stylish new hotel by the River Aire, with bold, modern furnishings, stylish bar and brasserie, contemporary French-style food and decent breakfasts, and helpful friendly service; disabled access

LINTON SE3646 **Wood Hall** *Trip Lane, Linton, Wetherby, West Yorkshire LS22 4JA (01937) 587271* **£140***, plus racing breaks; 42 spacious well furnished rms. Grand Georgian mansion in over a hundred acres of parkland by the River Wharfe; comfortable reception rooms, log fire, antiques and fresh flowers, and imaginative cooking in the no smoking restaurant; indoor swimming pool and health centre; disabled access; dogs welcome in bedrooms

MONK FRYSTON SE5029 **Monk Fryston Hall** *Main St, Monk Fryston, Leeds, West Yorkshire LS25 5DU (01977) 682369* **£109**, plus wknd and special breaks; 30 comfortable, recently refurbished rms. Benedictine manor house in 30 acres of secluded gardens with lake and woodland, an oak-panelled lounge and bar with log fires, antiques, paintings and fresh flowers, good honest food, and friendly helpful staff; disabled access; dogs welcome away from restaurant

OTLEY SE2143 **Chevin Lodge** *Yorkgate, Otley, West Yorkshire LS21 3NU (01943) 467818* **£110**, plus special breaks; 50 rms, some in log lodges deep in the woods. Built of Finnish logs with walks through 50 acres of birchwood (lots of wildlife), this comfortable hotel has its own leisure club, good food in lakeside restaurant, and friendly service; tennis and fishing; disabled access; dogs welcome in bedrooms

ROYDHOUSE SE2112 **Three Acres** *37–41 Roydhouse, Shelley, Huddersfield, West Yorkshire HD8 8LR (01484) 602606* **£80***; 20 pretty rms. In lovely countryside, this civilised former coaching inn has a welcoming atmosphere in its traditional bars, an exceptional choice of wines, well kept real ales, marvellous imaginative food in two restaurants, and particularly good breakfasts; specialist delicatessen next door; cl 25 Dec, 31 Dec–1 Jan

SCISSETT SE2408 **Bagden Hall** *Wakefield Rd, Scissett, Huddersfield, West Yorkshire HD8 9LE (01484) 865330* **£80**; 17 rms. Handsome hotel in 40 acres of parkland with its own 9-hole par 3 golf course, comfortable airy public rooms inc a bright conservatory bar, well prepared French and English food, and quietly efficient service; limited disabled access

SHEFFIELD SK3485 **Charnwood Hotel** *10 Sharrow Lane, Sheffield, South Yorkshire S11 8AA (0114) 258 9411* **£83**w, plus special breaks; 22 comfortable well equipped rms. Friendly extended Georgian house with peaceful lounges, conservatory, and freshly cooked, interesting food in both the Brasserie and elegant little restaurant; cl Christmas; disabled access

---

We welcome reports from readers

This *Guide* depends on readers' reports. Do help us if you can – in return, we offer a discount on the next edition to people who've helped us with reports for it. Tell us what you think about places already in it, and anything extra you think we should say about them. And send us your ideas for inclusion in the next edition: places to visit, eat at or stay in, attractive drives or walks, maybe even unusual shops you know of. Use the card in the middle, the report forms at the end, or just write – no stamp needed: *The Good Britain Guide*, FREEPOST TN1569, Wadhurst, E Sussex TN5 7BR. Or log on to www.goodguides.com

To see and do

Yorkshire Family Attraction of the Year

MIDDLESTOWN SE2416 **National Coal Mining Museum** (Caphouse Colliery, New Rd) The best of several new developments at this excellent site over the last year has been the scrapping of all entrance charges, making it an outstanding choice for families; you'll get a fascinating half-day glimpse of life as a miner, and it's completely free. They've also introduced a number of interactive displays, and much improved the visitor facilities, with a new café and shop. One thing that hasn't changed is the excellent underground tour, which takes you 140 metres (450 ft) down the pit, to find out first-hand the methods and working conditions of miners from the 1800s to the present. Very much the highlight of any visit, this hour-long tour is led by former miners, who have lots of exciting and evocative tales to keep children enthralled. You'll be issued with a hard hat and belt, and it's worth wearing sensible shoes and warm clothing, even in summer, when it can feel cold underground. The knowledgeable guides work hard to make sure everyone's comfortable – but obviously if you don't like dark confined spaces you'll be better off staying at the top. In school holidays and on the busiest weekends you'll need to arrive well before midday to get on to a tour; places are limited for safety reasons, so get there too late and you may find you won't be able to go down. There are quite a few things to see on the surface as well, including many of the original pit buildings, and plenty of the old machinery and equipment. Well organised displays give an intriguing insight into the miners' home lives, and there are several happily retired pit ponies. A good new indoor play area for under-5s should make up for the fact that they're not allowed to go underground. Meals, snacks, shop, disabled access (even under ground, though helpful to arrange it in advance) and excellent facilities; cl 24–26 Dec, 1 Jan; (01924) 848806; free.

ANSTON BROOK SK5184
Reached on foot from South Anston, this flows through a wooded valley that interrupts the monotony of the flat farmlands SE of Rotherham. It can be combined with a walk along the towpath of the Chesterfield Canal.

BATLEY SE2325
Bagshaw Museum (Wilton Park) Beautiful Victorian Gothic mansion in pleasant lakeside park, with one of those excellent miscellaneous collections based on the curio-hunting of an individual enthusiast. Shop, some disabled access; cl wknd ams, Good Fri, 24–26 Dec, and 1 Jan; (01924) 326155; free. The Old Hall at Heckmondwike (B6117), once Joseph Priestley's home, is interesting for lunch.

Skopos Motor Museum 🅳
(Alexandra Mills) It's worth the trek off the beaten path to visit this good varied collection of cars, in a pleasant airy building. Vehicles on display range from Edwardian Rolls-Royces to the tiny BMW Isetta, and the only surviving

Bramham. Shop, disabled access; cl Mon (though open most bank hols), Tues, 25–26 Dec, and 1 Jan; (01924) 444423; £2.50.

BRADFIELD SK2692
Attractive two-part village, with interesting church and good walks in great scenery. The old Strines Inn up in the hills has decent food (all day wknds and summer).

BRADFORD SE1632
Though horribly knocked about by heavy-handed civic designers in the 1960s and 1970s, and currently notorious for the riots of 2001, Bradford can still make you gasp at the stone buildings which survive from its zenith as one of Britain's finest Victorian cities. These are a staggering monument to the days when its wools, woollens and worsteds ruled the world: gigantic Renaissance-style woollen and velvet mills, the imposing Wool Exchange, the opulent city-centre cliffs of heavily ornate merchants' warehouses in Little Germany behind

the mostly 15th-c cathedral, and the florid exuberance of the municipal buildings such as the Gothic city hall, the neo-classical St George's concert hall, even the great Undercliffe cemetery with its sumptuous Victorian memorials (and sweeping Pennine views) – it's been called the most spectacular graveyard in Britain. For visitors, the vivid dash of diversity brought by its Asian immigrants is a plus, and for a meal you might prefer one of the multitude of Pakistani or Bangladeshi restaurants to useful pub lunch places such as the Fountain (Heaton Rd), Office (off City St) and Rams Revenge (Kirkgate).

Bolling Hall Museum (off Brompton Ave, S) Classic mainly 17th-c Yorkshire manor house, now home to the city's collection of local furniture. Shop, disabled access to ground floor; cl Sun am, Mon (exc summer bank hols) and Tues; (01274) 723057; free.

Cartwright Hall Art Gallery (Lister Park) Dramatic baroque-style building in attractive floral park, housing the *Brown Boy* by Reynolds and a good representative selection of late 19th- and early 20th-c paintings. Snacks, shop, disabled access; cl Sun am, and all day Mon (exc bank hols), and 24–26 Dec; (01274) 751212; free.

Colour Museum 🖾 (Providence St) Imaginative study of the use and perception of colour, with interactive displays on the effects of light and colour in general, and particularly the story of dyeing and textile printing. Shop, disabled access; cl Sun, Mon, and 23 Dec–1 Jan; (01274) 390955; £1.75.

Industrial Museum (Moorside Rd, Eccleshill) Former Victorian spinning mill well illustrating the growth of the worsted textile industry. Horse-drawn trams carry you up and down the Victorian street, which is complete with workers' cottages, mill owner's house and working Victorian stables with shire horses. Meals, snacks, shop, disabled access; cl Sun am, and all day Mon (exc bank hols), 25–26 Dec, 1 Jan, Good Fri; (01274) 435900; free.

National Museum of Photography, Film and Television 🖾 (Princes View) Eight interactive galleries take in everything from John Logie Baird to the toys from *Play School*. Among the three million items kept here are the world's first negative, very early television footage, and what's generally considered the first example of moving pictures – Louis Le Prince's 1888 film of Leeds Bridge. Wallace and Gromit and Morph explain the secrets of animation, and you can try your hand at operating a camera or reading the news. Other highlights are the intriguing photography gallery, which includes the cameras used to create the Cottingley fairies, and a stunning gallery showcases the latest digital technology, where you can experiment with virtual reality; also the cameras used on Ealing comedies and James Bond films. The five storeys high IMAX screen regularly shows 3D and other films, and more conventionally sized cinemas offer films from around the world. Guided tours, meals and snacks, excellent shop, good disabled access; cl Mon (exc bank hols and school summer hols), 25 Dec; (01274) 202030; free, IMAX cinema £5.80.

BRAMHAM SE4041

Bramham Park The garden here is really quite beautiful, very much in the grand style – Versailles comes to Yorkshire. Long prospects of ornamental lakes, cascades, temples, statuary, grand hedges and stately trees and avenues surround a classical Queen Anne house of great distinction, with lovely period furnishings and paintings. Snacks, small shop, some disabled access to gardens; house open by written appointment only (minimum group of six), gardens open daily Apr–Sept exc during horse trials (5–8 Jun), but best to check; (01937) 846000; grounds and gardens *£4. The Red Lion has enjoyable food.

BRODSWORTH SE5007

Brodsworth Hall and Gardens Grand house vividly illustrating life in Victorian times; the family that lived here closed off parts of the house as their fortunes waned, inadvertently preserving the contents and decor exactly as they were (right down to the billiard score-book). Richly furnished rooms, lots of marble statues, and busily cluttered servants' wing. The family commissioned some of the largest and fastest yachts of the Victorian era, and an exhibition charts the history of these splendid vessels. The marvellous formal gardens and parkland are gradually being restored. Meals, snacks, shop, some disabled access; cl am, Mon (exc bank hols), and all Nov–Mar (exc gardens open wknds); (01302) 722598; *£5.50; EH.

CARL WARK SK2581
On the edge of the Peak District, this hill fort is set handsomely in a great bowl fringed by gritstone outcrops, and offers a more interesting walk than most in South Yorkshire. The Fox House nearby (A6187/A625) has good value food.

CAWTHORNE SE2708
Cannon Hall Open Farm Unusual animals such as wallabies and llamas among the residents at this busy working farm; also baby animals throughout the year, with piglets born regularly. Good play areas, and mostly concreted so doesn't get muddy. Meals, snacks, shop, disabled access; cl 25 Dec; (01226) 790427; £2.25. Cannon Hall itself is now a museum with a mixture of local bygones, mounted butterflies and animals and so forth, and the grounds an attractive country park (£1.50 car park). The village is pleasant, and the Cherry Tree overlooking the park from High Hoyland has a small popular restaurant.

CONISBROUGH SK5198
Conisbrough Castle Mightily impressive 12th-c castle with uniquely designed 27-metre (90-ft) keep – circular, with six buttresses and a curtain wall with solid round towers. An added roof and floors re-create something of the original feel, and there's a good audio-visual show; special events in summer. Snacks, shop, limited disabled access; cl 24–26 Dec, 1 Jan; (01709) 863329; *£3.75; EH. Sir Walter Scott set much of *Ivanhoe* here, writing the novel while staying at the Boat at Sprotbrough nearby; then a riverside farm, it's now a good dining pub.

CUSWORTH SE5403
Cusworth Hall Museum (Cusworth Lane, just W of Doncaster) Excellent museum of South Yorkshire life, in an elegant 18th-c house. Displays on

mining, transport, costume and entertainment, and especially popular gallery of toys and childhood. Tearoom, shop, disabled access to ground floor only; cl Sun am, 25–26 Dec, 1 Jan and Good Fri; (01302) 782342; free.

DENABY MAIN SK4999
Earth Centre ⌨ Perhaps the most ambitious of all the country's environmental centres, this Millennium Commission project has witnessed the redevelopment over the last decade or so of more than 400 acres left derelict by the decline of the coal industry. Overlooked by mighty Conisbrough Castle and rarely busy, the centre aims to promote environmental issues in an enjoyable way through a range of attractions taking in an interactive nature trail (with pond-dipping, eco-friendly games and an area designed to stimulate all your senses along the way), galleries looking at the history and future of the planet's development, and specially themed gardens dotted with often bizarre-looking constructions; also a fun adventure playground inc a 16-metre (52-ft) play tower. Meals, snacks, shop, disabled access; cl 25 Dec; (01709) 512000; £4.50. You can stay here too. The Cadeby Inn has good value food.

DEWSBURY SE2522
Dewsbury Museum (Crow Nest Park, Heckmondwike Rd) Cheerful place for the child in everyone, with collection of toys dating back to the 1900s, a children's trail, and a re-created 1940s classroom, plus temporary exhibitions and events. Snacks, shop, disabled access to ground floor only; cl am wknds, 25–26 Dec and Good Fri; (01924) 325100; free. The station buffet in the town is famously good.

DONCASTER SE5802
Not really a great deal to attract visitors apart from its race meetings, but there is some fine architecture, especially around the High St and Market Pl, and a junk market on Weds.
Doncaster Museum and Art Gallery (Chequer Rd) Archaeology displays, local history and a good deal of natural history (the museum is undergoing refurbishment so some rooms may be shut). Shop, good

disabled access; Cl Sun am, 25–26 Dec, 1 Jan and Good Fri; (01302) 734287; free.

ELSECAR SK3899

Elsecar Heritage Centre (Wath Rd) Developing centre in restored industrial workshops, with a history centre where you can dress up and star in a Victorian melodrama, a beam engine, bottle museum, and craft workshops. On summer Suns a diesel loco runs to the Hemingfield Basin (£2.50). Meals, snacks, shop, disabled access; cl 25 Dec–2 Jan; (01226) 740203; free. The Elephant & Castle in Hemingfield has good fresh food.

GOLCAR SE0915

Colne Valley Museum (Cliffe Ash) Enthusiastic museum spread over three weavers' cottages, with hand weaving, spinning and clog-making in gas-lit surroundings, and re-created 1850s living room. Snacks, shop, occasional craft festivals, limited disabled access; open pm wknds and some bank hols; (01484) 659762; £1.20. The Scapehouse (High St) is a useful food stop, and there's a good year-round walk along the Huddersfield Canal's restored towpath between here and Marsden in *Last of the Summer Wine* country.

GOMERSAL SE2026

Red House Museum (Oxford Rd) Former cloth merchant's home which vividly re-creates the 1830s in its nine carefully furnished period rooms. Charlotte Brontë often stayed at the house, and it featured as Briarmains in her novel *Shirley*. The gardens have been restored in 1830s style, and the restored cartsheds have exhibitions on the Brontës and local history. Shop, disabled access to ground floor; cl am wknds, Good Fri, best to phone for opening times over Christmas; (01274) 335100; free.

GOOSE EYE SE0240

Interesting preserved village; good drives around here. The Turkey has decent food and brews its own beer.

HALIFAX SE0925

Another town with an impressive show of former textiles wealth, interesting to drive through when it's quiet on a summer evening or a Sunday, and surrounded by a splendid ring of moorland. The centre's been cleaned up and partly pedestrianised, which makes it pleasant to potter through, and there are several first-class attractions, with the town now going through something of an artistic renaissance. The medieval church has an extremely grand spire and fine carving: look out for Old Tristram, the life-size painted carving of a beggar which was used to collect alms. The Shears (Paris Gates, Boys Lane) down steep lanes among the mill buildings is a pub that embraces much of Halifax's past and atmosphere; the 17th-c waterside Shibden Mill (Shibden – off A58 via Kell Lane) is a lovely place for a meal.

Bankfield Museum (Ackroyd Park, Boothtown Rd) Collection of textiles, costume and contemporary crafts, as well as a regimental museum and display of toys. Snacks, shop, disabled access to ground floor only; cl Sun am, Mon (exc bank hols), and over Christmas and New Year; (01422) 354823; free.

Dean Clough Enormous carpet mill, faced with demolition when it closed down some years ago, but now well restored and home to a thriving complex of galleries and small businesses; best are the Crossley Gallery and Henry Moore Studio, the latter a great showcase for contemporary sculpture; (01422) 250250; cl 24–26 Dec, 1 Jan; free.

Eureka! (Discovery Rd) Remarkable hands-on museum designed exclusively for children; few places are as likely to spellbind anyone between around 3 and 12. Each of the four main galleries ostensibly explores one subject, but in fact covers a multitude of topics and ideas. Particular highlights are the broad-based Things Gallery, full of bright colours and images, the communications gallery (you can put your picture on a front page, save a yacht in distress, or read the TV news), and Living and Working Together, where children try their hand at grown-up activities like filling a car with petrol at the garage, working in a shop or bank, or making a meal in the kitchen. Meals, snacks, shop, disabled access; cl 24–26 Dec; (01422) 330069; £5.50.

Piece Hall (centre) This magnificent

Renaissance-looking galleried and arcaded building was put up in 1775 by the merchants of Halifax as a market for their cloth. It houses many specialist shops selling books, antiques and bric-a-brac, and an art gallery (cl Mon exc bank hols) and other exhibitions. Meals, snacks, shop, disabled access; cl 25–26 Dec and 1 Jan; (01422) 358087; free. There are market stalls in the Italianate courtyard on Sat, Thurs (second-hand), a few on Fri and Sun.

Shibden Hall & Folk Museum (Godley Lane, off A58 just E) Excellently refurbished 15th-c house, each room illustrating a different period from its history. In the barn a folk museum has an interesting collection of horse-drawn vehicles, while outside are reconstructed 19th-c workshops, a cottage and even a pub. Boating lake, miniature railway, play area and woodland walks in the 90-acre parkland. For many this is a real Halifax highlight. Snacks, shop, limited disabled access; cl Sun am, and 25 Dec–2 Jan; (01422) 352246; £3.50.

Wainhouse Tower 🏛 off A646 just W) This 75-metre (250-ft) folly offers good views if you can manage all those steps. Shop; usually open bank hols, Easter, Father's Day and the 2nd Sun in Sept, but best to check (01422) 393213; £1.50.

HAREWOOD SE3245

Harewood House & Bird Garden 🏛 (A61) The area's most magnificent stately home, inside and out. The 18th-c exterior is splendidly palatial, and inside is some glorious restored Robert Adam plasterwork. Fine Chippendale furnishings, exquisite Sèvres and Chinese porcelain, and paintings by Turner, El Greco, Bellini, Titian and Gainsborough. Capability Brown designed the 1,000-acre grounds, which have very pleasing lakeside and woodland walks, a spectacular formal cascade, an outstanding collection of rhododendron species and other more recently introduced Himalayan and Chinese plants, and the famous landscaped bird garden (you could spend half a day in just this part). Charles Berry's Terrace has an excellent gallery with contemporary art and crafts. Try to visit the 15th-c

church, with a splendid array of tombs, and a curious tunnel under the wall of the churchyard, so that servants could arrive unseen by sensitive souls. There's a first-class adventure playground. Meals, snacks, shop, disabled access; cl 3 Nov to mid-Mar (exc wknds Nov–Dec); (0113) 218 1010; £9 everything, £6.50 bird garden and grounds only (discount voucher excludes Sun and bank hols). The Harewood Arms opposite has good food, and just N Wharfedale Grange have **pick-your-own** fruit.

HAWORTH SE0237

A touristy village with plenty of craft shops, antiques shops and tea shoppes catering for all the people drawn here by the Brontës (spelt Brunty before father Patrick went posh). A visit out of season catches it at its best, though at any time the steep cobbled main street has quieter more appealing side alleys. Most of the family are buried in the churchyard, except Anne, interred in Scarborough. For the most evocative views and atmosphere go up to the moors above town, very grand and not much different from when the Brontës knew them – despite the Japanese footpath signs. The Old White Lion (West Lane) and the 17th-c Old Hall (Sun St) are good value for lunch. The A6033 is an interesting drive to Hebden Bridge, and there's a fine old moors road via Stanbury (with its nice Old Silent pub) over to the Colne Valley in Lancashire.

Brontë walks The Pennine moors around here are a favourite stamping-ground for walkers, with a good walk W through Penistone Hill Country Park to the much-visited **Brontë Waterfalls**, and on through a remote valley to Withins, the original **Wuthering Heights**. There are plenty of paths, though finding the way across fields frequently entails searching for unprominent stone stiles over the dry-stone walls.

Keighley & Worth Valley Railway Actually begins just N at Keighley (where you can connect with mainline trains) but is based here. Run by enthusiastic volunteers, the line was built to serve the valley's mills, and passes through the heart of Brontë country. The prettiest station is Oakworth (familiar to many from the film *The Railway Children*). Snacks, shop (open daily exc 25 Dec), some disabled access; steam trains (good buffet car) run wknds all year, Tues–Thurs last 2 wks Jun, daily July–early Sept, and most school hols; (01535) 645214 for timetable; £6 return.

Museum of Rail Travel ☒ (Ingrow Railway Centre, Station Rd) Collection of historic railway carriages and a steam locomotive; unusually displays focus on what rail travel was like for passengers, and you can sometimes watch restoration work taking place. Snacks, shop, disabled access; cl 25–26 Dec; (01535) 680425; £1.

Parsonage Museum ☒ The Brontës' former home has some 80,000 visitors a year (it was something of a tourist attraction even while Charlotte still lived here). The house is very carefully preserved, with period furnishings, very good changing exhibitions, and displays of the siblings' books, manuscripts and possessions inc the sisters' writing table. Shop; cl 24–27 Dec, 2–31 Jan; (01535) 642323; £4.80.

HEATH SE3519
Extraordinarily old-fashioned common with gipsy ponies alongside 18th-c mansions (and contrasting views over Wakefield); the gaslit Kings Arms here is good.

HEBDEN BRIDGE SD9927
Engaging small town deep in a valley below the moors, and stepped very steeply up the hillsides. The White Lion (Bridge Gate) has good value food all day. In summer there are horse-drawn barge trips along the canal basin; (01422) 845557. The hold of one barge in the marina has been converted into a **visitor centre** with a traditional boatman's cabin (cl Nov–Easter; free).

Hardcastle Crags A beauty spot above the wooded river valley, ideal for walks or a picnic. The Nutclough House on the way up also has decent food.

Heptonstall An interesting and ancient village, a crippling climb up a fearsomely steep cobbled lane above Hebden Bridge; Sylvia Plath is buried in the churchyard. The adjacent early 17th-c Cross Inn has good value hearty food. There's a rewarding scenic path

along Heptonstall Crags (the cliffs above the wooded valley of Colden Water). An exhilarating old high road leads out to Widdop and beyond (for fine views and walks), and another runs via Colden and Blackshaw Head.

HOLMFIRTH SE1408
Instantly recognisable as the setting for TV's *Last of the Summer Wine*, with evocative little alleys, several good pubs, and a handsome Georgian church.

Compo's World ☒ (Huddersfield Rd) An exhibition on *Last of the Summer Wine*, the longest-running comedy series in the world. Meals, snacks, shop; cl 25 Dec; (01484) 681408; *£1.50. The Rose & Crown (Victoria Sq) nicely fits the mood.

HUDDERSFIELD SE1416
There's a great sense of style in many of its buildings, especially around the station and central square, and much of the centre is now closed to traffic. The A640 W is a good moorland drive.

Huddersfield Narrow Canal
Running between here and Ashton-under-Lyne in Lancashire, most of this canal is now navigable. The highest in Britain, it rises 134 metres (440 ft) through 42 locks to Marsden, where the Standedge Tunnel is Britain's longest – over three miles. The **Standedge Visitor Centre** will tell you more about the canal's history, with interactive exhibitions, and you can go on a short guided boat trip; open daily in summer, ring for winter opening; (01484) 844298; £4.50 inc boat trip.

Jubilee Tower (Almondbury) Castle Hill is 275 metres (900 ft) high, overlooking the surrounding moors. Recently restored, this tower with its 165 steps gives unrivalled views, even over the Pennines and Peak District; open pm summer wknds and bank hols; £1.20. The Bowl nearby is a good food pub.

Tolson Museum (Ravensknowle Park) The myths and legends asssociated with Castle Hill are outlined in this former wool baron's mansion, which also has a look at the textile industry; there's a collection of horse-drawn vehicles, and a puzzle trail for the under-5s. Snacks, shop, disabled access; cl am wknds, phone for winter opening times; (01484) 223830; free.

ILKLEY SE1147

Owes its Victorian and Edwardian spaciousness and style to the mid-19th-c and later craze for hydropathic 'cures', which produced quite a rash of luxurious hydros using the town's pure moorland spring water. Their forerunner was the simple little bath-house built in the mid-18th c around the ice-cold spring up on the moor just S at White Wells – you can still follow the paths the infirm took by donkey. The group of quaintly shaped rocks known as the Cow & Calf up here also makes a pleasant short walk above the town. The church has three lovely Saxon crosses, and just beside it are traces of a Roman fort. There are a good few prehistoric remains around the town, the best known of which is the Bronze Age Swastika Stone, a symbol of eternity carved on a flat rock by a moorland path SE of the town, above wooded Hebers Ghyll; the stone is marked on the Ordnance Survey 1:50,000 map, at SE095469. Hebers Ghyll itself is a picturesque ravine with steep Victorian walkways, and the town with its attractive gardens and interesting shops makes a nice stop. Ilkley Moor S of the town has potential for satisfying high-level walks. Reliable lunch places are the Bar t'at (Cunliffe Rd), Cow & Calf (moors road SE towards Hawksworth) and Wheatley (Ben Rhydding).

Manor House Gallery & Museum (Castle Yard) One of the few buildings in town to predate the 19th c, an Elizabethan manor house built on the site of a Roman fort, with local history displays. Shop; cl Sun am, all day Mon (exc bank hols) and Tues, 25 Dec and Good Fri; (01943) 600066; free.

KEIGHLEY SE0542

(pronounced Keithly) A busy working town with a pleasant centre. The Grinning Rat near the 16th-c church is popular for lunch, and the newish Dalesway (Bradford Rd, Sandbeds) is a useful family dining pub.

Cliffe Castle Museum and Gallery (Spring Gardens Lane) This 19th-c mansion is now a museum with local natural history, and displays of minerals and fossils; also temporary exhibitions,

and some furnished rooms. Though quite close to the centre, it's set in a park well above the main road, with aviaries and greenhouses. Shop, disabled access to ground floor only; cl Sun am, all day Mon (exc bank hols), 25–26 Dec, Good Fri; (01535) 618231; free.

East Riddlesden Hall ⊞ (Bradford Rd, just NE) Interesting early 17th-c oak-panelled stone manor house with attractive plasterwork, period textiles and furniture. There's a medieval monastic pond, an orchard garden and herbaceous border (plants for sale), huge tithe barn, and children's quiz and play area. Meals, snacks, shop, some disabled access; cl am, and Mon (exc July–Aug), Thurs, Fri and all Nov–Mar; (01535) 607075; £3.60; NT.

LEEDS SE2934

Leeds is now a really rewarding place to visit, with something for all ages: its Royal Armouries Museum is an outstanding family day out, Tropical World is popular with children, and there's plenty more to fill a short stay. It's prosperous again these days (flourishing financial services industry), with bright young evening crowds around the bars and clubs of its compact and largely traffic-free centre, which has virtually a 24-hour café culture. By day it's ideal for exploring, with splendid covered arcades (Victorian, Edwardian and modern), and all sorts of interesting and engaging Victorian architectural details to spot. Shoppers and theatre-goers are well catered for – the former in the exuberantly Venetian/Oriental glass-roofed market, the biggest in Europe, and the latter by the West Yorkshire Playhouse (a useful meeting place with fine city views from its good café/bar) and the Grand (home of Opera North). The imposing town hall is perhaps the high point of Leeds's essentially Victorian centre; and there are good gardens and open spaces. Whitelocks (Turks Head Yard, off Briggate) is a marvellous old city tavern, very much a Leeds institution. The historic Waterfront area has been well developed for visitors in recent years.

Abbey House (opposite Kirkstall Abbey) You can wander freely through the re-created Victorian streets at this enjoyable museum, and right through some of the shops, inc their ironic conjunction of tavern, smoker's pipe maker and undertaker. There's an interactive gallery on childhood (some good games and interesting facts here), and another gallery shows what life would have been like as a medieval monk. Outside are gardens, a play area, and picnic tables. Shop, snacks, disabled access; cl all Mon, am Sat, 25–26 Dec, and 1 Jan; (0113) 230 5492; £3.

Armley Mills Industrial Museum ⓔ (Canal Rd) Once the largest woollen mill in the world, now a huge museum, its floors given over to a massive display of textile machinery. Also a printing gallery, reconstructions of a small 1930s clothing factory, a 1920s-style cinema, and demonstrations of railway locomotives (bank and summer hols, phone to check). Snacks and picnic area, shop, disabled access; cl Sun am, Mon (exc bank hols), 25–26 Dec, 1 Jan; (0113) 263 7861; *£2.

Corn Exchange (Call Lane) This impressive 1860s building is now filled with neat little specialist and designer shops, and has plenty of places for tea, coffee and so forth, as well as an excellent fresh continental bread stall.

Henry Moore Institute ⓔ (The Headrow) Over a footbridge is this delightful place, with temporary exhibitions of sculpture from Roman times to the present, displayed in quite an unusual building (they don't actually show anything by Henry Moore). Shop, disabled access, cl bank hols, 24–26 and 31 Dec, 1–2 Jan; (0113) 246 7467; free. Stays open late on Weds.

Kirkstall Abbey (off A65, 2m NW of centre) Built in the 12th c and in attractive grounds, this is one of Britain's best-preserved Cistercian monasteries; (0113) 230 5492; free.

Leeds City Art Gallery (The Headrow) Excellent collection of 20th-c British art, inc good watercolours and sculpture gallery with carefully chosen works by Henry Moore (he had his first exhibition here in 1941). Meals, snacks, shop, limited disabled access; cl Sun am and bank hols (stays open late on Weds); (0113) 247 8248; free.

Leeds City Museum Resource Centre (Moorfield Rd, out at Yeadon) Offering access to the excellent stored collections of the closed Leeds City Museum; the highlight is Natsef Amun (Keeper of the Bulls), an important Egyptian mummy which has been in the city for almost 200 years; also displays of local wildlife, minerals and fossils, and exhibits from ancient Greece and Rome. Shop, some disabled access (notice preferred); open by appointment only Mon–Fri; (0113) 214 6526; free.

Meanwood Valley Urban Farm ⓔ (Meanwood) Small working organic farm on regenerated waste land N of centre, with rare breeds, organic market garden, and environment centre. Meals, snacks, shop selling organic farm produce, good disabled access; cl Mon; (0113) 262 9759; *£1.

Middleton Railway ⓔ Running from Tunstall Rd to Middleton Park, this is the oldest running railway in the world and was the first to be authorised by Parliament in 1758. Later it was the first to succeed with steam locomotives, and in 1960 became the first standard-gauge line to be operated by volunteers. With a picnic area, fishing, nature trail and playgrounds as well as the shed with a large collection of industrial steam and diesel engines on display, there's plenty for families here. Snacks, shop, disabled access; diesel or steam trains most wknds and bank hols Apr–Christmas; (0113) 271 0320 or www.middletonrailway.org.uk for timetable; *£2.50 (discount voucher not valid for special events).

Roundhay Park (off A58) 700 acres of rolling parkland, well known for concerts and events. On Princes Avenue here the Canal Gardens are a very pleasant and peaceful corner of the city, with several national flower collections (inc dahlias and violas), lots of roses, and ornamental wildfowl; free. The Roundhay dining pub has very cheap food.

Royal Armouries Museum (Clarence Dock, Waterfront) When it opened a few years ago, run by a private company, this got off to a shaky start financially. Now run instead by the Royal Armouries itself, it's a far cry from the average military museum, showing the national collection of arms and armour in a radically different way; and it's now free (funded directly by the government). It's almost completely interactive, with hi-tech effects and touch-screen displays, and plenty of costumed demonstrations showing not just how weapons were made and used, but how they affected everyday life; children can try on costumes and helmets, or even test their aim with a crossbow. The building's design is stunning (don't miss the breathtaking Hall of Steel, with 3,000 pieces of gleaming arms and armour on the walls), but the most spectacular feature is outside: the country's only full-size authentically re-created tiltyard, with dramatic exhibitions of jousting, fencing, duelling, and hunting dogs and birds of prey. An inside display area often has martial arts displays, and there are demonstrations of traditional skills in the Craft Court. Meals and snacks, shop, good disabled access; cl 24–25 Dec; (0113) 2201999; free.

Temple Newsam House (5m E, S of A63) Capability Brown designed the wonderful two square miles of landscaped parkland and gardens in which this house stands, an extraordinary asset for any city. Due to reopen in the summer after major restoration, the house itself dates from Tudor and Jacobean times, and contains the city's very good collections of decorative and fine art, as well as an exceptional assemblage of Chippendale furniture. Rare breeds and a working organic farm in the grounds; picnic and play areas; grounds open daily (free), phone for house opening times and prices; (0113) 264 7321.

Thackray Medical Museum 🅯 (St James's Hospital, Beckett St) A surprising favourite not only for readers but also their children, this dynamic museum puts the emphasis more on social history than on science. But there are interactive displays on how the body works, and good reconstructions showing the progress of medical care in Britain, inc some deliciously gruesome parts on surgery before the development of anaesthetics. Children particularly like the part where they pick a character,

then discover their fate as they work their way around the museum. Meals, snacks, shop, disabled access; cl Mon (exc bank and school hols), 24–26, 31 Dec, 1 Jan; (0113) 244 4343; £4.40.

Thwaite Mills Watermill (Stourton, 2m S) This water-powered mill was the focus of a tiny island community perched between the River Aire – which drives the mill wheels – and the Aire & Calder Navigation. The restored Georgian mill-owner's house has displays on the site's history; guided mill tours every hour. Snacks, shop, disabled access; cl wkdys during school term-times, Mon (exc bank hols), am wknds, 25–26 Dec, 1 Jan; (0113) 249 6453; *£2.

Tropical World (Roundhay Park) Huge conservatory with the biggest collection of tropical plants outside Kew, along with all sorts of exotic trees, reptiles, fish, birds and butterflies, in careful re-creations of their natural settings. Meals, snacks, shop, disabled access; cl 25–26 Dec; (0113) 266 1850; £2.

LOTHERTON HALL SE4436 (B1217 Garforth–Tadcaster) Edwardian house with displays ranging from oriental art to British fashion, as well as paintings, silver and ceramics, and some lovely furnishings. The restored grounds are good for strolling, with a bird garden, an interesting bronze statue in the front rose garden, and a 12th-c chapel. Snacks and picnic area, shop, disabled access to grounds and café only; cl Mon (exc bank hols), am Sun, 24–26 Dec, and Jan–Feb; (0113) 281 3259; £2 house, grounds free, £2 car park. The Swan at nearby Aberford is popular for lunch.

LUDDENDEN SE0426 Interesting village with Brontë connections; the enormous Oats Royd Mill in the valley is a remarkable sight. The streamside Shoulder of Mutton down in Mytholmroyd (B6138) has bargain home cooking.

MALTBY SK5489 **Roche Abbey** (off A634 SE) A fine gatehouse to the NW and the still-standing walls of the S and N transepts are all that's left of this 12th-c Cistercian abbey, but they make an impressive sight. Snacks, shop, some disabled access; cl Nov–Mar; (01709) 812739; £1.70; EH. The Black Lion in attractive nearby Firbeck has enjoyable food, and lots of interesting photographs.

MIDDLESTOWN SE2416
National Coal Mining Museum See separate family panel on p.715.

MONK BRETTON SE3706
Monk Bretton Priory The red sandstone remains of an important 12th-c priory, with 14th-c gatehouse (restored), church and other buildings, as well as some unusually well preserved drains; EH; free. The ancient Mill of the Black Monks is pleasant at lunchtime (live music for young people most nights).

NORLAND MOOR SE0521
S of Sowerby Bridge, this gives walkers views from the Calderdale Way into adjacent Calderdale, with the Rochdale Canal along its foot.

NORTH ANSTON SK5284
Tropical Butterfly House (Woodsetts Rd) Friendly place with insects, reptiles, snakes, birds of prey and farm animals, besides the butterflies; they positively encourage you to touch as well as look. Also tractor trailer rides (exc winter) and new interactive display boards. Meals (in season and wknds), snacks, shop, disabled access; cl 24–26 Dec and 1 Jan; (01909) 569416; *£4.40. The Duke of Leeds over in Wales (Church St) does good value lunches, not Mon/Tues.

NOSTELL PRIORY SE4017
(off A638) This sumptuous Palladian mansion, with an additional wing built by Adam in 1766, has perhaps the best collection of Chippendale furniture anywhere, all designed for this house. Other highlights include the tapestry room, charming saloon, servants hall and great kitchen, and a remarkably intricate 18th-c doll's house also said to have been furnished by Chippendale. The most attractive grounds have woodland walks and a lovely rose garden; coarse fishing on the lakes. There's an interesting **medieval church** near the entrance, and occasional craft fairs in the stables. Snacks, shop, disabled access; cl am, plus Mon, Tues, and 4 Nov–22 Mar (exc wknds till 15 Dec), grounds also open

from 11am and wknds 2–17 Mar; (01924) 863892; house and gardens £4.50, grounds only £2.50; NT. The Spread Eagle has good value food.

OAKWELL HALL SE2127
(signed off A651/A652 S of Birkenshaw) Moated Elizabethan manor house, altered in the 17th c, and still furnished to give something of the atmosphere then; look out for the unusual dog gates at the foot of the staircase. Also period formal gardens, extensive country park with adventure playground, visitor centre and, for children, the Discovery Gallery – a hands-on exploration of the four 'elements', earth, air, fire and water. Snacks, shop, limited disabled access; cl am wknds (Discovery Gallery cl all am), Good Fri, best to phone over Christmas and New Year; (01924) 326240; £1.40 house (free Nov–Feb), visitor centre and Discovery Gallery free. The ancient Black Bull opposite the partly Saxon church in nearby Birstall has good cheap food.

OGDEN RESERVOIR SE0630
N of Halifax, this is well served with paths for walkers (inc a stretch of Roman road).

OTLEY SE2045
Archetypal Yorkshire market town on the River Wharfe with a most attractive atmosphere. The Rose & Crown (Bondgate) is good value for lunch.
The Chevin Behind the town, this is not a high hill, but gives walkers a grand view of Wharfedale.

RIPPONDEN SE0318
Rather austerely attractive, with medieval packhorse bridge; the B6113 and B6114 above here are interesting moors roads.

ROTHERHAM SK4091
Magna (off A6178, SW of centre; Templeborough) In an awesomely converted former steel works (2001 winner of the Stirling prize for architecture), this centre puts a colourful spin on the story of the steel industry. It has four themed pavilions based around the main elements used in steel-making: Earth, housed in the basement, re-creates the drama of working in a quarry, Air is an inflated structure, designed to look like an airship hovering over the main factory

floor, Water gives children plenty of excuses to soak their parents, and Fire, set around a giant live flame, uses audio-visual displays to illustrate how man has controlled fire for his benefit, as well as its explosive (and destructive) possibilities. Plenty of emphasis on hands-on activities and interactive experiences. Meals, snacks, shop, disabled access; cl 24–25 Dec; (01709) 720002; £7.99.

SALTAIRE SE1337
The pioneering industrial village Titus Salt developed in Shipley in the 1850s, now a World Heritage Site. Salt's beautifully thought-out classically designed village was so successful that even now it's a favoured place to live. It's well worth looking around, and you might want to try the antique **cable railway**. There's a splendid flight of locks on the Leeds–Liverpool Canal.

1853 Gallery (Victoria Rd) Named from the year when the magnificent mill it's housed in was built, with one of the largest collections of contemporary art in the country, inc around 300 works by David Hockney, especially some of his intriguing experiments with photography. Huge bookshop, disabled access; (01274) 531163; cl 25–26 Dec, 1 Jan; free. Some good smart shops, and a restaurant in the building too.

Victorian Reed Organ Museum (Victoria Hall, Victoria Rd) Unique, with some eye-opening exhibits, inc one organ no bigger than a family bible. If you're an organ-player you may get the chance to try some of those on display. Shop, limited disabled access (with notice); cl Fri, Sat, and Dec–Jan; (01274) 585601; £2.50.

SAXTON SE4736
Attractive village with decent pub; don't miss the magnificent church, where Lord Dacre is buried sitting on his war horse – the 1461 Battle of Towton site is just N. The Greyhound by the church is a charming unspoilt pub.

SHEFFIELD SK3281
A vast industrial city (and rather surprisingly, the greenest in England), redeveloped extensively in post-war years, and now being spruced up with heavy funding under urban renewal schemes. Projects to revitalise the heart of the city, and a cheerful new waterfront development called Victoria Quays, go hand in hand with a cultural life that's already thriving, and there are several places worth visiting – though needing a street map and quite a bit of journeying. Best to use the comfortably modern tram to get about; it runs out to the giant indoor shopping mall at Meadowhall. They hope to open the Winter Garden (the largest temperate glasshouse to be built in Britain for 100 years) by the beginning of 2003, as an attractive endpiece to the stunning Millennium Galleries. Besides Smith's of Sheffield, good value food can be found at the Bankers Draft (all day; Market Pl).

Bishop's House (Meersbrook Park, S Sheffield) Striking 15th- and 16th-c yeoman's house, now a good museum of social history. Limited disabled access; cl wkdys exc by appointment; (0114) 278 2600; free.

City Museum and Mappin Art Gallery (Weston Park) Firmly traditional in its approach, but with some interesting collections, inc fine cutlery and a splendid display of antique Sheffield plate. The excellent gallery features works by Renoir, Cézanne, Turner and even Walt Disney. Meals, snacks, shop, disabled access; cl Mon exc bank hol and 25 Dec; (0114) 276 8588; free.

Fire Police Museum 🔁 The history of fire-fighting shown in a Victorian fire/police station, with themed areas inc a reconstructed fireman's bedroom and a car crash scene, plus related artefacts and hands-on exhibits. In the engine house and courtyard you can see a variety of fire appliances from an 18th-c manual pump cart to a 1974 Angus Jaguar; there's also a model railway, play area and Fireman Sam video. Snacks, shop, disabled access to ground floor only; open Sun and bank hol Mon; (0114) 249 1999; *£2.50. The Fat Cat nearby in Alma St has good cheap food.

Graves Art Gallery (Surrey St) Well worth a visit, with some fine decorative art; cl Sun; (0114) 2782600; free. The Red Lion in nearby Charles St has good simple food.

Kelham Island Industrial Museum (around Alma St, signed from centre) Lively exploration of Sheffield's industrial development, with all sorts of buildings, workshops and machinery collections (inc formidable working engines), and traditional cutlery craftsmen at work. Snacks, shop, disabled access; cl Fri–Sat, and a few days at Christmas; (0114) 272 2106; £3.50. The Fat Cat here has really good cheap food.

Millennium Galleries (Arundel Gate) This elegant complex is the focal point of the city centre's redevelopment, with four exhibition spaces. Highlights include a metalwork gallery on the city's heritage, the Ruskin collection (previously at Norfolk St), and collections from London's Victoria & Albert Museum (which has been closely involved in the development); also changing craft and design exhibitions. Café, shop, disabled access; cl 24–26 Dec and 1 Jan; (0114) 278 2600; free, £4 for special shows. Nearby are new café-bars, cinemas and so forth.

Sheffield Bus Museum (Tinsley) Diverse collection of buses with related memorabilia and a big model railway. Snacks, shop; open pm wknds Easter–Christmas for restoration work, with special open days every couple of months when the displays are more lively; (0114) 255 3010; £1.

SOWERBY BRIDGE SE0623
Worth a stop if you're passing; turn down to the canal basin, which always has a lot going on.

STAINBOROUGH SE3103
Wentworth Castle Gardens A heritage lottery grant of around £9 million has recently been awarded to restore these Grade I gardens and the surrounding Stainborough Park. Mostly laid out in the 18th c with Victorian and Edwardian additions, the 40-acre gardens have national collections of rhododendrons, magnolias and camellias. Some disabled access (steep slopes); guided tours probably pm Tues and Thurs mid-Apr to end Aug, and some pm Suns, but phone to check; (01226) 731269; £2.50.

THORNTON SE1032
Brontë Birthplace (72 Market St) Born here rather than in Haworth, the Brontë siblings lived here till 1820. Re-created in Regency style and still lived in; the knowledgeable owner (a writer

herself) is happy to show you around. Shop, open pm Tues–Sun plus bank hol Mon Apr–Sept though best to check as the property is up for sale (01274) 830849; £3. The Ring o' Bells (Hill Top Rd, off B6145) is a good dining pub with great views.

THURGOLAND SE2900
Wortley Top Forge Built in 1640, this is one of the very few water-powered iron forges left anywhere in the world; there's a collection of steam and other engines, and a miniature railway usually runs when the forge is open; guided tours and a picnic site. Shop, phone for disabled access; open pm Sun and banks hols early Feb–late Nov; (0114) 281 7991; £2.

ULLEY SK4687
Pleasant walks around a reservoir, also good for fishing and watersports; the Royal Oak, in a lovely setting by the church, is a popularly priced dining pub.

WAKEFIELD SE3221
A number of handsome buildings include its cathedral, much restored in Victorian times but with some fine 15th-c masonry and carvings (and a marvellous spire – the tallest in Yorkshire), its rare 14th-c bridge chapel over the River Calder, some Georgian and Regency houses most notably around Wood St and St John's Sq, and its imposing civic buildings.

Wakefield Art Gallery (Wentworth Terrace) Good collection of 20th-c painting and sculpture, internationally famous for its galleries devoted to two famous local sculptors – Barbara Hepworth and Henry Moore. Shop; cl Sun am, all Mon, and a few days over Christmas and New Year; (01924) 305796; free.

Wakefield Museum (Wood St) Along with the unique collection of preserved animals and exotic birds gathered by local explorer Charles Waterton, and an exhibition on sports and games, this has plenty of opportunities for hands-on activities. Shop, good disabled access; cl Sun am, 25 Dec, 1 Jan; (01924) 305351; free.

Yorkshire Sculpture Park (West Bretton; A637 SE) Major contemporary sculpture carefully and imaginatively displayed in 500 acres of fine 18th-c landscaped parkland. There are 16 works by Henry Moore in the adjacent country park, often surrounded by grazing sheep, and there's a new visitor centre. Meals, snacks, shop, disabled access; cl 24–25 and 31 Dec; (01924) 830579; free (though £1.50 car parking charge).

WENTWORTH SK3898
Reckoned by some readers to be the prettiest village they've ever seen. The George & Dragon, with a craft and antiques shop nearby, has enjoyable food.

WITHENS CLOUGH RESERVOIR SD9822
S of Hebden Bridge, this has a path for walkers – and the more energetic can climb up to the prominent monument on Stoodley Pike, for the views. The nearby Hinchcliffe Arms has enjoyable food (not Mon).

WORSBROUGH SE3503
Worsbrough Country Park (A61) Hard to believe this was once a busy industrial area; the only sign of those days is the working corn mill, now the **Worsbrough Mill Museum** but still producing stoneground flour. Snacks, shop, some disabled access; usually cl Mon (exc bank hols), Tues, and mid-Dec to early Jan; (01226) 774527; 50p. About a mile away, **Wigfield Farm** is a hit with children, with traditional and rare breeds. Café and picnic area, shop, disabled access; cl 2 wks Christmas–New Year; (01226) 733702; £2. The peaceful 200 acres also include nature trails, and you can hire bikes (07811) 804991.

Other attractive or attractively placed villages with decent pubs include Appleton Roebuck SE5542, Askwith SD1648, Barkisland SE0420, Blackshaw Head SD9527, Boston Spa SE4345, East Morton SE1042, Esholt SE1840, Firbeck SK5688, Holme SE1006, Honley SE1312, canalside Kildwick SE0145, Ledsham SE4529 and nearby Ledston SE4328, Sowerby SE0423, Stanbury SE0037, Tickhill SK5993 (esp church and semi-ruined castle) and Warthill SE6755.

Other useful pubs in fine positions or with good views include Dick Hudsons on the Otley rd at High Eldwick above Bingley SE1240, the Castle overlooking the reservoirs nr Bolsterstone SK2796, Brown Cow by open-access woods at Ireland Bridge (B6429) nearer Bingley, Strines nr Strines Reservoir above Bradfield SK2692, Stanhope Arms on Windle Edge Lane nr Winscar Reservoir by Dunford Bridge SE1502, New Inn at Eccup SE2842, Cow & Calf up Skew Hill Lane at Grenoside above Sheffield SK3293, the Malt Shovel at Harden SE0838, Robin Hood at Pecket Well outside Hebden Bridge SD9928, the Cherry Tree on Bank End Lane at High Hoyland SE2710, Fleece at Holme SE1006, Buckstones on the A640 towards Denshaw high above Huddersfield SE1416, Blacksmiths Arms on Heaton Moor Rd at Kirkheaton SE1818, Shepherds Rest and Top Brink on Mankinholes Rd at Lumbutts SD9523 (bracing walks to Stoodley Pike monument), Hinchcliffe Arms at Cragg Vale, Mytholmroyd SE0126 (the B6188 S is a good moors road), Hobbit up Hob Lane, Norland SE0723, Grouse on Harehills Lane, Oldfield, nr Oakworth SE0038, Causeway Foot on the Keighley Rd by Ogden Reservoir SE0631, Waggon & Horses (A6033) and Dog & Gun (off B6141 towards Denholme, both nr Oxenhope SE0335, Pineberry on the A644 Keighley rd out of Queensbury SE1030, Brown Cow (A672) dramatically overlooking Scammonden Reservoir SE0215, Clothiers Arms in Station Rd, Stocksmoor, nr Shepley SE1810, White House on the B6107 or Rose & Crown up Cop Hill at Slaithwaite SE0813, Blue Ball nr Soyland SE0120, the Sportsmans Arms at Hawks Stones, Kebcote on Stansfield Moor SD9227, Ring o' Bells on Hill Top Rd at Thornton SE0933, Freemasons Arms on Hopton Hall Lane at Upper Hopton SE1918, Cross Keys overlooking the restored Rochdale Canal at Walsden SD9322, Delvers on Cold Edge Rd and Withens on Warley Moor Rd at Wainstalls SE0428, and Pack Horse at Widdop SD9333.

Where to eat

GOLCAR SE1015 **Weavers Shed** *86 Knowl Rd (01484) 654284* Warmly friendly restaurant-with-rooms in a converted cloth-finishing mill, with beams and flagstones, particularly good modern British cooking using home-grown fruit and vegetables and good local meat and fish, enjoyable breakfasts, and helpful staff; cl Sun, Mon, Sat am, 25 Dec–1 Jan; spacious attractive bdrms. £30/2-course menu £9.95

HALIFAX SE0726 **Design House** *(01422) 383242* Stylish modern restaurant in thriving carefully restored carpet mill complex, with enjoyable modern cooking to match; relaxed and friendly atmosphere, good service, and thoughtful wine list; cl Sun; disabled access. £25|£7

HAWORTH SE0237 **Weavers** *15 West Lane (01535) 643822* Charming evening restaurant made up of weavers' cottages, with lots of bric-a-brac, photographs, and spinning mementoes, delicious food, cheerful service, and a good loyal following; bdrms; cl Sun pm, Mon, 2 wks after Christmas. £25/2-course set menu £10.50

LEEDS SE3033 **Brasserie Forty-Four** *42–44 The Calls (0113) 234 3232* Originally a grain mill (below 42 The Calls, see *Where to stay*), this riverside restaurant is simply furnished with modern designs, and serves enjoyable British and Mediterranean food (very good value early evening set menu), and a good value wine list; cl Sat am, Sun, bank hols; partial disabled access. £25/3-course early bird meal £12.50

LEEDS SE3033 **Pool Court at 42** *42–44 The Calls (0113) 244 4242* Cleverly converted quayside grain mill (also incorporating Brasserie Forty-Four and the stylish hotel, 42 The Calls), this smart modern restaurant has a calm atmosphere, very accomplished enjoyable food with French leanings, lovely puddings, and an interesting wine list; cl Sat am, Sun; no babies; disabled access. £46

LEEDS SE2736 **Salvos** *115 Otley Rd, Headingley (0113) 275 5017* Welcoming Italian restaurant run by the same family for over 30 years, with good modern food (popular and interesting daily specials) and cheerful service; cl Sun; disabled access. £22/2-course rapido menu £5

LEEDS SE2933 **Sous le Nez en Ville** *The Basement, Quebec House, Quebec St (0113) 244 0108* Imaginative popular food in fashionable panelled basement restaurant with tiled floors and some exposed brickwork, a very good wine list, and efficient service; cl Sun, bank hols (but open Good Fri), 25 Dec, 1 Jan. £17.95|£8.95

RIPPONDEN SE0419 **Old Bridge Inn** *(01422) 822595/823722* Civilised medieval inn by pretty bridge over River Ryburn with three interesting rooms, well chosen pictures and prints, a big woodburning stove, and some no smoking areas; a dozen wines by the glass, real ales, and very popular cold buffet wkdy lunchtimes (best to book); children until 8pm; partial disabled access. £17.35/£8.95 2-course lunch|£5.75

SHEFFIELD SK3187 **Thyme** *34 Sandygate Rd (0114) 266 6096* Popular restaurant, newly enlarged and decorated, with a relaxed chatty atmosphere, stylish modern cooking using influences from all over the world, and a good wine list; cl Sun pm; disabled access. £34|£9

Special thanks to M Borthwick, J Black, Phil Skelton

LONDON

**Endless choice of things to see and do –
and many of the best bits are free**

Our top choice of places to visit includes the Imperial War Museum, the London Eye, the Tower of London, the Natural History and Science Museums, the British Museum, the National Gallery, a trip to Greenwich with all its attractions, the London Aquarium, Somerset House, the London Museum and the Horniman Museum. Most of these are free. And of course there are those crowd-pullers – the London Dungeon, Madame Tussaud's and Tate Modern; while the Victoria & Albert Museum's big art deco show will win it many new friends.

Then there are the 'must sees': the Houses of Parliament, Buckingham Palace, Westminster Abbey, St Paul's, Trafalgar Square, the parks, the street markets, the riverside, and the essential walk from Piccadilly Circus through Leicester Square to Covent Garden.

As well as all those obvious draws, there is a host of lesser-known places that delight the people who discover them. Prime examples, again mostly free, are the Sir John Soane's Museum, the National Army Museum, the Geffrye Museum, Firepower, 18 Folgate St, the Wallace Collection and the Museum of Childhood. And there are the special places further out, such as Kew Gardens and Richmond.

London is surprisingly easy to explore on foot. Quite a number of people lead guided walks. Original London Walks are consistently good and have a choice of more than ten a day. Usually starting from a tube station, walks last about two hours. You don't need to book, and they cost about £5; (020) 7624 3978 or www.walks.com.

Travelcards are good value tickets for the day, weekend or longer, valid on buses, tube and rail trains (not the morning rush hour). London's Tube is a quick and straightforward though often unpleasantly crowded way of getting around. Pocket tube and bus route maps are free from ticket offices. In the text, we have grouped things to see and do under the heading of the most convenient tube station, using the ⊖ symbol – or the ⇌ symbol if it's surface rail instead.

Where to stay

22 Jermyn Street Hotel *22 Jermyn St SW1Y 6HP (020) 7734 2353* **£272.05**; 5 rms and 13 suites – spacious with deeply comfortable seats and sofas, flowers, plants, and antiques. Stylish little hotel owned by the same family for over 80 years and much loved by customers; no public rooms but wonderful 24-hr service, helpful notes and suggestions from the friendly owners, in-room light meals, and a warm welcome for children (with their own fact sheet listing shops, restaurants, and sights geared towards them, free video library, old-fashioned and electronic games, and own bathrobes); disabled access; dogs welcome ☺

Basil Street Hotel *8 Basil St SW3 1AH (020) 7581 3311* **£232.65**, plus special breaks; 80 pretty, decent-sized rms. Handy for Harrods and Hyde Park, this very civilised, privately owned Edwardian hotel has a relaxed atmosphere, antiques, fine carpets and paintings in the public rooms, a panelled restaurant with reliably enjoyable food, afternoon teas in lounge, and ladies' club (named after a parrot who had to go when his language became inappropriate); helpful courteous service – many of the staff have been here for years; dogs welcome in bedrooms

Capital *22–24 Basil St SW3 1AT (020) 7589 5171* **£313**; 48 luxury rms with lovely fabrics, fine paintings, marble bthrms, and tempting extras. Exclusive little hotel nr Harrods with a warm welcome and log fire in reception, intimate panelled bar with good nibbles, a small lounge, exemplary service, and exceptional French-inspired food in chandelier-lit restaurant; disabled access; dogs welcome in bedrooms

Chesterfield *35 Charles St W1X 8LX (020) 7491 2622* **£264.37**, plus special breaks; 110 well equipped and newly refurbished pretty rms. Charming hotel just off Berkeley Sq, with particularly courteous helpful staff, afternoon tea in panelled library, a relaxed club-style bar with resident pianist, and fine food in attractive restaurant or light and airy conservatory; dogs welcome in bedrooms

Claridge's *Brook Street W1A 2JQ (020) 7629 8860* **£482**, plus luxury breaks; 203 excellent rms. Grand hotel long used by royalty and heads of state, with liveried footmen, lift attendants and valets, elegant and comfortable day rooms, and civilised colonnaded foyer where the Hungarian Quartet plays; lovely formal restaurant (now Gordon Ramsay at Claridge's) with fantastic food and wine and exemplary service; free tennis at Vanderbilt Racquet Club; disabled access

Claverley *13–14 Beaufort Gardens SW3 1PS (020) 7589 8541* **£120**, plus special breaks; 30 individually decorated rms, most with own bthrm. Friendly privately owned Edwardian house with comfortable lounge, panelled reading room, and good breakfasts in cheerful dining room

Connaught *Carlos Place W1Y 6AL (020) 7499 7070* **£400**, plus special breaks; 92 lovely, individually decorated rms inc 22 suites. A very special place with fine old-fashioned dignified values, elegant, restful day rooms filled with beautiful flowers and antiques, fine panelling, exemplary service, and outstanding food in the two formal restaurants; disabled access

Conrad London *Chelsea Harbour SW10 0XG (020) 7823 3000* **£180**; 160 luxury suites with a light and spacious living room area (many have sofa-beds so two small children could stay with parents at no extra cost). London's first 'suite hotel', tucked away in the quiet modern enclave of the Chelsea Harbour development and overlooking its small marina; enjoyable Mediterranean and Asian-influenced dishes in Aquasia restaurant and bar, friendly service, and health club; disabled access; dogs welcome (if small)

Covent Garden Hotel *10 Monmouth St WC2H 9HB (020) 7806 1000* **£309.13**; 58 big individual bdrms with smart bthrms. Stylish luxury hotel nr theatres, with wrought-iron staircase from foyer to panelled upstairs drawing room and library, richly coloured interesting furniture, and popular ground-floor brasserie; state-of-the-art screening room for film companies, and for hotel guests' film club; they are kind to children; limited disabled access

Durrants *26–32 George St W1H 6BJ (020) 7935 8131* **£192**; 92 well equipped rms, with own bthrms; the quietest are at the back. Managed by the same family for over 70 years, this surprisingly quiet central hotel, behind a delightful Georgian façade, has fine paintings and antiques, a clubby bar, and relaxing lounges; cosy panelled restaurant with essentially English cooking, a redecorated breakfast room, and helpful pleasant staff; disabled access

Goring *15 Beeston Place SW1W 0JW (020) 7396 9000* **£229.12**w, plus special breaks; 74 individually decorated rms, some with balconies overlooking pretty garden. Built in 1910 by the grandfather of the present Mr Goring, this family-run, impeccably kept and very English hotel has a particularly welcoming atmosphere (many staff have been there for years), very good cooking in the elegant restaurant, a super wine list, comfortable lounge for afternoon tea, airy cocktail bar, and staunchly loyal customers; disabled access

Halkin *5 Halkin St SW1X 7DJ (020) 7333 1000* **£270**w, plus special breaks; 41 stylish well equipped rms, with wonderful marble bthrms. Despite its Georgian exterior, the decor and furnishings here are ultra-modern but enjoyable, and there's a particularly good Thai restaurant overlooking the garden; fine breakfasts, and really charming staff; much liked by businessmen, too; disabled access; dogs if very well trained and by prior arrangement

Hazlitts *6 Frith St W1V 5TZ (020) 7434 1771* **£229.13**, plus special breaks; 23 rms with 18th- or 19th-c beds and free-standing Victorian baths with early brass shower mixer units. Behind a typically Soho façade of listed early Georgian houses, this well kept and comfortably laid-out little hotel has been completely restored this year; very handy for the West End; good continental breakfasts served in your bedroom, snacks in the sitting room, lots of restaurants all around; kind, helpful service; dogs by prior arrangement

Knightsbridge Green Hotel *159 Knightsbridge SW1X 7PD (020) 7584 6274* **£152**, plus special breaks; 28 no smoking suites with sitting room. Friendly family-owned hotel, carefully refurbished and neatly kept, with very good in-room breakfasts (no restaurant), bar service, free coffee and tea in lounge, and helpful efficient staff; disabled access

L'Hotel *28 Basil St SW3 1AS (020) 7589 6286* **£164.50**; 12 well equipped rms. Small family-owned French-style city hotel, nr Harrods, and set above the neatly kept well run Metro wine bar where continental breakfasts are served – as well as good modern French café food; friendly staff; disabled access; dogs by prior arrangement

Leonard *15 Seymour St W1H 5AA (020) 7935 2010* **£295**; 44 rms – mainly luxury suites – with fine paintings, antiques, lovely fabrics, fresh flowers, videos, satellite TV, and hi-fi system; smart 18th-c townhouse with marvellous staff, light modern meals all day in café bar, and compact exercise room; disabled access ☺

Meridien Piccadilly *21 Piccadilly W1V 0BH (020) 7734 8000* **£199**w, plus special breaks; 266 luxurious rms. The very best in modern French hotel-keeping, with attractive quiet public rooms, professional and friendly service, popular afternoon tea, marvellous food in the Oak Room restaurant, and free membership of the largest health club in a London hotel; one child under 12 free in parents' room; partial disabled access

Number Sixteen *16 Sumner Pl SW7 3EG (020) 7589 5232* **£176.25**; 40 individually styled rms, some with views of the garden. Four carefully refurbished townhouses with a relaxed, friendly atmosphere, a pretty and cheerfully decorated lounge, a book-filled library, honesty bar, lots of pictures, antiques, and bowls of fresh flowers, an airy conservatory overlooking the garden, and enjoyable breakfasts.

One Aldwych *1 Aldwych WC2B 4BZ (020) 7300 1000* **£283.50**w, plus special breaks; 105 luxury bdrms and suites with fresh fruit and flowers delivered daily. Close to theatres and Covent Garden, this fine Edwardian hotel has an impressive foyer with a giant statue of an oarsman in his boat, huge flower arrangements and contemporary paintings throughout, two bars, three restaurants, and helpful friendly staff; health facilities inc indoor swimming pool with underwater music; disabled access

Pelham Hotel *15 Cromwell Pl SW7 2LA (020) 7589 8288* **£229.12**, 51 rms and suites, individually designed combining antique furniture and modern decor. Luxurious Victorian townhouse nr South Kensington tube station and the museums, with a country house-type atmosphere, huge bowls of flowers, opulent decor and an open fire in drawing room, a cosy dark-panelled smoking room, and good modern British cooking in cheerfully decorated restaurant and wine bar

Rubens *39–41 Buckingham Palace Rd SW1W 0PS (020) 7834 6600* **£155**w, plus special breaks; 172 well equipped, individually furnished rms inc 12 luxurious suites. Opposite Buckingham Palace and nr Victoria Station, this attractive hotel has comfortable day rooms inc lounge with views of the Royal Mews, open fire in bar,

and library restaurant with fine international food
Swiss House *171 Old Brompton Rd SW5 0AN (020) 7373 2769* **£93**; 15 rms.
Festooned with ivy and flower boxes, this is a warmly friendly and good value
family-run hotel, relaxed and tidy inside, with very good buffet continental
breakfasts – English available, too; dogs welcome in bedrooms
Tophams Belgravia *24–32 Ebury St SW1W 0LU (020) 7730 8147* **£140**; 39 cosy
rms, 34 with own bthrm. Small, charmingly old-fashioned hotel made up of several
townhouses with a friendly country-house atmosphere, downstairs bar, attractive
lounges, good modern cooking in the elegant restaurant, and decent wines; cl
Christmas and New Year; partial disabled access
Trafalgar *25 Cockspur Street SW1Y 5BN (020) 7870 2900* **£158**w, plus special
breaks; 129 rms, many looking down over Trafalgar Sq (these are the ones that
make this notable). Handsome Cunard building rebuilt internally as stylish new
hotel (a Hilton, but not recognisable as such), minimalist but comfortable modern
decor and furnishings, big cool bar, friendly and informal but punctilious young staff

The West End

This area is world-famous for its shopping and window-shopping, from the
daunting bustle of Oxford St, through the bookshops around Charing
Cross Rd, the specialist food and cookery shops of Soho, and the elegant
stores of Regent St and Piccadilly, to the ultra-smart clothes shops of
South Molton St and Bond St. There are great opportunities for window-
shopping in the auction houses and fine art galleries. The West End is
synonymous with theatre; it's worth knowing that on Leicester Square a
half-price ticket booth sells off surplus tickets for that day's performances:
open around 12–2 pm for matinée tickets, then from about 2.30 pm for
evenings – there's usually a queue so it's worth getting there earlier.
Highlights here include the National Gallery and Trafalgar Square,
Piccadilly with the Royal Academy, the sumptuous Wallace Collection (in
an elegant remodelled 18th-c house), and colourful Covent Garden (the
London Transport Museum here is surprisingly good fun for families).
Chinatown is a vivid enclave, Neal St is a focus for rather alternative shops
and cafés, and there are staunchly old-fashioned institutions of Englishness
and English cooking like Rules or Simpsons – among an extraordinarily
eclectic crowd of other places to eat.

To see and do

BOND STREET ⊖
Handel's House This was Handel's
home for 36 years until his death in
1759; he composed the *Messiah* here,
and there's a display on his life and
work. The rooms have been
authentically refurbished and fitted out
as described in Handel's will, with
period instruments on show. Shop,
disabled access; cl Sun am, all Mon (exc
pm bank hols), 25–26 Dec, 1 Jan; (020)
7495 1685; £4.50. Note the
neighbouring blue plaque showing
where Jimi Hendrix lived.
Mayfair W of Regent St and N of
Piccadilly (and only the shortest of
strolls from them; Bond St and Green
Park tube stns are handy). This is mostly
a quietly discreet area of elegant town
houses, smart well established hotels,

and richly unobtrusive offices. Despite their famous names, Berkeley Sq and Grosvenor Sq don't have any special appeal for visitors. Bond St with its continuation New Bond St is the area's main street for shopping, though unless you want to spend a great deal of money on top-notch designer clothes and shoes, jewellery or oriental rugs this is likely to be confined to the window. Plenty of art and antiques galleries, and a good indoor antiques market (124 New Bond St). Aspreys is a remarkable place, famous for its opulent luxury goods and glittering with an awesome tonnage of gems and precious metals. Nearby is a charming life-size sculpture of Churchill chatting to Roosevelt on a bench – you can sit with them. Sotheby's auction rooms are fascinating to wander around. Other small and prestigious art galleries are dotted throughout Mayfair, particularly in nearby Dover St and (mainly contemporary) Cork St; Grays antiques market off 58 Davies St has hundreds of indoor stalls. South Audley St has Hobbs of Mayfair, a delicious smart delicatessen, and Goode's, a magnificent glass and china shop. Higgins in Duke St is the Queen's coffee-man. The best Mayfair pub is the Red Lion in Waverton St; the grander Audley (Mount St) is also good.

Wallace Collection (Hertford House, Manchester Sq – across Oxford St) Excellent art collection beautifully displayed in an elegant 18th-c house, improved and remodelled by the American architect Rick Mather, 100 years after it was first opened as a museum. It's visually very seductive, with probably the best collection of 18th-c French paintings in the world, inc luscious offerings from Watteau, Boucher and Fragonard. Also great Canalettos, fine works by Rembrandt, Rubens and Van Dyck, works by British painters, furniture (mostly 18th-c French), notable assemblage of Sèvres porcelain, and an amazing array of arms and armour, Oriental as well as European. It's rarely busy, and in places feels more like a historic home than a museum. There's a watercolour gallery and public library in the basement, and a café in the glass-covered sculpture garden. Meals, snacks, shop, disabled access (phone for parking); cl Sun am, 24–26 Dec, Good Fri, 1 Jan, May Day bank hol; (020) 7935 0687; free. The O'Connor Don (Marylebone Lane) is a civilised nearby place for a snack lunch.

CHARING CROSS ⊖ ≋

Trafalgar Square Many people think of this as the heart of central London (distances to and from central London used to be measured from the Cross on the Strand). For a long time it's certainly seemed at the heart of London's traffic, but that's all changed with the new scheme to confine the traffic to the S and E edges, making the square a great pedestrianised space in front of the National Gallery. Named for the naval victory of 1805, it was designed by Nash and completed in 1841; the fountains were added a century later, and recently there's been an enjoyable series of witty changing sculptures. The centrepiece, **Nelson's Column**, stretches up 56 metres (185 ft), its base guarded by four huge identical lions. Trafalgar Square wouldn't be the same without the innumerable pigeons, but at the moment a feud rages between Mayor Ken Livingstone, who wants to rid the square of these 'rats with wings' (you can no longer buy food for them here), and pigeon activists who continue to feed them.

National Gallery This magnificent building right on Trafalgar Square houses the national collection of western European painting, with around 2,300 pictures dating from 1250 to 1900. You'll enjoy it most if you're firm and restrict yourself to just a few of the galleries, rather than trying to see everything. It's hard to pick out highlights (the whole collection is worth studying), but don't miss the Sainsbury Wing, which gives perfect lighting and viewing conditions for its treasure-trove of early Renaissance works. It gets very busy, especially on a Sat, or at any time around the Impressionist works; 19 Feb–18 May, the biggest-ever Titian show is expected to draw the crowds. There's a hi-tech audio tour (by donation), with a commentary on every single picture in the main gallery. Meals, snacks, shop, disabled access; cl 24–26 Dec, 1 Jan and

Good Fri; (020) 7747 2885; free, charges for some exhibitions.

National Portrait Gallery (St Martin's Pl, just round the corner) Grandly illustrates British history, with paintings of kings, queens and other notable characters arranged in chronological order from the top floor (medieval) to the present. The immensely stylish Ondaatje wing includes Tudor and 20th-c galleries where Shakespeare rubs shoulders with the Rolling Stones, and a rooftop restaurant gives views across Trafalgar Sq and Whitehall. Meals, snacks, shop (where computer technology allows them to print you a poster of any painting in the gallery), disabled access; cl 24–26 Dec, 1 Jan and Good Fri; (020) 7306 0055; free, £6 for some special exhibitions.

St Martin-in-the-Fields This elegant church has frequent lunchtime and evening concerts; (020) 7839 8362 for programme. Unmistakable for its blue clock-dial – the only clock in this part of London that seems always to keep the right time – the church has a busy but very well liked coffee bar in its crypt, with frequent art exhibitions; also brass-rubbing centre, shop (inc all the Academy of St Martin-in-the-Fields CDs), and a daily market; all proceeds support the mission of the church, particularly the homeless – you're likely to see plenty of bodies huddled in shop doorways in the surrounding streets, a sadly common sight all over London, but especially obvious around here.

Theatres Theatres abound off Trafalgar Sq, with a group based around this end of Charing Cross Rd, and another up along the Strand. Marked out by the globe on top of the building, the Coliseum (St Martin's Lane) is the home of the English National Opera. You can usually get decently priced seats on the day, from 10am, if you do want to hear operas translated into English instead of the original; (020) 7632 8300. From June, it's closed for around six months, and when it reopens £41 million should have restored it to its 1904 glory. Almost next to the Coliseum, the Chandos is a good pub with food all day, down past the Post Office the underground Tappit

Hen is an atmospheric wine bar, and there's no end of smart little coffee shops and cafés near by – Gabys (30 Charing Cross Rd) does perfect hot salt beef sandwiches.

COVENT GARDEN ⊖

Partly pedestrianised, the former vegetable, fruit and flower market with its elegant buildings is now made over to smart café-bars, boutiques and stalls, such as those in the covered piazza, selling good but expensive handmade clothes and craft items. There's a bustling cosmopolitan atmosphere, and good street entertainers. The Jubilee Market specialises in different wares on different days. The many bars and restaurants are always lively at night, but again they're not cheap. One of the delights of this area is its range of unusual or specialist **shops**. In the streets around the Piazza, Knutz (Russell St) has everything for the practical joker, and Penhaligon's (Wellington St) sell lovely old-fashioned toiletries. On the other side of the market, N of the tube station, interesting shops are set in a labyrinthine network of attractively rejuvenated alleys and streets; you will get lost, but wandering around is great fun, and they all lead back to roughly the same area. Neal St is rewarding for its small craft and specialist shops, and Neal's Yard is full of healthy living – delightful in summer with its fresh paint and tubs of flowers; a multi-storey mini-mall here has a good airy atrium-effect basement coffee bar. Floral St has elegant and expensive clothes and shoe shops (plus the Tintin shop – paradise for the Tintin fan). The Africa Centre on King St may have exhibitions of African art and culture. No shortage of places to eat around here, but useful pubs for lunch or refreshment include the idiosyncratic modern Porterhouse on Maiden Lane (food all day), and the Lamb & Flag on Rose St, an attractive 300-year-old pub with good value snacks, its back room still much as Dickens described it.

London Transport Museum (The Piazza) On the site of the former Flower Market, this is a surprisingly fun attraction. You can race a tram and a bus, delve into feely boxes, design your own bus, and see why a steam train doesn't suit the Underground. The main show is quite traditional, but they don't mind if you climb aboard some of the buses, trams and tube trains, and there are good touch screens throughout. Costumed actors tell nostalgic transport tales, and there might be story-telling, face-painting or craft workshops in school hols. Snacks, interesting shop, disabled access; cl 24–26 Dec; (020) 7836 8557; £5.95.

Royal Opera House Beautifully restored and extended (at inordinate cost), and you can now look around the refurbished foyer areas and various exhibitions. Readers greatly enjoy the backstage guided tours, led by enthusiastic guides – interesting even if you're not an opera or ballet buff. Tours vary depending on what is happening on the day, and usually start at 10.30, 12.30 and 2.30 Mon–Sat, best to phone first; (020) 7212 9389; £8. A limited number of tickets for performances are available on the day, from 10am; (020) 7304 4000. There are lovely views across Covent Garden from the good (but not cheap) Amphitheatre restaurant.

St Paul's church The actors' church, full of interesting memorials to performers. Pepys watched the first-ever Punch and Judy show here in 1662. Outside its back gate, facing the covered market, the theatrical tradition continues, with jugglers, clowns, mountebanks and unusual musicians performing on the cobbles.

Theatre Museum (Russell St) Exhaustive look at events and personalities on the stage over the last few hundred years. Posters, puppets and props are among the permanent collection, which although astonishingly comprehensive is arranged a little confusingly; it's easy to find yourself going round backwards. The very good temporary displays leave the deepest impression: there are always free stage make-up demonstrations, and you can dress up in the costume workshops. Shop, disabled access; cl Mon and bank hols; (020) 7943 4700; free.

Theatre Royal (Drury Lane) The oldest working theatre in the world, first opened in 1663 (Nell Gwynn was one of its earliest performers), but rebuilt several times over the next few centuries. Tours show backstage features inc the intriguing hydraulic lift beneath the stage, still in use. Meals, snacks, shop, disabled access to theatre but not tour; tours 2.15pm and 4.45pm (exc Weds and Sat when tours are 10.15am and 12noon), best to check as there are no tours in between shows; (020) 7850 8793; £8.50.

LEICESTER SQUARE ⊖

All central London's attractions are within easy walking distance of here, with several of the more interesting theatres little more than five mins' stroll. The tube station's various exits are a favourite with Londoners stuck for a place to meet; hordes of them mill around anxiously looking for the friends they finally discover they've been standing next to for half an hour. Around the bustling edges of the pedestrian square, attractively cleaned up in recent years and usually with living statues and other free entertainment, are several huge cinemas, pricy but with excellent sound; you can see films more cheaply at the Prince Charles in Leicester Pl, leading off (where Notre Dame de France has an impressive Jean Cocteau mural). Marked out by its dramatic ornamental gate, **Chinatown** has developed its own character; the inviting supermarkets and shops along pedestrianised Gerrard St and in neighbouring streets are fascinating, with their weird and wonderful vegetables, strange squidgy things in little cellophane packets, and odd-smelling dried meats and fish. Plenty of authentic Chinese restaurants, as well as less convincingly adapted telephone boxes. Back by the tube station, this stretch of Charing Cross Rd is justifiably famous for its **bookshops**, specialist and general, new and second-hand, as are the side alleys between here and St Martin's Lane; Cecil Court is perhaps the best. Two distinctively designed pubs round here are the good value modern Moon Under Water opposite Blackwells on Charing Cross Rd, and the Salisbury on St Martin's Lane, a sumptuously Victorian pub, all red velvet and cut glass. Not far away towards Covent Garden is Stanfords

(Long Acre), the best map and guidebook shop in Britain; on the way, the upstairs Photographers Gallery (Gt Newport St) is always worth a look. Leicester Sq is very handy for Soho, described below under Tottenham Court Rd.

MARBLE ARCH ⊖

Striking in itself, it was originally a grand entrance for Buckingham Palace, moved here decades ago. Over the road **Speakers Corner** on the edge of Hyde Park is where every Sun morning you can still hear impassioned diatribes on all sorts of causes. Also on Sun you can see what's probably the longest free open-air art exhibition in the world, with the work of 300 artists and craftsmen laid out along the park railings on Bayswater Rd; the Swan opposite gives a pleasant break. The tube station – with so many exits it's a real initiative test finding your way out – is also handy for Oxford St.

Hyde Park Riding Stables (Bathurst Mews) Can organise horse-riding in the park; cl Mon; (020) 7723 2813; from £39 an hour.

OXFORD CIRCUS ⊖

The heart of the city's busiest shopping areas, crowded and noisy Oxford St to the left and right, and altogether nicer Regent St to the S. **Oxford St** doesn't have a lot of character, but is full of good stores such as Selfridges, John Lewis (the self-service restaurant is good for lunch), Marks & Spencer, the giant music shops HMV and Virgin Megastore, and the usual high street chains inc a new Allders (the first department store to be opened on Oxford St since 1930). South Molton St and St Christopher's Pl on either side of Oxford St are full of designer clothes shops and smart cafés. **Regent St** is one of the grandest streets in the whole area, with a splendid curve as it reaches Piccadilly Circus. A harmonious street of considerable character, with the fine shops definitely enhancing its appeal, even if all you want to do is browse. Liberty's is a splendid art nouveau timbered building full of gorgeous soft furnishings and clothes, oriental and leather goods, jewellery and a good gift department. Other high points include Mappin & Webb for fine china, glass,

and jewellery; Hamleys, a marvellous toy shop (not cheap, though); Aquascutum, great for expensive classic English clothes; and Waterford/Wedgwood, for china and glass in quite a wide range of prices. The Old Coffee House in Beak St around the corner from here, and Red Lion in Kingly St, are useful for lunch. Carnaby St, tucked away behind, has some rather florid men's shops and good street-fashion houses, but is mainly full of small boutiques with trendy accessories, leather goods and tacky souvenirs.

PICCADILLY CIRCUS ⊖

Another lively hub of London life, with famous streets radiating off in every direction, each quite different in character; handsome Piccadilly roughly to the W, the theatres of bustling Shaftesbury Avenue to the E, with smarter ones on Haymarket to the S, Regent St (£500 million is being invested in reinvigorating it over the next ten years) coolly curving N towards Oxford Circus, and of course the famous statue of Eros, where all the foreign students sit to be photographed. The streets around here are excellent for shopping. On opposite sides of the traffic islands in Piccadilly Circus are Tower Records, three floors of pop, classical and jazz (open till midnight), and Lillywhites, the long-established sports clothes and equipment store. On Piccadilly, Waterstones is the biggest bookshop in Europe, while friendly Hatchards further down is a nicely old-fashioned bookshop where the staff can still sometimes turn vague requests into actual books. Almost next door, Fortnum's (Fortnum & Mason) has superior if expensive clothes, as well as the foods for which they're world-famous. Nearby, the Burlington Arcade is an elegant Regency covered arcade of expensive but good shops (excellent cashmere and knife/scissors shops, for instance), with a delightful set of rules, still enforced, that stop people whistling, singing or running in its confines. The Ritz is gorgeously flamboyant inside: well worth the high price of having a frogged and liveried waiter bring you a cup of tea. Behind

Piccadilly's S side is Jermyn St, where among other splendid but top-of-the-range shops you can buy fine cheeses at Paxton & Whitfield's, briar pipes at Astleys, hand-made shoes at Tricker's, hand-made shirts from Turnbull & Asser, flat hats at Bates, old-fashioned toiletries at Floris, and a haircut or shave at Trumper's; the ground floor museum of deco watches and bijouterie at Dunhill's is well worth a look. The Red Lion in Duke of York St just off here is a little gem of a pub, with decent snacks (but very busy on wkdy lunchtimes). A landmark on Haymarket is one of the two branches of Burberrys the mac makers (the other's in Regent St).

Funland A surprise to find in the centre of London, and quite unexpected behind the preserved façade of the vast Trocadero building, this mammoth recently refurbished attraction is filled with state-of-the-art rides and games (as well as a cinema and 10-pin bowling alley). The myriad flashing and bleeping attractions all have individual charges.

Royal Academy of Arts (Burlington House, Piccadilly) Splendid building with excellent changing exhibitions for most of the year (such as *Aztecs* Nov–11 Apr 2003, the biggest show on them ever put together anywhere), then from early Jun to mid-Aug its famous (often notorious) Summer Exhibition. Meals, snacks, shop, disabled access; cl 24–25 Dec; (020) 7300 8000; admission charge varies – usually between £5 and £10. The £3 million transformation of the grand courtyard has made it an attractive setting for exhibitions of contemporary sculpture.

TOTTENHAM COURT ROAD ⊖
Soho Often heady mix of the tawdry and the fashionable, its coffee bars and cafés swarming with colourful young people in the evenings. Many of Soho's Georgian terraces are rather run-down, with peepshows and naughty video shops stuffed into basements and ground floors. But there are parts that have had much of their original quiet charm restored, like Soho Sq and Meard St, and it's still good for restaurants, and for shops connected with food or cooking. Old Compton St, central London's gayest street, has a good few interesting shops – Italian delicatessens (I Camisa is the best, with fabulous salamis), the Algerian Coffee Stores which also sells lots of fruit teas, and two cheap but good wines and spirits shops. Milroys in Greek St has a wonderful collection of hundreds of different malt whiskies. Berwick St still has a daily fruit and veg market, though it's being invaded by other stalls now; at Simply Sausages down here you can watch them making some of their 43 different varieties of sausage, which include vegetarian and seafood flavours. The little Dog & Duck in Frith St and Coach & Horses in Poland St (the *Private Eye* pub) are two of the nicest Soho locals; in Romilly St another Coach & Horses is also on the well known Soho characters' circuit, and Kettners, now part of the Pizza Express chain, is a very entertaining old building. The area as a whole forms a sort of square, with the tube stns at Leicester Sq, Piccadilly Circus, Tottenham Court Rd and even Oxford Circus all just as handy.

Westminster

This centre of court and government is a pleasant area to walk around, much of it with only light traffic, and with few shops to add extra people to the wide pavements. Westminster Abbey and Buckingham Palace are divided by St James's Park – a fine walk between the two. A tour of the Houses of Parliament during the summer recess is most rewarding, and the Tate Gallery (under its current alias Tate Britain) and Westminster Cathedral are other highlights. The Cabinet War Rooms and the Queen's Gallery are worth seeking out.

To see and do

GREEN PARK ⊖

The park itself is the smallest of the parks in Central London. It's not a formal garden but, watered by the Tyburn stream which runs below the park, stays genuinely green even in hot summers when London's other grassy spaces are dry and dusty. It's a short stroll to **Shepherd Market**, a colourful place where Mayfair lets its hair down, no longer a market but busy with cafés, good wine bars and a nice pub (the Grapes), and little lanes to wander down.

Clubland The area around St James's St and Pall Mall seems to have more gentlemen's clubs than anything else, but there is a good number of interesting upmarket **shops** too: hand-made shoes at Lobb's, hats at Lock's, fishing equipment at Hardy's, several cigar shops, and fine wines at Berry's, or Berry Bros & Rudd to give it its full name. This last is the only shop in London still to look both inside and out just as it did in the early 19th c (though they now have two more modern side rooms), and they are very helpful even if you want just one humble bottle. On Pall Mall Farlow's new country sports and expeditions outfitting megastore opens in spring 2003. Christie's auction galleries are on King St (the friendly Red Lion off here in Crown Passage is useful for a snack), and there are some other top-of-the-market antiques and book shops nearby, especially up Duke St.

Spencer House (St James's Pl) Overlooking Green Park, this gleaming townhouse was built for the first Earl Spencer in the mid-18th c. Its sumptuous rooms, restored to their full glory, were among the first neo-classical interiors in Europe. The garden, replanted with flowers and shrubs appropriate to the late 18th and early 19th c, is open on some days in spring and summer. Disabled access; house open for guided tours every Sun (exc Jan and Aug); (020) 7499 8620; *£6.

St James's Palace Though comparatively domestic-looking, this is exceptionally harmonious and carries a real feel of Old London. It's not open to the public (its apartments are used by members of the Royal Family and their officials) but is well worth strolling past. If you stand on the Friary Court, Marlborough Road side of the palace you can see the guardsmen leaving here at 11.05am to go to Buckingham Palace, and coming back at around 11.40pm.

PIMLICO ⊖

Tate Britain (Millbank and Atterbury St) Designed in classical style to house the collection of Sir Henry Tate, this building which we all still think of as the Tate Gallery houses the world's greatest collection of British art, marking its rise and fall from the Tudors to the Turner Prize, by way of Constable, Rossetti and Epstein to name but a few. A new wing has increased the display area by about a third, and the end of a rather controversial experiment galleries are again organised chronologically, rather than by theme. Rooms are devoted to artists such as Gainsborough, Hogarth, Sickert and Hockney, and more are given over to the art collected for the nation by the Tate in the late 20th c. Decent changing exhibitions, and a good hi-tech audio guide; the gardens have been redesigned to include sculpture courts. Two shops, disabled access through the new Manton entrance in Atterbury St; cl 24–26 Dec; (020) 7887 8000; free (exc for special exhibitions). A new river pier will open outside here sometime in 2003 allowing visitors to hop down the river to Tate Modern. Though the Tate Gallery restaurant is a particularly good one (with a witty mural by Rex Whistler), you might find the Morpeth Arms nearby useful, with its views of the glossy MI6 ziggurat across the river.

ST JAMES'S PARK ⊖

This is the best approach to the palace (you can get there more quickly, though less attractively, from Victoria). The oldest of London's Royal Parks, it was drained and converted into a deer park for Henry VIII, redesigned in the style of Versailles by order of Charles II (who often went for walks through it), and then reworked by Nash for George IV – this is the park which we see today, its relaxing lakeside environment particularly enjoyed by lunch-breaking office workers (and by hundreds of more or less exotic waterfowl), with a brass band in summer. It's beautifully floodlit at night, and on Sun traffic is barred from its roads. **The Mall** Running all the way along the top of the park, this 1,040-metre (⅔m) long ceremonial route was laid out from 1660 for Charles II, between the palace and the magnificent Admiralty Arch. Along it, as well as various grand buildings and government departments, are a couple of good contemporary art galleries, with various changing exhibitions at the **Mall Galleries** ((020) 7930 6844 for exhibition info; free to around £2.50), and a wonderfully informal little restaurant and bar at the ICA, which with exhibitions and cinemas too is an excellent place to spend several hours (cl am; (020) 7930 0493; £1.50 day membership, £2.50 at the wknd).

Buckingham Palace A marvellous position, surrounded by Royal Parks and looking commandingly along the stately Mall towards Admiralty Arch. At the grand front palace gates the guards still keep their unflinchingly solemn positions: you can watch the **changing of the guard** every day Apr–July (every other day in winter) at 11.30am; the ceremony may be late or even cancelled in exceptionally wet weather. **Buckingham Palace tour** Now firmly established as one of London's most visited attractions, usually drawing around 400,000 visitors in the eight weeks it's open. The main appeal is that this is where the Queen actually lives – her official London residence, and where she meets other Heads of State; the Royal Standard flies above it when she's home. But beyond that, while perhaps not the most satisfying of the Royal palaces, it does pile a magnificent series of opulent sights into your walk through the state rooms. Highlights include the beautiful Picture Gallery, 46 metres (150 ft) long and filled with paintings from the Royal Collection, the spectacular Grand Staircase, and the throne room with its

predominant impression of gold, red and splendour. Tours are unguided, and there aren't many clues to help you, so it's definitely worth buying the guide book. Theoretically you see everything at your own pace, but in practice you're likely to be carried along in the stream of other people, and you won't get much of a chance to linger. You leave the palace with a short walk through a section of the 42-acre gardens, with a good view of the Garden Front of the Palace and the 19th-c lake. Tickets are sold from an office opposite the palace by the entrance to Green Park, though it's advisable to book a day or two in advance, on (020) 7321 2233. Shop, disabled access (with notice); open early Aug–Sept; £11.50.

Guards Museum (Wellington Barracks, Birdcage Walk) Military ephemera spanning 350 years of Grenadier, Coldstream, Scots, Irish, and Welsh Guards regimental history. Shop with large collection of antique and modern toy soldiers, disabled access by prior arrangement; cl Christmas–Jan; (020) 7414 3271; £2.

Queen's Gallery (Buckingham Palace Rd) Recently redeveloped, and reopened by the Queen in May 2002, this former palace chapel is dedicated to changing exhibitions of items from the Royal Collection: perhaps paintings, prints, drawings and watercolours, furniture, porcelain, miniatures, enamels and jewellery. Disabled access (booking advised); cl 25–26 Dec; (020) 7321 2233; £6.50.

Royal Mews (Buckingham Palace Rd) Contains the State Coaches, private driving carriages and even sleighs of the Royal Family, as well as the immaculately turned out carriage horses. The longest painting in the Royal collection is here too, a 36-metre (120-ft) canvas depicting William IV's Coronation procession. Shop, disabled access; cl Oct–Mar; (020) 7321 2233; £5.

VICTORIA ⊖ ≷

RHS Lindley Library (80 Vincent Sq) The finest horticultural library in the world, as well as around 50,000 books (ranging from a 1514 edition of Pliny the Elder's *Historia Naturalis* to contemporary gardening manuals), it also provides a home for 21,000 paintings and drawings of plants, 1,500 periodicals, and a computer archive with access to 70,000 works; also drawings and exhibition room, darkroom, and good disabled access. Cl wknds and bank hols; (020) 7821 3050; free. The RHS hold regular flower shows filled with beautifully arranged displays by specialist nurserymen; (020) 7649 1885 for information; admission charge.

Westminster Cathedral (just off Victoria St) Completed in 1903, the red-brick Roman Catholic building is an astonishing structure, very un-English, with handsome mosaics and marble work in its richly ornamental interior. At night its black ceiling seems almost to disappear in the darkness. Its Byzantine splendour is welcome relief from the glassy governmental cliffs of Victoria St, and its tall tower gives great views over central London, and across to the London Eye (lift; £2); donations.

WESTMINSTER ⊖

Banqueting House (Whitehall) The only surviving part of the Palace of Whitehall, designed by Inigo Jones and built in 1619; it was a Royal residence until late that century. Charles I was executed here, and it was also the site of his son's restoration. The severely classical hall is pretty much all there is to see, but an entertaining audio tour and good audio-visual exhibition keep your interest for quite some time. The highlight is the wonderful ceiling painted by Rubens, commissioned by Charles I to glorify the Stuart monarchy. They've put mirrored tables underneath, so you can study the detail without straining your neck; don't lean on these though – they're on wheels and liable to speed off like errant supermarket trolleys. Shop; cl Sun, 22 Dec–2 Jan; (020) 7839 7569; £4. The partly 13th-c Silver Cross is an interesting old pub, the huge and very ornate Lord Moon of the Mall another useful refuge.

Cabinet War Rooms (King Charles St, just off Whitehall) An intriguing series of 21 rooms built to provide Sir Winston Churchill, the War Cabinet and his Chiefs of Staff with a safe place from which to plan their strategies during World War II. The Cabinet Room, Map Room and Prime Minister's Room were preserved intact from the end of the war, and the other rooms have been authentically restored since. Quite basic, they're very evocative, with sound-effects adding to the atmosphere. A museum dedicated to Churchill's life will open here in 2005. Shop, disabled access; cl 24–26 Dec; (020) 7930 6961; *£5.80, children free.

Cenotaph (Whitehall) Designed by Lutyens, this is a sombre reminder of last century's two World Wars, standing indomitably in the centre of the road. Initially it was planned as a temporary symbol, but strong public feeling led to the original wooden structure being replaced by the permanent stone version you see today.

Downing St Famous as the residence of the Prime Minister at No 10 and the Chancellor of the Exchequer at No 11 (the current incumbents have swapped to give Mr Blair and family more space). For long those were the street's only numbers, but a No 12 has recently emerged, housing more ministers. You can't get past the gates, but you can at least have a passing look at its surprisingly modest buildings.

Houses of Parliament Across the road from St Margaret's church, these buildings are now of course the main seat of British government, but until Henry VIII moved to Whitehall Palace in 1529, the site was the main residence of the monarch – when they answer the phone today they still call it the Palace of Westminster. The present 19th-c building was designed by Charles Barry, though the 'gothick' detail which has given so much life to what would otherwise be rather a tiresomely deadpan classical façade is by Pugin. One end of the extraordinary 286-metre (940-ft) structure finishes in a lofty Victorian tower (which flies the Union Jack when Parliament is in session), and the other in the clock tower which contains **Big Ben**, the 3½-ton bell whose sonorous hourly rings are one of the best-known sounds in the world. Inside, over two miles of passages link the central hall and two chambers – the Houses of Lords and Commons to the N and S of the building respectively. The Commons sits from 2.30pm Mon–Weds, all day from 11.30am–7.30pm Thurs, and 9.30am–2pm some Fri; to watch the antics from the Strangers' Galleries, you'll need to queue by St Stephen's Gate (on the left for the Commons, right for the Lords – rather appropriate in a way) – or arrange it first with your MP. A letter from your MP can also give access to what's called the Line of Route, going through both Houses and the Members' Lobby and Divisions Lobby, to Westminster Hall, from 1224 to 1882 the chief law court of the country. It witnessed such trials as those of Sir Thomas More and Charles I, and organising admission is worth the trouble even just to admire the magnificent hammer-beam roof, the earliest surviving example of its kind; alternatively you can book yourself in for a good (if rather hurried) guided tour during the summer recess, early Aug to late Sept. There are proposals to change the sitting hours radically, so check before you visit; (0870) 906 3773; £7.50. The Westminster Arms in Storeys Gate across the square is a good pub, and you're likely to see politicians in the imposing Albert up Victoria St.

Jewel Tower (Parliament Sq) Opposite the statue of Oliver Cromwell (whose attitude towards Parliaments when he was Lord Protector was not unlike that of Charles I – they were more trouble than they were worth), this 14th-c building has an exhibition on Parliament's history. It was originally a huge treasure chest for Edward III. Shop, cl 24–26 Dec, 1 Jan; (020) 7222 2219; £1.60; EH.

Mounting the Guard (Whitehall) A survival of the kind of Royal pageantry which once filled this area can be seen in this daily ceremony at Horse Guards Parade, 11am Mon–Sat and 10am Sun.

St Margaret's church (Parliament Sq) The official church of the House of Commons, worth a look particularly for its exceptional 16th-c Dutch stained glass; Sir Walter Raleigh is buried here.

Westminster Abbey Surely one of the most impressive pieces of architecture to survive from the Middle Ages: Edward the Confessor transformed it into the crowning place of English kings, and his body now lies in the great shrine of the present building, erected in the 13th c on the site of his original. Pretty much every king and queen up to George II is buried here; Henry VII's chapel is particularly impressive, and there are splendid tombs erected by James I for his mother Mary Queen of Scots, and his predecessor Elizabeth I, under whose orders Mary had been executed. Perhaps it's in revenge for this that Elizabeth was lumped in with her sister Mary I, with whom she never got on. The loosely named Poets' Corner takes in a wide range of cultural figures. There's a small medieval garden in the charming tranquil cloisters. Snacks, shop, disabled access, cl 25 Dec and Good Fri, and Sun (exc for services); £6; audio tour £2. If you like history the **museum** in the Norman undercroft shouldn't be missed – it has effigies of many ancestors of the Royal Family made from their death masks, and often wearing their own clothes; (020) 7654 4889; £2.50 (which also includes entry to the Chapter House and Pyx Chamber).

Westminster Central Hall This Edwardian building functions as a Methodist church and is also one of London's premier meeting places (the first United Nations Assembly was held here in 1946). The impressive Great Hall has a magnificent organ (free recital afternoons on the first Sun of each month), and the views from the Dome roof are terrific. Just turn up at the Visitor Services reception desk for a free guided tour; (020) 7222 8010.

Knightsbridge, Chelsea & Kensington

The three great South Kensington museums – all free now – have something for everyone, from the visually spectacular collections of the Victoria & Albert to the outstanding Natural History and Science Museums, both excellent for children. There's grandeur in Kensington Palace, the less-visited but free Leighton House, and across Hyde Park the magnificent Apsley House. Wellington Arch gives a different perspective on central London, and down towards the Thames, the free National Army Museum and the nearby Chelsea Physic Garden are both rather special. A placid grid of clean-cut, subdued Georgian terraced houses contrasts with the ostentatious bustle of the King's Rd in the S and the hubbub of the Portobello Rd market in the N.

To see and do

FULHAM BROADWAY ⊖
The best tube station for the clutch of good value **antiques shops** towards the bottom end of Fulham Rd. You can quickly cut through to the interesting series of more specialised shops on the New King's Rd, some of which yield unexpected treasures: lovely old clocks, imposing model ships, garden furniture, and ornaments going back to the 16th c. Two shops specialise expensively but magnificently in mirrors, and there's also Christopher Wray's enormous lighting shop which largely fuelled the vogue in faux Tiffany lamps and has almost any sort of lamp fitting you could possibly want. In the opposite direction is the unfrequented, rather melancholy tranquillity of the somewhat overgrown **Brompton Cemetery**.
Chelsea Harbour (Lots Rd) This modern development includes a striking modern covered mall (mainly luxurious soft furnishings specialists), with popular Deals Restaurant, the stylish Canteen, the smart but relaxed Matts café, and an adjacent marina. Children like the glass-sided lifts which swoop up into the big dome, and on Sun pms they often have jazz by the marina.
Chelsea World of Sport (Fulham Rd) Best if you're in a group, and

especially absorbing for young boys; sports enthusiasts will enjoy testing their skills on the 30 different challenges at this new attraction, and there's also a display on Chelsea Football Club. Meals, snacks, shop, disabled access; cl 25 Dec; (020) 7915 2222; £12.50, £10 if you book in advance.
HIGH ST KENSINGTON ⊖
Albert Memorial (Kensington Gardens) Restored to its former glory, a gleaming golden monument to Queen Victoria's beloved husband: intricate mosaics, classic high Victoriana, marvellously grand.
Holland Park One of London's lesser-known open spaces, a wooded park with peacocks, summer open-air theatre and airy restaurant.
Kensington Gardens Surrounding the palace, and well worth a wander, though less lush than neighbouring Hyde Park. There's a toy boats lake, playground, a fetching statue of Peter Pan, and a tree trunk carved with all sorts of little painted animals. On a sunny day you could be forgiven for thinking you'd stumbled on a beach club, as the grass is covered with prone bodies soaking up the sun.
Kensington Palace State Apartments (Kensington Gardens) Once-humble townhouse remodelled

by Sir Christopher Wren and then enlarged by William Kent, the birthplace of Queen Victoria, and principal private Royal residence until the death of George II. Princess Margaret and Princess Diana lived here, and it's still the home of Prince and Princess Michael of Kent. The state rooms are quite magnificent, with elaborate furnishings and decor, while other rooms are interesting for their comparatively restrained understatement and personal history. Make sure you look up at the ceilings: some are exquisitely painted, inc an effective trompe-l'oeil dome (a couple of the patterns transfer very nicely to stationery in the gift shop). There are pictures and furniture from the Royal collection, and this is home to the Royal Ceremonial Dress Collection, with items of Royal, ceremonial and court dress dating from the 18th c to today, inc a display of the Queen's dresses and Diana's evening gowns. There's a small formal sunken garden. Café in imposing Orangery, shop, disabled access to the dress collection only; cl 24–26 Dec; (020) 7937 9561; £10.

Kensington shops This is a good area for shopping, especially if you consider yourself young and fashionable. An unusual haven from the crowds is the **Roof Gardens** above BHS on the High St; these extraordinary gardens are often closed for private functions, so you'll need to check first on (020) 7937 7994; free. Their restaurant (open Thurs and Sat evenings) does very good food. Good food pubs in this area include the Windsor Castle (Campden Hill Rd; excellent courtyard garden) and (a walk up Kensington Church St, which has some interesting antique shops) the Churchill Arms – surprisingly good Thai food.

Leighton House (12 Holland Park Rd) This splendid 19th-c house is a uniquely opulent monument to High Victorian Art, its lavish decor and collections created by Lord Leighton, former President of the Royal Academy. The centrepiece Arab Hall has a fountain and an almost dazzling assemblage of Islamic tiles, and there's a fine collection of paintings by Millais, Burne-Jones, and Leighton himself. Shop; cl Tues, 25–26

Dec and 1 Jan; (020) 7602 3316; free.
Serpentine Gallery (Kensington Gardens) Often has some of London's most interesting exhibitions, concentrating on challenging modern and contemporary art, and younger artists. Bookshop; (020) 7402 6075 for programme; cl Christmas and New Year; free.

HYDE PARK CORNER ⊖
Apsley House The Duke of Wellington's elegant former home, designed by Robert Adam. It was known as Number One London, as it was the first house past a toll gate into London at the top of Knightsbridge. The magnificent building has been painstakingly restored; everything gleams and looks as good as new, and works by Correggio, Rubens and Velazquez, as well as outstanding silver and porcelain amassed by Wellington as gifts from grateful kings and emperors, are back in their original positions (not always to their best advantage). Sumptuous furnishings, decor and sculpture – inc a statue of Napoleon by Canova that has him looking quite different from the usual image. Shop, limited disabled access; cl Mon (exc bank hols), 24–26 Dec, 1 Jan, Good Fri, May Day bank hol; (020) 7499 5676; £4.50 inc audio guide.

Hyde Park These 340 acres used to be a Royal hunting park, and in 1851 were the site of the Great Exhibition. Now very much a city park, complete with cycle lanes, roller-bladers, summer sun-bathing and Serpentine boating lake: you can hire boats, or even swim in parts, and a water-feature memorial nearby to Diana Princess of Wales, possibly allowing paddling in its moat, is scheduled for completion in the next year. At the park's bottom corner is the relentless torrent of traffic around Hyde Park Corner; the subway can bring you up near the entertaining neo-baroque gates erected in honour of the late Queen Mother.

Wellington Arch Last occupied some 30 years ago as a police station, Decimus Burton's magnificent triumphal arch, somewhat stranded in the whirl of traffic around Hyde Park Corner, has been lavishly restored by English Heritage. You can walk through three floors of galleries (displays on the arch and other statues and monuments cared for by English Heritage) to the roof, for unusual views of Green Park and Hyde Park, or even to watch the mounted horse guards who pass through its columns daily at 10.30 and 11.30 (10.30 only on Sun). They kindly provide umbrellas if it's raining. Shop, disabled access; cl Mon (exc bank hols), Tues, 24–26 Dec, 1 Jan; (020) 7930 2726; £2.50.

KNIGHTSBRIDGE ⊖

Harrods (Knightsbridge) A wonderful place to browse, and has most things anyone could want – there's even a personal shopper available to help you choose. But it's the food halls that visitors to London really enjoy; they're divided into fruit and vegetables, an interesting delicatessen, grocery, meat, poultry, fish (the display of fresh fish at the end of the room is legendary), bread and cakes, flowers, and wines – and the downstairs pantry is not as expensive as you might think.

Sloane St Headed by Harvey Nichols, a long-standing fashion store now split into numerous famous-brand boutiques; its 5th-floor food store is superb, alongside a very good bar/restaurant. The street stretching down from here has had something of a renaissance recently, with international designers jostling to open very expensive new stores. In the handsome terraces beyond Sloane St can be found the charming Grenadier (Wilton Row; no food in the bar, but a snug little restaurant) and the surprisingly countryish Nags Head (Kinnerton St).

NOTTING HILL GATE ⊖

Portobello Rd Famous for its market – fruit and veg during the week, antiques and everything else on Sat from 5.30am, with most dealers there by 8am; with well over a thousand dealers you can still pick up a bargain. The quality and prices are higher at the Notting Hill end; it's more bric-a-brac as you get towards Ladbroke Grove. The Pelican in nearby All Saints Rd has good organic food.

SLOANE SQUARE ⊖

The heart of Chelsea, with Peter Jones, the mecca of the Sloanes, on the square itself (a sister department store of John Lewis, it's good value for money), and stylish kitchenware at David Mellor opposite. Just around the corner, the Antelope in Eaton Terrace is a useful lunch stop. King's Rd leading off the square used to be a mecca of trendiness in the 60s and 70s, but is now really just another shopping street. The bottom end of Sloane St has two interesting though expensive shops: Partridges, a fancy food shop, and the General Trading Company, with a fine collection of oddities, besides good-looking houseware, soft furnishings, antiques, glass and so forth.

Carlyle's House (Cheyne Row) The home of the writer from 1834 till his death, with lots of letters and personal possessions, and an early piano played by Chopin. There's a charming little Victorian walled garden. Cl am, also Mon (exc bank hols), Tues, Good Fri and Nov–Mar; (020) 7352 7087; £3.60; NT. The nearby Kings Head & Eight Bells, across a green and a busy road from the Thames, is almost villagey, with elegant Chelsea Old Church at the far end of the green. The grandiose 'Tudor' mansion facing the river here is in fact largely brand new.

Chelsea Physic Garden (Royal Hospital Rd) A real haven of peace, this was started in 1673 to study the plants used in medicine by the Society of Apothecaries. It's still used for botanical and medicinal research (there's a unique garden of medicinal plants), but is also full of lovely and unusual plants which thrive here in Thames-side London's warm micro-climate. Snacks, shop (inc rare plants grown here), disabled access; open pm Weds and Sun Apr–Oct, for the Chelsea Flower Show, and occasional other days; (020) 7352 5646; £4. The Coopers Arms in nearby Flood St has good food.

National Army Museum (Royal Hospital Rd) Surprisingly little visited but well and honestly presented – the history of the men of the British, Indian and colonial armies from the Battle of Agincourt to the present day, told with photographs, models, uniforms, prints and other mementoes inc the skeleton of Napoleon's horse and a lamp used by Florence Nightingale. Interactive exhibits test your map reading and rank recognition, there's an astonishingly detailed 70,000-man model of the Battle of Waterloo, and an interesting exhibition about the army of today. Portraits by Gainsborough and Reynolds, and the collections of the former Museum of the Women's Royal Army Corps. Snacks, shop, disabled access; cl 24–26 Dec, 1 Jan, Good Fri, May Day; (020) 7730 0717; free.

Pimlico Rd An interesting collection of antiques and other small shops (and Peter's Restaurant, a very good value all-day Italian-run café which has been a taxi-drivers' haunt for well over 30 years).

Royal Hospital (Royal Hospital Rd) Christopher Wren's most glorious secular building, which still houses over 400 Chelsea Pensioners. Disabled access; cl noon–2 pm, Sun am (though you can go to the full dress service in the Chapel at 11 am on Sun); (020) 7730 0161; free. The adjacent spacious Ranelagh Gardens are the site of the Chelsea Flower Show in May.

SOUTH KENSINGTON ⊖

Brompton Oratory (Brompton Rd) Roman Catholic, and heavily magnificent – sombre despite the pallor of its marble. The Swag & Tails round the corner in Fairholt St has good sensibly priced food.

Holy Trinity Brompton London's most fashionable church, at the forefront of evangelical Anglicanism. Its gardens lead you into a very peaceful corner of residential London, with a decent pub in Ennismore Mews (the Ennismore Arms, which does Sun lunches).

Natural History Museum (Cromwell Rd) One of the most appealing places for families in the capital, constantly updating or adding attractions, and with displays that could keep most visitors enthralled for a week. Picking out highlights of this wonderful place isn't easy. There's an entire gallery devoted to dinosaurs, with lots of touch-screen activities and information and the popular life-like replica robotic *Tyrannosaurus rex*. More gently evocative are the complete skeletons in the museum's main hall, a grand and noble sight below the intricately painted ceilings of the remarkable Romanesque building. The creepy-crawlies are another good bet: you can get a taste on their website (www.nhm.ac.uk), which every few seconds displays fresh images from their ant colony. The Earth Galleries are worth putting near the top of your list; there's an earthquake simulator, and you can see where real earthquakes have occurred in the last few days. An extensive new wing of the museum, the Darwin Centre, offers an interactive look at the museum's collection, with scientists at work, regular presentations by scientists, and live video link-ups to laboratories round the world, as well as displaying zoological exhibits (some packed away for over 100 years) from such famous expeditions as those of the *Beagle* and *Endeavour*, and from contemporary expeditions. Until May 2003 *Dino-Birds* explores feathered dinosaurs found in China (thought to link dinosaurs and birds as we know them); £5, and a terrific wildlife photography exhibition also runs till then. Remember to pick up one of the maps and guides as you go in, as it's a vast place, covering four acres. Meals, snacks, shops (one is dinosaur-themed), disabled access; cl 25–26 Dec; 020 7942 5000; free.

Royal Albert Hall (Kensington Gore) The home of the summer Promenade Concerts and many other concerts throughout the year; completed in 1871, this huge oval arena was built in honour of Prince Albert. Below its massive metal and glass dome a terracotta frieze shows Man's progress in arts and sciences down the ages. Before modern technology (in the form of giant suspended mushrooms) got to grips with its acoustics, the hall used to be famous for its echo – it was said that this was the only hall where you could hear the works of modern composers twice. Late 2003 should see the end of an eight-year £66.3m development programme; improvements include restoration of the building inside and outside, relandscaping of the gardens, creation of a new South Porch, and better pedestrian and disabled access.

Science Museum (Exhibition Rd) Amazing museum, with its splendid Wellcome Wing devoted entirely to contemporary science, medicine and technology. Other galleries look at subjects such as genetics, the internet and the future role of science, and *Grossology* gives children a graphic exploration of all the yucky bodily functions they seem to enjoy; there's also an IMAX cinema (£6.95). The area has been designed to hold fast-changing, interactive exhibitions with plenty of hands-on displays, workshops and demonstrations, and a multi-sensory activity area aimed at under-8s (but parents seem to love it too). Elsewhere in the museum, exhibits range from Stephenson's *Rocket* to the Apollo 10 space capsule, and there are newly landscaped gardens outside. They hold various special events, such as all-night camp-ins which enthral children 8–11 (£25 inc science shows, treasure hunts, workshops and breakfast – bring a snack and a sleeping bag). Meals, snacks, shop, disabled access; cl 24–26 Dec; 0870 870 4868; free (visitor numbers have nearly doubled since they dropped the admission charge).

Victoria & Albert Museum (Cromwell Rd) Britain's national museum of applied and decorative arts has one of the finest collections in the world; it was founded in 1852 by Prince Albert, and houses all manner of decorative arts, from all ages and countries. Visitor numbers have soared, much more than doubling since the recent dropping of the admission charge. The galleries run to over seven miles, inc a spectacular glass gallery (with touch-screen computer displays), a dazzling silver gallery, and the world's greatest collection of Constables. The magnificent new British Galleries display art and design from the Tudor age to the Victorian era, featuring designers from Chippendale to Adams to Morris and Mackintosh. The galleries combine modern displays, five restored period rooms and interactive technology. Highlights include James II's wedding suit, Canova's *Three Graces*, and the 5-metre (17-ft) high Melville Bed. The biggest-ever art deco exhibition (including a huge complete restored hotel foyer) will run 27 Mar–20 July. Meals, snacks, shop, disabled access; cl 24–26 Dec, late night opening Weds and last Fri of the month; (020) 7942 2000; free, charge for some exhibitions.

The City & East End

The City's most typical financial buildings are mainly Victorian and Edwardian, and its landmark churches are mostly elegant classical designs, but the ground-plan follows the narrow twisting streets and alleys of medieval times – though because of the Great Fire of 1666 only a handful of buildings are medieval or Tudor. Very few people actually live here: for each one that does, another 60 or 70 flood in each day to work here, then flood out again at night – when the area becomes virtually deserted, as it is at weekends. Originally, particular streets came to be associated with particular crafts and trades, and this is reflected in the street names – Carter Lane, Hosier Lane, Cloth Fair, Ropemaker St, Milk St, Silk St, Coopers Lane and so forth. The great City Livery Companies representing the various trades have effectively run local government in the City for 800 years or more, and it's only now that the franchise is being widened to allow more modern financial institutions a share in local government here. Many guilds have only a tenuous connection with the original crafts involved in their trades. But in Billingsgate Market, still controlled by the ancient Fishmongers Company, you can still see the fish trade being carried on in much the same way as ever (West India Dock Rd, early morning Tues–Sat). Though the halls of the City Livery Companies may have been rebuilt since they were first established in the Middle Ages, they still house some remarkable treasures. Some are open to visit, but only by prior arrangement: you'll have to book well ahead, through the City of London Information Centre, St Paul's Churchyard, EC4; (020) 7332 1456. Around splendid St Paul's and the Tower of London (a real winner with children), the layout is more open, and far less affected by the City's human tides. Excellent free museums include the Geffrye Museum, the Museum of Childhood, the Ragged School Museum, and the exhaustive Museum of London. 18 Folgate St makes for a most unusual guided tour and, due to open in spring, there's a new museum on the history of the docklands. Two of the river's most striking monuments, Tower Bridge and much further downstream the Thames Flood Barrier, both have enjoyable visitor centres. The liveliest glimpse of East End life nowadays is to be had on Sunday mornings in Brick Lane market.

To see and do

ALDGATE EAST ⊖
Brick Lane market London's biggest and most lively street market, a riot of colour, smells and sound, inc some very entertaining market patter. There are plenty of bargains for early risers (and things to avoid – we've even seen someone specialising in second-hand felt-tip pens). The community is largely Asian, so much of the food and other wares are quite exotic; Sun 5am–2pm. Once the haunt of Jack the Ripper, Whitechapel, the area around here, is still one of London's poorest areas.
Columbia St market Entirely devoted to garden and house plants, has bargains as it closes around 1pm on Sun.

BANK ⊖
Some of the City's finest buildings are around here, though with most you'll have to content yourself with looking at just the outside. Besides the Bank of England itself, handsome or interesting buildings include the neo-classical Custom House on Lower Thames St, Lloyds of London on Lime St, and the Renaissance-style Royal Exchange on Cornhill, with several proud columns in front.
Bank of England Museum (Bartholomew Lane) This neo-classical fortress does still contain oodles of gold – and you can handle a real gold bar in the small but interesting **museum**, which shows how computerised currency speculators work and lets you try your hand at being a dealer. Shop, disabled access with prior notice; cl wknds and bank hols; (0207) 601 5545; free.
Leadenhall market (Whittington Ave, off Gracechurch St) Victorian iron- and glass-covered market, vibrant with Cockney humour yet quite smart, and filled with seafood, game, fruit and veg; cl around 4pm and wknds. The Lamb's top-floor dining bar gives good views of the market activity.

BARBICAN ⊖
Could be called the north bank's equivalent to the South Bank Centre – certainly its aesthetic equal. This complex includes theatres, exhibition halls, galleries, and what some would say is the city's most comfortable cinema. There's often free entertainment in the foyers.
Museum of London (London Wall; Barbican tube station) No other city museum in the world is quite as comprehensive as this; anyone with just a passing interest in history will find it compelling. London's development is told through chronological reconstructions and period clothes, music and various remains, from a

medieval hen's egg to an early (and quite different) tube map – ever heard of the station called Post Office? The 18th-, 19th- and 20th-c sections have almost too much to take in. Excellent redeveloped galleries cover Roman London (the building adjoins a stretch of original Roman wall), remarkable research on a 14th-c Black Death cemetery near the Tower of London, the rich historical clues that have emerged from a Tudor rubbish dump, and now the World City gallery – London's history from the French Revolution through a reconstructed Victorian street to the outbreak of World War I. New for 2003, *London before London* takes you back to the days of Iron Age settlements and locally roaming elephants. Meals, snacks, shop, disabled access; cl Sun am, 24–26 Dec, 1 Jan; (020) 7600 0807; free.

BETHNAL GREEN ⊖
Museum of Childhood (Cambridge Heath Rd) This very special little museum houses the V&A's collection of toys, dolls, dolls' houses, games, puppets and children's costumes. Excellent programme of events and children's activities (most wknds and several school hols) – most completely free. Snacks, shop, disabled access; cl Fri, 24–26 Dec, 1 Jan; (020) 8980 2415; free.

DOCKLANDS ⊖
Once the heartland of Britain's trade-based Empire, these 8½ square miles have become the biggest redevelopment site in Europe, the old warehouses imaginatively converted into smart apartments and office blocks. 244-metre (800-ft) **Canary Wharf** is the great landmark; most of its floors are filled with offices, but there's now a busy covered shopping mall at ground level. A growing cluster of modern but contrasting towers around the central skyscraper is carefully set off by beautifully designed small public gardens, and the Thames-side walkways here have been enlivened by a swelling number of good café-bars and restaurants. Most parts of Docklands are reached and seen best by the **Docklands Light Railway**, which generally stays open even on Underground strike days; the best bit is

between West India Quay and Island Gardens, where you can get off and walk through the foot tunnel under the Thames to Greenwich. The Jubilee Line tube extension has brought with it some architecturally spectacular stations, the most eye-catching of which are Canary Wharf (designed by Sir Norman Foster) where you descend by escalator from the eyelid-like glass roof entrance to a vast naturally lit hall, and North Greenwich, with its roof cleverly complementing the adjacent Millennium Dome – now rather a pathetic landmark, as it stands abandoned, awaiting future redevelopment. Some docks have been brightly reworked and appeal to visitors: St Katharine's Dock (Tower Hill tube station is quite handy), which has a lively marina, a quite cheerful pastiche of a Victorian pub in the Dickens Inn, and lots going on, and Tobacco Dock, with an American-style factory shopping centre. Further E down the river is the gigantic closeable **Thames Flood Barrier**, built to protect the city from freak tides; a Visitor Centre on Unity Way, Woolwich SE18, has an exhibition on the construction of the barrier, a working scale model and a children's play area. Café, shop, disabled access; cl around 2 wks over Christmas and New Year; 020 8305 4188; £1.

Museum in Docklands Financial problems have obliged this new museum which is housed in a converted Georgian warehouse (once used to hold the West India Company's sugar, coffee and rum) at West India Quay to merge with the London Museum, and it's hoped it will open in February 2003. Twelve galleries (inc an interactive children's gallery) will document the area's history from Roman settlement, it's role as a hub of the colonial empire, to the closure of wharfs and dock systems between 1967–81 and its current regeneration; (020) 7001 9800.

FARRINGDON ⊖
Museum of the Order of St John (St John's Lane) Housed in a 16th-c gatehouse and 12th-c crypt, silver, paintings and furniture belonging to the medieval Order, and an interactive gallery covering its more modern

offshoot, the St John Ambulance. Shop, disabled access to ground floor; cl Sun, bank hol wknds; (020) 7324 4000; free, £5 donation requested for guided tours of the gatehouse and priory church on Tues, Fri and Sat at 11am and 2.30pm. The Eagle in Farringdon Rd/Bakers Row has outstanding food, and there's an excellent second-hand bookshop opposite the station.

St Bartholomew the Great church (West Smithfield) Mainly Norman, with a 16th-c gateway into the market precincts. Shop; cl Mon, pm Sat, lunchtime Sun; (0207) 606 5171; £3 donation. The nearby Bishops Finger is a pleasant retreat, and on wkdys you can get breakfast from 7.30 in the Butchers Hook & Cleaver – the name reminding that Smithfield is London's streamlined and updated wholesale meat market.

LIVERPOOL STREET ⊖ ⇄
18 Folgate St Guided tours of a quite remarkable house now named after the late Dennis Severs who made it such fun to visit – but be warned, this is no ordinary guided tour, and one far more suited to adults than children. It doesn't do the place justice to say that it's been furnished and decorated in period style – to all intents and purposes you are back in the 18th c, with candles and firelight flickering away, food and drink laid out on the table, even urine in the chamber-pots. Open 2–5pm first and third Sun of month (£8) and noon–2pm on the Mon following the first and third Sun (£5); (020) 7247 4013. Elaborate candlelit tours Mon evening (booking required); £12. Dirty Dicks (Bishopsgate) re-creates a traditional City cellar tavern, also fun for visitors.

MILE END ⊖
Ragged School Museum (Copperfield Rd) This canalside warehouse was one of the many 'ragged' (or free) schools set up by Dr Barnado in Tower Hamlets in the late 19th c. Displays concentrate on the school's history (there's a re-created Victorian classroom), life in the East End in the 1890s, and the work of the great philanthropist himself. An exhibition takes a detailed look at the area's social history over the last 200

years or so, through the eyes of local people inc a former waiter, and an usherette from the People's Palace theatre. Snacks, shop, disabled access to ground floor exhibition only; open Weds, Thurs, and pm first Sun of month (cl Christmas and New Year); (020) 8980 6405; free.

MONUMENT ⊖
Monument (Monument St) A fluted Doric column designed by Wren and Hooke at an exact height of 202 ft (62 metres) to mark the spot where the Great Fire of London began in 1666 – in Pudding Lane 202 ft from its base. The city views from the top are tremendous, though there are 311 spiral steps up. The viewpoint was designed as a cage to prevent people jumping off. Cl 24–25 Dec; (020) 7626 2717; £1.50.

OLD STREET ⊖
Geffrye Museum (Kingsland Rd; Liverpool St/Old St tube station) One of London's most friendly and interesting museums, yet least-known; 18th-c almshouses converted to show the changing style of the English domestic interior. Displays go from lovely 17th-c oak panelling and furniture through elegant Georgian reconstructions and Victorian parlours to the latest in interior design inc a contemporary loft-style dwelling, though not all is as it seems – out of sight inside the shell of a vintage radio for example there's actually a distinctly modern CD player. They've given the gardens similar treatment, showing trends in domestic horticulture through the ages, inc a notable herb garden. Excellent programme of exhibitions, special events, talks and activities. Well worth tracking down. Meals, snacks, shop, disabled access; cl Sun am, all day Mon (exc pm bank hols), 24–26 Dec, 1 Jan, Good Fri; (020) 7739 9893; free.

John Wesley's House & Chapel (49 City Rd) The father of Methodism had his house and chapel built here in 1778, and they're still much as they were then, with plenty of his personal possessions. You can see Wesley's tomb in the chapel, and the crypt has a museum on the history of Methodism. Shop, disabled access to museum only;

cl bank hols, Thurs 12.45–1.15pm, and limited opening Sun (when services); (020) 7253 2262; donations. The nearby Fox (Paul St) has good interesting food.

ST PAUL'S ⊖

Guildhall (off Gresham St) 15th-c, where the Court of Common Council, over which the Lord Mayor presides, administers the City of London. The Lord Mayor's Banquet is held in the great hall, hung with the banners and shields of the City's 102 livery companies. Underneath is the largest 15th-c crypt in the City; there's also a clock museum, library with unrivalled collection of City-related manuscripts and books. Disabled access; cl Sun Oct–Apr, and for civic occasions, phone to check (020) 7606 3030; book for guided tours on (020) 733 21460; free. The striking new **Guildhall Art Gallery** on the east side of Guildhall Yard displays about 250 works of art ranging from Royal portraits through period views of historic London to contemporary works, and temporary exhibitions. In 1988, Museum of London archaeologists unearthed London's only **Roman amphitheatre**, under Guildhall Yard (a black line across the yard marks its shape). Through a complex process the remains have now been integrated with the structure of the new art gallery, with excavations taking place at the same time as construction. You can now enter the amphitheatre by the route taken by gladiators and wild animals, and light displays complete missing sections of the structure – quite a convincing jump back 2,000 years. Shop; cl Sun am, 25–26 Dec, 1 Jan; £2.50, free Fri. The nearby Red Herring has good lunchtime food.

St Anne & St Agnes church (Gresham St) Particularly worth knowing for the Bach cantatas that grace its Lutheran services (usually second Sun in month); (020) 7606 4986 for programme.

St Mary le Bow church (Cheapside) With the famous Bow Bells; often Thurs lunchtime concerts, and possibly interesting Tues dialogues (the rector in conversation with a distinguished guest); cl wknds, and for a week after Christmas and Easter; (020) 7248 5139.

Williamsons nearby (off Bow Lane), well rebuilt in Jacobean style after World War II bomb damage, has food all day (and ornate wrought iron gates supposedly presented by William and Mary when the Lord Mayor lodged here).

St Paul's Cathedral Despite the attempts of brasher, taller modern buildings to take over, and now the completion of the controversial Paternoster Square development just NE, this masterpiece still asserts itself proudly as the area's real landmark, its unmistakable shape repeatedly looming out above the streets. Its huge dome is a pleasing shape after the stolid self-satisfaction of the Victorian and Edwardian masonry which dominates this area. Originally the cathedral was Gothic in style, with a towering 150-metre (500-ft) spire. It fell into disrepair and Wren was assigned to work on its renovation. He didn't relish the job, and no doubt was delighted when the Great Fire of London swept the old church away, allowing him to construct something entirely new. His mainly classical design is unlike any other cathedral in Britain, and took just 35 years to build. The setting for various State occasions, it's full of interesting monuments – the one to John Donne was the only complete figure to be salvaged from the Great Fire. Look out for the wonderful carving on the exterior – some of which is by Grinling Gibbons, who also did the choir stalls. Other highlights include the dizzying Whispering Gallery, the panoramic views from the top, and the crypt, full of tombs and memorials to notable figures from British history. Snacks, shop, disabled access; cl Sun, Good Fri, 25 Dec and for occasional services; (020) 7236 4128; £6. The City Pipe by the tube station is an enjoyable weekday wine bar, and the heavy-beamed Olde Watling (Watling St) was knocked up by Wren as a commissariat for his site workers.

TOWER HILL ⊖

Tower Bridge Experience Inside the landmark bridge, with wonderful views from its glass-covered walkways, 43 metres (142 ft) above the Thames, displays explore the bridge's historic links with the Tower. Lively multi-media shows are designed to leave you feeling proud to be British. The bridge is unusual not just for its design, but because it's still fully operational, raising the roadway from each side drawbridge-style to allow ships to pass; you can see some of the Victorian machinery that used to power this. Shop, disabled access; cl 24–25 Dec; (020) 7403 3761; *£4.50. The Anchor Tap (Horselydown Lane, almost directly below the bridge) has simple low-priced food.

Tower of London Picturesque classic castle, the most notable building to survive the Great Fire of London. A lot of fun to look at even superficially, it dates back to the late 11th c, though the site had been used as a defensive position by the Romans much earlier. It's witnessed all sorts of gruesome goings-on, with not even the highest or mightiest safe from imprisonment or even execution: Walter Raleigh, Lady Jane Grey and two of Henry VIII's wives spent their last days in the Tower.

There's a mass of things to see, inc enough medieval weaponry and armour to glut the appetite of even the most bloodthirsty, and not forgetting the Beefeaters and the ravens – you need a fair bit of time to see everything properly. The Jewel House shows off the Crown Jewels to dazzling effect; on the busiest days those tempted to linger are gently drawn along by moving floorways. Two towers that were part of Edward I's medieval palace are furnished in period style, and peopled with appropriately costumed helpful guides; one room in this part has been left untouched to show what a difficult job the restoration was. A reorganisation of the oldest part, the White Tower, has revealed that the inside of the fortress when built was much less imposing than was suggested by the formidable exterior – they were clearly just trying to intimidate the locals. You can also walk along the elevated battlements. Meals, snacks, shop, some disabled access; cl 24–26 Dec, 1 Jan; (020) 7709 0765; £11.50.

Bloomsbury, Holborn & Regent's Park

The British Museum is the outstanding attraction in Bloomsbury and Holborn, a civilised if slightly faded area of Georgian squares, gardens and courts between the City and Westminster – legal and academic London. Much less well known, the Sir John Soane's Museum is not to be missed, nor are the excellent art collections at Somerset House with its fountain-filled courtyard. The vast modern British Library at King's Cross has some intriguing exhibits, too, and the London Canal Museum combines nicely with a boat trip up the Regent's Canal to Camden. Bloomsbury merges into a smarter area to the West, over towards Marylebone (inc Madame Tussaud's), with Regent's Park (and the Zoo) on its N border; away from the shopping streets of Marylebone High St and Baker St this is largely residential, and the capital of private medicine and dentistry – a very rich little enclave, as the preponderance of smart new cars makes clear. Bloomsbury does have a large number of hotels, especially for the more budget-conscious visitor, though many are on the tawdry side. Ones which can be recommended include the Academy (17 Gower St WC1E 6HG (020) 7631 4115), the Morgan (24 Bloomsbury St WC1B 3QJ (020) 7636 3735) – both handy for the British Museum – and the George (60 Cartwright Gardens WC1H 9EL (020) 7387 6789).

To see and do

BAKER STREET ⊖

London Planetarium (Marylebone Rd) This shows off one of the most advanced star projectors in the world, and surround-sound gives their enjoyable presentations an added sense of realism. Make sure you get to each show on time – stragglers barely have a moment to find a seat before the lights are dimmed. Interactive displays too – you can even see how much you'd weigh on another planet. Meals, snacks, shop, disabled access, cl 25 Dec; (0870) 400 3000; best to phone for prices, joint ticket with Madame Tussaud's available. Opposite, the café of St Marylebone church has good value simple vegetarian meals.

Madame Tussaud's (Marylebone Rd) Almost half of overseas visitors place this famous waxworks museum at the top of their list of things to do in London, which explains why the queues can be so long and slow-moving (it definitely makes sense to phone in advance for queue-avoiding timed tickets), and perhaps why German TV presenters and Japanese sumo wrestlers crop up among more familiar simulacrums. Some of the models are uncannily realistic (some talk, and even breathe), others rather less so. Highlights are the famous Chamber of Horrors, and the entertaining Spirit of London finale – you sit in a black cab and are whisked through a cheery interpretation of the city's history. This part is excellently put together, and in places rather witty, but is over a little quickly – like the waxworks as a whole. As you can be in and out of the museum in little over an hour, you're paying more per minute here than practically anywhere else in Britain. Meals, snacks, shop, disabled access; cl 25 Dec; (0870) 400 3000; ticket prices vary according to times and seasons so best to phone, joint ticket available with the Planetarium.

Sherlock Holmes Museum (221b Baker St) To many people the world over, Baker St calls to mind only one thing – Conan Doyle's great detective. This famous address has various Holmes paraphernalia (avid readers enjoy recognising objects mentioned in the stories), and something of the atmosphere of the books re-created in a replica apartment; also waxwork models of characters from the stories, and you can look through replica period newspapers. Shop; cl 25 Dec; (020) 7935 8866; £6. There's a giant bronze statue of the super-sleuth outside Baker St station, and you can easily imagine Holmes in disguise in one of the 19th-c cubicles of the nearby Barley Mow (Dorset St).

GOODGE STREET ⊖

Pollock's Toy Museum (1 Scala St) Housed in a rather charming setting, a wide range of playthings from all over the world and from all periods, almost as if lots of enthusiastic children had just left them scattered through these little rooms. Mechanical and optical toys, teddy bears, furniture, board games and theatres, and a proper toy shop downstairs. Shop; cl Sun and bank hols; (0207) 636 3452; £3.

HOLBORN ⊖

Legal London A perfect example of the tranquil architecture of this area, Lincoln's Inn Fields is a large open space with trees and lawns surrounded by handsome houses, also tennis courts and summer band concerts; it's a pleasant place to spend a summer afternoon. Nearby, the Gothic **Royal Courts of Justice** are impressive, and you can also stroll through the gardens of **Gray's Inn**, said to have been laid out by Francis Bacon around 1600. This area really is legal London, and you'll usually find a good number of lawyers in the splendid Cittie of Yorke (22 High Holborn), an enormous and very atmospheric basement pub with little private booths down one side. Another fine pub in this area is the classic Lamb in Lamb's Conduit St.

Sir John Soane's Museum (13 Lincoln's Inn Fields) One of London's hidden highlights, built by the architect for his splendid collection of pictures, books and antiquities. It's most eccentric, full of architectural tricks and mirrors, which form a complex natural-lighting system for the antiquities covering most of the walls. There's a lovely picture by Turner and an Egyptian sarcophagus, but the highlights are Hogarth's acid series on *The Rake's Progress* and *The Election*. When you've seen them the guide swings open the hinged 'walls' and further treasures emerge inc choice Piranesi drawings and a scale model of the Bank of England. At the back of the Picture Room is a monument to his dog ('Alas, poor Fanny!'); you ring the bell to get in, and sign a visitors' book. The guides are very friendly and helpful, and the guidebook worthwhile. Shop, phone for disabled access; cl Sun, Mon, bank hols and 24–26 Dec; open first Tues evening of every month; (020) 7405 2107; free (donations welcome). The breakfast room of Soane's first house, no 12 next door, can also be visited.

KING'S CROSS ⊖ ⇌

British Library (Euston Rd) This vast modern library has good exhibition space for its national treasures (which range from the Magna Carta to Beatles' manuscripts, and Jane Austen's writing desk), and changes its displays frequently, as well as mounting special exhibitions (one on the Lindisfarne Gospels will run mid-May to Sept); also guided tours, and a good programme of events. The entrance courtyard has a gigantic bronze of a crouching seated Sir Isaac Newton, by Paolozzi after William Blake, and impressive entrance gates. Cl 24–26 Dec, and 1 Jan; (020) 7412 7332; free. The Euston Flyer over the road has decent food.

London Canal Museum (12–13 New Wharf Rd) The history of London's canal network is told in this former ice warehouse, with displays about the people who strove to make a meagre livelihood by living and working on them, the horses which pulled their boats, and the cargoes they carried. You can peer down into a huge ice well, where winter ice was once stored into summer; temporary exhibitions. Book and gift shop, disabled access; cl Mon exc bank hols, plus a few days over Christmas and New Year; (020) 7713 0836; £2.50. The Waterside on the Battlebridge Basin (York Way) has food all day.

REGENT'S PARK ⊖

(Great Portland St or Regent's Park tube station) Covering over 400 acres, this is the culmination of a glorious swathe of Regency terraces designed by John Nash, which can be seen almost all around it; the buildings of Park Crescent are among the finest. The park was originally intended to be the setting for a palace for the Prince Regent, after whom it was named: now, besides plenty of paths to stroll along, it includes the lovely Queen Mary's Rose Garden, the spectacular Avenue Garden (restored to its 1864 glory), a boating lake, bandstand concerts on summer Suns, and an open-air theatre where Shakespeare and other plays are performed in the summer (phone to book; (020) 7486 2431).

London Zoo (Regent's Park or Camden Town tube station) There are lions, giraffes and so forth, and the monkeys and sloth bears which use the famous Mappin Terraces as a sort of animal playground, but it's with smaller creatures that the zoo currently excels. Highlights include the Web of Life, a live animal exhibition housed in a glass building with a ventilation system inspired by termites' nests. This shows how animals adapt to different environments, and how new species evolve; animals chosen to illustrate this include sea-horses, a swarm of locusts, and organisms not normally visible to the naked eye, viewed in a micrarium. At the irresistible children's zoo, you can get right up to the animals (and help feed the pigs), and they've the biggest reptile house of any UK zoo; at the spellbinding Moonlight World day and night are reversed so you can watch nocturnal creatures such as vampire bats. The 1930s architecture of the penguin pool remains quite something. Meals, snacks, shop, disabled access; cl 25 Dec; (020) 7722 3333; £11.

Primrose Hill Once part of the same hunting park as Regent's Park, now popular strolling ground for this sober residential area. The modest rounded summit gives eye-opening views of the city.

Regent's Canal The canal offers an excellent walk from Little Venice to Camden Lock, passing by Regent's Park and Primrose Hill; boat cruises also operate along here – one-way tickets available. Jason's is one of several companies who now run along the stretch of Regent's Canal between Little Venice and Camden Lock; (020) 7286 3428; £6.95 return. Another, the London Waterbus Company, make a stop for passengers who want to get off at the zoo; (020) 7482 2660 for timetable.

RUSSELL SQUARE ⊖

British Museum (Great Russell St) Monumental 19th-c building housing spectacular collections of priceless man-made objects from all over the world, some of them over 3,000 years old. The range is staggering; some of the many highlights are the Elgin Marbles (or Parthenon Sculptures as some now call them), the wonderful and intriguing Egyptian galleries, the comprehensive galleries of Greek vases, the oriental antiquities, the Amaravati sculpture, and fascinating collections of non-Western art and culture. Don't try to take it in all at once – decide what interests you most and stick to that, or your head will start reeling with the extent of this treasure-house before you've got even a tenth of the way through. Try to arrive early as it can get very busy. Readers are full of praise for the Foster-designed Great Court, the largest covered public square in Europe; an uplifting place, it's home to an ethnographic collection, as well as cafés, restaurants and lecture theatres. The famous Reading Room now has a public reference library giving visitors access to exhibits not on show. Meals, snacks, shop, disabled access; cl 24–26 Dec, 1 Jan, and Good Fri; (020) 7323 8000; free exc for special exhibitions, museum tours £8. Ironically the museum's determination to stay free when other national museums rushed to charge for entrance meant that it has not got the grants they got when the government abolished their entrance charges. An income shortfall has led to some job losses and partial closures, but should be eased by their 2002 sale for £40 million of a nearby site they had bought for just £7 million in 1995 (for a planned textile museum which never materialised). Just up Gower St, Dillons is a first-class serious bookshop, and in Museum St the Coffee Gallery is good

for a light lunch or patisserie, while the Museum Tavern has food all day.

Dickens House Museum 🏛 (48 Doughty St) Dickens lived here during his 20s, and during that period wrote the *Pickwick Papers*, *Oliver Twist* and *Nicholas Nickleby*. The drawing room has been reconstructed to appear as it was then, and there are pictures, personal possessions and original manuscripts and first editions (in 2002 three first editions of *A Christmas Carol* were stolen from here). His wife's sister died here in 1837, an event which the writer later used as the model for the death of Little Nell in *The Old Curiosity Shop*. Shop, some disabled access; cl 25–26 Dec and 1 Jan; (0171) 405 2127; £4. Round the corner in Roger St the Duke of York has good interesting modern food.

TEMPLE ⊖

Dr Johnson's House (17 Gough Sq) A perfect example of early 18th-c architecture, just as Dr Johnson himself was a perfect example of 18th-c barbed, slightly flawed gentility. Between 1749 and 1755 he wrote his great *English Dictionary* here, and there are various memorabilia from his learned life on show. Shop; cl Sun and bank hols; (020) 7353 3745; £4. The passages and walkways around here are a good reminder of how London's streets used to be laid out; the 17th-c Olde Cheshire Cheese nearby is a splendid old tavern.

Middle Temple Hall Of all the Inns of Court, this is perhaps the most impressive, and it boasts many famous literary figures among its former members. Most of the buildings date from after the reign of Elizabeth I or the Great Fire, but the name points to an older history: the land was owned by the Knights Templar from about 1160. The hall is a fine example of Tudor architecture, with a double hammer-beam roof and beautiful stained glass. There is a table made from timber from Sir Francis Drake's *Golden Hind* – he was a member of the Middle Temple – while a single oak tree from Windsor Forest supplied the wood for the 9-metre (29-ft) long High Table. Open 10–11.30am and 3–4pm wkdys (exc bank hols, Easter week, Whitsun week, Aug and 2 wks at Christmas); (020) 7427 4800;

free. The Temple has an unusual round church. Up on Fleet St, the Old Bank of England is a spectacular pub conversion. **Somerset House** (Strand; on Sun when Temple Station is closed, Charing Cross is not far) Built as government offices in the later years of the 18th c (on the site of an earlier spectacular Royal palace; archaeological finds inc an early 17th-c silver river god mask are now on show), and for years the HQ of the Inland Revenue, this grand building designed by Sir William Chambers is now a great place to visit. It houses three major art collections, spread throughout several buildings surrounding a central paved courtyard with a stunning series of waterspouts. It's long been the home of the **Courtauld Gallery** (North Wing), an outstanding collection of Impressionist and Post-Impressionist paintings inc works by Monet, Renoir, Degas and Cézanne, also Michelangelo, Rubens, Goya and other masters; (020) 7848 2526; £5. Opened more recently, the **Gilbert Collection** (South Building) is a spectacular assortment of objets d'art (mostly gold and silver) made for the rich and famous over the past 500 years, from six jewel-encrusted gold snuffboxes owned by Frederick the Great of Prussia (valued at over £1m each) to a massive wine cistern weighing nearly 36kg (80lb), and even a pair of silver chamber-pots; (020) 7420 9420; £5. The **Hermitage Rooms**, on the ground floor of the South Building, house rotating exhibitions from the famous Winter Palace in St Petersburg, and furnishings attempt to re-create something of that museum's Imperial Russian splendour; (020) 7845 4630; £6. The River Terrace – open as a public promenade for the first time in 100 years – has an open-air café, restaurant and shop; all the galleries have full disabled access; Somerset House cl 25 Dec (free), all collections cl 24–26 Dec; (020) 7845 4600. In winter, the courtyard holds an ice rink, and in summer it's filled by quite an army of fountains – also outdoor plays and concerts then.

St Bride's church (Fleet St) A Wren masterpiece, its splendid steeple the influence for today's traditional three-tiered wedding cake; good Sun choir and frequent short lunchtime recitals; (020) 7427 0133 for programme. There's an interesting **museum** in the partly Roman crypt (cl bank hols; free). Caxton set up his first printing press alongside, and ever since St Bride's has been the parish church for anyone involved in the press. This was useful in the days when adjoining Fleet St was the hub of newspaperland; today it's really just a passage between the law courts and the City – but look out for relics of the newspaper kingdoms such as the black-glass former Daily Express Building. The nearby Old Bell is a nice old tavern.

South of the River

The south side of the Thames has perked up enormously in the last two or three years, with the elegant London Eye its centrepiece. Tate Modern on Bankside draws vast numbers of happy visitors, and the London Aquarium and an interesting Dali gallery (and from around April, the new Saatchi gallery, which will focus on large-scale shows by contemporary British artists such as Tracey Emin and Damien Hirst) are all in the grandiose building that used to house London's bureaucrats; there's a growing number of bars and cafés by the riverside walkway. Even the South Bank arts centre has a more lively and welcoming feel these days, with pleasant bars and so forth. Besides the aquarium, children particularly like the expensive London Dungeon, and older ones enjoy the marvellous Imperial War Museum, and HMS *Belfast*. Britain at War and the Design Museum are strong draws, and some of the gruesome surgical instruments at the Old Operating Theatre can send a shiver down your spine; a new Fashion and Textile Museum is also due to open in spring, and this year we've also added the London Fire Brigade Museum. Bankside's rich theatrical heritage has been well exploited over the last few years, with the magnificent reconstruction of Shakespeare's Globe Theatre. The best views of the Houses of Parliament are from the quiet riverside walk between Westminster Bridge and the ancient palace of the Archbishop of Canterbury by Lambeth Bridge. For an alternative way of seeing the sights, the unusual Frog Tours make quite a splash.

To see and do

London Family Attraction of the Year

LAMBETH NORTH ⊖ Imperial War Museum (Lambeth Rd; not far to walk from Waterloo or even Westminster) Now completely free, this top-notch museum exhaustively recounts masses of detail about the major conflicts of the 20th c, but the tone isn't at all gung-ho – the displays clearly bring home the everyday realities of war for the individual, and at times are deeply affecting. Adults and children alike can spend hours here, and there's an extraordinary amount of things to see; you can't possibly do the place justice in less than half a day, and even then you probably won't get round it all. As you go in you're met by dozens of tanks, guns, searchlights and rockets, dramatically displayed in a huge hall with planes hanging from the ceiling, and touch screens launching videos and archive films to put it all in context. Children love it in here, and they can pick up trails and quiz sheets to make it more fun as they go round. Most of the permanent exhibitions are downstairs, very much the heart of the museum, with comprehensive galleries on the First and Second World Wars, and on the conflicts since. Big cases show off everything from uniforms and weapons to posters, pictures and letters, with old newsreels and period music wherever you go. A highlight is the very well put together Trench Experience, which vividly re-creates the conditions faced by British troops in World War I. The Blitz Experience gives World War II London the same treatment. Other sizeable displays spread over the various floors look at the work of the Secret Services and the Merchant Navy, and there's an excellent (and often harrowing) art gallery. An acclaimed recent addition has been the huge Holocaust exhibition, the biggest and most moving exploration of this subject in the country. Among the original artefacts are a funeral cart from the Warsaw ghetto, letters written by an 8-year-old French Jewish boy before his betrayal and deportation to Auschwitz, and a section of a deportation railcar from Belgium. Several of this year's excellent temporary exhibitions will continue into 2003: Submarines, aimed very much at children, with periscopes to look through and plenty to climb on, runs until February, as does the full-scale re-creation of the suburban semi featured in Channel 4's *The 1940 House*. New in 2003 will be an exhibition looking at the work of wartime poets, and a major new gallery called Women in Uniform, which should help broaden the museum's appeal to girls. And by the time this book hits the shops they'll have opened a new gallery about Field-Marshal Montgomery. Extra activities for children in school holidays might include a Spy School Mission, or various crafts (with materials supplied). The place fills up quickly: get there when it opens to avoid the crowds. Meals, snacks, shops (inc a special shop for children), disabled access; cl 24–26 Dec; (020) 7416 5000; free.

BOROUGH ⊖

London Fire Brigade Museum
(Southwark Bridge Rd) Spotted for us
by readers, this less well known
museum looks at the history of
firefighting since 1666. As well as an
extensive collection of old fire
appliances and memorabilia, you can
find out about the personalities of
various fire brigade chiefs. The building
too is interesting – it was the home of
the first chief officer of the Metropolitan
Fire Brigade, and you might see recruits
training at an adjacent centre; guided
tours by appointment. Shop, limited
disabled access; cl wknds and bank hols;
(020) 7587 2894; £3.

ELEPHANT & CASTLE ⊖

Bermondsey market (Bermondsey
St/Long Lane) Get up very early on Fri
for the bargains: when the antiques
dealers start arriving around 5am, other
dealers literally pounce on the choice
items while they're being set out, and by
8 or 9am things are more ordinary. It's
probably the biggest primary source of
antiques and bric-a-brac in London, and
can be the most exciting.

LAMBETH NORTH ⊖

Florence Nightingale Museum (St
Thomas Hospital, Lambeth Palace Rd)
On the site of the first School of
Nursing, a re-created Crimean War
hospital ward, and exhibits of the Lady
with the Lamp. Shop, disabled access; cl
24 Dec–2 Jan, Good Fri and Easter Sun;
(020) 7620 0374; £4.80.

Imperial War Museum See separate
family panel on p.756.

Lambeth Palace (S end of Lambeth
Bridge) The official residence of the
Archbishop of Canterbury, with a
charming late 15th-c red-brick exterior.
The adjacent **Church of St Mary** has
the tombs of several archbishops, and
Captain Bligh of the *Bounty* is buried
here too. Just by the S gateway is a little
Museum of Garden History
founded as a memorial to the
Tradescants, father and son, gardeners
to Charles I and Henrietta Maria, with a
small area planted with plants grown in
their time. Snacks, shop, some disabled
access; cl mid-Dec to early Feb; (020)
7401 8865; free.

LONDON BRIDGE ⊖

Bankside This area is very much on
the up, with quite a bit of
redevelopment going on in the old
buildings, and plenty more to come.
Riverside promenades offer good
Thames and City views – Wren is said
to have watched the building of St Paul's
from here, and Pepys certainly did
watch London burning down in the
Great Fire, from near the interesting
old Anchor tavern. One of the best
cross-river views of St Paul's is from the
modern Founders Arms pub. The latest
landmark is the remarkable staggered
circular glass palace near Tower Bridge,
for the Mayor and Greater London
Assembly. A ramp leads to a glazed
viewing gallery and function room at the
top, where there are good views over
London (or if you prefer of the
assembly at work – phone for days;
(0207) 983 4100); the ground floor has
an exhibition area and coffee shop (cl
wknds), and the elegantly paved new
plaza is prettily lit at night. For centuries
this area was London's entertainment
centre, full of theatres, bars and
licensed brothels. In Clink St are the
medieval remains of the Bishop of
Winchester's palace, once said to be
the biggest building in Europe but now
reduced to a single wall and wistful rose
window. With fun children's activities
on board, a full-size replica of Francis
Drake's *Golden Hind* is moored nearby
(cl 26 Dec, but phone to check as it
occasionally closes for functions; (0870)
0118 700; £2.50).

Bramah Tea and Coffee Museum
(40 Southwark St, Bankside) Founded
by tea trader Edward Bramah, this is
almost scholarly but surprisingly
interesting, meticulously charting the
history of these two favourite
commodities: inc smuggling, tea
auctions, opium trading, the Boston tea
party and ceramics. Leaf teas and
ground coffee, snacks, shop, disabled
access; cl 25–26 Dec; (020) 7403 5650;
*£4.

Britain at War 🔲 (Tooley St) A
splendidly put together re-creation of
Blitz-hit London, from reconstructed
streets and air-raid shelters to a BBC
radio station and GI club. The special
effects are suitably dramatic, with lots
of smoke, smells and noise. Also
authentic period newsreels and front

pages, wartime shop windows and a bombed-out pub, and lots of fascinating little details. Shop, disabled access; cl 24–26 Dec; (020) 7403 3171; *£6.50.

Clink Prison Museum 15th-c prison, possibly the oldest in Britain, which gave its name *The Clink* to all the others. Now a museum, with some cell reconstructions, and hands-on displays, also a selection of the usual gory restraining and torturing devices. Shop; usually only cl 25 Dec and 1 Jan, but best to check (as we went to press they were fighting plans for closure to make way for a café); (020) 7403 6515; £4.

Design Museum (Butlers Wharf, by Tower Bridge) Intriguing museum dedicated to 20th- and 21st-c design, fashion, creative technology and architecture, with a permanent collection of design classics, and changing exhibitions. Snacks, interesting if pricey shop, disabled access; cl 25–26 Dec; (020) 7940 8790; *£6.

Fashion and Textile Museum Founded by Zandra Rhodes, this brightly coloured new museum will showcase the work of local and international fashion and textile designers, with rotating displays of vintage and modern designs. Kicking off with an exhibition on 'my favourite dress' (top designers send in their favourite outfits), it's due to open in March. Phone for opening times and prices; 020 7403 0222.

Globe Theatre The most famous of Southwark's 1600s theatres, Shakespeare's Globe has been reconstructed on its original site, where it was open from 1599 to 1642 (when the Puritans closed it down). It couldn't be more different from the West End: shaped like an O, the three-tiered open-topped theatre is 30 metres (100 ft) in diameter, seating audiences of 1,500 with a further 500 promenaders. Shakespeare's works are performed almost the way they were in the early 1600s – no spotlights, canned music or elaborate sets. Anyone who tells you the seats are uncomfortable has rather missed the point (and you can hire cushions). There are entertaining tours during the day, and displays on the Globes old and new – a

good substitute if you can't make a performance. An exhibition under the building looks at the life and works of Shakespeare. Very good café and restaurant with river views, shop, disabled access; tours daily, although there are no tours summer pms; (020) 7902 1500; £8. The 17th-c galleried George in Borough High St, back past London Bridge station, gives another idea of how the area's buildings used to look back then; NT.

Hays Galleria (off Tooley St) An old dock attractively converted into a shopping arcade, with several places to eat inc a good river-view pub, and a fascinating whimsical pirate-ship working sculpture by David Kemp.

HMS *Belfast* (E side of Southwark Bridge) Docked permanently in the pool of London, this is the only surviving example of the big-gun armoured warships built for the Royal Navy in the first half of the 20th c. This floating museum has sound and light displays re-creating life at sea, and there's masses to see among its nine decks, from the ship's gun decks to its sick bay. Snacks, shop, limited disabled access; cl 24–26 Dec; (020) 7940 6300; £5.80, children free.

London Dungeon (Tooley St) A sensationalised look at London's seamy underside, so only for unsqueamish children, with witchcraft, torture, black magic and death (inc a grisly Jack the Ripper section) all presented in ghoulishly life-like waxwork scenes. The Great Fire of London takes you back to the fury of that urban inferno, and the Judgement Day water ride treats you to a trip on an executioner's barge. The whole place is very atmospheric and well laid out, though parents may find the scariest thing about it is the price. Snacks, meals, shop, disabled access; cl 25 Dec (open later in the evenings mid-July to early Sept); (020) 7403 7221; £10.95.

Old Operating Theatre 🖼 (St Thomas St) The church of St Thomas has a unique restored 19th-c operating theatre in its roof (originally this space was deemed far enough from the rest of the hospital for patients' screams to be out of earshot), and a museum looking at the history of surgery and herbal medicine, with some particularly gruesome bits of surgical equipment on show; special events. Shop; cl 15 Dec–5 Jan; (020) 7955 4791; £3.75.

Southwark Cathedral 🖼 Off the busy main road and quite a contrast to the buildings cluttered all around it, this is well worth a look, with parts over 600 years older than the present late 19th-c nave. There are interesting memorials to William Shakespeare (whose brother is buried here) and the poet John Gower, and a chapel is dedicated to John Harvard, founder of the American university named for him, who was baptised here in 1607. An exhibition in the visitor centre uses touch-screen computers to show finds from recent excavations at the cathedral, while interactive tower-top cameras give views of London (you can contrast these with various views recorded from the 16th c onwards from the same viewpoint), and a mini-theatre has a film on the cathedral's history. Meals, snacks, shop, disabled access; cl 25 Dec, Easter Sun and Good Fri and occasionally during services; (020) 7367 6700; £2.50 suggested donation, £2.50 for audio guide, £3 exhibition (discount voucher valid for this).

Vinopolis 🖼 (Bank End, Bankside) Cavernous vaulted arches housing a celebration of all things Bacchic. A self-guided audio tour takes you around displays on the world's wine-growing regions, their culture and history, and afterwards you can sample five wines or champagnes from a choice of 200 (all of which feature in the exhibition). Restaurant, two shops, disabled access; cl 24–26 Dec, 1 Jan; (0870) 241 4040; £11.50, £10.50 if you book in advance.

SOUTHWARK ⊖

Tate Modern (Bankside) Standing proudly robust on the bank of the Thames opposite St Paul's Cathedral, this masterfully gentrified former power station is a salient landmark amid the cluster of new and exciting developments in this part of the city. Designed by Sir Charles Gilbert Scott in 1947 (the architect of Liverpool's Anglican Cathedral, Waterloo Bridge, and designer of the red telephone box), it stood derelict for nearly 15 years,

until the Tate Gallery acquired it in 1994. Today, its cathedral-like windows give splendid views over central London, and a series of stunning top-lit galleries provide perfect lighting for artworks. The collection covers every modern movement from Pop Art to Surrealism, with works by all the great modern artists inc Dali, Picasso, Matisse, and Duchamps, on permanent show. An insistence on themed displays does rather jumble things up so that the real gems can seem hidden among lesser stuff, and there tends to be too much emphasis on the merely trendy, but this is a great place. There are around three major loan exhibitions a year (one on the history of photography begins in the summer), as well as an education centre, auditorium, café with outdoor terrace and a restaurant with river views. Very good disabled access, but phone first; (020) 7887 8888; cl 24–26 Dec; free (exc special exhibitions). The stunning Millennium footbridge (at last reopened after anti-wobble works) makes access from the north bank of the Thames easier, and gives great views – worth a visit in its own right, for the unique sense it gives you of floating over the Thames, as it seems so very much less substantial than any other bridge.

WATERLOO ⊖ ⇌

BFI London IMAX (Waterloo Rd/York Rd roundabout) Britain's largest screen (the height of five double-decker buses), in an eye-catching cylindrical glass building, you can see 2D and 3D films. Café, disabled access; daytime and evening screenings; cl 25 Dec, 1 Jan, phone (020) 7902 1234, for details; £7.10.

Gabriel's Wharf (Upper Ground) One of quite a few projects to have sprouted along the river in recent years: a relaxed place, with a number of cheery designer and craft workshops, along with cafés, restaurants, and events.

Oxo Tower Wharf Offers great views over the city from the top of the lavishly restored art deco tower, with its landmark logo, cafés, bars and restaurants, designer shops and a temporary exhibitions gallery; cl 25 Dec, design shops also cl Mon; (020)

7401 2255; free.

South Bank Centre This stretch of the riverside, home to a string of externally unlovely but world-class theatres, concert halls, cinemas and galleries (not for nothing do they boast that it's the biggest arts complex), is to undergo a radical redevelopment over the next few years. Part of the project – funded in part by the Arts Council and Heritage Lottery Fund – aims to cheer up the surroundings by extending Jubilee Gardens, and adding an open-air performance space, and a new area for skateboarders. Other parts of the scheme include the renovation of the Royal Festival Hall (due to be completed in 2006), and the incorporation of shops and bars whose takings will contribute to the overall reconstruction. For the time being, annual open-air festivals, and the stalls of books going down to the river, bring quite a buzz on a sunny day. Inside there are frequent free performances and interesting small exhibitions in the foyers of the various halls. The National Theatre, as well as the excellent productions in its three different-sized auditoriums, has interesting artistic exhibitions, and guided tours behind the scenes; (020) 7452 3400 to book a tour (£5; cl Sun). The National Film Theatre has good themed screenings and events as well as a riverside café. Refurbishment is also planned for the Hayward Gallery which specialises in world-class art exhibitions. There are good places to eat – often accompanied by live music in the foyer of the Royal Festival Hall, which is London's premier concert hall; its river-view People's Palace is a good modern restaurant and bar. It's a short walk from here to the London Eye and other attractions in and around County Hall (a rather longer one to the Imperial War Museum); and now the shiny new Hungerford Bridge footway sweeps across the Thames from over on the Embankment.

WESTMINSTER ⊖

Dali Universe (County Hall) Devoted entirely to the great Spanish Surrealist, this is part of the exciting tourist development around County Hall. Most of the 500 works on display have never been exhibited in Britain before, and among them is the spectacular oil painting created for the set of Hitchcock's 1945 film *Spellbound*, and the infamous *Mae West Lips* sofa. Snacks, shop, disabled access; cl 25 Dec; (020) 7620 2420; £8.50. Outside, a series of fantastical Dali sculptures have certainly brought some artistic panache to the riverside walkway.

Frog Tours 🔲 (over the bridge at County Hall) First-time visitors to the capital won't find a better introduction than this quirky tour. What makes it so different is that after an hour or so of travelling past the best-known sights by road, you suddenly veer down a slipway near Vauxhall Bridge, and the distinctive vehicle takes to the water, rounding off the tour with a half-hour or so trip down the Thames. In their original form, the amphibious vehicles they use played a role in the D-Day landings. You'll probably need to book in advance, they run from 10am until dusk; cl Jan; (020) 7928 3132 to book; £15 adults. £10 children.

London Aquarium 🔲 (County Hall, a pleasant walk across Westminster Bridge from Westminster tube stn) One of Europe's biggest collections of underwater life; the main Atlantic and Pacific tanks are spectacular in their sheer size, giving great views of the sharks, stingrays and conger eels swimming round the Easter-Island style giant heads. The creatures (and occasional divers – often more entertaining than the fish) have plenty of room to swim about. The rest of the displays – arranged in different themed areas representing rivers, coral reefs and rainforests – are a more conventional size, so you may have to wait a couple of minutes to get right up to them. Some areas are fairly imaginative, making good use of sound and light effects, and of course the fish and sea life are quite spectacular, with breath-taking colours and patterns. Well sized touch tanks let you stroke a ray or gingerly handle a crab. To avoid the crowds at wknds and school holidays, try to come early or late in the day. Shop, disabled access; cl 25 Dec; (020) 7967 8000; £8.75. Great views of the Houses of Parliament and river from outside.

London Eye (County Hall) This gigantic steel wheel is the most successful and popular of the country's Millennium attractions, and the tickets are worth every penny. The wheel stands nearly 140 metres (450 ft) above the Thames – the fourth-tallest structure in London, three times the height of Tower Bridge. On a clear day, passengers can see up to 25 miles in each direction from its 32 glass capsules, although pre-booked tickets (the way to avoid queues) mean you can't guarantee perfect viewing conditions. Each rotation (or flight, as the operators British Airways insist on calling them) takes 30 mins, and tickets must be collected from County Hall 15–30 mins in advance – it's all very well organised. There's a coffee shop by the ticket office, and capsules are fully accessible by wheelchair (readers tell us the staff are helpful); cl 25 Dec, Jan; (0870) 5000 600; £9.50, children (must be accompanied by adults) £5.

Further Afield

We include here only those places which, despite being away from the centre, have so much to offer that it's well worth making the journey out to visit them. A trip down the Thames from Westminster is a fun way to begin a very full day out at Greenwich, now a thoroughly enjoyable destination for families. Its star attractions, the National Maritime Museum (you can see the museum's art collection at Queen's House) and the Royal Observatory, are free, you can also climb on board the *Cutty Sark*, visit the splendid art collection at Ranger's House and enjoy wonderful alternative views over the city from the park (ideal for picnics). Kew is also very appealing, with its memorable vistas and glorious glasshouses, as is the earlier grandeur of Syon House (attraction for children here too) in Brentford. Firepower over in Woolwich takes a lively look at the history of the artillery, and the outstanding Wetland Centre at Barnes not only provides a haven for thousands of birds, but looks after its human visitors too. Wonderfully regal Hampton Court Palace is a popular outing (the famous gardens are worth a visit in themselves). Richmond and Hampstead are pleasant places to potter in, and elsewhere attractions range from a backstage tour of the BBC to a visit to the Palladian villa at Chiswick.

To see and do

BARNES ⇌
Wetland Centre 🖼 4 miles from the heart of the city, this Wildfowl and Wetlands Trust reserve is an incredible feat of environmental transformation. A hundred acres of reservoir have been broken up and resculpted to create over 30 lakes, linked by 27 bridges. With 30,000 trees and countless aquatic plants, the centre is starting to attract wildlife from kingfishers through grebes, teal, plovers and herons to even bitterns now – not to mention newts. There are seven hides, and a three-storey viewing tower, but for those who like bird-spotting in comfort, a glass-walled observatory with views across the reserve relays live pictures via CCTV from the hides. A fun-looking discovery centre has lots of hands-on activities for children, with re-created wetland habitats. A visitor centre has

touch-screen displays on the wildlife seen at the reserve, along with a café and shop. It's all been designed to accommodate wheelchair access, and there's even a lift in the observation tower. At peak times, the centre provides a bus service from Hammersmith, Barnes, and perhaps other stations, to prevent traffic from disturbing the wildlife. Meals, snacks, shop, disabled access; cl 25 Dec; (020) 8409 4400; £6.75. The Bulls Head (Lonsdale Rd) is quite handy for cheap refreshment.

BRENTFORD ⇌
Syon Park ⬛ The London home of the Duke of Northumberland, this was built on the site of a medieval abbey and remodelled from its Tudor original by Robert Adam – it's widely considered to be one of his finest works. The ceiling by Cipriani and the magnificent Scagliola floor are particular highlights, but a visit here can keep the whole family entertained, with 40 acres of grounds to stroll around (landscaped by Capability Brown), Thames-side watermeadows, and a giant indoor adventure playground. Snacks, shop, disabled access to café and gardens only; house open Weds, Thurs, Sun and bank hol Mon (and all Easter wknd) mid-Mar to Oct, gardens open daily exc 25–26 Dec; (020) 8560 0882; house and gardens £6.95, gardens only £3.50. Also in the grounds is the **London Butterfly House** (shop, disabled access; cl 25–26 Dec; (020) 8560 0378; £4.95) and, with a range of endangered species, the **Aquatic Experience** (shop, disabled access; cl 24–26 Dec, 1 Jan; (0208) 8474730; £4).

CAMDEN TOWN ⊖
A Bohemian's idyll, with a very wide variety of unusual shops from radical bookshops to fashion workshops, and comic shops. Lots of restaurants and cafés too, and good delis serving the area's Italian and Greek communities. The area's biggest draw is its weekend series of lively **markets**, particularly the interesting craft, handmade fashion and other stalls around the attractively converted former warehouses of Camden Lock. There's also a covered market on Camden High St, the Inverness St market for fruit and veg,

and the Stables, where the best food stalls are to be found. Go and browse, but be warned about the huge crowds – the markets here draw 200,000 people every weekend.

Jewish Museum (129 Albert St) Excellent look at Jewish life, history and religion, with a particularly fine collection of ceremonial art, portraits and antiques, and various audio-visual displays. Shop, disabled access; cl Fri–Sat, all bank and Jewish hols; (020) 7284 1997; *£3.50. Another branch on East End Rd, Finchley, (020) 8349 1143, traces the history of Jewish immigration and has a moving exhibition on the Holocaust. The Princess of Wales up towards Primrose Hill (Chalcot Rd/Regent's Park Rd) does good bistro food.

CHISWICK ⇌
Chiswick House (Burlington Lane – A316) Surrounded by beautiful classical gardens (the first true example of English naturalistic landscaping), this fine Palladian villa was designed by Lord Burlington in 1728. Sumptuously decorated, with the lavish blue velvet room as a particular highlight; there's an exhibition and video on the house and gardens. Snacks, shop, phone for disabled access; cl Mon (exc bank hols), Tues, pm Sat, and all Nov–Mar; (020) 8995 0508; £3.30 inc audio tour. Chiswick Mall is an 18th-c Thames-side village, well worth a stroll.

ELTHAM ⇌
Eltham Palace (Court Yard) In attractive grounds on the site of an early 14th-c Royal palace, this splendid 1930s country house was built around part of a medieval hall erected for Edward IV. Re-created by English Heritage, the art deco interior reflects the glamour of its age. Teas, shop, disabled access; cl Mon (exc bank hols), Tues, Sat, 23 Dec–1 Feb; (020) 8294 2548; house and grounds £6.20, grounds only £3.60; EH.

GREENWICH ⇌
Now a World Heritage Site, this is the sort of place worth coming back to again and again. Once a favoured residence of the Royal Family, Greenwich has a long and illustrious maritime heritage, still reflected in the museums, boats and grand old ships you

can visit. On wknds, the covered market has arts and crafts, while outdoor markets on High Rd and Stockwell St have antiques, junk and second-hand books. You should be able to get boat trips from the pier up to Westminster (around £7.80 return). The Cutty Sark (Lassell St) and Trafalgar (Park Row) are good river-view dining pubs. Three of the most enjoyable places, the Queen's House, National Maritime Museum and Royal Observatory, are all free, and the Ranger's House now contains a fabulous art collection. A route booklet from the helpful Tourist Information Centre (£2) lets you follow one of five Millennium Heritage Trails – a pleasant way to spend a sunny afternoon.

Cutty Sark In dry dock not far from Greenwich Pier, this clipper built in 1869 was the fastest of her time – she once sailed 363 nautical miles in a single day. On board, you can visit the crew's and officers' cabins; there's an impressive collection of ships' figureheads, and children's display panels and activities. Shop, limited disabled access; cl 24–26 Dec; (020) 8858 3445; £3.90.

Fan Museum 🏛 (12 Crooms Hill) Unique changing collection of around 3,000 fans and related items from all over the world. They even do fan-making classes. Shop, disabled access (with notice); cl Sun am, all day Mon, 25 Dec, 31 Dec and Jan, but best to check; (020) 8305 1441; *£3.75.

Greenwich Park Wonderful views from this carefully landscaped park sloping down towards the river; it's a great place for a picnic. A herd of deer graze in a smallish area of woodland and wild flowers known as the Wilderness, and there's the largest children's playground in any Royal Park (as well as the preserved trunk of a tree in which the young Elizabeth I is said to have played).

National Maritime Museum (Romney Rd) Enclosed by a spectacular glass canopy roof, this is now one of the country's most impressive and enjoyable museums. The 20 galleries have displays on topics as diverse as passengers, piracy, deep-sea diving, sea power, and oceans and the environment. Hundreds of exhibits range from contemporary art and great battle-scene masterpieces, to Nelson's bloodstained coat and Prince Frederick's gilded Royal barge; you can see some of the thousands of exhibits not on display on computers, and there are plenty of hands-on activities. A temporary exhibition on Elizabeth I starts in Apr. It's all great fun and combines nicely with a visit to the Royal Observatory and Queen's House. Meals, snacks, shop, disabled access; cl 25–26 Dec, and parts may be closed in winter to prepare for temporary exhibitions; (020) 8312 6565; free.

Queen's House (Romney Rd) On the site of the original magnificent Royal palace, this early 17th-c house was the first Palladian-style villa in the country, designed by Inigo Jones for Anne of Denmark. Once the setting for balls and banquets, it's now used to show more of the National Maritime Museum's excellent maritime art collection; the first-floor galleries host changing art exhibitions, while the ground floor has a display on the house's architecture and the famous people associated with it. Disabled access; cl 24–26 Dec; (020) 8858 4422; free.

Ranger's House (Chesterfield Walk, Blackheath) This lovely stately home was the 19th-c official residence of the Greenwich Park ranger. Now on display here is the impressive life-time collection of Julius Wernher who built a fabulous fortune mining diamonds; treasures include Italian and Dutch Old Master paintings, 18th-c English paintings by Reynolds and Romney, Byzantine and medieval ivories, wonderful Renaissance bronzes, jewellery and majolica pottery, Sèvres porcelain and Limoges enamels. Shop, disabled access, cl Mon, Tues, and end Dec–Mar; (020) 8853 0035; £4.50. Blackheath and Greenwich Park opposite are civilised places, good for a pleasant stroll.

Royal Naval College This glorious group of buildings was designed initially by Wren in the 17th c, and then completed by Hawksmoor and Ripley – it's a magnificently preserved part of old London. Visitors can see an interesting chapel and a notable painted hall. You can find out more about the college at the visitor centre (handily, next to the good Tourist Information Centre). Meals, snacks, shop; chapel cl Sun am, 24–26 Dec; (020) 8269 4747; free. The view from across the river (there's a pedestrian tunnel under the Thames here) looks like an 18th-c print come to life.

Royal Observatory Greenwich (Greenwich Park) The original home of Greenwich Mean Time – standing as it does on the Prime Meridian of longitude zero. The brass line marking the meridian is still there set in the ground: standing over it with one foot in the western hemisphere and one in the east is irresistible. The Wren-built observatory was founded by Charles II in 1675, and now houses a comprehensive collection of historic instruments for time-keeping, navigation and astronomy. Good views from the top. The Time Ball is rather confusing – it can go down and up so fast you barely notice it. Shop; cl 24–26 Dec; (020) 8858 4422; free.

HAMPSTEAD ⊖ Prides itself on its villagey atmosphere, and off the main streets its maze of twisting lanes is very picturesque and seductively charming. It's home to artistes of all kinds, and well heeled Bohemians in general; in some streets a commemorative blue plaque on the front of the house is almost compulsory. Particularly attractive parts include early Georgian Church Row, and Squires Mount (where the Regency-looking house at the end on the left, in fact built in the 1950s, belonged to Richard Burton and Elizabeth Taylor). The gaslit Holly Bush, prettily tucked away up Holly Mount, is a good pub, as is the Flask in Flask Walk (a long-standing favourite of local actors).

2 Willow Road 🏛 The first Modern Movement house acquired by the National Trust. Designed and built by the architect Erno Goldfinger, it has a good range of work by the artists and intellectuals who lived around Hampstead in the 1930s – as well as the only working TV on show in any NT property. Guided tours from 12.15pm Sat only Mar and Nov, Thurs–Sat

Apr–Oct; (020) 7435 6166; *£4.50, joint ticket with Fenton House £6.50; NT.

Fenton House (Hampstead Grove) Fine William and Mary merchant's house in a walled garden, with oriental, English and European china and an exceptional collection of early keyboard instruments. Their period-music concerts on some summer evenings are well worth catching. Shop, disabled access to ground floor and garden; cl am, also Mon, Tues, and 3 Nov–Mar exc Mar wknds; (020) 435 3471; *£4.50; NT.

Hampstead Heath North London's best open space, with lakes, hilly prospects, and some wonderful views of the city skyline – Parliament Hill has a direction-finder pointing out various landmarks. On one edge the ancient Spaniards Inn, still as popular as when Dickens made it famous in the *Pickwick Papers*, faces an 18th-c toll booth notorious for the way its road-narrowing blocks the traffic here.

Kenwood House (Hampstead Lane) Achieved its present splendid proportions in the 18th c at the hands of Robert Adam. The refurbished rooms show off well the splendid collection of paintings, inc works by Rembrandt, Vermeer and Turner. The grounds are lovely, and summer concerts are idyllic when it's fine, with the music drifting across the lake, and sometimes a fireworks finale. Meals, snacks, shop, disabled access to ground floor only; cl 24–26 Dec, 1 Jan; (020) 8348 1286; free; EH.

Sigmund Freud's House 🏛 (20 Maresfield Gdns) Extraordinary collection of antiques from various ancient cultures, as well as Freud's library, papers and indeed his desk and couch. Shop, some disabled access; cl am, also Mon, Tues and 25 Dec and Good Fri; (020) 7435 2002; £4. A monumental seated statue of Freud by Oscar Nemon can be seen outside the Tavistock Clinic on nearby Belsize Lane.

HAMPTON COURT ⇌ **Bushy Park** Another Royal Park, formerly reserved for hunting. Wren laid out its famous double chestnut avenue, which runs from Teddington Gate to the great house.

Hampton Court Gardens
Elaborately landscaped, fine mix of
formal and informal (esp the
Wilderness, full of spring flowers),
bounded by deer park with golf course.
William III's quiet Privy Garden has
been restored to its intricate 1702
design, with fountains, stonework,
topiary and elaborate sand patterns cut
into lawn. The famous maze swallows
up 300,000 people a year, and the
annual flower show here is one of the
world's biggest. Open as palace; Privy
Garden and maze £3 each (unless you
are also visiting the palace, see below),
gardens free. The Kings Arms (Lion
Gate) is a decent food stop.
Hampton Court Palace An amazing
place, just as a Royal palace should be.
Begun by Cardinal Wolsey in the early
16th c, the house's splendour soon so
pricked Henry VIII's jealousy that
Wolsey felt compelled to present it to
his king in an attempt to appease him.
Successive monarchs have left their
architectural marks: the hammer-
beamed hall and kitchens were Henry's
addition, the Fountain Court was
designed by Wren for William and
Mary, and much comes from the work
of the Victorians (the chimneys mostly
date from then). The rooms have
managed to keep their distinctive styles,
from the starkly imposing Tudor
kitchens (themselves taking up 50
rooms) to the elaborate grandeur of
the Georgian chambers. The King's
Staircase is wonderfully over the top,
and the Picture Gallery has the finest
Renaissance works from the Royal
collection, inc Pieter Bruegel the Elder's
fascinating *Massacre of the Innocents*.
Look out too for the carvings by
Grinling Gibbons and the cartoons by
Mantegna in the Lower Orangery.
There are several excellent audio
guides you can pick up and listen to as
you go along, with no extra charge.
Meals, snacks, shops, disabled access;
cl 24–26 Dec; (0870) 752 7777;
£11 inc entry to Privy Garden and
maze.
River Thames There are pleasant
Thames-side walks around Hampton
Court, and summer cruise boats from
here back down to Westminster;
(0207) 930 4721; £12.

HIGHGATE ⊖
An easy walk across the Heath from
Hampstead, this dates largely from the
Victorian period and still keeps a
villagey atmosphere, centred as it is
around the High St. The village is
dominated by Highgate School (which
Betjeman attended and where T S Eliot
taught). There are lots of pubs in this
area, and some smart little cafés. The
Grove, a row of very elegant Victorian
houses, has been home to such diverse
musicians as Lord Menuhin and Sting.
Highgate Cemetery (Swains Lane)
The most impressive of a series of
landscaped and formal cemeteries
started in the early decades of Victoria's
reign on the then outskirts of the city,
very well restored over the last 20
years, and still in use. The cemetery has
the tombs of many household names
(inc Karl Marx), though the best thing is
the sheer atmosphere of the jumbled
trees, shrubs and crumbling ivy-
covered monuments. The E cemetery is
open all year (exc 25–26 Dec and
during funerals), the W by guided tour
only (not wkdys Dec–Feb), phone
before visiting; (020) 8340 1834;
separate charges for each.
KEW ⊖ ⇌
Kew Bridge Steam Museum
(Green Dragon Lane) Over the bridge
from the gardens, by the train station,
this splendid old pumping station
houses five Cornish beam engines – one
of which you can walk through while it's
working. Also a narrow gauge railway,
and surprisingly interesting exhibition
on the development of London's water
supply: there are peepholes into the
sewers. It won't engross unless you've
at least some interest in the subject – in
which case you'll find the engines prime
examples of their type. Wknd meals
and snacks, shop, some disabled access;
cl 20–26 Dec, Good Fri; (020) 8568
4757; £4.50 wknds and bank hols (when
engines in steam), £3.50 wkdys.
Kew Gardens Started in 1759 by
George III's mother as nine acres
landscaped by Capability Brown, by
1904 they had grown to cover 300
acres, with the foundations of the
present wonderful collection firmly laid.
The glasshouses include the magnificent
modern Princess of Wales range and

the remarkable restored Victorian Palm House, as well as an Evolution House with plants from up to 400 million years ago. The gardens near the entrance are largely formally arranged, and drift into attractively landscaped woodland, glades and tree collections further out. As well as a museum, there's a gallery, and jazz concerts on some evenings in July. A wonderful place you can come back to time and time again – always discovering something new. Meals, snacks, shop (great for unusual plant books), disabled access; cl 25 Dec, 1 Jan; (020) 8332 5655; £6.50. The Coach & Horses on the green has decent food. In summer you can come to Kew by cruise boat from Westminster – see the numbers we give for Hampton Court and Richmond.

OSTERLEY ⊖

Osterley Park House One of the most complete examples of Robert Adam's work, this elegant neo-classical villa was built on the foundations of a Tudor mansion. It's set in an estate that runs to over half a square mile, with pleasure grounds and 16th-c stables (still in use); changing art exhibitions in the Jersey Gallery. Meals, snacks, shop, disabled access; cl am, also Mon, Tues and Nov–Mar exc Mar wknds; (020) 8232 5050; £4.50.

RICHMOND ⊖ ⇌

Agreeable if much extended Thames village, Britain's most affluent corner, with lots of fine 18th-c houses esp around the Green and up Richmond Hill (a 1902 Act of Parliament protects the river and meadow view immortalised by Turner – the cows are now owned by a local preservation trust). There's a little local history museum in the Old Town Hall (cl Mon, plus pm Sun Oct–Apr; (020) 8332 1141; £2), and the riverside White Cross has decent food. The river here is really attractive for strolls, and there are summer cruise boats from here back down to Westminster, stopping at Kew (more fine riverside walks) on the way; (020) 7930 2062.

Ham House (Petersham) A pleasant two-mile walk W along the river from Richmond to this outstanding Stuart mansion (once at the centre of Restoration court life) with 17th-c

formal gardens, in a charming little old-world hamlet; there's a new exhibition on the development of the garden, and a video on the house. Snacks, shop, disabled access; cl am, also Sun–Tues and all Nov–Mar; (020) 8940 1950; £6, £2 garden only; NT. If you happen to be in Twickenham you can get a ferry across.

Public Records Office The national archive of records great and small, with anything from your great grandfather's marriage licence to cabinet papers once they've been released; efficient search mechanisms and helpful staff. The little museum showcases some of the most famous documents of the past 1,000 years; displayed according to themes, changing exhibits have included Shakespeare's will, Guy Fawkes's confession, a letter from Jack the Ripper, the Dam Busters' log book, and the deed poll showing Elton John's name change. The grounds have small lakes with ducks and fish. Meals, snacks, shop, disabled access; cl Sun, bank hol Sat and Mon, 2–7, 25–28 Dec, and 1 Jan, best to check; (020) 8876 3444; free, you need to bring ID (UK driver's licence, credit or bank card or passport).

Richmond Park The most country-like of all London's parks, with great rolling spaces and wildlife (inc herds of deer), model boats on Adam's Pond, and fishing in the 18-acre Pen Ponds. There's a good formal garden at Pembroke Lodge, and the Isabella Plantation's rhododendrons and azaleas are a must-see in season.

Strawberry Hill House It's hard to believe that this fanciful place, created by Horace Walpole, was once just a coachman's cottage. An outstanding example of an early Gothic Revival building, the exterior has hardly changed since additions by the Waldegrave family in the mid-19th c. Shop; tours (the rooms are just shells) leave at 2, 2.45 and 3.30 Suns May–Sept; (020) 8240 4224; £5.

STAMFORD BROOK ⊖

Fullers Brewery Tours The oldest brewery in London, with a comprehensive tour looking at its history, and demonstrations showing its mix of traditional methods and the latest technology; there's a pub on site. Tours (no under-14s) Mon, Weds–Fri, phone to book; (020) 8996 2063; £5.

WHITE CITY ⊖

BBC Backstage Tours 🏛 (Wood Lane) As it's a working studio, what you see depends on what is being produced on the day, but among other things you're likely to go to the BBC's News Centre, look into studios, and visit a dressing room; tours (no children under 10) last around 1½ hours and involve a fair bit of walking. Snacks, shop, disabled access; cl Sun, 24–26 Dec; phone to book; (0870) 603 0304; £7.95.

WOOLWICH ⇌

Firepower 🏛 (Royal Arsenal West, Warren Lane) In restored former Ministry of Defence research buildings, and part of the overall redevelopment of the Royal Arsenal, this new museum brings to life the history of artillery since Roman times: plenty of big guns and military vehicles, alongside uniforms, photographs, books and manuscripts. Lots to appeal to families, with interactive displays and so forth, and an audio-visual show gives an idea of what it felt like to be in the middle of a battle. Some of the displays have a more personal side to them, with recorded recollections of former servicemen and women, and a poignant show of medals. Meals, snacks, shop, disabled access; cl Mon (exc bank hols), Tues, phone for winter opening times; (020) 8855 7755; £6.50. A new Heritage Centre, combining the Borough Museum from Plumstead, and the local history library from Blackheath, is expected to open nearby in 2003.

More Specialised Expeditions

To see and do

ANGEL ⊖

Camden Passage This and the surrounding streets have a great collection of **antiques shops**, well worth the expedition if that interests you. The Duke of Cambridge (St Peter's St) has good food.

CHISLEHURST ⇌

Chislehurst Caves (entrance off Caveside Close nr the Olde Stationmaster, B264; nr Chislehurst railway station) 45-min lamplit tours of labyrinthine tunnels and passageways carved out of the rock over 8,000 years. They've been used by flint knappers, druids, and as an air-raid shelter during the war. Meals, snacks, shop; cl Mon and Tues (exc school hols), around a wk over Christmas; (020) 8467 3264; £4. The Olde Stationmaster is a good value family food pub.

COLINDALE ⊖

RAF Museum Hendon (Grahame Park Way) The story of flight from early times, with over 70 full-size aeroplanes, a lively Battle of Britain Experience, and an interesting examination of the impact of flight on history and politics. A highlight is the Fun 'n' Flight gallery, which has good hands-on exhibits (you can have a go at the controls of a modern jet trainer), and there are dramatic simulator rides (inc one which lets you imagine you're piloting a Red Arrow). Excellent for enthusiasts and flying-minded children, and warmly recommended by several of our contributors; special events throughout the year. An expansion to the museum, which comprises a new building and a hangar (dating from the early days of aviation), is due to open around Dec 2003 with new displays and more aircraft. Meals, snacks, shop, disabled access; cl 24–26 Dec, 1 Jan; (020) 8205 2266; free.

FOREST HILL ⇌

Horniman Museum (London Rd) This art nouveau building, home to eclectic, mainly ethnographic, collections with artefacts from every continent, now has a stunning new £13m extension. New galleries house the musical instrument collection (interactive computers let you hear what some of the extraordinary objects sound like), the world culture collection, thousands of hands-on exhibits, there to touch and try, and temporary exhibitions (one on puppets runs Feb–Oct). Also here are the African gallery (inc a fine group of mummies and Africa's largest mask), the natural history gallery (lots of stuffed animals), and an aquarium. Other improvements include a new entrance to the museum from the delightful 16-acre gardens (with friendly small farm animals – also from around the world). Children love it, and there's a good programme of events. Disabled access, new café; cl 24–26 Dec, gardens 25 Dec; (020) 8699 1872; free.

HIGHBURY & ISLINGTON ⊖
Estorick Collection of Italian Art (39A Canonbury Sq) This outstanding collection of modern Italian art includes fine futurist works by artists inc Balla and Boccioni, as well as later figurative works by Modigliani and Sironi; also temporary exhibitions. Meals, snacks, shop, disabled access; cl Mon, Tues, am Sun and over Christmas and New Year; (020) 7704 9522; £3.50. The appealingly villagey little Compton Arms (Compton Ave) has good value food.

HOMERTON ⇌
Sutton House 🏛 Built in 1535 by Henry VIII's Principal Secretary of State, it was then home to successive merchants, silk-weavers, Victorian schoolmistresses and Edwardian clergy. Although altered over the years, it remains essentially Tudor, and the oak-panelled rooms and carved fireplaces survive intact. An exhibition will tell you more about the house and its inhabitants, and there are changing art exhibitions, and special events. Café/bar, shop, disabled access to ground floor; cl am, also Mon–Thurs and Jan, best to check; (020) 8986 2264; £2.10; NT.

KNOCKHOLT ⇌
South London walks The SE fringes of London give way to surprisingly rural North Downs countryside, still within the London borough of Bromley, around Knockholt, High Elms and Downe; paths are plentiful and well maintained. Only the view over S London from behind Knockholt church shows how close you are to the capital. The nearby Three Horseshoes has good value food.

PADDINGTON ⊖ ⇌
Alexander Fleming Laboratory Museum (St Mary's Hospital, Praed St) The laboratory in which Alexander Fleming discovered penicillin by chance in 1928 has been reconstructed, and an accompanying display and video tell the story of the bacteriologist and the life-saving antibiotic. Shop; cl pms, all Fri–Sun, bank hols, and 25 Dec–1 Jan; (020) 7886 6528; £2.

SOUTHFIELDS ⊖
Wimbledon Lawn Tennis Museum 🏛 (Church Rd) The only museum of its type in the country, with trophies, pictures and other tennis memorabilia tracing the development of the game through the last century. Also highlights of past Wimbledon Championships, and an interesting display on the changes in tennis fashions. You can see the famous Centre Court outside, and they do behind-the-scenes guided tours (phone for details). Café, shop, disabled access; cl 24–26 Dec, 1 Jan and every day during the Championship fortnight (unless you've gone to watch the tennis); (020) 8946 6131; *£5.50. If you're in London during Wimbledon fortnight it's always worth popping along to the club in the early evening around 5.30 or 6 – lots of people leave then and their seats are resold cheaply.
Wimbledon Windmill Museum Around the common is an attractive old core, and a striking **windmill** on Windmill Rd (open Sat pm, Sun and bank hols Easter–Oct; (020) 8947 2825; £1). The common, with its ponds and windmill, is one of the best strolling grounds provided by South London's numerous commons and parks. The Fox & Grapes and Crooked Billet are pleasant common-side pubs.

ST JOHN'S WOOD ⊖
Lord's Tour 🏛 (St John's Wood Rd) Tours of the famous club and grounds, inc the space-age media centre (if not in use), the players' dressing room, and

the excellent MCC Museum, with an exhaustive collection of cricket memorabilia, such as the Ashes urn and 18th-c paintings of the game. Meals, snacks, shop, disabled access to most of the ground; tours usually daily at 12 and 2pm (and at 10am Apr–Sept) exc winter bank hols, and during major matches and preparation days, phone to check; (020) 7432 1033; £6.50. Down in Aberdeen Pl Crockers is a remarkably opulent Victorian pub with decent food.

TWICKENHAM ⇌

Marble Hill House In 66 acres of parkland overlooking the Thames, this Palladian villa was built for Henrietta Howard, mistress of George II; audio tours take you around the lavishly gilded rooms. Snacks, shop, disabled access to ground floor; cl Mon (exc bank hols), Tues and all Nov–Mar; (020) 8892 5115; £3.30. The riverside White Swan is pleasant for lunch.

Museum of Rugby (Rugby Rd) Combines tours of the 75,000-seat home of Rugby Union with an excellent museum of related memorabilia under the East Stand; interactive displays and period reconstructions illustrate the game's history, and there's plenty of footage from classic matches. Meals, snacks, shop, disabled access; cl Mon (exc bank hols), 24–26 Dec, Good Fri, and a day after match days; four tours a day (only two on Sun), best to book on (020) 8892 8877; £6, £3 for just museum (match days only, when there are no tours). The Turks Head (Winchester Rd) has decent food.

WALTHAMSTOW CENTRAL ⊖

William Morris Gallery (Lloyd Park, Forest Rd) William Morris lived here 1846–1858, and the house has an excellent collection of his work: fabrics, furnishings and wallpaper, much of it still fashionable today. Pre-Raphaelite works upstairs include pictures by Burne-Jones and Rossetti. The attractive grounds are ideal for picnics. Shop, disabled access to ground floor only (this is where the main exhibition is); cl 1–2pm, all day Mon, Sun (exc first Sun in month), and bank hols; (020)

8527 3782; free.

WANDSWORTH TOWN ⇌

Young's Brewery Tours Working museum of English brewing through the ages. Tours are usually Tues, Weds, Thurs and Sat (12 and 2pm), and last about 1½ hours, phone to book; (020) 8875 7005; shop; £5.50.

WARWICK AVENUE ⊖

Puppet Theatre Barge (Little Venice) This wonderful floating puppet theatre is moored here Nov–May, touring the Thames in the summer. They have performances for children on wknds and during the school hols, and on Sat evenings in summer there are productions for older children and adults. Snacks, they can accommodate up to three wheelchairs; phone in advance, box office (020) 7249 6876; *£7.

WEST DULWICH ⇌

Dulwich The village still is villagey, with imposing 18th-c houses, duckpond, good pub (Crown & Greyhound), and an almost rural feel (there's even a toll road). There are good walks, in Dulwich Park (best in rhododendron time), and through Dulwich Wood to adjacent Sydenham Hill Wood – the largest fragment of ancient woodland in inner London, and a most surprising place (just big enough to lose your way in), with woodpeckers among the oak and hornbeam trees. The best of the wood is a nature reserve fiercely guarded against developers by the London Wildlife Trust; a trail starts from the Crescent Wood Rd entrance on the Sydenham side. The nearby Dulwich Wood House (Sydenham Hill) is popular for food.

Dulwich Picture Gallery (between College Rd and Gallery Rd) This rather austere brick building, designed by Sir John Soane in 1811, was England's first public gallery when it opened six years later. It's home to an impressive collection of 17th- and 18th-c works by artists inc Rembrandt, Van Dyck and Canaletto. Café, shop, disabled access; cl Mon (exc bank hols) and 24–26 Dec, 1 Jan and Good Fri; (020) 8693 5254; £4, children free.

Where to eat

Alastair Little *49 Frith St W1 (020) 7734 5183* Starkly furnished small restaurant with a low-key atmosphere, particularly good modern British cooking from a sensibly short menu – plenty of strong flavours – enjoyable puddings, an interesting small wine list, and excellent service; cl Sat am, Sun, bank hols. £42 dinner, £34 lunch

Bank *1 Kingsway WC2 (020) 7234 3344* Large, modern brasserie between the city and Theatreland with interesting decor (the slanted glass decorations hanging from the ceiling are quite a sight), an open kitchen, and reliably good brasserie-type food from a very varied menu (as well as lunch and dinner, they also serve breakfasts, from 7am, pre-theatre meals, and wknd brunches inc a children's menu); there's another branch in Westminster and one in Birmingham; cl bank hols; disabled access. £35/2-course set meal £10.95

Bertorelli's *33 Floral St WC2 (020) 7836 3969* Cheerful, simply furnished Italian restaurant and slightly cheaper café, excellent for pre-opera meals (it's opposite the stage entrance to the Royal Opera House), with crisp white-clothed tables, exotic flower arrangements, quite a few mirrors, smiling unflappable service, fairly priced Italian wines, and a long choice of good enjoyable Italian food; cl Sun. £30 restaurant, £20 café

Bibendum *Michelin House, 81 Fulham Rd SW3 (020) 7581 5817* Magnificent art deco Michelin building housing a light and spacious restaurant with exceptionally good European-style cooking (more elaborate in the evening), marvellous wine list, and courteous well trained staff; the unpretentious downstairs oyster bar is a fine place for a lighter (and cheaper) meal; cl 24–26 Dec; disabled access. £60 dinner, £20 weekday lunch

Bishop's Finger *9–10 West Smithfield EC1 (020) 7248 2341* Swish little bar-cum-restaurant with fresh flowers on elegant tables set on polished bare boards, comfortably cushioned chairs under a wall lined with prints, distinctive food from an open kitchen, well kept real ales, a wide choice of wines, and friendly service; upstairs evening bar; cl Sat, Sun, bank hols; disabled access. £17|£6.75

Blue Elephant *4–6 Fulham Broadway SW6 (020) 7385 6595* Luxurious Thai food among waterfalls and exotic jungle greenery, with produce flown in weekly from Thailand; the set meals are better value; cl Sat am, 24–26 Dec; disabled access. £45|£10

Bluebird *350 King's Rd SW3 (020) 7559 1000* Former 1920s garage converted to Gastrodrome with smart supermarket, flower market, and kitchenware shop, and overlooked by the huge airy first-floor restaurant hung with kite-like artwork; bustling and busy atmosphere, lots of customers, and modern (not particularly cheap) cooking with plenty of shellfish; pre-theatre meals and wknd brunches; cl 25 Dec; disabled access. £40/2 courses £12.50

Bombay Brasserie *Courtfield Cl SW7 (020) 7370 4040* Grand colonial-style furnishings in big restaurant and conservatory, with good authentic Indian food using recipes from all over India (lots of vegetarian dishes), and courteous helpful staff; cheaper at lunchtime when there's a buffet; cl 25–27 Dec; children over 10; disabled access. £44/£16.95 buffet lunch

Browns *82–84 St Martin's Lane WC2 (020) 7497 5050* Spacious bar and restaurant in what was once the City of Westminster's County Courts; a good relaxed atmosphere, big mirrors and potted plants, bentwood seats, wooden tables, and panelling, helpful service, and enjoyable good value food; other branches in Bath, Brighton, Cambridge, Edinburgh and Oxford; disabled access. £31/2-course lunch £10.95 ☺

Café in the Crypt *St Martin-in-the-Fields Church WC2 (020) 7930 0089* Popular place under the lovely arches of the church with a relaxed atmosphere, good freshly prepared daily changing food; shop, free lunchtime concerts, candlelit evening concerts, brass rubbing; cl 25 Dec, pm Maundy Thurs, Good Fri am. £16|£6.75

Christopher's *18 Wellington St WC2 (020) 7240 4222* Fashionable place with high ceilings and rococo decor spread over three floors, enjoyable modern American cooking (good value pre- and post-theatre meals), cheery speedy service, and lots of American wines; there's also a branch in the Thistle Victoria Hotel at 101 Buckingham Palace Road; cl Sun pm. £30/pre-theatre 3-course meal £18.50

Chutney Mary *The Plaza, 535 King's Road SW10 (020) 7351 3113* Very good interesting Indian food (with some Anglo touches) in light conservatory and two dining rooms, plus a verandah bar, opulent decor, a good choice of drinks, and knowledgeable staff; only set lunch available on Sun; cl pm 25 Dec; some disabled access. £35/3-course set lunch £16

City Rhodes *The Merchant Centre, 1 New St Sq EC4 (020) 7583 1313* Airy light restaurant with plenty of reference to the well known TV chef, excellent and beautifully presented inventive British food using luxury ingredients (the puddings are wonderful), helpful efficient service, and an interesting if pricey wine list; cl wknds, Christmas, New Year, bank hols; disabled access. £55

Clarkes *122–124 Kensington Church St W8 (020) 7221 9225* Long established restaurant in two quietly decorated rooms, with consistently good and very popular Californian-style food (no choice), friendly staff, and an interesting choice of wines; cl Sun, 2 wks Aug, 2 wks Christmas; disabled access. £38

Cork & Bottle *44–46 Cranbourn St WC2 (020) 7734 7807* Basement wine bar we've liked for over 30 years, nr West End theatres – good food inc interesting salads, cold buffet and unusual hot dishes, excellent wines, and cheerful service; children at manager's discretion. £21.50|**£6.95**

Duke of Cambridge *30 St. Peter's St N1 (020) 7359 3066* Well furnished cornerhouse and London's first completely organic pub, with a big, busy main room, simply decorated and furnished, lots of chunky wooden tables, pews and benches on bareboards, a couple of big metal vases with colourful flowers, daily papers, good lighting, a warmly inviting atmosphere, and a steady stream of varied customers; a couple of smaller candlelit rooms for eating, a changing choice of well presented imaginative food, four organic real ales on handpump, organic lagers, and organic wines, many by the glass; cl Mon am, 25–26 Dec. £34|**£8**

Eagle *159 Farringdon Rd EC1 (020) 7837 1353* Particularly good Mediterranean-style food in popular stylish pub where open kitchen forms part of the bar, well kept real ales, lots of wine by the glass, properly made cocktails, a lively and chatty atmosphere (lots of young media folk), and simple furnishings; daily specials run out early, so get there early. £20.50|**£6**

Ebury Wine Bar *139 Ebury St SW1 (020) 7730 8206* Said to be London's first wine bar (established 1959) with a loyal following, an excellent list of wines by the glass, and very good modern cooking; they have another bar restaurant called Carriages opposite the Royal Mews in Buckingham Palace Rd, and Joe's Brasserie at 130 Wandsworth Bridge Rd; cl Sun am 1 May–31 Aug, 24 Dec–2 Jan. £35

Fire Station *150 Waterloo Rd SE1 (020) 7401 3267* Remarkable conversion of a former fire station with two chatty front rooms, plenty of wooden pews, chairs and long tables, some brightly red-painted doors, modern art on the walls, newspapers to read, very good imaginative food, a decent choice of wines, and well kept real ales. £26/2-course early-bird meals £10.95

Food For Thought *31 Neal St WC2 (020) 7836 9072* Long-established and consistently good unlicensed vegetarian restaurant in former banana ripening warehouse, with take-away service upstairs and communal eating at long tables downstairs – you can also eat at tables outside; no corkage (Oddbins is round the corner); cl Sun pm, Christmas and New Year, Easter Sun. £9.70|**£3.90**

Fortnum & Mason *181 Piccadilly W1 (020) 7734 8040* Famous store with elegant 4th-floor St James's Restaurant (must book), Fountain Restaurant (ground floor), Patio Restaurant, and Salmon and Champagne bar (mezzanine) doing good breakfasts, morning coffee, lunches, fine afternoon tea and pre-theatre meals; cl Sun, bank hols; disabled access. £38|**£14**

Gavroche *43 Upper Brook St W1 (020) 7408 0881* London was put on the eating map when this quietly decorated club-like restaurant was opened by the Roux brothers 30 years ago; exemplary classic French cooking with modern touches (lovely puddings and perfect cheeses, too), attentive and professional service from French staff, and a classy but expensive wine list (some reach four figures); the set lunch is real value; cl Sat am, Sun, bank hols, Christmas and New Year. £100/£40 set lunch

Gay Hussar *2 Greek St W1 (020) 7437 0973* Very long-standing Hungarian restaurant with bags of atmosphere (downstairs has the most), good generous authentic food (especially enjoyable on a cold winter's day), and friendly service; cl Sun, bank hols. £30|£10

Greenhouse *27a Hays Mews W1 (020) 7499 3331* In a mews hidden away in Mayfair, this upmarket restaurant is a mixture of traditional and modern decor, a larger bar, and a water feature in the garden; enjoyable modern English food (lovely puddings), and thoughtful wine list; cl Sat am, bank hols, 25–26 Dec. £45

Livebait's Café Fish *36–40 Rupert Street W1 (020) 7287 8989* Bustling restaurant on two floors with lots of fish prints, closely set tables on wooden floors, efficient, swift service, particularly good fresh fish including platters of shellfish, a good bustling atmosphere, and plenty of customers; mostly white wines; cl 25–26 Dec, 1 Jan; disabled access. £20.

Mon Plaisir *19–21 Monmouth St WC2 (020) 7836 7243* Rambling French bistro with super bustling atmosphere, good value well prepared food, decent wines, and friendly staff; good value pre-theatre menus; cl Sat am, Sun, bank hols, Christmas, New Year; disabled access. £36/3-course set lunch £15.95

Monte's *164 Sloane Street SW1 (020) 7245 0896* Fronted by TV chef Jamie Oliver, this is a clubby, somewhat formal restaurant open to non-members at lunchtime only; very good modern European cooking using the best organic produce, and a carefully chosen (if not cheap) wine list; cl Sun; children lunchtime only; disabled access. £30

Moro *34–36 Exmouth Market EC1 (020) 7833 8336* Simply decorated restaurant with smart bentwood chairs on bare boards, cream and green walls, side bar with high stools, open-plan kitchen, and thriving atmosphere; interesting modern cooking with Spanish, North African and Middle Eastern influences, a short, thoughtful wine list, and informal but punctilious service; cl Sat am, Sun, bank hols, 10 days over Christmas and New Year; disabled access. £30|£12

Nahm *Halkin Hotel, 5 Halkin Street SW1 (020 7333 1000)* Minimalist-style restaurant in modern, individual hotel, serving particularly good, often complex Thai food cooked by renowned Australian expert; stylish modern bdrms; cl Sat am, Sun, 24–26 Dec, 1 Jan; disabled access. £67|£18

Nobu *Metropolitan, 19 Old Park Lane W1 (020) 7447 4747* Chic and very fashionable first-floor restaurant overlooking Hyde Park, with innovative beautifully presented Japanese food touched with South American influences, helpful friendly staff, lots of sakis and good choice of wines; prices can quickly add up; cl Sat am, bank hols, Christmas; children over 10; disabled access. £75/set lunch £25

Odette's *130 Regents Park Rd NW1 (020) 7586 5486* Smart front dining room with lots of gilded mirrors, airy back conservatory, and slightly cheaper downstairs wine bar with good modern English and more unusual dishes, friendly service, and thoughtful wine list; cl Sun pm, Christmas and New Year; partial disabled access. £40/£12.50 2-course set lunch

Oxo Tower Restaurant & Brasserie *Oxo Tower Wharf SE1 (020) 7803 3888* Briskly modern brasserie and restaurant on 8th floor of South Bank redevelopment, light and airy, with busy open kitchen, lots of functional tables and chairs, and promptly served modern English food; what stands out, of course, is the panoramic view over the Thames and City – best in summer from tables on the outside terrace; cl 25–26 Dec; disabled access. Restaurant: 3-course lunch £28.50/ Brasserie: 2-course lunch £19.50

Petrus *33 St. James's Street SW1 (020) 7930 4272* Slightly formal but very popular spacious restaurant with complex and elegant French cooking, a fine wine list, and attentive, correct service; vegetarian dishes by prior notice only; cl Sat am, Sun, bank hols; children over 5. £75/3-course set lunch £26

Poons 27 Lisle St WC2 (020) 7437 4549 Atmospheric unlicensed and unmodernised Chinese restaurant with extremely good value tasty barbecued and wind-dried food; cl Good Fri, 24–26 Dec; late opening Sun till 5.15pm. £15|**£5.50**

Porte des Indes 32 Bryanston St W1 (020) 7224 0055 Grand and exotic Indian restaurant with wonderful flower arrangements, a huge marble waterfall, palm trees and potted plants, and jungle murals; good interesting dishes from 7 regions of India and some unique recipes from the resident French Creole communities of Pondicherry; cl Sat am, 24–27 Dec; disabled access. £50/lunchtime buffet £20

Portobello Gold 95–97 Portobello Rd W11 (020) 7460 4900 Enterprising pub with a brightly painted front bar, changing displays of art and photography on the walls, a nice old fireplace, cushioned pews, daily papers, and a laid-back atmosphere; the back, partly no smoking dining room has a mural of an exotic-seeming bay, a profusion of plants and trees, and comfortable wicker chairs, stained wooden tables, and a cage of vocal canaries; interesting food from a monthly changing menu, Sunday roasts served until 8pm, coffee and fresh pastries from 10am, real ales and a wide range of tequilas, 15 wines by the glass, a cigar menu, and polite, helpful young staff; bdrms; cl Christmas; children until 8pm. £18.50/2 courses £10|**£5.95**

Quaglino's 16 Bury St SW1 (020) 7930 6767 Fashionable restaurant with big stone staircase to antipasti bar overlooking huge dining room with flamboyantly painted pillars, fine flowers, highly modern attractive furnishings, and buoyant buzzing atmosphere; modern cooking and a good wine list; cl 25 Dec, 1 Jan; no children in bar in evening; disabled access. £40|**£11**

Rebato's 169 South Lambeth Rd SW8 (020) 7735 6388 Busy and attractive high-ceilinged bar with friendly barman and waiters, good choice of tapas (plenty of fresh fish), and lots of Spanish wines; also Spanish restaurant; cl Sat am, Sun, bank hols, Christmas. £23.95|**£4.95**

RSJ 13a Coin St SE1 (020) 7928 4554 Relaxed and friendly restaurant with fine modern British and Mediterranean cooking and exceptional Loire wines in simple surroundings; handy for the South Bank and popular for pre- and post meals; cl Sun. £25/2-course set lunch £15.95

Rules 35 Maiden Lane WC2 (020) 7836 5314 One of London's oldest restaurants (1798), smart and very British (a firm local favourite, as well as loved by tourists), with good English food inc fine seasonal furred and feathered game and oysters; an interesting history; cl 4 days over Christmas; partial disabled access. £51|**£16.95**

Simpsons in the Strand 100 Strand WC2 (020) 7836 9112 There are two restaurants here: Simply Simpsons upstairs has light pink Adam-style decor, serves contemporary British food, and has a smart casual dress code; cl Sun, 25 Dec. 2-course meal £16. Downstairs is Grand Divan which is much more formal (jacket and tie), with heavy wooden panelling and ornate plasterwork, a club-like atmosphere, and old-fashioned traditional English cooking inc nursery puddings, roasts carved as you want them at your table on silver-domed trolleys, and full English breakfast; cl Sat am, 25–26 Dec; disabled access. £45/2 courses £15

Sotheby's Café 34–35 New Bond St W1 (020) 7293 5077 Very small but very classy café with simple high-class food inc lovely puddings and good cheeses, a carefully chosen little wine list, and courteous staff; cl wknds, 2 wks Aug, Christmas, New Year; partial disabled access. £35|**£12.50**

Souk Litchfield St WC2 (020) 7240 1796 Basement restaurant with Moroccan decor – low vaulted ceilings, drapes, ceramic tiles and mirrors, banquettes with colourful cushions, pouffes, low wooden or brass patterned tables, and dim lighting and candlelight; generous and enjoyable Moroccan food, mint tea, and occasional belly-dancing; cl 25–26 Dec. £21

Square 6–10 Bruton St W1 (020) 7495 7100 Elegant slightly formal Mayfair restaurant with bold modern drawings on the walls, well spaced tables on the parquet floor, superb modern French cooking with plenty of strong flavours and beautiful presentation, wonderful puddings, a really fine wine list (at a price), and exemplary service; cl Sat and Sun am, 25–26 Dec, 1 Jan; disabled access. £55/2-course lunch £25

Tante Claire *Wilton Place SW1 (020) 7823 2003* Classic, civilised French restaurant in a wing of the Berkeley Hotel, with high French-style food using luxurious ingredients (and described in French only), correct, courteous service, and an exceptional (though not cheap) wine list; the set-price lunches are good value; jacket and tie required; cl Sat am, Sun, bank hols, Easter, Christmas and New Year; children over 7; disabled access. £70 dinner/£29 3-course set lunch

Tappit Hen *5 William IV St WC2 (020) 7836 9839* Cosy and atmospheric little wine bar, feeling very old-fashioned, with good snacks and good value wines – more for lunchtimes (when the smoked salmon sandwiches are lovely), though you can book for upstairs in the evening; cl Sat, Sun, bank hols; no children in evening. £23/2-course lunch £12.95

Wagamama *4 Streatham St WC1 (020) 7580 9365* You will have to queue to get into this trendy, simply furnished Japanese basement restaurant with its long tables and benches for communal eating; very friendly cheerful service, noisy informal atmosphere, good healthy food – raw salads, ramens (huge bowls of noodles with meat, vegetables and Japanese additions), rice dishes, sake, grape and plum wines, beer, and free green tea; exceptionally good value; no smoking; disabled access; cl 25–26 Dec; several other branches too. £25|£6

Zafferano *15 Lowndes St SW1 (020) 7235 5800* Many think this the best Italian restaurant in town – smart but relaxed, with carefully set tables, really first-class food (especially nice – and cheaper – at lunchtime), smart friendly staff, perfect coffees, and a good choice of Italian wines; cl 25 Dec. £37.50 dinner, £25.50 lunch

Special thanks to Jenny and Michael Back, Paul Kennedy, Roger and Jenny Huggins, B and K Hypher

---

SCOTLAND

Edinburgh is famously rewarding for a city holiday. And there's massive scope beyond that lovely city for all sorts of different breaks and holidays. We have sifted carefully through what Scotland has to offer, and creamed off the absolute tops. What's particularly good is that many of the hundreds of memorable places to visit are free. And we have tracked down over a hundred really nice places to stay in, often at most attractive prices, as well as eating places that do justice to Scotland's first-class raw materials.

To make all this manageable, we have divided the country into four areas.

South Scotland includes Edinburgh, Glasgow, and many of Scotland's most interesting places to visit, as well as some charming and very peaceful countryside. It's the best part to go to if you've never been to Scotland before.

East Scotland has a marvellous variety of scenery from Highland grandeur to placid lochs and rich valleys, from intimate fishing villages and sandy beaches to rugged cliffs. There's also a great variety of interesting places to visit, and the fastest roads run up this side.

West Scotland is on the whole less populated, with a glorious and intricate series of mountain and coastal landscapes. There are interesting family outings, though not nearly so many as in the South and East. We've defined this area as N of the Clyde and S of the Great Glen, with Loch Lomond (the focus of Scotland's new – and first – National Park) marking its eastern edge.

North Scotland, everything N of the Great Glen, has fewer places to visit (and fewer visitors – part of its charm for many). There is magnificent scenery on the W coast and on Skye, a quieter sandy E coast, and some wild and desolate places in the N.

Outside Edinburgh, Glasgow and areas within easy reach, many places close over winter – and others change to shorter winter opening hours in Sept, rather than Oct (the usual month for a change in England). For the scenery, the best time to visit is May and June, when the days are very long, the great gardens are at their best, the weather is generally at least as fine as in high summer, the roads (often narrow and twisting in the West and Highlands) are not yet clogged by summer crowds, and the northern midges are still on their best behaviour.

A three-hour drive will get anyone living N of Manchester or York well into South Scotland. Beyond that, you really need a longer stay to make the driving worth while. Rail and air, of course, bring Scotland much closer. The fastest trains, when they run on time, do the London–Edinburgh trip in around 4 hrs. Direct flights connect London and some regional airports with Edinburgh, Glasgow, Inverness and Aberdeen, with some local connections from there.

Visit Scotland have special offers (especially in autumn) on transport, accommodation and attractions; phone (0131) 332 2433 or take a look at their website www.visitscotland.com. Historic Scotland looks after most of the castles and abbeys we list. A good value Explorer ticket admits you to all their properties; £15 for 3 days out of five, £20 for seven days out of ten, or £23 for ten days out of 21 (you can get them from all HS properties, most Tourist Information Centres, or in advance on (0131) 668 8800

South Scotland

Edinburgh is a great holiday city, and the rest of South Scotland is bursting with a great variety of places to visit, from spectacular castles, mansions and gardens to lively discovery centres, bustling coastal towns, and lovely islands

An unbeatable place for a break, Edinburgh has a tremendous amount to offer everyone, from great galleries, museums and historic buildings, to plenty of lively family treats. Glasgow can't compare with it for beauty or poise, but also has lots to fill a visit, with a hi-tech new family science centre on top of some of Britain's most rewarding and varied museums and galleries.

Outside these two cities, there's a host of places with appeal for families. New Lanark is perhaps the pick of several absorbing excursions into the living past, with the Scottish Mining Museum in Newtongrange another real eye-opener. Budding young inventors will love a trip to the Big Idea in Irvine, and Motherwell has Scotland's biggest theme park. Galloway Forest Park is ideal when the weather is fine. Perky Largs (Vikingar! here is appealingly lively), and over on the E coast, Dunbar and Eyemouth make good seaside trips. The islands of Bute and Arran both tempt with enjoyable expeditions for a day or longer.

This part of Scotland has an abundance of ancient castles, romantic ruined abbeys, and some glorious gardens and grand houses to explore. Culzean is a great favourite, the opulent furnishings at Manderston near Duns have to be seen to be believed, and, newly opened to the public, Newhailes House near Musselburgh is unusual. Many other stately homes offer more entertainment (for all ages) than you might expect: romantic Traquair, Paxton House, Bowhill House near Selkirk, and Drumlanrig Castle by Thornhill are especially enjoyable.

The Borders hills are grand and relatively little-visited – peaceful get-away-from-it-all walking. A Freedom of the Fairways pass covers a round on the finest Borders golf courses. The gentler SW corner is one of Britain's friendliest areas, and a great place for utter relaxation.

Please let us know what you think of places in the *Guide*. Use the report forms at the back of the book, write us a letter or log on to www.goodguides.com.

Where to stay

AUCHENCAIRN NX8149 **Balcary Bay** *Auchencairn, Castle Douglas, Kirkcudbrightshire DG7 1QZ (01556) 640217* **£112***, plus special breaks; 20 rms with fine views. Once a smugglers' haunt, this charming and much liked hotel has wonderful views over the bay, neat grounds running down to the water, comfortable public rooms (one with log fire), a relaxed friendly atmosphere, good enjoyable food inc super breakfasts, and lots of walks; cl 1 Dec–1 Mar; disabled access; dogs welcome in bedrooms

BEATTOCK NT0603 **Auchen Castle** *Beattock, Moffat, Dumfriesshire DG10 9SH (01683) 300407* **£95**; 25 pleasantly decorated rms, most with own bthrms, some in Lodge. Smart but friendly country-house hotel in lovely quiet spot with a trout loch and spectacular hill views, good food, and peaceful comfortable bar; dogs welcome in bedrooms

CANONBIE NY3976 **Riverside** *Canonbie, Dumfriesshire DG14 0UX (013873) 71512* **£70**, plus special breaks; 7 chintzy rms, 2 in cottage. Civilised little inn with friendly owners, comfortable communicating bar rooms, open fire, attractive furnishings, good imaginative food using top-quality produce, a fine wine list, and marvellous breakfasts; cl first 2 wks Feb; partal disabled access; dogs welcome in bedrooms

CLARENCEFIELD NY0669 **Comlongon Castle** *Clarencefield, Dumfrieshire DG1 4NA (01387) 870283* **£110**; 12 rms. Magnificent 15th-c castle keep with 18th-c mansion house adjoining – suits of armour and a huge fireplace in oak-panelled great hall, good food in Jacobean dining room, and a relaxing drawing room; dungeons, battlements, archers' quarters and haunted long gallery; cl first 2 wks Jan

EDINBURGH NT2573 **Balmoral Hotel** *1 Princes St, Edinburgh EH2 2EQ (0131) 556 2414* **£230***, plus special breaks; 188 luxurious rms. In city centre and handy for visitor attractions. Splendid Victorian hotel with wonderfully opulent entrance hall, elegant day rooms, lovely flowers, particularly friendly helpful staff, and very good food in several restaurants; excellent leisure facilities; good disabled access; dogs welcome in bedrooms

EDINBURGH NT2473 **Bonham** *35 Drumsheugh Gdns, Edinburgh EH3 7RN (0131) 623 6060* **£195**, plus special breaks; 48 stylish, individually designed rms with all the latest technology, and some with views to the Firth of Forth. Chic town house in a quiet square, cleverly converted from a former maternity hospital (and then a university residence), with plenty of original Victorian features among more contemporary designs, lovely fresh flower arrangements, paintings by Scottish artists throughout, good modern cooking in oak-panelled restaurant (open to non-residents, too), and professional but friendly staff; disabled access

EDINBURGH NT2374 **Channings** *12–16 South Learmonth Gdns, Edinburgh EH4 1EZ (0131) 315 2226* **£185***, plus special breaks; 46 individually designed bdrms. Originally five Edwardian townhouses and now a stylish hotel on a quiet cobbled street overlooking private gardens; relaxed club-like atmosphere, comfortable lounges with open fires, contemporary wine bar and conservatory, and enjoyable modern French food in restful downstairs restaurant; cl Christmas

EDINBURGH NT2572 **Ellesmere Guest House** *11 Glengyle Terrace, Edinburgh EH3 9LN (0131) 229 4823* **£28**; 6 comfortable, spotless rms. Warmly friendly and homely guest house in a quiet spot overlooking Bruntsfield Links, with friendly helpful owners and good hearty breakfasts in combined no smoking dining room/lounge; children over 12

EDINBURGH NT2572 **Elmview** *15 Glengyle Terrace, Edinburgh EH3 9LN (0131) 228 1973* **£75***; 3 large rms. Quietly placed in fine Victorian terrace overlooking a park 15 mins' walk from the castle and centre; carefully maintained, elegantly furnished, good breakfast and welcome; no children

EDINBURGH NT2674 **Greenside** *9 Royal Terrace, Edinburgh EH7 5AB (0131) 557 0022* **£90***; 16 individually decorated rms. Family-run hotel in Georgian terrace with friendly atmosphere, big lounge, hearty breakfasts, and quiet terraced garden; disabled access

EDINBURGH NT2574 **Howard** *34 Great King St, Edinburgh EH3 6QH* *(0131) 315 2220* **£275**, plus special breaks; 18 luxurious rms inc 5 suites. Discreet hotel in three Georgian townhouses, with comfortable, elegant public rooms, and courteous friendly service; separate breakfast room and dining room though dinner can be served in your room by your butler. There are restaurants in their sister hotels, Channings and the Bonham; cl Christmas

EDINBURGH NT2776 **Malmaison** *1 Tower Pl, Leith, Edinburgh EH6 7DB* *(0131) 555 6868* **£141.50***, plus special breaks; 101 stylish rms with CD players and satellite TV. Converted baronial-style seamen's mission in the fashionable docks area of Leith with very good food in the downstairs French brasserie, cheerful café bar, gym, and friendly service; free parking; disabled access; dogs welcome in bedrooms

EDINBURGH NT2474 **Seven Danube Street** *7 Danube Street, Edinburgh EH4 1NN* *(0131) 332 2755* **£90**, 3 fine rms with plenty of extras. Quietly placed Georgian house with charming helpful owners, comfortable lounge, a relaxed homely atmosphere, marvellous breakfasts served at one big table, and small garden; no smoking; cl Christmas; dogs by arrangement

ESKDALEMUIR NY2595 **Hart Manor** *Eskdalemuir, Langholm, Dumfriesshire DG13 0QQ* *(01387) 373217* **£83***, plus special breaks; 4 recently refurbished rms. 19th-c shooting lodge with lovely views and fine hill-walking country all around; a warm, relaxed atmosphere in both the lounge and library, particularly good individual and totally home-made country cooking, a thoughtful wine list and choice of malt whiskies, and superb breakfasts; no smoking; cl Christmas; children over 12; dogs welcome in bedrooms

GATEHOUSE OF FLEET NX6056 **Cally Palace** *Gatehouse of Fleet, Castle Douglas, Kirkcudbrightshire DG7 2DL* *(01557) 814341* **£136** inc dinner, plus special breaks; 56 rms. 18th-c country mansion, a hotel since 1934, with marble fireplaces and ornate ceilings in the public rooms, relaxed cocktail bar, enjoyable food in elegant dining room (smart dress required), evening pianist and Sat evening dinner dance, helpful friendly staff, 18-hole golf course, croquet and tennis, indoor leisure complex with heated swimming pool, private fishing/boating loch; cl Jan, cl wkdys in Feb; disabled access; dogs welcome in bedrooms ☺

GIFFORD NT5367 **Tweeddale Arms** *Gifford, Haddington, East Lothian EH41 4QU* *(01620) 810240* **£65**, plus special breaks; 16 rms. Civilised late 17th-c inn in quiet village, with comfortable sofas and chairs in tranquil lounge, gracious dining room, wide choice of good daily-changing food, and charming service; cl 1st Jan; disabled access; dogs welcome in bedrooms

GLASGOW NS5965 **Babbity Bowster** *16–18 Blackfriars St, Glasgow G1 1PE* *(0141) 552 5055* **£70**; 6 clean simple rms, showers. Warmly welcoming rather continental place with decent breakfasts (served till late), attractively decorated airy bar, and a cheery first-floor restaurant which hosts a gallery as well as a programme of musical and theatrical events; cl 25 Dec, 1 Jan

GLASGOW NS5865 **Malmaison** *278 West George St, Glasgow G2 4LL* *(0141) 572 1000* **£120**; 72 smartly quirky very comfortable rms. Stylishly converted Scottish Episcopal church with Greek façade, striking central wrought-iron staircase, a relaxed contemporary atmosphere, friendly staff, enjoyable French food in attractive brasserie/bar; gym; disabled access

GLASGOW NS5567 **One Devonshire Gardens** *Glasgow G12 0UX* *(0141) 339 2001* **£244**; 29 opulent rms. Elegant cosseting hotel a little way out from the centre, with luxurious Victorian furnishings, fresh flowers, exemplary staff, and fine modern cooking in the stylish restaurant; dogs welcome in bedrooms

GULLANE NT4983 **Greywalls** *Duncar Rd, Gullane, East Lothian EH31 2EG* *(01620) 842144* **£240***, plus special breaks; 23 individually decorated rms. Overlooking Muirfield golf course, this beautiful family-run Lutyens house has antiques, open fires and flowers in its comfortable lounges and panelled library, very good food and fine wines in the restaurant, impeccable service, and lovely Gertrude Jekyll garden, all of a piece with the perfect design of the house; cl Nov–Mar;

disabled access; dogs welcome in bedrooms

INNERLEITHEN NT3336 **Traquair Arms** *Innerleithen, Peeblesshire EH44 6PD* *(01896) 830229* **£70**, plus special breaks; 15 comfortable rms. Very friendly hotel with interesting choice of good food in attractive dining room, cosy lounge bar, friendly service, superb local Traquair ale, and nice breakfasts; disabled access; dogs welcome away from restaurant

LOCKERBIE NY1283 **Dryfesdale Hotel** *Dryfebridge, Lockerbie, Dumfriesshire DG11 2SF (01576) 202427* **£85**, plus wknd breaks; 16 rms, 6 on ground floor. Relaxed and comfortable former manse in five acres of grounds, open fire in the homely lounge, good food in the pleasant restaurant, garden and lovely surrounding countryside, putting and croquet; cl 26 Dec; good disabled access; dogs welcome in bedrooms

MAYBOLE NS3103 **Ladyburn** *Kilkerran, Maybole, Ayrshire KA19 7SG (01655) 740585* **£120**, plus special breaks; 5 rms. Quietly set family home dating from the 1600s and set on the edge of the magnificent estate of Kilkerran; antiques, books and open fires in comfortable drawing room and library, good traditional Scottish/French cooking, and friendly staff; shooting and fishing can be arranged; newly refurbished self-catering flat also (children allowed here but not in main house); cl 2 wks Nov, 4 wks Jan–Mar

MELROSE NT5433 **Burts** *Market Sq, Melrose, Roxburghshire TD6 9PN (01896) 822285* **£94***, plus special breaks; 20 rms. Welcoming 18th-c family-run hotel close to abbey ruins in delightfully quiet village; coal fire in bustling bar, residents' lounge, consistently popular imaginative food, exceptional breakfasts; cl 26 Dec; dogs welcome

MELROSE NT5434 **Dunfermline House** *Buccleuch St, Melrose, Roxburghshire TD6 9LB (01896) 822148* **£50***, plus special breaks; 5 rms. Neatly kept Victorian terraced house nr abbey ruins, with good breakfasts and friendly owners

MINNIGAFF NX4165 **Creebridge House** *Creebridge, Newton Stewart, Wigtownshire DG8 6NP (01671) 402121* **£108***, plus special breaks; 19 rms inc 2 with four-posters. Attractive country-house hotel in three acres of gardens with a relaxed and friendly atmosphere, open fire in the comfortable newly decorated drawing room, cheerful bar, and big choice of delicious food inc fine local fish and seafood in the newly refurbished garden restaurant; cl 25 and 26 Dec; dogs welcome in bedrooms

NENTHORN NT6938 **Whitehill Farm** *Nenthorn, Kelso, Roxburghshire TD5 7RZ (01573) 470203* **£48***; 4 rms, 3 with shared bthrm. Comfortable farmhouse on mixed farm with fine views, big garden, log fire in sitting room, and good home cooking; no babies; cl Christmas and New Year; dogs welcome

PEEBLES NT2344 **Cringletie House** *Cringletie, Peebles EH45 8PL (01721) 730233* **£140**, plus special breaks; 14 pretty rms. Surrounded by 28 acres of garden and woodland and with fine views, very welcoming quiet turreted baronial mansion, delicious food using home-grown vegetables, extensive Scottish breakfasts, and excellent service; dogs welcome in bedrooms

PORTPATRICK NW9954 **Crown** *Portpatrick, Stranraer, Wigtownshire DG9 8SX (01776) 810261* **£72**, plus special breaks; 12 attractive rms. Atmospheric harbourside inn with rambling and interestingly furnished old-fashioned bar, airy art deco dining room, good food with an emphasis on local seafood, super breakfasts, and carefully chosen wines

PORTPATRICK NX0252 **Knockinaam Lodge** *Portpatrick, Stranraer, Wigtownshire DG9 9AD (01776) 810471* **£250** inc dinner, plus special breaks; 10 individual rms. Lovely very neatly kept little hotel with comfortable pretty rooms, open fires, wonderful food, and friendly caring service; dramatic surroundings, with lots of fine cliff walks; children over 12 in evening restaurant (high tea at 6pm); dogs welcome in bedrooms

QUOTHQUAN NT0140 **Shieldhill** *Quothquan, Biggar, Lanarkshire ML12 6NA (01899) 220035* **£160**, plus special breaks; 16 pretty rms. Partly 12th-c castle located in a fine setting with a comfortable oak-panelled lounge, open fires, library, and particularly good food in the no smoking restaurant, and warm friendly service; disabled access

SWINTON NT8347 **Wheatsheaf** *Main St, Swinton, Duns, Berwickshire TD11 3JJ* *(01890) 860257* **£85***, plus special breaks; 8 rms with baths or showers. Warmly friendly inn with exceptionally good food, a pleasantly decorated and relaxed main lounge plus small pubby area, new reception lounge, and no smoking front conservatory; garden play area for children; cl 25 Dec, 1 Jan, 2 wks Jan and 1 wk July; dogs welcome in bedrooms

UPHALL NT0571 **Houstoun House** *Uphall, Broxburn, West Lothian EH52 6JS* *(01506) 853831* **£125**, plus wknd breaks; 72 comfortable rms, quite a few in extension. 17th-c house divided into three distinct buildings: fine food in three panelled dining rooms, vaulted bars (one with a fire nearly all year), quiet lounge, lovely grounds, and leisure complex with swimming pool, sauna, gym, tennis courts and Italian bistro; disabled access

To see and do

ALLOWAY NS3318
Burns National Heritage Park 🅰
A key stop on the Burns Trail: the poet was born here in 1759. The associated local sites are grouped together under the above name. The introductory visitor centre the **Tam O'Shanter Experience** (Murdochs Lane) is a multi-media show bringing Burns's famous poem vividly to life. Up the road you can explore the tiny rooms of the poet's birthplace, thatched Burns Cottage, and an adjacent museum of his life has a good collection of manuscripts and letters. In the other direction, S of the centre, the **Burns Monument** was built in 1823 to a fine design by Thomas Hamilton Jr, and is adorned with characters from Burns's poems sculpted by James Thom. Meals, snacks, shop, disabled access; cl 25–26 Dec, 1–2 Jan; (01292) 443700; £5. The **Head of Ayr Farm Park** (Dunure Rd) is useful for restless children; snacks, shop, disabled access; cl mid-Oct to Mar; (01292) 441210; £4.50.

ARRAN NS0037
This rewarding island is just under an hour by ferry from Ardrossan, a popular public-transport day trip from Glasgow, with summer ferries from Claonaig on Kintyre too; (01475) 650100 for ferry enquiries. It has a marvellous variety of scenery from subtropical gardens to mountain deer forest, and has beautifully set and highly regarded golf courses. Brodick the main

settlement has several places to hire bikes. The Kingsley on Brodick esplanade has decent home cooking, and the Brodick Bar (Alma Rd) is simple good value. On the opposite side of the island near Machrie are several intriguing Bronze Age stone circles. Arran has a good circular walk up and down Goatfell, prominent for miles around, and you can follow the shore right around the N tip, the Cock of Arran. Up near here the waterside Catacol Hotel has decent food. There's a good walk on the W coast, from Blackwaterfoot to the King's Cave, which supposedly sheltered Robert the Bruce.

Arran Brewery 🅰 The island's first modern brewery, with rewarding views over Brodick Bay and Goatfell Mountain. A viewing gallery in the visitor centre looks over the microbrewery itself, and you can sample some of the beers you've watched being made. Shop, reasonable disabled access; cl winter Tues and Sun; (01770) 302353; £1.

Brodick Castle and Garden Fine old castle, in lovely surroundings between the sea, hills and majestic mountain of Goatfell. Partly 13th-c, and extended in 1652 and 1844, it's very fierce-looking from the outside, but comfortably grand inside – even a little homely in places. There are almost a hundred antlered heads on the walls of the main staircase. It's surrounded by magnificent formal gardens, with the highlight the woodland garden started in 1923 by the Duchess of Montrose, inc many lovely rare and tender rhododendrons. Adventure playground, plants for sale, meals, snacks, shop, limited disabled access; castle cl Nov–Mar, garden and country park open all year; (01770) 302202; £7; NTS.

BALCARY POINT NX8149
On the W side of sandy Auchencairn Bay, this makes for a good peaceful walk from the pretty village of Auchencairn. The Balcary Bay Hotel has good bar food, and lovely views from its terraces.

BALERNO NT1666
Malleny House Garden ⊞ (off A70) Charming gardens that are home to a national collection of 19th-c shrub roses (best in late Jun), as well as four clipped old yew trees – the survivors of a dozen planted exactly four centuries ago. Limited disabled access; (0131) 449 2283; around £2; NTS. The handsome Johnsburn House Hotel does good lunches.

BATHGATE NS9970
Cairnpapple Hill (just E of Torpichen, off B792) One of the most important prehistoric sites in the country, a stone circle and series of successive burial cairns that seems to have been used for around 3,000 years from neolithic times to the 1st c BC, and especially during the second millennium BC. Extraordinary views from this raw and atmospheric hilltop site, known locally as 'windy ways'; HS.

BEARSDEN NS5472
Roman Bath House (Roman Rd) Probably the best surviving visible Roman building in Scotland, built in the 2nd c for the garrison at Bearsden Fort, part of the short-lived Antonine Wall defences; free. The appropriately named 55BC (Drymen Rd) has decent food.

BIGGAR NT0437
Several good museums here.
Gasworks (Gasworks Rd) This striking old building is now a museum on the coal-gas industry; disabled access, open pm Jun–Sept; £1.
Gladstone Court Museum (North Back Rd) Houses an entire reconstructed village street; cl Sun am,

and all mid-Oct to Easter; (01899) 221573; *£2.
Greenhill Covenanters House ⊞ (Burn Braes, Biggar) 17th-c farmhouse originally at Wiston but moved piece by piece and reassembled here; cl am wknds, Mon–Fri by appointment, cl Oct–May; £1.
Moat Park Heritage Centre ⊞ Good local history collections, and the centrepiece of the town's several worthwhile museums. Shop, disabled access; cl Sun am, and mid-Oct to Easter; (01899) 221050; *£2.
Puppet Theatre (just off A702) Magical and different, with really big puppets that glow in the dark; when they're not doing shows (must book as very popular) they sometimes do backstage tours. Teas, shop, disabled access (phone first); cl 25 Dec, 1 Jan, and some winter Suns; (01899) 220631 for programme and booking; shows £5, tours £2.50.

BLANTYRE NS6958
David Livingstone Centre ⊞ (Station Rd, off A724) The birthplace of the famous explorer, with a museum on his life and work inc personal belongings. Adventure playground in the landscaped grounds. Meals, snacks, shop, disabled access; cl Sun am, Jan–Mar; (01698) 823140; £3.50. The Cricklewood at Bothwell (B7071) is a good dining pub.

BUTE NS0864
This popular Glasgow holiday island is a ½-hr ferry trip from Wemyss Bay/Skelmorlie; it has a mix of fresh air and ebullient summer entertainments. In Rothesay, the island's main town, the seafront Black Bull has good food. There's lovely open country in the N, its southern tip is rewarding too, and the West Island Way allows walks with great vistas all along the island's W side – you may see seals on the shore, and there's a bird hide suitable for wheelchairs at Kirk Dam NS0863. The waterfront Royal at Port Bannatyne has good home cooking, and the Kames Inn has grand sea views and food all day.
Bute Museum (Stuart St, Rothesay) Decent museum, worth a visit (shop, disabled access; cl winter Sun and Mon, Christmas and New Year; £1.50). The gents' at the harbour, built in 1899, has

ornate wall tiles and fine ceramic mosaic floors.

Monastery of St Blane NS0953 Ruined Norman chapel in a delightful spot, a short way uphill from the road – just sheep and the occasional walker.

Mount Stuart 🖼 (off A844, just E of Upper Scoulag) In this bracingly bleak landscape, the spectacular Victorian Gothic mansion is almost a shock; the elaborate rooms are splendidly over the top too. The 300 acres of landscaped grounds and woodland include several pretty gardens, as well as a pinetum of mature conifers and a nicely isolated stretch of sandy beach, reached via a lime avenue. Meals, snacks, shop, disabled access; cl Tues, Thurs, and Oct–Apr (exc wknds Oct and Apr); (01700) 503877; £7, garden only £3.50. Scotrail do a bargain ticket (£16) inc entrance and train, ferry and bus travel from Glasgow Central or Strathclyde stations.

Rothesay Castle 13th-c; shop; cl Sun am, and in winter Thurs pm and all day Fri; £2.20; HS.

Victorian Fern House and Gardens (Ascog Hall, S of Rothesay) The only one of its kind in Britain, restored and replanted with one of the most impressive collections of ferns to be found outside a botanic garden, inc many species from the southern hemisphere – one is thought to be over 1,000 years old. Cl Mon, Tues and all Nov–Easter; (01700) 504555; *£3.

CAERLAVEROCK NY0265

Caerlaverock Castle 13th-c, protected not just by its moat but by the wild swampy marshes around it – spruce plantations are being felled to bring the landscape back to its former look. It has an unusual triangular inner courtyard, and elaborate projecting tops for dropping missiles on assailants. Snacks, shop, some disabled access; cl 25–26 Dec, 1–2 Jan; (01387) 770244; £2.80; HS.

Wildfowl & Wetlands Trust The Caerlaverock salt marshes are a reserve with outstanding hide facilities and observation towers. Countless wildfowl flock here, especially barnacle geese; between Oct and Apr there are generally around 13,000 of them, very dramatic when they're all in flight.

Snacks, shop, some disabled access; cl 25 Dec; (01387) 770200; £4. The Nith at Glencaple has good value food.

CARDONESS NX5955

Cardoness Castle (A75) Well preserved 15th-c four-storey tower house, overlooking the Water of Fleet; interesting fireplaces. Shop; cl wkdys Dec–Mar; (01557) 814427; £2.20; HS. A mile NE, Gatehouse of Fleet has places to eat.

CARMICHAEL NS9338

Discover Carmichael Visitor Centre 🖼 (A73 N of Biggar) Among the eclectic attractions here are a collection of waxwork models of Scotland's heroes and heroines, various period re-creations inc a Victorian wash-house, a baby animal farm, free horse and cart rides, and an exhibition on wind energy, all within the attractive grounds of the Carmichael Estate. Also outdoor adventure play areas, buggy racing and a deer park walk; meals, snacks, farm shop specialising in home-reared meat, disabled access; cl Jan–Mar, Apr and May open by appointment; (01899) 308169; *£3.25.

CASTLE DOUGLAS NX7462

Threave Castle (off minor road Bridge of Dee–Townhead) The Black Douglas, Archibald the Grim, built this in the 14th c; four storeys high, it stands on an islet in the River Dee, so you have to get a ferry across (ring the bell and the custodian will come to get you). Shop; cl Oct–Mar; (07711) 223101; £2.20 inc ferry; HS.

Threave Garden (1m W off A75) The National Trust for Scotland's horticulture school, with plenty to see through the year in its walled garden, glasshouses and waymarked nature trails (the estate is 1,500 acres). If you're there in spring, don't miss the massed display of over 200 varieties of daffodil. 19th-c Scottish baronial Threave House is now also open to the public, showing the main rooms and a museum of country life. Meals, snacks, shop, some disabled access; visitor centre cl Jan–Mar; (01556) 502575; *£5, £8.50 inc house; NTS. The Royal Hotel has good value food.

CLARENCEFIELD NY0669

Comlongon Castle (B725) 15th-c, unusually well preserved, with interesting original features inc dungeons, kitchen, great hall and even privies. Cl 24–26 Dec and 1st 2 wks Jan; (01387) 870283; £2 – and see **Where to stay**.

COATBRIDGE NS7265

Summerlee Heritage Park (off W Canal St) Ambitious centre looking at the local iron, steel and engineering industries. Lots going on, spread over 25 acres of a former iron works; the working machinery creates a real feeling of authenticity. The site has Scotland's only working electric tramway. Snacks, shop, disabled access (but not to mine); cl 25–26 Dec, 1–2 Jan; (01236) 431261; free (tram 75p).

Time Capsule 🖴 (Buchanan St) Fun – swimming pools and leisure centre with a loose historic theme: water chutes whizz you through the origins of man, and a woolly mammoth holds court in the centre of the ice rink; cl 25 Dec, 1 Jan; (01236) 449572. *£4.20 waterworld, *£2.60 ice age.

COLDSTREAM NT8240

Hirsel Country Park Pretty lakeside and woodland walks (best May–Jun) through the huge Hirsel Estate (nearly 5 square miles), with Douglas highland cattle and various waterfowl (there's a hide by the lake); also a craft centre and gallery, and a little museum has displays on the estate. Tearoom and picnic area, shop, disabled access; *£2 per car.

CRAMOND NT1877

Charming preserved former fishing village, the once-humble cottages now snapped up by Edinburgh's professionals. The Cramond Inn has good value food.

Lauriston Castle Interesting, with mostly Edwardian decor and antiques. Shop, disabled access; open for guided tours only (not Fri), phone for times; (0131) 336 2060; £4.50.

River Almond walk W of Edinburgh, from the Cramond Brig Hotel on the A90, you can walk along the wooded valley to Cramond, cross the Almond by ferry, then go along the shore past Dalmeny House, and finish below the Forth Bridge at South Queensferry. There are frequent buses back to the start, and to Edinburgh.

CREETOWN NX4759

Gem Rock Museum 🖴 (Chain Rd)

Enormous private collection of gem stones and minerals, some displayed in an atmospheric crystal cave. Also a fossilised dinosaur egg and dung, and meteorites. Snacks, shop, disabled access; cl wkdys 23 Dec–31 Jan but open by appointment wkdys in Dec and Feb; (01671) 820357; £2.90.

CRICHTON NT3861

Crichton Castle (2½m SW of Pathhead) Not far from Edinburgh, but really remote-feeling, as it's reached only by a half-mile walk from the car park by Crichton church; medieval tower house, with grim external defences for an elegant late 16th-c Italianate interior courtyard; open Apr–Nov; (01875) 320017; £2; HS.

CULZEAN NS2310

Culzean Castle (pronounced 'Cullane') A day here is one of the most popular outings in the region. The 18th-c mansion is one of great presence and brilliance, and the grounds (nearly a square mile) are among the finest in Britain, lushly planted and richly ornamental, with woods, lake, an abundance of paths, bracing clifftop and shoreline walks, and an 18th-c walled garden. The house was splendidly refashioned by Robert Adam, and has been well restored to show off his work to full effect. Meals, snacks, shop, disabled access; house open Apr–Oct, and possibly some winter wknds, park open all year; (01655) 884455; £9; NTS. You can stay in rather smart self-contained apartments on the top floor.

DALKEITH NT3167

Edinburgh Butterfly & Insect World (Dobbies Nursery, off A720 at Gilmerton jnctn) Gloriously coloured exotic butterflies, as well as scorpions and tarantulas, bee garden, and rainforest frogs. Handling sessions mean you can get even closer to some of the animals. Meals, snacks, shop, disabled access; cl 25–26 Dec, 1 Jan; (0131) 663 4932; £4.35. The Sun (Lothianbridge – A7 S) has good value food.

DIRLETON NT5184

Dirleton Castle (A198) Grandly rebuilt after a siege in 1298, only to be destroyed again in 1650 – though you can still see plenty of the original squared 13th-c masonry. It has a charming garden planted in the 16th c, with ancient yews and hedges around a bowling green, and what is thought to be the longest herbaceous border in the world. Cl 25–26 Dec, 1–2 Jan; (01620) 850330; £2.80; HS. The Castle Hotel and Open Arms in this pleasant golfing village are both good for lunch.

DRYBURGH NT5932

Dryburgh Abbey (Dryburgh) Remarkably complete ruins in a lovely setting among old cedars by the River Tweed – its graceful cloisters are very peaceful. Walter Scott is buried here (and on the B6356 N the signposted Scott's View is idyllic). Shop, some disabled access; cl am Sun in winter, 25–26 Dec, 1–2 Jan; (01835) 822381; *£3; HS. The Buccleuch Arms at St Boswells is a civilised place for something to eat.

DUMBARTON NS4074

Dumbarton Castle (A82, Dumbarton) Perched on a rock 73 metres (240 ft) above the River Clyde, with dramatic views of the surrounding countryside. Most of what can be seen dates from the 18th and 19th c, though there are some earlier remains. Snacks, shop; cl noon–1.30pm, Thurs pm, all day Fri and Sun am throughout Oct–Apr; (01389) 732167; £2.20; HS. The Ettrick in the picturesque Clydeside village of Old Kilpatrick has good value food.

DUMFRIES NX9775

A pleasant red sandstone town, the biggest in the SW, with close Burns connections. The Globe Tavern (off High St) has two rooms still very much as they were when this was his regular haunt (Anna Park, a barmaid, bore his child).

Burns House (Burns St) Where he lived for the three years before his death; has original letters and manuscripts along with the chair in which he wrote his last poems and songs, and an upstairs window has his signature scratched in the glass. Shop; cl Sun am (all day in winter), winter lunchtimes and winter Mon, 25–26 Dec, 1–2 Jan; (01387) 255297; free.

Burns Mausoleum (St Michael's churchyard) The tomb of Robert Burns, his on-and-off wife Jean Armour, and their five sons; you can usually make an appointment to visit at the Burns House; free.

Museum and Camera Obscura 🔲 (Church St) In the tower of an 18th-c windmill, this has a camera obscura and local history. Shop, limited disabled access; cl 11–2pm, all day Sun and Mon Oct–Mar, plus am summer Sun, and all 25–26 Dec, 1–2 Jan; (01387) 253374; museum free, camera obscura £1.50.

Robert Burns Centre (Mill Rd) Exhibition and audio-visual display in handsome stone-built watermill, as well as an interesting scale model of the town at the time he wrote. Meals, snacks, shop, disabled access; cl Sun and Mon and lunch hours Oct–Mar; (01387) 264808; £1.50 for audio-visual exhibition

DUMGOYNE NS5282

Glengoyne Distillery You can go on a 50-minute guided tour of this prettily set 150-year-old distillery; cl am Sun, best to phone over Christmas; shop, some disabled access; (01360) 550254; £3.95 inc a taster.

DUNBAR NT6779

The harbour here is pretty, with some picturesquely jagged fragments of the medieval castle in the John Muir Country Park, and good walks nearby, along the cliffs and by the marshy inlets of Belhaven Bay; the harbourside Starfish has good seafood. Quite a few good clean beaches near here, notably Belhaven, nearby Whitesands Bay, and the one at Thorntonloch a few miles down the coast.

DUNDRENNAN NX7547

Dundrennan Abbey (A711) Ruined Cistercian abbey famous as the place where Mary Queen of Scots is thought to have spent her last night in Scotland. Cl am Sun and Thurs, and all day Fri in Oct (open wknds only Nov–Mar); (01557) 500262; £1.80; HS.

DUNS NT8054

Edin's Hall Broch Off the A6112 from Duns, this is one of very few such Iron Age strongholds in the Lowlands.

Manderston (2m E, off A6105) Splendidly lavish house built for the plutocrat racecourse owner Sir James Miller; he told the architect to spare no expense, so ended up with the world's only silver staircase. Other gloriously extravagant parts are the painted ceilings, and a ballroom decorated in Miller's racing colours. Also fine formal gardens, and an unusual biscuit-tin museum. Teas, shop, limited disabled access; open only Thurs and Sun pm mid-May to Oct; (01361) 883450; £6.50, £3.50 grounds only. The Wheatsheaf at Swinton isn't far, for a very good meal.

EAST FORTUNE NT5578

Museum of Flight (East Fortune Airfield, B1347) Scotland's National Museum of Aviation, with over 40 aeroplanes from a Spitfire to a Vulcan bomber, also Britain's oldest surviving aircraft (1896), and displays on famous flyers and air traffic control. Café, shop, disabled access; cl 25, 31 Dec, 1 Jan; (01620) 880308; £3.

EAST KILBRIDE NS6055

Museum of Scottish Country Life (Philipshill Rd, off A726 W) In 170 acres, this £9 million centre houses the rural life collection of the National Museums of Scotland, with galleries on the environment, rural technology, and people; there's also a picture gallery and film room, and they hold special events in the arena. A working farm owned by the same family for 400 years shows farming methods from the 1950s, when horses were still being used alongside machines. Meals, snacks, shop, disabled access; cl 25–26 Dec, and 1–2 Jan; (01355) 224181; £3, children and NTS members free.

EAST LINTON NT5875

Hailes Castle (minor rd SW) 13th/14th-c, another brief stopping point for Mary Queen of Scots; now in ruins, but lovely in spring, with wild flowers along the stream; free.

Preston Mill (B1407) One of the oldest working water-driven oatmeal mills left. It's a pretty spot with geese and ducks, and an old dovecote nearby. Shop, limited disabled access; cl am, also Tues, Weds and end Oct–start Apr; (01620) 860426; £3.50; NTS. The Drovers Inn has good food.

EDINBURGH NT2573

Edinburgh is one of Britain's most rewarding cities for visitors, whether you've been dozens of times before or are popping in for the first time. It always looks good, and there are lots of interesting places within a pleasant walk of each other. It's dominated by the ancient silhouettes of Edinburgh Castle on its castle cliff and of the long erratic line of tall, thin Old Town buildings stretched along beside it. Up here narrow streets and alleys with steep steps between them and courtyard closes leading off the **Royal Mile** have a real flavour of the distant past, with a good many interesting ancient buildings (and a lot of the city's antiquarian bookshops and other interesting specialist shops). But it's by no means stuck in the past, with for instance a stunning new dance studio set right into the castle rock. When the authorities decided to redevelop the city in the 18th c, they did it not by knocking down the medieval buildings, but instead by creating an entirely new part of the city, working from scratch. The resulting New Town is a masterpiece of spacious Georgian town planning, stretching out handsomely below the steep crag of Castle Rock and its medieval skyline. Walking tours in the evenings are often led by students, and the literary pub tour is particularly good fun; (0131) 226 6665; £7. New Town highlights are Charlotte Square, Moray Place, Ainslie Place and Randolph Crescent. The regular bus services have good value daily and weekly passes, and it is worth getting used to the public transport (the city council has plans, unpopular with residents, for a car toll). As in most cities, there's a hop-on hop-off tour bus, and the ticket gives discounts to some of the places to visit. The August Festival has great music and dance and a fun Fringe. The city's at its best then; if you do visit the festival, make sure you've got accommodation sorted out well in advance. Edinburgh's pubs and bars are a special delight, chatty places often of great character. Among the best for atmosphere are the Bow Bar (Victoria St), Bannermans Bar (Cowgate), Bennets Bar (Leven St), Café Royal and Guildford Arms (both W Register St), Cumberland (Cumberland St), Athletic Arms (Angle Park Terrace/Kilmarnock Rd) and Kays Bar (Jamaica St W); for food, we recommend the Abbotsford, Kenilworth and Milnes (all Rose St), Dome (George St), Starbank

(Laverockbank Rd), Braidwoods (West Port) and both Fishers and Ship on the Shore (The Shore, Leith). The corner lobby bar of the Balmoral Hotel is a relaxing spot at the hub of the town. For a fuller meal, the city has a remarkable number of good value bistro-style restaurants (as well as the places we mention in the **Where to eat section**). There are lots of good shops dotted around town, especially on or near Princes St – its tall, mainly Georgian buildings lining just the one side, giving an expansive view across the sunken gardens to the castle. Parallel George St has some superior shops, while Rose St, an alley between the two, has plenty of pubs and cafés. More bars around the Grassmarket and Lawnmarket, a lively area of the Old Town; Victoria St has interesting shops. Iain Mellis (Bruntisfield Pl) specialises in farm cheeses, and Valvona & Crolla (Elm Row) is a dazzling delicatessen.

Arthur's Seat Out beyond Holyrood in Holyrood Park is this saddle-back mountain, a great volcanic mass giving a wonderful panorama over the city, and a pleasant place for wandering, with a hill fort on top and the largely unspoilt Duddingston village below it (the Sheep Heid here is a good pub).

Blackford Hill Virtually a mountain within the city, giving walkers great views of Edinburgh.

Calton Hill Dominating the E end of Princes St, with magnificent views over the city. An unusual sight up here is a romantic Doric colonnade, intended to be a full replica of the Parthenon (until the money ran out).

Clan Tartan Centre (Leith Mills, Bangor Rd) Displays of various clans and their costume, computers that let you trace your own Scottish heritage, and a factory shop with good value Pringle knitwear and tweeds. Meals, snacks, shop, disabled access; cl 25 Dec, 1 Jan; (0131) 553 5161; free.

Craigmillar Castle (A68) On the city's SE outskirts, this is a seemingly impregnable 14th-c tower house (it did in fact fall to the English in 1544), within an impressive double curtain wall; lots to see, and a proper castle feel. Snacks, shop; cl all Fri, Thurs pm, Sun am, 25–26 Dec, 1 Jan; £2.20; HS.

Dynamic Earth (Holyrood Rd) This exemplary exhibition shows the story of the planet using hi-tech effects and state-of-the-art displays. It vividly relates the story of evolution using giant screens, dramatic sounds and commentary, and evocative smells, spread over eleven hugely different and often quite spectacular display areas. You can see a volcano erupt, experience an earthquake, watch animals swinging through trees in the rainforest, and take a helicopter flight over the glaciers of Scandinavia. The finale is a colourful film taking in images of storms, hurricanes, and sunsets, with a serious environmental message of course – but hearing it has rarely been so much fun; play area for younger children. Meals, snacks, shop, disabled access; cl Mon and Tues between Nov and Mar, and 24–26 Dec; (0131) 550 7800; £7.95.

Edinburgh Castle Perched on its hill above the city, this is a place of great magnetism; it's been a fortress since at least the 7th c, and excavations show there's been a settlement here for 4,000 years. The oldest building today is the beautiful St Margaret's Chapel, thought to have been built in the 12th c and little changed since. Other highlights include the apartments of Mary, Queen of Scots, Mons Meg (the 15th-c Belgian cannon with which James II cowed the Black Douglases), the Scottish Crown Jewels (centuries older than the English ones), and for romantics the Stone of Destiny or Scottish coronation stone; the polished natural rock protruding into the building also stays in the memory. Glorious views from the battlements, over the Firth of Forth to Fife beyond. You can wander around on your own, but the official guides are a great bonus – they leave from the drawbridge, several times a day. Meals, snacks, shop, mostly disabled access; cl 25–26 Dec; (0131) 225 9846; £8.50 (inc audio tour); HS. If you're around at lunchtime, look (and listen) for the firing of the One o' Clock Gun from the parapet.

Edinburgh Zoo (Corstorphine Rd; A8 W) Best known for its Penguin Parade most afternoons at 2.15 (Apr–Oct); there are plenty of other rare and odd-looking animals around the attractive grounds. Children enjoy the yew-hedge maze loosely themed around Darwin's theory of evolution; it has several fountains along the way that periodically shoot out jets of water (summer only). Extra events and activities in summer hols. Meals, snacks, shops, disabled access (though a little hilly); open every day (inc 25 Dec); (0131) 334 9171; £7.50.

Georgian House (Charlotte Sq) Archetypal New Town period house, part of Robert Adam's magnificent terrace along the N side. The rooms and servants' quarters have been refurbished in the style of 1800. Shop, disabled access to ground floor only; cl Jan–Feb; (0131) 225 2160; £5; NTS. Close by, nr Queen St, beyond a further strip of gardens, is another Georgian area with some interesting shops.

National Gallery of Scotland (The Mound) Fine neo-classical building with particularly good examples of most European schools and periods inc a £20 million Botticelli *Madonna and Child*, barely seen for over a century and acquired thanks to grants from the Heritage Lottery and the National Art Collections funds. Plenty of Scottish paintings too, with many great works by Ramsay, Raeburn, Wilkie and McTaggart. Few would dispute that it's one of Britain's best galleries. Look out for the rather incongruous portrait of one of the donor's dogs – it has to be hung here as a condition of the donation of other pictures. The gallery is being extended and will join on to the Royal Scottish Academy (closed for refurbishment until summer 2003) and will house an underground lecture theatre, restaurant and shop. The first exhibition will be a blockbuster Monet one, beginning Aug–26 Oct 2003. Shop, disabled access; cl Sun am, 25–26 Dec; (0131) 624 6200; free (exc major exhibitions).

Nelson Monument (Calton Hill) Best of all for the views of Edinburgh – if you can face the 31-metre (102-ft) climb to the top. Every day at 1pm (exc Sun) the time ball drops as the gun at the castle goes off. Shop; cl Mon am, Sun, 25–26 Dec, 1–2 Jan; (0131) 556 2716; £2.

Palace of Holyroodhouse

(Canongate) Imposing yet human-scale palace with its origins in the Abbey of Holyrood, founded by David I. Later the court of Mary Queen of Scots, it was used by Bonnie Prince Charlie during his occupation of Edinburgh, and is still a Royal residence for part of the year. The oldest surviving part is James IV's tower, with Queen Mary's rooms on the second floor, where a plaque on the floor marks where her secretary Rizzio was murdered in front of her. The throne room and state rooms have period furniture, tapestries and paintings from the Royal collection. Much more inviting than many English palaces, and this year a new gallery in an old church in the grounds has changing exhibitions of graphic art (separate charge). In summer a path through the palace gardens takes you back to the forecourt. Shop, limited disabled access by prior arrangement; cl Good Fri, 25–26 Dec, and occasional other dates (if the Queen is in residence, for example) – best to check on (0131) 556 7371; £6.50.

Royal Botanic Garden (Inverleith Row) A magnet for plant lovers, founded as a physic garden in 1670 at Holyrood, then transplanted here (just N of the centre) in the early 19th c. Covering 72 acres, it has various splendid themed areas, with a woodland garden, peat garden, arboretum, Chinese collection and the Glasshouse Experience, inc palm houses, fern house and aquatic house. Meals, snacks, shop, disabled access; cl 25 Dec, 1 Jan; (0131) 552 7171; free.

Royal Mile Between castle and palace at the heart of the Old Town (for most people Edinburgh's two must-sees) is this a largely medieval street, around which you'll find all sorts of interesting or historic houses and features, and quaint lanes leading off in all directions. The following places (down to the Museum of Edinburgh) are listed in order, as you go down the Mile towards Holyrood. Usefully, it's punctuated with cafés and bars in which to stop and work out your next move, starting with the old-world Ensign Ewart on the left as you leave the castle.

Camera Obscura (Castlehill) Up at the top of the Royal Mile, these 19th-c revolving lenses and mirrors create unique panoramas of the city as soon as the lights go down, with a good commentary; best on a sunny day. Shop; cl 25 Dec; (0131) 226 3709; £4.95.

Scotch Whisky Heritage Centre (Castlehill) Entertainingly illustrates the story of the national drink, starting off with a shortish journey in a barrel-shaped car through well put together sets and tableaux. The full tour is a useful introduction to the distilling process; if you haven't been to a real distillery it's a good substitute, and there's a decent sample and well stocked shop at the end. Meals, snacks, disabled access; cl 25 Dec; (0131) 220 0441; £6.95.

Gladstone's Land (Lawnmarket) Six-storeyed early 17th-c building, still with its arcaded front, and refurnished in period style. The walls and ceilings have remarkable tempera paintings. Shop; cl Sun am, and Nov–Mar; (0131) 226 5856; £5; NTS.

Lady Stair's House (Lady Stair's Cl, off Lawnmarket) Named after its 18th-c occupant, this partly 1622 building houses the **Writers Museum**, a collection of manuscripts and objects associated with Robert Burns, Walter Scott and R L Stevenson. Shop; cl Sun exc pm during Festival, 25–26 Dec, 1–2 Jan; (0131) 529 4901; free.

St Giles Cathedral (High St) The Royal Mile widens out briefly around Scotland's High Kirk, the city's most impressive ecclesiastical building, mainly 15th c, but dating from around 1120. Topped with an ornate crown-like tower, it has monuments to famous Scots from Knox (minister here until his death) to R L Stevenson. Cl am Sun, 26 Dec, 1–2 Jan; guided tours; free (donations welcome).

Parliament House (Parliament Sq) Just behind the cathedral, this was the seat of Scottish government until the Union of 1707, and now houses the supreme law courts of Scotland. Don't miss the fine hammerbeam roof in the hall. Snacks, some disabled access; cl wknds and public holidays; (0131) 225 2595; free.

John Knox House (High St) The oldest house on the Royal Mile, where the great reformer is supposed to have died. Now looking every bit of its 500 years, it still has its original timber galleries, oak panelling and splendid painted ceiling. Snacks, shop, disabled access to ground floor; cl Sun (exc July–Aug), 25–26 Dec, possibly closing from March 2003 for refurbishment, so best to check; (0131) 556 9579; *£2.25.

Museum of Childhood (High St) The first of its type and still one of the best, a charming collection of games, toys and dolls from all over the globe. Shop, some disabled access; cl Sun (exc pm during Festival and July–Aug); (0131) 529 4142; free.

Museum of Edinburgh (Canongate) 16th-c, with well refurbished galleries on glass, pottery and trade; other collections include Scottish pottery, Edinburgh silver, local history, and even Greyfriars Bobby's collar and bowl. The exhibits are thoughtfully – even artistically – arranged; also temporary exhibitions. Shop; cl Sun (exc pm during Festival), cl 25–26 Dec, 1–2 Jan; (0131) 529 4143; free. The Canons Gait nearby is a smart bar, and Cadenheads (number 172) sell some unusual whiskies .

Canongate Tolbooth (Canongate) This elaborate building houses an excellent social history exhibition, the People's Story, with reconstructions built very much around first-hand accounts of Edinburgh life. Shop, disabled access; cl Sun (exc pm during Festival), 25–26 Dec, 1 Jan; (0131) 529 4057; free.

Royal Museum/Museum of Scotland (Chambers St) A tremendous variety of collections, covering virtually anything you might care to poke around in, now shared between a gloriously light and spacious Victorian building, and its grand new counterpart next door. Children particularly enjoy the intricate working scale models of early engines, but it has something for everyone. Meals, snacks, shop, disabled access; cl Sun am and 25 Dec; (0131) 225 7534; free.

Royal Observatory 🖼 (Blackford Hill) An interactive science centre with hands-on exhibits about light, CD-Roms about space and astronomy, and Scotland's largest telescope showing a panoramic view of Edinburgh; info about the past and present work of the observatory, and new World in a Spin exhibition. Snacks, shop, limited disabled access; cl Christmas and New Year; (0131) 668 8405; *£3.50.

Royal Yacht *Britannia* Displays about the yacht and its Royal past in an onshore visitor centre, and a chance to explore five decks of the ship in which the Queen and Prince Philip cruised the world. Shop, disabled access; cl 25 Dec, 1 Jan; (0131) 555 5566; £7.75.

Scott Memorial (Princes St) After the castle, probably Edinburgh's most memorable building: remarkably ornate, with its handsome if mucky exterior (they've kept the dirt, as cleaning seemed more damaging). The crypt of the very handsome Gothic-Revival St John's episcopal church on Princes St has interesting vegetarian and vegan food.

Scottish National Gallery of Modern Art (Belford Rd) Breathtaking collection inc great works by Picasso, Barbara Hepworth and Lichtenstein. Meals, snacks, shop, disabled access; cl Sun am, 25–26 Dec; (0131) 624 6200; free (may be charges for temporary exhibitions). Across the road the **Dean Gallery** houses extensive collections of Dada and Surrealist art; Sir Eduardo Paolozzi's collection of prints, drawings, and the contents of his studio are here too, and there are changing modern art exhibitions. Cl Sun am, 25–26 Dec; snacks, shop, disabled access; free.

Scottish National Portrait Gallery (Queen St) The history of Scotland through a huge and varied collection of portraits in a variety of media. Meals, snacks, shop, disabled access; cl Sun am, 25–26 Dec; (0131) 624 6200; free.

Water of Leith W of the centre and well worth exploring, often very picturesque and ravine-like. By its banks is the quaint little Dean Village, surprisingly close to the heart of the city, yet unaffected by all the New Town building above it; further N you can leave the river and head into the Royal Botanic Garden. The river eventually winds down to Leith itself (a once prosperous and separate dockland area now swallowed up by the city, its waterfront reviving again with trendy bars and restaurants). The Scottish Malt Whisky Society (Giles St), dedicated to cask-strength top-quality malt whiskies, has a downstairs bar/restaurant.

ELLISLAND FARM NX9283

Ellisland Farm (off A76) Robert Burns lived here from 1788 to 1791, trying unsuccessfully to introduce new farming methods. There are displays of material associated with the poet (who wrote *Tam o' Shanter* and *Auld Lang Syne* while living here), and cattle and sheep wander around much as they must have done then. Lovely riverside walk. Shop, some disabled access; cl Sun am, and in winter cl all day Sun and Mon (though if you ring, you may find them open); (01387) 740426; *£2.50.

ESKDALEMUIR NY2597

Beautifully set mountain village, famous for its cruel winter weather; it also has an unexpected Tibetan Buddhist temple and monastery.

Southern Upland Way The longest of only three official long-distance paths in Scotland, this route makes a 212-mile coast-to-coast journey over the hills from Portpatrick to Cockburnspath. It's a good basis for day walks, for instance from this village, though large distances between places often make it hard to find focal points.

EYEMOUTH NT9464

Understated family holiday seaside town around busy but pretty fishing harbour, with a decent beach. The Ship overlooking the harbour has reasonable food.

Eyemouth Museum (Market Pl) Good local history museum in former church, with magnificent tapestry commemorating the terrible gale of 14 Oct 1881 which drowned 189 fishermen (139 from Eyemouth); cl Sun in Oct, cl Nov–Easter; *£2.

St Abbs A steep and pretty little seaside village nearby, with a sandy beach and old fishing harbour, little used now.

St Abb's Head The best of the E coast scenery for walkers; walk from Eyemouth or St Abbs, with a good path along the cliffs – noisily crowded with breeding seabirds in late spring, with high breezy walks, and a lighthouse. £1 parking, £1 visitor centre (cl Nov–Mar).

FERNIEGAIR NS7453
Chatelherault (Carlisle Rd) Originally built by William Adam as a hunting lodge and summer house for the Dukes of Hamilton; a grand avenue of trees once linked this restored hilltop building with Hamilton Palace (now demolished). The former kennels house a museum with displays on the history of the house, the local area and its wildlife. The Banqueting Hall and Duke's private bedroom can still be seen, and the grounds include restored Georgian gardens, woodland trails, rare white park cattle (much closer to wild ancestors than today's breeds), and a children's adventure playground. Ranger-led walks; meals, snacks, shop, disabled access; West Wing cl Fri; cl 25–26 Dec, and 1–2 Jan; (01698) 426213; free.

GALLOWAY FOREST PARK NX3672
Attractive and easily accessible, taking in around 100 lochs, 300 miles of river, great views, and many miles of forest, mountain and moorland. Many trees are fairly recent replantings, the original woodland having from the 15th c onwards rapidly fallen victim to the demand for timber. Many of the lochs are ringed by waymarked walks and trails, and there are plenty of scenic drives and cycle routes. Visitor centres (Apr–Oct only) at Kirroughtree, Glen Trool and Clatteringshaws all have exhibitions and information to help you make the most of the forests, inc details of where you can camp or fish, and the best places to spot wildlife. Stones mark 14th-c battles between Scotland and England, and the 1680s Killing Time, when Scottish covenanters were hunted down and killed in the government's attempts to impose bishops on the Scottish church.
Loch Trool NX4180 There are particularly attractive trails around the loch, with a good informative summer visitor centre nearby. A memorial stone commemorates a 1307 battle between Robert the Bruce and the armies of Edward I.
Merrick NX4285 The highest point in SW Scotland, a worthwhile but long and strenuous walk up from Glen Trool.
Wood of Cree NX3771 One of the best surviving stretches of ancient forest, with an RSPB reserve among its trees and marshes.

GLASGOW NS5865
There's a real zing and vitality about this proud city (Scotland's biggest), which is making great strides in its efforts to shake off its rather rough image, including embarking on a 10-year massive redevelopment of the waterfront. Besides the excellent art galleries and interesting museums, it houses the Royal Scottish National Orchestra (with a fine-sounding concert hall), the Scottish Opera and the Scottish Ballet. Though there are many places to see and visit, a snag for visitors is that they are scattered around this sprawling city, and often poorly signposted: the Burrell Collection, one of the most interesting places of all, is tucked away in the suburbs. Families will find it worth investing in a Day Tripper ticket, which allows virtually unlimited train and underground travel (£13 for two adults and up to four children). This also makes it easy to get out to the really attractive parks fringing the city (we list these after the other attractions here, starting with Greenbank Garden). Besides the restaurants and bars mentioned in **Where to eat**, Glasgow is full of places to eat out in, formal and informal; interesting and undaunting pubs and bars include the Auctioneers (St Vincent Pl), Blackfriars (Bell St), Bon Accord (North St), Cask & Still (Hope St) and Horseshoe (Drury St).
Art Gallery & Museum (Kelvingrove Park) Huge Victorian building with remarkably rich collection of paintings, esp strong in works by the French Impressionists, Post-Impressionists, and Scottish artists from the 17th c. Also sculpture, silver, porcelain, armour, ethnography and natural history. Meals, snacks, shop, disabled access; cl 25–26 Dec, 1–2 Jan, and will close for refurbishment in spring 2003; (0141) 287 2699; free.
Botanic Gardens (730 Great Western Rd) Sloping gently down to the River Kelvin, these are famous for their fantastic glasshouses, particularly the half-acre Kibble Palace, with its soaring tree ferns interspersed with

Victorian sculpture (they are hoping to do a major restoration this year). Snacks, disabled access; (0141) 334 2422; free.

Burrell Collection (Pollok Country Park, SW Glasgow) A couple of miles out in the suburbs, but not to be missed – and rarely too crowded. Splendidly and imaginatively housed in a modern building created to show its different parts to perfection, the huge collection – far too much to see at one go – includes Egyptian alabaster, Chinese jade, oriental rugs, remarkable tapestries, medieval metalwork and stained glass, even medieval doorways and windows set into the walls, as well as paintings by Degas, Manet and Rembrandt among others. Good meals and snacks, shop, disabled access; cl 25–26 Dec, 1–2 Jan; (0141) 287 2550; free (parking £1.50). See entries for Pollok Country Park and House below.

Pollok Country Park (SW) One of the best of the several parks and gardens you'll find around Glasgow, with waterside and woodland trails, rose garden, Clydesdale horses and highland cattle. Shop, snacks, disabled access; (0141) 632 9299; free.

Pollok House (Pollok Country Park) Treasures here include silver, ceramics and porcelain, but it's the paintings (for which the house was largely redesigned 100 years ago) that stand out, with a collection of Spanish masters such as Goya and El Greco cannily acquired in the mid-19th c when they were greatly undervalued. Meals, snacks, shop; cl 25–26 Dec, 1–2 Jan; (0141) 616 6410; £5 (free Nov–Mar).

Charles Rennie Mackintosh tours Sauchiehall St, a link between the museum/university quarter and the centre, is an ordinary shopping street, but well worth the walk for the ground-breaking designer and architect's most famous building, the Glasgow School of Art (Renfrew St, just off; the tours are highly recommended, (0141) 353 4526), and the decoratively mirrored Willow Tea Room (open till 5pm), furnished to his designs, too. Shop, some disabled access; cl Sun Sept–Jun, 25 Dec, 1 Jan; *£5. As well as other places we mention with Mackintosh connections, you can buy works after

him at the Glasgow Style Gallery on Gt Western Rd.

Clyde walks A walkway tracks along the cleaned-up Clyde waterfront, and planning permission has recently been granted for a £500 million 10-year regeneration of one central stretch – work has begun on a landmark new conference centre. The world's last ocean-going paddle steamer, *Waverley*, fresh in its 1940s splendour after a £4 million refit, makes summer runs from Anderston Quay; (0141) 221 8152 for times. Some Clydeside pubs well outside Glasgow with decent food and good sea views include the Cardwell at Cardwell Bay in Gourock and the Spinnaker there, and the Lookout down in Troon Marina.

Clydebuilt (Braehead Shopping Centre, off junctions 25a and 26 of M8) This extension of Irvine's Scottish Maritime Museum tells the story of Glasgow and the Clyde from the tobacco lords of the 17th c, through the city's days as a global centre for shipbuilding, right up to the present. Interactive exhibits let you steer your own ship, make a fortune as an ocean trader, and for a taste of the real thing you can take control of a real steam engine and go aboard the oldest Clyde-built vessel still afloat. Shop, disabled access; cl Fri, 25 Dec and 1 Jan; (0141) 886 1013; *£3.50.

Gallery of Modern Art (Queen St) Big newish gallery concentrating on living British artists – not just Scottish. Lively café-bar (open some evenings too), shop, good disabled access; cl 25–26 Dec, 1–2 Jan; (0141) 229 1996; free.

Glasgow Cathedral 12th-c, dedicated to St Mungo, the founder of the city. It's very well preserved, though most fittings date from the 19th c; best parts are the crypt, a gracefully vaulted affair built in the mid-13th c, and the Blackadder aisle; summer shop; cl Sun am, 25–26 Dec, 1–2 Jan; (0141) 552 6891; free. The spectacular Necropolis graveyard is interesting to wander around, and there's a fine overview from the cathedral. The area around here is the oldest part of Glasgow, though not the most interesting. **Glasgow Science Centre** 🔄 (Pacific

Quay) By far the largest Millennium project north of the border. There are three main attractions, the four-storey Science Mall, the remarkable 100-metre (328-ft) Glasgow Tower, and the IMAX theatre. All are extraordinary-looking: the Mall and the theatre are the only buildings in Europe apart from Bilbao's Guggenheim to be clad in shimmering titanium, while the tower is the only one in the world capable of revolving 360 degrees from the ground up. The most appealing part for families is the Science Mall, with hundreds of interactive and hands-on displays, a planetarium, and the Virtual Science Theatre. One floor concentrates on fairly basic science, with simple experiments and activities for children (and a soft play area for younger ones). The next floor up has slightly more complex activities showing science in action, all with touch-screen instructions, perhaps letting you build your own vehicle and race it round the building. Another floor has touch-screen displays on how science affects our lives, and dotted around are Discovery areas – small spaces where you can crack on with your own experiments. The Tower has multimedia displays and presentations on past and future developments in Glasgow, as well as splendid views from the top, and the IMAX theatre is Scotland's first. Meals, snacks, shop, disabled access; cl 24–25 Dec , 1 Jan; (0141) 420 5000. Definitely recommendable, but some grown-ups might feel miffed at having to pay more than children when all the seats etc are at child height, and given the high prices the glass surfaces could perhaps be cleaned even more frequently; also, we found some sections closed. You can buy individual tickets for each attraction: £6.50 for the Science Mall, and £5.50 for the Tower or the IMAX; but it's better value to get a double ticket (£9.50) or a triple ticket (£14).

House for an Art Lover (Bellahouston Park) Built to 1901 designs by Charles Rennie Mackintosh, with an exhibition of decorative rooms, and contemporary art exhibitions. Meals, snacks, shop, disabled access; exhibition cl every Fri, wkdys Oct–Mar (though best to check winter opening times), house cl 25–26 Dec, 1–2 Jan; (0141) 353 4770; *£3.50. The Empire Exhibition of 1938 was held on these 171 acres, which now comprise a Victorian walled garden and sweeping lawns.

Hunterian Art Gallery (Hillhead St) Dr Hunter bequeathed the core of fine paintings which form the basis of this beautifully hung collection. A grand range of works by Whistler, interesting and well chosen contemporary British art and sculpture, and an amazing re-creation of the home of Charles Rennie Mackintosh (cl 12.30–1.30pm), the designer/architect whose exuberant yet very disciplined and clean-lined art nouveau buildings stand out among the more traditional solidity of much of Glasgow. Shop, disabled access with prior notice; cl Sun; (0141) 330 5431; free.

Hunterian Museum (Gilbert Scott building, University Ave) Scotland's first public museum, housing the University collections of ethnographic, palaeontological and anthropological material, along with lots of archaeology, and a coin display. Shop, disabled access; cl Sun, public hols and 24 Dec–2 Jan; (0141) 330 4221; free. The exhibitions were also founded by Dr William Hunter, the 18th-c physician (see above).

Lighthouse (11 Mitchell Lane) One of the largest temporary exhibition spaces for architecture and design in Europe, with four exhibition floors, and a permanent Mackintosh Interpretation Centre with interactive displays and models – good views over the city from the Mackintosh Tower. Restaurants, cafés, shops, disabled access; cl 25–26 Dec, 1–2 Jan; free, £3 for the Mackintosh Centre and tower. The interesting Horseshoe round the corner in Drury St has cheap food upstairs.

McLellan Galleries (Sauchiehall St) Spacious and well lit, these have good changing art exhibitions. Snacks, shop, disabled access; cl 25–26 Dec, 1–2 Jan; (0141) 332 7521; free.

Merchant City The area around George Sq and Buchanan St was built on a grid plan in the 19th c, and visually has something in common with New York

City – Americans say they feel at home here. With its proud Victorian buildings cleaned back to their warm sandstone, this smart shopping quarter is the city's most comfortable area to stroll around. Guided walking tours leave the Tourist Information Centre on George Sq daily at 2.30 and 6pm Mon, Tues, Thurs and Fri, 2.30pm Weds and 10.30 and 2.30 Sun Jun–Sept, and there are also evening ghost tours, (0141) 772 0022; £5. The City Chambers here is a spectacular monument to 1880s civic pride, marble everywhere; free tours. The Counting House is a splendid pub in an opulent converted bank nearby. There are café-bars and bistros off Princes Sq, and antiques stalls in Victorian Village (W Regent St). On the SE edge of this area, between Gallowgate and London Rd past the Tolbooth, the Barras (barrows) is an entertaining wknd flea-market. With around 800 stalls it's one of the biggest covered markets in the world, great for bargains or just passing time; try the plump fresh clappie doos (mussels).

Museum of Transport (Kelvin Hall, Bunhouse Rd) Plenty of vehicles for the enthusiast, from trams to ships; a walk-through car showroom is arranged as if some were for sale, with original prices displayed on the windscreens. Meals, snacks, shop, disabled access; cl 25–26 Dec, 1–2 Jan; (0141) 287 2720; free.

Museum quarter NW of the centre, the West End, Kelvingrove and the University quarter have some elegant streets, the main concentration of museums, and the botanic gardens.

People's Palace (Glasgow Green) Very enjoyable social history museum looking at Glaswegians over the centuries, in a park just SE of centre. Disabled access; cl 25 Dec, 1–2 Jan; (0141) 5540 223; free. The museum's café is in the adjacent Winter Gardens, a massive conservatory with huge tropical plants.

Provan's Lordship (Castle St) Glasgow's oldest house, used by the Prebend of Provan – a canon of the cathedral. Dating from 1471, it's been carefully restored and furnished according to several period styles. Shop, disabled access to ground floor only; cl 25–26 Dec, 1–2 Jan; (0141) 553 2557; free.

Scotland Street School Museum Designed by Mackintosh, this spectacular building originally had a capacity of 1,250 pupils in 21 classrooms, and now houses a lively museum with displays on the history of education in Scotland from 1872 and reconstructed classrooms: Victorian, World War II, and 1950s–60s, also an Edwardian cookery room. New displays include the architectural history of the school and Mackintosh's designs, and the history of the school and local area including interactive displays and a photographic database. Audio-visual, activity programme and temporary exhibitions. Cl 25–26 Dec, 1–2 Jan; (0141) 287 0500; free.

Scottish Football Museum (Hampden Park) This enjoyably covers such themes as football's origins, women's football, fans, other games influenced by football, even some social history too. Lots of memorabilia (inc the world's oldest football ticket), audio-visual and hands-on displays, and they've reconstructed the 1903 changing room and press box from the original stadium. Best to book for the 45-min guided tours. Snacks, shop, disabled access; cl match days and for special events, and a few days over Christmas, phone to check; (0141) 616 6100; £5, tours £2.50.

St Mungo Museum of Religious Life (Cathedral Precinct, Glasgow) Unique collection of art from all the world's major religions – and some rather obscure ones too. Everything from an Egyptian mummy mask to Dali's *Christ of St John of the Cross*, and in the grounds Britain's only permanent Zen garden. Meals, snacks, shop, disabled access; cl 25–26 Dec, 1–2 Jan; (0141) 553 2557; free.

Tall Ship (Glasgow Harbour, 100 Stobcross Rd) Late 19th-c sailing ship, *Glenlee*, one of only five Clyde-built sailing ships still afloat; an interactive exhibition tells her story. The adjacent pumphouse houses a gallery, shop and café. Meals, snacks, shop, disabled access; cl 25–26 Dec, 1–2 Jan; (0141) 222 2513; £4.50.

Tenement House (145 Buccleuch St) One-floor late 19th-c flat well worth a visit for its vivid impression of life for many Glaswegians a century ago. The same woman lived here from 1911 to 1965 and in that time scarcely changed a thing; its time-capsule quality was preserved by a subsequent owner, and then the flat, still with its original furnishings and fittings, was left to the National Trust for Scotland. Open pm Mar–Oct; (0141) 333 0183; £3.50; NTS.

University of Glasgow Visitor Centre (University Ave) Interactive displays on the history and life of the university (founded in 1451), with tours around some of its grander features, such as the Lion and Unicorn Staircase, Bute and Randolph Halls and Memorial Chapel. Snacks, shop, disabled access; cl all day winter Sun, plus am summer Sun, and 2 wks over Christmas and New Year; (0141) 330 5511; visitor centre free, tours (2pm Mon–Sat May–Sept, Oct–Apr just 2pm Weds) £2. You can stay in some of the university buildings during vacations.

Greenbank Garden (Flenders Rd, Clarkston, off A726) Aims to encourage and help owners of small gardens, so has lots of different shrubs and flowers to spark ideas. Also garden and greenhouse designed to meet the needs of disabled gardeners, with advice on specially designed tools. Summer teas, shop, disabled access; cl 25–26 Dec, 1–2 Jan; house open Sun pm only Apr–Oct; (0141) 639 3281; £3.50; NTS.

Linn Park (Cathcart/Castlemilk) Lots to do – riverside walks, nature trails, golf course, as well as a ruined 14th-c castle, an adventure playground for the disabled (prior arrangement preferred), and an equestrian centre; (0141) 637 3096. Visitor centre open most wknd pms; (0141) 637 1147; free.

Mugdock Country Park (N Glasgow) Good strolling ground, with two castle ruins, a view over Glasgow, and an attractive loch.

Rouken Glen Park (Thornliebank) A place of great tranquil beauty, with a walled garden, gorgeous lawns, and woodland walks to a waterfall at the head of the glen.

Victoria Park (Victoria Park Drive N) Tree-lined park where the remains in the Fossil Grove, some of them 330 million years old, were discovered by workmen digging a path in the late 19th c.

West Highland Way Level walks from Milngavie can take in the early stages of the West Highland Way, which starts here. The determined can press on along glen routes all the way up to Fort William – the scenery getting better all the way.

GLENLUCE NX1858
Glenluce Abbey Ruined Cistercian abbey founded in the late 12th c, in beautiful surroundings. Limited disabled access; cl winter Sun am, cl winter wkdys; (01581) 300541; £1.80; HS.

GORDON NT6439
Mellerstain House 🖼 (just W, off A6089) William and Robert Adam both worked on this striking Georgian house, which has impressive plasterwork and furnishings, and paintings by Van Dyck and Gainsborough. Every great house in Scotland seems to have something that belonged to Bonnie Prince Charlie – this one has his bagpipes. Very pleasant terraced gardens and parkland, with fine views towards the distant hills. Meals, snacks, shop, limited disabled access; cl am, all day Sat, and Oct–Apr; (01573) 410225; *£5.50.

GREENOCK CUT NS2472
Part of an elaborate abandoned water scheme for Greenock below, this allows a level walk meandering around a hillside terrace giving views into the Highlands.

GRETNA GREEN NY3167
Old Blacksmith's Shop It's now tourists rather than runaway couples that flock to the 19th-c Old Blacksmith's Shop in this little Borders village. More people come here than to any other Scottish attraction outside Edinburgh, despite the fact that there's really very little to see. An exhibition centre looks at the once thriving marriage business. Cl 25–26 Dec, 1 Jan; (01461) 338224; £2.

GREY MARE'S TAIL NT1814
Spectacular waterfalls, a pretty walk from the A708 car park NE of Moffat, up a narrow glen. You can continue beyond them along Tail Burn to Loch Skeen.

HADDINGTON NT5173
A pretty market town; the comfortable

George and Maitlandfield House hotels, and the aptly named Waterside Inn, all have above-average food.

Lennoxlove (B6369 S) The Duchess of Lennox (La Belle Stewart) gave this old house its unusual name in memory of her dead husband. Among reminders of other members of her family are the casket and death mask of Mary Queen of Scots. In the grounds the Cadzow herd of white park cattle are said to be descended from the sacrificial cattle of the Druids. Meals, snacks, disabled access; open pm Weds, Thurs, Sun; cl end Oct–Easter; (01620) 823720; £4.25.

HAWICK NT5014

Drumlanrig's Tower (Towerknowe) Fearsome-looking 16th-c tower with state-of-the-art displays of Borders history, some quite gripping. Shop, disabled access; cl Sun am (all day Sat and perhaps Sun Oct–Mar); (01450) 373457; £2.50.

Hawick Museum and Scott Art Gallery (Wilton Lodge Park) There are newish craft and archaeology exhibitions at this museum, given a big boost by its appealing setting in a park with riverside walks and gardens. Shop, disabled access to ground floor; cl 12–1pm, am wkdys and Sun and all day Sat Oct–Mar, 8–9 Jun, 25 Dec–3 Jan; (01450) 373457; free.

HERMITAGE NY4995

Hermitage Castle Almost perfect from the outside, the well restored but very forbidding remains of a 14th-c Borders stronghold reeking of dire deeds. Shop, limited disabled access; cl am Sun and Thurs and all Fri Oct, and all Nov–Apr; (01387) 376222; £2; HS.

INNERLEITHEN NT3336

Robert Smail's Printing Works (High St) Fully restored Victorian printer's shop, with water-powered press; you can try your hand at metal typesetting and hand-print your own bookmark. Shop, limited disabled access; cl am in winter, cl all day Tues and Weds, cl am Sun in summer, cl end Oct–end Mar; (01896) 830206; £3.50; NTS. The Traquair Arms is the place to eat.

IRVINE NS2740

Big Idea 🖼 (Harbour St) In a huge sand-dune-shaped building on the tip of the Ardeer Peninsula, this giant inventors' workshop celebrates a century of Nobel Laureates as well as the creations and innovations of the last millennium. A pedestrian drawbridge leads you to a vast array of inventions from life-saving machines to utterly ridiculous contraptions, and hundreds of exhibits with which you can interact thanks to a specially designed electronic key. You're actively encouraged to come up with your own inventions, and best of all, after testing them out, you get to take the end product home. Café, gift shop, disabled access; cl 24–26 Dec and 1 Jan; (08708) 404030; £7.95.

Scottish Maritime Museum 🖼 (Gottries Rd) Down by the harbour, very much a working museum, with lots of restoration work on the good range of historic vessels. Snacks, shop, some disabled access (not to boats); cl Christmas–New Year; (01294) 278283; £2.50. The nearby Keys has decent food (all day wknds).

Vennel Gallery Art gallery and museum, and behind, a reconstruction of the Heckling Shop where, as a young man, an unwilling Burns tried to learn the filthy trade of flax dressing. Happily for him, during a New Year's Eve party his aunt knocked over a candle and burnt the building to ashes. Shop, disabled access; cl 1–2pm, cl Mon–Thurs; (01294) 275059; free.

JEDBURGH NT6420

Castle Jail and Museum (Castlegate) Now a local history museum; snacks, shop, disabled access; cl end Oct–Apr; (01835) 863254; £2.

Jedburgh Abbey The most complete of the ruined 12th-c Borders monasteries founded by David I, and an impressive sight despite its town setting. Imposing 26-metre (86-ft) tower, splendid W door, and audio-visual show in visitor centre. Snacks, shops, disabled access; cl Sun am Oct–Mar, 25–26 Dec, 1–2 Jan; (01835) 863925; £3.30; HS. The Pheasant has good food (and makes a point of having good value pheasant in season). Just off the A68 S of town are the mainly 16th-c ruins of Ferniehurst Castle.

Mary Queen of Scots House (Queen St) Charming 16th-c fortified dwelling where Mary had to prolong her 1566 stay because of a near-mortal fever (she was later to say she wished she'd died here). There's a good interpretation of her life. Shop; cl end Nov–start Mar; (01835) 863331; £3.

KELSO NT7035

Floors Castle 🏰 (1m NW) Magnificent building designed by William Adam in 1721, and much embellished in the next century. It's reputed to be Scotland's biggest inhabited house, with a window for every day of the year. Splendid collection of tapestries and French furniture, and wonderful walled garden (best July–Sept). Good home-made meals and snacks, shop, disabled access; cl end Oct–Easter; (01573) 223333; £5.50.

Kelso Abbey The greatest and wealthiest of the four famous Borders abbeys, though today not much of the building remains. Cobbles (Beaumont St) and the Queens Head (Bridge St) have good value food.

KILMARNOCK NS4339

Dean Castle (off Glasgow Rd) The castle is a magnificent collection of restored buildings dating from the 1350s. For 400 years it was the stronghold of the Boyds of Kilmarnock, and today it shows off important collections of arms and armour, musical instruments, tapestries and Burns's manuscripts. It's surrounded by 200 acres of woodland, with nature trails, deer park, riding and other activities. Snacks, shop; open pms Easter–Sept, wknds only in winter; guided tours from noon; (01563) 522702; free. The 18th-c Wheatsheaf in the pretty village of Symington on the other side of town has good original food.

KIPPFORD NX8355

Charming yachting place, usually plenty to watch in summer. The Anchor here is good.

LANGBANK NS3673

Finlaystone (A8, 1m W) Some say the garden here is the finest in Scotland – formal and walled, with woodland walks, adventure playgrounds, and picnic areas. The house has connections with Robert Burns and John Knox (unlikely partners), and there's a visitor centre with displays on the Clan Macmillan and Celtic art (open daily

Apr–Sept and winter wknds). Tearoom, shop, disabled access; gardens open all year; (01475) 540505; £3. The modern Langbank Lodge nearby has sensibly priced food (inc afternoon tea and scones) and incredible Clyde views.

LARGS NS2059

The pick of the traditional Clydeside resorts, with boats across the narrow strip of water to the island of Great Cumbrae. The pleasure steamer *Waverley* calls here in summer, and Nardinis (Esplanade) is a vintage tearoom – or rather tea palace, with acres of immaculate tables and smartly aproned motherly waitresses.

Vikingar! (Barrfields Centre, Greenock Rd) Lively look at the Vikings in Scotland, from their arrival to their defeat at the Battle of Largs. Very much an 'experience', with lots of interactive displays, and a multi-media show as the centrepiece. There's an adjacent swimming pool. Meals, snacks, shop, disabled access; cl wkdys Oct, Nov and Feb, all Dec and Jan; (01475) 689777; £4.

LAUDER NT5347

Thirlestane Castle (off A68 and A697) Stately yet charming castle with restored assemblage of pictures, interesting collection of old toys (some of which children can touch), some outstanding plasterwork in the 17th-c state rooms, woodland walk and picnic areas. There's an adventure playground and dungeon display. Snacks, shop; cl Sat, and Nov–May but open Easter; (01578) 722430; *£5.50, £2 grounds only. The Eagle and Lauderdale Hotel are useful for lunch.

LINLITHGOW NT0580

Blackness Castle Built in the 1440s, massively strengthened in the 16th c as an artillery fortress (walls up to 5.5 metres, 18 ft, thick), ship-shaped waterside Blackness became an ammunition depot in the 1870s. You can walk along the top of some of the walls, and climb up to the roof of the central tower. Cl Thurs pm, all day Fri and Sun am Nov–Feb; £2.20; (01506) 834807; HS.

House of the Binns (3m E, off A904) The home of the Dalyell family since 1612, with some splendid plaster ceilings and a fine collection of furniture and porcelain. Limited disabled access; cl am, all day Fri, and Oct–end Apr; (01506) 834255; £5; NTS.

Linlithgow Palace The birthplace of Mary Queen of Scots, a magnificently sombre lochside ruin. You can still see the chapel, great hall and a quadrangle with an impressive fountain. Shop, limited disabled access, cl 25–26 Dec and 1–2 Jan; (01506) 842896; £2.80; HS. In the town a pleasant old tavern, the Four Marys, is named for her maids-in-waiting Mary Carmichael, Mary Hamilton, Mary Beaton and Mary Seaton, with relevant memorabilia.

LIVINGSTON NT0366

Almond Valley Heritage Centre 🖾 (off A705) An innovative museum packed full of things to prod, sniff, shake and discover, plus working farm and watermill, play areas, narrow-gauge railway and trailer rides. Meals, snacks, shop, disabled access; cl 25–26 Dec, 1–2 Jan; (01506) 414957; *£2.80.

LOCHWINNOCH NS3558

Nature Centre (Largs Rd) RSPB nature reserve with fine views, good woodland and marsh nature trails, and three observation hides. Shop, complete disabled access; cl 25–26 Dec, 1–2 Jan; (01505) 842663; £2. The Mossend is a useful dining pub.

MELROSE NT5034

Abbotsford House (B6360 3m W) Set grandly on the River Tweed, this was the home of Sir Walter Scott until his death in 1832. You can still see his mammoth 9,000-volume library, and several of the historical oddities he liked to collect, like Rob Roy's sporran. Snacks, shop, disabled access; cl Sun am (Mar–May and Oct), plus all Nov to mid-Mar; (01896) 752043; £4.

Eildon Hills Above the town, these are splendidly compact, giving a very pleasing ridge walk along the top.

Melrose Abbey The ruins are among the finest in the country – best in moonlight, as Scott says (though he admitted he never saw them thus himself). Look out for the wonderful stonework on the 14th-c nave (and the pig playing the bagpipes). Archaeological investigations now leave little doubt that this was the burial place of Robert the Bruce's heart. Shop;

limited disabled access; cl Sun am Oct–Mar, 25–26 Dec, 1–2 Jan; (01896) 822562; £3.30; HS. Just opposite there are good views of the abbey and Eildon Hills from Harmony Garden (St Mary St), a tranquil walled garden around an early 19th-c house.

Priorwood Garden (Abbey St) Specialises in flowers suitable for drying, with a herb garden and display orchard illustrating apples through the ages. Shop, disabled access; cl Sun am and Jan–Mar; (01896) 822493; £2; NTS.

MERVINSLAW NT6713

Jedforest Deer & Farm Park (A68) Working farm with different breeds of deer as well as other animals inc hawks, owls and rare breeds. Good for children, and peaceful trails nearby. Also ranger-led activities and walks. Snacks, shop, some disabled access; cl Nov–Apr; (01835) 840364; £3.75.

MOTHERWELL NS7456

M & D's Theme Park In 1,500 acres of parkland, this is Scotland's biggest theme park, with more than 40 rides and attractions, and a large indoor entertainment complex (cl 25 Dec, 1 Jan) with a new bowling alley (£3.50), play area and arcade games. Meals, snacks, shop, disabled access; cl Nov–Mar; (01698) 333999; £12.50 for a day's wristband with unlimited rides.

MULL OF GALLOWAY NX1530 Beautifully unspoilt, Scotland's SW toe; good coastal walking.

MUSSELBURGH NT3272

Newhailes House (A6095 W) Once home to the influential Dalrymple family, this 17th-c house is now open after a 5-year restoration project. Unusual in that it has been conserved rather than restored (carpets remain faded and paint chipped), with impressive rococo interiors and fine furnishings. Once the largest in Scotland, the library drew praise from Dr Johnson (the books, currently in storage at the National Library, should be returned after further conservation work). The 80-acre grounds are being restored, and an old stable block has a visitor centre (free). Café, shop, disabled access; usually open pm Thurs–Mon, phone to book; (0131) 653 5599; guided tours £7.

NEW ABBEY NX9562

Criffel This summit gives walkers an

astonishing view of the English Lake District over the Solway Firth.

New Abbey Corn Mill The pretty village has a restored 18th-c corn mill; shop; cl 1–2pm all year, plus Thurs pm, all Fri, and Sun am Oct–Mar, 25–26 Dec, 1–2 Jan; (01387) 850260; £2.80; HS.

Shambellie House of Costume (A710) Dazzling displays of costume, thoughtfully arranged in appropriately furnished rooms. Snacks, shop; cl Nov–Mar; (01387) 850375; £2.50.

Sweetheart Abbey (A710) One of the most romantic ruins in the area, with a lofty arched nave open to the sky, and a touching story attached. Shop; cl Sun am, Thurs pm and all day Fri Oct–Mar, 25–26 Dec, 1–2 Jan; (01387) 850397; £1.80; HS.

NEW LANARK NS8842 (off A73) Now a UNESCO World Heritage site, this is Scotland's best example of an industrial village (founded in 1785), with plenty to keep families amused for a good chunk of the day. Many of the old millworkers' buildings (showing living conditions of the 1820s and 1930s) have been interestingly converted to modern accommodation, so it's very much a living village rather than a museum. The village store has an exhibition about Robert Owen's original store, and his house contains an exhibition on his work; there's also a hotel in a renovated 18th-c cotton mill (01555) 667200. The village can be busy at wknds; try to visit during the week if you can. There's a time travel ride at the visitor centre. Meals, snacks, shop, disabled access; cl before 11am, 25 Dec, 1 Jan; £4.95. In Lanark itself the Crown (Hope St) has a decent restaurant.

Falls of Clyde The countryside here is spectacular, with a short walk snaking around river cliffs through a verdant gorge to these falls that used to power the mill. A visitor centre here has lots of information on badgers; cl before 11am (midday in winter), and 25 Dec, 1 Jan. The falls are dramatic when the hydro-electric station upriver opens the sluices.

NEWTONGRANGE NT3363 **Scottish Mining Museum** (Lady Victoria Colliery, A7, Newtongrange) Easy to spend an interesting half-day here, exploring the highs and lows of the Scottish coal industry on two floors of displays, interactives and magic helmets, plus audio tour of the old mine workings interspersed with short films, and a coal face mock-up explained by an ex-miner; play area. Good value meals and home-baked snacks, good shop, disabled access; cl Christmas and New Year; (0131) 663 7519; *£4.

NORTH BERWICK NT5585 Prettily sited resort on the sands of the Firth of Forth, a holiday destination for nearly 200 years. Excellent shoreside walks along the sands between here and Aberlady, with stop-off possibilities at Dirleton and Gullane; seaside walks are helped by the good bus service connecting all the shoreside villages between here and Edinburgh, though the hinterland is dull. The arch topping volcanic Berwick Law is a whale's jaw.

Scottish Seabird Centre 🖼 (North Berwick Harbour) Each year over 150,000 seabirds (inc the largest colony of gannets in the world) return to the islands off this town, and remote cameras in the centre let you see the birds and wildlife up close in comfort; telescope deck, auditorium. Shop, café with wonderful views across the islands of Forth, disabled access; cl 25 Dec; (01620) 890202; £4.95. A good value family ticket covering two adults and two children is £13.50, and a Scotrail Edinburgh–North Berwick return inc entry to the centre is £7.50; phone (08457) 550033 for details.

Tantallon Castle (off A198 3m E) Formidable coastal stronghold of the Douglases, and mentioned by Scott in his poem *Marmion*. From the clifftop the red-walled ruins look across the Firth of Forth to the Bass Rock, making it one of the most majestically sited castles in Scotland; cl Thurs pm, all day Fri and Sun am Oct–Mar, 25–26 Dec, 1–2 Jan, best to check though; (01620) 892727; *£3; HS.

OLD DAILLY NS2401 **Bargany Gardens** (Old Dailly) Fine ornamental trees, woodland walks, rock garden and a lily pond enveloped by azaleas and rhododendrons; plants for sale. Mostly disabled access; open Sat–Mon May; (01465) 871249; *£2. The Kings Arms over at Barr (a pretty drive) has enjoyable food.

PAISLEY NS4863

Coats Observatory (High St)
Displays on astronomy, meteorology
and space flight. Shop, cl 1–2pm, and
Mon, best to check for Christmas
opening; (0141) 889 2013; free.

Paisley Museum and Art Gallery
(High St) Paisley is not just a place but a
pattern, so as well as a very wide range
of 19th-c art, the appealing museum has
a marvellous collection of antique and
more modern Paisley shawls, along with
the looms on which they were made.
Shop, some disabled access; cl Sun am
and all Mon (exc bank hols), 25–26 Dec,
1–2 Jan; (0141) 889 3151; free. The
Anchor (Glasgow Rd) does decent
lunches.

Sma' Shot Cottages You can see
two distinct periods in the town's
weaving history at this unusual
museum. Guides take you around a fully
restored and furnished mid-18th-c
weaver's cottage, and then across the
yard to a row of three cottages,
showing what life was like in the 1940s.
They've a working loom (occasional
demonstrations), and a local history
display. Tearoom, shop selling locally
produced crafts, limited disabled
access; open pm Weds and Sat
Apr–Sept; (0141) 889 1708; free.

PATNA NS4308

Dunaskin Open-Air Museum 🆔
(Dalmellington Rd) Well preserved
Victorian ironworks (employing up to
1,400 people at its 19th-c peak) in
attractive rolling countryside, with a
period cottage, reconstructed
manager's office, industrial machinery,
an audio-visual show about Ayrshire life
in the 19th and early 20th c, fun play
area based around the principles of an
iron furnace, and nature trails around
the site. Meals, snacks, shop, disabled
access; cl Nov–Mar; (01292) 531144;
£4.50.

PAXTON NT9352

Paxton House 🆔 (B6461) Built in
1758 by the love-struck Patrick Billie,
who hoped to marry an aristocrat at
the court of Frederick the Great; the
marriage never took place, but the
result was a splendid neo-Palladian
mansion, designed and later
embellished by the Adam family, and

furnished by the Chippendales; 18th-c
German/Prussian costume display. Also
woodland and riverside walks, highland
cattle, and adventure playground
designed by the Territorial Army.
Meals, snacks, shop, disabled access; cl
Nov–Mar but grounds open all year;
(01289) 386291; *£5, £2.50 gardens
only. Cantys Brig towards Berwick has
good food.

PEEBLES NT2540
Attractive if sedate Borders town, with
quite a lot for visitors; the Green Tree
has reasonably priced food, and the
Park Hotel does good bar meals (both
Innerleithen Rd).

Kailzie (B7062, 2m SE) Extensive
grounds with lovely old trees flanked by
azaleas and rhododendrons, formal
rose garden, walled garden, trout pond
and small art gallery; also children's play
area. Meals, snacks, shop, some
disabled access; restaurant and gallery
cl Nov–Easter; (01721) 720007; £2.50,
(£1 Oct–Apr).

Neidpath Castle (off A72 just W)
Spectacularly set, converted from the
original 14th-c tower in the late 16th
and early 17th c. There's a rock-hewn
well, small museum (children like the
mummified rat), period kitchen, and a
pit prison – not much chance of escape,
as some of the walls are 3½ metres
(11 ft) thick. Super views from the
parapets. Shop; cl am Sun and all mid-
Sept to Easter; (01721) 720333; £3.00.

PENICUIK NT2360
Edinburgh Crystal Visitor Centre
(Eastfield) Demonstrations of glass-
blowing, cutting and engraving, with an
exhibition on the crystal's history.
Meals, snacks, shop, disabled access;
tours daily, cl 25–26 Dec, 1–2 Jan;
glasshouse tours not available during
Christmas and New Year fortnight;
(01968) 675128; £3. They run a free
minibus service from Waverley Bridge
in Edinburgh (on the hour, Apr–Sept
only). The Horseshoe out on the
Peebles road is a civilised dining pub.

PENTLAND HILLS NT1558
Within easy reach of Edinburgh,
genuine uplands with some good high-
level walks and attractive reservoirs.

PORT LOGAN NX0942
Logan Botanic Garden 🆔 (off
B7065) A specialist garden of the Royal

Botanic Garden of Edinburgh, with a wide range of plants from the warm temperate regions of the southern hemisphere. Meals, snacks, shop; plant sales; cl Nov–Feb; (01776) 860231; *£3. The village itself has a natural sea pool where fat fish will eat from your fingers; the Inn does good food. Great sunsets here.

PORTPATRICK NW9954
Attractive harbour town, usually with something going on down by the water, and good food in the waterside Crown.

PRESTONPANS NT3874
Industrial Heritage Museum (B1348 Prestongrange Rd) Based around the oldest documented coal mining site in Britain. Steam and diesel locomotives, a Cornish beam engine, and displays on other local industries, from brick and pipe making to brewing and weaving. Lots going on, esp at wknds, and family workshops during the summer. Snacks, shop, some disabled access; cl late Oct–Mar (may be open Christmas week); (0131) 653 2904; free.

RHINNS OF GALLOWAY NX0650
This hammerhead of land in the extreme W of the area is largely empty even in high summer, a very peaceful place, with cliffs (especially on the S point), rocks and small coves.

RHINNS OF KELLS NX7274
This ridge has energetic hill walking from Forrest Lodge NW of New Galloway.

ROCKCLIFFE NX8453
Attractive yachting village, with a good peaceful walk to Castle Hill Point headland, and beyond by vast stretches of tidal sands.

SELKIRK NT4227
Bowhill House (off A708, 3m W) Outstanding collection of paintings, inc works by Canaletto, Van Dyck, Gainsborough and Claude, as well as impressive furnishings and porcelain, and memorabilia relating to Scott and Queen Victoria. Also restored Victorian kitchen, adventure playground, very active little theatre, and surrounding country park. Snacks, shop, disabled access; grounds cl am, all Fri (exc in July), and all Sept–late Apr; house open daily July only; (01750)

22204; *£4.50.
Selkirk Glass (off A7 just N) Demonstrations of paperweight-making. Meals, snacks, factory shop, disabled access; cl common riding day in June, 25–26 Dec, 1–2 Jan; (01750) 20954; free.
Sir Walter Scott's Courtroom (Market Pl) Low-key exhibition on Sir Walter Scott in the former courtroom where, as sheriff, he dispensed justice to the people of Selkirk. Shop, snacks, limited disabled access; cl Sun (exc pm Jun–Aug), am in Oct, and all Nov–Mar; (01750) 20761; free. The decorous town is good for bargain-hunting for the tweeds, woollens and cashmeres which are woven and knitted here; the Queens Head has freshly cooked food.

SMAILHOLM NT6334
Smailholm Tower (just S, signed off the B6404 NE of St Boswells) Classic 15th-c Borders tower house, very well preserved – all 17 metres (57 ft) of it. Display based on Scott's book *Minstrels of the Borders*, and an exhibition of dolls. Shop, limited disabled access; normally only cl Thurs pm, Fri and Sun am Oct–Nov, and wkdys Dec–Mar; (01573) 460365; £2.20; HS.

SOUTH QUEENSFERRY NT1378
Notable for its views of the two great Forth bridges on either side, with piers to potter on; the Hawes Inn, famous from *Kidnapped*, is still going strong. A well signposted cycle track links North Queensferry (over the bridge) to Edinburgh.
Dalmeny House 🏛 (B924, 3m E) Despite its Tudor Gothic appearance, this splendidly placed house dates only from the 19th c – there's a superb hammer-beamed roof, as well as fine furnishings, porcelain and portraits. Good walks in the grounds and on the shore. Snacks; open pm Sun–Tues July–Aug; (0131) 331 1888; *£4.
Hopetoun House (off B904, 2m W) This huge place is probably Scotland's best and certainly most palatial example of the work of William and Robert Adam. The magnificent reception rooms have a wonderful art collection with works by Canaletto and Gainsborough, while the superb grounds include a deer park and a flock of rare sheep. The rooftop gives

wonderful views. Meals, snacks, shop, some disabled access; cl Nov–Mar; (0131) 331 2451; £5.30, £2.90 grounds only.

Inchcolm Abbey Much-raided medieval ruins on a memorable island site in the Firth, reached by a 30-min ferry trip from South Queensferry; also from North Queensferry, weather permitting; cl Nov–Mar and wkdys in Oct; (0131) 331 4857; £9.95 inc ferry; HS.

ST MARY'S LOCH NT2320
A pretty spot for walks, tracked by the Southern Upland Way along its E shore; the Tibbie Shiels Inn is a handy stop.

STOBO NT1534
Dawyck Botanic Garden 🏛 (B712) Another specialist garden of the Royal Botanic Garden, particularly noted for its arboretum rich in mature conifers (inc a larch believed to have been planted in 1725), with notable Asiatic silver firs and many rarities. Snacks, shop; cl mid-Nov to mid-Feb; (01721) 760254; *£3.

STRANRAER NX0760
Castle Kennedy Gardens (A75, 4m E) Prettily set between two lochs (with lots of good walks around), these gardens were first laid out in the early 18th c, then after years of neglect were restored and developed in the 19th. They're particularly admired for their walled garden, rhododendron collection and flowering shrubs. Snacks, shop, limited disabled access; cl Oct–Mar; (01776) 702024; £3.

TARBOLTON NS4327
Bachelor's Club (off A77 S of Kilmarnock, and off A76, 7½m NE of Ayr) 17th-c thatched house where Burns and his friends formed a debating club in 1780. Shop; cl am, cl 27 Oct–Mar; (01292) 541940; £2.50; NTS. The Wheatsheaf over at Symington has good food.

THORNHILL NX8599
Drumlanrig Castle (off A76) Spectacular almost theatrical pink sandstone mansion built in the late 17th c, with a glory of fine panelling and furnishings (mainly Louis XIV), and splendid paintings by Leonardo, Holbein, Rembrandt and Murillo; you can see what's said to be Bonnie Prince Charlie's campaign kettle. Also craft

workshops, adventure playground, peacocks wandering over the lawn, working forge, and extensive woodland walks. Meals, snacks, shop, disabled access; cl Sun am, and Sept–Easter; (01848) 330248; £6.

TRAQUAIR NT3336
Traquair House (B709) The oldest inhabited and most romantic house in Scotland; no fewer than 27 English and Scottish kings have stayed here. The Bear Gates have remained closed since 1745 when Bonnie Prince Charlie passed through them for the last time – they won't open again unless the Stewarts regain their place on the throne. An 18th-c brewery still produces tasty beers (£4 for tastings, phone to book), and there's a brewery museum (and shop). Traquair is particularly popular with our contributors, and with a maze, new adventure playground, and antiques and craft shops as well as the house and gardens, there's plenty to see. Meals, snacks, shop, some disabled access; cl Jan–Mar and Nov–Dec (exc for pre-booked parties); (01896) 830323; £5.60, grounds only £2.50.

UDDINGSTON NS6960
Bothwell Castle Picturesquely set and extensive 14th-c ruin by the river, once the finest stone castle in the country and virtually impregnable; shop; Nov–Mar cl Thurs pm, all day Fri, Sun am; (01698) 816894; £2; HS.
Glasgow Zoo 🏛 (Calderpark) Open-plan zoo, specialising in cats and reptiles (snake-handling every day), with other rare mammals and birds, display barn, orienteering course, and wknd car boot sales. Events include falconry and parrot flying displays in summer. Snacks, shop, disabled access; cl 25 Dec; (0141) 771 1185; £4.

WANLOCKHEAD NS8713
Museum of Lead Mining (B797) Guided tours of an 18th-c lead mine, heritage trail and miners' cottages furnished in the styles of 1740 and 1890. You can have a go at panning for gold. Meals, snacks, shop, limited disabled access; cl Nov–1 April; (01659) 74387; £4.95. This remote village is Scotland's highest.

WHITHORN NX4736
Isle of Whithorn Picturesque

harbour with boat trips and lots of yachtsmen: the Steam Packet has good local fish.

Whithorn Dig Scotland's first-recorded Christian settlement was established here by St Ninian 1,500 years ago. There have been several churches on the site since, the last of the line the ruined 13th-c priory you can see today. Archaeologists have been hard at work here for some time. An excellent visitor centre and museum have plenty of the finds, with some fine Celtic crosses. Shop, disabled access; museum and visitor centre cl Nov–Easter (though you can still wander round the priory ruins then); (01988) 500508; £2.70; HS.

Other attractive villages with decent pubs include Ancrum NT6325, Gifford NT5368, Kirkcowan NX3260, Kirkcudbright NX6851 (particularly enjoyable), Lilliesleaf NT5325, Larkhall NS7651, Old Kilpatrick NS4673, Sorn NS5526, Straiton NS3804 and Symington NS3831.

Some **Clydeside pubs** with decent food and good **sea views** include the Cardwell at Cardwell Bay in Gourock NS2477 and the Spinnaker there, and the Lookout in Troon Marina NS3230.

Others with a decent bite to eat and particularly **well placed for walkers**, drivers or just strollers in these parts include the Murray Arms, Masons Arms and Angel at Gatehouse of Fleet NX5956, Golf Hotel and Old Clubhouse at Gullane NT4882, Breadalbane Hotel at Kildonan NS0231, Swan at Kingholm Quay NX9773, Border at Kirk Yetholm NT8328, Gordon Arms at Mountbenger NT3125 and Buccleuch Arms at St Boswells NT5931.

Where to eat

CROSSMICHAEL NX7366 **Plumed Horse** *Main St* (01556) 670333 In an unremarkable building, this simply but attractively decorated restaurant offers perfectly timed and presented modern cooking with quite an emphasis on absolutely fresh fish; especially good value set lunch, charming service, and a short wine list; cl Mon, Sat lunch, Sun pm, 2 wks Jan and 2 wks Sept; well behaved children welcome, disabled access. £34.45

EAST LINTON NT5977 **Drovers** *5 Bridge St* (01620) 860298 Comfortable 18th-c inn with prints and pictures for sale, cosy armchairs, a basket of logs by the woodburner, hops around the bar, very good interesting food (more elaborate in the evening), a good range of real ales, and partly no smoking upstairs restaurant; cl 25 Dec, 1 Jan. £28|£5

EDINBURGH NT2473 **Atrium** *10 Cambridge St* (0131) 228 8892 Next to Usher Hall and Traverse Theatre, unusually modern restaurant with wire sculptures, railway sleepers, dim lighting from glass torches, cheerful friendly staff, interesting wine list, and very good imaginative modern Scottish food – lunchtime two-course set menu, too; cl Sat lunchtime, Sun, Christmas and New Year; disabled access. £40/2-course lunch £13.50

EDINBURGH NT2776 **Fishers** *1 Shore* (0131) 554 5666 Bustling, lively bistro overlooking the Leith waterfront, with an informal, friendly atmosphere, a dark bar with a few tables and bar counter, and light airy dining room; exceptionally good imaginative fish dishes, enjoyable straightforwardish puddings, a well chosen fairly priced wine list, and genuinely helpful, quick, cheerful service. £30|£10

EDINBURGH NT2672 **Kalpna Indian Restaurant** *2–3 St Patrick Sq* (0131) 667 9890 Extremely good Indian restaurant with carefully cooked, very fresh and interesting vegetarian food, and polite efficient service; cl Sun pm, Christmas and New Year, disabled access. £15/£5 buffet

EDINBURGH NT2776 **Restaurant Martin Wishart** *54 Shore* (0131) 553 3557 In the smartened-up dockland area, this simply furnished and decorated restaurant with just a few tables on the stone floor, and modern paintings to bring some colour, offers a short set-price, weekly changing menu with exceptionally good modern French dishes; first-rate cheeses, lovely prettily presented puddings, a thoughtful wine list, and cheerful, knowledgeable service; cl Sun and Mon, Sat lunch, disabled access. £16.50

EDINBURGH NT2676 **Vintners Rooms** *The Vaults, 87 Giles St, Leith (0131) 554 6767* Bustling restaurant – a former fine old sale room, above ancient wine vaults; most enjoyable French provincial cooking plus more modern dishes, super puddings, and a good wine list; you can also choose to eat in the more informal bar; cl Sun, 2 wks from Christmas. £30/2 courses £11.50

GLASGOW NS5567 **Amaryllis** *1 Devonshire Gardens (0141) 337 3434* Gordon Ramsay has brought a trusted protégé from London to cook in this fine hotel's restaurant (it is an independent operation); simple furnishings and decor, delicious European cooking, and a marvellous, if not cheap, wine list; cl Mon, Tues and 1–2 Jan, disabled access (there are steps to the entrance). £35/£18 for 2 courses

GLASGOW NS5965 **Café Gandolfi** *64 Albion Street (0141) 552 6813* Named after the famous brothers who produced early cameras, this Merchant City favourite has the brothers' photographs of Italian restaurants and cafés in the Glasgow district during that period, interesting furniture and stained glass, imaginative and enjoyable modern Scottish cooking with international flavours using consistently high quality local produce, often organic, a thoughtful wine list, a relaxed informal atmosphere, and helpful friendly service; cl 25–26 Dec, 1–2 Jan. £21.50|£5

GLASGOW NS5965 **Rogano** *11 Exchange Pl (0141) 248 4055* Long-standing restaurant in splendid 1930s deco woodwork and chromium, with quite an emphasis on fish – vegetarian and meaty dishes, too; Café Rogano (downstairs) is open all day for lighter meals; cl 25 Dec, 1 Jan. £52|£9.50

GLASGOW NS5667 **Ubiquitous Chip** *12 Ashton Lane (0141) 334 5007* Friendly and informal restaurant (no chips, hence the name) in Victorian coach house with interesting modern Scottish cooking, outstanding wines (at fair prices), and no smoking areas; disabled access; cl 25 Dec, 1 Jan. Upstairs is cheaper. £30|£6

GLASGOW NS5865 **Yes** *22 West Nile St (0141) 221 8044* Stylish bustling restaurant with a relaxed, if fashionable, feel, very good modern cooking taking ideas from all over the world using first-class local produce, courteous service, and a short well chosen wine list; cl Sun. £23/2-course lunch £13.95

HADDINGTON NT5173 **Waterside** *1–5 Waterside (01620) 825674* A really lovely spot on a sunny day with a fine view across the water, this long two-storey white house has very good bistro-style food, a good range of wines and real ales in two plush rooms with a woodburner, and a more formal stripped-stone conservatory; cl 25 Dec, 1 Jan. £30|£6.95

LANARK NS8843 **Vigna** *40 Wellgate (01555) 664320* Imaginative Italian menu with good basics, more imaginative dishes, and lots of fresh fish; cl Sun am and 2 wks Jan. £35

LINLITHGOW NT0378 **Champany Inn** *Champany (01506) 834532* Wonderful Aberdeen Angus beef as well as lovely fresh fish (they also have their own smoke-house), home-made ice-creams, and good wines; cheaper bistro-style meals in their Chop and Ale House next door; main restaurant cl Sun (bistro open all week), 25–26 Dec, 1 Jan; disabled access. £30|£15

East Scotland

Plenty for all ages, from lively family outings to spectacular castles, richly varied scenery, and appealing seaside towns and villages

Excellent animal-oriented family outings include Blair Drummond's Safari and Adventure Park, the Highland Wildlife Park at Kincraig (also here, Working Sheepdogs is quite an eye-opener), and this year we've added the Auchingarrich Wildlife Centre in Comrie (and the nearby trout farm). There are deer to stroke near Cupar and Glenmore, and entertaining sheep shows at Aberfoyle; the aquarium at North Queensferry is one of the best in the country. Elsewhere, the Landmark Heritage & Adventure Park in Carrbridge is useful for keeping energetic children occupied, and there are acres of free fresh-air fun in Mintlaw and Bo'ness (good steam railway here too).

Out of a real wealth of terrific castles, we pick out the ones at Turriff, Crathes, Ballindalloch, Blair Atholl and Craigievar as especially breathtaking. Grand Haddo House in Tarves makes a busy outing, in Falkland there's a Renaissance palace, and Fort George holds good special events in summer. Leith Hall & Garden in Kennethmont has stunning grounds as well as elegantly furnished rooms (garden lovers should make a beeline for Kildrummy, Kemnay and Muthill too). There are lively museums in Oyne, Kingussie and Falkirk (the Falkirk Wheel is another interesting new draw here), and Kirkcaldy has a good art gallery.

This part of Scotland has plenty of interesting and attractive smaller towns and villages. Picturesque Stirling has quite a bit to offer families (its castle is great fun), and civilised St Andrews has a quiet charm. Riverside Inverness and Perth are attractive without being too touristy. The thriving city of Aberdeen has lots for visitors, and Dundee has several points of real interest including Sensation, our Scottish Family Attraction of the Year.

The best scenery here is in the N: both Highland, and the valleys – the well known Spey, Dee and Don, and lesser-known places such as the Angus glens of Glen Clova, Glen Esk and Glen Isla. Further S, the very pretty Trossachs are now part of Scotland's first National Park. The coast has appealing fishing villages in Fife's East Neuk, and a little-known but charming stretch from Nairn to Aberdeen, with good sands, quaint little coves and awesome cliffy crags such as Slains Castle and the nearby Bullers of Buchan.

Where to stay

ABERDEEN NJ9305 **Ferryhill House** *169 Bon Accord St, Aberdeen AB11 6UA* (01224) 590867 **£50**w; 9 rms. Well run small hotel with comfortable communicating spacious bar areas, well over 100 malt whiskies, real ales, friendly staff, a wide choice of food in bar and restaurant and lots of tables on neat well sheltered lawns

ARDEONAIG NN6634 **Ardeonaig Hotel** *Ardeonaig, Killin, Perthshire FK21 8SY* (01567) 820400 **£100**; 12 rms. Extended 17th-c farmhouse on S shore of Loch Tay with log fire in snug and lounge, library with fine views, and tasty, honest food using fresh local produce; salmon fishing rights on the loch – as well as fishing for trout and char – a drying and rod room, and boats and outboards; shooting, stalking and pony trekking can be arranged, lots of surrounding walks; cl 2 wks at Christmas and 2 wks early Jan; dogs welcome in bedrooms

AUCHTERARDER NN9211 **Gleneagles Hotel** *Auchterarder, Perthshire PH3 1NF* (01764) 662231 **£320***, plus special breaks; 275 individually decorated rms. Grand hotel in lovely surroundings with attractive gardens and outstanding leisure facilities: three championship golf courses (one designed by Jack Nicklaus), shooting, riding, fishing, health spa, tennis, squash, croquet and even falconry, lots of children's activities inc playroom with arts and crafts; comfortable, elegant high-ceilinged day rooms, a fine bar, exceptional service, pianists, enjoyable food using local produce (much is home-grown) in four restaurants, famous afternoon teas; disabled access; dogs welcome in bedrooms ☺

AVIEMORE NH8810 **Lynwilg House** *Aviemore, Inverness-shire, PH22 1PZ (01479) 811685* **£60**; 4 rms, 3 with shower. Attractive, quietly set 1930s-style house in four acres of landscaped gardens with open fire in spacious lounge, lovely breakfasts with their own free-range eggs and home-baked bread, super dinners using home-grown produce, and charming owners; plenty to do nearby; cl Nov–Dec; dogs welcome

BALLATER NO3696 **Auld Kirk** *31 Braemar Rd, Ballater, Aberdeenshire AB35 5RQ (01339) 755762* **£60**, plus winter breaks; 7 attractive rms, inc 2 family rms. 19th-c church converted to a hotel in 1990, still with bell tower, stained glass and exposed rafters; original pillared pine ceiling in newly refurbished restaurant, other public rooms with homely decor; cl 25–27 Dec, 1–4 Jan; dogs welcome in bedrooms

BALLATER NO3695 **Balgonie Country House** *Braemar Pl, Ballater, Aberdeenshire AB35 5NQ (01339) 755482* **£125***, plus special breaks. 9 pretty rms. Quietly set and spotless Edwardian house with fine views from four acres of mature gardens, particularly helpful friendly owners, fresh flowers, games and books in lounges, and most enjoyable food using the best local produce in charming dining room; cl 6 Jan–10 Feb; dogs by arrangement

BALQUHIDDER NN4318 **Monachyle Mhor** *Balquhidder, Lochearnhead, Perthshire FK19 8PQ (01877) 384622* **£85***; 10 rms with fine views overlooking Voil and Doine lochs, some newly redecorated. Remote 18th-c farmhouse/hotel six miles W of Balquhidder on 2,000-acre estate with prettily furnished rooms and good food using own game, cured meats and herbs; private fishing and stalking for guests; children over 12; cl Jan

BLAIRGOWRIE NO1244 **Kinloch House** *Blairgowrie, Perthshire PH10 6SG (01250) 884237* **£175***, plus special breaks; 20 individually decorated rms. Creeper-covered 19th-c country house in 25 acres of parkland with highland cattle and fine views; relaxed lounges, comfortable bar, pretty conservatory with lots of plants, and fine choice of carefully prepared food in an elegant dining room; popular sportsmen's room with own entrance, drying facilities, gun cupboard, freezer, game larder and so forth, and new fitness suite; cl 16–30 Dec; children over 7 in dining room; disabled access; dogs welcome in bedrooms

BRIDGE OF CALLY NO1551 **Bridge of Cally Hotel** *Bridge of Cally, Blairgowrie, Perthshire PH10 7JJ (01250) 886231* **£50**, plus winter breaks; 18 rms. In an acre of grounds along the River Ardle, this former drovers' inn is a friendly family-run place with good value home-made food using seasonal game in restaurant and comfortable bar; dogs welcome

CALLANDER NN6208 **Poppies** *Leny Rd, Callander, Perthshire FK17 8AL (01877) 330329* **£60***; 9 rms. Small private hotel with excellent food in popular and attractive candlelit dining room, comfortable lounge, helpful friendly owners, and seats in the garden; cl Jan; dogs welcome

DALCROSS NH7451 **Easter Dalziel Farm** *Dalcross, Inverness-shire IV2 7JL (01667) 462213* **£44***; 3 rms with shared bthrm. Early Victorian farmhouse on 210 acres of family-run mixed farm (beef cattle and grain) with friendly helpful owners, log fire in lounge, good Scottish breakfasts in big dining room and – when farm commitments allow – evening meal using own beef, lamb and veg; self-catering cottages, too; cl Christmas and New Year; dogs welcome

DUNBLANE NN7606 **Cromlix House** *Cromlix, Dunblane, Perthshire FK15 9JT (01786) 822125* **£215***, plus special breaks; 14 rms inc 8 spacious suites. Walking, loch and river fishing or shooting on 2,000 acres around this rather gracious country house; relaxing day rooms with fine antiques and family portraits, an informal atmosphere, very good food using local produce in two dining rooms, and

NK

Buckie
Findlater Castle
Banff Macduff
Fraserburgh
A98
✕ *Drybridge*
Fochabers
A90
A98
A90
Turriff
Mintlaw
Peterhead
A952
Craigellachie
Huntly
Tarves
Dufftown
NJ
Pitmedden
Forvie
A96
Kennethmont
Oyne
A90
Kildrummy
Bennachie
Kemnay
Balmedie Country Park
Alford
Craigievar
✕ Aberdeen
Peterculter
A93
Crathes
Ballater
Stonehaven
NO
Fettercairn
Edzell
A90
Kirriemuir
Montrose
Glamis
Meigle
Arbroath
Dundee
Broughty Ferry
A85
Tentsmuir Sands
✕ *Strathkinness*
✕ St Andrews
A91
Cupar
Peat Inn
Crail
✕
Falkland
Anstruther
St Monance
Pittenweem
Glenrothes
Elie
Kirkcaldy
FIRTH OF FORTH
Burntisland

0 Miles 20
0 Kilometres 32

NT
SOUTH SCOTLAND

courteous service; cl Jan; dogs welcome in bedrooms

DUNKELD NN9849 **Kinnaird House** *Kinnaird Estate, Dunkeld, Perthshire PH8 0LB (01796) 482440* **£365*** inc dinner, plus special breaks; 9 spacious individually decorated rms. 18th-c country-house hotel on 9,000-acre estate with deeply comfortable antiques-filled rooms, with lovely flowers, family mementoes and pictures, log fires, good creative food in no smoking dining room with early 19th-c frescoes, and a fine wine list; excellent fishing on River Tay and three hill lochs, and shooting; cl Mon–Weds during Jan–Feb; children over 12; disabled access

EAST HAUGH NN9656 **East Haugh House** *East Haugh, Pitlochry, Tayside PH16 5TE (01796) 473121* **£100*** inc dinner, plus special breaks; 12 rms, 5 in converted bothy, some with four-posters and one with open fire. Turreted stone house with lots of character, delightful conservatory bar, house-party atmosphere and very good food inc local seafood and game in season cooked by chef/proprietor; excellent shooting, stalking and salmon and trout fishing on surrounding local estates; cl 20–27 Dec; disabled access to one room; dogs welcome in bedrooms

ELGIN NJ2163 **Mansion House** *The Haugh, Elgin, Morayshire IV30 1AW (01343) 548811* **£130**, plus special breaks; 23 rms. Relaxed and friendly Scottish baronial mansion with pretty public rooms, fresh flowers, lovely food inc fine breakfasts, and good wine list; leisure club facilities inc swimming pool; disabled access

FINTRY NS6287 **Culcreuch Castle** *Fintry, Glasgow G63 0LW (01360) 860228* **£124***, plus special breaks; 13 individually decorated rms with lovely views. Central Scotland's oldest inhabited castle, nearly 700 years old, in beautiful 1,600-acre parkland, with log fires and antiques in public rooms, good freshly prepared food in candlelit panelled dining room, and a friendly relaxed atmosphere, play area; 8 modern Scandinavian holiday lodges, too; disabled access; dogs by arrangement

GLENDEVON NN9705 **Tormaukin** *Glendevon, Dollar, Clackmannanshire FK14 7JY (01259) 781252* **£90**, plus special breaks; 12 comfortable rms, some in converted stable block. Neatly kept 18th-c inn in good walking country, with loch and river fishing, lots of golf courses in reach, beamed dining room and softly lit bar, very good food using fresh local produce, and fine breakfasts, also a self-catering chalet; cl 4 days beginning of Jan; disabled access; dogs welcome in bedrooms

GLENROTHES NO2802 **Balbirnie House** *Markinch, Glenrothes, Fife KY7 6NE (01592) 610066* **£190***, plus special breaks; 30 rms. Fine Georgian country house in 400-acre park landscaped in Capability Brown style, with fresh flowers, open fires and antiques in gracious public rooms, extremely good inventive food, and a big wine list; disabled access; dogs welcome in bedrooms

GRANTOWN ON SPEY NJ0227 **Culdearn House** *Woodlands Terrace, Grantown on Spey, Morayshire PH26 3JU (01479) 872106* **£150** inc dinner, plus special breaks; 9 rms. Carefully run Victorian granite stone house with homely decor inc local watercolours, friendly chatty atmosphere, helpful owners, and enjoyable Scottish food; packed lunches on request; self-catering too; cl Nov–Feb; children over 10; partial disabled access

INVERNESS NH6245 **Bunchrew House** *Bunchrew, Inverness IV3 8TA (01463) 234917* **£155**, plus special breaks; 14 individually decorated rms. Friendly 17th-c mansion W of town by Beauly Firth with fine views and landscaped gardens, log fire in the elegant panelled drawing room, and traditional cooking using local produce and local game and venison; cl 22–26 Dec; dogs welcome in bedrooms

INVERNESS NH6343 **Dunain Park** *Inverness IV3 8JN (01463) 230512* **£158**; 13 rms inc 6 suites with own lounge. 19th-c Italianate mansion in six acres of well tended gardens and woodland, overlooking the River Ness and Caledonian Canal; charming owners, traditional homely decor with family photographs and china ornaments, log fires and fresh flowers, wonderful food using home-grown produce and local game, fish and Aberdeen Angus meat, generous breakfasts, and 200 whiskies; small warm swimming pool, sauna, lots of walks and golf courses nearby; disabled access; dogs welcome in bedrooms

KINCLAVEN BY STANLEY NO1437 **Ballathie House** *Stanley, Perth PH1 4QN (01250) 883268* **£160**, plus special breaks; 42 pretty rms, some luxurious and some in new building with river views from balconies. On a vast estate with fine salmon fishing on the River Tay (lodges and facilities for fishermen) and plenty of sporting opportunities, this turreted mansion has a comfortable and relaxed drawing room, separate lounge and bar, good enjoyable modern Scottish cooking, croquet and putting; disabled access; dogs welcome in bedrooms

KINNESSWOOD NO1703 **Lomond Country Inn** *Main St, Kinnesswood, Kinross KY13 9HN* (01592) 840253 **£70***; 10 comfortable rms, 8 in an extension. Attractive little inn in village centre with views across Loch Leven, open fires, informal bustling bar, well kept real ales, and good reasonably priced bar and restaurant food using local produce; disabled access; dogs welcome in bedrooms

KIRKTON OF GLENISLA NO2160 **Glenisla Hotel** *Glenisla, Blairgowrie, Perthshire PH11 8PH* (01575) 582223 **£50**; 6 rms. Attractively placed peaceful 17th-c coaching inn, prettily restored with natural unpainted wood throughout, happily unmatched furniture, bar with open fire and two real ales, good food, cheerful warm atmosphere; nice garden; cl 25–26 Dec; dogs welcome in bedrooms

NAIRN NH8756 **Clifton House** *Viewfield St, Nairn, Nairnshire IV12 4HW* (01667) 453119 **£100***; 12 individually decorated comfortable rms. Lovely, civilised, flower-filled old family hotel (the present owner has lived in this elegant Victorian house all his life and has been running it as a hotel since 1952), individually furnished with exquisite antiques, paintings and sculptures; extremely good food using local eggs, fish, meat and game, fine breakfasts with home-made jams, bread, and oatcakes, and an exceptional wine list; during the winter they stage some 20 concerts, plays and recitals; cl mid-Dec–mid-Jan; dogs welcome in bedrooms

PEAT INN NO4509 **Peat Inn** *Peat Inn, Cupar, Fife KY15 5LH* (01334) 840206 **£150***, plus special breaks; 8 luxurious suites. Famous restaurant with rooms: beams and white plaster walls, log fires and comfortable sofas, friendly service, fine food using the best local produce inc plenty of game and seafood, and excellent wine list; cl Sun/Mon, 25 Dec, 1 Jan; disabled access; dogs welcome in bedrooms

PITLOCHRY NN9162 **Killiecrankie Hotel** *Killiecrankie, Pitlochry, Perthshire PH16 5LG* (01796) 473220 **£190*** inc dinner, plus special breaks; 10 spotless rms. Comfortable country hotel in spacious grounds with splendid mountain views, mahogany-panelled bar with stuffed animals and fine wildlife paintings, cosy sitting room with books and games, a relaxed atmosphere, friendly newish owners, and excellent well presented, locally sourced food in elegant restaurant; cl 3 Jan–13 Feb; disabled access; dogs welcome in bedrooms

SCONE NO1526 **Murrayshall House** *Perthshire PH2 7PH* (01738) 551171 **£130***, plus special breaks; 41 rms inc 14 suites, plus lodge which sleeps 6. Handsome mansion in 300-acre park, very popular with golfers (it has two of its own courses); comfortable elegant public rooms, warm friendly staff, relaxed atmosphere, imaginative food, and good wines; disabled access; dogs welcome

SPEAN BRIDGE NN2891 **Letterfinlay Lodge** *Letterfinlay, Spean Bridge, Inverness-shire PH34 4DZ* (01397) 712622 **£80***, plus special breaks; 13 rms, most with own bthrm. Secluded and genteel family-run country house right on the edge of our East Scotland area and well placed for the west too, with extensive modern bar overlooking loch; elegantly panelled small cocktail bar, good popular food, friendly attentive service; grounds run down through rhododendrons to the jetty and Loch Lochy; fishing can be arranged; cl Nov–Mar; dogs welcome in bedrooms

SPITTAL OF GLENSHEE NO0672 **Dalmunzie House** *Glenshee, Blairgowrie, Perthshire PH10 7QG* (01250) 885224 **£100**, plus special breaks; 16 rms with own bthrm. Old-fashioned former Victorian shooting lodge, off A93, peacefully set in huge estate among spectacular mountains, plenty of walks within it, and own golf course; family-run atmosphere, enjoyable food using local produce, and tasty breakfasts; cl Dec; dogs welcome in bedrooms

STRATHKINNESS NO4516 **Fossil House & Cottage** *12–14 Main St, Strathkinness, St Andrews, Fife KY16 9RU* (01334) 850639 **£50**; 4 well equipped pretty rms with fresh flowers – particularly good family room. Once a smallholding, the two stone buildings here have a comfortable little guest lounge and sunny conservatory (no children in these two rooms), plenty of books, board games, videos, and lots of ornaments and fighter aircraft pictures, especially helpful friendly owners, really super breakfasts, and barbecue facilities in the garden; no smoking

TOMINTOUL NJ1718 **Argyle House** 7 *Main St, Tomintoul, Ballindalloch, Banffshire AB37 9EX* (01807) 580766 **£32***; 5 rms, most with own bthrm. Small family run guesthouse, originally a Temperance Hotel, and recently carefully renovated; library with books for guests to borrow, good breakfasts in dining room, and a genuine welcome from the friendly owners; lots to do nearby; dogs welcome in bedrooms

To see and do

Scotland Family Attraction of the Year

DUNDEE NO4029 **Sensation** (Greenmarket) This splendid new science centre – Tayside's flagship Millennium Project – focuses on the senses, with dozens of fun exhibits and interactive displays. It's been designed very much with younger visitors in mind: right from the planning stage, several local children have sat on a junior board, vetoing ideas they found too dull. So the emphasis is firmly on finding things out through lively activities rather than traditional displays: climbing round a giant head, for example (and sliding out through the nose), or discovering why a strange lump of goo goes hard and then breaks when it's squeezed. Touch-screen games vividly explain everything from germination, with individual seeds clamouring for attention while you decide what they'll need to make them grow, and body temperature, with the chance to see yourself as a thermal image to discover how hot or cold your various parts are. Along the way you can find out how plants turn light into food and know when to flower, and what the world looks like to a dog. They have extra activities in school holidays, good temporary exhibitions, and an enjoyable soft play area, where you can fire balls out of a cannon. Teenagers may not find it as engaging as their younger siblings (though there is an area with the latest computers and multimedia equipment), but most children will find plenty to keep them happy for a half day or so. The website – www.sensation.org.uk – has several online games, ostensibly to help develop keyboard skills. Meals, snacks, shop, disabled access; cl 25–26 Dec, 1 Jan; (01382) 228800; £5.50 adults, £3.99 children 4–15.

ABERDEEN NJ9305
Scotland's third-largest city, with a large active harbour, well worth pottering around; there's a popular farmers market (Belmont St, last Sat in month). The granite centre has wide, orderly streets not unlike Edinburgh's New Town in places, and parks. Leafy Seaton Park is famous for its 14th-c Brig (or bridge) o' Balgownie. The Ferryhill House Hotel (Bon Accord St), Royal Hotel (Bath St) and Athol (King's Gate, W of centre) are useful for lunch, and the Old Blackfriars (Castle St) has lots of character.
Aberdeen Art Gallery (Schoolhill) First-class collection of Scottish and English painting since the 16th c,

especially strong on contemporary works. Meals, snacks, shop, disabled access; cl Sun am, 25–26 Dec, 1 Jan; (01224) 523700; free.
Aberdeen Maritime Museum (Provost Ross's House, Shiprow) In the third-oldest building here (very striking), with very good displays on the city's nautical heritage. Meals, snacks, shop, disabled access; cl Sun am, 25–26, 31 Dec, 1–2 Jan; (01224) 337700; free.
Cruickshank Botanic Garden (St Machar Drive) Eleven acres first planted in the 19th c, and divided into various smaller gardens – rock, water, rose and herbaceous – as well as trees and shrubs and a small terrace garden.

Disabled access to most areas, cl am wknds May–Sept and all day wknds in winter; (01224) 272704; free.

King's College Founded in 1495, and very Oxbridge-like; the chapel is one of the most complete examples of a medieval collegiate church in Britain. A visitor centre outlines the history. Snacks (in barrel-vaulted former library), shop, disabled access; cl Sun, Christmas, New Year; (01224) 273702; free. It dominates the pedestrianised villagey High St of the Old Town (N of the centre, really too far to walk). Above the River Don, this part seems quite separate, and has other charming old streets, and attractive buildings.

Marischal Museum (Broad St) Housed in the splendid 19th-c neo-Gothic building of Marischal College, the Protestant rival to King's (the two were joined to form Aberdeen University in 1860); innovative displays of material from north-east Scotland, and from many parts of the world, strong on anthropology and archaeology; cl Sun am, all day Sat, 23 Dec–3 Jan, 1–6 July; (01224) 274301; free.

Provost Skene's House (Guestrow) Named after its most famous resident, a stately well restored 16th-c house with refurbished period rooms, remarkable painted ceilings and displays on archaeology and costumes. Snacks, shop; cl am Sun, 25–26 Dec, 1–2 Jan; (01224) 641086; free. The Illicit Still nearby has food all day.

Satrosphere [access] (Constitution St) Lively science and technology centre with over 100 hands-on exhibits, shows, workshops and special events. Gift shop, café with home baking and light lunches, disabled access; cl 25 Dec, 1–2 Jan; (01224) 640340; £5.

St Machar's Cathedral (Old Town) Austere mainly 15th-c church notable for its painted wooden heraldic ceiling. It's the only granite cathedral in the world; shop, disabled access; £2 suggested donation.

ABERDOUR NT1985
Aberdour Castle 12th-c castle extended and modified over 500 years; the first-floor gallery gives an idea of how it was furnished in 1650, and the interesting 17th-c walled gardens are being restored around an ancient sundial centrepiece. Snacks, shop, disabled access; cl Thurs and Fri pm in winter; (01383) 860519; £2.20; HS.

ABERFELDY NN8549
This quiet and pleasant small Highland shopping town has a fine 18th-c stone bridge designed by William Adam. There's a well restored watermill on Mill St (now closed), and just S of town the delightful verdant 1½ m walk along to the oak-lined Den and Falls of Moness inspired Burns's song *The Birks of Aberfeldy*. Close by in Weem, you can get a good lunch at the Ailean Chraggan. Also in Weem, **Castle Menzies** is a good example of a 16th-c fortified tower house; this was the stronghold and home of Chiefs of Clan Menzies for over 400 years; there's a small clan museum. Shop, disabled access; cl am Sun, and mid-Oct to Apr; (01887) 820982; £3.50.

Dewar's World of Whisky This makes an entertaining stop even if you don't like whisky (or aren't old enough to drink it). An audio guide takes you round the various displays (some interactive) in a 19th-c malting barn; also films, a couple of re-creations, and old adverts. Admission includes a guided distillery tour (not wknds, no disabled access) and a sample. Outside is a restored 1939 steam locomotive and a nature trail. Snacks, shop, disabled access; cl am Sun, wknds Nov–Mar, 2 wks Christmas–New Year; (01887) 822011; £3.95.

ABERFOYLE NN5200
Lots of woollen shops, and in the heart of Queen Elizabeth Forest Park (readers recommend the forest visitor centre; good walk suggestions), so lovely scenery around. You can hire bikes; (01877) 382614. The Inverard has decent food.

Scottish Wool Centre [access] The story of Scottish wool from sheep to shop, entertainingly told by a live sheep show in the amphitheatre (cl Nov–Mar; the centre itself is open all year). They have spinning demonstrations, and sheepdogs herd ducks around an intricate course. Meals, snacks, good shop, disabled access; cl 25 Dec; (01877) 382850; £3.

ALFORD NJ5815

Alford Valley Railway (A944)
Narrow-gauge passenger railway with
trips in one-mile section, and a good
static display at the station. Shop,
disabled access; trains usually in steam
wknds 1st Sun May–Sept, and daily pm
Jun–Aug; (019755) 62326; *£2.

Grampian Transport Museum 🎦
(A944) Big collection of vintage
vehicles, from horse-drawn carriages to
sleek sports cars including the unique
Craigevar Steam Express Tricycle;
exciting events all summer; children's
playground. Snacks, shop, disabled
access; cl Nov–Mar; (01975) 562292;
£4. The village has a new life-size
bronze statue of an Aberdeen Angus
bull, to mark its long association with
the breed, and the Forbes Arms at
Bridge of Alford has good food.

ALLOA NS8892

Alloa Tower (A907, 6m E of Stirling)
This beautifully restored 13th-c tower
is all that remains of the ancestral home
of the Earls of Mar. Although it was
splendidly remodelled by the sixth earl
before his exile after the 1715 Jacobite
uprising, the tower, its walls well over 3
metres (11 ft) thick, retains some rare
medieval features inc groin vaulting, a
complete timber roof, interior well and
underground dungeon. Also some
attractive furniture and fine paintings
inc works by Raeburn and Kneller.
Shop, disabled access to ground floor
only; cl am, and Oct–Mar ext Oct
wknds; (01259) 211701; £3.50; NTS.

ANSTRUTHER NO5603
Pretty East Neuk fishing village;
May–Sept (weather permitting) you can
get boat trips out to the nature reserve
of the Isle of May, summer home to
countless puffins and seals; (01333)
310103. The 16th-c Dreel does good
bar meals.

Scottish Fisheries Museum 🎦 The
many facets of fishermen's life are
portrayed in this museum, inc the
dangers they face at sea. There's an
excellent collection of models of old
fishing boats, with 16 full-sized vessels
displayed in a former boatyard and in
the adjacent harbour. Cl Christmas and
New Year; (01333) 310628; £3.50.

ARBROATH NO6441

Arbroath Abbey Substantial remains
of 12th-c abbey, connected with
Thomas à Becket and Robert the Bruce.
Shop, disabled access to ground floor
only; cl Thurs pm, Sun am and all day Fri
Oct–Mar, 25–26 Dec, 1–2 Jan; (01241)
878756; £2.50; HS.

AVIEMORE NH8912
Uncompromisingly modern ski-resort
village. There are plenty of places to get
something to eat in this sizeable tourist
development (the Olde Bridge is our
current recommendation).

Cairngorms A £15 million funicular
railway, the highest in Britain, takes you
up to the Ptarmigan Station just below
the summit of Cairngorm. If you can
tear yourself away from the view,
there's an exhibition on the history and
ecology of the mountain. Meals, snacks,
shop, disabled access; cl in bad weather,
best to check; (01479) 861261; £7.50.

Loch an Eilein A draw for walkers,
nestling beneath the Cairngorms; a
forest track encircles this delightful
little loch, with its castle romantically
placed on an isle – great echoes here.

Strathspey Steam Railway 10 miles
of great scenery between here and
Broomhill. Snacks (not Sat), shop,
limited disabled access; usually open
daily Jun–Sept, plus other dates and
wknds – best to ring for timetable;
(01479) 810725; *£8.40.

BALLATER NO4198

Cambus o' May Walks (A93 E)
Extensively quarried until the early
20th c, this pleasantly wooded area is
dissected by several walks inc one
around a small loch (with picnic area),
designed to accommodate wheelchairs.
If you're lucky, you might catch a
glimpse of red deer and capercaillie
among the mix of evergreens.

Old Royal Station (Station Sq) This
Victorian railway station has been fully
restored to how it would have been in
the days when Queen Victoria used it
on the way to nearby Balmoral.
Displays tell the history of its Royal
connections, and lifelike figures inhabit
the Royal Waiting Room. Restaurant,
Tourist Information Centre, disabled
access; cl Christmas and New Year
(013397) 55306; free.

BALLINDALLOCH NJ1736

Ballindalloch Castle Romantic castle
in a lovely spot in the heart of Speyside

whisky country, grandly enlarged around 1845, and still lived in by the Macpherson-Grants whose ancestors settled here in mid-16th c. Furnishings inside are cheerfully light, and there's a fine collection of 17th-c Spanish paintings. The Rivers Spey and Avon run through the grounds, which also include a large rock garden, and the oldest herd of Aberdeen Angus cattle in the world. Enjoyable afternoon teas, well stocked gift shop, disabled access to tearoom and ground floor of castle only; cl Sat, and Oct–Maundy Thurs exc by appointment; (01807) 500206; £4.50.

Glenlivet Distillery The first Highland malt whisky distillery to be licensed, and thought by many to produce the best; cl Sun am and Nov–Mar; (01542) 783220; £3.

BALMEDIE COUNTRY PARK NJ9820

Along a constantly shifting stretch of coast, this is splendidly bleak-feeling despite the closeness of Aberdeen. Visitor centre usually cl winter wknds, though best to check; (01358) 742396. The beaches are clean and safe.

BALMORAL NO2693

Balmoral Castle (off A93) The Royal Family's Highland residence. Prince Albert bought the property four years after he and Queen Victoria had first rented it in 1848, and had a new castle built here by 1855. You can't go inside, but you can explore the wonderful gardens and woodlands, and there are various exhibitions in the ballroom. Also pony trekking and pony cart rides. Snacks, meals, shop, disabled access; cl Aug to mid-Apr; (013397) 42334; £4.50.

BANFF NJ6963

Duff House This magnificent example of 18th-c baroque architecture has served as a ducal residence, hotel, sanitarium and prisoner-of-war camp in its time. It now houses a splendid collection of paintings and tapestries from the National Galleries of Scotland, hung in sumptuously furnished rooms inc Chippendale furniture designed like the house by Robert Adam. The extensive grounds laid out alongside the River Deveron are pleasant for strolling in, and include a mausoleum

and, rather quaintly, the 19th-c headstones of various dogs. Tearoom with very good home-made food, shop, good disabled access including lifts to gallery, cl Mon–Weds Nov–Mar, 25–26 Dec, and 1–2 Jan; (01261) 818181; £4; HS.

BEN VENUE NN4706

Allows some good mountain walks comparable in difficulty to some of the fells of the English Lake District.

BEN VORLICH NN6218

Good walking, for those used to pretty hearty fell walking.

BENNACHIE NJ6623

On the E edge of the Grampians near Inverurie, this is not that high but gives walkers tremendous views over lowland Grampian; the gently rolling moorland top has several colour-coded Forestry Authority trails (the lower slopes are forested).

BLAIR ATHOLL NN8665

Atholl Country Life Museum 🖼 Turn in at the White Horse for this friendly little **folk museum**, with some unusual exhibits inc the largest known trophy in Britain (awarded for shooting). Meals, snacks, shop, disabled access; open pm late May–end Sept, plus wkdy ams July–mid-Sept; (01796) 472215; *£3.

Blair Castle (off A9) Nestling among forests and heather-clad hills, this is Scotland's most-visited privately owned house, dating back to the 13th c, though largely renovated in the 18th. You can see 30 rooms, and there's an 18th-c walled garden. A display charts the history of the Atholl Highlanders – the Duke of Atholl's unique private army that turns out here for its annual parade in May. A piper outside most days in summer adds to the atmosphere. Meals, snacks, shop, disabled access to ground floor only; cl end Oct–beginning Apr (limited winter opening hours); (01796) 481207; *£6.50, £2 for grounds only. The Atholl Arms has good value food all day.

House of Bruar (A9) Country shopping complex with fine specialist foods and clothing; readers like it a lot.

BLAIR DRUMMOND NS7498

Safari and Adventure Park (A84) Wild animals in natural surroundings, with plenty of other activities included in the price, from gentle rides for younger children to the exhilarating Flying Fox slide over the lake. You can explore part of the water in pedal-boats, and boat trips circle Chimpanzee Island leaving the chimps to enjoy their natural habitat undisturbed; one of them made the news recently by stealing a keeper's mobile phone and making anonymous calls with it. Feeding times of lions, sea lions, and penguins are posted in the park. Meals, snacks, shop, disabled access; cl Oct–Mar; (01786) 841456; *£9 (£4.50 children 3–14) – not bad value if you bring a barbie and make a half-day of it. The Lion & Unicorn at Thornhill does good family lunches.

BO'NESS NS9981

Bo'ness & Kinneil Railway ☒ Re-creation of the days of steam complete with relocated railway buildings and Scotland's largest collection of locomotives and rolling stock. The 7-mile round trip takes you to the woodlands of the Avon Gorge at Birkhill, for tours of an old fireclay mine. Meals, snacks, shop, disabled access to railway only; trains usually run wknds Apr to mid-Oct, daily (exc Mon) July and Aug, and for special events in Dec, though you can see the locomotives all year; cl Jan, Feb, Nov; (01506) 822298; £7.50 mine and train, £4.50 train only. (Discount voucher not valid on special event days).

Kinneil Estate Includes the interesting if not extensive remains of a Roman fortlet, as well as a few later ruins and remains. The converted stables of adjacent Kinneil House have a museum on the site's history, with lots of local pottery. You can still see the workshop where James Watt developed the steam engine, and there are pleasant woodland walks and a new adventure playground. Shop, limited disabled access; cl am and all day Sun and bank hols; (01506) 778530; free.

BRAEMAR NO1491

One of the most beautifully set Highland villages; the Fife Arms (very much on the coach routes) is good for lunch. A steep path up Morrone takes the most determined walkers along a route used for a race in Braemar's famous Highland Gathering.

Braemar Castle ☒ (A93 NE) Highly unusual and charming interior. Snacks, shop; cl Fri (exc July–Aug), and all Nov–beginning of Apr; (013397) 41219; *£3.50.

Highland Heritage Centre (Mar Rd) Good, showing useful film on the area's history and scenery (inc an interesting look at the building of Balmoral Castle), and on the Gathering. Shops, disabled access; cl 25–26 Dec, 1–2 Jan; (01339) 741944; free.

Linn of Dee NO0689 Not far, giving long glen walks into the Cairngorms along Glen Dee and the Lairig Ghru.

BRODIE CASTLE NH9757

Brodie Castle (off A96) Handsome gabled castle with extensive art collection featuring 17th-c paintings of the Dutch school, English watercolours and French Impressionists. Before the National Trust for Scotland took it over in 1980 it had been the seat of the same family since 1160. Outside are woodland walks and wildlife observation hides, and beautiful daffodils in spring. Snacks, shop, limited disabled access; cl Tues, Weds and Oct–Mar; (01309) 641371; £5; NTS. Their occasional evenings of traditional Scottish music are good fun. The nearest really good place for a meal is the Clifton Hotel in Nairn.

BROUGHTY FERRY NO4630

Broughty Castle Museum (off A930 4m E of Dundee) 15th-c fort rebuilt in the 19th c to defend the estuary, now a local and natural history museum. Plenty of harpoons and whaling exhibits – whaling used to be one of Dundee's major industries. Snacks, shop; cl Mon Oct–Mar, Sun am, 25–26 Dec, 1–3 Jan; (01382) 436916; free. The Fishermans Tavern and Ship (fantastic view upstairs) are good.

BUCKIE NJ4366

Buckie Drifter ☒ Interesting fishing museum with a re-created 1920s quayside, and an interactive exhibition on the life of the herring, and the fishermen who depended on it; you can climb aboard a lifeboat, and there's a collection of marine paintings by Peter Anson. Restaurant with views of the harbour and the Moray Firth, shop, disabled access; cl Sun am and beginning of Nov–end Mar; (01542) 834646; £2.75.

BURNTISLAND NT2385

Once famous for shipbuilding (and shipbreaking), now a popular little resort, with an unusual octagonal church where the decision was made to produce the Authorised Version of the Bible in 1601.

CALLANDER NN6207

Quite a busy tourist town, popular in Victorian times thanks to the works of Walter Scott, and still remembered for its appearances in the original *Dr Finlay's Casebook*. The **Hamilton Toy Collection** (Main St) is worth a look if you're passing; usually cl Mon (exc bank hols and during Aug), am Sun, and end Oct–Easter; (01877) 330 004; £1.50. **Kilmahog Woollen Mill** (just N) Restored flax mill with 250-year-old working wheel, selling tweeds, tartans and other woollen gifts; also whisky tasting. Meals, snacks, shop; cl 25 Dec; (01877) 330268; free. The Lade Inn out here has good food.

Rob Roy & Trossachs Visitor Centre (Ancaster Sq) The story of Scotland's most whitewashed rascal (or brave supporter of the downtrodden, depending on your point of view), well told with hi-tech displays. Also information on the beautiful surrounding countryside. Shop, disabled access; cl 25–26 Dec and 1–2 Jan; (01877) 330342; £3.25.

The Trossachs The Highlands in microcosm, beloved by coach tours for their dense conifer forests, steep glens and beautifully framed lochs, and now part of Scotland's first National Park. Perhaps surprisingly, not brilliant for low-level walks unless you like forests; the route on to Callander Crags from Callander is one of the best. The Byre at Brig o' Turk is a good food stop.

CARRBRIDGE NH9022

Landmark Heritage & Adventure Park Good family day out, with exhibition on the microscopic world, well signposted forest trails (one through the tree-tops), a new covered, elaborate adventure playground (children 5–14), water-coaster, and Forestry Heritage Park with fully operational steam-powered sawmill (Apr–Oct). You can sometimes have a go at log-cutting and Lex the giant Clydesdale horse may be hauling logs to the mill. Great views from the top of the viewing tower. Meals, snacks, shop, disabled access; cl 25 Dec; (01479) 841614; *£7.45. The beautifully placed Dalrachney Lodge Hotel (nr junction A9/A95) does good lunches.

CASTLE CAMPBELL NS9699

Castle Campbell Once known as Castle Gloom, this late 15th-c castle was burned by Cromwell's enemies in the 1650s, but still has its courtyard, great hall and barrel roof, as well as splendid views from the tower. Snacks, shop; cl every Sun am, Thurs pm and all day Fri in winter, 25–26 Dec, 1–2 Jan; (01259) 742408; £2.80; HS. The Kings Seat in Dollar has good home-made food.

Dollar Glen An amazing short track takes you up through these spectacular 60 acres of Arthur Rackham-esque woodland – catwalks, rock overhangs, jungle-thick vegetation, and a swirling stream below. Take care, some paths are steep and narrow, and can be dangerous after rain. But this is a gripping approach to Castle Campbell.

CAWDOR NH8449

Cawdor Castle (B9090) Home of the Thanes of Cawdor since the 14th c, this splendid old house is one of the most entertaining as well as interesting places to visit in the whole area. Look out especially for the tree inside a tower and the freshwater well inside the house, as well as the more usual fine tapestries, furnishings and paintings (inc Dali's odd interpretation of the Macbeth tale). The grounds have several pretty gardens, craft and wool shops, nature trails, and a 9-hole golf course. Meals, snacks, shop, disabled access to ground floor only; cl mid-Oct to end Apr; (01667) 404615; £6.30, grounds only £3.20. The nearby Cawdor Tavern is good for lunch.

CLAVA CAIRNS NH7544

A group of circular burial cairns from around 1600 BC surrounded by three concentric rings of great stones, on the banks of the River Nairn.

COLLESSIE NO2712

Fife Animal Park (B937) Unique collection of ostriches, emus and rheas – they have birds of all ages, play areas, and animals such as lambs, pigs and wallabies. Meals, snacks, shop, good disabled access, only open Fri–Sun; may cl Oct–Apr; (01337) 831830; free. The Albert over in Freuchie has good value food.

COMRIE NN7919

Auchingarrich Wildlife Centre You can spend a whole day at this 100-acre park and, as much of it is under cover, it's enjoyable even if it's wet. As well as rabbits, pigs, sheep and highland cattle, they've animals such as raccoons (see them being fed at 2pm, otters feed an hour later), llamas, arctic foxes and emus; you can watch chicks being born in the hatchery, and a falconry centre has regular summer flying displays (50p). Lots of well thought-out play areas, and space for picnics and barbecues. Summer snacks, shop, disabled access; open daily Easter–Oct, best to phone in winter when parts are shut, and there's an honesty box; (01764) 679469; £4.75.

Deil's Cauldron Beauty spot reached by a signposted circular walk through Glen Lednock from Comrie (the Earthquake House at Comrie records tremors).

Drummond Trout Farm and Fishery Very friendly, especially good for first-time fishermen (if it's not too busy – they're happy to give you some tips); also see how a fishery works, and you can feed the fish. Summer snacks, picnic area (you can bring your own barbecue), shop, disabled access; cl a few days over Christmas and New Year (open till 10 in summer); (01764) 670500; £3.50 for 2 hours' fishing, £4 for 3.

CRAIGELLACHIE NJ2944

Speyside Cooperage Visitor Centre 🖾 (Dufftown Rd) Working cooperage and visitor centre, with viewing area to watch the craftsmen and a tasting area. Shop (wide range of wood goods), picnic area, disabled access to exhibition only; cl wknds, and Christmas/New Year; (01340) 871108; £2.95. The fine Telford-built bridge here opened in 1814, and carried traffic until 1973. The little Fiddichside Inn (Keith Rd) is a charmingly old-fashioned fishing pub.

CRAIGIEVAR NJ5609

Craigievar Castle (A980) Perhaps the most fairytale-romantic of the area's castles, this picturesque early 17th-c multiple tower dotted with erratically shaped windows soars to a mushrooming of corbels, turrets and crow-stepped gables. Inside, a warren of narrow staircases climbs through a rich series of ornately beamed and plastered rooms. The National Trust for Scotland are worried that too many people come here, so if you do decide to visit (and it is worth while), try to avoid busy times – it's not a place to absorb coach parties comfortably. Castle open pm only Apr–Sept, grounds open all year; (013398) 83635; £6.50; NTS.

Noah's Ark Country Activity Centre (off A980) You can help to feed and tend to the animals at this friendly place, attractively set just S of the castle. Snacks, shop, partial disabled access; cl Mon, Christmas and New Year weeks; (01339) 883670; £3.

CRAIL NO6107

One of the prettiest of the East Neuk fishing villages – the East Neuk being the local name for the E part of the Fife coast.

Secret Bunker 🖾 (B940 4m W) Beneath an innocuous-looking farmhouse is a network of underground rooms and corridors from where the government would have run Scotland in a nuclear attack. Meals, snacks, shop, disabled access; cl Nov–end Mar; (01333) 310301; £6.95.

CRATHES NO7596

Crathes Castle (A93) Beautiful 16th-c tower house with wonderful interiors – esp its ceiling paintings, filled with wise old sayings in a mixture of Scots and English. Best of all are the surrounding gardens, inc a four-acre walled garden with a remarkable series of carefully toned colour borders. Meals, snacks, shop, some disabled access; cl Nov–Mar; (01330) 844525; £8.50, £5 garden or castle (£1 car park); NTS. Scott Skinners (A93 towards Banchory) has good value food.

CRIEFF NN8621

A pleasant airy town, perched on the edge of the Highlands. A modern visitor centre has a pottery, plant centre, wildlife sculptures, and a new exhibition on cattle droving (01764) 654014; there's a Stuart Crystal factory shop on

Muthill Rd. The Knock of Crieff, a wooded hill just above, gives walkers a good viewpoint.

Glenturret Distillery (off A85 NW) Now with the new Famous Grouse Experience (a lively look at the history, marketing and production of this well known whisky), this is Scotland's oldest distillery, dating from 1775 and using the pure water of the Turret Burn. There's a statue of the distillery cat Towser, who died in 1987 but is still in the *Guinness Book of Records* as World Mousing Champion – challengers have 28,899 to beat. Meals and snacks, shop, some disabled access; cl 25–26 Dec, 1–2 Jan; (01764) 656565; guided tours £6.

CULLODEN NH7445
Culloden Battlefield (B9006) The bleak site of the gruesome massacre in which the 25-year-old Duke of Cumberland destroyed the Highland army of Bonnie Prince Charlie. On the moor a cairn marks this last bloody battle fought on mainland Britain. You can see the Graves of the Clans and the Wells of the Dead, as well as the Old Leanach Cottage around which the battle was fought, refurbished in period style. Meals, snacks, shop, disabled access; visitor centre cl 24–26 Dec, and first 2 wks in Jan; (01463) 790607; £5; NTS. The Snow Goose (E of A9/A96) does good food.

CULROSS NS9885
(off A985) Fascinating small town on the Forth, virtually unchanged since the 16th and 17th c. Until the 1930s this was because no one could afford any improvements, and since then its red pantiled-roofed houses have been carefully restored and preserved by the National Trust for Scotland (they are still lived in). There are the remains of a 13th-c abbey.

Culross Palace The laird's house was the first building the Trust purchased here. It's fully furnished in 17th-c style, and they've re-created a period garden. Guides are good at pointing out those small but fascinating details that make the difference between just another building and a real experience. Snacks, shop; cl am (exc Jun–Aug), wkdys in Oct, and all Nov–Mar; (01383) 880359; £5 inc audio guide; NTS. The price includes admission to the Trust's two other main properties here, the Town House (good visitor centre), and the Study, with a Norwegian painted ceiling in the drawing room.

CUPAR NO3711
Hill of Tarvit Mansionhouse (off A916 S) Rebuilt in 1906 with Edwardian-style interiors, French, chippendale-style and vernacular furniture, Dutch paintings and pictures by Raeburn and Ramsay, Flemish tapestries and Chinese porcelain and bronzes. Tearoom; cl am (exc July–Aug) and end Oct–Easter; (01334) 653127; house and grounds £5, grounds only £2; NTS.

Scottish Deer Centre 🏷 (Bow of Fife; A91 just W) You can stroke the deer and feed the young fawns at this friendly place. There are also nature and heritage trails, daily falconry displays, aerial walkways and observation platforms, and an adventure playground. Snacks, shop, disabled access; cl 25 Dec, 1 Jan; (01337) 810391; *£4.50. There's an adjacent holiday shopping courtyard.

DOUNE NN6901
Doune Castle (A84) 14th-c stronghold with two fine restored towers on the banks of the River Teith. Strong associations with Bonnie Prince Charlie and Walter Scott, and the Knights of Ni – the castle was used in the filming of *Monty Python and the Holy Grail*. Shop; from Nov–Mar cl Thurs pm, Sun am and all Fri, 25–26 Dec, 1–2 Jan; (01786) 841742; £2.80; HS. The village's bridge is said to have been built out of spite by James IV's tailor when the ferryman refused him passage. The Lion & Unicorn over in Thornhill is good for lunch.

DUFFTOWN NJ3240
Glenfiddich Distillery (A491, just N) The only Highland distillery where you can follow the entire whisky production process from barley to bottle – most other distilleries bottle elsewhere. Look out for the friendly distillery cat. Enjoyable tours and generous tastings, shop, disabled access; cl Sun am, winter wknds, 2 weeks over Christmas; (01340) 820373; free. Dufftown has a useful museum.

DULNAIN BRIDGE NH9823
Speyside Heather Centre (Skye of

Curr, off A95) Over 300 different types of heather in landscaped garden, along with an exhibition on its various uses, and gift shop inc wide range of heather-based goods. Home-made meals and snacks, garden centre, antique shop and gallery, disabled access; cl 25 Dec, reduced opening hours Jan–Feb; (01479) 851359; 75p exhibition.

DUNBLANE NN7801

Dunblane Museum This small town of ancient origin, its name now tragically familiar all over the world, is of ancient origin, with plenty of old buildings in its narrow streets, esp around the close of its elegant 13th-c cathedral. This incorporates a much older tower, and has a beautiful oval window that you can see only from outside. The museum which explains the interesting background is nearby (cl all day Sun, and Oct–early May; free). The Stirling Arms has good food.

DUNDEE NO3929

Beneath the straightforward modern wrappings of this bustling city, you can uncover signs of its distinguished heritage in a number of museums. You can watch sweets being made at Shaws Factory (Mains Loan; Weds pm only, (01382) 461435; free). The Chequers (South Tay St), Royal Oak (Brook St – Indian), Mercantile (Commercial St) and Number 1 (Constitution Rd) have all been recommended by readers for their food.

Camperdown Country Park (off A90) 400 acres of fine parkland with golf course, nature trails, woodland footpaths, and wildlife centre with indigenous animals from wolves and bears to wildcats. Also adventure play area themed around the defeat of the Dutch at the 1797 Battle of Camperdown. Snacks, shop, disabled access; cl Christmas and New Year; (01382) 432689; free, £2.20 wildlife centre.

Contemporary Arts Centre (152 Nethergate) £9m centre for contemporary art and film, with two galleries showing changing exhibitions, plus an arts cinema, print studio and activity room for workshops. The trendy Jute Café Bar here has good food; shop, disabled access; centre cl 25–26 Dec, 1–2 Jan, galleries cl Mon;

(01382) 606220; free.

Discovery Point (Docks) Excellent lively visitor centre with hi-tech displays on the Royal Research Ship *Discovery*, moored here, which was the first British purpose-built research vessel, commissioned for Scott's first expedition to the Antarctic; displays too on him and others who used the ship. Café, shop, disabled access; cl 25 Dec, 1–2 Jan; (01382) 201245; £6.25.

Frigate Unicorn (Victoria Dock) This 1824 vessel is the oldest British-built warship still afloat, now with an audio-visual show and a museum of naval life in her days in commission. Snacks, shop; cl Mon–Tues Nov–Mar, and 2 weeks at Christmas/New Year; (01382) 200893; £3.50.

McManus Museum and Art Galleries (Albert Sq) Important works by 19th-c Scottish and English artists, and a splendid hall with vaulted ceiling and stained glass; cl Sun am, 25–26 Dec, 1–2 Jan; (01382) 432084; free.

Mills Observatory 🖼 (Balgay Park) Exhibits on space research and astronomy, as well as a small planetarium (by prior arrangement or last Fri in month during winter), and splendid 10-inch refracting telescope. Shop; open Tues–Fri and pm wknd Apr–Sept; Mon–Fri 4–10pm and wknd pms in winter (exc 25–26 Dec, 1–2 Jan); (01382) 435846; free.

Sensation *See separate family panel on p.812.*

Verdant Works (Discovery Point, Riverside Drive) Award-winning look at the jute industry, once an important part of the local economy, with films and interactive displays. Shop, disabled access; cl 25 Dec, 1–2 Jan; (01382) 225282; £5.95.

DUNFERMLINE NT0987

Quite a prosperous light-industry town with a distinguished distant past – it was once Scotland's capital.

Abbot House (Maygate) Exhibitions and relics inc the shrine of St Margaret, and a replica sword that would have been used in the Battle of Bannockburn. Tours using audio-visual technology lead you through the labyrinth of corridors and the twists and turns of Scotland's turbulent past. Meals, snacks, shop; cl 25 Dec, 1 Jan; (01383) 733266;

£3. The cave that St Margaret used to pray in is 84 steps below the Glen Bridge car park (cl Oct–Easter; free).

Andrew Carnegie Museum 🖻 (Moodie St) Focuses on the man who from humble origins in this house made a fortune in Pittsburgh steel, then gave away over $350 million – all the while claiming he didn't believe in charity. Handloom weaving demonstrations the first Fri of each month, May–Oct. Shop, disabled access; cl am Sun, and Nov–Mar; *£2.

Dunfermline Abbey The remains of a Benedictine abbey and later church buildings are pleasantly set in quiet precincts away from the busy centre. The foundations of the original 11th-c church underlie the more elaborate Norman nave, and the grave of King Robert the Bruce is marked by a modern brass in the choir stalls. The Palace is the birthplace of Charles I. Snacks, shop; cl Sun am in Oct, plus Thurs pm and all Fri Nov–Mar, 25–26 Dec, 1–2 Jan; (01383) 739026; £2.20; HS.

Dunfermline Museum (Viewfield Terrace) Looks at the local manufacture of damask linen (open by appointment only but cl wknds; (01383) 313838; free).

Pittencrieff House Museum (Pittencrieff Park) Fine 17th-c mansion in gently rugged glen, with displays and paintings (cl 25–26 Dec, 1–2 Jan; free).

DUNKELD NO0242 Charming small town by the River Tay. The cathedral has the tomb of the notorious Wolf of Badenoch, Alexander Stewart (the illegitimate son of English King Richard II). There are pretty preserved cottages (NTS), and riverside forest walks through National Trust land around the waterfalls near the Hermitage, an 18th-c folly, and so-called Ossian's Cave. The Atholl Arms is a useful stop.

Beatrix Potter Garden & Exhibition A small garden next to the Birnam Institute re-creates the house of Mrs Tiggywinkle and Peter Rabbit's burrow (free); Beatrix Potter spent holidays here. The institute houses a café, and various exhibitions inc one on the author herself; (01350) 727674. Birnam is a tiny township, a 15-min walk from Dunkeld across the River Tay. Birnam Wood (of Macbeth fame) has a venerable oak, and there's plenty of stirring walking country around.

EDZELL NO5969

Edzell Castle (B966) Some unique features at this pretty old place – the walled garden planted here in 1604, and the charming series of heraldic and mythical sculptures that decorate the walls around it; these alternate with recesses for flowers and nests for birds. They claim to have captured on camera the castle's rather active ghost. Shop, snack, limited disabled access; in winter cl Thurs pm, all day Fri and Sun am, 25–26 Dec, 1–2 Jan; (01356) 648631; £2.80; HS. The Ramsay Arms in Fettercairn has decent food, and just N there's a lovely drive up Glen Esk, passing a wayside folk museum (tearoom, giftshop (01356) 670254).

ELGIN NJ2263 Shopping town of some poise, with some handsome ancient buildings and handy for the coast; Thunderton House has decent food.

Elgin Cathedral Founded in 1224, and known as the Lantern of the North and the Glory of the Kingdom because of its extraordinary beauty and fine-traceried windows. There's still quite a lot to see of the ruins: the 15th-c nave has some ancient Celtic cross slabs with Pictish symbols, and you can go inside the spires. A viewing platform in one of the towers gives unrestricted views. Shop, some disabled access; cl winter Thurs pm and all Fri, Sun am, 25–26 Dec, 1–2 Jan; (01343) 547171; £2.80; HS.

Elgin Museum 🖻 (High St) Refurbished thanks to a Lottery grant, with a world-famous fossil collection, Pictish stones and changing exhibitions; cl am Sun, all Nov–early Apr; £2.

Moray Motor Museum (Bridge St) Well worth a look, in a converted mill; shop, disabled access, cl Oct–Mar; (01343) 544933; £3.

Pluscarden Abbey 🖻 (nr Barnhill, 5m SW) Fascinating; built in the 13th c, it gradually fell to ruin, but was rebuilt this century by monks from Prinknash Abbey down in Gloucestershire – they now sing a rediscovered chant which may well have been sung by St Columba himself; shop; (01343) 890257; open from 4.45am; free.

Spynie Palace 🏛 (A941 2m N) Former residence of the bishops of Moray, the biggest tower house in Scotland, with good views over Spynie Loch. Shop, disabled access; cl wkdys Nov–Apr; 12.30–1.30; (01343) 546358; £2; HS.

ELIE NT4999
Attractive fishing village set around a broad bay – the beach is notably clean and safe (and has a good pub, the Ship, virtually on it).

FALKIRK NS8979
Callender House (A803 just E) This huge park, with woodland walks and lots of summer activities, includes Callender House, a striking old house used briefly as HQ by Oliver Cromwell. Remodelled in the 19th c to look like a French château, it's now a museum, with costumed guides interpreting its history. Part of the Antonine Wall, the Roman Empire's farthest frontier, runs through the grounds. Meals, snacks, shop, disabled access; house cl Sun Oct–Mar, 25–26 Dec, 1–2 Jan; (01324) 503770; house £3, park (open all year) free.

Millennium Link This brings nearly 70 miles of canal from Glasgow to Edinburgh back to life, rebuilding a link that was severed over 60 years ago when a flight of 19th-c locks was closed. The project (partly funded by Lottery money) has seen the removal of obstacles inc filled-in stretches and low bridges, and the refurbishment of locks, and newly opened is the spectacular Falkirk Wheel (Lime Rd, Tamfour Hill): a rotating boat lift as high as a nine-storey block of flats which will winch vessels weighing up to 600 tonnes up a 24-metre (80-ft) rise; £6.50. It has been designed by the same team of architects responsible for the new Scottish Parliament building, who consider it to be a form of contemporary sculpture; the visitor centre has information about the canal's restoration and the construction of the wheel; (01324) 619888; free but £2 car parking.

Rough Castle (6m W) One of the best-preserved sections of the Antonine Wall; not too much is left of the Roman fort that once stood here, but you can still see the ramparts and ditches; free.

FALKLAND NO2507
Falkland Palace & Garden Lovely Renaissance palace of the Stuart kings and queens, set below the Lomond Hills on the main street. Not all is as old as it looks, but it doesn't really matter – accurate restoration work has created a comfortably cosy and genuinely lived-in feel. Pleasant gardens and grounds, with the 1539 tennis courts said to be the oldest in the country. Shop; cl Sun am, and end Oct–Mar; (01337) 857397; £7, £3 garden only; NTS. Parts of the village are delightful and were Scotland's first conservation area. Kind Kyttock's Kitchen (Cross Wynd) is good for light lunches and afternoon teas, and the 17th-c Stag (Mill Wynd), opposite a charming green and round the corner from the medieval village square, has enjoyable food for most of the day.

FETTERCAIRN NO6573
The square has a magnificent archway erected to commemorate a visit by Queen Victoria, and the Ramsay Arms has decent food. The drive along the twisting and climbing B974 to Banchory is good, with spectacular views from Cairn o' Mount at the top – and when the water's high enough salmon jumping near the Dee bridge as you enter Banchory.

Fettercairn Distillery (Distillery Rd) One of Scotland's oldest licensed distilleries, with tours, tastings, and good audio-visual show. Shop, disabled access to visitor centre only; cl Sun, and Oct–Apr; (01561) 340205; free.

FINDLATER CASTLE NJ5467
This windswept cliff-edge ruin makes a good destination for a walk; walkers can enjoy other stretches of this coast around Banff, with the bus service along the main road a useful method of return. The Cullen Bay Hotel has good value food.

FOCHABERS NJ3359
Baxters Highland Village (A96 just W) Explores how the grocery shop set up by George and Margaret Baxter grew into a company whose food is now sold all over the world. Landscaped gardens and woodland walk; meals, snacks, good shops, some

disabled access; cl wknds and 24 Dec–4 Jan; (01343) 820393; free.

Folk Museum (High St) Very good; cl Oct–Mar, free. The Gordon Arms is a reliable food stop in this pleasant small town.

FORRES NJ0356

Dallas Dhu Distillery (2m S) Perfectly preserved Victorian distillery, which you can wander around on your own. Animatronic models explain what's happening, and there's an audio tour. Shop (nearly 200 different types of whisky), picnic area, disabled access; cl winter Thurs pm, Fri, Sun am, 25–26 Dec, 1–2 Jan; (01309) 676548; £3.30; HS.

Falconer Museum (Tolbooth St) Good fossil collection; cl Sun, Good Fri, May bank hol, 25–26, 31 Dec, 1–2 Jan (01309) 673701; free.

Sueno's Stone (E end of town) Mysterious 9th- or 10th-c stone that may have been erected to commemorate a forgotten battle. It's 6 metres (20 ft) high, carved with a cross on one side and groups of warriors on the other. In summer you can usually climb the Nelson Tower in Grant Park for good views of the Moray Firth; free.

FORT GEORGE NH7656

One of the finest examples of an 18th-c artillery building, one of three fortresses built after 1745, when the Hanoverians were taking no risks in keeping this area firmly under their thumb. Very big, with quite a bit to see and special events all year. A highlight is the Seafield Collection of arms and military equipment. Snacks, shop, disabled access; cl Sun am in winter, 25 Dec; (01667) 462777; £5; HS. Just off from the fort in the Moray Firth you may be lucky enough to see one of the very few inshore schools of dolphins around the British coast.

FORVIE NK0029

Forvie National Nature Reserve The fifth-largest sand dune system in Britain – and the one least disturbed by people, so lots of wildlife inc Britain's biggest colony of eider ducks. You have to stick to the footpaths and keep dogs on leads so as not to disturb the birds and other wildlife. Disabled access; visitor centre cl winter wknds; (01358) 751330; free.

FRASERBURGH NJ9967

Museum of Scottish Lighthouses (Quarry Rd) Based around a lighthouse working up to 1991 and dating from 1787; guided tours take you to the top and demonstrate how everything works. Snacks, shop, limited disabled access; cl 25–26 Dec and 1–2 Jan; (01346) 511022; £3.90.

GLAMIS NO3847

Glamis Castle (A94) The family home of the Earls of Strathmore, and the childhood home of the Queen Mother; a splendid creation, utterly suitable as the setting for Shakespeare's murder of Duncan in *Macbeth*. Notable features include the chapel with its painted panels and ceiling, and of course there are those stories about what's locked away in one of the towers. Meals, snacks, shop, limited disabled access; cl Nov–Mar; (01307) 840393; *£6.70. The Strathmore Arms is good for lunch.

GLEN ROY NN3088

The glen and its curious Parallel Roads (not actually roads but the tubmarks of a former glacier) can be seen from an easily walked track along its bottom, a spectacular 4-mile route from Brae Roy Lodge (return the same way).

GLENMORE NH9809

Cairngorm Reindeer Centre 🏕 (A951) Mingle with free-ranging reindeer in a pretty stretch of the Cairngorms; you can feed and stroke them. Guided walks leave the visitor centre every day, weather permitting, at 11am (plus 2.30pm May–Sept). Shop, disabled access to visitor centre only (reindeer here Easter–New Year); cl New Year–Feb half-term; (01479) 861228; *£6.

HUNTLY NJ5240

Huntly Castle The original medieval castle here was destroyed and rebuilt several times, once by Mary Queen of Scots. Rebuilt for the last time in 1602, the ruins are worth a look for their ornate heraldic decorations. Shop, disabled access; in winter cl Thurs pm, all day Fri and Sun am, 25–26 Dec, 1–2 Jan; (01466) 793191; £3; HS. In the square is a little local history museum, and a ski centre can teach you how to cross-country ski through the local forest. On the outskirts (Depot Rd, not far from Somerfields supermarket),

Deans Shortbread has a good factory shop.

North East Falconry Centre (Cairnie, off A96 N) Four flying displays a day in a richly meadowed glade, as well as a herd of red deer. Snacks, shop, disabled access; cl Nov–Feb; (01466) 760328; £4.25.

INNERPEFFRAY NN9018

Innerpeffray Library ⚅ Founded in 1680, this is Scotland's oldest free lending library; many rare and interesting books inc a particularly fine collection of Bibles. Snacks; cl 12.45–2pm, all day Thurs (by appointment only Nov–Feb), but always best to check; (01764) 652819; £2.50.

INVERNESS NH6645

The biggest town up here, and the main shopping town for the whole of the N of Scotland. It has an attractive riverside setting, and is a handy centre without being at all touristy. There's a little local museum and art gallery on Castle Wynd; cl Sun; snacks, shop; free. James Thins is a good book shop. Nicky Tams (Ness Bank Rd) has decent food, and the Blackfriars (Academy St) is good for local colour. From here the train across to Kyle of Lochalsh gives good Highland views – 2½ hours, the last minutes of which are much the best. There are even early-start day trips to the Orkneys; (01955) 611353. Or keep your feet on the ground, with good walks by a flight of locks on the Caledonian Canal from the Clachnaharry Inn just NW.

KEMNAY NJ7212

Castle Fraser (off A944) Once one of the grandest castles of Mar, the z-shaped building incorporates the remains of an earlier one, and there are excellent formal gardens. Snacks, shop; cl Weds and Thurs (exc July–Aug) and Nov–Easter, grounds open all year; (01330) 833463; castle £7, car park £1.60; NTS.

KENMORE NN7644

Scottish Crannog Centre Interesting reconstruction of a prehistoric loch dwelling. Shop, disabled access; cl Nov–Mar (exc for groups of 10 or more); (01887) 830583; £4.25. The attractive estate village is pleasant for a stroll, with a poem pencilled by Burns himself on a wall in the welcoming Kenmore Hotel.

KENNETHMONT NJ5430

Leith Hall & Garden In over 280 acres of interesting grounds, this mansion was home to the Leith family for over 300 years (their estate then ran to about 20 square miles), and the elegantly furnished rooms reflect their lives and tastes; an exhibition examines their long tradition of military service. The gardens are breathtakingly beautiful in Jun, and dotted elsewhere around the estate are ponds, nature trails, a bird hide, unusual semi-circular stables, and an ice-house. Staff are very friendly; snacks, shop; house cl am, Mon–Tues, Nov–Easter, grounds open daily; (01464) 831216; £7; NTS. Readers have enjoyed staying in the gateway lodge, and there's a flat in the mansion.

KILDRUMMY NJ4516

Kildrummy Castle Now in ruins, though still with its original 13th-c round towers, hall and chapel, as well as some later remains. Cl Sun am, Thurs pm and all day Fri Oct–Nov and all Dec–Mar; (01975) 571331; £2; HS.

Kildrummy Gardens (A97) Very beautiful indeed and of some botanical interest. There's an alpine garden in an old quarry, a water garden, walks in the woods, a video showing the changes through the seasons, and a small museum. Shop, snacks, disabled access; cl Nov–Mar; (01975) 571203/571277; £2.50. The ruins provide a spectacular backdrop.

KINCRAIG NH8305

Highland Wildlife Park ⚅ (B9152) Owned by the same charity as Edinburgh Zoo, this 180-acre wildlife park manages to seem a bit wilder than most animal attractions; perhaps it's because they specialise in species once native to the area, so you really get a feeling that the animals could have wandered out of the surrounding woods and mountains. You drive through the main reserve with red deer, wild horses, and enormous bison. The most exciting feature is the wolf territory, where a walkway takes you to a safe vantage point right in the heart of the enclosure. Plenty of rare breeds, inc the wild Przewalski's horses, one of the world's rarest mammals, and you may see red squirrels feeding in the forest; daily talks and wknd summer face-painting. Snacks and shop in visitor centre, disabled access; cl in bad weather, so best to check; (01540) 651270; £7

Working Sheepdogs You'll be amazed at how skilfully the sheepdogs work, in teams of up to eight, to manoeuvre sheep and even ducks at these 45-minute demonstrations. Shop, disabled access; cl 12–2, Sat, and Nov–Apr, phone to check; (01540) 651310; £4.

KINGUSSIE NH7500

Highland Folk Museum (Duke St) Return to the living conditions of the past in a reconstructed Isle of Lewis black house, mill and smokehouse; major exhibits provide an insight into the social history of the people of the Highlands; shop, disabled access; cl Sun, wknds Oct–Mar, Christmas and New Year (open for guided tours only in winter); (01540) 661307; £1. The Royal is useful for lunch (and brews its own beer); the town's pronounced Kinoossie.

Highland Folk Park (A86 E) On 85 acres, this reconstructed 18th-c settlement is the Folk Museum's younger but bigger out-of-town offshoot: you can see a Victorian water-powered sawmill, curling hut, pre-war school (with many original fittings) and clock-maker's workshop. Costumed guides help bring history to life, and vintage buses transport you round the site. Snacks, shop, audio-visual centre, disabled access, play area. Cl wknds Sept–Oct and all Nov–Mar; (01540) 673551; £5.

KINNOULL HILL NO1423

Just outside Perth, this offers walkers forest tracks and paths, and two folly 'castles' above the River Tay.

KINROSS NO1202

Kinross House Gardens 🖾 Rather fine and formal, with yew hedges, topiary, roses and herbaceous borders and fine views to Castle Island where Mary Queen of Scots was imprisoned. Disabled access; cl Oct–Apr; (01577) 862900; £2. The Muirs has good value food, as does the Lomond Hotel at Kinnesswood with its quiet views over Loch Leven.

Loch Leven Castle Reached by ferry, the islet fortress where Mary Queen of Scots was imprisoned for a while; she was rowed to freedom by a page boy, but only after she had been persuaded to abdicate in favour of her infant son. Shop; limited disabled access; cl Tues and Fri in Oct, cl Nov–Mar; (0131) 668 8800; £3.30 (inc ferry).

Loch Leven RSPB Visitor Centre 🖾 At the S end of the loch, with good facilities for watching the birds; in the winter the evening flights and sounds of the thousands of ducks and geese are very moving. Snacks, shop, disabled access; cl 25–26, 1–2 Jan; (01577) 862355; £3. The loch itself is serene rather than dramatic.

KIRKCALDY NT3093

This busy resort and shopping town (birthplace of the economist, Adam Smith) is not too interesting to visitors, but it has a decent museum and art gallery (see below), and there are some charming old wynds and houses in the eastern suburb of Dysart, which has its own picturesque little harbour. Between here and the main town is 15th-c Ravenscraig Castle, perhaps most notable for its symmetrical shape; great views over the Firth of Forth. Snacks, limited disabled access; free.

Kirkcaldy Museum and Art Gallery In the town's attractive War Memorial Gardens, this houses a superb collection of 18th- to 20th-c Scottish paintings inc perhaps the largest gathering of works by William McTaggart and the Scottish colourist S J Peploe outside the National Galleries of Scotland; also a local heritage museum, and changing exhibitions of art and crafts, photography and natural history. Snacks, shop, disabled access; cl Sun am, 25–27 Dec, 1–3 Jan; (01592) 412860; free.

KIRRIEMUIR NO3854

Barrie's Birthplace (Brechin Rd) The birthplace in 1860 of the writer of *Peter Pan*: the upper floors are furnished in the style of the period, and next door are displays relating to his work, both literary and theatrical. Teas, shop, disabled access; cl am Sun, and Oct–Mar exc Oct wknds; (01575) 572646; £3, combined with Camera Obscura close by, £5; NTS.

Gateway to the Glens Museum
(High St) This 17th-c townhouse has
displays on the town and the West
Glens of Angus inc hands-on activities,
touch-screen computers, a wildlife
diorama and town model. Shop,
disabled access to ground floor only; cl
Thurs am, all Sun, 25–26 Dec, and 1–2
Jan; (01575) 575479; free. The Drovers
in Memus is an attractive place for
traditional food.

LOCH EARN NN5924
With a trunk road alongside, not one of
Scotland's quieter lochs – and largely
given over to water-skiing and that sort
of thing. The Four Seasons at St Fillans
has good imaginative food and great
views. Lochearnhead offers a round
walk from along a nature trail into Glen
Ogle and back via the trackbed of an
abandoned railway.

LOCH ERICHT NN6284
Very peaceful but does involve foot-
slogging to make the most of it. The
road from Dalwhinnie on the A9 at the
N end runs along the foot of a steep
forested slope; the S end of the loch has
more varied scenery, but no road once
you reach the end of the little road off
the B846 at Bridge of Ericht.

LOCH KATRINE NN4009
A lovely stretch of water that inspired
Scott's *Lady of the Lake*, with a Victorian
steamer, named after the author, which
runs trips three times a day (twice on
Weds) in summer; (01877) 376316;
£6.50 am, £5.50 pm. The main approach
to the E end through the Trossachs
does bring a fair bit of summer traffic,
but the central part of the loch is served
by just a narrow back road, so is fairly
peaceful even then.

LOCH MUICK NO2984
Nestling below the dark summit of
Lochnagar, which Byron called 'the most
sublime and picturesque of the
Caledonian Alps', this has paths around
its shores, with a car park at the end of
the Glen Muick road from Ballater. It
was a favourite spot of Queen Victoria's.

LOCH RANNOCH NN6257
Among the quieter and more beautiful
lochs, wooded for much of its length.
There are peaceful walks from the back
road along the S shore.

LOCH TAY NN7745
Remarkably long, with the view seeming
to change moment by moment as the
clouds flit across the sky. It has a quiet
road along its S side. There are easy
walks at the E end of the loch, from
Kenmore (see above), along the banks
of the River Tay, or into the adjacent
forest to a viewpoint over the loch.

Ben Lawers This towering bulk, well
over 1,200 metres (nearly 4,000 ft),
dominates Loch Tay, and is an
interesting spot, with alpine wild
flowers not found elsewhere in Britain
and a quite different feel from other
Highland mountains; a steep road leads
up the side.

LOCH VOIL NN5220
Served by just a narrow back road, so
fairly peaceful even in summer; it's
famous for having Rob Roy's grave at
Balquhidder. It's worth keeping on the
road beyond the far end of the loch;
there's some striking scenery around
the picnic site at its end.

LOMOND HILLS NO2206
A level walk from the car park by the
road above Falkland gives some
pleasant rambles – not to be confused
with Loch Lomond, this upland gives
views over most of SE Scotland.

MACDUFF NJ7064
Macduff Marine Aquarium 🏆 (High
Shore) Huge central tank holding nearly
half a million litres, open to the sky – a
unique design. Emphasis on fish native
to the Moray Firth, with touch pools,
audio-visual presentation and dive and
feeding shows throughout the week.
Snacks, shop, disabled access, cl 25–26
Dec, 1–2 Jan; (01261) 833369; £4

MEIGLE NO2844
Meigle Museum Outstanding
collection of Pictish sculptured stones,
all found in or around the churchyard,
the largest well over 2 metres (8 ft) tall,
and formerly reputed to mark the grave
of Arthur's Guinevere. Shop, disabled
access; cl 12.30–1.30pm, and all end
Oct–Mar; (01828) 640612; £2; HS.

MINTLAW NJ9847
Aberdeenshire Farming Museum
In over 200 acres of lovely woodland
and farmland, criss-crossed with nature
trails and with plenty of wildlife, this
illustrates two centuries of farming
history, with seasonal open-air
demonstrations and tours. Meals,
snacks, shop, disabled access; park open

all year, museum cl Nov–Easter; open daily May–Sept and best to phone for times outside these dates; (01771) 622906; free.

MONTROSE NO6856
Montrose Basin Wildlife Centre
⌨ (A934) The enclosed estuary is a rich feeding ground for thousands of native and migrant birds, inc oystercatchers, curlews, pink-footed geese, and eider ducks. This centre has great views, interactive displays and high-powered telescopes. Snacks, shop, disabled access; cl 25–26 Dec, 1 Jan; (01674) 676336); £2.50.

MUTHILL NN8616
Drummond Castle Gardens (A822) Majestic formal gardens originally laid out in 1630 by the second Earl of Perth. Lovely views from the upper terrace, splendid early Victorian parterre, and centrepiece sundial designed and built by the master mason of King Charles I. Cl am and Nov–Apr (exc Easter wknd); (01764) 681257; £3.50. Muthill is a conservation village, and the Village Inn has enjoyable food.

NAIRN NH8856
A quiet, relaxed and rather discreet old-fashioned resort, with good clean sheltered beaches.

NEWTONMORE NN7199
Waltzing Waters (Main St) Readers spotted this wacky water, light and music show – a bit like liquid fireworks, with jets of coloured water and lights performing in time to music. Snacks, shop, disabled access; cl for 2 wks in Jan, limited show over Christmas, so best to check; (01540) 673752; £4.

NORTH BERWICK
Boat Trips Readers enjoy the boat trips from the harbour, for instance to see the puffins on Craigleith, go round the Bass Rock, or perhaps land on Fidra.

NORTH QUEENSFERRY NT1380
Deep-Sea World ⌨ The highlight of this elaborate aquarium is a spectacular underwater safari. Moving walkways carry you along a transparent viewing tunnel as long as a football pitch, surrounded by all kinds of underwater creatures in a million gallons of water; divers hand-feed the fish and even answer questions, using waterproof communication systems. The sea-horses are popular, and you can stroke

some of the creatures kept in the rock-pools (inc a shark), or pilot an underwater camera. There's a good programme of talks, activities and feeding displays, and the free behind-the-scenes tours give a good insight into the demands of looking after so many creatures, and an introduction to their successful breeding and conservation programmes. They also have a good collection of amphibians, taking in the world's most poisonous frog, and some snakes. Meals, snacks, shop, disabled access; cl 25 Dec; (01383) 411880; £6.95 (inc face-painting); they also offer 'try dives' to over-16s for £85; (01383) 411880.

OCHIL HILLS NS9099
A range of green mountains which rise without preamble from the lowland plain – a striking textbook example of the Highland Fault. A path from Tillicoultry up Mill Glen takes you to Ben Cleuch, the highest point of the range.

OYNE NJ6725
Archaeolink ⌨ This lively centre is a fun exploration of the past. A remarkable turf-roofed building houses an audio-visual presentation, there's an exhibition on myths and legends, and you can try out ancient crafts such as weaving, grinding and arrow-making. Outside are the remains of an Iron Age hill fort, a reconstructed Iron Age farm, a Roman marching camp and a sandpit play area, where younger members of the family can dig for the past. Meals, snacks, shop, disabled access, cl Nov–Mar; (01464) 851500; £4.25.

PERTH NO1223
Spaciously laid out along the broad River Tay; with an excellent specialist rhododendron nursery at Glendoick Gardens (A90). There are a couple of decent museums and galleries (the one in George St is well worth a visit; shop, disabled access; cl Sun, Christmas–New Year; free). Handsome St John's Kirk is where John Knox preached the 1559 sermon against idolatry that started the sacking of the Scottish monasteries. Greyfriars (South St) is good value for lunch – ironic, as the overfed Grey Friars monks were the first losers to Knox's followers.
Branklyn Garden ⌨ (Dundee Rd)

Only about 2 acres but seems much bigger, thanks to a remarkable planting of interesting rhododendrons, small trees, Asiatic primulas, meconopsis, lilies, Himalayan poppies and the like. Snacks, shop, disabled access; cl Nov–Mar; (01738) 625535; £3.50; NTS.

Caithness Glass (Inveralmond Industrial Estate, N edge) Displays of paperweight-making, with audio-visual theatre, collectors' museum and factory shop. Meals, snacks, shop, disabled access; cl 25–26 Dec, 1–2 Jan; (01738) 637373; free.

Huntingtower Castle (just W) The main thing to see is its interesting painted ceiling; in winter cl Thurs pm, Sun am and Fri, 25–26 Dec, 1–2 Jan; (01738) 627 231; £2.20; HS. The nearby Huntingtower House Hotel has a good restaurant, and a streamside garden.

PETERCULTER NJ7900
Drum Castle (off A93) Still looks out over what's left of the medieval forest granted to the Irvine family by Robert the Bruce. Mainly a much-altered Jacobean mansion, the house is based around a 13th-c keep, one of the three oldest tower houses in Scotland. There's a historic rose garden. Snacks, shop, limited disabled access; cl am (exc Jun–Aug), and all Nov–Easter, grounds open all year; (01330) 811204; £7; NTS. The Lairhillock Inn at Netherley a few miles S is good for lunch.

PETERHEAD NK1246
One of Europe's busiest fishing ports, with a bustling market and rejuvenated marina. There's a good local history **museum** on St Peter St (cl Weds pm, Sun, 25–26 Dec, 1 Jan; free) and a **heritage centre** (South Rd) with interactive displays on the fishing industry. Shop, meals, snacks, disabled access; may be cl winter wkdys, best to check (01779) 473000; £2.60.

Ugie Fish House (Golf Rd) Ancient place selling a good range of wild salmon and trout, caught from the adjacent river in season; cl Sat pm, all day Sun; (01779) 476209; free.

PITLOCHRY NN9458
An inland resort town for a good long time, beautifully set in fine countryside; a happy sort of place, with a comfortable feel, and lots of craft and speciality shops. There's lovely

woodland on the banks of man-made Loch Faskally, with walks and nature trails. TheMoulin Inn (which brews its own beer) and Old Mill have decent food.

Edradour Distillery (A924 E) Scotland's smallest distillery, founded in 1825 and virtually unchanged since Victorian times. Guided tours (exc Jan–Feb), tastings, shop, some disabled access; cl Sun am, all day Sun Nov–Dec, no tours mid-Dec to end Feb; (01796) 472095; free. There's another distillery on Atholl Rd.

Killiecrankie Visitor Centre (B8079 NW) Queen Victoria was just one of the people to have found this romantic spot beguiling, but it wasn't always so serene. In 1689 it was the site of a fierce battle when the Highlanders routed the troops of William IV, and a visitor centre tells the tale. Snacks, shop, disabled access; cl Nov–Mar; (01796) 473233; £1.60 for parking; NTS.

Pitlochry Power Station The visitor centre shows how the hydro-electric scheme works, and you may see salmon leaping up the fish ladder. Shop, disabled access to shop; cl end Oct–mid-Mar; (01796) 473152; £2.

Scottish Plant Collectors' Garden With a mix of traditional and modern, these extensive new gardens aim to celebrate 300 years of pioneer plant collecting. There have been more Scottish pioneer plant collectors than any other nationality, and information and stories about various collectors will be displayed on boards throughout the garden. There'll be permanent and touring sculptures on show, and outdoor performance areas; £3.

PITMEDDEN NJ8823
Pitmedden Garden (A920)
Originally planted in the 17th c and pretty much unchanged since, with sundials, fountains and pavilions in elaborate formal gardens. Snacks, shop, limited disabled access; cl Oct–Apr; (01651) 842352; £5; NTS. The Redgarth Hotel over at Oldmeldrum has decent food and good bedrooms.

PITTENWEEM NO5402
Attractive East Neuk fishing village, with some attractive crow-gabled houses (the gables in steps which seagulls rather than crows sit on here), and

quite an artists' colony now; the Aug arts festival is a growing draw, with 70 or more display areas.

Kellie Castle & Gardens (B9171) Fine example of 16th- and 17th-c domestic architecture, though parts date from the 14th c, with good collections of plasterwork, panelling and furniture. Also four acres of gardens inc a Victorian walled garden. Snacks, shop, disabled access to ground floor and gardens; cl am, Tues, Weds end Mar–end Sept, and all Nov–Apr, grounds open all year; (01333) 720271; £5, garden only £2; NTS.

PORT OF MENTEITH NN5700

Inchmahome Priory Famous as the refuge of the infant Mary Queen of Scots in 1543, this Augustinian priory was founded in 1238 on an island in the middle of the lake, and in spring and summer you can get a boat across. Robert the Bruce prayed here before the Battle of Bannockburn. Snacks, shop; cl Oct–Mar; (01877) 385294; £3.30 inc ferry; HS.

SCONE NO1126

Scone Palace (off A93) The seat of government in Scotland from Pictish times, though the current building is largely 16th-c behind an 18th-c castellated façade. It was the site of the Stone of Destiny – the famous coronation stone – until it was seized by the English in 1296 (it's now back in Scotland, at Edinburgh Castle). Good displays of porcelain, furniture, clocks and needlework, and the grounds are pleasant with formal gardens, pinetum, a maze and children's play area. Meals, snacks, shop, some disabled access; cl Nov–Mar; (01738) 552300; £6.35. Pronounced 'Scoon', by the way.

ST ANDREWS NO5116

This civilised university town doubles as rather a dignified seaside resort, with clean, safe beaches. It's outstanding for golfers, though to play on the hallowed greens of the Old Course, you'll need to ring the St Andrews Links Trust on (01334) 466666 before 2pm the day before you want to go, to enter a daily ballot; after that you'll have to tee up £105. There are a few interesting museums on the city's history, some quite lively, and a number of fine buildings belonging to Scotland's oldest

university – esp St Leonard's and St Mary's colleges. South St is worth strolling along: attractive riggs or small courts and alleys off, the ancient West Port gateway at the end, and Holy Trinity church where John Knox preached his first sermon in 1547. The Saltire, West Port and (a mile S) Grange are all good eating places. **Craigtoun Country Park** has a boating pond, children's play areas, activities such as crazy golf, a countryside centre and a mini railway; cl Nov–Feb; (01334) 473666; £3 (free Mar and Oct when there's less to do).

British Golf Museum ⊞ (Bruce Embankment) Fascinates anyone keen on the game, with up-to-date interactive and audio-visual displays going right through its 500-year history. Assorted memorabilia include lots of glamorous golfing gear. Shop, disabled access; cl Tues and Weds Oct–Easter, 25 Dec–1 Jan (limited winter opening hours); (01334) 478880; £3.75.

St Andrews Aquarium ⊞ (The Scores) Up-to-date surroundings for displays of tropical fish, sea-horses and resident seals. Meals, snacks, shop, limited disabled access; phone for winter opening, cl 25 Dec, 1 Jan; (01334) 474786; £4.85.

St Andrews Botanic Garden (just off Canongate) Around 18 pleasantly landscaped acres, with a good range of trees and shrubs, and several glasshouses. Disabled access; (01334) 477178; £2.

St Andrews Castle 13th-c, the scene of Cardinal Beaton's murder during a wave of anti-Catholic feeling in 1546. It was largely demolished in the 17th c, but some substantial ruins remain. The visitor centre has rare examples of medieval siege techniques, and a bottle dungeon hollowed out of solid rock. Shop, disabled access; cl 25–26 Dec, 1–2 Jan; (01334) 477196; £2.80; joint ticket with the cathedral £4; HS.

St Andrews Cathedral Impressive twin-towered Norman remains; till fervent locals sacked it in the 16th c this was the largest cathedral in Scotland. Shop, limited disabled access; cl 25–26 Dec, 1–2 Jan; (01334) 472563; £2.20, joint ticket with the castle £4; HS. Beside it the older Romanesque St

Rule's church is basically just a soaring thin tower built to guide pilgrims to the small shrine below which housed relics of St Andrew; if you can face over 150 steps it gives wonderful views from the top.

ST MONANCE NO5201

One of the most attractive East Neuk fishing villages, with an unusual fisherman's church and a restored 18th-c windmill (the Seafood Restaurant has good seafood and sea views).

STIRLING NS7994

Strategically placed on the Firth of Forth, this has just been granted city status: a very unstuffy place, with the university students putting quite a bit of buzz into the atmosphere. Dropping down the steep hill on which the castle stands is an attractive and interesting network of old streets, with a lot of character in their old-to-ancient buildings; the Church of Holy Rude was where Mary Queen of Scots and James VI were crowned as babies.

Argyll's Lodging Built by Sir William Alexander, founder of Nova Scotia, and then passed on to the Earls of Argyll, this is the finest surviving example of a 17th-c townhouse in Scotland. Used as an army barracks and hospital, and then a Youth Hostel, the main rooms have now been re-created to look as they would have done in around 1680. Shop; cl 25–26 Dec, phone for opening times over New Year; (0131) 668 8800; £3, £7 joint ticket with Stirling Castle.

Bannockburn Heritage Centre (A872 S) Plenty of information on Robert the Bruce's finest hour, inc an audio-visual show on the battle itself. Café, shop, disabled access; cl 23 Dec–20 Jan; (01786) 812664; £3.50.

Old Town Jail 🔳 (St John St) In season, actor-led tours take you through the preserved cells of this 19th-c jail (self-guided audio tour at other times), and there's an exhibition on prison life today. Shop, disabled access; cl 25–26 Dec, 1–2 Jan; (01786) 450050; £3.95.

Smith Art Gallery & Museum (Dumbarton Rd) Good changing exhibitions; cl Sun am, all day Mon, 25–26 Dec, 1–2 Jan; (01786) 471917; free.

Stirling Castle Provides magnificent

views from its lofty hilltop site. It became very popular with the Royal Family in the 15th and 16th c, and most of the buildings date from that period. It's great fun to visit, from the flame-lit medieval kitchen to the splendid Chapel Royal built by James VI (and I of England), and the Great Hall of James V's Renaissance palace. A huge new hammerbeam roof has been crafted here from 350 oak trees, and the restoration of the castle's lavish early 16th-c furnishings continues with on-site tapestry weaving. Snacks, shop; cl 25–26 Dec; (01786) 450000; £7 inc Argyll's lodging, parking £2; HS. There's a good visitor centre in a restored building next door, and Whistlebinkies (St Mary's Wynd), formerly part of the ancient castle stables, has decent food.

Wallace Monument (top of Abbey Craig, just NE) 67-metre (220-ft) Victorian tower with dramatic views from the open windy top of its 246 spiralling steps. Each floor has audio-visual displays, one on Sir William Wallace, another examining other Scottish heroes. There is a statue of Wallace as portrayed by Mel Gibson in *Braveheart* in the car park. Snacks, shop; cl 25–26 Dec, 1–2 Jan; (01786) 472140; £3.95.

STONEHAVEN NO8783

Dunnottar Castle (just S) On a precipitous sea-girt crag stands this the bleak and battered but still extensive and well preserved 14th-c ruin, used for the filming of Mel Gibson's *Hamlet*. It sheltered the Scottish Crown Jewels during the Civil War, but has seen much darker episodes in its time. Shop; cl Sun am in summer, Tues–Thurs in winter, 25–26 Dec, 1 Jan; (01569) 762173; £3.50.

Swimming Pool 🔳 This cheerful art deco open-air swimming pool is the only one of its kind in the country; olympic-size, and filled with salt water, it's heated to 29 deg C (84 deg F). They have floodlit night-time swims most Weds in the summer (10–12pm). Meals, snacks, shop, disabled access; cl Sept–May; (01569) 762134; £3.20.

Tolbooth Museum (Old Pier) Good local history museum in ancient tolbooth; cl am, Tues, Nov–Apr; (01771) 622906; free. This old fishing town has more seasidey but discreet Victorian streets in its upper part; the harbourside Marine Hotel has good reasonably priced food.

TARVES NJ8634

Haddo House (off B999) Wonderfully grand yet still very much a family home; designed by William Adam, and refurbished in the 1880s in the Adam Revival style, with fine furniture and art throughout. The chapel (regular services) has stained glass by Burne-Jones; both the house and adjacent hall host concerts and events throughout the year; (01651) 851770 for details. House open July–Aug only, shop cl Nov–Mar; (01651) 851440; £7; NTS. Charming terrace garden leads into 200-acre country park with waymarked trails, wildlife hides, visitor centre and events; (011651) 851489; free; Aberdeenshire Council. Tearooms serving light lunches and snacks; two shops with estate produce, crafts, gifts and souvenirs; children's play areas. Interesting medieval tomb in Tarves churchyard and stunning views from nearby outlook tower called the Prop of Ythsie. The Redgarth down in Oldmeldrum has decent food and gorgeous views to Bennachie.

Tolquhon Castle (off B999 S) Impressive remains of a 15th-c castle; cl Thurs pm, all day Fri and Sun am Oct, wkdys and am Sun in winter; (01651) 851286; £2.

Tolquhon Gallery Decidedly unstuffy, with contemporary Scottish art and crafts; cl all day Thurs, and wkdys Jan and Feb; (01651) 842343; free.

TENTSMUIR SANDS NO5024 Five miles of shore walking from Kinshaldy car park on the Fife coast; you may see common and grey seals on the sandbanks, and there are good clean beaches – shorter routes back through the forest.

TOMINTOUL NJ1618 Charming Highland village in attractive scenery, real whisky country; the welcoming Glenavon Hotel has decent food.

TURRIFF NJ7550

Delgatie Castle 🏰 Dating from 1050 – but like most Scottish castles rebuilt in the 16th c when the invention of

siege guns demanded greater fortification – some walls are up to 4 metres or more (14 ft) thick. There are fine 16th-c painted ceilings, an unusual turnpike stair built into a wall, and a bedchamber where Mary Queen of Scots spent three nights; displays on the Clan Hay. Excellent tearoom, shop; cl Nov–Mar; (01888) 563479; £3. You can stay here too.

Fyvie Castle (off A947) Each of the five towers of this magnificent castle was built in a different century by the family that lived here throughout; the oldest parts date back to the 13th c, and the whole building is one of the most fantastic examples of Scottish baronial architecture. Collections of armour and tapestry, and paintings by Raeburn, Romney and Gainsborough. Snacks, shop; cl am and Thurs, Fri mid-season, cl Nov–Easter; (01651) 891266; £7; NTS. The Towie Tavern does good food.

WHISKY DISTILLERIES NJ1943

Cardhu NJ1943 (B9102 nr Knockando) Working malt whisky distillery open for tours and tastings (cl wknds Oct–Easter, Sat Easter–Jun; £4).

Glen Grant NJ2749 (Rothes) Founded in 1840 by the brothers Grant, whose malt whisky was one of the first to be bottled and sold as a single malt. Guided tours, tastings, shop, some disabled access; cl Nov–Mar; (01542) 783318; £3.

Glencoyne NS5086 (A81 nr Killearn) Working malt whisky distillery open for tours and tastings; (01360) 550229.

Glenfarclas NJ2138 (Marypark) Producing one of the top malt whiskies, open for tours and tastings; cl Sun all year plus Sat Oct–May, and Christmas hols; £3.50.

Tomatin NH7929 Working malt whisky distillery open for tours and tastings; cl wknds exc summer Sats, best to phone; (01808) 511444; free.

Worthwhile inns in good spots for walkers, drivers or just strollers (besides those we've mentioned as places to eat at or stay in) include the lochside Achray at St Fillans NN6924, Bridge of Cally Hotel at Bridge of Cally NO1451, seaview Creel at Catterline NO8778, Loch Ericht Hotel at Dalwhinnie NN6384, Dores Hotel at

Dores by Loch Ness NH5930, Clachan overlooking pretty Drymen's green square NS4788, Anchor at Dunipace NS8083, Old Smiddy in the pleasant village of Errol NO2523, Hungry Monk at Gartocharn NS4286, Clova Hotel in Glen Clova NO3373, Guard Bridge Hotel at Guard Bridge NO4518, Old Mill at Killearn NS5285, Cross Keys at Kippen NS6594 (pretty village), Trossachs Hotel nr Loch Achray NN5106, Corriegour Lodge nr Altrua on Loch Lochy NN2390, Loch Tummel Hotel above Loch Tummel NN8460, Meikleour Inn at Meikleour NO1539 (handy for the 30-metre, 100-ft high beech hedge planted in 1746), Pennan Inn in the pretty seaside *Local Hero* village of Pennan NJ8465, Potarch Hotel at Potarch NO6097, Sheriffmuir Inn on wild Sheriff Muir NN8202 and Tomdoun Hotel at Tomdoun NH1501.

Where to eat

ABERDEEN NJ9305 **Babylon** *9 Alford Pl (01224) 595001* On the second floor of a former religious training college, recently refurbished bustling place with bold modern paintings, simple contemporary furniture on bare boards, a bar replacing the altar, innovative brasserie-style cooking, super puddings, and a decent little wine list; cl lunchtimes (exc Fri), Sun, Mon. £26.50|**£9.95**

ANSTRUTHER NO5603 **Cellar** *24 East Green (01333) 310378* Off a little courtyard nr the harbour, with beams, stone walls, and peat fires – and wonderful fresh fish, good wines; cl Mon–Tues lunchtime, maybe cl lunchtimes and Sun in winter. £30|**£12.50**

BLAIRGOWRIE NO1845 **Cargill's** *Lower Mill St (01250) 876735* Busy bistro, part of a complex with a crafts gallery and coffee shop, antiques warehouse and upholstery business; good varied food inc nice puddings, and several teas and coffees; bright helpful staff; cl Tues, cl winter Mon–Tues; disabled access. £28|**£7.95**

CUPAR NO3714 **Ostlers Close** *25 Bonnygate (01334) 655574* Cosy unpretentious much-liked restaurant with lovely food using the best local fresh produce, game and fish, and home-grown herbs, a reasonably priced wine list, and friendly owners; children over 6 but no children in the evenings; cl Sun–Mon, cl Tues–Thurs lunchtime, two wks Jan and Oct; £42 dinner/£11 lunch Fri–Sat only

DRYBRIDGE NJ4562 **Old Monastery** *(01542) 832660* Lovely views from former monastery – as well as very good fish, game and Aberdeen Angus beef, reasonably priced wines and friendly service; cl Sun, Mon, Tues, 3 wks Jan; £30 dinner, £20 lunch

FALKLAND NO2507 **Kind Kyttock's Kitchen** *Cross Wynd (01337) 857477* Popular well known tearoom nr village centre, with enjoyable light home-made meals and super afternoon teas; friendly staff; cl Mon, 24 Dec–5 Jan. £16|**£5**

KELTY NT1393 **Butterchurn** *Cocklaw Mains Farm (01383) 830169* In the courtyard of a farm, this popular restaurant has fine views over Loch Leven, and serves morning coffee, lunch, afternoon teas, snacks, and traditional high teas using fresh local ingredients; they also sell their own products to take away and have a craft and gift centre, farmyard pets for children, and walks and cycle trails; cl 25–26 Dec, 1–2 Jan; disabled access. £25|**£4.50**

KILMAHOG NN6008 **Lade Inn** *(01877) 330152* Well run place in lovely wooded surroundings with beamed and partly panelled main bar, Highland prints, no smoking room opening on to terrace and attractive garden, a wide choice of interesting bar food, decent wine list and real ales; disabled access. £24.50|**£6**

KINGUSSIE NH7501 **Cross** *Tweed Mill Brae, Ardbroilach Rd (01540) 661166* Converted 19th-c stone tweed mill by stream, now a no smoking restaurant-with-rooms, with a relaxed friendly atmosphere, extremely good eclectic Scottish cooking (evenings only) using the best local produce, excellent wine list, marvellous cheeses, and super breakfasts; bdrms; cl Tues evening, 1 Dec–28 Feb; children over 8; disabled access. £37.50 for 5 courses

PERTH NO1123 **Let's Eat** *77 Kinnoull St (01738) 643377* Very popular restaurant in what was the Theatre Royal; relaxed friendly atmosphere, enjoyable modern cooking inc proper old-fashioned puddings, and short selective wine list; cl Sun–Mon, 2 wks Jan, 2 wks July; disabled access. £27.50|£10

ST ANDREWS NO5016 **Vine Leaf** *131 South St* *(01334)* 477497 Warmly welcoming and attractively laid out dining room overlooking walled herb garden, super food (inc seafood, game and vegetarian dishes), unobtrusive service and decent wines; evenings only; cl Sun, Mon and Jan; disabled access. £30

ST FILLANS NN6924 **Four Seasons** *(01764)* 685333 Long white family-run hotel with wonderful Loch Earn views, generous helpings of very good Scottish food inc super fish and game dishes; lunchtime snacks, too; can eat in Tarken Bar, on terrace or in smarter restaurant; comfortable bdrms and chalets; cl 3 Jan–Mar; £35|£6.95

ST MONANCE NO5201 **Seafood Restaurant & Bar** *16 West End* *(01333)* *730327* Immaculate, snug and cosy inside, with seafaring models and mementoes on illuminated shelves, plenty of well polished light wood panelling, plainer locals' bar, very good modern cooking inc excellent seafood in no smoking back restaurant, and good bar food; cl Jan and Sun pm and Mon in low season. £30

STONEHAVEN NO8595 **Lairhillock** *(01569)* 730001 Relaxed and friendly extended 18th-c country pub with wide choice of good, popular and imaginative food, well kept real ales, lots of malt whiskies and wines, nice views from cheerfully atmospheric beamed bar, central fire in spacious lounge, and airy conservatory; cl 25–26 Dec, 1–2 Jan, restaurant cl Tues pm; disabled access. £35|£7.95

WEEM NN8449 **Ailean Chraggan** *(01887)* 820346 Small friendly inn with lovely views, very good food inc plenty of fresh fish and enjoyable puddings – you can eat in the bar or restaurant – and a very good wine list; comfortable bdrms; cl 25–26 Dec, 1–2 Jan, disabled access. £23.50|£8.95

West Scotland

**The very best of mainland Scotland's scenery,
with a glorious coast; few highlights for children**

Beautiful countryside is something that this area has plenty of, inland and on the coast. The best place to begin exploring Scotland's new National Park (which covers Loch Lomond and the Trossachs) is the impressive new visitor centre in Balloch, while roads winding slowly along the intricate coast make driving there a succession of glorious sea-and-mountain views.

Aside from coastal Oban (a pleasantly bustling town) and Inveraray (some interesting family attractions), places to visit are mostly low-key, suiting the relaxed pace of life. Families enjoy the good underwater centre at Barcaldine, Hill House in Helensburgh is a fine example of the work of Charles Rennie Mackintosh, and you can get a good sense of the past at the Auchindrain Township Museum. The cluster of ancient sites around Kilmartin is quite thought-provoking, and Mull (and nearby Iona) is well worth the journey. The great west coast gardens are at their peak in May and June.

Where to stay

ARDUAINE NM7910 **Loch Melfort Hotel** *Arduaine, Oban, Argyll PA34 4XG* (01852) 200233 **£118**, plus special breaks; 27 rms, gorgeous sea views. Comfortable hotel popular in summer with passing yachtsmen (hotel's own moorings), nautical charts and marine glasses in airy modern bar, own lobster pots and nets so emphasis on seafood, pleasant foreshore walks, outstanding springtime woodland gardens; disabled access; dogs welcome in bedrooms

BALLACHULISH NN0559 **Ballachulish House** *Ballachulish, Argyll PA39 4JX* (01855) 811266 **£120***, plus special breaks; 8 rms with views. Remote 17th-c house with a friendly atmosphere, elegant rooms, log fires, honesty bar, hearty helpings of good food using local fish and beef, and walled garden, croquet lawn; children over 10

CRINAN NR7894 **Crinan Hotel** *Crinan, Lochgilphead, Argyll PA31 8SR* (01546) 830261 **£210*** inc dinner, plus special breaks; 20 rms. Rather smart hotel by start of canal to Lochgilphead, marvellous views from stylish formal top-floor restaurant and bedrooms, nautical decorations in lounge bar, lots of local fish and large wine list; cl Christmas and New Year; disabled access; dogs welcome in bedrooms

DERVAIG NM4749 **Druimard Country House** *Dervaig, Tobermory, Isle of Mull PA75 6QW* (01688) 400345 **£125** inc dinner, plus special breaks; 7 rms. Peaceful Victorian country house with wonderful views across the glen and River Bellart, friendly helpful owners, comfortable lounge and conservatory, lots of pictures, books and magazines, good breakfasts, excellent food using the best local produce; the Mull Little Theatre is in the grounds; cl Nov–Mar; disabled access; dogs welcome in bedrooms

ELLANBEICH NM7417 **Inshaig Park** *Easdale, Oban, Argyll PA34 4RF* (01852) 300256 **£70***, plus special breaks; 6 rms. Solid family-run stone building on Seil island (bridge to mainland), a hotel since Victorian times, with stunning sea views, good food inc fresh local seafood, friendly bar and warm welcome; dogs welcome in bedrooms

ERISKA NM9041 **Isle of Eriska Hotel** *Ledaig, Oban, Argyll PA37 1SD* (01631) 720371 **£225**, plus winter breaks; 17 rms. In a wonderful position on small island linked by bridge to mainland, impressive baronial hotel with very relaxed country house atmosphere, log fires and pretty drawing room, excellent food, exemplary service, and comprehensive wine list; leisure complex with indoor swimming pool, sauna, gym and so forth, lovely surrounding walks, and 9-hole golf course, clay pigeon shooting and golf – and plenty of wildlife inc tame badgers who come nightly to the library door for their bread and milk; cl Jan; children over 5 in pool and evening restaurant (high tea provided); disabled access; dogs welcome in bedrooms

FORT WILLIAM NN0973 **Grange** *Grange Rd, Fort William, Inverness-shire PH33 6JF* (01397) 705516 **£80***; 4 rms with loch views. Charming Victorian house in quiet landscaped gardens with log fire in comfortable lounge, fine breakfasts in dining room overlooking Loch Linnhe, and helpful hard-working owners; cl Nov–Mar; children over 12

GIGHA NR6551 **Gigha Hotel** *Isle of Gigha PA41 7AA* (01583) 505254 **£90**, plus special breaks; 13 rms, most with own bthrm. Traditional family-run hotel, small and attractive with lots of charm, bustling bar (popular with yachtsmen and locals), neatly kept comfortable residents' lounge, and local seafood in restaurant; self-contained cottages too; dogs welcome in bedrooms

KILBERRY NR7267 **Kilberry Inn** *Kilberry, Tarbert, Argyll PA29 6YD* (01880) 770223 **£75***; 3 ground-floor no smoking rms. Homely and warmly welcoming inn on W coast of Knapdale with fine sea views, old-fashioned character, very good traditional home cooking relying on fresh local ingredients; cl mid-Oct to end Mar; disabled access

KILCHRENAN NN0422 **Taychreggan Hotel** *Kilchrenan, Taynuilt, Argyll PA35 1HQ* (01866) 833211 **£127***, plus special breaks; 19 rms. Civilised and extensively refurbished hotel with fine garden running down to Loch Awe, comfortable airy bar, attractively served lunchtime bar food, polite efficient staff, good freshly prepared food in no smoking dining room, careful wine list, dozens of malt whiskies, and pretty inner courtyard; no children; dogs welcome in bedrooms

KILFINAN NR9279 **Kilfinan Hotel** *Kilfinan, Tighnabruaich, Argyll PA21 2EP (01700) 821201* **£84***; 11 rms. Friendly former coaching inn, popular locally, in fine scenery with sporting activities such as shooting, fishing and stalking; very good traditional restaurant food often using own game and salmon, decent bar food, and log fires; children over 12

KILNINVER NM8727 **Knipoch** *Knipoch, Oban, Argyll PA34 4QT (01852) 316251* **£144**, plus winter breaks; 20 rms. Elegant very well kept Georgian hotel in lovely countryside overlooking Loch Feochan; fine family portraits, log fires, fresh flowers and polished furniture in comfortable lounges and bars, carefully chosen wines and malt whiskies, and marvellous food inc their own smoked salmon; dogs welcome in bedrooms

ONICH NN0461 **Allt-Nan-Ros** *Onich, Fort William, Inverness-shire PH33 6RY (01855) 821210* **£105***, plus special breaks; 20 rms, many with views over the gardens to the water. Victorian shooting lodge with fine Scottish food, friendly atmosphere, bright airy rooms, and magnificent views across Loch Linnhe and the gardens; cl 5 Jan–10 Feb; disabled access; dogs away from eating areas

PORT APPIN NM9045 **Airds Hotel** *Port Appin, Appin, Argyll PA38 4DF (01631) 730294* **£300*** inc dinner, plus winter breaks; 12 lovely rms – also, 4 cheaper rooms in Linnhe House 60 yds away. Instantly relaxing 18th-c inn with lovely views of Loch Linnhe and the islands of Lismore, blissfully comfortable day rooms, professional courteous staff, and charming owners; the food is exceptional (as is the wine list) and there are lots of surrounding walks, with more on Lismore (small boat every hour); cl 17–27 Dec, 6–31 Jan; dogs welcome in bedrooms

TARBERT NR8768 **Columba Hotel** *East Pier Rd, Tarbert, Argyll PA29 6UF (01880) 820808* **£73.90**, plus special winter breaks; 10 rms. In a peaceful position on Loch Fyne with views of the surrounding hills, this family-run hotel has log fires in the friendly bar and lounge, an informal and relaxed atmosphere, very enjoyable food using fresh local produce, and quite a few malt whiskies; cl 24–26 Dec; dogs welcome in bedrooms

TARBERT NR8571 **Stonefield Castle** *Stonefield, Tarbert, Argyll PA29 6YJ (01880) 820836* **£170** inc dinner, plus special breaks; 33 rms. With wonderful views and surrounding wooded grounds, this Scottish baronial mansion has comfortable public rooms and decent restaurant food; snooker room; dogs welcome in bedrooms

To see and do

ARDUAINE NM7910
Arduaine Gardens (A816) The seaside gardens here shelter behind extensive windbreaks, though the high viewpoint gives a superb view of coast and islands; almost subtropical, with many rarities beside the rhododendrons, azaleas, camellias and magnolias which flourish so in this part of the world. Disabled access, open all year; (01852) 200366; £3.50; NTS. The comfortable Loch Melfort Hotel, with great sea views, does good bar lunches.
AUCHINDRAIN NN0102
Auchindrain Township Museum (A83) The only communal tenancy township to have remained on its ancient site much in its original form. All the buildings have been excellently restored and simply furnished in period style, so you get a real feeling of stepping back into the past. Shop; cl Oct–Mar; (01499) 500235; *£3.80.
BARCALDINE NM9240
Scottish Sea Life Sanctuary 🖾 (A828) Lively underwater centre, with hi-tech face-to-fish-face displays of native marine life from sea-horses and jellyfish to sharks, and a new Otter Creek with a pair of North American river otters, deep-dive pools, streams and underwater views into their holt

(home). Also conservation exhibits of local loch creatures, and a rescue centre for dozens of playful abandoned seal pups; nature trails, and woodland adventure playground. Meals, snacks, shop, mostly disabled access; cl wkdys Dec–Feb exc school hols; (01631) 720386; £6.95. The Lochnell Arms and Falls of Lora down at Connel are reliable lunch stops.

BEN NEVIS NN1671

Though Britain's highest mountain, this is one of the more easily managed summits, with a long, safe path up: expect big crowds in season. Munro-baggers say it's far from being the best viewpoint mountain, though; a 'munro' is any 3,000-ft peak (914 metres), named for Sir Hugh Munro, who first tabulated them. The mountain is owned by a conservation charity. Just N on Aonach Mor, Britain's only mountain gondola carries visitors up 650 metres (2,150 ft) to Scotland's highest restaurant, and gift shops – the views are spectacular; cl for around 6 wks early Nov–late Dec, and in bad weather; *£7.50.

BENMORE NS1391

Younger Botanic Garden (A815) An outstation of Edinburgh's Royal Botanic Garden, with attractive woodland and glorious rhododendrons. Some enormously tall and magnificent conifers here, and a good many rarities. Nice views too. Meals, snacks, shop, disabled access; cl Nov–Feb; (01369) 706261; £3.

CAIRNDOW NN1710

Ardkinglas Woodland Garden (off A83) On a hillside overlooking Loch Fyne, the pinetum here includes one of Britain's tallest trees, a grand fir well over 61 metres (200 ft) and still shooting upwards, as well as the mightiest conifer in all Europe – a silver fir with a girth of over 9 metres (30 ft). Also rhododendrons, azaleas and other exotic plants, and daffodils and bluebells in spring. Open all year; disabled access; *£3. The same people run the Tree Shop (about 2m N at the top of the loch), which specialises in specimen trees, indigenous Highland trees, and shrubs. Also lots of well crafted woodware (inc some lovely toys and puzzles); meals, snacks, shop; (01499)

600263. Next door the Loch Fyne Oyster Bar is renowned for its fresh shellfish, which you can eat in the restaurant or buy in the shop; the Cairndow Hotel with a waterside garden is also good.

COLINTRAIVE NS0374

This attractive village spreads along the shore of the sea loch, with gorgeous views (for example from the well run Colintraive Hotel) across the narrow Kyles of Bute. There's a short ferry crossing to Rhubodach on Bute.

CORPACH NN1177

Caledonian Canal From Corpach there are straightforward towpath walks NE, up a flight of locks known as Neptune's Staircase, with mountain backdrops. There's good access to the locks from the Moorings Hotel (good value basement wine bar) at Banavie.

Treasures of the Earth ⌼ (Mallaig Rd) Good collection of gemstones, crystals and minerals, imaginatively displayed in carefully lit rock cavities. Shop, disabled access; cl Dec–Feb but best to phone; (01397) 772283; £3.50.

CRINAN CANAL NR7894

Cut through the nine miles at the top of the Kintyre peninsula at the end of the 18th c, to save coastal sailors many miles of dangerous waters; the end at Crinan is attractive, usually with one or two yachts or even a rare fishing boat waiting to enter the first lock, and the Crinan Hotel is a comfortable lunch stop. The canal towpath allows gentle strolls.

DUNOON NS1878

Brought in easy reach of Glasgow by frequent ferries from Gourock, this late Victorian resort has pleasant views from its fine long promenade; very busy in Aug. The local history museum (Castle Gardens) has re-created Victorian rooms. Shop, disabled access; cl Sun am and mid-Oct to Easter; £1.50; (01369) 701422.

FORT WILLIAM NN1174

A largely Victorian town, partly pedestrianised, that manages to combine its role as a regional centre with its other life as a holiday base, particularly for solid Ben Nevis which rises above it, and for the Caledonian Canal which leads on up into the Great Glen and eventually across to the North Sea. The Alexandra and Nevis Bank hotels are useful for food, as is the cheerful Grog & Gruel pub; the Nevisport is the place for walking and climbing chat. In summer you can take the Jacobite Express steam train on the **West Highland Line** from here – it goes right up into the Highlands and the views are quite superb (01463) 239026; cl Oct–Mar.

Inverlochy Castle (NE edge) Partly 13th-c ruins (usually under scaffolding), site of the 1645 battle between Montrose and the Campbells; free.

West Highland Museum ⌼ (Cameron Sq) Great on Jacobite relics: a secret portrait of Prince Charlie needs a curved mirror to decode it. Shop, limited disabled access; cl Sun (exc July–Aug), 25–26 Dec, 1–2 Jan; (01397) 702169; £2.

GIGHA NR6549

3 miles offshore, linked by frequent ferries from Tayinloan on the A83 down the W coast of Kintyre; the island (recently bought by the islanders with a sizeable loan from the Land Fund) is a perfect place for really getting away from it all. Apart from the small Gigha Hotel, there are rooms at the Post Office and other places, and you can hire bicycles to explore it properly. Try to see the strange old stones, some of which are supposed to have mysterious powers. Phone (01880) 730253 for ferry times.

Achamore Gardens Created by Sir James Horlick, who bought the island in 1944; a garden of woodlands filled with rhododendrons and azaleas, many plants brought from his home in Berkshire in laundry baskets. Lots of subtropical plants – the climate and soil are perfect for them. Snacks, shop, limited disabled access; *£2.

GLEN NEVIS NN1468

(nr Fort William) Probably the best-known Highland valley, with splendid gorge scenery for an easy long mile's walk to Steall Falls. The Pap of Glencoe and the succession of peaks in the largely unwooded Mamore Forest (access from the Glen) are interesting viewpoint summits; they don't need rock-climbing expertise, just reasonable fitness and plenty of time.

GLENCOE NN1557

The scenery around here is some of

Scotland's most beautiful and wild. It's understandably popular with walkers and climbers, who share it with deer, wildcats and golden eagles. The Clachaig and Kings House do food. A forest walk runs from the hospital by Glencoe village past a lochan (small loch) above Loch Leven.

Altnafeadh Good start for walks from the top of the glen. The West Highland Way takes a zigzag route N up the Devil's Staircase and through the mountains to Kinlochleven; another hill walk from Altnafeadh heads E up Beinn a' Chrulaiste, one of Glencoe's more manageable peaks.

Glen Etive Reached from Glencoe by a squelchy walk along glens (or a long track from the A82 E of Glencoe), with close-ups of mighty peaks for reward.

Glencoe Visitor Centre (A82; 1 mile out of village) Brand new visitor centre telling the story of the massacre of 1692, when billeted troops tried to murder all their MacDonald hosts, as well as useful local information and facts about the mountainside and local conservation. Meals, snacks, shop, disabled access; may cl Nov–Feb, but best to phone to check details; (01855) 811307; £3 expected price; NTS.

Lost Valley This secret Glencoe pasture-ground was used by the MacDonalds for stolen cattle in times of clan warfare; the walk involves an ascent from the Meeting of the Three Waters.

HELENSBURGH NS2983

Hill House (Upper Colquhoun St) In an area short of many great houses, this is a wonderful example of the work of Charles Rennie Mackintosh; there's an exhibition on his life, and the gardens have been restored to reflect features common to the architect's designs. Teas, shop; cl am, and all day Nov–Mar; (01436) 673900; *£7; NTS – it's one of their busier properties. The dignified resort town, attractively placed on the Clyde, has some good views from its broad streets.

INVERARAY NN0908

Beautifully placed and rather self-consciously elegant, this was built as an estate village in the 18th c, and is now a magnet for visitors. The Loch Fyne Hotel is pleasant for lunch, with stunning views; the George is popular too.

All Saints church The bell tower has the world's second-heaviest ring of ten bells, installed in 1931. Even if there's no-one ringing them you should be able to hear a recording. Shop; cl 1–2pm, all Oct–Apr; (01499) 302346; £2 for tower, exhibition free.

Argyll Wildlife Park 🔲 (Dalchenna; A83 SW) A collection of local or once-local animals (deer, foxes and wildcats) plus chipmunks, wallabies, racoons and so forth – with some eminently tame wild creatures wandering around. Snacks, shop, disabled access; cl Nov–Mar; (01499) 302264; £4.00.

Inveraray Castle Built in 1745, and still the home of the Duke and Duchess of Argyll, it has particularly impressive state rooms, and a striking hall. Snacks, shop, ground floor disabled access; cl 1–2pm (exc July and Aug), Sun am, and Nov–Mar; (01499) 302203; £5.50. Nearby woodland trails include a view over Loch Fyne from Dun na Cuaiche Tower.

Inveraray Jail (Church Sq) Excellent prison museum, with costumed guides and Katie the Governor's cow really bringing the place to life. You can sit and listen to trials, try your hand at hard labour, and even experience being locked up in the airing yards. Watch out for the animated surprises. Shop; cl 25 Dec, 1 Jan; (01499) 302381; *£5.10.

KILMARTIN NR8395

Dunadd Fort (3m S) This prehistoric hill fort was one of the ancient capitals of Dalriada from which the Celtic kingdom of Scotland was formed. Look out for the carvings nearby of a boar and a footprint, which probably mark the spot where early kings were invested with royal power.

Kilmartin church Plain and Victorian, but it has a stunning 10th-c cross; the graveyard has interesting carved medieval tombstones. The simple Kilmartin Hotel is useful for lunch. A short walk away, tracks link the well signed North, Mid and South Cairns (impressive prehistoric burial mounds – you can climb into the North one via trapdoor and ladder, to see sup-and-ring carvings), and the Templewood stone circles.

Kilmartin House Museum Explains the rich and intriguing archaeology of the area. Meals, snacks, shop, disabled access; cl 25 Dec, 1 Jan; (01546) 510278; *£4.50. The Forestry Commission are still thinking about reintroducing beavers to Scotland just a few miles S of here in Knapdale Forest.
KILMUN NS1781
Kilmun forest walks Rare conifers, an arboretum of great beauty, and some striking gum-trees.
LOCH LOMOND NS3884
Loch Lomond, with the Trossachs, have recently been designated a National Park (surprisingly Scotland's first – it's taken 50 years in the planning). Straddling the Highland–Lowland divide, the park covers 580 square miles, and in spite of being so close to Glasgow and on every coach company's hit list, the loch (Britain's largest freshwater lake) does have a serene beauty that seems unspoilt by the visitors. Wee birdies sing and wild flowers spring – and the water is often calm enough to reflect the mountains. The best views are from the narrower N end. Surprisingly, there aren't many paths: the shoreline track, partly metalled, on the quieter E side, comes closest to the water; the Oak Tree at Balmaha round here is a useful food stop. Cruises round the lake leave from Balloch, as well as from the pretty village of Luss, a good place to hire a boat for pottering about on the water (there's a visitor centre here too).
Lomond Shores Visitor Centre (Luss Rd, Balloch) This new £60 million visitor centre marks the southern gateway to the new National Park, and is a good place to start. As well as lots of displays (inc interactive ones) and information on the area, there are craft shops, restaurants serving Scottish food, and a film, *The Legend of Loch Lomond*, on a screen the size of a tennis court. Disabled access; cl 25 Dec; (01389) 721500; £5.95, £2 for just the viewing gallery at the top of the visitor centre. The reopened Balloch Hotel is a reliable nearby dining pub.
Balloch Castle Country Park This includes a visitor centre, woodland and meadow trails, walled garden, and fine views. Snacks, shop, limited disabled

access; cl Nov–Apr exc Tues and Thurs in Apr; (01389) 758216 (ranger service events (01389) 722600); free.
Ben Lomond The southernmost munro (or peak over 3,000 ft, 914 metres), and the first of 21 in the new National Park, with a good walk up from Rowardennan on the E shore. On a really clear day the views are remarkable, to Ben Nevis and the Highland mountains in the N, to the Irish coast in the W, and to the hills above Edinburgh in the E – with Loch Lomond itself laid out in special beauty below.
Conic Hill Less than half Ben Lomond's height but more accessible, a straightforward but rewarding climb from Balmaha at Loch Lomond's SE corner.
MINARD NR9799
Crarae Gardens (A83) After having had to close for a while for lack of funds and now owned by the NTS, these lovely gardens opened again in Apr 2002; they are noted for their rare ornamental shrubs and rhododendrons, azaleas and conifers, set in a beautiful gorge overlooking Loch Fyne. Snacks, shop, and interesting plant sales (summer only), limited disabled access; open all year; (01546) 886614; £2.50.
MULL NM5055
For most people this island takes a bit of getting to, but if you are within reach its unspoilt coasts are certainly a dramatic lure. There's a good ferry service from Oban and Lochaline (and in summer from Kilchoan). A couple of castellated mansions, one going back to the 13th c and another, 19th-c Torosay Castle, with attractive gardens (tearoom, shop, limited disabled access; open daily Easter–end Oct; £5), give some rainy-day scope. From May to Sept, the Mull Experience runs day trips from Oban to these attractions, inc return ferry travel and a trip on Mull's unique railway (£17, phone (01680) 812421 for details). The interior is less interesting than the coast, with brackeny moors and conifer plantations over much of it, though there is some mountainous hill walking in the S (as usual, not many defined paths).
Iona (off Mull) Lovely, filled with a

sense of spirituality as well as its tangible remains of ancient shrines; Scotland's first kings were buried here (as is former Labour leader John Smith).

St Columba Visitor Centre (Fionnphort) Visitor centre dedicated to the saint. The little coastal settlement overlooks Iona, and the boats go from here. The Keel Row has decent food.

OBAN NM8530

This bustling coastal town is a busy ferry port and a popular place for holidaymakers, with a good cheerful atmosphere; the Oban Inn is fun, and the Lorne has decent food inc fresh local fish. Besides the main ferries, there are boats to Lismore, which has shoreside walks and several castle ruins and antiquities, and (just a hop really) Kerrera, for more shoreside walks and a 12th-c ruined fort on its S cliff. A little way S at Cologin, the countrified Barn is useful for lunch, and often has evening folk music.

Dunstaffnage Castle (off A485 4m N) Beautifully set, this was once the prison of Flora MacDonald. It's now in ruins, but you can still see its gatehouse, round towers and massively thick walls. Shop, disabled access to visitor centre only; cl Thurs and Fri Nov–Mar; (01631) 562465; £2.20; HS.

Oban Rare Breeds Farm 🎫 (A816 Oban–Kilmore) In lovely countryside; you can meet, touch and feed the very visitor-friendly animals (inc llama and alpaca). Teas, shop, pets' corner, play and picnic areas, woodland walk, some disabled access; cl Jan to mid-Mar; (01631) 770608; £5.

PORT APPIN NM9045

An attractive little settlement, very peaceful, where you can pick wild blueberries by the roadside, catch a boat across to Lismore (shoreside walks), or just sit by the water keeping your eyes open for the seals that are so common around here. The Pier House has great seafood, and comfortable bedrooms. This is *Kidnapped* country,

with the scene of the Appin Murder not far off, and a monument marking where James of the Glens was wrongly hanged at Ballachulish to the N (the Ballachulish Hotel has decent food and wide views).

RIVER LEVEN NN1861

The glen gives a fine walk through semi-wooded terrain, from Kinlochleven to the dam of the gigantic Blackwater Reservoir – with an awesomely bleak view ahead of empty hills.

SEIL NM7819

This little island is linked to the mainland by a short bridge that people call the Bridge over the Atlantic. There's an attractive walk over to the anchorage on the far side which looks out to Jura; the Tigh an Truish overlooking the water has home-made food.

TARBERT NR8465

Pleasant and quite picturesque small harbourside town; the Tarbert Hotel, with comfortable bedrooms overlooking the harbour, does good local seafood.

TAYNUILT NN0031

Bonawe Iron Furnace (off A85) The most complete remaining charcoal-fired ironworks in Britain, worked until 1876. Iron produced here was used for the cannonballs for Nelson's ships. Shop; cl Sun am, cl Oct– Mar; (01866) 822432; £2.80; HS. The lockside Polfearn Hotel does good food.

Inns with decent food, in good places for drivers, walkers or strollers, include the Loch Shiel Hotel at Acharacle NM6867, Ardentinny Hotel by Loch Long at Ardentinny NS1887, Village Inn at Arrochar NN2903, Galley of Lorne at Ardfern NM8004, Bridge of Orchy Hotel at Bridge of Orchy NN2939, Four Seasons at Inchree NN0263 nr Onich, Kilchrenan Inn at Kilchrenan by Loch Awe NN0222, Portsonachan Hotel on the opposite side of that loch NN1227, Whistlefield Hotel by Loch Eck NS1493, Loch Gair Hotel on Loch Gair NR9190 and Oystercatcher at Otter Ferry NR9384.

Please let us know what you think of places in the *Guide*. Use the report forms at the back of the book, write us a letter or log on to www.goodguides.com.

Where to eat

CAIRNDOW NN1812 **Loch Fyne Oyster Bar** *Clachan Farm (01499) 600236*
Relaxed restaurant in converted farm buildings by Loch Fyne, serving good seafood
and smoked fish (they have their own smokehouse); reasonably priced wine list and
a warm welcome; cl 25–26 Dec, 1–2 Jan; disabled access. £20|**£9.50**
FORT WILLIAM NN1074 **Alexandra** *The Parade (01397) 702241* Popular
hotel in town square with meals and snacks in the Great Food Stop (open all day)
and evening restaurant; disabled access. £22|**£7.50**
KENTALLEN NN0259 **Holly Tree** *(01631) 740292* Super food in carefully
converted railway station, cosy public rooms, lovely shoreside setting (best to book
in winter); bdrms; cl Nov–Jan; disabled access. £26|**£6**
TAYVALLICH NR7487 **Tayvallich Inn** *Kintallen (01546) 870282* Simply
refurbished pub overlooking yacht anchorage with super local seafood (other
decent dishes too), dining conservatory (no smoking), and friendly service; cl Mons
Nov–Mar, 25/26 Dec and 1/2 Jan. £30|**£8**

North Scotland

**Sensational scenery in the west and on Skye, solitude in the north,
empty beaches on the east coast – some surprising gardens**

Families who enjoy the outdoors, and scrambling around the occasional
ruin, will enjoy this part of Scotland more than those who like plenty of
organised entertainment. The W coast has glorious vistas of sea,
mountains and islands, while long empty sandy beaches (and good golf
courses) make the E coast just right for a quiet summer holiday. The N
coast is relatively wild and empty: addictive to some people, harsh and
inhospitable to others. Skye is idyllic in good weather. The magnificent
mountain scenery of Torridon is perhaps the best place to spot local
wildlife, and a dolphin or whale-watching trip from Cromarty can be really
memorable.

You'll find splendid castles at Golspie (fine collections of furnishings and
art), Dornie (in a beautiful position), and on Skye, Armadale Castle (lovely
walks) and Dunvegan Castle (in the same family for 800 years). There are
interesting ruins in Drumnadrochit (children enjoy the monster stuff at
Loch Ness 2000 nearby), and at Kirkhill's Moniack Castle you can buy
traditional country wines.

An unexpected treat, interesting gardens here include Attadale
Gardens at Strathcarron, and Inverewe Gardens at Poolewe, the
Hydroponicum at Achiltibuie are thought-provokingly futuristic and, new
this year, we've added the recently created oasis at Kylesku (you get there
by boat). Craig Highland Farm is nice for children.

The Highlands offer ultra-tough mountain walking, but relatively few
easier routes on defined paths; shorter circular walks are few and far
between. Compared to the uplands of England and Wales there are few
obvious walking routes (OS maps show hardly any), and the scale of the
scenery is often so vast that you need to walk for hours before the views

change. The high peaks are mostly for the dedicated (and fit) enthusiast. There is an informal tradition of allowing general access to the mountains, but there are few rights of way, and areas are often closed for at least part of the grouse-shooting season (12 Aug–10 Dec), particularly its first few weeks, or the deer-stalking season (1 July–20 Oct for stags, 21 Oct–15 Feb for hinds).

We list some lovely places to stay in here, and their prices compare very favourably with equivalent places further south.

Where to stay

ACHILTIBUIE NC0208 **Summer Isles Hotel** *Achiltibuie, Ullapool, Ross-shire IV26 2YQ (01854) 622282* **£110***; 13 comfortable rms. Beautifully placed above the sea towards the end of a very long and lonely road; warm, friendly, well furnished hotel with delicious set menus using fresh ingredients (in which it's largely self-sufficient), a choice of superb puddings and excellent array of uncommon cheeses; pretty watercolours and flowers; cl mid-Oct–Easter; children over 6; dogs welcome in bedrooms

APPLECROSS NG7144 **Applecross Inn** *Shore St, Applecross, Strathcarron, Ross-shire IV54 8LR (01520) 744262* **£64***; 7 rms, all with breathtaking sea views over Sound of Raasay, some with shared bthrms. Gloriously placed informal inn with tables out by shore, simple comfortable and friendly bar, log or peat fire in lounge, small restaurant with excellent fresh fish and seafood; cl 25 Dec and 1 Jan; dogs welcome

AULTIVULLIN NC8267 **Catalina** *Aultivullin, Strathy, Thurso, Caithness KW14 7RY (01641) 541395* **£40***, plus special breaks; 1 suite with small fridge. Extended former croft on wild headland just a short walk from the sea; residents have own wing with private lounge and dining room but owners offer a friendly welcome, good breakfasts, and enjoyable 3-course meals – bring your own wine and they will serve you at whatever time you wish to eat; no children, no smoking

COLBOST NG2050 **Three Chimneys** *Colbost, Dunvegan, Isle of Skye IV55 8ZT (01470) 511258* **£175**; 6 chic but comfortable rms. Simple but very stylish no smoking crofter's cottages on the edge of a loch, with two cosy stone-walled dining rooms, open fires, warmly friendly helpful owners, exceptionally good imaginative food with a strong emphasis on fish (though plenty of game and vegetarian, too), super breakfasts, and a carefully chosen wine list; cl 2 wks in Jan, restaurant cl Sun lunchtime Oct–Feb

CROMARTY NH7867 **Royal** *Marine Terrace, Cromarty, Ross-shire IV11 8YN (01381) 600217* **£59.90***; 10 rms. Traditional waterfront hotel with friendly owners and staff, attractive lounges, bars and sun lounge, and Scottish dishes in dining room; gets very busy in summer; dogs welcome in bedrooms

DRUMNADROCHIT NH4731 **Polmaily House** *Drumnadrochit, Inverness-shire IV63 6XT (01456) 450343* **£115***, plus special breaks; 11 light, pretty rms. Very relaxing and homely hotel in 18 acres, with comfortable drawing room and library, open fires, and excellent food in the no smoking restaurant (wonderful packed lunches too); a happy place for families with well equipped indoor play area with lots of supervised activities, baby sitting and listening, hundreds of children's videos, plenty of ponies and pets, swimming pool, tennis, croquet, fishing, and boating; cl 4 days at Christmas; disabled access; dogs welcome in bedrooms ☺

GARVE NH3874 **Inchbae Lodge** *Garve, Ross-shire IV23 2PH (01997) 455269* **£70***, plus special breaks; 15 rms, some in chalet. Former hunting lodge in lovely Highland setting with comfortable homely lounges, winter log fires, small bar (liked by locals), and good fixed-price evening meals using fresh local produce; lots of wildlife, marvellous walks; cl Christmas; disabled access; dogs welcome

Cape Wrath
Balnakiel
Durness
Kinlochbervie
A838
Scourie
Kylesku
A838
Elphin
Knockan Crag
Achiltibuie
A837
Ullapool
Falls of Shin
A835
Falls of Measach
Beinn Eighe
A832
Torridon
Garve
Craig
Muir of Ord
Strathcarron
Kirkhill
Falls of Glomach
Drumnadrochit
Dornie
Glen Affric
Shiel Bridge
Glen Shiel
A87
Loch Ness
A82
Glenfinnan
Highland Line

NC

Aultivullin
Bettyhill
A836
Strathy Point
Melvich
Dunnet Head
Brough
Mey
Duncansby Head
John O'Groats
Auckengill
Wick
Lybster
A9
Helmsdale
Golspie
Tarbat Ness

ND

Evanton
Strathpeffer
Cromarty
MORAY FIRTH
A9

NH

A9

NN

EAST
SCOTLAND

WEST SCOTLAND

0 Miles 20
0 Kilometres 32

GLENELG NG8119 **Glenelg Inn** *Kirkton, Glenelg, Kyle, Ross-shire IV40 8JR* (01599) 522273 **£120*** inc dinner, plus special breaks; 6 individually decorated and comfortable rms, all with fine views. Overlooking Skye across its own beach, this carefully refurbished homely hotel has a relaxed bar, comfortable sofas and blazing fires, friendly staff and locals, good food using local venison, local hill-bred lamb and lots of wonderfully fresh fish and seafood, and quite a few whiskies; the drive to the inn involves spectacular views from the steep road (and the pretty drive to Glen Beag broch is nice); open in winter if pre-booked; disabled access; dogs welcome away from dining room

ISLE ORNSAY NG7012 **Eilean Iarmain** *Isle Ornsay, Isle of Skye IV43 8QR* (01471) 833332 **£120***, plus winter breaks; 17 individual rms (those in main hotel best), all with fine views. Sparkling white hotel with Gaelic-speaking staff and locals, big cheerfully busy bar, pretty dining room with lovely sea views, and very good food; disabled access; dogs welcome in bedrooms

ISLE ORNSAY NG7315 **Kinloch Lodge** *Isle Ornsay, Isle of Skye IV43 8QY* (01471) 833214 **£150**, plus winter breaks; 14 rms. Surrounded by rugged mountain scenery at the head of Loch Na Dal, this charming white stone hotel has a relaxed atmosphere in its comfortable and attractive drawing rooms, antiques, portraits, flowers, log fires, and good imaginative food; cookery demonstrations; children by arrangement; cl 22–27 Dec; dogs welcome in bedrooms

LAIDE NG8990 **Old Smiddy** *Laide, Achnasheen, Ross-shire IV22 2NB* (01445) 731425 **£70***; 3 pretty rms with thoughtful extras. Really welcoming charming no smoking cottage in lovely spot by sea and mountains, with blazing fire in comfortable homely lounge, and dining room with super breakfasts and delicious evening meals (using local and home-grown produce; bring your own wine); lots of outside pursuits; cl Nov–Easter; children over 12; dogs welcome

LYBSTER ND2436 **Portland Arms** *Lybster, Caithness KW3 6BS* (01593) 721721 **£72.50***; 22 comfortable rms. Staunch old granite hotel with really friendly staff, attractive dining room, generous helpings of good fresh food and fine breakfasts, small cosy lounge bar, and informal locals' bar; shooting/fishing can be arranged; cl 31 Dec–2 Jan; disabled access to ground floor

MELVICH NC8864 **Melvich Hotel** *Melvich, Thurso, Caithness KW14 7YJ* (01641) 531206 **£50***, plus special breaks; 14 rms with showers (also have 4 bthrms). Small traditional hotel in lovely spot with homely furniture and peat fires in the civilised lounge, cosy bar, very relaxing atmosphere, friendly owners and staff, good food (esp local seafood and wild salmon), and fine bay views

PLOCKTON NG8033 **Plockton Hotel** *41 Harbour St, Plockton, Ross-shire IV52 8TN* (01599) 544274 **£70***, plus special breaks; 10 rms, most with own bthrm, plus 4 in cottage annexe. Small notably friendly hotel (not to be confused with Plockton Inn around the corner), in a row of elegant houses by a shore lined with palm trees and flowering shrubs, looking over the sheltered anchorage to rugged mountains, with comfortably furnished lively lounge bar, separate public bar, enjoyable award-winning food in no smoking restaurant, good breakfasts, a good choice of whiskies, and attentive owners; good disabled access

POOLEWE NG8580 **Pool House** *Poolewe, Achnasheen, Ross-shire IV22 2LE* (01445) 781272 **£240**; 5 beautifully themed suites with remarkable Edwardian and Victorian baths 2½ metres (over 8 ft) tall inc canopied showers. On the shore by the River Ewe, this early 18th-c hotel, remodelled in the 19th by the founder of Inverewe Gardens and recently refurbished, has original panelling, fine doors and friezes uncovered; restful drawing room with open fire, fine antiques and sea views, delicious food with an emphasis on local seafood; plenty of walks and wildlife; cl Jan–Feb, parts of Dec

PORTREE NG4843 **Rosedale** *Quay Brae, Portree, Isle of Skye IV51 9DB* (01478) 613131 **£90***, plus special breaks; 23 rms, many with harbour views. Built from three fishermen's cottages with lots of passages and stairs, this waterfront hotel has two traditional lounges, small first-floor restaurant with freshly cooked popular food, lots of whiskies in the cocktail bar, helpful staff, marvellous views; cl

Nov–Easter; dogs welcome in bedrooms

RAASAY NG5537 **Isle of Raasay Hotel** *Isle of Raasay, Kyle, Ross-shire IV40 8PB* (01478) 660222 **£58***; 12 rms, the new owners plan to redecorate in 2003. Victorian hotel with marvellous views over the Sound of Raasay to Skye, popular with walkers and bird-watchers, home-made food with an emphasis on fresh fish; no petrol on the island; disabled access; dogs welcome in bedrooms

SCARISTA NG0192 **Scarista House** *Scarista, Harris, Isle of Harris HS3 3HX* (01859) 550238 **£135***, plus special breaks; 5 rms, some in annexe. Marvellously wild countryside and empty beaches surround this isolated small hotel with its antiques-furnished rooms, open fires, warm friendly atmosphere, plenty of books and records (no radio or TV), an impressive wine list, and good food in candlelit dining room using organic home-grown vegetables and herbs, hand-made cheeses, their own eggs, home-made bread, cakes, biscuits, yoghurt and marmalade, and lots of fish and shellfish; excellent for wildlife, walks and fishing; cl Christmas and occasionally in winter; dogs welcome

SCOURIE NC1641 **Eddrachilles** *Badcall, Scourie, Lairg, Sutherland IV27 4TH* (01971) 502080 **£80***, plus special breaks; 11 comfortable rms. Well run hotel in its own 320 acres overlooking Badcall Bay, with wonderful island views; popular with nature-lovers – bird sanctuary nearby, seals, fishing and walking; cl Nov–Feb; children over 3; partial disabled access

SCOURIE NC1544 **Scourie Hotel** *Scourie, Lairg, Sutherland IV27 4SX* (01971) 502396 **£80**, plus special breaks; 20 rms with views to Scourie Bay. A haven for anglers, with 36 exclusive beats on 25,000-acre estate; snug bar, two comfortable lounges and good food using plenty of local game and fish in smart no smoking dining room; cl mid-Oct to end Mar; dogs welcome

SHIEL BRIDGE NG9419 **Kintail Lodge** *Glenshiel, Kyle, Ross-shire IV40 8HL* (01599) 511275 **£80**; 12 good value big rms. Pleasantly informal and fairly simple former shooting lodge on Loch Duich, with magnificent views, four acres of walled gardens, residents' lounge bar and comfortable sitting room, good well prepared food inc wild salmon, and fine collection of malt whiskies; dogs welcome in bedrooms

SHIELDAIG NG8153 **Tigh an Eilean** *Shieldaig, Strathcarron, Ross-shire IV54 8XN* (01520) 755251 **£110**, plus special breaks; 11 rms. Attractive hotel in outstanding position with lovely view of pine-covered island and sea, kayaks, private fishing and sea fishing arranged, within easy reach of NTS Torridon Estate, Beinn Eighe nature reserve and Applecross peninsula; pretty woodburner in one of two comfortable residents' lounges with well stocked honesty bar, modern dining room with delicious food inc home-baked bread, warmly friendly owners; cl end Oct–Mar; dogs welcome in bedrooms

SKEABOST NG4048 **Skeabost Country House** *Skeabost Bridge, Portree, Isle of Skye IV51 9NR* (01470) 532202 **£105***, plus special breaks; 19 rms, 4 in annexe in Garden House. Smart and friendly little hotel in 29 acres of landscaped grounds on the shores of Loch Snizort; 9-hole 18-tee golf course and 8 miles of salmon and trout fishing; log fires, comfortable day rooms, friendly, helpful staff, and good, enjoyable food; disabled access; dogs by arrangement

STRONTIAN NM7961 **Kilcamb Lodge Hotel** *Strontian, Acharacle, Argyll PH36 4HY* (01967) 402257 **£115***, plus winter breaks; 11 rms. Warm friendly little hotel in 28 acres by Loch Sunart, with log fires in two lounges, carefully cooked food using fresh ingredients from organic kitchen garden, fine choice of malt whiskies in small bar, and a relaxed atmosphere; beach, fishing boat, four moorings and jetty; no children; disabled access in cottage; dogs welcome in bedrooms

TARBERT NB1301 **Leachin House** *Leachin, Harris, Isle of Harris HS3 3AH* (01859) 502157 **£90***, plus special breaks; 2 comfortable rms. Meaning 'house among the rocks', this neat and peaceful Victorian stone house on the loch shores (wonderful sunsets) is a haven for nature-lovers and walkers – guided trips to look for seals, otters and eagles, fishing, and fine wild flowers in spring and early summer; friendly helpful owners, interesting nautical memorabilia, open fire in the drawing room, and particularly good food using delicious local seafood and lamb, served around a communal table in dining room with original 19th-c hand-painted French wallpaper; cl 18 Dec–18 Jan; children over 10

TORRIDON NG8854 **Loch Torridon Hotel** *Torridon, Achnasheen, Ross-shire IV22 2EY (01445) 791242 £132**, plus special breaks; 20 comfortable rms. Built in 1887 as a shooting lodge in 58 acres at the foot of Ben Damph by Upper Loch Torridon, this turreted stone house has unusual ornate ceilings and panelling, log fires and innovative cooking; they also run the Ben Damph Lodge nearby; cl Jan; children over 10 in dining room; disabled access; dogs welcome in bedrooms

To see and do

ACHILTIBUIE NC0208
Hydroponicum 🖼 Bizarre indoor garden of the future – without any soil. Fascinating guided tours show how plants such as figs, lemons and bananas grow quite happily using the nutrients from the soil, but not the soil itself. Good home-made meals and snacks, shop; disabled access; hourly tours Easter–Sept (cl Nov–Easter); (01854) 622202; £4.75.

AUCKENGILL ND3664
Northlands Viking Centre (Old School) Interesting displays on how the Norsemen came from Scandinavia to Shetland, Orkney and Caithness, with a Viking longship and other relics. Shop, disabled access; cl Oct–May; (01847) 805518; £1.70.

BALMACARA NG8028
(A67) Huge crofting estate surrounding the Kyle of Lochalsh, with challenging walks through breathtaking scenery; you can still see traditional crofting at Drumbuie and Duirnish, and the NTS have a cottage that's enjoyable to stay in. The landscape is interspersed with lochs and impressive landmarks like the Five Sisters of Kintail (a fine target for hardened walkers) and Beinn Fhada. **Lochalsh Woodland Garden** (A87 3m E of Kyle of Lochalsh) Wonderful woodland gardens, with peaceful walks, collections of rhododendrons, hydrangeas, fuchsias and other plants, and views towards Skye. Open all year; (01599) 566325; £2; NTS. The Lochalsh Hotel has enjoyable simple bar food.

BALNAKIEL NC3967
The most NW part of mainland Britain, wild, remote and spectacular, with a little craft village (some bits cl Sun, and limited opening in winter; (01971) 511277; free).

BEINN EIGHE NG9963
One of the easier mountain ascents, with a well marked Mountain Trail making a circular route above beautiful island-studded Loch Maree.

BETTYHILL NC7062
Strathnaver Museum Good informative memorial to the notorious Highlands Clearances; limited disabled access; cl lunchtime, Sun, and Nov–Mar; (01641) 521418; £1.90. The churchyard has a finely carved 9th-c Celtic stone. The Bettyhill Hotel does decent food. Just S is a wonderful **nature reserve**, and the beach nearby is attractive.

CRAIG NG8233
Craig Highland Farm This conservation centre for rare breeds of domestic animals and fowl (some you can feed) is picturesquely set on the shores of Loch Carron; you might catch a glimpse of some wilder creatures too like seals, otters and pine martens, and at low tide you can walk across a coral beach to a heron sanctuary. Snacks, disabled access; cl Oct–Easter; (01599) 544205; £1.50.

CROMARTY NH7867
Dolphin Ecosse (Bank House) Boat trips to see the local bottlenose dolphins: they can't guarantee sightings, but nine out of ten of their trips do come across dolphins, and they point out various seabirds and local landmarks along the way. Very friendly and informal, and rated very highly by readers. Whale-watching trips too in Aug and Sept – best to book on (01381) 600323; shop, snacks, disabled access; *£20. A dolphin centre and shop are now open at Harbour Workshop, Victoria Pl (same phone number). Cromarty itself is a delightfully sleepy place with lots of unspoilt buildings in its

well restored core. The old courthouse (Church St) has a surprisingly good little museum; open May–Oct; (01381) 600245; £2.50. The friendly Royal Hotel has good value food and lovely views.

DORNIE NG8826

Eilean Donan Castle (off A87) Connected to the mainland by a causeway, and unforgettably beautiful. First built in 1220, destroyed in 1719, and then rebuilt at the beginning of the last century, it's perfectly positioned at the meeting point of Lochs Long, Duich and Alsh. Visitor centre with teas and shop, disabled access; The centre is cl late Nov–mid-Mar, but the shop stays open; (01599) 555202; £4. The Dornie Hotel has good reasonably priced food inc local seafood.

DRUMNADROCHIT NH5130

Loch Ness 2000 📷 (Drumnadrochit Hotel) Walk-through multi-media experience tracing the legend from its beginnings in Highland folklore to the scientific investigations of recent years, using the latest technology, laser animations and special effects. There's a kilt-maker on site, a new garden with fountain and waterfall, and boat trips run from Easter from the centre. Meals, snacks, shop, disabled access; cl 25 Dec; (01456) 450573; *£5.95.

Urquhart Castle (just SE) A stronghold since the Iron Age: the present 14th-c remains were once the biggest castle in Scotland, and there's still plenty to see. A piper plays here every day Jun–Sept. The new £5 million visitor centre tells the story of the castle and the people who lived here, with a display of artefacts, and a short film about the castle. Café, shop, disabled access; cl 25–26 Dec, 1–2 Jan; (01456) 450551; £5; HS. In the village the Fiddlers Elbow has enjoyable food.

DUNCANSBY HEAD ND4073 A grand spot on a fine day, with an absorbing cliff walk S for a good view of the spectacular Stacks of Duncansby, 60-metre (200-ft) offshore rock pinnacles.

DUNNET HEAD ND2074 Mainland Britain's furthest point N, with views to Orkney. Lovely on a clear early summer's day, with spring flowers in the close turf, and puffins pottering around – but wild and unforgiving when the weather changes.

DURNESS NC4067 Attractively placed near the beautiful sea loch Loch Eriboll, and also has atmospheric boat tours of the Smoo Cave and its underground waterfall; cl Nov–May; (01971) 511704; £3.

Cape Wrath In summer you can make an adventurous expedition to this stormy tip of coast, guarded by a lonely lighthouse, by boat across the Kyle of Durness and then along a very long rough track to the lighthouse itself; for details phone Mrs Mackay, (01971) 511343.

ELPHIN NC2110

Highland & Rare Breeds Farm (A835) Traditional Scottish farm animals close up, on a family-worked croft in attractive setting. They sell fleeces and hand-spun wool. Snacks, shop, some disabled access; cl Sept–Jun; (01854) 666204; £3.50.

EVANTON NH5864

Storehouse of Foulis In an attractive restored building on the shores of Cromarty Firth, this lively visitor centre takes a fresh look at the area's local heritage and maritime history. Café, shop, disabled access; cl 25 Dec, 1–2 Jan; (01349) 830038; *£3.50.

FALLS OF GLOMACH NH0125 Tremendous waterfall, Scotland's highest, eventually tumbling to a pool 230 metres (750 ft) below the crest of the ravine – a fine wilderness destination for walkers on Kintail, though not at its best in dry seasons.

FALLS OF MEASACH NH1978 With a mighty drop of 60 metres (200 ft), these are the highlight of the mile-long, sheer-sided Corrieshalloch Gorge, owned by the National Trust for Scotland and equipped with a little viewing platform. Readers warn us that the swaying suspension bridge across the gorge is not for the faint-hearted, though the views from it are spectacular.

FALLS OF SHIN NH5799 (B864 S) There's a good chance of seeing salmon leaping here in Jun or early July, esp if there's been a dry spell followed by rain so that the river is in spate.

GAIRLOCH NG8076

Gairloch Heritage Museum 📷

Enthusiastically run, perhaps the most enjoyable of the several heritage museums in the Highlands, with a hands-on exhibition. Meals, snacks, shop, disabled access; cl Sun, pm Oct, Nov–Mar exc by arrangement; (01445) 712287; £2.50. The Old Inn here is a good stop; Gairloch has a beach, and is a good base for hikers; the easy walk up Flowerdale Glen is interesting.

GLEN AFFRIC NH2124
One of the most majestic inland glens, with a walking route along its floor, and one of the largest surviving native pinewoods in Britain.

GLENFINNAN NM9080
Jacobite Monument (A830) Built in 1815 to commemorate the Highlanders who fought and died for Bonnie Prince Charlie, in a commanding position at the head of Loch Shiel. A visitor centre has exhibitions on the prince. Good snacks, shop, disabled access to most areas; visitor centre cl Nov–Mar; (01397) 722250; £2; NTS.

GOLSPIE NC8500
Dunrobin Castle (A9) Splendid castle – a gleaming elegantly turreted structure with views out to sea and gardens modelled on those at Versailles. The family home of the Earls and Dukes of Sutherland for longer than anyone can remember, the site was named after Earl Robin in the 13th c; he was responsible for the original square keep. Drastically renovated and enlarged to cope with a hugely bigger family in the 19th c, it has fine collections of furnishings and art, and a unique collection of Pictish stones; falconry. Snacks, shop; cl Sun am, and 16 Oct–31 Mar, gardens open all year; (01408) 633177; £6.25. The Sutherland Arms has reasonably priced food.

HELMSDALE ND0315
Timespan (Dunrobin St) Visitor centre with reconstructions of scenes from Highland history (with sound effects), art exhibitions and interesting herb garden. Riverside café, shop, disabled access; cl Sun am, Nov–Mar; (01431) 821327; £3.50.

JOHN O' GROATS ND3773
Gets its share of visitors under the mistaken impression that it's the most northerly point on mainland Britain. Increasingly developed for tourists, but

still a pleasant spot. The hotel on the harbour looking across to the Orkneys has decent food. A 90-min cruise spots seals, puffins and colonies of breeding guillemots, end Jun–Aug 2.30pm, (01955) 611353, £12; and longer boat trips go from here to the Orkney Islands, (01955) 677535.

KINLOCHBERVIE NC2156
Friendly village with decent beaches, mountains and scenery around; it's most lively around 6pm on Mon–Thurs (2pm Fri), when the fishing boats return to the pier and auction their catch. You can take boat trips round the harbour.

KIRKHILL NH5543
Moniack Castle 🏰 (A862) Former fortress of the Lovat chiefs, now producing traditional country wines and liqueurs, and interesting meat and game preserves, sauces and coulis, and breakfast preserves. There are tastings and tours, and an amusing video. Shop; cl Sun, 25 Dec, 1 Jan; (01463) 831283; *£2.

KNOCKAN CRAG NC2010
(13 miles N of Ullapool on A835), Open-sided visitor point with turf room looking over surrounding rocky landscape and hands-on interactivities, graphics, cartoons, sculptures, games, and poetry, all to do with rocks and how they tell of volcanoes, ice sheets, oceans and deserts; various routes and trails; open all year; free.

KNOYDART NG8100
A real Highland wilderness on the W coast, glorious roadless country that's irresistible to hardened walkers – given good weather, full equipment and strong legs. There is a ferry three days a week from Mallaig to Inverie, where the Old Forge is very hospitable (and open all day).

KYLESKU NC2333
Kerrachar Boat trips to this one-hectare garden, developed since 1995 on the site of a disused croft, take 30 mins and leave from the Old Ferry Pier 1pm Tues, Thurs and Sun mid-May to mid-Sept; phone to book; (01571) 833288; £12.50 inc an hour's visit to the garden and the ferry, children free; snacks, plant sales.

LOCH NESS NH5330
Drumnadrochit (see above) is the best place to begin exploring this striking 24-mile loch with the largest volume of

fresh water of any lake in the British Isles; up to 215 metres (700 ft) deep in places, so it's not hard to see why stories sprang up of what was hidden in its waters. You can generally take boat trips on the lake, some of them equipped with sonar for monster-spotting.

MALLAIG NM6797
Bustling fishing port, good for shellfish and prawns; from this most westerly mainland harbour you can take a ferry to the Isle of Skye, the Small Isles or Knoydart. The **Mallaig Heritage Centre** next to the station is worth a look if passing, and at **Mallaig Marine World** you can touch some of the fish; shop, disabled access; usually cl Sun Nov–Easter, a few days over Christmas, and 2 wks in Feb, best to check; (01687) 462292; £2.75. The seaview Marine Hotel does good bar lunches.

MEY ND2872
Castle of Mey Surprisingly homely inside, with a lovely traditional walled garden, this 16th-c Z-plan castle was bought by the late Queen Mother in 1952, and became her beloved northern home. She left specific instructions that it should become open to the public. Shop, limited disabled access (phone first); open daily (exc Mon, and am Sun) 24 May–2 Aug and 13 Aug–12 Oct; (01847) 851227; £5. The Castle Arms has decent food.

PLOCKTON NG8033
Idyllic waterside village, with palm trees along the village street; the TV series *Hamish Macbeth* was filmed here. The Plockton Hotel has good generous food, and readers recommend Off the Rails, a restaurant in a restored 19th-c railway station.

POOLEWE NG8681
Inverewe Gardens (A832)
Unmissable beautiful gardens full of rare and subtropical plants, with a magnificent background of mountain scenery. The Atlantic Drift is responsible for the special microclimate which lets these unusual plants flourish even though this is further N than Moscow. Guided walks wkdys at 1.30pm, mid-Apr to mid-Sept. Meals, snacks, shop, limited disabled access; visitor centre, well stocked shop and restaurant (cl Nov to mid-

Mar); (01445) 781200; £7; NTS.

RUBHA REIGH NG7391
Rubha Reigh Lighthouse Remote outpost several miles along a track N of Melvaig; they organise enjoyable walking holidays in the splendidly wild countryside around; tearoom open Tues and Thurs; cl Jan after New Year; B&B or hostel-style rooms – don't worry about the colour of the water, it's just peaty; (01445) 771263.

SKYE NG4829
After Lewis, the biggest of the islands off the Scottish coast, now linked to the mainland by a bridge, though the easier access doesn't seem to have spoilt the island's special air of romance. The coasts have plenty of opportunities for gentle pottering, and for finding quiet coves and bays, particularly on the W coast, where for instance Tarskavaig, or the good Stein Inn in the N, are lovely spots to watch the sun go down. The jagged teeth of the Cuillins mountain range to the SE of the centre are unforgettable. Besides places mentioned in **Where to stay** and **Where to eat**, the Misty Isle at Dunvegan, Sligachan Inn (A850/A863 in the middle of the island), Flodigarry Hotel nr Staffin (stunning views from this turreted mansion with Flora MacDonald connections), Ardvasar Hotel, Struan Grill at Struan and the waterside Old Inn at Carbost (handy for the Talisker distillery, which can be visited; (01478) 614306) all do decent food.

Armadale Castle, Gardens & Museum of the Isles [icon] NG6404 The castle was built for Lord Macdonald in 1815, and the surrounding 40 acres offer beautiful walks among gardens and woodlands. Sleat, this southern peninsula, is known as the Garden of Skye. There is a museum which helps to unravel the complexities of the area's history, and a gallery too. Very good restaurant, shop, disabled access; cl Nov–Mar; (01471) 844305; *£4.

Dunvegan Castle NG2449
Dramatically set on the sea loch of Dunvegan, this has been the home of the Chiefs of Macleod for 800 years; no other Scottish castle has been inhabited by the same family for so long. Among its relics is a lock of Bonnie Prince

Charlie's hair. Staying here inspired Walter Scott's *Lord of the Isles*. Good meals and snacks, shops; open daily; cl 25–26 Dec, 1–2 Jan; (01470) 521206; £6, £4 gardens only. There are several good self-catering cottages in the attractive grounds, and summer boat trips go from the jetty to a nearby colony of brown and great grey seals, £4.

Elgol NG5113 A peaceful spot for gorgeous sunset views. There are summer boat trips to the lonely and dramatic inlet of Loch Coruisk from Elgol. One of the island's most lovely shoreside walks runs from Elgol to Loch na Creitheach at the heart of the formidable Cuillins, a mecca for rock-climbers. The drive up to Torrin, around the head of the loch and past a ruined church and graveyard, is picturesque.

Museum of Island Life ⌷ NG2547 (Kilmuir) Worth a look; shop, snacks, disabled access; cl Sun, and end Oct–Easter; (10470) 552206; *£2.

Portree NG4843 Skye's busiest harbour, attractive and quite picturesque, though in summer it tends to swarm with visitors; the harbourside Pier Hotel is right in the thick of the action, the quieter Cuillin Hills on the outskirts has good value food in its conservatory. The Aros Experience (A87 just S) is worth a look for its displays on island life (and the restaurant does tasty chicken broth).

Quiraing NG4569 A fascinating tumbled rock mass, with a surprisingly manageable path through it.

Raasay (off Skye) Very peaceful island, an ideal place for gentle pottering without lots of competition from other visitors – and for some quite stiff hill walks if that's what you prefer.

Trotternish peninsula NG5163 Quite extraordinary rock scenery and formations like the Old Man of Storr; the Glenview Hotel at Culnaknock up here has good food, and in season the Flodigarry Hotel serves food all day.

STRATHCARRON NG9338

Attadale Gardens ⌷ (A890 towards South) Attractive gardens with excellent water gardens and winding woodland paths, sheltered by the surrounding hills and steep cliffs.

Started in the 1890s, they include rhododendrons, azaleas, bamboo, Himalayan poppies and primulas. The old sunken garden has been restored, and there is a kitchen garden and conservatory; nursery specialising in unusual plants for sale. Disabled access; cl Sun, and 1 Nov–1 Apr; (01520) 722603; *£3.

STRATHPEFFER NH4858 Originally a fashionable 19th-c spa resort (you can look round the beautifully restored Pump Room, by appointment (01997) 420124), this has quite a different feel from the rest of the area, with its rather continental appearance of dignified hotels and villas stepped up among its wooded slopes; some call it the Harrogate of the North. Up the A835 Rogie Falls are worth the short walk from the car park.

Highland Museum of Childhood ⌷ In restored Victorian railway station, telling the history of childhood in the Highlands among crofters and townsfolk, recorded by oral testimony, displays, photographs and video; fascinating doll and toy collections. Snacks, shop; disabled access; cl Sun am, and Nov–Mar; (01997) 421031; £1.50.

STRATHY POINT NC8269 (W of Thurso) With a lighthouse at the end of a narrow peninsula, a pleasant stroll along the little road from its car park.

TARBAT NESS NH9487 Jutting from the S side of Dornoch Firth, this is rather isolated, but worth the journey for the walk around the peninsula, from Portmahomack, past the lighthouse, and then along the S coast past a ruined castle to reach Rockfield.

TORRIDON NG9055

Torridon Countryside Centre (junction A896 and Diabaig road) Gateway to a huge area of nature reserve in stunning mountain scenery – some say the best in Scotland. It has displays on the scenery and wildlife, as well as a deer park and deer museum. Visitor centre cl Oct–Easter; £2; (01445) 791221; NTS. Nearby at the Mains there are herds of red deer and Highland cattle. Torridon is wonderful for challenging walks, and there are a few outstanding easier ones, based for example on Loch Torridon's shores. The Kinlochewe Hotel (A896 E) has decent food; to reach anywhere N of here by car from the S, incidentally, it's much quicker to go by Inverness than to make your way all the way up the W coast.

ULLAPOOL NH1294

A good centre, with quite a busy harbour, a lot going on for a small place – and good eating (besides the places we've picked out, the fish and chip restaurant is very good, with surprisingly presentable white wines, and the Ferry Boat is nice). The Museum and Visitor Centre on West Argyle St has local history displays; cl Sun, limited opening hours Nov–Feb; (01854) 612987; £3. You can get a ferry out to the Summer Isles.

WEST HIGHLAND LINE NM9080

A good way of seeing Highlands scenery between Fort William and Mallaig: steam trains in summer, year-round normal trains. The views are terrific.

WICK ND3650

This small harbourside town has attractive houses and a good early 19th-c church.

Caithness Glass Factory (Wick Airport Industrial Estate) Glass-making demonstrations (not wknds), and factory seconds. Meals, snacks, shop, disabled access; cl Sun Christmas–Easter; (01955) 602286; free.

Castle of Old Wick (just SE) Ruined four-storey square tower in dramatic clifftop setting, probably dating from the 12th/13th c.

Wick Heritage Centre In eight buildings by the harbour, this very good centre presents the history of the town; cl Sun, and all Oct–May; (01955) 605393; *£2.

This is a part of the world where inns doing a decent bite to eat are very much at a premium, and a welcome sight indeed after miles of empty road. Besides those listed elsewhere, ones we can recommend for their positions include the Aultbea Inn at Aultbea NG8689, Aultguish Hotel NH3570 on the A835 nr Loch Glascarnoch, Badachro Inn at Badachro NG7773, Royal Hotel at Cromarty NH7867, Northern Sands at Dunnet ND2170, Lock at Fort Augustus NH3709, Cluanie by the loch (walks and maybe eagles) in Glen Shiel NH0711, Glenuig Inn at Glenuig NM6676, Garvault Inn extraordinarily isolated on the B871 N of Kinbrace NC8732, Kylesku Hotel at Kylesku NC2234 (the boatman here has taken readers for fascinating 4-hour boat tours), Lewiston Arms at Lewiston NH5029, Loch Carron Hotel on Loch Carron NG9039, Glenuig Hotel at Lochailort NM7682, Inver Lodge Hotel overlooking Lochinver harbour NC0923, Scrabster Inn at Scrabster ND0970, Ben View at Strontian NM8161, Loch Maree Hotel at Talladale NG8970 and Ben Loyal Hotel at Tongue NC5957. Almost all have bedrooms.

Where to eat

BROADFORD NG6423 **Fig Tree** *(01471) 822616* Enjoyable home-made food inc fresh fish and vegetarian choices in friendly little place; cl Sun, Oct–Mar; disabled access. £15|£6.50

BROUGH ND2273 **Dunnet Head Tearoom** *(01847) 851774* Small traditional unpretentious cottage with good reasonably priced meals and snacks served by warmly friendly owners – fair choice of vegetarian dishes, fresh salmon, local seafood, and local beef; take your own wine; bdrms; open 3–8pm (last orders then), tearoom cl Oct–Mar, Weds; children must be well behaved. £15|£5

DUNVEGAN NG2351 **Macleod's Table** *The Castle (01470) 521310* Decorated with pine throughout, popular family restaurant with very reasonably priced generous morning coffee, snacks and full meals, and afternoon teas; friendly helpful staff; loch cruises, seal colony, castle gardens and craft shops; cl end Oct–mid-Mar; disabled access. £18|£6.

KINLOCHBERVIE NC2256 **Old School House** *Inshegra (01971) 521383* Very good food in old school building with school-related items like photographs, maps, notebooks on tables; home-grown vegetables, local fish and venison, enjoyable puddings, and very good service; bdrms in newish building; disabled access; cl 25 Dec, 1 Jan. £15|£5

MUIR OF ORD NH5251 **Dower House** *(01463) 870090* Very good modern cooking in attractive hotel restaurant, with fine wines, and friendly service; bdrms and lovely gardens; children over 5 in restaurant; cl 2 wks Nov and Christmas. **£43|£3.50**

ULLAPOOL NH1195 **Morefield Motel** *North Rd (01854) 612161* Big helpings of exceptionally fresh enterprisingly cooked fish and seafood (owners are ex-fishermen and divers), Aberdeen Angus steaks and roast beef, and vegetarian dishes in smart restaurant of basic hotel, also bar food; bdrms; disabled access. **£21.45|£7.50**

Special thanks to Dr and Mrs B W Marsden, Mrs Edna M Jones, Stuart Paulley, Mr and Mrs J Douglas, Mrs E M Jones, R V Elliston

WALES

Medieval castles are almost a Wales trademark, as are spectacular private railways (the one in Llanberis is Wales Family Attraction of the Year). But Wales has much more to offer families. Enjoyable days out run from dramatic show caves to grand houses and gardens, from animal parks to Celtic myth-making, from outstanding and very lively historic and industrial re-creations to some splendid boat trips. Prices of places to stay in and to visit are generally attractive, making Wales good holiday value.

North Wales has all sorts of family outings, stretches of attractive coast and some good summer holiday resorts. There are some nice towns to wander around, and lots of highly dramatic mountain scenery.

West Wales has a beautiful coastline, with a great coast path in the Pembrokeshire National Park. Even in bad weather, when upland areas are more or less a write-off, the coast preserves a gloomy magnificence. It too is a good family holiday area, with some interesting attractions, but its strongest appeal is to people who like to keep things simple.

Mid Wales has few organised attractions, though to many that is part of its appeal, with empty, scenic roads and little-frequented paths. Its most special parts include the Brecon Beacons National Park, the empty and lonely Cambrian Mountains (wonderful high-level drives here), and the Elan Valley lakes.

Considerably more built-up, South Wales has a good choice of excellent days out, and pockets of fine scenery, particularly on the coast of the Gower and along the Wye Valley.

We have mentioned a few of the Roman and prehistoric sites in which the area abounds. You can get more information from Cadw (Welsh Historic Monuments Commission), (029) 2050 0200, which is also responsible for the care of the great majority of the historic castles and other monuments here. If you plan to visit many of their sites, the Explorer Pass is good value (£15.50 for a week, £9.50 for three days – available from most of their sites). There are reciprocal rights for English Heritage and Historic Scotland cardholders – half price for the first year of membership, free thereafter.

North Wales

Memorable landscapes and plenty of good family outings

The richly varied landscape is a special draw in North Wales, from Snowdonia's majestic mountain expanses (excellent for a walking holiday) to the intricate and rather intimate scenery of Clwyd, the luscious Vale of Conwy, and the peace of Anglesey. The much less visited Berwyn Hills give memorable scenic drives. There are good long beaches and attractive traditional family resorts (Llandudno's our pick), yet it's easy to get away from the crowds even in high summer – particularly on the shores of the very welsh Lleyn Peninsula.

Readers thoroughly enjoy the tours of the slate caverns in Blaenau Ffestiniog and the slate museum above Llanberis is interesting too. You can head for even more underground entertainment, in the copper mine in Beddgelert, or the slate caverns in Harlech (there's a children's farm here too). At the Welsh Mountain Zoo in Colwyn Bay you'll be torn between the exotic animals and the tremendous views; other attractions for families who like animals include the friendly farms in Bodorgan and Brynsiencyn. For marine life, there's the nearby Anglesey Sea Zoo, and the Sea Life Aquarium in Rhyl; there are seabird centres at South Stack. The Greenwood Centre in Y Felinheli has more than enough to keep active children occupied.

Something you'll find plenty of in North Wales are magnificent castles and picturesque railways (the Ffestiniog from Porthmadog and the Snowdon Mountain Railway, our Wales Family Attraction, stand out). The castles at Caernarfon, Conwy and Harlech are particularly impressive: Bodelwyddan Castle and Plas Newydd at Llanfairpwllgwyngyll are charming. At beautiful Erddig in Wrexham and unusual Penrhyn near Bangor, you get a glimpse of life downstairs as well as upstairs. Ancient Chirk Castle has lovely gardens. If gardens are something you're interested in, don't miss one of Britain's greatest – glorious Bodnant (other charming grounds at Bodrhyddan Hall in Rhuddlan, and Plas yn Rhiw). The rescued buildings at Holywell are well worth a look.

Cheerful Conwy (plenty for families), pretty Beaumaris, and the fairytale holiday village of Portmeirion make pleasantly relaxed excursions. There is a splendid range of places to stay, and many are in superb countryside.

Where to stay

ABERSOCH SH3226 **Porth Tocyn Hotel** Bwlch Tocyn, Pwllheli, Gwynedd LL53 7BU (01758) 713303 **£102**, plus special breaks; 17 attractive rms, most with sea views. On a headland overlooking Cardigan Bay, a lovely place to stay – with a refreshingly sensible and helpful approach to families (though not solely a family hotel) – and carefully refurbished this year; very friendly hard-working owners and staff, several cosy interconnecting sitting rooms with antiques and fresh flowers, most enjoyable traditional cooking in the restaurant (lots of options such as light lunches, high teas for children as they must be over 7 for dinner in the restaurant, and imaginative Sun lunches), and a happy atmosphere; lots of space in the pretty garden, heated swimming pool in summer, hard tennis court; cl mid-Nov to mid-Mar; disabled access; dogs welcome in bedrooms ☺

BEAUMARIS SH6076 **Olde Bulls Head** Castle St, Beaumaris, Gwynedd LL58 8AP (01248) 810329 **£92***, plus special breaks; 13 rms with antiques and brass bedsteads. Partly 15th-c pub nr castle, with snug alcoves, low beams and open fire in quaint rambling bar, interesting decorations, popular brasserie, very good restaurant food (esp fish), fine wines, and cheery service; entrance to pretty courtyard closed by biggest single-hinged door in Britain; cl 25–26 Dec, 1 Jan; children over 7 in restaurant in evening

BEDDGELERT SH5948 **Sygun Fawr Country House** Beddgelert, Caernarfon,

Gwynedd LL55 4NE (01766) 890258 **£64**, plus special breaks; 9 rms. Spectacular scenery surrounds this secluded 17th-c hotel, with lots of surrounding walks; beams, stripped stone walls, inglenooks, and a restful atmosphere, a varied imaginative menu, antiques and an informal atmosphere in the restaurant, and 20 acres of mountainside and gardens; cl Jan; dogs welcome in bedrooms

BETWS-Y-COED SH7955 **Ty Gwyn** *Betwys-y-Coed, Gwynedd LL24 0SG (01690) 710383* **£56**, plus special breaks; 12 pretty rms, most with own bthrm. Welcoming and well run 17th-c coaching inn with interesting old prints, furniture and bric-a-brac, good food and friendly service; pleasant setting overlooking river and a very good base for the area; children free if sharing parents' room; cl Mon–Weds in Jan; disabled access; dogs welcome in bedrooms

BLAENAU FFESTINIOG SH7045 **Queen's Hotel** *1 High St, Blaenau Ffestiniog, Gwynedd LL41 3ES (01766) 830055* **£60**, plus special breaks; 12 individually decorated rms named after locomotives. By the famous narrow-gauge railway and surrounded by Snowdonia National Park, this most attractively refurbished Victorian hotel has real ales in convivial lounge bar, good all-day food in bistro (converts to more formal evening restaurant with imaginative dishes), and swift friendly service; lots to do nearby; cl 25 Dec

CAERNARFON SH5163 **Seiont Manor** *Llanrug, Caernarfon, Gwynedd LL55 2AQ (01286) 673366* **£140**, plus special breaks; 28 luxurious rms. Fine hotel built from the original farmstead of a Georgian manor house, in 156 acres of mature parkland; open fires and comfortable sofas in lounge, restful atmosphere in library and drawing room, imaginative food in restaurant's four interconnecting areas, and leisure suite with swimming pool, gym, and sauna; dogs welcome in bedrooms

CAPEL GARMON SH8156 **Tan-y-Foel Country House** *Capel Garmon, Llanrwst, Gwynedd LL26 0RE (01690) 710507* **£120***, plus special breaks; 6 comfortable rms. Charming partly 16th-c no smoking stone country house N of village, vibrant modern decor in lounge and breakfast room, warmly friendly relaxing atmosphere, very good robustly flavoured modern food in newly refurbished restaurant using the freshest produce inc local lamb, organic vegetables and home-made bread, interesting wine list; mature gardens and marvellous surrounding countryside; cl Dec, limited opening Jan; children over 7

CAPEL GARMON SH8155 **White Horse** *Capel Garmon, Llanrwst, Gwynedd LL26 0RW (01690) 710271* **£64***, plus midweek off-season breaks; 6 simple rms (those in newer part are quietest). Comfortable, homely, low-beamed inn with friendly atmosphere, winter log fires, very good home-made food in bar and cosy no smoking restaurant (some traditional Welsh meals), marvellous breakfasts, magnificent views, delightful surrounding countryside; cl 2 wks Jan; no children

CONWY SH7577 **Sychnant Pass House** *Sychnant Pass Rd, Conwy, Gwynedd LL32 8BJ (01492) 596868* **£70***; 10 rms. Victorian house in two acres among the foothills of the Snowdonia National Park; big comfortable sitting rooms, log fires, a relaxing, friendly atmosphere, and enjoyable food (the restaurant is open to non-residents, too); cl late Dec–Jan; disabled access; dogs welcome

DOLGELLAU SH7015 **Tyddynmawr Farmhouse** *Islawrdref, Dolgellau, Gwynedd LL40 1TL (01341) 422231* **£50***; 3 spacious rms. 18th-c farmhouse at the foot of Cadair Idris, with wonderful scenery, oak beams, log fires, and Welsh oak furniture, marvellous breakfasts with home-made bread, preserves and muesli, and warmly welcoming owners; cl Dec–Feb; no children

GELLILYDAN SH6939 **Tyddyn Du Farm** *Gellilydan, Blaenau Ffestiniog, Gwynedd LL41 4RB (01766) 590281* **£58***; 4 ground floor, private stable and long barn suites with jacuzzi baths, fridges and microwaves, one with airbath. 400-year-old farmhouse on working farm in the heart of Snowdonia, with beams and exposed stonework, big inglenook fireplaces in residents' lounge, and delicious candlelit evening meals; children can help with the lambs, goats, ducks, sheep and pony; fine walks, inc short one to their own Roman site; partial disabled access; dogs welcome ☺

LLANABER SH5919 **Llwyndu Farmhouse** *Llanaber, Barmouth, Gwynedd LL42 1RR (01341) 280144* **£64***, plus special breaks; 7 charming rms, most with own bthrm, some in a nicely converted 18th-c barn. Most attractive 16th-c farmhouse just above Cardigan Bay, with a warm welcome from friendly owners, big inglenook fireplaces, oak beams, little mullioned windows, relaxing lounge, enjoyable breakfasts, and good imaginative food in candlelit dining room; cl 25–26 Dec; dogs welcome in bedrooms

LLANARMON D C SJ1532 **West Arms** *Llanarmon Dyffryn Ceiriog, Llangollen, Clwyd LL20 7LD (01691) 600665* **£108***, plus special midweek breaks; 15 rms. Charming and civilised 16th-c inn with heavy beams and timbers, log fires in inglenook fireplaces, lounge bar interestingly furnished with antique settles, sofas in the old-fashioned entrance hall, comfortable locals' bar, good food, and friendly quiet atmosphere; the lawn runs down to the River Ceiriog (fishing for residents); disabled access; dogs welcome away from restaurant

LLANDRILLO SJ0337 **Tyddyn Llan** *Llandrillo, Corwen, Clwyd LL21 0ST (01490) 440264 £105*; 10 pretty rms. Restful Georgian house with fresh flowers and antiques in elegantly furnished and comfortable public rooms, charming staff, very good inventive food (using their own herbs) and three acres of lovely gardens; fishing on four miles of River Dee (ghillies available) and fine forest walks (guides available) – can arrange riding and shooting too; cl 2 wks Jan; dogs welcome in bedrooms

LLANDUDNO SH7979 **Bodysgallen Hall** Pentywyn Rd, Llandudno, Gwynedd LL30 1RS (01492) 584466 **£189***, plus special breaks; 35 deeply comfortable rms, 19 in hotel, the rest in cottages in grounds. Fine 17th-c house in its own parkland, with mullioned windows, oak panelling, lovely entrance hall and first-floor drawing room, open fires, very good imaginative food in no smoking dining room, and 18th-c walled rose garden and knot garden; tennis, croquet, swimming pool, sauna, solarium, gym and beauty salon; children over 8; disabled access

LLANDUDNO SH7882 **St Tudno** 15 North Parade, Llandudno, Gwynedd LL30 2LP (01492) 874411 **£156**, plus special breaks; 18 individually decorated rms, some with sea view. Opposite the pier, this well run, smart Victorian seaside hotel has genuinely helpful and friendly staff, Victorian-style decor in restful no smoking sitting room, a convivial bar lounge, relaxed coffee lounge for light lunches, and attractive no smoking garden-style restaurant with imaginative modern food; good wine list; small indoor pool

LLANERCHYMEDD SH4284 **Llwydiarth Fawr Farm** Llanerchymedd, Gwynedd LL71 8DF (01248) 470321 **£50***; 4 rms in main house, 2 cottage suites in grounds. Handsome Georgian farmhouse on 850-acre cattle and sheep farm, with a particularly warm homely atmosphere and welcome, comfortable lounge with antiques, log fire, books and lovely views, and very good home-made food using farm and other fresh local produce; terrace, lake for private fishing, nature walks, bird-watching; no smoking; cl Christmas

LLANFAIR D C SJ1355 **Eyarth Station** Llanfair Dyffryn Clwyd, Ruthin, Clwyd LL15 2EE (01824) 703643 **£48***, plus special breaks; 6 pretty rms. Carefully converted old railway station with quiet gardens and wonderful views, a friendly relaxed atmosphere, log fire in airy and comfortable beamed lounge, good breakfasts and enjoyable suppers in dining room (more lovely views), sun terrace and heated swimming pool, and lots of walks; cl Jan–Feb; disabled access; dogs welcome in bedrooms

LLANFIHANGEL-YNG-NGWYNFA SJ0815 **Cyfie Farm** Llanfihangel, Llanfyllin, Powys SY22 5JE (01691) 648451 **£60***, plus special breaks; 4 rms inc 3 suites with lovely views. Carefully restored 17th-c Welsh stone longhouse on 178 acres; timbered and beamed rms with fine family furniture, log fire in residents' lounge, hearty farmhouse cooking in attractive dining conservatory, and relaxed friendly atmosphere; cl Jan and Feb; children over 5

LLANSANFFRAID GLAN CONWY SH8075 **Old Rectory Country House** Llanrwst Rd, Glan Conwy, Colwyn Bay, Clwyd LL28 5LF (01492) 580611 **£199** inc dinner, plus special breaks; 6 deeply comfortable rms. Georgian house in pleasant gardens with fine views over Conwy estuary, Conwy Castle and Snowdonia; delightful public rms with flowers, antiques and family photos, delicious food of the highest restaurant standards, and marvellous wines; good breakfasts, warmly friendly staff; cl Dec–Jan, open wknd only Nov and Feb; children under 9 months or over 5; dogs in coach house only

LLANWDDYN SJ0219 **Lake Vyrnwy Hotel** Llanwddyn, Oswestry, Powys SY10 0LY (01691) 870692 **£115**; 35 rms, the ones overlooking the lake are the nicest – and quietest. Large impressive Tudor-style mansion overlooking lake from hillside in 40 square miles of forestry, with lots of sporting activities (esp fishing), log fires and sporting prints in the comfortable and elegant public rooms, relaxed atmosphere, bar, and good food using home-made preserves, chutneys, mustards and vinegars and produce from own kitchen garden; enjoyable teas too; dogs welcome in bedrooms

NANTGWYNANT SH6555 **Pen-y-Gwryd** Nantgwynant, Caernarfon, Gwynedd LL55 4NT (01286) 870211 **£62***, plus special breaks; 16 rms, some with own bthrm. In two acres, this cheery hotel is by the Llanberis Pass in Snowdonia National Park; warm log fire in simply furnished panelled residents' lounge, rugged slate-floored bar that doubles as mountain rescue post; lots of climbing mementoes and equipment, friendly, chatty games room (lots of walkers, climbers and fishermen), hearty enjoyable food, big breakfasts, and packed lunches; sauna in the trees and outdoor swimming pool, table tennis; private chapel; cl Nov–New Year and midweek Jan–Feb; disabled access; dogs welcome away from dining room

PORTMEIRION SH5837 **Portmeirion Hotel** *Penrhyndeudraeth, Porthmadog, Gwynedd LL48 6ER* (01766) 770000 **£147** in village (26 rms), **£172** in hotel (14 rms), and **£192** in Deudraeth Castle (11 rms), plus winter breaks. On the edge of an estuary and surrounded by beaches and woods (and traffic-free), this is a remarkable place; the hotel down by the water is quite luxurious – elegant rooms with marble, gilt, and rich colourful fabrics – while behind and in the steeply landscaped grounds above it is a well dispersed very colourful Italianate village, luscious to look at, inc all sorts of individualistic cottage bedrooms tucked into the hillside; very romantic when the day visitors have left, and lots to do; disabled access. See **To see and do**, below ☺

SARON SH4557 **Pengwern** *Saron, Caernarfon, Gwynedd LL54 5UH* (01286) 831500 **£56***, plus special breaks; 3 rms. In 130 acres running down to Foryd Bay, this spacious no smoking farmhouse has marvellous views of Snowdonia, and delicious food using local fresh produce; cl Dec–Jan

TAL-Y-BONT SH7669 **Lodge** *Tal-y-Bont, Conwy, Gwynedd LL32 8YX* (01492) 660766 **£72**, plus special breaks; 14 rms. Friendly little modern hotel in over three acres on the edge of Snowdonia, with open fire, books and magazines in comfortable lounge, generous helpings of popular food using lots of home-grown produce in no smoking restaurant, and good service; lots of walks; well behaved pets welcome; good disabled access; dogs welcome in bedrooms

TALSARNAU SH6135 **Maes-y-Neuadd** *Talsarnau, Gwynedd LL47 6YA* (01766) 780200 **£143*** inc 4-course dinner, plus special breaks; 16 luxurious rms. Looking out across Snowdonia, this attractive extended 14th-c mansion stands in eight acres of landscaped hillside; flowers, plants, antiques and open fires, peaceful atmosphere, very good food (herbs and vegetables from their own garden), friendly cats, and charming staff; disabled access; dogs welcome in bedrooms ☺

TREMEIRCHION SJ0771 **Bach-y-Graig** *Tremeirchion, St Asaph, Clwyd LL17 0UH* (01745) 730627 **£52***; 3 rms, 2 with brass beds. Wales's first brick-built house with a date-stone of 1567, in 200-acre dairy farm at the foot of the Clwydian Hills; inglenook fireplace in big lounge, home cooking using home-produced beef and lamb and own free-range eggs, and warm welcome; woodland trail, fishing; cl Christmas and New Year

To see and do

Wales Family Attraction of the Year

LLANBERIS SH5859 **Snowdon Mountain Railway** (A4086) A masterpiece of Victorian engineering, this is without a doubt one of the most spectacular railway journeys you could hope to go on – and certainly the most painless way to reach the top of Snowdon, the highest mountain in England and Wales. It's Britain's only public rack-and-pinion railway, its vintage Swiss steam or modern diesel locomotives following the route of an old pony track, and on a good day taking passengers on a 4½ mile journey that climbs to almost the very summit. That's no mean feat: barely any of the track is on flat ground, and at times the trains are hauled up 18% gradients. The journey lasts an hour, and the views along the way can be magnificent, in clear weather stretching over to the Isle of Man and the Wicklow mountains in Ireland. But the weather can be unpredictable, and chances are you'll find the summit swathed in clouds, if indeed you get that far: trains sometimes have to terminate at an earlier stop because of ice or strong winds, so it's worth ringing ahead to check conditions on the day – also, bear in mind that even then they can change quickly. And wrap up well – it's chilly up at the summit. Don't let that put you off: this really is a great adventure, and whatever the conditions at the top it feels as if you've entered wild, unexplored territory, spoiled only by the summit's inelegant café, one of the less successful works of Portmeirion architect Sir Clough Williams-Ellis (and perhaps a candidate for a Lottery-funded replacement). Make sure you bring your postcards: mail collected from the postbox up at the top is franked with a special stamp. There's no fixed timetable: trains generally leave when there are between 15 and two dozen people on board, so if there aren't many people about you may have to wait (and if there are you may have to queue). The service is more frequent in the summer holidays (usually every half hour) but they can sell out on busy days, so they recommend booking in advance, or at least arriving early. Your return journey is generally supposed to be on the same train you went up on, with a half-hour turn-around; they can't guarantee there will be room for you to go down on a different train. You can buy single tickets, though these are intended for those proudly fit people who choose to walk one way. The station at Llanberis has a small exhibition. Special events include their Teddy Bears picnic, when up to two children travel free provided they've brought their teddy. Café and shop at both ends, disabled access (helpful to ring in advance); trains run at least part of the way from mid-Mar to the start of Nov, but usually go to the summit only from May – as we say, best to ring first to be sure; (0870) 4580033; a return trip is £18 for adults, £13 for children under 15. Early birds can get a £3 discount by travelling on the day's first trains, at 9 and 9.30.

ABERFFRAW SH3270
Barclodiad y Gawres Some 5,000 years old, this 6-metre (20-ft) underground passage tomb at the top of the cliff has the finest British example of tomb carvings, which appear by the entrance and in the side chambers, shown up by a good torch; it's sealed, but you can ask for a key at the Countryside Centre, Aberffraw; (01407) 840845. Hard to believe now, but Aberffraw was once the capital of the North Wales kingdom of Gwynedd.

There are some lovely unspoilt coves and beaches nearby; the beach up the road at Rhosneigr is particularly good (and clean).
BANGOR SH5872
Quiet university town with a pedestrianised High St and a restored pier and yacht harbour that adds a lively touch in summer. The Bangor Museum and Art Gallery has exhibitions on local history and archaeology, and collections of Welsh furniture (open Tues–Sat (01248) 353368; free). The

Union and Nelson near the harbour have decent food. Well signposted from the A55 just before Bangor are the Aber Falls at Abergwyngregyn, the highest falls in Wales at just under 100 feet (30m).

Bangor Cathedral Founded 70 years before the one at Canterbury; the present building is restored 13th- to 15th-c, and has an interesting 16th-c carving of Christ bound and seated on a rock, as well as some fine Victorian stained glass; also, unique 14th-c Flemish statues. It is currently undergoing further restoration. Disabled access; cl Sat pm, wk after Easter; free, £2 suggested donation.

Bangor Museum and Art Gallery (Ffordd Gwynedd) Local history and archaeology, Welsh furniture, changing art exhibitions; shop; cl ams, Mon, Sun, 10 days at Christmas, and bank hols; (01248) 353368; free.

Penrhyn Castle (1m E) Splendid 19th-c neo-Norman fantasy built by a slate magnate: the interior is in suitably grand style, with quite remarkable – and often bizarre – panelling, decoration and furnishings. The 14 rooms that made up the kitchens and service rooms have recently been restored to look as they would have when the Prince of Wales stayed here in 1894. The cathedral-like great hall is heated by the Roman method of hot air under the floor, and one of the beds weighs over a ton – carved from slate. An unexpectedly rich collection of paintings includes works by Rembrandt and Canaletto. In the stableyard is a museum of unique early locomotives, and there's a walled garden and adventure playground. Snacks, shop, disabled access; cl am (exc July and Aug), all day Tues, and Nov–Mar; (01248) 353084; £6, garden only £4; NT.

BARMOUTH SH6115
Traditional seaside resort with a huge clean beach, a landtrain that runs the length of the promenade, and donkey rides; the Lifeboat Institute on the quay has some nice old memorabilia and is free. A 7m walk, good for bird-watchers, crosses the Barmouth bridge to Morfa Mawddach station, then follows the former railway track all the way along the river bank to Penmaenpool (see below); you can return across the toll bridge to Tai Cynhaiaf for the bus to Barmouth.

BEAUMARIS SH6076
Anglesey's most historic and attractive town faces across to the mainland. Apart from the obvious castle there are several characterful buildings, as well as a yachty waterfront, though the shingle beach is not suitable for swimming. The 15th-c church of St Mary and St Nicholas – easy to spot by its robust square tower – houses the stone coffin of Joan, daughter of King John and wife of the Welsh leader Llewelyn the Great. The Olde Bulls Head (dating partly from 1472) and Sailors Return are good for lunch.

Beaumaris Castle One of the most impressive and complete of those built by Edward I, despite the struggle over it with Owain Glyndwr in the early 1400s, and the plundering of its lead, timber and stone in later ages. Beautifully symmetrical, it took from 1295 to 1312 to build (though the money ran out before it could be finished). Shop, good disabled access; cl 24–26 Dec, 1 Jan; (01248) 810361; £3; Cadw.

Beaumaris Gaol Paints a vivid picture of the harshness of the 19th-c prison system, particularly in the dark, poky cells. Shop, very limited disabled access; cl end Sept–Easter exc by appointment, (01248) 810921; £2.75, £3.50 joint ticket with Courthouse.

Courthouse Remarkable survival, dating back to 1614 and still occasionally in use. You can stand in the dock and imagine you're just about to be sentenced. Shop, very limited disabled access; open as gaol; (01248) 811691; £1.50.

BEDDGELERT SH5948
Pleasant village base for the Snowdon area, with walks along the old railway track through the Aberglaslyn Pass, and W up to the summit of Moel Hebog (one of the easier peaks hereabouts); or easier still, follow Cwm Bychan NE up to a lowish pass, then down to Sygun Copper Mine for the quiet lane back. The comfortable Tanronen does good value food, and there's good Snowdonia walking around the Aberglaslyn Pass (A498 S).

Sygun Copper Mine (A498 NE)

Interesting tours through often spectacular underground mine workings, with magnificent stalactites and stalagmites, and traces of gold and silver in the copper ore veins. You're greeted by a wonderful view of the mountains when you come up at the end. Snacks, shop; cl Nov–Jan; (01766) 510101; £5.

BENLLECH SH5282

Beautiful clean beach, good even for toddlers – and at low tide you can walk round into Red Wharf Bay; several beach-side cafés and so forth.

BETWS-Y-COED SH7956

Touristy 19th-c inland resort village In a beautiful wooded gorge at the head of the Vale of Conwy. Surrounded by picturesque woodland walks, the village has over a century of catering to visitors behind it, though at peak times the crowds can dilute its appeal. One of the best strolls is along the old riverside railway track by the Afon Llugwy W: the raging Swallow Falls and Fairy Glen just W of the village itself are deservedly regarded as two of the area's finest beauty spots. Longer walks well worth taking in are SW through the woods to Llyn Elsi Reservoir, where mountain views open up and you can return via the Miners Bridge; and further afield NW in the mini lake district around Llyn Crafnant. W of the village, the bizarre Ugly House looks like a series of boulders thrown haphazardly together. The cottagey Ty Gwyn has good food, and the Pont y Pair and Waterloo Hotel are useful too.

BLAENAU FFESTINIOG SH6946

This straggle of village is dwarfed by the vast spoil slopes from the slate mines all around it – once the slate capital of Wales, now with the passing of the industry like a living museum.

Ffestiniog Pumped Storage Power Station (Tanygrisiau, off A496 S) Guided tours of the first hydro-electric pumped storage scheme in the country, with dramatic views towards the peaks of Snowdonia. Meals, snacks, shop; cl Sat, and end Oct–Easter; (01766) 830310; £2.75. From the information centre there's an attractive (if slightly hairy) drive into the mountains to Stwlan Dam, which also gives super views.

Llechwedd Slate Caverns (A470) The same company has been mining and quarrying slate here for over 150 years, and their well organised tours of the huge caverns bring the history of the site vividly to life; it's well worth doing both the underground rides. In Deep Mine, Britain's steepest passenger railway takes you 137 metres (450 ft) below the summit of the mountain. Next is a hard-hat walk through ten stunning subterranean chambers, each with a sound and light show illustrating the world of a Victorian miner. You need to be relatively agile (there are 61 steps going down, but 10 more on the way up if we counted right), and bring warm clothing even in summer. The highlight is an eerie underground lake, nicely lit to create atmospheric shadows on the water and the steep, craggy walls. The other tour (the Miners Tramway) explains more about the mining process: battery-powered trains take you around the Victorian workings, through splendid man-made caverns, some of which have tableaux or demonstrations of ancient mining skills. You get off at various points along the way, and the guides give useful talks. Outside you can explore the old buildings of Llechwedd village; the last residents left in the 1970s, but there's a Victorian pub (wholesome inexpensive food), and several shops stocking Victorian-themed goods which you can buy using period money; you can exchange your coins at the former bank, now a museum. Meals, snacks, shops, some disabled access with prior warning; cl 25–26 Dec, 1 Jan; (01766) 830306; both tours costs £11.50, just one is £7.50. The surface attractions are free.

BODELWYDDAN SH9974

Bodelwyddan Castle (off A55) The walled gardens surrounding this showy white limestone castle include a glorious mix of woodland walks, flowering plants, aviary and water features. The house (older than its 19th-c exterior suggests) has been very well restored as a Victorian mansion, with furniture from the Victoria & Albert, and paintings and photographs from the National Portrait Gallery. Plenty for children, inc a woodland adventure playground, and entertaining exhibitions of puzzles, games and optical illusions which they plan to extend next year. Snacks, shop, disabled access; cl Fri (exc July and Aug), plus Mon Oct–Apr, 25–26 Dec, 1 Jan; (01745) 584060; £4, grounds only £1.50. The Kinmel Arms at St George has good interesting food.

Bodelwydden Marble Church 19th-c, built entirely of locally quarried stone: an unusual and quite splendid sight.

BODORGAN SH4272

Henblas Park ⊞ (Junction 6, A55 – follow the clear signs) Good range of family activities, from sheep-shearing, falconry and farm animals, through dog and duck displays and indoor adventure playground, bouncy castle and ball pool to tractor rides and a neolithic burial chamber. Meals, snacks, shop, disabled access; cl Sat (exc bank hols) and Oct–Easter; (01407) 840440; £4.

BRYNSIENCYN SH4765

This Anglesey farming village stands close to some impressive prehistoric monuments. On the back road NW to Llangaffo are Caer Leb, with ramparts of a 3rd-century settlement, and Bodowyr chambered tomb. To the W by the A4080 there are more historic humps at Castell-Bryn Gwyn, dating from Neolithic times.

Anglesey Sea Zoo ⊞ (A4080 just S) Excellent collection of local marine life, in tanks specially designed to provide as unrestricted and natural an environment as possible. Also walk-through shipwreck, touch pools (school hols only), adventure playground; they sell home-made fudge and ice-cream, and their own good sea salt. Meals, snacks, shop, disabled access; cl beginning of Nov–spring; (01248) 430411; £5.95.

Foel Farm Park Friendly working farm with daily calf feeding, tractor rides, and home-made chocolate (on wkdys you can often see them making it). Restaurant, tearoom and ice-cream parlour, shop, disabled access; cl late Oct–Mar; (01248) 430646; *£4.50.

Pick-your-own (Gwydryn Hir farm) Pick fruit and veg (open Jun–Sept) while taking in the view of Snowdonia; also farm shop and butchery (open all year)

specialising in home-grown produce and home-made soups, jams and cakes; (01248) 430322.

Prehistoric burial chamber A couple of miles NW by the back road towards Llangaffo is what looks like a Stone Age hut, but is actually a burial chamber from which the covering earth has been eroded over the millennia.

CAERNARFON SH4763

Surviving lengths of its 13th-c town walls still crowd in its quaintly narrow streets (quaint, that is, unless you're trying to drive through them). The town harbour is busy with yachts in summer. The Hole in the Wall and Palace Vaults have good value food.

Air World ⊞ (Caernarfon Airparc, off A499 nr Llandwrog) They encourage you to climb aboard some of the helicopters and aeroplanes here; also a great many model aeroplanes, and pleasure flights. Meals, snacks, shop, disabled access; cl end Nov–beginning of Mar (exc by appointment); (01286) 830800; *£4.50.

Caernarfon Castle With its nine polygonal towers and walls of colour-banded stone, this was planned by Edward I as a Royal residence and seat of government for North Wales. Edward's son was born here and presented to the people, setting the precedent for future Princes of Wales. Exhibitions include the regimental museum of the Royal Welch Fusiliers, and an impressive audio-visual display. Shop; usually cl 24–26 Dec, 1 Jan; (01286) 677617; £4.50. In the square outside, around the statue of former PM David Lloyd George, there's a busy Sat market.

Inigo Jones Slateworks You can go on an audio tour of this working slate works (established in 1861 primarily to make school writing slates). A showroom displays slate and stone products, with exhibitions on calligraphy and the development of the slate industry, and there's a quiz for children. Snacks, shop, disabled access; cl Sun Oct–Easter, and 21 Dec–7 Jan; (01286) 830242; £3.80.

Segontium Roman Fort & Museum (A4085) Roman fort dating from AD78; excavations have exposed various rebuildings during its three centuries of importance, and a museum shows some of the finds. There's a tradition that Constantine the Great was born here (and the walls of the nearby castle used to be thought to be modelled partly on the walls of Constantinople). Shop; cl Sun am, 24–26 Dec, 1 Jan; (01286) 675625; free; Cadw.

CAPEL CURIG SH7258
Centrally located amid the Snowdonia highlands, but a bit dominated by the two main roads that cut through the village. This makes a useful starting point for walks up Moel Siabod and to the attractively landscaped reservoirs to the N. Cobdens has reasonably priced food, and Bryn Tyrch (A5 W) is strong on vegetarian and vegan dishes.

CHIRK SJ2938
The quiet little town, important as a staging post on the former road to Ireland, has something of a bypassed-by-time feel now; the Hand and (B5070 S) Bridge are quite useful for lunch.

Chirk Castle (just W) One of the lucky few of Edward I's castles to survive as an occupied home rather than fall to ruin. The exterior is still much as it was when built 700 years ago, with its high walls and drum towers, though there have been lots of alterations inside: most of the medieval-looking decorations were by Pugin in the 19th c, the elegant stone staircase dates from the 18th c, and the Long Gallery is 17th-c. The wrought-iron entrance gates are particularly fine, and the formal gardens are magnificent. Meals, snacks, shop, some disabled access; cl am, Mon, Tues, and Dec, Jan, Feb; (01691) 777701; £5.60; NT. It's right by a well preserved stretch of the earthworks of Offa's Dyke.

COED Y BRENIN SH7226
Forest Park & Visitor Centre
(Maesgwn) Excellent introduction to what translates as King's Forest, so called to commemorate the Silver Jubilee of King George V. Some beautifully varied sights and landscapes, as well as wildlife observation hides, and over 50 miles of walks. Snacks, shop, disabled access; cl wkdys Nov–Mar; (01341) 440666; free, £3 all-day parking.

COLWYN BAY SH8480

Made popular in the 19th c by wealthy Lancashire industrialists who retired here (though now rather run down in parts), this busy summer seaside resort has all that's wanted for a family beach holiday, though it's rather eclipsed by Llandudno just along the coast. The quieter end at Rhos-on-Sea has a puppet theatre; mainly open just school hols; (01492) 548166 for programme. The Rhos Fynach opposite the small harbour at this end, once Capt Morgan's home, does decent food, and the newly remodelled Pen-y-Bryn (Wentworth Ave) is now a good stylish place for a meal.

Welsh Mountain Zoo 🔞 (Flagstaff Gardens, Old Highway) Lots of exotic animals in natural-looking habitats, but what really distinguishes this 37-acre zoo from any other is the quite magnificent view over the bay. Also penguin parade and falconry displays. Meals, snacks, shop, mostly disabled access; cl 25 Dec; (01492) 532938; £6.85. In summer a free minibus service runs here from the town station.

CONWY SH7877
Cheerful old town dominated by its castle, the key part of the town's elaborate defensive system – 21 (originally 22) towers linked by walls some 9 metres (30 ft) high, still the most complete town wall in Wales, with craggy old town gates. You can walk along some parts, looking down over the narrow little streets that still follow their medieval layout. You can go on summer **boat trips**, and redevelopment of the aquarium by the quay should be complete this year. The Castle Hotel is a civilised place for lunch.

Aberconwy House 🔞 (Castle St) The only house in the town which survives from the 14th c, once the home of a prosperous merchant. Rooms are furnished in period style, and there's an interesting audio-visual show. Shop; cl Tues, and Nov–late Mar; (01492) 592246; £2; NT.

Butterfly Jungle 🔞 (Bodlondeb Park) Tropical butterflies and exotic plants and birds in a re-created jungle environment with rainforest surround-sound; picnic area. Shop, snacks, disabled access; cl Nov–Mar; (01492)

593149; £3.50.

Conwy Castle One of the best-known in Wales, and one of the most important examples of military architecture in the whole of Europe. Built for Edward I in 1283–9, it's very well preserved, still looking exactly as a medieval fortress should – despite the ravages of the Civil War and beyond. There's an exhibition on Edward and the other castles he built. The top of the turrets offer fine panoramic views; the most dramatic views of the castle itself are from the other side of the estuary. Shop; cl 24–26 Dec, 1 Jan; (01492) 592358; £3.50; Cadw.

Conwy Mountain Just W of the town, pleasant walking; not a real mountain but with views of Anglesey worthy of mountain status.

Conwy Suspension Bridge ⌷ Built by Telford in 1826, and restored by the National Trust, who have also opened up its toll house, with the rooms furnished as they would have been in the 19th c; shop; disabled access; cl Tues (exc July and Aug) and all Nov–Mar; (01492) 573282; £1. The other, tubular bridge was built by Stephenson in 1848.

Plas Mawr (High St) Elaborate Tudor mansion, carefully restored, its splendid plasterwork, flagstone floors and huge fireplaces all looking as good as new. Small shop; disabled access ground floor only; cl Mon (exc bank hols) and 27 Oct–27 Mar; (01492) 580167; £4.50 (no extra charge for audio tour).

Smallest House ⌷ Nicely placed on the quayside is Britain's smallest house, barely 2 metres (6 ft) wide and its front wall only 3 metres (10 ft) high. Squeezed into the two rooms (one up, one down) are all the comforts of home, or at least most – there's no lavatory. Shop, limited disabled access; cl Nov–Mar, Good Fri; (01492) 593484; 50p.

Teapot World ⌷ (Castle St) Splendidly zany collection of unusually shaped teapots from the last 300 years – everything from wigwams to cauliflowers. Shop; cl Nov–Easter; (01492) 593429; *£1.50.

CORWEN SJ0750

Derwen church (off A494 a few miles N) Interesting medieval building with an elaborately carved rood screen and loft, some old wall paintings, and an excellent Celtic cross in the churchyard.

Llangar old parish church (B4401 S) Built in the 13th c, with remarkable paintings of the seven deadly sins; it's visited from Rug chapel (and covered by the same ticket). The Crown in Corwen has good value food.

Rug chapel (1m N) 17th-c, not inspiring from the outside, but inside is a riot of colour, almost every available piece of woodwork covered with cheery patterns and paintwork. Cl Mon (exc bank hol wknds), Tues, Oct–Mar; nearby Llangar church is open 2–3pm on the same days; (029) 2082 6185; £2; Cadw.

CRICCIETH SH4937

Restrained resort with a good sheltered sandy beach. The Poachers Restaurant (High St) is good, and the Prince of Wales (The Square) is a reliable food pub.

Criccieth Castle 13th-c remains on a rocky, mounded peninsula above the little town, giving superb views over Tremadog Bay. Parts of the inner walls are well preserved, and there's an impressive gatehouse. A cartoon video looks at Gerald of Wales and other Welsh princes. Shop, disabled access; visitor centre cl late Sept–Mar; (01766) 522227; visitor centre £2.50; castle free; Cadw.

DENBIGH SJ0566

Built as a defensive town in the 13th c, with large chunks of the town wall still surviving, as well as (unusual for Wales) some fine arcaded buildings. A museum on the High St has interesting finds from nearby Bronze Age sites, and the riverside Brookhouse Mill is popular for lunch, as is the Lion out at Gwytherin (B5384 W).

Denbigh castle Largely ruined, but still impressive, with a trio of towers and superb archway in the 13th-c gatehouse; the figure on the summit is thought to represent Edward I. Among other remains are what's left of an ambitious church built by the Earl of Leicester, favourite of Elizabeth I. Museum and exhibition in castle and exhibition in Burgess Gate entrance. Snacks, shop, limited disabled access; cl

Oct–Apr; castle open all year; (01745) 813385; £2; Cadw.

DINAS MAWDDWY SH8513

Meirion Mill Nestling among riverside woods below the mountains on the S fringes of Snowdonia is this charmingly set woollen mill, in the grounds of the old Mawddwy railway station. Meals, snacks, shop (a huge range of country and outdoor clothing, sheepskin and woollen goods, crafts, and gifts), children's playground, disabled access; cl 25–26 Dec; (01650) 531311; free. Nearby is a picturesque packhorse bridge, and there's a scenic walk to so-called King Arthur's Stone at Camlan; the waterside Dolbrodmaeth has decent food.

DOLWYDDELAN SH7352

Dolwyddelan Castle Picturesquely set on a lightly wooded crag, these old ruins were reputedly the birthplace of Llewelyn the Great. You can still see a restored keep from around 1200, and a 13th-c curtain wall. Shop; cl 24–26 Dec, 1 Jan; (01690) 750366; £2; Cadw. The village church is attractive, and the Gwydr has cheap food.

FLINT SJ2473

Flint Castle Another fine 13th-c castle, the first built by Edward I to subdue the natives. Parts of the walls and corner towers survive, but the most impressive bit is the great tower or donjon, which is separated by the moat. Overlooking the River Dee, it has a role in Shakespeare's *Richard II*; usually open daily; free. The Britannia in nearby Halkyn is good for lunch, with fine Dee estuary views from its conservatory.

GRESFORD SJ3454

Gresford church Has some wonderful medieval stained glass, and its bells are often described as one of the Seven Wonders of Wales. A yew tree outside is reputed to be 1,400 years old. The Pant-yr-Ochain has very good food.

HARLECH SH5831

Harlech Castle Splendid-looking structure built in 1283–1289 by Edward I, its rugged glory the massive twin-towered gatehouse. It was starved into capitulation by Owain Glyndwr in 1404, and later dogged defence inspired the song 'Men of Harlech'. Before the sea retreated there was a sheer drop into

the water on one side, but it now stands above dunes, with wonderful views of Snowdonia from the battlements. Shop; cl 24–26 Dec, 1 Jan; (01766) 780552; £3; Cadw. The village around it has all that the crowds of summer visitors to the castle and the good beach could want. The riverside Victoria at Llanbedr does decent food. Some of the most sensationally remote scenery in Wales stretches inland E of Harlech, where a few tortuous roads wind past hill farms towards the splendidly isolated lake of **Llyn Cwm Bychan** SH6431. From the car park at the end of the road you can walk along a few miles of the **Roman Steps** (not Roman at all, but an old packhorse route paved with large stone slabs) that heads through some of the most challenging rock-strewn wilderness in the country (the Rhinogs); the summits need advanced scrambling skills, but the secluded little mountain lake of Llyn Du makes a nicely manageable objective instead (turn right off the main path at the top of the path).

Slate Caverns and Children's Farm Park Two separate attractions – self-guided tours of slate caverns, and a farm where they encourage children to help handle and feed the goats, lambs, pigs etc. They also have birds of prey, and a nature walk has spectacular views. Café, craft shop, disabled access to farm only; farm cl mid-Sept to early May £3, caverns cl mid-Oct to Easter, £3.40; (01766) 780247.

HOLYHEAD SH2482

Long-established fishing town on little Holy Island, now an unassuming resort with some burial chambers and ancient sites not far away. The Victorian breakwater protecting the harbour is Britain's longest. Across the old Four Mile Bridge at Valley the Bull has good value food.

HOLYHEAD MOUNTAIN SH2183

A dramatic hill giving good walks at the W tip of Holy Island, with an Iron Age fort and Roman watchtower site.

HOLYWELL SJ1977

Greenfield Valley Heritage Centre (A548) Farm museum, and an increasing number of buildings rescued from their original sites and rebuilt here. These include a 17th-c cottage, Victorian farmhouse, and a school, all furnished in period style. Also the remains of a Cistercian abbey and a good few relics of the Industrial Revolution. Snacks, shop, disabled access; cl 1 Nov–31 Mar; (01352) 714172; *£2.65. The partly 15th-c Llyn y Mawn at Brynford has good generous food (all day Sat).

St Winefride's Well Source of the holy spring that turned the spot into a centre of pilgrimage – it's supposed to have healing powers. There are pleasant walks from here through the valley to the coast.

LAKE VYRNWY SJ0119

This massive reservoir, created at the end of the 19th c, supplies Liverpool with 57 million gallons of water a day. It's an attractive spot, with a visitor centre and exciting 3D exhibition, a network of waymarked paths, cycle hire, bird hides and a sculpture trail. Shop (wknds only Nov–Mar), limited disabled access; (0121) 722 4563; free. The friendly Tavern Inn behind the hotel does enjoyable light meals, and has great views from its terrace.

LAVAN SANDS SH6473

(nr Aber) Much of the North Wales coast is built on or ribboned by roads, but this is a notable exception: walks by a vast stretch of tidal sands, with flocks of wading birds.

LLANALLGO SH4986

Din Llugwy ancient village Remains of a 4th-c village: a pentagonal stone wall surrounds two circular and seven rectangular buildings; free. The Parciau Arms at Marianglas is fairly handy for a meal.

LLANBEDR SH5526

Shell Island (Llanbedr) A causeway leads over the sands to this near-island, appropriately named – after winter storms and high tides it's excellent for beachcombing; there are also wild birds and flowers, and you can fish here. Snacks, shop; (01341) 241453; £5 per car.

LLANBERIS SH5760

Plenty of B&Bs, small hotels, shops and cafés for the summer visitors here for Snowdonia, and there are quite a few craft shops dotted along the High St. It's a popular area for film-makers, and parts of *Tomb Raider 2* have recently been filmed near here. Sherpa Buses run a good service up the mountain

(you can get it from several of the North Wales resorts). 3m out of town, on the A4809, is a modern working pottery; cl 2 weeks at Christmas; (01286) 871931; free.

Dolbadarn Castle (A4086, at the foot of Llanberis Pass) Built in the early 13th c by Llywelyn the Great – it has a fine round towered keep still standing up to 15 metres (50 ft); free; Cadw.

Electric Mountain 🖼 Various changing exhibitions, then a coach whisks you off for a tour of the spectacular Dinorwig pumped storage station (one of Europe's biggest), deep in the mountain. Best to book, (01286) 870636. Snacks, shop, disabled access (with notice); cl Nov–Easter exc some occasions in winter – phone; *£5.50.

Llanberis Lake Railway 🖼 (Padarn Country Park, off A4086) Steam locomotives dating from 1889 to 1948 chug 4m along the shore of Llyn Padarn: ideal for those who want the steam-train experience but don't want to spend too long getting it. Snacks, shop, disabled access; cl Sat (exc July–Aug), and all Nov–Feb; (01286) 870549 for timetable; £4.50. The station is in a super lakeside park with walks through ancient woodland.

Pen-y-Gwryd Hotel (Nant Gwynant, A4086/A498 SE) A great spot for Snowdon walks, and a base for generations of mountaineers; also a good place for lunch.

Snowdon Mountain Railway See *separate family panel on p.862.*

Welsh Slate Museum (Padarn Country Park, off A4086) This intriguing place, stepped steeply into the mountain, and once one of the biggest quarries in the country, is home to a working incline, and a row of reconstructed quarrymen's houses decked out in period furniture from the 1860s, 1900s and 1969. An exhibition on the story of slate is introduced by a 3D show and demonstrated by craftsmen; also children's activity centre. The quarry workshop has been preserved largely in its original state – complete with working craftsmen and machinery. Its water wheel is one of the largest in the world. Snacks, shop with locally designed slate items, disabled access; cl Sat during Nov–Easter;

(01286) 870630; free.

LLANDDANIEL SH5069

Bryn Celli Ddu (Llandaniel Fab)
Particularly well preserved Bronze Age
burial chamber, with stone slabs at the
entrance leading inside the mound to a
chamber with upright stones, inc a
replica of an incised stone; locked, but
key at nearby farmhouse; free. Take a
torch.

LLANDDWYN ISLAND SH3863
Really a peninsula, cut off only by the
highest of tides, grazed by soay sheep,
and with a tiny, remote settlement
consisting of a ruined church, some
sailors' cottages, a cannon and a
lighthouse. Reached by a satisfying walk
along a huge beach fringed by dunes and
the pine forest of Newborough Warren
from a car park in the forest (take
Llanddwyn road from Newborough
village).

LLANDUDNO SH7882
The main holiday town in the area, and
though it does have a long well
sheltered curve of good pebbly beach, a
prom and a range of resort
entertainments, it doesn't feel at all
brash. There are charming little shops
and boutiques, a well restored pier
(from which you can fish), and cable-
cars as well as the famously steep quaint
tramway up the massive Great Orme
headland which protects the main
beach – there's a quieter but more
exposed beach on the far side. You can
walk right up, too; a café on the way has
views to justify stopping. At the top
there's a 12th-c church, a visitor centre
with local geology, and more good
walking. On the way down a dry ski
slope also has a toboggan run. The
Kings Head by the tram station is a nice
stop, and the Queens Head at
Glanwydden, off the Colwyn Bay road,
does very good food.

Alice in Wonderland Centre 🏛
(Trinity Sq) Jolly exhibition devoted to
Alice in Wonderland, with life-size
animated tableaux; the real Alice
holidayed in Llandudno as a child. Shop,
disabled access; cl winter Suns, 1st 2
wks Nov, 25–26 Dec, 1 Jan; (01492)
860082; *£2.95.

Conwy Valley Railway Railtrack line
from Llandudno to Blaenau Ffestiniog,
through magnificent scenery, with

several useful stops en route.

Great Orme Mines 4,000-year-old
copper mine near the summit of Great
Orme, the biggest such site so far
discovered. It's also the only prehistoric
metal mine open to the public, with
displays of finds, and underground
walks through the cavernous workings
themselves; weather permitting, you
can sometimes see digs in progress.
Teas, shop; cl end Oct–1 Feb; (01492)
870447; *£4.50.

LLANELLTYD SH7219

Cymer Abbey (1½m NW of
Dolgellau, off A470) Remains of a 12th-
c Cistercian abbey, beautifully set in a
partly wooded valley; free; Cadw. The
George III at Penmaenpool is quite
handy for something to eat.

LLANFAIRPWLLGWYNGYLL
SH5372
The record books add another 39 letters
(gocherychwyrndrobwllllantysiliogogogo
ch) to this village's name, but locals cut
it even shorter, to Llanfair PG, or
Llanfairpwll. Excellent views of
Snowdonia and the Menai Strait from
the top of the Marquess of Anglesey's
Column, built in 1816 to commemorate
the military achievements of
Wellington's second-in-command at
the Battle of Waterloo. The nearby
village of Penmynydd was the ancient
home of the Tudor family. The
Liverpool Arms at Menai Bridge is the
nearest good place for lunch.

Plas Newydd 🏛 (A4080, 2m S)
Lovely mountain views from the elegant
18th-c former home of the Marquess of
Anglesey, known best for association
with Rex Whistler whose largest
painting is here; there is also an
exhibition about his work. A military
museum contains the campaign relics of
the first Marquess of Anglesey who
commanded the cavalry at the Battle of
Waterloo. A fine spring garden (the
rhododendron garden is open
Apr–early Jun), summer terrace, and
Australasian arboretum; a woodland
walk gives access to a marine walk on
the Menai Strait, and the adventure play
trail has been extended; boat trips from
the jetty (weather permitting). Meals,
snacks, shop, disabled access; cl Thurs,
Fri, all Nov–Mar; (01248) 714795;
£4.60; NT.

LLANGEFNI SH4576
Right in the centre of Anglesey, and its 'capital', with a big open-air market every Thurs and Sat.

Oriel Ynys Mon (Rhosmeirch, B5111 N) Excellent gallery with imaginative changing displays on the history of Anglesey, as well as a collection of wildlife paintings by C F Tunnicliffe. You can spend a surprising amount of time here. Meals, snacks, shop, disabled access; cl Mon (exc bank hols), 25 Dec–1 Jan; (01248) 724444; £2.50.

LLANGOLLEN SJ2142
Not special in itself despite a good few solid and gracious Georgian and Victorian villas; what makes it attractive is its charming valley setting above the River Dee. It has discreet hotels that cater for the generally older people to whom the area most appeals – though it comes vividly alive during the Eisteddfod. The strikingly converted riverside Corn Mill has interesting enjoyable food, and Abbey Grange, Royal and Wild Pheasant hotels are all pleasant for lunch, too.

Castell Dinas Bran The place for walkers to head for from Llangollen. This hill fort commands views over the vale and is close to the Panorama Walk (actually a surfaced minor road); walks can be linked to the canal towpath below.

Horse-drawn boat trips (Llangollen Wharf) Trips along the lovely Vale of Llangollen; meals and snacks at the Wharf Centre, shop, disabled access; cl Nov–Easter and may cl Thurs and Fri in Apr and Oct; (01978) 860702; *£4.

Llangollen Exhibition Centre 🏛 (Mill St) Masses of Dr Who costumes, models and props, spanning 30 years of TV; also 20 extensive working model railway layouts with lights and sound effects, from the 1920s to today. Includes entrance to Llangollen Museum and Toy Factory; snacks, shop; cl 25–26 Dec, 1 Jan and Weds in Nov, Jan and Feb (exc half-term); (01978) 860584; £5.95, both exhibitions £9.75.

Llangollen Railway (Abbey Rd) Runs eight miles, with steam and diesel trains from the pleasantly preserved station (being renovated as we went to press) to the village of Carrog up the Dee (the Grouse in a lovely setting above the

river does reasonably priced food all day); special events inc santa specials. Snacks, shop, special coach for the disabled (you have to book); cl Jan and Nov; (01978) 860951 for timetable; £8 full return fare, less for shorter trips.

Motor Museum and Canal Exhibition 🏛 Classic cars and motorcycles and an exhibition on the canal network. Snacks, shop, disabled access; cl Mon and Nov to mid-Feb; (01978) 860324; *£2.50.

Plas Newydd 🏛 Lady Eleanor Butler and Sarah Ponsonby, the Ladies of Llangollen, lived here 1780–1831. The beautiful house has stained glass, leather wall coverings and domestic paraphernalia of the period, and pleasant gardens. Shop; cl Nov–Easter; (01978) 861314; £2.50.

Pontcysyllte aqueduct (off A5/A539 E) The longest in Britain, very spectacular to cross – by boat or on foot; the Sun Trevor at Trevor Uchaf above here has good food and more views.

Valle Crucis Abbey (A542 2m N) Substantial remains of the early 13th-c abbey church, and some beautifully carved grave slabs. Shop, limited disabled access; cl late Sept to mid-Mar – you can still get into the abbey then, but not into the dormitory or exhibitions; (01978) 860326; £2; Cadw. The ruins stand at the bottom of the Horseshoe Pass, a nerve-wrackingly steep but extremely scenic mountain drive; the Britannia Inn just above the abbey has exceptional views.

LLANGWM SH9845
Ewe-phoria As well as seeing the sheepdogs put through their paces at these enjoyable shows, you can watch shearing demonstrations, and learn about 13 different breeds of sheep in their ram parade. The best time to visit is spring when there are lots of baby lambs (you may be able to feed them); picnic and indoor play areas. Meals, snacks, shop, disabled access; (01490) 460225; cl Mon (exc bank hols), Sat, and all Nov–Easter; £3.95.

LLANGYBI SH4241
St Cybi's Well Known to the Welsh as Fynnon Gybi, this has been reckoned to have healing properties for over a thousand years. Look out for the

corbelled beehive vaulting inside the roofless stone structure, which is ancient Irish in style.

LLANRWST SH7961

Pretty little town with old stone bridge over the Conwy river, said to be the work of Inigo Jones. Gwydir Chapel, added by the influential Wynn family to the parish church in the 17th c, has a stone coffin reputedly that of Llewelyn the Great, as well as a magnificent rood screen from the ruins of Maenan Abbey. The Wynns also constructed the nearby Gwydir Uchaf Chapel, with intriguing ceiling paintings.

Gwydir Castle Splendid Tudor courtyard house with later additions, partly built of Maenan Abbey stone after the Dissolution. The former ancestral home of the Wynn family, it is set in Grade I listed gardens in the Conwy Valley. Cl Nov–Feb, and some Sats for weddings; (01492) 641687; £3.

LLANUWCHLLYN SH8829

Bala Lake Railway 🚂 Some of the carriages on trains using this delightful 4½-mile route are open to the elements, which seems to make the views of the lake and mountains more vivid. The locomotives were once used to haul slate in the local quarries. Snacks, shop, disabled access (but no facilities); cl Oct–Easter, and Mon and Fri during April, May, June and Sept; (01678) 540666 for timetable; £6.70. The Eagles has good home-made food and nice views.

LLANYSTUMDWY SH4738

Lloyd George Memorial Museum (A497) Audio-visual displays and memorabilia relating to the life and times of Lloyd George. Between 1864 and 1880 he lived in nearby Highgate Cottage, with its shoemaking workshop, which has been restored to the way it was then, and has a Victorian garden; a new library has a collection of books about him. Shop, disabled access; cl Oct–May (exc Easter and May/Oct wknds), cl Sun in Jun; (01766) 522071; £3. The old-fashioned bar opposite is good value, and it's a short stroll from here to where he's buried.

Rabbit Farm (just off A497) Children enjoy this, with hundreds of rabbits (you can buy bags of food; 50p), as well as other small animals such as chipmonks, chinchillas, pygmy goats and guinea pigs; also pony rides, and picnic and play areas. Snacks, shop, disabled access; cl end Oct–Mar; (01766) 523136; £2.

LLEYN PENINSULA SH3235

Well worth carrying on to the very end of this long peninsula for the best of the cliff-top walks, starting W from Aberdaron, with fine windswept views from Mynydd Mawr (where there is a useful hilltop car park), and E of here is the spectacular bay of Hell's Mouth; the beaches along here have clean bathing water. For a stiffer walk, try Yr Eifl (the Rivals), a 563-metre (1,849-ft) mountain close to the N coast.

LLYN IDWAL SH6460

This superbly sited Snowdonia lake beneath Glyder Fach gives pleasant walks along a signed nature trail.

MENAI BRIDGE SH5571

The village takes its name from Thomas Telford's magnificent iron suspension bridge linking Anglesey to the mainland, the first such bridge in the world. The waterside Liverpool Arms has good value fresh food.

Butterfly Palace 🦋 (A5025) Exotic butterflies from all corners of the globe, as well as bird house, insectarium, reptile house, and adventure playground. Meals, snacks, shop, disabled access; cl Jan–Feb; (01248) 712474; £4.50.

MOEL FAMAU SJ1662

The highest point of the Clwydian Range, a bulging massif with clearly marked paths; walk up from the car park on the minor road E of Llanbedr DC through colour-coded forest trails or over open land, for views of much of Snowdonia, the edge of the Peak District and the Wirral. The Offa's Dyke Path returns over the moor S to the road, just after which it continues up the Iron Age hill fort of Foel Fennli, another fine viewpoint.

MOLD SJ2364

A very good theatre, and a richly decorated parish church built to commemorate the victory of Henry Tudor at Bosworth Field in 1485. The Druid out at Llanferres on the Ruthin road and the Bryn Awel on the Denbigh road are reliable dining pubs.

PENMACHNO SH7752

Ty Mawr Wybrnant (forest road

NW) Picturesque, lonely thick-walled medieval cottage, birthplace of Bishop William Morgan who first translated the Bible into Welsh (see St Asaph). Shop, disabled access; cl Mon–Weds, and Nov–Mar; (01690) 760213; £2. NT.
Ty'n-y-Coed Uchaf 🏠 Reached by a pleasant walk along the river from the Woollen Mill's car park, a fully furnished 19th-c farmhouse, good for showing the traditional way of life in this area. Cl am, also Mon–Weds, Sat and Nov–Mar; (01690) 760229; *£2; NT.

PENMAENPOOL SH6717
Its small waterside nature reserve has a very useful nature information centre pointing out promising places throughout this whole area, a good region for walks. One is the walk along the old railway track beside the Mawddach estuary to Fairbourne, giving magnificent views. The George III is a pleasant place for lunch.
Abergwynant Farm Trekking Centre 🏠 (A493, about a mile SW) Will take beginners out on ponies (experienced riders, too), over scenic routes. Snacks, disabled access; (01341) 422377; from £10 per hour, £15 for two hours. You can stay at the farm in self-catering cottages and flats; fishing.

PENMON SH6279
A tiny place near the NE corner of Anglesey, notable for its ruined priory. This was a Norman rebuild, but there are earlier Celtic crosses, a 17th-c dovecote and a hermitage well. From here it is well worth driving the final mile along the road to the car park at the cliff edge, for a fine view of Puffin Island, ½m offshore. Uninhabited apart from visiting cormorants, shags and seals, the island is known in Welsh as Ynys Seiriol, after St Seiriol whose monastic settlement is now a few scant ruins.

PORTHMADOG SH5638
Quite a busy shopping town of low slate-roofed houses, with a spacious harbour and long causeway road (5p toll) across the estuary. The Ship has decent food, and nearby Black Rock Golden Sands is one of the area's finest beaches.
Ffestiniog Railway (Harbour Station) The famous narrow-gauge railway opened in 1836 to carry slate from Blaenau Ffestiniog to Porthmadog by gravity. Closed in 1946, it reopened in 1955 and has gradually been extended to climb the 13½ miles to Blaenau Ffestiniog; in 2003 a they hope a further 7 miles will be opened and will join up with the sister Welsh Highland Railway at Caernarfon. Stop off at stations along the way for good walks and views. The railway links with the main-line Cambrian Coast Line, hugging the coast from Pwllheli to Machynlleth, with many stops along the way. Meals and snacks (good station bar with seats out on terrace), shop, some disabled access; cl 25 Dec and limited winter service, best to phone; (01766) 516073; full return fare £14.

Welsh Highland Railway (opposite main line station) Overshadowed by its more famous neighbour in size but certainly not in spirit, this enthusiastically restored line runs trains daily; a two-mile extension is still under way. Meals, snacks, shop, disabled access; cl Jan–Easter (but they run all-day courses then, which include driving a steam engine); (01766) 513402 for timetable or (0151) 608 1950; *£3.

PORTMEIRION SH5837
🏠 On the steep wooded shores of an inlet from Tremadog Bay, this fairytale 20th-c holiday village designed by Williams-Ellis is set in 175 acres of lush coastal cliff and woodland gardens. Quite charming, it's an italianate folly – pastel-washed cottages interlaced with grottoes and cobbled squares, a bell tower, castle and lighthouse, and long picturesque flights of steps zigzagging down to the water, which at low tide dries to miles of sand. Enveloping the village are the 60 acres of Gwyllt gardens, with fine displays of rhododendrons, azaleas, hydrangeas and subtropical plants; good wild woodlands, too. You have to pay a toll to enter the village, but once in can see the house where Noël Coward wrote *Blithe Spirit* and the locations for the cult TV series *The Prisoner*; children can play in the playground, on a make-believe schooner apparently moored by the hotel, or, tide permitting, on the beach. A lovely relaxing place, quite unlike anywhere else. Meals, snacks, shops (one specialising in Portmeirion

pottery), some disabled access; (01766) 770000; £5.30. No dogs – though there's a touching dog cemetery in the woods nearby.

Plas Brondanw (Llanfrothen, A4085 N of Penrhyndeudraeth) The ancestral home of Portmeirion's architect Sir Clough Williams-Ellis, you can visit the architectural garden he designed there – great views; open daily; (01766) 770228; *£2.50. The nearby Brondanw Arms has popular food.

PRECIPICE WALK SH7321

Signposted N of Dolgellau, this is an attractive Snowdonia walk.

PRESTATYN SJ0683

Bustling seaside resort standing at one end of the 168-mile walkable route of Offa's Dyke, marked by a stone pillar above the main beach. At Gwaenysgor in the hills just behind, the Eagle & Child has good value food and fine views. There are plans for a huge wind farm out at sea down the coast towards Rhyl.

PWLLHELI SH3231

Plas Glyn-Y-Weddw (Llanbedrog) Fine gallery in a stunning Victorian Gothic Grade II* mansion; tearoom, shop; cl Tues (exc July and Aug) and following bank hols, cl Jan; (01758) 740763; *£2. The nearby Glynyweddw Arms does enjoyable food.

RHIW SH2328

Plas yn Rhiw Charming if unassuming little manor house at the tip of the Lleyn Peninsula, with all the furniture and kitchen utensils exactly as they were originally; lovely gardens and woodland, inc a waterfall, spring snowdrop wood and subtropical specimens. Shop, very limited disabled access; cl Tues, plus Weds 23 Mar–13 May, cl wkdys Oct (open all week half-term), cl all Nov–Mar; (01758) 780219; £3.20; NT. The setting is lovely, overlooking one of the area's wildest coasts. The beautifully placed Sun over at Llanengan does decent food.

RHUDDLAN SJ0478

Bodrhyddan Hall 🏠 (A5151 Rhuddlan–Dyserth) Lovely doll's-house front, and some wonderfully elaborate fireplaces in the drawing room. Also formal French garden, a woodland garden with four ponds and a Palladian-styled summer house, and an interesting well-house built by Inigo

Jones. Teas (meals by appointment), disabled access to ground floor only; open pm Tues and Thurs Jun–Sept (or to parties by appointment at any time); (01745) 590414; *£4.

Dyserth church Partly 13th-c, with a Jesse window; not far from a plunging 18-metre (60-ft) waterfall.

Rhuddlan Castle Fine old castle, adapted by Edward I from an earlier Norman structure, to guard what was once a busy port (now a sleepy little town). Overlooking the river, it's a pretty spot. Shop, mostly disabled access; cl end Sept–Easter; (01745) 590777; £2.

RHYL SJ0081

Rather brash seaside resort; if you're passing with children, they'll enjoy the Terror Tomb, a walk-through ghost train

Seaquarium (East Parade) One of the very good sea life centres that we've described in several English resorts, with a dramatic Shark Encounter as well as the usual walk-through underwater tunnel. Meals, snacks, shop, disabled access; cl 25 Dec; (01745) 344660; £5.25.

SNOWDON SH6455

The highest mountain in England or Wales, Snowdon is the most famous of the diverse mountain shapes in Snowdonia National Park. This whole area has plenty of fine walking, both gentle and taxing, to fill a walking holiday. Snowdon itself has a number of ways up ranging from the easy path alongside the mountain railway (see Llanberis) to the enthralling Horseshoe Route, which makes its way along knife-edge ridges; the Pyg Track and Watkin Path are among the favourites. For a taste of the mountain without actually going up it, follow the start of the Miners' Track (from the Pen-y-Pass car park on the A4086), which really is a track as far as Glaslyn, the last of four lakes passed. The National Trust now owns large areas of the mountain, and is carrying out path improvements alongside careful conservation of the landscape – perhaps with eventual regeneration of some former oak forest.

SOUTH STACK SH2182

Seabird Centre The spectacular cliffs

near the lighthouse are full of seabird breeding colonies, and this RSPB reserve covering over a square mile has guillemots, razorbills and puffins (esp around May, Jun and July). Lots of colourful wild flowers too, and perhaps the odd seal. The visitor centre has CCTV of nesting birds; guided walks leave here at 2pm most Suns May–Aug. Visitor centre cl mid-Sept to Easter; (01407) 764973; free. The RSPB have now opened a second seabird centre at the lighthouse itself, which also has CCTV; cl Oct–Easter; (01248) 724444; £2. Nearby is a large group of the foundations of **hut circles**, probably around 2,000 years old, still with some visible traces of stone sleeping slabs.

ST ASAPH SJ0374

St Asaph Cathedral To match its tiny little city, this is the smallest in Britain, founded in 537. A column in the grounds commemorates its most famous cleric Bishop Morgan (see Penmachno) and his work translating the Bible into Welsh. A little museum has finds from the site, open by appointment; shop, disabled access; (01745) 583429; free. The Farmers Arms (The Waen) does proper food.

TAL-Y-CAFN SH7972

Bodnant Garden (off A470) Started in 1875 but improved in 1900, this garden is among Britain's greatest. Part of the 80-acre grounds have a beautiful woodland garden in a sheltered valley, notable for its rhododendrons and azaleas, while below the private house are five terraces in the Italian style, with a canal pool, reconstructed pin mill and an open-air stage on the lowest. Many fine rare plants inc unusual trees and shrubs. Meals, snacks, shop, disabled access (but it is steep in places); cl Nov to mid-Mar; (01492) 650460; £5.20; NT. The nearby Tal-y-Cafn Hotel is useful for lunch.

TAN-Y-BWLCH SH6945

Plas Tan-y-Bwlch 🏛 (off A487) The grounds of the Snowdonia National Park's environmental study centre have rewarding strolls through the gardens and extensive woodland; in places the paths cross the Ffestiniog Railway. Woods open all year, gardens summer only; (01766) 590324; *£2.50.

TRE'R CEIRI HILL FORT SH3744

Off B4417, just up the hill from Llanaelhaearn, a signed path leads to this evocative place, occupied from the Bronze Age through to the Dark Ages; a massive stone wall, lots of hut foundations, and fine views. At Morfa Nefyn nearby the Bryncynan and (overlooking a lovely sandy bay) Cliff Hotel do good lunches.

TREFRIW SH7863

Used to be a spa, and you can still see the wells on the N outskirts of the village (the water is said to treat rheumatism, indigestion, and homesickness). The village also has a 14th-c church; the Princes Arms has decent food.

Trefriw Woollen Mill (B5106) The same family have run this woollen mill for over 140 years; two hydro-electric turbines are driven by the fast-flowing Afon Crafnant, and there's a weaver's garden (best Jun–Sept). Weaving demonstrations and turbine house wkdys all year (even Nov–Easter when the mill itself is closed); hand-spinning demonstrations wkdys from spring bank hol to end Sept. Snacks, shop (selling traditional Welsh bedspreads and tweeds made here); cl Sun (exc Easter and spring bank hol, and July/Aug); no weaving over Christmas hols; (01492) 640462; free.

WREXHAM SJ3350

Mostly an industrial town, but its 15th-c church is worth a look, with its magnificent steeple. The A525 to Ruthin is a pleasant drive.

Bersham Heritage Centre & Ironworks (B5099/B5098 W) Well re-created 18th-c ironworks, with a good overview of other local industries, and occasional demonstrations of various traditional skills. Snacks, shop, limited disabled access; Heritage Centre open all year (exc 25–26 Dec, 1 Jan); Ironworks cl Sept–Easter, best to phone for opening hours; (01978) 261529; free.

Erddig (well signed S) Superb late 17th-c house, especially interesting for the way you can explore the life of those 'upstairs' and 'downstairs' equally as thoroughly; the gallery of servants' portraits is very touching. Enlarged and improved in the early 18th c, the house is filled with splendid original furnishings, inc a magnificent state bed in Chinese silk, and butler's pantry with silver collection. Restored outbuildings include a laundry, bakehouse, estate smithy and sawmill, and the surrounding parkland is very pleasant to stroll through. It's one of the most attractive places to visit in all of Wales. Meals, snacks, shop, some disabled access; cl Thurs, Fri (open Good Fri), and Nov–Mar, house also cl am; (01978) 355314; *£6.60, garden and outbuildings *£3.40; NT. The Cross Foxes at Overton Bridge, a few miles S, has good food.

Farm World (adjacent to Erddig) Well liked by readers, a 300-acre working dairy farm with all the necessary ingredients. Cl Nov–Feb; (01978) 840697; £4.45.

Y FELINHELI SH5367
Greenwood Forest Park (off B4366 NE of Caernarfon) This developing centre is an unexpected delight, taking a lively look at trees and wood from trunks and rainforests to Ethiopian wooden pillows. You can handle most of the exhibits, and there's 17 acres of woodland to explore. They've a giant 70-metre (230-ft) slide, longbow shooting, toddlers' play barn, and have recently added boat rides and mini tractors (£1). Lots is indoors, so enjoyable even if the weather isn't great. Teas and picnic areas, shop, some disabled access; usually cl Nov to mid-Mar; (01248) 671493; £3.95–£5.50. The Vaynol Arms at Pentir has good food.

Attractive villages, almost all with decent pubs and in general tending to appeal for their surroundings more than for the beauty of their buildings, include Betws-yn-Rhos SH9174, Cilcain SJ1865, Erbistock SJ3542, Halkyn SJ2172, Hanmer SJ4639, Llanarmon DC SJ1633, Llanarmon-yn-Ial SJ1856, Llanasa SJ1082, Llandwrog SH4456, Llanelidan SJ1150, Llangedwyn SJ1924 in the Tanat valley, Llanrhaeadr-ym-Mochnant SJ1326, Llansannan SH9466, Pontblyddyn SJ2761, Porth Dinllaen SH2741 (an idyllic seaside spot, but you have to walk to it) and St George SH9576; other pubs and inns in attractive areas or with notable views include the Porth Tocyn Hotel above the sea at Abersoch SH3226 (excellent clean beach for families), Castell Cidwm at Betws Garmon SH5458, Sportsmans Arms up on the A543 S of Bylchau SH9863, Bryn Tyrch at Capel Garmon SH8255, Grouse at Carrog SJ1144, T'yn-y-Groes at Ganllwyd SH7224, Three Pigeons at Graig Fechan SJ1454, Eagle & Child in the hilltop village of Gwaenysgor SJ0881, Druid at Llanferres SJ1961, Cross Foxes on the Dee at Overton Bridge SJ3643, Ship by acres of sand on the shore of Red Wharf Bay SH5281, Cwellyn Arms at Rhyd Ddu SH5753 (big playground), White Eagle on Holy Island at Rhoscolyn SH2676 and Caerffynon Hall at Talsarnau SH6236.

Where to eat

BEAUMARIS SH6076 **Sailors Return** *Church St (01248) 811314* Bright and cheerful, more or less open-plan pub, with a collection of car-shaped teapots, naval memorabilia and maps and old prints, comfortable furnishings in rich colours, a good mix of customers, well kept real ales, and enjoyable food inc daily specials; disabled access. £17.65

GRESFORD SJ3453 **Pant-yr-Ochain** *Old Wrexham Rd (01978) 853525* Stylishly decorated spacious pub in attractive grounds, with a gently upmarket atmosphere in the light and airy main room, a wide range of interesting prints and bric-a-brac, and a good mix of individually chosen country furnishings; open fires, a big dining area set out as a library, delicious food from a daily changing menu, a good range of decent wines, well kept real ales, and polite efficient service; one room is no smoking; children until 6pm. £24.65|**£7.25**

LLANBERIS SH5760 **Y Bistro** *43–45 High St (01286) 871278* Friendly no smoking restaurant (both rooms are no smoking) using the best local produce for its Welsh and English cooking – fine fish and enjoyable puddings; cl Sun, Mon; partial disabled access. £30

LLANDUDNO JUNCTION SH8180 **Queens Head** *Glanwydden (01492)*

546570 Busy but comfortable dining pub with a spacious and comfortable modern lounge bar, carefully prepared, generously served, imaginative food from a weekly changing menu (lots of fine seafood and tempting puddings), real ales, and decent wines; cl 25 Dec; children over 7. £22|**£4.95**

LLANGEDWYN SJ1924 **Green** *(01691)* *828234* Very well run ancient place in lovely spot in the Tanat Valley; lots of nooks, alcoves and crannies, a blazing log fire, a good mix of furnishings, pleasant upstairs no smoking restaurant, impressive range of tasty bar food, half-a-dozen real ales, and a good choice of malt whiskies and wines; attractive garden over road with picnic-sets by the river, and fishing permits; cl pm 25 Dec; disabled access. £21|**£5**

LLANRWST SH7961 **Ty-Hwnt-i'r-Bont** *(01492)* *640138* Charming little 500-year-old cottage by bridge, run by Holt family for 30 years, with nice old country furniture under the beams and joists, interesting knick-knacks, light lunches, home-made cakes, shortbread and scones for enjoyable afternoon teas, and quite a choice of teas, coffees and milk shakes; home-made mustards to take away, and old books and bric-a-brac upstairs; cl Mon (exc bank hols), cl end Oct–2 wks before Easter; partial disabled access. |**£4**

PWLLHELI SH3535 **Plas Bodegroes** *(01758)* *612363* Lovely Georgian manor house, aptly described as a restaurant-with-rooms, in tree-filled grounds and fronted by a 200-year-old beech avenue; comfortably restful rooms, enjoyable food using superb fresh local produce (esp fish) and very good wine list; bdrms; cl Mon, Dec–Feb, children welcomed but not encouraged. *£44*

RED WHARF BAY SH5281 **Ship Inn** *(01248)* *852568* Solidly built old pub looking over miles of cockle-sands, with enterprising bar food, big old-fashioned bars, coal fires, friendly cheerful service, no smoking dining room and cellar room, well kept real ales, quite a few whiskies, and plenty of seats outside. £28|**£6.95**

TY'N-Y-GROES SH7774 **Groes** *(01492)* *650545* Particularly well run family inn with wonderful views from airy no smoking conservatory, rambling low-beamed and thick-walled rooms with welcoming atmosphere and interesting old furnishings, winter log fires, a fine range of good traditional country cooking, well kept real ales, and efficient friendly service; stylish bdrms; cl 25 Dec; children over 10 in restaurant; disabled access (and one specially equipped bdrm). £25|**£8.50**

West Wales

Miles of beautiful unspoilt coastline, some splendid gardens and ruins, and ample opportunities for family fun; ideal for a relaxing break

This is open-air Wales at its cheerful best – a happy place for undemanding (and cheap) family holidays, and for relaxing short breaks. In this mood, there are plenty of places to visit and things to do, from the spectacular 2,000-acre Stackpole Estate, through numerous attractions at Pembrey Country Park, to the exotic creatures at St Florence. There are friendly farm animals at Begelly and Castle Morris (a good place to buy cheese), and in Gwbert you might catch sight of seals and even dolphins. Oakwood in Narberth is the only real theme park in Wales, and has one of the scariest rides we know. In Pumsaint you can have a go at panning for gold.

The National Botanic Garden of Wales at Llanarthne is now well worth a visit (good approach from the A48 – the approach from the A40 to this important national attraction is in serious need of improvement). And it's not just gardeners who are entranced by the haunting ancient garden among ruins at Llangathen.

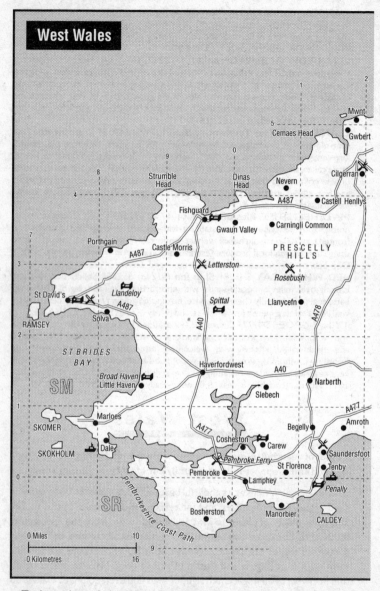

West Wales

Tenby with its sheltered sandy beaches is an enjoyable civilised small resort, ideal for a laid-back weekend, and St David's too is well worth a visit (good walks, and an excellent aquarium). From both theses places you can go on enjoyable boat trips; other boat trips to spectacularly wild Skomer (watch out for seals), Grassholme and Skokholm leave from Dale.

The coast is relatively gentle in the S, with level cliffs, sinuous estuaries and some lovely sandy beaches. In the W and N it's much more rugged. The Pembrokeshire Coast Path snaking around the intricate seaboard makes the most of it, as does the Celtic cycle trail, part of the national Sustrans network. The Millennium Coastal Park, the product of a remarkable environmental transformation, has increased the appeal of Llanelli and its outlying areas for visitors.

Where to stay

BROAD HAVEN SM8616 **Druidstone Hotel** *Broad Haven, Haverfordwest, Dyfed SA62 3NE* (01437) 781221 **£90***; 11 rms, some with sea view, shared bthrms. Alone on the coast above an effectively private beach with exhilarating cliff walks, this roomy and very informally friendly hotel, run by a very nice family, has something of a folk-club and Outward Bound feel at times; it's extremely winning and relaxing if you take to its unique combination of good wholesome and often memorably inventive food, slightly fend-for-yourself approach amid elderly furniture, and glorious seaside surroundings; self-catering cottages, two with wheelchair access; disabled access; dogs welcome ☺

CAREW SN0403 **Old Stable Cottage** *Carew, Tenby, Dyfed SA70 8SL* (01646) 651889 **£48***; 3 charming rms. Originally a stable and carthouse for the castle, this attractive place has an inglenook fireplace and original bread oven, a lovely sitting room with teak beams (probably from former shipyards), games room, conservatory overlooking the garden, and good Aga-cooked food; cl Dec–Jan inc; children over 3

CRUGYBAR SN6437 **Glanrannell Park** *Crugybar, Llanwrda, Dyfed SA19 8SA* (01558) 685230 **£90***; 7 rms. Surrounded by lawns and overlooking a small private lake, this peaceful hotel has two comfortable lounges and a small library, a well stocked bar, good varied food using fresh local produce where possible, and friendly helpful staff; excellent area for walks and esp bird-watching, also lots of wildlife, pony-trekking, and fishing nearby; cl Nov–Mar; children over 8; dogs welcome in bedrooms

FISHGUARD SM9736 **Gilfach Goch** *Fishguard, Dyfed SA65 9SR* (01348) 873871 **£54***; 6 rms. Traditional carefully modernised 18th-c Welsh stone farmhouse on 18-acre smallholding near Pembrokeshire coastal path, with sheep, donkeys, cats and fowl; lovely views, log fires, homely lounge, good country cooking, and a safe garden for children; cl Nov–Mar; partial disabled access

FISHGUARD SM9537 **Manor House Hotel** *Main St, Fishguard, Dyfed SA65 9HG* (01348) 873260 **£55***, plus special breaks; 6 comfortable rms, most with sea views. Georgian house with fine views of harbour from sheltered garden, a guests' lounge with books, an attractive, well planned basement restaurant with delicious home-made food using fresh local produce, and enjoyable breakfasts (and pre-dinner drinks), out on the terrace overlooking the sea in good weather; cl Christmas, Nov and part Jan; dogs welcome in bedrooms

GLYNARTHEN SN3049 **Penbontbren Farm** *Glynarthen, Llandysul, Dyfed SA44 6PE* (01239) 810248 **£86**, plus special breaks; 10 rms in converted stone farm outbuildings. Victorian farmhouse in lovely countryside with a little farm museum, and nearby beaches; period pine furnishings in bar, lounge and well liked restaurant, good honest country cooking and hearty breakfasts; cl 24–28 Dec; disabled access; dogs welcome in bedrooms

LLANDELOY SM8527 **Lochmeyler Farm** *Llandeloy, Haverfordwest, Dyfed SA62 6LL* (01348) 837724 **£40***, plus special winter breaks; 15 pretty rms with videos (they have a video library). Attractive creeper-covered 16th-c farmhouse on 220-acre working dairy farm; two lounges (one no smoking), log fires, traditional farmhouse cooking in pleasant dining room, mature garden, and Welsh cakes on arrival; can walk around the farm trails; cl Christmas and New Year; disabled access; dogs welcome in bedrooms

LLANELLI SS5499 **Llwyn Hall** *Llwynhendy, Llanelli, Dyfed SA14 9LJ* (01554) 777754 **£59**; 10 rms, 5 in main house. Attractively furnished and spacious country house hotel, with a welcoming, relaxed atmosphere, plenty of antiques, good enjoyable food from a varied menu, and very handy for the Wildfowl & Wetlands Trust, also in Llwynhendy; children over 10

PENALLY SS1199 **Penally Abbey** *Penally, Tenby, Dyfed SA70 7PY* (01834) 843033 **£120***, plus special breaks; 16 pretty rms, many with four-posters, and 4 in coach house. Gothick-style country-house hotel in five acres of gardens and woodland with fine views across golf course and Carmarthen Bay; open fire in comfortable lounge, little bar, conservatory, very good food in elegant candlelit restaurant, delicious breakfasts, small indoor swimming pool, snooker and croquet; disabled access

SPITTAL SM9822 **Lower Haythog** *Spittal, Haverfordwest, Dyfed SA62 5QL* *(01437) 731279* **£50**; 6 rms. Centuries-old farmhouse on working dairy farm in 250 acres of unspoilt countryside, with comfortable lounge, log fire, books and games, traditional breakfasts, good cooking in the dining room, and friendly owners; swing and slide in the garden, trout ponds in the woods; self-catering also; dogs welcome in bedrooms

ST DAVID'S SM7524 **Warpool Court** *St David's, Haverfordwest, Dyfed SA62 6BN* *(01437) 720300* **£140***, plus special breaks; 25 rms. Originally built as St David's cathedral school in the 1860s and bordering NT land, this popular hotel has lovely views over St Bride's Bay; Ada Williams's collection of lovely hand-painted tiles can be seen in the public rooms, food in the spacious elegant restaurant is imaginative (good for vegetarians too), and staff are helpful and friendly; quiet gardens, heated summer swimming pool, tennis, exercise room, table-tennis, pool and croquet; cl Jan; dogs welcome in bedrooms

To see and do

ABERAERON SN4562
The line of colour-washed houses facing the harbour is very pretty; there's a good craft centre here too, and the Harbourmaster is a useful food stop.
Llanerchaeron (2 miles E) Little-changed 1790s house by John Nash in a lovely, small-scale gentleman's estate, with a dairy, brewery and laundry among the service buildings – all subject to painstaking restoration by the National Trust. It now operates as a working organic farm, with estate walks, stables and walled gardens, and captivating views of the wooded valleys of the Aeron and Mydr. Cl Mon (exc bank hols), Tues, and all Nov–Mar; (01545) 570200; £4; NT.
AMROTH SN1508
Colby Woodland Gardens 🏠 (off A477) Beautiful woodland gardens in sheltered valley – very pleasant and colourful, esp in spring; a walled garden has a 'gothick' gazebo and colourful herbaceous plants. Snacks, gallery, shop; cl early Nov–Mar; (01834) 811885; £2.80; NT. In the village the 16th-c New Inn near the lovely beach has decent food inc local seafood.
BEGELLY SN1109
Folly Farm (A478) Busy working dairy farm, where you can watch the cows being milked in the milking parlour. There's a daily horse parade, pony and

donkey barn, pets to handle, and a circus workshop; also large indoor traditional fairground, good play areas, a pirate ship, and go-karts. Meals, snacks, shop, disabled access; cl Nov–Feb; (01834) 812731; £4.50. A working pottery is nearby, (01834) 811204; cl Oct (open half-term – Easter.
BOSHERSTON SR9394
Elegug Stacks (3m W) A pair of great rock pinnacles harbouring vast numbers of guillemots, herring gulls and kittiwakes. Unless the artillery ranges are in use (red warning flags, etc) you can get here by the coast path from St Govan's Chapel, or by a lonely road through the ranges. Just W is the Green Bridge of Wales, a fine natural arch.
St Govan's chapel (SE of Bosherston, towards St Govan's Head) A simple reroofed 14th-c ruin, dramatically set half-way down the sea cliffs, and reached via rough rock steps; the former holy well just below has now dried up.
Stackpole Estate & Bosherton Lakes E of Bosherston, this spectacular 2,000-acre estate is a real delight to wander through, with lily ponds, woodlands, cliffs, dunes and beaches offering a range of landscapes to suit every taste and mood. **Bosherston Lakes** make a particularly easy strolling-ground, with level paths

around them; a fine sight when the lilies are in bloom in summer; several car parks; free. At the S end you can cross dunes to emerge on to a large sandy beach, Broad Haven. Barafundle Bay is a lovely relatively undiscovered beach. Snacks (at Stackpole Quay); (01646) 661359; car park open Easter–Sept, £2 (free to NT members); NT. The Armstrong Arms does good food.

BURRY PORT SN4100

Pembrey Country Estate Good for families to unwind in, with 500 acres of woodland, pitch-and-putt, orienteering, adventure playground, visitor centre, dry ski slope, toboggan run, miniature railway and 8m of clean sandy beach (no dogs on one stretch in summer). Adjacent, Pembrey Burrows is a huge sweep of sands flanked by dunes and forest. Meals, snacks, shop, disabled access; park open all year exc 25 Dec, though most attractions cl winter; (01554) 833913; parking £3.20 (£5.30 July–Aug, £1.50 Oct–Mar, charges for some attractions).

CAREW SN0403

Carew Castle & Tidal Mill Magnificent Norman castle (the setting for the Great Tournament of 1507), with esp handsome ivy-clad SE tower. The mill is one of just four restored tidal mills in Britain, with records dating back to 1558. Shop, some disabled access; cl Nov–Mar; (01646) 651782; £2.80 both, £1.90 each. By the good Carew Inn nearby is the Carew Cross, an impressive 4-metre (13-ft) Celtic cross dating from the 11th c.

CARMARTHEN SN4120

Busy regional market town, according to legend the birthplace of Merlin, with the remains of a 13th-c castle, and on Priory St an unusual 2nd-c Roman amphitheatre. The Salutation along the A40 E in the pretty village of Pont-ar-Gothi (pleasant riverside walks) has good food.

Carmarthen Museum (Abergwili, just E) Good museum in a former palace of the Bishop of St David's, in seven attractive acres. Snacks, shop, disabled access to ground floor only; cl Sun, 25–26 Dec, 1 Jan; (01267) 231691; free.

Gwili Railway (Bronwydd, A484 N) Steam-train trips along 2½m of scenic standard-gauge branch line of the old Great Western Railway. Snacks, shop, mostly disabled access; cl Jan–Mar and Nov; (01267) 230666 for timetable; £4.50.

CARNINGLI COMMON SN0637

(S of Newport) Pleasant walks with some interesting views, on largely unspoilt moorland capped by ancient cairns and other antiquities.

CASTELL HENLLYS SN1138

Castell Henllys (signed off A487 E of Newport) Iron Age hill fort in beautiful countryside overlooking River Gwaun, with interesting reconstruction of three big conical roundhouses; the BBC fly-on-the-wall documentary *Surviving the Iron Age* (screened in 2001) was made here. Also a forge, smithy, primitive looms and herb garden. Snacks, shop, some disabled access; cl Nov–Mar; (01239) 891319; £2.80.

CASTLE MORRIS SM9032

Llangloffan Farmhouse Cheese ▣ (Llangloffan Farm, just N) Delicious traditional farmhouse hard cheeses are hand-made here, and cheese-making demonstrations run from 10am to 12.45pm (Mon–Fri Apr–Oct); also friendly animals, a museum-cum-tearoom, children's play area and a picnic spot. The farm shop sells samples of the cheeses, as well as home-made bread and other locally produced foods; cl Sun; (01348) 891241; £2. The excellent value fish restaurant at Letterston is handy.

CEMAES HEAD SN1249

Gives walkers good views over the mouth of the Teifi estuary and out over the Irish Sea.

CENARTH SN2641

National Coracle Centre ▣ (Cenarth Falls) Unique collection of small hand-made boats from all over the world; they may have demonstrations of how they're made, and there are also various tools used for poaching. A medieval bridge and a pretty waterfall provide the backdrop. Snacks, shop, disabled access; cl Sat, and all Nov–Easter; (01239) 710980; £3. In the appealing village, the beamed Three Horseshoes has decent food.

Newcastle Emlyn The attractive main street leads down to an ancient bridge; the Three Compasses has good value food.

CILGERRAN SN1943

Cilgerran Castle (off A484)
Picturesquely placed on a crag above
the River Teifi, these remains include a
pair of highly defensible round towers
dating to the first half of the 13th c, with
some earlier Norman origins; good
views from the towers and high walls,
though, as usual, you have to go up a
spiral staircase. Shop (not Sat), some
disabled access; (01239) 615007; £2.50;
Cadw. The ancient Pendre is very good
and remarkably cheap for lunch.

Welsh Wildlife Centre Covering
270 acres, this nature reserve is one of
the richest areas of wetland in the area
– the reed bed is the second biggest in
Wales. There are various trails, hides
and information boards; you'll probably
see more towards dusk, but even then
some bashful creatures might not
emerge. Meals, snacks, shop, disabled
access; cl Nov– Easter; (01239) 621600;
free, £3 car park.

CRUGYBAR SN6638
**Felin Newydd Watermill &
Gardens** 200-year-old watermill, still
capable of grinding flour; interesting
graffiti link it to the 19th-c Welsh
colonists of South America; attractive
gardens with chickens and ducks.
Snacks, craft shop and plant sales,
disabled access; cl Tues (exc school
summer hols), Weds, and Nov–Good
Fri; (01558) 650375; £2.

DALE SM8104
Dale Sea Safari Lots of varied boat
trips to the islands of Skomer,
Grassholme and Skokholm to see
wonderful seabirds, flowers, seals,
dolphins, and porpoises; sailing times
(usually Apr–Oct only); (0800) 028
4090; £20.

Grassholm The island has 30,000 pairs
of gannets: on a clear sunny morning
even from the coast you can see it's
white with them.

Skokholm This island has Britain's first
bird observatory, still tracking
migrations.

Skomer 720 acres of spectacular wild
scenery with countless birds (inc
breeding pairs of short-eared owls,
puffins and more than half the world's
population of Manx shearwaters) and
flowers, as well as seals playing on the
shore – perhaps common seals briefly
in Jun or July, more likely grey seals and

their pups in Sept and Oct; it's also
remarkable for the easily traced
remains of the Iron Age settlement
here – there's a well laid-out trail. The
Wildlife Trust West Wales has
accommodation on Skomer and
Skokholm (contact Mrs Glenister,
(01834) 870011), letting visitors see the
amazing spectacle of the thousands of
shearwaters leaving their nests in the
evening.

Dale peninsula At the entrance to the
huge natural harbour of Milford Haven,
with gentle level-topped terrain giving
walkers a bird's-eye view of the
shipping activities, reducing the giant oil
tankers to a pleasantly toy-like scale.
The waterside Griffin in Dale itself is
useful for something to eat (you can sit
out on the sea wall).

DINAS HEAD SN0039
A classic north Pembrokeshire
headland: the path circuiting it takes
about an hour's walking from the car
park. The Old Sailors has food from
sandwiches to local seafood inc
summer cream teas.

DREFACH FELINDRE SN3539
**Museum of the Welsh Woollen
Industry** Reopening summer 2003
after a £1.7 million facelift, this is a
working textile mill in the Teifi Valley.
Displays focus on the 19th-c heyday,
when this was an area known as the
Huddersfield of Wales, with 50 mills in
operation. Phone for opening times;
(1559) 370929; free.

FISHGUARD SM9537
Joined on to Goodwick, from where
ferries leave to Rosslare in Ireland,
Fishguard has narrow, winding streets
of cottages leading down from the
attractive upper town to the old
harbour (the Ship here has lots of
atmosphere). The Royal Oak was the
scene of the final surrender of the
French in a bungled attempt to invade
the mainland in 1797; the cannon fired
then still stand on the now ruined fort.

GWAUN VALLEY SN0034
Pretty walks along the lushly wooded
river either upstream or downstream
of Pontfaen.

GWBERT SN1648
**Cardigan Island Coastal Farm
Park** Most notable for its fine clifftop
setting overlooking Cardigan Island;

there are a good few friendly animals for children, as well as plenty of wild flowers, and a coastal walk to caves where seals breed (best Mar–Nov). You may even see dolphins leaping. Cl Nov to mid-Mar; (01239) 612196; £2.50.

HAVERFORDWEST
Castle Museum 🏛 An English stronghold throughout its history (repulsing an attack in 1405 during Owain Glyndwr's war of Welsh independence), most of the surviving stonework dates from the late 13th c. A little museum in the old Governor's House (it was a prison in the 18th and 19th c) has local history displays. Shop, disabled access to ground floor only (though you can see the upstairs rooms on computer); open Mon–Sat Easter–end Oct; (01437) 763087; £1. Georges (Market St) has a good choice of home-made food, with a Celtic arts shop in front.

KIDWELLY SN4007
Kidwelly Castle Remarkably well preserved, this fine castle was built as an earth-and-timber stronghold in 1106, and rebuilt in stone in 1270. Four massive towers, the tremendous gatehouse and much of the impressive outer walls still remain, with steps up to the battlements and turrets. From the walls, the narrow medieval street layout of Kidwelly itself is very obvious. Shop, some disabled access; cl 24–26 Dec, 1 Jan; (01554) 890104; £2.50 inc audio tour; Cadw.
Kidwelly Industrial Museum (Mynyddygarreg, NE; clearly signposted from A484 Kidwelly by-pass) Looks at two great Welsh industries, coal and tinplate. The original tinplate working buildings are still here, and there's an exhibition of coal-mining with pithead gear and a winding engine; children's play area and quizzes. Snacks, shop, disabled access; cl all Oct–May, and am wknds; (01554) 891078; free. The nearby Gwenllian Court Hotel has decent food.

LAMPHEY SN0101
Lamphey Palace (A4139) Ruined 13th-c palace once belonging to the Bishops of St David's. Shop; cl 25 Dec; (01646) 672224; £2.50; Cadw.

LAUGHARNE SN3011

The setting on the Taf estuary makes this a rewarding spot for wandering – past Laugharne Castle, Dylan Thomas's Boat House and along the cliff walk (known as Dylan's Walk); in the other direction there's a pleasant walk via Roche Castle. Thomas and his wife are buried in the village churchyard, their grave marked by a simple white cross. Browns Hotel (King St) seems not much changed since Thomas drank there; splendid second-hand bookshop opposite.
Dylan Thomas's Boat House (Dylan's Walk) Wales's best-known recent poet lived here while he was writing *Under Milk Wood*, and there are still some of his family photographs and furniture. The writing shed he used for so many poems is nearby. Snacks, shop; cl a few days over Christmas and New Year, limited hours in winter; (01994) 427420; *£3.
Laugharne Castle The ruin Dylan Thomas described as 'brown as owls' is a massive battlemented compilation of styles from 12th- to 16th-c; it has Victorian and Georgian gardens, and good views over the estuary. Cl Oct–Apr; (01994) 427906; £2.50; Cadw.

LITTLE HAVEN SM8512
Attractive village, with boats pulled up on to the sand, and a good base for seaside walks on the Pembrokeshire Coast Path. The Swan and Castle overlooking the bay do good lunches. There are some attractive sandy-floored rock coves to explore at low tide around here and the Druidstone Hotel to the N, with a good cliff walk N from there to the long sweep of sand and surf at Newgale Sands (food all day from the Duke of Edinburgh).

LLANARTHNE SN5320
National Botanic Garden of Wales (well signed from A48 – signing from the A40 needs improvement!) The first national botanic garden to be made in Britain for two centuries, this is developing around 18th-c Middleton Hall, in the heart of the attractive Tywi Valley. The centrepiece is the awesome Norman Foster-designed Great Glasshouse – made from 1,000 panes (controlled by computer to vary the climate in different parts) and big

enough to cover a football pitch. Plants in here come from as far afield as Southern California, Western Australia and the Canary Islands, and include Britain's rarest tree, the ley's whitebeam, of which there are only 11 known examples left in the wild. Outside, visitors are treated to a Mediterranean-style landscape with a 5-metre (16-ft) deep ravine, rock terraces, waterfalls and a lake (one of seven on the site). Highlights include a genetic garden and a physic garden displaying herbs and their medicinal uses around the world. The centre has a hands-on science centre and an audio-visual theatre. Meals, snacks, shop, good disabled access; cl 25 Dec; (01558) 668768; £6.95. The Golden Grove Arms (B4300) has good food.

LLANDEILO SN6222
An attractive sloping town; the Castle Hotel is home to some splendid beers, and past it the Plough at Rhosmaen is a favourite local dining pub.

Dinefwr Park (20 mins' walk from riverside lodge at S edge of Llandeilo; follow Dyfed Wildlife Trust path) Pleasant walks through wooded Capability Brown parkland around isolated, largely 13th-c castle and Newton House. Plenty of deer (a feature of the estate for over 1,000 years), but no trace of the medieval town which is known to have stood outside the walls. Meals, snacks, shop, disabled access; cl Nov–Mar; (01558) 823902; £3.20.

Gelli Aur Country Park (3m W, off B4300) Very relaxing: 60 acres of wooded parkland around a splendid mansion, with an arboretum, nature trails, and specimen trees and shrubs. Meals, snacks, shop, disabled access; cl 25–26 Dec, 1 Jan; (01558) 668885; £1.50 parking charge.

LLANELLI SS5099
Millennium Coastal Park 14 miles of coastline – once heavily scarred by industry – transformed into an attractive public park. Attractions between Loughor Bridge and Pembrey (where the Burry Port harbour is being restored) include several wetland nature reserves, a golf course designed by Jack Nicklaus, a national angling centre, a restored historic dockyard,

and the seafront promenade at Llanelli. Lots of public sculpture has been commissioned, gardens and community woodlands have been landscaped, and there are plenty of rewarding viewpoints over the estuary. The sites are linked by a continuous traffic-free cycleway/footpath which hooks up with the **Celtic Trail**, a 220-mile cycle route that winds its way across South and West Wales, from the Severn Bridge to the Pembrokeshire Coast National Park.

National Wetlands Centre for Wales 🖼 (Llwynhendy, 3m E) By Wales's main estuary for wildfowl and waders, with plenty of observation hides and special walkways, and home to thousands of spectacular ducks, geese and swans. Many of the birds will feed from your hand, and at their summer Duckery you can hear ducklings calling from inside their eggs. The Millennium Wetlands is a 250-acre reserve with a discovery centre as well. Meals, snacks, shop, disabled access; cl 24–25 Dec; (01554) 741087; £5.30.

Parc Howard Art Gallery & Museum In pleasant parkland, the largest collection of the distinctive local pottery in existence, as well as local history, and pictures by local artist J Dickson Innes. Snacks during school hols; shop; cl 1–2 pm, cl am all year at wknds, and 25–26 Dec, 1 Jan; (01554) 772029; free. The Stepney (Park St) is handy for lunch.

LLANGATHEN SN5822
Garden Lost in Time (Aberglasney) Exciting garden restoration project with six different gardens (including three walled ones) in nine acres, with at its heart, a unique and fully restored Elizabethan/Jacobean cloister and parapet walk. Meals, snacks, disabled access; cl 25 Dec; (01558) 668998; *£5.

LLANGRANOG SN3154
Attractive fishing village with a nice family beach backed by cliffs; there's a pleasant stroll to a headland to the N (otherwise, Cardiganshire lacks a coast path for much of the way). Further N Cwmtydu Cove is pretty – spectacular at sunset.

LLANSTEPHAN SN3410
Llanstephan Castle Sprawling 11th/13th-c ruin, majestically

overlooking the Tywi estuary and Carmarthen Bay from an isolated ridge high over the water. Impressive gatehouse with fine vaulted ceiling, and you can still see the slots for drenching intruders with boiling fat or lead. Disabled access; free.

LLANYCEFN SN1024

Penrhos Cottage (off B4313) There can't have been many housing problems around here if local tradition is to be believed; anyone who built a house overnight on common land was entitled to claim it, and this old cottage was such a one, frantically constructed by friends and family. Small shop, disabled access; open by appointment only; (01437) 731328; donations.

MANORBIER SS0697

Manorbier Castle Still in the hands of the family who have owned it for over 300 years, this impressive partly 12th-c fortress looking down to the beach has massive medieval outer walls and an early round tower, with a 13th-c chapel (where music is played) and other buildings, and more modern constructions within the walls. Self-catering house. Snacks, shop; cl Oct–Easter; (01834) 871394; £2.50. The quiet village is attractive, with a particularly good clean beach, and there's a striking view of the castle from the church. The Castle Inn (open all day in summer) is useful for lunch, and children are made very welcome at the friendly Chives tearoom. Springfields Farm (off A4139) has pick-your-own strawberries and a decent farm shop; (01834) 871746.

MARLOES SM7508

Marloes Deer Park Not actually a deer park, but a wild cliffy headland a couple of miles W, joined to the mainland by quite a narrow isthmus showing steep Iron Age defences; a place to watch birds (choughs breed here) and maybe seals on the offshore rocks. The Lobster Pot is a useful informal family pub, and the beaches are safe for bathing as well as gloriously remote.

Marloes peninsula Gentle terrain above the cliffs, giving views of Skomer Island, and memorable walkers' routes that need only minimal inland walking to complete the circuit.

MWNT SN1951

Tiny, idyllic chisel-shaped cove with a sandy beach, enclosed by sheer cliffs, beneath a whitewashed church and a NT car park at the end of a narrow lane NE of Cardigan.

NARBERTH SN1014

Pleasant small town standing on the imaginary Landsker line separating the Little England of South Pembrokeshire from the more properly Welsh areas to the N. The Angel has good food inc local fish and lamb.

Black Pool Mill ⊞ (Canaston Bridge, 3m W) Striking three-storeyed former corn mill with working machinery, and pleasant walks along the fish-filled river that powered it. Snacks, shop, some disabled access; cl Oct–Mar; (01437) 541233; £2.50. The nearby Bush has decent food.

CC2000 (Canaston Bridge, 3m W) 10-pin bowling, amusements and a reconstruction of TV's *Crystal Maze*; cl Sept–Apr exc school hols; (0870) 1240101; separate charges for individual attractions.

Cwm Deri Vineyard (Martletwy, off A4075 SW) Self-guided vineyard walk; 350 teddy bears hidden in a shed, and tastings of speciality wines, liqueurs and mead; winery and shop; picnic area. May be cl Sun am, wkdys Oct–Mar, and all Jan and Feb; (01834) 891274; free.

Llawhaden Castle 12th-c ruins, surrounded by a deep moat, with the remains of the 13th/14th-c bishop's hall, kitchen and bakehouse; free; Cadw.

Oakwood (A4075 W) Wales's premier theme park, with rides from the world's No 1 wooden roller-coaster Megafobia to the sky-coaster, Vertigo: you're strapped in a harness and winched to a height of up to 50 metres (165 ft), then free-fall at 70mph back towards the ground – just in time you'll start swinging like a frantic pendulum. A nightmare cross between bungee-jumping and a parachute drop, this obviously wouldn't suit everyone, so rather than bump up the entry price, there's an extra charge of £10 per person (3 flyers). There's a real mix of other things, with younger children having their own little roller-coaster (there's another medium-sized one aimed at families), carousels and the like, and a New Orleans-style Mardi

Gras party (early Jun). During the school holidays, the park stays open until 10pm and the evening ends with a spectacular firework and waterscreen light show. Meals, snacks, shop, disabled access; cl Oct–end Mar (exc school hols); (0845) 3455667; £12.25.

NEVERN SN0839
Interesting old riverside village with a medieval bridge over the Nyfer. The church has a tall 10th-c carved Celtic cross and other carved stones, some with Viking patterns, in the graveyard, where the massive yew trees are reputed to weep tears of blood if the priest is not Welsh-speaking. The Trewern Arms is handy for lunch.

Pentre Ifan Burial Chamber (SE towards Brynberian) One of the most impressive ancient monuments in Wales: a striking former long barrow with the enormous capstone still held up by three of the four surviving great upright megaliths. Great views over the Nyfer Valley.

PEMBROKE SM9801
Museum of the Home 🖼 (Westgate Hill) Intriguing private collection of all sorts of everyday objects from the past 300 years, in a pleasant domestic setting. No under-5s; open Mon–Thurs May–Sept; (01646) 681200; £1.20.

Pembroke Castle The birthplace of Henry VII and thus the Tudor dynasty, this impressive 13th-c castle is largely intact, and its endless passages, tunnels and stairways are great fun to explore. The 23-metre (75-ft) tower is one of the finest in Britain; there's also a brass rubbing centre (from £1.95, not Sat) and an exhibition on the castle and Pembroke yeomanry. Summer snacks, shop, disabled access; cl 24–26 Dec, 1 Jan; (01646) 684585; £3 (guided tours Jun–Aug exc Sat, 50p extra). The Pembroke Ferry pub by the water at the foot of the bridge over the estuary does good fresh fish.

PENDINE SN2307
Museum of Speed The hard flat sand on the beaches here made it a favourite spot for attempting new speed records; in 1926 J G Parry Thomas and his 27-litre car Babs set a short-lived land-speed record of 168 mph, but the careers of both ended the following year in a grisly accident. The car spent

the next 40 years buried in the sand but has now been restored, and in July and Aug (perhaps longer) forms the centrepiece of this small museum overlooking the beach. Also local and natural history. Shop, disabled access; cl 1–1.30pm, all Nov–Easter, Tues–Thurs Oct–beginning of June; (01994) 453488; free.

PORTHGAIN SM8132
Quaint small working harbour in tiny village carefully preserved by the National Park authorities, former granite and slate centre – bastions of former stone works still tower over water. The Sloop is a good pub, and there are fine coastal walks.

PRESCELLY HILLS SN0529
(Mynydd Preseli) Celebrated as the place from where the bluestones from Stonehenge were transported – either by man or by glacial action. Appropriately it has a primeval, windswept ruggedness, the gorse and heather clad upland dotted with Bronze Age cairns (most memorably, Carn Arthur) and an Iron Age hill fort. A fine path follows the length of the ridge E to W, though circular walks are a bit hard to devise. A layby a mile SW of Crymych (off A478 on the road to Mynachlog-ddu) makes a useful starting point.

PUMSAINT SN6640
Dolaucothi Gold Mines 🖼 (off A482) 2,000 years of gold-mining are the focus of this unusual mine, in use since Roman times; tours of both the Roman adits, Victorian, and 1930s workings, complete with miners' lamps and helmets. Visitor centre, woodland walks, and the chance to have a go at panning for gold. Stout footwear recommended. Meals, snacks, shop; site open Apr–mid-Sept. *£2.80; NT. Underground tours; (01558) 650177. Estate events – monthly walks and talks Apr–Sept; Roman and archaeology activity days for families, fishing, self-catering, B&B and cycle hire on the estate; (01558) 650707. The nearby Brunant Arms in fine scenery at Caio has good value food (inc prime Welsh black steak), and opposite the pub is a Roman fort and red kite information centre.

SAUNDERSFOOT SN1304

Relaxed extended seaside village, with a lighthouse on the spit sheltering the harbour and sandy beach; good fresh fish at the Royal Oak – which has heaters for its outside tables.

SLEBECH SN0215

Picton Castle Still lived in, and set in 40 acres of gardens, including a maze, woodland and walled gardens, gallery and garden shop. It started as a massive medieval castle, then during the 1750s the influential and philanthropic Philipps family attuned it to gracious living by adding lavish Georgian Gothic interiors with ornate plasterwork and fireplaces. Castle cl am, also Mon (exc bank hol), Sat and Oct–Mar, garden and gallery cl Mon exc bank hol and all Nov–Mar; 01437 751326; £3.95 castle (guided tour only), £4.95 castle, garden and gallery. **Slebech church** (off A40 5m E of Haverfordwest) Gloriously isolated ruined 12th-c church, formerly a temple of the Knights Hospitaller, by the tidal waters of the East Cleddau. Though there is a track from the main road, it's more enjoyable to turn down the A4075, take the next right turn and park by the mill, walk over the bridge and down the track through the woods above the river.

SOLVA SM8024

One of the prettiest villages on the coast, with a great deal of character. From the harbour a good interesting shortish path running E to Dinas Fawr, the opposite headland. This high crag (enclosed by the ramparts of an Iron Age fort) gives pretty views of the attractive little fishing village and the coast. The Cambrian Arms is a reliable dining pub.

ST DAVID'S SM7525

The cathedral here has had a community in residence around it for longer than any other in Britain, but thanks to the relative isolation of the place it's stayed undeveloped, so that St David's today is little more than a village – with lots of colourful flowers in spring. It's a good area for coastal walks, perhaps to ancient sites such as the neolithic burial chambers up by St David's Head to the S or over towards Solva, to St Non's Chapel, or W to St Justinian (another chapel here, looking over Ramsey Island). The cheerful

Farmers Arms by the cathedral gate has good value food. The beach at Whitesands Bay is good. In summer there are boat trips from the lifeboat station around or to rocky Ramsey Island, where seabirds nest in great numbers.

Bishop's Palace Impressive ruins, clearly once very grand: plenty of quadrangles, stairways and splendid arcaded walls, with all sorts of intricate and often entertaining details (like the carvings below the arcaded parapets). Atmospheric and tranquil, particularly out of season when you may have it largely to yourself. Shop, limited disabled access; cl winter Suns am, 24–26 Dec, 1 Jan; (01437) 720517; £2.50; Cadw.

Oceanarium (New St) Excellent insight into sea and shore life; highlights include the shark tank and rock pool. Talks and demonstrations for children during school hols. Snacks, shop, limited disabled access; cl 24–26 Dec; (01437) 720453; £3.

St David's Cathedral The Norman church had largely collapsed by the 15th c, and elaborate repairs had to be made; the resulting roof is an impressive lace-like oak affair, and oak features in most of the rest of the church too. There's a fine collection of Celtic sculptured crosses. Shop, disabled access; cl Sun am; free, though donation welcome.

St David's Open Farm (NE edge, off A487) Commercial farm with rare breed animals as well, and a network of grassy paths giving a view into most fields; playgrounds and picnic areas. Cl Nov–Mar; (01437) 721601; £2 suggested donation.

St Non's chapel (about ½m N) Reputed birthplace of St Non, the mother of St David; there are lovely sea views from the very scant ruins of the simple coastal chapel here, signed down a track from the useful St Non's Hotel, with a holy well nearby. The walk from St David's is pleasant.

TYF Adventure Organise well supervised abseiling, canoeing, rock-climbing and other activities – ideal for off-loading active children for the day (over-8s only); (01437) 721611.

ST FLORENCE SN0802

Manor House Wildlife Park

(B4318) Around 35 acres of wooded grounds and gardens with exotic birds, reptiles and fish, a pets corner, playground, model railway and falconry displays (2pm); also natural history museum. Meals, snacks, shop, disabled access; cl Oct–Mar; (01646) 651201; £4.50. The Old Parsonage Farm does quick family food. At **Heatherton Country Sports Park** (B4318 towards Tenby), you'll find a range of different activities from pitch-and-putt golf to karting and coarse fishing or archery; you can also book horseriding and paintballing, and they have a summer maize maze. Meals, snacks, shop, some disabled access; phone for details; (01646) 651055.

STRUMBLE HEAD SM8941
Remote, but well worth the drive from Fishguard through a maze of very minor roads. Beyond the car park the seas boil through the narrow neck cutting off the rock on which Strumble Head lighthouse stands. Down on the rocks there you quite often see seals even in the spring, though they're more common in late summer. The scenery typifies the rocky, big-dipper coastline of north Pembrokeshire: outstanding walking in both directions. Garn Fawr, 2m S, is a splendidly sited hill fort right by a car park, with a path leading W to join the coast path.

TALLEY SN6332
Talley Abbey (off B4302) Ruins of once-magnificent 12th-c abbey, still very fine, esp the two pointed archways; open daily; free. Cadw.

TENBY SN1300
Pleasantly restrained family seaside resort, with nice sheltered beaches and rock coves. It's a walled town, the splendidly preserved 13th-c wall still with many of its towers left, as well as a magnificent 14th-c arched barbican gateway; a moat used to run the whole length of what is now a tree-lined street. The medieval Plantagenet House has good interesting food.
Caldey Island boat trips Reached by summer boat trips from Tenby harbour (Apr–Sept, weather permitting, £7), still a monastic island, where the Benedictine monks have good shortbread and chocolates for sale, as well as herbs, more durable crafts and

old-fashioned perfume (for the sachets they hand-pick island gorse, which must teach endurance). Besides the modern abbey, there's a 13th-c church with a simple cobbled floor, still in use, on one side of the small cloister of the original priory; these ancient priory buildings (which you can see from outside but not enter) give a better sense of the past than almost anywhere else in West Wales. Sailing times from the Tourist Information Centre; (01834) 842404.
Dinosaur Park 🎫 (Great Wedlock Farm, Gumfreston – B4318 W) Family-run, in a rural setting: over 20 life-size dinosaurs in glades and swamps along a woodland trail; outdoor and indoor adventure playgrounds, an organised daily activity programme, pets, rides, and computer games. Restaurant, indoor and outdoor snack kiosks, and picnic facilities, shop, disabled access; cl Nov–end Mar; (01834) 842668; *£4.50.
Hoyle's Mouth Cave (off A4139 just SW, Trefloyne Lane towards St Florence; short path through wood on left after 500 yds) Running more than 30 metres (100 ft) back into the hillside, this spooky place has yielded Ice Age mammoth bones, as well as human tools dating back over 10,000 years. Take a torch, but don't go in winter – you'd disturb the hibernating bats.
St Mary's church Interesting 13th-c building with a huge steeple and a plaque commemorating a local invention that many of us use every day – the equals sign.
Tenby Museum and Art Gallery 🎫 Some remains of a 13th-c castle stand on the headland above the yachting harbour; this site houses a local history and geology museum, with prehistoric finds, and two art galleries with Augustus and Gwen John collections. Shop; cl winter wknds and Christmas week; (01834) 842809; *£2.
Tudor Merchant's House (Quay Hill) Fine example of gabled 15th-c architecture, with a good Flemish chimney and the remains of frescoes on three walls; small herb garden. Shop; cl every Weds and Sun am, all day Sat in Oct, and all Nov–Mar; (01834) 842279; £2; NT.

TRESAITH SN2751
Attractive coastal village down steep

roads, with a decent pub (and a waterfall to its beach).

Pubs and inns doing food that are noteworthy for their fine positions include the Black Lion at Abergorlech SN5833 (lots of good walks nearby), Forest Arms at Brechfa SN5230, Cresselly Arms by the water at Cresswell Quay SN0406, Ship at Freshwater East SS0298, Stanley Arms on the Cleddau estuary opposite Picton Castle at Landshipping SN0111 and Cennen Arms at Trapp SN6518. The Teifi Netpool at St Dogmaels SN1645 is handy for a walk along to Poppitt Sands.

Where to eat

ABERAERON SN4562 **Hive on the Quay** *Cadwgan Pl (01545) 570445* Cheerful harbourside place on the wharf, based around family honey business (their home-made honey ice-cream is delicious), with lunchtime buffet and popular café relying heavily on organic produce, and with quite an emphasis on fish from their own boat; also bee exhibition and shop; evening opening too during July seafood festival and in Aug; cl mid-Sept to Whitsun. £15.25|**£6.50**

CILGERRAN SN1942 **Pendre** *High St (01239) 614223* Ancient pub with massive stripped 14th-c medieval stone walls above a panelled dado in the original bar area, some beautifully polished slate flooring, and a comfortable lounge bar and restaurant area; astonishingly cheap and really good interesting food, well kept real ales, prompt welcoming service, and a small terrace with sturdy tables, with more in an enclosed play area; babies and well behaved young children lunchtime and early evening only; cl Sun. £12|**£1.75**

LETTERSTON SM9429 **Something Cooking** *Haverfordwest Rd (01348) 840621* Enthusiastically run and very friendly fish restaurant with truly outstanding fresh fish, served by neat uniformed waitresses – very reasonable prices too; cl winter Sun, 2 wks Christmas; disabled access. £17|**£4.99**

PEMBROKE FERRY SM9704 **Ferry Inn** *(01646) 682947* Former sailors' haunt by the water below Cleddau Bridge (not by the new ferry), with wide choice of very fresh fish dishes – non-fishy things too – nautical decor, good views, a relaxed pubby atmosphere, well kept real ales, decent malt whiskies, and efficient service; restaurant cl 25–26 Dec; disabled access. £17.50|**£3.95**

ROSEBUSH SN0729 **Old Post Office** *(01437) 532205* Quaint bistro with lots of local photos, farming tools and teapots on the ceiling, good value lunches, well prepared traditional cooking in the candlelit dining room, and coffee and afternoon tea; bdrms; cl Sun and Mon pm; some disabled access. £15|**£4.50**

SAUNDERSFOOT SN1304 **Royal Oak** *Wogan Terrace (01834) 812546* In a good spot in the village centre above the harbour, this very well run pub has friendly attentive staff, a buoyant atmosphere in the dining area and carpeted no smoking lounge bar, and enjoyable food inc eight or so fresh fish dishes (increasing to well over a dozen in summer), well kept real ales, 25 malts, an interesting choice of wines with a dozen by the glass, and seats outside, with overhead heaters for cold days; cl 25 Dec pm; children must be well behaved; disabled access. £20|**£4.95**

ST DAVID'S SM7525 **Morgan's Brasserie** *20 Nun St (01437) 720508* Smart little brasserie specialising in good fresh fish from a shortish menu, supplemented by daily specials and using good fresh local produce; friendly service, and good value wines; cl Sun (best to phone in winter before visiting), cl Jan, Feb; well behaved children welcome. £28

STACKPOLE SR9896 **Armstrong Arms** *Jason's Corner (01646) 672324* Charming rather Swiss-looking dining pub with neat oak furnishings and glossy beams in four rambling areas, good interesting hearty food (inc fresh local fish), well kept real ales, cheerful uniformed waitresses, and seats in the flower-filled garden; must book Sat pm, Sun am; cl Sun pm and Mon in Jan–Feb; disabled access. £20

Mid Wales

**Dramatic natural features, and great untouched landscapes
where you can walk or ride for hours without seeing anyone;
some spectacular steam trips too**

The sparsely populated heart of Wales is one the best parts of Britain for feeling you've escaped it all. It has very good walking, though much of it is so little-frequented you'll need careful map-reading to make the most of it. There are now two national trails – the Offa's Dyke Path (coast to coast up the Welsh border) and Glyndwr's Way (recently promoted to national trail status), running 121 miles from Knighton to Welshpool.

The roads are often completely empty, although the area's charms are beginning to make themselves well known to cyclists, and we have picked out some glorious Cambrian Mountain drives threading through moorland and forest, scarcely encountering a single building along the way. Most popular with walkers is the Brecon Beacons National Park: the western Black Mountain, the Brecon Beacons (with some memorable waterfalls in their southern reaches), and the eastern Black Mountains. The area's river valleys are among the finest in Wales: the friendly Usk, the rather more imposing Upper Wye, and above Aberystwyth, the beautiful Vale of Rheidol. We have tracked down some very comfortable places to stay in, with glorious countryside more or less on their doorsteps.

The friendly towns include a string of dignified slightly old-fashioned inland spa towns, with excellently restored historic buildings in Brecon (good annual jazz festival) and Presteigne. Llandrindod Wells is charming, and Hay-on-Wye is a joy for book lovers.

A good investment for families is the Dyfi Valley Pass (£13.50) which covers lively Celtica and the Centre for Alternative Technology (both in Machynlleth, there's a good art gallery here too), as well as the Arthurian legends in the caves of Corris (thrilling for children), and you get a 20% discount on the Talyllyn Railway in Tywyn. Other enjoyable family attractions include the intriguing caves at Craig-y-Nos, underground tours of the Llywernog Silver Lead Mine in Ponterwyd, and the friendly Borth Animalarium. Magnificent Powis Castle is well worth a visit, and there are haunting ruins in Carreg Cennen. Several steam railways pass through picturesque countryside

Where to stay

ABERDOVEY SN6196 **Penhelig Arms** *Terrace Rd, Aberdovey, Gwynedd LL35 0LT (01654) 767215* **£80***, plus special breaks; 14 comfortable rms, 4 impressively furnished rooms in annexe with fine harbour views. Carefully refurbished building in fine spot overlooking sea, with cosy bar, open fires, delicious food with emphasis on daily-delivered fresh local fish in no smoking restaurant, extensive (and fairly priced) wine list with 14 by the glass (champagne, too), splendid breakfasts, and charming friendly service; lovely views of Dovey estuary; cl 25–26 Dec; dogs welcome in bedrooms

ABERDOVEY SN6196 **Preswylfa** *Aberdovey, Gwynedd LL35 0LE (01654) 767239*
£60*; 3 super rms with lovely views. Friendly and relaxed Edwardian house in
pretty, mature garden, courteous genuinely helpful owners, period drawing room
with grand piano (all welcome to play), enjoyable evening meals (by arrangement)
using home-grown produce in dining room with fine views, and footpath leading to
village and beach (4 mins); no children

CHURCH STOKE SO2689 **Drewin Farm** *Church Stoke, Montgomery, Powys
SY15 6TW (01588) 620325* **£44***; 2 rms. Attractive 17th-c farmhouse with
panoramic views, warm welcome, comfortable beamed lounge, traditional cooking
in newly decorated dining room; Offa's Dyke footpath runs through the mixed farm
of sheep, cattle and crops; cl Nov–Feb

CRICKHOWELL SO2118 **Bear** *High St, Crickhowell, Powys NP8 1BW (01873)
810408* **£70**; 35 rms, the back ones are the best, and some have jacuzzis.
Particularly friendly coaching inn with calmly civilised atmosphere, excellent food
using local produce and home-grown herbs (some Welsh specialities), fine wines
and ports, well kept real ales, and prompt attentive service; lots of antiques, deeply
comfortable seats, and a roaring log fire in the heavily beamed lounge, and a partly
no smoking family room; children over 5 in restaurant; dogs welcome except in
dining room

CRICKHOWELL SO1719 **Gliffaes Hotel** *Gliffaes Rd, Crickhowell, Powys NP8
1RH (01874) 730371* **£115.50**, plus special breaks; 22 rms. Run by the same family
since 1948, this imposing house stands in 33 wonderfully peaceful acres, with fine
rare trees; enjoyably informal and relaxed atmosphere, comfortable big sitting
room, elegant drawing room, pleasant conservatory, glorious Usk Valley views
from terrace, good cooking, and cheerful staff; fishing, hard tennis court, golf
practice net, and a putting and croquet lawn; limited disabled access

EGLWYSFACH SN6796 **Ynyshir Hall** *Eglwysfach, Machynlleth, Dyfed SY20 8TA
(01654) 781209* **£160***, plus special breaks; 9 individually decorated, no smoking
rms, two with four-posters. Carefully run Georgian manor house in 14 acres of
landscaped gardens adjoining the Ynyshir coastal bird reserve, with particularly
good service, antiques, log fires and paintings in the light and airy public rooms,
extremely good food using home-grown vegetables, and delicious breakfasts; lots
to do nearby; cl 3 wks Jan; children over 9; disabled access to ground floor rms;
dogs welcome in bedrooms

GUILSFIELD SJ2110 **Lower Trelydan** *Guilsfield, Welshpool, Powys SY21 9PH
(01938) 553105* **£54***; 3 rms. Charming black and white farmhouse on beef cattle
and sheep farm, with lovely heavily beamed ceilings, fine antiques and comfortable
seating, a cosy licensed bar, warm and friendly atmosphere, and delicious
farmhouse cooking; pretty garden; also self-catering cottages; cl Christmas and
New Year; disabled access

HAY-ON-WYE SO2342 **Old Black Lion** *26 Lion St, Hay-on-Wye, Hereford,
Herefordshire HR3 5AD (01497) 820841* **£80**, plus special breaks; 10 individually
designed rms, some in modern annexe. Smartly civilised, recently refurbished old
hotel with low beams and panelling, convivial bar, wide choice of carefully prepared
food in bar and no smoking beamed restaurant, and an extensive wine list; close to
fishing (private salmon and trout fishing) and riding; cl 25–26 Dec; children over 5

KNIGHTON SO3371 **Milebrook House** *Stanage, Knighton, Herefordshire LD7
1LT (01547) 528632* **£82***, plus special breaks; 10 spacious, refurbished rms.
Charming 18th-c house in three acres surrounded by really unspoilt countryside
with River Teme trout fishing; log fires, residents' sitting room, bar (where light
lunches are served), and good sound cooking using home-grown vegetables;
children over 8; disabled access

LLANDEFALLE SO1034 **Trehenry Farm** *Llandefalle, Brecon, Powys LD3 0UN
(01874) 754312* **£40***; 3 rms. 18th-c farmhouse on 200-acre farm with lovely views
of Black Mountains and Brecon Beacons; inglenook fireplaces, beams, TV lounge
with board games, good food, and large garden with swing, slide and playhouse; self-

catering also; cl Christmas

LLANDEGLEY SO1263 **Ffaldau Country House** Llandegley, Llandrindod Wells, Powys LD1 5UD (01597) 851421 **£54***, plus special breaks; 3 rms. Carefully restored heavily beamed 16th-c country house with flower-filled landscaped gardens, log fire in comfortable lounge, residents' bar, upstairs sitting room with games and books, a peaceful atmosphere, enjoyable dinners (by arrangement) in charming dining room, and fine breakfasts; cl Jan; no children

LLANEGRYN SH5905 **Cefn Coch Guest House** Llanegryn, Tywyn, Gwynedd LL36 9SD (01654) 712193 **£48***, plus special breaks; 5 rms, most with own bthrms. Traditional coaching inn set in an acre of gardens with fine views over the Dysynni valley on the edge of Snowdonia National Park; beams, slate floors, stripped pine, and fresh flowers, Laura Ashley decor, pictures and woodburner in lounge, homely atmosphere, friendly owners, and enjoyable food; worth visiting the local church, famous for its wooden screen; cl Dec–Jan; no children

LLANGAMMARCH WELLS SN9447 **Lake** Llangammarch Wells, Powys LD4 4BS (01591) 620202 **£170***; plus special breaks; 19 charming, pretty rms with fruit and decanter of sherry. Particularly well run 1860 half-timbered hotel in 50 acres with plenty of wildlife, well stocked trout lake, clay pigeon shoots, tennis, and riding or walk their two friendly labradors; deeply comfortable tranquil drawing room with antiques, paintings and log fire, wonderful afternoon teas (in summer under the chestnut tree overlooking the river), courteous discreet service, fine wines and very good modern British cooking in elegant candlelit dining room, and liberal breakfasts; children over 7 in evening dining room; disabled access; dogs welcome in bedrooms ☺

LLANGORSE SO1329 **Trewalter** Llangorse, Brecon, Powys LD3 0PS (01874) 658442 **£52***; 3 rms. Only 10 mins from Hay-on-Wye, this charming and friendly Victorian house has panoramic views across to the Brecon Beacons, an open fire and plenty of games and books in comfortable sitting room, and good breakfasts; landscaped garden; watersports on lake by village; cl Christmas/New Year; children over 8

LLANWRTYD WELLS SN8746 **Carlton House** Dolycoed Rd, Llanwrtyd Wells, Powys LD5 4RA (01591) 610248 **£65***, plus special breaks; 7 well equipped rms. Warmly friendly owners run this comfortable Edwardian restaurant-with-rooms, and there's a relaxing little sitting room with plants and antiques, an attractive dining room with original panelling and log fire, exceptionally good modern British cooking using top-quality local produce (delicious puddings and home-made canapés and petits fours), super breakfasts with home-made bread and marmalade, and a thoughtful wine list; cl 10–28 Dec; dogs welcome in bedrooms

LLYSWEN SO1240 **Llangoed Hall** Llyswen, Brecon, Powys LD3 0YP (01874) 754525 **£145**, plus special breaks; 23 very pretty rms with luxurious touches. Fine Edwardian mansion beautifully converted into a first-class hotel with lovely house-party atmosphere, handsome hall, elegant and spacious public rooms with antiques, pictures, fresh flowers and views over the grounds, imaginative modern cooking in charming restaurant (non-residents most welcome), an excellent wine list, and very good Welsh breakfasts; marvellous surrounding countryside; children over 8

MONTGOMERY SO2296 **Dragon** Market Sq, Montgomery, Powys SY15 6PA (01686) 668359 **£75**, plus special breaks; 20 rms. Attractive black and white timbered small hotel with a pleasant grey-stone tiled hall, comfortable residents' lounge, beamed bar, restaurant using local produce; indoor swimming pool, sauna; dogs welcome in bedrooms

OLD RADNOR SO2559 **Harp** Old Radnor, Presteigne, Powys LD8 2RH (01544) 350655 **£58**; 5 pretty rms, most with own bthrm. 15th-c inn in superb tranquil hilltop position, with lovely views and good walks nearby; friendly attentive owners, traditional bars with good log fires, some slate flooring and antique settles, character dining room, good value home cooking inc good breakfasts, well kept ales; seats outside with play area; cl wkdy lunchtimes

PENNAL SN6799 **Gogarth Hall Farm** Pennal, Machynlleth, Powys SY20 9LB

(01654) 791235 **£50**; 4 rms. 17th-c house on working farm of suckler cows and sheep with marvellous views of Dovey estuary – guests welcome to walk around the farm; dining room and lounge, and enjoyable breakfasts and evening meals; babysitting available; self-catering also

PRESTEIGNE SO3164 **Radnorshire Arms** *High St, Presteigne, Powys LD8 2BE* *(01544) 267406* **£82**; 16 rms. Rambling handsomely timbered 17th-c hotel with old-fashioned charm and an unchanging atmosphere, elegantly moulded beams and fine dark panelling in the lounge bar, latticed windows, enjoyable food (inc morning coffee and afternoon tea), separate no smoking restaurant, well kept real ales, and politely attentive service; dogs welcome

RHAYADER SN9969 **Beili Neuadd** *Rhayader, Powys LD6 5NS (01597) 810211* **£47***; 3 rms with log fires, and newly converted stone barn with 3 bunkhouse rms. Charming partly 16th-c stone-built farmhouse in quiet countryside (they have their own trout pools and woodland), with beams, polished oak floorboards, and nice breakfasts in new garden room; self-catering also; cl Christmas; children over 8; dogs welcome in bedrooms

To see and do

ABERDOVEY SN6196
Attractive, restrained resort with very pleasant sheltered beaches but none of the crowds or tat they usually bring. Legend has it there's a lost city beneath the sea, inundated by the crashing waves in a great storm 1,500 years ago. Sometimes at night imaginative people can hear the mournful tolling of its bells. The Penhelig Arms Hotel, with tables out by the harbour walls, is an excellent food stop.

ABERYSTWYTH SN5981
Low-key resort, scarcely changed in 20 years, with long shingle beaches and sedate cliff railway to large camera obscura high above. Quite a scholarly university town, too, with a good museum, and one of the very few of Edward I's castles in this part of Wales. Yr Hen Orsaf (Alexandra Rd) has sensibly priced food all day. The university has a large agricultural college attached and, as well as the usual sheep, you may see llamas in some of the surrounding fields. There's a pleasant walk along the straight stretch of coast to Borth; you can use the train for the other half of a round trip.
National Library of Wales (Penglais Hill) Imposing neo-classical building looking over the town, with exhibitions of fine early Welsh and Celtic manuscripts and more modern art. Meals, snacks, shop, disabled access; cl Sun, bank hols, first full wk Oct, 25–26 Dec, 1 Jan; (01970) 632800; free.

Vale of Rheidol Railway (Alexander Rd) The town's main attraction for families, with steam trains for several miles along the picturesque twists of the Rheidol Valley to the dramatic beauty-spot gorge of Devil's Bridge. You can use the railway for attractive round-trip walks. Snacks, shop; trains run most days Easter–Oct; (01970) 625819 for timetable; £11 full return fare.

BERRIEW SJ1800
Andrew Logan Museum of Sculpture The only museum in Europe dedicated to a living artist, with witty sculpture, paintings and jewellery from throughout his career. Meals, snacks, shop, disabled access; cl am, and Mon, Tues and all Jan–Mar; (01686) 640689; *£2. The village is attractive, with the river tumbling over rocks below a high bridge, and enjoyable food in the Lion.
Glansevern Hall Gardens In parkland by the River Severn around a Greek Revival house, this 18-acre formal garden has some notable and unusual trees. Snacks, shop and plant sales, disabled access; open Fri–Sat and bank hol Mon May–Sept; (01686) 640200; £3.

BLACK MOUNTAIN SN8123
The westernmost range in the Brecon Beacons National Park – not to be confused with the Black Mountains to the E. Much of the high terrain is a long way from the road, so this part is more the preserve of the committed long-

distance walker. The craggy ridge known as Carmarthen Fan protrudes dramatically above the moors and provides the high point of a long but rewarding walk from the N.

BLACK MOUNTAINS SO2632 Making up the E part of the Brecon Beacons National Park, these finger-shaped ridges have steep-sided valleys between. Most of the best views are from the Offa's Dyke Path along the E flanks: the land eastwards slopes abruptly down to low-lying agricultural Herefordshire, and views far into England give you a feeling of true border country. Circular walks here tend to be long and hefty, often with two major ascents to get you up on to the different ridges, but the scenic Gospel Pass road from Hay-on-Wye lets you drive to within reasonable striking distance of Hay Bluff (670 metres, 2,200 ft). Twmpa (690 metres, 2,263 ft) is better known by its intriguing English name of Lord Hereford's Knob; though it's not itself on the Offa's Dyke Path, it is nearby, and you can combine it with Hay Bluff in a longer walk. Llanthony Abbey, with an unusual cellar bar, makes a beautiful objective in the valley below, where diligent map-reading is needed for a cross-fields route from Cwmyoy, with extensions on to the Offa's Dyke Path on the ridge to complete a satisfying circuit.

BORTH SN6086 **Borth Animalarium** 🔲 Just a short walk from this low-key resort's big beach (pebbly when the tide is in), this friendly little place packs in so much that it keeps children happy for a good half-day. Committed to conserving endangered animals, it has lemurs and small primates, wallabies, bats, parrots, owls, rheas, and a family of geoffreys cats; also iguana and crocodiles, perhaps snake-handling and pony rides. Daily demonstrations, good play and picnic areas, snacks, shop, disabled access; open daily; (01970) 871224; *£4.20

BRECON SO0428 Enjoyable and interesting small town despite too much traffic, with some fine old buildings around its main square and narrow streets. The striking Norman priory was grandly restored in the 19th

c and became a cathedral in 1923. Also the rather sad remnants of a castle, and a couple of decent little museums. The George (George St) has reasonably priced food all day and an attractive dining conservatory, and some of the highest peaks in the area are a short drive away.

Brecknock Museum and Art Gallery (Captain's Walk) Has the town's excellently preserved assize court with an interpretative exhibition, as well as plenty of love spoons and some interesting Celtic crosses. Extensive programme of art, craft, and historical exhibitions. Shop, disabled access; cl 1–2pm Sat, Sun Oct–Mar, Good Fri, 25–26 Dec, 1 Jan; (01874) 624121; *£1.

Brecon Beacons Mountain Centre (Libanus) Useful National Parks visitor centre; (01874) 623366; free. They can advise on local walks, inc how to get to the spectacular waterfalls near Glyn Neath, and from the centre there's free access to the surrounding area known as Illtud Common, with fine views of the Beacons and an Iron Age hill fort to make for; this can also be used as a starting point for walking up to Craig Cerrig-gleisiad a Fan Frynach national nature reserve SN9522, home to arctic/alpine flora and some 80 bird species.

Cantref Trekking & Riding Centre (Upper Cantref, just S) Can organise pony-trekking through this attractive landscape, and does farmhouse B&B too; ring Mrs Evans on (01874) 665223.

BRECON BEACONS SO0121 The highest land in Wales outside Snowdonia, this fine area for walking is crowned by a pair of graceful pointed summits connected by a short ridge that seems to be visible from most of South and Mid Wales. There's a magnificent high-level walk along the crest, which has massive drops on the N side. Pen y Fan (886 metres, 2,906 ft) is the highest Welsh summit outside Snowdonia, and the main E–W upland spine effectively stretches about 5m. The most popular walk up from Pont ar Daf, from the A470 to the W, is straightforward enough although there has been some serious footpath erosion, but the N approaches are

Mid
Wales

Fairbourne

Cadair
Idris

SH

Corris

Centre for Alternative Technology

Llanegryn

Pennal

Tywyn

Machynlleth

Aberdovey

Ynys Hir

Eglwysfach

Furnace

Ynyslas Nature Reserve

Borth

Plynlimon

Llandinam

Llanidloes

Aberystwyth

Ponterwyd

Rheidol

Devil's Bridge

Gilfach Nature
Reserve

Elan Valley

Rhayader

Strata Florida

Llandrindod Wells

Newbridge-on-Wye

Disserth

Llanafan Fawr

Builth Wells

Aberedw

WEST
WALES

SN

Llanwrtyd Wells

Llangammarch
Wells

River Wye

0 Miles   20
0 Kilometres   32

Pwllgloyw

Myddfai

Brecon

Black Mountain

BRECON
BEACONS

Carreg
Cennen

Craig-y-Nos

NORTH

more exciting and surprisingly little walked.

Brecon Beacons Waterfall Country A series of mighty waterfalls with few rivals in Britain grace the deep wooded gorges of the Nedd, Hepste and Mellte, just inside the southern Brecon Beacons park boundary (within easy reach of South Wales, too). An easy path leads along the River Nedd from Pontneddfechan, where the Old White Horse does enjoyable food.

Porth yr Ogof car park near Ystradfellte is convenient for the Mellte. Dire warning notices ward you off getting too close to the edge (it is certainly hazardously slippery), but you can accompany the river most of the way to its junction with the Hepste. Here, a path crosses the river by going behind the curtain of Sgwd yr Eira waterfall – a rock ledge holds you in safely, but it's an excitingly damp experience. Note the forest tracks may be closed during felling operations.

BUILTH WELLS SO0451
Pleasant small spa town, with good walks in attractive scenery. Just N, the knobbly upland of Carneddau has some bracing moorland tracks linking up Iron Age hill forts. To the S, the Seven Stars in Aberedw below the Radnorshire Hills has good value food.

CADAIR IDRIS SH7112
This great peak in the S of the National Park offers walkers various ways up its friendly slopes; for a really dramatic ascent, take the Minffordd Path from the car park E of Tal-y-llyn lake (A487); it rises past Llyn Cau, a striking lake in a huge glaciated scoop below the mountain. Good strolling and picnicking opportunities to the W near the car park by the little Cregennen Lakes above Arthog.

CARREG CENNEN CASTLE SN6619
Few castles can boast as excellent a setting as these old ruins (nr Trapp, SE of Llandeilo), dramatically dominating their limestone crag high above the river, and overlooking the unspoilt countryside towards the Black Mountains. Rebuilt in the 13th c (and again in the 19th – you can easily distinguish the new stonework), the castle has a mysterious passage in the

side of the cliff. Part of the reason readers like this so much is the friendliness of the staff. Meals, snacks, shop; cl 25 Dec; (01558) 822291; £3; Cadw. The Cennen Arms nearby has good simple food.

CORRIS SH7408

Attractive and nicely set beneath the towering crags of Cadair Idris, with lakes and pine forests in the surrounding valley. The whole village seems to be made of slate.

Corris Craft Centre (off A487 towards Corris Uchaf) Craft workshops inc working potter, toymaker, jeweller, leatherworker, and candlemaker, with a restaurant, shop, disabled access, picnic and play areas; best to check winter opening; (01654) 761584; free.

King Arthur's Labyrinth (Upper Corris, off A487 towards Corris Uchaf) Fun for families; a boat trip takes you to the heart of the underground tunnels and caverns, then it's a half-mile walk through passageways punctuated with scenes from the local version of the Arthurian legends. Wrap up well: it can get cold down here. Meals, snacks, shop; cl Nov to beginning of Apr (may open half-term Feb); (01654) 761584; £4.70.

CRAIG-Y-NOS SN8316

Craig-y-Nos Country Park Ideal for a picnic or a stroll: 40 acres of woodland, lake and meadow, landscaped and developed in the last century by the opera singer Adelina Patti. Interactive displays and exhibitions in the visitor centre. Shop, limited disabled access; cl 25 Dec; (01639) 730395; park free, though £2 parking. The Gwyn Arms nearby, open all day, has good generous food.

National Showcave Centre for Wales (A4067 just N) Fascinating series of caves, well lit to emphasise the extraordinary rock formations. The Cathedral Cave is the largest single chamber open to the public in any British showcave, while 3,000 years ago Bone Cave was lived in by humans. There's also a dinosaur park, Iron Age farm, shire horse centre, and artificial ski-slope, so lots to see. Meals, snacks, shops; cl Nov–Apr (open Feb half-term); (01639) 730284; £8. The Tafarn y Garreg just N does decent food.

CRICKHOWELL SO2118

Pleasant village-sized 'town', with an excellent inn in the Bear, and a fine ancient bridge over the Usk (which the popular Bridge End Inn overlooks).

DEVIL'S BRIDGE SN7477

Three bridges stacked one on top of another, with a dramatic waterfall far below, tucked away in a beauty-spot wooded gorge near the meeting of two rivers. Well marked paths supply the ingredients for a decent circular walk, taking in the former lead-mining village of Ystumtuen. The oldest bridge gave this place its name, when it was built by the Devil in order to trap an old woman into giving him her soul; she outwitted him. For the Vale of Rheidol Railway, see Aberystwyth entry. The entertaining Halfway Inn at Pisgah on the A4120 to Aberystwyth is good for lunch.

ELAN VALLEY SN9365

These four lakes W of Rhayader are the most majestic of the many man-made reservoirs in Wales. Built at the turn of the last century, they have weathered in well now – even the dams look good, and there are splendid valley and Cambrian Mountain views, especially from high-level trackbeds of the long-vanished railway. It's a good spot for bird-watching, particularly in summer, with red kites usually prominent – huge birds with forked tails, often flying above the lakes. The exciting drive beyond the reservoirs to Devil's Bridge follows an old drovers' route through the startlingly empty scenery of the Cambrian Mountains. The Elan Valley Hotel (B4518) has decent food.

Elan Valley Visitor Centre (Elan village) Good opening to this attractive area, with an audio-visual show and displays, and children's play area. Meals, snacks, shop, disabled access. Cl Nov to mid-Mar; (01597) 810880; free (£1 car parking charge). Outside is a statue of Shelley, who lived in a house now lost beneath the reservoirs. Walks from here include woodland walks and strolls along the old railway track by the water's edge – very attractive, and fine for wheelchairs, cyclists, and horse-riders.

FAIRBOURNE SH6112

Fairbourne & Barmouth Steam Railway (Beach Rd) Running the spectacular 2½m to the end of the peninsula and the ferry for Barmouth, this started life in 1890 as a horse-drawn railway used to carry building materials for the seaside resort of Fairbourne. Meals, snacks, shop; cl last wk Sept–Easter exc Oct half-term; (01341) 250362 for timetable; £6.10. The Fairbourne Hotel is quite useful for lunch, as is the 15th-c Last Inn on Barmouth Harbour. The attractively set George III along the estuary at Penmaenpool is quite handy too. Fairbourne and Barmouth both have good clean beaches.

FURNACE SN6895
On the edge of the woods are eerie ruins of Dyfi Furnace that gave the village its name. Now partly restored by Cadw as a monument, it's a rare example of an 18th-century charcoal-fired blast furnace, where iron ore was smelted; later on, the use of coke made such furnaces redundant. Free. Up the road at Derwenlas the Black Lion is a pleasant food stop.

HAY-ON-WYE SO2342
This pleasant small town has become a world centre for second-hand and antiquarian books. There is a growing number of print, junk and antiques shops too, as well as a rather jolly puzzle and teddy bear shop on Broad St. Hay Bluff nearby has lovely walks, and it's within easy reach of the Black Mountains, the Golden Valley over the English border, and the attractive unspoilt countryside just over the Gwent border that we've mentioned in the South Wales section. Kilverts and the Blue Boar have enjoyable food. Black Mountain Activities just up the road (technically in Herefordshire) can arrange all sorts of exertions; (01497) 847897.

KNIGHTON SO2872
Pleasantly hilly town with the ubiquitous Welsh-style clock tower. At the junction of two national trails, the Offa's Dyke Path and Glyndwyr's Way, so there are usually rucksack-clad hikers about. The George & Dragon (Broad St) is a useful stop.

LLANBISTER SO0974
Llananno church Remarkable, with an astonishingly elaborate rood screen that wouldn't be out of place in a cathedral.

Llanbister church Interesting, with a chimney instead of the usual tower, and presumably a warmer congregation.

LLANDRINDOD WELLS SO0661
A delightful Victorian period piece, with red and yellow brick hotels and turreted villas nestling in the green landscape. The former spa town is immaculately preserved with period shop fronts, imposing buildings on broad avenues and terraces, wrought-iron frills everywhere, elegant flower displays and Victorian parks, antique shop-fronts and little canopies along the shopping streets. It was clearly a resort for temperance – though there are places to drink, they're tucked discreetly away. The former spa pump room in Rock Park has been reopened, with a small museum about the spa alongside, there are sedate walks around a very old-fashioned boating lake, and a very helpful Tourist Information Centre is housed in the Old Town Hall. The Metropole Hotel generally does some food all day, and the 16th-c Llanerch has plenty of atmosphere.

Cefnllys Castle A good walk from the town to this impressively sited hill fort with a lonely church below, close to Shaky Bridge (no longer shaky); a nature trail here takes you along the banks of the River Ithon.

National Cycle Collection 🖭 (Temple St) Over 250 cycles, reconstructions of Victorian and Edwardian cycle shops, early lamp collections, displays on past racing stars, and artist exhibitions. Meals, snacks, shop, disabled access; best to ring for winter opening hours. (01597) 825531; *£2.50.

Radnorshire Museum (Temple St) Charming district museum, well worth a look, with a gallery showing varying exhibits from early Christian carvings to Victorian paintings. Shop; cl 1–2pm, Mon, Sun am Apr–Sept (all day Sun in winter), and Christmas bank hols; (01597) 824513; *£1.

LLANFAIR CAEREINION SJ1006
Welshpool & Llanfair Railway (A458) Colonial and Austrian steam locomotives are among the wide variety of engines that run along this pretty eight-mile line, and the

Welshpool end has a handsomely done station reconstruction. Snacks, shop, disabled access; cl wkdys mid-Sept–mid-Oct (open daily half-term), cl end Oct–Easter exc Dec Santa Specials; (01938) 810441 for timetable; £8.50. The Goat has good home cooking.

LLANIDLOES SN9584
Engagingly old-fashioned and surprisingly untouristy small town, with unique Elizabethan timbered market hall.

LLANWRTYD WELLS SN8746
Pleasant small spa town, said to be Britain's smallest town, with good walks in attractive scenery, also mountain bike hire. The nicely laid-back Neuadd Arms is the focus for all sorts of activities inc man v horse v mountain bike marathons, and bog-snorkelling championships.

MACHYNLLETH SH7400
Wide main street with tall, dark and handsome 19th-c clock tower and a very relaxed feel. The good value Dyfi Valley Days pass (see Celtica, below) covers several of the places to visit nearby, and the White Lion and Wynnstay Arms do enjoyable lunches.
Celtica Very enjoyable look at the history and legends of the Celts, in an 18th-c mansion. There's a traditionalish museum upstairs, but more fun is the lively walk-through exhibition on the ground floor, special effects bringing ancient villages and druids' prophecies vividly to life. Also a good themed indoor play area for under-8s. It's popular with school trips the last couple of weeks of term. Meals, snacks, good shop, disabled access; cl 24–26 Dec, 1 Jan; (01654) 702702; £4.95, joint ticket with other attractions inc Talyllyn railway, the Centre for Alternative Technology and King Arthur's Labyrinth £13.40.
Centre for Alternative Technology (A487 3m N) Reached by a water-balanced cliff railway with lovely views, the 7-acre display gardens are crammed with exhibitions, displays and information. The Centre is concerned with presenting solutions to environmental problems in an interesting and informative way, and shows sustainable ways of living through environmental technologies –

and how to save energy and money in your home. Wholesome vegetarian restaurant, good bookshop, partial disabled access; cl 25–26 Dec and mid-Jan; (01654) 705950/702400; £7. They do good value family tickets, and you can save 10% if you arrive by bus, bike or foot; you can also halve the cost of hiring a bike from Greenstiles (Heol Maengwyn); (01654) 703543.
Museum of Modern Art, Wales (Penrallt St) Lively place with six galleries inc works by Wales's top contemporary artists, a permanent collection of post-1900 art, and shows devoted to individual artists. Year-round recitals and performances in the adjacent auditorium (a former Wesleyan chapel converted into a centre for the performing arts 17 years ago) include the Aug Machynlleth Festival, with special events for children. Occasional snacks, shop, disabled access; cl Sun, 24–26 Dec, 1 Jan; (01654) 703355; free.
Parliament House Local history museum in 15th-c building, with a particular emphasis on the 1404 rebellion of Owain Glyndwr (it's on the spot where he held parliament); great events planned for the 600th anniversary next year. Brass rubbing centre, shop, disabled access; cl 12.30–1.30pm, Sun (exc bank hols), and all Oct–Easter; (01654) 702827; free.
MONTGOMERY SO2793
Tiny town, not much more than a handsome Georgian square, with great views from its castle perched above; the Bricklayers Arms (B4386) has good food mainly from local smallholdings, and the comfortable Dragon Hotel (Market Sq) is open all day. Montgomeryshire consists of the quintessential sheep-grazed lands of rural Wales – generally not prime walking country, with few major objectives for walkers, and fair distances between villages.
OFFA'S DYKE PATH SO2455
The major walkers' attraction in this part; on its coast-to-coast route pretty much along the Welsh border it takes in some very attractive hill-farm country between Hay-on-Wye and Knighton, inc the breezily open Hergest Ridge (access from Kington or Gladestry; in

the latter, the Royal Oak is a useful walker's pub) and some well preserved stretches of Offa's 9th-c boundary marker between Knighton and Kington. The George & Dragon in Knighton is worth knowing.

OLD RADNOR SO2559

Old Radnor church Handsome screen and roof, Britain's oldest organ-case and font; delightful hilltop surroundings, with beautiful views. The attractive Harp up in this peaceful spot has good home cooking.

PLYNLIMON SN7687

One of the big peaks of Mid Wales, this is the source of both the Wye and the Severn; its bog-strewn top doesn't make it the most appealing summit, but there are fine views of the range from two scenic roads – from Nant-y-moch Reservoir (at the end of a tortuous road off the A487 at Talybont, NE of Aberystwyth) and from the back road off the B4518 N of Staylittle, via Dylife towards Machynlleth.

PONTERWYD SN7281

Bwlch Nant-yr-Arian Forest Centre (A44 just W) Designated Kite Country centre, with feeding daily all year (3pm summer, 2pm winter); Explore the forest on the way-marked walks and enjoy breathtaking valley views. There's a mountain bike trail and a lakeside walk even wheelchairs can manage. Visitor centre (01970) 890694 with snacks, shop, disabled access; picnic areas and children's play area; cl Christmas period. Free (parking £1).

Llywernog Silver Lead Mine (A434 just W) A lively place, set against a beautiful sweeping mountainside backdrop. Regular displays of silver panning, an underground tour past sound and light tableaux in the caves and tunnels, and working water-wheels; you can try panning for fool's gold or dowsing for mineral veins; good trails. Wear sensible shoes in wet weather. Snacks, shop, some disabled access; cl Nov–Mar exc Oct half-term; (01970) 890620; *£5.95.

Mountain drive An eye-opening mountain drive runs from Ponterwyd N past the partly wooded Nant-y-moch reservoir below the slopes of Plynlimon, and on to Tal-y-bont.

PRESTEIGNE SO3164

Attractive former county town of Radnorshire, with some fine timbered houses and a handsome church. The handsome Radnorshire Arms is good value, and readers have enjoyed the Hat Shop restaurant, with its exhibitions by local artists.

Judge's Lodging 🏛 (Broad St) Good restoration of the judge's living quarters. Unlike in most historic reconstructions you can sit on the chairs and try out the beds for comfort. A lively audio tour leads you to trial in the Victorian court. Shop, disabled access to ground floor only; cl Mon and Tues Nov–23 Dec, cl 23 Dec–end Feb; (01544) 260650; *£3.95.

RADNOR FOREST SO2160

Open walking country for the most part, with conifers on the northern slopes. Walks include New Radnor to the modest summit of the quaintly named Whimble, and from the A44 between Llanfihangel-nant-Melan (where the Red Lion has decent food) and New Radnor to Water-break-its-neck waterfall (car park just above A44).

RADNORSHIRE HILLS SO1551

Away from Offa's Dyke, Radnorshire is less well known than it deserves to be, with old drovers' tracks providing some enjoyable escapist walking, and a reasonable network of field paths. There are few major objectives, but this part between Aberedw, Glascwm and Gladestry is all very pleasant walking.

RHAYADER SN9867

Gigrin Farm 🏛 (South Rd, just outside) Farm trail with excellent views and red kite feeding station with hides (the birds are fed daily at 2pm in summer); children's play area and picnic site. A new wetland site also has a hide, and you can watch badgers on CCTV. Also B&B, self-catering and camping. Snacks, shop, disabled access; cl 25 Dec; (01597) 810243; *£2.50; dogs welcome in bedrooms

Gilfach Nature Reserve (St Harmon, just N) Includes farmland virtually unchanged in 200 years in fine craggy mountain backdrops (look out for red kites); several well signed paths include the Monks' Trod and the nature trail from Gilfach Farm – leading across a defunct railway and close to the otter-populated River Marteg, eventually emerging on the A470 by Pont Marteg, a delightful shady place with a footbridge over the River Wye. Longhouse and visitor centre, snacks, shop, disabled access; cl Tues–Thurs May, Jun and Sept, and all Oct–Mar; (01597) 823298; free.

Welsh Royal Crystal (Brynberth Industrial Estate) Workshop tours; no glass-cutting demonstrations wknds or some wkdys, best to check first on (01597) 811005. Snacks, shop, disabled access; cl 25–26 Dec, 1 Jan; free. This is a pleasant little town, and the mainly 16th-c Triangle (B4518) has good food; we're also fond of the Lion Royal (West St).

RHEIDOL SN7079
Rheidol Hydro-electric Scheme (off A44 at Capel Bangor) Guided tours of power station with unexpected fish farm. Good nature trails, scenic lakes and reservoirs, trout fishing. Snacks, disabled access; cl Nov–Mar; (01970) 880667; free, fishing permits from £6.

STRATA FLORIDA ABBEY
SN7465
Little is left of this once-important centre of learning, exc the ruined church and cloister, but the surroundings are lovely. 14th-c poet Dafyd ap Gwilym is thought to be buried here. Teas, shop, disabled access; cl Oct–Apr; (01974) 831261; £2; Cadw. From Tregaron down the B4343 a steep road climbs through the pine forests into the mountains, eventually reaching the Llyn Brianne reservoir.

TALYBONT-ON-USK SO1122
Attractive village, with friendly boat hire on the Monmouthshire & Brecon Canal, opposite the Travellers Rest (generous food). It's on the Taff Trail waymarked path.

TRETOWER SO1821
Tretower Court & Castle (off A40) The medieval manor house dates from the 14th c, though it has been developed over the centuries; beside it is the substantial ruin of an 11th-c motte and bailey, with massively thick walls and a three-storey tower. Limited disabled access; cl Nov–Feb; (029) 2082 6185; £2.50; Cadw. The friendly Farmers Arms at Cwmdu has good

value food, or for an excellent lunch go to the Nantyffin Cider Mill.

TYWYN SH5800
Talyllyn Railway This railway journey gives glorious views, climbing from the little seaside resort up the steep sides of the Fathew Valley and stopping for passengers to get off and admire Dolgoch Falls and the Nant Gwernol Forest (there's a waterfall two mins away from the platform at this end). The 27in-gauge railway, the oldest of this gauge in the world, was built in 1865 to serve the slate mine at Abergynolwyn (where the Railway Inn does decent food in a lovely setting). Snacks, shop, disabled access with prior notice; cl Nov–mid-Feb (exc a few days around Christmas); (01654) 710472 for timetable; £9.50 full return. A museum at the Tywyn Station shows locomotives, wagons and signalling equipment whenever the railway is running.

WELSHPOOL SJ2106
Powis Castle (A483, 1m S) In magnificent gardens with splendid 18th-c terraces, this dramatic-looking castle was built in the 13th c, but far from falling into decay like so many others, has developed into a grand house. It's been constantly occupied since its construction, once by the son of Clive of India – there are displays about his father's life. Meals, snacks, shop; cl Mon, Tues (exc July–Aug), and Nov–beginning of Apr (castle and museum cl am); (01938) 551944 information line, (01938) 551920 property office; *£8, garden only £5.50; NT.

Powysland Museum and Canal Centre (Canal Wharf) Decent local history museum, with canal material too; disabled access; cl 1–2pm, Weds; (01938) 554656; *£1. The big Royal Oak Hotel has enjoyable bar food, and the main station is rather unusual.

YNYS HIR SN6895
(1m N). Intriguingly diverse RSPB reserve with reedbeds, saltmarsh, oak woods, freshwater pools and peat bogs, on low-lying land on the southern flank of the Dyfi estuary. Dragonflies, damselflies and butterflies as well as breeding woodland birds and wintering wildfowl. Daily until dusk; (01654) 781265.

YNYSLAS NATURE RESERVE
SN6094
(just N of Borth) A major scenic
highlight of the coast, with watery views
across the vast sands of the Dovey
estuary, lots of birds inc red kites, and
an important dune system, habitat for
orchids. You can walk round the tip of
land jutting into the mouth of the
Dovey and then along the shore.
**Attractive villages and small
towns** in the area, all with decent pubs,
include Berriew SJ1801, Llanafan Fawr
SN9655, Llanbedr SO2420, Llandinam
SO0388, Llangenny SO2417, Llanvapley
[SO3714 (Saxon churuch), Llyswen
SO1337, Myddfai SN7730 and
Newbridge-on-Wye SO0158. Other
pubs doing food that are particularly
worth noting for their positions include
the Neuadd Fawr at Cilycwm SN7540,
Admiral Rodney at Criggion SJ2915,
Farmers Arms at Cwmdu SO1823,
Dolfor Inn at Dolfor SO1187, White
Swan at Llanfrynach SO0725, Coach &
Horses above the canal at Llangynidr
SO1519 (lovely walks), Stables Hotel at
Neuadd Fawr SO2322 (good hill
walking), canalside Royal Oak at
Pencelli SO0925, Royal Oak at
Rhandirmwyn SN7843 and Goose &
Cuckoo at Rhyd-y-Meirch.
**Some unspoilt and humble rustic
churches in beautiful settings**
include Aberedw SO0847, Bleddfa
SO2168 (the Hundred House is a good
base for walkers), Disserth SO0358,
Llanbadarn-y-garreg SO1148,
Maesyronnen Chapel SO1740 NW of
Hay, and Rhulen SO1349.

Where to eat

CRICKHOWELL SO1920 **Nantyffin Cider Mill** *Talgarth Rd (01873) 801775*
Handsome pink-washed dining pub with striking raftered restaurant, smart relaxed
atmosphere, fresh and dried flowers, woodburner, comfortable tables and chairs,
beautifully presented imaginative food (much organic produce), excellent service,
well kept real ales, good wines and charming views; cl Mon; disabled access. £27.75
FELIN FACH SO0933 **Griffin** *(01874) 620111* Brightly painted opened-up
roadside restaurant with good imaginative modern cooking using only local
ingredients in two formally set out bare-boards or flagstoned no smoking front
dining rooms with big modern prints; back bar area with stripped furniture and
floors, mustard walls and bright blue dado, and leather sofas by the log fire; six good
house wines in three glass sizes, polite service, and no smoking area; comfortable
bdrms; cl Mon, last wk Jan, 1st wk Feb; children must be well behaved; disabled
access. £22.50|£7.90
HAY-ON-WYE SO2342 **Kilverts** *Bullring (01497) 821042* Friendly town pub
with an informal relaxed atmosphere in the airy high-beamed bar, candles on the
good mix of tables, some stripped stone walls and standing timbers, interesting
enjoyable food (esp the daily specials) from a thoughtful menu, well kept real ales,
local Welsh wines, and efficient easy-going service; bdrms; cl 25 Dec. £23.95|£6.95
LLANDRINDOD WELLS SO0561 **Llanerch** *High St (01597) 822086*
Welcoming low-ceilinged 16th-c inn with old-fashioned settles in cheerful beamed
main bar, communicating lounges (one no smoking), popular bar food, well kept
real ales, prompt service, peaceful mountain views from the back terrace, and
boules in the orchard garden; bdrms; cl 25 Dec, 1 Jan. £20|£5
LLOWES SO1941 **Radnor Arms** *(01497) 847460* Small, modest and very old
place with log fire in the bar, neat little cottagey dining room, enjoyable food (nice
puddings), friendly staff, and tables in imaginatively planted garden; cl Sun pm, Mon
(exc bank hols), 2 wks Nov, 1 wk Jun; well behaved children welcome; partial
disabled access. £23|£7
PWLLGLOYW SO0333 **Seland Newydd** *(01874) 690282* Popular with a good
mix of people, this friendly former pub (under new ownership this year) has a
comfortable lounge, a huge fireplace in the bar, and attractive no smoking dining
room with good modern cooking using the best local produce; good value little
wine list; bdrms; cl Sun pm, Mon, Tues am; disabled access. £29|£9.50
TYWYN SH5800 **Proper Gander** *High St (01654) 711270* Popular little pink tea

shop on two floors with morning coffee, lunches, and good afternoon teas, more elaborate evening restaurant, and good Sun lunch; no smoking. £20.90 dinner, £14 lunch|£6

South Wales

Plenty of outings for all ages, in rewarding variety

Cardiff is appealing to visitors, with some great attractions from the castle and engaging museum in its centre out to the hands-on science centre in the increasingly visitor-friendly Bay. The fascinating Museum of Welsh Life (enough here to keep children happy for most of the day) is just outside. Swansea has several places of interest, and the broad sands of the Gower peninsula are ideal for uncomplicated beach holidays. Monmouth is an attractive small town with good nearby walks, and there's a busy market in Abergavenny.

The re-creations and underground tours at the former coal mines in Trehafod and free Blaenavon are unforgettable experiences. Other excellent family attractions include busy Margam Park, magnificent Tredegar House in Newport, and the lively museum at Nelson. Historic buildings range from picture-book Castell Coch in Tongwynlais, and mighty Caerphilly Castle, to the first recorded Norman stone castle at Chepstow. There's no shortage of atmospheric ruins: we pick out especially the impressive Roman remains at Caerleon, and beautiful 14th-c Tintern Abbey, but there are many more.

The former coal-mining valleys north of Cardiff are not conventionally pretty, but are interesting to drive through. And even quite close to the built-up and industrialised areas are some unspoilt pockets of attractive scenery.

Where to stay

CARDIFF ST1974 **St David's Hotel & Spa** *Havannah St, Cardiff, South Glamorgan CF10 5SD* (029) 2045 4045 **£150**w; 132 well equipped, comfortable rms with ship-style balcony decks overlooking the water. Luxurious hotel on Millennium Waterfront with lovely views over the Bay, impressive and stylish public rooms with Italian furniture and lovely flower arrangements, imaginative food in Tides Marco Pierre White restaurant, and superb hydrotherapy spa with swimming pool and 14 treatment rms

GILWERN SO2413 **Wenallt Farm** *Twyn-wenallt, Gilwern, Abergavenny, Gwent NP7 0HP* (01873) 830694 **£48***; 8 rms. Friendly and relaxing 16th-c Welsh longhouse on 50 acres of farmland, with oak beams and inglenook fireplace in big drawing room, a TV room, good food in dining room, and lots to do nearby; cl Christmas; dogs welcome in bedrooms

GOVILON SO2513 **Llanwenarth House** *Govilon, Abergavenny, Gwent NP7 9SF* (01873) 830289 **£86***, plus special breaks; 5 spacious, comfortable rms. Fine family-run 16th-c manor house in quiet grounds, with gracious sitting room, log fires, antiques and fresh flowers, fine food using local game and fish and home-produced meat, poultry and garden veg in elegant candlelit no smoking dining room, and friendly helpful staff; lots to do nearby; croquet; children over 10; disabled access; dogs welcome in bedrooms

LLANFIHANGEL CRUCORNEY SO2917 **Penyclawdd Court** *Llanfihangel Crucorney, Abergavenny, Gwent NP7 7LB (01873) 890719 £80**; 4 period rms with mountain views. Interesting medieval manor house below Bryn Arw mountain in Brecon Beacons, with an Elizabethan knot garden, herb garden, Norman motte and bailey, and yew hedge maze; careful renovation, hidden heating and no electricity in dining room (breakfast by candlelight), as well as flagstones, beams and sloping floors, and a friendly relaxed atmosphere; children over 12

MONMOUTH SO5012 **Riverside Hotel** *Cinderhill St, Monmouth, Gwent NP25 5EY (01600) 715577 £68*, plus special breaks; 17 rms. Comfortable, warmly welcoming bustling hotel overlooking River Monnow and the 13th-c fortified gatehouse, with good value bar meals, extensive restaurant menu, a bustling lounge, and conservatory; disabled access; dogs welcome in bedrooms

MUMBLES SS6087 **Hillcrest House** *1 Higher Lane, Langland, Swansea, West Glamorgan SA3 4NS (01792) 363700 £77.50**; 6 individually decorated rms, each themed to represent a different country. Friendly white house with stone terrace two mins from beach yet handy for Swansea; informal welcoming atmosphere, thoughtful individual service, comfortable lounge with newspapers, and enjoyable breakfasts

OXWICH SS4986 **Oxwich Bay Hotel** *Oxwich, Swansea, West Glamorgan SA3 1LS (01792) 390329 £66**, plus special breaks; 13 rms. Comfortable hotel on edge of beach in a lovely area, with dedicated friendly staff, food served all day, restaurant/lounge bar with panoramic views, summer outdoor dining area, and a welcome for families; cl 24–25 Dec

PARKMILL SS5389 **Parc-Le-Breos House** *Penmaen, Swansea, W Glamorgan SA3 2HA (01792) 371636 £48*, plus special breaks; 10 rms. 19th-c former hunting lodge in 70 acres, down a long wooded drive; open log fire, relaxing lounge, games room, enjoyable meals using home-grown fruit and vegetables in period dining room, and helpful owners; pony trekking, and they can arrange all manner of water sports; wonderful walks and wildlife, and historic sites; partial disabled access

REYNOLDSTON SS4691 **Fairyhill** *Reynoldston, Swansea, West Glamorgan SA3 1BS (01792) 390139 £140**, plus special breaks; 8 rms. 18th-c hotel in 24 wooded acres with croquet, trout stream and wild duck on the lake; log fire in comfortable drawing room, cosy bar, lovely food in attractive dining room, hearty breakfasts, a leafy terrace, and personal friendly service; cl 1–16 Jan; children over 8

ST BRIDES WENTLOOG ST2982 **West Usk Lighthouse** *St Brides Wentloog, Newport, Gwent NP10 8SF (01633) 810126 £90*; 3 rms. Unusual ex-lighthouse – squat rather than tall – that was on an island in the Bristol Channel (the land has since been reclaimed); modern stylish furnishings, lots of framed record sleeves (Mr Sheahan used to work for a record company), informal atmosphere, good big breakfasts, and a Rolls-Royce drive to good local restaurant; flotation tank, aromatherapy and reflexology sessions, roof garden with palm trees, vines and a barbecue, and lots of nearby walks

TINTERN PARVA SO5200 **Parva Farmhouse Hotel** *Tintern, Chepstow, Gwent NP16 6SQ (01291) 689411 £74**, plus special breaks; 9 comfortable rms. Friendly stone farmhouse built in 17th c, with leather chesterfields, woodburner and honesty bar in large beamed lounge, books (no TV downstairs), and very good food and wine (inc wine using locally grown grapes) in cosy restaurant; 50 yds from River Wye and lovely surrounding countryside; dogs welcome in bedrooms

WHITEBROOK SO5306 **Crown at Whitebrook** *Whitebrook, Monmouth, Gwent NP25 4TX (01600) 860254 £90**, plus special breaks; 10 neat rms. Small modernised restaurant-with-rooms in beautiful Wye Valley, with friendly caring service, relaxed atmosphere, comfortable lounge and bar; small cosy restaurant with fine wines and excellent food combining Welsh ingredients and French style, very good breakfasts; cl 2 wks Christmas and New Year; children over 12; dogs welcome in bedrooms

To see and do

ABERDULAIS SS7799
Aberdulais Falls (A465) Since the 16th c this splendid waterfall has been used to power a range of industries from copper-smelting to tinplate. A magnificent water-wheel now generates electricity. Snacks, shop, disabled access (right to the top of the falls thanks to a lift powered by the electricity generated on site); cl Nov–Mar exc Mar wknds; (01639) 636674; £3; NT.

ABERGAVENNY SO2914
There are some attractive ancient buildings in Nevill St and particularly Market St, with its busy Tues market and smaller produce market on Fri. The **church** has a remarkable collection of memorials. The Coliseum (Lion St) has reliable straightforward food, while outside the Lamb & Flag (A40 NW) is also useful.
Abergavenny Castle 12th- and 14th-c remains inc the walls, towers and rebuilt gatehouse; the early 19th-c keep and adjoining house now contain a local history museum inc Victorian farm kitchen, saddler's workshop and 1950s grocer's, and the grounds are good for picnics. Shop, limited disabled access; cl 1–2pm, all day Sun (exc pm Nov–Feb), 24–26 Dec, 1 Jan; (01873) 854282; *£1.

BARRY ST1166
Lively seaside resort which, along with its jutting-out peninsula Barry Island, grew as a centre for the coal industry. Remains of 13th-c castle, and usual fairground attractions for children. The suburban Glenbrook (Dobbins Rd) has good value food.
Welsh Hawking Centre 🖾 (Weycock Rd) Cheery centre with over 200 birds of prey. Regular flying demonstrations (noon, 2.30pm, 4pm), baby birds (May–July), adventure playground, and animals for children to fuss. Snacks, shop, some disabled access; best to phone for winter opening; (01446) 734687; *£5.

BETTWS NEWYDD SO3605
Bettws Newydd church Largely unaltered from the 15th c, with a choir gallery and fine screen; the village is peaceful

BLAENAVON SO2509

The former centre for mining and ironwork in the Gwent valleys, this industrial village is now a World Heritage Site.
Afon Lwyd Valley Interesting example of post-mining land reclamation between here and Cwmbran New Town, with plantings designed for re-establishment of nature (and for pleasant walking).
Big Pit Mining Museum (B4248) This was a working pit for 200 years, until 1980, and the tour guides are all former miners; their anecdotes and expertise, and the underground atmosphere, make a visit here quite special. There are plenty of colliery workings to explore on the surface, but it's the hour-long pit tours that stand out; armed with a hard hat and lamp, you get into the pit cage and descend 90 metres (300 ft) into the inky blackness that was daily life for generations of local men. Wrap up warmly (even in summer) and wear sensible footwear. They don't allow under-5s, or anyone under a metre tall. Back on the surface there's a reconstructed miner's cottage, and an exhibition in the old pithead baths. The whole site takes around 2½ hrs to see properly. Meals, snacks, shop, disabled access (even underground, though you must book); usually cl Dec–mid-Feb; (01495) 790311; free.
Blaenavon Ironworks (North St) Appreciable ruins of five 1788–89 steam-powered blast furnaces, driven out of business by the advent of steel in the following century. A water-balance tower (which provided power to move materials around the site) and workers' cottages also survive. Site exhibition; open Apr–Oct; (01495) 792615; £2; Cadw. Tours through the Pontfaen Museum, Pontypool.

BRIDGEND SS9084
Bryngarw Country Park (just N) Unexpectedly tranquil refuge from the M4, with woodland walks, formal gardens, ornamental lakes and a Japanese garden. Playground, snacks, shop; usually only cl 25–26 Dec; (01656) 725155; free, (£2 parking wknds and bank hols, and school hols, Apr–Sept).
Ewenny Priory (just S) This riverside

ruin is one of the finest fortified religious buildings in Britain.

Newcastle (Newcastle Hill) Ruined 12th-c castle with surviving rectangular tower, richly carved Norman gateway and massive curtain walls; open daily; free; Cadw. The prosperous industrial town below isn't much of a place for visitors.

CAERLEON ST3490

Roman Fortress Baths, Amphitheatre & Barracks The site of the 50-acre Roman fortress of Isca, established in AD 75 as the permanent base of the 5,500-strong Second Augustan Legion. One of the best examples of an amphitheatre in the country, alongside impressive remains of the fortress baths, barrack blocks (the only examples currently visible in all Europe), and fortress wall. Shop, disabled access; cl 24–26 Dec, 1 Jan; (01554) 890104; £2; Cadw. Caerleon is reckoned in these parts to have been the site of the court of King Arthur. Near the Tourist Information Centre on the High St is a little art gallery, with various craft workshops in an 18th-c walled garden; the Hanbury Arms has generous food.

Roman Legionary Museum (High St) Gives some idea of the daily life of the garrison; quite a few hands-on activities at wknds and school hols. Shop, disabled access; cl am Sun, 24–26 Dec, 1 Jan; (01633) 423134; free.

CAERPHILLY ST1587

Caerphilly Castle One of the largest medieval fortresses in Britain, begun in 1268, with extensive land and water defences. Rising sheer from its broad outer moat, it's a proper picture-book castle, pleasing for this reason to the most casual visitor. It also enthrals serious students of castle architecture with its remarkably complex design of concentric defences. Look out for the incredible leaning tower, which appears ready to topple any second; audio-visual display and replica medieval siege engines; new visitors centre. Shop, disabled access to ground floor; cl 24–26 Dec, 1 Jan; (029) 2088 3143; £2.50; Cadw. In the oddly strung-out small town, the ancient Courthouse overlooking the castle has reasonably priced food.

CAERWENT ROMAN WALLS
ST4790

These massive walls, still some 4½ metres (15-ft) high in places, enclosed the large site of Venta Silurum – over 40 acres, enough for a sizeable town, though none of that's left now; free. The Carpenters Arms up in the attractive village of Shirenewton does good value food.

CALDICOT ST4888

Caldicot Castle (off B4245) Founded by the Normans, developed in Royal hands as a stronghold in the Middle Ages, restored as a Victorian family home, and now surrounded by 55 acres of parkland. It's a pleasant place for a relaxed afternoon, with hands-on activities and games for children, a new play area, picnic facilities and barbecue hearths; special events. Snacks, shop, limited disabled access; cl Nov–Feb; (01291) 420241; £3 inc audio tour.

CARDIFF ST1876

Cardiff's bustling centre, much of it pedestrianised, has a good friendly feel; there are several interesting Victorian covered shopping arcades, as well as modern ones, and near the medieval church of St John the Baptist, there's a two-storey Victorian market hall. The Cottage and Prince of Wales (both St Mary St) are useful for lunch, and in summer a lively place to head is Mill Lane, where lots of the cafés and bars have outside tables. Between Cardiff Castle and the River Taff, Bute Park, created by Andrew Pettigrew in the second half of the 19th-c, is one of the largest urban parks in Britain. The magnificent riverside Millennium Stadium is also surprisingly central (and dominates the city skyline from most approaches), and on match days the roar of the crowds can be heard right across the city; there are hourly tours every day; (029) 2082 2228; £5. The white neo-classical City Hall, flanked by the National Museum of Wales and the Law Courts, holds itself slightly aloof, and leads to formal Cathays Park, now dominated by the grand buildings of the city's university. Cyclists and walkers can take the Taff trail S to Cardiff Bay or N to the Brecon Beacons.

Cardiff Bay (Britannia Park) A space-age-style **Visitor Centre** tells of the

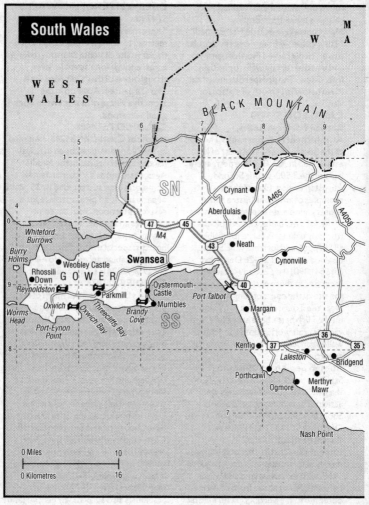

South Wales

WEST WALES

BLACK MOUNTAIN

M W A

SN

Crynant

Aberdulais

A465

A4058

Whiteford Burrows

Burry Holms

Rhossili Down

Weobley Castle

GOWER

Reynoldston

Parkmill

Oxwich

Threecliffs Bay

Oxwich Bay

Port-Eynon Point

Worms Head

Brandy Cove

Oystermouth Castle

Mumbles

SS

Swansea

M4

Neath

Cynonville

Port Talbot

Margam

Kenfig

Porthcawl

Ogmore

Laleston

Merthyr Mawr

Bridgend

Nash Point

0 Miles 10

0 Kilometres 16

continuing transformation of Cardiff's waterfront and docklands; shop, disabled access; cl 24–26 Dec; (029) 2046 3833; free. A newly created freshwater lake, separated from the sea by a 1,000-metre barrage (costing £191 million – one unforeseen consequence has been clouds of summer midges) – is fringed by new residential and commercial developments. At its heart is a hole in the ground where an innovative assembly building may one day embody the self-confidence of the Welsh assembly. Nearby the skeletal outline of the Millennium Centre, to

house the Welsh National Opera and other cultural organisations, gives some cause for hope that the centre of Cardiff Bay will not just be represented by the Mermaid Quay development, with its restaurants, cafés and bars which lead down to the waterfront. You can go on a boat ride (or a land train) to the barrage, and to Penarth Marina. In summer concerts are held outdoors in the Oval Basin, next to the magnificent Pierhead building.
Cardiff Castle (Castle St) Despite their fairytale medieval appearance, the main buildings are largely 19th-c, when

the Marquess of Bute employed William Burges to rebuild and restore the place, adding richly romantic wall paintings, stained glass and carvings. Some parts are much older, and in the grounds there's even a piece of a Roman wall 3 metres (10 ft) thick. The Norman keep survives, as does a 13th-c tower – these two look like proper castle architecture, perched on a little mound. Also two military museums. Snacks, shop; usually cl 25–26 Dec, 1 Jan only, though major development over the next five years may affect opening times – best to phone; (029) 2087 8100;

*£5.50 for full guided tour, *£2.75 grounds only.

Craft in the Bay (Lloyd George Ave) Demonstrations by potters, jewellers and glass workers, and a large gallery and shop; cl 25–26 Dec, 1 Jan; free.

Llandaff Cathedral (W of centre) Rebuilt several times; it includes some delightful medieval masonry, Pre-Raphaelite works, a marvellous modern timber roof, and a central concrete arch that you may think a mistake. The nearby green has an attractive collection of buildings around it, inc the good Black Lion.

Museum of Welsh Life (St Fagans, A4232 4m W) Excellent 100-acre open-air museum, with a variety of reconstructed buildings illustrating styles and living conditions throughout the ages. Buildings have come from all over Wales, and there are some remarkable exhibits, inc a homely gas-lit Edwardian farmhouse and a Celtic village. You can buy things from a period grocery store, ride on horse and cart or have a go at making your own pot. Also crafts, regular demonstrations and lots of seasonal events – there's plenty to fascinate here, and the grounds are pretty too. Meals and snacks (in 1920s tearoom), shops, limited disabled access; cl 24–25 Dec; (029) 2057 3500; free. The Plymouth Arms is very handy for good value food.

National Museum of Wales (Cathays Park) Lively, with interactive displays and exhibitions on subjects as diverse as ceramics, coins and prehistoric sea monsters. The East Wing has an impressive collection of paintings, with notable French Impressionists, and there's an excellent section on the evolution of the Welsh landscape. Meals, snacks, shop, disabled access; cl Mon (exc bank hols), 25 Dec; (029) 2039 7951; free.

Techniquest ⊞ (Stuart St) An excellent family excursion, with fun as well as interest at this hi-tech science centre; around 160 hands-on exhibits and activities, and a planetarium – all exceptionally well done. Snacks, shop, very good disabled access; cl 24–26 Dec, 1 Jan; (029) 2047 5475; *£6.50.

CHEPSTOW ST5294
A steep but civilised small town, still with its battlemented 13th-c town gate. Stuart Crystal have a workshop opposite the castle, and there's a working pottery on Lower Church St (cl Sun). The Castle View is useful for lunch.

Chepstow Castle The first recorded Norman stone castle, proudly standing on an easily defended spot above the Wye, overlooking the gorge, which here is spanned by a handsome Regency iron bridge. Splendid gatehouse with portcullis grooves and ancient gates, and exhibitions on siege warfare and the English Civil War, with models of the medieval lords and a Civil War battle scene. Shop, limited disabled access; cl 24–26 Dec, 1 Jan; £3. Cadw.

Chepstow Museum (Bridge St) Good local history in an elegant 18th-c house; shop, some disabled access; cl 1–2pm (exc July–Sept), Sun am, and 25–26 Dec, 1 Jan; £1.

COSHESTON SN0104
Upton Castle Gardens ⊞ (off A477 E of Pembroke Dock; signed from Cosheston) Lovely woodland gardens, surrounding a medieval castle (not open) with wide variety of trees and shrubs, formal terraces with herbaceous borders, and rose gardens. Picnic area; cl Sat and Nov–Mar. £1.20.

CRYNANT SN7904
Cefn Coed Colliery Museum ⊞ (A4109) On the site of former Cefn Coed Colliery, the story of mining in the Dulais Valley. It still has a steam winding-engine, though the winding gear is now run by electricity. Also a simulated underground mining gallery, boiler house and compressor house. Shop; cl Nov–Mar; (01639) 750556; free.

CWM DARRAN SO1203
(Rhymney Valley, nr Bargoed) Interesting example of post-mining land reclamation, which now provides a wide variety of habitats for wildlife and plants, with scenery ranging from the valley floor through forest areas to upland moors giving walkers superb views of the Brecon Beacons.

CWMBRAN ST2795
Greenmeadow Community Farm (1m W) Founded to protect one of the encroaching new town's last green areas, this friendly farm has a wide range of animals – traditional, rare and cuddly – as well as a deer enclosure, bluebell wood, and craft workshops. Meals, snacks, shop, disabled access; cl 25 Dec; (01633) 862202; *£3.50. Up towards Pontypool the canalside Open Hearth (Griffithstown) has good food.

CYNONVILLE SS8194
Afan Forest Park (A4107) 14 tranquil square miles of forest, with trails for walking or cycling (you can hire mountain bikes in summer) inc challenging mountain bike trails, picnic and barbecue areas, and visitor centre;

disabled access; (01639) 850564; free, parking from £1, miners' museum £1.20.

Welsh Miners Museum ☒ (Afan Forest Park) Illustrates life as a miner, with coal faces, pit gear and mining equipment among the displays. Meals, snacks, shop, disabled access; cl Christmas wk; (01639) 850564; £1.20.

EBBW VALE SO1508

Victoria Park (Victoria, A4046 2m S) The site of a former Garden Festival, still full of the lakes, gardens, wetlands and woodland. Pleasant walks and trails, woodland craft centre and owl sanctuary and some quite extraordinary sculptures, one made from 30,000 individually modelled clay bricks. Also a large factory shopping centre. Meals, snacks, shop, disabled access; centre cl 25 Dec; (01495) 350010; free (£1 summer land train).

GOVILON SO2414

Monmouthshire & Brecon Canal A walk along the Monmouthshire & Brecon Canal to Llanfoist SO2813 can tie in with a return along the track of the former Abergavenny–Merthyr Tydfil railway line, making a level 4 miles in all. On the lower section of the canal at **Goytre Wharf** (Llanover) there's a heritage and activity centre; meals, snacks, shop, disabled access; cl mid-Dec to early Jan; (01873) 881069; free, charges for activities. You can hire boats nearby.

GOWER SS4990

This peninsula stretching W of Swansea has quite a bit of off-putting ribbon development along the roads leading in, but it's well worth persevering. Once beyond this creeping urbanisation, it encapsulates on a small scale many different types of Welsh landscape, with lots of walking opportunities, and parts of the coast are lovely (the N coast though is attractive only at its western end). Busy in summer with quite a young feel in parts, though even the main places tend to be virtually empty out of season.

Brandy Cove This tiny cove makes an attractive destination for a walk down the wooded Bishopston Valley, perhaps from the good Joiners Arms.

Burry Holms Islet with ruined chapel and Iron Age fort; you can walk out

across the sands at low tide.

Mumbles Pleasantly unspoilt resort with a gallery collection of traditional Welsh love spoons (cl Sun; (01792) 360132), and a surprisingly active night-life; around 14 pubs line the stretch of Mumbles Rd near Mumbles Head, and Swansea students like to 'go mumbling' between them. Claudes Restaurant (Newton Rd) does good value set meals; the Park Inn (Park St) is also good value, with lots of photographs of the old Mumbles Railway.

Oxwich Bay Dunes and broad sands, presided over by Oxwich Point on its W side; good walking. It's also good for windsurfing – you can hire wet suits from a windsurfing school at Oxwich Bay – though the the water will never be more than what might euphemistically be called invigorating. The seaview Oxwich Bay Hotel has above-average food all day.

Oxwich Castle 16th-c courtyard house, luxurious in its day and built as a mock-fortified manor; now an atmospheric ruin. Shop, disabled access to ground floor; open Easter–end Sept; (029) 20826185; £2; Cadw.

Oystermouth Castle ☒ (Mumbles) Very complete ruins of the de Breose family castle, in a small park overlooking the bay. The gatehouse, chapel and great hall date from the 13th/14th-c. Cl Sept–Apr; (01792) 368732; £1; Cadw.

Port-Eynon Point Interesting, with a huge medieval rock-dove dovecot in the cliff (birds still use it), and cliff walks on either side; windsurfing below.

Rhossili Down This rounded windswept rough-cropped moorland seems a million miles from Swansea (yet as the crow flies is only about ten from the outskirts); it offers Gower walkers breathtaking coast views. From Rhossili walks can also take in the long surfers' sands of the bay. There's an informative NT visitor centre at Rhossili; cl Mon–Tues Nov–Dec, and wkdys Jan to mid-Mar.

Threecliffs Bay From the NT car park near Penmaen church a good walk follows the lane down to this lovely bay, then heads W along the coast as far as Nicholaston Farm to end with the mild ascent of Cefn Bryn, a rounded moorland hill giving breathtaking views

of both – or all three – Gower coasts.
Weobley Castle (Llanrhidian)
12th/14th-c fortified manor house with
an exhibition on the area's history, and
superb views. Cl 24–26 Dec, 1 Jan;
(01792) 390012; £2; Cadw. This is a
lovely spot above the estuary and its
long glistening cockle sands – full of
interest for walkers.
Whiteford Burrows An extensive
nature reserve, with sand dunes,
marshy slacks and pine trees – good
walks.
Worms Head Nature reserve where
you may see seals on the tidal rocks in
late summer; walks here can also take in
Mewslade Bay, where the south-facing
sands are enclosed by limestone cliffs.
The Worms Head Hotel with clifftop
views over Rhossili Bay has enjoyable
food.
KENFIG SS8081
Kenfig National Nature Reserve
(off A48 W of Bridgend) A thriving
medieval town till huge storms buried it
in sand (the only remaining trace is the
castle keep), this is one of the last
remnants of a huge dune system that
stretched for miles along the South
Wales coast; bird hides overlook a 70-
acre freshwater pool, and the little
visitor centre has a hands-on exhibition
(shop; cl am and 25 Dec; free). The
ancient Prince of Wales has good home
cooking.
LLANTHONY SO2923
Cwmyoy church (Llanthony Valley
road) Repeated landslips have left the
medieval church twisted, and its tower
leans at an angle that makes the Tower
of Pisa look positively sober.
Llanthony Priory Graceful ruins of
12th-c priory, the money for its
construction put up by Hugh de Lacey
when he decided he'd had enough of
being a bold bad baron and was thinking
of retiring into these lonely hills. It's a
very romantic spot, with nothing much
to disturb the peace. The remains cover
a variety of architectural styles; free.
The very ancient crypt bar below the
Abbey Hotel, right among the priory
buildings, is useful for a snack lunch – a
most unusual place. This is a good start
or objective for Black Mountains walks.
Partrishow church (nr Llanthony) A
remarkable building in the Black

Mountains, with a musicians' gallery and
a mural of a figure of Death wielding a
shovel.
LLANTILIO CROSSENY SO3914
Attractive village with a lovely view of
the 13th-c church from the former
moat of Hen Cwrt nearby; the Halfway
House and Hostry are good for lunch.
White Castle (NW) The remains of
the most substantial of the trio of
moated castles Hubert de Burgh built
to defend the Welsh Marches; £2;
Cadw. The other ruins stand at
Skenfrith (the Bell by an old mill here
has good value food) and Grosmont, an
attractive hillside village with another
13th-c church (the Angel here is also
good value).
LLANTRISANT ST0483
The **ancient church** in this attractive
hill town has a window by Burne-Jones.
Overlooking the Bullring in the centre
of the old town, the decent **Model
House Craft & Design Centre** has
around ten contemporary craft
exhibitions every year; shop; cl Mon
(exc bank hols); (01443) 237758; free.
LLANVAPLEY SO3614
Interesting village, with a church dating
from 860. The friendly Red Hart by the
cricket green has good food.
MARGAM SS8086
Margam Park (A48) Pretty country
park based around a splendid 'gothick'
mansion, its 850 acres full of natural and
historic features and various themed
areas, inc a scaled-down nursery-rhyme
village for young children. Also a ruined
abbey and Iron Age hill fort, marked
walks among the parkland and forests,
deer and cattle, a new light railway and a
good adventure playground. Meals,
snacks, shop, disabled access; usually cl
Mon and Tues Oct–Mar, 25 Dec;
(01639) 881635; free.
MERTHYR MAWR SS8877
Delightful village of thatched cottages,
bordered by meadows and woodlands.
Nearby Merthyr Mawr Warren is
Europe's largest sand dune system, a
site of special scientific interest; the
ruined 15th-c Candleston Castle stands
at the edge of the dunes.
MERTHYR TYDFIL SO0511
Brecon Mountain Railway (off
A465) This narrow-gauge railway starts
at Pant Station, 3m N of Merthyr Tydfil,

and runs for 3½m into the beautiful Brecon Beacons to the end of the Taf Fechan reservoir; there's a footpath to a picnic site with lovely panoramic valley views. Meals, snacks, shop, disabled access; cl Nov–Mar exc Dec; (01685) 722988 for timetable; £6.80. On a stretch of disused line nearby, the Ponsarn Viaduct is a striking sight, well worth a detour.

Cyfarthfa Castle (Cyfarthfa Park) Impressive early 19th-c castellated 'gothic' mansion, in beautiful gardens. Now restored to their full Regency glory, the state rooms contain a museum with displays on Egyptology and archaeology, also fine art and ceramics. Snacks, shop, disabled access; cl wknd ams and Mon Sept–Mar, 24–26 Dec, 1 Jan; (01685) 723112; free.

Garwnant Forest Centre (5m NW, off A470) Looking out over the Llwyn-On reservoir on the S edge of the National Park, carefully restored old farm buildings with displays on forestry, wildlife and conservation, and information on nature trails and cycle routes (you can hire bikes). They run some summer activities for children. Meals, snacks, shop, disabled access; (01685) 384060; £1 car parking charge.

Joseph Parry's Cottage (Chapel Row, Georgetown) The composer of Myfanwy was born here, and the ground floor has been restored and decorated in the style of the 1840s. Shop, disabled access to ground floor only; cl am, also Mon–Weds and all Oct–Mar; (01685) 723112; free. The Butchers Arms up at Pontsticill has good home cooking.

MONMOUTH SO5113
Attractive market town of considerable character; below the remains of the 12th-c castle where Henry V was born, and the 17th-c Great Castle House (built in its precincts with enormous blocks of masonry), the main Agincourt Sq is surrounded by handsome buildings, inc the imposing central Shire Hall with its arcaded market floor. The town nestles in the crook formed by the River Wye and the River Monnow, with a splendid 13th-c gatehouse bridge over the Monnow. The Punch House is the most enjoyable place here for lunch, and the Gockett (B4293 towards

Trelleck) is also useful.

Fairview Rock Lofty crag near the Biblins suspension bridge, making a good riverside walk from Monmouth, with a level track giving an easy route along the picturesque Lower Wye gorge.

Naval Temple and Round House A pair of whimsical Georgian buildings in grounds on top of the Kymin, the hill just E of Monmouth, commanding views over the Forest of Dean and Black Mountains. The Naval Temple is a delightful rustic conceit, built in 1800 to commemorate the admirals of the Napoleonic Wars, while the Roundhouse is a circular banqueting house. Roundhouse open Sun and Mon, Apr–Oct; (01600) 719241; *£2.10; NT.

Nelson Museum (Priory St) Tremendous collection relating to Nelson, inc letters, medals and best of all his fighting sword. Nelson has nothing to do with Monmouth, but the collection was originally put together by Lady Llangattock who lived nearby, and whose son was one of the founders of Rolls-Royce; also local history collections and temporary exhibitions. Shop, mostly disabled access; cl 1–2pm, Sun am, 24–26 Dec, 1 Jan; (01600) 713519; *£1.

NANTGARW ST1285
Nantgarw China Works Museum (Treforest Industrial Estate, off A470) For a brief period early in the 19th c, Nantgarw porcelain was among the finest in the world. They still make pots and clay pipes, and you can watch the craftsmen at work. Snacks, shop; cl Mon, plus winter Tues and Weds, mid-Dec to mid-Jan; (01443) 841703; free.

NASH POINT SS9168
The curious striped cliffs of the Glamorgan coast look over the Bristol Channel to Exmoor. It is worth getting down to shore level to see the cliffs in their full glory. The coast path provides a number of possibilities, inc walking E past the lighthouse to St Donat's Castle (now a college) and back.

NEATH SS7597
Borough Museum (Gwyn Hall, Orchard St) Includes finds from a nearby Roman fort and hands-on activities for children, inc using a Celtic loom and the chance to dress up as a

Roman soldier. Shop, disabled access; cl Sun, Mon (exc bank hols), 24–26 Dec, 1 Jan; (01639) 645726; free.

Gnoll Estate (B4434 NE) Enchanting landscaped grounds beautifully restored by the local council, with some lovely features; there's also an adventure playground, and you can fish in one of the four lakes. Snacks, shop, disabled access; cl 24 Dec–2 Jan; (01639) 635808; free.

Neath Abbey Remains of Cistercian abbey founded in 1130 by Richard de Grainville. Disabled access; free.

NELSON ST1196

Llancaiach Fawr 🔄 (B4254) Splendidly entertaining and carefully organised living history museum, the Elizabethan manor's Civil War days brought vividly to life by costumed guides who rarely step out of character – they even speak in 17th-c style. Children actually enjoy visiting a stately home when it's like this – there are no ropes or barriers (it's all firmly hands-on) and they can try on historic clothes, handle armour, or even languish in the stocks for a while. Extra activities summer wknds. Meals, snacks, shop; cl Mon Nov–Feb, and 24 Dec–2 Jan; (01443) 412248; *£4.50.

NEWPORT ST3187

Museum and Art Gallery (John Frost Sq) Worthwhile collections – inc a mass of teapots, and a display on the Chartist uprising. Shop, snacks, disabled access; (01633) 840064; cl Sun and bank hols; free. Newport has been raised to city status as part of the Jubilee celebrations, and down by the docks (B4237) its 1906 transporter bridge is now back in action – an extraordinary sight. Out at Bassaleg (A468 W) the Tredegar Arms has well cooked food.

Tredegar House (Coedkernew; off A48 SW) Magnificent 17th-c house and gardens in 90-acre landscaped park on the edge of this industrial town. The Morgans, later Lords Tredegar, lived here for five centuries, and the household's above and below stairs activities are well illustrated in the 30 or so rooms on show. In the grounds are self-guided trails, craft workshops, an Edwardian sunken garden, as well as boating and an adventure playground. Meals, snacks, shop, disabled access; cl

Mon and Tues, and Oct–Easter; (01633) 815880; £5.10. Past here on the B4239 the Lighthouse Inn at St Brides Wentlooge has good food upstairs, and great Severn views.

OGMORE SS8876

Ogmore Castle Three-storeyed 12th-c keep with a preserved hooded fireplace, a dry moat surrounding the inner ward, and a surviving 12-metre (40-ft) W wall. The setting of this ruin is attractive: odd to think that what this impressive fortress was built to defend was the row of stepping stones which still cross the river; free. The Pelican is good for lunch, and the cheery Three Golden Cups along the road at Southerndown gives sea views to Devon on a clear day. Just past it there's a car park by the interestingly preserved remains of the seaside gardens of entirely demolished Dunraven Castle, with walks by the cliffs over the sands and rock pools, and around to the fragmentary remains of an Iron Age promontory hill fort above the sea.

PARKMILL SS5489

Gower Heritage Centre Based round a 12th-c water-powered cornmill (you can still see it working), this developing centre includes a re-created mill cottage, farm museum, a display of coracles, blacksmith, wheelwright and pottery (you can have a go at making your own pot, £2) and hatchery; also picnic and play areas, and you can feed the fish. They have a puppet theatre and hold special events. Tearoom, shops, disabled access; cl 25–26 Dec, 1 Jan (but best to check as parts may be closed); (01792) 371206; £3.50.

PENARTH ST1971

An unspoilt seaside resort of some charm, with the usual attractions.

Cosmeston Medieval Village 🔄 (Lavernock Rd towards Sully) Living museum of medieval life, reconstructed on the site of an actual village which was deserted during the 14th c. Hens and sheep wander between the cottages. Meals, snacks, shop, disabled access; cl 25 Dec; (029) 20701678; *£3. It's in the Cosmeston Lakes country park, with lakes, woodland and wildlife.

Turner House (Plymouth Rd) Changing exhibits from the National

Museum of Wales; shop, disabled access to ground floor; cl all day Mon (exc bank hols), between exhibitions, and occasional lunch times; (029) 20708870; free.

PENHOW ST4290

Penhow Castle 🏰 (A48) The oldest lived-in castle in Wales, with tours of the restored rooms taking you from the 12th-c ramparts and Norman bedchamber through the 15th-c Great Hall with its minstrels' gallery to the Victorian housekeeper's room. There's a choice of several good audio tours, one specially for children, and others concentrating on a particular topic, such as the musical or domestic history of the building. You can stay here. Snacks, shop; cl Mon (exc bank hols), Tues, and all end Sept–Good Fri exc Weds and pm Suns, best to check; (01633) 400800; *£3.80. The 16th-c Rock & Fountain has popular food.

PONTYPOOL SO2801

Pontypool Museum (Pontypool Park, off A4042) The story of a typical South Wales valley, well shown in the Georgian stable block of Pontypool Park House. Snacks, shop, disabled access; cl Sat and Sun am, 24 Dec–7 Jan; (01495) 752036; £1.20 (though they have hopes of abolishing the entrance fee). The surrounding country park is a microcosm of the Welsh valleys scenery: patches of conifer plantation and rather scrappy moorland rising high above the industrial valleys – not exactly pretty, but its gruff sense of place appeals to some. The Open Hearth just below the canal at Griffithstown is good for lunch.

PORTHCAWL SS8176

Developing summer resort, with broad sandy beaches, well placed golf club, fairground, fishing from the pier, and what's said to be the largest caravan park in Wales; it's quieter on the W side of the harbour.

RAGLAN SO4108

Raglan Castle Quite magnificent ruins of 15th-c castle, particularly notable for its Yellow Tower of Gwent. Its intricate history is displayed in the closet tower and two rooms of the gatehouse. Shop, some disabled access; cl 24–26 Dec, 1 Jan; (01291) 690228; £2.50; Cadw. The Clytha Arms (Abergavenny road) has good food.

ST HILARY ST0171

Beaupre Castle Well preserved ruined Elizabethan courtyard mansion with an extraordinarily elaborate three-storey Italianate porch; free. The Bush is good for lunch, and the village with its thatched houses is pretty.

ST NICHOLAS ST0971

Dyffryn Gardens (off A48) These lovely Grade I Edwardian Gardens are currently being restored with help from a lottery grant. Small themed gardens and seasonal bedding displays help break up the 55 acres of rare plants and shrubs, and there's an arboretum and a visitor centre. Summer snacks, shop, limited disabled access; gardens cl 25–26 Dec, visitor centre cl Nov–Mar (when entry is free); (029) 20593328; £3.

SWANSEA SS6593

Largely post-industrial and commercial, so there are few buildings of any age or great appeal to visitors, but long sandy beaches have made it something of a family summer resort (and there's a good fresh-food covered market with cockles and laverbread). Among some high spots is the 1934 Guildhall, containing the Brangwyn Hall with its 16 huge British Empire murals painted by Sir Frank Brangwyn for the House of Lords – Wales's gain, as they were judged too controversial. There are some castle ruins (you can't go inside, but can see them from outside), inc a striking 14th-c first-floor arcade. The handsome **Dylan Thomas Centre** (Somerset Pl, Marina) is devoted to Welsh literature, with changing exhibitions as well as a permanent exhibition on Dylan Thomas. Restaurant and good bookshop café (you can peruse the books over your coffee), disabled access; cl Mon, and some bank hols; (01792) 463980; free, charges for events. From the marina, a cycle- and footpath takes you around the bay to Mumbles and Gowerton beyond. The Hanbury in Kingsway is popular for lunch, and the Bankers Draft (Wind St) and Potters Wheel (Kingsway) have good value food all day.

Egypt Centre (University Campus, off Oystermouth Rd) An important collection of Egyptian artefacts. Snacks, shop, disabled access; cl Sun and Mon, bank hols, Christmas–New Year; (01792) 295960; free.

Glynn Vivian Art Gallery & Museum (Alexandra Rd) Displays of porcelain from Swansea's all-too-brief but brilliant period of production between 1814 and 1824, and paintings, drawings and sculptures by British, French and, above all, Welsh artists – especially the locally born Ceri Richards. Good changing exhibitions. Shop, disabled access to ground and first floors; cl Mon (exc bank hols), 25–26 Dec, 1 Jan; (01792) 655006; free.

Plantasia (Parc Tawe) Tropical and desert plants in big futuristic landscaped glasshouse, also monkey house, reptiles and various creepy-crawlies. Snacks, shop, disabled access; (01792) 474555; cl Mon (exc bank hols), 25–26 Dec, 1 Jan; £2.75.

Swansea Museum (Victoria Rd, Maritime Quarter) The oldest in Wales, with local history and replicas of the oldest human bones found in Wales; shop, limited disabled access; cl Mon (exc bank hols), and a few days over Christmas and New Year; (01792) 653763; free.

TINTERN SO5300
Tintern Abbey (off A466) Remarkably well preserved, these 14th-c ruins were considered an essential spot for 18th-c artists and poets to visit, lying as they do in a lovely part of the steeply wooded Wye Valley. Wordsworth was just one of many to find inspiration here. Shop, disabled access; cl 24–26 Dec, 1 Jan; (01291) 689251; £2.50; Cadw. The Moon & Sixpence overlooking it and the river has good value food, and the ancient tucked-away Cherry Tree (signed off the main road) does bargain lunches. The Abbey Mill has been converted into a craft and visitor centre. Demonstrations, restaurant and coffee shop; cl 25–26 Dec; free. A visitor centre at Tintern Old Station can help you make the most of the surrounding hills and woodland; open Apr–Oct; free.

TONGWYNLAIS ST1382
Castell Coch (off A470) This spectacular triangular hillside landmark, designed in 1875 by William Burges for the Marquess of Bute, is actually based on a 13th-c castle in spite of its improbable appearance, like something by Disney out of Wagner – red sandstone, conical towers, drawbridge and portcullis. Though never finished, it's a very successful pastiche, and inside is just as impressive: an astonishingly elaborate mock-medieval idyll of gilt, gorgeous colours, statues, murals and carvings. The bedroom of Lady Bute is decorated on the theme of Sleeping Beauty. Shop, disabled access to ground floor only; cl 24–26 Dec, 1 Jan; (029) 2081 0101; £3; Cadw. The Black Cock up towards Caerphilly has enjoyable food.

TREHAFOD ST0290
Rhondda Heritage Park 🏛 (off the A470) Based around the last colliery buildings in the area, this well organised centre uses lively multi-media exhibitions to re-create the golden days of the coal-mining industry, evoking sights, sounds and smells from the life and work of the miners. The excellent underground tour showing what it was like to work a shift is uncannily realistic, and the twisting simulated trip back to the surface is a definite highlight. Other displays look at the wider social heritage of the valley, with art by locals, a re-created village street, and (Easter–Sept) an excellent themed adventure play area for children. A good excursion whatever the weather. Meals, snacks, shop, good disabled access (even underground); cl Mon Oct–Easter, and 25–26 Dec; (01443) 682036; £5.60.

USK SO3700
Gwent Rural Life Museum (New Market St) Interesting collection, housed in three old barns; one shows life in the Welsh Borders from Victorian times to World War II, inc a typical farmhouse kitchen, laundry and dairy, and the others have machinery and wagons; cl am wknds and all Nov–Mar; £2. The little town is attractive, with an interesting church and good river walks; the Nags Head is currently the best pub.

WYND CLIFF ST5297
This viewpoint gives walkers an extensive panorama, a short detour up steps. Elsewhere, the Wye Valley Walk between Chepstow and Tintern gives only occasional views down to the

river, which in this picturesque Lower Wye gorge makes the boundary between England and Wales. **Attractive villages or small towns**, all with decent pubs, include Bedwellty SO1600, Cowbridge SS9974 and Laleston SS8879. The church and churchyard of Llancarfan ST0570 are worth a look. Pubs or inns elsewhere which are particularly useful for their attractive surroundings or views include the Lamb & Flag out on the Brecon road from Abergavenny SO2515, Goose & Cuckoo at Rhyd-y-

Meirch SO2907 (follow Upper Llanover sign up narrow track off A4042 S of Abergavenny), Bridgend by the canal at Gilwern SO2414, Old Glais at Glais SN7000, Prince of Wales nr the sand dune nature reserve at Kenfig SS8383, Old House at Llangynwyd SS8588, Greyhound at Llantrisant ST3997, Brynfynnon at Llanwonno ST0295, Plough & Harrow at Monknash SS9270, Rowan Tree at Nelson ST1195, Halfway House at Talycoed SO4115, Trekkers at The Narth SO5206 and Fountain at Trelleck Grange SO4902.

Where to eat

CARDIFF ST1676 **Gallois** *6–8 Romilly Crescent (029) 2034 1264* Small and stylish split-level restaurant with a loyal following, bustling cheerful atmosphere, delicious imaginative food from a modern menu, a good wine list with ten by the glass, and helpful staff; good value lunch; must book; cl Sun, Mon, 3 wks Aug, Christmas–New Year; disabled access. £32

CARDIFF ST1974 **Izakaya Japanese Tavern** *Mermaid Quay (029) 2049 2939* Japanese tavern with views over Cardiff Bay, eating and drinking bars, more formal rooms with sunken tables, and colourful decor; a choice of up to 60 items with English descriptions, a relaxed atmosphere, and some fine sakes served warm or cold; cl 24 Dec–2 Jan; disabled access. £21|**£5.90**

COWBRIDGE SS9974 **Farthings** *54 High Street (01446) 772990* Attractively decorated restaurant with stripped stone and black beams, candles and soft lighting, partly flagstoned front part, spreading far back up one or two steps into a cosily divided area with French prints on white walls and mix of carpet and quarry tiles, good freshly made modern food including tender Welsh black steaks, elaborate cakes, well chosen wines at rather low mark-ups, and friendly informal service; cl Sun and Mon pm, 25–26 Dec, 1 Jan; disabled access. £15|**£2.95**

LLANDEWI SKIRRID SO3416 **Walnut Tree** *(01873) 852797* Simply furnished dining pub with a small white-walled bar, some polished settles and country chairs around biggish tables on its flagstones, and a log-effect gas fire; it opens into an airy and relaxed dining lounge with dark wooden chairs and tables; excellent modern food, and a tempting choice of wines (particularly good Italian ones). £32

PORT TALBOT SS7489 **Aberavon Beach Hotel** *Princess Margaret Way (01639) 884949* Popular modern hotel opposite wide sandy beach, with imaginative modern cooking in no smoking restaurant, thoughtful wine list, helpful staff, and attractive public rooms; all weather leisure centre; comfortable bdrms; good disabled access. £23|**£7.50**

RAGLAN SO3608 **Clytha Arms** *(01873) 840206* Fine old country inn with a tastefully and solidly comfortable bar, cheerful helpful staff, good carefully prepared food inc delicious puddings and good value Sun lunch in no smoking restaurant, log fires, well kept real ales, and neat garden; bdrms; cl Mon am (open bank hols), 25 Dec. £28|**£6**

USK SO3700 **Nags Head** *4–6 Twyn Sq (01291) 672820* Run by the same warmly welcoming family for 35 years, this relaxed old coaching inn has enjoyable interesting food inc plenty of seasonal game and well kept beers, with plenty of character in its traditional beamed bar, and (cl winter) a separate coffee bar; disabled access. £18.50|**£5**

Special thanks to Mr and Mrs P Smith, Michael and Jenny Back, Peter and Audrey Dowsett, Prof R Harrison

INDEX

This index includes the main places in the **To see and Do** sections.

926 ● INDEX

LONDON INDEX

REPORT FORMS

Please report to us: you can use the card in the middle of the book, tear-out forms on the following pages, or just plain paper – whichever's easiest for you. Or you can send reports on our web site www.goodguides.com. Please tell us what you think about places already in the *Guide*. And about other places worthy of inclusion. We try to answer all letters, and readers who send us reports will be offered a discount on forthcoming editions.

If you are recommending a new place to stay or eat in, the more detail you can give, the better. Imagine you're writing about it for the *Guide* itself, and put in the sorts of things you'd want to know yourself before deciding on a visit. A full address and telephone number is also an enormous help.

We'd also very much like to know about places you've enjoyed visiting – anything from a little village to a stately home, from a peaceful wood or a nature reserve or a stretch of unspoilt coastal cliff to a theme park or a zoo or a pleasure beach. Whatever it is, if you've enjoyed it, please tell us about it. We'll assume we can print your name or initials as a recommender unless you tell us otherwise.

When you write to *The Good Britain Guide*, FREEPOST TN1569, WADHURST, E Sussex, TN5 7BR, you don't need a stamp in the UK. The information you send us will be stored in our computer files.

We will reply to your letters but we would ask for your patience if there's a delay, particularly from June well into autumn, when we are fully extended getting the next edition to the printers. The end of May is pretty much the cut-off date for reasoned consideration of reports for the next edition – the earlier the better, if they're suggestions for new entries.

The Good Britain Guide: Endorsement Form

I have been to the following hotels/restaurants/attractions/places in *The 2003 Good Britain Guide* in the last few months, found them as described, and confirm that they deserve continued inclusion:

By returning this form, you consent to the collection, recording and use of the information you submit, by The Random House Group Ltd. Any personal details which you provide from which we can identify you are held and processed in accordance with the Data Protection Act 1998 and will not be passed on to any third parties.

The Random House Group Ltd may wish to send you further information on their associated products. Please tick box if you do not wish to receive any such information. ☐

PLEASE GIVE YOUR NAME AND ADDRESS ON THE BACK OF THIS FORM

Your own name and address (*block capitals please*)

Please return to:
>   *The Good Britain Guide*
>   FREEPOST TN1569
>   WADHURST
>   E. Sussex
>   TN5 7BR

The Good Britain Guide: Report Form

Please use this form to tell us about anything that you think should or should not be included in the next edition of *The Good Britain Guide*. Just fill it in and send it to us – no stamp needed.

ALISDAIR AIRD

☐ Please tick this box if you would like extra report forms

Report on *(its name)*

Its address:

Postcode: Telephone:

What is this? (e.g. *hotel, restaurant, garden, village, drive, walk*)

Description/why it appeals

BACK OF THIS FORM

Your own name and address (*block capitals please*)

Please return to:

   The Good Britain Guide
   FREEPOST TN1569
   WADHURST
   E. Sussex
   TN5 7BR